CROSSED FINGERS

Property of
INSTITUTE FOR WORSHIP STUDIES
Orange Park, Florida

Other Books by Gary North:

Marx's Religion of Revolution (1968, 1989)
An Introduction to Christian Economics (1973)
Puritan Economic Experiments (1974, 1988)
Unconditional Surrender (1981, 1988, 1994)
Successful Investing in an Age of Envy (1981)
The Dominion Covenant: Genesis (1982, 1987)
Government by Emergency (1983)
Backward, Christian Soldiers? (1984)
75 Bible Questions Your Instructors Pray You Won't Ask (1984)
Coined Freedom (1984)
Moses and Pharaoh (1985)
The Sinai Strategy (1986)
Conspiracy: A Biblical View (1986)
Honest Money (1986)
Fighting Chance (1986), with Arthur Robinson
Unholy Spirits (1986, 1994)
Dominion and Common Grace (1987)
Inherit the Earth (1987)
Liberating Planet Earth (1987)
Healer of the Nations (1987)
The Pirate Economy (1987)
Is the World Running Down? (1988)
When Justice Is Aborted (1989)
Political Polytheism (1989)
The Hoax of Higher Criticism (1990)
Tools of Dominion: The Case Laws of Exodus (1990)
Victim's Rights (1990)
The Judeo-Christian Tradition (1990)
Westminster's Confession (1991)
Christian Reconstruction (1991), with Gary DeMar
The Coase Theorem (1992)
Politically Incorrect (1993)
Salvation Through Inflation (1993)
Rapture Fever (1993)
Tithing and the Church (1994)
Leviticus: An Economic Commentary (1994)
Baptized Patriarchalism (1995)
Lone Gunners For Jesus (1995)

CROSSED FINGERS
How the Liberals Captured the Presbyterian Church

Gary North

Institute for Christian Economics
Tyler, Texas

Copyright, Gary North, 1996

The author hereby transfers the right to reprint this book in electronic form to anyone without further permission and without royalty payments. The author retains the exclusive rights to the printed version of the book. Anyone who downloads a copy of this book from a web site, bulletin board, or CD-ROM disk is authorized to print out one copy for his own personal use. If you don't want to tie up your printer, it is probably cheaper ($34.95) to buy a hardback copy if you want more than a couple of chapters. The electronic version is available at www.freebooks.com.

Library of Congress Cataloging-in-Publication Data

North, Gary.
    Crossed fingers : how the liberals captured the Presbyterian Church / Gary North
    p. cm.
    ISBN 0-930464-74-5 : $34.95
    1. Presbyterian Church in the U.S.A. – History – 19th century. 2. Presbyterian Church in the U.S.A. – History – 20th century. 3. Liberalism (Religion) – Presbyterian Church in the U.S.A. – History – 20th century. 4. Liberalism (Religion) – United States – History – 20th century. 5. Presbyterian Church – United States – History. 6. Modernist-fundamentalist controversy. 7. United States – Church history – 20th century. I. Title.
BX8937.N67 1996   95-194
285'.132'09 – dc20   CIP

Note to librarian: It would not hurt to add:

Briggs, Charles Augustus (1841–1913)
Machen, John Gresham (1881–1937)
Bryan, William Jennings (1860–1925)
Fosdick, Harry Emerson (1878–1969)
Rockefeller, John D., Jr. (1874–1960)

Institute for Christian Economics
P.O. Box 8000, Tyler, TX 75711

This book is dedicated to my parents

Sam and Peggy North

who financed its first draft, and

Morton Smith

the Machen of twentieth-century Southern Presbyterianism, who has seen all this before . . .at least once.

WARNING!

You will notice that every footnote that extends to the following page is indented on the following page. This is not my mistake; it is a long-term design flaw in the Ventura Publisher program. The latest version, 5.0, has not remedied it. Corel, which bought Ventura Publisher in 1994, has been told about the flaw by publishers, but nothing has been done to correct it. The updated version will solve it, we are told. (Real Soon Now.)

The flaw makes this book look goofy, but software designs are law in desktop publishing. There was no way for me to correct the glitch. Pasting over copy by hand is an anachronistic pain.

In using version 5.0, my typesetter has discovered that the program randomly adds lines of garbage when she opens up the document to make a simple alteration, such as deleting a word. To make one minor correction in chapter six, she spent one full day cleaning out the garbage, making any alterations a very expensive change! This has happened repeatedly.

So, we bought a copy of FrameMaker, now owned by Adobe. After trying to learn it for two months, my typesetter found that it "solves" the footnoting problem as follows: it will not split a footnote; it just pushes it to the next page, sometimes leaving an inch or two of blank space at the bottom of the previous page. This was what WordPerfect did back in 1980, before it was WordPerfect. (It was called S.S.I.). Today, 16 years later, FrameMaker is still afflicted with this defect. (My one consolation is that Adobe paid $500 million to buy the Frame Technology company in June, 1995, and by March, 1996, Adobe's stock value had fallen 40% as a result: *Wall Street Journal*, March 14, 1996, p. B4.)

No wonder academic books use endnotes today. Publishers can't find a PC typesetting program that automatically does footnotes, putting them at the bottom of the page without defects. Techies who don't know what a footnote is supposed to do now shape the academic publishing industry.

The software revolution will solve man's problems! (Real Soon Now.)

Table of Contents

Note to the Reader.................................... ix
Foreword... xii
Preface.. xxxi

Introduction... 1

Part 1: Orthodoxy and Its Discontents............. 33
Introduction to Part 1............................... 35
1. Theologies in Conflict........................... 40
Conclusion to Part 1................................. 95

Part 2: From Old School to New School............. 97
Introduction to Part 2............................... 99

Whose Legitimacy?
2. Old School vs. New School....................... 116

Whose Authority?
3. Authority: Biblical, Confessional, Ecclesiastical........ 146
4. Testing Orthodoxy's Will to Resist............... 197
5. The Last Heresy Trials, 1891–1900................ 247
Conclusion to Part 2................................. 285

Part 3: From Evangelicalism to Liberalism......... 307
Introduction to Part 3............................... 309

Whose Legality?
6. Shadow Government, Administrative Law........... 343

Whose Sanctions?
7. Darwinism, Democracy, and the Public Schools..... 427
8. The Revival of Rhetoric.......................... 470

9. The Auburn *Affirmation* and Its Aftermath............ 534
10. Princeton, Pensions, and Peace..................... 582
11. Conflict Over Foreign Missions..................... 643

Whose Inheritance?
12. Inheritance and Disinheritance..................... 707
Conclusion to Part 3................................. 757

Part 4: The Strategy of Subversion................... 795
Introduction to Part 4................................ 797
13. Theology, Strategy, Tactics........................ 800
14. Monopoly Returns and the Flow of Funds............ 844
Conclusion to Part 4................................. 881

Conclusion.. 885

Appendixes.. 941

Appendix A: H. L. Mencken's Obituary
   of Machen: "Dr. Fundamentalis".................... 942
Appendix B: How to Immunize Presbyterianism.......... 947
Appendix C: The Strange Legacy of the Westminster
   Assembly.. 974
Appendix D: Francis Schaeffer's Role in
   the Presbyterian Conflict......................... 999
Appendix E: Winners and Losers....................... 1008

Scripture Index...................................... 1024
Index.. 1027

Helpful Suggestions to Book Reviewers................ 1087
About the Author..................................... 1089

NOTE TO THE READER

The history of the rise, progress, and peculiar character of American Presbyterianism, has for some time been considered a great desideratum by many of the members of our denomination. There is certainly no other religious community, embracing such numbers and being so long in existence, who are exposed to the imputation of having practised such gross negligence in failing to preserve authentic documents of their proceedings, and who still remain in such entire ignorance respecting their own history, and the founders and fathers of their church.

William Hill (1839)[1]

Rev. Hill's lament is more valid today than it was then, since an additional century and a half have passed by. We still need a comprehensive multi-volume history of mainline American Presbyterianism and its numerous spin-off denominations. I use the word "we" advisedly. The market does not want it, no matter how much "we" need it. So, "we" are unlikely to get it. Yet we are fast approaching the fourth century of American Presbyterianism. Something is wrong.

The last major scholarly history of American Presbyterianism was written by Charles Hodge. His two-volume *Constitutional History of the Presbyterian Church* (1839) remains the most detailed history of eighteenth-century American Presbyterianism. It was as a challenge to that book that Rev. Hill wrote his 224-page response. Hodge correctly insisted that the *Constitutional History* was not a comprehensive history of the Church; it was a history of the national Synod. Church historian George Hutchinson relates that Hodge told his son A. A. Hodge that writing that book was the most difficult project of his career. No other scholar has attempted to write an equally comprehensive, heavily footnoted follow-up volume that picks up the story

---

1. Hill, *A History of the Rise, Progress, Genius, and Character of American Presbyterianism* (Washington City: J. Gideon, 1839), p. v.

where Hodge left off: 1788, the revision of the Westminster Confession. There were several popular Presbyterian histories written in the late nineteenth century, but no scholarly history.[2] The closest thing to a critical history is Robert Ellis Thompson's history, published in 1895: a century ago.

Pamphlets for Pastors

Rev. Hutchinson is the author of a detailed history of a denomination that no longer exists, the Reformed Presbyterian Church, Evangelical Synod (RPCES). That small denomination merged in 1982 with the Presbyterian Church in America (PCA). Hutchinson wants to write a scholarly history of the PCA. In his unsuccessful attempt to raise funds for this project, one pastor told him: "If you can boil the story down into a pamphlet, I'll read it." Such is the present intellectual condition of American Presbyterianism, which a century ago was known as the most intellectually militant Protestant denomination. Presbyterianism has fallen on soft times.

I did not write this book for that anonymous pastor or his sleepwalking peers. Any pastor who cares so little about the history of the Church to which he is covenanted by ministerial oath must believe that, to the extent that he is representative of other men of his caliber and commitment, he will not be remembered. His work on earth will leave no earthly trace, and even if it does, no one like him will ever read about it. *He who ignores the past expects to be ignored in the future.* He is therefore unlikely to commit the personal resources necessary to have a significant effect on the future.

Crossed Fingers is a monograph, fat though it is. It is not a history of Presbyterianism; it is a study of how the liberals captured one Presbyterian denomination: the main one. The story I have written here has not previously been told. There are books on the Presbyterian conflict. There are doctoral dissertations on it. But chronicles are not enough. We know that the liberals captured the Northern Presbyte-

---

2. Southern Presbyterians have E. T. Thompson's three-volume *Presbyterians in the South* (1973).

rian Church. But something was missing: a detailed study of *how* the liberals did it.

This book partially fills the gap. It was a large gap; that is why this is a very large book. Yet this book only surveys the highlights. Furthermore, there is no comparable book for any of the other mainline Protestant denominations, most of which have succumbed to the liberals' strategy of subversion. This void points to the present intellectual condition of American Protestantism. One thing is sure: conservative American Protestantism is not future-oriented. In this sense, it is lower class.[3] Lower-class people and movements do not shape history; they are carried along in the back of the bus in order to be milked by those future-oriented people and movements that do shape history.

I wrote this book for Christians who are tired of being milked, bilked, and forced to ride silently in the back of humanism's bus. If this is you, keep reading. Understand, however, that you are part of a small remnant: a person who is willing to pick up a book about one aspect of Presbyterian Church history. The final remnant will be even smaller: those who finish reading this book. Few are called; even fewer are chosen. But cheer up; there are words of comfort available: "Woe is me, my mother, that thou hast borne me a man of strife and a man of contention to the whole earth! . . . The LORD said, Verily it shall be well with thy remnant; verily I will cause the enemy to entreat thee well in the time of evil and in the time of affliction" (Jer. 15:10a-11).

---

3. On future-orientation and class position, see Edward C. Banfield, *The Unheavenly City: The Nature and Future of Our Urban Crisis* (Boston: Little, Brown, 1970), pp. 48-59.

FOREWORD

Almost every contemporary proposal to bring freedom into the church is simply a proposal to bring tyranny into the world. For freeing the church now does not mean freeing it in all directions. It means freeing that peculiar set of dogmas called scientific, dogmas of monism, of pantheism, or of Arianism, or of necessity. And every one of these ... can be shown to be the natural ally of oppression.

G. K. Chesterton (1924)[1]

In 1924, Chesterton converted to Roman Catholicism and wrote *Orthodoxy*, which was his testimony against modernism. He understood that the most dangerous of modernism's heresies are to a great extent merely extensions of heretical theologies that were rejected long ago by the early Church. Chesterton's insight here was that theology has implications for society. Heretical theology leads to political tyranny. Bad theology produces political oppression. The twentieth century stands as evidence of his contention.

Modernism is another gospel. This was Chesterton's contention; it was also the contention of his Protestant contemporary, John Gresham[2] Machen.[3] Both of them did their best to challenge modernism. Both of them wrote popular books for Christians in the pews. They died within a few months of each other. Chesterton did not live long enough to see the Roman Church engulfed by modernism; Vatican II began a quarter century after his death. Machen, however, did see modernism triumphant in his denomination, the Presbyterian Church in the United States of America. Seven months before he died, modernists persuaded the broad evangelical majority of that de-

---

1. Chesterton, *Orthodoxy* (Garden City, New York: Image, [1924] 1959), p. 125.
2. Pronounced GRESSum. I was told this by his nephew, Arthur W. Machen, Jr. Most of his followers today are unaware of this; they refer to him as GRESHam.
3. Pronounced MAYchen.

nomination that Machen had become disobedient to Church authority, and that for the sake of the peace, he should be removed from office.

'Twas a Famous Victory

Modernism has achieved a comprehensive cultural victory in our day. This has been a barren victory. Modernism has pushed the West to its moral and epistemological limits, especially the former. The crucial divisive issues in a civilization are ethical: right vs. wrong. Man's primary problems are moral, not intellectual. While it is no doubt true that the modern world is in a flight from truth,[4] this is because it is in a flight from God, His permanent law, and, above all, His permanent negative sanctions: hell and the lake of fire.

Modernism seeks solutions to man's ethical problems apart from an appeal to an authoritative God who has revealed Himself in the Bible in such a way that this revelation can be authoritatively assembled by men in terms of propositional truths. Without a permanent God to provide permanent standards, whirl becomes king. Modernism faithfully serves this king, though usually in the name of evolving linear progress. But in seeking historical progress autonomously, modern man has achieved its inversion, alienation.[5]

Because modernism has invaded every area of life, including the churches, whirl's dry rot of relativism has undermined those institutions that might otherwise act to prevent the looming crisis. This book is the story of how modernism invaded and then captured one denomination: the Northern Presbyterian Church.

An Old Problem

What Christians should recognize is that this has happened before, though in slow motion: the breakdown of classical civilization. The heresies that plagued the early Church were extensions of ancient Greek philosophy.[6] As faith in Greek moral philosophy steadily

---

4. Jean-Francois Revel, *The Flight from Truth: The Reign of Deceit in the Age of Information* (New York: Random House, 1991).

5. Robert A. Nisbet, *The Sociological Tradition* (New York: Basic Books, 1966), p. 6; ch. 7.

6. Cornelius Van Til, *Christianity in Conflict* (Philadelphia: Westminster

broke down, so did the civilization that had been constructed in terms of its categories.[7] The Roman world was viewed by its intellectuals as the product of either godless impersonal fate or godless impersonal chance, i.e., fatalism or anarchy.[8] The only way out of this philosophical dilemma seemed to be the assertion of an eternal tension between them: part fate, part chance, no final resolution. This tension we call dualism or dialecticism. It undermined Greek philosophy as thoroughly as it has now undermined modernism. The pantheistic monism of Greek continuity—the great chain of being[9]—was offset philosophically by the futile Greek dialecticism of form (idea) vs. matter. Similarly, modernism's materialistic monism—the world as mere matter in motion—is offset philosophically by the equally futile dialecticism of Kant's phenomenal/noumenal (science/freedom) dialecticism.[10] Matter vs. mind, fate vs. chance, law vs. change, necessity vs. freedom, science vs. personality, determinism vs. responsibility: modern man's updated versions of ancient Greek antinomies plague him every bit as much as they plagued the ancients. The relativist historian Carl Becker raised the issue in a rhetorical statement that was really not all that rhetorical: "What is man that the electron should be mindful of him!"[11] When men seek freedom and meaning in anything but the self-revelation of God in the Bible, they hit philosophical brick walls. And every once in a while, the crash takes down a whole civilization. Ours may be one of them. We are now facing a potential breakdown of monumental proportions.[12]

Seminary, 1962).

7. Charles Norris Cochrane, *Christianity and Classical Culture: A Study of Thought and Action from Augustus to Augustine* (New York: Oxford University Press, [1944] 1957).

8. *Ibid.*, p. 159.

9. Arthur O. Lovejoy, *The Great Chain of Being: A Study of the History of an Idea* (New York: Harper Torchbooks, [1936] 1965), ch. 2.

10. Richard Kroner, *Kant's Weltanschauung* (Chicago: University of Chicago Press, [1914] 1956).

11. Carl L. Becker, *The Heavenly City of the Eighteenth-Century Philosophers* (New Haven, Connecticut: Yale University Press, [1932] 1951), p. 15.

12. Pitirim A. Sorokin, *The Crisis of Our Age: The Social and Cultural Outlook* (New York: Dutton, [1941] 1957).

The answer to Greek rationalism is also the answer to modern rationalism: the biblical doctrines of the Trinity, the Creator/creature distinction, the bodily resurrection and ascension of Jesus Christ in history, and God's declaration of "Not guilty!" to His people on the judicial basis of this death and resurrection. This is the Bible's theme of *creation-fall-redemption*. Here is the answer presented in the creeds and councils of the early Church. God is in control; man isn't. God has sent a redeemer in history. This redeemer is not the State.

What Happened to Presbyterianism?

In 1924, the year *Orthodoxy* appeared, the conservatives' candidate won the Moderatorship of the General Assembly of the Presbyterian Church for the first and last time during what has come to be called the Presbyterian conflict. That conflict ended in June of 1936 with the defeat of the conservatives. On June 15, for the last time, an article on the Presbyterian conflict appeared on the front page of the *New York Times*. The headline announced: "Barring of 3 Philadelphia Pastors Brings Walkout by Presbyterians." The same page announced: "G. K. Chesterton, Noted Author, Dies." Somehow, these parallels seem fitting.

Move ahead two decades. In 1955, a book was published with the title, *What Presbyterians Believe*. I can think of no book with a more misleading title, given its date of publication. It was a study of the Westminster Confession of Faith (1647). It was written by a Calvinist minister, theologian, and philosopher, Gordon H. Clark. Clark was a member of the United Presbyterian Church of North America, which three years later would merge with the far larger mainline denomination, the Presbyterian Church in the United States of America (PCUSA), at which time Clark left the denomination. The United Presbyterian Church in 1955 was drifting into liberalism. It had been dabbling with liberalism for a quarter of a century. It had initiated discussions on a possible merger with the larger denomination in 1930, but then had voted not to follow through after the PCUSA voted for the plan in 1934. It was obvious in 1930 that the PCUSA's liberals had brought the conservatives under control. Nevertheless, from 1948 to 1958, Clark subordinated himself to the jurisdiction of men who did not believe in Calvinism, and who proved it in 1958 when they voted to join the PCUSA. Had Clark been more honest in selecting a title for his book, he would have called it *What a Handful of Presbyterians Believe*, or *What Presbyterian Officers Swear They Believe, But Rarely Do*, or even *What Presbyterians Believe in the Small Denomination I Abandoned as Hopeless in 1948 When I Joined This One*.[13] But he didn't. Instead, he pretended in public that he was not a minority voice, that he was not under the ecclesiastical jurisdiction of Presbyterians who did not believe. In this, he was not alone.

Today, there are millions of confessionally faithful but ecclesiastically compromised Church members and thousands of compromised pastors who are in a condition similar to Clark's in 1955. If anything, they are in a much worse condition: the mainline Protestant churches have become much more liberal since 1955. So has the Roman Catholic Church. Only the Southern Baptist Convention has reversed course: the most remarkable ecclesiastical reversal of the past three centuries.[14]

Church Government and Theology

America in the twentieth century has offered a three-fold ecclesiastical development.

> 1. Theologically conservative, creedal, hierarchical denominations grow more liberal as they grow larger and wealthier, thereby attracting the services of pastors who have been educated in state-funded and state-accredited colleges and universities.

> 2. Theologically liberal hierarchical denominations grow smaller as their members discover what their well-educated pastors actually believe.

> 3. Theologically conservative, non-creedal, non-hierarchical churches enjoy most of the growth. Their lack of formal academic requirements for the ministry inoculates them against the worst features of liberalism. Their freedom from hierarchical

---

13. He had been ordained by the Orthodox Presbyterian Church in 1944. See "Clark, Gordon Haddon," in *The Orthodox Presbyterian Church 1936–1986*, edited by Charles G. Dennison (Philadelphia: Committee of the Historian of the Orthodox Presbyterian Church, 1986), p. 330.

14. Paul Pressler and Paige Patterson deserve far more than this footnote for what they engineered, 1977 to 1990.

control allows the members to fund the theology they prefer, which is rarely liberal.

This has created an institutional dilemma for the leaders of theologically conservative, creedal, hierarchical churches. To grow, they apparently have only three choices: to go soft creedally, to go independent, or both. They must position themselves creedally somewhere in between Cotton Mather and *The Christian Century*. In no denomination has this dilemma been revealed more clearly than in American Presbyterianism, but it has happened in all of the large Protestant denominations.

Are you a well-catechized Presbyterian? If so, you are the member of a tiny minority group. People such as you have been in one of the following situations since 1960: (1) members of a large, wealthy, but shrinking denomination that has been taken over by liberals; (2) members of a medium-sized, officially Calvinistic, and growing denomination that has been taken over at the top by people who are more concerned with Church growth than theology, and who do not make it sufficiently difficult to penetrate by Arminians, neo-evangelicals, Scofieldians, and Baptists who happen to sprinkle babies and who want in on the deal;[15] (3) members of a tiny, hard-pressed Calvinist denomination that Arminians and liberals do not regard as worth the effort to take over. Putting it graphically, you're governed by ministers who believe the editorials in (1) *The Christian Century*, (2) *Christianity Today*, or (3) a denominational magazine printed on non-slick paper with no color pictures inside. It boils down to this: you've been sold out to liberals; you're being sold out to neo-evangelicals who will later sell you out to liberals; or you're not yet worth buying.

What you need is membership in a large and rapidly growing Presbyterian Church that is so costly to penetrate by neo-evangelicals that the liberals might as well concentrate on taking over the Missouri Synod Lutheran Church.[16] Sorry; this ecclesiastical product is not

---

15. The outstanding twentieth-century example is William Jennings Bryan. Billy Sunday comes in second.

16. If you're in the Missouri Synod Lutheran Church, you are in condition two, just barely. Had the denomination not cleaned house on Concordia Seminary in the mid-1970's, you would be in condition one.

only not available at the present time, it is not even in the early prototype stage.

What should a Presbyterian prototype look like? You cannot begin to answer this until you know what it had better not look like: the Presbyterian Church, U.S.A., in 1920.[17]

Rotten Wood

This book is about a conflict between two mighty religions, Christianity and humanism. It is also about a third religious tradition that was caught in the middle, whose adherents were forced by circumstances to decide which side to support: experientialism-pietism. Some of them were Christians; others were humanists. This book is about a number of confusions, both theological and institutional, and their subsequent clarification. It discusses heroes and villains, and it acknowledges that the vast majority of the participants were somewhere in between. This is true of every turning point in history except the rebellion of Adam and Eve, in which there were no innocent bystanders. It is the story of a turning point in the history of the United States.

This is a history of the liberals' strategy of infiltration and conquest of the Northern Presbyterian Church. A similar strategy was carried out in the public schools, the judiciary, the colleges, and the media, but this ecclesiastical battle was the most important battle of the war. It had to be won. Why? Because the fundamental covenantal issues of life are always at bottom *theological*, not political, educational, or economic. The public testimony of the Presbyterian Church was by far the most theologically rigorous testimony in the country—indeed, in the world. Humanists had to silence this denomination, for it was too influential. The capture of the most theologically articulate large conservative Protestant denomination in the United States was modernism's best-publicized ecclesiastical success story of the era. The strategy the modernists used to take over the Presbyterians was used, with modifications, to capture the other large denominations.

---

17. See Chapter 6, below.

This book is more than a history; it is a study in sociological patterns: how institutions and groups adjust in order to survive through history. This is why I focus on a few representative figures. I agree with C. Wright Mills: "No social study that does not come back to the problems of biography, of history and their intersections within a society has completed its intellectual journey."[18]

This book is also a study in what could be called ecclesiastical entomology: bugs. Specifically, it is a study of ecclesiastical termites: liberals. By 1921, these voracious termites had eaten away so much of the Presbyterian Church that Princeton Seminary's greatest living theologian, Warfield, shortly before he died called the entire denomination rotten wood.[19]

Beyond Presbyterianism

I wrote this book to be more than a monograph on one denomination's history. It is a representative case study of a much wider phenomenon. It provides an introduction to the whole question of theological liberalism in the churches, and how this came about. Church historian William Hutchison has described well the subject matter of this book: the presence and then the triumph of theological liberals in a denomination in which a large majority of the members did not regard themselves as liberals. Hutchison writes:

> The Protestant establishment can in fact be understood as a "broad church" that held together, and exercised whatever cultural authority it did enjoy, precisely because it retained the adherence, at all levels, of many besides liberals. While it is probably true that few who called themselves fundamentalists were able to remain comfortably in these churches after about 1930, all the evidence indicates that "liberal" was rarely a preferred term outside the theological seminaries and the more sophisticated periodicals. (During the time of neo-orthodox reaction against con-

---

18. C. Wright Mills, *The Sociological Imagination* (New York: Oxford University Press, 1959), p. 6.

19. Reported by J. Gresham Machen in a letter to his mother in 1921. Ned B. Stonehouse, *J. Gresham Machen: A Biographical Memoir* (Philadelphia: Westminster Theological Seminary, [1954] 1977), p. 310.

ventional liberalism—that is, between 1930 and 1960—such terminology was a bit suspect in those precincts as well.) Most establishment leaders and people, if forced to use limiting terms, were likely to designate their own positions as evangelical, confessional, progressive, or—calling on that all-time favorite among weasel words—moderate.[20]

I write for those Christians who fully recognize that in this, the final decade of the second millennium after the birth of Jesus Christ, His Church is in a full-scale war against an implacable enemy: humanism. There can be no permanent cease-fire. This book is written for those Christians who understand this and who are ready to act accordingly. Any other reader is entitled to come along for the ride, but he is not my target. Ethically self-conscious Christians are my targeted audience. Their needs and, more to the point, their vulnerability are my concern. There are still conservative Protestant denominations, and similar liberal strategies are still in effect. The problem is, the conservatives, then as now, have had no strategy.

This book is a strategy manual. It is a manual tracing how an earlier institutional battle was lost. It is not written in the spirit of detached academic inquiry. It is written in the spirit of institutional conquest: to recapture lost ground from the spiritual heirs of the invaders. When the invaders surrender cultural territory, we will regain it—not inside the four walls of liberal churches but in the culture at large. As for liberal churches today, let the dead bury the dead. Large brick churches in declining sections of town are not worth re-capturing. The heating and cooling bills alone would strap us.

Had it not been for the defection of earlier generations of Christians, we would not be in the place we are today: looking in from the outside on institutions that once belonged to God and His people rather than to the covenant-breakers who now occupy positions of institutional authority. But their authority is now fading. The flow of funds—a primary mark of authority—has begun to flow elsewhere.

---

20. William R. Hutchison, "Protestantism as Establishment," in Hutchison, ed., *Between the Times: The Travail of the Protestant Establishment in America, 1900-1960* (New York: Cambridge University Press, 1989), p. 14.

So has political power. From the foundation of the Federal (later National) Council of Churches in 1908, theological liberals exhorted theological conservatives to get involved in social action and politics. Now that conservatives have begun to do this, great is the anguish inside the hallowed halls of liberalism. God has granted the liberals their request, and like the Israelites after the quail feast in the wilderness (Num. 11), the liberals are now paying dearly for it. They do not have the votes. The Christian Right has the votes. The action today is in places like Colorado Springs and Orlando, not 475 Riverside Drive, New York City.

Liberals committed their strategic resources to capturing mainline Protestant churches at the peak of these churches' influence, 1920 to 1940. They have seen this influence wither away since 1960. They bought close to the top of the market and are now hanging on for eternal life to their portfolio, hoping against hope for a recovery. It has been a primary bear market for a generation, and today looks weaker than ever. The Protestant Establishment peaked with Dwight Eisenhower and his Secretary of State, John Foster Dulles (d. 1959). It has been all downhill since then.

Liberals still seek to recoup their losses however they can. If your church has assets, it is a potential target. If it also has the same judicial and educational structure that the Presbyterian Church had in 1869, it is surely a target. Your denomination has a large neon sign flashing brightly: "Come and get us!" Somebody will. In all likelihood, the subversion is already in progress.

I know, I know: "It can't happen to us." That's what they all say.

What Reading This Book Can Do for You

Do you want to recognize well in advance the tell-tale signs that your Church is moving away from orthodoxy toward theological liberalism? This book provides you with guide markers.

Do you want to find out what the most vulnerable and undefended parts of your Church are? This book identifies them.

Do you want to know how to patch up these undefended parts? This book shows you both how and how not to do this.

Do you want to spot the catch phrases of those who are actively infiltrating your Church or selling it out? This book provides them.

Do you want to understand the strategy of subversion that proved successful in the most spectacular Protestant takeover in modern American history? This book explains it in detail.

Do you want to know how those accomplices outside the Presbyterian Church cooperated with infiltrators inside to undermine and then capture the Church? This book reveals this mystery.

Do you want to identify the bait which the subversives used to hook the Presbyterian Church? This book shows you what to look for in your own denomination.

Do you want to know which deeply rooted Presbyterian ideals led to the institutional defeat of those who held them? This book identifies them.

Do you want to know what never works in any program to reform a Church's hierarchy? This book shows you how to avoid volunteering for a suicide mission.

Do you want to know what terrifies the infiltrators in the early stages of their invasion? This book shows you.

Do you want to know what terrifies them after they have completed the take-over at the top? Learn the secret in this book.

Do you want to know why the liberals' strategy of subversion always backfires on them in the next generation, or even sooner? This book shows you.

Do you want to learn the details of the strategy used by the conservatives who recaptured the Southern Baptist Convention, 1977–1990? (For that, you're going to have to pay more. There are limits on my generosity.)[21]

---

21. For a copy of my audiotape interview with the man who co-designed the strategy and then very quietly directed the conservatives' mobilization, send $10

Do you know why liberals and their queasy conservative allies will give this book hostile reviews or no reviews at all? (You do unless you have an IQ lower than Forrest Gump's.)

Who, What, Why, When, and Where?

My strategy for this book has forced me to answer a series of specific historical questions—a "package inquiry" which historians of the Presbyterian conflict have scrupulously avoided making in the past. They have not previously been dealt with in a single study.

What was the institutional and theological legacy of the Presbyterian reunion of 1869?

Why did the Northern Presbyterian Church cease all heresy trials after 1900?

What was the *theological* strategy of the liberals after 1900?

What was the *institutional* strategy of the liberals after 1900?

What is the proper role of historic creeds and confessions in the life of the Church?

Why did the Presbyterian Church, U.S.A., abandon its Confession as the means of screening its leadership?

What was the importance of seminary education in the liberals' capture of the Presbyterian Church?

What was the theological legacy of Princeton Seminary?

What was the theological legacy of Union Seminary?

What compromises in strategy was Machen forced to make, and why?

Why did people who initially "talked conservative" wind up going along with liberal Church leaders?

---

to ICE, P. O. Box 8000, Tyler, TX 75711. Ask for the **Southern Baptist Strategy Tape.**

Why did others who "talked Calvinistic" wind up going along with liberal Church leaders?

Did Machen's tactics destroy the Old School Presbyterian tradition?

How was a Baptist, John D. Rockefeller, Jr., involved in the Presbyterian conflict?

What You Have Not Been Told

I am not paid to write my theological books. I receive no book royalties. If a topic does not interest me, I do not pursue it. I pick my books' topics mainly out of personal curiosity: to find out how things work or how things happened.[22] I piece things together on my computer screen. I argue with myself on-screen. I do a lot of electronic erasing, despite how long some of my books are. Then, when I think I have the answers, I publish.

With respect to the origins, issues, and outcome of the Presbyterian conflict, I think I now have the broad outline of the answer. It took a long time for me to put the pieces together. As you read my answer, please keep in mind my original question: "What strategy did the liberals adopt in their successful attempt to capture the Northern Presbyterian Church?" Their strategy, I argue, was developed as part of a much larger process. Most scholars would call that process cultural. I call it covenantal.

My book is long, but it had to be. As I researched this topic, on and off, for over three decades, I kept uncovering things that I had never been told—not as a student at Westminster Seminary, not as a graduate student in American history, and not in any textbook on American Church history. The more I discovered, the more I wondered, "Why didn't someone tell me about this earlier?" Then I figured out why: nobody had known. A kind of collective amnesia set in after 1936, and even prior to 1936. The victims never did fully understand what had happened to them, and the perpetrators were not

---

22. Exceptions: those books that are replies to critics.

about to tell them or anyone else. The spiritual heirs of those on all sides of the Presbyterian conflict have not been told what happened.

Since 1963, graduate students have examined some of the more accessible records. Bits and pieces of the story have dribbled out in doctoral dissertations. In very recent years, academic books have appeared on the topic. But young men in graduate school and assistant professors seeking tenure are not supposed to tell a story in the way that a man my age, with no academic reputation to lose and access to enough foundation money to have his book published without an outside editor to tell him to "tone this down," is able to tell it.[23] So, I have told the story—as Cromwell is said to have told his portrait painter, "warts and all." I assure you, you have never read anything like it. But if you are a member of any hierarchical Protestant denomination with more than 50,000 members, some of it will, I predict, seem suspiciously familiar.[24]

Even if you are a pastor in the Orthodox Presbyterian Church, founded in 1936 when Machen and his tiny band of 4,200 people departed from the Presbyterian Church in the United States of America (PCUSA), you have never been told anything like the whole story of why and how your denomination came into existence. You may have read Edwin H. Rian's book, *The Presbyterian Conflict* (1940), which the OPC reprinted after I tipped off Rev. Charles Dennison that William B. Eerdmans Co. had failed to renew the book's copyright. Rian's book is incomplete, to say the least. You may even have read Lefferts Loetscher's book, *The Broadening Church* (1954). That book is also incomplete, though less incomplete than Rian's. Neither of them asked this crucial question: Was the Presbyterian conflict part of a much wider series of events that transformed American society? In short, was the Presbyterian conflict a microcosm—no, *the* microcosm—of the triumph of modernism in America, 1870 to 1940?

---

23. I must say, however, that Albert Frederick Schenkel's 1990 Harvard dissertation on how John D. Rockefeller, Jr., bought a controlling interest in America's Protestant Establishment, ventured courageously into a crucially important area that had been off-limits academically from the day that the proxy purchases began.

24. As any successful coach will tell you, if you find a play that works again and again, run with it until it quits working.

Why This Book Is So Long

In order to earn my living, I have had to master the techniques of direct-mail advertising. In this field, there are many rules to obey. Two rules are crucial. The ad writer must write the ad so as to cut off two negative reactions by the reader. One is a rhetorical question; one is a challenge. These two statements are legitimate, and if not dealt with in the text of the ad, the ad will fail. The two statements are:

So what?

Says you!

The historian also must pay close attention to these two statements. He must write every word to cut them off in advance. It is not sufficient for the historian to offer a narrative. For example, Will and Ariel Durant offered a gigantic narrative in their multi-volume *Story of Civilization*. But when the reader has finished the set—a highly unlikely prospect—he thinks to himself: "So what?" What were the lessons learned? No one can remember—not even the Durants.[25] Stories are not sufficient. They are necessary, but not sufficient. In this book, I tell a story. But on every page, I do my best to tell why this part of the story was significant. This makes the book longer than it would have been, had I just told the story.

I offer many direct citations from the record. This also has made the book longer. The more controversial the interpretation, the more necessary the documentation. When an author is presenting the case for losers in history, those educated by the winners are far more ready to say, "Says you!" To which I reply: "Says the record, if you pay close attention."

I would like to see a generation of institutional historians pay even closer attention to the record, and not just of the Presbyterian

---

25. See their slim, belated, and ignored book, *The Lessons of History* (New York: Simon & Schuster, 1968). They begin with this Darwinist presupposition: "History is a fragment of biology. . . . Therefore the laws of biology are the fundamental lessons of history" (p. 18). Try to find anyone who has read even one of their fat volumes who learned that lesson from it.

Church, U.S.A., but of all Seven Sisters: the mainline Protestant denominations that comprise the Protestant Establishment in America.[26]

A Brief History of This Book

What little I know about sociology I learned mainly from Robert Nisbet's lectures and graduate seminars. He made an important point a few years after I began writing this book: "History, it has been well said, yields her secrets only to those who begin with the present. The present is, in Alfred North Whitehead's phrase, holy ground."[27] The problem is, such ground does not stay holy for very long. The experience of writing this book over a period of three decades has driven home to me just how fleeting such holy ground is.

I began writing this book in the fall of 1962. I was a senior at the University of California, Riverside. In those days, UCR was the University of California's one exclusively undergraduate school. (There has been none since 1963.) It had about 2,000 students in 1962. All seniors were required to write a bachelor's thesis. I completed mine about the time Dallas Roark completed his Iowa State University Ph.D. dissertation on Machen. (It would have looked suspicious if mine had been turned in a year later, had anyone known of Roark's dissertation. I did not learn of it until three decades later.) My thesis advisors were Dennis Strong[28] and Jeffrey Burton Russell, who later did his best to teach me medieval history when I returned to UCR to begin my graduate studies in 1965. In between, I attended Westminster Theological Seminary in Philadelphia, from which I did not graduate.[29]

My original 1963 thesis was a conventional exercise in historiography. This book is not. It is neither a conventional work in Church

---

26. The phrase, "Seven Sisters," is William Hutchison's: "Protestantism as Establishment," in Hutchison, ed., *Between the Times*, p. 6. The Seven Sisters represent half of the members of the Federal and National Council of Churches: Congregationalists, Episcopalians, Presbyterians, Baptists, Methodists, Disciples of Christ, and Lutherans. *Ibid.*, p. 4.

27. Nisbet, *Sociological Tradition*, p. 5.

28. Strong complained that I had not attempted to explain the broader cultural relevance of the Presbyterian conflict. This book is my response, 33 years later.

29. I could see the handwriting on the wall. It went from right to left.

history nor a conventional study in applied sociology. It is a hybrid: a mixture of history, sociology, theology, and economics. I did not work on it from 1963 until I moved to Tyler, Texas, in 1980. My understanding of U.S. history had been expanded by earning a Ph.D. and doing a great deal of reading. I revised the manuscript in 1980; it more than tripled in size. Then I stopped working on it.

I began again in 1985 when Ray Sutton came up with his variation of Meredith G. Kline's suggested Old Covenant model.[30] His breakthrough alerted me to a possibility. Machen's thesis in *Christianity and Liberalism* (1923) was that there were two rival religions battling for control in America's mainline Protestant churches. Was this thesis true? If so, the theology of theological modernism-liberalism may have been a mirror-image replacement for the five-point structure of biblical covenant theology. I began looking at the documents to see if my suspicion could be verified. I discovered that there were numerous defenders of a five-point covenant theology of modernism. Then I stopped again. I returned to the project in 1992. I expanded the manuscript. But once again, I quit writing. I returned for the last time in December of 1993. I worked steadily for the next 20 months to complete it, also finishing *Leviticus: An Economic Commentary* (1994). The manuscript grew larger.

Missing Pieces in 1963

Beginning in 1985, I revised my manuscript in terms of a theological premise:

> *A covenant is a legally binding relationship between God and man that is established by taking an oath to which are attached sanctions, positive and negative.*

The centrality of the covenantal oath and its sanctions was fundamental to the continuing Presbyterian conflict from the days of the First Great Awakening. I did not understand this when I began to research this book's first draft in 1962. This is why I did not fully understand what the Presbyterian conflict was all about when I completed the initial draft in May of 1963, although I did understand that

---

30. The ICE published Sutton's book, *That You May Prosper*, in 1987.

Machen and his followers were defending theological orthodoxy against its enemies. I did not fully comprehend why Machen lost. It was not that there were more self-conscious enemies of orthodoxy than supporters in the Presbyterian Church in 1936, for the evangelicals outnumbered the liberals. It was rather that the enemies of orthodoxy had captured the instruments of ecclesiastical power by means of a strategy—a strategy that extended back for three centuries: an attack on the authority of the Bible in the name of the Bible.

In 1963, Henning Graf Reventlow had not written *The Authority of the Bible and the Rise of the Modern World* (1980), which traces the origins of the higher criticism of the Bible back to the reaction against English Puritanism, beginning in the 1630's. The Puritans had emphasized the Old Testament as a source of legitimate judicial standards.[31] Anti-Puritans developed an alternative approach. R. B. Mullin correctly identifies as Unitarian this literary-textual approach to the Bible.[32] This was the legacy claimed by liberals in the United States and greatly extended by them after 1875.

Also in the spring of 1963, I was unaware of Edmund Morgan's path-breaking insights that same year into the origins of the New England Puritans' doctrine of halfway covenant, another tradition stretching back to the 1630's: the elevation of religious experience to equality with creedal confession and personal ethics as an identifying mark of conversion.[33] This was the legacy adopted by minimal-creed Presbyterian conservatives. I was therefore unaware of the existence of three centuries of institutional precedents against Machen and his followers: a two-fold ancient heritage—higher criticism on the left and experien-

---

31. Reventlow begins his discussion of anti-Puritan higher criticism with a discussion of William Chillingsworth and the Anglican Great Tew circle of the late 1630's: literary critics who moved from considering the Old Testament's literary themes to questioning its judicial authority. Reventlow, *The Authority of the Bible and the Rise of the Modern World* (London: SCM Press, [1980] 1984), pp. 147–52.

32. Robert Bruce Mullin, "Biblical Critics and the Battle Over Slavery," *Journal of Presbyterian History*, 61 (Summer 1983), p. 211.

33. Edmund S. Morgan, *Visible Saints: The History of a Puritan Idea* (New York: New York University Press, 1963), pp. 99–105.

tialism on the right—that Machen's opponents could invoke against him.

Conclusion

Unread diet books on the shelf will not help a person to lose weight. Neither will a diet book that he reads while munching Fritos with bean dip. So, before you proceed any further, let me warn you:

> No man, having put his hand to the plough, and looking back, is fit for the kingdom of God (Luke 9:62).

> For which of you, intending to build a tower, sitteth not down first, and counteth the cost, whether he have sufficient to finish it? Lest haply [it happen], after he hath laid the foundation, and is not able to finish it, all that behold it begin to mock him, Saying, This man began to build, and was not able to finish (Luke 14:28-30).

> But be ye doers of the word, and not hearers only, deceiving your own selves. For if any be a hearer of the word, and not a doer, he is like unto a man beholding his natural face in a glass [mirror]: For he beholdeth himself, and goeth his way, and straightway forgetteth what manner of man he was (James 1:22-24).

Now, get out your yellow highlighter, your pen, and some note cards. It is time to begin stage one: reconnaissance. It will take you about 50 hours to complete this initial mission. That is a lot of time, and time is money. Not many people will make this large an investment. The problem is, whenever good people refuse to prepare themselves for the ecclesiastical battles that lie ahead, *righteousness loses by default*. This book offers a lot of evidence to prove this statement.

When you have finished, start thinking about what a revamped ecclesiastical prototype should look like. That will take you a lot more than 50 hours. Should some faithful Presbyterian tell you that no revamped prototype is necessary, ask him to sketch his plan for retrofitting one of the three existing Presbyterian models: liberal, neo-evangelical, or culturally invisible.

PREFACE

Historians begin with basic intentions, as do all persons who plan to reach an objective. Self-consciously or otherwise, they approach their work with some notion of what they expect to do with a topic. It is often difficult to ascertain the subtler aspects of purpose because at the outset the authors frequently do not realize what they intended to accomplish.

Henry Warner Bowden (1985)[1]

Let it never be said of me that (1) I do not realize what I intend to accomplish when I write a book or (2) there is anything subtle about my purposes. I am about as subtle as a high voltage cattle prod.

On the surface, this is a book about Church history: not one of the hot topics in any recent American generation's curriculum, even in theological seminaries. Within the field of Church history, the least interesting subdivision for most academic historians is denominational history. This book at first glance is a denominational history—a denomination that has yet to see its first full-scale scholarly history, almost three centuries after its founding in America. Worse; it is a large book that focuses on a relatively brief period in that denomination's history: 1869 to 1936. There is already another seemingly definitive book in the field, Lefferts Loetscher's *The Broadening Church* (1954), one of the most influential books in American Presbyterian Church history, not just as a secondary source but as a primary source.[2] It has become the standard account for non-Presbyterian Church historians. This brings me to one of my not-too-subtle purposes: to provide an antidote to that book.[3] Warning: like Ipecac, *Crossed Fingers* will upset many tummies prior to emptying them.

---

1. Bowden, "Ends and Means in Church History," *Church History*, 54 (March 1985), p. 75.
2. Cynthia M. Campbell, "*The Broadening Church*," *American Presbyterians*, 66 (Winter 1988), pp. 309–13.
3. Other purposes include: (1) to identify the central tenets of liberal Protes-

It is not just that I do not agree with the "spin" that Loetscher put on the events and debates he surveyed. It is that he, like so many Church historians, refused to look outside the Church at the broader sweep of political and intellectual affairs in which the Presbyterian Church was operating. It was as if these ecclesiastical events were taking place in an intellectual and cultural vacuum. It was as if the battle to control the Northern Presbyterian Church had not been the representative moral conflict of the era: where modernism challenged traditionalism in a struggle for the hearts, minds, and wallets of men.

Exclusion is the problem with all specialized histories. The historian asks: "Which events should be left out of my version of the story?" The problem of exclusion becomes acute whenever a central institution is perceived by the historian as a peripheral one. The specialist concentrates his attention on internal organizational affairs when external affairs were just as important. When this happens, the historian becomes an antiquarian wielding footnotes.

This surely is what happened to Edwin Rian (d. 1995), who wrote the Calvinists' version of *The Broadening Church*. He wrote *The Presbyterian Conflict* (1940) as an apologetic for a tiny minority group's secession in 1936, not as a discussion of the importance to American life of the pre-secession conflict. His book says: "See all the trouble we were compelled on principle to make!" (Seven years later, he changed his mind.)

Much the same can be said of Loetscher. He wrote his book as an apologetic to show why all the unpleasant theological conflict ended after the secession. His book says: "See all the unnecessary trouble those people made!" I do not think Loetscher came close to understanding how central to American thought, culture, and national politics the Presbyterian Church, U.S.A. was, 1869 to 1936.[4] If he did understand it, his book does not reflect this understanding.

---

tant theology prior to 1930; (2) to identify the liberals' strategy of subversion, 1875 to 1936; (3) to identify the weaknesses of the conservatives who opposed them; (4) to identify scoundrels and saints; (5) to follow the money.

4. It was re-named the United Presbyterian Church in 1958. Since 1983, it has been called PCUSA again.

Hart Attack

This book is also an attack on one aspect of D. G. Hart's 1994 biography of J. Gresham Machen. Dr. Hart's award-winning book is admirable with respect to chronicling the details of Machen's life—almost as good as his 1988 Ph.D. dissertation on the same subject. But it suffers from a fatal defect: it rejects Machen's analysis of the spiritual crisis of the Christian Church in his era. This was a very meaty bone to toss to the editors of Johns Hopkins University Press and their ideological colleagues.

Machen argued that there were two rival religions warring for control in the Protestant churches: Christianity and liberalism. These were not two sides of the same religion; they were two rival religions. Only one of them could win. In *Christianity and Liberalism* (1923), Machen identified theological liberalism as what we today would call the religion of humanism. The liberals, Machen implied (and said in private letters), were wolves in sheep's clothing. They were apostates. By 1936, almost no one believed Machen regarding the irreconcilable nature of the two religions except for the most self-conscious liberals and the nationally known skeptic, H. L. Mencken. Dr. Hart does not believe him, either. In this respect, he has not been alone. Approximately two million members of the Presbyterian Church, U.S.A., also refused to believe, 1923-1936.

Dr. Hart tries to persuade the reader that there was a distinction between cultural modernists (bad guys) and Presbyterian theological modernists (basically, well-meaning guys).

> . . . the use of a common adjective to describe both "modernist" Protestants and "modernist" intellectuals creates confusion. Except for the most radical fringe of Protestant "modernists," mainstream and liberal Protestants only sought adjustments to traditional Christianity. They wanted to preserve historic Protestant certainties and the privileged position of Protestantism in American culture. They thought they could reach this goal with tactical adaptations of the historic faith. Cultural modernism, by contrast, according to David Hollinger, was "resoundingly post-Biblical" and rejected inherited religious authority. Liberal Protestantism's confidence in a benevolent God and its optimism about finding a lasting solution to the problems of modern soci-

ety were "distant" from the intents of modernist writers and intellectuals.[5]

For this string of implausible assertions he offers no evidence. *Crossed Fingers* offers hundreds of pages of evidence that Machen was correct in his assessment of theological modernism, and Dr. Hart is wrong in his. In his own subtle academic way, Dr. Hart, the librarian at Machen's legacy, Westminster Seminary, is telling the hard-pressed heirs of those who lost the Presbyterian conflict that Machen had it wrong. In doing so, he is also telling the victors that their ecclesiastical predecessors had been correct. He is implying that Machen's inclusivist, peace-seeking critics were justified in asking Machen to be more reasonable, more charitable, and to sit down and shut up. He is implying that the liberals who attacked Machen's theology and drove him out of the Church were really not all that bad, and probably were provoked by Machen's exaggerated assessment of their theology and their intentions. After all, to quote Dr. Hart, they were only seeking "adjustments to traditional Christianity." They were only seeking ways "to preserve historic Protestant certainties."

If you believe this, I've got a bridge in Brooklyn to sell you. Or a seminary in Philadelphia.

Presbyterian modernist leaders were not only as morally corrupt as Machen said they were, they were a lot more corrupt than Machen ever said in public. They were thieves, charlatans, and liars who were not only in an alliance with cultural modernists; they were a major part of cultural modernism. They were, in fact, cultural modernism's Levites, ranking just below the Aaronic priests who officiated in the secular temples of higher education. Deception was fundamental to their strategy. Machen identified them as morally corrupt apostates inside the camp of the faithful. This is why he became their most feared and hated enemy after William Jennings Bryan died in 1925. They had to silence him, just as they had to silence Bryan. And they did.

---

5. D. G. Hart, *Defending the Faith: J. Gresham Machen and the Crisis of Conservative Protestantism in Modern America* (Baltimore, Maryland: Johns Hopkins University Press, 1994), p. 7.

Modernism Was a Unified Faith

Politically, American theological modernists were Progressives. Progressivism was itself deeply religious. Richard Hofstadter writes that "Progressivism can be considered . . . as a phase in the history of the Protestant conscience, a latter-day Protestant revival. Liberal politics as well as liberal theology were both inherent in the response of religion to the secularization of society."[6] The reason why the term "modernist" has been applied by historians to religious figures as well as to contemporary political activists and cultural innovators is that theological modernists shared Progressivism's faith. What was this faith? It was faith in Darwinian evolution, historical relativism, progress through science, the benevolent State, and the benefits of getting one's hands on other people's money—through political force, deception, or both. Sharing this faith, modernists inside and outside the Church repeatedly worked together to silence those Christians who challenged their claims of legitimacy, whether ecclesiastical or civil.

I cannot say what most of the liberal Presbyterian pastors believed or what they preached in their pulpits. No historian can. There are insufficient records. What I can do, and have done in this book, is to examine in detail the writings and careers of several representative theological modernists who exercised enormous influence inside and outside of the Presbyterian Church. The main ones were Charles A. Briggs, Henry van Dyke, and Harry Emerson Fosdick. Others who served in secondary roles were Henry Preserved Smith, Philip Schaff, Arthur C. McGiffert, Henry Sloane Coffin, William Adams Brown, and Henry P. Van Dusen. All but van Dyke served as members of Union Theological Seminary's faculty. If these men were not cultural modernists—political Progressives in clerical robes—then modernism was a vapor, a subject fit only for doctoral dissertations in third-rank universities. There was also one other key figure: Presbyterian ruling elder Woodrow Wilson. If he was not a cultural modernist, then modernism was not only a vapor, it has been a figment of the imagination of professors in the best universities.

---

6. Richard Hofstadter, *The Age of Reform: From Bryan to F.D.R.* (New York: Vintage, 1955), p. 152.

The United States prior to World War I was Protestant. To capture the country, modernists had to capture the mainline Protestant churches in the North. This they accomplished no later than 1940. They did it with a strategy of subversion. Modernists outside the Church had agents inside the Church who mouthed pious platitudes and invoked traditional pious phrases to keep the sheep calm and their shepherds confused.

Presbyterian modernism was self-consciously designed to deceive the theologically orthodox. Let me suggest an analogy given to me over three decades ago by the man who brought me to saving faith in Jesus Christ: "When you're a counterfeiter, you don't use triangular orange sheets of paper and then put a picture of Bob Hope in the center." Dr. Hart, like so many other trusting victims, got stuck with a large pile of counterfeit academic bills. I am not saying that he is now deliberately trying to stick his readers with these counterfeits. What I am saying is that he is passing them into circulation with abandon, and he has received lots of applause for his efforts from the spiritual heirs of the original counterfeiters.

From 1876 to 1936, one institution, more than any other, was the primary distribution center for counterfeit bills: Union Theological Seminary of New York. But, as we shall see, the center that actually designed American academic modernism's original phony plates was Johns Hopkins University, which awarded degrees to Wilson (Ph.D.), Machen (B.A.), and Hart (Ph.D.), and which also published Hart's book.

Winners and Losers

If there is one rule above all other rules governing the writing of history, it is this: *the winning side writes the popular history books*. Lefferts Loetscher wrote his book as a winner for the winners. Unlike other book-length scholarly studies of the Presbyterian conflict except Rian's *Presbyterian Conflict* (which he implicitly repudiated in 1947 when he returned to the Presbyterian Church, U.S.A.), my book is written from the point of view of the losers: the Calvinists who defended the Old School Presbyterian position. It is written from a position sympathetic to what became the largest lost cause in American Protestant Church history.

How large a lost cause? At the time of the Presbyterian reunion in 1869, the Old School had 2,381 ministers, 2,740 congregations, and 259,000 members.[7] The new school had 1,848 ministers, 1,631 congregations, and 173,000 members.[8] Each side had five seminaries.[9] In 1936, leaving behind thirteen liberal seminaries, approximately 100 ministers out of some 9,500, and about 4,200 members out of some two million, departed from the denomination to protest the de-frocking of their spokesman, J. Gresham Machen, who died soon thereafter: January 1, 1937. Fewer than ten ministers had their names erased from presbytery rolls or were suspended in 1936, but Machen was the most visible representative. At the end of the first General Assembly of the Orthodox Presbyterian Church[10] in 1936, the denomination had 44 ministers and 22 elders. A year after the original exodus, 14 ministers and three ruling elders left to begin forming a premillennial denomination, the Bible Presbyterian Church.[11] Of those theologians who remained in the Orthodox Presbyterian Church, none maintained the postmillennial eschatology of the Old Princeton. (John Murray did after 1963.) The new Church's leading philosopher, Cornelius Van Til, had never accepted the Old School's apologetic method, i.e., Scottish common-sense realism. By 1937, there was no identifiable institutional trace of Old School Presbyterianism in the North. This, in my judgment, constitutes a lost cause.

---

7. *Minutes of the General Assembly, 1869*, p. 498. Cf. *Presbyterian Re-union Memorial Volume, 1837–1871* (New York: DeWitt C. Lent & Co., 1870), p. 494.

8. *Presbyterian Re-union*, p. 503.

9. *Cyclopaedia of Biblical, Theological, and Ecclesiastical Literature*, edited by John M'Clintock and James Strong, 12 vols. (New York: Harper & Bros., 1894), VIII:535.

10. Called the Presbyterian Church of America until 1939.

11. Letter to the author from Charles Dennison, historian of the OPC: Jan. 12, 1994. The BPC came into existence in 1938. On the BPC's New School links, see George M. Marsden, "Perspective on the Division of 1937," *Pressing Toward the Mark: Essays Commemorating Fifty Years of the Orthodox Presbyterian Church*, edited by Charles G. Dennison and Richard C. Gamble (Philadelphia: Committee for the Historian of the Orthodox Presbyterian Church, 1986), ch. 18. This essay appeared originally as a four-part series in *The Presbyterian Guardian* (Jan.–April 1964). See also Marsden, "The New School Heritage and Presbyterian Fundamentalism," *Pressing*, p. 179.

The reader should know in advance that I do not come as an agent of Old School Presbyterianism. Why not? Because of my commitment to (1) six-day creationism,[12] (2) Calvin's defense of weekly communion,[13] (3) an affirmation of at least the Apostles' Creed or Nicene Creed for communicant membership, and the entire Confession plus proof of tithing as conditions of *voting* Church membership,[14] (4) a sacramental view of the ministry[15] as taught in the long-neglected Larger Catechism but not in Presbyterian tradition,[16] and (5) Van Til's presuppositional apologetics.[17] I regard Old School Presbyterianism as far too lax theologically and institutionally. In 1869, Old School Presbyterianism had been the entrenched right flank of American Protestantism. In 1937, it was gone.

A Question of Sanctions

The events collectively known as the Presbyterian conflict centered around five theological questions: (1) What is the nature of God and His relation to His Church? (2) What is the (representative) voice of God's authority in history? (3) What is the nature of law, e.g., the ecclesiastical judicial function of creeds and confessions? (4) On what legal basis, and in which jurisdiction, should Church discipline be brought against ordained ministers who are regarded as theologically deviant? (5) Which faction will become the dominant one in the Church's future? I have summarized these issues in five words: legitimacy, authority, legality, sanctions, and inheritance.

---

12. Gary North, *Is the World Running Down? Crisis in the Christian Worldview* (Tyler, Texas: Institute for Christian Economics, 1988).

13. John Calvin, *Institutes of the Christian Religion*, IV:XVII:43.

14. Gary North, *Tithing and the Church* (Tyler, Texas: Institute for Christian Economics, 1994), ch. 3.

15. *Ibid.*, chaps. 3, 6.

16. See Introduction, below: section on "Sacrament and Word," pp. 20–24.

17. Gary North, ed., *Foundations of Christian Scholarship: Essays in the Van Til Perspective* (Vallecito, California: Ross House Books, 1976). This apologetic approach argues that all men must argue from religiously held presuppositions, and that these presuppositions cannot be reconciled through so-called neutral reason. Men presuppose the source of truth.

I argue in this book that point four—Church sanctions—was the key institutional factor in the Presbyterian conflict. The other four points were important, but the outcome of the conflict was determined by point four: the imposition of negative sanctions.

Because the theological terminology of the Presbyterian conflict has seemed foreign to religiously pluralistic and secular historians, and even to Christians who have been educated by such historians, I begin with an analogy that will be very understandable to them, as well as to conservatives. I begin with that most hated of all groups in the post-1940 era, the Nazis. Here, not even the most dedicated ethical relativist has any doubts: we are dealing with evil, and we must discover institutional ways to deal with it, i.e., effective negative sanctions. (The best way for a college student to destroy in full public view any liberal college professor who defends ethical relativism is with this question: "Are you saying that there was no objective ethical difference between Adolph Hitler and Franklin Roosevelt?" If he says *no*, he loses the argument; if he says *yes*, he loses his job.)

Your Church, Their Target

What if a well-organized, dedicated group of Nazis has found an entry point to become ordained as ministers in your denomination? A prominent theological seminary that supplies candidates for the ministry has been quietly taken over by Nazis and Nazi sympathizers. What if other seminaries also have hired Nazi professors who hold advanced theological degrees? Should everyone else in the denomination consent quietly? Should you remain silent?

When challenged by critics, the Nazis take the following approach. First, they cry out for theological toleration. Isn't the modern Church broad enough to include men of many opinions? Second, they insist that they believe in the tenets of the Church, but in their own way. When they speak of the Holy Spirit, for example, they really mean the spirit of the *Volk* as it speaks to every man, but especially as it has spoken through great teachers. "It has spoken most eloquently in our era through one enlightened, illuminated man, Adolph Hitler. Two thousand years ago, the same Spirit spoke through Jesus Christ." Third, when anyone challenges their right to interpret the biblical doctrine of the Holy Spirit in this way, the Nazis reply that the Bible is not an infallible book. "It contains mistakes, although it was a meaningful revelation of God in the eras in which its parts were written. But its contradictory ideas should not be used as judicial standards for today." Fourth, if a critic then argues that the Church's Confession does not teach any such view of the Holy Spirit, the Nazis reply that the Confession is not to be applied in such a narrow fashion. "After all, it does not say that the Holy Spirit is not the spirit of the *Volk*, nor does it deny that Adolph Hitler was the Spirit's supreme mouthpiece in the twentieth century." (It was written over three centuries ago.) Fifth, if a pastor tries to take a Nazi minister into any Church court except the one that ordained him in the first place, the Nazi replies that the critic has no lawful jurisdiction over him; after all, his local presbytery ordained him. But, the critic replies, that presbytery is filled with Nazis and Nazi sympathizers. "You had better be able to prove that in a trial in my presbytery," replies the Nazi, smirking.

If a majority of ministers in the denomination also take a similar view of the Bible, toleration, progressive revelation in history, the Church's Confession, and its jurisdictions, even though they are not themselves Nazis, how could you remove that Nazi and his colleagues? What would you do to alert your fellow churchmen to the dangers of Nazi infiltration?

In short, if there are no negative institutional sanctions that can lawfully be imposed in terms of fundamental law, Constitutional law, and organizational by-laws, how can the Church (or any organization) protect itself from a takeover by its mortal enemies? This was the organizational question that confronted Old School Presbyterians from 1874 to 1936.

Strategy: Offensive or Defensive?

What I contend in this book is this: *the best defense is a good offense*. The conservative defenders of the Presbyterian Church from 1900 until 1922 had no institutional offense. They gave offense, but they had none. Calvinists and conservatives had chosen not to fight to the death the ordination of modernists from 1900 until 1922, so by 1922 they had no secure institutional power base when the modernists launched the next stage of their long-term offensive operations. Because the conservatives sought victory through publication and public rallies, they appeared to be the aggressors. A crucial tactic in the modernists' strategy of conquest was to appear as victims of the conservatives. The fact is, the conservatives were last-ditch defenders, the victims of a successful conspiracy. The invaders easily crossed that ditch.

This was not just a Presbyterian problem. Conservative leaders in American Protestantism had only a defensive strategy. The institutional and theological battles of the twentieth century were lost because the vast majority of those who called themselves Bible-believing Christians from 1900 to the mid-1970's were conducting holding actions. They had, at best, a stalemate mentality.[18] They did not believe that they could win the long-term earthly battle against Satan and his forces. In this respect, Machen was an exception, but his mild postmillennialism was not shared by his colleagues even at his own Westminster Seminary. Without a vision of victory, they lost the skirmishes that lasted three generations, 1901–1975. When it came to a battle for institutional control, conservative Christians were up against professionals, men who believed in power above all else. The conservatives could not win by taking a defensive stand, but they did not have an aggressive theology, nor did they know how to organize institutionally. This was not true of the modernists.

Very late in the Presbyterian conflict, a year after the Church-mandated reorganization of Princeton Seminary, Machen wrote an essay, "The Present Situation in the Presbyterian Church." It appeared in *Christianity Today* (May 1930).[19] He made this cryptic one-sentence summary of the crucial years, 1906 to 1920: "After the Cumberland union, the destructive forces labored for a time in the dark." Then he skipped to the Plan of Organic Union in 1920. Presbyterian Church historians also labor in the dark regarding this period.[20] What is needed is a detailed, multi-volume study of the archives of the boards and commissions of every mainline American Protestant denomination to see how the capture of power took place. We need a generation of doctoral dissertations on this topic. We will not get them soon.

---

18. Gary North, *Backward, Christian Soldiers?* 2nd ed. (Tyler, Texas: Institute for Christian Economics, 1988), ch. 11.

19. This was not related to the post-1955 magazine with the same name.

20. See Chapter 6, below.

I want to see many other books written about this diabolically brilliant and temporarily successful strategy, with each book dedicated to a detailed study of how the humanists captured a particular institution, but with every book governed by an integrating presupposition: *a conspiracy was operating in terms of a strategy of subversion*. We need book cases filled with such books. We need to understand that Christian historiography is necessarily *conspiracy history*, for all history is *covenantal history*. History is the manifestation of a war between two covenants. Only one covenant is sovereign: God's. Covenant-breakers conspire against it.

A Conspiracy View of History

Most historians dismiss disdainfully the conspiracy view of history. Most historians of any temporarily successful conspiracy have accepted one task above all others: to deny the legitimacy of any conspiracy view of history, humanistic or biblical.[21] They have devoted their careers to this assignment.

History is the unfolding of a conflict between the covenantal representatives of God and Satan. This conflict is intensely personal. History is not the product of impersonal forces. It is also not the product of great men, great ideas, or great armies. Most of all, it is not the product of random events. There is nothing either random or impersonal about history, which is the unfolding of God's sovereign decree in time. History incorporates ideas, social forces, great men, and not-so-great men. It involves a series of conspiratorial attempts by Satan's followers to overturn God's decree. What conventional historians deny, either implicitly or explicitly, is Psalm 2:

> Why do the heathen rage, and the people imagine a vain thing? The kings of the earth set themselves, and the rulers take counsel together, against the LORD, and against his anointed, saying, Let us break their bands asunder, and cast away their cords from us. He that sitteth in the heavens shall laugh: the Lord shall have them in derision. Then shall he speak unto them in his

---

21. Gary North, *Conspiracy: A Biblical View* (Westchester, Illinois: Crossway, 1986), ch. 6.

wrath, and vex them in his sore displeasure. Yet have I set my king upon my holy hill of Zion. I will declare the decree: the LORD hath said unto me, Thou art my Son; this day have I begotten thee. Ask of me, and I shall give thee the heathen for thine inheritance, and the uttermost parts of the earth for thy possession. Thou shalt break them with a rod of iron; thou shalt dash them in pieces like a potter's vessel. Be wise now therefore, O ye kings: be instructed, ye judges of the earth. Serve the LORD with fear, and rejoice with trembling. Kiss the Son, lest he be angry, and ye perish from the way, when his wrath is kindled but a little. Blessed are all they that put their trust in him.

On the surface, and for a time, some of these conspiracies appear successful. Herbert Schlossberg is correct: "The Bible can be interpreted as a string of God's triumphs disguised as disasters."[22] The cross of Jesus Christ is the obvious example. But conspiracies cannot remain successful. They are overturned in history. God overturns them by mobilizing His people.[23]

The Need for Institutional Historiography

In a 1976 article on William H. Roberts, who served as Stated Clerk of the General Assembly of the Presbyterian Church from 1884 until 1920, Bruce David Forbes made this observation: "To the author's knowledge, there exists no detailed, critical examination of the great changes in structure and function of the Presbyterian Church in the U.S.A. during this turn of the century period."[24] Yet institutional history is neglected by the historian at the peril of historical truth. As in modern warfare, battles for ecclesiastical control

---

22. Herbert Schlossberg, *Idols for Destruction: Christian Faith and Its Confrontation with American Society* (Westchester, Illinois: Crossway, [1983] 1993), p. 304.

23. The most obvious example in the twentieth century is the collapse of Communism in Europe, 1989-1991. From apparently total power to the pathetic *coup* of August 19-21, 1991, Communism collapsed in a drunken stupor. Today, Communism survives only in culturally bleak outposts: North Korea, Cuba, and the English departments of major American universities.

24. Bruce David Forbes, "William H. Roberts: Resistance and Bureaucratic Adaptation," *Journal of Presbyterian History*, 54 (Winter 1976), p. 413.

are fought and won mainly in the trenches of Church boards and committees, not overhead in the skies. The infantry captures and holds territory, not the air force. This is especially true in Presbyterianism, where national boards and committees count for more than they do in independent churches.

Institutional histories rarely focus on great moral or ideological confrontations, great battles fought, or great anything except boredom. Reading the minutes of ancient meetings, reports of forgotten conferences, and fading personal letters in poorly catalogued manuscript collections in major libraries is not most people's idea of a life well spent. Yet it is in such forgotten and long-neglected records that the historian finds the means of putting the flesh of institutional life back onto the bones of ideology and rhetoric. Pamphlets alone do not a revolution make. The quip of President Nixon's Attorney General John Mitchell is worth repeating: "Watch what we do, not what we say."[25] The higher the institutional stakes, the more important it is for someone to do the watching, at the time especially, but also in retrospect. This detailed archival research has not been done by those who have written about the Presbyterian conflict, including me. The best I can do here is to sketch a few areas of interest that may prove fruitful for future researchers.

We need multiple institutional histories of the Presbyterian Church written to throw light on the great conflict that beset it. But this is rarely the way institutional histories are written. They are usually written by the winners and their spiritual heirs, who have an incentive not to emphasize the existence of conflict, especially if the winners employed nefarious tactics. They are written to be boring, and they usually succeed. "Nothing crucial was going on here! I'll prove it." The losers do not get access to the files, and the losers' heirs are rarely interested. If the losers have failed to multiply and build up their own organization, the division of labor works against them: too few well-trained historians and too few potential book buyers.

---

25. He was only partially correct. The Watergate Committee listened to what they all said on the secret White House tapes, and Mitchell went to jail for what he did.

The capture of the Presbyterian Church—and, I suspect, all of the others—was made far easier for the liberals because nobody in the conservative camp was carefully monitoring the activities of the boards of the Church. I am not exaggerating: nobody. There were no published warnings until after World War I—two decades after the takeover had begun—and even then only with regard to foreign missions. No historian has made a detailed study of even one of the Presbyterian boards, 1890 to 1930, and I am aware of no representative example from any of the other Protestant denominations.

A series of detailed studies of the Presbyterian boards, especially the Board of Foreign Missions, should be written by a dozen enterprising Ph.D. candidates. This would require years in the archives and private collections of letters, as well as the annual reports of the boards (included in the second volume of the *Minutes of the General Assembly*). We need such projects done in the seven main Protestant denominations. Questions that need answers are these: (1) Where did the boards recruit most of their ministers and workers? (2) What screening process was used to sort through the candidates? (3) How many of those who got hired were ever fired, and for what reasons? (4) What percentage of the money sent to the boards got to the people in the field? (5) What was the theological perspective of the boards and committees, where such records exist? (6) What was the theological content of official pronouncements by the boards and commissions? (7) How closely did board members work with board members of comparable boards in other denominations? But life is short, funds are limited, and interest is nil. These dissertations will not be written. So, we must content ourselves with incomplete outlines of partial records that only hint at what went on behind closed doors.

Then there is the issue of personal financial considerations. No historian I have read has ever asked this question, let alone attempted to answer it: "What effects, if any, did the 1927 revision of the Church's retirement system have on the institutional loyalty of ministers, 1928-1936?" I decided that it was time for at least one historian to consider the relevance of the question. I found it very relevant.

There was more to this Presbyterian conflict than the traditional Presbyterian practice of writing pamphlets. But historians find it easier to summarize pamphlets and books than to follow the money. For most Church historians, including me, pamphlets and books are easier to read than yellowing accounting reports. Church histories reflect this preference. Were I a full-time historian, I would have done more digging around in dusty filing cabinets in Philadelphia's Witherspoon Building. But I have at least sniffed around some long-ignored areas.

The Minutes of the General Assembly

The annual General Assemblies were open forums. You might think that it would be possible to trace in the *Minutes of the General Assembly* the history of the great battle for control over the Presbyterian Church: great speeches, crucial votes, parliamentary maneuvering. This is not the case, however. Delwyn Nykamp's 1974 doctoral dissertation, which remains by far the most detailed study of the 1922-26 phase of the struggle, has warned the prospective researcher: "To the despair of the critic, however, official records contain little actual discourse and few clues to permit reconstruction of the events."[26] The *Minutes of the General Assembly* after 1900 reveal mainly what the various boards, committees, and commissions wanted revealed. The *Minutes* are sufficient only to indicate the general direction of the process of administrative centralization.

In one paragraph, let us briefly survey the growth of bureaucracy in the Church through the lens of a surrogate indicator: the growth of the *Minutes*. In 1789, the *Minutes* filled 16 pages, nine pages of which were actual minutes. A full decade of *Minutes* of the Old School denomination, 1848 to 1858, filled 586 pages. Statistical columns and boxes averaged six pages per year. All of 1865 to 1869 filled 535 pages. From 1870 to 1871, after the reunion, they filled 946 pages. In 1900, they filled 817 pages, but much of this material was statistical. In 1906, it was a 916-page volume. In 1907, the year after the arrival of 1,100 Cumberland Presbyterian congregations, the *Minutes*, including committee reports (Sections II-V, pp. 261-439) and statistics (Section VI, pp. 450-937), filled 1,077 pages, and the reports of the Boards filled a second volume: 1,432 pages. From that time on, the *Minutes* were a

---

26. Delwyn G. Nykamp, A Presbyterian Power Struggle: A Critical History of Communication Strategies in the Struggle for Control of the Presbyterian Church, U.S.A., 1922-1926 (Ph.D. dissertation, Northwestern University, 1974), pp. 12-13.

two-volume affair. Volume 1 contained reports from the Assembly's commissions and standing committees, which filled most of the 250 to 300 pages devoted to actual decisions. Information on debates in the General Assembly disappeared except as brief, fragmentary entries related to actions in response to committee reports. The rest of the first volume was filled with 500 or more pages of boxes of small-print statistical data from presbyteries, synods, and other Church entities. This section is a lasting testimony to W. H. Roberts, the Stated Clerk (senior permanent bureaucrat), who had been trained as a government statistician: highly detailed, no typographical errors, and utterly useless. We never find so much as a footnote in *The Journal of Presbyterian History* or *American Presbyterians* that refers to the statistical sections of the *Minutes*.[27]

From Christendom to Humanist Civilization

The Presbyterian conflict was part of a much larger process, which I call covenantal: a conflict between the kingdom of God and the kingdom of man. The Presbyterian conflict was an important American manifestation of a two-stage shift in the judicial worldview of the West. The first stage was the shift from covenant to contract (1690 to 1890). The second stage was the shift from contract to coercion (1890 to the present).

Calvinistic covenantalism had emphasized the presence of God as a sanctioning agent in the four supreme contracts in life: God and man; man and the Church; man and wife; and man as a citizen. The most profound defender of covenantal political theory was Johannes

---

27. Here is my suggestion to scholars who use the *Minutes of the General Assembly*. The Committee on Bills and Overtures was usually the most important committee at each General Assembly. Begin with the section on the overtures from the presbyteries. The early overtures reveal which issues were likely to be the most important at that year's GA. Then turn to the index to see to which committee an overture was assigned by the Committee on Bills and Overtures. Turn to the pages listed in the index to find out what the particular committee did in response to any overture. This is a bureaucrat's approach to historical research, but bureaucrats structured the *Minutes* to achieve their goals, not yours. One of their goals—in my view, the supreme goal—was concealment. In this sense, the *Minutes of the General Assembly* are like the *Congressional Record*.

Althusius (c. 1600), today an almost forgotten figure.[28] He was the great intellectual rival of Hugo Grotius, the Arminian natural law theorist, who receives at least a cursory discussion in most European history textbooks. The English Puritans and the Scottish Presbyterians sought a covenantal political theory, but the demise in 1559 of Cromwell's premature revolution ended this quest. The Presbyterians were then marginalized in Anglo-American culture for two generations, and by the time they emerged as a powerful cultural influence in North America after 1740, they had adopted the legitimacy of contractualism, humanism's alternative to covenantalism.

Contractualism removed God and biblically revealed law from the civil realm. There were two main versions of contractualism: Whiggism, represented by Locke's *Second Treatise on Government* (1690) and its economic legacy, Adam Smith's *Wealth of Nations* (1776); and Continental contractualism, beginning with Rousseau's *Social Contract* (1762). By 1790, civil contractualism was judicially operational at the national level in the United States, France, and England.

The second stage of the shift was from Whiggism to Social Democracy—in the United States, Progressivism. In political theory, this was marked by the replacement of philosophical individualism with some version of class theory, usually accompanied by an economic interpretation of history. In economic theory, this was marked by the supplementation or even replacement of voluntary contracts by state regulation. This shift in outlook took place within a single generation among the West's educated elite: from about 1890 to 1920. By 1936, the culmination year of the Presbyterian conflict, this political worldview was accepted by almost everyone. Evidence from that year includes fascism in Italy, national socialism in Germany, the first Presidential ratification year of Franklin Roosevelt's New Deal (a landslide), and the publication of John Maynard Keynes' *General Theory of Employment, Interest, and Money*—especially the now-forgotten

---

28. Johannes Althusius, *Politica*, trans. Frederick S. Carney (Indianapolis, Indiana: Liberty Fund, [1964] 1995). This is an abridged version of his *Politica methodice digesta* (1614). The translator also wrote a Ph.D. dissertation, The Associational Theory of Johannes Althusius: A Study in Calvinist Constitutionalism (University of Chicago, 1960).

German edition, with its introduction complimenting the total planning state.[29] Those who disagreed were relegated to the fringes of acceptable political discourse,[30] or in Germany and Italy, eliminated.

The transition from Christendom to humanist civilization can be understood in many ways, among which are these:

> From cosmic personalism to cosmic impersonalism
>
> From cosmic impersonalism to humanistic sovereignty
>
> From biblical revelation to epistemological neutrality
>
> From eternal sanctions to historical sanctions
>
> From covenant theology (1560 to 1659) to contractualism (1660 to 1890)
>
> From Newtonian political theory (1690 to 1776) to historicism (Rousseau to the present)
>
> From mechanism to organicism
>
> From predictability to process
>
> From absolutes to relativism
>
> From the discovery of truth to the search for truth
>
> From substantive justice to procedural justice
>
> From law to methodology

---

29. Keynes wrote: "The theory of aggregate production, which is the point of the following book, nevertheless can be much easier adapted to the conditions of a totalitarian state than the theory of production and distribution of a given production put forth under the conditions of free competition and a large degree of laissez-faire. This is one of the reasons that justifies the fact that I call my book a *general* theory." A side-by-side translation of the Preface in the original German edition is found in James J. Martin, *Revisionist Viewpoints* (Colorado Springs: Ralph Myles Press, 1971), pp. 203, 205. A modified version of the citation appears in *The Collected Writings of John Maynard Keynes* (New York: St. Martin's, 1973), VII, p. xxvi. It does not include his final sentence.

30. Justin Raimondo, *Reclaiming the American Right: The Lost Legacy of the Conservative Movement* (Burlingame, California: Center for Libertarian Studies, 1993), chaps. 1–6.

From creationism to Darwinism

From free market social Darwinism to reform social Darwinism

From status to contract (nineteenth century)[31]

From contract to status (twentieth century)[32]

From decentralization to centralization

From business partnership to corporation

From Whig political economy to Progressivism

From excise taxes to income taxes

From the gold standard to the Federal Reserve System

From open entry to government regulation

From price competition to professional licensing

From apprenticeship to certification by exams

From academic scholasticism to specialization (seminary to seminar; M.A. to Ph.D.)

From political spoils to Civil Service

From voluntarism to conscription

From morality to efficiency

This civilization-wide transformation can be represented by one phrase that encapsulates the incomparable mundanity of the move from the kingdom of God in history to the contemporary kingdom of man:

---

31. Henry Sumner Maine, *Ancient Law* (New York: Dorset, [1861] 1986), p. 141.

32. The reversal of the process described by Maine. The difference is that family connection undergirded ancient status; today, formal certification does. The West has moved from familism to the free market to bureaucracy.

From the Ten Commandments to *Robert's Rules of Order*

Conclusion

Machen's role in the battle, 1922–1936, was representative of numerous struggles between humanists and Christians for the control of the mainline denominations. The same slogans and tactics occurred again and again in different denominations and ecclesiastical groups. My hope is that this book will provide a case study of national and even international trends—theological, ecclesiastical, and educational. Let us learn from Machen's loss: we cannot win with a defensive strategy. Also, we cannot beat something with nothing.

Please keep this slogan in the back of your mind as you read this book: **toleration during wartime = surrender to the enemy**. Keep this in mind, too: **There is no substitute for victory**. If you find it difficult to apply these slogans to the institutional Church, apply them to World War II. Do they seem reasonable in that context? Then ask yourself: If German Protestant churches had not ordained theological liberals in the eighteenth and nineteenth centuries, would there have been a Hitler? Would there have been World War II? Germany lost World War II in its universities and churches long before Adolph Hitler arrived on the scene. A nation that still believed in the God of Martin Luther would not have surrendered to a master of confrontational rhetoric who required this verbal confession: "Heil [salvation] Hitler!"[33] Theological ideas have consequences.

---

33. Thomas Schirrmacher, "National Socialism and the Future of Germany," *Symbiotica*, 1 (Spring 1991), pp. 23–29. This is the journal of the Institute for Christian Economics—Europe.

"ROTTEN WOOD"

Dr. Warfield's funeral took place yesterday afternoon at the First Church of Princeton. . . . It seemed to me that the old Princeton—a great institution it was—died when Dr. Warfield was carried out.

I am thankful for one last conversation I had with Dr. Warfield some weeks ago. He was quite himself that afternoon. And somehow I cannot believe that the faith which he represented will ever really die. In the course of the conversation I expressed my hope that to end the present intolerable condition there might be a great split in the Church, in order to separate the Christians from the anti-Christian propagandists. "No," he said, "you can't split rotten wood." His expectation seemed to be that the organized Church, dominated by naturalism, would become so cold and dead, that people would come to see that spiritual life could be found only outside of it, and that thus there might be a new beginning.

Nearly everything that I have done I have done with the inspiring hope that Dr. Warfield would think well of it.

J. Gresham Machen (1921)[*]

---

[*] Letter to his mother (Feb. 19, 1921); cited in Ned B. Stonehouse, *J. Gresham Machen: A Biographical Memoir* (Philadelphia: Westminster Theological Seminary, [1954] 1977), p. 310.

INTRODUCTION

I take a grave view of the present state of the Church; I think that those who cry, "'Peace, peace,' when there is no peace," constitute the greatest menace to the people of God. I am in little agreement with those who say, for example, that the Presbyterian Church, to which I belong, is "fundamentally sound." For my part, I have two convictions regarding the Presbyterian Church. I hold (1) that it is not fundamentally sound but fundamentally unsound; and I hold (2) that the Holy Spirit is able to make it sound. And I think we ought, very humbly, to ask Him to do that. Nothing kills true prayer like a shallow optimism. Those who form the consistently Christian remnant in the Presbyterian Church and in other churches, instead of taking refuge in a cowardly anti-intellectualism, instead of decrying controversy, ought to be on their knees asking God to bring the visible Church back from her wanderings to her true Lord.

J. Gresham Machen (1932)[1]

J. Gresham Machen was involved in a great theological and institutional struggle, 1922–1936, as surely as Patrick Henry was about to become involved in a life-and-death military struggle in 1775 when he uttered these same words, "Peace, peace, when there is no peace," taken from Jeremiah 6:4. In neither conflict could there be any near-term peace. It both cases, it was a struggle for the conscience of the nation. In Machen's day, the United States was still perceived as Protestant, although this was being challenged by humanism in almost every area. In the 1920's and 1930's, the Presbyterian conflict frequently became front-page news, even in the normally sedate *New York Times*. Each May, when the General Assembly met, the press was there to cover the story, for a decade and a half. After Machen's ejection in 1936, however, what the General Assembly did was regarded as front-page news only once over the next decade, on June 1,

---

1. Machen, "Christianity in Conflict," in *Contemporary American Theology*, edited by Vergilius Ferm (New York: Round Table Press, 1932), I:272–73.

1937: "Nazis Denounced by Presbyterians." The media ceased to care what Presbyterians did.[2]

The Presbyterian Conflict

The Presbyterian conflict is generally dated from 1922 to 1936, but I do not follow this tradition. The timeline on the inside front and back covers presents my chronological account of the Presbyterian conflict. As the bold facing indicates, I think there is an underlying pattern to this chronology: five phases. These correspond to five clusters of covenantal disputes that divided Presbyterianism from almost from its beginning until 1936. Nevertheless, the book's chronological narrative is divided into two main sections, with 1900 as the dividing year: 1869 to 1900 and 1901 to 1936. In 1900, liberal theologian A. C. McGiffert left the denomination to escape a heresy trial. This was a major turning point in the history of the Presbyterian conflict.

The Church prior to the reunion of 1869 went through the first phase of the conflict: the battle over legitimacy. The reunion launched phase two: the battle over authority. This was the first phase of the liberals' conflict; it was phase two of the Presbyterian conflict. The year 1900 marks the end of phase one of the liberals' battle. It took

---

2. In June, 1994, the press was once again in attendance. A controversy had arisen over the November, 1993, "RE-imagining 1993" conference, sponsored by the World Council of Churches. At that conference, ecumenical feminist ministers (including a few witches) and laywomen called upon a female divinity, Sophia, during a pagan communion meal. This was media-worthy. See "Feminist Crusade Sparks Holy War," *Insight* (July 25, 1994). The Presbyterian News Service released a summary of the meeting (Presbynet, Dec. 23, 1993). The denomination paid $66,000 to help fund this $390,000 conference. Over 400 women from the PCUSA attended, including 22 leaders. Of the almost 2,200 in attendance (83 were men), Presbyterians constituted the largest group from any denomination. Presbyterian laymen briefly awakened from their traditional slumber to protest at the 1994 General Assembly. But the protest fizzled: the vote was 516 to 4 in favor of reconciliation. After the vote, delegates cheered, hugged, and wept. In protest, many congregations had withheld funds totalling $2.4 million; these funds were expected to be released. The Church's official statement upheld the Church's Reformed tradition, but it also affirmed the right to explore theological options. It supported those who had attended the conference. *National & International Religion Report* (June 27, 1994), p. 1.

two successive generations for the liberals to replace the conservatives: 1869 to 1900; 1901 to 1936.

The conservatives in the first period were comprised of two groups: Old School and New School Calvinists. The New School was increasingly dominant from 1869 to 1900. The transition from conservatism—increasingly an alliance between the Old School and evangelicalism-fundamentalism—to liberal dominance took until 1936. To grasp this transformation, a two-part division is necessary but not sufficient. There were three factions, not two—something that Machen emphasized before 1915 and in the final weeks of his life, but not in between. To delineate the silent majority's shift from support for conservatism to support for liberalism, 1901 to 1936, I have overlaid the two-part general division with four of the five subdivisions.

The Presbyterian conflict had five phases. The last two phases are those that generally are designated by historians as "the Presbyterian conflict." To narrow the definition in this way is to miss most of the story of that conflict: about three-fifths of it.

The Presbyterian conflict lasted from 1721 (the beginning of the two-century debate over strict vs. loose subscription to the Confession)[3] to November, 1936 (Machen's removal from the Independent Board for Presbyterian Foreign Missions). It began with the split between what soon became "Old" Presbyterians—Old Side and Old School—vs. "New" Presbyterians. The Old Presbyterians were creedalists; the New Presbyterians were experientialists. The split began in 1721 with the decision of the newly formed Presbyterian synod of three presbyteries to punish a minister's admitted fornication: a mere four-week suspension from the pulpit.[4] It ended with the deciding vote against Machen as president of the Independent Board being cast by an heir to the New School, his former friend and former presbyterial defense attorney, who had recently been caught in a sexual scandal

---

3. Jonathan Dickenson, *A Sermon Preached at the Opening of the Synod at Philadelphia* (1722); extracts in *The Presbyterian Enterprise: Sources of American Presbyterian History*, edited by Maurice W. Armstrong, Lefferts A. Loetscher, and Charles A. Anderson (Philadelphia: Westminster Press, 1956), pp. 26–27.

4. Leonard Trinterud, *The Forming of an American Tradition: A Re-examination of COLONIAL PRESBYTERIANISM* (Salem, New Hampshire: Ayer, [1949] 1978), p. 38.

and not disciplined for it.[5] His vote ended both the Old School and New School as identifiable movements.

The debate over subscription had begun in Scotland in the 1690's and was still going on in the 1720's.[6] In the new American Church, "loose subscriptionists" opposed any tightening of synodical authority, especially over the creedal requirements for ordination.[7] The strict subscriptionist party was led by the fornicator, John Cross, whose scruples regarding subscription were much more rigorous than they were in that other crucial area of applied theology. This party became the anti-revivalist "Old Side" in the 1730's.[8] The same debate over subscription is still going on in the Presbyterian Church in America. If there is one irreconcilable conflict in Presbyterianism—and not just in Presbyterianism—it is this one. "What is the judicial function of a confession of faith?" is still a burning ecclesiastical question.

The Five Phases

The conflict's initial stage, 1721 to 1868, had to do with legitimacy, which in turn was a debate over earthly institutional sovereignty. The debate was over these two crucial issues: (1) What are the marks of saving faith? (2) How does the Church extend the kingdom of God in history? These questions can be summarized by one question: *What are the marks of ecclesiastical sovereignty?* It was a debate over legitimacy, and the Presbyterian Church split twice over this question, in 1741 and 1837. Each side claimed: "I'm OK; you're not equally OK."

The second phase of the conflict, 1869 to 1900, was a debate over Church hierarchy and lawful authority. Institutionally, it was a debate over the limits of Church courts' authority over ministers. Ultimately, however, it was a debate over the earthly source of authority: the Bible. *Is the Bible the infallible and authoritative word of God?* If it

---

5. Charles G. Dennison, "Tragedy, Hope and Ambivalence: The History of the Orthodox Presbyterian Church, 1936-1962, Part 1," *Mid-America Journal of Theology*, 8 (Fall 1992), pp. 155-56.

6. Trinterud, *American Tradition*, pp. 39-42.

7. *Ibid.*, p. 43.

8. *Ibid.*, p. 63.

is not, then the constitutional documents of Presbyterianism—the Westminster Confession of Faith and its two catechisms—must be revised, for they identify the Bible as God's absolutely authoritative word. The debate over Confessional revision began in 1889 during a debate over biblical authority. The same man initiated both debates: Charles A. Briggs. He began the debate over the Bible in 1876; he began the debate over the authority of the Confession in 1885.

The third phase of the conflict, 1901 to 1921, was over judicial standards. It was this question: *What constitutes the Constitution of the Presbyterian Church?* It involved these questions: Should the Confession of Faith be revised? How extensive should this revision be? How broadly should its categories be interpreted? Finally, what kind of judicial structure should enforce these laws? This was the era of governmental consolidation in the Presbyterian Church.

The fourth phase of the conflict, 1922 to 1933, was over sanctions. It began in January of 1922. It began outside the Presbyterian Church: in the Kentucky legislature and the pages of the *New York Times*. It spread into the Church within three months. The question in this phase of the conflict was this: *Who has the votes to impose which sanctions?* What was initially a debate over State sanctions spread to the Church. It was in the middle of this struggle that the liberals visibly captured the General Assembly: 1926. The General Assembly re-defined Church sanctions in 1927, turning the denomination into functional Congregationalism.

The fifth and final phase of the conflict, 1934 to 1936, was a debate over inheritance: *Which organized group would retain control over the assets of the Presbyterian Church?* The battle had broken out over the question of liberalism in the foreign mission field, where it had also broken out in 1921. The moderates and liberals contained the outbreak in 1921 by a minor restructuring of the Church's appeals court system for foreign missionaries. In the final phase, they contained it by a major restructuring of Church law from Congregationalism to a hybrid system: centralized administrative Presbyterianism. This restructuring had been proposed in 1931, the year before the outbreak over foreign missions. Even before this restructuring was judicially sanctioned by the presbyteries in 1934, the liberals began the final imposition of negative sanctions. They claimed the inheritance. They collected.

A conflict always involves all five issues: legitimacy, authority-hierarchy, standards, sanctions, and inheritance-disinheritance. There will be winners and losers. *A conflict becomes visible when each side seeks to impose sanctions on the other.* While the focus of the battle shifts from one phase to the next, the battle is enjoined when the sides seek to impose sanctions. The conflict continues until one minority faction or the other persuades the less committed majority to accept the removal of the rival faction's public representatives. The removal of these representatives silences the majority. The majority prefers to remain silent prior to the visible outcome of the rival systems of sanctions: ". . . and the people answered him [Elijah] not a word" (I Kings 18:21b). Only in the final phase of a conflict does the majority speak out and impose corporate sanctions (I Kings 18:40). This is why I argue throughout this book that the crucial issue in the Presbyterian conflict was sanctions. The presence of the sanctions is what made it a conflict.

A National Spokesman

One of the ironies of the final two phases of the Presbyterian conflict was Machen's position as an ecumenical leader. He was not only the academic spokesman for Calvinistic Presbyterianism; he was also the unofficial intellectual spokesman for American fundamentalism in general, a position that he knew was confusing to many. He was not a fundamentalist, as he said repeatedly,[9] but rather an Old School Calvinist. He did not believe in man's free will, nor did he believe in premillennialism, two common marks of Protestant fundamentalism. But by default, he won the fundamentalists' mantle of authority. The fundamentalists had no figure of comparable influence nationally who could match wits and rhetoric with the representatives of theological and political liberalism. William Jennings Bryan was a Presbyterian ruling elder, but he was no theologian. Billy Sunday, the ex-baseball player and flamboyant revivalist, was a Presbyterian minister (teaching elder), but he was not regarded as a theological spokes-

---

9. Ned B. Stonehouse, *J. Gresham Machen: A Biographical Memoir* (Philadelphia: Westminster Theological Seminary, [1954] 1977), pp. 337–38.

man. In any case, Sunday's influence faded after 1917; he died in 1935. Bryan died in 1925.

For as long as fundamentalists were willing to fight modernism publicly, they relied on Machen to defend a common position. Machen understood his unique role. In 1926, he acknowledged his position as an ecumenical spokesman: "But in the presence of a great common foe, I have little time to be attacking my brethren who stand with me in defense of the Word of God."[10] His leadership ended only with his death on New Year's Day in 1937.

When Machen's voice was silenced—institutionally in June of 1936, and physically by his death seven months later—the conscience of both Northern Presbyterianism and fundamentalism was silenced. Carl Henry in 1947 wrote *The Uneasy Conscience of Modern Fundamentalism.* The title was evidence of a malaise. No one took Machen's place as a representative national figure who personally transcended the warring factions of conservative Protestantism until the final days of Billy Graham's three-week tent crusade in Los Angeles in 1949. At that point, William Randolph Hearst, the anti-Communist newspaper magnate and world-famous adulterer,[11] sent a memo to his reporters: "Puff Graham."[12] They did, and Graham became a celebrity overnight. He later became the best-known representative of a new ecumenism: neo-evangelicalism.[13] But unlike the fundamentalist ecumenism of Machen's day, Graham's was more broadly based. Unlike Machen, Graham's cooperation with the National Council of Churches, beginning with his New York City crusade in 1958, brought forth harsh criticism from fundamentalists.[14] Had fundamen-

---

10. Cited in *ibid.*, p. 338.

11. His consort was actress Marion Davies. This affair was made famous by Orson Welles' 1941 film, *Citizen Kane.* See W. A. Swanberg, *Citizen Hearst* (New York: Charles Scribner's Sons, 1961).

12. Marshall Frady, *Billy Graham: A Parable of American Righteousness* (Boston: Little, Brown, 1979), p. 201.

13. Historian George Marsden writes of neo-evangelicalism: "Close connections with Billy Graham gave this new leadership national impact and attention. For the two decades after 1950, the most prominent parts of this more narrowly self-conscious evangelicalism focused around Graham." Marsden, "The Evangelical Denomination," in Marsden, ed., *Evangelicalism and Modern America* (Grand Rapids, Michigan: Eerdmans, 1984), p. xiii.

14. William E. Ashbrook, *Evangelicalism: The New Neutralism*, 9th ed. (Men-

talists known in 1958 that John D. Rockefeller, Jr., had donated $75,000 to help fund that New York crusade,[15] more of them might have protested earlier.

A subculture without even one articulate, well-known spokesman has no national status; it is a ghetto phenomenon. This is what conservative American Protestantism became in 1937. Once the United States was visibly no longer seriously Christian, all the other contenders for moral authority began to rush in to fill the void, but the Presbyterian Church, U.S.A., having seen its day pass, was no longer a major contender. What its leaders and bureaucrats had done to Machen in full public view had identified the Presbyterian Church, U.S.A., as just another power-seeking, power-wielding special-interest group, and one without any legitimate claim to represent a higher authority. H. L. Mencken said as much in his laudatory obituary of Machen.[16]

Strict vs. Loose Subscription

This book is the story of a victory and a defeat. The victory went to men whose theological opinions were at odds with the creedal position set forth by the Westminster Confession of Faith and its Larger and Shorter Catechisms: the Presbyterian Church's official statements of faith.[17] These documents had been hammered out by English Puritans and Scottish Presbyterians in the midst of a national revolution. The Confession's public defeat in 1936 came to those few people in mainline Northern Presbyterianism who still believed in that historic Confessional position.

Yet this summary is too simplistic. The battle was not merely a dispute over personal belief; it was also a matter of verbal profession

---

tor, Ohio: Author, [1958] n.d.), pp. 10–17. *Billy Graham: Performer? Politician? Preacher? Prophet? A Chronological Record Compiled from Public Sources* (Wheaton, Illinois: Church League of America, 1982).

15. Peter Collier and David Horowitz, *The Rockefellers: An American Dynasty* (New York: Holt, Rinehart and Winston, 1976), p. 150n.

16. See Appendix A: "H. L. Mencken's Obituary of Machen: Dr. Fundamentalis."

17. A creed is one of the ancient statements of the Christian faith: Apostles', Nicene, Chalcedonian, etc. A confession is a later, more detailed summary of the Christian faith.

of faith. It was ultimately a matter of *judicial sanctions*. In 1901, the leaders on all three sides of the Presbyterian conflict had verbally and publicly professed faith in that historic Confessional position, despite the fact that none of them fully believed it. Having sworn a public oath to defend a standard they did not fully believe, the officers of the Presbyterian Church, U.S.A., had little incentive to use the denomination's courts to impose the oath's mandatory negative sanctions. *But without negative sanctions there can be no organization.* So, negative sanctions would eventually be imposed. These sanctions would be imposed in terms of a standard other than the Westminster Confession of Faith and its two catechisms. The institutional question became: *By what other standard?* The quest for this rival standard was the fundamental theme of the final three phases of the Presbyterian conflict, 1901–1936.

The problem of negative sanctions had been festering in Presbyterianism ever since the Westminster Assembly (1643–48). The Assembly had not produced the definitive ecclesiastical document that Parliament had expected and had asked for. The House of Commons in 1643 was divided between ecclesiastical independents and self-identified Presbyterians who had never been inside a Presbyterian Church. In addition, probably a majority of members of the House of Commons wanted Parliament to replace the King as head of the English Church or share his ecclesiastical sovereignty: the Erastians. Initially, the Assembly reflected these Parliamentary divisions, and by the time the Assembly's vocal malcontents left in 1645, their spiritual associates in Oliver Cromwell's New Model Army had become a growing political force in England.

From the beginning, the Assembly found that it had to compromise drastically on ecclesiology if it was to get Parliament to accept its recommendations, a political goal which it never did achieve. In that fruitless ecclesiastical compromise, the Assembly bequeathed a legacy of confusion to Anglo-Scottish-American Presbyterianism that is still not resolved in those secessionist Presbyterian Churches that take seriously at least some of the Assembly's documents.[18] The matter was resolved judicially in the Northern Presbyterian Church in 1936 when

---

18. See Appendix C: "The Strange Legacy of the Westminster Assembly."

the theological heirs of the Westminster Assembly were driven out by theological liberals who had individually sworn formal allegiance to the Westminster Confession of Faith, but who had mentally crossed their fingers when they made their confession.

Protecting the Vulnerable

The age-old debate between a strict interpretation of a standard and a loose interpretation was a big part of the Presbyterian conflict. To understand what was involved, consider a speed limit sign. It says "35" (either miles per hour or kilometers per hour). What if a man drives 36? Will he be ticketed by a policeman? Probably not. The policeman has limited amounts of time to pursue speeders. He has to chase the speeder, ticket him, and perhaps appear in court to defend his actions. In a world of limited resources, a person who speeds by driving 36 in a 35 zone is probably going to get away with it. If there are lots of serious speeders on the road, he *should* get away with it; the safety of the public is dependent on stopping the activities of those other, life-threatening speeders. Only if the community is willing to hire many, many policemen and judges can it afford to ticket speeders who drive 36.

Now consider someone who drives 55 in a "25" speed zone for young school-age children. Will a policeman pursue him? Without question. The speeder is putting children at risk. That speeder is a serious lawbreaker. To refuse to pursue him, a policeman would be abandoning the very essence of law enforcement. His own job would probably be at risk for malfeasance. A city that will not bring employment sanctions against a traffic policeman who steadfastly refuses to pursue such speeders is saying, in effect: "Our posted signs mean nothing. Drive as fast as you want, day or night." In other words, "Young children had better look out for themselves; we will not do it for them."

Strict subscription, like speed limits, is designed to protect the vulnerable person who is under the protection of the law. As surely as a seven-year-old child walking to school is protected by a speed limit sign *and a court system prepared to enforce it*, so is a resident in a country protected by the strict interpretation of a written civil constitution *and a court system prepared to enforce it*, and so is a Church member protected by strict subscription to a confession of faith *and a court system prepared to enforce it.*

Two conclusions follow: (1) law without sanctions protects no one; (2) law interpreted by loose construction protects no one predictably. This is as true in ecclesiastical matters as it is in highway safety matters.

The child is under the protection of the law, the posted limit, the police, and the court, even though he did not publicly swear an oath of allegiance to obey the law. The speed limit sign is for his protection: the person at greatest risk from speeders. When he becomes a driver, he will be expected to obey the law.

In the Bible, the widow, the orphan, and the stranger are identified as the most vulnerable people in the community. The civil law is supposed to protect them. The minor or resident alien today is protected by the national constitution, even though he did not publicly swear an oath of allegiance to it, as the person most at risk of government tyranny.

The visitor or the non-voting Church member is protected by the confession of faith, even though he did not publicly swear allegiance to it. It protects his soul from wolves in sheep's clothing: false shepherds. He will be expected to take a public oath to uphold the confession if he ever becomes a Church officer.

Then what about becoming a voting member? Here, Protestant Christianity refuses to follow the logic of strict subscription and affirmation. Very few churches require a voting member to do anything more than swear allegiance to a minimal statement of faith, perhaps a short historic creed. Presbyterianism, which requires its officers to affirm their acceptance of the most detailed theological confession in what used to be called Christendom, has almost no denomination-wide confessional requirement for a voting member. To receive baptism, he is constitutionally required to affirm only that he believes in Christ and will obey Him. There is zero theological content in this oath. Even this minimal promise is found only in the Larger Catechism (A. 166), which has never been used to prosecute anyone in the Presbyterian Church, U.S.A. This arrangement crippled the conservative forces during the Presbyterian conflict, as we shall see. Voting members could impose local Church sanctions on Church officers ("You're fired!"), yet they had never taken a public oath, nor did

Church law or tradition suggest that they had taken an implicit oath. Instead, a system of defensive Presbyterian Church sanctions and oaths was established in the seventeenth century in order to remove any judicial influence above the congregational level of non-oath-bound voting members. But conservative leaders, 1922 to 1925, relied heavily on support by conservative laymen during the Presbyterian conflict. This reliance doomed the conservative cause.

Freedom or Arbitrariness?

Loose subscriptionists are comparable to elected or appointed public officials who come before the voters in the name of greater freedom: loose constructionists of the Constitution. As law enforcers, they resent the tight controls placed on them by the law, especially constitutional law. Loose constructionists are not greatly concerned with the needs of those who are being protected by the strict enforcement of predictable, written law.

Let us return to the analogy of the speed limit. The loose constructionist announces his faith in the good judgment of the police and the courts. "The important thing is true safety, not adherence to arbitrary speed limits." He denies the legitimacy of posted speed limits. In the early stages, he may come as a representative of "oppressed" drivers who want to drive a lot faster.

Once the speed limit signs are removed, however, a policeman can arrest any driver he wants. He can make up the rules as he goes along. "Your honor, I say that this driver was not driving safely." Without a fixed speed limit to appeal to, who can successfully challenge this professional? The driver cannot say, "Your honor, I was driving 34 in a 35 zone."

Add to the dilemma a government that seeks to fund itself by collecting fines from speeders. The police have an incentive to impose arbitrary standards for the sake of the flow of funds. So, in later stages of the debate over posted limits, the loose constructionist may not be on the side of "oppressed" drivers; he may be ready to ticket anyone whenever the government's coffers are depleted of funds.

Question: Are posted speed limits a hindrance on our freedom as pedestrians and drivers, or are they the basis of freedom? The strict constructionist in civil law sees the posted signs *and the court's enforcement of those signs* as crucial elements of a free society. The same is true of strict subscription in ecclesiastical law. Strict subscription places strict limits on the decision-making ability of law enforcers, thereby increasing the freedom of those under this authority. Strict subscription increases the predictability of law enforcement. It reduces arbitrary power.

This argument appears to be all about stipulations: the proper interpretation of the law. Such a narrow interpretation of the subscription issue is incorrect. The argument is inevitably also about sanctions: the degree of arbitrary power allowed by the constitution to those who lawfully possess the institutional authority to impose sanctions. The debate is really over *the law enforcement system's protection of vulnerable innocents*. Jesus told Peter to feed His sheep, not eat them. Yet ecclesiastical shepherds, as with all shepherds, are economically dependent on the productivity of their sheep. How can the Church protect Jesus' sheep, who must fund the necessary shepherding system? This is what the strict subscription debate is all about. It is also what the flow of funds debate is all about.

The Subscription Battle in Church and State

Theological liberals were loose subscriptionists. Old School Presbyterians were strict subscriptionists. The evangelical New School majority was somewhere in between. The Presbyterian conflict was a battle over the degree of subscription *and the system of sanctions appropriate to defend subscription.*

This ecclesiastical battle paralleled an analogous and simultaneous battle in politics: the war between those who held to a strict interpretation of the United States Constitution vs. those who barely believed in the Constitution. These parallel institutional battles—covenantal battles—began at the same time and in the same place: in May of 1787, in the city of Philadelphia, where the Presbyterian Synod and the Constitutional Convention met separately to draw up a pair of antitheocratic constitutions.[19] In the Church, the debate was over Confes-

---

19. Gary North, *Political Polytheism: The Myth of Pluralism* (Tyler, Texas: Institute for Christian Economics, 1989), pp. 543–50. On the Presbyterian influence at the Constitutional Convention, see James H. Smylie, "We, the Presbyterian People: On Celebrating the Constitution of the U.S.A.," *American Presbyterians*, 65 (Winter 1987).

sional subscription; in politics, it was over Constitutional construction. Jeffersonians were strict constructionists; Hamiltonians were loose constructionists. The country was more with Jefferson than Hamilton in 1787. To get the Constitution ratified, the pro-Constitution politicians had to promise a Bill of Rights.

These parallel battles increased in intensity during the decades prior to the Civil War (1861–1865): in Presbyterianism, Old School (strict subscription) vs. New School (loose subscription); in politics, Democrats (strict construction) vs. Whigs[20] and then Republicans (loose construction). There was a civil war in the Church, which resulted in a split in 1837.

After the Civil War, there were two reunions, both consummated on terms laid down by the loose interpretationists: ecclesiastical (New School after the 1869 reunion)[21] and political (Republican Party after the 1865 reunion).[22] In politics, this resulted in the extension of Federal power, though checked after 1877 by the settlement over Reconstruction in the South.[23] In the Church, this was marked by the rise of the social gospel, though checked by the rise of premillennial pietism in the 1870's.[24]

Both of these subscriptionist battles went into high gear from the 1890's to the 1920's. Loose construction in politics is seen in the Progressive movement and, in rural areas, the Populist movement. Loose subscription in the Church is seen in modernism. The Populist influence was incarnated in the career of a Presbyterian ruling elder, a member of the Democratic Party, William Jennings Bryan (d. 1925);

---

20. English Whigs were ideological allies of American Democrats. American Whigs and Republicans were ideological allies of Wellington- or Disraeli-type English Tories.

21. See Chapter 2, below.

22. Harold M. Hyman, *A More Perfect Union: The Impact of the Civil War and Reconstruction on the Constitution* (New York: Knopf, 1973); George Mowry, *The Era of Theodore Roosevelt* (New York: Harper, 1958), chaps. 5–7.

23. C. Vann Woodward, *Reunion and Reaction: The Compromise of 1877 and the End of Reconstruction*, rev. ed. (Garden City, New York: Doubleday Anchor, 1956).

24. Timothy P. Weber, *Living in the Shadow of the Second Coming: American Premillennialism, 1875–1925* (New York: Oxford University Press, 1979).

the Progressive influence was incarnated in the career of a former Presbyterian ruling elder, a member of the Democratic Party, Woodrow Wilson (d. 1924).[25] Their careers destroyed the politics of strict construction. After 1912, the Democratic Party leap-frogged the Republican Party in its quest to remove the restraints of the Constitution.[26] Meanwhile, strict-subscription Presbyterian Confessionalists also retreated: the revision of the Westminster Confession in 1903. The twin battles culminated in the mid-1930's: the demise of the Old Republican order with the rise of Franklin Roosevelt's first New Deal (1933–36);[27] and the demise of the Old School in the Presbyterian conflict (1934–36).

Left, Right, and Center

As was the case in the great political-Constitutional battle, three main ecclesiastical viewpoints were involved: left, right, and center. (It is significant that in all major languages except Chinese, "left" is associated with opposition to traditional social and religious customs.[28] As historian James Billington writes concerning the French Revolution, "The subsequent equation of the left with virtue dramatized revolutionary defiance of Christian tradition, which had always represented those on the right hand of God as saved and those on the left as damned."[29])

Undergirding the left end of the spectrum was the *power religion*, represented by theological liberalism (modernism).[30] The liberals in the early stages demanded theological toleration: the annulment of

---

25. A third Presbyterian, Benjamin Harrison, was a Republican. He defeated Grover Cleveland for the Presidency in 1888, and lost to him in 1892. Cleveland, son of a Presbyterian minister and husband of a Presbyterian wife, never joined the Church.

26. Philip M. Crane, *The Democrat's Dilemma* (Chicago: Regnery, 1964).

27. Arthur M. Schlesinger, Jr., *The Age of Roosevelt*, 3 vols. (Boston: Houghton Mifflin, 1957–60), vol. 2, *The Coming of the New Deal*.

28. J. A. Laponce, "Spatial Archetypes and Political Perceptions," *American Political Science Review*, 59 (March 1975), p. 17.

29. James H. Billington, *Fire in the Minds of Men: Origins of the Revolutionary Faith* (New York: Basic Books, 1980), p. 22.

30. On the three viewpoints, see Chapter 1.

strict subscription. This camouflaged their commitment to power, which became clear only in the mid-1930's. Modernism justified its rejection of the judicially binding character of creeds and confessions on the basis of three arguments: an appeal to secular evolutionary science and reason (Darwinism), an appeal to historical change (historicism), and an appeal to individual experience (experientialism), by which modernists meant Christian man's autonomous judgment in defiance of explicit biblical revelation and the historic creeds.

Dominating the middle and also influencing the right were representatives of one variety of *experiential religion*, sometimes called pietism. Pietism's concern was with personal salvation, not theological precision. It placed heavy emphasis on personal evangelism, missions, and Church growth. With respect both to experientialism and Church growth, pietism was close to modernism. The capture of the Northern Presbyterian Church by the liberals was consented to by the evangelical experientialists, who had a numerical majority after 1906 and had been dominant psychologically since 1869. They, like the modernists, regarded themselves as inclusivists, although their inclusivism did not automatically mean the passive acceptance of modernist ministers until 1926. What they wanted was peace.

Leading the right intellectually, though rarely organizationally, were defenders of *judicial religion*: the judicial theology of Calvinism. These were the exclusivists, whose intellectual leader in the 1920's and 1930's was Machen. They were exclusivists in the sense that they wanted to exclude from the ministry men who were modernists. But they did not actually do anything to exclude them judicially, once modernists were ordained, after 1900.

Machen used a similar three-fold classification scheme in 1913: anti-supernatural, anti-cultural, and biblical cultural transformation. The first is liberalism; the second is fundamentalism (pietism); and the third is biblical Christianity. Machen denied the existence of a supposedly necessary dualism between Christianity and culture.[31] But he

---

31. Machen, "Christianity and Culture," *Princeton Theological Review*, 11 (1913), pp. 1-15; reprinted in *What Is Christianity?*, edited by Ned Bernard Stonehouse (Grand Rapids, Michigan: Eerdmans, 1951), pp. 156-69. Elsewhere, I have used a parallel three-fold division: power religion, escape religion, and dominion

dropped this classification scheme in 1915 in his inaugural lecture at Princeton Seminary, "History and Faith." Covenantally, the two-fold classification is correct: saved and lost. Strategically, the three-fold classification is more useful.

"Peace, Peace!"

Machen's three categories in 1913 were far more accurate, but far less rhetorically compelling, than his two categories in his 1923 book, *Christianity and Liberalism*. His later description of the division between Christianity and liberalism was accurate as far as it went, but it did not go far enough, as he was to learn after the liberals captured Princeton Seminary in 1929. What his analysis in 1923 did not acknowledge was that the middle ground, where about 80 percent of those in any organization normally reside, did not fit comfortably into his two categories. But by 1923, he was strategically dependent on a significant portion of that 80 percent, who were best described as pietists. Pietism limits the realm of meaningful faith to the realm of the heart, thereby truncating the commitment of those who hold it. Pietism is similar to Greek neoplatonism: escapist, world-renouncing, and mystical.[32] Pietism, like neoplatonism, has flourished during eras marked by a loss of optimism.[33]

By the time Machen wrote *Christianity and Liberalism*, several mainline Protestant denominations had been rent by controversy, with the liberals (modernists) challenging conservative believers for control over the ecclesiastical machinery. The Episcopal Church had gone liberal a generation earlier. The drift within his own denomination had concerned him at the time of his ordination in 1914.[34] He had for a time considered ordination in the Southern Presbyterian

---

religion. Gary North, *Moses and Pharaoh: Dominion Religion vs. Power Religion* (Tyler, Texas: Institute for Christian Economics, 1985), pp. 2–5.

32. R. J. Rushdoony, *The Flight from Humanity: A Study of the Effect of Neoplatonism on Christianity* (Nutley, New Jersey: Presbyterian & Reformed, 1973).

33. The loss of optimism by liberal theologians in the post-1918 era in Europe and in the United States in the 1930's was accompanied by the rise of neo-orthodoxy, which emphasizes an existentialist encounter with God at the expense of propositional truth.

34. Stonehouse, *Machen*, p. 221.

Church (PCUS). He had decided to go into the Northern Church because he was persuaded that there was still hope. By the time he realized that such hope was misplaced, he was publicly committed to a defense of the denomination. He refused to transfer to the PCUS, even when offered a seminary job in 1926, the year of victory for the anti-confessionalists in the General Assembly. He defended his ministerial oath by refusing to remain silent. He knew at least by 1935 that he would eventually be silenced. He may have known in 1929, with the takeover of Princeton Seminary. If he believed Warfield's warning, he knew in 1921.

The experientialists were willing to defend institutionally only the stripped-down fundamentals of America's Protestant evangelical faith: the inerrancy of Scripture, the virgin birth of Christ, Christ's substitutionary atonement, Christ's bodily resurrection, and the historic reality of Christ's miracles.[35] What Machen did not recognize soon enough was that most experientialists shared a common commitment that was even more precious to them than these theological fundamentals: the goal of institutional peace. By the early 1930's at least, Machen knew.[36] By this time, it was too late for conservatives to recapture the denomination. The advocates—both conservative and liberal—of pietism's religion of inner peace demanded that new men be given control of the denomination, which would then reflect this peaceful ideal. These new men came in the name of theological peace and institutional order. The pietists-experientialists were willing to pay a theological price to attain this goal, but as in the case of every economic transaction, they preferred to pay the lowest possible price. And like so many people who seek a below-market price, they wound up paying far more than they bargained for.

Crossed Fingers

The development of every organization is determined by the private confessions of those who gain control over the formal procedures

---

35. These were the criteria of the General Assembly's Doctrinal Deliverances of 1910, 1916, and 1923, reprinted in *Presbyterian Enterprise*, p. 281.

36. See his statement that begins this Introduction.

and sanctions that are used to defend the institution's official confession of faith. The historian's problem escalates when formal adherence to the confession was publicly made by all the participants. Some of them were lying or were self-deluded, but who?

In the year before his death on February 10, 1985, I spoke on the phone with Rev. Milo F. Jamison, who in 1933 became the first pastor to be thrown out of the denomination because of orthodoxy.[37] (I had first interviewed him about this in late 1962.) He told me the story of a fellow graduate of Princeton Theological Seminary who had just been ordained in the mid-1920's. Jamison knew that the man did not believe in the Westminster Confession of Faith. Jamison asked him: "How could you tell the examining committee that you believe in the Westminster Confession when you really don't?" The man answered: "I kept my fingers crossed." Jamison repeated the man's statement again, as if to affirm it categorically with a double witness.

But Jamison himself did not believe this historic Confession of Presbyterianism, nor had he believed it when their exchange took place. He was a premillennial dispensationalist.[38] When, in 1937, he was defeated for Moderator at the second General Assembly of the year-old Presbyterian Church of America, he immediately departed with Carl McIntire's secessionist group. He joined McIntire's Bible Presbyterian Church, founded in 1938, which revised the Westminster Confession's section on eschatology in order to make it conform to

---

37. He was the leader of a popular Bible study class held on or near the campus at UCLA in West Los Angeles. When other denominations that had campus ministries formed an interdenominational campus organization, Jamison refused to participate. Its creed was "cooperation without compromise." He was ordered by the Los Angeles Presbytery to bring his group in, but he still refused. Without a trial, the presbytery then erased his name from presbytery's rolls. This took place on January 24, 1933: "Jamison, Milo Fisher," *The Orthodox Presbyterian Church 1936–1986*, edited by Charles G. Dennison (Philadelphia: Committee for the Historian of the Orthodox Presbyterian Church, 1986), p. 339.

38. The notes in *The Scofield Reference Bible* (New York: Oxford University Press, 1909) provide the most popular introduction to dispensational theology. For a critical study of dispensational theology, see Oswald T. Allis, *Prophecy and the Church* (Philadelphia: Presbyterian & Reformed, 1945). For a defense, see Charles C. Ryrie, *Dispensationalism Today* (Chicago: Moody Press, [1965] 1988); Ryrie, *Basic Theology* (Wheaton, Illinois: Victor, 1986).

premillennialism,[39] although the denomination was not formally dispensational. Jamison left the Bible Presbyterian Church in 1968,[40] but in fact he spent his post-1933 career as the pastor of an independent Bible church that taught the *Scofield Reference Bible*. He did not discuss the Westminster Confession in the pulpit.[41] He was not a Calvinist.[42] He had crossed his fingers early.

This was Machen's dilemma: everyone on all sides of the Presbyterian conflict had his fingers crossed. The strategically relevant question was: On which issues?

Sacrament and Word

This book is my attempt to answer many questions regarding Presbyterian history. First and foremost, there are two judicial questions: (1) What does American Presbyterianism teach are the marks of a true Church? (2) What role have the Westminster Confession and the Larger and Shorter Catechisms played in American Presbyterianism? Until these questions are answered in terms of the historical record, the details of the rival camps' strategies will remain unintelligible.

Sacrament and Ministry

The Westminster Confession and the two catechisms do not define the following offices in terms of a judicial oath and its stipulations: minister, ruling elder, and deacon. The words "elder" and "deacon" do not even appear. The phrase "minister of the gospel" (WCF XXVIII:2) is used to describe what is today called the teaching elder in conservative Presbyterian circles and Minister of the Word and Sacrament in the Presbyterian Church, U.S.A. The words "teaching elder" do not appear in the Confession. The term "elder," meaning any offi-

---

39. George P. Hutchinson, *The History Behind the Reformed Presbyterian Church, Evangelical Synod* (Cherry Hill, New Jersey: Mack, 1974), p. 249. See *The Constitution of the Bible Presbyterian Church* (Collingswood, New Jersey: Independent Board for Presbyterian Home Missions, 1959), ch. XXXIII, p. 41.

40. "Jamison, Milo Fisher," *op. cit.*

41. My parents were members of his church in the 1960's.

42. As he told me in late summer, 1963, when I was about to leave California to attend Westminster Seminary in Philadelphia, "Don't let them sell you on covenant theology." They did, however.

cer not a "teacher," "doctor," or "deacon," does appear in the 1645 Form of Church-Government, under *Other Church-Governors*, but this document has had no binding legal authority in Presbyterianism.[43]

According to the Confession, only a minister can lawfully administer the sacraments (WCF XXVII:4; XXVIII:2). The word "minister" does not appear in the Confession in any ecclesiastical context other than the sacraments. *Judicially speaking, the Westminster Confession has a solely sacramental view of the ministry.* The Larger Catechism adds preaching (Q&A 158). Even here, far more space is devoted to the sacraments (Q&A 162–177) than to preaching (Q&A 158–160). *American Presbyterianism's Constitutional documents establish a predominantly sacramental basis for the ministry.* But I am aware of no Calvinist Presbyterian theologian or spokesman who has ever defended the sacraments as the primary judicial basis of the ministry.

A Church member is defined in these documents as someone who professes faith in Christ and promises to obey Him. This is the only Church oath mentioned in the Constitutional documents of Presbyterianism. This lone reference to a Church oath appears in the context of baptism (Larger Catechism, A. 166). *The only official Presbyterian Church oath is the oath of the lowly Church member.* This has been a major weakness of Presbyterianism. Presbyterians built a structure of Church government on something other than binding covenantal oaths, their stipulations, and precise negative sanctions. This has made it far easier for the enemies of the Confession to capture the Church in the name of the Confession: "No oath-bound stipulations; therefore, no negative sanctions."

Sacrament and Preaching

In the Presbyterian conflict from 1869 to 1934, the sacraments were rarely if ever mentioned in relation to the ecclesiastical battle underway. I do not remember reading anything in the writings of the Old School regarding the defense of the Church or the ministry as a defense of the sacraments. Modernists did mention the sacraments, 1934 to 1936, but only in relation to money: refusing to send money

---

43. *The Form of Church-Government*, in *Confession of Faith*, p. 402. See Appendix C, below: section on "A Transformed Scottish Legacy," pp. 993–95.

to an official ministry of the Presbyterian Church was said by the Church's hierarchy to be the equivalent of not taking the Lord's Supper. This was fully consistent with modernism's view of the true sacrament: power leading to control over Church assets. Yet even in this extreme case, the Old School did not respond by presenting a carefully constructed theological case to refute this obviously anti-Presbyterian, anti-Protestant theory of Church order.

The failure of the Old School to build its case against modernism in terms of the sacraments weakened its case—I believe fatally. The Old School called the ministry the *teaching eldership*, which the Confession does not mention. The Confession defines the ministry as the agency authorized to administer and therefore defend the sacraments. The Larger Catechism adds preaching. The judicial emphasis of the two documents is *sacrament first, preaching second*. Yet in terms of Presbyterian tradition, preaching has always come first, which has led to the establishment of higher education for ministers as the number-one priority and the main distinguishing mark of the minister. (The secondary mark is his membership in his presbytery rather than his congregation.) This allowed the worldwide capture of Presbyterianism by liberals through their capture of higher education: first in the colleges, then in the seminaries. (European Presbyterianism also did not escape; it fell earlier.)

The Old School defined the ministry in terms of preaching and the minister's *extra-Confessional* 1729 oath to uphold the Confession. This weakened its case again: ruling elders took the same oath, yet they were not permitted to preach in a vacant pulpit.[44] The vote of a ruling elder was equal to vote of a minister, yet the Old School was only peripherally concerned with the institutional defense of the ruling eldership. Nevertheless, the Old School had more supporters in the ruling eldership than in the teaching eldership, since ruling elders

---

44. A congregation with a vacant pulpit was to gather together for praying, singing, reading the Bible, and reading "the works of such approved divines, as the presbytery within whose bounds they are, may recommend, and they may be able to procure; and that the elders or deacons be the persons who shall preside, and select the portions of Scripture, and of other books to be read; . . ." *The Form of Government*, XXI; *The Constitution of the Presbyterian Church in the United States of America* (Philadelphia: Presbyterian Board of Publication and Sabbath School Work, 1904), pp. 387-88.

did not have to attend seminary. They avoided the gauntlet of theological liberalism after 1890. Eventually, ruling elders sided with the middle majority—peace-seeking, controversy-avoiding, evangelical ministers—and the modernist ministers who in fact controlled the Church. *This defection of the ruling elders ended mainline Presbyterian Calvinism.*

Prior to 1900, the Old School based its case entirely on the defense of the integrity of preaching, meaning the integrity of doctrine, meaning the defense of the Westminster Confession (unofficially modified by James Hutton's and Charles Lyell's uniformitarian geological time scale). After 1903, it had to base its defense on the 1903 revision of the Confession: watered-down Calvinism. After 1909, it had to base its case on the even more diluted five points of fundamentalism known as the Doctrinal Deliverance of 1910. *Each time, the Old School retreated judicially from the Westminster Confession.* It did not have to retreat from the two catechisms, since no one on any side ever appealed to their specifics as binding elements of Presbyterian creedalism. They were ignored by everyone throughout the entire period. This also weakened the case for Calvinism in American Presbyterianism.

Sacrament and Apostasy

The primacy of the sacraments in Presbyterian Confessional and judicial standards is rarely discussed by Calvinist Presbyterians. This has been a major weakness of Presbyterianism. Ultimately, the sacraments are the most important *judicial* issue ecclesiastically, and they have been understood as such ever since the Donatist controversy in the fourth century.[45] No Church that baptizes infants can escape this question: *What about the re-baptism of adults?* Specifically, must a person who was baptized as a child or as an adult in a heretical Church be re-baptized when he transfers his membership? Non-Anabaptist churches have answered *no* ever since the days of Donatism. In fact, answering *yes* has long been considered heretical by such churches. Then what about an apostate Church's baptism? If the person's bap-

---

45. Augustine, *On Baptism, Against the Donatists*, in *Nicene and Post-Nicene Fathers*, edited by Philip Schaff (Grand Rapids, Michigan: Eerdmans, 1979 reprint), vol. 4.

tism was administered under the authority of a Trinitarian creed, non-Anabaptist churches have always said that no re-baptism is authorized. What about baptism by a cult? Here the churches have re-baptized, since they regard the cult's baptism as invalid. The baptizing church's creed is what makes the difference.

So, an apostate Church is still a Church sacramentally if it maintains a Trinitarian creed. Its baptisms are valid. Then what, judicially speaking, constitutes apostasy? From a practical standpoint, how serious *judicially* is continuing membership in an apostate Church? Sacramentally speaking, it is less serious than being in a cult and no more serious than being in a heretical Church. But what about creedally? The apostate Church's official creed is not enforced. A Trinitarian Church will normally accept as a new member a person who has been excommunicated by a heretical or apostate Church because of his orthodoxy or his contumacy relating to orthodoxy. So, the creed is judicially valid with respect to legitimizing the sanction of baptism, yet operationally invalid with respect to the sanction of excommunication. Confusing, isn't it?

The implicit oath of every Presbyterian baptism is not enforced by an apostate Church's government. I say implicit oath, for the Westminster Assembly's 1645 Directory for the Publick Worship of God does not require the parents of a child about to be baptized to promise to rear the child in a Christian manner; the minister merely exhorts the parents regarding their obligations in this regard. The only time a parent speaks is to tell the minister the name of the child.[46] On the question of adult baptism, the Directory is silent. The familiar American Presbyterian practice of asking the parents or adults to confess publicly their faith and promise to be obedient is not mandated by the traditional documents of Presbyterianism.

Defining apostasy in terms of the *sacraments, creeds*, and *ecclesiastical sanctions* remains a very large unresolved theological problem for modern confessional churches. This is one reason why Machen's decision in 1936 to designate the Presbyterian Church, U.S.A., as apostate did not impress the two million members who remained behind.

---

46. *The Directory for the Publick Worship of God* (1645), in *The Confession of Faith* (Publications Committee of the Free Presbyterian Church of Scotland, 1970), p. 383.

The Authority of the Confession

American Presbyterianism has deferred any public discussion of the problem of the Confession's lack of ministerial oaths because it has invoked the authority of such secondary documents as the Westminster Assembly's Directory for the Publick Worship of God or The Form of Presbyterial Church-Government and of Ordination of Ministers. But the Confession did not identify these supplemental documents as judicially binding. The extraordinary and rarely discussed fact is, **the Westminster Confession does not mention its own judicial authority**, a fact to which liberals appealed again and again during the Presbyterian conflict. The Confession does not say how its stipulations are to be enforced. How could it? It does not mandate oath-bound stipulations for any Church office. It does not establish any system for bringing formal sanctions against those who serve as ministers, let alone the two offices it does not mention, ruling elders and deacons. All offices are governed by the Church's supplemental by-laws. No one wants to admit it publicly, but the fact of the matter is this: Henry Martyn Robert did more to shape modern American Presbyterianism than any Presbyterian minister ever did. It has been more important institutionally to have gained a mastery of *Robert's Rules of Order* (1876)—originally, an obscure self-published book—than either the Bible or the Westminster Confession.

The Westminster Confession and the two catechisms therefore cannot serve as stand-alone judicial documents, yet they alone have been regarded as the Constitutional documents of Presbyterianism. This anomaly led to a long series of Presbyterian conflicts over the supplemental by-laws, beginning with English Presbyterianism after 1660. In every case, Unitarians (or worse) keep inheriting the largest Presbyterian denominations.

The Unholy Alliance

It is not simply the liberal power religionists who oppose the imposition of more rigorous confessional formulations. Conservative, pietistic, experiential religion also generally adopts an officially nonconfessional covering. It proclaims: "All people who affirm the name of Jesus are working for the same God and for the same goals." This belief is naive; almost anyone in the West can "name the name of Jesus" and mean anything by it: Mormons, Jehovah's Witnesses, even

New Age mystics. This does not make him a Trinitarian. The naive view of the experientialists is remarkably close to the familiar anti-Christian creed of the universal salvationists: "We're all traveling different roads to the same God." Anyone who denies the tenets of this inclusivist faith is regarded as a nuisance, and if he continues to disrupt the institution, he so completely alienates the "peace-keepers" that they remove him from their presence.

Machen opposed the experientialism of modernism, and eventually the majority evangelical experientialists took offense at his incessant criticisms of modernism's anti-Confessionalism. Criticizing Harry Emerson Fosdick, the most famous theological modernist of his day, Machen wrote: "Doctrine . . . is not an explanation of human experience, but it is a system revealed in the Holy Scriptures by God. It is not the product of experience, but a setting forth of those facts upon which Christian experience is based."[47] In this, he was following Warfield, who had insisted that "if theology is the science of God, it deals not with a mass of subjective experiences . . . but with a body of objective facts. . . ."[48] In 1924, conservative experientialists perceived Fosdick as the chief disturber of the peace; in 1936, they perceived Machen as the chief disturber of the peace. They imposed negative sanctions on both men: mild in the first case, rigorous in the second.

Negative Sanctions

There must be negative sanctions. Excommunication and removal from ordained office are essential to the maintenance of any ecclesiastical creed or confession, and ultimately every organization has a process of excommunication, for they all have implicit creeds. The experientialists are not exceptions to this rule. They want peace so much, they are willing to fight for it. They want unity so much, they are willing to excommunicate creedalists in order to attain it. But note well: the removal of their enemies from their presence is rarely done in terms of the content of a formal statement of faith. It is done in the

---

47. Machen, "The Parting of the Ways—Part II," *The Presbyterian* (April 24, 1924), p. 6.
48. B. B. Warfield, "Apologetics," *The New Schaff-Herzog Encyclopedia of Religious Knowledge*, 12 vols. (Grand Rapids, Michigan: Baker, [1907] 1951), I:234.

name of institutional peace. Why? Because in the view of the experiential religion, formal confessions are only rarely worth enforcing, once members have made a formal profession of faith in the confession, no matter what they profess subsequently. Once inside the organization, no one is supposed to suffer involuntary removal based on the judicial content of his original confession of faith. It is not the theological and judicial *content* of the confession that is determinative for the experiential religion; it is rather the *formal act* of public verbal confession and the inner experience of personal healing that supposedly follows.[49] A critic who seeks publicly to impose Church sanctions on mild-mannered confessors who no longer believe the formal terms of their own public confessions of faith is regarded by experientialists as a disturber of the peace.

The power religionists understand this, so they initially confine themselves to a subversive undermining of men's faith in the theological content of the original confession. They maintain the traditional forms of worship while denying the judicial content thereof. They infuse old terminology with new meanings. The judicialists see both the hypocrisy and the institutional threat in this strategy. They mount a defense based on the judicial and theological content of the original confession. The power religionists then enlist the support of the experientialists in the name of the original act of verbal confession and the supposed lifetime immunities thereof: "Once confessed, always confessed!" In the most radical forms of the experiential religion, the original confessional act confers judicial immunity to every theological revision that follows. The power religionists use this to their advantage. In 1927, the General Assembly actually concluded that no Church court had the authority to de-frock a minister for any theological reason. It declared: "Once a minister, always a minister. . . ."[50]

The judicialists cannot in good conscience take such a view of Church sanctions. This is why they are rarely successful institutionally, once the experiential religion has been widely accepted in a

---

49. In fundamentalist circles, this outlook is codified by the slogan, "once saved, always saved." The act of "walking the aisle" after an "altar call" is regarded as definitive.

50. *Minutes of the General Assembly, 1927*, p. 68.

Church. To remove the power religionists, the judicialists must deny the legitimacy of the institutional mandate of the experiential religion: "Never hold anyone accountable for the content of his original confession."

Seeking an Alliance

Judicial religion is at war with both the power religion and the experiential religion. Similarly, the power religion is at war with judicial religion and experiential religion. The problem is, to conduct this two-front war, both sides must seek an alliance with the experientialists, since they have been in the majority in American Protestant churches. The history of the institutional Church in the twentieth century can be seen in terms of the shifting alliances of these factions. The experientialists may ally themselves with the judicial religionists against the power religionists, or they may ally themselves with the power religionists against the judicialists. They reserve the option of changing sides. The experientialists want institutional peace.

When power religionists do not possess a majority, they adopt the language of "peace, peace," in order to gain time to consolidate their institutional position. They can afford to cooperate with the experientialists, for the experientialists are no significant threat to their ultimate goal: the capture and maintenance of power.[51]

The experientialists are willing to cooperate with the power religionists in order to remove from their presence all those who proclaim the judicial theology of the dominion covenant.[52] Experientialists are embarrassed and shocked by the controversies that such judicial theology creates, and they are also horrified at the burden of additional responsibility that the dominion covenant places on them.[53]

---

51. The main exception in recent history is the Southern Baptist Convention. There, a tiny group of dedicated confessionalists worked for over a decade to mobilize the conservative majority, 1977–1990. They conservatives steadily recaptured the Convention's leadership and its boards. This took a systematic plan and detailed knowledge of the organization's rules.

52. In the Dutch Calvinist tradition, the dominion covenant is called the cultural mandate.

53. Gary North, *The Dominion Covenant: Genesis*, 2nd ed. (Tyler, Texas: Institute for Christian Economics, 1987).

They want to get judicial religionists and their message out of their midst, but being peaceful and non-controversial, experientialists hesitate to take the lead in purging the dominionist leaven from their presence. At this point, the power religionists offer their services, seemingly free of charge. It is an offer that the experientialists never seem to be able to refuse.

Machen's Strategy: Defending Confessionalism

Machen's burden—a burden he had inherited from the Presbyterian reunion of 1869—was to develop an institutional strategy that could be fought successfully in terms of the traditional or familiar confessions of his denomination. He believed that the war between modernism and orthodoxy is ultimately a dispute over the truth of the theological system presented in the Westminster Confession of Faith, the most theologically rigorous confessional statement in the history of Christianity. But he also knew that he could get very few of his denomination's leaders to admit this, let alone fight in terms of it. The Westminster Confession was judicially a dead issue by Machen's day, and he knew it. Another, weaker creed had replaced the older, rigorous Confession. This was Machen's fundamental dilemma, or better put, his fundamentalist dilemma.

What Machen learned to his dismay was that people who denied the importance of a distinctly Presbyterian Confession as the basis of institutional authority within Presbyterianism were the ones who held the balance of power in the Northern Presbyterian Church after World War I. Their "loving" wrath would be directed against whichever of the two principled factions—right or left, judicial religion or power religion—disturbed their cultural slumber. The power-seekers had recognized this trend as early as 1900, and they adopted a tactic of proclaiming "peaceful coexistence" until they had the power to exercise their will.

Conclusion

It is one of the oddities of history that those who proclaim the judicial religion almost never seem to recognize the nature of the war they are in until the final stages. For example, the Sanhedrin—the power religionists of Jesus' day—understood that He had promised to rise from the dead in three days. They supposed that His disciples also understood this prophecy, so they wanted Pilate to seal up the tomb so that the disciples could not break in and steal the body, and then proclaim that Jesus' prophecy had been fulfilled (Matt. 27:62-64). But the disciples had not understood Jesus, and they had scattered. No seal on the tomb was needed to keep out the disciples. Nevertheless, no seal was powerful enough to restrain Christ's resurrected body, and when the disciples finally recognized what Christ had accomplished, no seal could keep the gospel bottled up. They learned slowly, but they did learn.

Machen was a Westminster Confessionalist. He understood that a formal theological confession is like a stepping stone up the ramp of history toward the pinnacle of victory, either for covenant-breakers or covenant-keepers. Just as the Roman legions built a ramp up a mountain to the summit of Masada, so must the Church build its confessional ramp. If a Church stands firmly on any confessional stepping stone, it cannot ascend the ramp. Each step is crucial in the Church's ascent, but standing motionless on one step is not a legitimate substitute for making the ascent.

Machen knew that confessions must be revised periodically, but he did not know how this could be done faithfully in his era. By 1921, the Westminster Confession was a dead letter judicially. Only the five-point Doctrinal Deliverance of 1910 could rally the conservatives. So, he wound up having to step down several confessional steps: to a watered-down, five-point fundamentalist confession. The conservatives did not believe in the Westminster Confession, and they were willing to march forward only by retreating to a lower step. That is to say, they were not willing to march forward at all. They wanted to retreat, form a circle with the wagons, and be left in peace. But history is a covenantal battle which leaves no one in peace for long.

Machen tried to cooperate with the experientialists who were selling out his cause, but as the confrontation grew more intense, they dropped away from him, one by one. By trying to understand the battle in terms of a limited two-fold distinction—Christianity vs. liberalism—Machen never overcame the hatred that his proclamation of a Confessional religion had created in the ranks of the supposedly faithful.

Almost alone, Machen recognized that either Christ's creed or liberalism's creed would have to direct the Presbyterian Church. It would be a battle to the end to see one or the other triumphant. He announced his opinions openly, unlike his modernist opponents: "Mere concessiveness, therefore, will never succeed in avoiding the intellectual conflict. In the intellectual battle of the present day there can be no 'peace without victory'; one side or the other must win."[54] But his temporary theological allies—defenders of a watered-down creed and a religion of institutional unity at almost any price—understood better than he did who their long-term allies really were. The long-term institutional allies of the limited-creed faction were the modernists. The experientialists knew the modernists would leave them alone to be culturally irrelevant in peace, precisely because of this cultural irrelevance.

The experiential religion is a religion of *principled irrelevance in history*. The modernists understood this and used this knowledge to gain the votes to expel those who preached the relevance of the Bible and the historic creeds and confessions, however limited in scope their concept of relevance may have been. The liberals needed only votes—one of the two sacraments they recognize, the other being a legal claim on other people's money. Year by year after 1925, the pietists sold the modernists their votes for the promise of peace. After 1936, they kept their pulpits and then collected their pensions.

---

54. Machen, *Christianity and Liberalism* (New York: Macmillan, 1923), p. 6.

Part 1

ORTHODOXY AND ITS DISCONTENTS

Things that are false will accomplish a great many useful things in the world. If I take a counterfeit coin and buy a dinner with it, the dinner is every bit as good as if the coin were a product of the mint. And what a very useful thing a dinner is! But just as I am on my way downtown to buy a dinner for a poor man, an expert tells me that my coin is a counterfeit. The miserable, heartless theorizer! While he is going into uninteresting, learned details about the primitive history of that coin, a poor man is dying for want of bread. So it is with faith. Faith is so very useful, they tell us, that we must not scrutinize its basis in truth. But, the great trouble is, such an avoidance of scrutiny itself involves the destruction of faith. For faith is essentially dogmatic. Despite all you can do, you cannot remove the element of intellectual assent from it. Faith is the opinion that some person will do something for you. If that person really will do that thing for you, then the faith is true. If he will not do it, then the faith is false. In the latter case, not all the benefits in the world will make the faith true. Though it has transformed the world from darkness to light, though it has produced thousands of glorious healthy lives, it remains a pathological phenomenon. It is false, and sooner or later it is sure to be found out.

J. Gresham Machen (1923)[*]

---

[*] Machen, *Christianity and Liberalism* (New York: Macmillan, 1923), pp. 142–43.

INTRODUCTION TO PART 1

> *In the first place, Christianity may be subordinated to culture. That solution really, though to some extent unconsciously, is being favored by a very large and influential portion of the Church to-day. For the elimination of the supernatural in Christianity—so tremendously common today—really makes Christianity merely natural. Christianity becomes a human product, a mere part of human culture. . . . The second solution goes to the opposite extreme. In its effort to give religion a clear field, it seeks to destroy culture. This solution is better than the first. Instead of indulging in a shallow optimism or deification of humanity, it recognizes the profound evil of the world, and does not shrink from the most heroic remedy. . . . Therefore, it is argued, the culture of this world must be a matter at least of indifference to the Christian. . . . Are then Christianity and culture in a conflict that is to be settled only by the destruction of one or the other of the contending forces? A third solution, fortunately, is possible—namely consecration. Instead of destroying the arts and sciences or being indifferent to them, let us cultivate them with all the enthusiasm of the veriest humanist, but at the same time consecrate them to the service of our God.*
>
> J. Gresham Machen (1913)[1]

Machen's 1913 *Princeton Theological Review* essay was his 1912 lecture to the incoming students at Princeton Theological Seminary. In this lecture, he set forth an analytical framework for understanding modern theology. This framework is what his older contemporary, German sociologist Max Weber, called an ideal type,[2] and what

---

1. Machen, "Christianity and Culture," *Princeton Theological Review*, 11 (Jan. 1913), pp. 3-5.
2. Thomas Burger, *Max Weber's Theory of Concept Formation: History, Laws, and Ideal Types* (Durham, North Carolina: Duke University Press, 1976), Part IV; Rolf E. Rogers, *Max Weber's Ideal Type Theory* (New York: Philosophical Library, 1969).

Thomas Kuhn calls a paradigm.³ An ideal type is a model, a conceptual pattern that enables us to understand the details of historical reality. While it does not "do justice" to every fact perfectly, it enables us to understand the complex interrelationships of facts. It serves as the map of the forest; without it, we are blinded by the jumble of trees.

Machen in 1913 argued that there were three separate religious traditions battling for the hearts of Protestants: culturalism (modernism), anti-culturalism (pietism), and consecrationism (Calvinism). Each outlook was well represented in the Presbyterian Church. The interplay of these three theologies led to the resolution of institutional conflict in 1936. For purposes of understanding the Presbyterian conflict, his three-fold model is indispensable.

He abandoned this three-fold model a decade later in his book, *Christianity and Liberalism*, in favor of a two-religion model. In fact, he abandoned it as early as 1915 in his inaugural lecture, "History and Faith." His language in 1915 sounds very much like his language in the early 1930's. "Two conceptions of Christianity are struggling for ascendency [sic] to-day. . . . The Church is in perplexity. She is trying to compromise. She is saying, Peace, peace, when there is no peace. And rapidly she is losing her power. The time has come when she must choose."⁴ Machen wanted the Presbyterian Church to choose. In 1936, it did: against him. Machen believed that this battle was, above all, a battle over theology.

From the point of view of the Christian gospel, this two-fold analysis is correct: saved vs. lost, covenant-keepers vs. covenant-breakers. It was also tactically important for the conservatives' strategy in the 1920's, since his three-fold model told him that they had to get the votes of the pietist middle in the denomination. Calvinists had to rally the troops, and these troops included large numbers of covenant-keeping pietists. So, rhetorically speaking, the two-fold model was better for public consumption: good guys vs. bad guys. But Machen's public position in the 1920's and the first half of the 1930's—two religions

---

3. Thomas Kuhn, *The Structure of Scientific Revolutions* (Chicago: University of Chicago Press, 1962).

4. Machen, "History and Faith," *Princeton Theological Review*, 13 (July 1915), p. 351.

battling for control of the Church—made it difficult for him to explain to his followers why he kept losing. Covenant-breakers obviously did not comprise a majority in the Church. Covenant-keepers, mostly pietists and anti-culturalists, did. To have identified the pietists as a major part of the Church's problem would have alienated them. It would also have publicly acknowledged that Machen did not speak for the majority or anything like a majority. This is poor positioning for any leader in a battle for votes. So, until 1935, when he was clearly defeated and now had to prepare a remnant for an exodus out of the Church, he ignored his original three-fold analysis.

As an historian, I do not ignore it. I make very heavy use of it. I agree with Machen: the key issues of life are theological. His three-fold analysis is crucial for understanding the history of the defeat of the Calvinists in the Presbyterian Church. It is just as crucial for understanding the surrender of Christendom by the Christians. We must pay close attention to theology.

The Relevance of Theology

Modern man has little respect for theology and even less taste for it. Yet he indulges in it daily. He lives his life in terms of a series of implicit assumptions about God, man, law, sanctions, and time, as well as eternity. He is generally unaware of his implicit theology, but he always has one.

The average person is not a master of any intellectual specialty, but he is dependent on those who are. Men have always been dependent on priests. In our era, we have substituted new priesthoods for old, but we remain in the clutches of one priesthood or another: teachers, lawyers, physicians, scientists, military specialists, central bankers, software code writers, network television news anchormen, and so forth. Each has a system of initiation; each has a temple of some kind; each dispenses blessings and cursings. Modern man does not accept the fact that the debates among theologians have the same importance in his life, let alone in a culture's life, as the debates among scientists, but modern man is wrong. He relegates such matters to funerals, but funerals should remind him: ideas have consequences—eternal consequences.

Theology is complex. Even though most people do not understand this complexity, it makes a difference what they believe about

God, man, law, sanctions, and time. It made a tremendous difference for the West that Athanasius won in his long theological battle with Arius, namely, that with respect to the Second Person of the Trinity, *homoousion* (same essence) is true and *homoiousion* (like essence) is not. The extra "i" made all the difference theologically. Athanasius held that Jesus Christ was not of *like* essence as God the Father, but of the *same* essence.

The skeptic's familiar refrain—like the theological liberal's[5]—dismisses as silly those theologians who debated the cosmic importance of an "i," but such contempt is itself historically and theologically silly. That particular "i" is far more important than the "I" which begins so many of men's sentences. It is that missing "i" which defines Christianity. Churches through the ages have not been in agreement regarding the doctrines of man, law, sanctions, and eschatology (last things), but they have been agreed on one issue, which was declared in 325 A.D. at the Council of Nicea: *homoousion*. Our world is what it is because of that ancient confession. Yet we hear no discussion of this fact in the typical history class, even a class in Church history in a conservative theological seminary. How many pastors could present a plausible case to show why Christian society is different from non-Christian society because Christians believed *homoousion* rather than *homoiousion*?[6]

The modern world has continued to debate the old issues of the Council of Nicea, although with new terminology and new accents. The modern world is still tearing itself apart over the meaning of, truth of, and relevance of that missing "i" in *homoousion*. Modern man knows in his heart (Rom. 2:14-15) that without that "i," his capitalized "I" is subordinate to Jesus Christ. He resents this fact of eternal life. He wages multiple wars against it.

---

5. Presbyterian liberal Henry van Dyke dismissed this debate as meaningless. *The Bible As It Is* (New York: Session, 1893), p. 11.

6. Hint: because Jesus did not evolve into God; He was of the same essence as God from the beginning. Hint: because God has manifested Himself in history. R. J. Rushdoony, *The Foundations of Social Order: Studies in the Creeds and Councils of the Early Church* (Fairfax, Virginia: Thoburn Press, [1968] 1978), ch. 1.

Conclusion

From the 1720's until 1936, there was a war for the control of the Presbyterian Church. This war was theological. Machen's three-fold analysis provides a useful conceptual tool for understanding this war. But Machen did not offer a detailed theological analysis of the three camps. In Chapter 1, I do. I invoke Calvinism's covenant theology. I apply the biblical covenant model (a God-given ideal type) to the three factions of American Presbyterianism. To make sense out of the Presbyterian conflict, we have to understand the rival covenantal theologies.

1

THEOLOGIES IN CONFLICT

But we cannot understand at all what the New Testament says about heaven, unless we attend also to what the New Testament says about hell; in the New Testament heaven and hell appear in contrast. . . . There can be no greater mistake than to suppose that Jesus ever separated theology from ethics, or that if you remove His theology—His beliefs about God and judgment, about future woe for the wicked and future blessedness for the good—you can have His ethical teaching intact.

J. Gresham Machen (1925)[1]

The doctrine of hell is the starting point for any orthodox Christian theology of negative sanctions. Jesus warned: "And fear not them which kill the body, but are not able to kill the soul: but rather fear him which is able to destroy both soul and body in hell" (Matt. 10:28). Jesus assured His followers that God really does send to hell the souls of all covenant-breakers, Adam's disinherited sons (Luke 16:22–28). Only through personal faith in the substitutionary atonement of God's Son, Jesus Christ, the lawful heir of the kingdom, can anyone escape hell. "He that believeth on the Son hath everlasting life: and he that believeth not the Son shall not see life; but the wrath of God abideth on him" (John 3:36).

---

1. Machen, *What Is Faith?* (Grand Rapids, Michigan: Eerdmans, [1925] 1974), pp. 222, 224.

The New Testament teaches that after the general resurrection and the final judgment, God will send covenant-breakers, angelic and human (the contents of hell), into the lake of fire (Rev. 20:14–15). He will then torture them forever. Some soft-hearted Christians may think "torture" is too strong a word. The New Testament Greek word is translated "torment" (Luke 16:28). The meaning, however, is torture: God's deliberate imposition of pain and misery on covenant-breakers forever, not to cure souls or restore men to righteousness, but purely for the sake of vengeance. "Vengeance is mine: I will repay, saith the Lord" (Rom. 12:19). The God of the Bible is no buttercup, to quote Otto Scott.

To put this as mildly as I can, consigning men and women to screaming agony forever has to be regarded as an intolerant act on God's part. The issue of sanctions in history is the issue of the judicial toleration of one's enemies: how much toleration, for how long, for which people, and in what institutional arrangements. After the day of judgment, toleration ends forever. God announces for all men and angels to hear eternally: "No more common grace."[2]

The most important dividing issue in the Presbyterian conflict between conservatives and modernists was the doctrine of eternal sanctions: heaven vs. hell, followed by the New Heaven and New Earth vs. the lake of fire. There was not a lot of argument over heaven, however; the fundamental theological and judicial issue that divided liberals from conservatives, then as now, was the doctrine of hell. The dividing question became: Which group will exercise the positive ecclesiastical sanction of ordination and the negative ecclesiastical sanction of ministerial suspension in terms of which opinion regarding hell?

Presbyterianism's Official Doctrine of Hell

All ordained officers in the Presbyterian Church took an oath affirming the Westminster Confession. This Confession announced: "By the decree of God, for the manifestation of His glory, some men and

---

2. Gary North, *Dominion and Common Grace: The Biblical Basis of Progress* (Tyler, Texas: Institute for Christian Economics, 1987).

angels are predestinated unto everlasting life; and others are foreordained to everlasting death" (III:3). The Confession made it plain: only some men are elect. "The rest of mankind God was pleased, according to the unsearchable counsel of His own will, whereby He extendeth or withholdeth mercy, as He pleaseth, for the glory of His sovereign power over creatures, to pass by; and to ordain them to dishonour and wrath for their sin, to the praise of His glorious justice" (III:7). There were many ministers within the Presbyterian Church who did not believe this. Nevertheless, they took the oath. They lied. They looked their future associates in the eye and lied. Not one of them was ever de-frocked for this particular lie.

The issue here is the judicial limits of ecclesiastical toleration. If God refuses to tolerate covenant-breakers in eternity, should the Church's government tolerate those inside the Church who side with the covenant-breakers? If those who swore allegiance to the Confession in order to gain positions of authority inside the Church are in fact in agreement with those outside the Church on this, the crucial doctrine of eternal sanctions, shouldn't the Church's courts bring the negative sanction of de-frocking against those who falsely subordinated themselves by ministerial oath to the Church's authority? The crucial issue was sanctions.

Guarding the Sacraments

The priests and Levites of the Old Covenant had three primary tasks: to preach and teach God's word (Deut. 31:9–13; Neh. 8:13), to administer the sacrifices (Num. 3:6–9), and to defend the temple area from unauthorized trespassers who might cross the boundaries of the area of sacrifice (Num. 3:10). Each of these was a judicial task. These three judicial tasks have not changed in the New Covenant. The required sacrifices and sanctions have changed, but not the tasks.

In his *Institutes of the Christian Religion*, Calvin argued that the institutional Church has two identifying marks: the lawful preaching of the word and the lawful administration of the sacraments: baptism and the Lord's Supper. Implicit in his definition is a third mark: institutional discipline. Preachers who do not faithfully preach God's word are to be removed from office. Church members who do not confess the Christian faith and walk uprightly are to be kept away from the table of the Lord. The Church is therefore marked by three things: word, sacrament, and the judicial protection of both.[3]

The sacraments are the formal means of implementing God's ecclesiastical sanctions: positive and negative. Baptism is the New Testament's equivalent of circumcision. Baptism places a person under the dual sanctions of God: blessing and cursing. Kline calls baptism the oath-sign of the New Covenant.[4] The Lord's Supper (Holy Communion) also brings positive and negative sanctions. Paul warned the church at Corinth about God's negative sanctions against those who participate unworthily in the Lord's Supper: sickness and death (I Cor. 11:29–30). Thus, the Lord's Supper is the source of sanctions, just as the altar was under the Old Covenant. I am not implying that the New Covenant altar is a place of sacrifice; I am speaking of it as the place of *judicial confrontation between God and man*. Following Kline's lead, I call the Lord's Supper the *oath-renewal sign* of the New Covenant, just as Passover was in the Mosaic Covenant.

Who has the right to renew his oath? Only those who still are willing to confess—or whose legal representatives are still willing to confess on their behalf—their agreement with the terms of the oath. There is no lawful covenantal oath without terms (stipulations), just as their is no lawful covenantal oath without specified covenantal sanctions. Historically, the Church of Jesus Christ has specified the following terms for all adult (communing) members: the Apostles' Creed or one of the more detailed creeds, the Lord's prayer, and the Ten Commandments. These judicial standards have been basic to Church liturgy from very early days. The Church has not tolerated members who deny these confessional terms. The Church has, until quite recently, denied lawful access to the Lord's Supper those who have denied these standards. This is an aspect of the priestly guarding function.

---

[3]. A detailed study of Calvin's thought on the sacraments is by Ronald S. Wallace, *Calvin's Doctrine of the Word and Sacrament* (Tyler, Texas: Geneva Divinity School Press, [1953] 1982).

[4]. Meredith G. Kline, *By Oath Consigned: A Reinterpretation of the Covenant Signs of Circumcision and Baptism* (Grand Rapids, Michigan: Eerdmans, 1968), ch. 5.

Excommunication by the Church is the ultimate negative sanction in history, for God honors the excommunication in eternity (Matt. 18:18).[5] Execution by the State is a mild rebuke compared to this. He who is lawfully excommunicated by a Trinitarian Church is in worse condition than the heathen who never heard the gospel. From him to whom much has been given, much is expected (Luke 12:47–48).

A Strategic Blunder

The Presbyterian conflict was a conflict over two of Calvinism's marks of the Church: faithful preaching and faithful Church discipline. To my knowledge, no major participant in the conflict ever wrote so much as an article on the defense of the sacraments. This issue did not become a significant part of the public debate. It is also never mentioned by the many authors who have studied the Presbyterian conflict. The Confessionalists and the minimal-creed conservatives always argued that the most judicially significant issue is the theological content of preaching. In contrast, their modernist opponents always said that the fundamental judicial issue is lawful Church government: toleration (to 1933) and obedience (1934–36). But no one ever argued that the fundamental judicial issue is the defense of the sacraments. Like the dog that never barked in the Sherlock Holmes story, so is the missing issue of the sacraments in the Presbyterian conflict.

The conservatives—initially Old School Presbyterians, and later Old School and New School Presbyterians—always presented their case against their opponents in terms of the requirements (stipulations) of the preaching ministry. This was a fatal strategic blunder. The issue was not merely unfaithful preaching by ordained ministers; it was also

---

5. Calvin commented on Matthew 18:18: ". . . the latter applies to the discipline of excommunication which is entrusted to the church. But the church binds him whom it excommunicates-not that it casts him into everlasting ruin and despair, but because it condemns his life and morals, and already warns him of his condemnation unless he should repent. . . . Therefore, that no one may stubbornly despise the judgment of the church, or think it immaterial that he has been condemned by the vote of the believers, the Lord testifies that such judgment by believers is nothing but the proclamation of his own sentence, and that whatever they have done on earth is ratified in heaven." Calvin, *The Institutes of the Christian Religion* (1559), IV:XI:2. Ford Lewis Battles translation, 2 vols. (Philadelphia: Westminster Press, 1960), II:1214.

the question of who possesses lawful access to the sacraments and who does not.

The Plan of Salvation

Christianity affirms the existence of a supernatural Creator who calls ethically rebellious people to Himself (Matt. 20:16), regenerates them through His grace (Eph. 2:8-9), and makes them adopted sons (John 1:12). They become members of God's household. Christianity affirms that there is no other way to salvation except through faith in the substitutionary death and resurrection of Jesus Christ, the Son of God, who was both God and an ethically perfect man in one person. Christianity is a religion that preaches *redemption by the grace of the God of the Bible and no other*. It is an "all-or-nothing" religion. It acknowledges no middle position. It is at war—spiritual, doctrinal, and historical—with all other religions. It proclaims the existence of God's "non-negotiable demands,"[6] His call for "unconditional surrender."[7]

Machen recognized this from the beginning. He knew that Christ's Church is in a fight, not merely to the death, but to the day of judgment. This fight is a *fight to the second death*, for Satan and his followers (Rev. 20:14), and a *fight to life eternal* for Christians. Christians are supposed to understand that this fight is still in progress, as Machen warned his generation: "The type of religion which rejoices in the pious sound of traditional phrases, regardless of their meanings, or shrinks from 'controversial' matters, will never stand amid the shocks of life. In the sphere of religion, as in other spheres, the things about which men are agreed are apt to be the things that are least worth holding; the really important things are the things about which men will fight."[8]

But Machen's distinction between Christianity and liberalism was not enough, for the Christians were not united in his era in an organ-

---

6. Gary North, *Moses and Pharaoh: Dominion Religion vs. Power Religion* (Tyler, Texas: Institute for Christian Economics, 1985), ch. 10.

7. *Ibid.*, ch. 13; Cf. Gary North, *Unconditional Surrender: God's Program for Victory*, 3rd ed. (Tyler, Texas: Institute for Christian Economics, 1988).

8. Machen, *Christianity and Liberalism* (New York: Macmillan, 1923), pp. 1-2. Reprinted by William B. Eerdmans Co.

ized defense of the fundamentals of the faith. We need additional categories to make sense out of the Presbyterian conflict. I have selected two tripartite classification schemes: (1) power religion, (2) experiential religion, and (3) judicial religion; and the division of (1) Conservatism: Calvinist, (2) Conservatism: Arminian, and (3) Liberalism-Modernism. There were additional subdivisions, although I am limiting my discussion of these more subtle distinctions in order to help readers in their understanding of the split. What must be understood are the three religious worldviews.

1. Power Religion

This religious viewpoint affirms that the most important goal for a man, group, or species, is the capture and maintenance of power. Power is seen as the chief attribute of God, or, if the religion is officially atheistic, then the chief attribute of man or nature. This perspective is a perversion of God's command to man to exercise dominion over all the creation (Gen. 1:26-28).[9] It is man's attempt to exercise dominion in history apart from his covenantal subordination to the true Creator God. It invokes a transfer of sovereignty from the Creator to the creation.

Power religion denies the presupposition that God the Creator is absolutely sovereign over His creation. Because God is not absolutely sovereign, partially sovereign man must seek ways to bring order into his life and to the creation. Man then seeks order through power. The basic perspective of power religion is that knowledge is power. *Salvation is by knowledge*. This was the worldview of Greek philosophy and all occultism (with Pythagoras and even Socrates, who claimed that a *daimon* spoke to him,[10] as intermediaries). The less that God

---

9. Gary North, *The Dominion Covenant: Genesis*, vol. 1 of *An Economic Commentary on the Bible*, 2nd ed. (Tyler, Texas: Institute for Christian Economics, 1987).

10. In the *Apology* 31, he said: "You have heard me speak at sundry times and in divers places of an oracle or sign which comes to me, and is the divinity which Meletus ridicules in the indictment. This sign, which is a kind of voice, first began to come to me when I was a child; it always forbids but never commands me to do anything which I am going to do. This is what deters me from being a politician." *The Dialogues of Plato*, translated by B. Jowett, 2 vols. (New

has to do with the creation, the more sovereignty falls to man if man can exercise it through power. Mankind gains such sovereignty through representatives. In the reform social Darwinism of the Progressive era in the United States (1890-1920), this was understood as implying that a scientific elite would advise politicians in the techniques of scientific planning and management.[11]

What distinguishes the Bible's judicial religion from humanism's power religion is ethics. Is the person who seeks power doing so for the glory of God primarily, for himself secondarily, and only to the extent that he is God's lawful and covenantally faithful representative? If so, he will act in terms of God's ethical standards, which includes partaking in the Lord's Supper, and in terms of a Trinitarian profession of faith in God. The Church has long recognized this, establishing a dual requirement for membership: profession of faith and a godly life, which includes taking the sacrament of the Lord's Supper. This was Calvin's definition of the basis of Church membership.[12]

In contrast, power religion is a religion of *man's autonomy*. It affirms that "My power and the might of mine hand hath gotten me this wealth" (Deut. 8:17). It seeks power or wealth in order to make credible this claim. In the cosmic hierarchy of authority, there can be no meaningful, efficacious judicial appeal beyond mankind in history.

Some final authority always undergirds power. This authority comes from man and his institutions, the power religionist asserts. If there is any god above man, this god acts primarily through certain men, who are in turn agents of mankind. In short, *the god of the power religion possesses no voice of authority independent of man.* Harry Emerson Fosdick, Machen's opponent in the 1920's, stated this position clearly: "To be sure, God cannot be an individual to whom we cry.... What we are manifestly dealing with is a vital universe sur-

---

York: Random House, [1892] 1937), I:414.

11. See below, "The Five Points of Modernism," point three: "Ethics/Law," pp. 75-77. See also North, *Dominion Covenant*, Appendix A.

12. Calvin wrote: ". . . we recognize as members of the church those who, by confession of faith, by example of life, and by partaking of the sacraments, profess the same God and Christ with us." Calvin, *Institutes*, IV:I:8. Battles translation, II:1022-23.

charged with Creative Power. . . . That power has issued in spiritual life and in terms of spiritual life must be interpreted."[13] The spiritual life of man incarnates the impersonal power of the universe. "May the Force be with you (and especially with me)!"

Wealth and power are aspects of both power religion and dominion religion. Advocates of both of these rival religions regard wealth and power as valid visible manifestations of historical progress. This is why God warns His people not to believe that their autonomous actions have gained them their blessings: "But thou shalt remember the LORD thy God: for it is he that giveth thee power to get wealth, that he may establish his covenant which he sware unto thy fathers, as it is this day" (Deut. 8:18). Christians need to recognize that God's opponents also want visible confirmation of the validity of their covenant: a covenant with death. God warns all men that "the wealth of the sinner is laid up for the just" (Prov. 13:22b). The entry of the Israelites into Canaan was supposed to remind them of this fact: the Canaanites had built homes and vineyards to no avail; their conquerors inherited the land (Josh. 24:13).

Those who believe in power religion have refused to see that long-term wealth in any society is the product of ethical conformity to God's law. They believe in historical sanctions—blessing and cursing—but not the law of God. They have sought the blessings promised by God's covenant while denying the validity and eternally binding ethical standards of that covenant. In short, they have confused the fruits of Christianity with the roots. They have attempted to chop away the roots but preserve the fruits.

The strategy of the power religionists: "Bide your time until you've got the votes. Meanwhile, plead for peace, harmony, and the blessings of diversity." Their battle cry (until the final phase): "Toleration must be tolerated!"

---

13. Cited in Cornelius Van Til, *Psychology of Religion*, vol. 4 of *In Defense of the Faith* (Phillipsburg, New Jersey: Presbyterian & Reformed, [1961] 1971), p. 102.

2. Experiential Religion

Seeing that the exercise of autonomous power is a snare and a delusion, the proponents of experiential religion have sought to insulate themselves from the general culture—a culture maintained by power. They have fled the responsibilities of worldwide dominion, or even regional dominion, in the hope that God will excuse them from the general dominion covenant. They have abandoned the ideal of Christendom.

The basic idea lying behind experiential religion is the denial of the dominion covenant. The experientialist believes that the techniques of self-discipline, whether under God or apart from God (e.g., Buddhism), offer power over only limited areas of life. Experientialists attempt to conserve their limited power by focusing their ethical concern on progressively (regressively) narrower areas of personal responsibility. The experientialist believes that he will gain more control over himself and his narrow environment by restricting his self-imposed zones of responsibility. An example of this outlook is gnosticism. The ancient gnostic's concern was self, from start to finish; his attempt to escape from responsibilities beyond the narrow confines of self was a program for gaining power over self. It was a religion of works, of *self-salvation*. A man "humbled" himself—admitted that there were limits to his power, and therefore limits to the range of his responsibilities—only to elevate self to a position of hypothetically God-like spirituality.

Experiential religion proclaims institutional peace: "peace at any price." Ezekiel responded to such an assertion in the name of God: ". . . they have seduced my people, saying, Peace; and there was no peace" (Ezek. 13:10a). Experientialism elevates the goal of peace because experientialism has little interest in the systematic efforts that are always required to purify institutions as a prelude to social reconstruction. It does not cry, "Give me liberty or give me death." It rests on another choice: "Give me peace or give me death." God gives defeat to those who choose peace at this price.

Experiential religion calls for a flight from the world. Experiential religion's advocates may hide their real concern—the systematic abandonment of a world supposedly so corrupt that nothing can be done to overcome widespread cultural evil—by appealing to their moral responsibility of "sharing Christ to the world" or "building up the

Church" rather than rebuilding civilization, but their ultimate concern is *personal flight from responsibility*.

Experiential religion shares a theological affirmation with power religion: *religion without binding propositional truth*. The power religionist often speaks of religion as grounded in man's experience. He may mean *collective man*; with neo-orthodoxy, this may mean individual experience. Neo-orthodoxy is inherently pietistic, even though its advocates are usually power religionists.[14] Modernist experientialism moves all religions into the realm of comparative religion, comparative culture, and therefore cultural relativism. This supposedly allows the power religionist personal freedom from the responsibility of having to conform to the specifics of any religion, especially if he regards himself as the vanguard of the next evolutionary phase of religion. This form of experientialism denies the uniqueness of any one doctrine or rite for all time and places. "There have been many saviors, many gospels." In contrast, the pietistic experientialist grounds his faith in his unique personal experience. He may or may not claim that this experience is universal. The Zen Buddhist does not; a Christian mystic may. If he claims that this experience is available to anyone, as the Christian fundamentalist does, he nonetheless has to admit that this experience cannot be put into words. It must be felt in order to be appreciated; it is nonpropositional.

A New Gnosticism[15]

Experiential religion is creedal, but in a gnostic sense: relegating matter and time to the realm of second-best or even to the realm of evil. Through experientialism, gnosticism seeps back into the Church. Gnosticism's goal is inner peace through an escape from time and from judicial confrontations in time. Gnosticism is Christianity's ancient rival. It keeps returning in new garb. Rushdoony has pointed

---

14. Barthians derive their power religion from their liberal politics; theologically speaking, however, neo-orthodoxy insists that God has not spoken in such a way as to enable men to derive permanent propositional creeds and theologies. Neo-orthodoxy places faith in Kant's noumenal realm, not his phenomenal realm.

15. Philip J. Lee, *Against the Protestant Gnostics* (New York: Oxford University Press, 1987).

out that gnosticism has generally been hostile to creeds. "Creeds too obviously revealed its departure from and hostility to the faith. It was much more effective to affirm the Apostles' Creed and to re-interpret in terms of Gnosticism. This, from Gnosticism on through neo-orthodoxy, has been a favored method of heresy."[16] This was precisely the strategy adopted by the modernists in the Northern Presbyterian Church after 1900: proclaiming that they believed the words of the Westminster Confession, they re-interpreted the meaning of its words and declared the opposite after ordination.

Gnosticism is a rival religion, the religion of humanism. "Gnosticism was in essence *humanism*, the glorification of man. In humanism, man makes himself ultimate by undercutting the ultimacy of God. The vaguer the doctrines of the Father, Son, and Holy Ghost were made, the more clearly man emerged as the sovereign, and man's order as the ultimate order."[17] This description characterizes the theology of the liberal humanists who captured the Presbyterian Church. The minimal-creed experientialists found it too expensive to deal judicially with this form of gnosticism; they shared too many presuppositions with it. Calvinism was a threat to both groups.

There are two institutional forms that are appropriate to individualistic experiential religion: separatism and inclusivism. Separatism is the way of the ecclesiastical independents. Inclusivism is the way of the denominationalists. The strategy of the separatists: "Make a stink and then leave." The battle cry of the separatists: "Come out from among them!"[18] The strategy of the inclusivists: "I'll think about it tomorrow." The battle cry of the inclusivists: "There must be no battle cries!"

---

16. R. J. Rushdoony, *Foundations of Social Order: Studies in the Creeds and Councils of the Early Church* (Fairfax, Virginia: Thoburn Press, [1968] 1978), p. 11.

17. *Ibid.*

18. Carl McIntire and his followers were separatists. They voted Machen off of the Board of Trustees of the Independent Board for Presbyterian Foreign Missions in late 1936. The following June, they walked out of General Assembly of the one-year-old Presbyterian Church of America when their candidate, Rev. Jamison, failed to win the Moderator's position.

3. Judicial Religion

Both forms of experientialism—mysticism and pietism—are opposed to judicial religion, for judicial religion announces both the universality of its claims and the uniqueness of its message. It announces: *one way*. Biblical Christianity proclaims the sovereignty of God, the reliability of the historic creeds and confessions, the necessity of standing firm for principle, and the requirement that faithful men take risks for God's sake. It proclaims that the one-time sacrifice of Jesus Christ on Calvary was a judicial act. His righteousness is imputed judicially to fallen men by the grace of God. Imputation is God's *judicial declaration*: "Guilty as charged!" to the sons of Adam; "Not guilty!" to the adopted sons. The theological doctrine of justification by grace through faith is a judicial doctrine.

Because covenant-keeping man's salvation is grounded in God's judicial declaration, he is responsible before God to keep God's ethical commands (I John 2:3-4). The Church must be kept pure by preaching which is faithful to the Bible, by the faithful administration of the sacraments, and by the defense of both doctrine and sacrament through discipline: the removal from ordained office of false preachers and the excommunication of covenant-breaking members. In short, *judicial religion mandates judicial sanctions*: in Church, State, and family. The battle for judicial religion begins in the Church, for the Church is the place where the whole counsel of God is to be preached. Judgment must begin at the house of God (I Pet. 4:17).

We can see the difference between Eastern Orthodoxy and Western Orthodoxy in the term for the rites of baptism and the Lord's Supper. In the Western Church, baptism and the Lord's Supper are called sacraments, from the Latin word *sacramentum*: the enlistment oath taken by a Roman soldier.[19] (Calvin, however, rejected the theological relevance of the grammatical origin of the word,[20] thereby separating the Reformed sacramental tradition from oath-taking. This

---

19. "Sacrament," *Cyclopaedia of Biblical, Theological, and Ecclesiastical Literature*, edited by John M'Clintock and James Strong, 10 vols. (New York: Harper & Bros., 1894), IX:212.

20. Calvin, *Institutes*, IV:XIV:13; Battles edition, p. 1288.

has led to an operational emphasis in Reformed churches on the liturgical importance of preaching over the Lord's Supper.) In the Eastern Church, these rites are called *mysteries*. Neither term is used in the New Testament to describe these rites. Usage stems from the differing emphases of the two traditions. The Eastern Church is primarily mystical; the Western Church is primarily judicial.

Both the power religion and the experiential religion have become mystical and antinomian as they have abandoned the creeds and confessions. Protestant and Catholic power religionists have proclaimed Barthian "Christ encounters," while Protestant experiential religion has moved into mysticism and tongues-speaking. Both forms of experientialism dismiss creedalism as rationalistic and legalistic. Both proclaim: "No creed but Christ, no law but love."

Judicial religion is always *openly, forthrightly creedal*; it has a public theology. The very existence of the creed testifies to the fact that God has dealt with men through revelation that can be summarized accurately in terms of propositional truth. Experiential religion emphasizes creeds only to the extent that they can promote a traditional sense of subordination to God that stimulates a religious experience. Power religion is officially anti-creedal. "All creeds are relative," it proclaims, but it keeps this mental reservation: "except the legitimacy of power and power that legitimizes." Every worldview has a creed, even if its permanent creed states that "there is no permanent creed." *Creeds are inescapable concepts*. It is never a question of "creed vs. no creed"; it is a question of *which* creed.[21]

The strategy of the judicialists: "Make a fight until we win or they kick us out." The battle cry of the judicialists: "All or nothing!"

The Content of Theological Systems

I have adopted the Bible's five-point covenant model as a grid to understand the rival theological positions in the Presbyterian conflict. Other models are no doubt possible and useful, but this one enables us to be sure that we have not missed anything really crucial. The five

---

21. Rushdoony, *Foundations of Social Order*, pp. 1–2. Cf. Rushdoony, *Systematic Theology*, 2 vols. (Vallecito, California: Ross House, [1978] 1994), I, ch. 1.

points of the biblical covenant are: (1) the transcendence of God, which also involves His universal presence; (2) hierarchy in the creation, with the word of God governing man, and with man as God's representative agent over the creation; (3) ethics based on God's twofold revelation of His standards to man: special revelation (the Bible) and general ("natural") revelation; (4) the covenantal oath as the judicial basis of legitimacy in Church, State, and family, in which God's eternal and historical sanctions are invoked: positive and negative; (5) succession in history based on covenantal inheritance and disinheritance.[22] The acronym for this system is THEOS, the Greek word for God: transcendence, hierarchy, ethics, oath, succession.

1. The Five Points of Calvinism[23]

The familiar five points of Calvinism were not arranged this way by John Calvin. They came in response to a theological challenge by the Dutch theologian Jacob Arminius, whose name perseveres as Arminianism. In the late sixteenth and early seventeenth centuries, he offered a rival theology to Calvinism.[24] He died in 1609. The Synod of Dort (1616–19) was held by Calvinists to refute him and his followers, known as the Remonstrants. The Calvinists adopted a five-point alternative. They affirmed the total depravity of man, the unconditional election of the saints by God's predestinating sovereignty, Jesus Christ's particular redemption of the elect (unfortunately popularized as "limited atonement"), God's irresistible grace in each redeemed person's election, and the perseverance of the saints' salvation until their bodily death. In English, the acronym for this theology is TULIP.

The five points of Dort summarize Calvin's soteriology (doctrine of salvation) for the individual. Calvin taught that God is absolutely sovereign. There is nothing that happens in history outside the decree

---

22. Ray R. Sutton, *That You May Prosper: Dominion By Covenant*, 2nd ed. (Tyler, Texas: Institute for Christian Economics, 1992). First edition: 1987.

23. David N. Steele and Curtis C. Thomas, *The Five Points of Calvinism: Defined, Defended, Documented* (Phillipsburg, New Jersey: Presbyterian & Reformed, [1963] 1979).

24. Carl Bangs, *Arminius: A Study in the Dutch Reformation* (Nashville, Tennessee: Abingdon, 1971).

of God. This is Calvin's doctrine of predestination. Some men are saved; others are lost; God is absolutely sovereign over both. This is taught most clearly in the Bible in the ninth chapter of Romans, in Paul's discussion of the love of God for Jacob and His hatred for Esau before either of them had been born or had done good or evil. Paul wrote: "And not only this; but when Rebecca also had conceived by one, even by our father Isaac; (For the children being not yet born, neither having done any good or evil, that the purpose of God according to election might stand, not of works, but of him that calleth;) It was said unto her, The elder shall serve the younger. As it is written, Jacob have I loved, but Esau have I hated" (Rom. 9:10-13). It was Calvinism's interpretation of this passage that Arminius objected to.[25] Elect individuals, Calvin taught, are elected by God's grace before the foundation of the world; they do not have the option of resisting this saving grace. They remain the saints of God throughout eternity. An elect person cannot "backslide"—modern Arminianism's term—into damnation.

The five points of Calvinism correspond to the five points of the biblical covenant model.

1. Total depravity/*Ethics* (man's)
2. Unconditional election/*Oath* (God's)
3. Limited atonement/*Hierarchy* (representation)
4. Irresistible grace/*Transcendence* (sovereignty)
5. Perseverance of the saints/*Succession*[26]

Calvinism is far more than these five points. Calvin's writings constitute a comprehensive, rigorous theological system that deals with society in general, the Church, and the State. His Bible commentaries cover those topics that the Bible covers. The five points are a stripped-down summary of Calvinism that is limited to soteriology. This summary reveals little of Calvin's theology in general, nor does it explain Calvinism's enormous impact on Western society. When

---

25. *Ibid.*, ch. 14.
26. North, "Publisher's Preface (1992)," *That You May Prosper*, p. xvi.

these five points are presented as the essence of Calvinism, the resultant Calvinism takes on the character of Arminian pietism: souls-only salvation rather than the comprehensive redemption of society as part of the Great Commission. Such a view ignores Book IV of the *Institutes*, the largest section of the *Institutes*, which is devoted to the institutional Church.

2. The Five Points of the Westminster Confession

The five points of the biblical covenant can be found in many of the Confession's sections, but I concentrate here on those points that became sources of controversy during the Presbyterian conflict.

1. The Absolute Sovereignty of God

Chapter III, *Of God's Eternal Decree*, announces: "God from all eternity, did, by the most wise and holy counsel of His own will, freely, and unchangeably ordain whatsoever comes to pass. . ." (Sec. 1). This decree was not based on His mere foresight of the future (Sec. 2).

God is identified as the sovereign Creator. God created the world "of nothing" in six days: Chapter IV, *Of Creation* (Sec. 1). In Chapter VIII, *Of Providence*, the Confession extends the implications of creationism: "God the great Creator of all things doth uphold, direct, dispose, and govern all creatures, actions, and things, from the greatest even to the least, by His most wise and holy providence. . ." (Sec. 1). This providence extended even to the rebellion of angels and men, "and that not by a bare permission. . ." (Sec. 4).

2. The Word of God

God was represented visibly in history by Jesus Christ: *Of Christ the Mediator*, Chapter VIII. Jesus Christ is both God and man (Sec. 2). He was conceived by the Holy Ghost and was born of a virgin, "of her substance" (Sec. 2). Christ reveals to His elect, "in and by the Word, the mysteries of salvation. . ." (Sec. 8).

What is this word? The Bible. Chapter I, *Of the Holy Scripture*, insists on biblical authority. Section 2 lists the books of the Bible. Section 3 rejects the Apocrypha. Section 4 insists: "The authority of the Holy Scripture, for which it ought to be believed, and obeyed, dependeth not upon the testimony of any man, or Church; but wholly upon God (who is truth itself) the author thereof: and therefore it is to be received, because it is the Word of God."

The Bible is the sole fixed authority over man in history: "The whole counsel of God concerning all things necessary for His own glory, man's salvation, faith and life, is either expressly set down in Scripture, or by good and necessary consequence may be deduced from Scripture: unto which nothing at any time is to be added, whether by new revelations of the Spirit or traditions of men" (Sec. 6). This law is unchanging. It does not evolve.

The Hebrew and Greek texts, "being immediately inspired by God, and, by His singular care and providence, kept pure in all ages, are therefore authentical; so as, in all controversies of religion, the Church is finally to appeal unto them" (Sec. 8).

The Bible is the voice of authority in history: "The infallible rule of interpretation of Scripture is the Scripture itself. . ." (Sec. 9).

3. Ethics/Law

Chapter XIX deals with law, *Of the Law of God*. It begins with Adam's covenant of works: "God gave Adam a law, as a covenant of works, by which He bound him and all his posterity, to personal, exact, and perpetual obedience. . ." (Sec. 1). This law has continued as "a perfect rule of righteousness; and, as such, was delivered by God upon Mount Sinai, in ten commandments, and written in two tables..." (Sec. 2). The laws of God given to Israel were moral, ceremonial, and civil. The ceremonial laws are abrogated (Sec. 3), as are many of the civil laws of Israel (Sec. 4). "The moral law doth for ever bind all, as well justified persons as others, to the obedience thereof. . ." (Sec. 5). This law, "as a rule of life informing them of the will of God, and their duty, it directs and binds them to walk accordingly" (Sec. 6).

This law is directed to the consciences of men: *Of Christian Liberty, and Liberty of Conscience*, Chapter XX. Under the New Testament, "the liberty of Christians is further enlarged, in their freedom from the yoke of the ceremonial law. . ." (Sec. 1).

Men's consciences are free to obey God's revealed will: "God alone is Lord of the conscience, and hath left it free from the doctrines and commandments of men, which are, in any thing, contrary to His Word; or beside it, in matters of worship." The conscience is therefore bound under God's word, His Bible. This adherence to the written word is the ethical basis of men's freedom of conscience. The

Bible is finally authoritative in history, not men's pronouncements. What is prohibited is "an absolute and blind obedience" to men's pronouncements (Sec. 2). But men are not to resist lawful powers "upon pretence of Christian liberty" and thereby "resist the ordinances of God" (Sec. 4). Churches have lawful authority to call such men to account; so does the civil magistrate (Sec. 4; see also Chapter XXX, *Of Church Censures*).

4. Oath/Sanctions

The Confession deals with oaths in relation to lawful authority: *Of lawful Oaths and Vows*, Chapter XXII. It discusses oaths as formal acts of swearing: testifying to the truth of some event (Sec. 1). The Confession does not discuss oaths in relation to the establishment of a covenantal bond in family, State, or Church. There is no formal affirmation of the biblical doctrine of sanctions imposed by God on the basis of an oath taken by man. It does not discuss the sacraments as oath-signs.

Election is an aspect of oaths, since God swore an oath to Abraham to seal His covenant with him (Gen. 15). "By the decree of God, for the manifestation of His glory, some men and angels are predestinated unto everlasting life; and others foreordained to everlasting death" (Sec. 3). The numbers in each group cannot be increased or decreased (Sec. 4).

With respect to election, "those predestinated unto life, and those only" are called by God to salvation. This is the teaching of Section 1 of Chapter X, *Of Effectual Calling*. This election includes infants. There is no automatic salvation for all infants. "Elect infants, dying in infancy, are regenerated, and saved by Christ, through the Spirit. . ." (Sec. 3). The Confession is silent regarding non-elect infants, but the language is precise: elect infants are saved.[27]

---

27. If all infants were said to be elect, then abortion would be the most effective evangelism program possible. Heaven would fill up through murder. If all infants were automatically damned, the Christian parents of dead infants and miscarried infants would be grief-stricken. Thus, we are not told by God which infants are saved and which are not. There is no concept of the so-called age of accountability in the Confession.

With respect to sanctions, Chapter XXXII deals with the intermediate state in between a man's death and the last judgment: *Of the State of Man after Death, and of the Resurrection of the Dead.* Souls of the righteous, "which neither die nor sleep, having an immortal substance, immediately return to God who gave them. . . . All the souls of the wicked are cast into hell, where they remain in torments and utter darkness, reserved to the judgment of the great day" (Sec. 1).

Chapter XXXIII, *Of the Last Judgment,* says that the righteous will go into everlasting life, but the wicked "shall be cast into eternal torments. . ." (Sec. 2). Men should be "always watchful, because they know not at what hour the Lord will come. . ." (Sec. 3).

5. Succession/Inheritance/Kingdom

Chapter XVII, *Of the Perseverance of the Saints,* denies that saved people can ever "finally fall away from the state of grace, but shall certainly persevere therein to the end, and be eternally saved" (Sec. 1). This perseverance does not depend on "their own free will, but upon the immutability of the decree of election. . ." (Sec. 2).

The saints are members of Christ's Church: Chapter XXV, *Of the Church.* The Confession says that the visible Church, "catholic and universal under the Gospel . . . is the kingdom of the Lord Jesus Christ, the house and family of God, out of which there is no ordinary possibility of salvation" (Sec. 2). This equation of the Church with the kingdom of Christ evades the issue of Christendom: the wider influence of the gospel in history.

The Confession is generally silent regarding eschatology, except as it applies to death and the last judgment. Only in the Larger Catechism does a broader ideal of the kingdom appear, in the discussion of the Lord's Prayer:

> Q. 191. *What do we pray for in the second petition?*
>
> A. In the second petition, (which is, *Thy kingdom come,*) acknowledging ourselves and all mankind to be by nature under the dominion of sin and Satan, we pray, that the kingdom of sin and Satan may be destroyed, the gospel propagated throughout the world, the Jews called, the fullness of the Gentiles brought in; the church furnished with all gospel-officers and ordinances, purged from corruption, countenanced and maintained by the

civil magistrate; that the ordinances of Christ may be purely dispensed, and made effectual to the converting of those yet in their sins, and the confirming, comforting, and building up of those that are already converted: that Christ would rule in our hearts here, and hasten the time of his second coming, and our reigning with him for ever: and that he would be pleased so to exercise the kingdom of power in all the world, as may best conduce to these ends.

This application of the Lord's Prayer instructs Christians to call on God to extend His kingdom in history. In this sense, the prayer is postmillennial in intent. It is also theocratic, calling on the civil magistrate to defend the Church. The Larger Catechism does not say that God will answer this prayer in history, but it does require that all Presbyterians pray it.

3. The Five Points of Old Princeton's Theology

The Calvinism of Princeton Seminary from 1812 to 1929 was Old School Calvinism. This was more consistently Confessional than New School Calvinism. But it deviated from the Westminster Confession in key areas.

1. The Absolute Sovereignty of God

With respect to the Calvinistic doctrine of predestination, Princeton was orthodox. But there was an important defection from the Confession: the six-day creation. Charles Hodge, who attacked Darwinism as atheism in 1874,[28] never accepted the six-day creation. In his early years, he had defended the "gap theory": a long but indeterminate period between Genesis 1:1 and 1:2. By 1871, he had switched; he defended an age-day theory.[29] In volume 1 of his *Systematic Theology* (1871), he self-consciously abandoned hermeneutical literalism in the name of scientific facts. "It is of course admitted that, taking this ac-

---

28. Charles Hodge, *What Is Darwinism? And Other Writings on Science and Religion*, edited by Mark A. Noll and David N. Livingstone (Grand Rapids, Michigan: Baker, 1994), pp. 63–157.

29. Jonathan Wells, "Charles Hodge on the Bible and Science," *American Presbyterians*, 66 (Fall 1988), pp. 159–61.

count by itself, it would be most natural to understand the word [day] in its ordinary sense; but if that sense brings the Mosaic account unto conflict with facts, and another sense avoids such conflict, then it is obligatory on us to adopt that other. Now it is urged that if the word 'day' be taken in the sense of 'an indefinite period of time,' a sense which it undoubtedly has in other parts of Scripture, there is not only no discrepancy between the Mosaic account of the creation and the assumed facts of geology, but there is a most marvelous coincidence between them."[30] In short, the authentic facts are scientific; we must interpret the Bible to fit these facts. He ended his discussion of the creation with this surrender to process philosophy: "And so if it should be proved that the creation was a process continued through countless ages, and that the Bible alone of all books of antiquity recognized this fact, then, as Professor Dana[31] says, the idea of its being of human origin would become 'utterly incomprehensible.'"[32] After Charles Hodge died, Princeton Seminary's faculty became far worse on the question of the evolutionary time scale.[33]

How an age-day theory that places the creation of the earth on day one and the creation of the stars on day four will help Christians become more scientifically acceptable, Hodge never explained. The longer the ages separating the so-called days, the more scientifically ludicrous the theory becomes.

The Creator/creature distinction is fundamental to Calvinism. By compromising on this distinction by abandoning both the Bible and the Westminster Confession on the six-day creation, the Princetonians surrendered to Charles Lyell's vast uniformitarian time scale.[34] This was a weak reed to rest on. Lyell in the early 1860's had returned to

---

30. Charles Hodge, *Systematic Theology*, 3 vols. (Grand Rapids, Michigan: Eerdmans, [1871]), I:570–71.

31. James Dana, author of *Manual of Geology*, was Stillman Professor of Geology and Natural History at Yale University: *ibid.*, I:571n.

32. *Ibid.*, I:574.

33. Daryl Freeman, The Attitudes of the Princeton Theologians toward Darwinism and Evolution from 1859–1929 (Ph.D. dissertation, University of Iowa, 1969).

34. Uniformitarianism assumes that today's rates of geological and biological change have remained unchanged throughout history.

the evangelical faith of his youth.[35] He had resisted Darwin's use of his theory, despite the fact that he had encouraged Darwin to publish in 1858. He had become a theistic evolutionist: God uses evolution for his purposes.[36] But in the 1867 edition of his *Principles of Geology*, Lyell could no longer maintain his resistance to Darwinism. He publicly surrendered to the evidence favoring natural selection, which he said established "a strong presumption in favour of the doctrine."[37] This progression of intellectual seduction has marked evangelical Christianity's continual flirtation with uniformitarianism.

2. *The Word of God*

The Princetonians defended the full authority of the Bible, but in a unique way: by denying the Westminster Confession's plain teaching on this subject and then proclaiming their allegiance to the true meaning of the Confession. This same argument was employed by the modernists on many occasions: denial in the name of a truer conformity.

B. B. Warfield adopted the lower criticism of the Bible: the supposedly neutral methodology of assembling the texts of the Bible. He argued that the preservation of Scripture affirmed by the Confession was achieved through scientific collation of extant texts.[38] In contrast, the Confession says that the manuscript copies were kept pure by God (I:8). If the Confession is incorrect, then what is needed is an explicitly biblical theory of the imperfect copies and their proper reconstruction, not a theory of neutral linguistic methodology. Warfield defended lower criticism as God's way of preserving the pure text.[39]

---

35. William Irvine, *Apes, Angels, and Victorians: The Story of Darwin, Huxley, and Evolution* (New York: McGraw-Hill, 1955), p. 139.

36. Ronald W. Clark, *The Survival of Charles Darwin: A Biography of a Man and an Idea* (New York: Random House, 1984), p. 134.

37. See the extract in *Darwin: A Norton Critical Edition*, edited by Philip Appleman (New York: Norton, 1970), p. 324.

38. Theodore P. Letis, "B. B. Warfield, Common-Sense Philosophy and Biblical Criticism," *American Presbyterians*, 69 (Fall 1991).

39. See Chapter 3, below: section on "Lower Criticism and the Westminster Confession," pp. 163-68.

The Princetonians developed a theory of the original manuscripts of the Bible. These manuscripts no longer exist. They were inerrant. There have been errors added in subsequent copies, but we have a sufficiently reliable Bible to make authoritative judgments based on its authority. This theory was contrary to the Confession (I:8).

3. Ethics/Law

The Princetonians did not break with the Confession on this point. The Confession affirms the permanence of the moral law. They were not evolutionists, nor were they ethical relativists. They defended systematic theology as a science of permanent propositional truth.

4. Oath/Sanctions

The Princetonians were defenders of the Confession's doctrine of the final judgment. They viewed the gospel as God's only means of bringing salvation from eternal torment to otherwise doomed sinners.

There was one strategic surrender, however, which left the Princetonians helpless against the accusation that they had quietly abandoned the Confession. With respect to the question of God's absolute sovereignty in election, the Old School no longer defended the idea, presumed though not explicitly stated in the Confession, that there can be non-elect infants.

The doctrine of final sanctions raises the legal issue of formal Church sanctions. The Princetonians, like the Old School generally, believed that modernist pastors should be de-frocked. They believed in heresy trials. But after 1874, they never actually recommended specific trials of named heretics. They upheld the legitimacy of negative Church sanctions; they just never invoked them.

5. Succession/Inheritance/Kingdom

The Princetonians were postmillennialists. This probably includes Geerhardus Vos, who was somewhat obscure on the subject (as he was on many others).[40] They believed that Christendom would be

---

40. Vos, "Eschatology of the New Testament," *International Standard Bible Encyclopedia* (1915), reprinted in *Redemptive History and Biblical Interpretation: The Shorter Writings of Geerhardus Vos*, edited by Richard B. Gaffin (Phillipsburg,

extended across the face of the earth in history. Warfield asked: "Are They Few That Be Saved?"[41] He answered in the negative. They were strongly opposed to premillennialism's doctrine of the bodily return of Christ to set up a kingdom prior to the final judgment.

The Princetonians were not ecumenists. They did not view the near-term future as a period of legitimate unity among evangelical churches. There can be unity among Christians, they taught, especially in the battle against modernism, but they resisted any alteration of the Confession, which meant that they could not accept Church unity in their day. The other churches would have to adopt the Confession in order for the Princetonians to accept ecclesiastical ecumenism: Church union as distinguished from temporary alliances.

4. The Five Points of Evangelicalism/Fundamentalism

The conservative evangelicals who constituted a majority of the Church after 1900 were heirs of the New School. They were not rigorous Calvinists, although ministers did have to proclaim allegiance to the Confession. After 1910, they became indistinguishable from fundamentalists in the denomination.[42]

1. The Sovereignty of God

The revision of the Confession in 1903 watered down the Confession's absolute predestination. The revision announced the love of God for all mankind, a revision of Chapter III, which affirms the foreordination of cursed men and angels to everlasting death (Sec. 3). The revision also stated that "no man is condemned except on the ground of his sin." This evaded the question of original sin and the

---

New Jersey: Presbyterian & Reformed, 1980), ch. 2. See especially his comments on the conversion of the Jews, pp. 35, 41.

41. *Lutheran Church Review* (1915), reprinted in *Biblical and Theological Studies* (Philadelphia: Presbyterian & Reformed, 1952), ch. 12.

42. Historic premillennialism teaches that the Church will go through a future great tribulation before Jesus comes again to set up His earthly kingdom. The broad majority of dispensational fundamentalists believe that the Church will be removed ("raptured") out of this world before the seven-year tribulation period begins. Also, historic premillennialists do not think that a restored political Israel will be the central focus of Christ's thousand-year earthly reign on earth; dispensationalists do.

total depravity of man, which the Confession says did not take place by God's "bare permission" (IV:4). It therefore tampered with the Confession's doctrine of the absolute sovereignty of God. Historically, this position has been known as four-point Calvinism.

2. The Word of God

The Bible is the revealed word of God in history. Its testimony is sure. On this point, the evangelicals agreed with the Princetonians. The Princetonians were regarded by evangelicals and fundamentalists as the premier defenders of the Bible. But the Princetonians had abandoned the Confession's statement on the purity of the existent manuscripts, especially those used to produce the King James Version. Some fundamentalists may have regarded this as a sell-out, but they did not go into print about it.

3. Ethics/Law

The conservatives were not defenders of situation ethics. The practical question facing them was this: Did the boundaries of theology and the Confession necessarily exclude modernists from the Church? Over this question and the question of Church sanctions the four later phases of the Presbyterian conflict were fought. Some experientialists sided with Machen in the 1920's; others didn't. Most of them refused to join him in 1936. The few who did set up the Bible Presbyterian Church in 1938.

4. Oath/Sanctions

Evangelicals believed in the Confession's doctrine of hell. They saw evangelism in terms of the offer of escape from hell and the gaining of eternal life. This was a major point of theological contact between Princeton and the broader Church.

The 1903 revision announced the universal salvation of infants. This compromised the Confession's teaching on elect infants. It was intended to; the whole denomination had abandoned the Confession's implication that there are non-elect infants.

The question of God's eternal sanctions leads to the doctrine of Church sanctions. Should those pastors who refuse to affirm the doctrine of hell or other key doctrines be de-frocked? Prior to 1900, the New School did believe this in principle, but they had to be strongly provoked by a modernist spokesman to persuade them to take steps to remove him. After 1900, the Presbyterian conflict was fought in terms of this question: What institutional price is reasonable and legitimate to pay in order to achieve the de-frocking of modernists? Answer: a price lower than the "market" called for.

5. Succession/Inheritance/Kingdom

Some conservative leaders after 1915 were defenders of ecumenism.[43] Most were not. But the arrival in 1906 of 1,100 congregations from the Cumberland Presbyterian Church did water down the hard-core resistance to further union. General Assembly standing committees on Church union continued throughout the 1906–1936 period.

Many Presbyterian conservatives after 1910 were premillennialists, and so had no hope in an earthly kingdom prior to Christ's visible return to earth in power. Others—probably very few—were amillennialists, who also had no faith in an earthly visible kingdom prior to the final judgment. Conservatives were united on the question of the bodily return of Jesus.

Theological Modernism: Darwinism for Vague Theists

What was theological modernism? It was secular modernism with the addition of a god who does not interfere with Darwinian evolution. There is no need to identify every theological nuance of modernism, every outworking of its creed. It is only necessary to identify those features without which modernism would not have been modernism. There were five such features, corresponding to the five points of the biblical covenant model. These are: the rejection of the doctrine of God as the absolutely sovereign Creator; the acceptance of higher criticism of the Bible; the acceptance of ethical, creedal, and theological relativism; the rejection of the doctrine of final judgment; and the acceptance of ecclesiastical ecumenism.

The modernist denied the existence of the God of the Bible, but in the initial stages of the confrontation, he was wise enough not to announce this openly. He covered his theology with the language of orthodoxy. He needed to conceal his institutional strategy: the capture

---

43. For example, J. Ross Stevenson and Charles Erdman of Princeton Seminary. Both sided with the modernists after 1920.

of a particular denomination or ecclesiastical association without losing the ownership of the buildings or the financial support of existing members. Nevertheless, there were key theological doctrines that he either had to reject or modify beyond the point of recognition. He began his attack where the Bible also begins: with the story of the creation.

The heart of modernism was its historicism, which included Darwinism. Had Darwinism not swept the intellectual world after 1859, theological modernism would not have taken the form that it did. There were two forms of Darwinism in the social sciences in the late nineteenth century. From the 1860's until the early 1890's, the dominant interpretation in the United States was that of "society as nature." These Darwinists, usually called the social Darwinists, promoted the laissez-faire economy in the name of scientific Darwinism. The two most important figures in this movement were England's Herbert Spencer and Yale University's William Graham Sumner. They applied Darwin's principle of nature's unrestricted and unplanned competition to society. The model was the free market. Nature is not planned by a guiding agent; therefore, society should not be planned by a guiding agent. In the words of Scottish social evolutionist Adam Ferguson a century earlier, society is the product of human action, not human design.[44] This form of social Darwinism was rejected by political Progressivism and by theological modernism.

Ward's Progressivism

Free market social Darwinism was challenged in the early 1880's, most notably by the self-educated American scholar and dedicated atheist, Lester Frank Ward.[45] He argued that man's presence in nature has at long last introduced an element of teleology: a planning agent. Unplanned nature has produced planning man. Mankind represents an evolutionary leap of being. Man's mind is capable of planning. There-

---

44. F. A. Hayek, *Studies in Philosophy, Politics and Economics* (Chicago: University of Chicago Press, 1967), ch. 6.
45. Samuel Chugerman, *Lester Frank Ward: The American Aristotle* (Durham, North Carolina: Duke University Press, 1939). Chapters 13 and 14 were prophetic of liberal fads to come: "The Feminist," "The Environmentalist."

fore, scientists who understand the laws of evolution can direct the process, including social evolution. Society needs such planned progress in order for mankind to compete successfully against other species. Ward published his theory in 1883 in a two-volume work, *Dynamic Sociology*. The specified targets of Ward's invective were Christianity and traditional social Darwinism. His was a reform social Darwinism: the Darwinism of scientific planning by an elite. This vision is central to twentieth-century liberalism. The decentralized social evolutionism of the eighteenth-century Scottish Enlightenment and nineteenth-century free market social Darwinism was transformed by the American Progressives, as well as by Communists, Italian fascists, and German National Socialists in Europe. The vision of the French Revolution and its Napoleonic fulfillment—top-down, State-planned social rationalism[46]—came to fruition in reform social Darwinism.

Dynamic Sociology attracted little attention initially,[47] but by 1900 Ward's views had become the dominant outlook within the Progressive movement.[48] Ward has been called the father of the American concept of the planned society.[49] This assessment is accurate. This Darwinian vision of social planning undergirded the modernists' confidence in the doctrine of progress. While confidence in the creativity of objective, rational thought began to wane visibly after World War I, especially among European intellectuals,[50] it was still strong enough in the United States to overcome traditionalists in politics and theology, especially after the Great Depression began in 1929. This confidence is evident in the words of University of Chicago political scientist Charles E. Merriam, who became a crucial figure in American

---

46. F. A. Hayek, *The Counter-Revolution of Science: Studies in the Abuse of Reason* (Indianapolis: LibertyPress, [1952] 1979).

47. Lawrence Cremin, *The Transformation of the School: Progressivism in American Education, 1876–1957* (New York: Vintage, 1964), p. 98.

48. North, *Dominion Covenant: Genesis*, pp. 297–318.

49. Clarence J. Karier, *Shaping the American Educational State: 1900 to the Present* (New York: Free Press, 1975), p. 139. Cf. Sidney Fine, *Laissez-Faire and the General Welfare State: A Study of Conflict in American Thought, 1865–1901* (Ann Arbor: University of Michigan Press, 1956), pp. 253–64.

50. H. Stuart Hughes, *Consciousness and Society: The Reorientation of European Social Thought, 1890–1930* (New York: Vintage, 1958), ch. 10.

social science after 1923 through his connection with the Rockefeller-funded Social Science Research Council.[51] In 1925, he called on other scholars "to contribute to the new politics which is to emerge in the new world: that of the conscious control of human evolution toward which intelligence steadily moves in every domain of human life."[52]

Salvation as Moral Reform

The impact of Darwinism on late nineteenth-century religious thought can be seen in an essay written by Rev. James Maurice Wilson, Canon of Worcester, in a 1925 essay, "The Religious Effect of the Idea of Evolution." Wilson was a modernist, one who fully understood the theological implications of Darwinism and Darwin's impact on Wilson's theological peers. Darwin had delivered them from Trinitarian orthodoxy by providing a scientific basis for believing in the religion of man. Man must become the focal point of religion, Wilson said, for "it is only in the study of man's nature that we can hope to find a clue to God's Purpose in Creation. Herein lies, as I think, the great service that the idea of evolution is rendering to theology."[53] Darwin had freed man from the biblical God. "The evolution of man from lower forms of life was in itself a new and startling fact, and one that broke up the old theology. I and my contemporaries, however, accepted it as fact. The first and obvious result of this acceptance was that we were compelled to regard the Biblical story of the Fall as not historic, as it had long been believed to be. We were compelled to regard that story as a primitive attempt to account for the presence of sin and evil in the world. . . . But now, in the light of the fact of evolution, the Fall, as a historic event, already questioned on other grounds, was excluded and denied by science."[54]

---

51. See Chapter 6, below: section on "Rockefeller's 'Baptism' in 1910"; subsection on "Firm Foundations," pp. 378-81.

52. Charles E. Merriam, *New Aspects of Politics*, 3rd ed. (Chicago: University of Chicago Press, [1925] 1970), pp. 59-60. That this book was reprinted in 1970 by its original publisher indicates that it was regarded as a classic.

53. James Maurice Wilson, "The Religious Effect of the Idea of Evolution," in *Evolution in the Light of Modern Knowledge: A Collective Work* (London: Blackie & Son, 1925), p. 492.

54. *Ibid.*, pp. 497-98.

Understandably, the rejection of the doctrine of the ethical rebellion of man against God at a particular point in human history necessarily transformed that generation's interpretation of Christianity. "The abandonment of the belief in a historic 'Fall' of a primeval pair of human beings has removed one of the great obstacles to the acceptance by our generation of the Christian Faith which had required that belief. Yet taken by itself it certainly tends to create, as well as to remove, a difficulty. For if there was no historic Fall, what becomes of the Redemption, the Salvation through Christ, which the universal experience of Christendom proves incontestably to be fact? How does Jesus save His people from their sins? *He makes men better.*"[55] Man now becomes a co-worker with a vague, undefinable god who does not judge. "It is the sins of the world and our sins that He who died on the Cross is taking away, by making us better. Salvation is not then thought of as an escape from hell; but as a lifting us all out from living lives unworthy of us. Religion so conceived is not the art of winning heaven, but the effort to become better and to work with God."[56] Here we have it: "Religion so conceived is not the art of winning heaven." More to the point, *religion so conceived is not the art of avoiding hell.* This, in my view, is the heart of modernism in all of its forms: the denial of hell. For modernism, the crucial issue was eternal sanctions.

5. The Five Points of Modernism

I have selected Shailer Mathews (1863–1941) as the representative modernist. He was a Baptist. He served as president of the Northern Baptist Convention in 1915, while he was also serving a four-year term as president of the Federal Council of Churches (1912–16). He was a defender of the social gospel. He ended his academic career as Dean of the Divinity School of the University of Chicago. To the extent that Presbyterian theologians and leaders expressed views similar to those expressed by Mathews, they were modernists.

---

55. *Ibid.*, pp. 498–99.
56. *Ibid.*, p. 501.

1. The Non-Sovereignty of God

The theology of modernism is process theology in a generic sense. The modernist must first challenge the doctrine of an absolutely sovereign God in order to make his position theologically plausible. Once any aspect of God's sovereign control over His creation is denied, no matter how minor this aspect may initially appear, the retreat from biblical orthodoxy has begun. What modernism denies is the Bible's absolute Creator/creature distinction. This is no minor aspect of God's sovereignty.

The Bible presents God as the Creator: "In the beginning God created the heaven and the earth" (Gen. 1:1). The doctrine of God's creation of the universe out of nothing is the doctrine that must be rejected. That God did this in six literal 24-hour days is anathema for the modernist. This creation account removes every trace of process (evolution) and substitutes God's spoken word: "And God said, Let there be. . . ." God literally *spoke* the universe into existence, day by literal day. First there was nothing; then there was something. The discontinuity between nothing and something was absolute. It is this radical discontinuity that the modernist had to deny. In place of the radical discontinuity of Genesis 1 he put continuity: *process*.

At issue is the question of ultimate sovereignty: *God vs. process*. Rushdoony is correct when he writes that "creation is described by all of Scripture as a creative *act* of God, in six days, and thus it must be understood as *act not process*. Every attempt to read process into the creation account, to turn the days into ages and make room for 'scientific' interpretations, is a surrender to process philosophies and an abandonment of a sovereign God. . . . The creative acts are not only perfect and final: they are totally supernatural. This is their offense."[57]

Mathews announced, "The modern age is primarily scientific and controlled by the conception of process."[58] Darwin's *Origin of Species* established "a new intellectual age."[59] Process philosophy has affected

---

57. Rousas J. Rushdoony, *The Biblical Philosophy of History* (Nutley, New Jersey: Presbyterian & Reformed, 1969), p. 3.
58. Mathews, *The Gospel and the Modern Man* (New York: Macmillan, 1912), p. 36.
59. *Ibid.*, p. 38.

the doctrine of God: ". . . God as immanent in this process rather than an extra-mundane monarch."[60] Process governs the cosmos; there are no God-miracles in the sense of imposed breaks in the "causal, genetic process."[61]

The messianic religion of Jesus was based on the sovereignty of God, he admitted. "Sovereignty was an analogy, but it was the most inclusive analogy under which the ancient world which shaped our ecumenical orthodoxy undertook to set forth the conception of God."[62] This concept no longer is acceptable to man. "We do not look to Him to find any likeness to the oriental monarch, but regarding Him as immanent Life . . . the source and guide of all progress."[63]

2. The Non-Word of God

"To the orthodox, Christianity was based upon the Bible as authority."[64] It was this viewpoint that modernism challenged. "The Fundamentalist movement was orthodoxy struggling to preserve not merely its doctrines but the inerrant authority of the Bible. To succeed it had to oppose science and other elements of a developing culture."[65] Science means evolutionary process.

From process, the modernist moves to historicism, i.e., the historical method: the scientific study of the biblical texts. "This historical method is of first importance throughout the entire field of investigation, but in the region of religion it is all but revolutionary."[66] Higher criticism is the result.

Higher criticism is now triumphant: ". . . there is no serious attempt to refute its conclusions by its own methods."[67] (This should come as no surprise; its method presumes its conclusions: an histori-

---

60. *Ibid.*, p. 43.
61. *Ibid.*, p. 46.
62. *Ibid.*, pp. 81–82.
63. *Ibid.*, p. 82.
64. Mathews, *New Faith for Old: An Autobiography* (New York: Macmillan, 1936), p. 277.
65. *Ibid.*, p. 278.
66. Mathews, *Gospel & Modern Man*, p. 42.
67. Mathews, *The Faith of Modernism* (New York: AMS Press, [1924] 1969), pp. 38–39.

cally relative, textually fragmented Bible that must be judged by the canons of secular literary analysis.) "The Modernist believes in studying the Bible according to accredited historical and literary methods."[68] (The accreditation system was and still is controlled by modernists.) Methodology, he said, has supplanted authority. "The substitution of scientific method for reliance upon authority is characteristic of our modern religious thought. . . [T]he methods of science are more conclusive than is authority, for authority itself is in question."[69] Anyone who has not been instructed by these methods cannot correctly understand Christianity. "The inability of the uninstructed to understand Christianity has always been asserted by dogmatic authority. What the Modernist is doing is, therefore, nothing new."[70] Therefore, the true orthodox Christian is the modernist—a familiar refrain of the liberals. "The Modernist rather than the champion of verbal inerrancy is a true successor of such fathers of orthodoxy"[71] as Clement of Alexandria, Chrysostom, Ambrose, Augustine, Aquinas, Luther, Calvin, Wesley, and others.[72]

The modernist challenges the Bible's unchanging authority in history, i.e., the only source of fundamental law. Higher criticism invokes the processes *of* history to challenge the absolute sovereignty of God's revelation of Himself *in* history. Higher criticism appeals to the human aspect of God's revelation of Himself, i.e., individuals in history. These individuals made mistakes with respect to this revelation, we are told—mistakes that the Bible's internal evidence does not always identify and correct. The Bible's account of what prophets said and did is flawed, we are told, just as any human document of comparable detail must be flawed. Therefore, the uniquely divine character of the Bible is denied. This leads to a necessary conclusion: a denial of the permanently binding judicial authority of the laws revealed in the

---

68. *Ibid.*, p. 43.
69. Mathews, "Scientific Method and Religion," in Mathews, *Contributions of Science to Religion* (New York: Appleton, 1924), p. 381.
70. Mathews, *Faith of Modernism*, p. 46.
71. *Ibid.*, p. 47.
72. *Ibid.*, p. 46.

Bible. The techniques of higher criticism produce a specific kind of ethical system: evolutionary.[73]

If God has not revealed Himself authoritatively in history, how can anyone speak authoritatively in His name? Who, then, speaks for God? *By what authority?* This is point two of the covenant: authority or representation. Furthermore, the modernist asks, by what standard does this person speak? This is point three: law. What sanctions are permanently appropriate to a law-order that is a product of history? This is point four: sanctions. Finally, how or why can subsequent revisions of the judicial boundaries—the enforcer's laws and sanctions—be themselves bounded by the judicial boundaries of the original revelation? This is point five: succession.

Higher criticism is inherently evolutionary, not in the biblical sense of the working out of fundamental principles—i.e., progressive sanctification (Phil. 2:12)—but rather morally open-ended. This is why modernism has no doctrine of *definitive sanctification* in history (II Cor. 5:17–18) to provide *judicially binding moral boundaries* to progressive sanctification. It has no doctrine of final sanctification: God's final judgment (I Cor. 3:12–15).

Once Darwinism has undermined men's faith in the absolute decree of God over creation, it is a simple step to undermine the morally binding character of the Bible. This is why higher criticism works in tandem with evolution. Higher criticism undermines the judicial authority of the Bible by an appeal to the historical origin of the texts: the autonomy, and therefore the sovereignty, of historical process. After the Bible's judicially binding authority as fundamental law is undermined by an appeal to historical process, the creeds and confessions lose their binding constitutional authority within the Church.

When the transcendent fixed anchor of authority of the Bible in history is removed, authority begins to drift. It is not that authority disappears. Rather, a new voice of authority is substituted for the old one. For the modernists, the voice of authority was science. Mathews wrote an essay titled, "Science Justifies the Religious Life."[74] Higher

---

73. Gary North, *The Hoax of Higher Criticism* (Tyler, Texas: Institute for Christian Economics, 1989), ch. 3.
74. Mathews, *Contributions of Science to Religion*, ch. 17.

criticism was presented by modernists as a scientific approach to the Bible.

Science has created a new priesthood. Modernists sought to cloak themselves in the robes of scientific authority, which is why they heralded scientific methodology as the road to truth. They infused their writings with the terminology of science. But in doing so, they abandoned permanence, for science as a vocation is always changing. As Max Weber wrote in 1919, "In science, each of us knows that what he has accomplished will be antiquated in ten, twenty, fifty years. . . . Every scientific 'fulfillment' raises new 'questions'; it *asks* to be 'surpassed' and outdated. Whoever wishes to serve science has to resign himself to this fact."[73] Nothing proves this better than the fate of modernism, which had begun to fade in 1936, the year Mathews wrote his autobiography and the year Machen was de-frocked.

3. Evolving Ethics/Law

In modernism, the supernatural Creator God of the Bible is pulled down from high heaven. He is dragged by nature and nature's theologians into the natural processes of history. His absolute sovereignty over nature is denied by the modernist.

If God lacks full control over the affairs of His creation, then process governs history. If process governs history, then men are not bound by fixed theological, moral, and judicial standards in history. Creeds lose their binding nature in Church history. Situation ethics becomes process theology's ethical standard. This has been a major goal of modernism: to escape permanent ethical standards in history. Modernists believe that a denial of God's fixed ethical standards will enable them to escape permanent negative sanctions in eternity. Thus, they adopt some version of evolution. The most common variety of evolutionary speculation in the West is Darwinism.

The immutable modernist doctrine of the evolution of the message found in the anonymously edited biblical texts leads to the equally immutable doctrine of ethical relativism. If the word of God

---

73. Max Weber, "Science as a Vocation" (1919), in *From Max Weber: Essays in Sociology*, edited by H. H. Gerth and C. Wright Mills (New York: Oxford University Press, 1946), p. 138.

itself has evolved, then the standards announced by that authority also must have evolved. When we ask, "By what authority?" we are necessarily also asking, "By what standard?" The modernist answers: By an evolving authority and an evolving standard. As Mathews put it, "Christians have never had a static system of philosophy or a finished theology."[76] "A theological pattern of unchanging content has never existed. . . . When a pattern no longer expresses a religious value or serves as the symbol of a group attitude, it should be and has been abandoned."[77]

Theologies reflect the Church. They change when the Church's historical conditions change. "We must look beneath and through the Creeds and Confessions to the attitudes and convictions, the needs, temptations and trials, the prayer and rites, in a word, the actual religious life of the ongoing and developing Christian group."[78] Historical study allows us to recognize that "the permanent element of our evolving religion resides in attitudes and convictions rather than in doctrines."[79] Therefore, "The first duty of the student of Christianity is to seize firmly the historical fact that it is the *concrete religious life of a continuous, ongoing group rather than various doctrines in which that life found expression.*"[80] Mathews' outlook moves theology from heaven to earth, from God to the Church, from individual confession—"I believe"—to group living. "*Our new world cannot be made Christian by reliance upon inherited patterns, but upon Christian attitudes and convictions embodied and expressed in the Christian group's life.*"[81] "Any study of Christianity must take into account the development of the social process which gave rise to the situations in which doctrines were developed. . . . Strictly speaking, there is no history of doctrine; there is only the history of the people who made doctrines."[82] Historical process replaces God's law as well as permanent

---

76. Mathews, *Faith of Modernism*, p. 3.
77. *Ibid.*, pp. 72, 73.
78. *Ibid.*, p. 58.
79. *Ibid.*, p. 76.
80. *Ibid.*, p. 61.
81. *Ibid.*, p. 83. Emphasis in original.
82. Mathews, *The Atonement and the Social Process* (New York: Macmillan,

propositional truth—except, of course, the permanent propositional truth of this proposition.

4. *The Denial of Eternal Negative Sanctions: Hell*

Mathews and the other modernists were relativists, both ethically and creedally. They denied the permanent binding nature of law. But if the covenant's stipulations change, then there can be no binding oath to God. If there is no binding oath to God, then there are no permanent sanctions for having broken it.

As I have written elsewhere, the doctrine of evolution must be seen primarily as a justification for denying the final judgment.[83] The language of hell, unlike almost every other biblical doctrine, cannot be evaded by prevarication, qualification, and obfuscation. The New Testament's language of eternal torment is clear. The modernist wants to scrap the doctrine of hell above all other doctrines. Thus, the doctrine of hell becomes a convenient touchstone of orthodoxy—perhaps the most useful of all biblical doctrines to identify and then remove self-professed Trinitarians who are in fact heretics or apostates. Hell is taught in the New Testament; hell is mentioned in the creeds; hell is discussed in the Westminster Confession, but hell is not found in the theology known as liberalism or modernism. The doctrine of hell is as useful a judicial screening doctrine today as it would have been a century ago and will be a century from now. No one has put the modernists' rejection of hell any better that Will and Ariel Durant did in their brief volume, *The Lessons of History*:

> In one way Christianity lent a hand against itself by developing in many Christians a moral sense that could no longer stomach the vengeful God of traditional theology. The idea of hell disappeared from educated thought, even from pulpit homilies. Presbyterians became ashamed of the Westminster Confession, which had pledged them to a belief in a God who had created billions of men and women despite foreknowledge that, regard-

---

1930), pp. 10-11.
83. Gary North, *Is the World Running Down? Crisis in the Christian Worldview* (Tyler, Texas: Institute for Christian Economics, 1988), pp. 63-64.

less of their virtues and crimes, they were predestined to everlasting hell.[84]

The denial of final judgment is *the* identifying mark of theological liberalism. Every other doctrine, every other tradition, and every other institutional alteration must be sacrificed on the altar of this new confession: God does not announce a permanent declaration of "guilty as charged" beyond the grave. He does not resurrect any person and give him a perfect body only to cast that body into the eternal torture chamber of the lake of fire (Rev. 20:14-15). This, above all other creeds, traditions, strategies, and tactics, must be affirmed by the modernist. If there is a hell, then the modernist knows what lies ahead. This must not be, so therefore it cannot be, he concludes. Those who preach otherwise must be removed from the presence of the modernist. There will be no final judgment, no eternal separation of the sheep from the goats, and anyone who preaches otherwise must be temporally separated from the presence of modernists. Separation is an inescapable concept. It is never a question of separation vs. no separation (e.g., ecumenism). It is always a question of who gets separated from whom by whom.

The broad conservative majority believed in hell. To deny the existence of a literal hell was to deny the evangelical faith. This created a problem for modernists. They could not publicly deny hell and stay inside the Church. Mathews, like so many modernists, was guarded in his language rejecting hell. In his autobiography, he announced: "From the scientific point of view immortality ceases to be an element of religious faith and takes its place among those hypotheses whose tenability depends upon available evidence. Heaven and hell have been repeatedly re-defined but among intelligent persons they no longer bulk as the basis for morality."[85] So, anyone who believes in hell has thereby identified himself as an unintelligent person. Mathews offered the tenuously held opinion that survival apart from the body after

---

84. Will and Ariel Durant, *The Lessons of History* (New York: Simon & Schuster, 1968), pp. 47-48.

85. Mathews, *New Faith for Old*, p. 234.

death "seems more probable than that life is purely mechanistic."[86] The idea that hell is a place where people are burned eternally is a valid figure of speech, but today we reject such "medieval pictures of punishment. . . ."[87]

Mathews was self-conscious in his rejection of the doctrine of hell. Hell, he said, disappears when the doctrine of God's absolute sovereignty disappears, i.e., point one of modernism's covenant theology. "The abandonment of divine sovereignty means the abandonment of the entire political pattern. Human guilt is the correlate of divine sovereignty and cannot survive its disappearance. And with the disappearance of sovereignty as a literal attribute of God and of guilt on the part of man, the need of satisfying the divine honor or punitive justice also disappears and the death of Christ no longer gets significance as expiation, satisfaction, or vicarious suffering."[88]

If there is no Creator God who creates and sustains the universe in terms of His sovereign decree, and if there is no final judgment by this God, then all there can be is historical process.[89] If there is neither *definitive* nor *final* sanctification, then all there can be is *change*: history without a sovereign, permanent decree. The only temporal boundaries for reality are the impersonal Big Bang at the beginning of time and entropy's impersonal heat death of the universe at the end. Neither has anything to do with ethical standards or eternal judgment. Life is then just a question of entropy: the irrevocable loss of heat—cosmically meaningless heat.[90] Better this, the liberal says, than eternally meaningful heat (Rev. 20:14–15).

If God's final judgment beyond history does not provide meaning to life, then what is the meaning of life? The modernist wrote rambling pages to deal with this problem, but he always came to a dead end. He kept affirming progress in this world as the meaning of life. But a moving standard is not a standard. Weber understood the impli-

---

86. *Ibid.*, p. 235.
87. Mathews, *Faith of Modernism*, p. 90.
88. Mathews, *Atonement & Social Process*, p. 182.
89. The Hindu would say that even this is *maya*, an illusion. All there is for him ultimately is impersonal timelessness: the divine unity of all life.
90. North, *Is the World Running Down?*, ch. 2.

cation of such a view: the death of meaning. "And because death is meaningless, civilized life as such is meaningless; by its very 'progressiveness' it gives death the imprint of meaninglessness."[91]

5. Succession/Inheritance/Kingdom

The kingdom of God is re-defined by modernists to be the kingdom of man, meaning collective man. It was not random that Mathews was also a socialist and a defender of the social gospel.[92] The social gospel was the product of social Darwinism: specifically, the collectivist or Progressive branch, which had been pioneered by Lester Frank Ward.

Mathews did not write much about ecclesiastical union, which is not surprising: he was a Baptist. His interest was in the effects of union: political and social rather than ecclesiastical. He took the standard line of the modernists in the early phase of their conflict with fundamentalism: a plea for tolerance. There should be a place for both the fundamentalists and the modernists. What will unite the two wings? A "common campaign of evangelicalism."[93] He saw the missionary movement as the model: cooperation between churches and parachurch ministries. "In some particulars, notably in the matter of Church coöperation, it is even breaking the road to Christians of all lands."[94] That the debate over foreign missions was the issue that finally split the Presbyterian Church is not surprising. It was here that liberals and ecumenists had infiltrated the churches. The call to evangelize the world had attracted many missionaries—perhaps thousands—whose theologies were closer to Mathews' than Moody's.

Thus ended Mathews' lesson. On ecumenism, he was not a representative modernist—too little said in print. We must consider the implication of his call for evangelism. A call for ecclesiastical unity based on evangelism can go only so far before the question arises: Is there unity of belief? If there is none, then what becomes of the call for

---

91. Weber, "Science as a Vocation," p. 140.
92. Mathews, *The Individual and the Social Gospel* (New York: Missionary Education Movement, 1914).
93. Mathews, *Gospel and Modern Man*, pp. 325–26.
94. Mathews, *Individual*, p. 69.

ecclesiastical unity? If there is no final judgment by God, then there is no legitimacy for institutional barriers that permanently exclude from the churches those who confess the modernist's unification faith. But the fundamentalists rejected this faith. As time went on, and the modernists gained majorities in the denominations, the only institutional barriers that were regarded as legitimate by modernists were those that separated the hell-preachers from the unification-preachers. The hell-preachers had to be isolated, cast out into the outer darkness of fundamentalist independency or sectarian denominations, leaving their fixed capital behind for others to inherit.

Once this surgical removal has taken place within the ever-expanding boundaries of the increasingly institutionalized Church, there must be no suggestion of *permanent* boundaries on theological expression. There may be temporary restrictions on self-expression for the sake of propriety, i.e., for the sake of the ultimate institutional integration—the omega point of ecumenical unification—but these are merely tactical considerations, not strategic goals. No one is to be removed from the presence of those who preach the ultimate integration of heaven and hell except those who refuse to preach this integration. A few premature enthusiasts of "ecumenism now" may have to be institutionally isolated from time to time—for the sake of selling the ecumenical program to the theologically unenlightened laymen in the pews who must finance it—but not removed by Church law or institutional sanctions.

Creedal religion that excludes is to be replaced by creedal religion that includes. As time goes on, the modernist believes, the many expressions of man's belief in God will be and must be absorbed into a single organization that will make room for even more bizarre expressions of this common faith. Every responsible person will find a place in the universal democratic Church. All views will be accepted, as long as each confession allows for all views to be accepted. All practices that are the outcome of such views must be accepted: "faith in action." In other words, nothing human is foreign to modernism! Except orthodoxy.

Factions and Functionaries

The liberals were liberals; they sought power in terms of modernism's five-point creed. They were Progressives. They were also promoters of a religion deeply opposed to Christianity. Their goal was simple: to capture an institution that belonged to their enemies. It is not difficult to understand their motives. They were men who coveted the ecclesiastical robes of authority, but who did not have the capital to construct their own ecclesiastical empire. Their goal was to steal the institutional Church without suffering a revolt by the donors. They wanted the robes of ecclesiastical authority, just as they wanted the robes of academic authority (tenured professorships) and the robes of judicial authority. *They wanted access to other people's money*—people who did not believe what they believed. This has been the goal of twentieth-century liberalism, political and theological: *build a new world order with old world money*. The implementation of this plan was pioneered by Presbyterian Woodrow Wilson, who did it first with Presbyterianism's Princeton University, then with the U.S. government, and suffered a stroke while he was campaigning to do it with the world.

Making sense of the modernists' Presbyterian opponents is more difficult. By 1936, a majority of the evangelicals wanted peace at the price of orthodoxy. Prior to 1926, when they believed that they might be able to win the fight, more of them had stood up to challenge the liberals. Conservatives remained in the Church, they claimed, in order to "fight from within," but there is no trace of any significant battle after 1936, i.e., after Machen and the hard-liners had departed.[95] How, then, are we to understand the varying motivations of the conservatives, 1922–36? I think it helps to single out key figures of the battle in advance, in order to identify the ecclesiastical forces that they represented. (This is the accepted methodology of "federal" theology or "covenant" theology: the quest for the representative head.)

Henry van Dyke was the most prominent modernist in the Presbyterian Church. In 1893, before Briggs was convicted of heresy, van Dyke set forth the modernists' new strategy of verbal conciliation; he

---

95. Lefferts A. Loetscher, *The Broadening Church: a study of theological issues in the presbyterian church since 1869* (Philadelphia: University of Pennsylvania Press, 1954), p. 155. This, in fact, is the thesis that Loetscher's book was written to prove: once Machen was out of their midst, there never was another Church-disrupting theological controversy.

chaired the Confession revision committee that prepared the revision of 1903; he defied the conservatives, taunting them to put him on trial in 1913 (they refused); he walked out on Machen in 1923 in a masterful display of press agentry; and he helped revise the Presbyterian hymnal in the early 1930's. He died in 1933. He served as a large-church pastor, as an English professor at Princeton University, as the U.S. Ambassador to the Netherlands in World War I, and was one of the most popular literary figures in the world. He understood the Presbyterian governmental system, and the only battle he ever lost was his support for creedal revision in 1889, which he won in 1903.

In sharp contrast was William Jennings Bryan, the consummate loser in American history. Defeated three times in his attempt to win the Presidency as the Democrat nominee, defeated in his attempt as Secretary of State to keep Wilson neutral prior to America's entry into World War I, defeated in his quest for Moderator of the Church in 1923, and defeated in 1925 in the most celebrated trial of his era, Bryan never won a battle he entered into. He was a fundamentalist, a Populist political radical, and an "old time religionist."[96] He was in no sense a Calvinist, but he was a vociferous opponent of theological liberalism. As a ruling elder, he exercised indirect influence over other ruling elders, but like the vast bulk of the denomination's elders, he was not involved in the Church's day-to-day operations. He was no match theologically or institutionally for his opponents. When he died, publicly humiliated, in July of 1925, having been pilloried by the world press because of his defense of the State of Tennessee in the famous Scopes "monkey trial," his followers were scattered—indeed, the whole fundamentalist world was scattered.[97]

Clarence E. Macartney was the most prominent Calvinist preacher in the United States, the conservatives' representative large-church pastor. In the early years of the battle, he stood firm with Machen, but when push came to shove in 1936, he revealed himself as a representative of the peace-seekers, the defenders of the religion of non-con-

---

96. Lawrence W. Levine, *Defender of the Faith: William Jennings Bryan: The Last Decade, 1915-1925* (New York: Oxford University Press, 1965).

97. See Chapter 9, below: section on "1925-26: The Visible Turning Point," subsection on "The Dividing Line: The Scopes Trial," pp. 572-75.

frontation. He did what every large-church Presbyterian pastor did: he surrendered. He had been an "exclusivist" in the 1920's, and had led the fight in 1923 and 1924 against the modernists, but when the modernists and inclusivists gained total power in the Church, he recognized that a continued defense of exclusivism would mean that he would be excluded by them, rather than they by him. He capitulated. He retained his pastorate but lost most of his influence outside his congregation.

Machen articulated the theological case for the hard-pressed remnant that attempted to defend traditional Calvinism. From the outset, he was in the minority, theologically speaking. He recognized early in the battle that he could win at that late date only if he downplayed the rigorous theological distinctions of his Church's Confession, since so few of his conservative colleagues still believed in it. Theologically, he was an "exclusivist" who was forced to fight his institutional battle as a "semi-exclusivist."

Robert E. Speer, a layman in name only, served as secretary of the Board of Foreign Missions, 1891 to 1937: from the end of phase two through phase five of the Presbyterian conflict. He became the most respected person in the denomination. He was a representative of the great bland evangelical majority, the archetypal "warm Christian" with "warm feelings" for all "men of good will" who preach any sort of gospel whatsoever, just as long as the name of Jesus (but not necessarily His theology) is mentioned occasionally. He was *the* representative inclusivist. Today, he would be referred to as a neo-evangelical. His chosen role was to serve *initially* as a mediator between the warring factions, and his presence calmed the majority of conservatives who believed that peace was preferable to the Westminster Confession. It was not surprising that they chose peace, for very few of them in the 1920's still believed in the Westminster Confession. Their lack of belief made them implicit allies of the modernists. Also like the modern neo-evangelical, once his work of mediation was over, and the creedal religionists were driven out, he sided openly with the liberals, whose agent theologically and institutionally he had been from the beginning. This two-fold role—mediator and theological agent for the liberal wing—was crucial to the takeover by the liberals.

Finally, there was Lewis Mudge, Speer's college classmate, who became the denomination's Stated Clerk in 1921 and supervised the expulsion of the conservatives, 1933–36. He was the archetype of the Church functionary who owes his position to the Church's institutional structure rather than to a specific congregation. He was the beneficiary of the power religion, a faceless bureaucrat who became the liberals' senior hatchet man.

What Is a Covenant?

A covenant is an incorporative union based on a judicial bond under God established by a self-maledictory oath that calls down God's negative sanctions on the party who violates the terms of the oath.[98] There are only four biblical covenants: individual (salvation), familial, ecclesiastical, and civil.[99] None of them rests on experience. All of them rest on a legally binding oath before God which calls down God's blessings for obedience and God's curses for disobedience.

We begin with the personal covenant between God and a new convert. The Christian must believe in Christ's work on the cross as his legal substitute, and then obey Him. The Westminster Confession puts it this way: "Christ hath purchased redemption, . . . effectually persuading them [His people] by His Spirit to believe and obey, . ." (IX:8). The old hymn, "Trust and Obey," has it right. *Experience is optional.* Conversion may be marked by a special experience, but this experience is not what establishes personal salvation (definitive), sustains it (progressive), and completes it (final). God's grace is the sole source of salvation, not men's feelings. God's grace is *judicial*: His declaration throughout time and eternity, that on the basis of the death and resurrection of His Son, Jesus Christ, an elect individual is officially "not guilty." This is Calvinism's highly judicial view of Christ's substitutionary atonement.

Christ died for man as a perfect sacrifice, a propitiation to God for man's sin. This is the official declaration of both Catholicism (certainly from Anselm's day in the twelfth century, this has been the case) and Protestantism. Christian theology in the West is judicial.

---

98. Sutton, *That You May Prosper*, ch. 4.
99. This four-fold division structured Richard Baxter's monumental Puritan study of ethics, *A Christian Directory* (1673).

Because the implications of this fact are not well understood with respect to the institutional Church, perhaps they will become clearer with respect to the family.

Judicial Bond, Not Feeling

A Christian marriage does not rest legally on the fact of two people having fallen in love. Divorce is not biblically justified because they subsequently "fall out of love." So, if the grounds for marriage are not a shared experience (love), and the grounds for divorce are not a shared experience (hate), then the grounds of marriage are not experiential. *The grounds of marriage are judicial: a binding oath of mutual loyalty*. God declares that there is only one legal way out of a marriage: the death of one of the partners, either physically or covenantally.[100] The marriage vow (oath) in most Church traditions makes this clear: "Till death do us part."

A judicial bond is equally the basis of civil citizenship. I was born inside the geographical boundaries of the United States. This makes me a U.S. citizen until one of three things takes place: (1) my death, (2) my renunciation of my citizenship and its transfer to another jurisdiction,[101] or (3) the revocation of my citizenship by a civil court based on a the decision of a jury to convict me of having committed a felony. Until then, I have the right to vote in U.S. elections. I am entitled to certain legal rights pertaining to U.S. citizenship. I may or may not get all tingly because I am a U.S. citizen; I am nevertheless a U.S. citizen. Prior to the Vietnam War, there were still patriotic parades and speeches every Fourth of July in the United States. Such events are rare today, and far less grand. This does not mean that Americans' citizenship is any less legal. The experience of citizenship is not the basis of citizenship. A civil covenant, *as with all other covenants*, is judicially grounded, not experientially grounded.

Christians understand these aspects of the civil covenant, but they do not apply this knowledge to the personal and ecclesiastical covenants. They do not recognize that God has established only three

---

100. Ray R. Sutton, *Second Chance: Biblical Blueprints for Divorce and Remarriage* (Ft. Worth, Texas: Dominion Press, 1987).

101. In state and local jurisdictions, this is done automatically by moving out of the jurisdiction.

ways out of a local church covenant: death, letter of transfer, or excommunication. As for the basis of marriage, the debate goes on within the churches. The widespread prevalence of divorce among Church members in good standing indicates that experientialism has moved from the personal covenant to the marriage covenant. Marriage is no longer viewed as grounded in a covenant with sanctions.

In the Westminster Confession of Faith (1647),[102] there is not a word on the necessity of an experience for salvation or for Church membership—not in the chapter on the covenant (VII), or effectual calling (X), or justification (XI), or saving faith (XIV), or repentance unto life (XV), or the Church (XXV), or the communion of saints (XXVI). In the chapter on effectual calling, we are warned that "Others, not elected, although they may be called by the ministry of the Word, and may have some common operations of the Spirit, yet they never truly come unto Christ, and therefore cannot be saved; . . ." (X:4). But like the New England Puritans in 1636, New Side (eighteenth century) and New School (nineteenth century) Presbyterians added experience as one criterion of Church membership, if not making it an explicit requirement, then at least an unofficial requirement. This led to the capture of the denomination by its enemies in 1936: three centuries after the New England Puritans stepped onto the slippery slope of experientialism.

De-emphasizing the Covenant

The Church from time to time has de-emphasized the judicial foundation of its covenant. It has emphasized experience over confession. As I explain in the Introduction to Part 2, the century-long confusion introduced by the New England Puritans' insistence on personal testimony of a conversion experience as a condition for local church membership led to the doctrine of halfway covenant, then to Solomon Stoddard's open communion practices, and finally to the First Great Awakening, which destroyed the Puritan holy commonwealth ideal. The Puritan emphasis on experience eventually undermined Puritanism's covenant theology.

---

102. It was completed by the Assembly in 1647 with the inclusion of the Bible support texts.

The problem with a religious experience is that it cannot be defined in propositional terms. At best, its physiological symptoms can be described in retrospect. *A religious experience surely cannot be defined judicially.* But all four biblical covenants are defined judicially, and *only* judicially. More important, the subsequent policing of all covenants must be in terms of known judicial standards. For example, the fact that a husband has had "a profound and spiritually moving" sexual encounter with someone other than his wife in no way restores their broken marriage covenant. Only his wife's acceptance of him can restore it. But in an age filled with adulterers, this judicial concept of the marital covenant repulses many people, including some Christians. It is much the same for Church covenants, and has been for centuries. The fact is, there was no way to distinguish judicially between a personal conversion experience in Boston in 1636, or during the First Great Awakening in 1736, or during the Second Great Awakening in 1836, or after reading a chapter in Karl Barth's *Church Dogmatics* on the "Christ encounter" during seminary in 1936.[103] But because the Presbyterian Church after 1869 refused to specify in its Form of Government that membership in the Presbyterian Church was exclusively legal—profession of faith and outward righteousness—and in no way based on experience, those who had read *Church Dogmatics* (or at least classroom lecture notes based on it) and who believed what they read, eventually captured the Presbyterian Church. The evidence of this is the 1967 revision of the Westminster Confession of Faith.

Defining Terms

In examining the doctrinal controversies that took place in Northern Presbyterianism, I have had to employ a number of terms that, without careful definition, could easily lead to confusion. The meanings of "conservative," and at the other end of the theological spectrum, "liberal" or "modernist," have fairly precise connotations, but what is the difference between a "fundamentalist" and an "orthodox"

---

103. Anyone who has tried to read a page or two of *Church Dogmatics* will find it difficult to believe that this "spiritual discipline" could produce a mystical experience.

churchman? Is it proper to designate both of them as "conservatives"? Without some attempt to define these words on my part, or at least to show how I have used them, they would lose their ability to make meaningful differentiations, and would thus become superfluous at best, misleading at worst.

From 1869 until approximately the second quarter of the twentieth century, a theologically orthodox Calvinist Presbyterian and a theological conservative seemed similar. But there were differences, and these differences ultimately led to the defeat of the conservative wing.

A central doctrine of Calvinism is the doctrine of the *Trinity*, which implies the sovereignty of God. Equal in importance is the doctrine of *creation*: the Creator/creature distinction.[104] Yet these are not exclusively Calvinist doctrines. So, the distinguishing doctrines of Calvinist theology are not its central doctrines. This is true of every Christian denomination or group. It is what distinguishes sectarianism from cults.

An Old School Presbyterian, being a Calvinist, put emphasis on the authority and sovereignty of God rather than on the will of man in the process of salvation: definitive (declarative), progressive, and final. A New School Presbyterian who was more in the tradition of Arminianism emphasized man's free will in accepting God's free grace. Both should be classified as conservatives. The Calvinist holds as the central feature of the doctrine of salvation the miraculous work that Christ performed at the cross, a literal historical event that serves as the sole basis of personal regeneration. The Arminian, however, is willing to discuss saving faith as a voluntary good work of man in response to God's free offer of the gospel—a work that can be forfeited by a subsequent "bad work" of disbelief. Both these streams of traditional Christian thought held to a miraculous, supernatural faith, and in this unity they were opposed to the theological liberalism that denied the supernatural nature of Christianity.

---

104. Machen's colleague at both Princeton and Westminster, Cornelius Van Til, reconstructed Calvinist philosophy in terms of these two doctrines. In this sense, his theology is radically theocentric.

1. Conservatism: Calvinist

What were the distinguishing features of Old School Calvinist theology? First, the doctrine of God's absolute predestination, including the work of salvation: God's sovereign grace. Second, judicialism: personal confession over personal experience as the basis of Church membership. Third, the doctrine of Confessional separatism: Presbyterian supremacy among ecclesiastical traditions. Fourth, the doctrine of hierarchical Church authority: hostility to parachurch or interdenominational missionary activity. Without these four theological principles, the Old School-New School conflict would not be understandable.

The problem for a Northern Presbyterian Calvinist after World War I was that his Church no longer really held to the Confession that he proclaimed. How could he engage in a successful battle to purge the Church of the modernists without the support of the vast majority of members and elders who were not willing to make a stand in terms of the Confession? There was only one way: to adopt a watered-down creedal position that the Arminians would accept, but which could not easily be accepted by the modernists. But if Calvinists adopted this strategy, they could preserve at best a conservative Church. *By 1910, there was no reasonable expectation that they could preserve a Calvinist Church*. That Church was gone. The Calvinists could at best reclaim it in the name of a broad, ecumenical fundamentalism. To achieve more than this, they would be forced to adopt the infiltration tactics of the modernists. But their public profession of the Westminster Confession made this strategy morally unacceptable and practically useless. Besides, such a strategy would have deceived no one. Everyone knew where the Calvinists stood. This stand was no longer acceptable to a majority of Northern Presbyterians.

2. Conservatism: Arminian

Any conservative Protestant in 1910 would have believed in the virgin birth of Christ, His divinity, the infallibility of the Bible, and the existence of a personal God. He would also have held the position that through faith in Christ, and in Him alone, can an individual gain his personal salvation, and thereby escape the horrors of an eternal, literal hell. But the theological battle for the Northern Presbyterian Church in this era was not over what the typical conservative churchman believed in. It was what he privately and silently *refused* to believe in: Calvinism. With the entry into the Church in 1906 of 1,100 Cumberland Presbyterian congregations—decidedly not Calvinistic—the Church quietly abandoned its judicially enforceable commitment to Calvinism.

What the Arminian conservative did not believe in was the Westminster Confession of Faith, with its doctrine of predestination-election. Yet the denomination officially was committed to this Confession. What the Arminian conservative had to deal with was the problem of denying ordination to liberals who personally did not believe in any of the Confession's distinctive theological premises, but who said they believed that it does represent what the Bible teaches. These well-trained, self-conscious hypocrites did not believe even remotely in what the Bible teaches. The essence of the conservative Arminian's problem was that he did not believe in many parts of the Confession, but he, too, had publicly affirmed that he believed in it as an accurate representation of the Bible's teaching. The liberal-modernist churchman was a bigger liar than the conservative Arminian, but it was always a question of comparative degrees of lying. And as modernist theologian Charles Briggs had pointed out in 1889, even the staunchest of the Princeton Calvinists had abandoned some of the Confession's doctrines, most notably the possibility of infant damnation.[105]

How could the conservative Arminians purge out the liberals without condemning themselves, unless the denomination adopted a non-Calvinist creedal formulation that would be specific in those areas of theology that the liberals could not easily affirm? And if conservative Arminians attempted a Confession-based purge, wouldn't their efforts be compromised by guilt and indecision because of their own hypocrisy? To ask these questions is to answer them. This book records how they answered these questions, and when.

3. Liberalism-Modernism

The theological liberal is a much more difficult person to describe. From 1874 to 1936, liberal Protestant belief could range from an ac-

---

105. Charles Augustus Briggs, *Whither?: A Theological Question for the Times*, 3rd ed. (New York: Charles Scribner's Sons, [1889] 1890), pp. 133–37.

ceptance of many of the tenets of traditional Christianity to thoroughgoing Darwinism. A liberal theologian desired to make his theology conform to accepted scientific truth and human reason, i.e., he was willing to sacrifice the former for the sake of the latter.

Most of those who could be classified as liberals insisted that they were not concerned with overthrowing the established churches, but only with modifying the faith so that it would be more applicable, in their eyes, to the scientific world in which they found themselves. Criticizing the society around them, one by one they arrived at a rejection of the old ecclesiastical order: an institution that resisted the material and social changes that they believed their society needed to preserve the dignity of its citizens. They were ready to demand "equal time" for a broader, more humane theology. This broad theology would eventually prove to be very broad indeed.

Their leaders knew better. They had no intention of allowing equal time for the Westminster Confession of Faith in the life of the denomination, for they well understood that this Confession does not allow a concept of equal time. The Confession is exclusivist—Protestantism's greatest masterpiece of theological intolerance. Liberals such as van Dyke intended to allow no time for it whatsoever. They also knew that their own exclusivist goal—a purge of the Confessionalists—would take decades to achieve. Their commitment to such a time frame gave them what proved to be an overwhelming competitive advantage against their opponents.

Drawing Some Lines, Erasing Others

Anyone in 1869 who accepted any of the findings of higher criticism, e.g., the non-Mosaic authorship of the Pentateuch, was, in the eyes of conservative theologians, theologically suspect. The authority of the Great Commission of the Church (Matt. 28:18–20) was based on the Holy Scriptures; any challenge to the latter was a challenge to the former. This was always a fundamental point of contention. A social reformer such as Bryan who held to the traditional doctrines of Christianity, and who accepted at least the testimony of the New Testament on the teachings and crucifixion of Christ, if not the whole Bible, was considered a theological conservative. Conversely, a political conservative who was willing to accept the Church as a fine institution, but devoid of any messianic mission—a proclaimer of Jesus of

Nazareth, but not Jesus the Christ—would have been placed in the modernist camp by theological conservatives.

In the late nineteenth century—or in the case of the Presbyterians, in the early twentieth century—these two streams of theological opinion began to merge within denominations, and even within individual believers. Thus, a man or a denomination might reject the infallibility of the Bible, yet accept Christ as Savior. Another might voice the traditional dogmas of Christendom, yet reinterpret them to mean something far different from what had been intended when they were categorized and written down. The distinction between conservative and liberal, at least in the middle ground between the extremists in each faction, became increasingly fuzzy, since so many on each side could be found who were in partial agreement with the other.

The vocal modernists were distinguished by their refusal to be bound by traditional theological dogmas. Far more dedicated to Progressivism's social ethics than to theological formulas, they were the active proponents of social reform within any congregation. Few after 1900 saw Christ as a uniquely divine figure; He was merely a great teacher, a man who had best exhibited that divine spark which flickers in every man's soul. Men, in this view, should be most concerned about this earthly life, and not about their eternal destinies, and therefore should devote the major portion of their lives to the earthly, material salvation of themselves and their fellow humans. Modernists were, and still are, best represented by the ecumenical Unitarian theology that is proclaimed at Union Theological Seminary in New York City.[106]

Conclusion

Each of the three groups in the Presbyterian Church, U.S.A., sought institutional peace, 1869–1936. The modernists sought *peace through institutional power*: anyone who could get himself ordained could and should remain a minister in good standing—without qualification prior to 1934, but after 1933 only so long as he conformed to

---

106. Southern Presbyterians also had a Union Seminary in Richmond, Virginia. It was conservative in Machen's era.

the dictates of the hierarchy, which was now modernist-dominated. The experientialist majority sought *peace through avoiding confrontational rhetoric*: with the liberals in charge, with the orthodox in charge, or with the fundamentalists in charge, just so long as they were allowed to build up their congregations. They did not want to stir up trouble. They did not want to take sides. In the 1870–1925 period, the experientialists would sometimes join with the judicialists against the modernists. After 1925, they steadily joined with the modernists against the judicialists. Why? Because the judicialists wanted *peace through separation*: the voluntary departure of the modernists from the Church. They recognized that Christianity was at war with the theological liberalism of their day. They saw that the liberals would eventually capture the Church if they remained in the Church. They understood that there cannot be a neutral ecclesiastical-confessional position that gives free reign to both Christianity and liberalism. They were outvoted after 1925, but they did achieve their goal of peace through separation: they were expelled in 1936.

The judicial aspect of this conflict began in 1729, when the New York Synod and the Philadelphia Synod joined together to form a single Presbyterian denomination. That decision was abandoned twice, in 1741 and again in 1838, and ratified twice, in 1758 and 1869. But the breach was never healed to the satisfaction of both sides. The theological war between New York and Philadelphia did not end until 1936, when representatives of the third theology, foreign to both, gained their victory. They threw out the handful of leaders who opposed them. The crucial issue was sanctions.

CONCLUSION TO PART 1

The visible Church should strive to receive, into a communion for prayer and fellowship and labor, as many as possible of those who are united to Christ in saving faith, and it should strive to exclude as many as possible of those who are not so united to Him. If it does not practise exclusion as well as inclusion, it will soon come to stand for nothing at all, but will be merged in the life of the world; it will soon become like salt that has lost its savour, fit only to be cast out and to be trodden under foot of men.

J. Gresham Machen (1925)[1]

Inclusion and exclusion: here are the two sanctions of the Church. Membership and excommunication, ordination and suspension: the Church must have both. The question for Machen was: Which group would announce the Church's standards and impose the Church's sanctions?

There were three major schools of theological opinion in the Presbyterian Church, U.S.A., after the mid-1870's: Old School Calvinism, New School Calvinism, and modernism. Each theology was covenantal; each had its representative five points. Each group also had its own strategy and tactics.

The Old School's theology was judicial and rested on a commitment to the 1788 Confession of Faith. Its members believed in the two catechisms, but these documents were not enforced by Church sanctions. The Old School was the heir of Puritanism's confessional Calvinism.

The New School's theology was officially Calvinistic, but its primary emphasis was experiential and evangelical. It was an heir of American revivalism. It tended toward cooperation with other ecclesiastical groups and even with what would today be called parachurch

---

1. Machen, *What Is Faith?* (Grand Rapids, Michigan: Eerdmans, [1925] 1974), p. 155.

groups. New School Calvinism drifted into fundamentalism after 1909.

Modernism was even more ecumenical. Modernists defended their position in terms of the language of New School experientialism and evangelism, but their experientialism and evangelism were not tied to the theological categories of the Westminster Confession.

The Old School had a view of Church sanctions more rigorous than the New School's, which in turn was more rigorous than the modernists until the 1930's. But Old School members refused to press formal charges against modernists after the Swing heresy case of 1874.[2] This left the initiating authority to New School members.

New School members refused to press charges against modernists after 1900. This left the Presbyterian Church devoid of effective Church sanctions in the area of theological confession for a generation, 1901 to 1934. Officially, Church sanctions for theological confession ended in 1901; the trials of the 1930's were officially conducted for reasons other than theology. So, after 1900, the Northern Presbyterian Church seemed to have no ecclesiastical sanctions. But no institution can exist apart from sanctions. So, in order to see what happened to the Presbyterian Church after 1900, we must examine in detail the substitutes for formal ecclesiastical sanctions. First, however, we must examine Church's theological sanctions prior to 1901.

---

2. See Chapter 3, below: section on "'General' Patton's Battles," subsection on "The Swing Case," pp. 180–83.

Part 2

FROM OLD SCHOOL TO NEW SCHOOL

... There is a widely prevalent theory, that truth may be of the feelings as well as of the intellect; that it may not only come thus from two independent sources, but may be contradictory so that what is true to the feelings may be false to the intellect and *visa versa*; and that as moral character and so Christian life are rooted in the voluntary nature, of which the feelings are an expression, the Christian life may be developed and, some say, would better be developed, without reference to such intellectual conceptions as doctrinal statements.

This theory is radically false. There is no knowledge of the heart. Feeling can give knowledge no more than can excitement. As Prof. Bowen has well said, "Feeling is a state of mind consequent on the reception of some idea." That is, it does not give knowledge; it presupposes it. There must be knowledge by the head before there can be feeling with the heart.

Once more you see the point. The religion of the heart and the theology of the head cannot be divorced. Unless the heart be disposed toward Christ, the head cannot, because it will not, discern the truth of Christ. As our Lord said, "It is only he who wills to obey God, whose heart is right toward Him, who shall know the doctrine whether it be of Him." On the other hand, zeal in Christ's cause will be strong and abiding in proportion as the faith from which it springs and by which it is nourished is intelligent. Zeal without knowledge is dangerous and short-lived.

William Brenton Greene, Jr. (1906)[*]

---

[*] Greene, "Broad Churchism and the Christian Life," *Princeton Theological Review*, 4 (July 1906), pp. 311-13.

INTRODUCTION TO PART 2

> *The controversies which have so long agitated the Presbyterian Church have, at length, resulted in separation. It would not be easy to state, in a manner satisfactory to both parties, the points of difference between them. It may, however, be said, without offence, that the one party is in favour of a stricter adherence to the standards of the church, as to doctrine and order, than the other.*
>
> Charles Hodge (1839)[1]

In 1839, Charles Hodge's two-volume *Constitutional History of the Presbyterian Church* was published. He completed it in the year following the 1837–38 break-up of the Presbyterian Church into two denominations. Old School Presbyterians had taken control of the General Assembly of the original denomination in 1837. They ejected four New School synods. The split came a year later when the four synods and sympathizing congregations seceded to start a new denomination. This was not the first time the American Presbyterians had divided. In 1741, Old Side and New Side Presbyterians separated along similar lines as they did in 1838, reuniting in 1758.

These controversies had originated outside of American Presbyterianism. They originated in American Congregationalism and, to a lesser extent, English Presbyterianism. Puritan Congregationalism had begun to break up in the 1720's as a result of a 50-year debate over the legitimate basis of Church membership, and therefore also over what constitutes a legitimate Church. This conflict had not been resolved when it spread into Presbyterianism as early as 1721. The debate, first and foremost, was a debate over the proper role of confession, both personal and ecclesiastical. A similar debate over the role of

---

1. Hodge, *A Constitutional History of the Presbyterian Church in the United States of America*, 2 vols. (Philadelphia: Presbyterian Board of Publication, [1839] 1851), I:1.

ecclesiastical confession came to a head in English Presbyterianism in 1719.

The retreat from Puritanism in England began with the restoration of Charles II to the throne in 1660. In 1662, the King imposed the Act of Uniformity that mandated conformity to the Church of England. Some 2,000 pastors refused to sign; they were then ejected from their pulpits and Church schools.[2]

English Presbyterianism also suffered from the Act of Uniformity. Its ministers lost their appointments. In response, they abandoned the Westminster Confession and its catechisms, which they regarded subsequently as the symbols of oppressive Scottish Presbyterianism. As one historian has put it, "Creeds had become detestable. . . ."[3] In the mid-1670's, the Unitarian controversy began. It continued for the next generation. In 1719, at a combined meeting of Baptists, Independents, and Presbyterians, the Church voted against adopting the Westminster Confession by a vote of 57 to 53, with the Presbyterians voting with the majority. The feeling of the time was expressed by this slogan: "The Bible won by a majority of four."[4] No; the Unitarians had won, and they soon took over the Church.

The Bible vs. the creeds: the sentiment exhibited by this slogan was to become the theological foundation of the anti-creedalists in all subsequent battles over orthodoxy until the Presbyterian Church suspended Machen and his clerical supporters in 1936. The theological Unitarians and their evangelical supporters always defended themselves in the name of the Bible. This defense was taken at face value by the Presbyterian majority for the next two centuries, and the victories went, step by step, to the Unitarians and the creed-minimizing evangelicals who made the way straight before them.

---

2. Iain Murray, *The Puritan Hope: A Study in Revival and the Interpretation of Prophecy* (Edinburgh: Banner of Truth Trust, 1971), p. 107. See also *Banner of Truth* (June 1962), pp. 1–32.

3. Frederick Maurice, *The Life of Frederick Denison Maurice*, 2 vols. (New York: Charles Scribner's Sons, 1884), I:2.

4. *Ibid.*, I:3. The primary source document of this historic debate is *An Authentic Account of the Several Things Done and Agreed Upon by the Dissenting Ministers Lately Assembled at Salters' Hall* (1719).

Calvinism, Experientialism, and Secularism

The history of the secularization of the American republic is the history of a process of substitution: personal experience in place of judicial confession as the basis of Church membership. This began in Puritan New England, probably by 1636, when the churches began requiring candidates for membership to relate the experience of their salvation. Without this confirming experience, the candidate's request was denied.

The second generation of Puritans, unlike their parents, had been baptized in Calvinist churches. They had not run Archbishop Laud's Arminian gauntlet, nor had they fled to New England. They could not easily identify such an emotional point of conversion in their lives. They could therefore not become local church members. This created a problem: Should their children be baptized? If so, on what legal basis? New England theologians invented a new theology in order to authorize the baptism of the children of the baptized but noncommunicant children of the first generation: the halfway covenant.[5] But these baptized grandchildren of the founders were not authorized to take communion. Then when could they take communion, and on what basis? Only after they became full-covenant members: experiential confession. The halfway covenant's solution was in fact only a one-generation deferral of the problems raised by experientialism.

The great irony—rarely if ever mentioned in monographs on the halfway covenant—is that the 1662 Synod's standards for halfway covenant membership were the same as those for full membership in European Calvinist churches: *profession of faith in Christ and an outwardly obedient life*. Calvin had declared that "we recognize as members of the church those who, by confession of faith, by example of life, and by partaking of the sacraments, profess the same God and Christ with us."[6] The Synod declared: "Church members who were admitted in minority, understanding the Doctrine of Faith, and publickly professing their assent thereto; not scandalous in life, and sol-

---

5. Edmund S. Morgan, *Visible Saints: The History of a Puritan Idea* (New York: New York University Press, 1963), pp. 99-105.

6. John Calvin, *Institutes of the Christian Religion* (1559), I:IV:8. Ford Lewis Battles, translator, 2 vols. (Philadelphia: Westminster Press, 1960), II:1022-23.

emnly owning the Covenant before the Church, wherein they give up themselves and their children to the Lord, and subject themselves to the Government of Christ in the Church, their Children are to be baptized."[7] In any Continental Calvinist church, this would have entitled New England's halfway covenant, non-communing members and their children to access to the communion table. But not many churches in New England accepted this theological solution until 1675, nor did most of those people outside the local churches, who continued to refuse to join even as halfway (non-communing) members. Only after the one-year Indian war known as King Philip's War broke out in 1675 did Church membership grow.[8]

Stoddard and the Lord's Supper

This theological anomaly could not persist indefinitely. In the late seventeenth and early eighteenth centuries, Solomon Stoddard, Jonathan Edwards' maternal grandfather, popularized the reversal of the Calvinist conception of closed communion—Church members only. He adopted open communion in 1677 as a means of bringing into the Church those excluded by the halfway covenant's ban. Several ministers in Connecticut had already pioneered this practice.[9] Because exclusion from the communion table is the meaning of excommunication, open communion undermines Church discipline by removing the Church's primary negative sanction. Stoddard was consistent: he opposed formal Church discipline.[10] He had to; he opposed

---

7. "Result of the Synod of 1662," *The Creeds and Platforms of Congregationalism*, edited by Williston Walker (New York: United Church Press, [1893] 1960), p. 328.

8. Robert G. Pope, "New England versus the New England Mind: The Myth of Declension," in *Puritan New England: Essays on Religion, Society, and Culture*, edited by Alden T. Vaughan and Francis J. Bremer (New York: St. Martin's, 1977), ch. 18.

9. Robert G. Pope, *The Half-Way Covenant* (Princeton, New Jersey: Princeton University Press, 1969), ch. 4.

10. Paul R. Lucas writes: "Stoddard's complaint went far beyond New England Congregationalism to the whole Protestant Reformation, in which New England represented but one isolated outpost. As he often wrote, he was a soul-winner, and he rejected not only New England's, but also the Reformed tradition's, seventeenth-century preoccupation with church discipline. That was Stoddard's significance for his time, a fact overlooked by most modern scholars." Paul R. Lucas, "'An Appeal to the Learned': The Mind of Solomon Stoddard," in

the very doctrine of a Church covenant.[11] A somewhat less intense opposition to Church discipline subsequently characterized his spiritual heirs: New Light Congregationalists, New Side Presbyterians, and New School Presbyterian evangelists.[12] Where he differed with them was in his rejection of the requirement that members give evidence of an experiential conversion. "No man can look into the heart of another, and see the workings of a gracious spirit."[13]

Those confessors who had been lawfully entitled to the Lord's Supper by Calvin's standards, but not New England's, now gained access, but only at the expense of the judicial character of this sacrament. Stoddard believed that the communion meal could increase a sinner's receptivity toward the gospel. Stoddard's rejection of Calvinism's doctrine of the Church covenant was coupled with a judicial downgrading of the Lord's Supper from a rite of covenant renewal and a mark of full Church membership to a technique of evangelism with no threatened supernatural sanctions attached to it.

The First Great Awakening

In the experientialist Puritanism of Cotton Mather, we can see the origins of the split between Confessionalists and experientialists during the First Great Awakening.[14] This familiar Christian dualism had long been present in New England, ready to divide into rival forms of religion.[15] Stoddard became the first American revivalist,[16] but he would not be the last.

Puritan New England, pp. 326–27.

11. Stoddard, *The Doctrine of Instituted Churches Explained and Proved from the Word of God* (1700), p. 8.

12. These distinctions will become more clear later in this book. When you read "New," think "experiential."

13. Stoddard, *The Falseness of the Hopes of Many Professors* (1708), p. 11.

14. Richard F. Lovelace, *The American Pietism of Cotton Mather: Origins of American Evangelicalism* (Grand Rapids, Michigan: Christian University Press, 1979).

15. James W. Jones, *The Shattered Synthesis: New England Puritanism Before the Great Awakening* (New Haven, Connecticut: Yale University Press, 1973).

16. Harry S. Stout, *The New England Soul: Preaching and Religious Culture in Colonial New England* (New York: Oxford University Press, 1986), pp. 99–101.

The arrival of Dutch Reformed pastor Theodore Frelinghuysen in 1720 in the New Jersey area is generally assumed by historians to mark the beginning of the First Great Awakening. It spread from him to Presbyterian Gilbert Tennent in the mid-1720's. Jonathan Edwards, beginning in 1734, became part of the Awakening.[17] It accelerated rapidly after 1740.[18] Revivals and revivalists fanned out across the land. The theology of revivalism retained the New England Puritan assumption that a unique experience is the mark of salvation and the basis for assessing one's status as a saint. The ecclesiastical implications of this theology now became clear: it divided congregations into saints and non-saints professing a formally sound theology but supposedly without a work of salvation in their lives.

Itinerant preachers—George Whitefield was the most capable—would come into a town, preach in the open air, gain converts out of local congregations, and leave behind divided congregations. In 1741, the Presbyterian Church split into two branches, Old Side (ecclesiastical traditionalists) vs. New Side (revivalists). This breach was not healed until 1758, after the Great Awakening had cooled. Congregationalists also split: Old Lights vs. New Lights. The "old" and "new" terminology continued into the nineteenth century.

But New England's theocratic order had more than one oath-bound covenant. There was also the civil covenant. Fragmenting ecclesiastical structures undermined the Puritan concept of the Trinitarian, oath-bound holy commonwealth, including Christian politics. The older theocratic order of New England began to erode in the face of this new experiential theology.[19]

---

17. H. Shelton Smith, Robert T. Handy, and Lefferts A. Loetscher, eds., *American Christianity: An Historical Interpretation With Representative Documents*, 2 vols. (New York: Charles Scribner's Sons, 1960), I:311–12.

18. Alan Heimert, *Religion and the American Mind: From the Great Awakening to the Revolution* (Cambridge, Massachusetts: Harvard University Press, 1966), Part 1; Heimert and Perry Miller, eds., *The Great Awakening: Documents Illustrating the Crisis and Its Consequences* (Indianapolis: Bobbs-Merrill, 1967); Leonard J. Trinterud, *The Forming of An American Tradition: A Re-examination of COLONIAL PRESBYTERIANISM* (Salem, New Hampshire: Ayer, [1949] 1970).

19. Richard L. Bushman, *From Puritan to Yankee: Character and the Social Order in Connecticut, 1690–1765* (New York: Norton, [1967] 1970), Part 4.

Old Side, New Side

The erosion of the older Puritan Calvinism raised a new question: If not biblical law, then what? Casuistry—the application of biblical moral principles to personal decision-making and ecclesiastical judgments—died out as a discipline after 1700.[20] Newtonianism replaced it as an ideal. Paralleling revivalism was the universal acceptance of Newtonian natural law philosophy in the name of Christianity. This theologically unstable amalgam of the Bible and Arian-Socinian-Unitarianism had been baptized by Cotton Mather as early as 1721 in his book, *The Christian Philosopher*. The vision of a world under God's law was powerful; that this law-order could be known without any appeal to the Bible seemed even more powerful because it was more universal in its appeal. The Unitarian implications of such a universe were not recognized by the Christians who adopted it. That a Unitarian had discovered it was one of the secrets Newton and his circle kept suppressed. (So was Newton's extensive pursuit of alchemy.)[21] Newtonianism seemed to make possible a common-ground physical science, which hinted of a common-ground political science. The holy commonwealth ideal was replaced in New England within one generation by a secular imitation.

The American Revolution

Two decades after the 1758 reunion, the Presbyterians were overwhelmingly supporters of the American Revolution. An agent of the Earl of Dartmouth, the Lord Privy Seal, informed him that "Presbyterianism is really at the bottom of this whole conspiracy."[22] Horace Walpole put it even more memorably: "Cousin America has eloped with a Presbyterian parson."[23] The Presbyterians became political

---

20. Thomas Wood, *English Casuistical Divinity During the Seventeenth Century* (London: S.P.C.K., 1952), pp. 32–36.

21. Betty J. T. Dobbs, *The Foundations of Newton's Alchemy; Or, "The Hunting of the Green Lyon"* (Cambridge: Cambridge University Press, 1977).

22. Cited in Trinterud, *American Tradition*, p. 250.

23. Cited in Martha L. Stohlman, *John Witherspoon: Parson, Politician, Patriot* (Louisville, Kentucky: Westminster/John Knox Press, 1976), p. 15. For a case study, see John Murray Smoot, Presbyterianism in Revolutionary Pennsylvania: Constitution and Freedom (Ph.D. dissertation, St. Mary's Seminary and Univer-

Whigs, and they remained so after the war ended.[24] The supreme representative of their resistance to England was Rev. John Witherspoon, the president of the College of New Jersey (later Princeton University), who signed the Declaration of Independence and who served in the Continental Congress.[25]

In 1787-88, American Presbyterians revised the Westminster Confession of Faith in order to make it conform to the political pluralism that also lay behind the U.S. Constitution,[26] which was being ratified at the same time that the presbyteries were voting for the revision of the Confession. The Presbyterians removed that clause in Chapter XXIII:3 which had authorized the civil magistrate to call a synod for advice.[27] This was one of the last traces of the theocratic Calvinism of the Scottish Covenanters—or Calvin's theocratic Calvinism, for that matter. (The final trace was the Confession's assertion that the failure to take an oath to a lawful authority is a sin [XXII:3]. That provision was abandoned in the 1903 revision, and Machen's Orthodox Presbyterian Church did not restore it in 1936.) From that time on, Presbyterians became defenders of a secularized republican order. They believed that God's civil covenant could be made on a common-ground confessional basis, without a mandatory covenantal civil oath, operat-

---

sity, 1982).

24. William Livingston, a Presbyterian, was the governor of New Jersey in 1790, when he observed that the American clergy were "almost all universally good Whigs." Livingston, "Observations on the Support of the Clergy," *American Museum* (1790), p. 254; cited in Heimert, *Religion and the American Mind*, p. 1. He had been known as "the American Whig" as early as 1768. See Edwin S. Gaustad, *A Documentary History of Religion in America to the Civil War* (Grand Rapids, Michigan: Eerdmans, 1982), pp. 247-48.

25. Varnum Lansing Collins, *President Witherspoon: A Biography*, 2 vols. (Princeton, New Jersey: Princeton University Press, 1925), I, ch. 6; II, ch. 1. Henry W. Coray, "John Witherspoon," *Heroic Colonial Christians*, edited by Russell T. Hitt (Philadelphia: Lippencott, 1966).

26. Article VI, Section III makes illegal any religious test to hold Federal Office, which by 1961 had been extended down to the lowest civil office in America: notary public. The Supreme Court case was *Torcaso v. Watkins*.

27. Gary North, *Political Polytheism: The Myth of Pluralism* (Tyler, Texas: Institute for Christian Economics, 1989), pp. 543-50; Edwin S. Gaustad, *Faith of Our Fathers: Religion and the New Nation* (New York: Harper & Row, 1987), p. 113.

ing under a providential natural law order that did not mandate Trinitarian confession. Obedience to this natural order, they believed, would bring national prosperity.[28] This was the liberal worldview of English Whig politics, and no group in America was more dedicated to defending it than the Presbyterians.[29]

A Shortage of Presbyterian Ministers

Let me remind the reader: the word "shortage" should not be used without considering its necessary analytical corollary, "at the price offered."

After the Revolutionary War, the Presbyterians began to lose their direct influence in American society, although they retained special influence among the educated elite. In the seven years before the outbreak of the Revolutionary War, the College of New Jersey had sent 75 men into the ministry. Over the next eighteen years, it sent only 39, an average of two men per year. At the same time, the population of the middle and southern states, where Presbyterianism was strongest, rose from 1.75 million in 1783 to 2.75 million in 1790.[30] Two new pastors per year could hardly be expected to keep pace with this population growth, let alone carry the gospel to other regions, especially the Western territories, which were growing even faster. As members moved west or south, older congregations gradually died off.[31] Yet W. W. Sweet began his 1936 collection of Presbyterian Church primary sources with this observation: "No church in America, at the close of the War for Independence, was in a better position for immediate expansion than was the Presbyterian."[32]

What went wrong? From the point of view of Presbyterian tradition, nothing. From the point of view of maintaining the Church's

---

28. Fred J. Hood, Presbyterianism and the New American Nation, 1783-1826: A Case Study of Religion and National Life (Ph.D. dissertation, Princeton University, 1968), ch. 2.

29. The American Whig Party was far less ideological and far more pragmatic than the Whig movement in England.

30. Trinterud, *American Tradition*, p. 265.

31. *Ibid.*, p. 266.

32. William Warren Sweet, *Religion on the American Frontier, 1783–1840*, vol. II, *The Presbyterians* (New York: Cooper Square, [1936] 1964), p. 3.

dominant position in the United States, everything. The problem was the Presbyterian tradition of an academically certified ministry. It was restricting the supply of ministers. During the War, there had been a growing demand for Presbyterian ministers. In 1783, the Synod refused to permit the licensing of men who had not received a liberal arts education, which meant the Latin classics. In 1785, the Synod even went so far as to recommend a two-year divinity degree beyond the four-year liberal arts degree. This was postponed for a year and then rejected in 1786.[33] Nevertheless, it indicates what the commitment of the denomination was.

A related problem was that a growing number of graduates of the College of New Jersey ceased to go into the ministry. In the 1770's, nearly half of the college's graduates went into the ministry. It fell to 21 percent during the Revolutionary War and 13 percent in President John Witherspoon's final decade, 1784-94. From 1803 to 1806, it was nine percent.[34] Ashbel Green, who drew up the plan for Princeton Seminary in 1811 and who became the president of the College in 1812, pled before the General Assembly in 1805: "Give us ministers."[35] On the supply side of the economic equation, this shortage was the institutional price of the old Presbyterian tradition of a formally educated, institutionally certified pastorate. This price grew ever-higher over the next century until the Presbyterian seminaries all fell to the humanists and modernists, and Machen was de-frocked. The Northern Presbyterian pastorate was very well educated in 1936; it just wasn't Calvinist.

The Second Great Awakening

Even before the Constitution and the revised Westminster Confession were ratified, sparks of the Second Great Awakening had begun.[36] A decade later, it began in earnest. For the next half century or

---

33. *Ibid.*, pp. 8-9.

34. Mark A. Noll, *Princeton and the Republic, 1768-1822* (Princeton, New Jersey: Princeton University Press, 1989), p. 172.

35. *Ibid.*, p. 170.

36. The key figure was a New School Presbyterian minister, James McGready, heir of the New Side tradition. See John B. Boles, *The Great Revival, 1787-1805: The Origins of the Southern Evangelical Mind* (Lexington: University of Kentucky Press, 1972), ch. 4; Ernest Trice Thompson, *Presbyterians in the South*,

more, revivals again swept the nation.[37] So did the demand for pastors. Calvinist churches could not respond fast enough to this demand. Their educational requirements for ordination to the ministry were too high. Methodists and Baptists did not labor under equally tight constraints. They could more easily meet the new demand. Arminianism became the dominant theology of the nation by 1860.

Arminianism Takes Over

Church historian Winthrop S. Hudson has estimated that in 1776, at least 90 percent of the churches in the colonies were in the Puritan-Calvinist-Reformed tradition.[38] A century later, this was no longer even remotely the case. Edwin Scott Gaustad's detailed study of the geography of American denominationalism reveals just how overwhelming this transition was. In 1780, in the middle of the Revolutionary War, there were slightly under 495 Presbyterian congregations in the United States.[39] In that year, there were 457 Baptist congregations. There were also 749 Congregational churches and 406 Anglican congregations.[40] There were so few Methodist congregations that Gaustad does not list them. The nation was predominately Calvinist in 1780, especially since most Baptists accepted the Philadelphia Confession of Faith, a version of the Westminster Confession. The Philadelphia Association of Bap-

---

3 vols. (Richmond, Virginia: John Knox Press, 1973), I:130–34.

37. Whitney R. Cross, *The Burned-over District: The Social and Intellectual History of Enthusiastic Religion in Western New York, 1800–1850* (New York: Harper Torchbooks, [1950] 1965); Paul E. Johnson, *A Shopkeeper's Millennium: Society and Revivals in Rochester, New York, 1815–1837* (New York: Hill & Wang, 1978); Anne C. Loveland, *Southern Evangelicals and the Social Order, 1800–1860* (Baton Rouge: Louisiana State University Press, 1980); Donald G. Mathews, "The Second Great Awakening as an Organizing Process, 1780–1830," *American Quarterly*, 21 (1969), pp. 23–43. The second wave of revivals, 1840–58, along with the rise of perfectionism, can be discussed as an extension of this awakening. See Timothy L. Smith, *Revivalism and Social Reform: American Protestantism on the Eve of the Civil War* (Gloucester, Massachusetts: Peter Smith, [1957] 1976).

38. Winthrop S. Hudson, *The Great Tradition of the American Churches* (New York: Harper & Bros., 1953), p. 47.

39. Edwin Scott Gaustad, *Historical Atlas of Religion in America* (New York: Harper & Row, 1962), p. 4. See also Figure 17, p. 21.

40. *Ibid.*

tists had adopted it in 1742.[41] This was the most important Baptist association in the colonies prior to the Revolution.[42] But after the Revolution, more and more Baptists adopted Arminianism.

In 1820, there were 2,700 Baptist congregations, 2,700 Methodist congregations, 1,110 Congregational, 600 Episcopal, and 1,700 Presbyterian.[43] Many of these Presbyterian congregations were Cumberland Presbyterians, which were more Arminian in perspective. Hudson writes that "the Calvinism of the other denominations was becoming so diluted as to be unrecognizable."[44] By 1860, there were 12,150 Baptist congregations, 19,883 Methodist congregations, 6,406 Presbyterian, 2,145 Episcopal, and 2,234 Congregational. To this must be added 2,100 Disciples of Christ congregations, the Arminian Campbellites.[45] The nation had become Arminian. By 1900, there were almost 50,000 Baptist congregations, almost 54,000 Methodist congregations, 15,452 Presbyterian, 5,604 Congregational (now liberal), 6,264 Episcopal (now liberal). There were over 10,298 Disciples congregations: two-thirds of the number of Presbyterians.[46]

As the revival spread, the Methodists expanded in number, while Presbyterians, Congregationalists, and Episcopalians for the most part remained on the Eastern seaboard, still hampered by their requirements of formal education and unable to supply the ministers needed to consolidate institutionally the fires of the revivals. Those who did venture west were often sponsored by some missionary society, not a denomination or association.[47] The camp meetings had become almost the exclusive property of the Methodists: 400 in 1811 alone.[48] One

---

41. *Dictionary of Christianity in America*, edited by Daniel G. Reid (Downers Grove, Illinois: InterVarsity Press, 1990), p. 895.
42. Edwin Scott Gaustad, *A Religious History of America* (New York: Harper & Row, 1966), p. 97.
43. Gaustad, *Atlas*, p. 43, Figure 31.
44. Winthrop S. Hudson, *Religion in America* (New York: Charles Scribner's Sons, 1965), p. 179.
45. Gaustad, *Atlas*, p. 43, Figure 32.
46. *Ibid.*, p. 44, Figure 33.
47. Hudson, *Religion in America*, pp. 146–50.
48. *Ibid.*, p. 140.

Presbyterian missionary in Kentucky put it this way: "I at length became ambitious to find a family whose cabin had not been entered by a Methodist preacher. In several days I traveled from settlement to settlement on my errand of good, but into every hovel I entered I learned that a Methodist missionary had been there before me."[49]

The Roots of Revivalism

The great irony of this development was that the revival that preceded the Great Awakening had broken out in 1787 at two Presbyterian colleges in Virginia, Hampden-Sydney and Washington. These revivals led about three dozen men into the Presbyterian ministry. They fanned out into the Western Carolinas, Kentucky, and Tennessee for a decade.

Some historians date the Second Great Awakening in 1797. No one argues that it began any later than the camp-meeting revival in Logan County, Kentucky, in 1800.[50] It spread eastward and northward, continuing for at least the next four decades. It reached Yale College in 1802, when President Timothy Dwight preached a series of chapel sermons. One-third of the student body professed a conversion. This led the "Old Calvinists" in New England Congregationalism to accept revivalism.[51] In 1801, Presbyterians and Congregationalists agreed to a Plan of Union which made possible cooperative evangelism and church-planting efforts in the West.

The revivalists modeled their ministries after the New Light Congregationalists of the previous century. The shining example was Presbyterian Charles Finney's self-conscious imitation of Jonathan Edwards' preaching techniques. But there was this difference: in the earlier awakening, men waited for the movement of the Holy Spirit. In this one, preachers adopted "means" to move men to make decisions for Christ.[52] The Presbyterian congregations that did participate in these frontier revivals were either Cumberland Presbyterians, whose commitment to Calvinism was at best tangential, or those that

---

49. *Ibid.*, p. 147.
50. *Ibid.*, p. 135. Cf. pp. 137–40.
51. *Ibid.*, pp. 135–36.
52. *Ibid.*, p. 136.

were part of the New School wing of the denomination, most notably Finney, who left the denomination in 1836 to join the Congregationalists. The mark of the revivalists was the elevation of experientialism at the expense of Calvinist theology, just as it had been a century before. Robert V. Remini, perhaps the leading historian of the Jacksonian era, has described the excesses: "As the revivals grew in number and intensified in enthusiasm, they frequently ended in orgies of excess, with men and women weeping, tearing their hair, crouching on all fours and barking like dogs to 'tree the devil,' and rolling on the ground in a display of repentance."[53] The Great Awakening overwhelmed Calvinism in the churches; the public schools overwhelmed it in the classrooms. The pietist-humanist alliance of the First Great Awakening—revivalism plus Newtonian political pluralism—moved to the next stage. This time, Calvinism survived only inside Presbyterian churches.

Political Repercussions

Once again, the debate over experientialism vs. judicial confession split the Presbyterian Church. In 1837, the Old School General Assembly ejected four New School (revivalists) synods. The New School established its own denomination in 1838.

Once again, politics experienced a revolutionary transformation, just as it had a century earlier. The major political result of the Second Great Awakening was the abolitionist movement. Abolitionism had become a judicial matter first among the Quakers, prior to the American Revolution.[54] It spread to the Presbyterian Church in 1815 but was then bottled up, as we shall see: the Bourne case. It spread a decade later to the Congregationalists.[55] But the "field grade officers" of the abolitionist movement after 1830 were mostly New England

---

53. Robert V. Remini, "A Prophet Without Honor, a Review of *The Kingdom of Matthias*, by Paul E. Johnson and Sean Wilenz," *Atlantic Monthly* (Feb. 1995), p. 108.

54. David Brion Davis, *Slavery and Human Progress* (New York: Oxford University Press, 1984), pp. 107–108.

55. Bertram Wyatt-Brown, *Lewis Tappan and the Evangelical War Against Slavery* (Cleveland, Ohio: Press of Case Western Reserve University, 1969).

Unitarians, despite the fact that the troops were mostly northern Trinitarians. Because of the Unitarians' emphasis on political action as the ultimate strategy for abolition, the Civil War transferred moral authority to the Unitarians and to politics. (So did the curricula of the public schools, beginning in Massachusetts: Horace Mann's legacy.)[56]

Each time that experientialism was substituted for confession, especially Calvinist confession, as the basis of Church membership, the process of secularization increased. Authority moved, step by step, from Calvinism to Arminianism to Unitarianism to secularism. In no denomination was this transformation more visible than the Presbyterian Church, U.S.A.

Conclusion

Hodge's *Constitutional History* was not merely a work of history; it was also a work of contemporary polemics. He devoted hundreds of pages to the Old Side-New Side controversy. He had nothing good to say about the New Side's anti-creedalism and its anti-Church authority outlook and actions, although he did acknowledge that the doctrinal profession of the leaders of the New Side was orthodox.[57] But he argued that the result of the revival was the decline of religion after the initial enthusiasm in the early 1740's, according to Jonathan Edwards and other pastors who had been participants.[58] False doctrines abounded.[59] The revival was not all evil, Hodge concluded, but many serious evils accompanied it.[60]

Hodge wrote this book during the Second Great Awakening. Like his Old Side forefathers and Old School brethren, he defended the lawful authority of the courts of the Presbyterian Church to exercise control over both the theological message and the mode of preaching

---

56. *Horace Mann on the Crisis of Education*, edited by Louis Filler (Yellow Springs, Ohio: Antioch Press, 1965), parts II, III. Cf. R. J. Rushdoony, *The Messianic Character of American Education: Studies in the History of the Philosophy of Education* (Nutley, New Jersey: Craig Press, 1963), ch. 3.
57. Hodge, *Constitutional History*, II:47.
58. *Ibid.*, II:54–56.
59. *Ibid.*, II:56–58.
60. *Ibid.*, II:100–101.

by its ordained officers. The Old School was more "high Church" than "low Church"[61]—liturgically more formal with respect to the boundaries of lawful worship. Formal worship must be conducted within narrow judicial boundaries, the Old School believed, and these boundaries are overwhelmingly Confessional. The subscription statement to the Westminster standards required by faculty members at Princeton Seminary was much more rigorous than the vow taken by ministers.[62] The New School, in contrast, emphasized the importance of the results of worship—the conversion of sinners—even, if necessary (and it usually seemed necessary to their most prominent spokesmen), at the expense of both Confessional rigor and the Church's judicial authority. The Old School emphasized the sovereignty of God and the theocentric nature of worship: "God's work done in God's way for the glory of God." The New School emphasized the salvation of men as the primary goal of the Church's Great Commission (Matt. 28:18–20).

Underlying this dispute was a disagreement over method: the glorification of God primarily through adherence to forms—creedal confession and Church authority—vs. the glorification of God primarily through the harvesting of souls, meaning men's experience and their profession of simple faith in the saving work of Christ. In the New

---

61. Lefferts A. Loetscher makes the same distinction in *The Broadening Church: a study of theological issues in the presbyterian church since 1869* (Philadelphia: University of Pennsylvania Press, 1954), p. 1. It was made long before Loetscher by the New School, which dismissed the Old School as "the High Church Party." *A History of the Division of the Presbyterian Church in the United States of America by a Committee of the Synod of New York and New Jersey* (New York: Dodd, 1852), p. 80. It was revived by a modernist defender of Charles Briggs and Union Theological Seminary: G. L. Prentiss, *The Union Theological Seminary in the City of New York: Its Design and another Decade of its History* (Asbury Park, New Jersey: Pennypacker, 1899), p. 214. This distinction undergirds the study by Ki-Hong Kim, Presbyterian Conflict in the Early Twentieth Century: Ecclesiology in the Princeton Tradition and the Emergence of Presbyterian Fundamentalism (Ph.D. dissertation, Drew University, 1983). The premier statement of the Old School's view of the Church is Charles Hodge, *Discussions on Church Polity, from the Contributions to the "Princeton Review"* (New York: Charles Scribner's Sons, 1878), published shortly after his death.

62. Princeton's subscription statement is reprinted in Edwin H. Rian, *The Presbyterian Conflict* (Grand Rapids, Michigan: Eerdmans, 1940), pp. 61–62.

School, experientialism was emphasized above formal worship, good works above precise confession. The New School prevailed; the Old School united with the New School on its terms in 1869. This was a surrender.

The long-term victors were the modernists. The modernists within the Presbyterian Church after 1870 initially emphasized the New School's downgrading of institutional authority, and they used the language of personalism (feeling) in contrast to impersonalism (government). In 1931, they switched. They proposed a new Form of Government to tighten institutional control, which was ratified in 1934. Modernists restructured key features of the New School and Old School traditions, changing them radically. The personalism of the New School became a very different kind of personalism in modernism: the personalism of *Confessional indeterminacy*. The formalism of the Old School became a very different kind of formalism in modernism after 1930: the formalism of *centralized authority*.

Phase 1: Whose Legitimacy?

2

OLD SCHOOL VS. NEW SCHOOL

> *With the woeful departures from sound doctrine, which we have already pointed out, and the grievous declensions in Church order heretofore stated, has advanced step by step, the ruin of all sound discipline in large portions of our Church, until in some places our very name is becoming a public scandal, and the proceedings of persons and Churches connected with some of our Presbyteries, are hardly to be defended from the accusation of being blasphemous.*
>
> Testimony and Memorial (1837)[1]

So announced the Old School wing of the Presbyterian Church at a meeting held prior to the 1837 General Assembly at which the Old School majority expelled four New School presbyteries. In the eyes of the Old School's members, this was necessary in order to re-establish the purity of the Presbyterian Church: theologically, judicially, and structurally. Loose subscription to the Westminster Confession would have to go, along with those who defended loose subscription.

The crucial dividing issue was theology—specifically, soteriology: the doctrine of salvation. What is the way of salvation? Rev. Albert Barnes, around whom the controversy had centered, had stated accu-

---

1. Reprinted in *The Presbyterian Enterprise: Sources of American Presbyterian History*, edited by Maurice W. Armstrong, Lefferts A. Loetscher, and Charles A. Anderson (Philadelphia: Westminster Press, 1956), p. 155.

rately in 1829: "All men have some scheme of salvation."[2] The Presbyterian Church asked the question: "What constitutes valid evidence that a person is regenerate and therefore lawfully a Church member?" On this point, Old Side and New Side Presbyterianism had divided in 1741. The Old Side had sided with Calvin: profession of faith and an outwardly holy life. The New Side had added experientialism. The same division marked Old School and New School Presbyterians in the first half of the nineteenth century. But there were additional divisions: some theological (Calvinism vs. Arminianism), some institutional (Church hierarchy vs. parachurch ministries), and one moral (the legitimacy of chattel slavery).

These debates were ultimately a debate over the legitimacy of the institutional Church. The question was: "What constitutes a legitimate Presbyterian Church?" The division of 1741 indicated that there had not been agreement on this point. The division of 1837–38 indicated that this question had not been resolved by the re-unification of 1758.

New School Presbyterianism was closely associated with the revivals of the Second Great Awakening, just as the New Side a century earlier had been associated with the First Great Awakening: phase one, part one of the Presbyterian conflict. In both cases, there was a tendency toward an ecumenism based on shared experience.[3] It was this ecumenism—financial support of parachurch ministries and union with Congregationalism on the Western frontier—that finally drew the fire of the Old School.

The Purity of the Church

Old School Presbyterians launched a series of heresy trials in 1830, beginning with the first trial of Albert Barnes of Philadelphia and ending in 1836 with Barnes' second trial.[4] Barnes was acquitted both times. Barnes was a revivalist.

---

2. Barnes, "The Way of Salvation" (1829), in *ibid.*, p. 146.

3. On the First Great Awakening's ecumenical impulse, see Edwin Scott Gaustad, *The Great Awakening in New England* (Chicago: Quadrangle, [1957] 1968), ch. 7.

4. Jacob Harris Patton, *A Popular History of the Presbyterian Church in the United States of America* (New York: Mighill, 1900), ch. 41.

Barnes' 1829 sermon, "The Way of Salvation," triggered the first of these judicial actions. He said: "No man is compelled, against his will, to be saved. The work of salvation, and the work of damnation, are the two most deliberate and solemn acts *of choosing*, that mortal man ever performs."[5] The theological question at issue here is the uniquely Calvinistic assertion of God's absolutely sovereign transformation of each person's will prior to any solemn act of man's choosing, but Barnes did not mention this. His sermon revealed its Arminian roots. "The Christian scheme, then, claims that God, by his spirit, renews all that will be saved."[6] The Arminian Christian scheme, yes; not the Westminster Confession's scheme: "Man, by his fall into a state of sin, hath wholly lost all ability of will to any spiritual good accompanying salvation: so as, a natural man, being altogether averse from that good, and dead in sin, is not able, by his own strength, to convert himself, or to prepare himself thereunto" (IX:3). God, "by His grace alone, enables him freely to will and to do that which is spiritually good" (IX:4b). Barnes had abandoned the Westminster Confession on this point. He was not alone, which was why he could not be convicted for heresy. He was brought to trial in 1830, cleared by the General Assembly in 1831, tried again in 1835, and again was cleared by the GA in 1836. In between, Lyman Beecher had also been tried and cleared in 1835. This led to the division of the Church in 1837.

Revival leader Charles Finney left Presbyterianism in 1836, the year after he had assumed the presidency of Oberlin College (a summer assignment).[7] Throughout his ministerial career, beginning in 1824, he repeated the standard defense of the New Side a century before, and what was to become the standard defense of the modernists half a century later: the negative effects of negative Church sanctions. Criticisms of the revivals were being offered, he said, by men who were themselves spiritually unproductive. "*Ecclesiastical difficulties* are calculated to grieve away the Spirit, and destroy revivals. It has

---

5. Barnes, "The Way of Salvation," *Presbyterian Enterprise*, p. 147.
6. *Ibid.*, p. 148.
7. Keith J. Hardman, *Charles Grandison Finney, 1792–1875: Revivalist and Reformer* (Syracuse, New York: Syracuse University Press, 1987), pp. 310–11. Paperback reprint by Baker Book House.

always been the policy of the devil to turn off the attention of ministers from the work of the Lord to disputes and ecclesiastical litigations. . . . When will these ministers and professors of religion who do little or nothing themselves, let others alone, and let them work for God?" He cited Jonathan Edwards' painful ecclesiastical experience with his congregation, just as he cited Edwards on so much else.[8] This "grieved Spirit" approach had been Gilbert Tennent's criticism of Old Side Presbyterianism in 1740, although without Tennent's vitriol.[9]

The charges against each of the accused revivalists were dismissed on appeal in every case. The Old School then gave up on the Church's existing court system.[10] The Old School at the 1837 General Assembly, which it controlled, annulled the 1801 agreement known as the Plan of Union, which had created joint Congregationalist and Presbyterian missionary activities and joint acceptance of each other's pastors in local congregations in the western territories.[11] The General Assembly then expelled four New School Synods.[12] Over 550 congregations and over 500 ministers in the New School were removed from the rolls.[13] This was the First Great Expulsion. The judicial issue, argued Old School theologian Robert Breckenridge in 1843, had hinged on the absence of ruling elders in the churches formed by the 1801 Union. "They had no ruling elders and therefore were not Presbyterian."[14] The issue, therefore, was "church order," he said. "Upon this ground, more than any other, it was triumphantly carried through the

---

8. Charles G. Finney, *Lectures on Revivals of Religion*, 2nd ed. (New York: Revell, [1835] 1868), p. 276.

9. Gilbert Tennent, "The Danger of an Unconverted Ministry" (1740), in *The Great Awakening: Documents Illustrating the Crisis and Its Consequences*, edited by Alan Heimert and Perry Miller (Indianapolis, Indiana: Bobbs-Merrill, 1967), ch. 9.

10. Winthrop S. Hudson, *Religion in America* (New York: Charles Scribner's Sons, 1965), p. 164.

11. *Presbyterian Enterprise*, pp. 102–104.

12. Robert Hastings Nichols, *Presbyterianism in New York State: A History of the Synod and Its Predecessors* (Philadelphia: Westminster, 1963), p. 131.

13. Sidney E. Ahlstrom, *A Religious History of the American People* (New Haven, Connecticut: Yale University Press, 1972), p. 468.

14. Robert L. Breckenridge, "Presbyterian Government: Not a Hierarchy, but a Commonwealth" (1843), in *Paradigms in Polity*, edited by David W. Hall and Joseph H. Hall (Grand Rapids, Michigan: Eerdmans, 1994), p. 519.

great Assembly, through the church at large, and through the civil tribunals of the country."[15] *Not theology but Church order*: so also would the modernists declare in the Second Great Expulsion of 1936.

New School vs. Negative Sanctions

The important point is this: the conservatives in the New School would not vote to convict those ministers who deviated from the Westminster standards. They publicly defended creedal orthodoxy, but they consistently refused to impose negative ecclesiastical sanctions in order to defend this professed orthodoxy. This crucial covenantal fact is what the Old School decided to ignore in 1869. Because of this, the Northern Presbyterian Church abandoned Calvinist orthodoxy within two generations of the reunion. The denomination ignored the fundamental principle of law that had been set forth in Puritan New England two centuries earlier: "*The execution of the law is the life of the law.*"[16] By failing to enforce the Confessional standards, they allowed their theological enemies to bury these standards and inherit the denomination. It was symbolic of what was to come when, in the spring of 1870, the reunited Church's representatives met in Philadelphia in Barnes' church.[17] He died that same year, victorious. He had served faithfully as a Director of Union Seminary in New York.[18] It was through Union, more than any other institution, that the Presbyterian Church, U.S.A., was lost to modernism.

In the 1890's, the modernists appealed back to the heresy trials of Barnes and Beecher, a sour memory in the minds of New School members, and a cause of the 1837–38 split. This rhetorical appeal was used to gain support from the spiritual heirs of the New School.

---

15. *Ibid.*

16. "Book of the General Laws and Liberties Governing the Inhabitants of the Massachusetts, 1647," in *The Foundations of Colonial America: A Documentary History*, edited by W. Keith Kavenaugh, 3 vols. (New York: Chelsea House, 1973), I:297.

17. "Barnes, Albert," *Dictionary of American Religious Biography*, p. 31. Finney died in 1875.

18. Channing Renwick Jeschke, The Briggs Case: The Focus of a Study in Nineteenth Century Presbyterian History (Ph.D. dissertation, University of Chicago, 1966), p. 127.

Theologically, Barnes had been Arminian; theologically, the modernists were apostate. This difference was immense. But the modernists' rhetorical appeal was a useful tactic in confirming the prejudices of those who did not think that ministerial oaths should invoke the threat of negative institutional sanctions. The modernists would seek protection under the umbrella of the New School's view of the Confession: devoid of negative sanctions. After 1900, this umbrella never again leaked at the General Assembly level.

Independent Agencies

Another major division between Old School and New School was their conflict over independent religious organizations. The Old School believed that such efforts as missions and charity should be under the judicial authority of the Church. The New School disagreed. In 1837, Charles Hodge and fellow Old School members strengthened the Board of Home Missions and organized a Board of Foreign Missions.[19] (These attitudes were reversed in the disputes a century later, when Machen and his clerical supporters were suspended for supporting an Independent Board for Presbyterian Foreign Missions.)[20]

In 1835, two years before the split, at a pre-General Assembly meeting, members of the Old School prepared the "Act and Testimony." It rejected the legitimacy of support by Presbyterian Church funds of interdenominational missions. The target was the American Home Mission Society. The "Act and Testimony" complained that congregational funds were being sent to this agency. This money "ought to come into the treasury of the body, to which its possessors belong; . . . The Assembly's own Board of Missions, created by herself, governed by herself, and amenable to herself, finds a great and powerful rival in her own house, with whom she comes into perpetual collision."[21] The issue was judicial: the rival organization "feels no

---

19. Ki-Hong Kim, Presbyterian Conflict in the Early Twentieth Century: Ecclesiology in the Princeton Tradition and the Emergence of Presbyterian Fundamentalism (Ph.D. dissertation, Drew University, 1983), p. 85.
20. This reversal is the subject of Kim's dissertation.
21. "The Acts and Testimony Convention," *Presbyterian Enterprise*, p. 151.

obligation to our courts. . . ."[22] (In 1933, Machen and his allies formed the Independent Board for Presbyterian Foreign Missions, and in 1935, Machen's presbytery convicted him of disobedience for refusing to support the denominational Foreign Missions Board.)

There was also the issue of educating pastors. Money was being sent to the legally independent Presbyterian Education Society in preference to the Assembly's Board of Education. This, too, was perceived as a threat. The Act warned that "no Church can be safe—safe in her doctrinal standards—safe in her ecclesiastical polity—safe in her financial operations—safe in the independence of her ministry, if that ministry are [sic] dependent upon an independent foreign body; and especially, if their houses and lands, their libraries and furniture, are under bonds."[23] (In 1929, Machen and his allies founded Westminster Seminary, a judicially independent institution for educating Presbyterian ministers.)

Something fundamental had changed in the Old School's position, 1869 to 1929. What had changed was a shift in confession. After 1903, the Presbyterian Church, U.S.A., was no longer covenantally a Calvinist denomination. It refused to enforce the Westminster Confession and its catechisms in its courts. This refusal destroyed the Old School's case for conformity to the 1835 "Act and Testimony." By 1935, the Old School had become, by 1835 Old School standards, a movement committed to New School organizational practices. Meanwhile, the New School members, in alliance with modernists, had adopted the Old School's position in 1835: "Conform to the Church's missions program." The Old School threw out the New School in 1837. (The New School and the modernists threw out the Old School and the separatists in 1936.)

The Old School and New School became separate denominations in 1838. This split was not healed institutionally until 1869.[24] The primary reason offered by the Old School to justify the split in 1837 was the New School's lack of conformity to Church discipline and

---

22. *Ibid.*, p. 152.

23. *Ibid.*

24. The reunion legally took place when the presbyteries ratified it in November, 1869. The first General Assembly meeting of the reunited denomination took place in May, 1870.

Church order.[25] The shoe would be on the other foot 99 years later. In 1936, however, theological error was not offered as the basis of proper Church discipline; in 1838, it was: "The impossibility of obtaining a plain and sufficient sentence [in Church courts] against gross errors. . . ."[26]

Abolitionism and Biblical Exegesis

Revivalism was part of the dispute, and so was theology. So was the question of congregational financial support for independent agencies. So was Church discipline. But the crucial issue was abolitionism. Because of this difference, the Old School felt compelled to crawl back to the New School in 1869, begging for acceptance. The Old School never recovered from that act of filial subordination.

The Bourne Case

If any event sealed the fate of American Presbyterianism, it was the de-frocking of English immigrant George Bourne by his Lexington, Virginia, presbytery in 1815. He had been ordained in 1812. In 1805, he had been the co-publisher of the Baltimore *Evening Post*; it failed that same year and was sold to Hezekiah Niles, one of the prominent newspaper publishers of the day.[27] He then worked for several years as an author. He began preaching in a start-up congregation near Harrisonburg, Virginia, in 1810. He was ordained in 1812.

In 1815, he presented an overture to the General Assembly raising the question of whether Presbyterians who owned slaves could be Christians. The Assembly refused to act. Upon his return home, his presbytery voted his deposition. In 1816, he published *The Book and Slavery Irreconcilable*, the most critical American anti-slavery book of its day. The theological importance of the book was that Bourne identified slaveholding as a sin. In his protest in 1815, he cited I Timothy 1:10, which links whoremongers, homosexuals, and man-stealers. The

---

25. "Testimony and Memorial," *ibid.*, pp. 153–56.
26. "Testimony and Memorial," Point 1, "In Relation to Church Discipline." *Ibid.*, p. 153.
27. John W. Christie and Dwight L. Dumond, *George Bourne and The Book and Slavery Irreconcilable* (Historical Society of Delaware and the Presbyterian History Society, 1969), pp. 5–6.

Larger Catechism cites this verse (A. 142) in listing crimes against the Ten Commandments.

The 1816 General Assembly retroactively removed this reference from his protest on procedural grounds.[28] The reason for this was that the Church's *Constitution* (1806) had added a detailed critique of man-stealing, but this passage had never been voted on by the presbyteries. This meant that it was not legally binding in a Presbyterian court. Part of the passage read: "The word he [Paul] uses in its original import, comprehends all who are concerned in bringing any of the human race into slavery, or in detaining them in it. . . . Stealers of men are all those who bring off slaves or freemen, and keep, sell, or buy them. To steal a freeman, says Grotius, is the highest kind of theft."[29] This note was eliminated in editions of the *Constitution* published subsequent to 1816.[30] This undercut Bourne's protest, for the Bible's man-stealing passage and the 1806 statement had been the central pillars of his formal protest and his book. What the Scriptures taught and what the Larger Catechism's biblical citation implied, the Church dismissed on a technicality, burying the topic for the next half century. But is was ultimately the Old School that was buried.

The Synod of New York had gone on record as early as 1787 as favoring gradual abolition. First, however, slaves had to be educated. Church members who own slaves should educate them with the goal of their emancipation. Masters should also give them property to start out. The Synod used the phrase "abolition of slavery."[31] Overtures to the General Assembly regarding the legitimacy of slave ownership were submitted in 1793 and 1795. These overtures were not voted on by the presbyteries, and so had no force of law. The Church did not vote to label slavery a sin. The retroactive expurgation of the 1806 addendum in 1816 was regarded by the Old School as having expurgated the Bible. If the formal Constitutional documents of the Presbyterian Church were now silent, or at least the damning 1806 extension, then God must be

---

28. Andrew E. Murray, "*The Book and Slavery Irreconcilable,*" *American Presbyterians*, 66 (Winter 1988), p. 230.

29. Christie and Dumond, *George Bourne*, p. 18.

30. *Ibid.*, p. 26.

31. Reprinted in Gaius Jackson Slosser, ed., *They Seek a Country: The American Presbyterians* (New York: Macmillan, 1955), p. 217.

equally silent. *The Constitution of the Church was elevated procedurally above the Bible.* From this time on, the Bible was regarded by the Old School as judicially irrelevant on this issue, and remained so.

Never did the Old School deal with the biblical passages on slavery in relation to the South's practices: no legal marriages for slaves; the widespread legalized adultery—no negative sanctions—and fornication of white owners with slave girls; the absence of any appeals court above the masters, either Church or State, contrary to Exodus 18 and Matthew 18:15–18; the absence of any State-legislated means for a slave to buy his way out; legalized maiming of slaves, contrary to the Mosaic law;[32] and the annulment of the inter-generational slave law of Leviticus 25:44–46 by Jesus' fulfillment of, and therefore annulment of, the Mosaic law's jubilee year (Luke 4:18–21).[33] The Old School sat as the three pagan monkeys sit: hear no evil, see no evil, and speak no evil. Evil rejoiced in the South. This silence delivered the North after 1860 into the hands of the Unitarian-abolitionist crusaders. After 1865, it delivered the South into Reconstruction's judicial revolution against the Constitution and social Darwinism's revolution against Christendom. Evil rejoiced in the North. It is still rejoicing.

On appeal, Bourne's de-frocking was reversed temporarily by the 1817 General Assembly, but in 1818 his presbytery's sentence was allowed to stand. Amazingly, the 1818 Assembly also voted to approve a statement opposing slavery as "a gross violation of the most precious and sacred rights of human nature" and "utterly inconsistent with the law of God, which requires us to love our neighbors as ourselves. . . ." But the Assembly equivocated. Having identified slavery as being in opposition to God's law, it did not call on slaveholders to emancipate their slaves immediately.[34] Bourne had. Church officials recommended gradualism, but they threatened no sanctions for a refusal to comply.

---

32. On the extent of the maiming, Congregationalist Theodore Weld's *Slavery As It Is: The Testimony of a Thousand Witnesses* (1839) was eloquent.

33. On the evils of the South's slave system, see Gary North, *Tools of Dominion: The Case Laws of Exodus* (Tyler, Texas: Institute for Christian Economics, 1990), pp. 232–44.

34. It is reproduced in Christie and Damond, *George Bourne.*, pp. 60–63.

Bourne subsequently became a full-time abolitionist, calling for immediate emancipation years before William Lloyd Garrison appeared on the scene.[35] Garrison borrowed heavily from Bourne from 1828 on, but he never acknowledged the degree of his dependence.[36] Neither have the historians, who generally begin their discussions of anti-slavery in America with the Unitarian crusade of the 1830's.[37] Bourne is long forgotten by most Americans, and is rarely mentioned in history textbooks, but if anyone deserves the distinction of being the first American to demand immediate abolition, it is Bourne.

Negative sanctions had been applied to Bourne by the Old School. After 1818, any Presbyterian pastor in the South knew that he would be fired and possibly de-frocked if he spoke out against slavery.[38] Negative sanctions would be applied to abolitionist pastors, not to slave-holders. In 1845, the Old School General Assembly announced that petitions asking the Church to declare slavery a sin "do virtually require this judicatory to dissolve itself, and to abandon the organization under which, by the Divine blessing, it has so long prospered. The tendency is evidently to separate the northern from the southern portion of the Church; a result which every good citizen must deplore, as tending to a dissolution of the Union of our beloved country, of which every enlightened Christian will oppose as bringing about a ruinous and unnecessary schism between brethren who maintain a common faith." The vote was 168 for, 13 against, 4 excused.[39]

---

35. Forrest G. Wood, *The Arrogance of Faith: Christianity and Race in America from the Colonial Era to the Twentieth Century* (New York: Knopf, 1990), pp. 296–97. Marsden's account refers to him as James Bourne. George M. Marsden, *The Evangelical Mind and the New School Presbyterian Experience: A Case Study of Thought and Theology in Nineteenth-Century America* (New Haven, Connecticut: Yale University Press, 1970), p. 91.

36. Christie and Dumond, *George Bourne*, pp. 78–80; ch. 6.

37. Typical is *Slavery Attacked: The Abolitionist Crusade*, edited by John L. Thomas (Englewood Cliffs, New Jersey: Prentice-Hall, 1965), a collection of primary source documents. The book begins with an 1830 essay by William Lloyd Garrison. Bourne's name is nowhere mentioned.

38. Wood, *Arrogance of Faith*, pp. 303–304.

39. *Minutes of the General Assembly, 1845*, p. 16. A contemporary history and reprinting of these pronouncements, from 1787 on, as well as the pronouncements of numerous other Protestant denominations, is David Christie, *Pulpit Politics; or, Ecclesiastical Legislation on Slavery in its Disturbing Influences on the American Union* (Cincinnati, Ohio: Faran & McLean, 1863). The passage is also

But the war came anyway, and when it ended, so had the legitimacy of the now-disunited Old School in the North.

The New School General Assembly in 1846 passed an anti-slavery Declaration, but it did not declare slave-owning a sin. It also condemned excessive pressures in the Church against slavery: ". . . we do at the same time condemn all divisive and schismatic measures, tending to destroy the unity and disturb the peace of our churches, and deprecate the spirit of denunciation. . . ." It then adopted an Old School-like judicial reticence: "As a court of our Lord Jesus Christ, we possess no judiciary authority. We have no right to institute and prescribe tests of Christian character and church membership not recognized and sanctioned in the sacred Scriptures, and our standards by which we have agreed to walk. We must therefore leave this matter with the sessions, presbyteries and synods—the judicatories to whom pertains the right of judgment—to act in administrative discipline as they may judge it to be their duty, constitutionally subject to the General Assembly only in the way of general review and control."[40] In short, with respect to slavery, the New School went officially Congregational. Congregations in New York could continue to bring slave-owners to justice, since there were none; congregations in Virginia could continue to ordain slave owners if they so chose. All very nice, and all very non-Presbyterian. This was state's rights for Presbyterianism. Only after the departure of the Southern New School in 1857 did the Northern New School gain the courage to become abolitionists. But this head start on the Old School gave them the late-blooming moral legitimacy they used to lure back the Old School on New School terms in 1869.

The vaunted neutrality of the Old School was a delusion; in 1861, it also proved to be a snare. There was no neutrality possible on this issue. Old School Presbyterians in the North would surely refuse to veto presbyterial de-frockings of Southern ministers. This transferred authority over the slavery question to the Southerners. The mark of judicial authority is the ability to impose negative sanctions. Southern regionalism prevailed in Old School Presbyterianism's courts until the secession of 1861; it continued to prevail morally until 1864, when the

---

reproduced in Slosser, ed., *They Seek a Country*, p. 222.
40. Cited in Slosser, ed., *They Seek a Country*, p. 226.

Northern Old School at last identified slavery as a sin.[41] They blamed the South for everything: "Under the influence of the most incomprehensible infatuation with wickedness, those who were the most deeply interested in the perpetuation of slavery have taken away every motive for its further toleration. The spirit of American slavery . . . threatens not only our very existence as a people, but the annihilation of the principles of free Christian government; and thus has rendered the continuance of negro slavery incompatible with the preservation of our own liberty and conscience."[42] Or, as a cynic in the South might have put it: "The Bible is still silent on the morality of slavery, but on July 3 and 4, 1863, Gettysburg and Vicksburg were noisy in their moral clarity." The General Assembly did not quote the Bible, following its long tradition regarding slavery as biblically irrelevant.

In the Southern Old School, slavery survived as judicially valid until the surrender at Appomattox Court House. Then, with the exception of Robert Dabney's 1867 *A Defense of Virginia [And Through Her, of the South]*, which included a defense of slavery,[43] the Old School in the South developed collective amnesia about the peculiar institution and its role in the coming of the war. The entire region became afflicted with the same amnesia. The supreme issue in retrospect became legal, not economic; Constitutional, not moral. It became, in the title of the two-volume work written by Alexander H. Stephens, the former Vice President of the Confederacy, *A Constitutional View of the Late War Between the States* (1867, 1870).[44] State's rights in general, not state's rights to defend chattel slavery, became the retroactive moral justification of secession. This outlook led to the South's "Jim Crow" racial segregation laws against blacks within a generation. It took another round of coercive Federal intervention, 1957 to 1970, to reverse this system and its mentality. Parts of the Old

---

41. Lewis G. Vander Velde, *The Presbyterian Churches and the Federal Union, 1861–1869* (Cambridge, Massachusetts: Harvard University Press, 1932), pp. 126-29.

42. *Ibid.*

43. The book was reprinted in 1969 by the Negro University Press. For a critique, see North, *Tools of Dominion*, pp. 190n, 234-35.

44. See R. J. Rushdoony, *The Nature of the American System* (Nutley, New Jersey: Craig Press, 1965), ch. 2.

South, like the Old School, perished in 1865, but it took over a century to remove the parts that remained.

By thumbing its collective nose at the Bible in the name of a legal technicality, the Old School in 1818 set a precedent that would destroy its last remaining traces in 1936, when another Presbyterian majority thumbed its nose at the Bible on the basis a revised Book of Discipline. As it turned out, the Old School perished before Jim Crow did.

Christian Abolitionism

In 1832, England abolished slavery in its colonies. This was the culmination of a lifetime of dedicated political organization and pressure by William Wilberforce and his Clapham group.[45] In the name of Christianity, Wilberforce had challenged the moral authority and legal right of slavery and its continued existence.[46] But it was the Society of Friends (Quakers), not Trinitarians, who first made the abolition of slavery a theological issue, beginning in the late 1750's and escalating in the 1770's.[47]

The New School became increasingly abolitionist, especially after the division of 1837.[48] But its move toward abolitionism was nevertheless gradual. The 1839 New School General Assembly attempted to defer Church conflicts over abolitionism by transferring the responsibility to deal with slavery to the presbyteries.[49] In a Presbyterian Church, this only delays the day of judgment: some disgruntled loser in a local presbytery trial will eventually appeal the case.

After 1846, when the political issue of the extension of slavery into newly created states became the most potent political issue of the day, anti-slavery men became far more influential in Northern

---

45. Ernest Marshall House, *Saints in Politics: The Clapham Sect* (London: George Allen & Unwin, 1974).

46. Garth Lean, *God's Politician: William Wilberforce's Struggle* (Colorado Springs, Colorado: Helmers & Howard, [1980] 1987).

47. David Brion Davis, *The Problem of Slavery in Western Culture* (Ithaca, New York: Cornell University Press, 1966), pp. 329-32.

48. Marsden, *Evangelical Mind*, ch. 4.

49. Victor B. Howard, *Conscience and Slavery: The Evangelical Calvinist Domestic Missions, 1837-1861* (Kent, Ohio: Kent State University Press, 1990), p. xii.

churches. Churches became sectional institutions.[50] Northern churches resisted the openly pro-slavery position of the Southern churches. Theology, not the tracts of the abolitionists, is what mobilized them.[51] As Howard writes: "Historians have tended to view the concept of free soil too narrowly to mean free labor. Free labor was a part of a concept that also included free religion and free schools unhampered by the institution of slavery."[52] One Democratic newspaper, the *Cleveland Plain Dealer*, adopted the following rhetoric: "Those old blue bellied Presbyterians that hung the witches and banished the Quakers"—actually, Massachusetts Congregationalists had done this—"are determined to convert the people of this region into a race of psalm singers, using the degenerate dregs of the old puritans remaining here to drive the Democracy out."[53]

New School members in the South withdrew in 1857. This freed the New School in the North from any remaining taint of slavery. In 1858, the Southern New School Assembly petitioned the Old School for membership, but the latter did not respond favorably. The Old School, which was heavily represented by Presbyterians in the South, also refused to stand with Wilberforce's tradition. Instead, it stood on the judicial and moral sidelines. *The Presbyterian*, an Old School magazine, professed "a stubborn neutrality" in 1856.[54] Members of the Old School, most notably the faculty of Princeton Seminary, were convinced that the Church had nothing authoritative to say against "moderate, humanitarian" slavery. Slavery was not seen as being inherently immoral. This had been the universal view of the Church International until the late eighteenth century. This Church tradition seemed quite safe in 1837. So did U.S. Constitution's tradition. They weren't.

The Old School's Position: **Adiaphora**

The Old School bet its moral legitimacy and its survival on two things: (1) the U.S. Constitution of 1788, which had established a

---

50. *Ibid.*, p. xiii.
51. *Ibid.*, p. xiv.
52. *Ibid.*
53. *Editorial, Cleveland Plain Dealer* (28 Nov. 1856); cited in *ibid.*, p. 148.
54. Cited in *ibid.*

compromise with the slave states on this issue, and (2) a strategy of ignoring Old Testament texts, especially Leviticus 25:44-46, which authorized inter-generational slavery: part of the jubilee law.[55] But the jubilee law was not in force after the fall of Jerusalem in A.D. 70. Traditional Jewish and Christian expositions of biblical texts had accepted the moral legitimacy of the institution of permanent chattel slavery,[56] yet without the jubilee law, it had no textual support. Refusing to separate from the Southerners over this issue—no one doubted that an abolitionist stand would have split the Old School—the Northerners relegated the institution of chattel slavery to *adiaphora*: things supposedly judicially indifferent to the faith. Slavery was supposedly a political matter, not ecclesiastical.[57] In effect, the northerners in the Old School said of slavery: "While we've never actually owned slaves, and while we don't personally believe in slavery, we don't think the Church or State should legislate against it. We should not infringe on the slave owner's freedom of choice. The slave owner is sovereign over his own household."[58] Only after Lincoln's Emancipation Proclamation announced semi-abolitionism in 1863—abolitionism for states currently in rebellion against the United States—did the Old School reverse itself in the North, but without offering any biblical justification for this reversal. For its theological silence, pre-War and post-War, Old School Presbyterianism in the North paid with its life, denominationally speaking, in 1936.

The Old School was not alone. Prior to the War, the Congregational Calvinist scholar Moses Stuart of Andover Seminary in 1835 appealed to Leviticus 25:44-46 as the proof text that refuted the Christian abolitionists' claim that slavery is sinful in itself.[59] Yet Stuart per-

---

55. Gary North, *Leviticus: An Economic Commentary* (Tyler, Texas: Institute for Christian Economics, 1994), ch. 31: "Slaves and Freemen."

56. Davis, *Problem of Slavery*, chaps. 3, 4, 7; Davis, *Slavery and Human Progress* (New York: Oxford University Press, 1984), ch. 6.

57. The most comprehensive defense of this position was Rev. John Robinson's *The Testimony and Practice of the Presbyterian Church in Reference to Slavery* (1852).

58. The problem was: Who would speak representatively in court for the slaves?

59. Robert Bruce Mullin, "Biblical Critics and the Battle Over Slavery," *Journal of Presbyterian History*, 61 (Summer 1983), pp. 215. Cf. J. H. Giltner, "Moses

sonally regarded slavery as an institution that should and would gradually fade away without legislative pressure. His position was morally ambiguous.[60] During the War, *Bibliotheca Sacra*, the Andover journal, published three essays by Elijah P. Barrows, whose exegetical strategy was to ignore the Old Testament texts on slavery and then claim that the New Testament's ethic was against it. He moved from the biblical texts to an alleged Gospel spirit.[61] This was close to the Christian abolitionists' pre-Civil War view. Charles Hodge took an even more neutral position than Stuart's prior to the War: slavery as not sinful in itself, but subject to legislative reforms to do away with certain evil aspects of slavery as then practiced.[62] In 1865, he insisted that his views, and the views of the *Princeton Review*, had not changed on the issue of slavery since 1836, either morally or politically.[63] Psychologically, he could vote against the guilt-induced reunion of 1869; no other theologian did.

Secession in early 1861 and the outbreak of war in April led to the departure of the Southerners from the Old School. The Old School General Assembly in May imposed a loyalty oath to the Union, which Hodge opposed but few others in the North did; it passed 156 to 66. Hodge denied that the General Assembly had the authority to decide a political question.[64] In 1861, on this issue, Hodge was a voice crying in the wilderness. Representatives of the Southern churches met on December 4 in a local congregation in Augusta, Georgia, to establish a Confederate Presbyterian Church.[65] The pastor of that congregation was Joseph Ruggles Wilson,[66] the father of five-

---

Stuart and the Slavery Controversy: A Study in the Failure of Moderation," *Journal of Religious Thought*, 18 (1961), p. 31.

60. *Ibid.*, pp. 216–17.

61. *Ibid.*, p. 220.

62. *Ibid.*, pp. 218–19.

63. Charles Hodge, "The Princeton Review on the State of the Country and of the Church," *Princeton Review*, 38 (1865), p. 637; cited in Jack B. Rogers and Donald K. McKim, *The Authority and Interpretation of the Bible: An Historical Approach* (New York: Harper & Row, 1979), p. 276.

64. Ernest Trice Thompson, *Presbyterians in the South*, 3 vols. (Richmond, Virginia: John Knox Press, 1973), I:564–65.

65. *Ibid.*, II:14.

66. John M. Mulder, *Woodrow Wilson: The Years of Preparation* (Princeton,

year-old Thomas Woodrow Wilson, who would later become a ruling elder in the PCUSA.[67] In 1864, they joined the New School seceders to create the Presbyterian Church in the United States (Southern Presbyterians). The secession of the Confederacy counted for more in Southern Presbyterianism than the theological issues of the Old School-New School division. Politics and the preservation of a slavery-based social order counted for more than ecclesiology.

That same year, the Northern Old School reversed itself on abolitionism, identifying slavery as a sin, indicating that politics and the preservation of the Union was more important than its previous theology of slavery as *adiaphora*. This left the Old School in the North high and dry theologically. Its members had felt compelled, as pastors during full-scale wars always do, to support the war effort, and therefore they also had to support the North's stated causes of the war: the illegitimacy of secession (1861) and the illegitimacy of slavery (but only in Confederate states) (1863). Hodge wrote five *Princeton Review* essays critical of Southern slavery, calling for its abolition, but still he refused to say that the Bible condemns slavery. He appealed to nationalism instead.[68] By 1864, politics, in both the North and the South, had overcome theology. With respect to the irreconcilable respective war aims, Presbyterian theology had become *adiaphora*. By 1869, so had Northern Old School concerns of 1837–68.

The General Assemblies from 1865 to 1867 announced policies that required the public repentance for any Old School pastors in the South to gain admission to the Church. The General Assembly of 1865 instructed presbyteries to question all prospective pastors regarding their views regarding the "atrocious rebellion." He must "confess and forsake his sin before he shall be received."[69] The 1866 General Assembly elected as Moderator R. L. Stanton, author of *The Church*

New Jersey: Princeton University Press, 1978), p. 3.

67. His father once bragged to a barber: "My son, Woodrow, has been made Ruling Elder in the Presbyterian Church. I would rather he held that position than be President of the United States." Spoken for many of us! See Josephus Daniels, *The Life of Woodrow Wilson, 1856–1924* (Philadelphia: Winston, 1924), p. 359.

68. Mullin, "Biblical Critics," pp. 221–22.

69. Vander Velde, *Presbyterian Churches*, p. 199.

and the Rebellion (1864), which had identified the Old School pastors as "the leading spirits of the rebellion."[70] Once installed, he told the Assembly that the war had been "the offspring of heresy, corruption, and all unrighteousness."[71] These and similar statements drove the border state churches into the Southern Presbyterian Church. Vander Velde, a University of Michigan historian with no ecclesiastical axe to grind, describes these assemblies as reflecting "the spirit of revenge and vindictiveness."[72] They made impossible any reconciliation in that generation with Southern Presbyterianism. Vander Velde summarizes the shift:

> Perhaps most significant of all, by 1866 the Church had come under the domination of what had once been regarded a contemptible group of radicals—men who for years had been agitators against slavery, against control of the Church by the East, and in favor of reunion with the New School Church. With its first two objectives virtually accomplished, this group, firmly in the saddle in 1866, gave the New School brethren an illustration of the completeness of its patriotism by its drastic handling of the case of the Presbytery of Louisville. . . . Sternly anti-slavery, vindictively aggressive in its patriotism, critically watchful of the "loyalty" of its ministers, openly currying favor with the New School brethren, distinctly Northern in its geography and Western in its control, the Old School Church of 1866 was a very different body from that to which the outbreak of the Civil War had brought such a serious crisis.[73]

These radical pronouncements and actions also had the effect of retroactively undermining the legitimacy of the pre-1864 Old School in the North, especially Charles Hodge and the Princetonians, who had led the battle to defer the Church's discussion of slavery as a sin, and who still refused to retract its pre-1864 position. Princeton's legiti-

---

70. *Ibid.*, p. 221.
71. *Ibid.*, p. 222.
72. *Ibid.*, p. 279.
73. *Ibid.*, p. 333.

macy was never completely restored. This fact was to shape the next two generations of the Northern Presbyterian Church.

Meanwhile, the New School General Assembly of 1866 issued a platform promoting the Freedman's Bureau and the political Reconstruction of the South.[74] It was time "to set aside all partisan aims and low ambitions . . . to the end that our Christian and Protestant civilization may maintain its legitimate ascendency. . . ."[75] Christendom would be advanced by the program of radical Republicans. This optimistic faith did not survive Reconstruction (1866–1877), and with it went the ideal of Christendom.

The Abandonment of the Ideal of Christendom

This war-induced theological surrender led to the emasculation of Old School Presbyterianism after the reunion. The Bible had not changed, but the Old School's beliefs regarding slavery had changed. Mullin writes of the Unitarians' response to the Calvinists' exegetical ambivalence on slavery: "Bound by their dogmatic presuppositions and their belief that the Bible contained a perfect moral law, they were unable to deal with the biblical ambivalence towards slavery. The obvious solution . . . was to abandon the belief in the infallibility of Scripture, and instead to acknowledge the historical relativity of the biblical record."[76] Escalating after 1875—but not in the South—this ambivalence led to the acceptance of the premises of biblical higher criticism. In the first half of the nineteenth century, a handful of theologians in New England began to accept the claims and methodology of higher criticism.[77] This increasingly Unitarian-dominated region became the academic headquarters of abolitionism. But it was only after 1875 that higher criticism gained a significant hearing in the North.

The South took a different approach: a world-rejecting experiential pietism that separated the Bible from social and political concerns.

---

74. *Ibid.*, pp. 358–59.
75. Cited in *ibid.*, p. 359.
76. Mullin, "Biblical Critics,", p. 222.
77. Jerry Wayne Brown, *The Rise of Biblical Criticism in America, 1800–1870: The New England Scholars* (Middletown, Connecticut: Wesleyan University Press, 1969).

Politics became *adiaphora*, or worse.[78] The Southern Old School theologian, James Henry Thornwell, had long favored this view of the institutional Church. Benjamin Palmer reaffirmed it in his opening sermon at the first General Assembly in 1861.[79] This outlook dominated the Southern Church for the next two generations. The social gospel was not welcome in the Southern Presbyterian Church in 1900; the Church was committed to a narrow pietism. The mission the Church, said Robert Ferris, editor of the *St. Louis Presbyterian* and the Permanent Clerk of the General Assembly, is not to reform men or corrupt societies; it is not to advance civilization. Its only task is to save souls.[80] This anti-cultural relevance resolve collapsed briefly in 1914 with respect to the Prohibition amendment.[81] The only other social issues that drew criticism from the General Assembly were these: (1) sabbath desecration (Sunday newspapers; running trains on Sundays to deliver the mail on Mondays);[82] (2) "worldly amusements" (dancing, card-playing, theater);[83] anti-lottery legislation;[84] and easy divorce (adultery and desertion only).[85] These were traditional fundamentalist social evils, with Scottish sabbatarianism as a substitute for the traditional anti-tobacco plank. The General Assembly in 1908 did recommend that employers and parents honor existing child labor laws.[86] That was the extent of its official concern on any economic issue. This was moralism rather than social transformation.

---

78. Cambellite David Lipscomb, publisher of the *Gospel Advocate* and author of *Civil Government*, is an example. Before the Civil War, he was a follower of Horace Greeley and a believer in the power of democracy. He believed that the United States had been the first nation founded on the principles of Jesus. After the war, he warned Christians not to vote, lest they pollute themselves with this-worldly politics. Robert E. Hooper, *Crying in the Wilderness: A Biography of David Lipscomb* (Nashville, Tennessee: David Lipscomb College, 1979), pp. 55–59; ch. 8.
79. Thompson, *Presbyterians in the South*, II:16.
80. He said this in 1888. *Ibid.*, III:261.
81. *Ibid.*, III:262.
82. *Ibid.*, II:225–26.
83. *Ibid.*, II:229–30. These positions the General Assembly officially held to, though without much enthusiasm.
84. *Ibid.*, II:233.
85. *Ibid.*, II:237–38.
86. *Ibid.*, II:243.

The South, having staked its legitimacy as a Christian social order on the armed defense of chattel slavery, suffered psychologically from its military defeat. Its commitment to slavery had been smashed on the battlefield; so had any pre-war commitment to the ideal of Christendom. A Christian social order was henceforth defined in terms of what Christians as individuals do not do, not what their civil representatives say or do in the legislature or court house. A different JC became the politically correct god of the New South: Jim Crow replaced Jesus Christ.

In North and South, the West's ideal of Christendom disappeared after 1865. The kingdom of God either became so immersed in history that it became indistinguishable from culture (modernism), or else it became so transcendent that it lost its judicial authority over culture (fundamentalism). This was a battle between two ideals, both announced in the name of Jesus Christ: the worldwide kingdom of man vs. the pietist ghetto. As they became more consistent over the next century, each side in the fundamentalist-modernist conflict developed the implications of its faith. *The modernists believed in history but not in God; the fundamentalists believed in God but not in history.* From about 1865 until about 1975, this pattern was only intermittently reversed in fundamentalism, the anti-alcohol crusade, 1900 to 1933, and Bryan's campaign against Darwinism in the public schools, 1921 to 1925, being the only major exceptions.[87] The voters' reaction against Prohibition in 1933, following the orchestrated reaction

---

87. After 1975, a growing number of fundamentalists in the United States began to abandon their world-rejecting pietism. They began to get involved in politics. The origin of the Christian Right can be dated from this period. Factors responsible for this reversal included these: (1) the reaction against the secularization and academic decline of the public schools and the rise of the Christian school and home school movements; (2) a growing awareness that legalized abortion is not *adiaphora*; (3) the Presidency of Jimmy Carter, who ran as an optimistic Baptist political outsider and turned out to be a national malaise-preaching Trilateral Commission political insider. The shift of charismatic author Bob Slosser is representative: he co-authored *The Miracle of Jimmy Carter* (Logos Books, 1976) and ghost-wrote Pat Robertson's *The Secret Kingdom* (Thomas Nelson Sons, 1982). The fundamentalist leaders' dispensational theology also began to slip into the shadows. Cf. Gary North, "The Intellectual Schizophrenia of the New Christian Right," *Christianity and Civilization*, 1 (1983), pp. 1–40.

against Bryan by the chattering class, sent American fundamentalism even deeper into its ghetto. The name adopted by one Baptist splinter group describes fundamentalism's cultural mind-set after 1933: Hard Shell.[88]

War and the Spirit of Unity

Once the Civil War began, the 1837 division appeared in retrospect to have been a mistake. In 1862, the Old School General Assembly passed a resolution proposing a "stated annual and friendly interchange of commissioners between the two General Assemblies."[89] The New School received this resolution with pleasure at its May, 1863 General Assembly.[90] At the 1864 Old School General Assembly, an unofficial group of ministers began working for reunion. This was the year that the General Assembly declared slavery to be sinful. They understood what would have to be done to achieve reunion: the resurrection of a spirit of unity. New School leader William Adams subsequently wrote: "Reunion cannot be accomplished, nor is it to be desired, without the restoration of a spirit of unity and fraternity. We believe this spirit exists, and is constantly increasing."[91] National unity during wartime was placing great pressure on regional ecclesiastical divisions. The affairs and needs of the respective civil governments had become the affairs and needs for regional churches. Civil government became the model for regional groupings within the denominations: a sure mark of theological crisis in the Church. When the desires of politicians determine the agendas of the churches, society has moved away from the ideal of Christendom and toward the ideal of humanism's Savior State.

Vindication and Exclusion

With the defeat of the South in 1865, the North's New School seemed vindicated politically and judicially. (The South's had merged

---

88. Yet since 1975, Aesop's story of the tortoise and the hare seems to be coming true. The fast-start modernists are spending more and more time napping.

89. William Adams, "The Reunion," *Presbyterian Re-union Memorial Volume, 1837–1871* (New York: DeWitt C. Lent Co., 1870) p. 249.

90. *Ibid.*

91. *Ibid.*, p. 250.

with the Old School in 1864.) The U.S. Constitution was amended over the next three years to stamp out all traces of the old slave system, and the South was placed under Reconstruction. Slavery became, in retrospect, the lost cause. The regional civilization that had been built on it was gone with the wind.

The North's Old School had always maintained that the Church should not get involved in the political cause of abolition. It rejected the claim of the New School that abolition was a legitimate moral cause. With the total victory of abolition, and with the public acceptance by almost everyone, even in the South, that slavery had in fact been immoral and therefore its defense a deservedly lost cause,[92] the Old School found itself outside the mainstream of American Christianity. Its embarrassment was no doubt compounded in 1867 by the publication of Dabney's wartime manuscript, *A Defense of Virginia*. Dabney had served Confederate General Thomas "Stonewall" Jackson as his chaplain, his aide-de-camp, and later as his biographer.[93] He was unreconstructed in 1867, both theologically and socially. He was a Southern Presbyterian and had been a leading Old School theologian prior to 1861. But in 1864, his recommendation of ecclesiastical union with the Southern New School carried the day.[94] His previous theological objections to the New School had been overcome by his commitment to a dying Confederacy: the common cause of both schools in the South.

The presence of Southern representatives in the Old School had kept that wing from opposing slavery. Only with their departure in 1861 could moderates on the slavery issue begin to think of reunion

---

92. The date of this transformation in the South was late 1864, when the Confederacy began considering an offer to the slaves: join the army and receive your freedom after the war. Once this was even contemplated politically, the slave cause was doomed. To make such an offer meant that black slaves were men, and men want and deserve freedom. See Richard E. Beringer, Herman Hattaway, Archer Jones, and William N. Still, Jr., *How the South Lost the Civil War* (Athens: University of Georgia Press, 1986), ch. 14. After the War, they write, "Few southerners ever admitted a desire to restore slavery, but thousands confessed relief that war had destroyed the peculiar institution." *Ibid.*, p. 361.

93. Thomas Cary Johnson, *The Life and Letters of Robert Lewis Dabney* (Richmond, Virginia: Presbyterian Committee of Publication, 1905), ch. 13.

94. *Ibid.*, p. 287.

with the New School. In the *Re-union Memorial Volume*, Old School representative Samuel Miller tried to put as good a face as he could on the Old School's earlier position, going so far as to write: "Sometimes it has been intimated, that pro-slavery tendencies on the part of the Old School were among the most influential causes of the division of 1838. No allegation could be more entirely opposed to historical truth."[95] But this self-serving assertion was denied by William Adams, a New School pastor who served as Chairman of the Joint Committee for reunion in 1867, 1868, and 1869.[96] He served for many years as a professor at Union Seminary. He wrote in the same volume that "the existence of slavery had more to do with the division of the Church than has generally been supposed; and that its entire extinction has been among the many causes which have made the Reunion of the two Northern Assemblies more easy and more certain."[97] While the documents of the division indicate that slavery had not been a factor officially, it was an underlying point of contention, and this division of opinion increased over the next two decades, especially after the Southern New School seceded from the New School in 1857. The New School in 1869 was quite open about this division; its members recognized their advantage.

What was the Old School to do? Only by joining with the New School could it re-enter the American ecclesiastical mainstream. But if it joined, it would return as the erring brother who had initially opposed the victorious forces of national unity, social reform, and abolition. The Old School was in no position to bargain after 1865. It would have to join on the judicial terms established by the New School.

"Welcome Home, [Prodigal] Brethren!"

Jonathan Stearns was a leader of New School Presbyterianism. He was a member of the Board of Directors of Union Seminary.[98] He

---

95. Samuel Miller, "Historical Review of the Church (Old School Branch)," *Re-union Memorial Volume*, p. 23.
96. William Adams, "Reunion," *ibid.*, pp. 260, 285, 296.
97. *Ibid.*, p. 249.
98. G. L. Prentiss, *The Union Theological Seminary in the City of New York: Its Design and another Decade of its History* (Asbury Park, New Jersey: Penny-

could afford to be magnanimous: "And now the long and troubled drama of New and Old School is at length finished. The seal is on the past, and the future, with its responsibilities, opens before us. And now, forgetting the things that are behind, all the grudges, all the alienations and rivalries of the past, and reaching forth to those things which are before, what have we, but to press towards the mark for the prize of the high calling of God in Christ Jesus?"[99] This sounded suspiciously like Lincoln's Second Inaugural address, after the electoral rout of the Democrats: "With malice toward none; with charity for all; with firmness in the right, as God gives us to see the right, let us strive on to finish the work we are in. . . ."

Stearns wrote a victory essay disguised as a conciliation essay. His view of Church sanctions was that of the New School, namely, that fights over theology are almost always a liability to the denomination. So, he recommended, let us forgive and forget. Since the reunion had been established on the basis of the New School's principles, the Old School would subsequently have no institutional alternative but to forgive; whether or not Old School members would forget was institutionally irrelevant to the New School. The issue was Church sanctions, and the New School had forever removed themselves from this threat as a condition of unity. Or so it seemed in 1869. In 1936, the threat reappeared: the modernists were not bound by the unofficial terms of the Old School's surrender.

A Question of Confession

The New School's defenders had always maintained that their members were full subscriptionists.[100] They made the same defense in the years immediately prior to the reunion. But the problem had not been the New School's confession; it had been the New School's unwillingness to bring negative ecclesiastical sanctions against those who were self-consciously Arminians. The reunion of 1869 necessarily

---

packer, 1899), pp. 21–22.
99. Stearns, "Historical Review," *Re-union Memorial Volume*, pp. 101–102.
100. See, for example, the New School defense: *A History of the Division of the Presbyterian Church in the United States of America by a Committee of the Synod of New York and New Jersey* (New York: Dodd, 1852).

came at the expense of the Old School's far stricter construction of the Westminster Confession and its view of Church discipline. This de-emphasis of judicial standards is always the institutional result, at least temporarily, when a more rigorous, more tightly knit organization joins with a less rigorous organization. The less rigorous organization will refuse to unify with the more rigorous organization unless all members of the new organization are promised immunity from subsequent trials based on the standards of the more rigorous faction. *The lowest common denominator of the less rigorous faction becomes the highest judicial standard for the courts of the new organization.* It will then take great diligence on the part of the stricter faction to keep the standards from drifting even lower. Loetscher is correct: "Once again in 1869, as in 1758, the Presbyterian Church was restoring unity not by resolving its differences but by ignoring and absorbing them."[101]

Men whose theology had been denounced as heretical by Old School members in the 1830's were now honored brethren. "The result was, of course, that the theological base of the Church (especially of the former Old School branch of the Church) was broadened and the meaning of its subscription formula further relaxed. . . . it would be increasingly difficult to protect historic Calvinism against the variations that might undermine its essential character."[102]

Theology without sanctions becomes mere opinion. The reunion of 1869 spelled the institutional death of the ecclesiastical views of Charles Hodge and Princeton Seminary. Those views could be publicly expressed, but they could no longer be defended through Church discipline except in the rarest of cases—after 1900, in none. After 1878 (the McCune case), the New School would not allow such enforcement without extreme rhetorical provocation from a modernist. The price of union had been the triumph of the New School's position; otherwise, they would not have voted to join with the Old School. Their view of Church order became the new institutional standard. The New School won the battle. It did not win the war, however;

---

101. Lefferts A. Loetscher, *The Broadening Church: a study of theological issues in the presbyterian church since 1869* (Philadelphia: University of Pennsylvania Press, 1954), p. 8.

102. *Ibid*. Loetscher, a liberal, approved of this development.

that victory went to the modernists. This transfer of power took a little over two generations: 1869–1936.

The Presbyterian conflict's later phases was a war between Calvinist orthodoxy at one end of the theological spectrum and theological modernism at the other. Typically, no more than ten percent of the members of any organization are committed to either end of the spectrum. The war is always for acceptance by the 80 percent in between. Presbyterian orthodoxy of the Old School (1838–1869) is relatively easy to define: Calvinistic, creedal, and hierarchical. But after the reunion of 1869, this commitment to Calvinism and creedalism began to fade in Northern Presbyterianism. This was the theological legacy of the New School. This decline of respect for the Westminster Confession led to the denomination's capture by the modernists in 1936.

The Price of Unity

The story of the decline of Presbyterian orthodoxy is the story of the decline of respect for the Confession and also the courts of the Church, to the extent that they imposed negative sanctions to enforce the Confession. Charles Hodge fought the reunion right down to the final vote.[103] The Old School's theology was taught at Princeton Seminary, and Hodge vigorously defended this theology. An historian a decade after the union wrote: "One may well doubt whether any other Christian communion of equal size has ever excelled it as to unity in the reception of an evangelical creed of such extent as the Westminster Confession and Catechisms."[104] But the vote was so overwhelming in 1869—unanimous in the New School's assembly; 285 to 9 in the Old School's[105]—that it was futile to continue the fight.

George Marsden, who was trained at Westminster Seminary before earning his Ph.D. in history at Yale, argues that the New School had become more conservative since 1838.[106] On abolition, it became

---

103. Charles Hodge, "The General Assembly," *Princeton Review*, 39 (July 1867); Hodge, "Presbyterian Reunion," *ibid.*, 40 (Jan. 1868). The second essay was more moderate in tone.

104. "Presbyterian Churches," in *Cyclopaedia of Biblical, Theological, and Ecclesiastical Literature*, edited by John M'Clintock and James Strong, 12 vols. (New York: Harper & Bros., 1879), VIII:535.

105. Marsden, *Evangelical Mind*, p. 225.

106. *Ibid.*, ch. 11.

conservative through military victory. Its 1838 position on abolition had not identified slavery as a sin, nor had its 1846 declaration, which is why Southern New School churches stayed on board until 1857. But at the 1866 General Assembly, it took a position favoring Reconstruction, including universal suffrage for blacks: the radical Republican position. There was nothing conservative about its politics. Then what about New School theology? There was no fixed pattern. The New School's theological heirs were sometimes modernists (e.g., the Union Seminary faculty after 1890) and sometimes fundamentalists (e.g., the Bible Presbyterian Church). The issue I am raising here is ecclesiology. The New School may have affirmed the Confession as a tactic for gaining entry into, and control over, the larger Old School Presbyterian communion, but the deciding issue was not verbal affirmation; it was its willingness to conduct heresy trials in the name of the Confession.[107] After 1900, the New School's resolve collapsed. The unwillingness to prosecute ministers in heresy trials was *the* New School ecclesiastical tradition. It was interrupted significantly for only one decade, 1891–1900, and only because of one man's rhetoric: Charles A. Briggs.

Without the threat of negative sanctions, the Confession and the catechisms steadily became museum pieces. The modernists' strategy was to defend the legitimacy of verbal profession at the time of one's ordination, but deny the moral legitimacy of Church sanctions to defend the integrity of these professions. This was a strategy that the New School had already established as a *de facto* policy of the denomination in 1869. It was to lead, step by step, decade by decade, to the capture of Northern Presbyterianism by the modernists.

Conclusion

Historians generally refer to two distinct traditions in American Presbyterianism at the time of the reunion of 1869 between the Old School and New School: the "exclusivists" and the "inclusivists."[108] Those men in favor of an inclusive, less dogmatic Church could appeal to the New School tradition; conversely, those favoring an exclu-

---

107. "Watch what we do, not what we say."
108. A representative study is Loetscher's *Broadening Church*.

sive, doctrinal organization had the history of the Old School supporting them. Institutionally, it was not so much a question of a new Church structure over an older form, but rather a question of *which tradition to select*, the Old School's theological exclusivism or the New School's theological inclusivism. The New School's tradition gained legitimacy after 1869. The question, "Whose legitimacy?" was answered with the reunion. It had taken a century and a half for Presbyterians to decide. Five years later, modernist minister David Swing would re-open the question again.

The Old School lost its judicial case as early as 1869. (It lost its moral case in 1818: the Bourne Case.) The merger with the New School downgraded the denomination's commitment to a systematic enforcement of the Westminster Confession. This was a replay of the Presbyterian union of 1758. From 1869 on, the Old School was fighting a rear-guard action, defensive rather than offensive.

A defensive strategy is inappropriate for those who proclaim a religion of victory. It was the liberals and modernists in the 1901–36 period who believed in victory and who took systematic steps—institutional and propaganda steps—to achieve it. As Shailer Mathews announced in the two-sentence opening paragraph of *The Faith of Modernism* (1924): "The world is being reconstructed. Can Christians aid?" These men were not fighting a rear-guard action. A Confessionally compromised Old School Calvinism and a peace-seeking New School evangelicalism proved to be unsuited for the kind of full-scale battle that had to be fought after 1875. The liberals determined the battlefields and the weapons. They controlled the initiative. They set the agenda. The historic results of the Presbyterian conflict prove that law apart from the willingness to impose appropriate sanctions is impotent. The crucial issue was sanctions.

Phase 2: Whose Authority?

3

AUTHORITY: BIBLICAL, CONFESSIONAL, ECCLESIASTICAL

> *Presbyterianism has made provision for an ever-fresh resort to that fountain of truth. It does not require us to receive the Confession of Faith as infallible. It does not tie us up to those precise words and forms of expression; it does not require us to subscribe to every proposition contained in it, but only to receive it as containing, according to its true intents and original meaning, the system of doctrines taught in the Scriptures. There is no dispute now between the two parties (whatever there may have been once), in regard to that matter. True, it would be hard to find in the Confession any other than a pretty strong Calvinism; but Calvinism is not that iron thing which some have supposed it. None of us takes it as such; none of us preaches it as such. We mean to have all reasonable liberty. But, in the union or out of it, we mean to maintain and teach the doctrines of the Confession.*
>
> Jonathan F. Stearns (1870)[1]

Rev. Stearns, a New School man, articulated the opinion of his wing of Presbyterianism: "Calvinism is not that iron thing which some have supposed it." Orthodox theology, Stearns implied, no

---

1. Jonathan F. Stearns, "Historical Review of the Church (New School Branch)," *Presbyterian Re-union Memorial Volume, 1837–1871* (New York: De Witt C. Lent & Co., 1870), p. 336.

longer possessed an ecclesiastical rod of iron to defend itself from its enemies. He represented the winning side at the beginning of a long retreat by the Old School. But in winning, he and his associates committed institutional suicide. They did so by swallowing repeated doses of a slow-acting poison. Their mortal enemies had deliberately re-labeled the bottle and had disguised its contents by adding an organic extract of their favorite flavor: *experientialism*. It took two generations for this poison to complete its work. The antidote was the Old School's judicial theology, but it tasted like castor oil to the New School. Rarely would they swallow it, and then only under extreme internal discomfort caused by an inadvertent overdose of the poison. When the source of their temporary discomfort was purged, they returned to their old habits.

The Civil War settled the ecclesiastical debate over the legitimacy of chattel slavery. It was that settlement on approximately 10,400 battlefields that sanctioned the re-unification of the Northern Presbyterian Church. It took more than a century for the North-South division to be healed denominationally, and the healing balm was neo-orthodoxy.

The unification of the Presbyterian Church in 1869 settled another old issue: What constitutes the mark of a true Christian? The Old Side and Old School had answered: profession of faith and an outward life obedient to God's moral standards; nothing else. The New Side and New School had added: experience of salvation. Unification made it clear that the New School's definition could no longer be excluded from the Church by the Old School through the imposition of the sanction of wholesale removal (1837) or retail excommunication (one trial at a time).

The unification did not settle the other divisive issue: the structure of authority over missions, education, and other kingdom work. The Old School had demanded hierarchical control; the New School had defended what would today be called parachurch ministries. Judicially, it was this issue that led to the final phase of the Presbyterian conflict in 1933 to 1936. But in that case, the Old School had reversed its position and was defending the position of the New School in 1836.

Cosmic Personalism and Judicial Representation

The Bible teaches that all of history is personal. It is also representational. A sovereign God is represented by His people and His angels, and a non-sovereign Satan is represented by his people and his angels. Adam represented God to the creation and mankind before God. The serpent represented Satan to Adam and the serpent species before God. Adam's fall condemned mankind judicially. Jesus, the second Adam (I Cor. 15:45), represented God to humanity and His people before God. His triumph restored His people judicially. There is no escape from the doctrine of representation. All authority is necessarily hierarchical.[2] All authority is necessarily personal.

More than any other theology in history, Calvinism is a theology of judicial representation. Calvin taught this clearly,[3] but the Puritans made it the bedrock foundation of their theology. The Puritan system was called Federal Theology. It was based on the biblical concept of judicial representation: Adam representing fallen mankind in the covenant of works;[4] Jesus Christ representing redeemed mankind in the covenant of grace.[5] The doctrine of imputation[6] was fundamental to original Presbyterianism's concept of soteriology (salvation): Adam's fallen humanity is imputed by God judicially to all men;[7] Christ's perfect humanity is subsequently imputed judicially by God to the elect.[8]

The biblical doctrine of representation requires that a covenantal representative speak in the name of God: in Church, State, and family. The Church's representative is ordained by the Church to speak authoritatively. Having spoken, he must then be able to enforce this

---

2. Ray R. Sutton, *That You May Prosper: Dominion By Covenant*, 2nd ed. (Tyler, Texas: Institute for Christian Economics, 1992), ch. 2.

3. See especially his comments on Romans 5:12–19. John Calvin, *Commentaries on the Epistle of Paul to the Romans* (Grand Rapids, Michigan: Baker, [1539] 1979), pp. 199–213.

4. Larger Catechism, A. 22.

5. *Ibid.*, AA. 31, 32.

6. *Theological Essays Reprinted from the Princeton Review* (New York: Wiley & Putnam, 1846), chaps. 6–8.

7. Westminster Confession of Faith, VI:3.

8. *Ibid.*, XI:1; Larger Catechism, A. 71.

word. Church government is the means by which the representative's word is formally enforced, modified, or overturned by a higher representative. Sanctions—point four of the biblical covenant model—are brought to bear in specific cases in order to enforce the representative's word: point two.

The theological debates that shook the Northern Presbyterian Church from 1874 to 1900 centered on questions of authority. The primary issue was the authority of the Bible. This was the debate over higher criticism, as well as the non-debate over lower criticism. The secondary issue was derivative: What is the authority of the Westminster Confession of Faith, which proclaims "the infallible truth and divine authority" of the Bible in Chapter I, Section 3?

The Source of Authority

The source of law in any society is the god of that society.[9] This god is said to be the source of law because it is said to be the source of origins. The battle between evolutionism and creationism is a battle over the question of law in every realm. It is equally true to say that the battle over law—revealed, natural, and social—is today a battle over evolutionism vs. creationism. Any study that deals with the twin ideas of law and origins independently of each other is misleading.

The battle over the integrity of the Bible is a battle over law, for it is a battle over the nature of God and His revelation of Himself in history. The two-part question is this: What is the source of law, and how do we gain knowledge of it? Point three of the biblical covenant model—law—points us backward to point two (authority) and forward to point four (judgment).

For over a century in the West, this deeply theological debate over authority, law, and judgment has been framed in terms of two related issues: (1) Darwinian evolutionary process and modern science vs. the Bible; (2) historical criticism of the Bible vs. inerrancy.[10] The debate is over the source of authority and man's judgment in history:

---

9. R. J. Rushdoony, *The Institutes of Biblical Law* (Nutley, New Jersey: Craig Press, 1973), p. 5.

10. See Charles Hodge, *Systematic Theology*, 3 vols. (Grand Rapids, Michigan: Eerdmans, [1871]), I, ch. 6: "Inspiration."

historical process or the Bible. Should men use history to judge (interpret) the Bible or should they use the Bible to judge (interpret) history? How should men interpret the facts of history: in terms of history or in terms of the Bible? How should men interpret the Bible: in terms of history or in terms of the Bible? *The supreme authority is self-authenticating and self-judging: either history or the Bible.* The debate is between historicism and biblical infallibility.

Chapter I of the Westminster Confession contained the following provisions:

> IV. The authority of the Holy Scripture, for which it ought to be believed, and obeyed, dependeth not upon the testimony of any man, or Church; but wholly upon God (who is truth itself) the author thereof: and therefore it is to be received, because it is the Word of God.

> VIII. The Old Testament in Hebrew (which was the native language of the people of God of old), and the New Testament in Greek (which, at the time of the writing of it, was most generally known among the nations), being immediately inspired by God, and, by His singular care and providence, kept pure in all ages, are therefore authentical; so as, in all controversies of religion, the Church is finally to appeal unto them.

The Confession set forth the Presbyterian Church's official position regarding the source of authority: the Bible. The Bible is the fundamental law of the Church. The authority of the Church rests on the authority of the Bible. To attack the authority of the Bible is to attack the authority of the Church.

The Revival of Idolatry

Man worships two kinds of idols: idols of nature and idols of history.[11] The nineteenth century saw a revival of both of these idols. The idol of nature had been worshipped furtively in the shadows of the mechanistic world of Newtonianism ever since the late seven-

---

11. Herbert Schlossberg, *Idols for Destruction: Christian Faith and Its Confrontation with American Society* (Westchester, Illinois: Crossway, [1983] 1991), p. 11.

teenth century. But mechanism has not been nearly so powerful a metaphor as organicism. Nisbet is correct: "There has never been a time in Western thought when the image of social change has not been predominantly biological in nature."[12] Within half a century of Newton's death, the idol of nature was dressed up once again in its familiar organic wardrobe: Rousseau's naturalism.[13] So attired, it was brought into the public square by the French Revolution. "The true priest of the Supreme Being," Robespierre declared in June of 1794, justifying the Festival of the Supreme Being, "is Nature itself; its temple is the universe; its religion virtue; its festivals the joy of a great people assembled under its eyes to tie the sweet knot of universal fraternity and to present before it [Nature] the homage of pure and feeling [*sensible*] hearts."[14]

The idol of history had been worshipped by the Enlightenment, both right wing and left wing. Adam Ferguson's social evolutionism and the Continental Enlightenment's faith in rational progress were equally devoted to the idol of history, although faith in natural law was never absent,[15] especially in France.[16] It was in Darwinism that the two idols were fused into a single, intellectually compelling cosmology. This cosmology remains the dominant intellectual alternative to Christianity in the West.

Historicism

In the worldview known as historicism, the laws of history are derived from history and change with history. Law becomes a function of history. There is no unchanging metaphysical order above history or outside of history that somehow provides structure to history. History and its laws are autonomous. Man is bounded by history, and

---

12. Robert A. Nisbet, *Prejudices: A Philosophical Dictionary* (Cambridge, Massachusetts: Harvard University Press, 1982), p. 274.

13. Paul Johnson, *Intellectuals* (New York: Harper & Row, 1988), p. 3.

14. Cited in Simon Schama, *Citizens: A Chronicle of the French Revolution* (New York: Simon & Schuster, 1989), p. 831.

15. Louis I. Bredvold, *Brave New World of the Enlightenment* (Ann Arbor: University of Michigan Press, 1961), ch. 2.

16. Lester G. Crocker, *Nature and Culture: Ethical Thought in the French Enlightenment* (Baltimore: Johns Hopkins University Press, 1963), ch. 1.

only by history. There can be no legitimate appeal beyond history. Rushdoony is correct: such an outlook leads to tyranny. "Humanistic law, moreover, is inescapably totalitarian law. Humanism, as a logical development of evolutionary theory, holds fundamentally to a concept of an evolving universe. This is held to be an 'open universe,' whereas Biblical Christianity, because of its faith in the triune God and His eternal decree, is said to be a faith in a 'closed universe.' This terminology not only intends to prejudice the case; it reverses reality. The universe of evolutionism and humanism is a closed universe. There is no law, no appeal, no higher order, beyond and above the universe. Instead of an open window upwards, there is a closed cosmos. There is thus no ultimate law and decree beyond man and the universe. Man's law is therefore beyond criticism except by man. In practice, this means that the positive law of the state is absolute law. The state is the most powerful and most highly organized expression of humanistic man, and the state is the form and expression of humanistic law. Because there is no higher law of God as judge over the universe, over every human order, the law of the state is a closed system of law. There is no appeal beyond it. Man has no 'right,' no realm of justice, no source of law beyond the state, to which man can appeal against the state. Humanism therefore imprisons man within the closed world of the state and the closed universe of the evolutionary scheme."[17]

Historicism as an ideal for understanding man can be found in Rousseau's writings: his timeless suggestion that no natural law order stands outside man, independent of the history of man's institutions.[18] But its academic form is more closely associated with nineteenth-century German academia. Historicism was given tremendous new impetus by Darwinism, which views all of nature as evolving: the product of historical forces. In Darwinism, the category of static natural law

---

17. R. J. Rushdoony, "Humanistic Law," introduction to E. L. Hebden Taylor, *The New Legality* (Nutley, New Jersey: Craig Press, 1967), vi–vii. Rushdoony revised this statement slightly, and I reproduce here his final version.

18. Andrzej Rapaczynski, *Nature and Politics* (Ithaca, New York: Cornell University Press, 1987), Part 3; Arthur M. Melzer, *The Natural Goodness of Man: On the System of Rousseau's Thought* (Chicago: University of Chicago Press, 1990), ch. 8.

disappears. Nature is defined in terms of evolutionary processes. Nature is thereby freed from all supernaturalism, i.e., anything beyond nature's domain. The wholly natural processes of the universe are understood to be closed to God, but they are open to man, who can understand these processes. Natural selection provides direction to life even though nature seeks no ends. Man, as the only form of life that can direct the impersonal forces of nature toward his own ends, becomes the sole source of meaning and teleology in nature, the source of cosmic personalism. Nature is governed by the laws of history, but only man can understand them—or at least certain specially trained or gifted men. Man becomes the source of progress in Darwinism—the only being capable of defining progress, discovering progress, and directing progress.

Historicism's faith in man's ability to discover the laws governing nature, including man, is a deeply flawed faith.[19] It proclaims a source of understanding and perhaps even predictability—historical laws—that are themselves in constant flux. But the faithful believed that this obvious contradiction, as old as Hericlitus' flowing river of history, could be overcome by additional historical research and more attention to methodology—a characteristically Germanic academic faith. The historicist treated the laws of history as a chef without a recipe might explain the art of cooking stew: if the stew tastes odd, add more ingredients; it might just work out. This time, anyway. For the cook. And if someone else does not like how it tastes, he can add more ingredients from his pantry. "Everyman his own cook," but without a recipe that can be proven scientifically to be valid for as long as water boils in a small pot.

The end result of historicism's relativism is today's politically correct academic methodology known as deconstruction: the affirmation of texts without context, i.e., texts only for me, here and now—a denial of the relevance of the past. But this existentialist dead-end was not foreseen by those enthusiastic pilgrims travelling down historicism's highway in the late nineteenth century. The road signs provided by the Bible and by the tradition of natural law—medieval and

---

19. Karl Popper, *The Poverty of Historicism* (New York: Harper Torchbooks, 1957).

Newtonian—had not yet been blown down by the hurricane winds conjured up by historicism and its two lineal descendants, nationalism and Marxist revolution.

The Old School's Task

The historicist worldview became increasingly dominant in nineteenth-century intellectual circles.[20] This development offered a crucial challenge to Old School theologians. They had to explain the permanent authority of the Bible to a society that was increasingly ready to accept the theology of historicism, which rests on the presupposition that the only law is the law of change. If the Bible is bounded by time, how can it be immune from the temporal relativism of historical process? If it was written by men in one era, how can it be authoritative in another era or in any society outside of the one to which it was revealed? Here is a variation of the ancient debate between Parmenides and Heraclitus, which the Greeks never successfully answered: "If law is constant, what role can it play in a world in which everything is in flux? Where are the points of contact between unchanging law and ceaseless flux?" Liberal theologians asked: "Is the Bible such a point of contact? If so, how?"

The triumph of historicism in the late nineteenth century established the intellectual task for the Old School theologians: to refute the ethical relativism of organicism-historicism without relying on the static cosmic impersonalism of traditional mechanism-Newtonianism. The fate of the Presbyterian Church would be determined by the answers that its leaders would adopt and by their ability to persuade its voting and paying members. Old School Presbyterians were regarded as the best equipped theologians in this intellectual battle. This was the opinion of their supporters from outside Presbyterianism and also by the higher critics. If the Old School's handful of academic lead-

---

20. This is the starting point of Mark Stephen Massa, S.J., *Charles Augustus Briggs and the Crisis of Historical Criticism* (Minneapolis, Minnesota: Fortress Press, 1990), ch. 1. Isaiah Berlin speaks of "a new historical vision" and its "dominant influence over much of the political and intellectual life of the West...." Berlin, "Foreword" (1972) to Friedrich Meinecke, *Historism: The Rise of a New Outlook* (London: Herder & Herder, [1936] 1972), p. ix.

ers—Charles Hodge, A. A. Hodge, B. B. Warfield—could be judicially isolated on this question, the higher critics would score a crucial victory. If they could not be isolated, then the Presbyterian higher critics would face a major problem: how to remain inside the denomination in order to carry on their work of evangelism for Darwinism.

The larger issue was the integrity of God's revelation of Himself in written form. A subordinate but important issue was Presbyterian law. The first and longest chapter in the Confession is *On the Holy Scriptures*. The Westminster Assembly placed the Church under the authority of the Bible. In legal terminology, the Bible served the Westminster Confession as fundamental law. The Confession itself was therefore the Constitution of the Presbyterian Church.[21] Like the U.S. Constitution, which identifies the source of its authority—"We the People"—the Westminster Confession identifies the source of its authority: the written text of Scripture.

Confessional Authority and Historical Change

In order for this hierarchical legal relationship to be believable, it was mandatory for the Presbyterian Church to be willing to revise the Confession periodically. If it did not do so, then operationally the Confession would take on the character of fundamental law. But the Westminster Assembly stated categorically that no Church's testimony can be equal to the Bible's: "The authority of the Holy Scripture, for which it ought to be believed, dependeth not upon the testimony of any man, or Church; but wholly upon God (who is truth itself) the author thereof; and therefore it is to be received, because it is the Word of God" (I:4).

If the Confession remained static, then any new theological insights derived from the Bible would create problems for the Church. They would have to be ignored, actively suppressed, or unofficially

---

21. Technically, the American Church defined the Constitution as all of the subordinate standards: *The Constitution of the Presbyterian Church in the United States of America: Being Its Standards Subordinate to the Word of God, Viz. The Confession of Faith, The Larger and Shorter Catechisms, The Form of Government, The Book of Discipline, and the Directory for the Worship of God, as Ratified by the Synod of New York and Philadelphia in the Year of Our Lord 1788* (Philadelphia: Presbyterian Board of Publication and Sabbath School Work, 1904).

adopted despite the Confession's statements to the contrary. Thus, to the extent that widespread belief within the Presbyterian Church deviated from the Confession, the integrity of the Confession would be undermined. It would no longer serve as Constitutional law, i.e., the legal basis of Church sanctions.

A theological confession is like a speed limit sign posted on a two-lane highway. As time goes on, the road may be widened to four lanes and then six lanes. Car design is improved, so cars can go faster without seriously reducing passenger safety. The old speed limit becomes outdated. Even careful drivers begin to ignore the sign. If the speed limit is not raised and the sign is not replaced, the incongruity between the new historical reality and the posted speed limit destroys the authority of traffic laws in general. The sign becomes a museum piece, a quaint reminder of horse-and-buggy days gone by. No jury will predictably convict a speeder who exceeds the sign's posted limit. To make sure that some speed limit is enforceable on the highway, the highway department will have to raise the speed limit. Otherwise, original sin being what it is, too many people will drive too fast to be safe. But exactly how fast is "safe"? Auto manufacturers will sometimes overestimate the safety of their products. So will highway engineers. The speed limit may be raised too high by the authorities. A lot of people will then be injured.

The modernists wanted no enforceable limit on any road. They wanted to limit the authorities to mere persuasion. Meanwhile, they were all test-driving new roadsters. A lot of innocent people were about to get run over, and a lot of deadly car crashes would soon take place. But the Confession still read "25" on certain six-lane highways.[22]

Challenging the Old School

There is progress in history. This includes creedal progress. This is why Presbyterians affirmed that the Westminster Confession was superior to previous confessional statements. But belief in general is not the same as action in the present. The Old School did not seek Confessional revisions in a denomination dominated by New School

---

22. For example, the Pope as the Antichrist (XXV:6). Hardly anyone in the Presbyterian Church paid attention to that sign by 1900.

members. The Old School therefore found itself in a dilemma: some of its beliefs had changed. The Confession says that only elect infants go to heaven (X:3). Old School theologians by the late nineteenth century believed that all infants are elect. This discrepancy between the strict language of the Confession and actual belief was used by modernists against the Old School and against the judicially binding authority of the Confession.

There was another way to undermine the judicial authority of the Confession: undermine the judicial authority of the Bible. The Westminster Assembly had declared that the texts of the Bible, "being immediately inspired by God, and, by His singular care and providence, kept pure in all ages, are therefore authentical" (I:8). How pure is pure? If there are errors in the existing texts, then this statement by the Confession regarding their preservation in history is called into question. At the very least, defining "pure" becomes mandatory. But if the historical texts were copied faithfully, and errors have nevertheless been found, this calls into question the meaning of "immediately inspired." Inspiration no longer means absolutely accurate, and without absolute accuracy, the judicial authority of the Bible is undermined. This moves the source of law away from the Bible as God's authoritative word to man and his authoritative word. This is where higher critics of the Bible want to move it.

The battle for the Bible was therefore a battle for the authority of the Westminster Confession. The Presbyterian higher critics had a two-fold goal: (1) undermine the judicial authority of the Bible as fundamental law; (2) undermine the judicial authority of the Westminster Confession as constitutional law. The Old School sought to affirm both positions. Both sides understood how high the stakes were: the future of the Presbyterian Church and, more broadly, the future of whatever traces remained of Christendom in American Protestant thought.

The Claims of Higher Criticism

The claims of Old Testament higher critics always begin with the supposed fact that Moses did not write the Pentateuch. Genesis 1, with its story of the six-day creation, must be jettisoned. So must Genesis 7: Noah's worldwide flood. It was a rejection of the higher critics' thesis of the later, multiple authorship of the Pentateuch that was at the heart of Old Princeton's view of inerrancy. This public battle began in 1881 in the pages of a newly established scholarly journal, *The Presbyterian Review*.

The Old School understood that the authority of the New Testament rests on the Mosaic authorship of the Pentateuch. Jesus said: "For Moses said, Honour thy father and thy mother; and, Whoso curseth father or mother, let him die the death" (Mark 7:10). "Now that the dead are raised, even Moses shewed at the bush, when he calleth the Lord the God of Abraham, and the God of Isaac, and the God of Jacob" (Luke 20:37). "And beginning at Moses and all the prophets, he expounded unto them in all the scriptures the things concerning himself" (Luke 24:27). "And he said unto them, These are the words which I spake unto you, while I was yet with you, that all things must be fulfilled, which were written in the law of Moses, and in the prophets, and in the psalms, concerning me" (Luke 24:44).[23] To undermine the Mosaic authorship of the Pentateuch is inevitably to undermine the authority of Jesus Christ. The American opponents of higher criticism recognized this threat, despite the repeated assurances of the critics that they were fully committed to Christ.[24] For those Christians who were committed to the New Testament's authoritative revelation of Jesus and His words, there would be grave problems with higher criticism.

Higher Criticism's Interpretation of the Bible

Traditional higher critics have been masters of grammar—too clever by half, as the English cleverly say. For example, they believe they have found two grammars (usages) in the book of Isaiah, so they

---

23. I have taken these proof texts from O. T. Allis, *The Five Books of Moses* (1943). Allis was the most articulate defender of the Princeton apologetic against higher criticism. He served as Assistant Professor of Hebrew at Princeton from 1910 to 1929, and then served as professor at Westminster Seminary from 1929 until 1936.

24. This resistance was far less true of Christians in England in the late nineteenth century, who tended to accept higher criticism of the Old Testament but not of the New Testament. Mark A. Noll, *Between Faith and Criticism: Evangelicals, Scholarship, and the Bible in America*, 2nd ed. (Grand Rapids, Michigan: Eerdmans, 1986), p. 71.

conclude that there were two Isaiahs: one who wrote Isaiah 1–39, and another who wrote what followed. (These days, their computers find three Isaiahs.) They have used grammar as a way to undermine men's faith in the unity of the biblical text. (A later generation of higher critics has searched for literary unity in the texts, a remarkable reversal of methodology, but not of conclusions, i.e., the Bible is still not acceptable as the authoritative word of God.)

They have also used history to undermine men's faith. They rely on the historical documents of non-Hebrew societies, especially chronologically impaired Egypt,[25] to criticize the Bible's chronology. As a result, they have produced a convoluted, incoherent jumble of dates for biblical events and texts. On the basis of this monumental jumble, they conclude that this or that passage in this or that text of the Bible was written hundreds of years later than the author of the text claimed. Later authors must have added materials to old texts, or else they wrote forgeries that claimed to be old. (Note: a higher critic never uses the pejorative word *forgery* when describing what would, in any other setting, be called a forgery. There is a very good reason for his verbal reticence: he is a subversive. He is a Trojan horse—I can use imagery, too—not a battering ram. His goal is to steal the inheritance, not burn it down.) This later-author methodology is applied without exception to every passage in which the writer made a prediction that was clearly fulfilled—above all, the book of Daniel: prophecies regarding three future empires (Dan. 2:37–45; 8).

The higher critics are generally self-conscious evolutionists. They assume that social law changes as societies advance over time. They are ethical relativists with respect to time.[26] This is a fundamental tenet of their theology, for their number-one goal is to deny God's final judgment, hell, and the lake of fire. Therefore, they attack the Bible's revelation of a permanent judicial standard by which God will bring His wrath against covenant-breakers throughout eternity.

---

25. Peter James, *Centuries of Darkness: A challenge to the conventional chronology of Old World archaeology* (New Brunswick, New Jersey: Rutgers University Press, 1993), ch. 10.

26. Gary North, *The Hoax of Higher Criticism* (Tyler, Texas: Institute for Christian Economics, 1989), ch. 3.

Higher critics present God's law, and therefore biblical theology—the progress of God's revelation in the Bible—as an evolutionary process.

Finally, they appeal to biblical symbols. This is the academic discipline known as biblical theology. (Not symbolic theology: the nineteenth-century phrase "symbolic theology" referred to the formal study of Church creeds.)[27] The discipline of biblical theology in America was originally a subset of higher criticism. Charles A. Briggs gave his ill-fated 1891 Inaugural Address[28] on the occasion of his having been appointed to an endowed chair in biblical theology at New York's Union Seminary. Shailer Mathews in 1936 summarized the importance of the introduction of the modernists' version of the discipline of biblical theology: "This was really an introduction of historical relativity into theological thought."[29] Biblical theology for the higher critic was crucial: a means of undermining the unity of systematic theology—the theology established by examining specific theological texts of the Bible and comparing them with other texts. This method is dismissed by the higher critic as "proof-texting." The texts are assumed by the higher critic to have no unity because they were written by different men, just as they are assumed by the orthodox theologian to possess unity because they came from God. There is no way to reconcile these rival assumptions. No supposedly neutral methodology can unify them. The two operating methodological assumptions are irreconcilable.

Higher Criticism in the United States

The cauldron of higher criticism had been bubbling in Germany[30] for almost a century by the 1870's. Then it overflowed into Anglo-American churches. In the mid-1870's, several men on both sides of the Atlantic began to announce their views in public lectures

---

27. When Briggs used the word "symbols" in his 1889 book, *Whither?*, he meant "creeds."

28. See Chapter 5, below.

29. Shailer Mathews, *New Faith for Old: An Autobiography* (New York: Macmillan, 1936), p. 27.

30. Germany as a political entity appeared in 1871. I am using the term culturally.

Authority: Biblical, Confessional, Ecclesiastical 161

and articles to academic audiences. The debate surfaced in a special way: a debate over Church sanctions. It was not until 1879 that the first institutional sanctions were applied, but not in Presbyterianism; the Baptists have that honor.

The existence of a looming institutional conflict over higher criticism in Anglo-American churches began to surface between 1875 and 1880. The modernist leader, Washington Gladden, remarked in his 1909 *Recollections* that in 1875, Congregational ministers in Massachusetts were aware of higher criticism, and were both shaken and in agreement with it, but "there was still great timidity in admitting so much in the hearing of the public."[31] The conflict over higher criticism appeared in Presbyterian circles in 1881, escalated for two decades, and then receded until 1922. It was almost like a naval campaign. A few submarine scouts put up their periscopes, 1875-76. They fired a few torpedoes and were fired upon, 1876-83. The surface ships' guns grew strangely silent, 1884-91. Then, provoked by a trio of subs, they sank two and chased away a third, 1893-1900. Then the war seemed to end. But a growing fleet of modernist Presbyterian subs remained submerged beneath the waves, 1900-22. The fleet's main center of production was Germany, but Union Seminary became the most prominent U.S. contractor.

A defensive intellectual campaign against German higher criticism had been intensifying in Northern Presbyterian circles since the 1830's. From 1800 to 1850, the targets were outside the denomination and generally outside the country. Between 1829 and 1850, *Princeton Review* published seventy articles against higher criticism, and the rate increased after 1850.[32] But it was a Baptist, C. H. Toy, who was the first American to lose his job for his stand. The Baptist Theological School of Louisville accepted Dr. Toy's resignation in 1879.

---

31. Cited in William R. Hutchison, *The Modernist Impulse in American Protestantism* (Cambridge, Massachusetts: Harvard University Press, 1976), p. 76. The pagination is the same in the Oxford University Press paperback edition.

32. Jack B. Rogers and Donald K. McKim, *The Authority and Interpretation of the Bible: An Historical Approach* (New York: Harper & Row, 1979), p. 279.

The Toy Case

Toy had received his bachelor's degree from the University of Virginia had studied at the University of Berlin in the same period as Briggs had: the mid-1860's. (He shared both alma maters with Briggs.) He had begun to teach higher criticism, quietly, in his classes around 1877.[33] In 1869, he had told his students that he was a Darwinist. The seminary covered up for him, fearing to disturb donors.[34] Toy wrote an essay for the *Sunday School Times* in 1879 in which he claimed that two authors had written Isaiah. Immediately, a Reformed Church of America publication, *The Christian Intelligencer*, attacked the essay and the *Sunday School Times*. This is what first brought the problem to the attention of the Baptist public. Toy defended his beliefs as being consistent with the Fundamental Principles of the seminary, but he also submitted his resignation, which the Board of Trustees accepted.

A year later, he was hired by Harvard University as a professor of Hebrew. The president of Harvard, Charles Eliot, had originally invited W. Robertson Smith, a Scottish higher critic who was under attack by his denomination, to fill the position, but Smith decided to go to the English Cambridge instead of the American Cambridge. Toy's upward academic mobility was neither normal nor random for Southern Baptist professors. It indicated a commitment on the part of Harvard University's leaders to endorse publicly, as powerfully as possible, Harvard's challenge to Christian orthodoxy. At Harvard, Toy came clean. As soon as he arrived, he announced that he wished to be known as a theist, not a Christian.[35] His charade ended when his funding changed. His public confession now matched his true faith.

Harvard was not alone. The Yale Divinity School began its visible drift into modernism in 1881, when newly appointed Professor Benjamin Bacon began promoting higher criticism. A former Congrega-

---

33. Pope A. Duncan, "Crawford Howell Toy: Heresy at Louisville," in *American Religious Heretics: Formal and Informal Trials*, edited by George H. Shriver (Nashville, Tennessee: Abingdon, 1966), p. 64.

34. *Ibid.*, p. 65.

35. Roger Finke and Rodney Stark, *The Churching of America, 1776–1990: Winners and Losers in Our Religious Economy* (New Brunswick, New Jersey: Rutgers University Press, [1992] 1994), p. 183.

tionalist minister, Bacon rejected the literal account of the story of Jesus' feeding of the five thousand, using three different German critical scholars as support: Paulus, Strauss, and Bauer.[36] In 1886, he was joined by George Barker Stevens, who rejected the doctrine of Christ's substitutionary atonement.

Higher criticism surfaced in the United States almost overnight. It had simmered in New England[37] and off-shore since the turn of the century; German university-trained seminary professors brought it back with them. Between 1880 and 1900, it gained a foothold in the major universities and the mainline denominations' seminaries.[38] By 1929, it reigned supreme academically everywhere in the North except Princeton Seminary.

Lower Criticism and the Westminster Confession

The problem posed by the higher critics was also posed by the technical subdiscipline of lower criticism, which deals with the textual analysis of the Bible in contrast (supposedly) to historical or literary criticism of the texts. The question of textual accuracy was therefore basic to the Princetonians' discussion of what comprises the authoritative canon of Scripture. There were tens of thousands of variant texts. As early as 1713, the deist Anthony Collins had used John Mill's collection of 30,000 New Testament textual variants to argue for replacing Trinitarianism's revealed religion with natural religion.[39]

The Revised Version of the English Bible appeared in 1881. This became the first major wedge of lower criticism into the American

---

36. Roland H. Bainton, *Yale and the Ministry: A History of Education for the Christian Ministry at Yale from the Founding in 1701* (New York: Harper & Bros., 1957), pp. 214-15.

37. Jerry Wayne Brown, *The Rise of Biblical Criticism in America, 1800-1870: The New England Scholars* (Middletown, Connecticut: Wesleyan University Press, 1969).

38. Ira V. Brown, "The Higher Criticism Comes to America, 1880-1900," *Journal of the Presbyterian Historical Society*, 38 (Dec. 1960).

39. [Anthony Collins], *Discourse of Free-Thinking. . . .*; cited in Theodore P. Letis, "B. B. Warfield, Common-Sense Philosophy and Biblical Criticism," *American Presbyterians*, 69 (Fall 1991), p. 175.

Church scene. Prior to this, lower criticism had been confined mainly to institutions of higher learning in the northeast.

Warfield and Lower Criticism

Warfield, the Old School's most distinguished theologian from the late nineteenth century until his death in 1921, was a defender of lower criticism. He did not accept as authoritative the *textus receptus* or received text on which the King James translators had based their work. He was the first Princetonian to break decisively with the *textus receptus*. This was the text which the Westminster Assembly had relied on.

The founder of Princeton, Virginia's Archibald Alexander, like Charles Hodge after him, followed Turretin by appealing to the judicial authority of extant copies. By Alexander's day, there were 60,000 textual variants.[40] Charles Hodge, unlike Alexander, studied in Paris and Germany (1826–27), leaving his wife and two children behind,[41] but this experience did not shake his faith. He did not import German methods back to Princeton. Warfield studied in Germany in 1876.[42] Letis writes: "Warfield, on the other hand, was the first professor at Princeton to allow his Common-Sense Philosophy the role of reconstructing the text according to the canons of German criticism."[43] This meant that he accepted the fundamental presupposition of higher criticism: the legitimacy of treating a biblical text as if it were like any other human text, subject to the autonomous canons of textual criticism.[44] He was persuaded that the "facts" of Scripture will prove the Bible's infallibility to any neutral investigator.[45]

Warfield in 1886 became the first American to write a textbook on German techniques of lower criticism.[46] In the meantime, he had

---

40. Letis, *ibid.*, p. 177.
41. McKim and Rogers, *Authority and Inspiration*, p. 275.
42. Letis, pp. 180–81.
43. *Ibid.*, p. 176.
44. *Ibid.*, pp. 176–77.
45. *Ibid.*, p. 181. Letis quotes his 1878 inaugural lecture at Western Theological Seminary.
46. Warfield, *Introduction to the Textual Criticism of the New Testament*, published first in England. Letis, pp. 180, 189.

published an article dismissing the last verses of the gospel of Mark.[47] This was the German higher critical view of Mark's text.[48] In 1881, he gave a favorable review to Wescott and Hort's critical Greek text, praising their "scientific method." This review appeared in *The Presbyterian Review* (1882), the academic journal that led to the undermining of the Old School's cause.[49] Union Seminary professor Philip Schaff, later to stand firm behind Briggs' higher critical views, invited Warfield to explain his views in Schaff's *Companion to the Greek Testament and English Version*.[50] By adopting Wescott and Hort's methodology, Warfield baptized the methodology of higher criticism: judging the accuracy of the existing biblical texts by means of independent critical-logical standards. Briggs, the co-editor of *Presbyterian Review*, immediately wrote Warfield a letter insisting that he and other higher critics such as W. Robertson Smith used the same methodology as that employed by Wescott and Hort.[51]

By adopting this common-ground textual methodology, Warfield had to admit that existing texts of the Bible contained errors. But the Westminster Confession had asserted God's unique providential maintenance of the texts through history. This, he concluded, meant that the efforts to restore the best texts by Wescott and Hort were part of this providential work of God. They were "instruments of providence in preserving the Scriptures pure for the use of God's people."[52] He was grasping at straws; lower criticism is simply not in conformity to the express language of the Westminster Confession. He had to admit that some members of the Assembly were defenders of the *textus receptus*.[53] He argued that the Assembly accepted the idea that some

---

47. Letis, *ibid.*, p. 181. The essay was published in the *Sunday School Times* (Dec. 2, 1882).
48. *Ibid.*
49. See below: "Princeton's Crucial Tactical Error," pp. 170–77.
50. *Ibid.*, p. 182.
51. Briggs to Warfield, 10 March 1882: *ibid.*, p. 183.
52. Warfield's posthumously published, *Critical Reviews* (Oxford University Press, 1932), p. 36; cited in Letis, p. 184. Cf. Warfield, "The Doctrine of Holy Scripture" (1893), *The Westminster Assembly and Its Work* (Grand Rapids, Michigan: Baker, [1931] 1991), p. 239.
53. Warfield, *Westminster Assembly*, p. 239.

copies of the transmitted texts contained errors.[54] True enough, but this did not solve his strategic problem: Assembly members' individual beliefs and the Confession's language did not support the common-ground methodology of modern lower criticism.

The question then became: On what Confessional basis could he and the Old School theologians who followed his leadership take a *judicial* stand against the higher critics? The answer is self-evident: they could not. They did not. They could not appeal to the Confession. They would have to appeal to standards not part of the Church's judicial tradition. The best they could do was to assert that their use of the same common-ground methodology was better than the higher critics' use of it. This moved the debate out of the courts and into the journals.

A generation later, Princeton's William P. Armstrong was still defending Wescott and Hort's theory of the text's history.[55] He tried to contrast lower criticism with higher criticism's historical and literary criticisms. He acknowledged that there can be no higher criticism apart from *a priori* presuppositions, "an ultimate theory of truth" and "an ultimate philosophy of history."[56] Having made this crucial methodological point, a few pages later he abandoned it. In what must be regarded as the terminal stage of academic verbal restraint run amok, he wrote this ponderous sentence regarding the separation of hypothesis from factual investigation in higher criticism: "It should, however, be possible to keep the two things separate or at least to recognize and discount the influence of principle in the phenomenal or factual sphere while freely admitting and indeed maintaining that this issue must be determining in the ultimate appreciation or evaluation of the facts, in their explanation and in the final estimate of their significance."[57] (Anyone who seeks to conduct a life-and-death intellectual battle with this sort of constipated academic rhetoric is going to lose the battle, as indeed Armstrong did. He remained behind at Princeton

---

54. *Ibid.*, p. 240.
55. William P. Armstrong, "Gospel History and Criticism," *Princeton Theological Review*, 12 (1914), p. 432.
56. *Ibid.*, p. 435.
57. *Ibid.*, p. 442.

after the reorganization of 1929.) A loose English translation is this: "The assumption of the non-supernatural nature of the Bible's existing texts ought to be able to be separated from the otherwise productive techniques of higher criticism." Funny thing, though; they never are. They are like Siamese twins who share a heart: any attempt to separate them will prove fatal to both.

To argue as Armstrong did is to surrender the case for biblical supernaturalism. Supernaturalism must be assumed from the beginning and defended till the end, in the same way that naturalism is assumed and defended. To assume neutrality regarding supernaturalism as an operating initial hypothesis of any investigation is to surrender your methodology to covenant-breakers. Once surrendered, it cannot be reclaimed. Logically, you cannot go from the autonomous mind of man (neutral methodology) to the absolute sovereignty of the God of the Bible. The Princetonians, including Machen, never understood this. They were blinded by the Scottish common-sense, anti-supernatural methodological presuppositions.

Rival Presuppositions

The higher criticism of the Bible begins with a presupposition: the texts of the Bible must be examined with the same tools of analysis as any other text. Oxford's classical scholar Benjamin Jowett put it this way: ". . . the same rules apply to the Old and New Testaments as to other books."[58] Historian Forrest G. Wood has echoed Jowett: "Since I was obliged to observe the canons of scholarship I did not have the luxury of accepting on faith an inerrant Bible and thus was left only with the premise that Christianity itself, the Way and the Word, was man-centered—that man created God in his image. . . ."[59] The assumption of an inerrant Bible is not a matter of luxury; it is a matter of warfare: the conflict between covenant-keepers and covenant-breakers. The problem for Princeton was that lower criticism begins with the

---

58. Jowett, "On the Interpretation of Scripture," in *Essays and Reviews* (London: John Parker & Sons, 1860), p. 337; cited in Noll, *Faith and Criticism*, p. 65.

59. Forrest G. Wood, *The Arrogance of Faith: Christianity and Race in America from the Colonial Era to the Twentieth Century* (New York: Knopf, 1990), p. xx.

same presupposition that higher criticism does regarding a non-inerrant Bible: the assertion of a common methodology for interpreting all literature.

In stark contrast to Princeton's methodological presupposition of neutrality, Westminster Seminary's professor of apologetics Cornelius Van Til always began with the presupposition that the Bible is the word of God and therefore judges all rules. Its testimony to its own authority cannot be challenged, for there is no higher standard in history above the Bible. "The light of Scripture is that superior light which lightens every other light. It is also the final light."[60] Speaking of self-proclaimed autonomous man, he wrote: "But in whatever guise he may appear, the self-authenticating man assumes that he is to be the judge. The vision originates with him. In his eyes he is the judge and the supreme court. He alone knows what can or cannot be. . . . But where is the constitution by which even the chief judge of the supreme court must judge? The answer is that this constitution has to be written by the chief judge himself."[61]

Higher criticism and biblical presuppositionalism are mutually irreconcilable. There is no intellectual common ground on which a mutually agreed-upon settlement can be based. But if this is true, then what becomes of lower criticism? Can it be reformulated to make it conform to biblical presuppositionalism? So far, no one has tried in a systematic fashion. In any case, Warfield's version did not break with the liberals' presupposition of a common-ground methodology. In this sense, Warfield was in a weak position to deal with Charles Briggs.[62]

Two Forms of Experientialism

In 1866, Charles Briggs (1841–1913) went to Germany to study, where he was taught the techniques of higher criticism. At the heart

---

60. Cornelius Van Til, "Nature and Scripture," in *The Infallible Word* (Grand Rapids, Michigan: Eerdmans, 1946), p. 257. This was a Westminster Seminary symposium.
61. Van Til, *The Case for Calvinism* (Nutley, New Jersey: Craig Press, 1964), p. 135.
62. In researching the Briggs case, I relied on a multi-volume collection of articles on Briggs that Warfield assembled. This set resides in the rare book collection of the Speer Library at Princeton Seminary.

of higher criticism from the seventeenth century until today has been what higher critic Edgar Krentz has called *methodical doubt*.[63] But Briggs always defended his method as scientifically beyond doubt. Five months after arriving in Germany, in January, 1867, Briggs wrote home to his uncle, a Princeton Seminary graduate,[64] to tell him about a moving experience which his initiation into higher criticism had produced in him: "I cannot doubt but what I have been blessed with a new—divine light. I feel a different man from what I was five months ago. The Bible is lit up with a new light."[65] Formerly a defender of the Old School's view of the Bible, he now recognized that he had been "defending a lost cause."[66]

In a way, Briggs' spiritual life encapsulates the transformation of the Presbyterian Church, 1858 to 1936. He always regarded his emotional experience in November, 1858, in his sophomore year at the University of Virginia, as a mark of conversion. This took place during what has sometimes been called the Third Great Awakening.[67] He had grown up under the instruction of an Old School mother. His father had never joined a local church and found Presbyterianism too formal, but he was an evangelical.[68] The son never repudiated his 1858 experience; it remained a formative factor throughout his career.

He did not return to the University of Virginia in the fall of 1860. He never graduated from there or anywhere else. He never again was willing to place himself under final academic sanctions. This is suspicious behavior for a man who challenged everyone throughout his career to answer his arguments, and then denied to his dying day that anyone ever had successfully done so. The General Assembly gave

---

63. Edgar Krentz, *The Historical-Critical Method* (Philadelphia: Fortress Press, 1975), pp. 10–16.

64. Massa, *Briggs*, p. 28.

65. *Ibid.*, p. 37. Also cited in Max Gray Rogers, "Charles Augustus Briggs: Heresy at Union," in *American Religious Heretics*, p. 90.

66. Briggs, *The Higher Criticism of the Hexateuch* (New York: Charles Scribner's Sons, 1892), p. 62; cited in *ibid*.

67. J. Edwin Orr, *The Fervent Prayer: The Worldwide Impact of the Great Awakening of 1858* (Chicago: Moody, 1974).

68. Massa, *Briggs*, pp. 26–27.

him an "F" in 1893; he kept insisting that he should have earned an "A."

After his equally experiential conversion to higher criticism in Germany, he was determined to persuade the Presbyterian Church that evangelicalism and higher criticism are reconcilable. Each methodology had produced an experiential conversion in his life. But in his academic writings, there is no trace of his experientialism. As he learned in his old age, his followers had never experienced what he had in 1858. They were uninterested in the evangelical Christianity of his youth. He failed utterly—perhaps monumentally—in his attempt to ram biblical criticism and historicism down the throats of New School Presbyterian experientialists, let alone Old School Calvinists. His writings produced only modernists. He was unsuccessful in persuading his liberal disciples of the need for experiential conversion—not unsurprising, given the fact that he never mentioned this necessity in his writings. To refer to him, as Massa does, as "an evangelical critical scholar" is misleading.[69] He was a scholar, and he was surely evangelical for biblical criticism, but he was in no sense an evangelical, i.e., a proponent of a judicially based gospel that categorically announces men's eternal damnation apart from saving faith.

In 1867, he saw Old School biblical interpretation as a lost cause. A man who announces that he had been defending a lost cause has already adopted a new cause. Briggs' illuminating experience, coupled with his new view of the Bible, led him to commit his life to this new cause: the subversion of the Old School tradition, which he dismissed as dogma. But dogma is an inescapable concept. It is never a question of dogma vs. no dogma. It is always a question of *which* dogma. When we read of a case in which "man bites dogma," it is always because he has adopted another dogma.

Princeton's Crucial Tactical Error

Upon his return from Germany, Briggs served for a few years as a pastor and then became a faculty member at Union, teaching Hebrew. (He is still known to seminary students as one of the triumvirate who

---

69. *Ibid.*, p. 158.

wrote the standard Hebrew lexicon: Brown, Driver, and Briggs.) Briggs understood his crucial role within Presbyterianism. In 1900, he said that in Presbyterian circles, he had been the first to call for freedom of inquiry for higher critics, in his 1876 inaugural address as a professor of Hebrew. He said that his opinions first excited public attention in his article, "Right, Duty, and Limits of Biblical Criticism," published in *The Presbyterian Review* in 1881.[70] In short, he knew exactly what he was doing from 1876 forward.

He had taken the lead in establishing *The Presbyterian Review*[71] in 1880, a cooperative effort supported by all six Northern Presbyterian seminaries.[72] He had originally encouraged Union Seminary's president, William Adams Brown, to suggest to Princeton's A. A. Hodge the creation of the journal.[73] Hodge became the co-editor. This seemingly innocuous venture in scholarly publishing would soon undermine the Old School's institutional defense of the Westminster Confession. It is not an exaggeration to say that this decision ultimately doomed the Old School. This is why Lefferts Loetscher devoted an entire chapter to *The Presbyterian Review*.[74] This is why Channing Jeschke began his 1966 doctoral dissertation on the Briggs case with a chapter on *The Presbyterian Review*. Massa argues that the publication of the first issue in January, 1880, "marked an important moment when the spiritual crisis of the Gilded Age entered the public (and published) arena."[75] The battle between Calvinism and historical criticism would be waged publicly in this journal. This created a strategic problem for the Princetonians.

---

70. Charles Augustus Briggs, *General Introduction to the Study of the Holy Scriptures* (Grand Rapids, Michigan: Baker, [1900] 1970), pp. 286–87.

71. A New School journal with the same name had ceased using the name in 1863 when it joined with the *American Theological Review*. Stearns, "Historical Review of the Church," *Presbyterian Re-union Memorial Volume*, p. 97.

72. Lefferts A. Loetscher, *The Broadening Church: a study of theological issues in the presbyterian church since 1869* (Philadelphia: University of Pennsylvania Press, 1954), p. 30.

73. Massa, *Briggs*, p. 51.

74. Loetscher, *Broadening Church*, ch. 4.

75. Massa, *Briggs*, p. 53.

The Strategic Problem: Ecumenical Methodology

The strategic problem for the Princetonians was the ecumenical character of the new journal, which was at odds with the Confessional exclusivism of the Old School. Briggs had requested and had received Princeton's surrender in advance. Hodge represented Princeton; Briggs represented Union. Each of the two managing editors could veto any article recommended by the other.[76] This meant that there had to be some sort of epistemological common ground between them, if the journal was ever to be published. One possible methodological framework was what Briggs believed in: *historicism*. Princeton's theologians also believed in common ground: *common-sense empiricism*. Briggs believed in the relevance of the testimony of the facts of history, while the Princetonians believed in the testimony of reason grounded in both historical and scientific facts. Both sides could appeal to fact and history on methodologically equal footing, or so it seemed. Each side believed it had the stronger case in terms of this common ground. But the historicism of the era was against the Princetonians, who still proclaimed an unchanging theology—a fixed "recipe" beyond time, yet somehow in time. Hodge and his successor as managing co-editor, Francis L. Patton, never seemed to suspect that their failure to veto Briggs' articles on higher criticism and on the Westminster Assembly, as well as articles recommended by Briggs, would transfer the Northern Presbyterian Church into the hands of the modernists half a century later. Only Warfield opposed the project from the beginning,[77] but he was not yet on Princeton's faculty.

According to Briggs' highly suspect testimony in 1891, the Princeton faculty had asked him his views regarding higher criticism. "I stated that I did not accept Verbal Inspiration and Inerrancy and that I was in accord with the movement of Higher Criticism. The Princeton faculty agreed to unite with the Union faculty in the enterprise...."[78]

---

76. Channing Renwick Jeschke, The Briggs Case: The Focus of a Study in Nineteenth Century Presbyterian History (Ph.D. dissertation, University of Chicago, 1966), p. 8.

77. *Ibid.*, p. 10.

78. Statement prepared for G. L. Prentiss, *The Union Theological Seminary in the City of New York: Its Design and another Decade of its History* (Asbury Park,

For whatever reason, by consenting to work with Union and Briggs on this basis, the Princetonians cooperated in the baptism of higher criticism. From that time forth, they could never successfully challenge higher criticism as heretical, for orthodox men cannot defend cooperating in joint academic ventures with heretics. Conclusion institutionally: a joint venture cannot be heretical.

The "Equal Time" Doctrine

Briggs continued: "Toward the close of 1880 the Princeton representative stated that it was necessary that Scotland's W. Robertson Smith case should be discussed in the *Review*, and that the conservatives demanded the right to speak their minds on it. It was then resolved that both ideas should be heard on the Higher Criticism."[79] This was not even close to the truth.[80] Briggs had volunteered for the assignment through Brown. The Princetonians had hesitated, fearing it would give Briggs an opportunity to defend Smith's views.[81] This is exactly what he did, yet the Princetonians allowed it to be published. Briggs ended the essay with a plea for toleration of "legitimate differences." This, of course, was a defense of Smith's right to teach his views without any threat of negative ecclesiastical sanctions, and equal rights for Briggs.

The Princetonians wanted to reply. This request led to two years of published debates—eight articles—on higher criticism.[82] But the Princetonians had already dug their own grave: first, by consenting to co-edit the journal; second, by accepting Briggs' request to write the Smith essay; third, by not vetoing it. Now they demanded "equal time." Briggs accepted the offer. And why not? The "equal time" doctrine always pleases any minority movement in the early stages of its subversion of an organization. The doctrine of pluralism and open debate is always invoked against the majority, which can impose nega-

---

New Jersey: Pennypacker, 1899), pp. 328-29.

79. *Ibid.*, p. 329.

80. Rogers was deceived by Briggs' misrepresentation, and says that the initiative to publish the essays on higher criticism came from the conservatives, not from Briggs. Rogers, "Briggs," *American Religious Heretics*, p. 92.

81. Massa, *Briggs*, pp. 56-57.

82. *Ibid.*, pp. 58-59.

tive sanctions. Only when the subverters are in the majority does "equal time" lose both its appeal and its authority in their eyes.

Briggs' second article in the series, "A Critical Study of the History of the Higher Criticism with Special Reference to the Pentateuch," published in January, 1883, defended Smith's methodology. Francis Patton replied in the following issue. Nothing had been settled, but this fact was now in full public view. Massa writes: "Thus had the *Presbyterian Review*, with the close of the 'Robertson Smith debate' in the spring of 1883, both announced and abetted a conflict that would mark the history of American evangelicalism for the next half century. . . . Beneath those conflicts lay an ineffable but pervasive sense that the very possibility of divine communication with humankind was now deeply problematic, problematic in a way that had no precedent in the Christian tradition."[83]

The Princeton Apologetic

Why had the Princetonians initiated this institutionally suicidal (because co-published) exchange of views? Because they were defenders of a particular method of apologetics, i.e., the philosophical defense of the faith. This method officially appealed only to the facts: empiricism, an appeal to pure factuality. They viewed truth as inductive, not deductive. Charles Hodge insisted that "in theology as in natural science, principles are derived from facts, and not impressed upon them."[84] This was Scottish common-sense rationalism, and it was basic to nineteenth-century conservative apologetics. This had been Princeton's approach from its founding.[85]

Conservative Willis J. Beecher of Auburn Seminary presented a classic statement of this empiricist apologetic position: "That the critical inquiry into the nature of the Scriptures may be independent, it must reject all evidence which is based on the assumption that the Books are inspired, just as it rejects that which is based on the assump-

---

83. *Ibid.*, p. 67.
84. Hodge, *Systematic Theology*, I:13.
85. On Scottish common sense realism at Princeton Seminary, see Noll's "Introduction" in *The Princeton Theology, 1812–1921: Scripture, Science, and Theological Method from Archibald Alexander to Benjamin Breckenridge Warfield*, edited by Mark A. Noll (Grand Rapids, Michigan: Baker, 1983), pp. 30–33.

tion that they are not inspired. While it is in progress it has nothing to do with inspiration."[86] This is the ever-popular cloak of academic neutrality. This methodology played into the hands of the higher critics from the beginning. If valid, this principle of neutral investigation meant that higher critics had the right—indeed, the moral obligation—before God to conduct their research apart from any assumption that they were dealing with unique texts in history: the verbally inspired word of God. They could ignore the Confession's doctrine of inspiration while conducting their research and publishing its results.

Hodge and Warfield had announced at the beginning of the debate, "Nevertheless we admit that the question between ourselves and the advocates of [modern criticism], is one of fact, to be decided only by an exhaustive and impartial examination of all the sources of evidence, i.e., the claims of the Scriptures themselves."[87] Problem: there are many potential sources of evidence in the world of "theologically neutral" scholarship that lie outside the Bible itself. The defenders of higher criticism would appeal to them extensively.[88]

This approach to the Bible led the Princetonians to make at least two crucial compromises in the series: adjusting the genealogies of Genesis to accommodate an ancient age for the earth (William Henry Green); and interpreting Genesis as supporting (or at least not denying) a kind of theistic evolution (Warfield).[89] Surely, these were examples of quietly importing evidence from outside the Bible into the exegesis of biblical texts—the most dangerous evidence of all: Darwinian conclusions.

---

86. Beecher, "The Logical Methods of Professor Kuenen" *Presbyterian Review*, 3 (Oct. 1882), p. 704; cited in Noll, *Between Faith and Criticism*, p. 25.

87. Hodge and Warfield, "Introduction," *Presbyterian Review*, 2 (1881), p. 247; cited in *ibid*, p. 18.

88. People sometimes ask Christian Reconstructionists: "Why are you so committed to the presuppositional apologetics of Cornelius Van Til?" The catastrophic failure of the Princetonian apologetic after 1883 is one answer. It made a successful offensive strategy impossible. The Princetonians were forced to respond to the agenda of the higher critics and then the modernists. What Briggs did or did not do (1889-93), what Fosdick did or did not do (1922-24), what Speer did or did not do (1932-36) determined the boundaries of the three major outbursts of the Presbyterian conflict.

89. *Ibid*., p. 24.

Too Little, Too Late

In 1884, Briggs wrote a *Presbyterian Review* article on the decision of the Europe-based Alliance of Reformed Churches to revise their various confessions. This article brought the divisive issue of Confessional revision into American Presbyterianism.[90] A year later, his book, *American Presbyterianism*, offered a little-disguised justification for such a revision based on the Church's history.[91] By the end of the decade, Briggs was leading the forces calling for a revision of the Westminster Confession. In 1888, he wrote "A Plea for an American Alliance of the Reformed Churches," his first public call for organic Church union. *Presbyterian Review* repeatedly served him as a highly useful tool for bringing his ideas before the Church.

The Presbyterian Review carried on until October, 1889. Warfield, who became co-editor earlier that year, had thrown down the gauntlet by refusing to publish Briggs' summary of the 1889 General Assembly.[92] Warfield had always opposed the joint venture. It was now unlikely to survive. But it was Union Seminary's faculty—not Princeton's—that voted to discontinue it.[93] Union's faculty had achieved their goal: equal time for higher criticism.

In 1893, Princeton's William Henry Green in effect conceded much of Briggs' argument by writing a lengthy critique of Briggs' book, *The Higher Criticism of the Hexateuch* (1892). Green had served as the Moderator of the 1891 General Assembly at which Briggs' new appointment at Union had been vetoed. He began his essay with a reference back to Briggs' 1883 *Presbyterian Review* essay, updated and reprinted in the new book. He surrendered the hermeneutical high ground in his second paragraph by accepting criticism as a legitimate procedure: "There is a distinction between the Higher Criticism *de jure* and the Higher Criticism *de facto*. Critical investigations may rightly be conducted and lead to correct conclusions; or they may be based on wrong principles, follow wrong methods, and lead to false

---

90. Massa, *Briggs*, pp. 71–72.
91. *Ibid.*, p. 75.
92. *Ibid.*, p. 81.
93. Loetscher, *Broadening Church*, p. 39.

conclusions." He accepted Briggs' statement in an 1881 *Presbyterian Review* essay that "Biblical criticism is represented by two antagonistic parties—evangelical critics and rationalistic critics."[94] On the next page, Green asked of Briggs' version of higher criticism: "Is it Biblical or anti-Biblical?" In so doing, Green publicly accepted the legitimacy of higher criticism as a method of inquiry: someone else's version might be biblical.

Briggs: The Point Man

In the infantry, the point man walks ahead of his platoon. If he draws fire from the enemy, or if he steps on a land mine, his fellow soldiers are warned of trouble ahead. Charles Briggs was the point man—the visible representative—in the Presbyterian modernists' strategy from 1876 to 1893. At each stage, he would press the issues, both theologically and rhetorically. But the radical nature of his theology always trailed the combativeness of his rhetoric until 1891. He used his rhetoric to test the Old School's will to resist. Each time that he was successful, he would then increase the pressure both rhetorically and theologically. By the time his rhetoric undermined him, his theology was firmly in place in the denomination. When he was deposed in 1893, it was because of his rhetoric.

Thus, there were only three Presbyterian casualties—"identifiable hits"—among modernism's supporters during the 1890's: Briggs, H. P. Smith, and McGiffert. All three ended their careers on the payroll of Union Seminary. This was a small price for the modernists to pay for establishing a judicially unassailable beachhead in Northern Presbyterianism's seminaries. The confrontational rhetoric of the higher critics ended by 1900; so did the heresy trials. This was important for American Protestantism because the Presbyterian Church was the denomination in the North that had made the most determined effort to root out higher criticism through public trials. The Lutherans did not have to resort to trials, they were so conservative; the Baptists could not use them, since their polity was not hierarchical; and Episcopalians

---

94. William Henry Green, "Dr. Briggs' Higher Criticism of the Hexateuch Examined," *Presbyterian and Reformed Review*, 4 (1893), p. 34.

were tolerant. The Methodists also conducted a few trials, but did so quietly. It was the conservative Presbyterians who became the representatives of orthodoxy in the public arena.[95]

Briggs' Strategy of Subversion

By 1876, Briggs had taken responsibility for introducing the program that would subvert the ultimate Calvinist standard, the Bible: higher criticism. Higher criticism in the nineteenth century promised to enhance the "true spirit" of the Bible by denying the authority of the letter of biblical texts. Briggs had escaped censure. He used *The Presbyterian Review* to begin the great debate series in 1881. Patton came on as co-editor, to be followed by Warfield in 1889. Briggs' strategy seemed letter-perfect. He remained the constant factor on the editorial board.

In *Biblical Study* (1883), Briggs presented a mild case for higher criticism as a legitimate methodology. This book marked the move of higher criticism out of the seminary classroom and into a wider American audience.[96] With *Whither?* (1889), he moved to the third and fourth stages of the strategy of subversion: a direct confrontation in the name of the spirit of the Confession (point three) against the denominational courts' right to enforce the letter of the Confession (point four). If his primarily rhetorical strategy proved successful, the institutional inheritance was assured (point five). It would be a replay of English Presbyterianism, which had abandoned the Westminster Confession in 1662 and went Unitarian in 1719.

Here was Briggs' strategy of Confessional subversion: to defend the Westminster Confession verbally, but then point to a few widely shared deviations from the Confession in his day. Then he identified the Princetonians as interlopers: "The Westminster system has been virtually displaced by the teachings of the dogmatic divines."[97] The Princetonians' orthodoxy was not Confessional, he said. In fact, no

---

95. Walter F. Petersen, "American Protestantism and the Higher Criticism," *Wisconsin Academy of Sciences, Arts and Letters*, 50 (1961), p. 325.

96. *Ibid.*, pp. 321-22.

97. Briggs, *Whither? A Theological Question for the Times*, 3rd ed. (New York: Charles Scribner's Sons, [1889] 1890), p. 223.

group completely accepts the Confession. "The Presbyterian Church is not orthodox, judged by its own standards. It has neither the old orthodoxy or the new orthodoxy."[98] In short, all contemporary orthodoxies are equally unorthodox, but some orthodoxies are worse than others: Princeton's.

This attack on the Westminster Confession in the name of the Confession paralleled the strategy of the higher critics: an attack on the document in the name of the document. First, point out a few errors in the existing texts. Then argue that these errors make no difference to "the fundamentals of the faith." Once accepted, this camel's nose of acceptable error soon resulted in a tent full of camel: *the denial of the judicially binding nature of the document as a whole.* Anyone who did not want to share his tent with this camel would have to leave, either voluntarily or involuntarily (in 1936).

Higher criticism, if accepted, would leave only tradition and experientialism as the foundations of the Church covenant. Traditionalism was highly suspect in a Protestant denomination. Experientialism, on the other hand, had always been regarded by New Side and New School churchmen as having at least equal status with the Confession. This was never formally stated in a revision of the Confession, but it was psychologically accepted and therefore institutionally defended. It had been the basis of both reunions: 1758 and 1869. This made it difficult for New School churchmen to challenge the modernists theologically; meanwhile, the dominance of New School churchmen within the courts made it difficult for Old School churchmen to challenge the modernists institutionally. The modernists, led by Briggs as their representative, felt ready by the late 1880's to test the coalition against them: they called for Confessional revision.

Rhetoric or Theology?

In Chapters 4 and 5, I show that it was not primarily Briggs' theology that led to his de-frocking. Rather, his rhetoric led to his de-frocking. Had he restrained his rhetoric, he would never have been brought to trial. His theology was the Church's legal justification for

---

98. *Ibid.*, p. 224.

his trial; it was not the cause. This is what the Union Seminary faculty argued in 1891; for the most part, I agree. Briggs escalated his confrontations from 1876 to 1893. This process of escalation involved both theological deviation from the Confession and offensive rhetoric. It was his rhetoric that triggered the explosion. I need to add, however, that the gun's rhetorical hammer would have gone "click" had the chamber not been loaded with Briggs' heretical opinions. This was the heart of the crisis of Northern Presbyterianism after 1880: conservatives could not easily mobilize the Church's court system to remove betrayers of the faith. In order for them to be removed, they had to become flagrant betrayers of the faith: rhetorically offensive rather than merely theologically offensive.

The real threat to Presbyterianism was not Briggs' rhetoric; it was his theology, which was grounded in higher criticism. It was not his repeated misuse of logic for rhetorical purposes that constituted his primary transgression; it was his higher criticism, grounded in his complete rejection of biblical Christianity in the name of Christianity. He insisted that he and his modernist peers could maintain Christianity while rejecting its theology. Higher critics and their intellectual predecessors for over three centuries have made the following claim: "Christianity can be maintained apart from a biblically integrated, biblically derived theology." This claim is a lie. It is a modern version of Satan's rhetorical question to Eve, "Hath God Said?", all dressed up in a black academic robe.

The question was: Who would become the Old School's point man? That task fell to Francis L. Patton.

"General" Patton's Battles

The most influential Old School leader in the Briggs era was Francis L. Patton. He was a theologian, but he was also a major participant in Presbyterian politics. He was the only Old School theologian in the Presbyterian conflict who had any experience in ecclesiastical organization.

The Swing Case

Patton, while a young seminary professor at Northwest Seminary (later renamed McCormick Seminary), had been brought to Chicago in 1873 to become the editor of *Interior*, a weekly journal financed by

Cyrus H. McCormick, the wealthy Calvinist inventor of the mechanical reaper.[99] From that position, he immediately began attacking modernist theologian Washington Gladden, a Congregationalist. In 1874, Patton began attacking a local Presbyterian pastor, David Swing.

Swing was a very popular preacher, with a congregation containing several thousand members. He was popular with his New School-dominated presbytery. But he made a tactical error: he went into print. He repeatedly attacked the idea of the authority of theological creeds; he discussed them as culturally determined and therefore immersed in history.[100] He contrasted spiritual religion with a religion of things and words; the former succeeds the latter.[101] "In our day the empire of words still lingers. The churches are still wedded to quantity more than to quality, but wedded by bonds that are growing weaker under the uprising of the 'inner life' philosophy."[102] The implication was that the creeds are morally relative and judicially irrelevant. They have no judicial authority.

For a time, the creeds did prove to be judicially irrelevant; his presbytery did nothing to stop him. He then escalated his rhetoric. He announced confidently that heresy-hunting was a thing of the past. Heresy-hunters, he said, are "the most useless and forlorn men who have lived since the world began . . . living for a certain assemblage of words just as the miser lives for labeled bags of gold."[103]

Patton, a recent arrival to the presbytery, formally brought charges against Swing for having deviated from the Westminster Confession. This was an important trial. It should have been easy to convict him if the presbytery was committed to creedalism, for Swing had made many public statements opposing the continuing authority of all creeds. Swing even defended himself at his trial by repeating his

---

99. John Frederick Lyons, "Cyrus Hall McCormick, Presbyterian Layman," *Journal of Presbyterian History*, 39 (March 1961), p. 23.

100. Hutchison, *Modernist Impulse in American Protestantism*, pp. 52–54, 57.

101. David Swing, "A Religion of Words" (1874); reprinted in *American Protestant Thought in the Liberal Era*, edited by William R. Hutchison (Lanham, Maryland: University Press of America, 1968), p. 47.

102. *Ibid.*, p. 50.

103. Cited in Hutchison, *Modernist Impulse*, p. 54.

arguments that "A creed is only the highest wisdom of a particular time and place. Hence, as in States, there is always a quiet slipping away from the old laws without any waiting for a formal repeal." As if to prove Swing's point, the presbytery cleared him by a margin of three to one.

Patton was denounced during the trial as an outsider—the inevitable fate of those who challenge the previous decisions of any local bureaucracy. This ever-present potential accusation would henceforth inhibit all critics from outside any presbytery from bringing formal charges against someone inside, especially someone who, unlike Swing, had not gone into print. One defender of Swing, Dr. Arthur Swazey, reminded his fellow presbytery members that Swing had worked among them for years, and no one had found anything wrong. Then, he said, "a stranger comes in here, and for reasons that are largely partisan, invites us to denounce him."[104] Patton was not part of the club, the local old-boy network. It was therefore his job to keep quiet about one of the most successful of the old boys. This rejection of criticism from outside a presbytery was an important factor in the immunity of liberals, once ordained, from further prosecution.

Patton's charges against Swing were poorly conceived. There were 28 accusations when ten clear-cut violations, especially relating to Swing's view of creeds, if well argued, might conceivably have persuaded the presbytery.[105] After the presbytery had closed ranks around Swing and voted him innocent, Patton announced that he would appeal to the General Assembly. Swing then resigned from the denomination. He did so, he said, "to secure to the Synod and to the Assembly that peace which can lead to a calm review and restatement of doctrine . . . without the stormy passions that gather around 'accuser' and an 'accused.' "[106] Notice the assumption: *the peace of the Church is dependent on the absence of heresy trials.* That is to say, the "true peace" of the Church is dependent on the creedalists' willingness

---

104. Cited in *ibid.*, p. 66.
105. *Ibid.*, p. 60.
106. Loetscher, *Broadening Church*, p. 14.

to ordain as ministers and seminary professors—i.e., sanction positively—men who denied the judicial authority of the creeds. Put differently, the "true peace" of the Church is supposedly achievable only by ignoring institutionally the negative sanctions that are inescapably associated with a lawful covenantal oath. This call for "true peace" would become the modernists' battle cry in every denomination. They cried "peace, peace," and after 1900, there was peace. But it came at a price: the abandonment of Confessional orthodoxy.

The first heresy trial after the 1869 reunion had not been conclusively settled. The Swing trial, in Hutchison's words, had been "the first great controversy of the New Theology,"[107] but it was not to be the last. The national press had covered the trial in great detail.[108] This, too, would be a characteristic feature of Presbyterian trials in the future, ending only after Machen's expulsion from the Church in 1936.

After 1874, Patton rose rapidly as a leader in the presbytery and the denomination. He was elected moderator of the General Assembly in 1878. It was at this General Assembly that William McCune saw his presbytery's "not guilty" declaration overturned by the General Assembly by a four-to-one vote.[109] This is evidence that Swing's decision to resign was wise. He probably would have lost on Patton's appeal.

Patton at Princeton University

In 1888, at the time of his resignation as co-editor of *Presbyterian Review*, Patton became the president of the College of New Jersey, which was re-named Princeton University under his administration (1896).[110] By the end of his career, he had become known as "the grand old man of Presbyterianism."[111] He could have made all the

---

107. Hutchison, *Modernist Impulse*, p. 75.
108. *Ibid.*, pp. 70–71.
109. Loetscher, *Broadening Church*, p. 17.
110. Henry Wilkinson Bragdon, *Woodrow Wilson: The Academic Years* (Cambridge, Massachusetts: Belknap Press of Harvard University, 1967), p. 214.
111. "Patton, Francis Landey," *Dictionary of American Religious Biography*, edited by Henry Warden Bowden (Westport, Connecticut: Greenwood Press, 1977), p. 357.

difference in the Presbyterian conflict, and far more than this: in the history of the world. He could have applied negative sanctions in a crucial incident, as we shall see, but he refused.

Patton succeeded the popular evangelical and theistic evolutionist James McCosh.[112] Patton did nothing as president to stop the growth of modernism and humanism on the Princeton campus, let alone reverse it. He taught theology and ethics, but continued to teach McCosh's Scottish common-sense rationalist apologetics.[113] Under Patton, Princeton's academic reputation lagged far behind Harvard, Yale, and other major universities, at least in the opinion of the Princeton faculty.[114] Any remaining traces of orthodox Christianity were understood by the academic community in general and on campus as inhibiting the academic reputation of the campus. So, despite Patton's failure to halt the drift toward secularism, the progressives engineered a revolt against him in 1902. He had not gone fast enough in the process of secularization to suit them.

This drift was part of the transformation of higher education in the United States: from Christianity to humanism.[115] In 1876, Johns Hopkins University opened a graduate school based on the German model.[116] This institution would soon become the model for the American university: secular, specialized, and pluralistic. The university model would subsequently re-shape seminary education in the

---

112. J. David Hoeveler, Jr., *James McCosh and the Scottish Intellectual Tradition: from Glasgow to Princeton* (Princeton, New Jersey: Princeton University Press, 1981), chaps. 6, 8, and 9; Joseph E. Illick, III, "The Reception of Darwinism at the Theological Seminary and the College at Princeton, New Jersey, II," *Journal of Presbyterian History*, 38 (1960), pp. 234–43. See also McCosh's book, *Development: What It Can Do and What It Cannot Do* (1883); extract in *The Presbyterian Enterprise: Sources of American Presbyterian History*, edited by Maurice W. Armstrong, Lefferts A. Loetscher, and Charles A. Anderson (Philadelphia: Westminster Press, 1956), pp. 235–39.

113. Hardin Craig, *Woodrow Wilson at Princeton* (Norman: University of Oklahoma Press, 1960), p. 38.

114. *Ibid.*, pp. 66–67. Craig is friendly towards Patton.

115. George M. Marsden, *The Soul of the American University: From Protestant Establishment to Established Nonbelief* (New York: Oxford University Press, 1994); Lawrence R. Veysey, *The Emergence of the American University* (Chicago: University of Chicago Press, 1965).

116. Noll, *Between Faith and Criticism*, p. 12.

Authority: Biblical, Confessional, Ecclesiastical 185

United States. The era of the self-taught seminary professor with an honorary doctorate would end within a generation.[117] Each faculty member would soon be expected to run the humanist academic gauntlet. Some of the pluralistic ideals of that gauntlet would be imported into the seminary. That same year, 1876, was also the year of Briggs' first inaugural address, in which he first publicly defended higher criticism. Noll is correct: the two phenomena, higher criticism and the professionalization of academic life, were part of the same process. The new scholarship and the New Theology were parallel developments.[118] Both were forms of evolutionary humanism, although Noll avoids calling them this. He makes another important point: theological seminaries, invented in the early decades of the nineteenth century, had been the only graduate schools in the United States until after the Civil War.[119] After Johns Hopkins began to issue Ph.D. degrees, this changed rapidly. The Ph.D. degree would, over the next century, become the "union card" for admission to college faculties.[120] Patton fought this development; he wanted undergraduate education only. The faculty wanted a graduate school.[121] He wanted a Christian college; the vocal members of the faculty wanted nonsectarianism, i.e., secular education.[122]

Patton resigned as president in 1902, becoming the president of Princeton Seminary (not legally connected to the university), an office

---

117. John M. Mulder and Lee A. Wyatt, "The Predicament of Pluralism: The Study of Theology in Presbyterian Seminaries Since the 1920s," in *The Pluralistic Vision: Presbyterians and Mainstream Protestant Education and Leadership*, edited by Milton J Coalter, John M. Mulder, and Louis B. Weeks (Louisville, Kentucky: John Knox Press, 1992), p. 39.

118. Except for a handful of Hegelians, everyone on campus before 1900 claimed to be a defender of empiricism, i.e., inductive reasoning; everyone claimed that he was appealing only to the facts. The higher critics invoked German empiricism, while the conservatives invoked Scottish.

119. Noll, *Between Faith and Criticism*, p. 14.

120. In 1969, the Ph.D. glut emerged, and then the union card in the social sciences entitled many of its holders to drive cabs for a living.

121. Paul C. Kemeny, "President Francis Landey Patton, Princeton University, and Faculty Ferment," *American Presbyterians*, 68 (Summer 1991), pp. 114-15.

122. *Ibid.*, pp. 116-17.

that carried very little executive authority in 1902.[123] He had been forced out by a circle of trustees who had persuaded—it had not taken much persuading—political science professor Woodrow Wilson to draw up plans for a new system of rule by executive committee. Wilson had referred in a private meeting with two trustees to discuss what he had called "the sinister influence" at Princeton.[124] Against Wilson's advice, Patton was then named by the Trustees as a member of the new Executive Committee, with former U.S. President Grover Cleveland (who lived in the town of Princeton) named as chairman.[125] Wilson had been hired under Patton's tenure (1890), had been praised publicly by Patton,[126] and had not been fired by Patton despite Wilson's frequent absences from campus throughout the decade due to his highly profitable off-campus speaking schedule.[127] Wilson showed no gratitude in 1902 for Patton's toleration of Wilson's behavior.[128]

Patton not only refused to fight this coup, he actually named his successor to the presidency of the university: Wilson.[129] Two positive factors motivated him to leave: first, $31,500 in severance pay,[130] a huge sum in 1902; second, he was completely deceived by Wilson regarding Wilson's supposed commitment to conservative theology. Wilson's father had been the Stated Clerk of the Southern Presbyterian Church from 1865 to 1898, a man noted for his conservative views.[131] As the new president, Wilson suspended Bible instruction

---

123. Edwin H. Rian, *The Presbyterian Conflict* (Grand Rapids, Michigan: Eerdmans, 1940), p. 64.

124. Kemeny, "Patton," p. 111.

125. Bragdon, *Wilson*, p. 276.

126. *Ibid.*, p. 205.

127. *Ibid.*, p. 230.

128. Years later, Wilson remarked to Rev. Clarence E. Macartney that Patton was the best extemporaneous speaker he had ever heard. When Macartney related this to Patton, Patton replied: "That's the first time I ever heard Wilson say anything good of me." Clarence E. Macartney, *The Making of a Minister* (Great Neck, New York: Channel, 1961), p. 122.

129. Bragdon, *Wilson*, p. 207.

130. John M. Mulder, *Woodrow Wilson: The Years of Preparation* (Princeton, New Jersey: Princeton University Press, 1978), pp. 156-57.

131. James H. Smylie, "Stated Clerks and Social Policy: American Presbyterians and Transforming American Culture," *American Presbyterians*, 67 (Fall 1989), pp. 192-93.

from 1902 to 1905. This was a direct assault on Patton, who had used the money from a legacy to the college to endow a chair in English Bible for his own son.[132] Wilson was self-conscious in his humanism. The only trace of conservatism was his racism; he refused to allow any black to enroll at Princeton, even telling one applicant to apply to Brown University, since it was Baptist.[133] (Wilson was a friend of Thomas Dixon, author of the trilogy of novels defending the original Ku Klux Klan. Dixon called on him in 1915 to elicit his support in promoting *Birth of a Nation*, the D. W. Griffith movie based on *The Clansman*, the first book of his trilogy. Wilson was ecstatic after viewing a private showing. "It's like writing history with lightning, and my only regret is that it is all so terribly true.")[134]

The assumption at the time was that there had been three rivals to Wilson for the presidency, but one, the best-selling literary figure and liberal Presbyterian clergyman Henry van Dyke, always insisted that he had no desire for the position.[135] In 1910, Wilson was elected Governor of New Jersey. In 1912, he was elected President of the United States. In 1919, he went to the Versailles peace conference as its supposed conscience. The terms of the Versailles Treaty led to World War II. Wilson had also been instrumental in the creation of the League of Nations, which became the model for the United Nations Organization. If Patton had fought Wilson's nomination, throwing his support to one of Wilson's rivals, Wilson would probably have lost. The world would be a very different place. As Macartney put it over five decades later, "Thus do great issues turn on the hinges of apparently small events."[136]

Yet Patton, by far, was the most effective strategist the Old School produced after 1869. This indicates the magnitude of the Old

---

132. Kemeny, "Patton," p. 118.
133. Mulder, *Wilson*, pp. 174–75.
134. David M. Chalmers, *Hooded Americanism: The First Century of the Ku Klux Klan, 1865–1965* (Garden City, New York: Doubleday, 1965), pp. 26–27.
135. Tertius van Dyke, *Henry van Dyke: A Biography* (New York: Harper & Bros., 1935), pp. 222–27.
136. Macartney, *Making of a Minister*, p. 123.

School's problem. The Old School had no long-term strategy; their opponents did.[137]

Two Years to Immunity

There was an aspect of the modernists' victory that has escaped attention by historians of the Presbyterian conflict. The modernists understood that history does not move backward. This means that judicial precedents are rarely reversed. One of these precedents is silence. Presbyterian law, like American civil law, operates on the premise that a person is innocent unless proven guilty. Silence can become an operational precedent even if it is not a legal precedent. This means that if any one of these modernist doctrines could be presented within the denomination and not be identified by the courts as heretical, this doctrine would remain as a permanent part of the denomination's acceptable range of theological opinion.

The modernists understood point two of the covenant: personal representation. They understood point four: sanctions. They understood point three: standards. If the representative who first articulated the new doctrine subsequently escaped negative sanctions, the doctrine entered the Church's pantheon of acceptable standards.

This meant that if the person who introduced the initially vulnerable doctrine was not brought under discipline in a short period of time after his confession became public, it would not matter if certain members of the denomination later identified the doctrine as heretical. The critics' opinions would then be judicially irrelevant—privately held opinions. This is how the New School regarded the distinctive ideas of the Old School: mere opinion. So, if an idea could be presented as being opposed to an Old School particular, the New School would probably not prosecute the person who introduced it. A fundamental strategy of the modernists was to present their ideas as challenges to Old School doctrines in the name of "true" Calvinism and "true" Presbyterianism.

---

137. See Chapter 13, below: section on "The Modernists' Five Steps to Victory," pp. 805-808.

Once the new idea was introduced, the Old School would have only a year or two to bring formal charges against the suspected heretic.[138] If the idea gained circulation without a formal protest, it became virtually unchallengeable in a Presbyterian Church court after two years, although the length of this provisional period was not known with any degree of certainty in 1876. This was the basis of the modernists' ratchet strategy. This strategy was to get the five points of modernism[139] into public debate, one by one, for a brief but unknown period of time. After that, only inflammatory rhetoric would produce a negative judicial response, and the response would have to be limited to the condemnation of one person's particular expression of the idea, not the idea itself. The debate would hinge on rhetoric, not theology.

What became clear only in retrospect is that members of the Old School did not understand the institutional limits under which they operated, especially the time constraints. They did not understand that they had approximately two years to make a formal complaint against an idea. *If they limited their complaints to intellectual disputation, they would lose the war.* Academic disputation apart from a formal protest in a Church court would doom the Old School's defense. An intellectual attack apart from formal negative sanctions was, judicially speaking, the implicit acceptance of the denominational legitimacy of the substance of the modernists' case: one opinion among many. But the Old School's leadership was almost entirely academic. The ecclesiastical dominance of theologians is a fundamental tradition of Presbyterianism. The Old School leaders had no strategy. Their *ad hoc* tactic, case by case, was to challenge their modernist enemies within the denomination, but only in academic journals. This tactic not only failed, it legitimized the modernist position as a privately held opinion, judicially immune: one opinion among many.

---

138. A traditional one-year limit applied to the General Assembly's veto of a newly appointed seminary professor: the next General Assembly after the appointment.

139. See Chapter 1, above: section on "The Five Points of Modernism," pp. 70–81.

The Modernists' Theory of Church Sanctions

The covenantal issue of sanctions is the key to a correct understanding of the Presbyterian conflict. Theology is not sufficient to win an ecclesiastical struggle; there must also be sanctions. The Old School never offered a developed theology of oath-bound Church sanctions. This put them at a disadvantage.

Presbyterian modernists had to deal with sanctions. This required a theory of sanctions. This theory was applied *ad hoc*, and it seems to have been developed *ad hoc*. It was a three-stage position after the McCune trial (1878): (1) evade negative institutional sanctions (1878-1900); (2) seek positive institutional sanctions (1901-1933); deploy negative institutional sanctions (1934-1936). The first stage required a public theology that invoked democratic pluralism: the illegitimacy of negative institutional sanctions against those holding the five points of modernism. The second stage involved the steady infiltration and capture of the highest offices of the denomination, especially academic positions in the seminaries. This required a public theology based on excellence in personal performance: above all, institutional teamwork. This is pluralism with a corollary: a principle of identification based on the inequality of commitment to the team effort. Its implicit slogan: "All theologies are equal, but some are more equal than others." Any theology that did not foster teamwork was said to be suspect. The final stage required a public theology that invoked bureaucratic authority: negative sanctions against those who would disrupt the team. "Disrupting the team" was defined operationally as any attempt to impose negative sanctions against modernists.

Safe and Unsound

In 1892, Union Seminary withdrew from the jurisdiction of the Presbyterian Church. A year later, Briggs was de-frocked for heresy by the General Assembly. He nevertheless remained on the faculty at Union as its most prominent and internationally respected member, and in 1899 was ordained by the Protestant Episcopal Church.[140] From that time on, he could write or say anything he pleased without

---

140. "Briggs, Charles Augustus," *Dictionary of American Religious Biography*, p. 67.

fear of another heresy trial. In 1900, he offered this evaluation of his experience: the Presbyterian Church could not silence him. He retained his influence in the Church through his Union card.

> The Presbytery of New York acquitted me of these charges, not on the ground that I did not hold these opinions, for I distinctly asserted these opinions, and gave ample proof of them in my *Defense*, but on the ground that these opinions did not conflict with Holy Scripture or the Westminster Confession. But the General Assembly of the Presbyterian Church in the United States of America found me guilty of heresy in these two particulars, as well as in others. . . . The General Assembly went no further. There are other scholars who agree with Henry P. Smith and myself, and who remain unchallenged. The General Assembly could not prevent Professor Smith or myself from pursuing our researches, nor have they stayed the hands of other scholars.[141]

The General Assembly could not control what a pair of defrocked seminary professors taught in a legally independent seminary, but it could have removed positive sanctions from any seminary that employed either of them or anyone else who espoused their views. The denomination required most candidates for the teaching eldership (ministers) to attend seminary. A teaching elder is the only Presbyterian Church officer who possesses the authority to administer the church's positive sanctions: the sacraments.[142] The seminaries possessed the authority to screen candidates for the teaching eldership: positive sanction ("pass") and negative sanction ("fail"). The General Assembly challenged this authority when it imposed a new rule, 1895 to 1897: no ordination of graduates of seminaries outside of the Church. The Assembly never actually enforced this policy, which was reversed in 1897.[143] The General Assembly had no authority in this area in its capacity as a legislative entity. Ordination is a presbytery's function. But the Church's leaders were as helpless before the ideol-

---

141. Briggs, *General Introduction*, pp. 288–89.
142. Westminster Confession of Faith, XXVII:4.
143. Loetscher, *Broadening Church*, p. 70.

ogy of academic freedom after 1869 as their Puritan predecessors had been since the days of Oliver Cromwell.[144]

Higher Criticism in America, 1875 to 1900

In 1878, Julius Wellhausen's seminal book appeared in Germany: *Prolegomena to the History of Ancient Israel*. It appeared in an English translation in 1885. He presented the now-familiar JEDP theory of multiple authorship of the manuscripts of the Pentateuch.[145] When this idea became prominent in the 1890's, the focus of concern on both sides of the debate was the Book of Genesis.[146] This is understandable: the crucial theological issue, God's sovereignty, was being debated through a surrogate issue, creation vs. evolution. Darwin had preceded Wellhausen and his peers by a decade and a half. The comparative explosion of academic interest in higher criticism followed Darwin, although the presuppositions of higher criticism had begun during the Puritan revolution in England.[147] Joseph S. Buckminster, a Congregationalist, had introduced biblical criticism to the United States early in the century, but there was only scattered interest in it until a decade and a half after Darwin's book appeared. Darwinism was the primary impetus.

In his survey of the early higher critics in America, Thomas Olbricht refers to a book by William Newton Clarke, *Sixty Years with the Bible*, published in 1917 by Charles Scribner's Sons, which published so many modernist authors. Clarke was a Northern Baptist and a professor of New Testament at Baptist Theological Seminary in

---

144. The Puritans recognized that the rationalistic curriculum of Oxford and Cambridge was a threat to their worldview. They also recognized the power possessed by these universities: the power to train members of the clergy. Yet they could not dislodge the curriculum, 1649–1660. John Morgan, *Godly Learning: Puritan Attitudes towards Reason, Learning and Education, 1560–1660* (New York: Cambridge University Press, 1986), Conclusion. This, despite the fact that Cromwell became Chancellor of Oxford. Antonia Fraser, *Cromwell: The Lord Protector* (New York: Knopf, 1974), pp. 379–80, 455, 621–22.

145. The Jahwist, Elohist, Deuteronomist, and Priestly forgers.

146. Thomas H. Olbricht, "Rhetoric in the Higher Criticism Controversy," in *The Rhetoric of Protest and Reform, 1878–1898*, edited by Paul H. Boase (Athens, Ohio: Ohio University Press, 1980), p. 267.

147. Reventlow, *Authority of the Bible*, ch. 1.

Toronto (1883) and later a professor of theology at Colgate University (1890–1912). Like generations of young people reared in Christian homes, his crisis began through reading books devoted to uniformitarian geology. He remained a six-day creationist until he read *Origin of Species*. As he wrote in 1917, "my experience with it is interesting, and worth recording, because it was precisely the reproduction in miniature of the experience of the Christian world in those first years of evolutionary doctrine."[148] He became a higher critic only in the late 1880's: first Darwin, then higher criticism. That he defended the Bible as a "guide to Jesus" was irrelevant.[149] The question was: Who is Jesus, and will He send to hell those who reject His substitutionary atonement?

Olbricht identifies *The Presbyterian Review* as the first journal associated with higher criticism.[150] The decision of the Princeton faculty to go ahead with the project was crucial, not just for the controversy within the Northern Presbyterian Church but for American Christianity generally.

The Popular Press

The notorious skeptic Robert Ingersoll gave a lecture, "Some Mistakes of Moses," and had it printed in 1879.[151] In response, Brooklyn's popular Presbyterian pastor, T. DeWitt Talmage, gave lectures to large audiences in 1882.[152] Talmage began by surrendering the six-day creation.[153] These sermons were printed in 300 weekly newspapers. Ingersoll then replied with a book of almost 450 pages.[154]

---

148. Clarke, *Sixty Years*, p. 56; cited in Olbricht, "Rhetoric," p. 267.

149. Hart thinks that Clarke and other mild-mannered higher critics, including the consummate academic infiltrator in American higher education, Moses Coit Gilman, were not self-conscious underminers of the faith. Such naiveté this late in the battle is astonishing. Gilman did his work well. D. G. Hart, *Defending the Faith: J. Gresham Machen and the Crisis of Conservative Protestantism in Modern America* (Baltimore, Maryland: Johns Hopkins University Press, 1994), p. 40.

150. Olbricht, "Rhetoric," p. 269.

151. *The Works of Robert G. Ingersoll*, 7 vols. (New York: Ingersoll League, 1933), VI:13–270.

152. Olbricht, "Rhetoric," p. 270.

153. *Ibid.*, p. 273.

154. Ingersoll, *Works*, vol. 5.

Ingersoll began his speech with an appeal to religious freedom. Next, he castigated Andover Seminary for requiring its faculty members to affirm the statement of faith every five years. He described them as failed preachers who state "the most absurd propositions with faces solemn as stupidity touched by fear." He called for a new ministry devoted to escaping the evils of this world rather than the next. Olbricht points out that the social gospel movement promoted just such a view of the ministry a few years later. Modernism agreed with Ingersoll's basic criticism on the seminary and the Bible. Olbricht adds: "A nascent movement begins slowly, winning a few at a time."[155]

Olbricht properly identifies higher criticism's date of entry into the thinking of the American Church: 1875.[156] He does not mention Briggs' 1876 Inaugural Lecture. In the 1880's academic debate began, and by 1890, two rival positions could be seen. The debate spread into the popular press. By 1900, the lines had hardened between higher critics and their critics. "After the turn of the century, pulpit discussion of these critical matters once again became cursory and superficial. Neither side felt an obligation to communicate with the other, nor prolong the earlier disputes."[157] The rhetoric ended, but not the division.

Conclusion

The battle over the Bible was a battle over point two of the biblical covenant: authority. What stands as the Church's link between God and man: the unchanging Bible or the evolving word of man? The battle over the higher criticism of the Bible was an international phenomenon, but nowhere were the institutional stakes recognized more clearly than in the Presbyterian Church. The Princetonians did their best to stem the tide academically, but their chosen arena for waging this war—in a cooperatively edited denominational academic journal—was the operational means of their defeat. By allowing the

---

155. Olbricht, "Rhetoric," p. 271.
156. *Ibid.*, p. 285. The same year is identified by Petersen, "American Protestantism," p. 321.
157. *Ibid.*, p. 286.

debate to take place within a co-edited journal that allowed their representative to veto any article, they baptized higher criticism as an academically legitimate academic methodology.

Their rationalistic, inductionist methodology had made it difficult for them to resist Briggs' call for a fair and open discussion of the facts. But because of the near-monopolistic authority of seminaries to train candidates for the Presbyterian teaching eldership, a published debate over higher criticism became far more than a strictly academic debate among skilled professionals. It was a public admission that belief in the techniques of higher criticism was legitimate within the theological boundaries of the Church. *Higher criticism became a matter of academic debate rather than Church sanctions.* This was an admission by the Old School that the Westminster Confession's statements regarding the absolute ecclesiastical authority of the Bible were arguably incorrect. Once they became arguably incorrect, they were no longer automatically a matter of Church censure. *The issue of Church sanctions then moved from theology to rhetoric.*

Several factors undermined the Old School in this battle. First and foremost was its empiricism, i.e., its faith that a neutral study to hypothetical brute factuality can bring men to the knowledge of the truth. This belief led Warfield to embrace the methodological assumptions of higher criticism in his acceptance of the techniques of lower criticism. Second, the tactical error of the Princetonians in cooperating in *The Presbyterian Review* allowed that journal to become an outlet for higher criticism as "one view among many." This presented an academic umbrella of open discussion for a view that would eventually transfer control over the denomination to the modernists. Third, the Old School refused to acknowledge that its leading theologian after 1890, Warfield, had departed from the plain language of Chapter I of the Westminster Confession: God's providential preservation of pure biblical texts. It also refused to acknowledge that its view of creationism was not Confessional, nor was its view of the universal salvation of infants dying in infancy. The Old School refused, therefore, to recognize that their resistance to Confessional revision made them vulnerable to the criticism that their defense of the Confession's standards as the basis of imposing Church sanctions was self-serving and judicially arbitrary. This appearance of judicial arbitrariness transferred the strategic initiative to the modernists.

The war over the Bible, the Westminster Confession, and the future of the Church was enjoined after 1875; there was no going back. Shailer Mathews summed it up in 1936: "To the orthodox, Christianity was based upon the Bible as authority."[158] To the modernists, Christianity was based upon man's evolving word as authority. Men could cry, "Peace, peace," but there would be no peace until one side expelled the other. The crucial issue was sanctions.

---

158. Mathews, *New Faith for Old*, p. 277.

4

TESTING ORTHODOXY'S WILL TO RESIST

> *The Christian Church ever contains the **body** of truth. At times, when God wishes to lead them into higher truth, he **reveals** the truth to certain men chosen of him. They being called in a **special** sense & occupying a higher & more advanced position than the Church, may be **rejected**; but God's particular people will rally around the **called** of God. . . . I now stand **firm** on all the received doctrines of the Church, & I defy any man to show that I do not. In the Church I will remain & teach the doctrines of the Church, & call upon men to **advance** to the higher life of sanctification. I have no reason to believe that the Church will not receive me. I shall remain in & with the Church until it takes the sin upon itself of **casting** me out, which God grant may never happen. I feel assured that the world needs this light.*
>
> Charles A. Briggs (1867)[1]

From his days as a student in Berlin, when he wrote this letter to his uncle, Charles Augustus Briggs had a sense of destiny about his career—far more "Augustus" than "Charlie" or "Chuck." His attitude could be described as bordering on the messianic. It is clear why he was willing to adopt the strategy that made him famous and led to his de-frocking in 1893, i.e., his escalating rhetoric. He was more con-

---

1. C. A. Briggs to Marvin Briggs, 8 Jan. 1867; cited in Channing Renwick Jeschke, The Briggs Case: The Focus of a Study in Nineteenth Century Presbyterian History (Ph.D. dissertation, University of Chicago, 1966), p. 139.

cerned about transforming the Presbyterian Church in terms of the processes of evolutionary growth—he called this process *sanctification*—than about the threat of Church sanctions.

He gained a great advantage, beginning in 1874: his employment by Union Seminary. Union had provided men with shelter from the rigors of Old School orthodoxy from its founding. The minutes of its founding meeting for January, 11, 1836, announced: "It is the design of the Founders to provide a Theological Seminary in the midst of the greatest, and most growing community in America, around which all men, of moderate views and feelings, who desire to live free from party strife, and to stand aloof from all extremes of doctrinal speculation, practical radicalism, and ecclesiastical domination, may cordially, and affectionately rally."[2] This was the hope of the Arminian New School moderates—such as Albert Barnes, who served as a Director for thirty years[3]—in 1837. The result within 50 years was the opposite: Union became the center of controversy in the Presbyterian Church and the nation because of the radical, extreme, doctrinal speculations of its faculty.

Beyond Negative Sanctions

Sheltered by Union, Briggs' number-one tactic was to demand freedom of inquiry. This tactic remained the central feature of the modernists' strategy in every denomination until they gained control of the seminaries and the courts. Freedom of inquiry meant both academic freedom and pulpit freedom. First and foremost, it meant *the freedom to write or teach higher criticism without fear of Church sanctions*. In a footnote regarding his 1876 address,[4] Briggs in 1900 referred the reader back to an earlier passage in his book, where we read: "Let us not be so presumptuous, so irreverent to the Word of God, so unbelieving with reference to the inherent power of convincing and assuring seekers for the truth, as to condemn any sincere and candid inquirer as a heretic or a rationalist, because he may differ from us on

---

2. *Ibid.*, p. 128.
3. *Ibid.*, p. 127.
4. Charles Augustus Briggs, *General Introduction to the Study of the Holy Scriptures* (Grand Rapids, Michigan: Baker, [1900] 1970), p. 287n.

such questions as these!"[5] His terminology regarding potential critics was both fervent and religious: "presumptuous," "irreverent to the Word of God." There must be no negative institutional sanctions; all objections must be limited to persuasion. We must trust "the inherent power of convincing." In other words, to exclude from a seminary faculty anyone who teaches that the word of God is fallible is itself an act of irreverence against the word of God.

True orthodoxy is here defined as the toleration of ideas that undermine orthodoxy. Briggs would adopt this same rhetorical strategy in his 1889 book, *Whither?* What is clearly illogical—the possibility of orthodoxy (straight speaking) without sanctions (straight shooting)—he defended with what appeared to be the rhetoric of orthodoxy. This did not save him, but it provided cover for those who shared his opinions and who were willing to abandon his frontal assault tactics.

Briggs was calling for the destruction of Confessional Presbyterianism. The whole point of requiring a subscription to a creed is to invoke sanctions. There can be no valid covenantal oath without the threat of negative sanctions for the violation of its stipulations. The oath is the invocation of sanctions: a self-maledictory oath. Ordination to the ministry is by covenantal oath. While the Adopting Act of 1729 allowed a man to express disagreement with the Confessional standards of the denomination, it did not authorize such a personal confession without the threat of sanctions. A presbytery had the right and the responsibility before God to screen out all those candidates whose confessional deviation its members regarded as too radical. What Briggs wanted was different: *confessional immunity*. He wanted to be able to violate the stipulations of his original oath as a Presbyterian minister, but without fear of negative sanctions. This was the thesis and theme of his 1885 book, *American Presbyterianism*, in which he called for a Church that contained both conservative and progressive forces. Such an inclusivist Church would be "vastly higher than any of the elements of which it is composed. . . ."[6]

---

5. *Ibid.*, p. 26.
6. Briggs, *American Presbyterianism: Its Origin and Early History* (New York: Charles Scribner's Sons, 1885), p. 373.

He wanted theological innovation without negative sanctions. In this regard, he had a lot in common with Adam. He also had a lot in common with modernists in every American Protestant denomination. As Hutchison has pointed out, what the modernists wanted was a series of "reasonably complete victories unaccompanied by controversy or unpleasantness. . . ."[7] From 1879 to about 1883, this is generally what they experienced. From 1883 to 1891, however, religious journals became more guarded.[8] The modernists had to adjust their strategy and their rhetoric. "Others besides Briggs became, during the 1880s, conscious of battle lines and in some measure willing to form ranks behind them."[9] Briggs had become the point man for the whole movement. It was his self-appointed task to test the opposition by drawing the fire of the most theologically skilled conservatives in Protestantism.

Briggs understood the risks of becoming a theological pioneer, which in his era meant becoming a theological commando. He noted in 1900 that "It is only within recent years that any general interest in the matters of Higher Criticism has been shown in Great Britain and America. This interest has been due chiefly to the labors of a few pioneers, who have suffered in the interest of biblical science."[10] He singled out Samuel Davidson, who was dismissed from his position as professor of Biblical Literature at the Lancashire Independent College at Manchester. The reason? He had been on the faculty since 1842, but he had at last gone into print with his views in 1856, in Horne's *Introduction to Scripture*. "This stayed the progress of criticism in Great Britain for some years."[11] Briggs understood: negative sanctions work.

Another "late bloomer" was W. Robertson Smith, who had taught Hebrew at the Free Church College of Aberdeen. In the famous ninth edition of the *Encyclopedia Britannica*, he went into print with his

---

7. William R. Hutchison, *The Modernist Impulse in American Protestantism* (Cambridge, Massachusetts: Harvard University Press, 1976), p. 105.
8. *Ibid.*
9. *Ibid.*, p. 106.
10. Briggs, *General Introduction*, p. 285.
11. *Ibid.*, p. 286.

views. The particular volumes appeared in 1875 and 1880. Then, in 1881, he published *The Old Testament in the Jewish Church*, which for the first time popularized the phrase "higher criticism."[12] That same year, he was removed from his post, but acquitted of heresy—the outcome of a series of judicial procedures that had begun in that remarkable year, 1876.[13] His dismissal was for the sake of harmony.[14] This contest, Briggs said, "gained liberty of opinion in Great Britain." Smith was immediately hired to teach at Cambridge University.[15] Smith's teacher, A. B. Davidson, held the same views, but was left undisturbed by the University of Edinburgh. One year later, in 1882, the General Assembly of the Free Church chose another known higher critic, George Adam Smith, to succeed as Principal of Glasgow a man who had opposed Robertson Smith.[16] (There were a lot of higher critics named Smith, which was appropriate, for they forged a new worldview.) There was no question which way the theological wind was blowing. The weather vane of institutional sanctions was pointing positive for higher critics. There were more higher critics than heresy trials to remove them. The sanctions did not set precedents. Confrontational rhetoric, as always, could prove risky, but the underlying modernist theology was increasingly safe.

In 1881, Briggs began what became a crucial series on higher criticism in *Presbyterian Review*. The next year, the General Assembly warned against the appearance of higher criticism in the seminaries. These methods "tend to unsettle faith in doctrine and divine origin and plenary inspiration of the Scriptures," the Assembly said.[17] It repeated its warning in 1883 upon receipt of complaints from five pres-

---

12. Jack B. Rogers and Donald K. McKim, *The Authority and Interpretation of the Bible: An Historical Approach* (New York: Harper & Row, 1979), p. 278.

13. Mark A. Noll, *Between Faith and Criticism: Evangelicals, Scholarship, and the Bible in America*, 2nd ed. (Grand Rapids, Michigan: Eerdmans, 1986), p. 16.

14. Briggs, *General Introduction*, p. 286.

15. Iain Murray, *The Forgotten Spurgeon*, 2nd ed. (Edinburgh: Banner of Truth Trust, [1978] 1986), p. 141. This was a replay of C. H. Toy's experience two years earlier: from a Baptist college to Harvard University in one jump. The magnitude of the jump, however, was less in Smith's case.

16. Briggs, *General Introduction*, p. 286.

17. Cited in Rogers & McKim, *Authority and Interpretation*, p. 351.

byteries. But it took no judicial action and threatened no sanctions. It reminded the presbyteries that this was their responsibility.[18] Initiative remained at the local level.

Escalating Rhetoric: 1883–1909

Rhetoric is the art of persuasion. Those who suggest a new interpretation of the past or a new way of interpreting the present must use rhetoric if they are to gain converts. In a suggestive essay, Leland M. Griffin has proposed a three-stage theory of rhetoric in a movement. First, there is the early period when men are becoming dissatisfied with prevailing interpretations. Second, there is a crisis period in which the outcome of the confrontation is unclear. Third, there is the consummation stage where one side or the other wins support of the targeted audience.[19] The three stages are doubt, institutional crisis and confrontation, and consolidation. A decade after this essay was published, Thomas Kuhn introduced a similar thesis regarding the history of science: the concept of the paradigm shift.[20] Briggs' career offers a classic example of the function of rhetoric, as well as its limits.

In 1883, Briggs' *Biblical Study* appeared. It was a 500-page introduction to higher criticism.[21] It was rhetorically subdued. The chapter on higher criticism was mainly historical. Briggs was laudatory regarding higher criticism. "No one need fear criticism, save those who are uncertain in their knowledge, for criticism leads to certitude."[22]

The book used conservative language, but the reader waited in vain for any reference to the doctrine of salvation as a judicial declaration of God, i.e., the doctrine of imputation, of Christ's mediatorial sacrifice as a legal substitute. On inspiration, Briggs wrote: "The Inspiration of the Word of God is a highly important doctrine, but it must not be so greatly emphasized as to lead us to neglect other and still

---

18. *Ibid.*, p. 352.
19. Leland M. Griffin, "The Rhetoric of Historical Movements," *Quarterly Journal of Speech*, 38 (April 1952).
20. Thomas Kuhn, *The Structure of Scientific Revolutions* (Chicago: University of Chicago Press, 1962).
21. Briggs, *Biblical Study: Its Principles Methods and History*, 3rd ed. (New York: Charles Scribner's Sons, [1883] 1890).
22. *Ibid.*, p. 81.

more important aspects of the Bible."[23] "The Scriptures are indeed means, not ends. They are to bring us to God, to assimilate us to Christ, to unite us in organic union with Him."[24] What was he getting at? His concluding paragraph hints at his goal: "The Word of God does not cease to be the Word of God when wrapped in other than Scripture language. Hence it is that the Christian becomes a living epistle (2 Cor. iii.3), and the Church, as a body of such epistles, a means of grace, conveying divine grace in another form to the world."[25] This, in a chapter titled, "The Scripture as a Means of Grace." His language seemed to raise men and the institutional Church to the status of divine revelation. That is to say, this language lowered the written word to the status of men. And that, in the final analysis, is what higher criticism is all about.

Biblical Study was well received by the American religious press. The review in *Presbyterian Review* was critical: Briggs had gone too far. The review in *Unitarian Review* was also critical: Briggs had not gone far enough. The other reviews were generally favorable.[26]

In 1885, Briggs laid another foundation stone in his strategy of subversion. He published *American Presbyterianism*, which argued that the Old Side tradition in colonial America represented a deviation from the true Presbyterian tradition. He called them Protestant scholastics, just as he called the Princetonians. This book tested the degree of resistance on the part of the Old School, and it also was designed to gain at least private acceptance by New School churchmen. Briggs understood who the one enemy was that could offer serious resistance to him and his modernist peers: the Old School. If he could silence them, the New School experientialists would be far less equipped—creedally, psychologically, or judicially—to resist the modernists, let alone expel them from the denomination. The book did not lead to his censure. He was then ready for the next test: *Whither?* (1889). No institutional response was forthcoming. After that came his Inaugural Address of 1891. That led to his de-frocking in 1893.

---

23. *Ibid.*, p. 411.
24. *Ibid.*, p. 426.
25. *Ibid.*, p. 428.
26. Hutchison, *Modernist Impulse*, pp. 106–107.

Sixteen years after this setback, he felt free to write: "The modern mind cannot accept any such absolute infallibility, either in the Bible, the Church or the Reason, as the older authorities maintained."[27] Then where must we seek the infallible truth? Within ourselves. "The only religious experience that is authoritative and infallible is that which the conscience and the religious feeling give us, in innate, *a priori*, immediate decisions, the voice of God Himself within us, where doubt and uncertainty are impossible."[28] The only infallibility, then, is in the religious experience of the individual. Here alone does God speak to man infallibly. But He does not speak in words, creeds, and catechisms. The modernist transfers authority from God and His Bible to the individual and his "immediate decisions." An existentialist god speaks only through a non-cognitive encounter with existentialist man. Karl Barth was to extend this theology of non-cognitive encounter in 1919 in his commentary on Paul's epistle to the Romans, but the worldview of theistic existentialism was already widespread within modernism before Barth began to write.

Did Briggs reject reason? No more than he rejected mysticism. He elevated the authority of reason to the status of equality with the Bible and the Church. Reason, he said, is as effective as the other two authorities in producing the non-cognitive encounter with the god of existentialism. "The historian recognizes that men have found God in the Bible, the Church and the Reason. . . . It is the opinion of Christian scholars that Socrates and pure-minded heathen have ever found God in the forms of the Reason. Why should any deny that modern Rationalists, and seekers after God among the people, who are fenced off from Bible and Church by the exactions of priest and ecclesiastic, find God enthroned in their own hearts."[29] Notice that the culprits are "priest and ecclesiastic," who "fence off" the "seekers after truth." These culprits place judicial boundaries around the Church, which is an affront to modernism. Judicial boundaries, not man's original sin, are what keep pagans from coming to God, Briggs insisted.

---

27. Briggs, *Church Unity: Studies of Its Most Important Problems* (New York: Charles Scribner's Sons, 1909), p. 243.
28. *Ibid.*, p. 226.
29. *Ibid.*, p. 322.

This was not Paul's message at Mars Hill (Acts 17), but Briggs rejected Paul's theology. Too great a reliance on Paul was a weakness of the Westminster Confession of Faith, he said. He found that 667 proof texts of the Confession were from Paul's epistles and the epistle to the Hebrews, whereas only 248 were from the gospels and 247 from other New Testament writers. "Thus the Confession is built on the words of Paul rather than the words of the Lord Jesus. It is Pauline rather than comprehensively Christian."[30] It was this commonly held modernist heresy—placing Paul in opposition to Jesus—that Machen challenged in his 1921 lectures and book, *The Origin of Paul's Religion*. Machen saw exactly what the affront of Paul was and is: its exclusivism. "The oriental religions were tolerant of other faiths; the religion of Paul, like the ancient religion of Israel, demanded an absolutely exclusive devotion. . . . Amid the prevailing syncretism of the Greco-Roman world, the religion of Paul, with the religion of Israel, stands absolutely alone."[31]

Briggs was heretical to the core. He had been heretical from his days as a student in Germany. But it took until 1909 for his public confession to match his private confession. He had guarded his words with the rhetoric of deception prior to 1891, although not so carefully that a denomination truly committed to the Westminster standards would not have de-frocked him before 1891. Outside of the Presbyterian Church, his ideas were being received favorably.[32] Inside the Episcopal Church, he had not been threatened with sanctions. In 1899, he decided to escalate his rhetoric and his theological challenge.

Briggs' Articulation of Modernist Theology

Men confess their true religion. Over time, progressive confession is normal. As men work out the implications of their faith, their lives become more consistent with their presuppositions. Cornelius Van Til called this process epistemological self-consciousness, but what his the-

---

30. *Ibid.*, p. 311.
31. Machen, *The Origin of Paul's Religion* (Grand Rapids, Michigan: Eerdmans, [1921] 1947), p. 9.
32. Hutchison, *Modernist Impulse*, p. 109.

ology really taught was *ethical* self-consciousness.[33] This process of progressive confession applies both to individuals and collective groups, especially the two ethically divided groups: the saved and the lost, covenant-keepers and covenant-breakers.

I have already presented the five points of modernism: a denial of God's absolute sovereignty; an affirmation of the legitimacy of higher criticism; the acceptance of evolution; the denial of God's negative sanctions, beginning with the doctrine of hell; and ecumenism. In *Whither?* (1889), Briggs presented a fully developed version of this theology, but in the name of historic Calvinism. He got away with this judicially. That he got away with it in 1889 indicates the magnitude of Machen's problem in 1923.

Briggs wrote the book, he said, because the 1889 General Assembly had called for a discussion at the presbytery level of the possibility of revising the Confession.[34] This pressure had come in 1888 from the Nassau Presbytery on Long Island, New York.[35] Briggs wanted revision.[36] So did many New School members, including James McCosh.[37] Briggs' colleague at Union, Philip Schaff, regarded the move toward creedal revision as a sign that the Old Calvinism was dying out; another sign was the move toward ecumenism.[38] Schaff announced that he knew of no Presbyterian minister who believed in limited atonement (particular redemption), one of the five points of Calvinism.[39] He called for revision. The Old School's leaders did not.[40] But the

---

33. Gary North, *Dominion and Common Grace: The Biblical Basis of Progress* (Tyler, Texas: Institute for Christian Economics, 1987), pp. 103–106.

34. Briggs, *Whither? A Theological Question for the Times*, 3rd ed. (New York: Charles Scribner's Sons, [1889] 1890), p. ix.

35. Lefferts A. Loetscher, *The Broadening Church: a study of theological issues in the presbyterian church since 1869* (Philadelphia: University of Pennsylvania Press, 1954), p. 41.

36. Briggs, "Revision of the Westminster Confession," *Andover Review*, 13 (Jan. 1890).

37. James McCosh, *Whither? O Whither? Tell Me Where* (New York: Charles Scribner's Sons, 1889), p. 18. McCosh identified himself as a New Light man (p. 17).

38. Philip Schaff, *Creed Revision in the Presbyterian Churches* (New York: Charles Scribner's Sons, 1890), p. 1.

39. *Ibid.*, pp. 13–14.

40. Francis L. Patton, *The Revision of the Confession of Faith* (1889?). This

revision that Briggs wanted dwarfed anything ever proposed in the history of American Presbyterianism, even as late as 1967. *Whither?* was his manifesto. Overnight, it became a best-seller.[41]

Those favoring Confessional revision suggested numerous minor revisions. No revisions received a sufficient number of votes from the presbyteries. The revision movement went into hibernation for almost a decade after 1893, the year of Briggs' de-frocking. But *Whither?* remains the classic statement of Presbyterian modernism during that crucial era in Presbyterian history. For this reason, we need to examine it in detail.

Readers are about to be introduced to more information about Charles Briggs' theology than any normal person would want to know. I cite his words in great detail for three reasons. First, Briggs was a representative modernist theologian of his era, and unquestionably he was *the* representative *de-frocked* Protestant modernist of his era. He had a national audience. A major book publisher, Charles Scribner's Sons, published volume after volume of his writings. What he said was important because he was a representative figure.

Second, and far more important, readers need to understand that modernism is a consistent theological system, one which offers a mirror image of biblical orthodoxy. Modernism is not just a series of seemingly random attacks on the details of traditional Christianity. By citing Briggs extensively, I can show from the details of his theology that *we are dealing with a coherent system of covenant theology,* not just a series of unconnected criticisms of orthodoxy. The details of his system would not have been that important, had there been no underlying theological system; his overall theology itself was very important. So was his use of rhetoric. Prior to 1891, each time Briggs escalated his rhetoric, he was left undisturbed by the courts of the Presbyterian Church. The Church did not acknowledge judicially—the only acknowledgment that truly mattered—the theological threat posed by Briggs' theology until Briggs presented a flagrant rhetorical challenge in 1891.

---

booklet does not identify its publisher or date of publication.

41. Mark Stephen Massa, S.J., *Charles Augustus Briggs and the Crisis of Historical Criticism* (Minneapolis, Minnesota: Fortress Press, 1990), pp. 79-80.

Third, in order to defend my thesis—that Briggs' rhetoric was the cause of his de-frocking far more than his theology—I need to show how flagrantly heretical his published theology was in 1889. The best way to show this is to quote him verbatim. But I must do more than quote numerous passages. I must show that he presented a rival theology of the covenant. Modernism is a perverse covenant theology. This is what the Presbyterian Church, like mainline Protestantism in general, failed to understand and respond to judicially in time to save itself.

1. The Not-So-Sovereign God

Calvinism, more than any other Christian theology, affirms the absolute sovereignty of God. Briggs came in the name of Calvinism. He therefore had a problem. He had to disguise his attack on God's sovereignty. He did this brilliantly. It was a two-level attack. The first level was rhetorical: *a rhetoric of deception* rather than a rhetoric of confrontation. The second stage was part deceptive rhetoric and part philosophy: a defense of *dialectical humanist philosophy* in the name of Christian freedom.

1. The Attack on "Protestant Scholasticism"

This was a continuation of his thesis in *American Presbyterianism*. Briggs drew a distinction between the Calvinism of John Calvin and the Westminster Confession on one side, and the Calvinism of his opponents at Princeton Seminary on the other. He called the Princetonian version scholastic Calvinism.

This was a rhetorical argument. By equating the Westminster Confession with Calvin's theology, and by equating Princeton's theology with medieval scholasticism, Briggs sought to prejudice the case against Princeton's theology: to make it appear to be in conflict with Calvin. This was a debating ploy. In the mid-1960's, however, Briggs' liberal heirs in the Presbyterian Church abandoned Briggs' rhetorical subterfuge regarding the Westminster standards, substituting a subterfuge of their own. The Church in 1967 published other Calvinist confessions, as well as the German Evangelical Church's Barth-inspired Theological Declaration of Barmen (1934), in a *Book of Confessions*. It also revised the Westminster Confession to make it conform to neo-orthodoxy, and it abandoned the Larger Catechism altogether—where the Westminster Assembly's judicial theology had been spelled out in greatest detail.[42] All of this was the result of a 1956 overture from the Amarillo Presbytery suggesting a revision of the archaic language of the Shorter Catechism.[43] As it turned out, the Shorter Catechism was the one 1647 document left untouched by the 1967 revision. The man most responsible for the 1967 revision, Princeton Seminary professor Edward Downey, announced in 1964: "While Westminster is thus a post-Reformation statement, it is by no means a modern one. It derives from an age of scholastic theology, of preoccupation with authority and law, of churchly and political absolutism."[44] Whenever a liberal Presbyterian theologian wants to evade some aspect of Anglo-American Calvinism's judicial theology, he chants Briggs' mantra: "Scholasticism, scholasticism, scholasticism...."

Briggs' criticism of Princeton's theology was not entirely rhetorical, however, i.e., effective but logically spurious. From the days of the founding of Princeton Seminary in 1812, Archibald Alexander and his successors had assigned Francis Turretin's massive *Institutio Theologiae Elencticae* (1674) to all students.[45] It was available only in Latin.[46] This screened out candidates for the Presbyterian ministry who were not fluent in Latin and also able to survive the rigors of a systematic theology that had been self-consciously modeled along the lines of Roman Catholic scholasticism. Charles Hodge modeled his three-volume *Systematic Theology* (1871-73) after Turretin's work, which was adopted at Princeton because too few college graduates in 1870 could read Latin. (Testifying to the reality of Presbyterian pride in the for-

---

42. It was reintroduced with the 1983 merger with the Southern Presbyterians.

43. Jack Rogers, *Presbyterian Creeds: A Guide to The Book of Confessions* (Philadelphia: Westminster Press, 1985), p. 209.

44. Cited in *ibid.*, p. 211.

45. On the influence of Turretin at Princeton, see Rogers & McKim, *Authority and Interpretation*, ch. 5: "The Development of Reformed Scholasticism in America." On Turretin's method, see *ibid.*, pp. 172-84. For a critique of their thesis with respect to the supposed uniqueness of the Princetonians' theory of inspiration, see John D. Woodbridge, *Biblical Authority: A Critique of the Rogers/McKim Proposal* (Grand Rapids, Michigan: Zondervan, 1982), chaps. 7, 8.

46. Only in 1992 did the first of three volumes appear in English.

mally educated ministry, the requirement that every minister be able to read and write in Latin at one stage in his career—early—was not removed from the Form of Government. It had been there since the Westminster Assembly's non-binding Form of Church-Government [1645].[47] Every candidate had to present "A Latin exegesis on some common head in divinity."[48] This remained in the list of requirements despite the fact that almost no one could do it and presbyteries could not enforce it. Only in 1911 did a majority of presbyteries vote to eliminate this requirement and substitute a bachelor's degree or master's degree.[49])

There is no doubt that Turretin was committed to a doctrine of the word-for-word inspiration of the Bible. What Briggs and his successors[50] have tried to do is link the scholastic method of logic—held in disrepute by most Protestants in 1889—with the doctrine of biblical inerrancy. His successors have even adopted his pejorative phrase: Reformed scholasticism.[51] Modernists wanted both to sink together. Briggs announced his strategy in the Preface: "This book is polemical. It is necessary to overcome that false orthodoxy which has obtruded itself in the place of the Westminster orthodoxy. I regret, on many accounts, that it has been necessary for me to attack so often the elder

---

47. *The Form of Church-Government*, in *The Confession of Faith* (Inverness: Publications Committee of the Free Presbyterian Church of Scotland, 1966), p. 413.

48. *The Form of Government*, XIV:iv:1. *The Constitution of the Presbyterian Church in the United States of America* (Philadelphia: Presbyterian Board of Publication and Sabbath School Work, 1904), p. 373.

49. *Minutes of the General Assembly, 1911*, pp. 197-98.

50. Such as Rogers & McKim: *Authority and Interpretation*, pp. 348-61. I would also add Ernest Sandeen: "The Princeton Theology: One Source of Biblical Literalism in American Protestantism," *Church History*, 31 (Sept. 1962).

51. Rogers & McKim, *Authority and Interpretation*, Part II: "Contemporary Response: Reformed Scholasticism in America and the Recovery of Alternatives in the Reformation Tradition." These Reformation "alternatives" are entirely spurious—an invention of deliberately rigged scholarship—as Woodbridge's refutation proves. I do not remember ever reading a line-by-line critique of a rival scholar's book that is more complete, more utterly devastating than Woodbridge's *Biblical Authority*. He is polite. He never uses such phrases as "fraud," "faked evidence," and "morally corrupt pseudo-scholarship." He merely provides evidence that leads to such conclusions.

and younger Hodge, divines for whom I have the greatest respect and admiration."[52] He also announced: "This book is irenical."[53] It wasn't, and saying it was did not make it so, except in the minds of his theological allies, then and now. "Irenical" means low-key language, a spirit of calm discourse. It may be an appropriate style when you are conducting a frontal assault on an enemy who has the votes. It is also an appropriate rhetorical smoke screen to announce your irenical disposition when you are about to toss a verbal stink bomb at your enemies, which is exactly what *Whither?* did.

Briggs maintained the rhetoric of toleration: the myth of judicial neutrality. He assured everyone: "The author does not wish to exclude from the Church those theologians whom he attacks for their errors. He is a broad churchman. . . . He rejoices in all earnest efforts for Christian unity, not only in Presbyterian and Reformed circles, but in the entire Christian world."[54] This became the official battle cry—irenic, of course—of the modernists within Northern Presbyterianism . . . until they had the votes to isolate the orthodox party. At that point, if the orthodox men protested, or worse, threatened to withhold their tithes and offerings, they were thrown out. Ironically, of course.

2. A Philosophical Substitution: Dialecticism

Briggs refused to discuss predestination in *Whither?* Nevertheless, the doctrine of predestination undergirds the other four points of the biblical covenant: the inerrancy of Scripture (the voice of authority that represents God in history), the comprehensive law of God, God's absolutely just final judgment, and the perseverance of the saints in history. Briggs' goal was to substitute four other doctrines: higher criticism for biblical inerrancy, evolution for biblical law, a second-chance theory of the "intermediate state" for final judgment, and minimal-creed ecumenism for the expansion of the kingdom of God in history.

---

52. Briggs, *Whither?*, p. ix.
53. *Ibid.*, p. x.
54. *Ibid.*

To accomplish this, he had to undermine the doctrine of God's absolute sovereignty over creation and history. He could not successfully appeal to the traditional language of Arminianism, i.e., "free will." This would have alerted every reader to his break with Calvinism. Instead, he turned to the categories of Kantian and post-Kantian philosophy. Instead of invoking the familiar Arminian argument regarding the conflict between God's predestination and man's free will, he spoke of a conflict between mechanism and personalism. These are the categories of Immanuel Kant: phenomenal vs. noumenal, science vs. freedom.[55] But in Kant's system these are dialectical categories; we do not choose one or the other. Both exist together in unresolved tension. Briggs, however, asked his readers to de-emphasize "mechanism" in favor of "personalism."

Again and again, Briggs contrasted objective truth with subjective truth. He favored the subjective. As Alan Pontier has written of Briggs' theology, "Doctrine is placed against religious vitality; evidences for verbal inspiration are placed against the witness of the Holy Spirit; and the 'orthodoxism' of nineteenth century conservatives is placed against the mysticism in Germany."[56] Pontier cites *Biblical Study*: "It is the mystic element that needs above all things to be revived in the British and American churches. It brings people face to face with the Bible and with the Divine Spirit working in and with it, so that they need no mediating priesthood of theologians, no help of apologetics or of Biblical polemics to convince them of the authority of the Bible and enable them to maintain it against all cavilling."[57] The intense rationalism of the techniques of higher criticism was balanced in Briggs' theology by the intense irrationalism of mysticism; his was a dialectical theology. This emphasis on the irrational was to culminate a generation later in the humanist, Kantian, dialectical theology known as neo-orthodoxy. This theology captured Princeton Seminary

---

55. Richard Kroner, *Kant's Weltanschauung* (Chicago: University of Chicago Press, [1914] 1956).

56. Alan Ross Pontier, A Survey of American Criticism of Inerrancy During the Last Century, master's thesis, Covenant Theological Seminary (1983), p. 9.

57. Briggs, *Biblical Study*, p. 123; cited in *ibid.*, p. 120.

within a few years after Machen and his colleagues resigned in protest in 1929.[58]

Briggs began by dismissing A. A. Hodge's doctrine of God. He wrote of Hodge's conception: "The doctrine of the living God is passed over altogether. This neglect of the doctrine of the living God has resulted in making the God of most dogmaticians an abstraction, a bundle of attributes, and in external and mechanical conceptions of His decrees and their execution. The immutability of God has been elaborated at the expense of His activity, His sovereignty at the cost of His deity."[59] He made no attempt to explain why God's sovereignty is necessarily antithetical to His deity; he simply asserted that this is the case, and then went on. He had scrapped Calvinism and had substituted . . . what? Existentialism? A precursor of neo-orthodoxy? He did not elaborate. But whatever it was, he called his system orthodoxy.[60]

He then quoted from an earlier article of his in *Presbyterian Review*, in which he had argued that the translation of Jahveh as *Lord* is a mistake. In all English translations and in Jewish rabbinical theology, *Jahveh* "has been associated with an undue stress upon the sovereignty of God. The Old Testament revelation in its use of Jahveh emphasized rather the activity of the ever living personal God of revelation."[61] His rhetorical strategy is visible: his use of such pejorative words as "mechanical" and "Rabbinical theology."

He did not say what the sovereignty of God is, only what it is not: whatever A. A. Hodge said it is. All Briggs said was this: "The doctrine of God needs to be enriched at the present time by the enthronement of the idea of the living God to its supreme place in Biblical theology, and the dethronement of the idea of divine sovereignty from its usurped position in dogmatic theology."[62] He then insisted

---

58. See Chapter 10, below: section on "The New Princeton", pp. 638-41.
59. Briggs, *Whither?*, p. 93.
60. *Ibid.*, ch. 2: "Orthodoxy."
61. *Ibid.*, p. 93.
62. *Ibid.*, pp. 93-94. By biblical theology, he had in mind that theology which teaches that God's revelation progressed in history, meaning changed in theological form and content. Before Geerhardus Vos came to Princeton in 1893, biblical theology meant the presupposition of higher criticism: historically bounded, evolving revelation.

that "The Westminster divines state this doctrine in its true fundamental position, but the later dogmaticians have changed the Westminster doctrine."[63] For obvious documentary reasons—the absence of evidence—he did not attempt to show exactly how or where the Westminster divines had enthroned God's living acts and dethroned the doctrine of God's sovereignty. Yet he expected to get away with this astounding theological assertion, which he did.

Briggs' rhetorical strategy has been used ever since: contrasting the Bible's predestinating God and His unbreakable decrees with a living, "personal" God. Almost seventy years after *Whither?*, G. Ernest Wright and Reginald Fuller adopted it in their higher critical study of what was purported to be the God of the Bible: *The Book of the Acts of God* (1957).[64] The modernists' Kantian god in his historically bounded but purely free acts is contrasted with the biblical God and His sovereign decree over history. The acts of this Kantian god are always discussed within the framework of man's social evolution, not the biblical God's sovereign decree. The acts of this god are not sovereign acts governed by his decree over creation; rather, they are acts that can only be interpreted by men in terms of their knowledge and perception. Man's evolving word replaces God's definitive written word as the voice of authority in history.

Yet even Briggs eventually had to confront the theological reality of Presbyterianism: the Westminster Confession. He wrote: "The most difficult doctrine in the Westminster standards is the doctrine of the 'divine decree.'"[65] Difficult in what sense? Difficult for Briggs: the threat of negative sanctions. The Confession's doctrine of the divine decree made things *strategically difficult* for a heretical theology professor in an ostensibly Calvinist seminary. As it turned out, he got away with it. He was never brought to trial for his Kantian doctrine of god, nor was anyone else.

---

63. *Ibid.*, p. 94.

64. I discuss this book in *The Hoax of Higher Criticism* (Tyler, Texas: Institute for Christian Economics, 1989), ch. 2: "The Techniques of Higher Criticism."

65. Briggs, *Whither?*, p. 97.

The Westminster divines were Calvinists, not Arminians, he had to admit. They were fighting the Arminians, so the categories of the Confession are "sharp, hard, polemical, and exclusive; . . ." Their polemics had led them into error: "At the same time it is my opinion that in this respect the Westminster divines went too far in their polemics." This really is a shame, he insisted, for their polemical definitions "have kept multitudes from uniting with the Presbyterian Church."[66] At this point, Briggs had reduced the Calvinist theology of the Westminster standards to mere polemics, and therefore not essential as a test of faith. Yet a few pages earlier, he had elevated his own polemics to the state of theology: presenting the Westminster divines as proto-existentialists, lovers of contingent freedom. This back-and-forth strategy between theology and rhetoric—his rhetoric of deception—could be used, and has been used, by other modernists to confuse their critics.[67] The bottom line was always the same: *ecumenism*, a growing Church without a fixed theology or negative sanctions against heretics. Trinitarian theology had to be scrapped in order to attain this.

Briggs preached the Fatherhood of God, as do all ecumenists: "The Fatherhood of God is one of the most precious doctrines of the Scriptures, . . . the people have been deprived of its comfort, until recent times, by the neglect of it in the teachings of so-called orthodox divines."[68] First, notice his use of the pejorative phrase, *so-called*. This was dual rhetoric: confrontation and deception. His rivals, this rhetoric implied, were not truly orthodox. Second, what the modernist refuses to accept, or even suggest, is that the biblical doctrine of the Fatherhood of God has a crucial judicial aspect to it: His disinheritance of His first son, Adam, and all those born to Adam except those adopted covenantally by His second Son, Jesus Christ. The Fatherhood of God for the modernist is the doctrine of "universal Fatherhood,"[69] not sovereign Adoptionhood. The modernist refuses to accept the doctrine of man's original disinheritance, and therefore he rejects the doctrine of spiritual adoption solely by grace. The disinher-

---

66. *Ibid.*
67. See my comments on Wright and Fuller in *Hoax*, ch. 2.
68. Briggs, *Whither?*, p. 143.
69. *Ibid.*, p. 145.

iting God of the Bible is as foreign to modernism as the Creator God of the Bible is.

The modernist has a doctrine of god. His god is not the sovereign God of the Bible, the Creator and Sustainer of everything there is. His god is the god of Kant: hidden in the noumenal realm—the realm of mystical, non-rational encounter between god and man—and never revealing himself as the master of history. He is a god who does not bring final judgment, either, for he is not sovereign. He is not the predestinating God of John Calvin and Martin Luther.[70]

2. The Not-So-Authoritative Bible

Having considered Briggs' view of sovereignty, we come to the question of authority. The Bible is the sole source of final authority in history, the Reformers had insisted: *sola Scriptura*. Briggs' task in *Whither?* was to prove that his view of the Bible was consistent with the Reformers' view and with the Westminster Confession. He did not cite the Reformers or the Confession on the question of the infallible authority of the Bible. Had he done so, he might have forfeited his illegitimate authority as a Calvinist theologian. He did cite Charles Hodge, A. A. Hodge, and Warfield to prove that they had not discovered a source of authority for the canon of Scripture. He concluded: "The inspiration, the canonicity, and the authority of the Bible depends, therefore, upon the results of the Higher Criticism."[71]

Briggs on the Reformation

The heart of higher criticism's thesis is that men wrote the Bible: fallible men. The heart of Princeton's defense was the insistence that these men were not fallible in their capacity as God's living vessels when writing the texts of Scripture. Briggs did not challenge the Princeton view directly in *Whither?*; instead, he deflected any consideration of the Princetonians' argument by referring to the Reformers. He assured his readers that the Reformers were not anxious about the fact of human authorship.[72] "The great Reformers found no difficulty

---

70. Martin Luther, *The Bondage of the Will*, translated by J. I. Packer and O. R. Johnston (London: James Clarke, [1525] 1957).
71. Briggs, *Whither?*, p. 84.
72. *Ibid.*, p. 87.

in recognizing anonymous and pseudonymous writings in the canon of Scripture."⁷³

He provided no evidence for this statement except for a footnote reference to another book by Briggs published in 1883, *Biblical Study*.⁷⁴ In that book, he had written: "How the reformers would have met these questions [regarding higher criticism] we may infer from their freedom with regard to traditional views in the few cases in which they expressed themselves."⁷⁵ He cited Luther's rejection of the Epistle of James—not an example to persuade Calvinists.⁷⁶ He cited Calvin's denial of Paul's authorship of the Epistle to the Hebrews—not an earth-shaking discovery, since the epistle does not say who wrote it.⁷⁷ He cited Calvin's belief that someone besides David edited Psalms. "These questions of authorship and date troubled the reformers but little; . . ."⁷⁸ He then moved to the Westminster Confession. "The Confession does not define the human authors and dates of the various writings."⁷⁹ This should not come as a shock, since the Westminster Confession merely lists the canonical books by name without comment (I:2). There is nothing else in *Biblical Study* on the subject of the Reformers' view of higher criticism, yet this is what Briggs presumably expected his readers to accept as evidence of the legitimacy of higher criticism. This was a thin thread to hang from, rather like the spider in Jonathan Edwards' sermon.

The Reformers did not have to deal with higher criticism. The Westminster Assembly was not aware of such speculation, either. So, whatever they thought about the human authorship of the Bible, they did not assume that the texts were fallible. But because the Confession did not specifically deny the fundamental thesis of higher criticism—deny it in advance of its academic development—Briggs felt safe in saying that the Confession does not challenge higher criticism. The

---

73. *Ibid.*, p. 88.
74. *Ibid.*
75. Briggs, *Biblical Study*, p. 165.
76. *Ibid.*
77. *Ibid.*, p. 166.
78. *Ibid.*
79. *Ibid.*, p. 167.

silence of the Confession regarding higher criticism was, in Briggs' logic, the judicial equivalent of its acceptance of higher criticism.

Not only did Briggs offer comparatively few examples of the Reformers' supposed acceptance of fallible portions of the Bible, the evidence was completely against him. But nobody called his bluff on this point during his lifetime. Reu's comprehensive book, *Luther and the Scripture*, did not appear until 1944. Woodbridge's detailed refutation of Rogers and McKim—and, by extension, of Briggs—did not appear until 1982. The historical evidence leaves no room for honest doubt: the Princetonians' defense of biblical inerrancy was no new doctrine, but an extension of what the Church had held from the beginning. Briggs and his successors were unwilling to admit what in fact was the case, namely, that by virtually all the historical evidence, their position on higher criticism had been opposed throughout the history of the Church.[80] They have refused to say forthrightly what the historical evidence reveals: they are, at the very least, heretical. They have never been confident enough to announce, as representatives of Queer Nation have announced: "We're here. We're queer. Get used to it." They have been closet heretics (or worse) seeking tenure or its equivalent.

The Original Texts

The defenders of biblical inerrancy had to appeal to the original texts of Scripture because all existing texts are copies, and faithful copies have retained errors that had been introduced by earlier copyists. The originals were called *autographs* by the Princetonians. Princetonians defended the perfection of these missing texts.[81] Contrary to Briggs, Sandeen, Rogers, and McKim, the strategy of the Princetonians was not unique to them; others had taken the same position earlier in nineteenth-century America.[82] The Princetonians could hardly appeal to the continuing infallibility of copyists—infallibility equal to the original word of God given to the prophets. Infallibility was a one-

---

80. Woodbridge, *Biblical Authority, op. cit.*
81. Charles Hodge, *Systematic Theology*, 3 vols. (Grand Rapids, Michigan: Eerdmans, [1871]), I:151–82. Patton wrote a defense of the position in the year of the reunion: *The Inspiration of the Scriptures* (Philadelphia: Presbyterian Board of Publication, 1869).
82. Woodbridge, *Biblical Authority*, pp. 122–28.

time event per text. There were also practical considerations. As Noll says, "If the Bible contained errors of fact in history, science, or the accounts of its literary origins, it could not be relied upon to describe the relationships between God and humanity, or the way of salvation, or the finality of divine law."[83]

The higher critics scoff at all this: the only texts that we have are copies. We cannot improve on them. We must use them. We must defend them. The modernists adopted a rhetorical device: identifying the conservatives' appeal to missing texts as an assault on *the* Bible, *our* Bible, the Bible filled with errors. Their conclusion: men no longer need to take literally the Bible's presentation of the relationships between God and humanity, the way of salvation, or the finality of divine law.

In this regard, Briggs adopted another tactic that was basic to the Presbyterian modernists' strategy: *strict adherence to the language of the Confession, whenever convenient.* He argued that the Westminster Confession does not contain a specific statement defending the verbal, plenary inspiration of the Bible, i.e., inerrancy of the original manuscripts (the autographs). The Confession speaks of inspiration, but not *verbal* inspiration. It does not mention inerrancy.[84] Such ideas are "extra-confessional, substituting false doctrines for the real faith of the Church...."[85]

We do not have the originals, he said, and we never will.[86] We know that the existing texts contain errors. "The presumption, therefore, in regard to errors in the best texts, is that they were also in the original documents. It is sheer assumption to claim that the original documents were inerrant."[87] The Reformers "did not hold to the inerrancy of the original autographs."[88] He cited Samuel Rutherford, but the citation says only that the documents we now have are imperfect.[89] He cited Richard Baxter, and the citation does indicate that Baxter temporized: "The Scripture is like a man's body, where some parts

---

83. Noll, *Between Faith and Criticism*, p. 23.
84. *Ibid.*, pp. 63–64.
85. *Ibid.*, p. 64.
86. *Ibid.*, p. 68.
87. *Ibid.*
88. *Ibid.*, p. 69.
89. *Ibid.*, p. 70.

are but for the preservation of the rest, and may be maimed without death: . . ."[90] But one analogy from one seventeenth-century Puritan who did not attend the Westminster Assembly and who later served as Charles II's chaplain is surely not proof.

Briggs' Judicial Strategy

What Briggs' appeal to the Confession's silence proves is that confessions do need periodic revisions in order to meet new battles that earlier generations did not recognize. Briggs also proved that by imposing the strict terms of the Confession, courts could not prove categorically that the Confession taught the Princetonians' concept of inerrancy. The judges would have to determine, as Briggs said they should determine, what is consistent with the underlying theology of the Confession, and what is not.

Briggs' judicial strategy throughout *Whither?* was to argue that any change in doctrine since 1647 constitutes a formal breaking of the Presbyterian Church's Constitution. Had the argument been accepted by the denomination, it would have opened the door for every shade of opinion, closing the door to all heresy trials prior to a full-scale revision of the Confession—in all likelihood, a political impossibility. Here was the primary institutional goal of *Whither?*: to remove the threat of heresy trials. Briggs did not succeed in his own case, but after 1900, there were no further successful heresy trials in the Presbyterian Church, U.S.A.[91]

He then went on the offensive, as if to scare away any critic, namely, any theologian at Princeton. His contempt was visible: "If he find any comfort in verbal inspiration and the inerrancy of the Scriptures, we have no desire to disturb him, provided he hold these errors as private opinions and do not seek to impose them upon others. But fidelity to the truth requires that we should state that they are not only extra-confessional, but that they are contrary to truth and fact, and that they are broken reeds that will surely fail any one who leans

---

90. *Ibid.*, p. 71. The citation is from *The Catechising of Families* (1683), p. 36.
91. San Francisco Theological Seminary professor Thomas Day was asked by the California Presbytery to resign in 1911, which he did. The case never went to trial. Clarence B. Day, "The Thomas Day Heresy Case in the Synod of California," *Journal of Presbyterian History*, 46 (June 1968).

upon them, and that they are therefore positively dangerous to the faith of ministry and people."[92] In short, there is no legitimate basis for imposing negative ecclesiastical sanctions against higher critics. Anyone who would attempt to do this is a person spreading ideas that are "positively dangerous to the faith of ministry and people." These theologians have mixed "wood, hay, straw, and stubble with the fine gold, as the standard of orthodoxy, and have presumed to set it up as a bulwark against the vast and profound discoveries of modern science."[93] "They are the true successors of the Pharisees. . . . Such pretended orthodoxy is real heterodoxy."[94] If this is irenic, then *Mein Kampf* is an etiquette manual.

So, once again, we are confronted with the reality of Briggs' confession. He was claiming to be a representative of the orthodox wing in the denomination; the Princetonians were the true heretics. He did not use the dreaded H word: *heresy*. He used *heterodoxy* instead. But Briggs' polemics make it clear in retrospect: orthodoxy is an inescapable concept. It is never a question of orthodoxy vs. no orthodoxy. There is only the question: *Whose* orthodoxy? What was orthodoxy for Briggs? "It is meek, lowly, and reverent. It is full of charity and love."[95] And anyone who disagreed with this was obviously full of wood, hay, straw, and stubble, irenically speaking.

3. Evolution

The modern evolutionist teaches that there are two areas governed by the processes of evolution: natural (impersonal) and historical (personal). These correspond to the two idols of man: nature and history. Nature evolves, we are assured, and man's institutions also evolve. Therefore, human law evolves. This means ethics. Here is the underlying message of all evolutionist philosophies: *the denial of God's immutable law*. The covenant-breaker seeks to break the chains of God's immutable, Bible-revealed law. If this cannot be done, the covenant-breaker faces God's eternal negative sanctions. *Escaping God's final*

---

92. Briggs, *Whither?*, p. 90.
93. *Ibid.*, p. 14.
94. *Ibid.*, p. 15.
95. *Ibid.*, p. 7.

judgment is the number-one goal—rarely admitted—of every evolutionist system, whether humanistic or theistic.

Briggs was an evolutionist. He adopted a two-part strategy to prove his case: first, defend the idea of evolution in nature by an appeal to science; second, apply evolution to human thought and institutions, meaning law. For the first 104 pages of *Whither?*, Briggs presented himself as a defender of the Westminster standards. On page 105, he dropped his mask. He came to the foundational doctrine of his religion: *the doctrine of origins*. From pages 105 to 107, he dealt with the doctrine of creation. He refused to compromise in any way. He did not mince words. He did not guard his rhetoric. He openly rejected the Confession's teaching. "The doctrine of creation has changed greatly since the Confession was composed. All the profound discoveries of modern science in geology, astronomy, chemistry, biology, and archaeology, have opened up new problems that were not in the minds of the Westminster divines. Accordingly, there are many different views on this subject now existing in the Presbyterian Church."[96]

He was correct on all points. Only one theologian, Charles Hodge, had publicly rejected Darwinism as atheism, in his book, *What Is Darwinism?* (1874), published 15 years after *Origin of Species* and three years after *Descent of Man*.[97] No other major Presbyterian theologian had joined him. None of that generation ever did.

Rev. James McCosh, president of the College of New Jersey (1868–88), was a theistic evolutionist. Yet Charles Hodge was the senior trustee at the College when it hired him; he preached the welcoming sermon.[98] Francis Patton agreed with McCosh on this point. He succeeded McCosh as president (1888–1902), and became president of Princeton Seminary in 1902. Also in the McCosh camp were War-

---

96. *Ibid.*, p. 105.

97. See Joseph E. Illick, III, "The Reception of Darwinism at the Theological Seminary and the College at Princeton, New Jersey, I," *Journal of Presbyterian History*, 38 (1960), pp. 152–65.

98. J. David Hoeveler, Jr., *James McCosh and the Scottish Intellectual Tradition: from Glasgow to Princeton* (Princeton, New Jersey: Princeton University Press, 1981), p. 230.

field, A. A. Hodge, and W. G. T. Shedd, who taught systematic theology at Union.[99] Princeton had capitulated on the crucial doctrine of origins.[100] Darwin's extended time scale met little resistance from American evangelicals.[101]

McCosh had greatly influenced Henry van Dyke, Class of 1872, who went on to become the incarnation of the liberal movement in the Presbyterian Church. He was convinced that McCosh's evolutionary outlook could become the basis for a new philosophical defense of the faith.[102] He was correct, but the faith so defended was no longer that of the Westminster Confession, or even the Apostles' Creed. This is why he became a loyal defender of Briggs and an advocate of Confessional revision.

Briggs had to challenge the Confession, for on this point, it is not silent. It specifies a six-day creation (IV:1). He felt safe, however. The six days of creation specified by the Confession are no longer subscribed to by most Presbyterian scholars, he said. "The doctrine of development has the field. . . ."[103] On this point, Briggs was confident that he would not be challenged by the Princetonians. Briggs then escalated his argument. A higher authority than the Confession has spoken: modern science. "Modern science takes exception to the 'six days' and 'made of nothing' in their connections in this definition and in their historical interpretation."[104] He moved from the discarded authority of the Confession to a new source of authority, modern science. No matter what the Princetonians said, had it not been for

---

99. Gary Scott Smith, *The Seeds of Secularization: Calvinism, Culture, and Pluralism in America, 1870–1915* (Grand Rapids, Michigan: Christian University Press, a subsidiary of William B. Eerdmans, 1985), p. 98.

100. Deryl F. Johnson, The Attitudes of the Princeton Theologians Toward Darwinism and Evolution from 1859–1929 (Ph.D. dissertation, University of Iowa, 1968).

101. David N. Livingstone, "B. B. Warfield, the Theory of Evolution and Early Fundamentalism," *Evangelical Quarterly*, 58 (Jan. 1986); Livingstone, *Darwin's Forgotten Defenders: The Encounter between Evangelical Theology and Evolutionary Thought* (Grand Rapids, Michigan: Eerdmans, 1987).

102. Tertius van Dyke, *Henry van Dyke: A Biography* (New York: Harper & Bros., 1935), p. 37.

103. Briggs, *Whither?*, p. 105.

104. *Ibid.*

modern science—not just Darwinism—Christians would still side with Augustine, rejecting as ridiculous any suggestion that the world is much over 6,000 years old.[105] Briggs knew it, and they probably did, too.

He correctly linked two doctrines: the six-day creation and *creatio ex nihilo*. He wanted to destroy men's faith in both doctrines. He believed that if the conclusion of nineteenth-century science (and Aristotle's science)[106] is ever accepted by Christianity—that there was never a time when emptiness preceded matter—then the Confession's doctrine of God's creation of the world out of nothing (III:1) will end. Briggs correctly observed, regarding the eternality of matter, that "the Confession leaves no room for this opinion. . . ."[107] Furthermore, "It is now conceded by many Biblical scholars"—he named none—"that the Old Testament does not teach creation out of nothing, and that the Westminster divines misinterpreted the first chapter of Genesis when they found that doctrine there."[108] The logic of his argument is clear: the Confession is wrong regarding creation—not just the six-day creation, but creation out of nothing.

How could Briggs evade the charge of having abandoned Presbyterianism? Two ways: (1) nobody in a position of influence in the orthodox camp believed in the Confession's statement on six-day creation; (2) the link between the doctrine of the six-day creation and the doctrine of creation out of nothing. Anyone who refused to affirm the first doctrine was in no position to affirm the second. It is illogical to cite the Confession's authority on one issue while rejecting its authority on the other. Briggs was safe.

He did not write all this explicitly. Instead, he relied on rhetoric to defend his theology. This time, it was two-stage rhetoric: the rhetoric of a personal challenge and his familiar rhetoric of deception. His rhetorical device was to leave two things unsaid but implied. First, an implied challenge: since the Princetonians had given up the six-day creation, they could say nothing about Briggs' failure to accept the

---

105. Augustine, *The City of God*, XVIII:40.
106. Aristotle, *Physics*, VIII.
107. Briggs, *Whither?*, p. 106.
108. *Ibid.*

Confession's standard. He was therefore willing to risk taking the second rhetorical step, although he never expressly stated what he was arguing: he implicitly tied the six-day creation (abandoned by Princeton) to the doctrine of creation out of nothing (still the linchpin of the Princetonian's view of the absolute sovereignty of God and His providential decree). He rejected the second doctrine by rejecting the first. Who would challenge him in a denominational court? Since no Princeton theologian except Charles Hodge had publicly attacked Darwin, and Hodge was dead, who would be willing and able to challenge Briggs' rejection of *creatio ex nihilo*? Briggs threw down this challenge: "It is impossible at present to hold Presbyterian ministers and professors to the exact statements of this Westminster definition."[109]

2. The Evolution of Man

His section on "The Doctrine of Man" follows "creation," as well it should. He rejected the Westminster Confession's statement on original sin. "The Westminster divines did not sufficiently appreciate the ethical development of mankind . . . they left little room for the doctrine of the development of sin."[110] This sounds safe: he was not denying original sin exactly; he was accentuating progressive sin, the covenant-breaker's equivalent of the covenant-keeper's progressive sanctification. But by appealing to progressive evil, Briggs was implicitly dropping two correlative doctrines: man's original (definitive) sin and God's final judgment of sin.

Bear in mind: *the ultimate objective of evolutionist systems is to refute the existence of God's immutable law, thereby negating the threat of final judgment.* On the next page, Briggs wrote: "It is not so easy as it used to be to think that for any act of sin, however small its importance, relatively speaking, the sinner must suffer hell-fire forever, unless redeemed by the grace of God."[111] He was careful not to mention James 2:10: "For whosoever shall keep the whole law, and yet offend in one point, he is guilty of all." So, he concluded, "The Westminster

---

109. *Ibid.*
110. *Ibid.*, p. 108.
111. *Ibid.*, p. 109.

Standards leave this field of the doctrine of sin entirely unworked. Modern German theology has made great progress in this direction, but this progress has not been shared in by British and American dogmaticians."[112] (It must have been comforting in 1889 to know how much progress German theology had made in explaining away original sin. It was less comforting from 1933 to 1945.)

Without a doctrine of creation out of nothing, there can be no Christian concept of permanently binding revealed law. Without a sovereign Creator God to establish and reveal permanent laws, all laws become subject to change. As he insisted, "The doctrine of development has the field. . . ."[113] *Process theology replaces judicial theology.* Briggs struck decisively at what was unquestionably the soft underbelly of Princeton's theology: its abandonment of the Confession's doctrine of the six-day creation, without which it becomes very difficult—I would say impossible—to defend the Confession's doctrine of creation out of nothing except on a modern, post-Heisenberg basis.[114] This left the process god of modernism as the manager of nature, not the Bible's sovereign Creator and Sustainer.

Modernism reduces all law to process. In modernist theology, man no longer faces a sovereign Creator who lays down the law. He faces instead a merciful co-worker in the creative process. Side by side, they battle the realm of nature—mechanistic, yet somehow organic; mathematically constrained, yet evolving—in order to establish their mutual freedom. Together they can develop situation ethics. The only final judgment, if any, is the mutually experienced heat death of the universe.[115]

4. Escaping Final Negative Sanctions

Toward the end of *Whither?*, Briggs revealed his deep repugnance to the Bible's doctrine of hell. Protestantism, he said, "has so pressed

---

112. *Ibid.*
113. *Ibid.*, p. 105.
114. I have in mind physicist Alan Guth's "inflation" theory of the Big Bang: the possibility of random creation out of nothing. See Gary North, *Is the World Running Down? Crisis in the Christian Worldview* (Tyler, Texas: Institute for Christian Economics, 1988), p. 22.
115. *Ibid.*, ch. 2.

the awfulness of the doctrine of the eternal damnation of the heathen world, exceeding the Christian world by hundreds of millions, that the older doctrine of the damnation of all heathen has been abandoned, and efforts have been made to find some mode of relief by which some or many of the heathen may be saved by the grace of God."[116] He adopted the passive voice as a rhetorical device. The older doctrine of hell has been abandoned. *By whom?* Efforts have been made to find some mode of relief. *By whom?* What is obvious from his single sentence is this: he and other Presbyterian modernists had already abandoned the doctrine of final judgment. They had not yet come up with a Confessionally acceptable justification for their switch.

Why such concern by modernists over the details of Presbyterian theology? If the modernists had already abandoned the doctrine of hell, why didn't they just leave the Presbyterian Church and join the Unitarians? Because they wanted the vast benefits of Presbyterian Church membership and seminary leadership. *They wanted the inheritance, despite their confessional status as the disowned sons of God.* They were concerned about theology only to the extent that they were concerned about Church discipline and God's final discipline. Briggs had already made up his mind about hell. What he needed was a way to sell the conservatives on a creedally acceptable rejection of hell, so that he and his colleagues could remain in the denomination, converting others to the old heresy of universal salvation, or near-universalism.

The Damnation of Infants

The longest section of *Whither?* that deals with the Westminster Confession discusses one of the most obscure doctrines of the Confession. Briggs' section is titled, "Damnation of Infants." He devoted over 16 pages to this topic. There was a reason for his allocation of space.

The Confession teaches that elect infants go to heaven: Chapter X, *Effectual Calling* (Sec. 3). The Assembly believed that the infants

---

116. Briggs, *Whither?*, p. 286.

born to non-Christians are damned from birth unless specially regenerated. If they die as infants, they perish eternally. One commissioner, Anthony Burgess, had written a book in which he stated that "many thousand thousands of pagan-infants are damned. . . ."[117] The third committee reporting to the Assembly had originally selected the phrase "elect of infants," not "elect infants."[118] Briggs reprinted lengthy passages from the Westminster Assembly's commissioners to prove that they believed this doctrine (pp. 122-32).

Why bother? Because Briggs had spotted a weakness in the Princetonians' position, from Archibald Alexander to his own day. The Princetonians had succumbed to popular opinion: *all* infants go to heaven. Therefore, to make this opinion fit the Confession, they had to conclude that *all infants are elect*. In 1869, A. A Hodge wrote: "It is not intended to suggest that there are any infants not elect. . . . [W]e have good reason to believe that *all* infants are elected."[119] He did not offer this "good reason"; he surely did not refer to Esau in the womb, condemned by God as hated. The Bible says that some unborn infants are hated by God, while others are loved by God. The examples are Jacob and Esau, both in the same womb (Rom. 9:10-13). God hated Esau from the beginning, before Esau had done good or evil.[120]

Briggs quoted several passages from their writings to this effect. Then he responded: "The Presbyterian churches have departed from their standards on this question, and it is simple honesty to acknowledge it."[121] He was quite correct on both scores: the Presbyterian Church had departed, and the Princetonians should have acknowledged it. But if they were to acknowledge this now, Briggs imagined, he would have them trapped again.

---

117. *Ibid.*, p. 122.
118. *Ibid.*
119. A. A. Hodge, *The Confession of Faith* (Edinburgh: Banner of Truth Trust, [1869], 1992), pp. 174-75.
120. This amazes modern man, including most modern Christians. But the astounding theological fact is that God loved Jacob from the beginning, despite original sin.
121. Briggs, *Whither?*, p. 135.

The fact is, if Christians believe that God has surely elected all infants, then their only "guaranteed effective" evangelism programs would be abortion and infanticide (prior to a hypothetical and indeterminate "age of accountability"). This would get every slain infant into heaven, something no theologian or Christian—even the most radical postmillennialist—ever expects to happen with every adult. So, if the chief goal of the Church is to get people saved—the standard view of the modern, pietistic, man-centered Church—then infanticide and abortion are the most appropriate methods of attaining this goal, *if* all infants are saved by grace. It was this very argument that undermined the position of Union Seminary's professor Shedd. He adopted the view that all infants are elect; only at some later age do they become accountable. One of his students asked him in the classroom if that made Herod one of the great benefactors of his day, since he killed so many small children, guaranteeing their salvation. According to Shedd's successor, liberal theologian William Adams Brown, this question divided the class. The smaller group followed Shedd's "uncompromising Calvinism, while the majority made up their minds that theology was an impossible subject and turned eagerly to the studies which were offered them in other classrooms."[122] (This, of course, is pure rhetoric; seminary students, like all students, rarely turn eagerly to studies in any classroom.) On the other hand, if all infants go to hell, what becomes of covenantal promises to Christians regarding their children? Does infant baptism promise only negative sanctions? What a grim doctrine that would be![123]

Briggs had a method to his madness. The Confession also includes in the "elect infant" category "all other elect persons who are uncapable of being outwardly called by the ministry of the Word" (X:3). This seems a covenantally reasonable conclusion from the "elect infants" premise: the God of grace in history makes certain allowances. His grace is, after all, *free* grace. But these unique and specified exceptions were vital to Briggs' theory of final judgment. He wanted to

---

122. William Adams Brown, *A Teacher and His Times: A Story of Two Worlds* (New York: Charles Scribner's Sons, 1940), p. 77.

123. The Church formally adopted the "all infants are elect" view in the revision of 1903 (X:3).

include virtually everyone else in history *and beyond history*. Many pages later, he got to the point: "If the divine grace may be applied to the millions of infants dying daily, why not millions of adult heathen?"[124] He left it as a question, but he added that it "must be answered before there can be any comfort or stability in modern theology."[125]

The Middle [Intermediate] State

There is another important question: What about life after death? What about the so-called "middle state"? Can adult heathens be converted to saving faith in Jesus Christ after their individual deaths? To get the question answered, Briggs insisted—no, *demanded*—that the Church should guarantee liberals a kind of safe-passage certificate: "The middle state must be opened up in the discussions that are in progress. There must be the fullest liberty in this debate."[126] After all, the conservatives had already abandoned the Confession's unstated implication that non-elect infants go straight to hell. "Those who claim to be conservatives in their departures from the Confession have no right to censure those who recognize themselves as progressives."[127] Then he decided to drive home his point as offensively as possible: "In some respects the conservatives are the greater sinners."[128] Here it is again: "All theologians are equally sinful, but some are more sinful than others: the conservatives."

He argued that beyond the grave, covenant-breakers get to reassess the claims of the gospel. Only at the final judgment will they run out of time to reassess and be saved. He took this theological approach: affirming the doctrine of the Christian's progressive sanctification, he extended it to heathen who die as heathens. "Sanctification is a work that is carried on by God in a gradual process until perfect holiness has been attained by man."[129] This process applies to covenant-break-

---

124. Briggs, *Whither?*, p. 221.
125. *Ibid.*
126. *Ibid.*, p. 222.
127. *Ibid.*
128. *Ibid.*
129. *Ibid.*, p. 147.

ers, too, he insisted, for the Confession "does not say that man is made perfect at the moment of death. The progress in sanctification goes on after death in the middle state, until it is perfected there, and man is prepared for the final judgment."[130]

What does the Larger Catechism say? "They who, having never heard the gospel, know not Jesus Christ, and believe him not, cannot be saved, be they never so diligent to frame their lives according to the light of nature, or the laws of that religion which they profess; neither is their salvation in any other, but in Christ alone, who is the Saviour only of his body the church" (Answer 60). Is there hope for those who die out of God's covenant? The Larger Catechism says: "Whereas the souls of the wicked are at their death cast into hell, where they remain in torments and utter darkness, and their bodies kept in their graves, as in their prisons, till the resurrection and judgment of the great day" (Answer 86b).

Briggs expected the denomination to allow him and his fellow-universalists to debate this openly without threat of the negative sanction of de-frocking. Well, why not? Since he had abandoned the Bible's doctrine of hell in the name of Presbyterian orthodoxy, why should he be punished in a Church court? If God will not bring negative sanctions against heathens after their death, why should the Presbyterian Church bring negative sanctions against liberals on seminary faculties?

One year after the third edition of the book was published, in the aftermath of his 1891 Inaugural Address, Briggs was asked by Union Seminary's Board to defend himself regarding his view of the intermediate state. The Board asked: "Do you believe that the issues of this life are final and that a man who dies impenitent will have no further opportunity of salvation?" Briggs answered: "Yes."[131] That is to say, *Briggs lied.* This was the problem with Briggs. When he was caught, he lied. It did not matter what he had written; a lie might get him off

---

130. *Ibid.*
131. Max Gray Rogers, "Charles Augustus Briggs: Heresy at Union," in *American Religious Heretics: Formal and Informal Trials*, edited by George H. Shriver (Nashville, Tennessee: Abingdon, 1966), p. 102. See also G. L. Prentiss, *The Union Theological Seminary in the City of New York: Its Design and another Decade of its History* (Asbury Park, New Jersey: Pennypacker, 1899), p. 544.

the hook, so he lied. Situation ethics was Briggs' ethics; he was an evolutionist. He was determined to remain in good standing with the denomination in order to continue its subversion. Union Seminary cooperated with him. Even after he was de-frocked in 1893, he remained on the Union faculty.

The problem with the conservatives and even the Old School was that they thought the best of Briggs' motives. When it came to heresy in general, they were ready to do battle, but when it came to individuals, they had to guard their tongues. It would have been regarded as slanderous for them to say that Briggs was a liar. He was a wolf in sheep's clothing, but the Old School could not or would not say this. They were trapped by standards of etiquette and also by the fact that they had jointly published his essays. In a critical review in Warfield's scholarly journal, Talbot W. Chalmers insisted: "But he [Briggs] has said nothing that has not been said before, only in previous cases it was said by those who were outside the evangelical pale."[132] The Old School's problem was that Briggs had said much of it first in *The Presbyterian Review*. The Princeton co-editors had refused to veto any of Briggs' essays until Warfield did in 1889.

Chalmers also cooed over Briggs' good faith: "No one who has any personal acquaintance with the author of this Inaugural Address will for one moment doubt his entire sincerity and good faith."[133] On the contrary, Briggs was sincerely attached to bad faith, which matched his bad theology.[134]

---

132. Talbot W. Chalmers, "The Inaugural Address of Professor Briggs," *Presbyterian and Reformed Review*, 2 (1891), p. 498.

133. *Ibid.*

134. Yes, I know: my saying such a thing in print is considered bad form in academic circles, which is one reason why Christianity's orthodox academic representatives always seem to lose their battles: we are not allowed to call a spade a spade. Our opponents hold us to tight rhetorical standards when they review our books; then they indulge in slander and rhetorical misrepresentation when they write about us. As an example, consider Westminster Seminary graduate and theological defector Edward J. Carnell's description of fundamentalism: "*Fundamentalism is orthodoxy gone cultic.*" Carnell, *The Case for Orthodox Theology* (Philadelphia: Westminster Press, 1959), p. 113. Or this, regarding fundamentalism's ideological thinking. "Ideological thinking is rigid, intolerant, and doctrinaire; it sees principles everywhere, and all principles come in clear tones of white and black; it exempts itself from the limits that original sin places on his-

Schaff: Defender of Briggs' Views

Also on the Union faculty was Philip Schaff, who four decades earlier had taught the same doctrine of the intermediate state that had trapped Briggs, forcing Briggs to lie. Like Briggs, Schaff also renounced this view when he was tried in 1846 by his denomination, the German Reformed Church. He renounced it on the grounds that the Bible does not tell us enough about the intermediate state to make a sure judgment one way or the other.[135] In other words, he retracted his view on the grounds that no one can say what happens to a sinner's soul immediately after he dies, especially those conservatives who believe in hell. Schaff insisted that "the whole subject of the Middle State of the heathen, and of infants universally is involved in great obscurity, nor can ever be made properly the subject of doctrinal and symbolical teaching."[136] With this theologically feeble defense, he was able to escape conviction, but he was still speculating in the classroom about the intermediate state in 1859-60.[137] By then, such speculation was safe; after 1847, there was never again a heresy trial in that denomination.[138]

Schaff formally resigned from the faculty at Mercersberg in 1865.[139] He joined the Union faculty in 1870.[140] He literally sat at Briggs' side throughout the trials.[141] He defended Briggs with the same argument that Briggs had used to defended his views in *Whither?*: on the grounds that Briggs was in fact more orthodox that his critics.[142]

---

tory. . ." (p. 114). This book was published by the publishing arm of the Presbyterian Church, U.S.A. Carnell's words were quoted as sociologically authoritative in a doctoral dissertation written to show that Machen and his colleagues were given to rhetorical excess. Delwyn G. Nykamp, A Presbyterian Power Struggle: A Critical History of Communication Strategies in the Struggle for Control of the Presbyterian Church, U.S.A., 1922-1926 (Ph.D. dissertation, Northwestern University, 1974), p. 73.

135. George H. Shriver, "Philip Schaff: Heresy at Mercersberg," Rogers, *American Religious Heretics*, p. 44.
136. Cited in *ibid.*, p. 45.
137. *Ibid.*, p. 46.
138. *Ibid.*, p. 47.
139. *Ibid.*, p. 49.
140. *Ibid.*, p. 50.
141. *Ibid.*
142. *Ibid.*

He had called for creedal revision in 1890. "The old Calvinism is fast dying out," he had announced. "We need a theology and a confession that will . . . prepare the way for the great work of the future—the reunion of Christendom in the Creed of Christ."[143] Schaff did not defend Briggs because he had become senile or merely because he believed in academic freedom; he defended Briggs because Briggs was an ecumenist.

Schaff rejected heresy trials in the name of Constitutional pluralism, both ecclesiastical and civil: "Heresy trials seem to be an anachronism in our age and country which allow the largest religious liberty consistent with public order and peace."[144] He cited the trial of Albert Barnes half a century earlier, who was cleared.[145] Conclusion in 1892: "This is not an opportune time to stop the legitimate progress of theological investigation and science." The Presbyterian Church "is orthodox and conservative enough, and can afford to be tolerant and liberal without running any risk."[146] In short, no further negative sanctions.

As for the doctrines of inerrancy and the original autographs of the Bible, "These are human fictions contradicted by undoubted facts, and make it impossible to defend the Bible against the objections of critics, historians, and scientists." Then he added the familiar phrase of every humanist-trained Christian academic who finds himself squirming as a certified professional under the pressure of biblical revelation: "It is not a manual of geology, or biology, or astronomy, or chronology, or history, or science."[147]

Schaff died in October, 1893. The circumstances of his death were like Machen's: on the road to defend his faith. "As if to illustrate the priority of ecumenism, he attended the World Parliament of Religions in Chicago, against medical advice, and spoke one last time about the

---

143. Philip Schaff, *Creed Revision in the Presbyterian Churches* (1890), cited in Loetscher, *Broadening Church*, p. 42.
144. Philip Schaff, "Other Heresy Trials and the Briggs Case," *Forum* (Jan. 1892), p. 621.
145. *Ibid.*, pp. 623-24.
146. *Ibid.*, p. 633.
147. *Ibid.*

reunion of Christendom which had shaped so many of his pursuits."[148]

5. Ecumenism

Here we come to the institutional bottom line. Here is the institutional heart, mind, and soul of modernism. (The theological heart, mind, and soul is the denial of hell; this is what gives modernists their confidence in pursuing the rest of their program. They share this theology of no eternal sanctions with humanists everywhere.) *Briggs was above all an ecumenist.* This idea had dominated his thought from the very beginning of his career.[149] His impulse had manifested itself publicly in 1884 with his call for all Presbyterian and Reformed denominations to unite in their foreign missions activities.[150] This theme—the need for ecumenical foreign missions—became the starting point for many discussions of ecumenism in the 1890's and beyond: ecumenism's wedge. In the case of the Rockefeller-sponsored Laymen's Inquiry of 1932 and its controversial report, *Re-Thinking Missions*, a battle over this thesis led to the final battle in the Presbyterian conflict.

Chapter 9 of *Whither?* is "Barriers." Barriers to what? Church union. These barriers were: the divine right of Church government,[151] subscription to elaborate creeds,[152] uniformity of worship,[153] and traditionalism.[154]

Briggs rejected any church hierarchy that possessed sanctions: "The first great barrier to Christian union is the theory of *submission to a central ecclesiastical authority claiming divine right of govern-*

---

148. "Schaff, Philip," *Dictionary of American Religious Biography*, edited by Henry Warden Bowden (Westport, Connecticut: Greenwood Press, 1977), p. 394.
149. Richard L. Christensen, "Charles Augustus Briggs: Critical Scholarship and the Unity of the Church," *American Presbyterians*, 69 (Fall 1991). Cf. Christensen, The Ecumenical Orthodoxy of Charles Augustus Briggs: Critical Scholarship in the Service of Church Unity (Th.D. dissertation, Union Theological Seminary, Richmond, Virginia, 1992).
150. *Ibid.*, p. 154.
151. Briggs, *Whither?*, p. 226.
152. *Ibid.*, p. 239.
153. *Ibid.*, p. 248.
154. *Ibid.*, p. 258.

ment."¹⁵⁵ Translated into his immediate concerns, he resented a General Assembly that could penetrate the protective judicial boundary of the New York Presbytery. But he could not very well say this. Instead, he used the rhetoric of deception to deflect his readers' focus: "This is the great sin of the Roman Catholic Church, . . ." What he wanted was congregationalism, for the pastor is the sole common denominator: "All Christian churches have pastors, and they cannot work without them. Here is the basis for union."[156] A pastor must be ordained by a bishop.[157] This is all the government the Church needs. Yet on the very next page, he abandoned the bishop. Not all churches accept bishops. All churches accept pastors. "Apart from this single church officer there is no agreement whatever."[158]

Then exactly where is the Church's judicial unity lodged? Briggs did not say. Not in this book. Not while he was still officially a Presbyterian. He was sure of only this: "The power of the General Assembly ought to be confined to a very few matters, and those of general interest, such as the Constitution of the church and its general work."[159] What about its role as the supreme court of the denomination? What about trying accused heretics? Silence. Rhetorical silence.

What about creeds? They are a hindrance. The "great verities of Protestantism" are "vastly more important than those particular doctrines that distinguish the Lutheran, Calvinistic, and Arminian systems."[160] But on what judicial or creedal basis should we limit ourselves to Protestantism? What about Roman Catholicism and Eastern Orthodoxy? With Rome, he said, there should at least be an alliance. "On all these practical questions of Christianity it is of the highest importance that the Roman Catholic Church and Protestant Churches should make an alliance."[161] He did not use the word "union."

---

155. *Ibid.*, p. 226.
156. *Ibid.*, p. 230.
157. *Ibid.*
158. *Ibid.*, p. 231.
159. *Ibid.*, p. 233.
160. *Ibid.*, p. 240.
161. *Ibid.*, p. 272.

Judicially, there was no question about his long-term vision: "The work of Christian Union"—notice that "Union" is capitalized—"is a work which begins in every family, and which rises in greater and greater sweeps of influence until it covers the nation and the Christian world and is absorbed in the innumerable company about the throne of God and the Lamb."[162]

The Rhetoric of Deception

In Chapter 10, "Thither," he spelled out his vision. His vision was worldwide ecumenism. To palm this off as Presbyterian orthodoxy, he returned to his rhetorical strategy of deception. First, he affirmed his commitment to an undefined something that he called "original Protestantism." Second, he rejected "Protestant scholasticism," meaning Presbyterian orthodoxy. "We have seen that there is a drift in modern Christianity away from the Standards of the Reformation and the Symbols of the 16th and 17th centuries; . . . We have also seen that the barriers between the denominations, erected chiefly in the 17th century, have been broken through, and to a large extent, broken down, and that the great spirit of Christian unity is moving over the troubled waters to bring peace and order out of the confusion and chaos of sects."[163] This rhetorical strategy rested on a deliberate misrepresentation: the identification of denominationalism—of "sectarianism"—with the seventeenth century ("Protestant scholasticism") rather than the era of the Reformation.

This he knew was a lie. Not to have known that the Reformation split the unity of Christendom and then produced the original break-up of Protestantism—Calvinist, Lutheran, and Anabaptist wings—well before 1535 would have made him an ignoramus. He knew also that his peers knew it was a lie. He had already admitted that the sixteenth century had been a century of creedal revision and extension when he adopted the traditional usage of theologians and spoke of the creeds as symbols.[164] These symbols are the Apostles' Creed and the Creeds of

---

162. *Ibid.*, p. 265.
163. *Ibid.*, p. 266.
164. On the use of the term "symbol," see "Symbol" and "Symbolical Books" in *Cyclopaedia of Biblical, Theological, and Ecclesiastical Literature*, edited by John

the Ecumenical Councils. There was no symbolical advance during the Middle Ages. The sixteenth and seventeenth centuries were centuries of great symbolical progress."[165] Then why did he resort to this obvious lie? Because this lie was basic to his strategy of subversion. It was a convenient lie, rhetorically speaking. If he could escape Church censures by means of this blatant misrepresentation of the past, this could then become the acknowledged precedent for the modernist takeover of the Presbyterian Church.

Briggs was confident about the ecclesiastical future. There will eventually be ecumenical union. This is guaranteed by the progress of science and reason. "The chief reasons of difference are imperfect knowledge and an indisposition to follow the truth sincerely and wholly without regard to consequences. A higher knowledge will remove the differences."[166] What we have to understand, he said, is that creeds do not define churches. "The symbols of the Churches do not define them. . . ."[167] Neither do majorities in Church courts define churches. "The faith of the church cannot be determined by majorities in ecclesiastical courts or by the dictation of ecclesiastical demagogues or of these little popes in different denominations."[168]

Briggs' rhetoric of deception was the irenical aspect of his frontal assault on the Old School and his end-run around the New School. He denied creedalism. He denied the legitimacy of Church courts. He therefore denied the legitimacy of negative Church sanctions. This was fundamental to the Presbyterian modernists' pre-1931 strategy. He had defended in print all five points of modernism. If he could get away with this kind of challenge to authority, then seemingly nothing would stand in the way of the modernists in their strategy of subversion. He did get away with it. But as Solomon warned, pride goeth before destruction. Briggs, as we shall see, did not take Solomon seriously.

M'Clintock and James Strong, 12 vols. (New York: Harper & Bros., 1879), X:65–68.
165. Briggs, *Whither?*, p. 19.
166. *Ibid.*, p. 276.
167. *Ibid.*
168. *Ibid.*

"What Will It Take to Provoke Them?"

Machen's critics in the 1920's and 1930's—as well as those liberal critics who have subsequently reviewed his role in the Presbyterian conflict—refer to his sharp rhetoric and uncharitable spirit. Yet Machen rarely named names or called specific opponents to account. Briggs did. Again and again, he identified and dismissed his opponents as not being true Presbyterians. Referring to Warfield and A. A. Hodge's views on the Bible's inspiration, he added: "Other scholars, wiser and greater than they, deny it and do not affirm it."[169] They are walking down "a path of error."[170] He dismissed "Dr. Hodge's private opinion" which "is not Presbyterian doctrine."[171] Hodge "changes the order of salvation in an Antinomian direction."[172] Here was a man whose theology constituted one long repudiation of the Calvinism of the Westminster Confession, especially its doctrine of final judgment, yet he saw fit to label his opponents as non-Confessional. And in 1889 and 1890, he got away with it.

Because of its confrontational rhetoric, as Christensen has argued, *Whither?* became an immediate best-seller, going through three printings in a year.[173] What was the response of the Presbyterian Church to *Whither?* A collective yawn. A theological and rhetorical frontal assault of this magnitude did not create a firestorm of protest, contrary to another recent observer.[174] Briggs, understandably, grew more confident. He was willing to take another step to escalate the confrontation. He would test the Old School once again.

A New Professorship

The opportunity for the next test came with his elevation at Union to a new professorship, an endowed chair in biblical theology, in 1890. He stated his views on the Bible once again in his Inaugural Address of January 20, 1891. The address was titled, "The Authority

---

169. *Ibid.*, pp. 64-65.
170. *Ibid.*, p. 86.
171. *Ibid.*, p. 95.
172. *Ibid.*, p. 139.
173. Christensen, "Briggs," *American Presbyterians, op. cit.*, p. 158.
174. Donald G. Dawe, "*Whither?*" *ibid.*, 66 (Winter 1988), p. 284.

240   CROSSED FINGERS

of Holy Scripture." In it, he presented his views regarding the higher criticism of the Bible.

The oddest thing about this address was that he had not originally intended to deliver it. He had intended to speak on biblical geography, but he was pressured to speak about higher criticism by the president of the Board of Directors, Charles Butler, who had donated the enormous sum of $100,000 to endow the new chair in Biblical Theology.[175] Butler was one of the original founders of the seminary in 1836, as well as a founder of New York University (50 years on its Council), and he was chairman of both boards until he died in 1897.[176] Briggs complied with his request. As he said later, Butler had told him that "under the circumstances forced upon us at this time, it was necessary to select a theme that would vindicate the seminary and myself in the matters under debate."[177] To speak of Union as being forced to do anything was hyperbole; Union was doing all of the forcing, and had been doing it for over a decade.

The Seminary's leaders may nevertheless have seen themselves as the victims of some growing though institutionally silent conspiracy; conspirators sometimes view themselves as victims. Jeschke writes: "A sense of crisis had been growing for some years among those responsible for the administration of the Seminary's affairs. For the most part, it was the result of the aggressive liberalism of Briggs's writings, and to a lesser degree of [Francis] Brown's, and the mounting feeling in the Church was that these men were dangerous." This was a strange feeling, given the fact that Briggs had yet to receive any meaningful opposition institutionally. Opposition was confined to book reviews in denominational magazines, where there were supporters as well as detractors. Jeschke continues: "The processes of change at Union had been accelerated during the decade of the 1880's under the same influences that were at work in other areas of American life affecting a

---

175. "Statement of Dr. Briggs," Prentiss, *Union*, p. 332. On the size of the donation, see Jeschke, Briggs Trial, p. 291. He cites the original published version of the Address: *The Edward Robinson Chair of Biblical Theology in the Union Theological Seminary, New York* (Union Theological Seminary, 1891), pp. 1-3.

176. Prentiss, "Biography of Charles Butler," *ibid.*, p. 502.

177. *Ibid.*, p. 332.

general cultural revolution."[178] Butler seems to have wanted Briggs to get it all into the open. Briggs was ready to do exactly that.

A New Level of Rhetoric

This time Briggs pulled no punches. His evolutionary premises were forthright. His rhetoric was masterful. This time, it was the rhetoric of direct confrontation: no pretended irenicism. No more Professor Nice Guy. He at last crossed over the boundaries of acceptable Presbyterian discourse. It had taken him since 1876 to do this, for the theological boundaries on all sides had kept moving outward.

One of the more rhetorically memorable passages in his address was his identification of the patriarchs as a bunch of felons. "The ancient worthies, Noah and Abraham, Jacob and Judah, David and Solomon, were in a low stage of moral advancement. Doubtless it is true, that we would not receive such men into our families, if they lived among us and did such things now as they did then. We might be obliged to send them to prison, lest they should defile the community with their example."[179]

He also spelled out in graphic detail the implications of the higher criticism of the Bible. His conservative critics could hardly misread his position this time.

> It may be regarded as the certain result of the science of the Higher Criticism that Moses did not write the Pentateuch or Job; Ezra did not write the Chronicles, Ezra, or Nehemiah; Jeremiah did not write the Kings or Lamentations; David did not write the Psalter, but only a few of the Psalms; Solomon did not write the Song of Songs or Ecclesiastes, and only a portion of the Proverbs; Isaiah did not write half of the book that bears his name. The great mass of the Old Testament was written by authors whose names or connection with their writings are lost in oblivion. If this is destroying the Bible, the Bible is destroyed already. But who tells us that these traditional names were the

---

178. Jeschke, Briggs Trial, p. 292.
179. Briggs, *The Authority of Holy Scripture: An Inaugural Address*, 2nd ed. (New York: Charles Scribner's Sons, 1891); reproduced in Briggs, *Inaugural Address and Defense, 1891/1893* (New York: Arno Press, 1972), p. 56.

authors of the Bible? The Bible itself? The creeds of the Church? Any reliable historical testimony? None of these! Pure, conjectural tradition! Nothing more! We are not prepared to build our faith for time and eternity upon such uncertainties as these. We desire to know whether the Bible came from God, and it is not of any great importance that we should know the names of those worthies chosen by God to mediate His revelation. It is possible that there is a providential purpose in the withholding of these names, in order that men might have no excuse for building on human authority, and so should be forced to resort to divine authority. It will ere long become clear to the Christian people that the Higher Criticism has rendered an inestimable service to this generation and to the generations to come. What has been destroyed has been the fallacies and conceits of theologians; the obstructions that have barred the way of literary men from the Bible. Higher Criticism has forced its way into the Bible itself and brought us face to face with the holy contents, so that we may see and know whether they are divine or not. Higher Criticism has not contravened any decision of any Christian council, or any creed of any Church, or any statement of Scripture itself.[180]

He continued: "I shall venture to affirm that, as far as I can see, there are errors in the Scripture that no one has been able to explain away; and the theory that they were not in the original text is sheer assumption, upon which no mind can rest with certainty." He rejected the doctrine of inerrancy. "It is a ghost of modern evangelicalism to frighten children."[181] To compare the orthodox party's concern over the critics' assertion of errors in the Bible with youthful fears of the bogeyman was rhetorically clever; it was also risky.

Then he went on the verbal offensive against traditionalists in the denomination. He invoked military imagery. "We have undermined the breastworks of traditionalism; let us blow them to atoms."[182] The battle has begun he said. It is a battle over inheritance. At stake are

---

180. *Ibid.*, pp. 33–34.
181. *Ibid.*, p. 35.
182. *Ibid.*, p. 41.

"the most sacred things of our religion. . . ." The "defenders of traditionalism" now confront "the critics, a victorious army, determined to capture all its sacred treasures and to enjoy its heavenly glories."[183]

What of creeds and theology? They are nothing compared to the love of God. "The love of God to the world is more important than all the systems devised by men. It will shine forever as the central sun of the universe, when all the creeds and theologies have been buried in the oblivion of the eternities."[184] In short, there are no fixed theological standards (point three of modernism's covenant theology), including the Westminster Confession. There will come a day, and now is (he thought), without negative sanctions (point four) against those ordained officers who reject the confessions of this world. "The old methods of building on selected texts and isolated passages, which you will find in all the creeds and in all the dogmatic systems, is about to pass away."[185] This sweeping rejection of proof texts obviously included the 1647 proof texts of the Westminster Confession.

He returned once again to his beloved doctrine of the Middle State: the period that each person will experience between his death and the final resurrection. He knew this sounded like the doctrine of purgatory, and he did not shrink from saying: "The Roman Catholic Church is firmer here. . . ."[186] He then dismissed the traditional Church doctrine that each man suffers God's judgment immediately after his death: a "bugbear."[187]

He went on: "Most of the ethical provisions of the Pentateuchal codes were of local and temporal validity. . . ."[188] On this point, there were many conservatives who agreed with him, although their rhetoric on this point was more subdued. But he would soon alienate even them with a defense of rationalism. "I rejoice at the age of Rationalism, with all its wonderful achievements in philosophy."[189] He ended

---

183. *Ibid.*
184. *Ibid.*, p. 49.
185. *Ibid.*, p. 62.
186. *Ibid.*, p. 54.
187. *Ibid.*
188. *Ibid.*, p. 58.
189. *Ibid.*, p. 66.

his lecture with a ringing call to action: "Criticism is at work with knife and fire. Let us cut down everything that is dead and harmful, every kind of dead orthodoxy, every species of effete ecclesiasticism, all merely formal morality, all those dry and brittle fences that constitute denominationalism, and are the barriers to Church Unity."[190]

At long last, Briggs' rhetoric had caught up with his theology. The burning fire came, but it was not the fire of higher criticism. It was a firestorm of outrage inside the Presbyterian Church, U.S.A. He finally woke up his critics.

Conclusion

What was remarkable about Briggs' career up until 1891 was his immunity from serious criticism. No matter how radical his language in his rejection of the Westminster standards, no one in the Presbyterian Church demanded a retraction. His forthright heretical statements were regarded as judicially inoffensive: "one man's views among many." He had long been persuaded that the Church in the broadest sense needed to abandon the judicial authority of its creeds and confessions, thereby jettisoning almost two millennia of theological and creedal development. In the name of growth, of sanctification, Briggs was ready to substitute a Darwinian evolutionary worldview for Church tradition. This frontal assault on the theological integrity of the Presbyterian Church received only academic responses, and not many of them. The academic Calvinists did not regard Briggs as a major threat. In the year Briggs died, Henry Preserved Smith went so far as to herald Briggs as a conservative,[191] and as late as 1987, a Dallas Seminary Th.D. dissertation described him as "broadly orthodox, affirming the historically fundamental doctrines of the faith against the onslaughts of liberalism."[192] This echoed the assessment of Smith, Handy, and Loetscher, who argued in 1963 that Briggs was "remark-

---

190. *Ibid.*, p. 67.
191. H. P. Smith, "Charles Augustus Briggs," *American Journal of Theology*, 17 (Oct. 1913), p. 497.
192. M. James Sawyer, Jr., Charles Augustus Briggs and the tensions in late nineteenth century American theology (Th.D. dissertation, Dallas Theological Seminary, 1987), Abstract, concluding words.

ably conservative" but had a "caustic style" which caused the reaction.[193] Briggs is still immune to serious criticism.

Charles Augustus Briggs, more than any Christian intellectual in American history, deserves to be called "underminer of the faith." He was the point man for modernism who devoted his entire career to persuading Christians that the Bible is untrustworthy and has always been untrustworthy, and that modern science is eminently trustworthy. He was the ultimate wolf in sheep's clothing, yet historians still see him as a wounded lamb even after he devoured half the flock. The only vaguely redeeming feature of his life of active, defiant subversion is that he later had serious doubts regarding the orthodoxy of those who served with him on Union's faculty after 1895. The convicted heretic was concerned over the public confessions of the unconvicted heretics he had trained.

Every member of Union's faculty was required to sign the following pledge regarding the Westminster Confession: "I do solemnly promise that I will not teach or inculcate anything which shall appear to me to be subversive of said system of doctrines, or the principles of said Form of Government, so long as I shall continue to be a Professor in the Seminary."[194] In 1904, the Seminary eliminated this requirement.[195] Its confession caught up with its practice. By 1890, Union Seminary was clearly involved in a sham: broken vows, crossed fingers, and subversion. But the denomination seemed powerless to do anything about it.

Briggs' career demonstrates that the Old School had become a spent force judicially by 1890. Its national leaders did not publicly demand a heresy trial for Briggs. Any such suggestion would have to come from others within the denomination. What this meant was that the Old School, short of an unexpected change within the Church, had lost its judicial salt. It could no longer serve as a barrier to the

---

193. H. Shelton Smith, Robert T. Handy, and Lefferts A. Loetscher, eds., *American Christianity: An Historical Interpretation with Representative Documents*, 2 vols. (New York: Charles Scribner's Sons, 1963), II:276.

194. Cited in Robert T. Handy, "Union Theological Seminary in New York and American Presbyterianism, 1836-1904," *American Presbyterians*, 66 (Summer 1988), p. 116.

195. *Ibid.*, p. 121.

spread of heresy outside the Princeton Seminary campus. Its members could no longer persuade the New School that a serious threat was posed by any given scholar or cleric. Such persuasion would have to come from outside the Old School. The initiator's rhetoric of confrontation—theological arguments clearly would not be sufficient—would have to trigger any organized resistance. Such rhetoric would have to be on an unprecedented scale, given Briggs' existing degree of immunity in 1890. So, he escalated his rhetoric once again. In 1891, he at last met a wall of resistance. It had taken a decade and a half. His rhetoric had finally roused the sleeping giant. The twin questions now would be: How roused and for how long? The crucial issue was sanctions.

5

THE LAST HERESY TRIALS, 1891–1900

The views propounded by Dr. Briggs in his Inaugural are not new. They have all been stated by him in one or another of his published works, in articles in the Presbyterian Review, during his ten years' editorship, and in more recent contributions to other periodicals. Moreover, for the past ten years, Dr. Briggs has been teaching Biblical Theology in the seminary, and has been expounding to successive classes of students the statements for which he is now arraigned. The present excitement is, as we believe, due, largely, to the tone of the Inaugural Address, to certain unguarded expressions, and to an impression that the transfer of the author to the Chair of Biblical Theology would be subject to the veto of the general Assembly.

So concluded the faculty of Union Theological Seminary in 1891, shortly after the General Assembly vetoed Charles Briggs' election to the newly created chair of Biblical Theology.[1] The faculty insisted that the decisive issue in the widespread outrage over Briggs' 1891 Inaugural Address had been his rhetoric—"unguarded expressions"—not higher criticism or biblical theology, the new academic 'subdiscipline built in terms of higher criticism. This line of reasoning rested on an unstated assumption: if the issue really had been theology, Briggs would have been formally charged with heresy at least a decade earlier, and possibly as early as 1876. The Inaugural Address had to be

---

1. "Statement of the Faculty of Union Theological Seminary," reprinted in G. L. Prentiss, *The Union Theological Seminary in the City of New York: Its Design and another Decade of its History* (Asbury Park, New Jersey: Pennypacker, 1899), pp. 545–46.

peripheral theologically, the faculty concluded. Half a century later, Briggs' former colleague, William Adams Brown, was still echoing this defense. "That a man who had been teaching theology for sixteen years, in one of the leading institutions of the Church, and whose orthodoxy had never been questioned, could have been tried and convicted of heresy, by the highest court of his Church, for continuing to teach what he had been teaching before, seems incredible."[2] This seems incredible only if you refuse to consider the importance of rhetoric. But, theologically speaking, Union had a good point. Briggs should have been tried for heresy in 1876. That his opponents had waited so long indicates that something more than theology was involved: an inability to impose negative sanctions.

Union Seminary's Judicial Challenge

The unstated implication of Union's announcement should have been obvious to all parties: Briggs' critics within the denomination should not bring formal charges against him *or anyone else* for heresy regarding the theological issues he had been discussing in print since 1876. If the evangelical New School members in the Presbyterian Church had agreed, this would have led to the judicial triumph of modernism in the Presbyterian Church, U.S.A., at least three decades early.

Institutionally speaking, the faculty's declaration was correct: for over a decade, Briggs had gotten away with Confessional murder—or at least attempted murder—without any threat to his ordination or his academic position. Analytically, the faculty's statement was also correct: it was the tone of the Inaugural Address that had initiated the response. This tone reflected an aggressive challenge to his opponents to do anything about it at this late date—the assumption of judicial immunity. Finally, the analysis was ecclesiastically correct: theology apart from institutional sanctions is institutionally peripheral.

The denomination's previous inaction regarding Briggs' published works on theology did seem to indicate that his theology was of no

---

2. William Adams Brown, *A Teacher and His Times: A Story of Two Worlds* (New York: Charles Scribner's Sons, 1940), p. 96.

concern judicially. The judicial question then became: Was Briggs' lecture still theologically peripheral in 1891, i.e., immune to judicial action? If so, then the failure of the denomination's courts to bring Briggs and his theological peers at Union (or anywhere else) to trial a decade or more earlier had granted them and their ideas a kind of permanent "king's x" within the denomination. The modernists announced: "You had your opportunity, and you missed it. You will never be allowed another opportunity. The statute of limitations is in force: your time is up." The Presbyterian modernists' defensive tactic after 1890 rested on the widespread acceptance of this argument within the churches generally. Briggs in his public defense appealed to just this line of reasoning. After 1900, this line of reasoning became universally accepted in Northern Presbyterianism, Methodism, and Episcopalianism. The statute of limitations was literally invoked by the court in 1935 to silence Machen during his trial.[3]

Lefferts Loetscher, a Briggs apologist in a later generation, admits that "Some of the language of the address was inexcusably careless.... His selection of Martineau, a Unitarian, as an illustration did gross injustice to his own extremely high view of the Person of Christ." (This, I think it is safe to say, is a very obscure detail to single out as a representative example of the rhetorical excesses of the Inaugural Address.) He then asks: "Why did he do it? Even Dr. Briggs's most intimate papers do not fully explain his motives—if indeed they were ever fully rationalized."[4]

Briggs' Motivation

There are at least three reasons why he did it. First, he had a particular view of his calling. He regarded his task as near-messianic, as his 1867 letter to his uncle indicated.[5] He saw himself as the point man for modernism within the Presbyterian Church, and, like Machen's representative role from January 1, 1924[6] to January 1, 1937

---

3. See Chapter 12, below: section on "Machen's Trial," pp. 734–39.
4. Lefferts A. Loetscher, *The Broadening Church: a study of theological issues in the presbyterian church since 1869* (Philadelphia: University of Pennsylvania Press, 1954), p. 51.
5. See the quotation at the beginning of Chapter 5.
6. See Chapter 8, below: section on "Machen Becomes a National Spokes-

for American fundamentalists, Briggs in 1891 had become the point man for modernism generally. It was his job as point man to test orthodoxy's will to resist, just as it later became Machen's job to test modernism's will to resist.

Second, men have a tendency to confess their true beliefs. Briggs' lecture was a highly concentrated polemic. It drew attention to what he had been teaching for many years. In effect, it announced to the world: "I have made it to the top, and I have done so by promoting all these ideas. I have beaten the ecclesiastical system." Personally speaking, this implicit announcement would soon prove premature. As events after 1900 would prove, he had beaten the system theologically, but not rhetorically.

Third was Briggs' career strategy: the upward ratchet. Every time he had escalated the ratchet of heresy, he had gotten away with it, beginning with his Inaugural Address in 1876. He had toyed ("Toyed") with the Old School since 1876 in much the way that Hitler would toy with the European powers, 1933–38. Easy successes made them both reckless. Briggs used his 1891 Inaugural Address as just one more upward move of the ratchet of heresy, but this time his rhetoric brought forth resistance. Massa summarizes the implications of the Address: it "announced to the culture at large that the shared religious world view upon which a continued united identity among evangelicals depended had indeed collapsed, and that the civil war was well in progress."[7]

He refused to stop. Even after he was charged with heresy, Briggs continued to escalate his rhetoric, a tactic that a recent defender says was "probably quite calculated. . . ."[8] If it was not calculated, Briggs should be regarded as one of the most naive leaders in Church history. Nothing else in his career suggests such naiveté. Briggs immediately wrote an article for the *North American Review*, a widely read national periodical. He confidently dismissed his opponents as those

---

man," subsection on "Van Dyke Strikes Again," pp. 505–508.

7. Mark Stephen Massa, S.J., *Charles Augustus Briggs and the Crisis of Historical Criticism* (Minneapolis, Minnesota: Fortress Press, 1990), p. 86.

8. William R. Hutchison, *The Modernist Impulse in American Protestantism* (Cambridge, Massachusetts: Harvard University Press, 1976), p. 94.

about to be crushed by the combined forces of modern life. "We stand at the heights of the last [note: he did not say "latest"] of the great movements of Christendom. . . . It must be evident to every thinking man [note: his intellectual opponents must not have been thinking men] that the traditional dogma has been battling against philosophy and science, history and every form of learning. . . . There can be little doubt but that the traditional dogma is doomed. Shall it be allowed to drag down into perdition with it the Bible and the Creeds?"[9] His opponents had offered in response only "castles in the air, schoolboys' bubbles. . . ."[10] These schoolboys included the two Hodges, Warfield, and Patton.

There may have been a more arrogant, confrontational man than Charles A. Briggs involved in the Presbyterian conflict, but if there was, his public rhetoric did not reveal the fact. Yet Massa, Briggs' most prominent biographer, refers to his "irenic efforts on the lecture platform"[11] and his casting of "a distinctly irenic light" on ecumenical issues.[12] Briggs had many public characteristics, but the ability to sustain irenicism for an entire essay was not among them. Massa later refers to Briggs' "bellicose personality" that "alienated people."[13] Massa should have written that Briggs repeatedly promised irenicism, but then failed to deliver on his promise. Massa also refers to the "stridency of Hodge and Warfield's arguments"[14] and the "ultraconservative cabal" that "seized control of the northern church. . . ."[15]

(Historiographical note: the Presbyterian conflict was part of a much wider ecclesiastical conflict. The spiritual heirs of the victors have written the academically baptized accounts of this conflict. What the liberals—I include Jesuit Massa—have done for over four decades in writing their lock-step accounts of the Presbyterian conflict is to

---

9. Briggs, "The Theological Crisis," *North American Review* (1891), pp. 101, 103. Cited in Massa, *Briggs*, p. 91.
10. "Theological Crisis," p. 114; *ibid.*, p. 92.
11. *Ibid.*, p. 117.
12. *Ibid.*
13. *Ibid.*, p. 123.
14. *Ibid.*, p. 61.
15. *Ibid.*, p. 119.

paint the victorious modernists as irenical, peaceful, and just plain jolly good fellows in search of a judicially fair deal. They have also labeled the conservatives as strident. This same mythology was part of the Presbyterian conflict itself. The historians are merely extending the received mythology into our own day.)

Reactions to the Inaugural Address

The religious press reported on the Inaugural Address. The press was hostile.[16] Many of the denomination's leaders were outraged. But the most amazing statement of all came from Auburn Seminary's Allen Macy Dulles, John Foster's father: he reproved Briggs for his "ambiguous attitude" and "vague teaching."[17] (In 1924, Professor Dulles gave his son advice on how to conduct the defense of that other rhetorical confrontationalist, Harry Emerson Fosdick.)[18]

Very few seminary professors immediately came to Briggs' defense. Those few who did speak out in favor of Briggs in 1891 found themselves outvoted. One of them, James A. Craig, adjunct professor of Hebrew at Lane Seminary, lost his job for his outspokenness. Edward L. Curtis spoke out at McCormick Seminary; the following May he left McCormick and succeeded William Rainey Harper at Yale,[19] who had departed to become president of the Rockefeller-funded University of Chicago.

By 1891, the modernists had representatives on Presbyterian seminary faculties. They had already provided a wedge for the institutional legitimacy of higher criticism. Once on a faculty, a higher critic could not easily be removed if he did not go into print or employ Briggs-level rhetoric. They would soon learn a lesson from Briggs' experience: keep your nose to the grindstone and your opinions out of print. Their continuing presence in Presbyterian seminaries would

---

16. Loetscher, *Broadening Church*, p. 52.
17. *Ibid.*
18. Chapter 10, below: section on "The 1924 General Assembly: Fosdick, Part II," subsection on "John Foster Dulles," pp. 552-57.
19. Channing Renwick Jeschke, The Briggs Case: The Focus of a Study in Nineteenth Century Presbyterian History (Ph.D. dissertation, University of Chicago, 1966), pp. 304-305.

make it operationally unlikely for presbyteries to be able to dam up a constant stream of indoctrinated graduates.

Union's conservative systematic theologian W. G. T. Shedd[20] sent a letter to the Board of Directors stating his total opposition to the Inaugural Address, saying that had he not retired from Union a year earlier, he would retire in protest now. This was a blow to the seminary, since the directors had been unable to secure a replacement for Shedd and had asked him to return.[21] (After the untimely deaths of his two named replacements in 1891, including Henry van Dyke's father, Shedd was replaced by modernist theologian William Adams Brown. No conservative would ever again hold the position.)

The Union Seminary faculty was split, although members did close ranks prior to the General Assembly of 1891. An iron law of all institutions—families, bureaucracies, and to a much lesser extent, profit-seeking enterprises—is this one: attacks from outsiders must be resisted, for any suggestion that someone inside the organization needs to be disciplined or removed is an implicit assault against the autonomy of the institution. In the case of a bureaucratic agency, such a criticism implies that the bureaucrats had made a mistake in the first place by refusing to screen out the deviant member, and also by refusing to remove him subsequently. Loetscher is correct: the issue was turf-protection. "If the seminary were to retain the power to decide its own future, it must close ranks before the Assembly of 1891."[22] The seminary could not admit what had been obvious to anyone who had bothered to read *Whither?*: Briggs was a heretic, and the seminary should have fired him in 1889. It really should have fired him in 1876. It hadn't; hence, the seminary had to form a circle with the wagons, with Briggs safely inside the circle. So would the New York Presbytery, for the same reasons.

The Seminary publicly demonstrated its commitment to Briggs by immediately publishing the Inaugural Address. This was in preparation for a fight at the Detroit General Assembly. It issued a second

---

20. Henry Warner Bowden, "W. G. T. Shedd and A. C. McGiffert on the Development of Church Doctrine," *Journal of Presbyterian History*, 49 (Fall 1971).

21. Jeschke, Briggs Case, p. 298.

22. Loetscher, *Broadening Church*, p. 53.

edition the following March. This edition was reprinted five times within three months, with a sixth in October, 1891, and a seventh in February, 1893.[23] The question was: Would the Seminary submit if the General Assembly vetoed Briggs' appointment to the chair in Biblical Theology?

The 1891 General Assembly: Detroit

Briggs must have known he was in trouble when the General Assembly elected Princeton's William Henry Green as Moderator. Massa describes the election as "carefully choreographed" by the confessionalists well ahead of time, although he offers no evidence.[24] After it ended, Union's president, Thomas Hastings, complained of a "Princeton conspiracy" to take revenge against *Whither?*[25] This was a self-serving rhetorical tactic: deliberately ignoring the magnitude of the entire conservative wing's outrage against the Inaugural Address. "It's only those narrow-minded, revengeful Princetonians. They're troublemakers!" For the next nine years, there would be a lot of troublemakers.

The Veto

One of the few gains that the Old School had made in the 1869 reunion was the right of the General Assembly to veto seminary professorships. The GA had to do this at the meeting following the appointment; if it failed to do so, the appointment stood (unless Machen was the nominee).[26] The Old School had always asserted this authority; the New School had not: its seminaries were legally independent. The New School seminaries consented in 1870 to come under this new control. At the 1891 General Assembly, the Standing Committee on Theological Seminaries unanimously voted to remove Briggs from his new professorship in Biblical Theology. This decision was accepted by the General Assembly, 449 to 60.[27] A negative sanction had at last been imposed on Briggs and Union Seminary. Or had it?

---

23. Jeschke, Briggs Case, p. 306.
24. Massa, *Briggs*, p. 95.
25. *Ibid.*, p. 96.
26. See Chapter 10, below.
27. *Ibid.*, p. 54.

The Standing Committee refused to state the reasons for recommending the veto. Francis Patton, its chairman, said that its reason for remaining silent was that there was going to be a trial in the Presbytery of New York, and the Committee did not want to appear prejudicial. Patton thereby shifted the terms of the debate from negative sanctions (heresy) to positive sanctions (approval). He asked the General Assembly to decide whether Briggs is "a man who you are ready to say ought to be sanctioned for a position of official theological teaching?"[28] The Committee, like the General Assembly, voted *no*, i.e., the members did not choose to sanction the appointment. The General Assembly voted to accept the Committee's report. So, the Church did not actually impose negative sanctions in the name of negative sanctions. It had merely refused to impose positive sanctions—a kind of suspended judgment regarding the theological content of Briggs' Inaugural Address. Its veto was defended in terms of a refusal to vote *yes*. This verbal tap-dancing around the judicial issue of heresy indicated that the Church still wanted to avoid an all-out confrontation with Briggs and Union Seminary.

Who Is Hounding Whom?

At this General Assembly, Dr. Bartlett, a graduate of Union Seminary, defended the veto of Briggs' appointment. He made one of the most rhetorically clever speeches ever recorded in the history of Presbyterianism. He called for negative sanctions: a veto on Briggs' appointment. The Presbyterian Church, he insisted, was not actively hounding a heretic; on the contrary, the heretic had been hounding the Church for a decade. This hound had to be silenced if the integrity of the Church was to be defended. Prentiss reprinted the speech in his book-long defense of Union Seminary.

> . . . Now, I say that any society has a right to have some defined rules, and after a Church has been pursued for more than ten years on this question, I say it is to be commended for longsuffering patience and for tender mercy and for quietness and peace. The implication has always been that there is heresy being

---

28. *Minutes of the General Assembly, 1891*, p. 97; cited in Jeschke, p. 308.

sought; that this is an age of thumbscrews and all that species of humbug. In this case it does not apply. Every Church is free, but the Church must be free enough to decide the question independently and fairly.

I like Professor Smith's dog story. It was a good one, and it reminded me of one that I will tell you. We had a bench show in Washington this winter and there were several $3,000 and $4,000 and I believe one $5,000 dog exhibited there. One day this $5,000 dog got out.[29] He was a rather ferocious fellow, though very expensive, and running down the street he seized one of my fellow-citizens in a convenient place in the back (laughter,) and his owner, who was chasing him, cried out to the citizen who had been seized: "Don't injure that dog, you might spoil him, and he is a very valuable dog"—and all the while the dog was gnawing away, and the poor man had the impression that he was not in any great danger of injuring the dog, but that the dog was in great danger of injuring him.

And so it is. We have been pursued and finally caught, and we wish for them to make the apology. Who has made this disturbance? Is it the Presbyterian Church, through spies and queer and double construction chasing a man down to convict him of heresy? The Church is forced to regard it, and we simply say: Let go. Let us alone. And if the time has come when you must go out from the beautiful land of Egypt under the repression of this awful Pharaoh—the Presbyterian Church—we say, go, and take all your intimate friends with you. (Laughter and applause.)[30]

Evading the Sanctions in 1891

Sanctions are an inescapable concept. It is never a question of "sanctions vs. no sanctions." It is always a question of *whose* sanctions. Who will impose them, in terms of which judicial standards? If the Old School could not get the New School to impose negative sanctions, then the modernists would eventually impose them on both

---

29. With gold at $20 per ounce in 1891, this was a 250-ounces dog. Valuable!
30. Prentiss, *Union Theological Seminary*, pp. 108–109. Paragraphs added.

wings. Charles Briggs in 1891 had at last forced the Presbyterian Church to consider this inescapable reality. It had taken a decade and a half of his escalating rhetoric to force this decision on the denomination. His deviant, anti-Confessional theology had been insufficient for the task; only his rhetoric had accomplished it. Yet even in 1891, the Church refused to impose negative sanctions officially; it merely refused to impose positive sanctions.

Would Union Seminary comply with the decision of the General Assembly? Would it remove Briggs from the chair in Biblical Theology? No. In June, the Board of Directors voted to keep Briggs in the position. The vote was 22 to 2.[31] G. L. Prentiss wrote an open letter, "To Whom It May Concern," which was published in the *New York Evangelist* (June 11, 1891). In it he chided Patton for his refusal to "strike a blow for justice, for sacred scholarship, for reasonable liberty, both of thought and teaching, and for the highest interests of Christian truth...."[32] The sacredness of scholarship had been substituted by modernists for the sacredness of the Bible.

In April, 1891, a committee of the New York Presbytery voted to try Briggs for heresy, but the presbytery dismissed the case that November, 94 to 39.[33] The presbytery then produced a document saying that it did not endorse his views, but he should be allowed to remain in the ministry.[34] In short, no further negative sanctions. Briggs received congratulatory notices from the following ecumenical modernists: Washington Gladden, A. C. McGiffert, W. Robertson Smith, C. H. Toy, William Rainey Harper,[35] and Newman Smyth.[36]

---

31. Jeschke, Briggs Case, p. 309.

32. Cited in *ibid.*, p. 311.

33. Loetscher, *Broadening Church*, p. 55. Jeschke devotes Chapter 8 of his dissertation to this trial, the 1892 General Assembly's decision to remit to the New York Presbytery, the second trial and acquittal, and the decision of the 1893 General Assembly to de-frock Briggs.

34. *Ibid.*, pp. 55–56.

35. On Harper's liberalism and great importance for higher education in America, see George M. Marsden, *The Soul of the American University: From Protestant Establishment to Established Non-Belief* (New York: Oxford University Press, 1994), ch. 14.

36. Massa, *Briggs*, p. 99.

The 1892 General Assembly: Portland, Oregon

The presbytery committee that had brought charges then appealed to the General Assembly in 1892. The General Assembly voted to require the New York Presbytery to try the case. The General Assembly's "Portland Deliverance" asserted: "Our Church holds that the inspired Word, as it came from God, is without error. The assertion of the contrary cannot but shake the confidence of the people in the sacred Books. All who enter office in our Church solemnly profess to receive them as the only infallible rule of faith and practice. If they change their belief on this point, Christian honor demands that they should withdraw from our ministry."[37]

An appeal to the Christian honor of the modernists in order to persuade them to withdraw was the height of naiveté. If the conservatives would not impose negative sanctions, why should modernists leave? What was the benefit of leaving? They would then have to fund their operations with money raised from their own supporters. They would no longer be able to get their hands on other people's money. That is always a chilling thought to minorities in any organization. For Progressives, however, it was more than a chilling thought: it was a denial of their religion.

The modernists were power religionists, willing to lie about the Bible, willing to lie about what they said about the Bible, willing to swear a judicially binding oath to a Confession they did not believe. There was only one effective way to deal with them: negative sanctions. This the General Assembly still vaguely understood in 1892; it did not a decade later. Opponents of the infallible Bible, the General Assembly said, "have no right to use the pulpit or the chair of the professor for the dissemination of their errors until they are dealt with by the slow process of discipline. But if they do so act, their Presbyteries should speedily interpose, and deal with them for violation of ordination vows."[38] Speeding up Presbyterian justice sounds

---

37. "Portland Deliverance," *The Presbyterian Enterprise: Sources of American Presbyterian History*, edited by Maurice W. Armstrong, Lefferts A. Loetscher, and Charles A. Anderson (Philadelphia: Westminster Press, 1956), p. 249.

38. *Ibid.*

easy to achieve, but it is not. Imposing Presbyterian Church sanctions is far more complex a matter than Warfield indicated in his summary of the 1892 Assembly: ". . . in judicial proceedings as well as in morals and mathematics, the shortest line between two points is usually the straight one."[39] Straight, yes, as in straight up the side of a cliff. The Old School had abandoned its grappling pegs and hooks in 1869, and had very few ropes.

The Deliverance announced: "They should withdraw from our ministry." A contextually judicial word, *should*. But attached to a legally binding *should* must be another pair of words: *or else*. Without them, *should* moves from the realm of law to the realm of suggestion. What was the General Assembly's threatened negative sanction against all presbyteries—New York's especially—that chose to ignore its warning? It mentioned none. The General Assembly was unwilling to threaten every ordained supporter of Briggs with removal from office.

The General Assembly could act as a court of final appeal, but it could not act as a legislative body. The 1892 General Assembly had no authority to bind the General Assembly of 1893 or any future General Assembly. The judicial character of any future Assembly would be decided by political mobilization: *votes*. A General Assembly possessed no legislative authority over the presbyteries; the presbyteries had not voted on this Deliverance. A two-thirds majority of the presbyteries was required to establish a new judicially binding theological position. Had the General Assembly submitted its Deliverance to the presbyteries in 1892 and received ratification in 1893, the character of the denomination might have been retained. Such was not to be.

Union Seminary's board voted in October, 1892, to renounce the 1870 agreement. It pulled out of the denomination. And nothing happened, except that the General Assembly announced that it would no longer be responsible for what was taught there.[40] In short, no further negative sanctions on Union. But what about Briggs?

---

39. Benjamin B. Warfield, "The One Hundred and Fourth General Assembly," *Presbyterian and Reformed Review*, 3 (1892), p. 531.

40. Loetscher, *Broadening Church*, p. 55.

Briggs' Second Defense in Presbytery

In mid-December, 1892, Briggs defended himself on the floor of the New York Presbytery. He defended the Inaugural: "No one has yet been able to show that any statement made in the Address is erroneous. When it is clear that I was wrong, I will confess it and retract—not before."[41] He never retracted a word, even after his defrocking in 1893.

He appealed to his writings, from his first Inaugural Address of 1876 to his lectures on "The Bible, the Church, and the Reason" in 1891. "My views of the Bible, of Biblical Theology, and of the Higher Criticism have remained unchanged in essence. They have become more mature. That is all."[42] This was not altogether accurate. The extent of his modernism in his published works became ever clearer and ever more radical over time. *Whither?* was far more radical theologically than *Biblical Study*; the 1891 Inaugural Address was more radical than *Whither?* He had been using his theological ratchet, escalating each successive deviation from orthodoxy. But claiming that there had been no significant theological change, 1876 vs. 1891, was a clever rhetorical device. If believed, it would have made his critics look like either slow-reacting dullards or arbitrary tyrants.

He insisted on his rights: "The defendant has not asked for toleration. He claims his rights under the constitution of his Church to teach anything and everything that he has ever taught."[43] In short, he argued, because the Church's courts had remained silent, 1876–90, they must remain silent now. The precedent had been set. Higher criticism is now beyond negative ecclesiastical sanctions.

He denied that the Adopting Act of 1729 requires subscription to every aspect of the Confession and catechisms.[44] He then moved from "not completely binding" to "not binding at all." Eleven pages later, he concluded: "It is doubtful, therefore, whether subscription to the

---

41. *The Defence of Professor Briggs Before the Presbytery of New York* (New York: Charles Scribner's Sons, 1893); reprinted in Briggs, *Inaugural Address and Defense, 1891/1893* (New York: Arno Press, 1972), p. xvii.
42. *Ibid.*, pp. xvii–xviii.
43. *Ibid.*, p. xviii.
44. *Ibid.*, p. 7.

Westminster Confession in any form is allowed by the Confession itself; and it may be argued with plausibility that subscription is against the doctrine of the three standards."[45] This was another instance of his familiar tactic of setting the Confession against the Confession. The Confession becomes a non-binding non-compact without negative sanctions; in fact, it was never intended to be the legal basis of a Church covenant. He treated the Confession as he treated the Bible: just another judicially impotent document. Modernism's situation ethics extends to the judicial foundations of the Church covenant. Then he added the ultimate insult to American Presbyterianism: "So thought the English Presbyterians. . . ."[46] Indeed they had, and by 1719, they had become a Unitarian denomination.

Briggs again appealed to his previous writings: his 1876 Inaugural, *Biblical Study*, and *Whither?* As a rhetorical *coup de grace*, he appealed to his 1883 essay on the authorship of the Pentateuch, published in *Presbyterian Review*. That journal had been co-published by Princeton Seminary, and everyone knew it. Yet, he said, his accusers were unwilling to refer to these earlier writings; they were prosecuting him only for the 1891 Inaugural. "If my Inaugural be heretical, all those other writings are still more heretical."[47] Here it was: an unstated challenge to the Princetonians to bring him to trial a decade after he had published his views in a journal for which Princeton was responsible. It was an unanswerable challenge. The General Assembly ignored it. He was condemned in 1893 only for his 1891 Inaugural.

"Not Guilty"

The New York Presbytery, in January of 1893, decided to clear Briggs, in spite of the hostility of the Church at large. Loetscher concluded from this that the decision showed a desire for "the subordination of unresolved theological differences to the necessities of cooperation for the successful prosecution of the church's work. It implied a shift in emphasis in the Calvinistic doctrine of the Church."[48] This

---

45. *Ibid.*, p. 18.
46. *Ibid.*
47. Briggs, *Defence*, p. 20.
48. Loetscher, *Broadening Church*, p. 59.

evaluation was correct concerning the New York Presbytery, but the 1893 General Assembly, to be held in New York City, had another opportunity to remove Briggs.

By upholding Briggs, the New York Presbytery announced publicly that from this point forward, there would be no escaping theological conflict within the denomination. This presbytery was going to become home base and a point of entry for modernists. One or the other side would win this denominational conflict. One side would have to persuade the other, or, barring persuasion, one or the other would eventually bring negative sanctions against the other.

The modernists could be reasonably sure that Briggs was going to be condemned by the 1893 General Assembly. The conservatives obviously had the votes. The question was: Could others affirm publicly what Briggs had affirmed and still escape the negative sanctions that faced Briggs? Put another way, was it Briggs' rhetoric that had brought him down or his theology? The modernists' strategy of subversion would hinge on the answer. Without a clear answer to this question, they could have no clear strategy. They had to have a clear answer. To get it, they began to test the conservatives' will to resist Briggs' theology even before the 1893 General Assembly met.

Van Dyke's Test

Henry van Dyke was a member of the New York Presbytery. He was pastor of the Brick Church. He openly supported Briggs. Prior to the 1893 General Assembly, in January, he had preached a sermon, *The Bible As It Is*. He professed contentment with his own ignorance. He professed contentment with the existing Bible. He pleaded for an end to meaningless controversy and a return to practical religion.[49] There must be an end to heresy trials.[50] As for the theory of inerrancy of the original autographs, it constituted a new test of orthodoxy, yet it is contrary to the Confession. The Confession speaks of the equality of today's Bible and the originals.[51] The theory is incapable of proof; the autographs do not exist. But, tolerant liberal that he was,

---

49. Henry van Dyke, *The Bible As It Is* (New York: Session, 1893), pp. 9–13.
50. *Ibid.*, p. 17.
51. *Ibid.*, p. 24.

he condescendingly wrote that "we ought to be patient in toleration of the Inerrancy theory, as a private opinion, even though it is unconfessional."[52] But as a test of orthodoxy, the theory is unconstitutional.[53]

Van Dyke then issued a challenge. This challenge was to serve from then on as the moral justification of the modernists' decision to remain within the Church. The Portland Deliverance had spoken of the need for Christian honor: the liberals should leave. Van Dyke countered: "It is our duty not to withdraw from the Presbyterian Church. Christian honor requires us to remain."[54]

To achieve this goal, he recommended a strategy of peace and quiet: "It is our duty to study to be quiet and to mind our own business." In short, no negative sanctions. He understood that Briggs' rhetoric of confrontation had unleashed the forces of conservatism, which threatened the liberals' takeover of the denomination. This rhetorical excess should not happen again. "Let us speak carefully, kindly, considerately. Let us beware of the fatal adjectives. . . ."[55] This became the new rhetorical strategy for the Presbyterian liberals, 1893 to 1922. (Thirty years later, on December 31, 1923, he issued to the press an incomparably vitriolic attack on Machen. This act constituted his formal abandonment of his 1893 strategy.) Meanwhile, liberals must appeal to the Church's Constitution and the rights thereof.[56]

Van Dyke called a meeting of others who agreed with him. On February 17, he released a statement to this effect, *A Plea for Peace and Work*, signed by 235 ministers.[57] It defended "plain Christianity," and argued that theological controversy would hinder the work of the Church. It claimed that a majority in the Church wanted only peace and work. It closed with an appeal to Christian liberty, peace, unity, and missions. In short, no further negative sanctions.[58]

---

52. *Ibid.*, p. 25.
53. *Ibid.*, p. 26.
54. *Ibid.*, p. 29.
55. *Ibid.*, pp. 29-30.
56. *Ibid.*, p. 30.
57. *Presbyterian Enterprise*, p. 254.
58. Van Dyke's long ministry, more than any other, was the incarnation of

Van Dyke, who would become the most notable literary stylist in the Presbyterian Church, was already a master of rhetoric. He was also a master of deception. In 1891, he had appropriated the language of conservatism to describe the platform of modernism. He re-defined orthodoxy as freedom from institutional sanctions. "Liberty first. And why? Because without liberty there is no true orthodoxy. A man cannot be taught to believe and think right without liberty. Orthodoxy must flourish in an air of freedom. . . . That is the position of a conservative."[59] This became a familiar claim of modernists regarding true orthodoxy: a system of belief devoid of negative sanctions . . . until 1934.

The 1893 General Assembly: Washington, D.C.

The General Assembly suspended Briggs from the ministry, overturning the presbytery's action. The vote was 295 (to sustain the whole of the prosecutors' case), 84 (partial support), to 116 (opposed).[60] The GA also reaffirmed its previous year's declaration on inerrancy.[61] Only the New York Presbytery voted not to retry.[62] But the General Assembly brought no sanctions against Union Seminary. It did not revoke Union's authority to train Presbyterian ministers. The Assembly declared: ". . . the Assembly disavows all responsibility for the teaching of Union Seminary. . . ."[63] The New York Presbytery would remain free to ordain graduates from Union. In short, no further negative sanctions.

Presbyterian modernism in the years of the Presbyterian conflict. It illustrates the formal commitment of liberals to a Church without negative sanctions until such time as they might gain full administrative control. He died in 1933, just as the liberals were restructuring the Church's machinery in order to bring formal sanctions against the Calvinists who opposed the takeover. Their primary target was Machen. It is one of those ironies of history that van Dyke was related to Machen; he was known to the family as Uncle Henry.

59. Cited in Tertius van Dyke, *Henry Van Dyke* (New York: Harper & Bros., 1935), p. 129.
60. Massa, *Briggs*, p. 108.
61. Loetscher, *Broadening Church*, p. 61.
62. *Ibid.*, p. 60.
63. Jeschke, Briggs Case, p. 353.

Double Jeopardy

In his defense before the 1893 General Assembly, Briggs had raised the issue of double jeopardy. He said that the General Assembly had no authority to reverse the "not guilty" decision of the New York Presbytery.[64] Had he persuaded the General Assembly on this point, this would have overturned traditional Presbyterianism. Final ecclesiastical authority would thereby have been transferred back to the presbytery in every case in which the presbytery cleared a man. This would have made the presbytery the legal equivalent of a jury under common law, as well as the ordaining executive. It would have fused executive and judicial authority in one institution: the presbytery. It would have broken Presbyterianism's chain of appellate courts. It would have transformed the denomination into a hybrid of Congregationalism and Presbyterianism. (This subsequently took place, 1927–1933.)[65] By refusing to honor Briggs' argument, the General Assembly maintained the traditional hierarchical appeals court structure of Presbyterianism. This meant that a presbytery could not automatically serve as an entry point for heresy for as long as the General Assemblies of the Church continued to convict heretics.

The General Assembly ignored Briggs' argument. The crucial institutional question then became: Would future General Assemblies maintain the traditional Presbyterian structure by continuing to allow appeals from minorities within presbyteries that had formally cleared heretics, and continue to de-frock those cleared by these presbyteries?[66] Would the Briggs case become a legally binding judicial precedent in the Church's courts? That is, would future General Assemblies *predictably* hand down decisions against those who preached what Briggs had preached in 1891? The future of the Church would depend on the answer to this question.

---

64. *Ibid.*, p. 349.

65. See Chapter 10, below: section on "The 1927 General Assembly," subsection on "No More Heresy Trials," pp. 611–14.

66. The practical question regarding appeals from outside the offending presbytery never arose from a case within Northern Presbyterianism. The soft judicial underbelly of traditional Presbyterianism would remain soft: a unanimous presbytery would remain autonomous.

Theories or Judicial Standards?

During the 1893 General Assembly, 87 men presented a signed protest. They took Henry van Dyke's line. The protest rejected the General Assembly's assertion of the infallibility of the Bible in its original form, referring to this doctrinal position as "a certain theory of inspiration." (This word—*theory*—would be used again in 1923 in the Auburn *Affirmation* to dismiss the virgin birth of Christ.) The protest denied that the Westminster Confession asserts any such theory. The signers defended their position as being the truly conservative one. The theory of inerrancy is not reverent regarding the Bible "Because it is disparaging the Bible we have, and endangering its authority under pressure of a prevalent hostile criticism."[67] Notice the familiar modernist assertion: the "real critics" of the Bible are the Princetonians, not the modernists, for the Princetonians criticize the post-autograph texts as being imperfect. This rhetorical tactic was used throughout the modernist controversy: painting the orthodox party as the heretics and the higher critics as defenders of the biblical text.

The 87 protesters publicly took Briggs' position on higher criticism, but not one of them was ever brought to trial for having signed this protest. This inaction of the General Assembly and the presbyteries to which the signers belonged meant that the Briggs trial was an incident rather than a judicial precedent. The Briggs case did not become a judicially representative case. Eighty-seven men who agreed with Briggs, but whose rhetoric was subdued, got away with it. They learned an important lesson: "If you keep your rhetoric subdued, you can occupy your pulpit." Without the threat of negative judicial sanctions, capturing the denomination was just a matter of time and organization, which the modernists knew they had and the Old School did not. The 87 had tested the conservatives' will to resist judicially. There was not much will remaining. After 1900, there would be less.

Smith and McGiffert

In subsequent years, two other ordained Presbyterian ministers, both seminary professors, were brought to trial for heresy. One was

---

67. "Eighty-Seven Protest Inerrancy," *Presbyterian Enterprise*, p. 250. *Minutes of the General Assembly, 1893*, pp. 167–68.

convicted by his presbytery, and his conviction was upheld by the General Assembly. The other was cleared by the New York Presbytery. The case was appealed by a critic within the presbytery, but the accused resigned before the General Assembly could try the case.

Smith

Henry Preserved Smith had become a higher critic during the time of the *Presbyterian Review* series. He had written one of the more controversial articles in the series. Like Briggs, he had studied in Germany: Berlin (1872–74) and Leipzig (1876–77). He had been professor of Old Testament at Lane Seminary since his return from Leipzig.[68] He and another faculty member, L. J. Evans, immediately backed Briggs' 1891 inaugural in their own 1891 address, *Biblical Scholarship and Inspiration*.[69] Smith's presbytery brought charges against him. He was tried in late 1892, and he was convicted of heresy. He was ordered not to preach or teach his views. But the Lane Seminary trustees voted in 1893 not to accept his resignation and to keep him on the faculty.[70] The faculty member who had originally complained about Smith had his chair cancelled at the same meeting.[71] In short, *no further negative sanctions against modernists, but sanctions against those who criticize them*. This was to be the experience of Machen and the conservatives, beginning with the reorganization of Princeton Seminary in 1929.

The General Assembly of 1893 protested both acts of the seminary. The seminary's trustees backed down and accepted Smith's resignation, but they sent a protest to the General Assembly for having interfered.[72] Academic turf was going to be defended, at least verbally.

Smith appealed his conviction to his Synod, lost, and then appealed to the General Assembly. He lost there, too, in 1894. The issue

---

68. "Smith, Henry Preserved," *Dictionary of American Religious Biography*, edited by Henry Warden Bowden (Westport, Connecticut: Greenwood Press, 1977), p. 410.
69. Loetscher, *Broadening Church*, p. 63.
70. *Ibid.*, p. 65.
71. *Ibid.*, p. 66.
72. *Ibid.*

was inerrancy, and Smith lost. For one last time, negative sanctions were successfully applied to a Presbyterian modernist.

Smith went on to publish several books on Old Testament higher criticism. He became a professor of Old Testament at Amherst College, his alma mater. Later, he taught at Meadville Seminary, and he ended his career as a professor and librarian at Union Seminary. In 1926, the year after he retired and the year before he died, his last book appeared: *The Heretic's Defense*. It was a fitting year: in 1926, the liberals visibly took over the Presbyterian Church.

McGiffert

Arthur Cushman McGiffert was a Church historian. He studied at Berlin (1885-86) and received his Ph.D. from Marburg University (1888). He taught at Lane and had been a strong supporter of Smith. He was not tried by his presbytery. He accepted a chair in Church history at Union after leaving Lane in 1893. In 1897, his book appeared, *A History of Christianity in the Apostolic Age*. The book led to a complaint at the 1898 General Assembly. This resulted in a heresy trial. The New York Presbytery condemned some parts of the book, but it refused to bring sanctions against him. One elder, the clerk of the presbytery, then filed charges against him. The presbytery declined to act. The elder appealed to the General Assembly in 1900. The outcome appeared obvious: McGiffert would lose the case. He quietly asked to resign from the denomination. This request was granted. The man who filed charges then dropped them with the acceptance of the General Assembly.[73]

McGiffert served as President of Union from 1917-1926.[74] He was a dedicated modernist. He was also the most accomplished Presbyterian defender of historicism's worldview. His biographer comments:

> One basic hypothesis found in most of his works was that historical change makes religious teachings relative to differing circumstances. Late in life he came to the point of saying there was no continuing essence or variation on common themes in

---

73. *Ibid.*, pp. 71-74.
74. "McGiffert, Arthur Cushman," *Dictionary of American Religious Biography*, pp. 271-72.

Christian history at all. No creed or doctrinal formulation remains in force very long because changed conditions bring about new questions which men should be free to answer as they are led. He also gave historical backing to the widespread view that religion consists primarily of experiences which deal meaningfully with contemporary problems. Blended with that pragmatic approach to spiritual affirmation were definitions of Jesus as an exemplar of human virtue and thoughts of salvation as a social rather than a personal process.[75]

This was not only historicism, it was the theological creed of modernism in the Progressive era: no definitive revelation by God in history, no authoritative creeds, evolutionary process, experientialism, Jesus as a moral example, and social salvation rather than personal.

What the historians of the Presbyterian conflict rarely mention is the truly astounding fact that Briggs, in the midst of McGiffert's heresy trial maneuvering, decided to complain to the Union Seminary Board about McGiffert's doctrinal irregularities. The president of Union, Francis Brown (co-author of Brown-Driver-Briggs), appealed to him not to do this, and Briggs relented, but he did not change his mind about McGiffert. Briggs had taught McGiffert. Massa says that this reflects "Briggs' growing personal fears about the evangelical integrity of his intellectual children."[76] It was King Canute all over again: "Thus far, and no farther!" Nevertheless, the tide of modernism rolled in, covering Union Seminary and the Protestant Establishment which Union served. It has yet to roll out.

The Will to Resist

The Presbyterian system is based on both creed and court. To prosecute a Presbyterian heresy trial successfully takes a great deal of research, careful theological argumentation, lots of time, the ability to pay no attention to increasingly vocal opposition against "needless bickering," and the overcoming of normal institutional inertia. This price was regarded as too high by the denomination after 1900. The

---

75. *Ibid.*, p. 272.
76. Massa, *Briggs*, p. 151.

denomination's leaders refused to admit publicly that views hostile to the judicial integrity of Scripture and hostile also to the reliability of the Confession are not random opinions, that such opinions are part of another religion—a religion at war with Christianity. It matters little whether "warm Christian" evangelists held such opinions or "cold academic rationalists." These views have predictable and disastrous consequences for the Church. The Presbyterian Church's leadership after 1900 rejected perhaps the most fundamental fact of civilization, namely, that ideas have consequences. They have consequences because men attach sanctions to them. The leadership rejected the idea that negative sanctions are worth the effort in order to defend positive ideas. They refused to acknowledge the connection between Presbyterian law and God's cosmic model: hell.

Briggs, Smith, and McGiffert had tested the will of the Church to resist. They had met resistance. With Briggs' and Smith's de-frocking and the departure from the denomination by McGiffert, the modernists adopted a new strategy: patience. There would be no further rhetorical confrontations until Harry Emerson Fosdick launched a new phase of the battle in 1922.

The Woodrow Case

This case was representative of the Church at large in the final decades of the nineteenth century: a war between conservatives and liberals which was won officially by the conservatives but in fact was lost by them. The details of this case reveal how long it took to convict an evolutionist, how divided opinion was, and how negative sanctions had no effect.

In the Southern Presbyterian Church, James Woodrow (1828–1907) was dismissed from South Carolina's Columbia Seminary in 1888 for teaching evolution.[77] Woodrow had received his Ph.D. from Heidelberg University, *summa cum laude*. When he returned to teach at Oglethorpe University in Atlanta in 1856, he became the first

---

77. James Woodrow, "Evolution" (1884), in *Darwinism and the American Intellectual: A Book of Readings*, edited by R. J. Wilson (Homewood, Illinois: Dorsey, 1967), pp. 58–70.

The Last Heresy Trials, 1891–1900 271

teacher in Georgia's history to hold the Ph.D.[78] Church historian Winthrop Hudson comments on his de-frocking: "A placid and undisturbed orthodoxy continued to prevail throughout the South as a whole."[79] The Woodrow case was more complex than this.

Woodrow had remained silent on the subject of evolution until he published in 1873 an attack on Robert Dabney's *Assaults on Physical Science*. Dabney had attacked Darwin and Huxley. Such critical opinions, Woodrow insisted, would produce infidelity.[80] It was the same old line: anti-Darwinism leads to infidelity. No charges were brought against Woodrow at this time, but it was obvious where he was headed.

He ceased writing on the topic for over a decade, although he was asked repeatedly to write on it.[81] By 1884, the board of Columbia Seminary was having doubts about his orthodoxy on this point. It asked him to state his views. He responded in a paper: the Bible is not a textbook of science, and its inconsistencies with science did not undermine its authority regarding religious truth. Evolution speaks only of the mode of creation; it is not in conflict with creation. God created man's body through evolutionary processes.[82] The board voted eight to three to support him.[83] The three formally protested. In the fall of 1884, the issue began to be debated in presbyteries.[84]

The Committee on Theological Seminaries of the South Carolina Synod cleared him. Two members objected.[85] The debate on the floor lasted five days. One professor, C. R. Hemphill, reminded the synod that there was a time when a majority of Christians believed in a six-day creation and Noah's flood. No longer, he said; he was correct

---

78. Allen P. Tankersley, *College Life at Old Oglethorpe* (Athens: University of Georgia Press, 1951), p. 39.
79. Winthrop S. Hudson, *Religion in America* (New York: Charles Scribner's Sons, 1965), p. 281.
80. Ernest Trice Thompson, *Presbyterians in the South*, 3 vols. (Richmond, Virginia: John Knox Press, 1973), I:458.
81. *Ibid.*, II:460.
82. *Ibid.*, I:462–63.
83. *Ibid.*, II:468.
84. *Ibid.*, II:470.
85. *Ibid.*, II:471.

with respect to Presbyterians. But the synod voted, 50 to 45, not to allow the teaching of evolution at the seminary.[86] Then it unanimously expressed its support for Woodrow.[87] This kind of dialecticism was typical of the era; the courts had difficulty making up their collective minds.

The Seminary's Board was soon replaced; the new board was antievolution. It invited Woodrow to offer reasons why he should not be dismissed. He refused. The Board then fired him. The debate in the denomination's press went on.[88] The Church's press was strongly opposed to him, except for the journal he owned (*The Southern Presbyterian*) and one other.[89] Thompson summarizes: "None of those who publicly defended Dr. Woodrow announced himself as an evolutionist, but they apparently agreed with Dr. John B. Adger, who denounced as intolerable [Columbia Seminary professor] Dr. Girardeau's view that a theological professor was not free in his classrooms to inculcate views contrary to the Standards of the church."[90]

He still refused to resign.[91] The Synod of South Carolina agreed with him, by a vote of 82 to 50, and denounced the Board's action as unconstitutional. The synods of South Georgia and Florida agreed. The Synod of Georgia, under whose jurisdiction his presbytery (Augusta) operated, agreed with the Board. The Board reaffirmed its decision: please resign, it said. This was in December, 1885.[92] He refused. He had already asked his presbytery to try him.[93] He was acquitted in a preliminary hearing in 1886. This decision was appealed by a member of the presbytery's court to the General Assembly. A formal presbytery trial was scheduled to take place after the General Assembly met in 1886.[94]

---

86. *Ibid.*, II:473.
87. *Ibid.*, II:473–74.
88. *Ibid.*, II:475.
89. *Ibid.*, II:477.
90. *Ibid.*, II:478–79.
91. *Ibid.*, II:476.
92. *Ibid.*, II:479.
93. *Ibid.*, II:476.
94. *Ibid.*, II:480.

Debate at the General Assembly took five days.[95] The Assembly voted 137 to 13 to reject his views. Then followed three more days of debate and another rejection.[96] At his subsequent trial by his presbytery, he was cleared. The presbytery then formally protested the Assembly's decision against him. But the Synod of Georgia backed the Seminary, 56 to eight, and instructed the Board of the Seminary to call for his resignation. It sustained the 1885 complaint against the Augusta Presbytery. So, Woodrow announced that he would appeal the case back to the General Assembly. The Synod of South Carolina then informed Woodrow that it believed he should resign. Would he do so? He replied by telegram: no, I won't.[97]

Meanwhile, the confusion had so disrupted the Seminary that it had suspended operations for the academic year, 1886-87.[98]

His appeal to the General Assembly against the Synod of Georgia was not sustained in 1888. God made man directly from the dust of the ground, the General Assembly announced.[99] Then Columbia Seminary fired him—no letter of resignation needed. This had taken four years.

The story was not over. Woodrow then requested a transfer to the Charleston, South Carolina, Presbytery, where he was also teaching at the University of South Carolina. Charleston refused to accept him. The General Assembly decided in 1889, contrary to its own rules (Paragraph 277), to allow him to remain a member in good standing of the Augusta Presbytery despite the fact that he had moved to Charleston.[100]

In summary, his presbytery had sustained him in 1886. The Synod of Georgia then identified his ideas as heretical; his presbytery ignored the Synod. The 1888 General Assembly then pronounced his views as

---

95. *Ibid.*, II:481.
96. *Ibid.*, II:482.
97. *Ibid.*, II:483.
98. *Ibid.*, II:484.
99. *Ibid.*, II:485.
100. T. Watson Street, "The Evolution Controversy in the Southern Presbyterian Church With Attention to the Theological and Ecclesiastical Issues Involved," *Journal of Presbyterian History*, 37 (Dec. 1959), pp. 243-44.

heretical; his presbytery ignored this. The Charleston Presbytery did not want him, so the General Assembly of 1889 allowed him to remain a minister in good standing in the Augusta Presbytery; it did this by self-consciously violating the Church's structure of presbyterial authority. End of case, 16 years after his public attack on Dabney. Conclusion: the wheels of Southern Presbyterian justice ground slowly, but they ground exceedingly coarse.

His nephew and namesake Woodrow Wilson no doubt was pleased. Nevertheless, Uncle James had been dismissed by Columbia Seminary. Wilson had written to his future wife: "If uncle J. is to be read out of the Seminary, Dr. McCosh ought to be driven out of the church, and all private members like myself ought to withdraw without waiting for the expulsion which should follow belief in evolution."[101] But McCosh died in great esteem, and Wilson did not withdraw. By the time Wilson left Princeton in 1910, theistic evolution was regarded by the faculty as reactionary. They imbibed their Darwinism straight.

The story was still not over. In 1894, with Woodrow now serving as president of the University of South Carolina, the Charleston Presbytery accepted him as a member. In 1901, he was elected Moderator of the Synod of South Carolina. At his retirement from teaching at the University, the board of directors of Columbia Seminary adopted resolutions retroactively affirming his piety and his theological orthodoxy. It repealed all of its former actions against him. "When he died a year and a half later—aged 78—the old controversy was all but forgotten."[102] It remains forgotten today. Specialized textbooks in American Church history still present the case as if he had lost. They make him into a martyr. If he was, he was a unique martyr: not only did he avoid being eaten by the lions, they came to revere him as their beloved tamer.

---

101. Arthus S. Link, ed., *The Papers of Woodrow Wilson*, III:217; cited in J. David Hoeveler, Jr., *James McCosh and the Scottish Intellectual Tradition: from Glasgow to Princeton* (Princeton, New Jersey: Princeton University Press, 1981), p. 278.

102. Thompson, *Presbyterians*, II:488.

Other Cases

In the Methodist Church, in 1904, there was a second attempt to de-frock theology professor Borden Parker Bowne of Boston University. He had studied in Paris, Halle, and Göttingen in the mid-1870's. He was on the Boston University faculty from 1870 to 1910. This attempt failed.[103] The next year, 1905, the last successful attempt by the Methodist Episcopal Church to stamp out heresy took place, when the bishops exercised their authority to have higher critic Hinckley G. Mitchell removed from Boston University's faculty.[104] In 1908, the Judiciary Committee of the Methodist General Conference removed the authority of the bishops to oversee the orthodoxy of professors in the denomination's theological schools.[105] There would never again be a significant investigation by the Methodist Church into the alleged heresy of one of its ministers.[106]

The Congregationalist conservatives succeeded in 1885 in ousting E. C. Smyth—another higher critic named Smith (almost)—from Andover Seminary for his views on higher criticism. He was reinstated in 1892, and no other Andover Seminary liberal was ever ejected for his beliefs.[107]

In 1905, Edward Curtis was appointed acting dean at Yale Divinity School. He had previously taught at McCormick Seminary in Chicago, but the conservatives there had resisted him. He was a strong defender of higher criticism, the author of the commentary on Chronicles in the *International Critical Commentary*.[108] Yale clearly had completed its move into modernism.

---

103. Harmon L. Smith, "Borden Parker Bowne: Heresy at Boston," *American Religious Heretics: Formal and Informal Trials*, edited by George H. Shriver (Nashville, Tennessee: Abingdon, 1966), ch. 4.
104. *Ibid.*, p. 151.
105. *Ibid.*, p. 153.
106. *Ibid.*, p. 150.
107. Mark A. Noll, *Between Faith and Criticism: Evangelicals, Scholarship, and the Bible in America*, 2nd ed. (Grand Rapids, Michigan: Eerdmans, 1986), p. 27.
108. Roland H. Bainton, *Yale and the Ministry: A History of Education for the Christian Ministry at Yale from the Founding in 1701* (New York: Harper & Bros., 1957), p. 179.

276   CROSSED FINGERS

The Episcopal Church de-frocked Dr. Algernon Crapsey in 1906. In the midst of the 1924 flap over Fosdick in several Protestant denominations, he called the Fosdick dispute a disgrace.[109]

Almost, But Not Quite: 1895-97

The General Assembly of 1895 voted to require candidates for the ministry to be graduates of only those Presbyterian seminaries that were in submission judicially to the General Assembly.[110] This was an attack on Union Seminary. The General Assembly spoke for the Church. If it was willing in its capacity as the Church's supreme court invariably to revoke the ordinations of those who graduated from non-approved seminaries, then minority complaints from the presbyteries would be successful. The generation-long purge would begin. Presbyterian seminaries would be brought to heel by threatening the removal their indispensable positive sanction for students: a union card for Presbyterian ordination. Union's Presbyterian union card would end. This might have become the crucial institutional decision by the conservatives in the history of the Northern Presbyterian Church after 1869, but it was not to be. This rule was reversed by the 1897 General Assembly.[111] The presbyteries were acknowledged as sovereign in matters of ordination. This was a replay of a similar pair of battles in 1738-40 and 1834, when the New Side and the New School, respectively, repelled Old Side and Old School attempts to control ordination from the General Assembly level.[112] In short, no further negative sanctions against liberal seminaries.

Briggs Pushes Up the Ratchet Again: Ecumenism

Briggs became a minister of the Protestant Episcopal Church in March of 1898.[113] He sent out a press release that announced: "I with-

---

109. "Dr. Crapsey Calls Dispute a Disgrace," *New York Times* (Jan. 10, 1924), p. 4.
110. Loetscher, *Broadening Church*, p. 70.
111. *Ibid.*
112. Delwyn G. Nykamp, A Presbyterian Power Struggle: A Critical History of Communication Strategies in the Struggle for Control of the Presbyterian Church, U.S.A., 1922-1926 (Ph.D. dissertation, Northwestern University, 1974), pp. 42-43.
113. His bishop introduced the printed version of George William Douglas'

hold the reasons for this decision in the interests of peace and quietness."[114] Ah, yes: Professor Peace and Quiet. Just what Union needed: a world-famous rhetorical confrontationalist who had now cast doubts publicly on the integrity of the Presbyterian Church. "The board was not amused," Massa writes.[115] Yet he remained on the faculty of Union.

In 1909, he published *Church Unity*, in which he called for a new unified Christianity. There was no significant idea in this book that had not been present in *Whither?* in 1889, but his claims had escalated. He explicitly argued that Modernism (capital "M") was in the process of undermining the Roman Catholic Church, and would bring it out of its medievalism. (He was correct, but this process took half a century to begin and about a decade to complete, once begun.)[116] This, in turn, would make possible a unification of Christian denominations.[117]

> It is evident to intelligent observers [the modernist's familiar rhetorical appeal to the court of culturally meaningful public opinion—imbeciles and fundamentalists need not apply] that Christianity is passing through a process of change which is

---

sermon at Briggs' ordination with these words: "The Coptic Church keeps her Scriptures imprisoned in a silver casket, which her votaries kiss; in the same way, a modern fetichism, which has dishonored the Bible while claiming to be its elect guardian, has shut it up, these many years, within the iron walls of a dreary literalism; robbing it, thus, alike of interest and of power. The Book is a literature; priceless, incomparable, and most precious; but still a literature, and it must accept, and those who love and reverence it must accept for it, the conditions of its existence." Henry C. Potter, "Introduction," *Sermon Delivered At the Ordination of Charles Augustus Briggs, D.D., and Charles Henry Snedeker* (New York: Macmillan, 1899), pp. 6–7.

114. Massa, *Briggs*, p. 125.
115. *Ibid.*
116. Joaquin Sáenz y Arriaga, *The New Post-Conciliar Montinian Church*, trans. Edgar A. Lucidi (La Habra, California: Edgar A. Lucidi, 1985); cf. Malachi Martin, *The Jesuits: The Society of Jesus and the Betrayal of the Church* (New York: Simon & Schuster, 1987). For a representative primary source, see *A New Catechism: Catholic Faith for Adults* (New York: Herder & Herder, 1967). It was released by the bishops of the Netherlands in 1966.
117. Briggs, *Church Unity: Studies of Its Most Important Problems* (New York: Charles Scribner's Sons, 1909), ch. 15.

gradually transforming it. Provincial, denominational, national and racial types of Christianity are confronted as never before in Christian history with other great historic religions of the world; with various races and peoples unknown to those who formulated the current doctrines and organized the existing institutions of Christianity, and the Church is obliged to adapt itself to these new conditions and circumstances to a greater degree. The Christianity of former days is passing, modern types of Christianity are springing up and asserting themselves, and we are obliged to ask what the Christianity of the future will be. . . . Modernism, however much discord it may seem to produce, is really gradually dissolving the discord of Christianity and preparing the way for the Reunion of Christendom.[118]

To achieve this unity, the creeds must be altered, especially passages suggesting negative eternal sanctions. The Nicene Creed pronounced damnation against those who refused to assent. "They ought never to have been used with the Creed. They may be appropriate as the judgment of the Council, but they are not proper in public worship."[119] That is to say, the pronouncement of negative sanctions *may* have been appropriate for that one Church council back in 325, but not in the continuing worship of the Church.

He went on to quote the late Philip Schaff, whose 2,500-page history of the creeds ("symbols") is one long call for the creation of some future universal creed that will provide "future harmony"[120] and "union and concord among the different branches of Christ's kingdom."[121] Schaff had said of the Canons of Dort that they were like the Lutherans' Formula of Concord: precise language, consistent and necessary developments (implied qualification: for their day). "Both prepared the way for a dry scholasticism which runs into subtle abstractions, and resolves the living soul of divinity into a skeleton of formulas and distinctions. Both consolidated orthodoxy at the expense

---

118. *Ibid.*, p. 426.
119. *Ibid.*, p. 305.
120. Philip Schaff, *The Creeds of Christendom*, 3 vols. (Grand Rapids, Michigan: Baker Book House, [1931] 1990), I:4.
121. *Ibid.*, I:11.

of freedom, sanctioned a narrow confessionalism, and widened the breach between the two branches of the Reformation."[122]

Briggs predicted "a crisis in which all of the forces of Christianity will come into play in order to give birth to a new age of the world in which the discord of Christendom will die away, and concord will live and reign and express its new faith and new life in a Creed, a choral praise to the triune God. . . ."[123] The new Christendom would be more like a choir than a civilization.

But the hard questions remained: Who will write the music, select the music to be performed, choose the singers, and direct the choir? And who will pay the performers?

The Rhetoric of Deception Revisited

A new Catholicism is coming. "The Coming Catholicism will be *orthodox*."[124] But who are the orthodox? He said there were two parties battling for control of Christianity: the Modernists and the Medievalists.[125] The Medievalists defend the *form* of doctrine, the "philosophical formula" of faith. Then Briggs once again invoked rhetoric: "The letter of these doctrines is dead, the living substance is wrapped in grave clothes. . . . Lazarus must come forth into the realities of the modern world."[126] This will make the old formulas live again. "This is not to destroy the doctrines, it is rather to make them live again."[127] All this is offered in the name of orthodoxy: "It is not to substitute error and heresy for the doctrinal judgments of Christianity. It is to banish all error and heresy, due chiefly to misconceptions and misstatements of the theologians, by letting the pure, unadulterated, undefiled truth shine forth from the new candelabra upon which the ancient lamps of orthodoxy are now being placed."[128] This is Orwellian

---

122. Cited in Briggs, *Church Unity*, p. 308. The quotation appears in *Creeds of Christendom*, I:515.
123. *Ibid.*, p. 314.
124. *Ibid.*, p. 447.
125. *Ibid.*, p. 448.
126. *Ibid.*
127. *Ibid.*
128. *Ibid.*, pp. 448–49.

newspeak, four decades before *Nineteen Eighty-Four* was published: heresy is orthodoxy, received doctrines are error.

Men want to confess their faith. Now that no negative sanctions could affect him, Briggs made his public confession. He was in 1909 what he had been in 1876: a modernist. "Modernism is the embodiment of the *Zeit-Geist*, the spirit of our age, that our Lord is using to mediate between the past and the future of his kingdom." Modernists, not their adversaries, are the true conservatives: "The Modernists, who have been smitten by the Roman Catholic and Protestant Churches alike, are for the most part, not radicals, but conservatives. . . ."[129] If you support attacks on modernists, you are the true radical. "The attack of the ecclesiastics upon conservative Modernists, in every case, has strengthened the hands of the radicals and stayed the hands of those scholars who were mediating the reconciliation of the Church with the modern world, and the advance of the Church to a higher and better future, by the use of the more comprehensive and efficient methods of modern thought and modern life."[130] Here was the deceptive rhetorical appeal that he had employed for over three decades to thwart the logic of confessional orthodoxy. He and his peers were the true conservatives, the true enemies of radicalism in the Church. They were also the true agents of true progress. Truly.

A Vision of Victory

He ended the book with this messianic vision: "When once the great fundamental Catholic principle of Holy Love has become the material principle of entire Christianity, it will fuse all differences, and, like a magnet, draw all into organic unity about that centre where Love itself most truly reigns. Nothing in this world can stand against such a Catholic Church. She will speedily draw all mankind into the kingdom of our God and Savior."[131]

From 1903 to 1907, he actively sought a reuniting of Protestantism with what he mistakenly regarded as a liberalizing Roman Catho-

---

129. *Ibid.*
130. *Ibid.*, p. 441.
131. *Ibid.*, p. 451.

lic Church.[132] This liberalizing movement was short-lived (1890 to 1907).[133] It did not revive until the papacy of John XXIII (1958 to 1963), after which it transformed the Church in about three years—a process dwarfing the capture of the Protestant mainline churches in both its speed and intensity. Not surprisingly, Briggs in 1907 did not win any Protestants to this new cause, which soon became a distinct embarrassment to his liberal allies. He had gone too far this time. Liberal Protestants, then as now, recognized who would be Jonah and who would be the whale in any ecumenical consummation with Rome.

What we see in the confession of Briggs as he grew bolder over the years is the systematic working out of a religious viewpoint. That viewpoint was not Christianity; it was humanism. This perspective was present in *Whither?*, when he was still a member of the Presbyterian Church, U.S.A. His chapter in *Whither?*, "Thither," had become a full volume.

The difficulties that the orthodox wing experienced in removing Briggs from the Church pointed to a looming problem—a problem that would henceforth plague the Northern Presbyterian Church: *defenders of Christian orthodoxy could not rally a majority of the Church's leaders in a full-time policing of its ranks.* They could not apply negative sanctions.

Conclusion

Leland Griffin's theory of the three stages of rhetoric in historical movements—doubt, institutional crisis and confrontation, and consolidation[134]—applies well to the rhetorical battle over higher criticism in the United States. Applying his theory reveals the organizational error of the Confessionalists. The initial stage of rhetoric, marked by self-doubt by higher criticism's pioneers, was in the 1870's and 1880's. Briggs had made the transition psychologically a decade earlier in Germany, but he was not ready to go public with this until his 1876

---

132. Massa, *Briggs*, pp. 132–35; ch. 6.
133. *Ibid.*, p. 127.
134. Leland M. Griffin, "The Rhetoric of Historical Movements," *Quarterly Journal of Speech*, 38 (April 1952).

Inaugural Lecture. When he did, he became the higher criticism movement's point man in the Presbyterian Church. The second stage, which is marked by an institutional crisis, erupted in 1891 with his second Inaugural Lecture. The third stage, consolidation, did not occur until after 1925.

Mark Noll, in his study of the history of higher criticism and its effects on American evangelicals, has summarized the 30-year period, 1870–1900. He notes that "A distinctly evangelical approach to the study of Scripture, involving a self-conscious stance toward biblical criticism, did not emerge in America until the last third of the nineteenth century.... In 1870 most Americans, including most academics, agreed on *what* it meant for the Bible to be the Word of God. By 1900, Christians contended with each other as to *how* the Bible was the Word of God. And the academic world at large asked *if* it was."[135] We can see this change encapsulated in the transformation of Princeton University: from the accession of James McCosh to the presidency in 1868, through the presidency of Francis Patton, 1888–1902, ending with the presidency of Woodrow Wilson, 1902–10.

The turn of the century saw the peak in membership of the Unitarians, the Universalists, and the Society of Friends. The decline which they experienced after 1900 reflected the new opportunities for liberal clerics in the mainline Protestant denominations. The New Theology of modernism had secured major gains in most denominations by 1900.[136] The primary exception in the North was the Presbyterian Church, U.S.A. On the surface, it appeared as though the modernists had been routed. But had they? Only if negative sanctions continued to be applied. But would they?

It was clear in 1900 that if a major case of heresy arose, the New School would probably prosecute the case. But for such a case to be tried, it would almost certainly have to be the result of an offensive attack by the defendant. The New School would not initiate proceedings without extreme provocation, meaning rhetorical excess. To gain judicial immunity for modernism, the modernists needed only to

---

135. Noll, *Between Faith and Criticism*, p. 11.
136. Hutchison, *Modernist Impulse*, p. 113.

avoid rhetoric that might initiate a confrontation. As long as the men who held views that were openly contrary to the Westminster Confession also held their peace, the New School would protect them. After all, the 1837 split had come following the New School's successful defense of Albert Barnes against an Old School attack. This is why Union Seminary historian George Prentiss linked together Albert Barnes, Briggs, and Smith in his 1899 apologetic of the Seminary: "For, at the best, an American heresy trial, like that of Albert Barnes, or like those of Charles A. Briggs and Henry Preserved Smith, is a pitiable thing in the sight of heaven and earth."[137] This argument was rhetorical, not theological: covering the apostasy of modernism with Barnes' beloved Arminian umbrella. This same rhetorical tactic had been used in 1891 by Rev. Israel Hathaway on the floor of the General Assembly, when he spoke in defense of Briggs: "Let us not make history so that our children will have to apologize for our position as some have in their position toward Albert Barnes."[138]

After the creedal reformulation of 1903 and the entry of 1,100 Cumberland Presbyterian congregations in 1906, modernists would gain additional protective cover from the growing influence of the New School. If the modernists avoided a deliberate confrontation, initiated by one of their own, they would be allowed to remain in the Presbyterian Church. The modernists got the message.

One modernist who might have caused trouble was Thomas Day, a graduate of Union and a disciple of Briggs. He was a seminary professor at the San Francisco Theological Seminary, 1899–1911. The California Synod asked him to resign in 1911. He complied.[139]

Because the conservatives had not driven out the modernists by 1900, both sides de-escalated. The conservatives decided that the war was basically over; the modernists switched their strategy to accommodate this illusion. This rhetorical de-escalation on both sides marked two facts: the victory of the conservatives in the courts, 1893–1900, and the victory of the modernists in avoiding further tri-

---

137. Prentiss, *Union Theological Seminary*, p. 323.
138. *Ibid.*, p. 113.
139. Clarence B. Day, "The Thomas Day Heresy Case in the Synod of California," *Journal of Presbyterian History*, 46 (June 1968).

als. The modernists avoided harsh rhetoric and thereby gained immunity for their ideas as well as a continuing flow of funds. Their willingness to reduce their rhetoric was shared by other higher critics in America; this was not just a Presbyterian phenomenon. It marked the end of the conservatives' willingness or ability to pursue higher critics in Church courts, at least in the North.

Protestant modernists then began the long process of burrowing into the bureaucracies of the mainline denominations. They had no further need of rhetoric on higher criticism, which would still be taught in the seminaries. The theological lines had been drawn. The takeover of the Church's agencies of positive sanctions would commence: missions (domestic and foreign), ministerial relief (pensions), and social concern—the central agencies of evangelism and healing. The modernists would establish their credentials as men of good will—healers—but they would finance this healing process with other people's money, i.e., with money donated by faithful laymen, most of whom did not share liberal views. Negative sanctions against representative conservatives would come later. What was crucial to the liberals' strategy after 1900 was that negative sanctions would not be applied to anyone until the process of infiltration was complete. Their key word would continue to be *toleration*. The crucial issue was sanctions.

CONCLUSION TO PART 2

We are conscious that in pronouncing the errors in question to be unscriptural, radical, and highly dangerous, we are actuated by no feelings of narrow party zeal; but by a firm and growing persuasion that such errors cannot fail, in their ultimate effect, to subvert the foundations of Christian hope, and destroy the souls of men. As watchmen on the walls of Zion, we should be unfaithful to the trust reposed in us, were we not to cry aloud and proclaim a solemn warning against opinions so corrupt and delusive.

General Assembly of 1837[1]

The acts of 1837 deposed no minister and excommunicated no Church member. They declared no man and no set of men unworthy of Christian communion. It would indeed have been a monstrous iniquity for the Assembly to excommunicate thousands of Christians of whom they knew nothing, and who had been neither accused nor convicted of any offense. The imputation of any such purpose to the General Assembly is a gross calumny against that venerable body.

Charles Hodge (1840)[2]

Well, which was it? It was both. *Judicially*, Hodge was correct in his assessment: the General Assembly, dominated by Old School Calvinists, excommunicated no one in 1837 or 1838. Deposing just one minister, let alone excommunicating hundreds of them, is a long, drawn-out, and expensive judicial procedure. Extending the right boot of fellowship to four synods at a single General Assembly is far cheaper. Yet *theologically*, there can be little doubt: the Old School majority in the 1837 General Assembly was motivated by theological

---

1. *Circular Letter, Minutes of the General Assembly, 1837,* p. 504.
2. Hodge, *Princeton Review* (1840); reprinted in Hodge, *Discussions on Church Polity* (New York: Charles Scribner's Sons, 1878), p. 222.

concerns. It did throw out four New School synods, and did so on a legal technicality: the supposedly unconstitutional nature of the Plan of Union of 1801, which had allowed presbyteries to bring together in one ecclesiastical body Congregationalists and Presbyterians.

The General Assembly made it plain in 1837 that the ejection of the four New School synods rested on a very definite theological foundation: the heretical nature of certain unnamed individuals who were hiding under the ecclesiastical umbrella of the Plan of Union and who were undermining the Presbyterian Church. The Assembly said just that, as we shall see. It was this publicly known fact that Hodge chose to ignore three years later. He claimed that the Assembly's decision was strictly judicial and in no way theological. A similarly preposterous assertion was echoed a century later in 1936 by a majority in the Church when it suspended a handful of Calvinist ministers—and it was no less a falsehood then.

A Strategy of Verbal Subversion

The language of the General Assembly was judicial-constitutional in its 1837 *Pastoral Letter to the Churches Under the Care of The General Assembly*. But this document was immediately followed in the *Minutes* by a *Circular Letter* issued by the General Assembly and signed by the Moderator and Stated Clerk who had signed the *Pastoral Letter*. The language of the *Circular Letter* was deliberately inflammatory. It spoke of the interests of the Church—specifically, the missions boards—as having been subjected to "humiliating and degrading perversions" by those who had established parallel boards outside the control of the General Assembly. (This would also become the formal cause of the Calvinists' ejection in 1936.) It spoke of "doctrinal errors" which had gained an "alarming presence in some of our judicatories."[3] These errors were Arminian in theology, which the *Circular Letter* identified as "another gospel"—the terminology used by Paul to justify his anathema, a judicial condemnation of false doctrine worthy of excommunication (Gal. 1:6-11). The *Circular Letter* also identified their opponents' strategy: a strategy of subversion based on the misuse of

---

3. *Minutes of the General Assembly, 1837*, p. 503.

words. This declaration would prove amazingly prophetic after 1875, when the modernists began to employ the same strategy. The Old School in 1837 summarized what would become the crisis of the reunited Church at the end of the century. It was a long document, but it is important, not just for what it said about the past but about the future. The author understood the strategy of ecclesiastical subversion.

> The advocates of these errors, on their first appearance, were cautious and reserved, alleging that they differed in words only from the doctrines as stated in our public standards. Very soon, however, they began to contend that their opinions were really new, and were a substantial and important improvement on the old creed of the church; and, at length, that revivals of religion could not be hoped for, and that the souls of men must be destroyed, if the old doctrines continued to be preached. The errors thus promulg[at]ed were by no means of that doubtful or unimportant character, which seems to be assigned to them even by some of the professed friends of orthodoxy. You will see, by our published acts, that some of them affect the very foundation of the system of gospel truth, and that they all bear relations to the gospel plan, of very serious and ominous import. Surely, doctrines which go to the formal or virtual denial of our covenant relation to Adam; the native and total depravity of man; the entire inability of the sinner to recover himself from rebellion and corruption; the nature and source of regeneration; and our justification solely on account of the imputed righteousness of the Redeemer, cannot, upon any just principle, be regarded as "minor errors." They form, in fact, "another gospel;" and it is impossible for those who faithfully adhere to our public standards, to walk with those who adopt such opinions with either comfort or confidence.
>
> It cannot be denied, indeed, that those who adopted and preached these opinions, at the same time declared their readiness to subscribe to our Confession of Faith, and actually professed their assent to it, in the usual form, without apparent scruple. This, in fact, was one of the most revolting and alarming characteristics of their position. They declared, that in doing this, they only adopted the confession *"for substance,"* and by no means intended to receive the whole system which it contained. Upon this principle, we had good evidence that a number of Presbyter-

ies, in the ordination and reception of ministers and other church officers, avowedly and habitually acted. And hence it has not been uncommon for the members of such Presbyteries publicly and formally to repudiate some of the important doctrines of the formulary which they had thus subscribed; and even, in a few extraordinary cases, to hold up the system of truth which it contains as "an abomination;" as a system which it were to be "wished had never had an existence." No wonder that men feeling and acting thus should have been found, in some instances, substituting entirely different Confessions of Faith in place of that which is contained in our constitution. Who can doubt that such a method of subscribing to articles of faith is immoral in principle; that it is adapted to defeat the great purpose of adopting confessions; and that, if persisted in, it could not fail to open the door of our church wider and wider to the introduction of the most radical and pestiferous heresies, which would speedily destroy her character as an evangelical body.[4]

It was not just Arminianism that alienated the Old School. It was also the political implication of this Arminianism, the "ever restless spirit of *radicalism*, manifest both in the church and in the state," which "has driven its deep agitations through the bosom of our beloved church. . . . It is ever the same levelling revolutionary spirit, and tends to the same ruinous results. It has, in succession, driven to extreme fanaticism the great cause or revivals of religion, of temperance, and of the rights of man."[5] The phrase, "the rights of man," was a code phrase that obviously referred to abolitionism, but its historic origins harkened back to the French Revolution and the atheism of Thomas Paine. "It has aimed to transmute our pure faith into destructive heresy, our scriptural order into confusion and misrule. It has crowded many of our churches with ignorant zealots and unholy members; driven our pastors from their flocks; and with strange fire[6] consumed the heritage of the Lord, filling our churches with confu-

---

4. *Ibid.*, pp. 503-4.
5. *Ibid.*, p. 507.
6. A rhetorical reference to the false sacrifice by Nadab and Abihu (Lev. 10:1-7).

sion, and our judicatories with conflict; . . ." Thus did the Old School dismiss the New School's claim of Calvinist orthodoxy.

Déjà Vu

These New School Arminians had pioneered a strategy of verbal deception which was adopted by modernists after 1875. But unlike the General Assembly of 1837, the post-1869 General Assemblies refused to remove from their ranks in one fell swoop all of the offending parties as well as their allies, whether active or passive, by means of a single surgical operation. The Old School in 1837 chose not to initiate a series of heresy trials, which they would have lost. By refusing to identify specific individuals as heretical and deserving of Church discipline, the Old School accomplished its goal with a minimum commitment of scarce judicial resources.

In the 1920's, their spiritual heirs adopted half of this strategy: a self-conscious refusal to name anyone as heretical or to launch formal trials against anyone. To demand a heresy trial was risky. Presbyterian law mandated that a person bringing a false accusation against a member would in turn become subject to censure for slander.[7] But unlike the General Assembly of 1837, the conservatives of the 1920's did not have the votes to remove from their presence all of the heretics and most of their sympathizers in one comprehensive judicial housecleaning. Geography was against them: the deviants were no longer confined to specific synods. The climate of opinion—the spirit of the times or Zeitgeist—was also opposed to them: pluralism. But most important, the structure of the Church was opposed to them: bureaucracy. The termites had multiplied. The wood was rotten.

A Marriage Apparently Not Made in Heaven

Analogies are always dangerous if taken too literally, but they are useful heuristic devices. In 1869, the Presbyterian Church, U.S.A., was like a couple who had been married to each other twice, had been divorced twice, and were ready to get married again. A marriage coun-

---

7. *The Book of Discipline*, II:14. *The Constitution of the Presbyterian Church in the United States of America* (Philadelphia: Presbyterian Board of Publication and Sabbath School Work, 1904), p. 395.

selor would not be optimistic about the proposed third union, especially since each party was convinced that his or her cause had been correct and the other's wrong.

As in marriage, the two sides came into the union as judicial equals. Each had the power to say *no* to the other prior to the union. In terms of democratic theory, the Old School should have been dominant politically, being significantly larger, but this proved not to be the case. The functional question in 1869 was this: Which party was entering the union on the other's terms? There was no doubt about this: the Old School. They had bet wrong on the most divisive political issue in American history: chattel slavery. Their public image was linked, if not to slavery, then at least to the forces of ethical and political reaction that had refused to challenge the now-defunct evil institution to mortal combat. They had implicitly announced that this issue was *adiaphora*, i.e., one not spoken to authoritatively by Scripture. The issue of slavery was none of the Church's business, they had dogmatically maintained. Yet in the United States, 1830–1865, no political issue had been more relevant. Thus, the Old School had in effect announced: "The Bible is irrelevant in this matter, and therefore so are we."[8] Theirs had been a massive failure of leadership, although this failure was not confined to Old School Presbyterians.[9]

Continuity and Discontinuity

The Old School needed to put all this behind it: judicially and psychologically. But its members were unwilling to do this through public confession and repentance.

The reunion offered a seemingly painless way to do this: to immerse the Old School's separate identity in a new denomination with the old name. Continuity would be provided by the denomination's name and Confessional standards; discontinuity would be provided by

---

8. Anyone who wonders how theologians of the caliber of the Old School could be this out of touch ethically for so long need only search for official statements against abortion issued by conservative Protestant theological seminaries and denominations. Warning: don't spend too much time in your search.

9. C. C. Goen, *Broken Churches, Broken Nation: Denominational Schisms and the Coming of the American Civil War* (Macon, Georgia: Mercer University Press, 1986), ch. 5.

Conclusion to Part 2

the presence of the New School within the new (old) denomination. But there was a high price tag on this disguised discontinuity: *judicial subordination*. The Confession was verbally the same; the New School's leaders repeatedly said that they believed it without qualification. It was this affirmation that broke the will to resist on the part of all of the Old School leaders except Charles Hodge, who believed the New School could not be trusted, and who turned out to be correct. The New School's leaders lied about their intentions as representatives of the whole faction. They swore allegiance to the Confession, but they held the reunion's first meeting in the congregation of the man whom they had refused to de-frock for Arminianism in 1837: Albert Barnes. The reunion was based on crossed fingers.

This meant that the Church's judicial enforcement structure would not be the same as it had been in the Old School. There would be the form of Calvinist orthodoxy but not the substance thereof. The New School's standards would dominate in most Church courts, and the New School had systematically refused to convict Arminians of deviation from the Confession. It should have been clear where this would lead, but only Charles Hodge had the fortitude to make the prediction in part. His colleagues did not believe him. They wanted the reunion more than they wanted to think through its judicial implications.

In 1869, the Old School was willing to return, hat in hand, bare head lowered, as the now publicly humiliated prodigal son. Its members swallowed their pride, but far more important, swallowed their judicial suspicions, in order to make possible what was to be, in retrospect, stage one in a program of Presbyterian ecumenical union. Cumberland Presbyterian churches were next: 1906. The Old School was swallowed by the New School. Old School members surrendered their ecclesiastical inheritance to their long-time opponents. The New School's spiritual heirs surrendered this grand inheritance to the modernists in 1936, when they silently consented to the modernists' public disinheritance of the tattered remnants of the Old School and a few New School premillennialists.

The Old School would not admit in 1869 that they had made a catastrophic error in ethical and political judgment: slavery as *adiaphora*. In short, *the Old School was unwilling to repent in public.* (The New School remained politely quiet, as a wise suitor should.) Old

School members were either silent about the matter or else they denied it, which was an exercise in self-delusion. Meanwhile, the South's partisans were playing this same psychological game of denial. Alexander Stephens, the former Vice President of the Confederacy, denied in 1870 that slavery had been the primary cause of the War; Constitutional issues had been.[10] This self-induced memory loss in the South was widespread.[11] But there was a high price to pay there, too. The Presbyterians' antebellum moral and cultural leadership in the South was surrendered at Appomattox Court House and never regained. The same was true of Old School's leadership in the reunited Northern Church.

With the reunion of 1869, the New School Presbyterians began a process of absorbing the Old School. The Old School's representatives—Charles Hodge excepted—had not understood how far this absorption process could lead. They learned only after 1900. The New School represented a theological tradition that favored a Confessionally broader-based Church and growth through evangelism. Their evangelism techniques had been established during the two Great Awakenings. They were experientialists more than they were Confessionalists.

New School members were willing to confess allegiance to the Confession, but unless strongly provoked by modernists, they were not willing to enforce its details on any ordained minister who had acknowledged its authority, once, at his ordination. Their Confessional assumption was "once confessed, always confessed." This would become official policy at the General Assembly in 1927. New School members had grown tired of squabbling over the details of Calvinist theology in 1838, and they remained tired. They could be mobilized into action if the rhetoric of the modernists grew flagrant enough, as it became in the 1890's, but after 1900, the modernists avoided rhetorical confrontations for two decades, and the New School retreated

---

10. Alexander H. Stephens, *A Constitutional View of the Late War Between the States*, 2 vols. (Philadelphia: National Publishing Co; Chicago: Ziegler, McCurdy, 1870), I:10.

11. Richard E. Beringer, *et al.*, *Why the South Lost the Civil War* (Athens: University of Georgia Press, 1986), ch. 16.

once again, calling for Church union with other, more Arminian Presbyterian churches. They could be mobilized against disturbers of the peace in the Church after 1900, but not by appeals to the Westminster Confession. The key issue after 1900 was peace, not the Westminster Confession.

Representative Cases

The multi-level heresy trials of Charles Briggs had absorbed enormous quantities of resources. Three General Assemblies, 1891-93, had devoted most of their concern to Briggs and the issues he represented. In 1894, the General Assembly had an open-and-shut case: Henry Preserved Smith formally supported Briggs. The decision was easy. But McGiffert had also publicly supported Briggs in 1893. He was brought to trial in 1898 on another issue. This pointed to trouble in the future. Would the New School's decade of enthusiasm for heresy trials remain?

McGiffert's resignation in 1900 ended General Assembly heresy trials. What must be recognized is something that books about the Presbyterian conflict and American Church history rarely or never point out clearly. Only three men were convicted of heresy in the Presbyterian Church, U.S.A., during the nineteenth century: William McCune in 1878, Briggs in 1893, and Smith in 1894. Still, these were important events—representative cases, just as convictions by a civil court are. Few crimes are ever solved; few criminals are arrested; few cases get to court; few of those that get to court result in convictions. But people who are convicted serve as warnings and deterrents to others who might be willing to break the law. *The tree of orthodoxy is watered by periodic heresy trials.* After 1900, the mainline Protestant churches ceased watering the tree of orthodoxy, just as European Protestantism ceased watering it in the nineteenth century. The twentieth century's mainline Protestant churches were the desiccated result.

From 1900 on, a majority of the ministers in the Presbyterian Church, U.S.A., decided that for the sake of peace, and for the spread of the gospel, there should be no further trials of heretics. There would be trials *by* heretics, 1935-36, but no trials *of* heretics. These later trials would be conducted in the name of institutional peace and obedience, not theology.

The General Assembly of 1893 did not agree with the modernists' main institutional argument, namely, that theology—meaning *orthodox* theology—is a hindrance to the life of the Church. It removed Briggs from the ministry. The following May it did the same with Henry Preserved Smith. But those 235 signers who agreed with Henry van Dyke's *Plea for Peace and Work* manifesto had only just begun to fight in 1893. They learned how to fight far more effectively after 1900. They learned to fight within the institutional restraints imposed by the majority: peacefully. They learned to work quietly in terms of the official rules, which, as the majority members of the Church boards after 1915, they increasingly wrote. In 1936, they won. They imposed negative sanctions—not an incident, but a precedent. They never had to impose them again.

The Liberals Resolve to Fight

Those who do not understand the power religion may ask, as Nathaniel Weyl asked in the early 1940's:[12] How could the modernists remain in a denomination whose Confession they rejected? This was not a problem theologically for them; their religion was *the religion of democracy*. Democracy was the reigning religion of the intellectuals during this era, as it is in our own.[13] Thus, what was basic to the modernists' agenda was the capture of institutional power and wealth through democratic means: voting the institutional legacy of orthodoxy into their own inheritance. Voting was their equivalent of the Lord's Supper.[14] The modernists recognized that in order to gain and

---

12. See Chapter 13, below: section on "Capturing the Robes," p. 804.

13. See, for example, the writings of the prolific modernist author Charles Fergusson, especially *The Religion of Democracy: A Memorandum of Modern Principles* (New York: Funk & Wagnalls, 1900); *The Affirmative Intellect: An Account of the Origin and Mission of the American Spirit* (New York: Funk & Wagnalls, 1901). Cf. William Rainey Harper, "The University and Democracy," in *The Trend in Higher Education* (Chicago: University of Chicago Press, 1905). Harper was the president of the University of Chicago. He described the modern university as prophet, priest, and sage. Harper was a friend of John D. Rockefeller, Sr., and had been installed by him as president. It was Harper who had advised John D. Jr. to attend Brown University in 1893: Peter Collier and David Horowitz, *The Rockefellers: An American Dynasty* (New York: Holt, Rinehart and Winston, 1976), p. 83.

14. In modern politics, voting really is the judicial equivalent of the Lord's

keep a majority, they had to capture the denomination's seminaries and its permanent bureaucratic boards. They also had to avoid the negative sanction of de-frocking.

Control of the seminaries was the key tactic. First, seminaries established the extreme limits of acceptable theological discourse: from Princeton to Union. By making them ever-more liberal, the modernists could move the denomination's center farther to the left, since Princeton was increasingly isolated after 1869. Second, seminaries trained the next generation of ministers. This would, over time, lead to victory: the sacrament of voting. Third—rarely mentioned by historians—a seminary professor was employable elsewhere, especially in the fields of Hebrew linguistics and Church history. This meant that there was little economic risk to a modernist if he was convicted of heresy. He could move to Union Seminary or to a humanist university. He would not suffer a permanent loss of income or prestige. The modernists had allies in the colleges. The personal cost of this tactic in the strategy of conquest was low.[15]

A Crucial Feature of the Liberals' Strategy

Liberals, both political and theological, have long honored a institutionally crucial rule, one which has governed both their ecclesiastical politics and their civil politics for over a century, and perhaps longer: *take care of your wounded*. This practice has been fundamental to their success. Crawford H. Toy was immediately hired by Harvard. W. Robertson Smith was immediately hired by Cambridge and would have been hired by Harvard. Briggs and McGiffert (in 1898) were already on the faculty at Union, a safe haven. Only Henry Preserved Smith suffered a few years of academic unemployment before he was hired by Amherst and later by Union. Knowing that they would be protected, they could afford to take greater risks. They could, when necessary, adopt confrontational rhetoric. For two decades, they

---

Supper: the public imposition of periodic sanctions, positive and negative, for or against oath-bound legal representatives in a covenantal institution—the civil government. Voting is an act of covenant renewal in the civil covenant.

15. Economics teaches that when the cost of anything drops, more of it will be supplied, other things remaining constant.

avoided this: 1900–1922. Briggs' rhetoric had established the battle lines; after 1900, the tactic moved from open confrontation to quiet infiltration: van Dyke's announced strategy in 1893.

When it came time to test again the defensive lines of orthodoxy by means of an escalation of rhetoric, an eminently protected point man did so: Harry Emerson Fosdick. A rich liberal Baptist with the resources of an even richer Baptist behind him—John D. Rockefeller, Jr.—he was not seriously threatened by any negative sanctions available to the Presbyterian Church.

The conservatives have never been strongly committed to the liberals' policy of taking care of their wounded. Even if they had been equally committed as the liberals in the 1930's, they were not equally well funded. The threat of theological disinheritance would, in the 1930's, come face to face with the threat of personal economic disinheritance. The exodus was small.

The Old School's Dilemma

A dilemma confronted the Old School theologians, 1869–1900. The New School gave an official affirmation to the historic confessions of Presbyterianism. They had sworn loyalty to them as the basis of the reunion of 1869. The Old School had voted overwhelmingly to accept this profession of faith at face value. Once the reunion was sealed, there was nothing that the Old School could do to challenge New School members regarding their commitment except to beg them to enforce the stipulations of the Confession against the most notorious heretics. This the New School would occasionally and sporadically do, but only under pressure—not pressure from the Old School, but rather from the modernists. This pressure had to be rhetorical, not merely theological. The 1870's produced only one conviction, William McCune, and his deviation was interdenominationalism, not modernism as such. If a specific modernist adopted confrontational rhetoric, as Briggs did, the denomination could be rallied temporarily to silence him. But there was no *operational* precedent set by a successful heresy trial, except this: confrontational rhetoric might, under certain limited circumstances, again provoke the denomination. But there was no meaningful theological precedent. Briggs was condemned because of his rhetorical excesses, not his theological excesses. Heresy was necessary but not sufficient to gain a conviction. This was never admitted in public, but it was the case. If *Whither?* could not get a seminary professor de-frocked, a mild-mannered modernist pastor had very little to fear, especially if he did not go into print with his views. There would be no further negative sanctions against rhetorically prudent men.

Without the willingness on the part of court members to impose negative sanctions, no one in the denomination could be sure that those who took ministerial oaths believed what they were saying. In fact, everyone could be certain that no one took the judicial content of his oath so rigorously as the seventeenth-century divines had intended when they debated them, 1643–47. Briggs had made this much clear: on certain issues, even the Old School's leaders had departed from the Confession, the "elect infants" clause being his favorite example. So, it was all a matter of degree. Every minister had mentally crossed his fingers on ordination day. This made them unwilling to prosecute others who had done the same thing, except for the most flagrant violations of the Confession—*flagrant* here defined as *rhetorically excessive*. This transferred the authority to set the agenda to the modernists. Their rhetoric would set the agenda.

Uncrossed Fingers

There are three ways to reduce the amount of finger-crossing. The Old School rejected two of them. First, encourage candidates to state their objections during their cross-examination by the ordination committee, but then tell each of them that his objections are no problem. That is, refuse to impose negative sanctions at the beginning of the judicial process. Let unofficial word get around to all seminary students in any institution that this is the new policy.

This approach would have been unacceptable to every presbytery except the New York Presbytery, which does seem to have adopted something like this after 1900. Certain traditions still had to be honored. However, the New School would have accepted as valid a great many more doubts on the part of candidates than the Old School did. There was no way around this new reality after 1869. The question was: How tightly would any given presbytery screen its candidates for the ministry? It was the Old School's job to say, "just a little bit tighter." They had to press as hard as they could without provoking a reaction from the New School.

Second, revise the Confession so that hardly any Presbyterian could object. The problem here is that there is always a "lowest common denominator" problem. "Lowest common denominator" always means "lowest at this point in time." Lower the common denominator today, and some of those who gain entry tomorrow will work to pull it even lower. The bell-shaped curve will never be eliminated in history. There will always be somebody on the far end of the spectrum who is having doubts. Similarly, the number of "true believers" in any organization is limited. Growth adds to the number of less rigorous creedalists. So, one creedal downgrading tends to lead to another, other things remaining constant.[16] Weaken the theological content of the ministerial oath, and those on the outer edge of the definition will try again to get inside. Candidates will still be tempted to cross their fingers. The Old School feared the slippery slope that seemed to lay ahead of every creedal revision. These fears proved fully justified after 1900.

The third way to reduce finger-crossing is to impose far more rigorous sanctions after ordination than those imposed after 1869. This is what the Old School wanted, but they did not have the votes. One reason why they did not have the votes is the economic reality of heresy trials: they absorb lots of resources, especially time. They go on for years. Also, the person who initiates one must be willing to disrupt "the club." Unlike a bishop, whose job is to impose sanctions on those under his jurisdiction, and who is not perceived as having overstepped his authority by initiating an investigation, men who are perceived as equals (teaching elders), let alone inferiors (ruling elders), are resented by many of their peers when they initiate sanctions against another ordained man. The accusers are saying implicitly that the screening committee had been too lax, unless the defendant comes out publicly and admits that he changed his views after his ordination. This is not likely; his best defense is to claim allegiance to "true" Presbyterianism, just as Briggs did. The accused will not admit that he changed his views, especially when he probably didn't. He came in as

---

16. Social theorists cannot speculate scientifically without *ceteris paribus*. Unfortunately, *ceteris paribus* is impossible: "You cannot change just one thing."

a closet heretic, and he must be proved to be a heretic in a court—several courts, in fact, for almost everyone convicted by a Presbyterian court will appeal this negative judgment unless he withdraws from the denomination before a court hands down a final decision.

The *operational* definition of "heretic" will then be shaped by the amount of resources that the denomination is willing to allocate to prove heresy in a representative number of cases.[17] Nevertheless, not every heretic must be brought to trial and convicted in order to reduce the amount of heresy and the degree of heresy. Convictions are representative; not every heretic can be identified and removed. The institutional question is rather: Is the likelihood of conviction high? If it is, then setting a judicial precedent is sufficient to silence many of them or persuade them to leave quietly. As the economist-legal theorist F. A. Hayek says, the test of a legal system is the number of trials that never go to court because the guilty parties know they are likely to be convicted. The larger the number of these non-trials, the more efficient the legal order.[18]

The Ordination Examination

Presbyterian government made it less expensive in time, trouble, and embarrassment to reject ministerial candidates than to conduct successful heresy trials after their ordination. The highest return on the Old School's investment of resources in restricting heresy was here: the candidate's examination. There was only one cost-effective way for the Old School to protect the theological integrity of the ministerial oath after 1869: to insist on the right of the presbyteries' examination committees to use the Confession to cross-examine the candidates. Here is where the Old School needed to test the seriousness of the New School regarding the latter's public affirmation of the Confession. This should have begun in 1870. Had the Old School

---

17. For a detailed study of how New England Puritans shifted the definitions of deviant behavior in terms of how much they were willing to pay to enforce public sanctions, see Kai T. Erikson, *Wayward Puritans: A Study in the Sociology of Deviance* (New York: Wiley, 1966).

18. F. A. Hayek, *The Constitution of Liberty* (Chicago: University of Chicago Press, 1960), p. 208. Hayek took his degree in law, as did all graduates in economics at the University of Vienna in his day.

insisted on this, Briggs would never have been ordained. The Old School had to go on the offensive in 1870 in order to defend the "gate": the point of entry. They had to do this in such a way that the New School would not—could not—object. They had to persuade the New School to impose negative sanctions in terms of the Confession and the catechisms. If the New School refused, then their verbal profession was a either sham or self-delusion.

The New School was not committed to the Confession to the degree that the Old School was. There was little likelihood that the New School would consent to a cross-examination that was based on Old School rigor. The cry of "Yes, yes, we all believe that; let's get this over with!" would have drowned out efforts by Old School members to screen each candidate by the Confession's explicit standards. This was a fact of institutional life. The Old School had to adjust to the new reality. The Old School did adjust. The problem was, it adjusted by remaining on the defensive. It did not develop an effective offensive strategy at the presbytery level.

The Old School needed a single representative doctrine from the Confession which would screen out their enemies. But who was the enemy? Not the New School. Not after 1869. The enemies of both schools were the modernists. The representative screening question had to be acceptable to the New School but an outrage to all modernists. It had to be so specific that no amount of verbal weaseling on the part of the candidate would let him escape. Better yet, it would affront his sense of justice; he would publicly proclaim his opposition.

A Representative Question

The Old School's problem was this: isolating the joint enemy of both schools, modernism. By the time of the reunion, one of the chief tenets of modernism had already spread to the College of New Jersey: evolution. The arrival of James McCosh in 1868 to become the college's president should have alerted them to what was coming.[19]

---

19. J. David, Hoeveler, Jr., *James McCosh and the Scottish Intellectual Tradition: From Glasgow to Princeton* (Princeton, New Jersey: Princeton University Press, 1981), ch. 6.

Darwin's initial presupposition—long time frames—had come from Charles Lyell's *Principles of Geology*. This idea had already breached the gates at the College and Princeton Seminary. The six-day creation was no longer publicly defended by the Old School's leaders. Charles Hodge rejected the doctrine. A. A. Hodge and Warfield adopted an indeterminate time in the past for the date of the creation. Warfield wrote: "The question of the antiquity of man has itself no theological significance. It is to theology, as such, a matter of entire indifference how long man has existed on earth. . . . The Bible does not assign a brief span to human history; this is done only by a particular mode of interpreting the Biblical data, which is found on examination to rest on no solid basis."[20] Charles Briggs could easily have written such a statement. Because the Old School had given up the Confession's precise language on the six-day creation, the Confession's creation statement was no longer available for screening candidates, despite its obvious use in dealing with modernists. "Six literal days, sir, just as the Confession says. Do you believe this? Yes or no?" Had he answered no, using some version of creative evolution, the presbytery would still have ordained him. This section was useless to the Old School; they were not ready to de-frock both Hodges and Warfield. But in terms of strict Confessionalism, all three deserved defrocking.

The Old School needed a substitute, one that would screen out modernists as well or better than the doctrine of the six-day creation, yet not backfire on them. That substitute doctrine was available: *the doctrine of eternal torment.* The Larger Catechism was clear, tightly worded, and anathema to every modernist: "Whereas the souls of the wicked are at their death cast into hell, where they remain in torments and utter darkness, and their bodies kept in their graves, as in their prisons, till the resurrection and judgment of the great day" (Answer 86b). The Bible is equally clear (Rev. 20:14–15). Then, pressing the issue, what about those who never hear the gospel? Answer: "They who, having never heard the gospel, know not Jesus Christ,

---

20. Benjamin B. Warfield, "On the Antiquity of the Human Race," *Princeton Theological Review*, 9 (Jan. 1911); reprinted in Warfield, *Biblical and Theological Studies* (Philadelphia: Presbyterian & Reformed, 1952), pp. 238–39.

and believe him not, cannot be saved, be they never so diligent to frame their lives according to the light of nature, or the laws of that religion which they profess; neither is their salvation in any other, but in Christ alone, who is the Saviour only of his body the church" (Answer 60). Such detailed specifics as these were why the Presbyterian Church in 1967 officially abandoned the Larger Catechism as a test of orthodoxy.

By screening every candidate for the eldership by means of the doctrine of eternal torment, Old School members could have positioned themselves as dedicated promoters of evangelism and Church growth rather than as last-ditch defenders of a narrow conception of the Confession—narrow compared with New School conceptions. The Old School had surrendered in 1869. That war was over. The Old School's strategic question after 1869 was this: How much of the Confession could be preserved as the outer defense against the systematic and continual assault by modernism? No one foresaw in 1869 that five years later, a higher critic of the Bible would be teaching at Union Seminary: Briggs. The Old School was still looking over its collective shoulder at the latent Arminianism of the New School instead of looking ahead at the forces of apostasy that were virtually at the gates. As is so often the case with generals, the Old School's generals were fighting the last, lost war: 1837–69. They were still on the defensive. They were still in retreat. Eventually, they would lose.

Weak Links

In the *Presbyterian Re-union Memorial Volume* (1870), Rev. John Hall announced this principle of ecclesiology: "The measure of the strength of a machine is the strength of its weakest part. It is prudent for a besieged city to look to its defences where the line is most easily penetrable. And it is wise for a church to make good any position which it is right to hold, preparatory to successful aggressive effort."[21]

It is ironic that this warning was announced by Rev. Hall, for his career, perhaps more than any other conservative minister in his generation, was representative of the Presbyterian Church's unsolved

---

21. John Hall, "The Future Church," *Presbyterian Re-union Memorial Volume, 1837–1871* (New York: De Witt C. Lent & Co.,1870), p. 462.

problem of weak links. As a newly arrived immigrant pastor from Northern Ireland in 1867, he was instrumental in bringing James McCosh to the College of New Jersey in 1868. As president of the Board of Home Missions, he tried to mediate between two wings of the Church.[22] The problem was, he did not work to suppress the third faction: modernism. When, at the General Assembly of 1895, the General Assembly was ready to move against modernists who were under the authority of the Board of Home Missions, Hall's speech turned back this, the first and last major attempt by the denomination to deal with this functionally autonomous board.[23] A defender of biblical inerrancy, he opposed the proposed revision of the Westminster Confession in 1889. Yet he defended Charles Briggs' right to preach what Hall knew was opposed to the Confession. He denounced heresy trials as useless.[24] In his capacity as a member of the Board of Trustees of Union Seminary, he devised the legal justification that Union adopted when it pulled out of the Church in 1892. Then he resigned in protest when it did.[25] He served as pastor of New York City's Fifth Avenue Presbyterian Church, retiring in 1898. In the next phase of the Presbyterian conflict, modernist Henry Sloane Coffin occupied that pulpit. Finally, Hall's son, a professor at Union, wrote his father's biography.

Hall was a man caught between two great theological movements, each pulling hard on Presbyterianism's chain: modernism and Calvinism. Hall chose not to acknowledge that modernism was a substantial threat to Christianity in general and the Presbyterian Church in particular. He and other Presbyterian conservatives like him could not keep the chain connected. They themselves were the weak links. The institutional question after 1900 was this: How much of the chain would each side retain after it snapped? The answer came in 1936.

---

22. Thomas C. Hall, *John Hall: Pastor and Preacher* (New York: Revell, 1901), p. 235.
23. *Ibid.*
24. *Ibid.*, pp. 286–89.
25. *Ibid.*, pp. 281–84.

Conclusion

In the era prior to the final institutional turning point in 1934—the new Form of Government—Presbyterian modernists, like the other denominations' modernists, invoked the theology of pluralism: broad churchmanship without the institutional threat of negative sanctions. They were theological inclusivists during any period in which they did not control the Church's institutions. The Church's theological boundaries were not to be policed by anyone possessing the authority to impose sanctions, they insisted. Those anti-pluralists who might seek to exclude others from crossing the institutional boundaries and enter the Presbyterian Church without abandoning the humanist idols in their suitcases had to be disarmed. Defenders of the Church's theological perimeters could be allowed shout the traditional, "Halt! Who goes there?", but only for tradition's sake, and only during ordination examinations. They were not actually supposed to enforce the fading "No Trespassing" signs that were posted on the roads leading from the seminaries to the pulpits. Surely there were to be no evictions after the installation ceremony.

On May 2, 1900, the New York Presbytery ordained Henry Sloane Coffin.[26] That was, as it turned out, an auspicious event. He had been McGiffert's pupil and would succeed him as the president of Union in 1926, a position which he then held for two decades. This was the new reality of Northern Presbyterianism.

If the conservatives agreed to these rules, then all that remained necessary for the modernists to capture the Church—or any hierarchical Church—was to capture the seminaries. After 1900, this is exactly what the Presbyterian modernists did, culminating in the capture of Princeton Seminary in 1929.

In the meantime, there would be a series of inclusions and attempted exclusions. What was significant was that these would not be enforced in terms of the Westminster Confession of Faith, as had also been the case with Swing (almost), McCune, Briggs, Smith, and McGiffert (almost). What the Old School had surrendered in 1869

---

26. Bradley J. Longfield, *The Presbyterian Controversy: Fundamentalists, Modernists, and Moderates* (New York: Oxford University Press, 1991), p. 85.

would never be recovered: the institutionally enforceable Confessional boundary markers of 1788.

Foreign Missions

In 1893, Briggs' colleague and public supporter Philip Schaff put in his final public appearance. In his address, "The Reunion of Christendom," he called for a federal union of American Protestantism. This Chicago meeting was the first in a series of conferences attended by representatives of Protestant world missions. It was followed by the first meeting of the Foreign Missions Conference of North America. These missions conferences were to set the tone for the next generation of evangelicals and liberals: the quest for Christian unity in missions.[27] The future of the Presbyterian Church would be determined by the success of two rival impulses: the narrowing impulse of Confessional purity and the broadening impulse of the evangelical alliance.

In 1900, America's most prominent promoter of world missions, John R. Mott, wrote a book, *The Evangelization of the World in Our Time*. As the chairman of the Student Volunteer Movement and the intercollegiate secretary of the YMCA, Mott exuded Protestant America's confidence in the future in the final year of the nineteenth century. His ecumenical foreign missions vision spread to the Presbyterian Church, in large part because of the efforts of Mott's eloquent partner in the SVM a decade earlier, Robert E. Speer, who served as the secretary of the Presbyterian Foreign Missions Board, 1891–1937. Their cooperation continued in the 1890's, culminating in the Ecumenical Conference on Foreign Missions, held in New York City in 1900.[28] It was at this conference, attended by representatives of 162 worldwide missions boards, that the word *ecumenical* can be said to have first entered the modern Protestant vocabulary.[29] This was not

---

27. Eldon G. Ernst, *Moment of Truth for Protestant America: Interchurch Campaigns Following World War I* (Missoula, Montana: American Academy of Religion, 1972), pp. 17–18.

28. John F. Piper, "Robert E. Speer: His Call and the Missionary Impulse, 1890–1900," *American Presbyterians*, 65 (Summer 1987), p. 107.

29. William C. Ringberg, "Benjamin Harrison: The Religious Thought and Practice of an American President," *ibid.*, 64 (Fall 1986), p. 186.

some small affair. At the conference, former President and Presbyterian elder Benjamin Harrison spoke, as honorary chairman. So did President William McKinley and Vice President Teddy Roosevelt. It seemed to mark a new era. Robert T. Handy writes: "Tensions between liberals and conservatives were somewhat sublimated in the partnership of piety, progress, and civilization which, it was confidently believed, was preparing the way for the kingdom itself."[30]

Mott's book raised two questions for American Protestantism. First, was there really a possibility of evangelizing the whole world in one generation? Second, what should be the theological message brought to the non-Christian world by Protestant missionaries? World War I and its immediate aftermath ended most Americans' confidence in Mott's vision of victory. The final phase of the war in Northern Presbyterianism would be fought over the second question: the theology of missions. And fought it was. Sanctions were imposed in 1936. The crucial issue was sanctions.

---

30. Robert T. Handy, *A Christian America: Protestant Hopes and Historical Realities*, 2nd ed. (New York: Oxford University Press, 1984), p. 116.

Part 3

FROM EVANGELISM TO LIBERALISM

It is sometimes said that although one way of salvation is by means of acceptance of the gospel there may be other ways. But this method of meeting the objection relinquishes one of the things that are most obviously characteristic of the Christian message—namely, its exclusiveness. What struck the early observers of Christianity most forcibly was not merely that salvation was offered by means of the Christian gospel, but that all other means were resolutely rejected. The early Christian missionaries demanded an absolutely exclusive devotion to Christ. Such exclusiveness ran directly counter to the prevailing syncretism of the Hellenistic age. In that day, many saviours were offered by many religions to the attention of men, but the various pagan religions could live together in perfect harmony; when a man became a devotee of one god, he did not have to give up the others. But Christianity would have nothing to do with these "courtly polygamies of the soul"; it demanded an absolutely exclusive devotion; all other Saviours, it insisted, must be deserted for the one Lord. Salvation, in other words, was not merely through Christ, but it was only through Christ. In that little word "only" lay all the offense. Without that word there would have been no persecutions; the cultured men of the day would probably have been willing to give Jesus a place, and an honorable place, among the saviours of mankind. Without its exclusiveness, the Christian message would have seemed perfectly inoffensive to the men of that day. So modern liberalism, placing Jesus alongside other benefactors of mankind, is perfectly inoffensive in the modern world. All men speak well of it. It is entirely inoffensive. But it is also entirely futile. The offence of the Cross is done away, but so is the glory and the power.

J. Gresham Machen (1923)[*]

---

[*] Machen, *Christianity and Liberalism* (New York: Macmillan, 1923), pp. 123-24.

INTRODUCTION TO PART 3

It is required of all officers in the Presbyterian Church, including the ministers, that at their ordination they make answer "plainly" to a series of questions which begins with the two following: "Do you believe the Scriptures of the Old and New Testaments to be the Word of God, the only infallible rule of faith and practice?" "Do you sincerely receive and adopt the Confession of Faith of this Church, as containing the system of doctrine taught in the Holy Scriptures?"

If these "constitutional principles" do not fix clearly the creedal basis of the Presbyterian Church, it is difficult to see how any human language could possibly do so. Yet immediately after making such a solemn declaration, immediately after declaring that the Westminster Confession contains the system of doctrine taught in infallible Scriptures, many ministers of the Presbyterian Church will proceed to decry that same Confession and that doctrine of the infallibility of Scripture to which they have just solemnly subscribed!

J. Gresham Machen (1923)[1]

Machen, as with previous Old School members, could not overcome the "crossed fingers" problem: ministers who publicly swore their commitment to the Confession, but who then defied its stipulations in teaching or preaching. These ordained men were not held judicially accountable to the terms—theologically precise terms—of their oaths. The Presbyterian court system had abandoned any defense of the Confession. The system of government declared by the Form of Government and the Book of Discipline no longer was being enforced.

Parallel Governments

No later than 1910, there was a well-organized shadow government inside Northern Presbyterianism. This shadow government had

---

1. Machen, *Christianity and Liberalism* (New York: Macmillan, 1923), p. 163.

its own rules, its own confession, and its own system of sanctions. Unless temporarily convenient to it, or unless forced upon it, this government would not abide by the written Confession and constitution of the Church.

This shadow government was shielded by the New School's tradition of resisting heresy trials. The New School in 1870 was not ready to enforce the Westminster Confession on a systematic basis, any more than it had been in 1837. Prior to the reunion, only Charles Hodge understood that the Old School would have to consent to a two-government system: official and unofficial, formal and substantive. New School ministers were confessing to a Confession that they had no intention of systematically enforcing in Church courts. This made possible an operating alliance between the modernists' shadow government and the New School.

Another aspect of this hidden government was the seminary system. As I have said earlier, from 1812 to 1871, Princeton had officially required that its incoming students be able read Latin well enough to read Turretin. But by the time of the reunion, this requirement had become a sham. Many students in 1870 could not read Turretin; instead, they read Hodge's lecture notes on Turretin, which were heavily, though not exclusively, based on Turretin. So, Hodge decided to put his notes in print: *Systematic Theology* (1871–73). Yet for another generation, the Church officially continued to pretend that every ordained man could read Latin fluently. Only in 1911 did the Church's presbyteries vote to substitute a bachelor's degree or master's degree in place of Latin.[2]

Presbyterianism officially placed the authority of ordination in the hands of the presbytery. But before he could be ordained, the candidate had to read Latin fluently (a sham by 1870) or earn an advanced academic degree (1911–), be a graduate of a seminary, and have a knowledge of Greek and Hebrew, all of which required formal education that the presbytery did not offer. Functionally, Presbyterianism after 1812 transferred the bulk of the ordination process to college professors (four years) and seminary professors (three years). Yet Presbyterians pretended that the presbytery was still in control: a one-

---

2. *Minutes of the General Assembly, 1911*, pp. 197–98.

hour (or less) exam. In short, a dual government system—separate sanctions—was in operation for ordination after 1812. It would be possible to argue that this tradition had begun through the transformation of New Side leader William Tennent's informal seminary of the late 1720's, which became the Log College in 1735,[3] which in turn became the College of New Jersey (1746). The college degree became mandatory for ordination.

Secular Education in America

The Calvinist seminary was the first institutionally separate graduate school in the United States: Andover (1808) and Princeton (1812). Beginning in 1876, Johns Hopkins University pioneered the secular graduate school in America. It was, in Marsden's words, "the virtual cradle of modern academic thought in America. . . ."[4] It was under the direction of Daniel Coit Gilman, who had arrived after completing his work in consolidating the University of California. He had been its second president, the man who shaped it. Gilman's first major public act was to bring Thomas Huxley, known as "Darwin's bulldog" and a champion of the recently invented term "agnosticism," to address the school in the fall of 1876, seven months after its official opening.[5] Johns Hopkins was committed to technical excellence, using the German educational model. Johns Hopkins, in turn, became the model for America's graduate schools. As Marsden summarizes this development: "Technical specialization almost inevitably meant that there would be vast realms separated from direct religious influences. . . . That meant that the universities themselves, as well as the vast majority of their disciplines, were defined according to the new professional scientific basis for which religion was considered irrelevant."[6] There was no protest from the Christian public, which had already accepted

---

3. Cited in Leonard Trinterud, *The Forming of an American Tradition: A Re-examination of COLONIAL PRESBYTERIANISM* (Salem, New Hampshire: Ayer, [1949] 1978), p. 63.

4. George Marsden, "J. Gresham Machen, History, and Truth," *Westminster Theological Journal*, 42 (Fall 1979). p. 159.

5. George Marsden, *The Soul of the American University: From Protestant Establishment to Established Nonbelief* (New York: Oxford University Press, 1994), pp. 151–52.

6. *Ibid.*, p. 156.

what Marsden calls "The larger tendency of modernity," i.e., "methodological secularization."[7] Seminaries did not escape this outlook. In 1876, Briggs delivered his first inaugural address promoting higher criticism; a decade later, Warfield was promoting lower criticism. Both forms of criticism rested on common-ground, religiously "neutral" principles of investigation.

The center of interest at Johns Hopkins in the 1880's was the weekly seminar conducted by Herbert Adams. This meeting was not called a seminar; it was called a Historical Seminary. In attendance at this Seminary were some of the major Progressive intellectuals, including Richard T. Ely (economics), J. Franklin Jameson (history), and Woodrow Wilson, who as a student was its scribe.[8] This Seminary was secular to the core.

Two Constitutions

In 1883–84, Wilson, still a graduate student, wrote a book, *Congressional Government*. It was published in 1885. He submitted it as his Ph.D. dissertation at Johns Hopkins. It was accepted. In it, he identified the crucial distinction between the "constitution of the books" and the "constitution in operation."[9] That distinction would soon become fundamental in both the U.S. government and Presbyterian government. In 1887, the first U.S. regulatory commission was established, the Interstate Commerce Commission. A new bureaucratic structure was imposed on the Constitutional order. This structure would allow a new hierarchy based on economic self-interest to gain control over the consumers' flow of funds through government regulation of the market.[10] Under Wilson, 1913–1921, this regulatory system would be extended as never before. The hidden Constitution would replace the written one.[11]

---

7. *Ibid.*

8. Ray Stannard Baker, *Woodrow Wilson: Life and Letters* (New York: Doubleday, Page, 1927), *Youth, 1856–1890*, pp. 178–79.

9. Woodrow Wilson, *Congressional Government: A Study in American Politics* (Gloucester, Massachusetts: Peter Smith, [1956] 1973), p. 30.

10. Gabriel Kolko, *The Triumph of Conservatism: A Reinterpretation of American History, 1900–1916* (New York: Free Press, [1963] 1977).

11. Arthur S. Miller, *The Secret Constitution and the Need for Constitutional Change* (Westport, Connecticut: Greenwood, 1987), ch. 1. Miller discusses the reality of the elite Establishment's control over this secret Constitution. The

Paralleling this development, a similar transformation took place in the Presbyterian Church. The Foreign Missions Board became both the model and the wedge. It raised funds outside of normal Church channels. This semi-independent structure of recruiting and funding was soon augmented by Dwight L. Moody's Northfield missions conferences, which in the late 1880's began attracting hundreds of young men who dedicated themselves to the foreign mission field. This Collegiate Great Awakening re-shaped foreign missions in the denominations.[12]

The modernists, who were political Progressives, established a shadow Presbyterian government by strengthening and extending the Church's system of permanent boards. When the Church added new layers of bureaucracy after 1908, modernists steadily sought and received employment in them. These agencies resembled the U.S. government's regulatory commissions in their independence from the legislative authority, i.e., the General Assembly. Progressives used the same system of infiltration and capture in both civil and ecclesiastical government. In both cases, they benefited from executive alternatives to legislative authority. This is the judicial process known as administrative law. It is undermining the Western legal tradition.[13]

In 1908, the Church established a new administrative bureaucracy: the Executive Commission, which would run the Church in between General Assemblies. This was the Church's major step in the creation of a shadow government. The shadow government had achieved invisible supremacy by 1920.[14]

Dead Letters and Hidden Agendas

Ministerial oaths are the judicial basis of ordination. A covenant oath for which no institutional sanctions can be invoked is judicially a

---

him develop his thesis.

12. See Chapter 14, below: section on "Foreign Missions and Ecumenism."

13. Harold J. Berman, *Law and Revolution: The Formation of the Western Legal Tradition* (Cambridge, Massachusetts: Harvard University Press, 1983), pp. 33-41.

14. See Chapter 6, below: section on "The Interchurch World Movement, 1919-1921," pp. 392-403.

dead letter, whether in Church, State, or family. The oath-taker may, for sentimental or other personal reasons, adhere to the terms of the oath, but it no longer has the force of law behind it. *If Presbyterian ministerial oaths were in fact dead letters institutionally after 1900, then historic Presbyterianism was equally a dead letter.* The defining characteristics of Presbyterianism then became ecclesiastical rather than theological: tradition over confession, form over content. Yet this was not really the case, either, for there is always confession; there is always content. *What had changed was the judicial character of the oath's content.* The Confession's words remained, but new interpretations were now in effect. *A hidden Confession had replaced the written Confession.* The new Confession governed the boards and permanent bureaucracies of the Church, where decisions regarding the Church's operations were increasingly being made.

A Larger Problem

The problem of modernist ministers who taught doctrines opposed to the Westminster Confession was part of a more general problem: conservative ministers who paid no attention to the Confession. The modernists defied the Confession; a majority of the conservatives by 1910 simply ignored it. They had publicly sworn an oath to uphold the Confession and the two catechisms, but they were interested in other things. To hamper the modernists, let alone see them de-frocked, Machen had to gain the votes of Confessional indifferentists. This was Machen's dilemma because it had been the Old School's dilemma since the reunion.

Machen knew that the Church's operational confession had changed. He understood that this had undermined historic Presbyterianism. But he could not prove his case theologically to the satisfaction of the vast middle that held the sanction of the vote. Very late in the Presbyterian conflict, he was trying to reclaim the denomination from its long-term theological deterioration, but without any institutional means to enforce the formal terms of ministerial oaths. Machen and his supporters were judicially offense-less. After the Scopes trial in 1925, they became increasingly defenseless.

So, Machen made the best of it. He incorporated this institutional defenselessness into his overall strategy, especially after Princeton Seminary was restructured in 1929. He adopted a method of proof which was more than academic and rhetorical; it was institutional. He decided to force his opponents to throw him out for pressing the case for Confessional orthodoxy. This would, he believed, publicly demonstrate his theological case against them. He would force them to demonstrate that they had abandoned the Confession.

They always refused to admit that this was the case. (Their defenders still do.) They denied that he was being thrown out for theological reasons. They argued that the issue was exclusively administrative: a matter of institutional authority and mandatory obedience irrespective of the details of formal theology. But this was nonetheless a theological statement: an affirmation of the power religion. In 1935 and 1936, men who had long denied the legitimacy of imposing sanctions to defend the Westminster Confession's stipulations applied sanctions against those who did affirm its authority. There is no escape from sanctions. The question in 1936 was this: *By which confession*—the official one or the unofficial one? This was the battle over point three of the covenant, stipulations. There was another battle, however: over point two.

Rival Theologies: Representation

Representation is point two of the biblical covenant. The covenantal questions are these: Who speaks for God in any organization? Who has the authority under God to enforce God's law in a particular organization? In short, to whom do subordinates report?

Ecclesiastical ordination is based on judicial representation. The question arises: Who is being represented? The Old School Presbyterians answered: God primarily, the Church's members secondarily. This ordination process is itself representative; it must be screened through men who are themselves ordained, and who are bound by the terms of the Church covenant. This view of Church officers is fundamental to Presbyterianism. The New School did not officially disagree, although the New School's emphasis was on personal experience and minimal confession rather than the detailed terms of the Confession of Faith and the Form of Discipline's sanctions.

Power and the General Will

The modernist disagreed with Presbyterianism's judicial basis of representation, but they could not do so publicly. Their view of God was radically different. Their god was the evolving god of spiritual process. This god reveals himself continually through mankind, which is continually evolving. There is no definitive revelation of a sovereign God to men in history, the modernists insisted. The people are sovereign, for they speak for the modernists' god; they manifest this god. There is no radical Creator/creature distinction in modernism, for there is no doctrine of definitive personal creation. Modernism is process theology, not creationist theology. Briggs did his best to equate his process theology with the traditional Calvinist doctrine of progressive sanctification,[15] but this was a tactic, not a serious theological position. Briggs' theology had no doctrine of the definitive imputation of Christ's perfect humanity as the judicial basis of personal salvation.

The people do incarnate god, modernism teaches, but they are an inchoate mass. They do not speak with a unified voice. Borrowing from Rousseau's political terminology, we could say that the people are the source of the General Will, but they do not express it. They themselves need representation. The sovereign people must be represented in a democracy, including the Church, but by whom? This was the institutional problem for the modernists.

The Church's answer was *formal*: representation by those who have been ordained. But the crucial figure in American Presbyterianism after 1926 was Speer, and he had never been ordained. The *substantive* answer as to who should represent the people's Church was ethical. The spokesman whose word must be obeyed is he who represents the interests of that sub-group which most faithfully voices the General Will, i.e., the spirit of the age, the climate of public opinion—the "best" opinions, of course. The spirit of the age in the 1920's was clearly not Calvinist. Thus, Presbyterian representation, while formally Calvinistic ("four-point Calvinism" after 1903), would have to be based on some other factor. For the modernists, this other factor was the ability to gain and maintain power, which in Rousseau's political theology is the meaningful manifestation of the General Will.

---

15. Briggs, *Whither? A Theological Question for the Times*, 3rd ed. (New York: Charles Scribner's Sons, [1889] 1890), p. 147.

Nisbet is correct: "It is political religion which Rousseau extols. . . ."[16] This religion has become the dominant religion of the modern world's intellectual and spiritual leaders.

Atonement vs. Moral Example

There was no way to reconcile Presbyterianism's judicial concept of representation with modernism's. Evolution and Christianity do not mix. The Confession's doctrine of progressive sanctification was undergirded by a theology of *definitive judicial representation*: Jesus Christ, in His judicial office of perfect humanity (the second Adam) died in place of His elect, i.e., *died representatively*. His perfect humanity is imputed judicially in history by God to the elect. ". . . God in justification imputeth the righteousness of Christ. . ." (Larger Catechism, Answer 77). This means that man's progressive sanctification is judged continually by God in terms of the fully complete, final sanctification achieved by Jesus Christ at His resurrection in history. Jesus Christ's achievement was in no way evolutionary; it was the very antithesis of evolution or process. By overcoming death in history, He definitively proved that the ultimate evolutionary process—life inevitably leading to death[17]—is not binding on man or the cosmos, both of which can be redeemed by God's grace.

The broad evangelical wing of the Church accepted the doctrine of judicial imputation, though not in its full Calvinist rigor, e.g., Jacob's pre-birth election but not Esau's. The modernists did not accept any of it. Thus, two irreconcilable doctrines of representation were operating inside the Presbyterian Church. Each view was an extension of a particular theology. The evangelicals proclaimed the God who declares all of His people "Not guilty!" in history on the judicial basis of the ethically completed work of Christ in history. The redeemed will escape God's final judgment at the end of time. In contrast, the modernists proclaimed a process divinity indistinguishable from the

---

16. Robert A. Nisbet, "Rousseau and the Political Community," in Nisbet, *Tradition and Revolt: Historical and Sociological Essays* (New York: Random House, 1968), p. 25.

17. Ultimately, the heat death of the universe: the triumph of entropy. Gary North, *Is the World Running Down? Crisis in the Christian Worldview* (Tyler, Texas: Institute for Christian Economics, 1988), ch. 2.

cosmos, one who does not bring final judgment in eternity, or if he does, few if any people are condemned (Briggs' view). Jesus supposedly did not act as man's representative judicial agent; rather, He acted as a moral example. All men can become what Jesus was. In the outline of his final sermon, which he preached at age 80 in 1931, Henry van Dyke wrote: "Man is sinful but not damned. Needs to be saved and can be saved. . . . Jesus is messenger of this forgiving love. . . . Truth as Jesus sees it is not static. Dynamic, unfolding, advancing."[18]

Sanctions

The crucial issue was sanctions. The Calvinists proclaimed the biblical God who will bring final judgment. The modernists refused to proclaim such a God; they did not believe in a literal hell. But if there is no hell, then the institutional Church does not possess the authority to declare someone outside the realm of special grace. This means that there can be no lawful excommunication based on a person's legal condition of being visibly lost and in danger of hell. *The Church cannot lawfully declare in history what cannot become a reality in eternity.*

Then on what judicial basis can a minister be removed from his pulpit? The modernists answered technically: "Only if his presbytery says he must, and the deciding issue must not be his theology." But this answer was a smoke screen, one which still blinds the eyes of Church historians. Theology is an inescapable concept. It is never a question of theology vs. no theology. It is always a question of *which* theology.

Rival Strategies: Representation

Because their theologies of representation were different, the two main camps operated in terms of rival views of Church court authority. The modernists did not publicly operate in terms of their view

---

18. Tertius van Dyke, *Henry van Dyke: A Biography* (New York: Harper & Bros., 1935), p. 412. He preached it four places: (1) Seal Harbor, Maine; (2) Bar Harbor, Maine—both located on Mount Desert Island, the enclave of America's Establishment; (3) the Brick Church in New York City, where he had been the pastor; and (4) First Church, Princeton, where he had walked out in 1923 because of Machen's preaching, notifying the press of his decision.

until after 1930; their strategy prior to 1930 was a strategy of subversion. Their goal was to subvert the Church's system of authority and sanctions, negating it until they could capture it.

The Debate Over Judicial Precedent

What was the role of judicial precedent? When a court handed down negative sanctions, to what degree would future courts be bound by this decision? In other words, to what degree was a prior decision *representative judicially* for future decisions?

Two views of law were at war in the Church. The modernists viewed Church law much as they viewed Mosaic law: as a series of isolated declarations cobbled together by an unprovable theory of providential judicial unity. Such judicial unity does not exist in the biblical texts, they insisted. Such unity is mythical. Belief in such unity is the product of pre-scientific mind-set. Those who would enforce such a view of law are clearly not to be trusted. The moral law was not revealed by an unchanging, sovereign God. Law evolves; ancient law has no moral authority. Law is based on present power, not past precedent.

For as long as the conservatives controlled the Church's courts, the modernists refused to acknowledge the courts' authority to make anything except retroactive decisions in specific trials. They denied that one General Assembly's decision could lawfully bind any future General Assembly. They were formally correct. The Church's rules limited the General Assembly's authority. Only with two-thirds of all the presbyteries voting to change the Church's theological standards, or a majority to change the Form of Government, could new standards be adopted or applied.[19] But this rule only applied to the General Assembly acting as a legislative body. As a supreme court, its rulings served as precedents, which is why the Church periodically published updated compilations of its rulings, the *Digest of the Acts and Deliverances of the General Assembly*.

The conservatives' theory of law rested on a non-evolutionary view of history. They viewed New Testament law and the Ten Com-

---

19. *The Form of Government*, XXIV:I, II, *The Constitution of the Presbyterian Church in the United States of America* (Philadelphia: Presbyterian Board of Publication and Sabbath School Work, 1904), pp. 389–90.

mandments as part of an unchanging moral order created by God. They believed in judicial precedents by the Church's courts. The Church's goal is to establish a judicial order that is in conformity to the Bible's moral and judicial requirements. Precedents should be honored. As with the Confession of Faith, judicial precedents should not be abandoned without major cause.

They concluded that if a man preaches what another man has been de-frocked for, he should also be de-frocked by the courts. Thus, the Church officially de-frocked Smith in 1894 because of Smith's declaration that he believed in the opinions voiced by Briggs. The conservatives believed in *declaratory representation* by individuals and courts.

If the supreme court's declaration of judgment does not bind future lower courts, and if it does not influence future supreme court decisions, then the rule of law collapses. *Without legal predictability, every institution's survival is threatened.* If one court decision sets no binding pattern on future decisions, every case will be appealed. The organization will be drained by the costs of endless adjudication. This undermines the rule of law. While the supreme court can change its mind under extraordinary circumstances—the Old School's 1864 reversal on slavery was a case in point—the preponderance of authority must rest with precedent.

Furthermore, without binding legal precedents, those disputants going before a judge cannot be sure what he will decide. Disputes are unlikely to be settled before they go into court, since each side has an equal opportunity to win, i.e., random. *A court unbound by precedent can become arbitrary and even tyrannical.* Given the fact of original sin, it will become arbitrary and tyrannical if more power is transferred to it or arrogated by it. To reduce the arbitrary power of the courts, conservatives defended judicial precedent. The Whig political tradition still prevailed in conservative circles.

The Modernists' Judicial Strategy

The rule of law can be undermined by the courts in two ways: (1) courts can ignore precedents, or reinterpret them into oblivion, thereby producing either legal chaos or judicial tyranny; (2) courts can refuse to try or convict, thereby producing either institutional chaos or tyranny by informal, extra-judicial institutional arrangements. In the first case, the courts' activity is the source of the problem; in the second case, the courts' inactivity is the source of the problem. The liberals on occasion promoted each of these possibilities.

The modernists understood Presbyterian law and tradition. They understood what they would have to do to deflect attacks against them. They understood what was necessary to take control of the Church's institutional structure. After 1900, they adopted a two-step judicial strategy at the national level: defensive and offensive. First, the *defensive judicial strategy*: reduce or eliminate the ability of the General Assembly, as a gathered annual body, to initiate anything judicially enforceable. Their strategy was to deny the legitimacy of all binding legislative declarations by the General Assembly. They became defenders of the initiating authority of the presbyteries. Second, the *offensive judicial strategy*: gain control over the supreme court, i.e., the General Assembly, through a new system of bureaucratic representation for the Assembly. Once accomplished, they could then reassert the power of the General Assembly. In short, "Power taketh away, and power giveth back; blessed be the name of power."

The General Assembly represented the Church once a year for one week in May. The supreme strategic goal of the modernists was to create a system of representation for the General Assembly in between the annual meetings, and then staff it with their representatives. They could not do this through a system of bishops. They had to do it by adding new layers of bureaucracy. This is the traditional Presbyterian way.

If this could be accomplished, their representatives could act in the name of the General Assembly in between the annual meetings, rewrite the Form of Government, persuade the General Assembly to vote favorably on the alteration at an annual meeting, submit it to the presbyteries, persuade the presbyteries to vote for it, and then re-introduce judicial precedent with a vengeance, conducting a coordinated series of trials. I know of no secret planning committee that sat down in 1901 to create this plan of infiltration, but the nature of Presbyterian law and Presbyterian tradition, as well as Progressive politics, mandated that the modernists use bureaucracy rather than personal rule (episcopacy) in their capture of the denomination. The structure of the Form of Government made it clear what they had to do: (1) avoid heresy trials at the presbytery level and (2) gain full-time administrative control in the name of a national representative assembly that met only once a year.

If they could avoid heresy trials, they would not need to fear Church sanctions. They could believe whatever they wanted, and even preach it, assuming they did so in a judicious, mild-mannered way. They did not feel morally bound by previous precedents, for they did not believe in God's final judgment, the doctrine of judicial imputation, or the lawful authority of the Church to make such judicial declarations in the name of an absolutely sovereign God. They did not believe that such a God has granted to men a uniquely holy book which speaks authoritatively in His name. They did not believe in binding universal unchanging law. If they could avoid negative sanctions, in any way, at any cost, they could remain in the Church as faithful representatives of the god of process. They felt no moral obligation to leave. They felt a moral obligation to stay.[20]

The Conservatives' Judicial Strategy

Conservatives could thwart the modernists by an offensive use of the courts to screen out new heretics and remove previously ordained ones. This initiatory authority existed only at the presbytery level. The General Assembly could not initiate heresy trials. So, the General Assembly would have to content itself by instructing presbyteries. But this instruction could not be judicial except in the sense of *guaranteeing the outcomes of future trials initiated by the presbyteries and appealed to the General Assembly*.

The conservatives got the opportunity to use the General Assembly as an appeals court only once: in the Fosdick case, 1923-24. They issued a series of declarations through the General Assembly (1910, 1916, 1923) about what lower courts should do, but the presbyteries ignored these recommendations. The conservatives acted as though the General Assembly were the supreme legislative body rather than the supreme judicial body. As a judicial body, just like the U.S. Supreme Court, it was also an unofficial but inevitable legislative body,

---

20. Cf. Henry van Dyke, *The Bible As It Is* (New York: Session, 1893), p. 29. See Chapter 5, above: section on "Briggs' Second Defense in Presbytery," subsection, "Van Dyke's Test," pp. 261-63.

but only in its capacity to declare judicial precedents that govern lower courts and all legislative assemblies. First, the General Assembly could initiate offensive actions by voting on overtures that would then be sent to the presbyteries for ratification. Second, the General Assembly could encourage offensive presbyterial action by issuing predictable final judgments in heresy trials. Both approaches required the cooperation of the presbyteries: to ratify changes in the Form of Government and to initiate heresy trials.

The second strategy was the easiest. It took only one elder to initiate a heresy trial, and he could appeal the results if the suspect was then declared innocent. But after 1900, only the Fosdick case produced a final decision by the General Assembly, and the decision was theologically indecisive.

The conservatives refused to pay the price of defending the Church from its enemies. They contented themselves with rhetorical gestures, the main one being their repeated calls for over four decades for the liberals to leave the Church. The liberals replied, schoolboy-like: "Make us!" The issue was negative sanctions. The conservatives refused to apply them.

The liberals were seeking power in the name of evolutionary ethics. Their strategy of subversion was based on process theology, which included ethics. Because the conservatives never really understood this application of modernism's process theology, they regarded the modernists as unethical men. By the standards of the Westminster Confession and the Bible, modernists *were* unprincipled men: wolves in sheep's clothing. But in terms of situation ethics, they were wiser than the children of light. The conservatives did not recognize this fundamental ethical separation. *There is no common ethical system joining Christians and modernists. There is only temporary common procedure.* Progressives became the masters of procedure in every field and in almost every influential national institution after 1900. They captured the robes of authority: representation.

This lack of common ethical ground is why the conservatives' insistence that the modernists leave the Presbyterian Church fell on judicially deaf ears. This demand merely amused the liberals. Why should they leave? The modernists were Progressives. They believed in democracy as a process. They also believed in bureaucracy as a structure promoting reform. They believed in reform, but they believed that reform comes only because a dedicated elite operates self-consciously within the democratic process to guide it.

The modernists saw themselves as representatives of an open-ended future that faces no final judgment other than what is common to all existence: the impersonal heat death of the universe. Conservatives saw themselves as representatives of a sovereign God who will bring final judgment. There was no common theological ground between them. There was only a common system of courts: civil and ecclesiastical. The modernists understood this far better than the conservatives did. They acted accordingly.

An Open-Ended Process

Modern democracy is open-ended. It is not based on a judicial concept of a covenantal oath taken by citizens before a God who threatens negative corporate sanctions against them if they corporately violate the legal terms of the covenant (Ex. 19). In this sense, modern democracy is based on the theology of modernism: "no representative sanctions in history imposed by a God who threatens final sanctions in eternity."

The Old School had always accepted this view of political democracy. They were Whigs, as theologically conservative American Presbyterians had always been. Machen said over and over that the judicial standard of political democracy does not apply in a voluntary institution. He argued again and again that the democratic standards of civil government must not be imported into the Church. He pointed to the oaths of Presbyterian ministers as evidence of the difference between secular democratic civil government, which he accepted, and Church government. If his opponents ever understood this argument, they must have silently thought to themselves, "Says you." His view of the limits of political democracy—the boundary wall of separation between Church and State—meant nothing to his opponents. They were Progressives. They recognized no limits to democracy as a methodology. Theirs was the religion of democracy. They imported their religion into the Church. They would not be bound by theological precedents. They saw themselves as representing the future, not the past. In modernism's theology, the future is not bound by past legal or theological precedents. There was therefore no moral reason for any modernist to leave except through formal expulsion.

Machen was in a bind. He believed in Church court precedents. He also believed that the Church's highest court, the General Assembly, did speak authoritatively in history. It spoke either for God or for covenant-breaking man. This became increasingly clear to him as he was squeezed by the modernists and their judicially silent evangelical allies. By 1936, he would decide whether the Church was apostate in terms of the General Assembly's decision against him. He concluded this because he at long last recognized the institutional significance of point two of the biblical covenant—representation—and point four: sanctions. He understood that the General Assembly's decision would be a representative decision. It would speak to the whole world in terms of a covenant. The question was: Whose covenant?

The Effects of Crossed Fingers

Only fanatics and highly principled people are willing to remain on what is clearly the losing side institutionally. This reality of human nature pointed to a time in which the average local church member, elder, and minister would knowingly adopt the tactic that the modernists adopted regarding the Confession: *crossed fingers*. They had been doing this since 1869 on what they regarded as minor issues. They would eventually have to do this with respect to major issues. If the long retreat from Confessional orthodoxy could not be reversed and turned into a successful offensive campaign, then the bulk of the conservative troops would eventually profess covenantal allegiance to a Church that opposed the fundamentals of their faith. They would eventually argue, as Machen heard them argue, that "the Presbyterian Church is fundamentally sound." Everyone would keep his fingers safely crossed, no matter how far from the Westminster Confession of Faith the might Church stray.

The modernists also adopted the tactic of crossed fingers. But there was a fundamental difference between the modernists and their opponents with respect to crossed fingers. The modernists were crossing their fingers as an offensive tactic which was part of a larger strategy, namely, to steal the inheritance left to their heirs by Confessionalists who had built the American Presbyterian Church for two centuries. They adopted crossed fingers to help advance their strategic plan to become the winning side. They did not adopt the tactic of crossed fingers as a way to remain forever on the institutional sidelines in a lost cause. For a modernist, crossed fingers are a way of life: *situational ethics*. Crossed fingers are part of a systematic strategy: *inheritance*. For a Calvinist Presbyterian, crossing his fingers represents personal moral compromise and institutional retreat. Crossing his fingers will eventually debilitate his will to resist. To preserve his self-esteem, he will have to re-define both his personal confession and his cause.

Most Calvinists in the Presbyterian Church, U.S.A., became progressively debilitated, 1901-1936. Therefore, they went through the painful process of re-defining their confession and their cause.

Darwinism, Progressivism, and Democracy

The 1890's saw the rise of the Progressive movement in the United States. It was Darwinist to the core. There had been a shift in the application of Darwinism in the 1880's, most powerfully presented by Lester Frank Ward in his two-volume *Dynamic Sociology* (1883) and reinforced a decade later by Benjamin Kidd's *Social Evolution* (1894).[21] The individualistic Darwinism of Herbert Spencer and Yale's William Graham Sumner had become passé in Progressive intellectual circles. Spencer's famous phrase, "the survival of the fittest," no longer was understood by Progressives as the survival of the most competitive individuals within a species. It now meant the survival of the more powerful species. Species man, through the impersonal forces of unplanned and unplanning nature, has made an evolutionary leap of being: the human brain.

The reform social Darwinists believed that some men possess a unique knowledge of the laws of evolution. These men—meaning an elite group of scientists—can now direct the environment, including race, and also including social forces, along progressive paths. Apart from such planning, society (like nature) is too wasteful. The State should therefore adopt the recommendations of the planners.[22] This

---

21. Arthur A. Ekirch, Jr., *Progressivism in America* (New York: New Viewpoints, 1974), ch. 2.

22. For a detailed discussion of this shift in Darwinism, see Gary North, *The Dominion Covenant: Genesis*, 2nd ed. (Tyler, Texas: Institute for Christian Economics, 1987), Appendix A.

reversed the anti-State, pro-free market worldview of the previous generation of Social Darwinists.[23] Arthur S. Link, who dedicated his career to a study of Woodrow Wilson, has summarized the new outlook: "By 1900 the ideal of an individualistic society had given way, at least in the minds of many intellectuals and political leaders, to the concept of a society organized for collective action in the public interest."[24]

The Progressive movement was dedicated to reform: of education, State, and society, which included the institutional Church. What was not emphasized by historians until late in the twentieth century was the influence of Calvinism in the early lives of several of the founders of Progressivism. In his aptly titled book, *Ministers of Reform*, Robert M. Crunden writes of these founders: "They routinely noted [in their autobiographies] the pervasiveness of Calvinist influences in their homes and made few objections to their import. They frequently rebelled as soon as they were old enough to succeed, yet they remained devoted to their parents and tolerant of discipline as an inevitable part of their emotional worlds."[25] Crunden does not make it clear that the roots of this Calvinist heritage were in New School Presbyterianism and New Light Congregationalism. He understands, however, that "The political heritage that informed this religious heritage was usually abolitionist."[26] The archetypical representative of the Progressive movement—its very incarnation—was Woodrow Wilson. Unlike most children who grew up in the South, Crunden observes, he became a Progressive.[27] What Crunden does not explain is that Calvinist Presbyterianism in the South had been dominated by Old School theologians until long after the Civil War. Wilson joined the Northern Church.

---

23. Herbert Spencer, *The Man versus the State* (Indianapolis, Indiana: Liberty-Classics, [1884] 1982); William Graham Sumner, *What Social Classes to Owe Each Other* (Caldwell, Idaho: Caxton, [1883] 1961). Reprinted, Yale University Press, 1925, 1934.

24. Arthur S. Link, *Woodrow Wilson and the Progressive Era, 1910–1917* (New York: Harper & Bros., 1954), p. 1.

25. Robert M. Crunden, *Ministers of Reform: The Progressives' Achievement in American Civilization, 1889–1920* (New York: Basic Books, 1982), p. 3.

26. *Ibid.*

27. *Ibid.*, p. 9.

The relationship between political/social Progressivism and theological modernism was not a one-way affair. Each of these reform movements shared common roots in New School/New Light Calvinism. Modernism was a rival theological system to both Old School and New School Calvinism. Progressivism was a rival political system to Whig political Calvinism, of which Machen was the last nationally prominent representative.

Darwin Replaces Newton

The Newtonian worldview was essentially mechanical. In Newtonianism, mathematics rules the cosmos. To the extent that physics became the ideal model for men's social theories, the quest for social order became the quest for fixed laws. Natural law was seen as above historical processes, bringing order to these processes. This worldview collapsed under the weight of Progressivism's version of social Darwinism. No better statement of the transformation can be found than Woodrow Wilson's 1908 book, *Constitutional Government of the United States.*

In 1906, Woodrow Wilson wanted to run for President in 1908 as the Democratic Party's nominee. He had an ideological problem. He had been a Hamiltonian throughout his classroom career: a believer in a strong central government.[28] The Hamiltonian vision was associated with the Republican Party generally, and after 1909, with Theodore Roosevelt's Progressives specifically.[29] This was not the tradition of the Democratic Party in 1906. The Jeffersonian-Jacksonian tradition was laissez-faire. Bryan's radical Populism had abandoned this tradition, but Populism was totally hostile to any elitist oligarchy—the essence of Hamiltonianism and, in Bryan's eyes, the Republican Party. The Democratic Party had nominated conservative lawyer Alton B. Parker in 1904, a defender of the gold standard, who lost so badly to Roosevelt that some of the Party's leaders were ready to abandon the old Andrew Jackson-Grover Cleveland-Whig liberalism tradition. Bryan despised this tradition; he called it "Clevelandism."[30] Bryan was

---

28. This was the assessment of his student, Raymond Fosdick: *Chronicle of a Generation: An Autobiography* (New York: Harper & Bros., 1958), p. 50.

29. Link, *Wilson*, p. 19.

30. Cited in Paolo E. Coletta, *William Jennings Bryan*, 2 vols. (Lincoln: Uni-

correct when he wrote in a letter, immediately after Parker's defeat, "The defeat was so overwhelming that we are not likely to hear much more—for some years at least—of the reorganizers. The Democratic Party will now have a chance to become a real reform party."[31] Regionally, the Democratic Party was moving toward Progressivism throughout the first decade of the twentieth century, even in the South,[32] but the national party did not clearly position itself as Progressive until after Taft's defeat of Bryan in 1908.[33]

So, to win the 1908 nomination, Wilson publicly had to switch. He switched four times in four years: from Hamiltonianism to Jeffersonianism (1906); from Jeffersonianism to Progressivism (1907); back to limited Jeffersonian government (the New Jersey governor's campaign of 1910); and back to Progressivism (the day after he won the governorship). In 1906, speaking at a Jefferson Day dinner of the National Democratic Club, he extolled Jeffersonian ideals of the little man's rights.[34] His speech defended laissez-faire economics. This speech was well received by an audience of "Old Democrat," Grover Cleveland types who, like Wilson, was opposed to Bryan's Populism. But Wilson had been opposed to Bryan in the name of Hamilton; the conservative Democrats had been opposed to Bryan in the name of Jefferson.

Bryan won the party's nomination for a third time in 1908, so Wilson's subtle moves to win the nomination had failed. Wilson had to wait another four years. In 1907, Wilson openly moved from laissez-faire Jeffersonianism to Progressivism. He wrote *Constitutional Government*, a thinly disguised fat campaign tract, published the next year. It praised the Presidency as the central political office: head of the party. This was a self-conscious break from the Constitution's view of the office. The Constitution does not mention political par-

---

versity of Nebraska Press, 1964), I, *Political Evangelist*, p. 319.
31. *Ibid.*, I:352.
32. Dewey Grantham, *Southern Progressivism: The Reconciliation of Progress and Tradition* (Knoxville: University of Tennessee Press, 1983).
33. David Sarasohn, *The Party of Reform: Democrats in the Progressive Era* (Jackson: University of Mississippi Press, 1989).
34. Henry Wilkinson Bragdon, *Woodrow Wilson: The Academic Years* (Cambridge, Massachusetts: Belknap Press of Harvard University, 1967), pp. 339–41.

ties, and the Framers had hated political factions in 1787. Wilson, having switched to Progressivism, had to undermine this older political faith. He turned to Darwin as the solution. The Founders had been Whigs because they had been Newtonians, he correctly argued. This Newtonian Whig worldview is incorrect, he insisted, and so is the Constitutional order that assumes it. "The government of the United States was constructed upon the Whig theory of political dynamics, which was a sort of unconscious copy of the Newtonian theory of the universe. In our own day, whenever we discuss the structure or development of anything, whether in nature or in society, we consciously or unconsciously follow Mr. Darwin; but before Mr. Darwin, they followed Newton. Some single law, like the law of gravitation, swung each system of thought and gave it its principle of unity."[35]

The checks and balances built into the Federal government by the Constitution are now a hindrance to effective political action, he said. This language of balances reflects mechanism. We need to overcome this mechanical way of thinking, Wilson said:

> The trouble with the theory is that government is not a machine, but a living thing. It falls, not under the theory of the universe, but under the theory of organic life. It is accountable to Darwin, not to Newton. It is modified by its environment, necessitated by its tasks, shaped to its functions by the sheer pressure of life. No living thing can have its organs offset against each other as checks, and live. On the contrary, its life is dependent upon their quick cooperation, their ready response to the commands of instinct or intelligence, their amicable community of purpose. Government is not a body of blind forces; it is a body of men, with highly differentiated functions, no doubt, in our modern day of specialization, but with a common task and purpose. Their cooperation is indispensable, their warfare fatal. There can be no successful government without leadership or without the intimate, almost instinctive, coordination of the organs of life and action. This is not theory, but fact, and displays its force as fact, whatever theories may be thrown across its

---

35. Woodrow Wilson, *The Constitutional Government of the United States* (New York: Columbia University Press, [1908] 1961), pp. 54–55.

track. Living political constitutions must be Darwinian in structure and in practice.[36]

This was the Progressives' worldview: the State as a centralized agency of reform in which sufficient political power is concentrated to overcome the economic power of large corporations. The State becomes society's coordinator, like the central nervous system-brain connection: organic.

State Planning

Liberalism in America after 1900 meant State planning, especially through bureaucratic centralization and Federal regulation. This worldview was shared by theological modernists. It was the basis of the social gospel of the Federal Council of Churches. Political reform was to be achieved through the establishment of bureaucracies that would control business. This would be financed by money collected from taxpayers.

This view of political centralization was mirrored after 1900 in the hierarchies of the churches, including the Presbyterian Church, U.S.A. The denomination consented to a centralization of power in agencies run by boards that were nearly independent, not merely from lay control but even from the General Assembly. Only if a scandal arose within a bureaucracy and gained public attention was the authority of a board likely to be challenged, which happened only once, in 1932–33, with the Board of Foreign Missions. These agencies were staffed by nearly permanent employees. Their jobs were not quite so secure as jobs were in the U.S. government. Government employees had Civil Service protection. Employees of the Church's bureaucracies were more vulnerable. *The Presbyterian liberals' primary protective strategies were secrecy and the avoidance of confrontational rhetoric.* Few documents are less rhetorical than bureaucratic reports.[37]

The worldview of Progressivism was based on the possibility of social healing through the centralization of political power, funded by

---

36. *Ibid.*, pp. 56–57.
37. Anyone who doubts this should spend a day reading sample passages from the thousand-plus pages of board reports published annually after 1906 in Volume 2 of the *Minutes of the General Assembly*.

other people's money.[38] This worldview became the operating standard for theological modernists, who were committed to the goals and means of the Progressive movement.

Machen rejected this worldview, both as an Old School Calvinist and a nineteenth-century Whig political liberal. He was a political liberal of the New South. There was more of the post-1815 John C. Calhoun in his politics than of Daniel Webster or Henry Clay. He did not trust the State.

The Progressives viewed democracy as an open-ended process, just as they viewed natural forces. Evolution reveals itself progressively, but its revelations are always bounded by time. There is no ultimate truth higher than evolution. This outlook was applied to democracy. The masses will always lag behind the insights of the scientific elite. Ward had announced in 1883: "The knowledge which enables a very few to introduce all the progressive agencies into civilization tends not in the least to render the mass of mankind, though possessing equal average capacity for such service, capable of contributing any thing to that result. On the contrary—and this is a fact of capital significance—this inequality in the distribution of knowledge actually tends in no small degree to render a considerable amount of the knowledge prejudicial to the true interests of society."[39] The fundamental issue then becomes: Who in society is best able to discern these "true interests"? *The scientific elite.* As with Rousseau's General Will, which is revealed clearly to all men only in the hypothetical absence of society's many non-political institutions, and which can be perceived in the real world only by political rulers,[40] so are the true interests of society in Progressive thought. Social science became the Progressives' proposed key to understanding—a social science informed by historical understanding, i.e., historical process and the forces of social and cultural evolution.[41]

---

38. Ekirch, *Progressivism in America*, Parts 3, 4.

39. Lester Frank Ward, *Dynamic Sociology; or Applied Social Science*, 2 vols. (New York: Appleton, [1883] 1907), II:535.

40. Nisbet, "Rousseau," *Tradition and Revolt*, ch. 1.

41. Morton White, *Social Thought in America: The Revolt Against Formalism* (Boston: Beacon Press, 1957).

Democracy and Bureaucracy

Max Weber wrote his studies of bureaucracy and power during the Progressive era. He understood that bureaucracy accompanies mass democracy.[42] He also understood the new principle of representation: someone must speak and act in the name of the masses, modern society's sovereign. "The *demos* itself, in the sense of a shapeless mass, never 'governs' larger associations, but rather is governed. What changes is only the way in which executive leaders are selected and the measure of influence which the *demos*, or better, which social circles from its midst are able to exert upon the content and the direction of administrative activities by means of 'public opinion.'"[43] This observation applied to the Presbyterian Church.

Political democracy rejects the rule of old elites, such as nobles who hold their power by birth. By substituting self-certifying bureaucracy for rule by nobles, the democratic order creates another rival to democracy. The bureaucrats resist public opinion whenever that opinion is opposed to the expansion of bureaucratic power. "Thereby democracy inevitably comes into conflict with the bureaucratic tendencies which have been produced by its fight against the notables."[44] Couple this tendency to resist public opinion with a view of social evolution which elevates the scientific planner to the position of representative of the progressive future—the vanguard of the next evolutionary leap of being—and there is built into bureaucracy an antidemocratic theology of administrative process.

The Primacy of the Examination System

Modernism's god is the god of evolutionary process. This god speaks only through evolving mankind, and really only through the uniquely ordained representatives of evolving mankind. This ordination is not based on a covenant oath; it is based on the successful completion of an examination system. But this is what the Old School

---

42. Max Weber, *Economy and Society: An Outline of Interpretive Sociology*, edited by Guenther Roth and Claude Wittich (New York: Bedminster, 1968), p. 983.
43. *Ibid.*, p. 985.
44. *Ibid.*

had also concluded: the functional sovereignty of the seminary examination system. Thus, functionally and judicially, the Old School was not in a strong position to stop the flood of theologically lax candidates for the ministry that was coming out of the seminaries. In 1914, Princeton Seminary graduated 29 students. This constituted 14 percent of the 200-plus graduates of the thirteen Northern Presbyterian seminaries, not counting Union.[45] The Old School was being swamped. Contrary to a 1992 study of the catalogues of Presbyterian seminaries,[46] Old School theology survived in the 1920's only at Princeton. The other formally Old School seminaries did not move overnight from Hodge, Strong, and Shedd to Barth, Brunner, and the two Niebuhrs in the 1930's. In between there was the Progressives' version of modernism. The transformation took three decades.[47] That the catalogues did not announce this theological shift until the 1920's is evidence that the modernists' strategy was in effect: *no public confrontation.*

The seminaries surrendered piecemeal. First, they hired men in the Old Testament department who taught higher criticism. Second, they quietly began to hire modernists in other departments, since the modernists' historicist methodology had already been accepted by the Old Testament department. This process was well underway by 1900. Union was the model, not Princeton. Third, the seminaries welcomed neo-orthodoxy in the 1930's and 1940's. The supreme irony here is that by the time the modernists captured the Northern Presbyterian Church in 1936, modernism was itself becoming passé; the existentialism of neo-orthodoxy and the political realism of Reinhold Niebuhr were rapidly replacing it.

---

45. *Minutes of the General Assembly, 1914*, pp. 328–68.

46. John M. Mulder and Lee A. Wyatt, "The Predicament of Pluralism: The Study of Theology in Presbyterian Seminaries Since the 1920s," in *The Pluralistic Vision: Presbyterians and Mainstream Protestant Education and Leadership*, edited by Milton J Coalter, John M. Mulder, and Louis B. Weeks (Louisville, Kentucky: John Knox Press, 1992), ch. 1.

47. Lefferts A. Loetscher, *The Broadening Church: a study of theological issues in the presbyterian church since 1869* (Philadelphia: University of Pennsylvania Press, 1954), pp. 77–82.

Throughout the period surveyed in this book, a stream of ministers was coming into the Presbyterian Church from other, less theologically rigorous denominations. From 1870 to 1926, over 5,100 of the 16,615 ordained ministers were received from other denominations. The percentage rose steadily after 1900: from almost one-third during the entire period to almost 39 percent, 1922–26.[48] The liberals had only to be patient. Time and seminary education were on their side.

Other People's Money

American Progressives had a strategy, which culminated in 1913 with the Sixteenth Amendment (the Federal income tax), the Seventeenth Amendment (the direct election of U.S. Senators), and the establishment of the Federal Reserve System, a quasi-public central bank relatively free from interference by Congress or the President that would possess a monopoly over the nation's monetary policy. Their strategy was to impose their agenda through the use of other people's money. The British Fabians achieved the income tax in 1911. Their forebears in 1694 had set up the Bank of England, the model for all successive privately owned, publicly sanctioned central banks.[49] Now it was America's turn.

The Progressives understood that the average citizen did not agree with their view of scientific management by an educated elite through government coercion. William Jennings Bryan's opposition to the Eastern Establishment, from his 1896 Democratic presidential nomination until his death in 1925, reminded them that an anti-elitist Populist political movement opposed them. The Populists also wanted extensive government controls, but not if the wealthy elite would benefit. The Progressives understood that individuals would not voluntarily finance all of the social programs that were dear to the hearts of most Progressives. The Progressives' strategy was to finance their

---

48. Herman C. Weber, *Presbyterian Statistics Through One Hundred Years, 1826–1926* (n.p.: The General Council, Presbyterian Church in the U.S.A., 1927), p. 103.

49. John Brewer, *The Sinews of Power: War, Money, and the English State, 1688–1783* (New York: Knopf, 1989).

projects through money collected by law from people who would not volunteer these funds. Like the Populists, Progressives needed to reach directly into the wallets of the citizenry in order to fund their reform schemes. The Sixteenth Amendment achieved this goal even though, technically speaking, it was never properly ratified by voters[50]—a judicial "oversight" that academic historians have never bothered to explore.

The Presbyterian Debate Over Economics

Presbyterian liberals were Progressives. The pronouncements of the Federal Council of Churches, founded in 1908, reflected the Progressives' political agenda: the social gospel of the Council's 1908 Social Creed of the Churches. (John D. Rockefeller, Jr., personally contributed five percent of the first year's budget.)[51] A modified version of these pronouncements was presented to the 1910 General Assembly as a report of the Special Committee on Social Problems, appointed by the 1909 General Assembly. This report was presented in the same year as the theologically conservative five-point Doctrinal Deliverance. The report did not explicitly call for the State to enforce child labor laws, shortened hours for women, and sabbath laws, but the State's action was implied.[52] It did not name the Federal government as the proper agency of enforcement. So, the report was ambivalent: a statement of social and economic goals without any mention of how this should be accomplished. The Assembly voted to approve it. From 1912 to the mid-1920's, conservatives resisted or de-fanged such pronouncements except for those associated with Prohibition and sabbath laws.[53] But they did not have the votes to stop these pronouncements completely.

---

50. This thesis, accompanied by photographic reproductions of the primary source documentation, is presented by Bill Benson and M. J. Beckman, *The Law That Never Was* (South Holland, Illinois: Constitutional Research Assn., 1985); cf. *XVI: The Constitution's Income Tax Not Ratified* (Washington, D.C.: American Liberty Information Society, 1985).

51. Albert F. Schenkel, *The Rich Man and the Kingdom: John D. Rockefeller, Jr., and the Protestant Establishment* (Minneapolis, Minnesota: Fortress Press, 1995), p. 182.

52. *Minutes of the General Assembly, 1910*, pp. 230–32.

53. Gary Scott Smith, "Conservative Presbyterians: The Gospel, Social Reform, and the Church in the Progressive Era," *American Presbyterians*, 70 (Sum-

Presbyterian liberals wanted to achieve in ecclesiastical affairs what the Federal government achieved through the income tax: *administrative centralization without loss of funding through the defection of those paying the bills*. They had a model: the Episcopal Church. They saw what Episcopalian liberals had achieved through administrative centralization. This process had accelerated after the withdrawal of the Calvinists from the denomination in 1873 to establish the Reformed Episcopal Church, which, like the Presbyterian Church, was headquartered in Philadelphia. When Briggs needed a place of refuge, he was ordained by the Episcopalian Church. After that, he could write *Church Unity* without fear of retaliation.

The Conservatives' Response

The most vocal Presbyterian opponent of Progressivism's economic ideas in these years was Princeton Seminary's William Brenton Greene, Jr., professor of apologetics (1893–1926), who wrote a hundred-plus book reviews opposing the social gospel.[54] But short book reviews by one man in an in-house academic journal did not constitute a successful defense. Greene and his associates did not offer an alternative economic framework in the name of the Bible. In fact, they denied that such an alternative existed. There was no systematically biblical, exegetical, conservative Protestant alternative to the baptized left-wing humanism of the Federal Council and its theological equivalents. There was only baptized right-wing humanism: Scottish Enlightenment sociology, i.e., some variant of nineteenth-century political liberalism. Greene presented this view; so did Machen in the 1920's.

In 1914, Greene issued a challenge to the social gospel in the name of New Testament ethics, but it was merely the familiar defense of nineteenth-century Whig individualism combined with Christian pietism. He complained: "Sociology is a more popular study than theology and the reason is that it puts its stress not in individual regeneration but on

---

mer 1992), pp. 93–96.
54. Earl William Kennedy, "William Brenton Greene's Treatment of Social Issues," *Journal of Presbyterian History*, 40 (1962), pp. 92–112.

social reformation."[55] He began with the assumption that all the Mosaic laws governing society are judicially annulled today. Then he said that their underlying "sociological principles" are still sound.[56] He suggested no way to get from these sound principles to actual civil legislation. (Neither had any of his ideological predecessors.) Furthermore, "Our Lord was anything rather than a social reformer or a teacher of sociology."[57] So far, he had offered no alternative to the modernists' Progressivism.

Greene openly rejected the Federal Council's 1908 Social Creed of the Churches.[58] The Bible does not pass judgments on such topics, he insisted, so the Church should not. "The authority of the Bible does not cover every sociological question."[59] Yet his silence with regard to what questions it does cover implied that it covers no sociological question. The minister's great work, he concluded, "is not to agitate even for the social principles laid down in the Bible." Rather, he is to preach the gospel. Greene ended his essay with this announcement: "This is the supreme and the most comprehensive lesson of the Bible regarded as *the* text-book in Sociology."[60] In short, the Bible is judicially silent on social issues, so the minister ought to be silent, too.

What Greene really was saying was that the Bible is *not* a textbook in sociology. Sociology is judicially independent of the Bible. The great issues of sociology, meaning social theory, are not really so great; they are *adiaphora*: things indifferent to the faith. Greene was arguing against the Federal Council's manifestoes in the same way that Hodge and other Old School theologians had argued against abolitionism: by steadfastly avoiding an appeal to the texts of the Bible in search of an alternative worldview. This theological defense failed miserably with respect to abolitionism and therefore also with respect to the Old School's authority in the nation after 1865 and in the North-

---

55. William Brenton Greene, Jr., "The Bible as the Text-Book in Sociology," *Princeton Theological Review*, 12 (Jan. 1914), p. 7.
56. *Ibid.*, pp. 13–14.
57. *Ibid.*, p. 19.
58. *Ibid.*, p. 21.
59. *Ibid.*
60. *Ibid.*, p. 22.

ern Presbyterian Church after 1869. It failed equally miserably with respect to modernism's Progressivism. It was not Greene's Calvinist Whig theology that prevailed over the old modernism; rather, what prevailed was the new existential modernism of Barth and Brunner and the left-wing political realism of Reinhold Niebuhr.[61]

The Presbyterian conservatives tried to defeat something with nothing. This defensive effort was doomed. The spirit of the age was contrary to the older non-interventionist political liberalism: the politics of Grover Cleveland. It was contrary to the older free market social Darwinism. Increasingly, so was the spirit of the Presbyterian colleges, whose younger faculty members had earned advanced academic degrees from secular universities. The liberals had only to bide their time in order to win. Eventually, a younger generation of university-trained seminary professors would replace the dwindling and aging Old Guard, which held forth only at Princeton by 1914. Only one younger faculty member at Princeton publicly articulated Greene's views: Machen, who became an assistant professor of New Testament in 1914. Few Presbyterians outside of the Princeton campus had heard of him until the first week of 1924. It was Henry van Dyke's resignation from the First Church of Princeton and his press release on December 31 that catapulted Machen into the limelight.

Follow the Money

Events are not the product of vast impersonal forces. Ours is not a cosmically impersonal universe. Mobs usually have leaders;[62] movements always do. Movements also have financial supporters. Theological modernism from 1910 to 1936 and beyond did, too. Most of these supporters were simple people who put their weekly offerings into collection plates, not recognizing that their money was being used to undermine the confessionally Christian worldview they had grown up with.

---

61. Donald B. Meyer, *The Protestant Search for Political Realism, 1919–1941* (Westport, Connecticut: Greenwood, [1960] 1973).

62. There are few groups more dangerous than a mob without a leader. A law-enforcement officer must then somehow create one in order to deal with the mob. This, at least, was Wyatt Earp's opinion, to whom I defer in such matters.

But there was another source of the funding, one who understood early what Franklin Roosevelt would later call pump-priming: spending money strategically in order to get far more money flowing. That man was John D. Rockefeller, Jr. He and his two employees —Frederick Gates, who had advised father,[63] and, beginning in 1920, Raymond Fosdick—spent enormous sums of money, 1910 to 1960, to redirect American religious, intellectual, and industrial life, and foreign policy. They were remarkably successful, yet they have received very little credit or blame. This was also part of their plan. I can do no better than to quote my colleague from our graduate school teaching assistantship days, Charles Harvey, who wrote a series of articles in 1982—insufficiently appreciated—on the Rockefeller connection: "The obscurity of Rockefeller's role is partly due to his artful circumspection as heir to the world's largest industrial fortune and the controversies surrounding its formation. The oversight is also due, one suspects, to the aversion of historians to what might seem a vulgar economic determinism or even a conspiracy thesis. Yet, as with a number of other major developments in the first half of the twentieth century, to ignore Rockefeller is to miss much of the inside story."[64]

This is why I do my best to follow at least some of the Rockefeller money in the following chapters.

Conclusion

After 1900, the modernists adopted a new strategy. It was based on the infiltration and strengthening of the bureaucracies and boards of the Church. They understood the threat of de-frocking; they respected power. Power is what they respected above all. They decided that discretion was the better part of valor. They were willing to bide their time, publicly testing the climate of ecclesiastical opinion occasionally but not continually. They did not depart from the Church

---

63. Gates had been the educational secretary of the Northern Baptists. Charles E. Harvey, "John D. Rockefeller, Jr., Herbert Hoover, and President Wilson's Industrial Conferences, 1919-1920," in *Voluntarism, Planning and the State: The American Planning Experience, 1914-1946*, edited by Jerold E. Brown and Patrick D. Reagan (Westport, Connecticut: Greenwood, 1988), p. 28.

64. *Ibid.*, p. 25.

even though Briggs and Smith had been de-frocked and two had resigned before their trials in the General Assembly: Swing in 1874 and McGiffert in 1900. They did not regard the Church's courts as representing a sovereign God in history. They believed in a god who reveals himself progressively only through the processes of history. If they could remain in the Church and gain control over its judicial agencies, they could someday impose sanctions in terms of their values. They would thereby reveal themselves as this evolving god's representatives in history.

The modernists had a theology. This theology was attractive and powerful. Even Machen, the most astute of their opponents, did not fully understand the extent of this theology's comprehensive claims. We know that he did not understand it because he kept repeating the naive, sanctionless request of the 1892 General Assembly: modernists should avoid violating their consciences and leave the Church. But they were not violating their consciences. They were Progressives. Such an act of voluntary withdrawal was regarded by the modernists as worse than cowardice: it was foolishness. They saw Church government as an open-ended evolutionary process. Their goal was the capture of America's greatest ecclesiastical treasure: colleges, seminaries, church buildings, a stream of income from donors, a prestigious denomination's reputation, and perhaps even political influence. Resign? Were their opponents fools?

Machen knew that modernism had a radically different view of God, propositional truth, and the Church, but he did not understand that it also had a radically different view of representation and sanctions. He fought his war on points one, three, and five of the five covenantal battlefields: theology proper (the doctrine of God); propositional truth (creedalism); and succession, meaning Church growth as an aspect of the expansion of God's kingdom in history. He understood very well that modernism had a rival view of the earthly future: the kingdom of God vs. the ecumenical kingdom of man. The battle over succession in Machen's day was the two-front battle over ecumenism: home missions (ecclesiastical ecumenism vs. personal evangelism) and foreign missions (universalism-ecumenism vs. personal evangelism). But he did not pay close attention to the modernists' theology in points two and four: representation and sanctions. Here was where the modernists chose to concentrate their efforts,

1901–1936, for in these two areas of the covenant the issues of power are settled in history. As power religionists, the modernists paid very close attention to points two and four. It was here that the battle would be won or lost, especially point four: sanctions. The crucial issue was sanctions.

Phase 3: Whose Legality?

6

SHADOW GOVERNMENT, ADMINISTRATIVE LAW

> *For five or six years, through overtures, committees of investigation, public addresses, newspaper articles, and private conversations, the Presbyterian Church has been voicing its desire for simplification, unification, and centralization, and also for cooperation, solidarity, and mutuality.*
>
> Minutes (1911)[1]

> *The leading inquiry in the examination of any system of government must, of course, concern primarily the real depositaries and the essential machinery of power. There is always a centre of power: where in this system is that centre? in whose hands is self-sufficient authority lodged and through what agencies does that authority speak and act?*
>
> Woodrow Wilson (1885)[2]

When he wrote this, Wilson was a 29-year-old graduate student at Johns Hopkins University in Baltimore, where he was frequently a

---

1. *Minutes of the General Assembly, 1911*, p. 151.
2. Wilson, *Congressional Government: A Study in American Politics* (Gloucester, Massachusetts: Peter Smith, [1956] 1973), p. 30.

guest in the Machen household.³ This was his first published book, *Congressional Government*. He submitted it in 1886 as his Ph.D. dissertation. It was accepted. He joined Princeton University a few years later. He became a ruling elder in Second Presbyterian Church, an office he would hold in the Presbytery of New Brunswick during most of the period in which Machen refused ordination by that same presbytery because of his theological doubts. Woodrow Wilson had no doubts about theology or anything else.⁴

From 1900 to 1920, there was no clear-cut answer in the Presbyterian Church to Wilson's question: "In whose hands is self-sufficient authority lodged and through what agencies does that authority speak and act?" By 1920 the answer was clear to anyone who cared to look: in the bureaucracies of the Church, including the Executive Commission, which spoke for the General Assembly at least 51 weeks every year. This 1908 creation was the crucial institution for the modernists. If they could take control over it, they would capture the Church. By 1920, they had. Warfield in 1921 knew that the battle was lost, but Machen refused to quit. His time of trial had not yet come. Beginning on December 31, 1923, it would. On that day, Henry van Dyke sent a letter of temporary departure to the trustees of First Presbyterian Church, vowing not to return until Machen ceased preaching there. He sent copies to the press.⁵

In acknowledgment of the dawning of a new liberal era, the social gospel liberals who edited the Disciples' magazine, *The Christian Oracle*, in 1908 changed its name to *The Christian Century*. The century soon proved to be anything but Christian. As accurate forecasting goes, the original magazine was not much of an oracle.⁶ But from

---

3. Ned B. Stonehouse, *J. Gresham Machen: A Biographical Memoir* (Philadelphia: Westminster Theological Seminary, [1954] 1977), p. 72.

4. He died in 1924, a broken, beaten man, absolutely confident that the U.S. Senate had been wrong about the League of Nations, and that he had been completely correct.

5. See Chapter 8, below: section on "Van Dyke Strikes Again." Van Dyke was the crucial modernist in the Presbyterian conflict.

6. In 1962, the magazine did it again. At the peak of the American Protestant Establishment's control over the religious scene—a drastically shrunken scene since 1908—its editor wrote: "Today, as a new era dawns, God is using the power

1908 to 1920, it did seem as though Protestant liberalism in America was destined for an era of ever-greater victories. In just two decades, 1901 to 1920, Presbyterian liberals were able to reverse what had appeared to be an overwhelming victory by the conservatives in 1900.

The institutional question had been representation. What did Briggs and Smith represent in 1900? Victory or defeat? The two sides had differing assessments. The conservatives were ready to "put all that behind us; we won." The liberals were ready to do the same thing; they had lost. The conservatives believed they had proved their point. Meanwhile, by remaining inside the Church, the liberals believed they could eventually prove their point. But both sides agreed: the trials of the 1890's should be put behind. And because of this readiness to "put all that behind us," the Presbyterian Church was publicly captured in 1936 by the spiritual heirs of the losers of the 1890's. The leaven of modernism steadily replaced the leaven of orthodoxy.

Theology as a Trifle

In 1901, Robert E. Speer, secretary of the Board of Foreign Missions, spoke eloquently, as he usually spoke, to the General Assembly. He defended the priority of foreign missions and the non-priority of doctrinal "trifles." He implored his audience: "Oh, my friends, our Church needs a supreme world purpose, such as this of which I have been speaking, that will forbid our trifling away the time of God, playing with details while men die."[7] Thirty-five years later, one year before Speer retired, Machen was publicly de-frocked because of his effort to bring minimal-creed orthodoxy to Speer's Board and, through it, to the Church. In the aftermath of that experience, Machen wrote: "But I am bound to say that I think such doctrinal

---

of ecumenical faith and experience to add a new dimension to churchmanship in Asia, Africa and Latin America, as well as in Europe and America." Harold E. Fey, "Preface," in Fey and Margaret Frakes, eds., *The Christian Century Reader* (New York: Association Press, 1962), p. 7.

7. Speech to the General Assembly, "The Speedy Bringing of the World to Christ," cited in James A. Patterson, "Robert E. Speer, J. Gresham Machen and the Presbyterian Board of Foreign Missions," *American Presbyterians*, 64 (Spring 1986), p. 59.

advance to be just now extremely unlikely. We are living in a time of widespread intellectual as well as moral decadence, and the visible church has unfortunately not kept free from this decadence.... Intellectual and moral indolence like ours does not constitute the soil out of which great Christian creeds may be expected to grow."[8]

Machen's words reflected not only his own defeat, but the defeat of Old School Presbyterianism, 1901 to 1903, while he was a student at Princeton Seminary. Machen understood what that defeat meant and how it was manifested: by the Confessional revision of 1903 and its aftermath. Yet even he and his followers retained two of these changes in 1936: the elimination of the Confession's statement that to refuse to take an oath to a lawful agency is a sin (XXII:3), which was the last trace of theocratic language in the 1788 American revision, and the identification of the Pope as the Antichrist (XXV:6),[9] which had been the most widely shared Protestant doctrine during the Reformation. Even in eras in which confessions supposedly should not be revised, confessions can be properly revised. This was a major theological problem for Machen and the Old School: they, too, had crossed their fingers.[10]

Speer as the Model Bureaucrat

The opening years of the twentieth century were marked by a shift of theological opinion within the Presbyterian Church: the devaluing of the Westminster standards and all other judicially enforceable creeds. This period was also marked by the beginning of the restructuring of the Presbyterian Church's administrative machinery. The model for this restructuring was the Board of Foreign Missions. Speer, secretary of that Board from 1891 to 1937, was the embodi-

---

8. Machen, "The Creeds and Doctrinal Advance" (1936), in *Scripture and Confession: A Book About Confessions Old and New*, edited by John H. Skilton (Nutley, New Jersey: Presbyterian & Reformed, 1973), p. 156.

9. Report of the Committee of the Constitution, *Minutes of the Second General Assembly of the Presbyterian Church of America* (Nov. 12-14, 1936), pp. 13-14.

10. This problem is not confined to ecclesiology; it is fundamental to every tradition and every constitution. History moves forward. New traditions appear. Constitutions are revised. New precedents are set. But God retains the final veto in terms of permanent standards.

ment of the institutional development, while Henry van Dyke incarnated the theological transformation. Because of Speer's commitment to minimal-creed missions work and ecumenical missions work, he became a spokesman for the minimal-creed umbrella under which van Dyke and his fellow liberals operated safely.

Speer was present at the creation of the Federal Council of Churches in 1908.[11] Its organizers had been working at the national level since the 1901 conference held in Philadelphia: the National Federation of Churches. There had been a series of local and regional conferences throughout the 1890's. The Inter-Church Conference of 1905 was the penultimate step.[12] Historian Sidney Fine writes of the Federal Council that it "was not only a product of the social-gospel movement but became, in effect, the institutional embodiment of the social gospel point of view in American Protestantism. Significantly, the social creed that it adopted in 1908 and amended in 1912 was in perfect accord with the legislative objectives of Progressivism."[13] In 1920, Speer was elected president of the Council for a four-year term. His fervent plea to the General Assembly in 1923 saved the Federal Council from a cut-off in funding by the Southern Presbyterian Church; the General Assembly had almost voted to secede. A year later, the PCUSA voted for the first time to fund the FCC: $25,000.[14]

Speer's language was always pietistic and conciliatory, but his four decades of pleas echoed Henry van Dyke's 1893 manifesto, *A Plea for*

---

11. In that same year, the Northern Baptist Convention was formed, with Henry Pratt Judson, president of the University of Chicago, as its first president. Judson conferred with Rev. Frederick Gates, Rockefeller's money-distributor, on numerous matters. Albert F. Schenkel, *The Rich Man and the Kingdom: John D. Rockefeller, Jr., and the Protestant Establishment* (Minneapolis, Minnesota: Fortress Press, 1995), pp. 35-36.

12. C. Gregg Singer, *The Unholy Alliance* (New Rochelle, New York: Arlington House, 1975), p. 19.

13. Sidney Fine, *Laissez Faire and the General-Welfare State: A Study of Conflict in American Thought, 1865-1901* (Ann Arbor: University of Michigan Press, 1956), p. 381. The 1908 social creed itself was the product earlier in the year of the General Conference of the Methodist Episcopal Church: "The Social Ideals of the Churches." See Samuel McCrea Cavert, *On the Road to Christian Unity: An Appraisal of the Ecumenical Movement* (New York: Harper & Bros., 1961), p. 31.

14. Singer, *Unholy Alliance*, p. 59.

Peace and Work. Speer faithfully hewed the modernists' wood and carried their water. When theological liberals sought an evangelical whose presence would legitimize their undermining of orthodox Christianity, they repeatedly turned to Speer.[15] For over four decades, he helped raise their money, gave them employment, and protected their interests. He did all this as a favor—no strings attached.

Speer walked down the center of the highway between liberalism and orthodoxy, but he always walked in the direction of liberalism. No truck travelling toward orthodoxy ever flattened him, and the liberals granted him the right-of-way. In the name of evangelicalism, Speer baptized Progressivism. But he did not do this alone. He had help from the most important teaching elder in phases three and four of the Presbyterian conflict, a man who began his career as an Old School man.

Roberts' Rule of Order

The Church's slow but sure administrative centralization after 1880 made the Stated Clerk of the denomination an increasingly influential figure. This position was filled from 1884 until his death in 1920 by William H. Roberts, a theological conservative.[16] There is no doubt regarding his conservatism. He was fired by Lane Seminary for his stand against higher criticism. The Trustees in 1893 simply abol-

---

15. See, for example, the symposium edited by Ralph H. Gabriel, *Christianity and Modern Thought* (New Haven, Connecticut: Yale University Press, 1924). Speer wrote Chapter 9: "Christianity and International Relations." The editor wrote in his Foreword regarding fundamentalism's "demagogic appeals" (p. viii). He announced triumphantly: "It seems fairly clear that liberal Protestantism is shaking off this inherent tendency ["to conserve the traditions of antiquity and to retard advance"] and is putting itself in the way to assume a new leadership in a new world" (p. xi). Furthermore, "the result seems destined to be Protestant unity." He spoke of "the passing of the Fundamentalists," and proclaimed "a new faith out of which will have been refined those encumbering superstitions and doctrinal antagonisms which are the inheritance of ignorance" (p. xii).

16. On Roberts' long career, see Bruce David Forbes, "William Henry Roberts: Resistance and Bureaucratic Adaptation," *Journal of Presbyterian History*, 54 (Winter 1976). The Stated Clerk of the Southern Presbyterian Church, 1865-1898, was also a conservative, Joseph Ruggles Wilson, the father of Woodrow and the brother-in-law of James Woodrow. Roberts was a friend of the Wilson family.

ished the Chair of Practical Theology that he occupied.[17] Yet he did more to further the cause of liberalism than Lane's Henry Preserved Smith ever did.

In 1894, the year of Smith's conviction, the office of Stated Clerk became a full-time position.[18] Roberts became the chief legal officer and chief financial officer of the denomination.[19] He became the Church's statistician, a task for which he was well trained, having worked as a statistician for the U.S. government early in his career.[20] He was appointed automatically to the most important committees. He also became the Church's representative in the various Reformed ecumenical organizations.[21] Perhaps most important from the point of view of the historian, the Stated Clerk edited the *Minutes of the General Assembly.*[22] He was succeeded in the office of Stated Clerk in 1921 by Lewis Mudge, Speer's classmate from Princeton University. Under Mudge, the centralization process was completed in 1936.[23]

In 1905, Roberts became the permanent chairman of the Inter-Church Conference, which organized the Federal Council of Churches.[24] In 1908, he became the acting president of the Council,[25] and in 1911 became the first secretary of the Council's newly created Commission on Evangelism.[26] His 1908 welcome speech before the Federal Council invoked the postmillennial vision of Princeton's theology in front of an assembly of social gospel advocates who were

---

17. *Ibid.*, p. 412.
18. *Ibid.*, pp. 414–15.
19. *Ibid.*, pp. 415–16.
20. *Ibid.*, p. 417.
21. Richard W. Reifsnyder, "Presbyterian Reunion, Reorganization and Expansion in the Late Nineteenth Century," *American Presbyterians*, 64 (1986), p. 33.
22. James H. Smylie, "Stated Clerks and Social Policy: American Presbyterians and Transforming American Culture," *ibid.*, 67 (Fall 1989), p. 193.
23. Smylie says not a word about Mudge, who served from 1921 to 1938. He served as Stated Clerk Emeritus until his death in 1945, and he served as Acting General Secretary of the Board of Education, 1938–40. *Minutes of the General Assembly, 1945,* p. 99.
24. *Minutes of the General Assembly, 1906,* p. 134.
25. Smylie, "Stated Clerks," p. 194.
26. Singer, *Unholy Alliance,* p. 79.

ready to immanentize the kingdom in the name of Progressivism. We must, he said, "hasten the day when the true King of Men shall everywhere be crowned as Lord of all. The Council stands for the hope of organized work for speedy Christian advance toward world conquest. . . . It is marvelous how the presence of the common enemy in heathen lands has brought Christian men to realize their need of unity in thought and work."[27] This was the ecumenical vision of Presbyterianism's most entrenched bureaucrat.

Forbes has put it well: the bureaucratization and centralization of the Presbyterian Church paralleled the bureaucratization and centralization of American society generally. "Some historians' preoccupation with the activist and the social gospel applications of American ecumenism, especially that of the Federal Council of Churches, has led to neglect of important institutional implications. The example of William Henry Roberts suggests that the organizing, consolidating impulse of ecumenism may have been more closely related to the bureaucratic, regularizing trends within the nation as a whole then [than] we have previously recognized."[28] Roberts served both as the midwife and nursemaid of this administrative process, making life far easier for the liberals whose theology was formally anathema to his, but whom he never bothered to challenge once he had accepted his job as chief bureaucrat. By 1920, when death removed him from the job, the takeover of the administrative machinery by the liberals was complete.

The Pressure to Revise

There had been a brief movement favoring the revision of the Confession, 1889-91. This effort had failed. The Briggs affair erupted in 1891, followed by Smith's conviction in 1894 and then the resignation of McGiffert in 1900, a year that became a turning point for the denomination, although no one recognized it at the time.

---

27. Cited in Robert T. Handy, *A Christian America: Protestant Hopes and Historical Realities*, 2nd ed. (New York: Oxford University Press, 1984), pp. 148-49. Handy lists the social gospel leaders involved in the work of the Council (p. 149).

28. Forbes, "Roberts," p. 417.

The removal of these three modernists, two by court action, was accomplished because of their offense against the Bible and biblical truth, not because of a concerted effort by the courts to defend Calvinistic sections of the Confession. Confrontational rhetoric had sunk Briggs, not ministerial concern over a defense of the Confession. The trials had revealed that the Confession was institutionally vulnerable. The modernists wasted no time in calling this vulnerability to the attention of the Church. They had the cooperation of the New School.

When a Church decides not to impose sanctions to enforce a creed, it will either revise its creed or ignore it forever. But Presbyterianism in 1900 could not abandon the Confession, so it would have to be revised. In 1900, the next wave of pressure to revise the Confession began. The General Assembly was petitioned by over three dozen presbyteries to begin consideration of revision. The Old School recognized this for what it was: an attempt to depart from the rigor of the Confession. Once again, the Old School was on the defensive. The liberal agenda regarding Confessional revision had returned to center stage: exactly where it had been in 1889, as if nothing had happened in between.

The Old School's defense would depend on their ability to persuade ruling elders that they should defend the Confession with the same enthusiasm that they defended the Bible. With respect to the reliability of the Bible, the ruling elders were generally in agreement with the Old School. But the Old School had a problem: confessions are man-made documents. Members of the Old School could not defend the Confession with the same confidence that they could defend the Bible. As for the two catechisms, relatively few Presbyterians were familiar with them. The last major commentary on the Shorter Catechism was Congregationalist Samuel Willard's *Complete Body of Divinity* (1726). The Larger Catechism has had only one major commentator.[29] The two catechisms were museum pieces, especially the Larger Catechism. People paid public respect to them; they did not pursue

---

29. Thomas Ridgeley, *A Body of Divinity*, 2 vols. (New York: Robert Carter & Bros., [1731–33] 1855). Reprinted by Still Waters Revival Books, 1993.

heretics by means of them. The Old School might have screened ministerial candidates with the Larger Catechism's answers 60 and 86b on final judgment, but the day of pursuing previously ordained and rhetorically discreet heretics never arrived.

Revision and Re-definition

In 1901, a 25-man committee under the chairmanship of Henry van Dyke was assigned the task of making recommended revisions in the Confession. That the New School majority would trust van Dyke with this responsibility indicates that the transition away from Calvinism was well advanced. He was widely regarded as the leader of Briggs' forces in 1893.[30] He was the pastor of New York City's Brick Church. He was a liberal who, more than any other liberal, was active in the middle three phases of the Presbyterian conflict, from his support for creedal revision in 1889 to his work in revising the Presbyterian hymnal in 1933, the year of his death. Beginning in 1889, during the first move to re-write the Confession, he had affirmed the salvation of all dying infants, the love of God for the whole world, and Christ's atonement for all mankind.[31] He announced the Pelagian doctrine that "no man is lost save for his own sins," a denial of the doctrine of original sin. "Is this Calvinism? I do not know. I do not care. It is Christianity."[32] He was, of course, lying through his teeth for rhetorical purposes. He was a careful scholar of Calvin. He knew that he was no Calvinist. Not long afterward, he offered a prize of $100—worth over $2,000 in today's money—to anyone who could show that Calvin ever affirmed that all children dying in infancy are automatically elect.[33] No one challenged him; he was correct regarding Calvin's silence. Van Dyke denied the Confession's doctrine that Christ died to save only the elect (III:6), i.e. particular redemption (limited atonement). He prepared a non-binding statement on the Church's faith. Neither biblical inerrancy nor reprobation was mentioned.

---

30. Tertius van Dyke, *Henry van Dyke: A Biography* (New York: Harper & Bros., 1935), p. 132.
31. *Ibid.*, p. 124. This was from a January 27, 1890 sermon.
32. Cited in *ibid.*, p. 125.
33. *Ibid.*, p. 126.

His Committee's report sailed through the 1902 General Assembly in two hours of debate.[34] There were only two dissenting votes.[35] In that same year, he was elected Moderator of the General Assembly.[36] He also served as the primary editor of the revised The Book of Common Worship, which the 1906 General Assembly accepted, though not without heated debate. (When asked in the early 1930's what rule the committee should follow at a meeting at which he was unable to attend, he replied: "Eliminate all hymns that mention hell; Hell is nothing to sing about."[37])

In 1903, the committee's proposed revisions were ratified by the presbyteries. There were four changes. *First*, a missions-related affirmation that God loves humanity in general and seeks the salvation of all mankind—a denial, in other words, of God's "double predestination" of fallen mankind to either heaven or hell (III). The Old School correctly saw this as a move toward the Arminian doctrine of general redemption. It was a move against the L in TULIP: limited atonement, meaning particular redemption. *Second*, there was an affirmation that all infants who die are elect (X:3). This the Old School had accepted long before. It was a denial of Paul's express teaching regarding God's hatred of at least one unborn infant, Esau (Rom. 9:10–13). *Third*, a denial that the Pope is the Antichrist (XXV:6). *Fourth*, dropping the statement that it is sinful to refuse a legal oath (XX:3). All in all, this constituted a weakening of the 1788 faith, but these changes were not of the same theological magnitude as the universal "crossed fingers" strategy regarding the six-day creation. The Old School had capitulated to geological science on the six-day creation; quibbling over the L in TULIP was hardly worth the effort. The Old School could live with these changes, but it could not prosper.

The proposed revisions received very little opposition from the Old School. Princeton Seminary ran a single article in its new journal, *The Princeton Theological Review*, two and a half pages long, written

---

34. Robert Hastings Nichols, *Presbyterianism in New York State: A History of the Synod and Its Predecessors* (Philadelphia: Westminster, 1963), p. 196.

35. Van Dyke, *Van Dyke*, p. 269.

36. *Ibid.*, p. 223.

37. Hugh T. Kerr, "Henry van Dyke," *American Presbyterians*, 66 (Winter 1988), p. 295.

by a very minor Hodge, Edward B., who opposed all the changes, although "We have no particular zeal about the proposed change in the action relating to the Pope."[38] His rhetoric was appropriate for a scholarly journal: formal, subdued, clinical. It was not appropriate, however, for a last-ditch defense of historic Presbyterianism by the Old School.[39]

The Old School was now boxed in by the "love of God" revision: an obvious denial of Calvinism's doctrine of particular redemption. The Church in 1903 adopted what is commonly known as four-point Calvinism. It was possible for most New School Calvinists to accept such a doctrine, and had been since at least 1837, but not the Old School. Old School fingers would now have to be crossed.[40] (One of the first acts of Machen's newly formed Presbyterian Church of America was to rescind this clause of the 1903 revision, which led to a rhetorically mischievous headline in the November 25, 1936, issue of *The Christian Century*: "Dr. Machen's Church Drops the Love of God.")

Word Games

While the new position on universally elect infants allowed the Old School to uncross its collective fingers, the "love of God" plank

---

38. Edward B. Hodge, "The Proposed Amendments and Additions to the text of the Confessions," *Princeton Theological Review*, 1 (1903), p. 283.

39. This journal and its cousin, edited by Warfield, *The Presbyterian and Reformed Review*, were mild-mannered academic affairs. They published articles on New Testament and Old Testament studies, Church history (mainly biographies), studies of the Confession, and similar topics. Typical is Frederick W. Loetscher's article, "Schwenckfeld's Participation in the Eucharistic Controversy of the Sixteenth Century," *Princeton Theological Review*, 4 (July 1906). George Hopkins' essay in the January, 1901, issue of *The Presbyterian and Reformed Review* may not be typical, but it reflects a kind of self-conscious otherworldliness: "Whether Angels Can Love." One rare exception was an article by Princeton Seminary's William Brenton Greene, Jr., "Broad Churchism and the Christian Life," *Princeton Theological Review*, 4 (July 1906). I discuss his article below.

40. In 1923, the Christian Reformed Church accepted a similar creedal revision that spoke of "the favorable attitude of God toward mankind in general." Westminster Seminary's Cornelius Van Til would later write a book defending this revision: *Common Grace* (Philadelphia: Presbyterian & Reformed, 1947). But this revision led to a split in the denomination. The Protestant Reformed Church understood the threat to Calvinist orthodoxy posed by the revision; its 1924 Synod rejected it.

forced a re-crossing, and on what appeared to be a much more fundamental issue. But it really was the same issue. If God universally loves infants, and every person begins as an infant, it takes no advanced training in logic to conclude that God does extend His love to mankind in general. Only as infants grow older—how old, no four-point Calvinist theologian wants to say—do they come under God's condemnation.

From 1903 forward, the Old School found itself in a condition similar to the modernists in the denomination. To remain in the denomination, the Old School would now have to find a way to re-define God's universal love, making its interpretation different in theological substance from the New School's, but identical in verbal profession. Even Warfield was reduced to playing this verbal game in 1904: "It would not be true to say that either the Declaratory Statement or the whole mass of the revision accomplished in 1903 in any way or to any degree modifies our doctrinal system: though it may possibly be true that some elements of truth not always recognized as provided in our doctrinal system are emphasized in it."[41]

The Old School wanted to remain inside the denomination, but to do so, its members had to consent to a verbal modification of a fundamental implication of Calvinism's doctrine of particular redemption: God's unique love for His people and His hatred of everyone else.[42] They could remain in the denomination in the hope of capturing it; the modernists also remained in order to capture it. Unlike the Old School, however, the modernists had a strategy to achieve their goal.

There was a conscience problem here. The modernists' self-justification since Briggs' *Whither?* had been to stress that the Old School's fudging on the Confession was judicially the equivalent of disbelieving whole portions of it. With respect to the Westminster Assembly of 1643-47, the Old School's fudging was hardly minor, but compared to Briggs' fudging, it was minor. Crossing one's fingers was a mere tactic for the modernists, not a moral issue. But the Old School had always

---

41. B. B. Warfield, "The Proposed Union With the Cumberland Presbyterians," *Princeton Theological Review*, 2 (April 1904), p. 298.
42. Gary North, *Dominion and Common Grace: The Biblical Basis of Progress* (Tyler, Texas: Institute for Christian Economics, 1987).

presented its moral case against the modernists because of this modernist tactic. "State your objections publicly or get out," the Old School had insisted. The Old School would now be at a psychological disadvantage in any confrontation with the modernists. They had stated their theological objections; the New School had outvoted them; yet the Old School's members stayed right where they were.

All three factions in the denomination were playing the same game of "let's pretend" regarding the 1788 standards, let alone the 1647 standards. The modernists thought this was clever; the New School was too interested in Church growth and institutional peace to care; but the Old School found itself with its moral confidence missing. Unlike the members of the Christian Reformed Church who would depart on principle to form the Protestant Reformed Church in 1924 after the CRC added the plank on God's favor toward mankind in general in 1923, the Old School decided in 1903 to remain in the denomination by continuing to play the game. But how could the Old School speak judicially as self-conscious Calvinists in future denominational assemblies? Its members couldn't. This is why 1903 marks the institutional end of the Old School's resistance in the name of Confessional Calvinism. In 1910, they would invoke a new, watered-down confession.

Four-Point Calvinism with Arminian Sanctions

Prior to 1903, it was not yet clear that the Westminster Confession could no longer be enforced in the denomination through the imposition of negative Church sanctions. After 1903, this became more clear. In 1903, the Presbyterian Church became a four-point Calvinist denomination.

The revised Confession only hinted at what was a much deeper change. It established a new low for the lowest common denominator. Practically, the Confession could no longer be enforced, although no one was sure of this until 1936. The issue was Church court sanctions, not the precise terminology of the revised Confession. The 1903 Westminster Confession remained the denomination's official standard until 1967, but it would be naive and utterly misleading to say that the denomination was Calvinist in, say, 1962, just because the 1903 version of the Westminster Confession was still on the books. Thus, Longfield's comment is misleading: "Though doctrinal interpretation can always be a matter of debate, it seems clear that the confessional revision of 1903 hardly made the Presbyterian Church an Arminian body."[43] Longfield mistakes form for content. The primary judicial issue after 1869 was not the Calvinist content of the Westminster Confession; the primary issue was sanctions: the judicial penalties undergirding the ordination oath and readily enforceable by Church courts. After 1869, no one was ever publicly challenged in a Presbyterian court for having denied any uniquely Calvinist doctrine in the Confession. The judicial rule is unbreakable: *no sanctions—no oath*. The Calvinism of the Confession had been a dead letter since the reunion.

Secession or Dilution?

Why didn't the Calvinists secede in 1903? There were two legal precedents for a split: 1741 and 1837–38. The historian can only speculate. Whatever the reason, it must have had something to do with their psychological acceptance of this downgrading of theology and an upgrading of their expected benefits for remaining inside. They were not being openly forced out, unlike the tiny band that would depart in 1936. They were only being asked (implicitly) to continue to cross their fingers, just as everyone had been doing for a generation. In 1903, the Arminian majority publicly shoved the crossed-fingers tactic down the collective throat of the Old School, to see if the Old School would gag. No one gagged. The game of "let's pretend" continued: "Let's pretend that this denomination is still defined judicially by the Westminster Confession of Faith. Let's pretend that its courts will occasionally bring negative sanctions against ministers who preach against the Confession's clauses." The price of remaining inside the Church seemed small. It proved to be huge: the eventual capture of the denomination's assets by the modernists. This inheritance went to those who rejected the Confession.

A person with theologically crossed fingers cannot make a fist. To fight with crossed fingers, you must be prepared to poke out your

---

43. Bradley J. Longfield, *The Presbyterian Controversy: Fundamentalists, Modernists, and Moderates* (New York: Oxford University Press, 1991), p. 24.

opponent's eyes. The modernists were prepared to do just this, since they had survived inside Presbyterianism only by throwing sand in their opponents' eyes. The Old School refused to poke out anyone's eyes, but they could not make a collective fist. The Old School ceased to fight for its theology after the 1903 Confessional revisions. At most, its members would support the majority evangelicals who did not define their theology in terms of the Confession. This permanent back-up position indicates that the overwhelming numerical majority which the Old School had enjoyed in 1870 had evaporated by 1903. Refusing to enforce its unique tenets when it had the votes, 1870 to 1900, the Old School had lost both its sense of responsibility for the life of the Church and its ability to recruit large numbers of men dedicated to its tenets.

Dilution: The Cumberland Petition

In 1903, the Old School may have entertained some hope for the recapture of the denomination, or hope at least that things would not get any worse. If so, they were deluded; things got worse almost immediately. At the 1903 General Assembly, several presbyteries of the Cumberland Presbyterian Church made an overture to reunite with the Presbyterian Church, U.S.A.[44] This would heal a split that had begun in 1810 and had become official in 1813. That split had been forthrightly doctrinal; the Cumberland Presbyterians had regarded the Presbyterian Church as too Calvinistic. The Cumberland Presbyterian Church had not changed its opinion of Calvinism. What had changed was the public confession of the Presbyterian Church. Warfield saw what was coming: another series of excruciating—for Old School members—redefinitions of words. "It is distressingly easy for signatories of differing traditions to attach differing interpretations to documents they sign in common."[45]

Warfield had speculated in 1904 that perhaps the union would come about because the Cumberland Presbyterians had at long last abandoned their Arminianism.[46] Ho, ho, ho; and, we might add, ha,

---

44. Warfield, "Proposed Union," *PTR* (1904), p. 295.
45. *Ibid.*, p. 302.
46. *Ibid.*, pp. 315–16.

ha, ha. As surely as the Old School had capitulated to the New School in 1869 and again in 1903, so did the Presbyterian Church capitulate to the Cumberland Presbyterians in 1906. The lowest common theological denominator was lowered again. After 1906, any successful institutional defense against modernism could be made only in terms of Arminianism's theology. Again, the issue was sanctions: a Church is defined by the oath-bound confession that it is willing to defend through the imposition of judicial sanctions.

The documents were signed in 1906. Over 1,100 Cumberland Presbyterian ministers joined the Church,[47] increasing the number of ministers from 7,848 to 9,031.[48] Something in the range of 90,000 Cumberland Presbyterians entered the Church; 54,000 remained behind.[49] Yet the actual number of Presbyterian churches began a long decline, from over 11,000 in 1907 to just under 10,000 in 1908, and from there to 9,565 in 1926.[50] This was due to consolidation, since the number of total members continued rising. The number of ministers with churches remained in the range of 6,000.[51] Some 23 percent of ordained Presbyterian ministers were not employed as ministers after 1910; others were employed as chaplains, missionaries, and teachers.[52] Only about 45 percent of ordained ministers were employed as pastors after 1910.[53] This means that an amazing number of churches could not afford a full-time pastor. Even as late as 1926, there were almost 2,000 vacant pulpits.[54]

The Sovereignty of the General Assembly

One Old School member, Rev. John Fox, filed a protest against the 1904 General Assembly during the meeting. Patton supported this

---

47. Herman C. Weber, *Presbyterian Statistics Through One Hundred Years, 1826–1926* (n.p.: The General Council, Presbyterian Church in the U.S.A., 1927), p. 88.
48. *Ibid.*, p. 30.
49. John T. Ames, "Cumberland Liberals and the Union of 1906," *Journal of Presbyterian History*, 52 (Spring 1974), p. 18.
50. Weber, *Presbyterian Statistics*, p. 31.
51. *Ibid.*, p. 89.
52. *Ibid.*, p. 109.
53. *Ibid.*, p. 108.
54. *Ibid.*, p. 94.

protest. Fox claimed that the proposed reunion was based on the General Assembly's claim earlier in the meeting that it possessed the authority to interpret the Confession. The General Assembly had stated that the 1903 revision had created a new state of judicial affairs with respect to the Cumberland Church: ". . . such agreement now exists between the systems of doctrine contained in the Confessions of Faith of the two Churches as to warrant this Union—a Union honoring alike to both." Such authority, Fox insisted, did not exist at the General Assembly level. The General Assembly replied by saying it did possess such authority.[55] But did it? The future of the denomination would hinge on just this claim.

Prior to 1934, the modernists denied that the Assembly possessed such initiatory legislative authority. It could not "lay down the law." Technically, this interpretation was correct. In reality, the Assembly-as-Supreme-Court could indeed lay down the law merely by predictably enforcing the Confession and by standing ready to try on appeal an endless stream of lower court cases. This the Calvinists proved unwilling to do even before 1900: a defense of Calvinism. When it became clear in 1936 that the modernists were willing to do exactly this, they captured the denomination. They did not have to prosecute streams of cases, because their opponents knew they were quite willing to do this if necessary. Like a man who does not have to fight because he is ready to fight, so were the Presbyterian liberals after 1936.

Alliances vs. the Broadening Church

The doctrines which the Old School shared with Arminians were far more rigorous judicially than modernism's evolutionary creed. After 1906, Calvinists and Arminians shared a common enemy within the camp. Meanwhile, modernists were working within the denomination quietly but steadily. There would be no replay of Briggs' confrontational rhetoric until 1922.

Despite the conservatism of the Presbyterian Church and its reputation as being reactionary in social questions, it was the first Ameri-

---

55. Charles E. Quirk, The "Auburn" *Affirmation* (Ph.D. dissertation, Iowa University, 1967), pp. 21–22.

can Protestant denomination to pursue an active social gospel program through the efforts of a paid secretary in one of its national boards. In 1903, the year of the revision, Rev. Charles Stelzle was appointed to head up the newly created Workingmen's Department (later changed to the Presbyterian Department of Church and Labor), a part of the Church's Board of Home Missions. He was an active proponent of Christian socialism at the turn of the century.[56] He advocated that the Church recognize the good points of socialism, and that "the working classes should be informed that the church does not endorse the present social system." He wrote this in *Christianity's Storm Center*, published in 1907, the year after the Cumberland reunion.[57] He resigned in 1912 due to budget cuts.[58] By then, the General Assembly had formally affirmed its commitment to the social platform of the Federal Council of Churches.[59] Stelzle was then hired by the Council.[60] There had been one brief attempt by his presbytery to examine his socialistic views, but the committee assigned to investigate him recommended that the matter be dropped, which it was. Stelzle reminded the denomination of this in 1915.[61]

A Question of Boundaries

One Princetonian did articulate his opposition to a denomination broad enough to encompass modernism. In an article presumably written before the Cumberland reunion became official and published in *The Princeton Theological Review* (July 1906), William Brenton Greene identified the broad Church movement as ecumenist, anticreedal, and sinful. He had commented a decade earlier on the connec-

---

56. Henry F. May, *Protestant Churches and Industrial America* (New York: Harper Torchbooks, [1949] 1967), p. 207.

57. Charles H. Hopkins, *The Rise of the Social Gospel in American Protestantism, 1865-1915* (New Haven, Connecticut: Yale University Press, 1940), pp. 234-35.

58. "Stelzle, Charles," *Dictionary of American Religious Biography*, edited by Henry Warden Bowden (Westport, Connecticut: Greenwood Press, 1977), p. 429.

59. See below: "Showdown in 1910," pp. 368-73.

60. Willard H. Smith, "William Jennings Bryan and the Social Gospel," *Journal of American History*, 53 (June 1966), p. 47.

61. *Minutes of the General Assembly, 1915*, pp. 168-69.

tion between Briggs and the movement toward a broader Church.[62] He contrasted what he called broad churchism with a federation: the first is anti-creedal; the second is pro-creedal. He pulled no rhetorical punches. He asserted his belief that "Broad Churchism is one of the great foes of Christian living; . . . The Broad Church attitude of mind is essentially sinful. . . . First, it tends toward mental suicide." It cannot make distinctions, he said.[63] "The other and the more significant aspect of the sinfulness of the Broad Church attitude is that it expresses indifference to God and thus is a direct insult to Him Himself."[64] It is "rooted in indifference to truth in general and to religious truth in particular."[65] This was a foretaste of what Machen would preach and write in the final two phases of the Presbyterian conflict, but it was not typical of Old School rhetoric in the first two decades of the twentieth century.

Greene and his colleagues would soon face a problem: in order to resist successfully the broad Church vision of men such as Stelzle, a new alliance—Greene called it a federation—would be required. The arrival of the Cumberland Presbyterians had already broadened the denomination. The question then became: How broad was the new Confessional boundary? To keep an effective restraining force against another extension of this boundary, the Old School would have to form an alliance with those who did not share its commitment to the Westminster Confession. It was no longer a question of a conservative ecumenical alliance, which Greene supported; it was now a question of saving the denomination from the acids of modernism.

To consummate this alliance, the Old School had to pay a price: the abandonment of any lingering hope of using the Westminster Confession as a test of orthodoxy. This judicial situation had in fact been the institutional reality since 1869, but only a few modernists would say this in public. The Old School after 1906 could not admit publicly that it had agreed in principle to this intra-Church alliance. It

---

62. Greene, "Broad Churchism and the Briggs Case," *Presbyterian Journal* (May 18, 1893).
63. Greene, "Broad Churchism and the Christian Life," *PTR* (1906), p. 309.
64. *Ibid.*, p. 310.
65. *Ibid.*

was the old problem of the lowest common denominator. The Old School had already joined a theologically less rigorous group, the New School; it therefore had to sacrifice a commitment to the enforcement of the old standards. But its members never had admitted this. To have admitted this would have meant committing theological suicide in public. It would have been an admission that Charles Hodge had been correct about the New School and the reunion of 1869. It was too late for that in 1906. So, members of the Old School would once again have to cross their fingers in silence. They preferred this slow strangulation of Calvinism to jumping out of the ecclesiastical window. In 1936, their spiritual heirs—vastly reduced in number and strength by this legacy of compromise—were publicly pushed out of the window.

The Great Restructuring: 1908

The Cumberland reunion was an institutional turning point for Northern Presbyterianism: the most important institutional turning point since 1869. The arrival of so many Cumberland Presbyterians offered an opportunity for the liberals to extend their control. The reunion justified a major alteration of Presbyterian government. The call for this alteration began in 1906, the year of the reunion. Each denomination had its own boards. Shouldn't they be consolidated?

Before the 1906 General Assembly convened, six overtures endorsed by 114 presbyteries,[66] known collectively as the Cleveland Overture, had been circulated. This overture called for consolidation of the benevolent agencies of the Church as well as "additional improvements in the administrative agencies of the Church. . . ."[67] The twin issues were money and the consolidation of the boards. The issue of consolidation would not be settled until the 1924 General Assembly, when the boards were finally restructured. The issue of the allocation of money never did get settled.[68] In 1906, the General Assembly

---

66. *Minutes of the General Assembly, 1906*, p. 82.
67. *Ibid.*, p. 83.
68. David G. Dawson, "Mission Philanthropy, Selected Giving and Presbyterianism," *American Presbyterians*, 68 (Summer 1990).

created a Special Committee on Administrative Agencies. It reported back in 1907.

One problem, the committee said, was this: "The Boards are not provided for in our Form of Government, but have been born of sheer necessity."[69] This had long been the most important institutional problem facing American Presbyterianism, the one which had split the Church in 1837: the debate over parachurch missions. The boards, like Presbyterian seminaries and colleges, had no official position in the original Presbyterian system of hierarchical authority. These institutions had grown up outside of the formal authority structure of the Church. From the day that the College of New Jersey had opened its doors in 1746, this structural indeterminacy had allowed the acids of academic humanism to invade the Church, just as they had been doing since the invention of the university in the twelfth century.[70] President John Witherspoon had announced in 1776: "Every question about forms of church government is so entirely excluded that . . . if they [the students] know nothing more of religious controversy than what they have learned here, they have that Science wholly to begin."[71] The College's ecumenical spirit was unmistakable.

The committee's statement raised a two-fold question of hierarchy and sanctions: the enforcement of covenantal oaths. The boards had an added degree of immunity from sanctions, either formally or operationally. Legally, they were chartered as separate organizations with their own boards of trustees, and often with their own sources of funding outside the General Assembly. So, *judicial sovereignty* was completely outside the presbyteries, and *economic sovereignty* was clouded. Yet Presbyterian law lodges primary sovereignty in the presbytery, to which ministers belong. Two crucial institutional questions are these: "Who's in charge here?" (sovereignty) and "To whom do I report?" (authority). The Presbyterian structure of government did

---

69. *Minutes of the General Assembly, 1907*, p. 80.
70. Friedrich Heer, *The Medieval World: Europe, 1100–1350* (New York: World, 1961), chaps. 9, 10.
71. Cited in Leonard Trinterud, *The Forming of an American Tradition: A Re-examination of COLONIAL PRESBYTERIANISM* (Salem, New Hampshire: Ayer, [1949] 1978), p. 256.

not provide clear answers in the case of the boards. The Church lost its ability to answer the third institutional question: "What are the rules?" It also lost the ability to deal with the fourth institutional question: "What do I get if I obey or disobey?" (sanctions).

Representation

Another problem, the committee said, was that there was no agency to speak for the Church. The Moderator has no executive functions. The Committee complained: "How different this phase of our organization is, when compared with the political government of our country and with the organization of other Churches...."[72] This problem was an aspect of point two of the covenant: representation in between the annual General Assembly meetings. "In episcopally organized churches there is not a day in the year in which executive officers are not charged with the responsibility of oversight of the Church at large and in each subdivision of it, and they are ready to improve opportunities for advancing the interests of the Church as these opportunities arise. In our Church, on the other hand, it is only the individual church that is thus completely organized."[73] Being Presbyterians, they could not call for bishops. Being Presbyterians, they called for more bureaucracy.

This is the recurring dilemma of Presbyterian government: the question of representation. There is an anomaly above the local congregation, where the pastor speaks for the local church. There is no comparable representative above the congregational level. There is no spokesman. But in a large organization, there must be spokesmen, each with authority to speak representatively. Even during the annual General Assembly, most questions cannot be answered by a formal vote. So, the crucial institutional question is this: "How should each bureaucratic unit within the Presbyterian Church sanction a spokesman who is himself under sanctions of that unit?" That was what the 1907 General Assembly tried to answer. Its answer—the committee's recommended answer—restructured the Presbyterian Church.

---

72. *Minutes of the General Assembly, 1907*, p. 81.
73. *Ibid.*

The 1907 General Assembly sent down a proposal to the presbyteries authorizing the creation of Executive Commissions at the presbytery, synod, and General Assembly levels. This was passed by the presbyteries in 1907–8 by a vote of 156 out of 279,[74] a close but irreversible majority, as subsequent events proved. The Form of Government was amended. But no rules governing the actual structure of these Executive Commissions had been included in the original proposal. The General Assembly would decide how the system would look at the General Assembly level. If this was not binding legislative authority by the General Assembly, then nothing is.

The Committee on Administrative Agencies proposed in 1908 that the GA's new Executive Commission be composed of eight ministers and seven ruling elders, each with a term of three years, with the terms overlapping. The Stated Clerk would be the Secretary of the Executive Commission. He would be the primary source of organizational continuity. This is why two men, Roberts and his successor Lewis Mudge, would become crucial figures in the Presbyterian conflict. No paid agents of the boards or commissions could serve, nor could any General Assembly permanent officer be a member.[75]

The Flow of Funds

The suggested list of the Executive Commission's duties was as follows: (1) receive financial reports; (2) prepare a tentative annual denominational budget; (3) consult with boards and permanent agencies on how to collect the funds.[76] Notice the primary frame of reference: *budgeting and collecting*. Then an open-ended clause was added: "To discharge such other executive or administrative duties as the General Assembly may from time to time require; and from time to time to recommend to the General Assembly such action concerning the needs or work of the Church as the Commission may deem wise."[77]

With this seemingly innocuous clause, the Presbyterian Church, U.S.A., was definitively transformed the moment the General Assem-

---

74. *Minutes of the General Assembly, 1908*, p. 206.
75. *Ibid.*, p. 156.
76. *Ibid.*
77. *Ibid.*, p. 157.

bly voted to accept the committee's report: May 28, 1908. The General Assembly's one-week-per-year body now had a permanent head: the Executive Commission. Initiative immediately shifted to the top. It never shifted back. The Form of Government now allowed a comprehensive series of Executive Commissions at the synod and presbytery level.[78] These became shadow bureaucracies that were easier for the central Executive Commission to coordinate. The committee's report recommended that the General Assembly instruct the presbyteries to appoint their own Commissions, and also instruct them "to cooperate with the Executive Commission of the General Assembly, in any way within their power, to secure from all the churches their fair share of contributions needed for the work of all our Boards."[79] Thus arrived *the politics of the fair share*,[80] announced two years before England adopted an income tax and five years before the United States did. (The Church sets the pattern for the State.) The next year, this rule was added: "It is made the duty of the Executive Commission to recommend to the General Assembly annually the amount of money that should be appropriated to each Board and other Permanent Agency for a given year; . . . ."[81]

Control over the budget is one of the crucial marks of sovereignty in any organization. The ability to collect the revenues mandated in the budget is even more crucial in non-market institutions.[82] The Executive Commission possessed the first mark of sovereignty: budgeting; it did not possess the second. Laymen still held the purse strings. The Presbyterian conflict was fought by conservatives in the name of theology, and by liberals in the name of institutional peace (pre-1934) and institutional authority (post-1933); but the chief spoils of victory were the hierarchy's moral access to laymen's purses, followed by a flow of funds.

---

78. *Ibid.*
79. *Ibid.*
80. Gary North, "The Politics of the 'Fair Share,'" *The Freeman*, 43 (Nov. 1993).
81. *Minutes of the General Assembly, 1909*, p. 91.
82. In market institutions, consumers are sovereign: they supply the funds. Gary North, *The Sinai Strategy: Economics and the Ten Commandments* (Tyler, Texas: Institute for Christian Economics, 1986), pp. 163–65.

No Resistance, 1908-1925

There is no indication that the conservatives strongly opposed this restructuring, organized against it, or even recognized what it might mean for the Church. There was no public resistance to it until 1926, when the Presbytery of Chester, perhaps the most conservative presbytery in the denomination, submitted an overture calling for a return to "the same condition that existed before the Executive Commission was created in 1908."[83] Too late; 1926 was the year that the liberals took complete control of the General Assembly.

Conservatives chose to fight over the issue of theology; the crucial institutional issue, however, was sanctions—in this case, economic sanctions: positive and negative. The issue after 1908 was control over the flow of funds.

Showdown in 1910

In 1909, the New York Presbytery again became the center of theological conflict when three men were ordained over the objections of a determined minority. The minority appealed to the General Assembly in 1910. The response to that appeal would lay the judicial foundations of Machen's struggle in the mid-1920's.

The three men had refused to assent to the doctrine of the virgin birth of Christ. They responded to their critics by saying that they did not actually deny the doctrine; they just were "not prepared to affirm it with the same positiveness as for some other doctrine."[84] (I wonder what that other doctrine might have been.) The General Assembly dismissed the complaint against them—*no further negative sanctions*—but instructed the Committee on Bills and Overtures to prepare a statement for governing future licensures by the presbyteries.

Here is the problem: *the General Assembly was not authorized to accept or dismiss a complaint.* It was authorized only to demit the complaint back to the presbytery. It could also instruct the Presbytery of New York to conduct a heresy trial. By doing this, the General As-

---

83. *Minutes of the General Assembly, 1926*, p. 25.
84. Cited in Lefferts A. Loetscher, *The Broadening Church: a study of theological issues in the presbyterian church since 1869* (Philadelphia: University of Pennsylvania Press, 1954), p. 97.

sembly would have created a way to render judgment in the case if someone in the New York Presbytery appealed to the Synod of New York, and from there to the General Assembly. That is, the only way the General Assembly could act authoritatively in such a matter was to launch the process of heresy trials by commanding the New York Presbytery to hold a trial. The General Assembly refused to do this. Instead, it pretended that it had initiatory legislative authority.

The Assembly had taken this position in 1904 when it asserted its authority to interpret the Confession, a claim unsuccessfully challenged by Old School minister John Fox. But the General Assembly had no legal authority to instruct the presbyteries to do anything other than hold trials. A majority vote of the presbyteries could initiate a change in procedural requirements; a two-thirds majority was required for any doctrinal change. The General Assembly could try cases; it could not officially serve as a legislative body. Only by a determined willingness to try cases and hand down consistent, predictable judgments could it become, functionally, a legislative body. But it refused to try the three cases. It pretended that it was a legislative body. In the 1920's, this tactic would explode in the faces of the conservatives with the Auburn *Affirmation*. Had the three been defrocked in 1910, the conservatives might have been given an extra generation of control. As it turned out, they had only a decade remaining to them.

The Doctrinal Deliverance of 1910

The General Assembly adopted a five-point doctrinal statement that came to be called the Doctrinal Deliverance of 1910. These five points were announced as "necessary and essential" doctrines—the same language as found in the 1729 Adopting Act that had created the Church. The five points were: the inspiration of the Bible by the Holy Spirit, error-free; the virgin birth of Jesus; the atonement; the bodily resurrection of Christ; and the historical reality of Christ's miracles.[85] There was nothing distinctively Calvinistic about any of them. They were reaffirmed by the General Assembly in 1916 and 1923.

---

85. *Minutes of the General Assembly, 1910*, pp. 273-74. Reprinted in *The Presbyterian Enterprise: Sources of American Presbyterian History*, edited by Maurice

This Deliverance was evidence of fundamental changes that were going on within the denomination. First, it was a statement that "fundamentalists"—this term first appeared a decade later—and theologically moderate evangelicals could accept. It was in no sense visibly Calvinistic. Second, it indicates that some presbyteries were still having trouble with ordained men, or candidates for ordination, who were verbally accepting the Westminster Confession, but only with mental qualifications that enabled them to hold heretical views of the fundamentals of the faith. This was a strategy of concealment condemned as "Jesuitical" by over three centuries of Protestants. The presbyteries supposedly needed a supplemental creed to assist them in their screening task. The obvious question was this: If the most rigorous and detailed Confession in Church history could not serve as a screening device, what difference would five common-ground fundamentalist paragraphs do to improve things?

Crossed fingers had undermined the presbyteries; they were no longer strongly committed to the original Westminster standards. The New School men were uncomfortable with using them as screening devices. So were the Cumberland Presbyterians. As far as there is any public record, no Northern Presbyterian spokesman after 1859 believed the Confession in the area of creationism. The ecclesiastical unions of 1869 and 1906 had brought men into the denomination who were opposed to the 1788 standards of the Westminster Confession, or at least its more rigorously predestinarianism elements. The orthodoxy of the Old School had been diluted in 1869 and then swamped after 1906. A "broadening Church" was in fact what they had worried about in 1869, and had finally capitulated to in the name of Christian unity. Thus, in order to provide the presbyteries with theological ammunition that they would be both willing and able to use—"short and sweet," as the saying goes, or "down and dirty," from the modernists' perspective—the General Assembly announced the Doctrinal Deliverance.

The problem faced by the conservatives after 1906 was how to call a halt to a further extension of this broadening process. A denomina-

---

W. Armstrong, Lefferts A. Loetscher, and Charles A. Anderson (Philadelphia: Westminster Press, 1956), p. 281.

tion that had been broadened sufficiently to include both the New School and the Cumberland Presbyterians could not easily be limited, as a matter of principle, to exclude others whose views were even farther away from historic Presbyterianism. The bulk of the conservatives were now unwilling to declare as judicially binding the more predestinarian and "exclusivist" aspects of the Westminster standards—for example, the eternal hatred by God of all unbelievers. Without a willingness to be bound by these "exclusivist" restrictions, they could not bind others, should these others be equally willing to affirm their faith in the Confession as a whole while not believing in numerous propositions of the Confession. They could vote on an *ad hoc* basis to keep this or that candidate out of a particular presbytery, but any invocation by evangelicals and outright modernists of "Church unity above creedal details" could hardly be rejected by Presbyterians who were themselves unwilling to affirm the more exclusivist aspects of historic Calvinism. They had made the Confession more inclusive in 1903, and this in the long run made the denomination inclusivist. Ideas do have consequences for the operation and development of institutions.

The Social Deliverance of 1910

There was a second Deliverance at the 1910 General Assembly. It has been neglected in most histories of the period. It has not been capitalized by the historians, indicating its supposed secondary importance. But it deserves to be capitalized, for it served as a window into the Church's future. Attendees voted to accept a 14-point Deliverance submitted by the Special Committee on Social Problems, which had been set up in 1909.[86] This Deliverance was a re-written version of the Federal Council of Church's 1908 program for social reconstruction. The Presbyterian version called for, among other things, "a more equitable distribution of wealth" and "the abatement of poverty."[87] Then the General Assembly directed the Board of Publication and Sabbath-school Work to print and distribute 10,000 copies of this Deliverance.[88] So, the liberals' social agenda was ratified by the same

---

86. *Minutes of the General Assembly, 1909*, p. 47.
87. *Minutes of the General Assembly, 1910*, p. 231.
88. *Ibid.*, p. 233.

General Assembly that established the five-point evangelical Deliverance. This platform was reaffirmed in 1913[89] and 1914.[90]

Also in 1910, the General Assembly approved a report that announced: "All these new questions can not be solved by one Church alone, nor one denomination alone. There must be a combination of the Churches—a united, persistent effort to lift society, in both Church and State, or the Republic is doomed. Realizing this, the Church bodies formed the Federal Council of the Churches of Christ in America, popularly called the Inter-Church Federation. The work of the Inter-Church Federation is the rousing in all our churches and citizens to the solving of the great religious and social problems of our day."[91]

I argue that 1910 was a significant theological turning point in Northern Presbyterian history—the result of the 1906 institutional turning point: the arrival of Cumberland Presbyterians. (The next major turning point was again institutional rather than theological; it took place in 1920, as we shall see.) The five-point Deliverance marked the judicial advent of what would become known as fundamentalism, as distinguished from New School Calvinism. So far, mine is a conventional interpretation. But 1910 was a turning point for the nation, not just for the Presbyterian Church. I need to explain why in greater detail than is customary in a Church history. The events of Church history do not take place in a vacuum.

Beginning sometime around 1910, Protestant Church expansion began a slow decline. More congregations were dissolved or merged, 1910 to 1940, than were organized.[92] After 1910, the evangelicalism of the Sunday School movement also began to fade; it was replaced by social entertainment activities.[93] This transformation had begun in the YMCA a decade earlier.[94]

---

89. *Minutes of the General Assembly, 1913*, p. 69.
90. *Minutes of the General Assembly, 1914*, p. 28.
91. *Minutes of the General Assembly, 1910*, p. 285.
92. Winthrop S. Hudson, *The Great Tradition of the American Churches* (New York: Harper & Bros., 1953), p. 209.
93. *Ibid.*, p. 210.
94. *Ibid.*, p. 207.

There were two other important events in 1910 that would leave their mark on the Presbyterian Church.

Henry Sloane Coffin Makes His International Debut

The month following the General Assembly meeting, a World Missionary Conference brought 1,200 attendees together in Edinburgh. This was the first of the great international ecumenical meetings that were to lead, almost five decades later, to the formation of the World Council of Churches. It is generally regarded a milestone in the modern ecumenical movement. "Here was born the kind of international and interdenominational Christian co-operation that has increasingly characterized the twentieth century," wrote W. R. Hogg in 1952.[95] It was a conference attended by missions agency bureaucrats, not missionaries—a point made in a contemporary account by one of the attendees.[96] Its predecessor was the 1900 missions conference in New York City. Church historian R. H. Nichols says that New York Presbyterians were conspicuous in both conferences.[97] The Edinburgh conference's main organizer was J. H. Oldham,[98] but its co-organizer was also its chairman, John R. Mott, who, along with Speer, his friend and associate of the late 1880's, became the leading voice of Protestant world missions through the 1930's. It is significant that throughout this period, Mott was John D. Rockefeller Jr.'s paid ecumenical agent.

At the Edinburgh conference, Presbyterian liberal Henry Sloane Coffin spoke on "The Finality of the Christian Ethic."[99] This was representative of the Presbyterian Church's future, for Coffin was a

---

95. William Richey Hogg, *Ecumenical Foundations* (New York: Harper & Bros., 1952), p. 130.

96. Charles Clayton Morrison, "The World Missionary Conference," *Christian Century* (July 7, 1910); reprinted in *Christian Century Reader*, p. 140. He called them "missionary specialists." Speakers included England's Arthur Balfour and America's William Jennings Bryan. *Ibid.*, pp. 141, 142.

97. Nichols, *Presbyterianism in New York State*, p. 182.

98. This, at least, according to Samuel McCrea Cavert, who worked with Oldham and Mott. Cavert, *On the Road to Christian Unity*, p. 23n.

99. Morgan Phelps Noyes, *Henry Sloane Coffin: The Man and His Ministry* (New York: Charles Scribner's Sons, 1964), p. 106.

defender of Darwinian evolution—a theological denial of ethical finality. The next year, Coffin's book appeared, *Social Aspects of the Cross*, a clear statement of the social gospel. It was published six years prior to Walter Rauschenbusch's *A Theology for the Social Gospel*.[100]

In 1910, a new hymn book appeared, edited by Coffin and Ambrose White Vernon, minister of a Congregational Church. The hymnbook was titled, *Hymns of the Kingdom of God*. They announced in the Editor's Note that their strategy had been "to include only hymns which are poetically beautiful, which express normal and healthy spiritual experience, contain no divisive theology, and are specifically Christian in religion."[101] Here was the rallying cry of the inclusivists and the liberals from 1910 to 1926: *experience and unity*. Men must express themselves liturgically. The older hymns were too constraining theologically and judicially for the liberals. While this 1910 hymnal never became popular, Coffin's biographer insists that it had "a profound influence upon other hymnals introduced to American churches. . . ."[102]

Establishment Credentials

Who was Henry Sloane Coffin? He was an heir to a famous fortune, the furniture firm of W. and J. Sloane & Co. His brother William, at the time of his death in 1933, was president of New York City's Metropolitan Museum of Art,[103] an extremely influential position in American culture. This Museum is an institution secured by and dominated by America's "old money."[104] Henry in 1910 was the pastor of New York's Madison Avenue Church. He was to become

---

100. *Ibid.*, p. 146.
101. Cited in *ibid.*, p. 107.
102. *Ibid.*, p. 108.
103. *Ibid.*, p. 202.
104. In his study of America's elite, a member of this elite, Nelson Aldrich, Jr., writes: "Trusteeships are also famously hereditary, at least as hereditary as family business. Even in a city like New York, a place famously hazardous to old fortunes, as late as 1979 the board of the Metropolitan Museum reserved seats for the Morgan family, the Astor family, the Whitney family, the Rockefeller family, and (the so-called media seat) the Sulzberger family. Morgan's seat was in its fourth generation in the line of descent." Aldrich, *Old Money: The Mythology of America's Upper Class* (New York: Knopf, 1988), p. 220.

the patriarch of a long line of liberal ministers. He was a graduate of Yale University (1897). In his student years he met evangelist Dwight L. Moody, who devoted considerable attention on the young man at Moody's famous Northfield Conferences in Massachusetts.[105] But something changed in Coffin's thinking before he was ordained in 1900. He would no longer be congenial to Moody's theology.

In 1896, he was one of the 15 junior-year students "tapped" to join Skull & Bones (also called The Order). His father had been a member.[106] His biographer does no more than mention this "tapping." Founded in 1832, this highly influential Yale secret society remained invisible to all but its members and Yale students until a 1977 article appeared in *Esquire* magazine. It remained invisible to most Americans until George Bush, a member, was elected President of the United States in 1988.[107] Bush was not the first Bonesman to be elected President, however; William Howard Taft was the first. He later served as Chief Justice of the U.S. Supreme Court—the only person ever to hold both offices. Taft's father had been a co-founder of the Order and served as President Grant's Secretary of War and his Attorney General, as well as Minister to Austria and Ambassador to Russia under President Arthur.[108]

The Bones connection has been an important launching pad for many stratospheric careers in American history.[109] Its initiatory rites

---

105. Noyes, *Coffin*, p. 25.

106. *Ibid.*, pp. 26–27.

107. Newspaper cartoonist Gary Trudeau featured Bush's Skull & Bones connection in several of his *Doonesbury* cartoon strips in 1988. Trudeau is a Bones member. Duncan Maxwell Anderson, "The Club," *Success!* (May 1987), p. 57.

108. See Antony C. Sutton, *America's Secret Establishment: An Introduction to The Order of Skull & Bones* (Billings, Montana: Liberty House, 1986), p. 8.

109. A brief list of influential members: Andrew Dickson White, the first president of Cornell University, author of the enormously influential anti-Christian book, *A History of the Warfare of Science with Technology in Christendom* (1896), and the first president of the American Historical Association; Daniel Coit Gilman, the second president of the University of California (1872–75), the first president of Johns Hopkins University (long tenure: 1875–1901), and the first president of the Carnegie Institution (1902–1905); William Graham Sumner, the right-wing Social Darwinist and sociology professor at Yale; Henry R. Luce, founder of Time-Life Corp.; Averell Harriman, one of the six "wise men" who superintended U.S. foreign policy after 1933, and partner of Brown Brothers,

and meetings are held in the organization's exclusive on-campus building, shaped as a tomb.[110] (Scroll and Key and Wolf's Head are Yale's two other senior secret societies.) Its initiation rites involve sitting overnight in a coffin, and at least three Coffins have done so: Henry's father, Henry, and William Sloane Coffin, his nephew ('49). Those who are initiated into Skull & Bones move rapidly into what can be called the American Establishment, but Coffin's family connections placed him in the Establishment before he was initiated.[111]

In 1916, Coffin was asked to assume the job of president of Union Seminary. He declined.[112] Authur C. McGiffert, unharmed by his near-conviction of heresy in 1900, took over.[113] Coffin accepted a similar offer in 1926, and he retained this post until 1945.

In 1917, Coffin served as Chairman of the Committee of the Board of Home Missions.[114] This indicates that the liberals' takeover was very nearly complete.

Harriman, a major investment banking firm; Prescott Bush, later a U.S. Senator, George Bush's father, who was a member of the Harriman organization; Henry L. Stimson, another of the wise men, who served as Theodore Roosevelt's Secretary of War, Herbert Hoover's Secretary of State, and Franklin Roosevelt's Secretary of War, continuing to serve under Harry Truman; Robert Lovett, whose family had been in the Order through several generations, a member of the Harriman organization, another of the wise men, Secretary of Defense under Truman; Robert A. Taft, the conservative U.S. Senator in the 1940's and 1950's; William F. Buckley, Jr., founder of *National Review*; Winston Lord, the sixth in his family to be initiated, the former Chairman of the Council on Foreign Relations and the U.S. Ambassador to Mainland China; the Bundy brothers, McGeorge (president of the Ford Foundation) and William; J. Richardson Dilworth, who in the 1970's managed a large share of the Rockefeller fortune. See Sutton's *America's Secret Establishment* for details. Brown Brothers, Harriman pays Skull and Bones' tax bill. Ron Rosenbaum, "Last Secrets of Skull & Bones," *Esquire* (Sept. 1977), p. 85.

110. A 1970 made-for-TV movie, *The Brotherhood of the Bell*, seems to have been modeled on Bones. One scene takes place in a bedroom with a Yale pennant on the wall—the only reference in the movie to a non-fictional university.

111. The starting point for any serious study of the American Establishment is Philip H. Burch, Jr., *Elites in American History*, 3 vols. (New York: Holmes & Meier, 1980).

112. Noyes, *Coffin*, p. 180.

113. In 1931, the McGiffert Hall dormitory for married students was completed at Union. It had been financed by John D. Rockefeller, Jr. *Ibid.*, p. 200.

114. *Minutes of the General Assembly, 1917*, p. 179.

Rockefeller's "Baptism" in 1910

The third event in 1910 may seem minor; it was in fact one of the most important events of the twentieth century. In 1909, the pre-election year propaganda of the Republican Party in New York City had charged Tammany Hall Democrats with having allowed organized prostitution to flourish in the city. (That anything this obvious could have become part of a political campaign in 1909 indicates the unpredictability of politics.) A judge of the Court of Sessions, Thomas O'Sullivan, a Tammany man, called a grand jury together. The grand jury then elected John D. Rockefeller, Jr., as its foreman, which he immediately protested to the judge, who let the election stand. Rockefeller reluctantly accepted. He then threw himself into the project with fervor. The jury was supposed to sit for a month; it sat for six months. The judge, frightened of the outcome, refused to take the jury's formal presentment in public. Eventually, it was accepted; it returned 54 indictments. Rockefeller was widely praised in newspapers around the nation for his work. This experience persuaded Rockefeller of the importance of his presence in the field of moral reform. In 1910, at age 36, John D. Jr., severed his tie with the family business and began a life of philanthropy and the subsidizing of science.[115]

The report called for a commission to study the whole subject of prostitution. Rockefeller decided to form this commission independent of politics. He established the Bureau of Social Hygiene in 1911, the first of the charitable-social organizations founded by the heir of the Standard Oil fortune. (This was the year that the Federal government broke up the Standard Oil Trust.) In searching for men to serve on the Bureau, he located a recent graduate of Princeton University, a young lawyer named Raymond Fosdick, the younger brother of liberal Baptist preacher Harry Emerson Fosdick.[116] At that time, Raymond Fosdick was a minor New York City official. Rockefeller hired him in 1913 at $10,000 a year[117]—in the range of $200,000

---

115. John Ensor Harr and Peter J. Johnson, *The Rockefeller Century* (New York: Charles Scribner's Sons, 1988), p. 87.

116. On the grand jury episode, see Raymond B. Fosdick, *John D. Rockefeller Jr.: A Portrait* (New York: Harper & Bros., 1956), pp. 137–39.

117. Daryl L. Revoldt, Raymond B. Fosdick: Reform, Internationalism, and

a year today, in an era in which income taxes were miniscule. Fosdick would become, in historian Charles Harvey's words, "the chancellor of the Rockefeller philanthropic empire."[118] Nothing would ever be the same in the United States—in religion, education, state and local government, medicine, foreign policy,[119] and even nuclear physics.

Firm Foundations

For example, the Rockefeller Foundation funded Niels Bohr's laboratory in Copenhagen.[120] One result of this was the atomic bomb. Another example: the hiring of Beardsley Ruml to run the Laura Spelman Rockefeller Memorial Fund in 1922. He had previously been employed as an assistant to the president of the Carnegie Corporation. He was 26 years old.[121] From 1923 on, he ran the Rockefeller-funded Social Science Research Council, along with his academic colleague, University of Chicago political scientist Charles E. Merriam. Through this organization after 1928, Ruml funded large segments of the American social science community to promote the ideology of the government-regulated economy. As Donald Fisher writes: "A bargain was struck between social scientists, Rockefeller philanthropy, and the State that has since become an accepted part of the way we organize social life."[122] In 1954, the Reece Committee investigations on tax-exempt foundations concluded: "The Social Science Research Council is now probably the greatest power in the social science research field."[123] Ruml later became the first dean of the social science depart-

---

the Rockefeller Foundation (Ph.D. dissertation, University of Akron, 1982), p. 75.

118. Charles E. Harvey, "John D. Rockefeller, Jr., and the Social Sciences: An Introduction," *Journal of the History of Sociology*, IV (Fall 1982), p. 13.

119. Edward H. Berman, *The Influence of the Carnegie, Ford, and Rockefeller Foundations in American Foreign Policy: Ideology and Philanthropy* (Albany: State University of New York Press, 1984).

120. Harr and Johnson, *Rockefeller Century*, p. 169.

121. Donald Fisher, *Fundamental Development of the Social Sciences: Rockefeller Philanthropy and the United States Social Science Research Council* (Ann Arbor: University of Michigan Press, 1993), p. 32.

122. *Ibid.*, Preface.

123. *Tax-Exempt Foundations, Report*, House of Representatives, 83rd Congress, 2nd session, Report 2681, Dec. 16, 1954 (Washington, D.C.: U.S. Government Printing Office, 1954), p. 47. Cf. pages 47–51.

ment at the University of Chicago. He drafted part of the Social Security Act in 1935, and he was the driving force in 1942 behind the introduction of Federal income tax withholding, which began in 1943.[124] He was on the board of the New York Federal Reserve Bank from 1937 to 1947; he served as chairman during the final six years. This was the dominant Federal Reserve Bank. As Chairman, he announced to the American Bar Association in 1945 that with the creation of a central bank (1913) and the suspension of gold payments (1933), the United States no longer needs to levy taxes for revenue purposes. Taxes have become means of redistributing wealth among groups and to express public policy "in subsidizing or in penalyzing various industries and groups."[125] He then dutifully called for the abolition of the corporate tax and the imposition in its place of any alternative.[126]

By a quiet, respectful, professional, and bureaucratic distribution of enormous amounts of money, Raymond Fosdick bought off the nation's potential critics of Rockefeller's interests: pastors, intellectuals, politicians, and publicists. Had he remained a minor New York City employee doing the same kind of work, he would have been called a bag man.

Rev. Frederick Gates served John D., Sr., in a similar capacity, helping him to give away close to $500 million by 1915,[127] the equivalent of about $10 billion today. Gates was a theological liberal and strongly anti-Calvinist. He shepherded John D., Jr., from 1901 to 1917 in the creation of the Rockefeller foundations.[128] He retired in

---

124. Patrick D. Reagan, "The Withholding Tax, Beardsley Ruml, and Modern American Public Policy," *Prologue: Quarterly of the National Archives*, 24 (Spring 1992), p. 23.
125. Beardsley Ruml, "Taxes for Revenue Are Obsolete," *American Affairs*, 8 (Jan. 1946), p. 36.
126. *Ibid.*, pp. 37–39.
127. Rounding figures to the nearest million, here are the expenditures. Rockefeller Foundation: $183 million; General Education Board: $129 million; Laura Spelman Rockefeller Memorial Fund (named after John D., Sr.'s wife): $74 million; Rockefeller Institute for Medical Research: $61 million; University of Chicago: $40 million. Total: $487 million. Ferdinand Lundberg, *The Rockefeller Syndrome* (Secaucus, New Jersey: Lyle Stewart, 1975), p. 150.
128. Schenkel, *Rich Man and Kingdom*, pp. 38–39.

1923, to be replaced by Raymond Fosdick. Gates had served as the Executive Secretary of the American Baptist Education Society in the late 1880's and the 1890's.[129] The liberals' infiltration strategy was not confined to the Presbyterian Church.

The ability of private philanthropic agencies to absorb and then productively distribute such gigantic sums is highly limited. Those people who gain initial control over the funds have an opportunity to become influential, even powerful. There is a strong compulsion—indeed, a fiduciary responsibility—of the administrators to conserve the assets, which means conserving jobs, influence, and power. The division of labor being what it is, only certain types of people are psychologically suited to submerge themselves in such an organization: those who prefer anonymity to visible power and ideological crusades, i.e., organization men. What has happened to every major tax-exempt foundation established by an extremely rich patron, from Andrew Carnegie to billionaire Presbyterian Calvinist J. Howard Pew (d. 1973), has been consistent to the point of monotony: bureaucrats have inherited control, meaning people trained in America's prestigious academic institutions and others brought in through personal connections to those who gained initial control. To the extent that they have espoused any theology, they have been liberals and modernists. Writes W. A. Nielson in an academic study of foundations: "Big foundation boards are a microcosm of what has been variously called the Establishment, the power elite, or the American ruling class."[130] Board members sit on multiple boards.[131] As for the staffs, at least in recent years, "The field has a particular attraction for the well-educated, the idealistic, and perhaps the insecure."[132] Prior to the 1960's, the major foundations were all to the left politically.[133] (Today, a few are conservative.)

---

129. *Ibid.*, p. 37.
130. Waldemar A. Nielson, *The Big Foundations* (New York: Columbia University Press, 1972), p. 316.
131. *Ibid.*, pp. 317–18.
132. *Ibid.*, p. 325.
133. See the series issued by the Capital Research Center, Washington, D.C.: *Patterns of Corporate Philanthropy* (1987, 1988, 1990).

What the large foundations are, the permanent boards of the Northern Presbyterian Church and the other major denominations became even earlier, beginning early in the twentieth century.

Rockefeller's initial contact with Fosdick in 1910 was to have enormous impact in the 1920's on the Presbyterian Church and American fundamentalism generally. But before this, Rockefeller had discovered and promoted John R. Mott and ecumenism.[134] It was Mott, as head of the YMCA, who chaired a national interfaith fundraising drive, the United War Work Campaign, inaugurated by President Wilson, to send money to Europe to keep U.S. servicemen from falling into immoral behavior.[135] This drive raised a staggering $170 million, the largest voluntary offering in American history.[136]

1913: Testing the Conservatives' Will to Resist

In 1913, President Wilson appointed his old Princeton colleague Henry van Dyke as the U.S. Ambassador to The Hague (Netherlands and Luxembourg). As historian Henry F. May described this appointment, van Dyke was one of three U.S. Ambassadors who were "the perfect representatives of progressive culture."[137] He was also a perfect representative of theological modernism. A vignette indicates van Dyke's theological commitment. In 1917, when America entered World War I, van Dyke was 65 years old. He called Secretary of the Navy Josephus Daniels. In his diary (December 15, 1917), Daniels recorded the following "playful" exchange:

> Dr. Van Dyke wished to know if there was not some service he could render. Yes. Chaplain in Reserve Corps. Send for Frazier [a Navy Chaplain—ed.] Are you less than 40? F "Looks like 38." "I was 38 once." Must examine you in theology. F & I both

---

134. Charles E. Harvey, "Speer Versus Rockefeller and Mott, 1910–1935," *Journal of Presbyterian History*, 60 (Winter 1982). Speer was less of an ecumenist than Mott, but he never formally broke with Rockefeller.

135. Harvey, "Social Sciences," p. 5.

136. Schenkel, *Rich Man and Kingdom*, p. 52.

137. Henry F. May, *The End of American Innocence: A Study of the First Years of Our Own Time, 1912–1917* (Chicago: Quadrangle, [1959] 1964), p. 356. The other two were Brand Whitlock, Progressive novelist and reformer (Brussels), and Walter Hines Page (London).

Methodists. Do you believe in Calvinism? I do not. "You have passed."[138]

In his son's version of this exchange, Daniels asked him if he believed in Calvinism, and van Dyke answered: "No, and I never did."[139]

Like Coffin, Henry van Dyke was part of the American Establishment, but he was far better known to the general public than Coffin because of his literary efforts. By 1927, his *Story of the Other Wise Man* (1902), had sold 800,000 copies in English and had been translated into the major European and Far Eastern languages.[140] He could even boast, had he chosen to, that he bought his Seal Harbor home on the Establishment's enclave, Mount Desert Island, even before John D. Rockefeller, Jr., and Edsel Ford bought theirs.[141]

Van Dyke's Challenge

In 1913, the year Wilson appointed Henry van Dyke, Tertius van Dyke, his son, was ordained to the ministry by the New York Presbytery. So were three others. All were graduates of Union.[142] These men held liberal views regarding the authorship of the Bible, and they had said so publicly. A minority of New York presbyters protested the presbytery's authorization of these ordinations.

Henry van Dyke preached at his son's ordination. He publicly identified himself as someone holding the same views on the Bible that his son and the other three men held. He then challenged anyone to bring him to trial for heresy. "Heresy-trials are the delight of the ungodly and the despair of religion. . . . Do not try it on eager-hearted seminary boys. Try it on a grown man who stands with them in the liberty wherewith Christ made us free."[143]

No one accepted the challenge of a man who was a nationally respected literary figure, whose numerous books and stories had a

---

138. *The Cabinet Diaries of Josephus Daniels, 1913-1921*, edited by E. David Cronin (Lincoln: University of Nebraska Press, 1963), pp. 250-51.

139. Van Dyke, *Van Dyke*, p. 350.

140. *Ibid.*, p. 390.

141. William Adams Brown, *A Teacher and His Times: A Story of Two Worlds* (New York: Charles Scribner's Sons, 1940), p. 149.

142. Quirk, Auburn *Affirmation*, p. 31.

143. Van Dyke, *Van Dyke*, p. 279.

ready market, many of which are still in print, six decades after his death. Van Dyke's challenge and the Church's failure to respond judicially established the new terms of the debate under the 1910 Doctrinal Deliverance. Because the conservatives remained silent, van Dyke's challenge publicly transferred the initiative into the camp of the modernists. They would subsequently set the pace, not the conservatives. This had been true operationally since the 1880's. This was the first time, however, that any major figure had taunted the conservatives in public by calling for his own trial. It was a rhetorical master stroke. It would not be his last.

This brings us back to my original point. The ecclesiastical issue cannot be limited to the judicial content of publicly professed theology. The issue is always *theology enforced by judicial sanctions*. If the courts of the Presbyterian Church were not prepared to de-frock, let alone excommunicate, even one representative member of the faction that refused to abide by the Confession's standards, then the Church was no longer covenantally Calvinistic. Everyone knew this by 1903, although none of the Calvinists would admit it. They should have known it in 1869. The Church did have Calvinists in it, but it was no longer covenantally Calvinist. Similarly, if the Church's courts were unwilling to enforce the watered-down creedal standards of the 1910 Doctrinal Deliverance, then the Church was no longer covenantally conservative and evangelical. An oath without sanctions is not a covenantal oath. There can be no covenant without an enforceable oath. The crucial covenantal question after 1913 was this: *Whose oath would the Church enforce?* The Church might have conservative evangelicals in it—even a majority of them—but it was no longer covenantally evangelical.

This had obviously become the case by 1913. The public challenge by van Dyke proved it. He had successfully tested the conservatives' will to resist. They had none. They were unwilling to bring formal charges against him. Like the alcoholic who claims that he can stop drinking at any time, so were the conservatives who claimed to be in control of the Presbyterian Church. They had the votes outside of the New York Presbytery, but they refused to use them. They were not yet the equivalent of the alcoholic who can no longer maintain his sobriety for a full day, but they were the equivalent of hard drinkers who choose not to stop while they still can. It was clear where they were headed, but like hard drinkers, they refused to face what they had already become and were fast becoming. Their opponents knew, and they took full advantage of the conservatives' blindness and lack of will.

The Covenant Lawsuit

The fact of covenantal faithfulness is not established solely by preaching the ethical and judicial terms of God's covenant. Covenant faithfulness is demonstrated institutionally through the imposition of covenant sanctions. The prophets did not come before Israel with a message of God's holy love alone or God's holy law alone. They came with a warning: obey God's law and receive positive covenant sanctions (Deut. 28:1-14); disobey His law, and He will bring negative covenant sanctions (Deut. 28:14-68). The threat of negative sanctions within 40 days was Jonah's message to Nineveh. This is why the fundamental issue of the gospel of Christ's salvation cannot be separated from the issue of covenant sanctions in both history and eternity. This is what the covenant theologians at Princeton should have affirmed more clearly than anyone, but from 1880 on, they never mentioned this in relation to the heretics within the denomination. They missed a fundamental aspect of Christ's ministry: Christ, as the ultimate Prophet, brought a covenant lawsuit against Old Covenant Israel.[144] Paul then brought this same covenant lawsuit against the gentiles. The message was the same: repent or be damned. This is the New Testament's gospel.

It is never enough to bring this lawsuit against those outside the institutional Church. If Machen's thesis is correct—Christianity and liberalism are rival religions—then it was mandatory that covenant-keepers within the Church bring lawsuits against ordained covenant-breakers within the Church. This, a majority of the conservatives would not do from 1900 to 1923. By failing to do so, they were institutionally denying the truth of Machen's thesis.

The humanists at the *New York Times* understood the crucial nature of these events. The *Times* published reports on the 1913 ordina-

---

144. David Chilton, *The Days of Vengeance: An Exposition of the Book of Revelation* (Ft. Worth, Texas: Dominion Press, 1987).

tion controversy.[145] When some conservatives challenged Union Seminary at the 1913 General Assembly, but failed to get the votes, the *Times* reported this.[146] Minority protests within the New York Presbytery took place after subsequent ordinations in 1914 and 1915, all dutifully reported by the *Times*.[147] John Fox called for the General Assembly to investigate the New York Presbytery.[148] Nothing came of his protest.

When news hit the press in 1916 that the New York Presbytery had licensed three more candidates for the ministry who would not affirm the virgin birth, protests against Union Seminary came from a dozen other presbyteries.[149] The 1916 General Assembly did not prosecute. An anti-Union Seminary candidate for Moderator of the General Assembly was defeated by a moderate.[150] But there was one presbytery that clearly understood the principle of sanctions: Cincinnati. It understood that the main problem was not Union Seminary; it was the presbytery that kept ordaining Union's heretical graduates. Cincinnati submitted an overture accusing the New York Presbytery of "being guilty of long-continued disloyalty, and being persistently disobedient to the General Assembly. . . ." It called for removing the New York Presbytery from the Church "if no other methods will prevail."[151] This suggestion was not taken seriously by the Committee on Bills and Overtures, which dismissed this overture and the others by taking the New York Presbytery's side. It was all a mistake made

---

145. April 15, 1913, p. 5; April 18, 1913, p. 6. Cited in Quirk, Auburn *Affirmation*, p. 31n.

146. May 20, 1913, p. 5. Cited in *ibid.*, p. 32n.

147. April 14, 1914, p. 3; June 9, 1914, p. 6; April 13, 1914, p. 7. Cited in *ibid.*, p. 33n.

148. Fox, *Does the Presbytery of New York Need Visitation?* (New York: n.p., 1915); *New York Times* (May 1, 1915), p. 13. Cited in *ibid.*, p. 33.

149. *New York Times* (April 18, 1916), p. 13; (May 9, 1916), p. 9; (May 16, 1916), p. 4; (May 20, 1916), p. 8. *Ibid.*, p. 36.

150. *New York Times* (May 19, 1916), p. 22. *Ibid.*, p. 37.

151. *Minutes of the General Assembly, 1916*, p. 58. The Presbytery of Chester presented a similar overture in 1925, with the same result. *Minutes of the General Assembly, 1925*, p. 20.

"on the basis of exaggerated and misleading newspaper reports."[152] (When caught red-handed, blame the media.)

Princeton's Seminary's New President

In 1913, Francis Patton resigned as president of Princeton Seminary. Warfield served as the interim president. J. Ross Stevenson was elected to replace him the following year. Stevenson had been on the Board of Directors since 1902. Machen opposed Stevenson's candidacy from the beginning. He thought Stevenson would be worse than Charles Erdman, a faculty member, and he had opposed Erdman.[153] Both Erdman and Stevenson later served as delegates to the Federal Council of Churches in 1916.[154] Stevenson was an ecumenist, an associate of Mott and Speer, who had spoken at the 25th anniversary of the Student Volunteer Movement in 1911.[155] Stevenson had been a pastor, and he was perceived by the Board—favorably—as having pastoral concerns rather than theological ones. The Old School professors agreed with this assessment; they opposed him for this reason. There had been pressure from students for over a decade to shift the curriculum from the rigorous theological training favored by Warfield to pastoral training.[156]

This had always been a major problem for the Old School: Princeton's rigorous curriculum kept it from graduating many ministers. By 1914, it was the last of the Old School seminaries that actually taught Old School doctrines. With 9,500 ministers in the denomination, and with 256 ordinations in 1914,[157] Princeton's influence had to fade. Only 29 seniors graduated from the seminary in 1914; total enrollment was 154 students.[158]

---

152. *Ibid.*, p. 130.
153. Stonehouse, *Machen*, p. 216.
154. *Minutes of the General Assembly, 1916*, p. 35.
155. J. Ross Stevenson, "Contribution of the S.V.M. to the Home Church," *Student Volunteer Movement after Twenty-Five Years* (n.p., n.d. [1911]).
156. Ronald Thomas Clutter, The Reorientation of Princeton Theological Seminary, 1900–1929 (Th.D. dissertation, Dallas Theological Seminary, 1982), ch. 4.
157. Weber, *Presbyterian Statistics*, p. 30.
158. William O. Harris, Librarian for Archives and Special Collections, Princeton Theological Seminary, to the author: Sept. 10, 1992.

The Board of Directors in 1914 set up a committee to consider curriculum changes. The committee was divided. One group wanted to cut back on the number of theology courses.[159] This had been the opinion of the Board's Supervising Committee in 1909. Warfield had opposed this, and he opposed the new suggestion. He then counter-offered: add an extra year of Greek for the woefully trained new students, but don't give them any academic credit.[160] The Committee discussed the possibility that some elective courses be allowed for graduation. There were none in 1914. Warfield opposed this suggestion.[161] His commitment to academic training, like the entire Old School's commitment to a formally educated ministry, was leading to the triumph of the rival schools, whose young ministers were the products of an increasingly secularized system of college education. Warfield preferred "extinction by swamping" to curriculum revision. His Old School colleagues at Princeton generally agreed, although they did agree to allow some electives for seniors. Thus, the defeat of the Old School at Princeton was only a matter of time—as it turned out, 15 years.

An Unenforceable Faith

Beginning in 1910, the year after the publication of the *Scofield Reference Bible*, and continuing to 1915, Lyman Stewart and his brother Milton, two wealthy businessmen in southern California, published a series of twelve pamphlets called *The Fundamentals: A Testimony to the Truth*.[162] The series grew to 90 essays, written by 64 authors. Lyman Stewart was a California Presbyterian layman and millionaire oil man (Union Oil Co.), as well as a dispensationalist.[163]

---

159. Clutter, Reorientation, p. 95.
160. *Ibid.*, p. 98.
161. *Ibid.*
162. *The Fundamentals: A Testimony to the Truth*, edited by R. A. Torrey, A. C. Dixon, *et al.*, 4 vols. (Bible Institute of Los Angeles, 1917). This set has been reprinted by Baker Book House in Grand Rapids.
163. Stewart was also the founder of the Bible Institute of Los Angeles, the predecessor of Biola College. He also contributed $1,000 to help publish the *Scofield Reference Bible* (1909). Ernest R. Sandeen, "Toward a Historical Interpretation of the Origins of Fundamentalism," *Church History*, 36 (1967), p. 78.

The Fundamentals defended theological conservatism. It was from the title of this series that Curtis Lee Laws, a Northern Baptist editor, coined the term *fundamentalists* in 1920.[164] These booklets were enormously popular in conservative circles; over three million copies were sold or distributed.[165] They were conservative in theology. Several were written by Calvinists, some of whom were Presbyterians, and even Presbyterian moderates, e.g., Charles Erdman and Speer. The former battled Machen in the 1920's; the latter in the 1930's.

A conservative manifesto, "Back to Fundamentals," had begun circulating within the denomination in the spring of 1915. The conservative magazine, *The Presbyterian*, ran a copy of it.[166] Liberal journals opposed it: *The Presbyterian Advance* and *The Continent*. But the major challenge came from James Snowden, editor of *The Presbyterian Banner*. He told the manifesto's signers to put up or shut up: either make their complaints official in the Church's courts or drop the whole thing.[167] This was an echo of van Dyke's challenge in 1913.

The reaction in *The Presbyterian* was typical of the conservative responses to every challenge after 1900. The editor refused to present evidence of specific heretical opinions expressed by specific individuals.[168] Quirk has summarized this strategy: "Throughout the lengthy controversy discussed in the remainder of the study, leading militant Presbyterians tended to stress the efficacy of formal testimonials to the Christian faith, and to shun heresy proceedings."[169] In short, no further negative sanctions.

---

164. Curtis Lee Laws, *Watchman-Examiner* (July 1, 1920); cited in LeRoy Moore, Jr., "Another Look at Fundamentalism: A Response to Ernest R. Sandeen," *Church History*, 37 (June 1968), p. 196. See Gabriel Hebert, *Fundamentalism and the Church* (Philadelphia: Westminster Press, 1957), pp. 17–27.

165. George M. Marsden, *Fundamentalism and American Culture: The Shaping of Twentieth-Century Evangelicalism, 1870–1925* (New York: Oxford University Press, 1980), p. 119.

166. *The Presbyterian* (April 22, 1916), pp. 18–19. Cited in Quirk, Auburn Affirmation, p. 39.

167. *The Presbyterian Banner* (April 29, 1916), p. 6. Cited in *ibid*., p. 40.

168. *The Presbyterian* (April 29, 1915), p. 5; (May 6, 1915), p. 4. Cited in *ibid*., pp. 40–41.

169. *Ibid*., p. 41.

Sanctions Must Come Early

At the 1916 General Assembly, the Committee on Bills and Overtures handed down two judicially significant recommendations. First, the report advised against making harsh judgments against ministers in good standing. Second, it advised presbyteries against licensing candidates who would not support the Church's doctrinal standards.[170] Putting these two recommendations together, an alert conservative would have concluded the following: once inside the "club," a minister was going to be protected by the club.

The only hope of the conservatives was to screen out the liberals at the presbytery level. This had been the unofficial reality ever since the reunion of 1869. The screening had to come at the ordination examination. The Presbytery of New York had long made a mockery of this restriction. What was rarely discussed at the time was the fact that once ordained, a minister could easily transfer without restriction. The receiving presbyteries rarely protested. This was a major failing of the Presbyterian system. Once certified by a seminary, a presbytery's teaching elders found it difficult to oppose a man's ordination. Once ordained, the man was nearly immune from rejection should he ever transfer to another presbytery. The Presbyterian Church refused to quarantine its diseased presbyteries. No one could accuse any presbytery of being diseased without facing possible court action in his own presbytery, for the accused presbytery (a high authority) could protest formally to the critic's presbytery (a high authority) to bring sanctions against the critic.

The 1916 report affirmed this: criticisms against ministers should not be accompanied by harsh judgments. "This man is heretical" surely is a harsh judgment. So, the 1916 General Assembly made it official: *there would probably be no successful restriction of heresy and outright apostasy within the Church*. From Union Seminary to ordination by the New York Presbytery and into the whole denomination: the modernists' organizational transmission belt had been baptized and offered the Lord's Supper.

The report repeated the fundamentalistic five-point Doctrinal Deliverance of 1910. The assembly accepted this report unanimously.

---

170. *Ibid.*, p. 37.

While this appeared to be a partial victory for the conservatives, it was in fact their unofficial decision to surrender. Without sanctions against ministers, and without sanctions against any presbytery for its continuing ordination of liberal candidates for the ministry, the 1916 Deliverance was as dead a letter as the 1910 Deliverance.

From 1913 on, the long-term future of the Church would be determined by the faction that could avoid negative sanctions while preparing to bring sanctions against its rivals. It was not sufficient to avoid sanctions; it was necessary also to prepare to bring sanctions: *no sanctions—no covenant.* Those who held van Dyke's views did not yet have the votes to de-frock those who opposed their views, but they were free to remain inside the Church, free to work to achieve such judicial domination. If this remained the case, and if they could eventually bring sanctions against their rivals, they would inherit the Church.

Parachurches and Ecumenism

Two distinct theological movements came to the forefront in the second decade of the twentieth century. One was the movement toward Church unity, in part stimulated by the First World War, and in part by the desire to increase the effectiveness of joint social programs. The other movement was the independent evangelical Christian associations, represented by Bible conferences, Bible colleges, and evangelical meetings that were held throughout the nation. The Student Volunteer Movement, co-founded by John R. Mott in 1888, was an early representative of this type of organization. So was the YMCA. These were independent agencies that were organized, for the most part, by men who were unwilling to work within established denominations, although they were not hostile to working with others who belonged to established churches, so long as there was some agreement doctrinally between the individual men involved.

The first movement, Church union, affected even the Presbyterians. This was another ecumenical dead end in which John D. Rockefeller, Jr., was involved, beginning in the planning stages in 1919.[171]

---

171. Schenkel, *Rich Man and Kingdom*, p. 183.

Schenkel, whose indispensable book is devoted to Rockefeller's religious views and financial contributions, concluded: "There was Rockefeller money behind virtually every interdenominational movement in the first half of the twentieth century."[172]

World War I

World War I had a decided effect upon American churches. They united temporarily in a display of patriotism, although each denomination maintained its sovereignty and formal independence. This development was well within the tradition of American revivalism, for from the beginning, as Rushdoony has put it, "Revivalism was undenominational and very often anti-denominational. It was not greatly concerned with reviving the church, in many instances, but rather with reviving America. Its cry was, 'Save America.' Hence its interdenominationalism and intense patriotism."[173] This new unity was analogous to the unity of the North during the Civil War. As had been the case in the 1860's, this new sense of Christian unity came at the expense of doctrinal clarity. Disputes within and among churches were at a minimum, but when the trials and tribulations of the war were over, the seeds of unrest still existed. The liberal elements in the denominations were ready to reassert themselves more forcefully than ever. They had gained time to infiltrate the boards and bureaucracies. They would now be far more difficult to dislodge.

Typical of the wartime effort to create religious unity was the General War-Time Commission, which sought to coordinate the work of Protestant, Catholic, and Jewish programs related to the war. It was formed on September 20, 1917. Its Chairman was Robert E. Speer; its General Secretary was William Adams Brown, a prominent self-proclaimed liberal Presbyterian professor at Union Seminary. In his autobiography, Brown correctly subtitles one section: "The General War Time Commission as an Experiment in Interchurch Cooperation."[174] Indeed, it was. The Commission was the creation of the

---

172. *Ibid.*, p. 181.
173. Rousas John Rushdoony, *This Independent Republic: Studies in the Nature and Meaning of American History* (Fairfax, Virginia: Thoburn Press, [1964] 1978), p. 107.
174. Brown, *Teacher and His Times*, p. 237.

Federal Council of Churches; it worked closely with the War Department. The Council also created a parallel organization, the National Committee on the Churches and Moral Aims of the War, which held meetings in three hundred cities and towns, drawing a million attendees. One of its themes was the need for the creation of a post-war international assembly of nations.[175]

The Interchurch World Movement, 1919-21

The turning point for the Presbyterian Church came in 1920. The liberals inside the Church's bureaucratic hierarchy acted after 1920 as though they knew that they were in control, which in fact they were. While the publicly visible turning point for the General Assembly came in 1926, the fate of the denomination had been sealed administratively six years earlier. It was sealed by the liberals' victory over the issue of funding the Interchurch World Movement, an organization which today only a handful of specialized Church historians have ever heard of. But it was to shape the terms of the Presbyterian conflict in the 1930's.

On November 11, 1918, the Executive Committee of the Board of Foreign Missions of the Presbyterian Church issued a call for a meeting of Protestant leaders which would plan for a united effort to fund world evangelism.[176] On December 17—a suspiciously brief time for any meeting this large to have been spontaneously assembled—135 representatives of various Protestant missions agencies met in New York City at the Foreign Missions Conference of North America. Speer opened the exercises.[177] At that meeting, they set up an Executive Committee of 15, including John R. Mott (chairman), which announced the formation of the Interchurch World Movement on February 6, 1919. Presbyterian William Foulkes was Vice-Chairman of the Executive Committee.[178] He soon became General Secretary of the

---

175. Singer, *Unholy Alliance*, p. 45.
176. Handy, *Christian America*, p. 161.
177. Eldon G. Ernst, *Moment of Truth for Protestant America: Interchurch Campaigns Following World War I* (Missoula, Montana: American Academy of Religion & Scholars' Press, 1972), p. 51.
178. *Ibid.*, p. 62.

Presbyterian Church's newly created New Era Movement, which would launch a huge fund-raising effort, 1919–24, which freed the Church's boards from direct financial control by the congregations.

The Interchurch World Movement was an experiment in ecumenism—the last major one, as it turned out. Brown described it in retrospect two years later, after the project had gone bankrupt: "But they had seen a vision—the vision of a united church uniting a divided world, and under the spell of what they saw all things seemed possible. Difficulties were waved aside, doubters were silenced."[179]

In January, 1920, the Prohibition amendment went into effect. This seemed to prove that the churches had the power to change society through coordinated action.[180] Political power is a heady thing, especially for those who have been kept out of the political dialogue for a generation or more. The Progressives had allowed fundamentalists inside the corridors of power, briefly, for the sake of the numbers they could bring into the voting booths on this, the main post-war issue on which Progressivism and fundamentalism shared an agenda. Power intoxicates some people even as alcohol intoxicates others. The Progressives were well into their addiction. So, this seemed to be an auspicious time for fund-raising. The post-War enthusiasm for reform had not yet cooled. The economic recession of 1920–21 had not yet hit. The Progressives' hangover had not yet arrived. The speakeasy had not yet replaced the vote-easy.

In January, 1920, John D. Rockefeller, Jr., formally joined the organization when 1,700 religious leaders gathered at Atlantic City for the World Survey Conference. At least 140 boards representing 34 Protestant denominations sent representatives. So did 20 parachurch organizations. Rockefeller addressed the group, claiming that it would "become the greatest force for righteousness in the whole world."[181] The IWM's proposed religious survey would bring efficiency, economy, and scientific grounding to the church, he prophesied. Coopera-

---

179. W. A. Brown, *The Church in America: A Study of the Present Condition and Future Prospects of American Protestantism* (1922), p. 119; cited in Handy, *Christian America*, p. 162.
180. Handy, *ibid.*, p. 164.
181. Cited in Schenkel, *Rich Man and Kingdom*, p. 131.

tion is the key, he said. This would require centralized ecumenical leadership.[182] In trying to raise a $50 million to $100 million endowment from his father—who turned down the request—he waxed eloquent regarding the potential of the IWM: "As I see it, it is capable of having a much more far-reaching influence than the League of Nations in bringing about peace, contentment, goodwill and prosperity among the peoples of the earth."[183] That was a great deal to expect from an organization whose main job would be to conduct religious surveys.

He expected a repetition of the enormous fund-raising effort of the United War Work Campaign, conducted immediately after the armistice, which had raised $170 million.[184] Political reaction and recession would soon dash these hopes, taking with them over a million dollars of his money, plus a million from his father.[185]

The stated goal of the Interchurch campaign was to raise money from the general public and from within the denominations. The first effort failed. The second effort was successful, but most of these funds stayed inside the denominations. The IWM ran a massive operational deficit as a result. A majority of the IWM's money came from the denominations in the form of loans, for which they had borrowed from the banks.[186] The churches funded the IWM, the central organization, expecting it to become self-sufficient through public donations. What they received for their investment was a national fund-raising drive, which is what they had asked for. This campaign may have helped them with their own intra-denominational fund-raising—it helped the Presbyterians—but the financial benefits of the IWM campaign were at best indirect.

At the end of the week-long fund drive in April, 1920, it was clear that the effort was a failure. As a member of the IWM's Executive

---

182. *Ibid.*

183. J. D. Rockefeller, Jr., to Rockefeller, Sr., 21 April 1920. Cited in Charles E. Harvey, "John D. Rockefeller, Jr., Herbert Hoover, and President Wilson's Industrial Conferences of 1919-1920," in *Voluntarism, Planning, and the State: The American Planning Experience, 1914-1946*, edited by Jerold D. Brown and Patrick D. Reagan (Westport, Connecticut: Greenwood, 1988), p. 36.

184. Schenkel, *Rich Man and Kingdom*, p. 52.

185. *Ibid.*, p. 140.

186. Ernst, *Moment of Truth*, p. 79.

Committee, Rockefeller had promised to underwrite the effort to the tune of a million dollars. But because of the pivotal role of his underwriting pledge, which encouraged an all-out effort, this pledge now appeared to be a potential open-ended liability of huge proportions. By May, the IWM employed over 2,600 people in an office building in New York City.[187] While the total IWM effort gained pledges of $176 million, half of the originally announced goal,[188] almost all of the money actually raised—there was never any formal accounting—remained inside the denominations that had raised it. On June 28, 1920, the IWM suspended operations, taking with it almost three million dollars of Rockefeller money—Junior, Senior, and assorted Rockefeller foundations.[189]

In April, 1920, Raymond Fosdick resigned from his job as the American Under Secretary General of the League of Nations and returned to the United States. Fosdick in 1919 and 1920 was travelling in high circles, which as a result of the international contacts generated by the Paris Peace Conference were becoming much higher for all concerned. His career had obviously soared since that fateful meeting with Junior in 1910. At the League of Nations, he had worked closely with 31-year-old Jean Monnet. As Fosdick put it at the time, he and Monnet were working in 1919 to lay the foundations of "the framework of international government. . . ."[190] This was no idle boast. Over the next six decades, Monnet became the driving force behind the creation of the European Common Market and the New European order. His connections to the American Establishment had made this possible.[191] He died in 1979.

---

187. *Ibid.*, p. 91.

188. Charles E. Harvey, "John D. Rockefeller, Jr., and the Interchurch World Movement of 1919–1920: A Different Angle on the Ecumenical Movement," *Church History*, 51 (June 1982), p. 205n.

189. Ernst, *Moment of Truth*, pp. 144–45.

190. Fosdick to his wife: July 31, 1919; in Fosdick, ed., *Letters on the League of Nations* (Princeton, New Jersey: Princeton University Press, 1966), p. 18.

191. Francois Duchene, *Jean Monnet: The First Statesman of Interdependence* (New York: Norton, 1994), p. 63; Richard J. Barnet, *The Alliance: America-Europe-Japan* (New York: Simon & Schuster, 1983), ch. 3.

Upon his return to the United States in 1920, Fosdick and two partners set up a new law firm in New York City. This was not what one would call a high-risk career move for Fosdick. He immediately signed up his first (and only) client: Junior.[192] Fosdick's primary initial task was to unsort the mess at the IWM. He did the necessary legal work to transform retroactively Junior's potentially open-ended guarantee into a one-time gift.[193] One result of this gift was that Rockefeller wound up the owner of the IWM's field survey materials on social needs and opportunities. From that time forward, Fosdick steered Junior toward projects in the social sciences.[194] The value of these assets was estimated by Fosdick to be over $2 million.[195] This collection was the origin of Rockefeller's Institute of Social and Religious Research (ISRR).[196] In 1932, one of its publications led to the final battle in the Presbyterian conflict: *Re-Thinking Missions*. The IWM became in retrospect a major factor in the rise of the Rockefeller empire in the social sciences.[197]

Consolidating the Presbyterian Bureaucracy

Presbyterians Speer, Foulkes, and James M. Speers had been high officials in the IWM. So had Presbyterian ruling elder Robert Lansing,[198] who had served as Secretary of State under Wilson from Bryan's resignation in 1915 until early 1920. Other prominent supporters included Thomas Marshall, the Vice President of the United States; Secretary of the Treasury McAdoo, Wilson's son-in-law; Mrs.

---

192. Raymond B. Fosdick, *Chronicle of a Generation: An Autobiography* (New York: Harper & Bros., 1958), p. 215.
193. Harvey, "Different Angle," p. 206.
194. Harvey, "John D. Rockefeller, Jr., and the Social Sciences," *op. cit.*, p. 9.
195. Harvey, "Different Angle," p. 207.
196. This was different from the SSRC: Social Science Research Council. The ISRR was formed in 1923: Harvey, "Social Sciences," p. 10. So was the SSRC: *Encyclopedia of the Social Sciences*, edited by Edwin R. A. Seligman, 15 vols. (New York: Macmillan, 1933), IX:299.
197. Harvey, "Social Sciences," pp. 1–31.
198. Eldon G. Ernst, "Presbyterians and the Interchurch World Movement—A Chapter in the Development of Protestant Unity in Twentieth-Century America," *Journal of Presbyterian History*, 48 (Winter 1970), p. 242. Lansing was John Foster Dulles' uncle.

Wilson; Senator (and soon to be President) Warren G. Harding; and General Pershing.[199] It would have been difficult for Presbyterian laymen or ministers to criticize the mission of the IWM, given the presence of these high-level connections. Only when the enormous bills came due in 1920 did Presbyterian critics briefly appear. Their failure marked the transfer of power in the denomination to the liberals.

At the 1919 General Assembly, the Executive Commission presented a report on the Interchurch World Movement. The Commission assured attendees that the IWM was not an ecclesiastical movement or effort at Church union.[200] The Commission also proposed that the General Assembly create a new denominational fund-raising agency, New Era Movement, whose director would be Foulkes.[201] Funds raised in the Church would go through the New Era Movement to the Church's boards. These assurances were offered:

> 4. That the cooperation shall be upon the condition that funds raised by the Presbyterian Churches and Agencies shall be paid to and distributed through the regular channels of the Presbyterian Church.
>
> 5. That no financial obligations for the administrative expenses of the Interchurch Movement shall be incurred by any of our Boards or Agencies without the authorization of the General Assembly or its Executive Commission.[202]

The key word in Point 5 was *or*. Debts would have to be approved by the General Assembly *or* the Executive Commission, meaning the permanent administrative unit created by the 1908 restructuring of the Church. This gave the Executive Commission a blank check. It soon wrote the check.

---

199. *Ibid.*, pp. 242–43.
200. *Minutes of the General Assembly, 1919*, p. 224.
201. He resigned in October, 1924. *Minutes of the General Assembly, 1924*, pp. 103–104. This was the year that the Church's consolidation went into effect; the New Era Movement had ceased to exist as the consolidating agency of benevolences.
202. *Minutes of the General Assembly, 1919*, p. 224.

This was not the first discussion of the New Era idea. In 1918, the New Era Extension Program had been announced to the General Assembly in a classic statement of the social gospel: "WHEREAS, This supreme crisis in the spiritual history of mankind presents itself largely in the forms and terms of physical needs, of combat with social vices, or readjustment of social relations and economical conditions, and, in our country especially, of the necessity of achieving a higher moral and spiritual, as well as political unity of the diverse elements of our population."[203] The fulfillment came in 1919, when the 27-member New Era Movement was voted into existence by the General Assembly. Nine members would be from the Executive Commission; nine from the boards; nine from the Church at large.[204] This structuring was crucial and also representative of the liberals' consolidation of power: representatives of the permanent agencies of the Church were in control at all times by a vote of 18 to 9.

Financially, the New Era Movement proved to be a bonanza. Funds raised for home missions rose from the $2 million level of 1916–19 to over $3 million in 1920, $3.7 million in 1921, $3.8 million in 1922, and over $4 million in 1923. Funds raised for foreign missions paralleled home missions almost exactly: from $2 million a year in 1917–19 to $3.5 million in 1920, $4.2 million in 1921, around $3.8 million in 1922 and 1923, and $4.6 million in 1924.[205]

Administratively, the New Era Movement also proved to be a bonanza. It was as a result of the New Era Movement's five-year campaign that financial independence for the major Church boards was achieved. Funds were increasingly funneled from a central collection agency into the boards. The boards became less and less dependent on the direct giving of individual members and congregations. This inevitably reduced the economic authority of donors over the boards, for the New Era Movement was operated as a central committee of bureaucrats. "He who pays the piper calls the tune." In this sense, the joint timing of the creation of the New Era Movement and the IWM was significant. The hoped-for fund-raising effort by the IWM had augmented the work of the New Era Movement, as well as similar

---

203. *Minutes of the General Assembly, 1918*, p. 67.
204. *Ibid.*, p. 55.
205. Weber, *Presbyterian Statistics*, pp. 117–19.

agencies within the other participating denominations. The IWM failed; the New Era Movement did not, at least from the point of view of the Church's increasingly independent boards.

The Executive Commission in 1919 did note the existence of "a state of doubt among the members with regard to the wisdom of our Church entering the proposed Interchurch World Movement at the present time. . . ."[206] It sought to overcome these doubts. It voted "to call together representatives of the Boards and Agencies in joint conference. . . ."[207] It promised to report back at the 1920 General Assembly. It then added this ominous warning regarding the IWM:

> We are also informed that the present organization has already incurred a debt, in an amount of which we have no information. This may of course be provided for without any contribution from us. We cannot tell without investigation. It is also reported to us that the said organization is now operating under heavy expense. As to this also we have no definite knowledge.
>
> . . . [B]ut we suggest that there can be no intelligent action without either the submission to us of definite and acceptable plans, or sufficient time to inquire whether they exist; and we suggest that on a project so important, the facts even when known, must be carefully weighed and considered.[208]

The bills came due a year later. The Executive Commission announced that it had incurred an obligation for its share of the IWM's budget. It had extended credit to the IWM.[209] The IWM had taken loans from banks, and these had been co-signed by the denominations.[210] The total debt of the IWM was $6.5 million.[211] The Northern Baptists were in debt $1.5 million. They agreed to pay.[212] The General Assembly's debt to the IWM's bankers was a million dollars. To this

---

206. *Minutes of the General Assembly, 1919*, pp. 224–25.
207. *Ibid.*, p. 225.
208. *Ibid.*, pp. 227–28.
209. *Minutes of the General Assembly, 1920*, p. 145.
210. Ernst, *Moment of Truth*, p. 79.
211. *Ibid.*, p. 146.
212. *Ibid.*, p. 149.

was added an additional $650,000 debt to the New Era Movement.[213] On top of this was interest owed to the boards, whose treasuries had been raided to advance the money. This announcement at the 1920 General Assembly came at the beginning of a major recession. At 6%, this debt was still building a year later.[214] In 1922, the General Assembly still owed $371,000 on its IWM debt.[215]

The IWM had coordinated a campaign that had raised a lot of money within the denominations, but this campaign had been, in Ernst's words, a moment of truth. Its public failure, he believes, marked end of Protestantism as a religious force in America.[216] I would say, rather, that the events of 1925 in Dayton, Tennessee, marked this end—the impotence of fundamentalism—but the IWM's failure was a harbinger: the impotence of theological modernism. Without the use of coercive force by the civil magistrate, theological modernism could fund its vision for America only by relying on donations from inside each denomination, for use only in that denomination. The Protestant ecumenical impulse among the laity was visibly dead in 1920. It never revived. But the ecumenical bureaucracies within the Presbyterian Church kept pushing their agenda. For a bureaucracy, nothing succeeds like failure.

Deflecting the Protests

There were dozens of protests from presbyteries in 1920, presented in the traditional form of overtures. Overtures 1 to 12 were collectively a call to reverse the action of the Executive Commission in indebting the Church for the IWM.[217] Overtures 13 to 55 were more moderate in tone but still critical.[218] The Executive Commission appeared to be in trouble. If it really was in trouble, a decade of centralization by the administrative machinery was at risk.

---

213. *Minutes of the General Assembly, 1920*, p. 218.
214. *Minutes of the General Assembly, 1921*, pp. 172–73.
215. *Minutes of the General Assembly, 1922*, p. 31.
216. Ernst, *Moment of Truth*, p. 171.
217. *Minutes of the General Assembly, 1920*, p. 26.
218. *Ibid.*, p. 27.

But the overtures led to no action. The Executive Commission proposed, and the General Assembly ratified, the payment of the million dollars to the IWM. No further payments would be made, the Executive Commission promised.[219] This was an easy concession to make, since the IWM was in the process of being shut down by May of 1920. Yet even here there was a loophole: if the IWM was reorganized, the Executive Commission was authorized to contribute $100,000 for the 1920–21 year.[220]

In February, 1920, the Pittsburgh Presbytery had sent a letter to the Executive Commission complaining about the IWM plus the New Era Movement's budget of $2.8 million. Was this $3.8 million total obligation constitutional? "May not such authorization of the use of benevolent funds, given through the ordinary denominational channels, be beyond the power of the Assembly? May it not, indeed, be considered a diversion of funds, that have been sacredly confided to the Assembly, for other uses?"[221] This was indeed the question—one of the two key institutional questions in the battle for the Presbyterian Church: *the flow of funds*. (The other was the question of judicial sanctions.)

The senior bureaucrat of the Church, Stated Clerk William H. Roberts, responded with a classic bureaucratic runaround in a letter dated February 18. Pittsburgh had asked: Did the Executive Commission act constitutionally in obligating the Church with such debt? Roberts answered: the Executive Commission has no authority to make such pronouncements on the Church's constitution. So, if the presbytery wants to gain such information, "the proper course for it to pursue would be to take the matter to the proper higher judicatory under the regulations of the Constitution of the Church."[222] In short, gentlemen, you can jump into Presbyterianism's legendary judicial morass! But this leap was exactly what the conservatives had been self-consciously avoiding since 1900.

---

219. *Ibid.*, p. 175.
220. *Ibid.*, p. 176.
221. *Ibid.*, p. 219.
222. *Ibid.*, p. 220.

This was one of Roberts' last pronouncements as Stated Clerk. He was too sick to attend the General Assembly, and he died before the end of the year. He had held this crucial post since 1884. Under Roberts, an Old School man originally, liberals gained control. Roberts, more than any other figure, had been the visible incarnation of the Presbyterian system, and the liberals steadily captured it under the protection of his formal adherence to the rules. The two Roberts became the liberals' crucial allies: William H. and *Robert's Rules of Order*.

The Committee on Bills and Overtures smugly dismissed mild-mannered overtures 13 to 55: ". . . it recommends that the Assembly and the Church be requested to acquaint themselves with the constitution of the Executive Commission."[223] In short, "Buzz off, critics; we bureaucrats are in control!" And they were.

Capitulation: The Green Light

The 1920 General Assembly then voted to authorize the Executive Commission's proposed budget of $45 million, with $22 million specifically "certified to the Executive Committee of the Interchurch World Movement as that part of the budget of the Presbyterian Church in the U.S.A. to be secured through the united simultaneous campaign."[224] Of course, this money would remain inside the denomination, but the underlying issue was legitimacy: gaining legitimacy from the IWM and granting legitimacy to it. Would the Church's Executive Commission receive its 1920 budget authorization from the General Assembly under the broader umbrella of the IWM ("legitimacy from")? Also, had its decision to give the IWM a million dollars in the interim been a legitimate expenditure ("legitimacy to")? The Executive Commission proposed this justification of $22 million in expenditures, knowing full well that the IWM was in the process of going into receivership to Rockefeller. In short, they insisted that the Presbyterian Church should raise this money for its own uses under the umbrella of the IWM, thereby retroactively legitimizing an ecumenical, Rockefeller-backed project that was virtually bankrupt at the

---

223. *Ibid.*, p. 202.
224. *Ibid.*, p. 244.

time. The General Assembly did what the Executive Commission proposed.

The critical overtures had completely failed. Resistance had failed. From this point on, the Church's senior bureaucrats never looked back. Their access to a percentage of the flow of funds was henceforth assured. *This was the critical institutional and political turning point in the victory of the liberals in the Presbyterian Church.* It took place two years before the advent of what has been called the Presbyterian conflict. The Church in 1920 helped to bail out Rockefeller's IWM; four years later, he reciprocated by bailing out the liberals' lone casualty in the next phase of the Presbyterian conflict: Harry Emerson Fosdick.

The organizational goal of goals was control over the flow of funds.[225] The New Era Movement paid lip service to individual responsibility by insisting that "scrupulous care shall be taken to carry out the intent of the original donors of funds." But then these words were added: "That individuals, churches, Presbyteries and Synods be urged to follow the percentages approved by the Executive Commission."[226] If the Executive Commission's recommendations were accepted, the pooling of funds would more and more reflect the allocational decisions of the Executive Commission. The Executive Commission, not the laity that dutifully paid the bills, would be in control. The goal, in short, was bureaucratic control over other people's money.

Church Union

The movement toward national unity and institutional centralization that occurred after the Civil War pushed the Old School and New School back into each other's arms. Similar pressures recurred in the years following World War I. The price of interdenominational union was the same: a lowering of doctrinal standards.

The 1919 General Assembly sent a Committee on Church Cooperation and Union to a national ecumenical convention that was proposing church union.[227] The 1920 General Assembly adopted the

---

225. See Chapter 14, below.
226. *Ibid.*, p. 143.
227. *Minutes of the General Assembly, 1919*, p. 154.

Committee's plan for organic union. The Presbyterian Church was to unite judicially with 17 other denominations, all designated as "Evangelical," a category broad enough to include the Protestant Episcopal Church, the Society of Friends (Quakers), and the Five Years' Meeting of the Friends in America.[228] The plan called for the creation of the "United Churches of Christ in America." The president of the Ad Interim Committee of the organization was going to be the Stated Clerk of the Presbyterian Church, William H. Roberts.[229] This new organization was to be a federal union, with denominations retaining their legal autonomy, i.e., "their autonomy in purely denominational affairs."[230] This plan had to be approved by two-thirds of the Church's presbyteries.

The proposed form of administration, however, resembled the administrative outline of the Presbyterian Church after the reorganization of 1908. The Preamble to the Plan of Union announced: "The United Churches of Christ in America shall act through a Council and through such Executive and Judicial Commissions, or Administrative Boards, working *ad interim*, as such Council may from time to time appoint and ordain."[231] For example, the Council would consolidate all missionary activities. But how? The Preamble did not say for sure, but it suggested the possibility of uniting the missionary boards.[232] The Committee on Church Cooperation and Union "heartily" recommended the adoption of the Plan of Union.[233]

What was called organic union was in fact *covenantal* union. Problem: every lawful covenant is established by taking a sanctions-bound oath to uphold a particular set of stipulations. There are no lawful covenants without judicial terms. Machen understood what this proposed union would mean: a watering down of the judicial terms of the faith. He wrote to his mother: "The Preamble of the Plan of Union sets forth the things in which all the constituent churches are to be agreed. Everything else is regarded as of secondary importance. The

---

228. *Minutes of the General Assembly, 1920*, p. 118.
229. *Ibid.*, p. 122.
230. "Preamble," *ibid.*, p. 119.
231. *Ibid.*
232. *Ibid.*, p. 120.
233. *Ibid.*, p. 121.

Preamble is studiously vague: a man could subscribe to the creed contained in it without believing in the essentials of the Christian faith."[234] The majority report of the Committee on Church Cooperation and Union was signed by the president of Princeton Seminary, J. Ross Stevenson.[235]

Machen Appears on the Scene

This was the prelude to a battle that erupted over the control of Princeton after the 1926 General Assembly, but Machen could not foresee this in 1920. Machen went public with an attack on the Plan of Union in *The Presbyterian* (June 10, 1920). He focused on the creedal issue.[236] Over the following year, *The Presbyterian* published articles critical of the union by Princetonians Warfield, W. B. Greene, C. W. Hodge, and O. T. Allis.[237]

Machen's opposition was two-fold. First, the judicial basis of the union was vague. This was a judicial criticism. Second, the author of the Preamble was a liberal, indicating that churches and ministers with similarly liberal views would not be threatened by the union. This was a question of the least common theological denominator. Machen's opposition was therefore both theological and judicial. He was not opposing cooperation with other churches; he was opposing an oath-bound covenantal union in which the oath was not expressly Bible-based and specific in its commitment to fundamental doctrine.

I stress this because numerous critics of Machen, in his day and ever since, have argued that his opposition to this union was inconsistent with his later cooperation with fundamentalists and other conservative evangelical organizations. This criticism is misleading. The issue in 1920 was not the legitimacy of alliances, which are permitted by the Bible (Gen. 14:13); the issue was the theological basis of Church covenants. Alliances are not covenants. Alliances are not created by means of a self-maledictory (negative sanctions-invoking) oath before

---

234. Cited in Stonehouse, *Machen*, p. 305. The Preamble is reprinted by Stonehouse: pp. 305–306.

235. He later claimed to have opposed it in presbytery.

236. *Ibid.*, pp. 306–307. Machen wrote other articles on this issue for *The Presbyterian*: January 20, 1921, and March 17, 1921.

237. *Ibid.*, p. 307.

God.[238] Machen never spelled out this distinction by means of covenantal language, for he rarely used covenantal language, but his hostility to Church union was based on his understanding that the fundamental issue was covenant law, not cooperation as such.

The Division at Princeton Begins

The presbyteries had to approve the union. They voted it down prior to the 1921 General Assembly, 150 to 100,[239] but not before Princeton's Charles Erdman came out in favor of it in front of the student body.[240] Machen a week later spoke against it before the student body.[241] It was clear that the conservatives were facing a growing opposition when a hundred presbyteries favored joining an organization whose preamble had been composed primarily by a liberal in another denomination.[242] It was also clear that the Old School's only remaining seminary was facing a revolt within its own faculty—a revolt led by its president, Stevenson.

Six years later, Erdman testified to a committee that was investigating the disputes at Princeton Seminary. He said, "The 1920 discussions on the Plan of Union was the dividing point in this seminary." He hastened to add that his position, which was also Stevenson's, was "misinterpreted, and has become the ground of endless suspicions."[243] From 1926 to 1936, these suspicions were proven to have been well grounded.

Did the presbyteries' vote in 1920–21 call a halt to the Church union movement? Hardly. The Committee on Church Cooperation

---

238. Gary North, *Healer of the Nations: Biblical Blueprints for International Relations* (Ft. Worth, Texas: Dominion Press, 1987), ch. 9: "Alliances Are Not Covenants."

239. *Minutes of the General Assembly, 1921*, p. 42.

240. Stonehouse, *Machen*, pp. 311.

241. *Ibid.*, p. 312.

242. The author was George W. Richards, a defender of Schleiermacher and Ritschl. Machen pointed this out in *The Presbyterian* (Jan. 20, 1921). *Ibid.*, pp. 308, 312.

243. Cited in Delwyn G. Nykamp, A Presbyterian Power Struggle: A Critical History of Communication Strategies in the Struggle for Control of the Presbyterian Church, U.S.A., 1922–1926 (Ph.D. dissertation, Northwestern University, 1974), p. 453.

in 1921 declared that the negative vote by the presbyteries had all been a big mistake, that the actual overture had merely been "a referendum," not "a final act." (Why a referendum voted by the presbyteries would not have been final, the Committee did not say.) This clarification had been made by the General Assembly of 1920, the Committee insisted; unfortunately, both copies of this clarification somehow disappeared, so it was not recorded in the 1920 *Minutes*. This clarifying information had not been sent to the presbyteries.[244] The presbyteries had misinterpreted this vote as "a hastily and ill-conceived scheme for super-government subversive of the sanctity and property rights of our Church. . . ."[245] The Committee therefore ignored the negative vote. It kept working. Stevenson was still serving as chairman of the Special Committee on Church Cooperation and Union in 1922.[246] It received a renewal of its 1918 authorization in 1923, becoming a permanent department known as the Council on Organic Union.[247] This was two decades after the establishment of the original Committee on Church Cooperation.[248] Obviously, 1903 had been a busy year, not just for creedal revision. The new reality was clear by 1920: once established, it proved impossible to de-fund a Church agency.

The Liberal Takeover in 1920

From the restructuring of 1908 until 1920, the liberals consolidated their control in the Church's administrative agencies. By 1918, they felt sufficiently secure to propose the New Era Movement, which passed in 1919. That year, the General Assembly also authorized a committee to study the possibility of the ordination of women, which reported back in 1920 with a recommendation to the General Assembly to submit to the presbyteries a plan to ordain women.[249] The General Assembly voted to submit this overture to the presbyter-

---

244. *Minutes of the General Assembly, 1921*, p. 83.
245. *Ibid.*, p. 84.
246. *Minutes of the General Assembly, 1922*, pp. 78ff.
247. *Minutes of the General Assembly, 1923*, pp. 296-99.
248. *Ibid.*, p. 296.
249. *Minutes of the General Assembly, 1920*, pp. 127-31.

ies, which was defeated, 129 to 125.[250] The fact that the General Assembly had authorized this vote is indicative of how far things had moved away from historic Presbyterianism. (Women were authorized to become ruling elders in 1930.) Also in 1920, the flare-up over the Interchurch World Movement was easily contained. The liberals' main setback in 1920 took place outside the General Assembly at the presbytery level: the failure of the Assembly's proposed Plan of Union.

The 1920 General Assembly also voted its moral support of the work of something called the World Alliance for International Friendship, which in turn had supported the work of the National Committee on the Churches and the Moral Aims of the War. This committee had sent out a postcard survey to the ministers of America, asking them their opinion of the following resolution: support for the League of Nations, calling on the U.S. Senate to ratify the treaty exactly as President Wilson was demanding, "without amendments or such reservations as would require resubmission of the Treaty to the Peace Conference and Germany." Of 16,125 ministers responding, all but 805 supposedly had responded favorably.[251] The World Alliance had called for "that spirit of goodwill which we desire to foster until it ripens into the general recognition of the brotherhood of nations."[252] The General Assembly added its vote of approval to this humanist manifesto, which was laying the foundations of world government. At the heart of the General Assembly's motivation was politics: "Presbyterian Churches were repeatedly urged to write letters to their Senators urging them to take a stand in ratification of the League Covenant. . . ."[253] The denomination's connection with the World Alliance became permanent.[254] By 1920, liberals had gained uncontested control over the Church's administrative machinery. This was exactly two decades after Arthur C. McGiffert had left the Church in the face of a heresy trial.

---

250. *Minutes of the General Assembly, 1921*, p. 44.
251. *Ibid.*, p. 45.
252. *Ibid.*, p. 46.
253. *Ibid.*, p. 44.
254. Cf. *Minutes of the General Assembly, 1923*, pp. 47–50.

The presbyteries overcame the 1920 General Assembly on two issues: the ordination of women and the Plan of Union. From that point on, the General Assemblies were able to get most of their overtures passed by the presbyteries. Unless some outside issue intruded, the General Assemblies were henceforth under the control of the Stated Clerk, the Executive Commission, and representatives of the boards, whose incarnation was Speer. When the 1920 Executive Commission escaped censure for its million-dollar funding of Rockefeller's Interchurch World Movement, its members knew that their day had dawned. They wasted no time.

There would soon be another challenge to this consolidation, however. It did not come from inside the Church. An outsider arrived to stir the pot. When it did not overflow, the liberals knew for sure that they had won control over the Church's executive system. As with the United States government after the defeat of Herbert Hoover in 1932, control over the executive agencies meant the ability to set most of the legislative agenda, to the extent that the General Assembly could have a *de facto* legislative agenda. Then all they would have to do was control the General Assembly's judicial function. That was not secured defensively until 1926, and not secured offensively until 1934.

But first, they had to get by the next challenge.

The Warning About Missions

Twice in the Presbyterian conflict, the dividing issue was liberalism in foreign missions: 1921 and 1932–36. The first battle began in 1921, when fundamentalist oilman Milton Stewart funded a tour by fundamentalist leaders of foreign missions in China.[255] The Stewarts were old rivals of the Rockefellers in Pennsylvania and later in California.[256] In 1921, Milton Stewart also anonymously donated $1.7 million to the Northern Baptist Convention, which then pledged that its missionaries would adhere to fundamentalist theology. This enraged

---

255. Colby and Charlotte Dennett, *Thy Will Be Done: The Conquest of the Amazon: Nelson Rockefeller and Evangelism in the Age of Oil* (New York: HarperCollins*Publishers*, 1995), p. 24.

256. *Ibid.*

John D., Sr., who had Junior inform every denomination and missionary society that had been receiving Rockefeller funds that there would be no further gifts if their missionaries were forced to espouse fundamentalism. This action, Senior told Junior, was designed "to forestall, if possible, the ill effect that their still treacherous action may have on the final carrying out of our ideas."[257]

That same year, an orthodox Anglican scholar-lecturer, W. H. Griffith Thomas, unleashed an attack on modernism within China's various mission agencies, including the Presbyterian missionary enterprise in China.[258] His account of his experiences shows that the mission field in China was already divided between defenders of higher criticism and conservatives. He raised a crucially important point in what I regard as the most insightful one-sentence evaluation in the post-1869 phases of the Presbyterian conflict, or, for that matter, in the history of the entire fundamentalist-modernist conflict:

> I also urged the importance of taking care lest Liberalism should be intolerant, because as long as conservatives are silent there is an outward appearance of unity, but when they begin to speak out on behalf of their own position, they are said to be causing division, though, in reality, the cause of division is the introduction of the new views.[259]

In one sentence, he identified the most important rhetorical tactic of the liberals from 1874 on: their accusation that the conservatives were the intolerant faction, disrupting the unity of the Church. Typical of this misrepresentation was Shailer Mathews' evaluation in his 1936 autobiography, that the fundamentalists' "language was often intemperate and their actions were repeatedly open to ethical criticism."[260] He did admit, however, that "they made no recourse to

---

257. Cited in *ibid.*, p. 25.
258. W. H. Griffith Thomas, "Modernism in China," *Princeton Theological Review*, 19 (Oct. 1921), pp. 630–71; reprinted with its original pagination in *Modernism and Foreign Missions: Two Fundamentalist Protests*, edited by Joel A. Carpenter (New York: Garland, 1988).
259. *Ibid.*, p. 632.
260. Shailer Mathews, *New Faith for Old: An Autobiography* (New York: Macmillan, 1936), p. 278.

force. . . ."²⁶¹ (That was why they lost.) The liberals' spiritual heirs, who have written all of the textbooks and most of the monographs, have repeated this argument ever since, to great effect. They have persuaded at least two generations of observers that rhetorical aggression and theological intolerance have been the morally incriminating monopolies of the conservatives. (This reiterated accusation has psychologically disarmed the conservatives, especially seminary professors, who have adopted a polemical style more suitable to after-dinner discussions regarding the careers of retired editors of scholarly journals.)

He also referred to a newly formed organization in China made up of missionaries: the Bible Union of China, which was interdenominational. It had begun after his departure from China. Its *Bulletin* spoke of "destructive critical views of the Bible, which teaching has been gradually introduced into some mission centres in China."²⁶² By the time he wrote his essay, the Union had over 600 members and was growing rapidly.²⁶³ He complained that *The Continent*, a liberal Presbyterian magazine, had blamed him for the creation of the Union, which it described rhetorically as "another bit of mischief."²⁶⁴ He said that he had received opposition from several YMCA workers, who said his lectures were dividing the missionaries.²⁶⁵ This was further confirmation of the 30-year problem with the YMCA missionary efforts under Mott: they tended toward liberalism.

What is clear from Griffith Thomas' extensive quoting from publications in China is that the China mission field had been sharply divided for years, and the participants on both sides recognized this. In his essay, he named specific Chinese teachers and visiting American lecturers who opposed the creeds or taught higher criticism. He identified liberal textbooks in use on the field. More of his essay is devoted to reprinted materials than to his own comments. But he was circumspect in his refusal to name a single liberal missionary.

---

261. *Ibid.*
262. Cited in Griffith Thomas, "Modernism in China," pp. 634–35.
263. *Ibid.*, p. 636.
264. *Ibid.*, p. 637.
265. *Ibid.*, p. 638.

412   CROSSED FINGERS

His was not the first warning on foreign missions. In 1918, a book by Northern Baptist theologian A. H. Strong, *A Tour of the Missions*, had warned about the growing modernism of Baptists on the foreign missions field. Strong had been the president of Rochester Theological Seminary for four decades, retiring in 1912. He had accepted higher criticism. He believed in the creeds, but he also believed that the Church should not bother to enforce them.[266] He had pressured John D. Rockefeller, Sr., into creating the University of Chicago.[267] His *Systematic Theology* went through eight editions, and the eighth edition in 1980 was in its 30th printing.[268] He had appointed Walter Rauschenbusch and other modernists to the faculty, although he had also hired conservatives.[269] He had been attacked as an incipient Unitarian during the 1890's. He announced in 1899 that "Christ is the principle of evolution."[270] Yet he also believed in timeless truth.[271] He was, in short, theologically schizophrenic, and his life's work has long puzzled American Church historians.[272] But this schizophrenia made him a successful college president: balancing rival worldviews in his mind, he could balance rival worldviews in his departments. He had defended his faculty's academic freedom, and he had raised so much money for the school's endowment that the school became immune to economic reprisals. He served as a mediator between "robber barron" donors who, as usual, were happy to subsidize their mortal enemies,[273] and social gospel socialists on his faculty. But by the time of

---

266. Grant Wacker, "The Dilemmas of Historical Consciousness: The Case of Augustus H. Strong," in *In the Great Tradition: In Honor of Winthrop S. Hudson, Essays on Pluralism, Voluntarism, and Revivalism*, edited by Paul R. Dekar and Joseph D. Ban (Valley Forge, Pennsylvania: Judson, 1982), pp. 223, 227.
267. *Ibid.*, p. 225.
268. *Ibid.*
269. *Ibid.*
270. Augustus H. Strong, *Christ in Creation and Ethical Monism* (Philadelphia: Griffith & Rowland, 1899), p. 10. Cited in *ibid.*, p. 227.
271. *Ibid.*, p. 229.
272. *Ibid.*, p. 226.
273. Wrote Joseph Schumpeter in 1942: "Perhaps the most striking feature of the picture is the extent to which the bourgeoisie, besides educating its own enemies, allows itself in turn to be educated by them. It absorbs the slogans of current radicalism and seems quite willing to undergo a process of conversion to a creed hostile to its very existence. Haltingly and grudgingly it concedes in part

his retirement, he had begun to have serious misgivings about what was going on in the Church. His trip to the missions field in 1916 and 1917 convinced him that his suspicions had been correct.[274] He proposed a three-part strategy in 1921, the last year of his life: purge the schools, rectify missions work, and adopt a confession of faith.[275] He was too late by three decades.

Challenge and Response

Griffith Thomas spoke in a series of lectures throughout the United States. He claimed that Presbyterian missionaries were giving aid to distinctly liberal activities of social reform and de-emphasizing the traditional Church message, but his accusations against the Board of Foreign Missions went unheeded, even by most of the conservatives. As was true in his *Princeton Theological Review* article, he refused to name specific missionaries when challenged to do so by one of the Foreign Mission Board's officers.[276] As an outsider, he was wise enough to recognize the nature of Presbyterian government: a judicial quagmire from which it took years to extricate yourself, assuming that you named only one name. He refused to rush in where Old School Presbyterians feared to tread.

Predictably, he was attacked publicly for having made his general accusation. This had been the liberals' strategy ever since Henry van Dyke's challenge in 1913: "Put up or shut up; prosecute or hold thy peace." Anyone who criticized any aspect of the Church's operations for liberalism had to be ready to inaugurate a full-fledged heresy trial to the bitter end. No one was. Griffith Thomas was therefore caught in the same web that had entangled Presbyterian conservatives for a decade: the inability to impose negative sanctions. But he at least had an excuse: he was not a Presbyterian.

---

the implications of that creed. This would be most astonishing and indeed very hard to explain were it not for the fact that the typical bourgeois is rapidly losing faith in his own creed." Schumpeter, *Capitalism, Socialism and Democracy*, 3rd ed. (New York: Harper Torchbooks, [1942] 1962), p. 161.

274. Moore, "Another Look at Fundamentalism," *op. cit.*, p. 198.
275. *Ibid.*, p. 200.
276. Loetscher, *Broadening Church*, p. 104.

Without a concerted judicial attack by the conservatives, nothing would be done by the bureaucrats who ran the Foreign Missions Board, since to admit that there were theological heretics under their jurisdiction would be to call attention to screening problems within the Board. The General Assembly of 1921 asserted that there was "nothing to disturb the confidence of the General Assembly in the Board of Foreign Missions and in the great body of its Christian missionaries." It did instruct the Board of Foreign Missions to conduct an examination of these reports.[277] To no one's surprise, the Board that had sent them onto the mission field found nothing seriously amiss with anyone. *The Presbyterian*, the publishing arm of the conservatives, did state that the investigation should have been conducted by a mixed group and not the Board, but that is as far as the criticism went.[278]

Erdman, a long-time member of the Board, defended the Board vigorously. Speer, secretary of the Board, was even more vociferous it its defense. He rejected the recent formation of the Bible Union of China, an independent missionary organization dedicated to conservative theology.

> If differences of interpretation of opinion do come, my friends, I do not believe that the principle of exclusion and separation and division is the right principle by which to deal with them. Much less, to set up organizations that divide the Body of Christ, that establish extra-Scriptural tests using in those tests words that are not in the New Testament. By what right do we erect barriers with words that the New Testament, itself, never uses?[279]

This is a familiar inclusivist argument against invoking theology as a screening device. If taken literally, it would have to exclude use of the word "Trinity." By adopting this argument, he implicitly rejected

---

277. *Ibid.*, p. 107.
278. *Ibid.*
279. Speer, "Are the Missionaries in China Trustworthy?" Address to the Presbyterian Social Union, March 28, 1921; cited in James Alan Patterson, Robert E. Speer and the Crisis of the American Protestant Missionary Movement, 1920–1937 (Ph.D. dissertation, Princeton Theological Seminary, 1980), p. 131.

the 1910 Doctrinal Deliverance and its reaffirmation by the 1916 General Assembly. He used a line of argument that would appear in late 1923 in the Auburn *Affirmation*.[280]

"Peace in Our Time"

By 1927, when he was elected Moderator of the General Assembly by acclamation, and perhaps a decade earlier, Speer had become the most widely respected lay leader in the Presbyterian Church. As secretary of the Board of Foreign Missions since 1891, he was also the best known representative for Protestant denominational missions in the United States.[281] He was a brilliant debater. He had graduated valedictorian from the College of New Jersey (Princeton) in 1889, just ahead of his lifetime friend and fellow Church bureaucrat, Lewis Mudge,[282] who became the Church's Stated Clerk in 1921 and held this crucial position until 1938. Speer was an early disciple of evangelist Dwight L. Moody. Immediately after graduation in 1889, he became a highly successful recruiter for the newly created Student Volunteer Movement, visiting 110 campuses and bringing in 1,100 students in one academic year, 1889-90.[283] Then he quit. In 1891, he became secretary for the Board of Foreign Missions, a position he held for the next 47 years; he retired in 1937 on his 70th birthday. He was never ordained to the ministry.[284] If there is a model of the modern Protestant ecclesiastical bureaucrat, Speer was the original.

He was a premillennialist, but he was also an ecumenist. Longfield writes: "At times it almost seemed as if Speer equated the gospel with the message of the oneness of humanity."[285] He was present at the first meeting of the Federal Council of Churches in 1908, where he delivered an address, "Christian Unity on the Foreign Missions Field."[286]

---

280. See Chapter 9, below.
281. Mott was less known as a promoter of denominational missions than as an ecumenist and a defender of interdenominational missions.
282. Patterson, Speer, p. 5.
283. *Ibid.*, p. 16.
284. *Ibid.*, p. 22.
285. Longfield, *Presbyterian Controversy*, p. 196.
286. Patterson, Speer, p. 25.

He was elected president of the organization for a four-year term in 1920.[287] In his study of the Federal Council of Churches, historian C. Gregg Singer comments: "Widespread criticism of the Federal Council from conservatives within the denominations was infrequent until after 1920, when the Council became involved in radical movements of various kinds on a wider scale than it had been during the years from 1908 to 1917."[288]

Unlike Machen, Speer was a strong advocate of the Volstead Act, i.e., Prohibition. He had joined several anti-alcohol organizations while in college.[289] Also unlike Machen, he was a supporter of American intervention into World War I. He called it "a just and necessary war."[290] He took quite seriously the National Security League's messianic claim that the United States was fighting for "FREEDOM FOR ALL FOREVER."[291] He referred to this as one of "the clear moral aims of the war." The Church must get behind "the great ideal ends which the President has stated. . . ."[292] The war offered a tremendous opportunity: the creation of an international government. "We have our opportunity through the war to effect an organization of the nations which should bring them under such a just and mutually helpful order as binds in closer bonds the widely varied interests of our American Union."[293] The problem here was "the resistance of nationalistic individualism to the spirit of world brotherhood and to the common interest of humanity."[294] To overcome this, we need two things: "One is a new spirit of universalism. . . . The other necessity is some instrumentality of international association by which the gains of a world peace in righteousness may be won and held without sacri-

---

287. *Ibid.*, p. 26.
288. Singer, *Unholy Alliance*, p. 28.
289. Patterson, Speer, p. 29.
290. Robert E. Speer, *The Christian Man, the Church and the War* (New York: Macmillan, 1918), p. 7.
291. *Ibid.*, p. 51.
292. *Ibid.*
293. *Ibid.*, p. 78.
294. *Ibid.*, p. 89.

fice of national personality."[295] This is true Christianity, for "Jesus Christ was and is a principle of unity."[296]

A year later, Speer continued this theme of a new moral order through a new world order. He argued in a post-War chapter titled, "The War Aims and Foreign Missions": ". . . the great ideas and principles of the missionary enterprise were taken over and declared by the nation as its moral aims in the war."[297] He waxed eloquent in 1919 about a coming new world order: "And above all as time went on men realized that they were in this struggle for the sake of what lies ahead of us, for the hope of a new human order—an order of righteousness and of justice and of brotherhood."[298] Men must now commit themselves to furthering a new international order, "the ideals of human brotherhood, of international justice and service, of peace and good will."[299] In 1919, this was rhetoric unmistakably promoting President Wilson's crusade for the League of Nations. That same year, he wrote in the *Federal Council Bulletin*: "What we speak of today as the League of Nations is an indispensable and unavoidable implicate of all our Christian faith and endeavor in the world." This, in an essay appropriately titled, "From World War to World Brotherhood."[300]

Speer worked with John D. Rockefeller, Jr., from at least 1913[301] until the end of his career. This, despite the fact that he eventually lost confidence in the bureaucrats at the Rockefeller Foundation. He wrote to his daughter in 1926: "I think the professional Rockefeller Foundation people are not especially interested in religious enterprises and I know they do not care for missionary enterprises. . . ." Then he added: "Don't whisper this to anybody else, however."[302] Rockefeller

---

295. *Ibid.*, p. 91.
296. *Ibid.*, p. 95.
297. Speer, *The New Opportunity of the Church* (New York: Macmillan, 1919), p. 89.
298. *Ibid.*, p. 93.
299. *Ibid.*, p. 109.
300. Speer, in *Federal Council Bulletin*, 2 (June 1919), p. 103; cited in Handy, *Christian America*, p. 161.
301. Charles E. Harvey, "Speer Versus Rockefeller and Mott, 1910-1935," *Journal of Presbyterian History*, 60 (Winter, 1982), p. 285.
302. Cited in Patterson, Speer, pp. 81-82.

418   CROSSED FINGERS

had great confidence in Speer as a spokesman for ecumenism. He wrote to Speer in 1920, after Speer's election as president of the Federal Council: "Surely there must be many people throughout the country who have believed firmly in the principle of federation but who have not had the fullest confidence in some of the personnel, and therefore have withheld their support and cooperation. As I may have perhaps said to you, this has been our own position. Your coming into the leadership of the movement will go far toward removing that obstacle and will inspire general confidence and bring about increased support of the enterprise throughout the country."[303]

Room for All

Speer was opposed to debates over theology. Longfield says that he was a disciple of Horace Bushnell, the mid-century Congregational pastor-theologian who sought to reconcile Calvinism and Arminianism by returning to the Apostles' Creed.[304] In 1901, Speer addressed the General Assembly on the matter. "For the Church to spend her whole strength on that battlefield is to war with phantoms. . . ."[305] His biographer comments: "Recognizing a threat to the stability and efficiency of the large missionary program he had carefully nurtured for many years, he naturally sought to protect the interests of his Board in the face of precisionist sniping."[306] This was the problem of the denomination generally: the national boards were havens from orthodoxy. Modernists could hide there knowing that the institutional response of the boards would be to shield those inside from theological critics outside.

Church historian Lefferts Loetscher, whose liberal sympathies pervade his book on the history of the era, has given us a description of Speer that needs to be considered very carefully. This thumbnail biographical sketch offers us the very essence of the inclusivist—the seemingly well-meaning defender of a "warm Christian faith" whose ac-

---

303. Rockefeller to Speer, Dec. 4, 1920; cited in Schenkel, *Rich Man and Kingdom*, p. 189.
304. Longfield, *Presbyterian Controversy*, pp. 189-95.
305. Cited in Patterson, Speer, p. 127.
306. *Ibid.*

tions, step by step, turned the denomination over to its covenantal enemies. No one could successfully question such a man's orthodoxy. He seems just as orthodox as anyone, and what a marvelous fellow, too! This figure is and has been absolutely indispensable to the modernists in the capture of formerly conservative churches. Loetscher regards Speer as the key figure in the Church after 1920.

> Dr. Speer, who was at this juncture thrust into the controversy, was, in the coming decade and a half, to do more in forming the theological policy of the Presbyterian Church than perhaps any other individual. After a career as football hero and near head of his class at the College of New Jersey, he had been snatched from his course at Princeton Seminary to be secretary of the Presbyterian Board of Foreign Missions. Almost immediately he had become one of the three or four principal leaders of a great forward thrust made by American Protestant foreign missions. In recruiting missionary volunteers, in formulating and directing missionary strategy, in moving popular audiences, he was unsurpassed. He had contributed to *The Fundamentals* and many of his deepest religious beliefs were very conservative, but as one who had been a broad reader and a leader in large practical affairs since early manhood, he could not accept any view of Christian "essentials" which would commit the Church to a detached and irrelevant existence. His theory, like his life, was intensely dynamic. "I wish," he told a correspondent in China at this time, "we could get up such a glow and fervor and onrush of evangelical and evangelistic conviction and action that we would be swept clear past issues like the present ones so that men who want to dispute over these things could stay behind and do so while the rest of us could march ahead, more than making up by new conquests for all the defections and losses of those who stay behind."[307]

In short, if we can just stop arguing about theology, and start marching forward, everything will go well for evangelism. But those who want to debate theology are retarding factors in this march into the future. This is what Loetscher means by a "dynamic faith." It is

---

307. Loetscher, *Broadening Church*, pp. 105-106.

also the faith of the evolutionist and the situation ethics advocate. It is the faith of the humanist. Without a strong commitment to some form of creedalism, the conservative is helpless to challenge such a position successfully, whether in politics in ecclesiastical affairs. Understandably, Speer was opposed to creedalism and systematic theology generally. In 1894, at a Student Volunteer Movement convention, he had warned them: "Don't preach a system of truth. What good is a system of truth anyhow? Don't preach salvation; don't preach redemption. Preach a Saviour. Preach a Redeemer. What is wanted is not more truth; it is a Divine Person. What is wanted is not a larger doctrine; it is the advent of Divine Life."[308]

Speer was a consummate bureaucrat who would become the master of the denomination, the "first among equals." He saw the problem facing those who, like himself, wished to de-emphasize theology. The General Assembly was in charge of the boards of the denomination. This included the Foreign Missions Board. The General Assembly at this time was conservative—more conservative than some of the presbyteries that had ordained the missionaries sent out by the Board. So, there was a distinct threat of negative sanctions against liberals on the mission field. But Speer would soon plug this threat. He exercised what Loetscher calls "truer statesmanship. . . . Dr. Speer therefore cast his powerful influence on the side of decentralization and pluralism—in constitutional terms, on the side of leaving full theological jurisdiction over the missionary in the hands of his presbytery."[309] This remained the tactic of the liberals until 1931: decentralizing power away from the General Assembly.

What he did was to announce the policy of having the Board of Foreign Missions receive complaints against a missionary, and then pass along the complaint to the missionary's home presbytery. This was certainly Presbyterianism in action: the locus of authority remained with the ordained man's presbytery back in the United States. The problem was, the presbytery was at least 10,000 miles away from the mission field in China. Loetscher was correct: the Presbyterian

---

308. Cited in Longfield, *Presbyterian Controversy*, p. 187.
309. Loetscher, *Broadening Church*, p. 106.

Church's administrative machinery "had never been completely integrated into the sixteenth-and seventeenth-century pattern of government by four ascending judicatories."[310] Where did the missionary fit into the four courts: congregation, presbytery, synod, and General Assembly? No one knew. This gave Speer the opportunity to define a new chain of command.

Speer had spotted an institutional escape hatch for liberal missionaries who were under fire from conservatives, either at home or abroad. The foreign missionary was in a kind of judicial "no man's land" in between his foreign congregation and his American presbytery. He was not a member of the foreign congregation; teaching elders were members of presbyteries. From the days of the Second Great Awakening, the problem of missionaries had plagued the Presbyterian Church. The debate over who had lawful authority over missions had split the Church in 1837. This split did not resolve the secondary debate over which court had lawful jurisdiction over the foreign missionary. It was not resolved in the 1860 General Assembly debate between Charles Hodge and James H. Thornwell (see below, pages 927–29). It was ultimately the question of the locus of authority in enforcing the ministerial oath. The Presbyterian court of final jurisdiction was the court of original jurisdiction; it was located far from the witnesses. Speer made effective use of this unresolved jurisdictional problem. It remained unresolved until 1936.

Lengthening the Chain of Command

Speer's deft move was perfect from the point of view of the modernists. Not only would the inherent bureaucratic resistance by each presbytery protect liberals in these presbyteries, it would then move these heretics to the four corners of the earth, where it would be virtually impossible for anyone to monitor their preaching other than other missionaries in the same area, which might mean hundreds of miles away. These other missionaries would not be part of a regional presbytery in that country. Thus, to bring negative sanctions against another missionary, the complaining missionary would have to complain through his own presbytery back in the United States. From

---

310. *Ibid.*

there the complaint would go to the defendant's presbytery, then up to the chain of appeals—synod, General Assembly—then back to the defendant's presbytery. These trials would be conducted 10,000 miles away from the mission field.

It would be obvious to any conservative on the mission field that the government was too distant for the any reasonable expectation of success. Because the denomination never established a permanent system to create geography-based presbyteries on the various mission fields, and because it assented to Speer's recommendation to avoid placing the authority over missionaries in the common agency of government—the Foreign Missions Board itself—the Presbyterian Church, U.S.A., effectively removed all threat of negative sanctions from anyone on the mission field. The result in 1932–33 would be the Pearl S. Buck affair.[311] There were many more missionaries on the field who shared her liberal theological views. The only reason why she became a target of conservatives is because she went into print: the public rhetoric factor.

As Machen and his supporters learned, beginning a decade later, Speer's commitment to decentralization was a temporary tactic, not a permanent principle. It was an *ad hoc* move to insulate liberal missionaries from conservative critics, both at home and on the field. It was a decision to isolate the influence of orthodox theology: at the presbytery level. This could be done only if the General Assembly could be stripped of all authority to impose negative sanctions on anyone who was not under its immediate authority. The boards had become institutional shields for liberals.

This policy of strengthening the presbyteries at the expense of the General Assembly was later abandoned by the inclusivists, after they took control of Princeton Seminary in 1929. The seminary was legally under the General Assembly's authority—an Old School policy. Once that test of power proved to be a total success, the tactic of decentralization was abandoned by the inclusivists, and a policy of comprehensive centralization of power over the presbyteries replaced it. Speer was part of this reversal. Well did Loetscher put it: from 1921 to 1936,

---

311. See Chapter 11, below.

Speer did more "in forming the theological policy of the Presbyterian Church than perhaps any other individual."[312]

In 1924, Princeton's Old Testament scholar Robert Dick Wilson visited the Far East. He returned and issued a basically favorable report on what he had seen. "It is my belief that the ordained missionaries of our church are as true to the teachings of the Confession and as loyal to the Word of God as the ministers at home are."[313] This report ended public criticism of the Foreign Missions Board for almost nine years. Wilson could not be written off as a compromiser. He was so dedicated to Old School Presbyterianism that in 1929 he left Princeton at the end of his career and joined the faculty at Westminster. (A very similar report appeared in *The Presbyterian* in 1935, written by fundamentalist pastor Donald Gray Barnhouse. It had a very similar effect under similar circumstances.)

Final Administrative Consolidation

In 1922, the General Assembly approved a plan to consolidate its 16 Church boards into four. Such a consolidation had been discussed publicly since 1906, the year of the first discussions regarding the 1908 restructuring. The report of the Special Committee on Reorganization and Consolidation of Assembly Agencies was presented. This Committee had been appointed at the turning-point General Assembly of 1920. The very title of the Committee is revealing: *Assembly* Agencies. The report, accepted **unanimously** (bold face in the original) by the Committee, filled the 1922 *Minutes* from page 149 to 181.

The report proposed the creation of a new organization, the General Council, which would coordinate missionary and benevolent operations.[314] But that was only the beginning. "The General Council shall discharge such other duties as the General Assembly shall from time to time require and authorize."[315] *Other duties*: here was an open-ended authorization, and it would soon be exercised.

---

312. Loetscher, *Broadening Church*, p. 105.
313. Wilson, "Friendly Advice to the Foreign Board," *The Presbyterian* (Oct. 25, 1923), p. 9; cited in Patterson, Speer, p. 135.
314. *Minutes of the General Assembly, 1922*, p. 178.
315. *Ibid.*

The Council's Chairman would be chosen for five years by the Council, "subject to the approval of the General Assembly."[316] *The General Assembly would henceforth no longer initiate anything of significance regarding the central agency that would represent it.* Attendees could merely exercise the veto. The Stated Clerk would also be a permanent member. If passed by the presbyteries, this overture would consolidate the denomination's bureaucracy. It passed overwhelmingly in 1923-24: 222 to 26, with 6 taking no action.[317] The presbyteries that voted for it included the conservative strongholds: Chester, Philadelphia, and New Brunswick (Machen's). At the 1924 General Assembly, the General Council recommended a seemingly minor alteration: a name change in the Form of Government from "Executive Commission(s)" to "General Council(s)." This was to be substituted at every level: General Assembly, synod, and presbytery.[318] The General Assembly approved of the alteration. This overture was also passed overwhelmingly by the presbyteries, 1924-25, and the same three conservative presbyteries voted for it.[319] So much for official concern over the administration of benevolences as the justification for the General Council. The consolidation of the hierarchy was now complete. Here is the significant fact: these changes were initiated by the only two post-war General Assemblies in which the conservatives were supposedly dominant, 1923 and 1924.

In 1926, Chester Presbytery submitted Overture 7, "On Dissolving the General Council," which called for a return to the pre-1908 General Assembly.[320] More than any other action in the entire history of the Presbyterian conflict, this overture reveals naiveté on an unprecedented scale. It justifies the application of an old phrase, "They never saw it coming." From the creedal revision of 1903 until the liberals' administrative juggernaut blind-sided them at the 1926 General Assembly, the conservatives never saw it coming.

---

316. *Ibid.*
317. *Minutes of the General Assembly, 1924*, p. 137.
318. *Ibid.*, p. 105.
319. *Minutes of the General Assembly, 1925*, p. 61.
320. *Minutes of the General Assembly, 1926*, p. 25.

Conclusion

The Old School's problem after 1869 was simultaneously theological and judicial. The judicial battles were lost, step by step: 1869 (reunion), 1903 (creedal revision), and 1906 (the Cumberland churches' invasion). The 1908 restructuring of the Church's administrative machinery had almost been defeated by the presbyteries. The 1910 General Assembly passed the fundamentalists' five-point Doctrinal Deliverance, but it also passed the Social Deliverance modeled after the Federal Council of Churches' 1908 statement. The five-point Deliverance, which had zero authority judicially, was the last major defeat for the liberals until 1920, when Church Union and the ordination of women elders were voted down. With each judicial defeat came a theological setback for the conservatives. Five-point Calvinism became judicially unenforceable in the courts in 1903. In 1910, what little remained of four-point Calvinism after the 1906 arrival of 1,100 Cumberland Presbyterian congregations was formally replaced creedally by something not distinguishable from common-ground fundamentalism: the five-point Doctrinal Deliverance.

Meanwhile, the modernists had learned their lesson from Briggs. From 1900 until 1922, they guarded their pens and tongues while they systematically infiltrated the agencies and boards. By 1920, their work was administratively secured from reversal. As Quirk writes of the Old School, "Exclusivists were not particularly prominent in the structure of boards and agencies, and they expressed concern about the growth of Church machinery, of professional programs, and the soundness of the missionary enterprises of the Church."[321] This is the familiar progression in every denomination: those who want to preach a conservative gospel enter the pulpits and stay there. Those who want jobs more than they want theological commitment enter the bureaucracy. *The larger the bureaucracy, the weaker its theology.* It takes a systematic and permanent effort for conservatives to retard this development.[322]

---

321. Quirk, Auburn *Affirmation*, p. 56.
322. Only once has it been reversed in the twentieth century: in the Southern Baptist Convention, 1977–1990. The Missouri Synod Lutherans slowed the drift

The modernists hid in the shadow of the New School's experiential-based, minimal-sanctions theology. They found that this shadow grew much broader in 1906 when Cumberland Presbyterians came in. This step-by-step downgrading of theology was exactly suited to their plans. If they could avoid giving rhetorical offense, they could continue their work unimpeded judicially. For example, Rev. Stelzle's version of the social gospel was controversial, but he was neither a theologian nor a seminary professor. He was a social activist who worked with the poor—an unrepresentative figure who resigned his position in 1912.[323] (He was representative in one sense, however: he was subsequently hired by the Federal Council. The liberals took care of their fallen wounded.) Meanwhile, the General Assembly ratified the social program of the Federal Council in 1910, 1913, and 1914. The modernists bided their time. They could afford to be patient.

The conservatives' rhetoric was mild because they did not want to provoke a fight. They called for the modernists in general (never by name) to leave the denomination, but that was the extent of it. This attitude of forbearance played into the hands of the modernists. Like a dim-witted mother who refuses to use a scrub brush on her muddy child because of her fear that this scrubbing might hurt the little tyke too much, so was the typical Presbyterian conservative in regard to the condition of the Church. Most of them preferred to slumber in peace. Anyone in their camp who betrayed this happy-face theology by adopting confrontational rhetoric risked being treated in the same way that Briggs was treated. It had not been his theology that had doomed him; it had been his rhetoric. Hostile rhetoric—or even the unproven accusation of hostile rhetoric—would bring forth negative sanctions. The crucial issue was sanctions.

---

into liberalism in 1975 and may have reversed it in 1992. The Convention voted 580 to 568 to replace the more liberal president with a conservative. *Christian News* (July 20, 1992), p. 23. But the fight continues.

323. George H. Nash, "Charles Stezle: Social Gospel Pioneer," *Journal of Presbyterian History*, 50 (1972), pp. 206-28.

Phase 4: Whose Sanctions?

7

DARWINISM, DEMOCRACY, AND THE PUBLIC SCHOOLS

Christians do not object to freedom of speech; they believe that Biblical truth can hold its own in a fair field. They concede the right of ministers to pass from belief to agnosticism or atheism, but they contend that they should be honest enough to separate themselves from the ministry and not attempt to debase the religion they profess. . . . It is time for Christians to protect religion from its most insidious enemy.

William Jennings Bryan (1922)[1]

With these words, the Great Commoner, three times the Democratic Party's nominee for President of the United States,[2] former Secretary of State under Woodrow Wilson,[3] and the most famous ruling elder in the Presbyterian Church, U.S.A.,[4] launched in the *New York Times* an attack on Darwinism and on the liberal clergymen who held Darwin's views on human evolution.

---

1. Bryan, "God and Evolution," *New York Times* (Feb. 26, 1922), VII, p. 10.
2. 1896, 1900, 1908.
3. He had resigned in 1915 in protest against Wilson's violations of neutrality in support of the British in World War I. He resigned on June 7, 1915, exactly one month after the sinking of the *Lusitania*. LeRoy Ashby, *William Jennings Bryan: Champion of Democracy* (Boston: Twayne, 1987), pp. 159–60.
4. Wilson was no longer a ruling elder.

Bryan's *New York Times* article was a warning shot to Presbyterian liberals, although he did not identify his own denomination as a source of the problem. Over two decades of relative public peace within the Church were about to be brought to a close. A new era of doctrinal, personal, and rhetorical confrontation was about to begin. It would last for a decade and a half, and would end with the exodus of the most doctrinally Calvinistic members of the denomination and the creation of two new ecclesiastical organizations by those members: the Orthodox Presbyterian Church[5] in 1936 and the Bible Presbyterian Church in 1938.

As we shall see, however, Bryan's challenge to theological liberals was peripheral to his challenge to the American Establishment in the broadest sense. This battle would soon extend far beyond the narrow confines of the institutional Church.

Editors Bearing Gifts

As a politician, he should have been suspicious of any request by the editors of the *New York Times* to give him free space on page 1 of Section VII of the Sunday edition. He should have asked himself: "What's the catch?" The offer was bait, and he bit. He had little choice: to have refused would have played into the editors' hands. "We gave him a chance to respond, but he did not." Three years later, the hook attached to this bait led to the destruction of his reputation and the beginning of a half-century rout of the fundamentalist movement in America.

The editors had an agenda. It was initially defensive, for Bryan had an offensive agenda. His agenda had only recently been manifested by political events. Politics, not theology as such, was what caught the *Times*' attention. Publishing Bryan's essay also offered the added benefit of being able to sell Bryan's publisher advertising space for Bryan's recently published book, *In His Image*.

Bryan in 1921 had been invited to deliver the annual Sprunt lectures at the "other" Union: Union Theological Seminary of Richmond, Virginia, a conservative Southern Presbyterian seminary.[6] In

---

5. Originally called the Presbyterian Church of America.
6. The book became a best-seller: over a hundred thousand copies. Bradley

1920, Machen delivered the lectures there that became *The Origin of Paul's Religion* (1921). In October, Bryan delivered his lectures, which were published as *In His Image*.[7] Chapter 4, "The Origin of Man," was subsequently published as a separate book, *The Menace of Darwinism*.[8]

The revival of confrontational rhetoric came from outside the Presbyterian Church. Political modernists initiated it. Theological modernists inside the Church merely followed the lead of their colleagues on the outside. Modern readers may be amazed at the level of vituperation. It is important to understand that basic to the strategy of the liberals has been the promulgation of a lie, still repeated: "The conservatives were guilty of excessive rhetoric." Theological conservatives were subsequently blamed by modernists and their spiritual heirs, who have written the history books, for what the modernists in fact adopted as a primary tactic: a level of confrontational rhetoric beyond the limits of acceptable public discourse, i.e., acceptable to liberals when used by conservatives, which the conservatives in fact did not use. What prompted this revival of rhetoric was a political issue that went to the very heart of the American experiment in the separation of Church and State: control over the content of public education.

Bluegrass Democracy

Between 1921 and 1929, 37 anti-evolution bills were introduced into state legislatures.[9] These bills forbade the teaching of evolution in taxpayer-funded schools. In 1917, this demand had been made before the Kentucky legislature, and in 1921, a rider to this effect was attached to an appropriations bill in South Carolina.[10] Kentucky began to debate such a law in early January, 1922. Bryan addressed a joint session of the legislature on January 19, devoting the second half of

---

J. Longfield, *The Presbyterian Controversy: Fundamentalists, Modernists, and Moderates* (New York: Oxford University Press, 1991), p. 57.
7. New York: Revell.
8. New York: Revell, 1922.
9. Lawrence W. Levine, *Defender of the Faith: William Jennings Bryan: The Last Decade, 1915-1925* (New York: Oxford University Press, 1965), p. 276.
10. *Ibid.*, p. 277.

his speech to the question of teaching Darwinism in the public schools and universities supported by government funds. Representative George Ellis introduced such a bill a few days later.[11] Soon, Bryan received invitations to speak before the legislatures of Tennessee, Arkansas, Georgia, Mississippi, Ohio, Wisconsin, West Virginia, and Florida.[12]

This threat of the removal of tax subsidies for Darwinian evolution was regarded by modernists as a sword of Damocles over their collective heads. At the public university level, this was indeed a major threat. At the public school level, this threat was not yet a major threat, for American high schools rarely taught Darwinism. High school textbooks did not discuss Darwin's thesis to any appreciable degree, nor did they promote creationism. This was still true in the centenary of Darwin's *Origin of Species* in 1959. Hermann J. Muller, Nobel laureate in physiology, complained in *The Humanist* in 1959, "One Hundred Years Without Darwin Are Enough."[13] We must bring the truths of Darwinism to the little child, he said.[14] But the public school textbook publishers in the United States were too fearful of losing sales to promote Darwinism. "Are we then to allow the urge for profits to keep our children and, through them, all our people benighted and a hundred years out of date in their world view?"[15] What was true in 1959 was even more true in 1922.

The modernists knew that the vast majority of the nation did not accept Darwinian evolution in 1922. This is why they greatly feared democracy on this issue, and feared Bryan above all, for he still could rally large numbers of the Democratic Party's troops, millions of whom who were in the pews of conservative churches on Sunday morning.

---

11. *Ibid.*
12. *Ibid.*, p. 278.
13. Reprinted in *Darwin: A Norton Critical Edition*, edited by Philip Appleman (New York: Norton, 1970), p. 544–51.
14. *Ibid.*, p. 548.
15. *Ibid.*, p. 550.

The Attack Begins

On February 2, the *Times* ran a story, "Darwinian Theory Stirs Up Kentucky." Support for the bill was evenly divided in the state, the *Times* asserted, with rural areas favoring it and cities against it. The battle had been going on for months, the story reported; then Bryan came to speak. The ex-commissioner of education told the press: "Such legislation belongs to the dark ages." He asked rhetorically: Why not teach the flat earth or a stationary earth?[16] These two themes—medievalism and the flat earth—were to be invoked repeatedly in the attacks that followed.

On the same page, the *Times* reprinted a letter from Columbia University's president, Nicholas Murray Butler. Butler served as president of Columbia from 1901 to 1945. He had been the founder of the Industrial Education Association, which later established Columbia Teachers College, the most influential teachers institution in the United States. He served as Chairman of the Carnegie Endowment for International Peace from 1925 until 1945. He won the Nobel Peace Prize in 1931.[17] In short, he was a major figure in American education. He had written his letter to the president of the University of Kentucky, who had issued a national plea for assistance.

Butler's rhetoric never dealt seriously with Bryan's argument, namely, that the voters of a state can legitimately determine what their tax money is spent for. Butler's rhetoric was entirely specious. "The bill, as you describe it, seems to me to lack vigor and completeness. It should, I think, be amended before passage to include in its prohibition the use of any book in which the word evolution is defined, used or referred to in any way. It might even be desirable to include a prohibition of books that use any of the letters by which the word evolution could be spelled, since in this way some unscrupulous person might, by ingenious effort, evade the salutary provisions of the law." He then compared the bill with Soviet tyranny: "I take it for granted that the introducer of the bill is in close communion with

---

16. *New York Times* (Feb. 2, 1922), p. 12.
17. *Grolier's Encyclopedia* (1990): "Butler, Nicholas Murray."

the rulers of Soviet Russia, since he is faithfully reproducing one of their fundamental policies." This was all rhetoric and no logic.

Democracy Has Limits

The next day, the *Times* ran an editorial that did not shy away from the implications for democracy posed by the bill. The *Times* repudiated democracy. It invoked the flat-earth analogy. "Kentucky Rivals Illinois" began with an attack on Illinois' Wilbur G. Voliva, founder of the flat earth movement. Next, it switched to Kentucky. "Stern reason totters on her seat when asked to realize that in this day and country people with powers to decide educational questions should hold and enunciate opinions such as these." To banish the teaching of evolution is the equivalent of banishing the teaching of the multiplication table.[18]

Three days later, the *Times* followed with another editorial, appropriately titled, "Democracy and Evolution." It began: "It has been recently argued by a distinguished educational authority that the successes of education in the United States are due, in part at least, 'to its being kept in close and constant touch with the people themselves.' What is happening in Kentucky does not give support to this view."[19] The Progressives' rhetoric of democracy was nowhere to be found in the *Times*' articles on Bryan and creationism, for the editors suspected that Bryan had the votes. For the Progressives, democracy was a tool of social change, not an unbreakable principle of civil government; a slogan, not a moral imperative. Though often cloaked in religious terms, democracy was merely a means to an end. What was this end? Control over other people's money and, if possible, the minds of their children.

The Divinization of Man by Default

Then the writer got to the theological heart of the matter: the divinization of man by default. Two theologians had sent telegrams to the president of the University of Kentucky complaining that Bryan's views dishonor God and man. "This will pain Mr. Bryan, who seems to hold that it is dishonorable to man as well as to God that man

---

18. *New York Times* (Feb. 3, 1922), p. 14.
19. *Ibid.* (Feb. 6, 1922), p. 12.

should have been created mediately out of the dust of the earth." But Bryan's creationist point was only that it dishonors God to identify hypothetically impersonal forces of nature—the only forces Darwin and his heirs believe in prior to the advent of purposeful man—as the source of creation.

This was only the beginning. In the Sunday supplement for February 5, John M. Clarke was given an opportunity to comment on the Kentucky case. He was the Director of the State Museum at Albany. His rhetoric returned to the important theme of the weakness of democracy in the face of ignorant voters. I cite the piece at length because readers are unlikely to have a copy of this article readily at hand, and when it comes to rhetoric, summaries rarely do justice to the power of words. It began:

> Our sovereign sister Kentucky, where fourteen and one half men in every hundred can neither read nor write, is talking about adding to the mirth of the nation in these all too joyless days by initiating legislation to put a end to that "old bad devil" evolution. Luther threw an ink bottle at one of his kind; the Kentucky legislators are making ready to throw a statute which will drive this serpent of the poisoned sting once and for all beyond the confines of the State, and not a school wherein this mischiefmaker is harbored shall have 1 cent of public moneys.

He identified as the source of this bill "the distinguished Chautauqua savant, William Jennings Bryan," a sneer at both Chautauqua and Bryan. Chautauqua was the major lecture circuit for the nation. Founded by a pair of Methodists in 1874, Chautauqua soon became America's most successful early experiment in adult education prior to World War I. By 1918, 300,000 people were enrolled in 10,000 local circles, receiving an informal but structured education.[20] It had been run by the theological modernist, William Rainey Harper, from 1883 to 1897. (Beginning in 1892, he also organized the Rockefellers' University of Chicago.)[21] Chautauqua openly promoted the science of

---

20. Theodore Morrison, *Chautauqua: A Center for Education, Religion, and the Arts in America* (Chicago: University of Chicago Press, 1974), p. 65.

21. George Marsden, *The Soul of the American University: From Protestant Establishment to Established Nonbelief* (New York: Oxford University Press, 1994),

evolution.[22] So, Clarke's sneer against Chautauqua was social, not ideological.

Invoking Old Testament language, Clarke predicted that the legislators "will smite the enemy hip and thigh." Why not amend the state's constitution and make the idea of evolution illegal? Again, he returned to the theme of the threat of democracy:

> When the majority of the voters, of which fourteen and a half out of each hundred can neither read nor write, have settled this matter, if they are disposed to do the right thing they will not stop at evolution. There is a fiction going about through the schools that the earth is round and revolves around the sun, and if Frankfort [Kentucky] is to be and remain the palladium of reason and righteousness, this hideous heresay [heresy] must also be wiped out.

Here it was again: the flat earth. It has been a favorite rhetorical device used against biblical creationists for a long time. The claim that pre-Columbus medieval scholars regarded the earth as flat, it turns out, is entirely mythical—a myth fostered in modern times. Jeffrey Burton Russell, the distinguished medieval historian, has disposed of this beloved myth of the flat earth.[23] The modernists who have invoked this myth have not done their homework.

They have also not done their homework on medieval science in general, which was extremely sophisticated. This has been proven by the French historian of science and theoretical physicist, Pierre Duhem (1861–1916), whose ten volumes on the subject are exhaustive: *Le système du monde*. The first five volumes were in print in 1917; the second five volumes appeared in 1954–59. In between, the French academic community and publishing world suppressed their publication because they undermined one of the most cherished myths of the Enlightenment, namely, that medieval science was "medieval." The story

---

p. 241.

22. Samuel Christian Schmucker, *The Meaning of Evolution* (Chautauqua, New York: Chautauqua Press, 1913).

23. Jeffrey Burton Russell, *Inventing the Flat Earth: Columbus and Modern Historians* (New York: Praeger, 1991).

of this exercise in humanist academic censorship has been written by his biographer, physicist and historian Stanley Jaki.[24] Even today, the only favorable references to Duhem that I have ever seen, other than in Jaki's writings, are two brief sentences in Robert Nisbet's *History of the Idea of Progress* (1980).[25]

The theological issue for Clarke was, ultimately, the divinization of man by default, and the divinization of nature: capital N. "It may be that the conception of the continuity and unity of life from its starting point on earth up to the climax it has reached in man does magnify the place of humanity in the scheme of Nature. The doctrine of evolution predicates this, teaches that out of the struggles of the ages man has stepped forth as the supreme result, not a finished product, far from that, but with always the glory of a growing hope for something better beyond. It would seem as though no more inspiring thought could be imparted to youth. . . ." Here was a vision of autonomous man's progress, and Bryan was calling this into question. Bryan believed in progress, and democratic progress above all; he just did not believe in man's autonomy.

The Rural Masses

Then it was back to the rhetoric of contempt for the masses, and the elevation of the scientific elite. "It would seem reasonable to assume that the demonstration of the fundamental doctrine of all Nature, inorganic as well as organic, might well be left to those who have brought to bear upon it the highest intellectual refinements. But it is a pleasing thought to fancy the erudite Nebraskan in academic cap and—gown, of course; we almost said bells, inspiring the Democratic majority of Kentucky to vote that Evolution isn't so! and to penalize any one who dares say it is! It is by such means as this that civilization advances and America assures her own high place among

---

24. Stanley L. Jaki, "Science and Censorship: Hélène Duhem and the Publication of the 'Système du monde,'" *Intercollegiate Review* (Winter 1985-86), pp. 41-49. Cf. Jaki, *Uneasy Genius: The Life and Work of Pierre Duhem* (Boston: Martinus Nijhoff, 1984).

25. Alexander Koyré refers to him—last name only—as an anti-Newtonian, but without naming his books. Koyré, *From the Closed World to the Infinite Universe* (Baltimore, Maryland: Johns Hopkins University Press, [1957] 1970), p. 100.

the cultured nations of the world."[26] The allusion to cap and bells—the clown's costume in the medieval world—was not all that clever, but it surely revealed Clarke's contempt for Bryan, his democratic politics, and his Christianity.

On February 9, another *Times* editorial cited the Louisville *Courier-Journal* as having identified Bryan as the initiator behind the bill. Bryan had raised up "ignorant fanatics" who had "intimidated" legislators. The *Times* warned: "Kentucky is not the only State in the Union, by any means, for whose village theologians the name of Darwin is still one with which to scare children. . . ." A nice rhetorical flourish: "village theologians." Here was a theme that carried through subsequent *Times* editorials to the media's coverage of the Scopes trial three years later to the screenplay of *Inherit the Wind*: rural Americans as ignorant fanatics, and the readers of urban newspapers as intelligent people. The *Times* identified the *Courier-Journal* as the spokesman for "intelligent Kentuckians."[27]

Challenging the Flow of Funds

In his *New York Times* essay, Bryan thanked the editor for having invited him to contribute. He need not have bothered. If ever there was a set-up, it was this.

After surveying at some length why he did not believe that Darwin's hypothesis was scientifically correct (Darwin's theory of sexual selection, already a scientific embarrassment in Bryan's day, was one reason),[28] he got to the heart of the matter from his point of view: democratic politics. "The Bible has in many places been excluded from the schools on the ground that religion should not be taught by those paid by public taxation. If this doctrine is sound, what right have the enemies of religion to teach irreligion in the public schools? If the Bible cannot be taught, why should Christian taxpayers permit the teaching of guesses that make the Bible a lie?" This surely was a

---

26. Clarke, "Evolution and Kentucky," *New York Times* (Feb. 5, 1992), VII, p. 12.
27. *Ibid.* (Feb. 9, 1922), p. 16.
28. The theory which comprised Part II of *Descent of Man*, which in turn constituted over half of the book.

legitimate question, one which has yet to be answered in terms of a theory of strict academic neutrality. But Paxton Hibben, in his 1929 biography of Bryan (Introduction by Charles A. Beard), dismissed this argument as "a specious sort of logic. . . . [Government-funded] schools, he reasoned, were the indirect creations of the mass of citizens. If this were true, those same citizens could control what was taught in them."[29] *If this were true*: the subjunctive mood announced Paxton's rejection of Bryan's premise—spoken on behalf humanist educators, from Horace Mann in Massachusetts to this week's multi-million dollar battle over selecting state-approved high school textbooks. When it comes to a threat to their self-accredited monopoly over public education, humanists can spot a "specious" argument at 300 yards. They reply, in rigorous logical fashion, "Citizens are morally and legally obligated to pay us to teach their children whatever we want to teach them, especially if they should disagree with what we teach."

Christians fund denominational colleges, Bryan pointed out. They pay to have their view of religion taught. He then raised a suggestion that, more than any other, was as welcome to the modernists, both political and theological, as a looking into a mirror was to Bela Lugosi's Dracula: "If atheists want to teach atheism, why do they not built [build] their own schools and employ their own teachers?" This was the heart of the matter, and remains so. He repeated this argument in his Preface to *The Menace of Darwinism* (p. 6). The thought of self-funding has always been abhorrent to liberals. Accepting rich men's money, yes; access to tithers' money and taxpayers' money, yes; but liberals avoid self-funding at all costs because it costs so much.[30]

A year later, in a speech to West Virginia lawmakers, Bryan argued that scientists had no rightful claim on the taxpayers' money. It is not an infringement on freedom of speech for a state legislature to

---

29. Paxton Hibben, *The Peerless Leader: William Jennings Bryan* (New York: Farrar and Rinehart, 1929), p. 371.

30. It leads to such debacles as Seminex, the Seminary in Exile, the short-lived port in the storm for liberals after they were fired by Concordia Seminary in the mid-1970's.

refuse to fund ideas that taxpayers oppose. He then uttered the words, more than any other words, that describe why education has been a political battle zone for two centuries around the world: "The hand that writes the pay check rules the school."[31] It was this doctrine, more than any other, which professional educators had to destroy through court action, since they found it embarrassing to oppose it publicly, given liberalism's official commitment to democracy. Clarence Darrow's defense strategy at the Scopes trial in 1925 was to get the jury to declare Scopes guilty, so that the defense lawyers could appeal the decision to a higher court and get it reversed. This same strategy undergirded the secularization of American public education after 1960—which at last overturned the state laws that made possible the Scopes decision.

Other People's Money

The supreme judicial issue was this: control over other people's money. Bryan's attack was a direct shot at the heart of the modernist worldview and program, both political and theological modernism. The central assertion of modernism, from Lester Frank Ward's *Dynamic Sociology* (1883) to the present, is this: the moral authority and legal right an educated elite that understands the processes of Darwinian evolution to commandeer the instruments of political coercion, as well as public funds gained through the threat of State coercion, in order to guide scientifically the evolution of the social order. This was American Progressivism's main agreed-upon doctrine. It was also the non-negotiable demand of theological liberals, who applied modernism's doctrine of the commandeering of State assets to Church assets, irrespective of the theological confessions of laymen whose money funded the Church. The divisions that arose within modernism were many, but they all had to do with the political battle over the distribution of the loot.

If Bryan was successful in this political project, modernism could lose the war. Modernists understood, just as Unitarian Horace Mann had understood in the 1830's, that the public school system is Amer-

---

31. Cited in Levine, *Defender of the Faith*, p. 278.

ica's only established Church.[32] "Perhaps the most striking power that the churches surrendered under religious freedom was control over public education," writes Church historian Sidney Mead.[33] Bryan was threatening to reclaim this power and reclaim America's future by means of the method that Ward had said is the best way to control other people's thinking: by excluding certain ideas from discussion in the public schools.[34] Ward called this the *method of exclusion* (his italics). "This, however, is the essence of what is here meant by education, which may be regarded as a systematic process for the manufacture of correct opinions."[35] Bryan assumed that in what he called a fair fight, the Christians would win. By excluding both creationism and Darwinism from the public schools, he believed that the Christians would win the debate. This was naive on his part, for the assumption of educational neutrality with respect to the Bible is inherently antitheistic, but the modernists were determined not to permit Bryan's test.

The debate over Darwinism in the public schools was an aspect of the politics of plunder. The politics of plunder came early in America, and it came at the very heart of the Puritan society: the State's establishment of Church and school. Here was where the *flow of ideas* would be controlled through control over the *flow of funds*. The New England Puritans had imposed this control system by 1647. Ward had merely extended the Puritans' strategy in the name of Darwinism. New England in 1635 made local church attendance compulsory, and in 1638 legislated compulsory financial support of these churches.[36] In 1642, the General Court of New Haven established a local school; Hartford followed this example and allocated funds for its school.[37] In

---

32. Sidney E. Mead, *The Lively Experiment: The Shaping of Christianity in America* (New York: Harper & Row, 1963), p. 68.

33. *Ibid.*, p. 66.

34. Lester Frank Ward, *Dynamic Sociology; or Applied Social Science*, 2 vols. (New York: Appleton, [1883] 1907), II:547-48. See Chapter 10, below: section on "Machen's Plea for Pluralism," pp. 625-28.

35. *Ibid.*, II:548.

36. Lawrence A. Cremin, *American Education: The Colonial Experience, 1607-1783* (New York: Harper & Row, 1970), p. 152.

37. *Ibid.*, pp. 180-81.

1647, the General Court of Massachusetts passed a law mandating that every town of 50 or more inhabitants establish a school, and that tax money be used to pay for these schools if parents refused.[38] Connecticut imitated this statute in 1650.[39] Residents, in short, were threatened with civil violence if they refused to support Church and school with their money and their persons, whether or not they believed in what was being taught. They had to attend Church, and their children had to attend school, or the State would impose negative sanctions. While the compulsory local church attendance laws were not systematically enforced in New England after 1650,[40] the other elements of coercion remained. With the coming of disestablishment laws from 1776 through the 1820's, the churches were cut out of the distribution of the loot, but increases in both the level of funding and the level of coercion associated with the public schools in the nineteenth century more than offset this minimal ecclesiastical deliverance from civil bondage.

America's schools followed the theological path which the churches of New England travelled. The schools began as Calvinist strongholds; the *New England Primer* is representative. The First Great Awakening and the American Revolution moved them from Puritanism into pietistic nationalism; the Second Great Awakening reinforced this. In Massachusetts in the 1830's, Horace Mann moved them into Unitarianism. In Bryan's day, the war was fought between an implicit common-ground Unitarian theism, disguised as Protestant culture, and Darwinian modernism. Bryan, in the name of the Bible, was trying to retain the traditional classroom theism of Unitarianism; his opponents were trying to move the schools into secularism. The doctrine of evolution was the touchstone on both sides of the battle.

To seek to replace what is taught in taxpayer-supported schools is to seek to replace the existing Establishment. An Establishment understands this threat. It fully understood in 1922. The American Establishment in the 1920's was modernist: theological, political, or both. It

---

38. *Ibid.*, pp. 181–82.
39. *Ibid.*, p. 182.
40. Carl Bridenbaugh, *Cities in the Wilderness: The First Century of Urban Life in America, 1625–1725* (New York: Capricorn, [1938] 1964), p. 106.

was evolutionist in its view of the origin of man. Bryan had to be stopped. In 1925, he was stopped. But the trap was set in early 1922.

Professional Educators Protest

The barrage of ink began again. On March 2, this headline announced a story on the annual convention of the National Education Association, the teachers' union: "Paint W. J. Bryan as a 'Medievalist.'" He had adopted, the convention was told, "methods of the Dark Ages. . . ." Columbia University economist E. R. A. Seligman again invoked the flat earth analogy: "Now, if we are going back to childhood, let's go all the way. Let's teach that the earth is flat and that the sun moves around it." He then recommended the creation of an exhibit that features the dinosaur and other extinct animals as proofs of evolution. (A decade later, Seligman served as Editor-in-Chief of the influential *Encyclopedia of the Social Sciences*.)

Dr. Frank Spaulding, dean of Yale's graduate school of education, brought up the crucial issue of sanctions. To resort to politics in order to keep the doctrine of evolution from spreading reveals a "wavering faith." (Rhetorical question: Is this also true of today's Darwinians, who have used the Supreme Court to remove every trace of creationism from public school curricula? Real question: Or is it a matter of sanctions, without which no worldview can become operational?) Then he invoked Briggs' ancient argument: the true Christians are the liberals. True Christianity is open to the teaching of evolution in the public schools. Bryan's methods are wrong. "Such methods lead away from the true spirit of the Bible."[41]

So much for the "creation in the public schools" debate, a familiar one in our own day. There was to be no debate. The issues have not changed: control over tax money by the educational establishment, the public's suspicion of the good judgment of that establishment, the theoretical possibility of neutral education, the presuppositions of science, and Christian dreams of reforming tax-supported education. In short, so much for one more familiar battlefield of the politics of plunder.

---

41. *New York Times* (March 28, 1922), p. 12.

It is now time to dig up one of the best-suppressed stories in American history. This, you will not find in the textbooks. It will not take much brainpower to figure out why.

Eugenics and the American Establishment (Pre-Hitler)

Henry Fairfield Osborn's response to Bryan was prominently featured on page 2 of the March 5 Sunday supplement. It is important to understand who he was and what (and who) he represented. He was one of America's earliest trained evolutionists, having studied under Thomas Huxley ("Darwin's bulldog").[42] In 1922, he was president of the Museum of Natural History in New York. He was professor of zoology at Columbia University. More important, he was a leading eugenicist, dedicated to the proposition that the scientific breeding of men is both possible and desirable. He had been a co-founder of the pro-eugenics Galton Society in 1918.[43] Galton, the originator of eugenics, was Darwin's cousin. He had been knighted in 1908 and in 1909 had been awarded the Copley Medal, the highest honor of Britain's prestigious Royal Society.[44]

Eugenics and Nordic Supremacy

Another co-founder was his lawyer friend, Madison Grant,[45] author of the then-famous (and now infamous) book, *The Passing of the Great Race*, published by Scribner's in 1916,[46] which by 1921 was in its fourth edition. It was a defense of the Nordic master race theory. Osborn wrote the prefaces to the first and second printings, which were retained in subsequent editions. This was reciprocated by Grant, who identified Osborn as one of the two men whose works he

---

42. Julian Huxley, *Memories* (New York: Harper & Row, 1970), p. 82.
43. Its full title was The Galton Society for the Study of the Origin and Evolution of Man.
44. Daniel V. Kevles, *In the Name of Eugenics: Genetics and the Uses of Human Heredity* (New York: Knopf, 1985), p. 57.
45. Donald K. Pickens, *Eugenics and the Progressives* (Nashville, Tennessee: Vanderbilt University Press, 1968), p. 53.
46. On the impact of this book, see Allan Chase, *The Legacy of Malthus: The Social Costs of the New Scientific Racism* (New York: Knopf, 1977), pp. 166–71.

relied upon most heavily. The other was economist William Z. Ripley, who wrote *The Races of Europe* (1899).[47]

Osborn's 1916 Preface made plain his views: in European history, "race has played a far larger part than either language or nationality in moulding the destinies of men; race implies heredity and heredity implies all the moral, social, and intellectual characteristics and traits that are the springs of politics and government."[48] Grant's book is a "racial history of Europe," which, Osborn insisted, "There is no gainsaying that this is the correct scientific method of approaching the problem of the past."[49] He called this methodology "modern eugenics."[50] The book is about the "conservation of that race which has given us the true spirit of Americanism. . . ."[51] In the second printing (1917), he made himself perfectly clear: ". . . the Anglo-Saxon branch of the Nordic race is again showing itself to be that upon which the nation must chiefly depend for leadership, for courage, for loyalty, for unity and harmony of action, for self-sacrifice and devotion to an ideal. Not that members of other races are not doing their part, many of them are, but in no other human stock which has come to this country is there displayed the unanimity of heart, mind and action which is now being displayed by the descendants of the blue-eyed, fair-haired peoples of the north of Europe."[52] With the passing of the great race, the whole world faces a crisis: ". . . these strains of the real human aristocracy once lost are lost forever."[53]

In Chapter 4, "The Competition of Races," Grant warned against the reduced birth rate of successful, wealthy races. It leads to "race suicide" when the encouragement of "indiscriminate reproduction" is heeded by the "undesirable elements."[54] Altruism, philanthropy, and sentimentalism are a threat because they "intervene with the noblest

---

47. Madison Grant, "Introduction," *The Passing of the Great Race*, 4th ed., revised (New York: Charles Scribner's Sons, 1921), p. xxv.
48. *Ibid.*, p. vii.
49. *Ibid.*, p. viii.
50. *Ibid.*
51. *Ibid.*, p. xix.
52. *Ibid.*, p. xi.
53. *Ibid.*, p. xiii.
54. *Ibid.*, p. 47.

purpose and forbid nature to penalize the unfortunate victims of reckless breeding," which leads to "the multiplication of inferior types."[55] He then made his point clear: "Mistaken regard for what are believed to be divine laws and a sentimental belief in the sanctity of human life tend to prevent both the elimination of defective infants and the sterilization of such adults as are themselves of no value to the community. The laws of nature require the obliteration of the unfit and human life is valuable only when it is of use to the community or race."[56]

There is now scientific hope in this regard: "A rigid system of selection through the elimination of those who are weak or unfit—in other words, social failures—would solve the whole question in a century, as well as enable us to get rid of the undesirables who crowd our jails, hospitals and insane asylums. The individual himself can be nourished, educated and protected by the community during his lifetime, but the state through sterilization must see to it that his line stops with him or else future generations will be cursed with an ever increasing load of victims of misguided sentimentalism."[57]

This book became a best-seller in the United States when Adolph Hitler was a corporal in the German Army. Chronology here is important.

Grant, in turn, wrote the Introduction for fellow eugenicist Lothrop Stoddard's book, *The Rising Tide of Color Against White World Supremacy*, published by Scribner's in 1921, the year that Scribner's published the fourth edition of Grant's book, one year before the company published Stoddard's *The Revolt Against Civilization: The Menace of the Underman*. (Scribner's was systematically cashing in on a rising tide of color: green.) In his Introduction, Grant informed his readers, "The backbone of western civilization is racially Nordic. . . . If this great race, with its capacity for leadership and fighting, should ultimately pass, with it would pass that which we call civilization. It would be succeeded by an unstable and bastardized population where worth and merit would have no inherent right to leadership and among which a new and darker age would blot out our racial inheri-

---

55. *Ibid.*, p. 48.
56. *Ibid.*, p. 49.
57. *Ibid.*, pp. 50–51.

tance" (pp. xxix–xxx). Wherever they looked, backward or forward, eugenicists saw a dark age. Christianity gave us the old one; Asians, Jews, southern and eastern Europeans, and Negroes threaten to give us a new one. The Nordic race is just barely hanging on for dear life: ". . . competition of the Nordic with the alien is fatal, whether the latter be the lowly immigrant from southern or eastern Europe or whether he be the more obviously dangerous Oriental against whose standards of living the white man cannot compete" (pp. xxx–xxxi). German translations of Grant and Stoddard were read widely years before the Nazis came to power in 1933.[58]

Eugenics was a widely received faith among American Progressives after 1900. Walter Truett Anderson has described the origins of eugenics in the United States from the early years of the century. "America's gates swung open for eugenics. Lavish support came forth from the wealthy families and the great foundations. [Charles] Davenport established a research center—the Station for the Experimental Study of Evolution—with a grant from the Carnegie Institution of Washington, and later added a Eugenics Record Office with grants from the Harriman and Rockefeller families."[59] Davenport's Station was set up in 1904.[60] The Eugenics Record Office was established in 1910 with money from Mary Harriman, Averell's sister. Over the next decade, she put at least $500,000 into the project.[61] John D. Rockefeller, Jr. donated money to it.[62] He also gave money to start the American Eugenics Society,[63] which was co-founded by Osborn.[64]

---

58. Karl Holler, "The Nordic Movement in Germany," *Eugenical News* (Sept.–Oct. 1932); cited in Chase, *Legacy of Malthus*, p. 635. The translated edition was published in 1925, as was Lothrop Stoddard's *Revolt Against Civilization*. Robert Proctor, *Racial Hygiene: Medicine under the Nazis* (Cambridge, Massachusetts: Harvard University Press, 1988), p. 99.

59. Walter Truett Anderson, *To Govern Evolution: Further Adventures of the Political Animal* (New York: Harcourt Brace Jovanovich, 1987), p. 153.

60. Kevles, *Eugenics*, p. 45.

61. *Ibid.*, pp. 54–55.

62. *Ibid.*, p. 55.

63. *Ibid.*, p. 60; cf. John Ensor Harr and Peter J. Johnson, *The Rockefeller Century* (New York: Charles Scribner's Sons, 1988), p. 454.

64. Harr and Johnson, *Rockefeller Century*, p. 456..

It was organized in 1923. It published *A Eugenics Catechism* in 1926, which included this insight: "Q. Does eugenics contradict the Bible? A. The Bible has much to say about eugenics. It tells us that men do not gather grapes from thorns and figs from thistles. . . ."[65]

Eugenics and Forced Sterilization

The eugenics idea had political consequences. In 1907, Indiana passed the first compulsory sterilization law in America.[66] States passed laws against marriages between people who were "eugenically unfit." By the late 1920's, 28 states had passed compulsory sterilization laws; some 15,000 Americans had been sterilized before 1930. This figure rose by another 15,000 over the next decade.[67] (In 22 states, Federally restricted versions of these laws still existed in the mid-1980's.)[68] This was also the era of laws against interracial marriage; 30 states passed such laws between 1915 and 1930.[69] (These laws no longer exist.)

The U.S. Supreme Court, in *Buck v. Bell* (1927), upheld Virginia's model sterilization law, which was carried out on 19-year-old Carrie Buck. By a vote of 8 to 1, the Court upheld this before the girl was sterilized; her guardian had opposed the action. The Court included Progressives William Howard Taft and Louis Brandeis, who voted to uphold. The lone dissenter was Pierce Butler, a conservative, who wrote no opinion.[70] The Court's opinion, written by justice Oliver Wendell Holmes, announced: "We have seen more than once that the public welfare may call upon the best citizens for their lives. It would be strange if it could not call upon those who already sap the strength of the state for these lesser sacrifices. . . . Three generations of imbeciles are enough."[71] Holmes was the justice most closely associated with the ideal of evolutionary law, whose book, *The Common Law*

---

65. Kevles, *Eugenics*, p. 61.
66. In England that year was formed the national Eugenics Education Society. *Ibid.*, p. 59.
67. Proctor, *Racial Hygiene*, p. 97.
68. Kevles, *Eugenics*, p. 111.
69. Anderson, *To Govern Evolution*, p. 155.
70. Kevles, *Eugenics*, p. 111.
71. *Ibid.*

(1881), had articulated this ideal. Here was political modernism in action: the State as biological predestinator.[72]

There was no vocal opposition. Writes Kevles: "*Buck v. Bell* generally stimulated either favorable, cautious, or—most commonly—no comment. Few if any newspapers took notice of the impact of the decision on civil liberties in the United States."[73] Carrie's daughter Vivian, who died young of an intestinal disorder, went through second grade. Her teachers regarded her as very bright.[74]

Virginia also sterilized Carrie's sister Doris in 1928. She found out about this 52 years later. The physicians had told her that the operation was to remove her appendix. When she found out, she broke down and cried. "My husband and me wanted children desperately. We were crazy about them. I never knew what they'd done to me."[75] Obviously, the woman was a hopeless imbecile; she should have said, "My husband and I," and she used an indefinite pronoun reference: "they." No children for her! The U.S. Supreme Court, the state of Virginia, and Progressive Darwinian science agreed: "The Bucks stop here."

The United States became the model for pre-Nazi German racial hygienists after World War I.[76] The Nazis merely applied on a massive scale a program that their liberal predecessors had recommended. A decade before Hitler came to power, G. K. Chesterton predicted what was coming in Germany. He explained why in his book, *Eugenics and Other Evils* (1922). He called eugenics "terrorism by tenth-rate professors."[77] The influence of the eugenics movement in Germany accelerated after Hitler came to power in 1933. Sterilization had been illegal

---

72. No more eloquent or flagrant example of this new American Progressive religion can be found than the book written by Alex Carrel, a 1912 Nobel Prize winner in "medicine or physiology" and an employee of the Rockefeller Institute, *Man the Unknown*, co-published by Harper & Brothers in 1935.

73. Kevles, *Eugenics*, p. 112.

74. *Ibid.*

75. Stephen Jay Gould, *The Mismeasure of Man* (New York: Norton, 1981), p. 336.

76. Proctor, *Racial Hygiene*, p. 98.

77. Cited in George Grant, *Grand Illusions: The Legacy of Planned Parenthood*, 2nd ed. (Franklin, Tennessee: Adroit, 1992), p. 94.

in Germany prior to Hitler; he changed the law in July, 1933.[78] Two million people were ordered sterilized by the Nazi's Eugenics Courts as eugenically unfit, 1933 to 1945.[79]

In 1939, the year of the "Duty to be Healthy," the Nazi program of sterilization went to the next phase: "mercy killings" of mentally and physically handicapped people who were incarcerated in hospitals and mental asylums. One estimate is that some 200,000 people were killed in this way during World War II. Physicians superintended the massacre.[80] Proctor writes: "For several years [prior to 1939], German health officials had campaigned to stigmatize the mentally and physically handicapped as people with 'lives unworthy of living.' Films like 'Erbrank' ('The Genetically Diseased') portrayed well-groomed, white-coated psychiatrists patronizing ill-kempt patients cast as human refuse. . . . Propaganda efforts of this sort were important, for though the operation was both secret and illegal (a euthanasia law was drafted but never approved), there was an obvious need to deflect potential opposition—especially from the churches."[81] The Nazis understood in 1939 what the humanist media in the United States had understood in 1922: churches could have become a major threat to their genetic ideal and program of forced sterilization for genetic purposes. As it turned out in both countries, however, churches remained mute on the issue.

In 1921, Osborn had used the Museum to host the Second International Congress of Eugenics.[82] At that Congress, he had announced: "The right of the state to safeguard the character and integrity of the race or races on which its future depends is, to my mind, as incontestable as the right of the state to safeguard the health and morals of its people. As science has enlightened government in the prevention and spread of disease, it must also enlighten government in the pre-

---

78. Proctor, *Racial Hygiene*, p. 101.
79. Chase, *Legacy of Malthus*, p. 135.
80. Michael Burleigh, *Death and Deliverance: "Euthanasia" In Germany, c. 1900–1945* (New York: Cambridge University Press, 1995). This book is too recent to have received academic reviews regarding its evidence.
81. Robert N. Proctor, "Review of Burleigh's *Death and Deliverance*," *New York Times Book Review* (Feb. 5, 1995), p. 3.
82. Chase, *Legacy of Malthus*, p. 277.

vention of the spread and multiplication of worthless members of society, the spread of feeble-mindedness, of idiocy, and of all moral and intellectual as well as physical diseases."[83] Sanctions must be applied.

Osborn in 1922 was safely inside Rockefeller's charmed circle. He became one of John D. Rockefeller, Jr.'s advisors on conservation issues after he and Madison Grant created the Save-the-Redwoods League in 1919, which Rockefeller supported.[84] When Junior would bring his boys to visit the Museum of Natural History, Osborn would sometimes personally conduct their tour.[85] The Osborn family's connection to the Rockefellers went back to the days of John D., Sr.[86] Junior put Frederick Osborn, Henry's nephew, on the board of the Rockefeller Institute in 1938. It was through Frederick that the Rockefellers were drawn away from eugenics and into the population control movement.[87] (Liberalism's faith in population control has replaced its earlier faith, equally confident, in the now-politically incorrect eugenics movement as a means of reducing the number of those who, in Grant's words, "are themselves of no value to the community." Between 1965 and 1976, the Rockefeller and Ford foundations poured $250 million into population control projects.)[88]

"Good Cop, Bad Cop"

The *Times*' editors adopted a version of the "good cop, bad cop" prisoner interrogation technique: a seemingly mild-mannered sterilizer began the public disemboweling of Bryan, and a hard-nosed sterilizer completed the operation.

Osborn's rebuttal to Bryan was rhetorically dispassionate. This made it unique among the *Times*' anti-Bryan articles. Instead of citing evolutionary dogma for Bryan, Osborn emphasized dead religious thinkers who supposedly had accepted evolution. One surely had: the

---

83. Cited in *ibid.*, p. 278.
84. Harr and Johnson, *Rockefeller Century*, pp. 212–13.
85. *Ibid.*, p. 212.
86. *Ibid.*, p. 457.
87. *Ibid.*
88. Julian Simon, *The Ultimate Resource* (Princeton, New Jersey: Princeton University Press, 1981), p. 293.

nineteenth-century eccentric (and chaplain to Queen Victoria) Charles Kingsley. He is more famous as the author of *Water Babies* than for his theology. Kingsley had written a letter to F. D. Maurice proclaiming his commitment to evolution. The orthodoxy of his theology can be judged by another letter that he wrote to Maurice in 1863 to describe his new discovery that "souls secrete their bodies, as snails do shells. . . ."[89] Kingsley's social theories were racist to the core. After visiting Ireland during a famine, he wrote: "I am daunted by the human chimpanzees I saw along that hundred miles of horrible country. I don't believe they are our fault. I believe that there are not many more of them than of old, but that they are happier, better and more comfortably fed and lodged under our rule than they ever were. But to see white chimpanzees is dreadful; if they were black, one would not feel it so much, but their skins, except where tanned by exposure, are as white as ours."[90]

Osborn also cited Augustine at some length on how nature should teach us truth. He was unaware of, or deliberately ignored, the fact that Augustine wrote in the *City of God*: "For as it is not yet six thousand years since the first man, who is called Adam, are not those to be ridiculed rather than refuted who try to persuade us of anything regarding a space of time so different from, and contrary to, the ascertained truth?"[91] Then he told Bryan that evolution is one kind of truth, religion another kind. If Bryan had entertained any doubts about his critics' opposition to the Bible's account of creation, Osborn's article would have cured him. But one citation was calculated to do real harm: Osborn's reference to the influence in his life of Princeton University's James McCosh, who had indeed been an evolutionist. Invoking the beloved McCosh was a good tactic in dealing with a conservative Presbyterian. Bryan, however, regarded theistic

---

89. Cited in William Irvine, *Apes, Angels, and Victorians: The Story of Darwin, Huxley, and Evolution* (New York: McGraw-Hill, 1955), p. 142.

90. Cited in Thomas Cahill, *How the Irish Saved Civilization: The Untold Story of Ireland's Heroic Role from the Fall of the Roman Empire to the Rise of Medieval Europe* (New York: Talese-Doubleday, 1995), p. 6.

91. Augustine, *City of God* (New York: Modern Library, 1950), XVIII:40, p. 648.

evolution as "an anesthetic which deadens the pain while the patient's religion is being gradually removed . . . a way-station on the highway that leads from Christian faith to No-God-Land."[92]

On the whole, Osborn's essay was mild-mannered and polite. That was bait. Then came a hook. His article ran over to page 14, where it occupied a few inches in the middle of the page. Filling page 14 was a large headline and a long article by Princeton University's E. G. Conklin. The headline was prophetic of liberal rhetoric yet to come: "Bryan and Evolution. Why His Statements Are Erroneous and Misleading—Theology Amusing If Not Pathetic."

Dr. Conklin was one of the prominent biologists of the day.[93] He was quite familiar with Grant's *Passing of the Great Race*, having footnoted it in 1921 as his only source in a chapter on "Modern Races and Man."[94] It did not seem to bother him that Grant was a lawyer with no formal training in biology, genetics, anthropology, or any other natural science. Conklin followed this with references to Stoddard's *Rising Tide of Color* in his chapter, "Hybridization of Races."[95] He also cited Osborn's *Contemporary Evolution of Man*.[96]

Conklin was a defender of what he called the religion of evolution.[97] As he said, "the greatest and most practical work of religion is to further the evolution of a better race."[98] "To a large extent mankind holds the power of controlling its destiny on this planet."[99] (C.S. Lewis warned in *Abolition of Man* that when we say that man must control man's destiny, this means that some men must do the controlling, while others must be controlled.) He concluded his book with a section insisting that "the religion of evolution is nothing new, but is the old religion of Confucius and Plato and Moses and especially Christ which strives to develop a better and nobler human race and to

---

92. Bryan, "Preface," *Menace of Darwinism*, p. 5.
93. Kevles, *Eugenics*, p. 88.
94. Edwin Grant Conklin, *The Direction of Evolution* (London: Oxford University Press, 1921), p. 35n.
95. *Ibid.*, pp. 38n, 39n.
96. *Ibid.*, p. 54n.
97. *Ibid.*, ch. 10.
98. *Ibid.*, p. 241.
99. *Ibid.*, p. 245.

establish the kingdom of God on earth."[100] It was an inspirational thought, how Moses and Jesus always seemed to be on the side of modernism, inside or outside the Church, despite modernism's denial of the literal truth of the Bible's account of Moses and Jesus—or perhaps because of this discrepancy.

As part of this kingdom-building effort, Conklin believed that the State should either segregate or sterilize citizens suffering from inherited defects, who presumably carry unfavorable genes.[101] Society needs intelligent guidance, he said. He then adopted the passive voice, which evaded the famous question posed by Lenin: "Who, whom?" "In time, under intelligent guidance, the worst qualities of the race might be weeded out and the best qualities preserved. This is the goal toward which intelligent effort should be directed. This should be the supreme duty of society and of all who love their fellow man."[102] He ended this book with a quotation from the founder of the idea of eugenics, Galton.

In his *Times* article, Bryan had referred to the hypothesis of evolution as a guess. Conklin responded that it was a guess in the way that the law of gravitation is a guess. Then, in a tone more suitable for pre-Heisenberg science, let alone pre-Kuhn,[103] he announced that this guess "is supported by all the evidence available, which continually receives additional support from new discoveries and which is not contradicted by any scientific evidence. . . . In the face of all these facts, Mr. Bryan and his kind hurl their medieval theology. It would be amusing if it were not so pathetic." (The next time that all the evidence supports any proposed scientific hypothesis will be the first.) "Bryan and his kind" were surely not Conklin and his kind: theologians of State-enforced sterilization. "Bryan and his kind" were pathetic.

---

100. *Ibid.*, p. 246.
101. Conklin, *Heredity and Environment in the Development of Men*, 6th ed. (Princeton, New Jersey: Princeton University Press, 1930), p. 309. The first edition was published in 1917.
102. *Ibid.*, p. 348.
103. Thomas Kuhn, *The Structure of Scientific Revolutions* (Chicago: University of Chicago Press, 1962).

Osborn and Conklin were representative of scientific opinion in their day. Osborn in 1928 wrote a Foreword to *Creation by Evolution: A Consensus*, an anthology published by Macmillan.[104] Conklin in that volume waxed eloquent about the superiority of the facts of evolutionary development over "prescientific" concepts of acts of creation—"vastly more wonderful," in fact.[105] He attacked fundamentalists. This appeared in his concluding remarks in a chapter on embryology, which is evidence that theology was never far from his mind.

These men were dedicated eugenicists. When, after World War II, it became clear just how seriously the Nazis had taken these ideas, eugenics fell completely out of favor with the public. This decline had begun in the mid-1930's, for obvious political reasons.[106] In 1940, the Carnegie Institution shut down the Eugenics Record Office.[107] The surviving founders of the supposed academic discipline of eugenics just stopped talking about it. They were not penalized retroactively in any way for having advocated the monstrous policy of forced sterilization. There were no negative sanctions applied. Osborn became the founder of the Conservation Foundation in 1947, which Rockefeller's son Laurance helped launch.[108] He died in 1969, no longer quoted as an authority, but with his reputation intact. Yet in 1922, he and Conklin were used by the *Times* to launch the scientific and rhetorical assault against American fundamentalism. To this day, their representative victim, Bryan, is regarded as a scientific ignoramus. But Bryan's view of creation never led to the forced sterilization of anyone.

Bryan vs. Eugenics

Bryan recognized that a ruthless hostility to charity was the dark side of Darwinism. Had Darwin's theory been irrelevant, he said, it

---

104. *Creation by Evolution*, Edited by Frances Mason.
105. *Ibid.*, p. 79.
106. Daniel J. Kevles, "Genetic Progress and Religious Authority: Historical Reflections," in *Responsible Science: The Impact of Technology On Society*, edited by Kevin B. Byrne (New York: Harper & Row, 1986), p. 43. Cf. Kevles, *Eugenics*, ch. 11.
107. Kevles, *Eugenics*, p. 199.
108. Peter Collier and David Horowitz, *The Rockefellers: An American Dynasty* (New York: Holt, Rinehart and Winston, 1976), p. 401.

would have been harmless. "This hypothesis, however, does incalculable harm. It teaches that Christianity impairs the race physically. That was the first implication at which I revolted. It led me to review the doctrine and reject it entirely."[109] He cited the notorious (and morally inescapable) passage in Darwin's *Descent of Man*: "With savages, the weak in body or mind are soon eliminated; and those that survive commonly exhibit a vigorous state of health. We civilized men, on the other hand, do our utmost to check the process of elimination; we build asylums for the imbecile, the maimed, and the sick; we institute poor-laws; and our medical men exert their utmost skill to save the life of every one to the last moment. There is reason to believe that vaccination has preserved thousands, who from a weak constitution would formerly have succumbed to small-pox. Thus the weak members of civilised societies propagate their kind. No one who has attended to the breeding of domestic animals will doubt that this must be highly injurious to the race of man."[110] He could have continued to quote from the passage until the end of the paragraph: "It is surprising how soon a want of care, or care wrongly directed, leads to the degeneration of a domestic race; but excepting in the case of man himself, hardly any one is so ignorant as to allow his worst animals to breed."[111] It is significant that Darwin at this point footnoted Francis Galton's famous 1865 *Macmillan's* magazine article and his book, *Hereditary Genius*.

Darwin in the next paragraph wrote that sympathy, "the noblest part of our nature," leads men to do these racially debilitating things.[112] Bryan replied: "Can that doctrine be accepted as scientific when its author admits that we cannot apply it 'without deterioration in the noblest part of our nature'? On the contrary, civilization is measured by the moral revolt against the cruel doctrine developed by Darwin."[113]

---

109. Bryan, *In His Image*, p. 107.

110. *Ibid.*, pp. 107–108.

111. Charles Darwin, *The Descent of Man* (New York: Modern Library, [1871], p. 501.

112. *Ibid.*, p. 502.

113. Bryan, *In His Image*, p. 109.

Darwin was taken very seriously by many Progressives on the matter of charity. In her book, *The Pivot of Civilization* (1922), Margaret Sanger criticized the inherent cruelty of charity. She insisted that organized efforts to help the poor are the "surest sign that our civilization has bred, is breeding, and is perpetuating constantly increasing numbers of defectives, delinquents, and dependents."[114] Such charity must be stopped, she insisted. The fertility of the working class must be regulated in order to reduce the production of "benign imbeciles, who encourage the defective and diseased elements of humanity in their reckless and irresponsible swarming and spawning."[115] Swarming (like insects), spawning (like fish): here was marvelous zoological rhetoric from the lionized founder of Planned Parenthood. "If we must have welfare, give it to the rich, not the poor," she concluded.[116] "More children from the fit, less from the unfit: that is the chief issue of birth control."[117]

Bryan's challenge to the science of evolution seemed to threaten the continuation of the Nordic aristocracy in America by obstinately denying the theoretical basis of eugenics and proclaiming that all men are made in God's image. The dedicated eugenicists who were called in by the *Times* in 1922 to refute him were defenders of both Darwin and Galton; they wanted to push Darwinism to its logical conclusion. Over the next two decades, they did. So did Adolph Hitler, beginning eleven years later. When Hitler's experiment in applied Darwinism failed politically, Bryan's critics very quietly took this section of *Descent of Man*, as well as their own public careers in defense of eugenic sterilization, and dropped them down the Orwellian memory hole, where the data still rest in peace alongside the long-forgotten moral critique by Bryan, who had opposed Darwin on principle on this, the only known practical application of Darwin's thesis. Bryan is still pictured as a scientific buffoon in the history textbooks, and his detractors are still pictured as the fearless defenders of autonomous science.

---

114. Margaret Sanger, *The Pivot of Civilization* (New York: Brentano's, 1922), p. 108; cited in Grant, *Grand Illusions*, p. 27.
115. Sanger, *ibid.*, p. 115; cited in Grant, *ibid.*
116. *Ibid.*, p. 96; cited in Grant, *ibid.*, p. 28.
117. Sanger, "Birth Control," *Birth Control Review* (May 1919); cited in Grant, *ibid.*, p. 27.

And what of the 30,000 Americans who were forcibly sterilized in the name of Darwinian science? Long dead, long forgotten, and therefore no longer a potential embarrassment.

Accomplices of Theological Modernism

In the same March 5 issue, a true master of supercilious rhetoric published his response in the form of a review of Bryan's *In His Image*. Here, in one paragraph, is the finest statement of the older modernism's view of the relationship between religion and science that I have ever read. Any modern reader who wonders why theological conservatives in the 1920's regarded theological modernism as a threat to everything they believed in need only consider the following:

> It is not generally recognized that, parallel with the great march of science during the last sixty years, religion, so far from retrogressing, has also advanced; and that never before in the history of the world has the interest in the spiritual side of life been keener, nor the quality of religious thought finer and nobler. Religion, indeed, has also been undergoing an evolutionary process and adapting itself to modern ideas, modern conditions and modern needs. Many dogmas have been discarded and the essential truths of religion and morality separated from the obsolete husks which formerly surrounded them. Not the least part of this progressive movement has been carried on by theologians and professional teachers of religion. Naturally, from the standpoint of crude and outmoded beliefs the new faith looks like a collection of heresies. The primitive religionist still imagines that to accept the truths of science is to become an "infidel"; and, since there still survive those who hold this restricted view, an occasional recrudescence of pre-Darwinian superstition is to be expected.[118]

On March 10, the Kentucky anti-evolution bill failed by one vote in the House.

On March 14, Bryan replied in a letter to the editor. He referred only to Osborn and Conklin. "They dodge the real question and refuse to state how much of the Bible they regard as consistent with

---

118. Austin Hay, "The Crusade Against Darwinism," *New York Times Book Review and Magazine* (March 5, 1922), p. 5.

Darwin's hypothesis. But as far as evidence can be drawn from what they do say, it is evident that they regard the discovery of the bones of a five-toed horse as a greater event than the birth of Christ."[119]

The next day, the editors responded, and in this response, we see the arrogance of urban men who know they possess great influence because they buy ink by the truck load. They had contempt for small-town Protestant America: "Nominally addressing The Times, Mr. Bryan really, of course, was advertising himself as a purveyor of exactly such ideas as he knew would be received with most favor in the towns where his lectures are regarded as wonderful expressions of wisdom, piety, and virtue."[120] Dayton, Tennessee, was such a town.

Two days after the defeat of the Kentucky bill and two days before Bryan's letter to the editor was published came another shot at him in the *Times*, as we shall see.[121] But first, we must consider Bryan's political career: what he believed and what he accomplished.

A David Without a Stone

Bryan faithfully served the rural Populists in the Democratic Party as a kind of stoneless David for three decades, from 1896 to 1925, although his political career had begun earlier. He had moved the Democratic Party from the pro-gold standard, low-tariff, balanced budget, limited government political party it had been prior to 1897—the party of Grover Cleveland—to the Populist-Progressive party that it became under Woodrow Wilson.

Bryan was the greatest master of political rhetoric of his generation. In 1907, 300,000 people paid to hear him. He could earn $25,000 in a summer of lectures[122] in an era in which the average urban worker earned well under $1,000 a year.[123] His "cross of gold" speech against the supposed evils of the traditional gold standard, delivered at the 1896

---

119. *New York Times* (March 14, 1922), p. 14.
120. *Ibid.* (March 15, 1922), p. 18.
121. See Chapter 8, below.
122. David Sarasohn, *The Party of Reform: Democrats in the Progressive Era* (Jackson: University Press of Mississippi, 1989), p. 36.
123. Contemporary estimates (journalistic guesses), cited in George E. Mowry, *The Era of Theodore Roosevelt, 1900–1912* (New York: Harper & Row, 1958), p. 3.

Democratic national convention, remains the most important political speech in American history. It launched his national career, enabling him and his brother Charles, the first master of the political mailing list, to transform the American political system by creating a Democratic Progressive party, which would be countered by Teddy Roosevelt after 1901 in his creation of a Republican Progressive party. Yet Bryan could not win. No matter what battle he entered, he always lost. Even when his Progressive political reform programs won out, which many did, others were given credit for these victories.[124] It was ominous that he had decided to launch an attack on modernists and evolutionists.

Political Radical, Theological Conservative

It is one of the peculiar ironies of history that Bryan became the spokesman for conservative American Protestantism, 1921-25—almost as surprising as the fact that he was a Presbyterian. Politically, he was a radical; theologically, he was ill-equipped. His father had been a Baptist; his mother was a Methodist. He had wanted to be a Baptist preacher from his youth, but he was afraid of water. He witnessed his first Baptist immersion at age six and never got over it. This is why he joined the Presbyterian Church at age fourteen.[125] What is significant is that he joined the Cumberland Presbyterian Church.[126] It was revivalistic and Arminian.

His political radicalism seemed antithetical to his theology. Political columnist and historian Garry Wills has called his campaigns the most leftist ever conducted by any major party Presidential candidate in American history.[127] In the 1920's, Bryan criticized American churches for their indifference toward profiteering, business monopolies, and industrial injustice.[128] His view of business he called "applied

---

124. David D. Anderson, *William Jennings Bryan* (Boston: Twayne, 1981), pp. 190-91.
125. Levine, *Defender of the Faith*, p. 246.
126. Hibben, *Peerless Leader*, p. 48.
127. Garry Wills, *Under God: Religion and American Politics* (New York: Simon & Schuster, 1990), p. 99.
128. Levine, *Defender of the Faith*, p. 253.

Christianity" in a 1919 address of that title. In that same year, he declared that "we should drive all the profiteers out of the Presbyterian Church so that when they go to the penitentiary, they will not go as Presbyterians."[129] In a 1920 speech on state constitutional reform, Bryan denied that he was a socialist. He then called for a new Nebraska constitution that would "authorize the state, the counties and the cities to take over and operate any industry they please.... The right of the community is superior to the right of any individual."[130] He distrusted the bureaucracy in Washington, so he advocated that these controls on business be imposed by state and local governments.[131] In terms of his political beliefs, Bryan was an advocate of the social gospel. He corresponded in a friendly manner with such social gospel leaders as Washington Gladden, Shailer Mathews, Charles Stelzle, and Progressive economist Richard T. Ely.[132] In 1919, he praised the Federal Council of Churches with these words: "It is, in my judgment, the greatest religious organization in our nation."[133]

He was a believer in pure democracy and majoritarian wisdom. He believed that democracy "is a religion, and when you hear a good democratic speech it is so much like a sermon that you can hardly tell the difference between them."[134] He insisted that "the love of mankind is the basis of both,"[135] an Arminian view. To defend this religious vision, Bryan offered as clear a statement of religious humanism as anything ever issued by the American Humanist Association: "Have faith in mankind.... Mankind deserves to be trusted.... If you speak to the multitude and they do not respond, do not despise them, but rather examine what you have said.... The heart of mankind is sound; the sense of justice is universal. Trust it, appeal to it, do not

---

129. Cited in *ibid.*, p. 252.
130. *The Commoner* (Feb. 1920), pp. 8-9; cited in *ibid.*, p. 195.
131. *Ibid.*, p. 196.
132. Willard H. Smith, "William Jennings Bryan and the Social Gospel," *Journal of American History*, 53 (June 1966), pp. 45, 47. On Ely's connection to the social gospel, see Benjamin G. Raider, "Richard T. Ely: Lay Spokesman for the Social Gospel," *ibid.*, pp. 61-74.
133. *The Commoner* (May 1919), p. 11; cited in Smith, *ibid.*, p. 48.
134. *The Commoner* (Oct. 28, 1904), p. 2; cited in *ibid.*, p. 42.
135. *Ibid.*, p. 43.

violate it."[136] Levine has summarized Bryan's political beliefs: "During the very years when Bryan stood before religious gatherings denouncing evolution he also went before political rallies to plead for progressive labor legislation, liberal tax laws, government aid to farmers, public ownership of railroads, telegraphs, and telephones, federal development of water resources, minimum wages for labor, minimum prices for agriculture, maximum profits for middlemen, and government guarantee of bank deposits."[137] Yet by 1922 he was fast becoming the most visible defender of theologically conservative Protestantism in the United States.

Bryan, more than any other figure in American history, had unleashed the forces of the politics of plunder. He had appealed to the rural masses and had cried out against the Eastern Establishment. He had brought the culture wars of the Populist Party into the mainstream. But three times he had lost, and in the persons of Teddy Roosevelt, William Howard Taft, and Woodrow Wilson, the Eastern Establishment had its revenge, both on him and on the Cleveland wing of the Democratic Party. The shift from Whig politics to Progressivism had undermined "Clevelandism," but it had also undermined Populism. Only in 1933, after the election of Franklin Roosevelt, would Progressivism and Populism at last fuse nationally. Whiggism died with Cleveland, but it was Bryan who had killed it; Roosevelt, Taft, and Wilson had participated only as pall-bearers at the funeral.

The Scopes Trial and Its Aftermath

Bryan called on modernists to resign voluntarily from the ministry, since they did not believe in the tenets of Christianity. This had been a familiar, though incredibly naive, theme of the conservatives ever since the 1892 General Assembly,[138] and would remain so. Machen used it repeatedly. Not one of those who took this line was ready publicly to identify the modernists for what they were, judi-

---

136. Cited in Levine, *Defender of the Faith*, p. 218.
137. *Ibid.*, p. 364.
138. The "Portland Deliverance." See Chapter 5, above: section on "The 1892 General Assembly: Portland, Oregon," pp. 258–59.

cially speaking: covenantally disinherited sons who were attempting to steal the lawful inheritance of the true sons of the covenant. Such language would have been regarded as rhetorically inappropriate by the vast majority of those whose inheritance was at risk. Instead, conservatives adopted different forms of confrontational rhetoric—less judicial but nonetheless inflammatory. The Church would not tolerate such verbal challenges after 1925. That is to say, the victorious modernists who visibly gained control in 1926[139] would not tolerate rhetoric aimed against them. Because they held all the largest spears after 1926, they did not need rhetoric to achieve their goal. Their goal was power, and no later than 1926, they had definitively attained it in the General Assembly. Over the next decade, they would progressively apply what they had definitively achieved.

Confession Without the Confession

Bryan's leadership on the anti-evolution front placed him in a peculiar position. He was not a six-day creationist. That is to say, he was typical of all Presbyterian conservatives; he had abandoned the Westminster Confession on this point (IV:1). His position became public knowledge in 1925 when Darrow cross-examined him during the Scopes trial. Late in the exchange, Darrow asked him if he believed that the world was created in six days. Bryan startled his audience: "Not six days of twenty-four hours."[140] The creation might have lasted

---

139. I believe they had gained definitive control by 1920, when the Church did nothing to those officials who had indebted it to pay the bills of Rockefeller's Interchurch World Movement.

140. Ray Ginger, *Six Days or Forever: Tennessee v. John Thomas Scopes* (New York: Oxford University Press, [1958] 1974), p. 171. Darrow asked him if he accepted the date of creation (Bishop Ussher's estimate) of 4004 B.C. Bryan said he had never made such a calculation. Darrow: "What do you think?" Bryan: "I do not think about the things I don't think about." Darrow: "Do you think about the things you do think about?" Bryan: "Well, sometimes." *Ibid.*, p. 169. The prosecuting attorney realized that this testimony had thrown his case off-track; he told Bryan that he would not allow him to testify the next day. The next day, July 21, the judge expunged it from the record. Darrow protested, and asked the judge to call in the jury to deliver a guilty verdict. *Ibid.*, p. 175. The judge complied. Darrow told the jury to convict Scopes, so that a higher court could settle the case. The jury did. *Ibid.*, pp. 176–77.

millions of years, but he did not want to commit himself on this point, he told Darrow.[141]

Bryan was not alone in this desire. Even Machen held to some sort of theistic evolution scheme. He revealed his views in private letters; in public he refused to comment on this subject.[142] Most Presbyterian conservative leaders had been studiously avoiding a fight with evolutionists for at least six decades. They had all abandoned the Confession's explicit words. This greatly hampered them. Bryan received little public support on this issue from conservative Presbyterian leaders.[143]

It was fundamentalists outside the Presbyterian Church who supported Bryan in this battle. Because of this, he gained a reputation after 1921 for being a fundamentalist, which in fact he was, rather than a Calvinistic Presbyterian, which he was not. He was Arminian to the core. His view of God's election was framed in political terms. He said that the best description of the doctrine of election he had ever heard was offered by a Georgia Presbyterian preacher. "It's just this way—the voting is going on all the time; the Lord is voting for you and the devil is voting against you, and whichever way you vote, that's the way the election goes."[144] This was the state of Presbyterian theological conservatism in the fourth phase of the Presbyterian conflict.

In retrospect, the Scopes trial was a strange event. First, it was a widely covered media event: 200 reporters, 65 telegraph operators, and a Chicago station's radio broadcasts of the trial—the first American trial ever broadcast by radio.[145] Second, the jury was excluded from the trial's technical debates.[146] Third, neither Bryan nor the American

---

141. *Ibid.*, p. 173.

142. Longfield, *Presbyterian Controversy*, pp. 69–70.

143. An exception was Clarence E. Macartney, who was a vociferous opponent of evolution. *Ibid.*, pp. 70–72.

144. *The Commoner* (Feb. 17, 1905); cited in Willard H. Smith, *The Social and Religious Thought of William Jennings Bryan* (Lawrence, Kansas: Coronado, 1975), p. 174.

145. Henry M. Morris, *A History of Modern Creationism* (San Diego: Master Book Press, 1984), p. 63.

146. *Ibid.*

Civil Liberties Union wanted it to be conducted as a criminal trial. Bryan offered in advance to pay any fine imposed on Scopes.[147] After the trial, Scopes, who never testified at the trial, told one reporter that he had not been present in the classroom on the day that evolution was covered in the textbook, and that he had feared being put on the witness stand, where he would have had to admit this.[148]

Bryan died in Dayton on Sunday, July 26, five days after the trial ended. That morning he had led a local Southern Methodist congregation in prayer.[149] Its minister conducted the final services,[150] which was appropriate; Bryan had been far closer to John Wesley's Arminianism than to Presbyterianism's Calvinism. His reputation had been destroyed during the trial and posthumously by H. L. Mencken, who was the author of *The Philosophy of Friedrich Nietzsche* (1908). Mencken, following Nietzsche, was a promoter of the pre-Progressive social Darwinism: the survival of the fittest individual. He had written: "There must be a complete surrender to the law of natural selection—that invariable natural law which ordains that the fit shall survive and the unfit shall perish. All growth must occur at the top. The strong must grow stronger, and that they may do so, they must waste no strength in the vain task of trying to lift up the weak."[151] Nietzsche's philosophy was an extension of Darwinism, and Bryan opposed both, as he wrote in *In His Image*.[152] This is not how the public remembers the Scopes trial, however. As usual, the winners wrote the press releases and the screenplay.

The effect of the trial devastated fundamentalism as a cultural force. Henry M. Morris, a dispensationalist, six-day creationist, and the founder of the modern Creation Science movement, writes: "One of the most disappointing aspects of the Scopes trial was its intimidating effect on Christians. Multitudes of nominal Christians capitulated to theistic evolution, and even those who retained their belief in crea-

---

147. Wills, *Under God*, p. 100.
148. Ginger, *Six Days*, p. 180.
149. *Ibid.*, p. 192.
150. *Ibid.*, p. 193.
151. Cited in Wills, *Under God*, p. 102.
152. Bryan, *In His Image*, pp. 123–24, 126.

tion retreated from the arena of conflict, using the fiction that it was somehow unspiritual to be involved in such controversies and urging each other to concentrate instead on 'soul-winning,' and 'personal Christianity,' with a great emphasis also on the soon return of Christ. The schools and government and society in general were, to all intents and purposes, simply abandoned to secular humanist control, and they have been firmly under that control ever since."[153]

Picking Up the Fallen Torch

A year after Bryan died, Northern Baptist fundamentalist leader William Bell Riley wrote a book, *Inspiration or Evolution?* Riley had long been one of the major spokesmen for American fundamentalism, and this mantle of authority increased after Bryan's death. He was the main spokesman for the World's Christian Fundamentals Association until it faded in 1930.[154] Riley delivered the memorial address at the Great Commoner's funeral.[155] His biographer calls him "the chief executive of the fundamentalist movement. . . ."[156]

In 1917, he wrote *The Menace of Modernism*, in which he pointed out the obvious: theological modernists had allies in the academic community. He fully understood this aspect of the modernists' strategy of subversion—perhaps better than any fundamentalist leader of his day. He also understood the uses of rhetoric. He once wrote that conservative ministers had about as much chance of being invited to speak at a state university as to be heard in a Turkish harem.[157]

In the Foreword to *Inspiration or Evolution?*, Riley echoed Bryan's 1922 warning about evolution in the public schools, which was not surprising, since he had been preaching the same theme since 1922.[158] "But the public schools of America and the denominational schools are alike dependent for personal and financial patronage upon tax pay-

---

153. Morris, *History of Modern Creationism*, p. 67.
154. William Vance Trollinger, Jr., *God's Empire: William Bell Riley and Midwestern Fundamentalism* (Madison: University of Wisconsin Press, 1990), p. 33.
155. *Ibid.*, p. 50.
156. *Ibid.*, p. 33.
157. Cited in *ibid.*, p. 35.
158. *Ibid.*, p. 48.

ers, millions of whom are the best citizens of America. This book is addressed particularly to this class, and is intended as 'A call to arms!' If we silently and indolently endorse the destructive doctrines to which this volume calls attention, we will deserve the fate that is certain to befall both Church and State. The munitions of war for the Christian citizen are his voice and vote. He who does not employ both to preserve the democracy of America and the integrity of her true churches is a traitor to both country and Christ."[159] He fully understood that Bryan had been correct, that control over education by the taxpayers was crucial to rolling back the theory of evolution.

But it was not just public education that was under siege; it was Christian education, especially higher education. The book reprinted a speech he had delivered in 1921 at the Third Annual Conference on Christian Fundamentals. He identified William Rainey Harper as having been the chief proponent of theological modernism in higher education. Harper, he said, had been the main figure in the creation of an "Academic Octopus."[160] Harper had been the academic director of the Chautauqua program, and he became the first president of the Rockefellers' University of Chicago. Riley recognized the crucial role of the Rockefellers in American higher education. It was with a million-dollar grant in 1902 that the process began. "With this bait he saw the fish begin to rise from every denominational pool, and on October 1, 1905, he increased the wabbler by $10,000,000.00. This grant stirred every pond."[161] In 1907, he added another $43 million. Riley identified the key agency: Rockefeller Senior's General Education Board, chartered by the U.S. Congress in 1903.[162] Here is how the deed was done, according to Riley:

> The standardization of the colleges of the South is now sought. Let them consent to it, as we have already consented in the North, and see what will be the effect in the instance of a single college. A school, for example, that has a million dollar

---

159. W. B. Riley, *Inspiration or Evolution* (Cleveland, Ohio: Union Gospel Press, 1926), p. 5.
160. *Ibid.*, p. 164.
161. *Ibid.*, p. 173.
162. *Ibid.*

endowment accepts the standardization scheme and agrees to receive from the "Foundation Fund" through the "General Board of Education" $50,000 more. The moment that amount goes from the Rockefeller Fund, entire control of that institution as to curriculum, faculty, and board, passes practically into the hands of fifteen men living in and about New York, chief of whom is John D. Rockefeller, Jr., and in all fundamental matters the entire institution must consult the judgment of this fifteen, which, when it is remembered that John D. Rockefeller, Jr., is the real representative of these million, means the judgment of this one.[163]

This was an exaggeration; no college surrenders that degree of sovereignty. Faculties are made up of people who guard their autonomy in the classroom. But there was a surrender: the acknowledgment of the legitimacy of a more standardized curriculum, as well as professional academic standards for new faculty members. Also, there was the lure of further money. The Rockefeller money would be seen as a down payment. There was a price to pay for additional funding.

Riley saw in 1921 what a pair of pro-Rockefeller biographers admitted openly in 1988: "It would be difficult to overstate the value of the work the GEB did in the ensuing half century. Ironically, it seems largely forgotten today.... To understand the GEB, one must see it as an agency of change, one of such remarkable accomplishments that it is scarcely an exaggeration to refer to it as revolutionary."[164] One of its major accomplishments was "reforming college administration and developing professional standards for graduate education throughout the United States...."[165] Furthermore, "the work was done very quietly, with great circumspection and skill, for the good reason that, like any agent of change, the GEB was up against some form of established opposition in each of its successive missions...."[166] By the time it was voluntarily shut down in 1960, the year Junior died, it had expended $324 million on its many projects.[167] Some $208 million had

---

163. *Ibid.*, p. 176.
164. Harr and Johnson, *Rockefeller Century*, p. 70.
165. *Ibid.*
166. *Ibid.*, p. 71.
167. *Ibid.*, p. 75.

gone into higher education.[168] But setting standards for lower-level schools was also part of the plan. The GEB was the main factor behind the creation of the public school system in the South, through the funding of one professorship in education in every major state university in the South, and through lobbying in every state capitol. From a few hundred schools in 1900, the South's public school system grew to thousands in the 1920's.[169] For seven decades, we have needed a detailed study of the origin of higher education's accreditation octopus, but as yet such a book has not been published. Riley was on target. His suggestion that the GEB was the source of the secularization of Christian higher education has not been followed, either by the tenured recipients who are still profiting from the system of accreditation or the victims, who still send their best and brightest into the system for final certification.

Conclusion

Bryan launched the final phase of his long public career with his attack on Darwinism as a false religion. *In His Image* (1922) could have been ignored by the media and the Establishment had Bryan not understood the political implications of his confession. He understood that the public schools were the established Church in the United States, and that the teaching of Darwinism had to be stopped in public school classrooms. He understood this as surely as Darwinists today understand that creationism must not be taught in public school classrooms. He believed that because public schools are funded by taxes, voters have final authority over what is taught there. (He was incorrect; the U.S. Supreme Court has this authority, short of a Constitutional amendment to the contrary.) Bryan realized that if voters continued to defer to the educational experts, including scientific experts, the schools would remain in the hands of the educated elite that produces the textbooks. Bryan had devoted his public career to challenging elites. He ended his career just as he had started, but on a far more fundamental issue than the gold standard vs. free silver. This issue was

---

168. *Ibid.*, p. 79. The two main figures in distributing the funds in the early years were Jerome Greene and Abraham Flexner.

169. *Ibid.*, p. 76.

at the heart of the debate between biblically revealed religion and modernism: the question of origins.

The Establishment recognized the severity of this challenge from the moment that Bryan's speech before the Kentucky legislature led to a bill to outlaw the teaching of evolution in taxpayer-supported schools. Gaining and maintaining control over these schools had been the most important tactic of Unitarianism and then modernism since the days of Horace Mann.[170] Bryan was threatening the most sacred cow in liberalism's pantheon of sacred cows. In January and February of 1922, the *New York Times* published one rhetorically savage article after another in order to lay the foundation of what would become America's most important religious battle in the 1920's. This battle ended in July of 1925 in Dayton, Tennessee. With it ended also the conservatives' influence in both the Presbyterian Church and the Northern Baptist Church.

Bryan in 1922 wanted his followers to gain control over the allocation of political plunder. He had been campaigning on this platform for three decades. He understood that modernist Progressives were now in control of the political process nationally. He was taking the fight to the hustings, where he had always had his greatest influence. Yet Bryan had delivered the Democratic Party into the hands of the Progressives. Like the sorcerer's apprentice, he now strove to reverse what his oratory and his brother's mailing lists had conjured. By challenging the modernists' right to override local democracy through the imposition of compulsory Darwinism in the public schools, he was invoking the last flickering traces of the Protestants' ideal of Christendom. He was invoking point four of the covenant—economic sanctions—in the name of point five: succession.

Bryan's opponents recognized this threat and feared it. They had a major tactical problem. His arguments rested forthrightly on an official principle of American democracy, namely, that he who pays the tax-collecting piper should call the political tune: "No taxation without representation!" Bryan was a staunch defender of Progressivism's

---

170. R. J. Rushdoony, *The Messianic Character of American Education: Studies in the History of the Philosophy of Education* (Nutley, New Jersey: Craig Press, 1963).

principle that the State has both the moral authority and moral obligation to confiscate wealth from one group in order to give it to another group. But he had always been more of a Populist than a Progressive. He believed that the State should confiscate the wealth of a minority—the rich—in the name of the majority, not in order to fund some elite group, and surely not a humanistic elite of Bible-scorning educational bureaucrats, with the hard-earned money of God-fearing Americans. He appealed to majority rule. This was a powerful appeal.

To refute him, his opponents had to downplay the obvious: they were taxing the political majority—Christians—in order to educate all children in terms of religious principles at odds with what most parents believed. They were not merely stealing money; they were stealing hearts and minds as well. (The Progressives' power religion strategy was re-stated clearly half a century later by an American general in Vietnam: "When you've got them by the ——, their hearts and minds will follow.") So, unable to defend their compulsory education program in terms of the democratic principle of majority rule, these professed democrats resorted to the negative sanction of ridicule and misrepresentation: flat earth, medievalism, etc. The rhetorical standard which they established in the public press would soon be adopted by their allies inside the Presbyterian Church against Bryan and his ecclesiastical allies. Inside the Church, as well as outside, the crucial issue was sanctions.

8

THE REVIVAL OF RHETORIC

Upon the Christian doctrine of the Cross, modern liberals are never weary of pouring out the vials of their hatred and their scorn. Even at this point, it is true, the hope of avoiding offence is not always abandoned; the words "vicarious atonement" and the like—of course in a sense totally at variance from their Christian meaning—are still sometimes used. But despite such occasional employment of traditional language the liberal preachers reveal only too clearly what is in their minds. They speak with disgust of those who believe "that the blood of our Lord, shed in substitutionary death, placates an alienated Deity and makes possible welcome for the returning sinner." Against the doctrine of the Cross they use every weapon of caricature and vilification. Thus they pour out their scorn upon a thing so holy and so precious that in the presence of it the Christian heart melts in gratitude too deep for words. It never seems to occur to modern liberals that in deriding the Christian doctrine of the Cross, they are trampling upon human hearts.

J. Gresham Machen (1923)[1]

Machen in 1923 quoted verbatim from a sermon. That sermon was fast becoming the most important sermon preached by any American pastor in the twentieth century. The historical context of that sermon was the battle over Darwinism. It was a follow-up to the

---

1. Machen, *Christianity and Liberalism* (New York: Macmillan, 1923), pp. 119–20.

preacher's article against Bryan which appeared in the *New York Times* on March 12, 1922.

The published attacks on Bryan by March 5 had been deemed insufficient by the editors of the *Times*. They wanted an even bigger gun. The previous attacks had been conducted by well-known secularists. This was not enough. Bryan was a Presbyterian. The Presbyterian Church had two million members and almost ten thousand pastors. First, the editors needed a prominent fellow-Presbyterian to respond. Second, the editors also needed a Baptist, the largest American Protestant association. Finally, they wanted a pastor whose name was known to literate Americans generally and to *New York Times* readers specifically. They got all three in one man: Harry Emerson Fosdick.

The Senior Pastor of the American Establishment

Harry Emerson Fosdick (1878-1969) was a Baptist minister with a unique distinction: he was the associate pastor of New York's First Presbyterian Church. This congregation had been formed in 1918 as an amalgam of three other Presbyterian Churches. This had been an era of war-inspired Church unity. Fosdick also served Union Seminary as professor of practical theology from 1915 until 1934.[2] He became the most famous radio preacher of his era—the original electronic preacher. He began his Sunday morning broadcasts in 1923.[3] Later, he preached free of charge for NBC's "National Vespers," 1927-1946,[4] a radio program sponsored by the Federal Council of Churches.[5] His book royalties did not suffer as a result of his radio broadcasts. He wrote nearly 50 books and 1,000 printed sermons.[6] His weekly audience was estimated at well over two million people in 1946.[7] He received 134,827 letters, October 1944 to May 1945.[8] In

---

2. "Fosdick, Harry Emerson," *Dictionary of American Religious Biography*, edited by Henry Warden Bowden (Westport, Connecticut: Greenwood Press, 1977), p. 163.
3. Robert Moats Miller, *Harry Emerson Fosdick: Preacher, Pastor, Prophet* (New York: Oxford University Press, 1985), ch. 20.
4. *Ibid.*, p. 384.
5. *Ibid.*, p. 386.
6. *Ibid.*, p. viii.
7. *Ibid.*, p. 385.
8. *Ibid.*, p. 386.

order to preach Sunday afternoons on "National Vespers," he had to forsake the Park Avenue Baptist Church's once-a-month afternoon communion services. Fosdick ceased taking communion from 1927 until 1931, when the newly built Riverside Church re-scheduled its communion services.[9] His biographer justifiably asserts: "In this century . . . no American Protestant minister has exceeded the prominence of Harry Emerson Fosdick."[10]

He was a liberal who, like his biographer, equated biblical orthodoxy with mindlessness: "Fosdick believed that it was possible to be a Christian in the twentieth century without throwing one's mind away. . . ."[11] He was a founder of psychological pastoral counselling,[12] and his best-selling book, *On Being a Real Person* (1943), was an early representative of "the power of positive thinking" school of theology, made famous a decade later by Rev. Norman Vincent Peale.[13] But he, unlike Peale, was never subject to a verbal barb such as Adlai Stevenson's quip, "I find Paul appealing and Peale appalling." His prestige among liberals was too great. He was also "up to his hips in the vast mental health movement. . . ."[14] But more to the point, he was up to his hips in the Rockefeller empire, which also financed much of the research cost for Miller's laudatory biography.[15]

His adult life, says his biographer, was a revolt against the "Calvinist ethos" of his childhood, i.e., the doctrine of hell.[16] He had become an evolutionist in his freshman year of college. His liberalism steadily increased until his suicide attempt in 1902, half way through his second year at seminary, his first at Union, where he also took

---

9. *Ibid.*, p. 383.
10. *Ibid.*, p. vii.
11. *Ibid.*
12. *Ibid.*, pp. 252–69.
13. *Ibid.*, pp. 273–80. This phase of his ministry began in 1923 with the publication of *Twelve Tests of Character*, essays that had appeared in the *Ladies' Home Journal*. In this book he cited an old Chinese proverb: "You cannot carve rotten wood." *Ibid.*, p. 274. That he would use a phrase so similar to Warfield's "you can't split rotten wood" is ironic.
14. *Ibid.*
15. *Ibid.*, p. xiv.
16. *Ibid.*, pp. 7–8.

philosophy courses at Columbia University.[17] After his recovery, he never looked back. He graduated from Union in 1904 with an A+ average.[18] Like Machen, he did not earn a doctorate; like Machen, he served in the YMCA in World War I;[19] like Machen, he wrote and preached for the average person; and like Machen, he was always known as "Dr."[20]

A Man With Connections

If any man has ever deserved the title, Senior Pastor of the American Establishment, it was Fosdick. He had been appointed as a member of the Board of Trustees of the Rockefeller Foundation in 1917, the year of its reorganization.[21] That was the year that John D., Jr., became the chairman of its Board.[22] He rubbed shoulders with Charles Evans Hughes, John D., Jr.'s old Sunday School teacher, who had just barely lost the 1916 Presidential election to Woodrow Wilson, and who became Secretary of State in 1921 and Chief Justice of the U.S. Supreme Court in 1930. Also on the Board was the head of Sears, Roebuck: Julius Rosenwald. Fosdick's younger brother Raymond had served as Wilson's Associate Secretary General of the League of Nations in Europe.[23] Raymond had studied under Wilson at Princeton.

In the first two weeks of June, 1922, a few months after his response to Bryan, Fosdick gave commencement addresses at the following institutions: Bryn Mawr College, Crozer Seminary, George Washington University (after spending the morning with Supreme Court

---

17. *Ibid.*, p. 44. He received an M.A. in political science from Columbia in 1908, having studied under economists John Bates Clark and E. R. A. Seligman, and sociologist Franklin Giddings. *Ibid.*, p. 64.

18. *Ibid.*, p. 49.

19. Unlike Machen, he had been an avid interventionist prior to the War. *Ibid.*, ch. 5. Machen had opposed America's entry into it.

20. *Ibid.*, p. 292.

21. John Ensor Harr and Peter J. Johnson, *The Rockefeller Century* (New York: Charles Scribner's Sons, 1988), p. 146.

22. Raymond B. Fosdick, *The Story of the Rockefeller Foundation* (Long Acre, London: Odhams Press, 1952), p. 37.

23. Raymond Fosdick, *Chronicle of a Generation: An Autobiography* (New York: Harper & Bros., 1958), p. 190.

Justice Brandeis), Ohio University, and the University of Rochester. Add to this a pair of baccalaureate addresses (Ohio University, Radcliffe College) and the invocation at Smith College, plus a morning sermon at Harvard University and a lecture at Ohio Wesleyan University.[24] He spoke at the memorial service for Woodrow Wilson in 1924.[25] In 1937, he conducted the funeral of John D. Rockefeller, Sr. He offered the benediction at Rockefeller, Jr.'s funeral in 1960.[26] He sponsored David Rockefeller's membership in the exclusive Century Club of New York.[27] In the years of the Presbyterian conflict, Fosdick was a regularly appearing author in the *Atlantic Monthly*, *Harper's*, and *Ladies' Home Journal*. Beginning in 1923, he began a long association with *Reader's Digest*: over 60 articles, making him the number-one contributor in his era.[28] It is not too much to say (and several Church historians have said it) that Fosdick was the most influential preacher in America in between the eras of Billy Sunday and Billy Graham.[29] Andrew Blackwood, who taught homiletics at Princeton Seminary, once said of Fosdick's abilities: "If any young man wishes to learn what to preach, he may look elsewhere; if he would learn how, let him tarry."[30]

He earned in this era at least $25,000 a year, placing him in the upper four-tenths of one percent of American income.[31] The average pastor earned under $1,000 in 1918;[32] fewer than 2,000 of America's 170,000 pastors earned over $3,000.[33] His salary from his congregation was only a small fraction of $25,000: perhaps 20 percent. Lecture fees

---

24. Miller, *Fosdick*, pp. 102–103.
25. *Ibid.*, p. 101.
26. *Ibid.*, p. 318.
27. *Ibid.*, p. 317.
28. *Ibid.*, p. 104.
29. *Ibid.*, pp. 336–37.
30. *Ibid.*, p. 339.
31. *Ibid.*, p. 312. Fosdick cited this figure himself in a 1945 letter to Rockefeller (p. 468).
32. This figure from the Interchurch World Movement survey of 1920; reported in Richard Hofstadter, *The Age of Reform: From Bryan to F.D.R.* (New York: Vintage, 1955), p. 151n.
33. Supposedly, 1,671: *ibid*.

and book royalties constituted the bulk of his income. He was the most audible American pastor of his day: the voice of the literate American public. His books were translated into 50 languages.[34] Meanwhile, the average Presbyterian pastor was generally thought to earn $1,200 a year in the 1920's, before the Great Depression hit, but some lay missionaries earned less.[35] Like Machen, who was also independent financially, he could preach what he believed without fear of being fired. But Union was not about to fire Fosdick. Shortly before the 1923 General Assembly, at which phase four the Presbyterian conflict publicly erupted, Fosdick wrote to his brother Raymond to ask Rockefeller to give Union money as part of Union's $4 million fundraising drive. Rockefeller gave a million dollars, and he gave another three million over the years.[36]

The president of Union in the period of Fosdick's participation in the Presbyterian conflict was A. C. McGiffert.[37] With respect to Fosdick's influence on campus, consider the remarks of John C. Bennett, who entered Union in 1926 and became one of the most prominent modernists of the twentieth century. He later became president of Union. He described Fosdick's course on practical theology. Fosdick, he said, "did more than anyone else to bring the results of critical study of the Bible to that whole generation. . . . It is hard to exaggerate what a source of emancipation it was for thoughtful people of that period to learn that the Bible was not a book of Fundamentalism."[38] Fosdick's classes were so popular that tickets had to be issued to allocate seats.[39] This explains why the *New York Times* approached Fosdick to respond to Bryan.[40]

---

34. Miller, *Fosdick*, p. 69.
35. *Minutes of the General Assembly, 1928*, p. 252.
36. Albert F. Schenkel, *The Rich Man and the Kingdom: John D. Rockefeller, Jr., and the Protestant Establishment* (Minneapolis, Minnesota: Fortress Press, 1995), p. 180.
37. Fosdick served under four Union presidents: Francis Brown, McGiffert, Henry Sloane Coffin, and (for one year) Henry P. Van Dusen. Miller, *Fosdick*, p. 328.
38. *Ibid.*, p. 321. It is one of those oddities of history that Bennett taught R. J. Rushdoony at the Pacific School of Religion in the early 1940's.
39. *Ibid.*
40. *Ibid.*, p. 115.

His role in the next phase of the Presbyterian conflict was appropriate for another reason: a year before, in the midst of the brief American flurry of interest over liberal missions in China, Fosdick had been in China addressing missionaries.[41] In 1922, he exposed to full public view the fact that the same theological divisions were undermining Protestantism in America.

Briggs' Rhetorical Strategy Revived

Let us begin with the *Times* headline: "**Attacks W. J. B.** Preacher Says Bryan Article Injury to Bible—God Infinitely Grander Than Occasional Wonder-Worker." This was Briggs' old ploy: positioning modernism as the religion that honors the Bible, with conservatism as dishonoring. The headline writer had read the article carefully; he understood what Fosdick was saying.

Fosdick challenged Bryan on three points: his rejection of a generally established scientific principle; his inappropriate use, in Fosdick's view, of the Bible as a measuring rod of scientific truth; and his narrow view of education. "Indeed, the real enemies of the Christian faith, so far as our students are concerned, are not the evolutionary biologists, but folk like Mr. Bryan who insist on setting up artificial adhesions between Christianity and outgrown scientific opinions, and who proclaim that we cannot have one without the other." Folk like Mr. Bryan: a catchy phrase. (Mr. White Liberal, try using this phrase the next time you speak before an audience of blacks: "What is it you folks want?" It doesn't sound appropriate, does it? It sounds condescending, doesn't it? If ever a man was condescending, it was Harry Emerson Fosdick.) He dismissed Bryan's "special form of medievalism" which Bryan wants to "be made authoritative by the state, promulgated as the only teaching allowed by the schools." By this time, the word "medieval" had been attached to Bryan and his campaign by the political modernists; Fosdick was simply following their lead. Almost prophetically, his conclusion warned Bryan of "a long, long road to travel before he plunges the educational system into such incredible folly...."[42]

---

41. Harry Emerson Fosdick, *The Living of these Days: An Autobiography* (New York: Harper & Bros., 1956), pp. 135-36.
42. *New York Times* (March 12, 1922), VII, p. 13.

This had been the argument of Charles Briggs a generation earlier: blame the defenders of an inerrant Bible as the true threats to Christianity. The true defenders of the faith are therefore those progressives who are ready and willing to fuse Darwinism and higher criticism with the language of orthodoxy. This strategy had cost Briggs his Presbyterian ordination, but primarily because of his excessively confrontational rhetoric. The liberals had avoided such rhetorical confrontations for a generation. Fosdick decided that it was time to launch a challenge to those in the denomination who still defended at least an outline of Confessional orthodoxy. He did this in the name of a stronger, truer Christianity. But he did so only after the rhetorical precedent had been set by political modernists outside the Church.

American Church historian Edwin Scott Gaustad[43] writes of higher criticism that "it was still possible in 1922 to hold that such criticism was chiefly constructive, that Christianity ended up both purer and stronger, and that one's faith was firmer than before."[44] That is to say, it was possible for an ordained minister to make such arguments in public and avoid being de-frocked in most Protestant denominations. The question in 1922 was: Did this generalization include the Northern Presbyterians?

The theological issue of higher criticism was the same as it had been in Briggs' day: the authority of the Bible (point two of the covenant). The institutional issue was also the same: Could a Presbyterian leader escape negative sanctions—point four—if he went into print with such ideas? The lines of battle were again drawn. Briggs had escaped censure for 15 years, 1876–1891. He kept escalating his rhetoric until he was prosecuted. Fosdick also escaped censure: for three months. Nothing happened. So, it was time to escalate the rhetoric once again.

"Shall the Fundamentalists Win?"

On May 21, 1922, Fosdick delivered the most important sermon of his career, or perhaps of any twentieth-century preacher's career:

---

43. And my Ph.D. dissertation advisor.
44. Edwin Scott Gaustad, "*Did* the Fundamentalists Win?" *Daedalus* (1982); reprinted in *Religion in America: Spiritual Life in a Secular Age*, edited by Mary Douglas and Steven Tipton (Boston: Beacon Press, 1983), p. 171.

"Shall the Fundamentalists Win?"[45] It immediately thrust him into the limelight of denominational politics and national prominence. It acted as a catalyst to the latent controversy within the Church. It was this sermon which gave widespread circulation to Curtis Lee Laws' term *fundamentalist*, despite the fact that the printed version did not include this word in its title, *The New Knowledge and the Christian Faith*.

Essentially, the sermon was the familiar liberal plea for tolerance within the denomination for those whose faith was less orthodox than the strict Calvinism of the Westminster Confession. He went beyond this, however; he inserted a statement that biblical inerrancy and the virgin birth are not necessary doctrines of the Christian faith. This was a direct challenge to the Doctrinal Deliverance of 1910, not just to the Calvinists in the denomination.

He began with praise for Gamaliel, who cautioned the Pharisees to show tolerance for the Christians (Acts 5:34–39). This was a clever beginning: he equated the fundamentalists with the Pharisees. He hastened to add: "All Fundamentalists are conservatives, but not all conservatives are Fundamentalists. The best conservatives can often give lessons to the liberals in true liberality of spirit, but the Fundamentalist program is essentially illiberal and intolerant."[46] He understood the division within the conservative ranks: conservatives who were willing to fight for what they believed because they regarded it as fundamental, and conservatives who would not fight because they did not regard their theology as sufficiently distinctive to be worth creating a public disturbance to defend.

The Five Points of Modernism

Fosdick's sermon revealed all five points: the non-sovereignty of God in history, the non-authoritative Bible, the judicial standard of evolution, the denial of legitimate negative sanctions (although he did not mention hell), and ecumenism, although the ecumenical aspect of the sermon was muted—implied but not stated clearly. The sermon

---

45. Gaustad asks rhetorically: ". . . has any one paid as much attention to any sermon since?" *Ibid.*, p. 169.

46. Harry Emerson Fosdick, "Shall the Fundamentalists Win?" in *American Protestant Thought in the Liberal Era*, edited by William R. Hutchison (Lanham, Maryland: University Press of America, 1968), p. 172.

was a warning against conservative theology as the basis of the liberals' doctrine of the Church. Its unstated assumption was that liberal theology should be allowed to spread within the denomination. He used the rhetoric of toleration to deny the legality of oath-bound ordination. This was always the public position of theological liberals in the mainline denominations until they gained control over the courts. After they had gained control, a new rhetoric of oath-bound confession—the confession to obey the Church's courts—was substituted for the rhetoric of toleration.

1. God's sovereignty over history and the processes of history. Fosdick said that Jesus may not have been born of a virgin. That is, His conception did not break with the normal historical processes of conception. In short, in terms of Jewish law, *Jesus was a bastard*: conceived before marriage. Either the Bible's account of Joseph's surprise is false—he was in fact Jesus' biological father—or else he thought he had been betrayed by Mary. But Fosdick was not so unwise as to put his bastard Christology this graphically. He had to proceed with caution.

Fosdick was making a fundamental liberal point: Jesus' sovereignty over history was not uniquely manifested by God's miraculous act of generation which clearly identified Jesus as God incarnate. Fosdick called this issue "the vexed and mooted question of the virgin birth of our Lord." There is one point of view which affirms the virgin birth, he said, but there are many people in evangelical churches who disagree with this view. He insisted that Christianity is not unique in its affirmation of a virgin birth. "Many people suppose that only once in history do we run across a record of supernatural birth. Upon the contrary, stories of miraculous generation are among the commonest traditions of antiquity. Especially is this true about the founders of great religions." He listed Buddha, Zoroaster, and Lao-Tsze.[47] His examples were weak. The sacred texts of Zoroastrianism make no such claim, and the story of Buddha's virgin birth came centuries after his era and is expressly opposed to his teaching—facts well known to students of comparative religion in Fosdick's day.[48] The

---

47. *Ibid.*, p. 174.
48. "Virgin Birth," *Encyclopaedia of Religion and Ethics*, edited by James Hastings, 12 vols. (Edinburgh: T. & T. Clark, 1921), XII:624.

point is, the New Testament teaches Jesus' virgin birth; it is not the product of accretions from later folk religion.

His acceptance of the possibility of a non-virgin birth for Jesus was a direct assault on the Westminster Confession, which announces that Jesus was "conceived by the power of the Holy Ghost, in the womb of the virgin Mary, of her substance" (VIII:2). If Fosdick was correct, is Jesus sovereign over history? Where and what is the evidence? If not the virgin birth, then what is the alternative? If He was not the son of God through incarnation, then He was a Jewish bastard. In what sense is a heretical dead Jewish bastard sovereign over history? The modernists much preferred to conduct worship on behalf of the memory of a dead Jewish bastard than on behalf of a living sovereign God who brings final judgment. The bulk of their parishioners agreed.

2. The inspiration and authority of the Bible. He admitted that some Christians defend the inerrancy of Scripture.[49] He called this a "static and mechanical theory of inspiration."[50] Then he asserted that the Bible's view of God as "an Oriental monarch, fatalistic submission to his will as man's chief duty, the use of force on unbelievers, polygamy, slavery—they are all in the Koran. . . . All of these ideas, which we dislike in the Koran, are somewhere in the Bible."[51] But these Old Testament ideas changed in the New Testament. He implied that revelation is progressive, *and is still going on*: ". . . finality in the Koran is behind; finality in the Bible is ahead. We have not reached it. We cannot compass all of it. God is leading us out toward it."[52] This was another assault on the Westminster Confession, which identifies the Bible as "The supreme judge by which all controversies of religion are to be determined. . ." (I:10).

3. Fixed vs. evolutionary standards. He appealed to science, meaning evolutionary science. "A great mass of new knowledge has come into man's possession: new knowledge about the physical universe, its origin, its forces, its laws; new knowledge about human history and in

---

49. Fosdick, *op. cit.*, p. 175.
50. *Ibid.*, p. 176.
51. *Ibid.*
52. *Ibid.*

particular about the ways in which ancient peoples used to think in matters of religion and the methods by which they phrased and explained their spiritual experiences; and new knowledge, also, about other religions and the strangely similar ways in which men's faiths and religious practices have developed everywhere." Of course, some Christians have been unable to integrate this new knowledge into their thinking. "They have been sure that all truth comes from the one God and is his revelation." Unmentioned here was the Westminster Confession's explicit statement: "The whole counsel of God concerning all things necessary for His own glory, man's salvation, faith and life, is either expressly set down in Scripture, or by good and necessary consequence may be deduced from Scripture: unto which nothing at any time is to be added, whether by new revelations of the Spirit or traditions of men" (I:4). Fosdick made Christianity and modernity correlative, i.e., *dialectical*: "We must be able to think our modern life through in Christian terms, and to do that we also must be able to think our Christian life through in modern terms."[53] But some men refuse to accept this. They establish fixed boundaries around the truth: ". . . the Fundamentalists are driving in their stakes to mark out the deadline of doctrine around the Church, across which no one is to pass except on terms of agreement."[54]

4. *Sanctions*. This was *the* judicial issue for liberals in all the denominations, and still is. It surely was for Fosdick. "Here in the Christian Church today are these two groups, and the question which the Fundamentalists have raised is this, Shall one of them drive the other out? Do we think the cause of Jesus will be furthered by that?"[55] The fundamental issue was sanctions. This is why he called the sermon: "Shall the fundamentalists win?" Notice: he recognized only two groups, fundamentalists and everyone else. Machen the next year based *Christianity and Liberalism* on the same two-fold division.

5. *Eschatology: premillennial kingdom vs. ecumenical*. What about Christ's second coming? That language meant something very differ-

---

53. *Ibid.*, p. 172.
54. *Ibid.*, p. 173.
55. *Ibid.*, p. 177.

ent for early Christians, he argued. They did not understand it as evolutionary. "No one in the ancient world had ever thought, as we do, of development, progress, gradual change, as God's way of working out His will in human life and institutions."[56] In the evangelical churches today there are differing views of the second coming, he noted. He dismissed premillennialism and premillennialists: "They sit still and do nothing and expect the world to grow worse and worse until He comes."[57] He contrasted this with Progressivism's secularized postmillennialism, which proclaims that "development is God's way of working out His will."[58] In music, painting, and architecture, we see progress. He did not mention biblical (i.e., Princeton Seminary's) postmillennialism or amillennialism—the traditional views of a majority of those who have defended historic Calvinism.

Rhetoric vs. the Facts

The fundamentalists plan to drive their enemies out of the Church, he insisted. The problem was, there was no evidence of this at the national level, and had not been since 1900 when McGiffert departed.[59] Bryan had suggested that liberals voluntarily depart. Machen would soon do the same. But Fosdick was using rhetoric, not logic, to mobilize his listeners.

Fundamentalists, he implied, will thwart the ecumenical impulse by their endless theological quibbling. It is a matter of "penitent shame that the Christian Church should be quarreling over little matters when the world is dying of great needs."[60] Here is the contrast: the quarreling, nit-picking Christian Church (not just the Presbyterian Church) vs. the great needs of the whole world. As a Baptist, he did not use the words "Church union," but the implication was clear: to meet the needs of a big world, the Christian Church should stop debating theology. Rhetorically, he asked: Should the Church "in the

---

56. *Ibid.*
57. *Ibid.*, p. 178.
58. *Ibid.*
59. Seminary professor Thomas Day had been asked to resign from the California Synod in 1911, which he did. See Chapter 5, above, Conclusion.
60. *Ibid.*, p. 180.

face of colossal issues, play with the tiddly-winks and peccadillos of religion?"[61] This was an echo of Speer's 1901 address to the General Assembly, where he warned against "trifling."

He hastened to add, as every minister who wants to keep his job should add, that he was not talking about anyone in his congregation. "Never in this church have I caught one accent on intolerance. God keep us always so and ever increasing areas of the Christian fellowship; intellectually hospitable, open-minded, liberty-loving, fair, tolerant, not with the tolerance of indifference, as though we did not care about the faith, but because our major emphasis is upon the weightier matters of the law."[62] Thus ended the lesson.

This was very strong rhetoric. Fosdick's implication was clear: the fundamentalists were not "intellectually hospitable, open-minded, liberty-loving, fair, tolerant." This sermon was reminiscent of Briggs' rhetoric in his 1891 Inaugural Address, both theologically and rhetorically. It, too, would soon provoke a negative reaction. In his case, at least, his prophecy would come true: after 22 years, the conservatives tried to remove a preacher from his pulpit.

Who Was Behind it?

The sermon became famous in theologically liberal circles within a few weeks. It was published in *The Christian Century* (June 8) and *The Christian Work* (June 10). But this was just the beginning. A layman in Fosdick's congregation, Ivy Lee, approached him. He asked: Would Fosdick consent to a reprinting of the sermon? Fosdick agreed, and soon thereafter Lee sent 130,000 copies to ministers and laymen throughout the nation.[63] The original title had been toned down; it was now called *The New Knowledge and the Christian Faith*. After it had been mailed, Fosdick announced that all this had been done without his knowledge.[64] Over 30 years later, however, Fosdick admitted

---

61. *Ibid.*, pp. 180–81.
62. *Ibid.*, p. 182.
63. Miller, *Fosdick*, p. 116.
64. Edwin H. Rian, *The Presbyterian Conflict* (Grand Rapids, Michigan: Eerdmans, 1940), p. 30.

in his autobiography that Lee had come to him and had asked permission to publish it.[65] That is to say, he had lied in 1922.

Someone had put up the money to print and mail 130,000 copies of this sermon. At the time, it was not clear who had done this. Also, the title had been changed. Why? Fosdick never publicly admitted why: because John D. Rockefeller, Jr., had suggested the change. Rockefeller had written to Lee: "The object in circulating this sermon is to get the views therein expressed widely read and not stir up discord. The title which I suggest is clear and accurately descriptive,—at the same time it does not breathe controversy. . . . This is merely a suggestion; whatever Raymond Fosdick thinks wise, and perhaps he will care to take up with the matter with his brother, will be satisfactory to me."[66] What interest did Rockefeller have in all this? Considerable: he was putting up the money to mail it.[67] This expenditure was part of his lifetime strategy to win American Protestantism to ecumenism and theological liberalism, a plan that he supported with over one hundred million dollars.[68] Much of this was spent during an era in which the dollar was worth at least ten times more than it is today.

Lee and Rockefeller had been close since 1914. Lee handled Rockefeller's public relations activities.[69] They shared memberships in three exclusive clubs: the Broad Street Club, the University Club, and the Recess Club.[70] They also shared a commitment to an ecumenical theology.[71]

Raymond Fosdick

In his letter to Lee, Rockefeller deferred to Raymond Fosdick. Why? Because Rockefeller was in the process of putting Fosdick in

---

65. Fosdick, *Living of These Days*, p. 146.
66. Quoted in Miller, *Fosdick*, p. 117.
67. *Ibid.*
68. This is the estimate of Schenkel, *Rich Man and Kingdom*, p. 2.
69. Ray Eldon Hiebert, *Courtier to the Crowd: The Story of Ivy Lee and the Development of Public Relations* (Ames, Iowa: Iowa State University Press, 1966), ch. 11.
70. Schenkel, *Rich Man and Kingdom*, p. 202.
71. Rockefeller's major public statement of faith was a 1918 article, "The Christian Church—What of Its Future?" *Saturday Evening Post* (Feb. 9, 1918).

charge of the distribution of his fortune. Also, Raymond was the author's brother. Raymond Fosdick had known Rockefeller since 1910.[72] Rockefeller had hired him prior to World War I to study European and American police systems in their control of prostitution.[73] Then Newton D. Baker, Wilson's Secretary of War and a former Progressive mayor of Cleveland, sent Fosdick to the Mexican-U.S. border towns during General Pershing's futile 1916 expedition into Mexico to capture the bandit Pancho Villa. Fosdick's task was to study ways to keep American troops morally pure. He spent five weeks on that assignment.[74]

Also in 1916, Fosdick persuaded Rockefeller to establish the Institute for Government Research, which shortly thereafter was re-named the Brookings Institution.[75] It was re-named for Robert S. Brookings, a businessman. Brookings was a defender of a government-business partnership which would control free market competition.[76] This was a continuing theme among the industrial magnates and great financiers of the Progressive era.[77] It was the big business application of Lester Frank Ward's vision of Darwinian scientific planning. Brookings called for "intelligent public supervision designed to protect the public and the trade from grasping and intractable minorities."[78] That is, *established* big businesses can continue to prosper if price-competitive newcomers are kept out of the market. "So we know from sad experi-

---

72. See Chapter 6, above: section on "Rockefeller's 'Baptism' in 1910," pp. 377-81.

73. R. Fosdick, *Chronicle*, ch. 7.

74. *Ibid.*, p. 137. Cf. Murray N. Rothbard, "World War I as Fulfillment: Power and the Intellectuals," *Journal of Libertarian Studies*, 9 (Winter 1989), p. 93; Charles E. Harvey, "John D. Rockefeller, Jr., Herbert Hoover, and President Wilson's Industrial Conferences, 1919-1920," in *Voluntarism, Planning and the State: The American Planning Experience, 1914-1946*, edited by Jerold E. Brown and Patrick D. Reagan (Westport, Connecticut: Greenwood, 1988), p. 29.

75. Peter Collier and David Horowitz, *The Rockefellers: An American Dynasty* (New York: Holt, Rinehart and Winston, 1976), p. 142.

76. Antony Sutton, *Wall Street and FDR* (New Rochelle, New York: Arlington House, 1975), pp. 77-79.

77. Gabriel Kolko, *The Triumph of Conservatism: A Reinterpretation of American History, 1900-1916* (New York: Free Press, [1963] 1977).

78. Robert S. Brookings, *Industrial Ownership* (New York: Macmillan, 1925), p. 56.

ence that blind or ignorant competition has failed to make its reasonable contribution through earnings to our national economic needs."[79] At the bottom of the Great Depression, he called for "a new co-operative epoch with social planning and social control. . . ."[80] (The Brookings Institution remains true to its namesake's ideological outlook. It is still one of the most influential think tanks in Washington. In 1988, it was the recipient of $677 million in donations. The *Forbes* index of the largest 250 American corporations, placed Brookings ninth in a list of 225 recipient organizations. The Council on Foreign Relations was tenth.)[81]

In 1917, Fosdick was appointed by the government to head two commissions, each called the Commission on Training Camp Activities, one run by the Army, the other by the Navy.[82] Its slogan was "fit to fight."[83] Rockefeller's Bureau of Social Hygiene paid his salary.[84] It had been doing so since 1913.

In 1919, he was named by Wilson as an Associate Secretary-General of the League of Nations. After he resigned in 1920 to become Rockefeller's advisor, he became a prime mover in the creation of the Foreign Policy Association and an organizer of the Council on Foreign Relations (1921). Write Horowitz and Collier: "It was Fosdick who got Rockefeller involved and interested in the question of the realignment of global power that would begin to take place in the decade after World War I."[85] Beginning in 1936, Raymond served as president of the Rockefeller Foundation for a dozen years; he also wrote the only authorized biography of John D., Jr.[86]

---

79. Brookings, *Economic Democracy* (New York: Macmillan, 1929), p. 4.

80. Brookings, *The Way Forward* (New York: Macmillan, 1932), p. 6.

81. Thomas J. DiLorenzo, *Patterns of Corporate Philanthropy* (Washington, D.C.: Capital Research Center, 1990), p. 25.

82. Fosdick, *Chronicle*, ch. 8; Rothbard, p. 92.

83. *Ibid.*, p. 147.

84. Charles E. Harvey, "John D. Rockefeller, Jr., and the Social Sciences: An Introduction," *Journal of the History of Sociology*, IV (Fall 1982), pp. 4, 26, note 31.

85. Horowitz and Collier, *Rockefellers*, p. 142.

86. Raymond Fosdick, *John D. Rockefeller, Jr.: A Portrait* (New York: Harper & Bros., 1956). Rockefeller wrote in 1951 that Fosdick "had more to do than anyone else with planning and developing the work of the Foundation and its

Raymond Fosdick was a scoffer where his brother professed tolerance. He described his religious upbringing in a pietistic Baptist household: ". . . we were brought up on the crude theology which characterized my grandfather's era. Yet I cannot remember either my father or my mother talking to us about damnation or hell-fire or the rest of the horrendous doctrine which was the bulwark of the church."[87] Baptism by total immersion was "an archaic and dismal initiatory rite."[88] "Such a religious environment as surrounded us in our early youth could have led either to morbidity or to a rebellious cynicism."[89] From his teen years, he attended two Baptist churches each Sunday. His father earned extra money singing in the evening at a rival congregation. One minister was a liberal, the other a conservative. The family would discuss both sermons at the Sunday evening dinner table. This turned him and his siblings into relativists. "Out of this conflict we children began to realize that even in the field of religion, ideas and concepts have no final and conclusive form. All systems of theology 'have their day and cease to be'; they are as transient as the cultures they are patterned on."[90] He used his growing influence with Rockefeller for half a century, 1910–1960, to do whatever he could to direct that liberal Baptist layman's immense fortune into moral reform projects, social science research projects, and other secular pursuits. His faith was in the kingdom of man, which he once referred to as "the kingdom of Social Righteousness."[91] When the time was ripe, he and Ivy Lee unleashed the power of his brother's sermon.

My reason for mentioning Raymond Fosdick's background is two-fold. First, because previous historians, especially Church historians, have ignored it. This was especially true when I began this project in 1962, when only a few Church historians paid any attention to the

---

related organizations. . . ." Rockefeller, "Foreword," to Fosdick, *Story of the Rockefeller Foundation*.
87. Fosdick, *Chronicle*, p. 15.
88. *Ibid.*, p. 17.
89. *Ibid.*
90. *Ibid.*, p. 18.
91. Letter to Woodrow Wilson (1912), cited in Daryl L. Revoldt, Raymond B. Fosdick: Reform, Internationalism, and the Rockefeller Foundation (Ph.D. dissertation, University of Akron, 1982), p. 69.

Presbyterian conflict, and none paid attention to the Rockefeller connection. Second, the reader should understand that the Presbyterian conflict was not some minor affair on the fringes of American life. It was a battle for the heart and soul of the nation. It was the primary battlefield of a larger war over the theological content of Protestantism's confession in what was then a self-consciously Protestant nation. Beginning in 1923, Machen, a little-known assistant professor in New Testament literature and theology, sounded the rallying cry of a frontal assault against a well-entrenched and well-funded enemy: the American Establishment—not just the religious Establishment, which today is a comparatively minor affair in the United States, but the American Establishment in the broadest sense.

Rockefeller was wrong about both reasons for changing the title of Harry Fosdick's sermon. First, the pamphlet stirred up more controversy than any printed sermon in American history. Second, despite the name change, the sermon has always been remembered by its original title: "Shall the Fundamentalists Win?"

The Master of Public Relations

That Ivy Lee initiated the mailing is also significant. Lee was no ordinary layman. He is generally regarded as America's first full-time public relations specialist.[92] Even if he wasn't the first, it was his genius at self-promotion that has persuaded historians to regard him as such. He worked independently for the largest industrial corporations

---

92. The only other figure of comparable early influence in this field was Edward Bernays (1891–1995), the son of Sigmund Freud's sister-in-law Minna. Bernays wrote more on the theory of public relations than Lee did. On the whole subject, see Marvin Olasky, *Corporate Public Relations* (Hillsdale, New Jersey: Lawrence Erlbaum, 1987). An early student of both Bernays and Lee was Herbert Hoover, who began using public relations techniques as early as 1912. Craig Lloyd, *Aggressive Introvert: A Study of Herbert Hoover and Public Relations Management, 1912–1932* (Columbus: Ohio State University Press, 1972), p. 70. Hoover in this period was a Rockefeller agent who worked closely with Raymond Fosdick. See Charles E. Harvey, "John D. Rockefeller, Jr., Herbert Hoover, and President Wilson's Industrial Conferences of 1919–1920," in *Volunteerism, Planning and the State: The American Planning Experience, 1914–1946*, edited by Jerold E. Brown and Patrick D. Reagan (Westport, Connecticut: Greenwood, 1988), ch. 2.

in America, including the Rockefeller interests. It has long been asserted that it was Lee who came up with the famous strategy of having the elderly John D., Sr., hand out dimes to children, which the old man actually enjoyed doing—30,000 dimes, according to one account.[93] This story of Lee as the developer of this technique is probably not true,[94] but Lee did encourage the old man to create opportunities for the press to photograph him when he did this.[95] It was Lee who, in a speech to the American Railway Guild in May of 1914, the month John D. Rockefeller, Jr., hired his services for the first time,[96] set forth this principle of modern public relations: "The people now rule. We have substituted for the divine right of kings, the divine right of the multitude. The crowd is enthroned. This new sovereign has his courtiers, who flatter and caress precisely as did those who surrounded medieval emperors."[97] The man who would represent the crowd must flatter it.

Lee was the son of a liberal Methodist minister.[98] He had attended Princeton University, where he had come under the influence of Wilson, as had Raymond Fosdick.[99] Lee was the man who engineered the Rockefellers' public relations response to the 1914 Ludlow, Colorado, massacre, in which eleven wives and two children of striking United Mine Workers had been suffocated or burned to death in a fire that had started accidentally when they fled in panic from the state militia, which had begun shooting at them.[100] The miners had been striking

---

93. Collier and Horowitz, *Rockefellers*, p. 70.
94. Hiebert, *Courtier to the Crowd*, p. 115.
95. Harr and Johnson, *Rockefeller Century*, p. 158.
96. Hiebert, *Courtier*, p. 97.
97. Cited in *ibid.*, page following the title page. On the same page, Hiebert quotes Abraham Lincoln's August 21, 1858, debate with Stephen A. Douglas: "Public sentiment is everything. With public sentiment nothing can fail; without it, nothing can succeed. Consequently, he who molds public sentiment goes deeper than he who enacts statutes or pronounces decisions."
98. Harr and Johnson, *Rockefeller Century*, p. 129. Hiebert describes the father as having taken "a middle position between the evolutionists and the biblicists...." Hiebert, *Courtier*, p. 226.
99. Collier and Horowitz, *Rockefellers*, p. 118. On Wilson's influence on Fosdick, see Fosdick, *Chronicle*, ch. 3.
100. Revoldt, *Raymond Fosdick*, p. 342.

490   CROSSED FINGERS

against a company in which the Rockefellers were heavily invested.[101] Because of this early work for the Rockefellers, he gained the epithet "poison Ivy."[102] Lee was a key participant of the American Establishment. He was one of the original hundred founders in 1921 of the Council on Foreign Relations,[103] a private, then-secretive association that has exercised strong and continuing influence over the American political agenda.[104] He served as a publicist for the Establishment. Theologically, he was a liberal and an ecumenist.

A member of Fosdick's Presbyterian congregation, Lee in 1922 provided his services to Junior, who wanted publicity for the newly

---

101. Lee recommended forthrightness with the press and the miners. He told John D., Jr., to set up grievance committees. The whole operation was supervised by W. L. Mackenzie King, a devout Presbyterian and Rockefeller employee who had lost his position as Minister of Labor for Canada. Horowitz and Collier, *Rockefellers*, pp. 119–22. He left Rockefeller's employment in 1921 to become Prime Minister of Canada. He served three terms: 1921-26, 1926-30, 1935-48. The most detailed account of King's career as a Rockefeller employee was written by King's aide at both the Ministry of Labor and the Rockefeller Foundation, F. A. MacGregor: *The Fall and Rise of Mackenzie King* (Toronto: Macmillan, 1962). See also Harr and Johnson, *Rockefeller Century*, pp. 130–44.

102. Hiebert, *Courtier*, p. 107. Socialist novelist Upton Sinclair used the name in his book on the press, *The Brass Check* (1919): *ibid.*, p. 298.

103. Harr and Johnson, *Rockefeller Century*, p. 156. The CFR's major publication is the quarterly journal, *Foreign Affairs*. One of the original organizers, Whitney H. Shepardson, in 1960 wrote a brief history of the origins of the CFR. He traced it to Britain's Institute for International Affairs and to the "Inquiry Group," which advised President Woodrow Wilson's advisor E. M. House before and during the 1919 peace conference in Paris. Shepardson, "Early History of the Council on Foreign Relations," reprinted for the Council's 50th Anniversary Dinner (1972); reprinted in *Freemen Digest* (1980), pp. 136–38.

104. The two key elitist organizations in the 1920's were the Council on Foreign Relations and the Carnegie Endowment for International Peace. The central figure, who served on each board, was Elihu Root, who had served as McKinley's Secretary of War and Theodore Roosevelt's Secretary of State. Philip H. Burch, Jr., *Elites in American History*, 3 vols. (New York: Holmes & Meier, 1981), II:250. The standard biography of Root is Philip C. Jessup, *Elihu Root*, 2 vols. (n.p.: Archon, [1938] 1964). Root persuaded Herbert Hoover to name Henry Stimson as his Secretary of State: Richard N. Current, *Secretary Stimson: A Study in Statecraft* (New Brunswick, New Jersey: Rutgers University Press, 1954), p. 43. On Root's influence on Stimson, who served in the cabinets of four presidents, see Geoffrey Hodgson, *The Colonel: The Life and Wars of Henry Stimson, 1867-1950* (New York: Knopf, 1990).

formed Park Avenue Baptist Church, where Rockefeller was a member.[105]

Lee had experience in direct-mail promotions. He had used the Princeton University alumni list to mail copies of a university lecture series. It produced excellent results (presumably, donations). He suggested to Rockefeller to have an independent laymen's committee serve as a front for the mailing.[106] He assured Rockefeller that mailing the sermon would lead to the "building of a firmer and stronger foundation upon which the work of the church in this country might proceed."[107] Lee remained as a public relations agent for Rev. Fosdick throughout the 1920's. As Fosdick's biographer notes, because of this connection, "virtually everything he said was given a 'play.'"[108]

Which Side Will Win?

Fosdick's original title for the sermon correctly identified the institutional issue: *sanctions*. One faction might win; its rivals would therefore lose. There were two rival views of Christianity present within the Presbyterian denomination and Protestant denominations generally, he argued. As a liberal, he argued the position that there could be institutional coherence without a victory by either side. This was nonsense, as the next 14 years would demonstrate: a victory for theological toleration would be a defeat for the fundamentalists and Calvinists.

The sermon was a plea for tolerance. Decades later, Fosdick later admitted that "If ever a sermon failed to achieve its object, mine did."[109] The sermon produced "an explosion of ill-will," he said in retrospect. He offered this explanation for the drastic effects that the sermon caused: "Since the liberals had no idea of driving the fundamentalists out of the church, while the fundamentalists were certainly

---

105. Hiebert, *Courtier*, p. 225. Lee's price was quite cheap, given his importance to the Rockefellers: a monthly retainer fee of $1,000. Sometimes, John D., Jr., would give him extra money for a project. *Ibid.*, p. 116.
106. *Ibid.*, p. 227.
107. Cited in *ibid.*, p. 228.
108. Miller, *Fosdick*, p. 252.
109. H. E. Fosdick, *Living of These Days*, p. 145.

trying to drive the liberals out, the impact of this appeal fell on the reactionary group."[110]

Fosdick was being too modest—or too clever. The sermon was a calculated risk. If it created no opposition, the tolerance-seeking modernists would inherit. If it was challenged, he could position himself (with Lee's masterful assistance) as a wounded lamb, an honest man seeking only tolerance. Where was this wave of conservative opposition to theological liberalism in 1922? Where was the strategy of defrocking? Nowhere. The *New York Times* essay by Bryan was the first widely circulated piece of anti-liberal rhetoric that the Presbyterian Church had seen from a conservative Presbyterian in over two decades, and he had called upon modernists to resign, not for conservatives to begin heresy trials. In any case, Bryan was a layman. The explosion came only after Fosdick's sermon was sent out.

His sermon proposed the removal of negative sanctions from ecclesiastical affairs. This suggestion appeared to rest on a broad-minded theology of open-endedness. This was an illusion; no theology is open-ended. A theology insists that God is one thing; He therefore cannot be something else. There is also the issue of eternal sanctions. The Christian doctrine of final judgment and eternal, irreversible sanctions is surely the most closed-end theology imaginable. There was no way for liberals to escape a theological confrontation if they publicly denied the Church's doctrine of final judgment. None of the liberals in the Presbyterian Church had been willing to admit this fact publicly from David Swing forward, nor had their peers in the other mainline denominations. The modernists' strategy was to foster the illusion of "tolerance vs. intolerance," when in fact they knew that the conservatives could not acquiesce to liberalism's doctrine of universal salvation. The liberals wanted to move the denominations into Unitarianism-Universalism, but this would take time. And money. Other people's money: Rockefeller's and the laity's.

Fosdick's explanation for the failure of his call to toleration was typical of liberals who resent the creeds of Christendom. For him, tolerance was the fundamental law of the church: *creeds without negative sanctions*. This belief was an extension of liberalism's most impor-

---

110. *Ibid.*

tant theological point: *eternity without negative sanctions*. Fosdick rejected all Church creeds; he detested all Church sanctions. "Fosdick openly boasted of never having repeated the Apostles' Creed in his life," his biographer reports.[111] Yet he was a pastor in a denomination that required for ordination formal subscription to the most rigorous Christian creed in history, the Westminster Confession of Faith and its two catechisms. As one secular newspaper editor put it, "It is not exactly ethical for a vegetarian to accept employment from a meat packer and urge a diet of spinach upon all who come asking for meat."[112] The capture of the Presbyterian Church by its theological enemies rested from the beginning on this "vegetarian" strategy, and more: a challenge to the moral legitimacy of any "meat packers" who might seek to remove these vegetarians from the payroll.

Fosdick wrote to his father in January, 1923: "I really think we are going in the end to get the two things that we want most to get: namely, a real victory for liberalism, while at the same time we are holding together the Presbyterian church without a split."[113]

Lippmann vs. Fosdick

The man who saw this clearly and described the nature of the conflict more concisely than anyone in his generation was not J. Gresham Machen. It was Walter Lippmann, the most influential columnist in America from the era shortly after the First World War until the Vietnam War.[114] (A few years after Machen's death in 1937, Lippmann would buy a summer home in the Establishment's enclave, where the Machens had also resided each summer: Seal Harbor, Mount Desert Island, Maine. He lived there in the summers until 1972; he died in 1974. His ashes were scattered off the Maine coast.)[115]

Lippmann was a Jew by birth and an atheist by confession. In his book, *American Inquisitors* (1928), he wrote a dialogue on the Chris-

---

111. Miller, *Fosdick*, p. 118.
112. Unnamed; cited in *ibid*.
113. Cited in *Ibid*., p. 120.
114. Carroll Quigley, *Tragedy and Hope: A History of the World in Our Time* (New York: Macmillan, 1966), p. 939; Ronald Steel, *Walter Lippmann and the American Century* (New York: Vintage, 1981).
115. Steel, *Lippmann*, pp. 385, 594-95, 598.

tian doctrine of salvation—the escape from God's eternal negative sanctions—a doctrine separating the modernists from the fundamentalists. It was clear to Fosdick that his target was Fosdick:

> Modernist: We can at least discuss it like gentlemen, without heat, without rancor.
>
> Fundamentalist: Has it ever occurred to you that this advice is easier for you to follow than for me?
>
> Modernist: How so?
>
> Fundamentalist: Because for me an eternal plan of salvation is at stake. For you there is nothing at stake but a few tentative opinions, none of which means anything to your happiness. Your request that I should be tolerant and amiable is, therefore, that I submit the foundations of my life to the destructive effects of your skepticism, your indifference, and your good nature. You ask me to smile and commit suicide.[116]

Fosdick got even a year later with a critical *New York Post* book review of Lippmann's *Preface to Morals*, chiding Lippmann for his "naive and medieval" view of theism.[117] But it was not Lippmann who was naive; it was Fosdick. Humanists such as Lippmann and H. L. Mencken understood what was at stake institutionally.[118] They recognized that Machen was correct: Fosdick was preaching a view of God that could not be reconciled with the Bible's doctrine of hell. But the crucial institutional issue was not formal theology as such; the issue was sanctions: the ability of one side or the other to drive its opponents from the denomination in terms of one of two creeds, either the Westminster standards or toleration. The question indeed was: Shall the fundamentalists win? The answer was clear: not if they conducted a strictly defensive campaign. Without negative sanctions, there could be no victory.

---

116. Cited in Miller, *Fosdick*, p. 177.
117. *Ibid.*
118. See Mencken's obituary of Machen: Appendix A, below.

The Conflict Escalates

Upon receipt of Fosdick's pamphlet, Clarence E. Macartney wrote "Shall Unbelief Win?" which was published in *The Presbyterian* (July 13, 1922), the conservative denominational magazine. In October, Macartney attended a Philadelphia Presbytery meeting at the home of John Wanamaker, the wealthy merchant. The issue was Fosdick. He introduced in executive session (closed to non-members of the presbytery) a proposed Address to the New York Presbytery from the Philadelphia Presbytery, asking the other presbytery to see to it that the preaching in the First Church be in conformity to the standards of the denomination. At the next meeting of the Philadelphia Presbytery, this Address was sent to every member of the New York Presbytery. The Philadelphia Presbytery also adopted an overture to the General Assembly requesting the same thing, which was sent to the Clerk of the General Assembly.[119] Phase four of the Presbyterian conflict had clearly begun.

Under the leadership of Macartney, the Philadelphia Presbytery was to remain the leading orthodox presbytery. It was joined by 14 other presbyteries in making this request. Since every ordained minister in the Presbyterian Church had to subscribe to the Confession "as containing the system of doctrine taught in the Holy Scriptures," Macartney, a strict Calvinist, believed that Fosdick's pronouncements had overstepped the limits of the Confession, and therefore deserved censure. In his mind, and in the minds of many other orthodox Presbyterians, such preaching could not be tolerated, especially from a minister who had never been licensed by the Church.

Macartney was generally regarded as the most gifted preacher in the conservative camp, the only man whose reputation for preaching matched Fosdick's. He later wrote a famous book of sermon illustrations. In his autobiography, he describes what happened after he introduced his Address-Overture:

> I had expected, of course, criticism and scoffing, and that the old cry and accusation, "heresy hunter," would go up. But what

---

119. Clarence E. Macartney, *The Making of a Minister* (Great Neck, New York: Channel Press, 1961), pp. 184–85.

surprised me was the intemperate and bitter abuse which poured forth. At the meeting of the Presbytery when the overture was adopted, I thought for a moment that one of the Presbyters was going to make a physical assault upon me. The letters of abuse poured in like a flood. I have preserved these letters in my files, and I call them, the "Liturgy of Execration." The so-called Liberals and Modernists certainly did not live up to their vaunted reputation and their claim of "sweetness and light."[120]

Liberals had worked long and hard after 1893 to create an illusion: their mild-mannered, gracious responses to rhetorically outrageous accusations by conservatives. The conservatives positioned themselves as defenders of the faith. This was a powerful appeal. To counter it, the liberals positioned themselves as defenders of the peace. I regard this as the liberals' most successful rhetorical ploy.[121] By repeating it endlessly, they eventually persuaded the majority of confrontation-avoiding pietists that it was the liberal faction that had long been the victim of "un-Christian" verbal abuse by their opponents. In a phrase attributed to Winston Churchill—as so many great phrases are—"If you get the reputation for rising at dawn, you can sleep till noon."

The 1923 General Assembly

The General Assembly met at Indianapolis in May of 1923, exactly one year after Fosdick had delivered his sermon. It was obvious from the beginning that the session would be a hot one, for the conservatives were championing as their candidate for Moderator none other than the Great Commoner himself, Bryan. His opponent, Dr. Charles F. Wishart, president of the College of Wooster, was known as a conservative theologically, but he was far from it, as events would prove. He won the election on the third ballot, just barely, by a margin of 24 votes out of some 800.[122]

This had been a showdown from the opening gavel of the General Assembly. Wishart had known Bryan for almost three decades, since

---

120. *Ibid.*, p. 186.
121. Another was to position themselves as the "true" defenders of the Confession and the Bible, with the orthodox wing as the "less than true" defenders.
122. Rian, *Presbyterian Conflict*, p. 32.

the time as a young man he had journeyed to Nebraska in 1896 to meet him after Bryan's presidential nomination by the Democratic Party. Bryan had spoken in Wishart's church two decades later. But the two were at odds with each other before the General Assembly began. Bryan had attacked in print one of Wooster's professors and a member of Wishart's church, Horace Mateer, for Mateer's open espousal of evolution. Mateer wrote an anti-creation book in 1923, *Evolution versus Special Creation*, in response to Bryan, who had spoken in 1921 at a Wooster chapel service for over two hours attacking evolution. This conflict was public knowledge within the Church's leadership. The vote for Moderator served as a kind of referendum.[123] Wishart, who had presented his candidacy in the guise of moderation, later wrote to Harry Fosdick: "I am convinced that most of the harm in our denomination has been made possible through one man, Mr. Bryan."[124] The feeling was mutual; six months after the General Assembly, Bryan was still complaining about Wishart's faculty.[125]

By 1923, the denomination had visibly begun to divide along theological lines. As Bryan said later in the conference, after the defeat of his proposal to ban money from the Educational Fund going to any instruction that taught Darwinism or evolution, "I have had experience enough in politics to know a machine when I see it, and the machinery in control of this Assembly works perfectly. The so-called liberals have everything their own way."[126] He exaggerated, given the subsequent decision of the Assembly regarding the re-affirmation of the five points of faith of the Doctrinal Deliverance of 1910 and 1916, but after 1925, his words were quite appropriate. But by that time, he was dead. He never got to see the liberals' machine in action, its wonders to behold.

---

123. L. Gordon Tait, "Evolution, Wishart, Wooster, and William Jennings Bryan," *Journal of Presbyterian History*, 62 (Winter 1984), esp. pp. 309–12.

124. Miller, *Fosdick*, p. 121.

125. *The Presbyterian Advance* (Nov. 15, 1923); cited in Willard H. Smith, *The Social and Religious Thought of William Jennings Bryan* (Lawrence, Kansas: Coronado, 1975), p. 185.

126. Louis W. Koenig, *Bryan: A Political Biography of William Jennings Bryan* (New York: Putnam's, 1971), p. 614.

The Fosdick Case

The chief issue of the General Assembly was the Fosdick case. It was first considered by the Committee on Bills and Overtures. All but one member of the 22-man committee recommended that the case be sent back to the New York Presbytery for further study and action. Judicially, this responsibility lay with Fosdick's presbytery. The minority report of one, however, accepting the Philadelphia overture and also calling for a reaffirmation of the Doctrinal Deliverance of 1910, was adopted by the Assembly, 439 to 359.[127] The New York Presbytery's representatives had voted 12 to three against the majority. The three "yes" votes came from ruling elders. Among the "no" voters was William Foulkes, the New Era's director. The New Yorkers' "no" voters were joined by Moderator Wishart and Vice Moderator Chapman.[128]

The battle against the Committee's report had been led by Bryan and Macartney. Macartney's statement opposing the majority report was rhetorical. "Fathers and brethren, this majority report is a masterpiece of whitewash. The man who wrote it ought to get a job as an interior decorator." But Macartney knew that the stakes were high: "This was only a skirmish—a whispering in the mulberry tree. The storm is coming, and you can't keep it back with pusillanimous compromises."[129] (He was correct; the storm came, and in 1936, he battened down the hatches, bid Machen a fond farewell, and pulled the covers up over his head.)

This 1910 doctrinal statement, compared to the Westminster Confession, was a pale affirmation of orthodoxy. It said nothing of predestination, creation, human depravity, or the covenant. It affirmed five beliefs: (1) the infallibility of the Bible, (2) the virgin birth, (3) Christ's substitionary atonement, (4) the reality of the resurrection, and (5) the reality of Christ's miracles.[130] Because this affirmation of faith had not

---

127. "Presbyterians Ban Views of Fosdick, Bryan Leading," *New York Times* (May 24, 1923), p. 1.
128. *Ibid.*
129. *Ibid.*, p. 6.
130. *The Presbyterian Enterprise: Sources of American Presbyterian History*, edited by Maurice W. Armstrong, Lefferts A. Loetscher, and Charles A. Anderson

been approved by two-thirds of the presbyteries, it did not constitute a binding decision in Church courts, as the conservatives were to discover at the 1927 General Assembly.

Even more disturbing for the conservatives was the divided support of the clergy. Lefferts Loetscher points out that the majority vote came from the elders of the Church (ruling elders), not from the clergy (seminary-trained teaching elders), since the latter group divided almost evenly on the issue, but the ruling elders supported it, three votes to two. According to Loetscher, the board members and officers of the Church were almost unanimously opposed to the action taken.[131] In other words, the higher up the bureaucratic chain of command, the stronger was the opposition to any kind of orthodox or conservative affirmation.

The Presbyterian (June 14, 1923) surveyed the results of the Assembly's vote on the provisions of the 1910 Deliverance. What the author found shocked him, but should not have at this late date: "Whenever the name of a man connected with the offices and Boards and organized activities of the church was called, a defiant 'No' was the response." Even more amazing to him, "The foreign missionaries, who of all persons might have been expected to cast a ringing vote for an overture which declared the honor of Jesus Christ, voted against it."[132] Three decades of Speer's leadership were showing. The conflict over missions would flare up again in late 1932, as it had in 1921. But more significant organizationally was the vote of board members and paid bureaucrats. There, the battle was already over. The modernists had won.

Liberal attendees issued a four-part protest. The first one revealed the heart of the conservatives' problem: the self-justification of the local presbytery. "We protest against the action taken because it was

---

(Philadelphia: Westminster Press, 1956), p. 281.

131. Lefferts A. Loetscher, *The Broadening Church: a study of theological issues in the presbyterian church since 1869* (Philadelphia: University of Pennsylvania Press, 1954), p. 112.

132. Cited in Delwyn G. Nykamp, A Presbyterian Power Struggle: A Critical History of Communication Strategies in the Struggle for Control of the Presbyterian Church, U.S.A., 1922–1926 (Ph.D. dissertation, Northwestern University, 1974), p. 184.

based upon allegations made by one presbytery in regard to conditions in another Presbytery, which are not substantiated by the evidence."[133] Not substantiated? Fosdick's sermon had been sent to 130,000 people. If this was insufficient evidence, then Presbyterianism had standards of evidence higher than those applying to angels.

A Brief Digression on Sources

The reader may have noted that I cite secondary sources for many of the events of the General Assembly's actions during this period. This is not because I have not consulted the *Minutes of the General Assembly*. The problem is that by the time this phase of the Presbyterian conflict broke out, the *Minutes* had long since ceased to record the details of the debates on the floor of the General Assembly. Two fat volumes for each year were filled with committee reports and statistics, not debates—and sometimes not even the numerical results of voting. This itself is an indication of the shift in power from the General Assembly to the denomination's permanent boards.

As an example, consider Bryan's motion on the floor of the General Assembly to prohibit the funding of any school by the Presbyterian Church if that school taught Darwinism as a fact. The *New York Times* reported on the front page that he spoke for an hour, and the session went on for three hours. Bryan's opponents succeeded in watering down the proposal, destroying its impact. The headline blared: "Bryan Loses Fight to Ban Darwinism in Church Schools: Presbyterian Assembly Defeats His Anti-Evolution Resolution After a Hot Debate."[134] The *Minutes* record the event in this passionless bureaucratic manner: "In the discussion of a resolution presented by the Hon. William Jennings Bryan, a member of the Standing Committee on Education, the following took part. . . ."[135] There follows a list of nine men's names and their presbytery memberships. No mention of the nature of Bryan's resolution appears. The *Minutes* then reprint the substitute motion, which carried. The substitute motion presented a vague instruction to synods and presbyteries to "exercise careful over-

---

133. *New York Times* (May 25, 1923), p. 10.
134. *Ibid.* (May 23, 1923), p. 1.
135. *Minutes of the General Assembly, 1923*, p. 211.

sight" over instruction in institutions receiving money from the Church, and to "withhold official approval"—money was not mentioned—from any school "which seeks to establish a materialistic evolutionary philosophy of life, or which disregards or attempts to discredit the Christian faith."[136] Since every Presbyterian modernist would deny doing either, this resolution would keep the flow of funds flowing. But the *Minutes* reveal little of what was at stake, or even what was going on.

The Far More Important Issue

All of the histories of the Presbyterian conflict focus on the 1923 General Assembly meeting because of the fireworks over Bryan, Macartney, and Fosdick. Yet the *Minutes*, true to their bureaucratic slant, reveal few signs of any contention. It is as if nothing significant were happening on the floor of the General Assembly. And, from the point of view of the liberals, who by now had captured complete control over the boards, nothing significant *was* happening. What really was significant received no attention from the press, either secular or denominational. In 1923, the Presbyterian Church was set up for a total reorganization by the liberals.

The most recent move to reorganize the Church had begun in 1920, the year of triumph by the liberals. A Special Committee on Reorganization and Consolidation of Assembly Agencies was appointed by the General Assembly. It reported back in 1921 and again in 1922.[137] The final report was approved by the General Assembly on May 21, 1923—exactly one year to the day after Fosdick preached "Shall the Fundamentalists Win?" to his congregation. Typically, the *Minutes* record nothing about the debate (if any) or the vote tallies.[138] If approved by a majority of the presbyteries, the eleven boards of the denomination would henceforth be consolidated into four. Church finances would be centralized into one collections agency—in the name of "economy."[139] The Office of the General Assembly would become

---

136. *Ibid.*, p. 212.
137. *Minutes of the General Assembly, 1922*, pp. 146–81.
138. *Minutes of the General Assembly, 1923*, p. 58.
139. *Ibid.*, pp. 61–62.

the General Council with control over executive commissions.[140] A final layer of bureaucratic representation would be laid down over the operations of the General Assembly.

Having been approved by the General Assembly, the report was then sent down to the presbyteries for ratification. The voting went on throughout the year prior to the 1924 General Assembly. At that Assembly, Macartney was elected Moderator. This is regarded by historians of the Presbyterian conflict as the one clear-cut General Assembly victory by the conservatives. Yet in the first year of the Fosdick case, the presbyteries approved the restructuring of the Church by a vote of 222 to 26, with six taking no action.[141] Philadelphia (Macartney's) voted *yes*. This is evidence that the conservatives, as late as 1924, did not have a clue regarding the process of infiltration and capture that had been going on since 1906. They would not receive another opportunity to learn from their mistakes.

The New York Presbytery

The 1923 General Assembly sent the Fosdick case back to the New York Presbytery. The New York Presbytery took no action, in defiance of the order of the General Assembly, except to adopt a protest against the General Assembly's actions in the first place.[142] A few weeks later it went so far as to license two men, Henry Van P. Dusen (later to serve as president of Union Seminary)[143] and Cedric Lehman, neither of whom was willing to affirm the virgin birth of Christ, the second point of the Doctrinal Deliverances of 1910, 1916, and 1923. The stage was set for continued antagonism on the floor of the General Assembly of 1924.

---

140. *Ibid.*, pp. 62, 97–101.
141. *Minutes of the General Assembly, 1924*, p. 137.
142. Rian, *Presbyterian Conflict*, p. 37.
143. Decades later, Van Dusen edited a collection of articles and addresses of John Foster Dulles: *The Spiritual Legacy of John Foster Dulles*, published in 1959 by Westminster Press, the book publishing arm of the Presbyterian Church, U.S.A. He wrote *The Vindication of Liberal Theology* (New York: Charles Scribner's Sons, 1963). From Briggs to Van Dusen, Charles Scribner's Sons served as the primary book publisher for modernist Presbyterians.

Lehman's statement is important because he said publicly exactly what he was doing. What he was doing was what all of the modernists coming into the ministry had been doing since 1875: crossing their fingers. *The Presbyterian* (June 21, 1923) reported what took place on the floor of presbytery:

> He, on being questioned, asserted that he could not affirm belief in the bodily resurrection of Christ. Asked how he could repeat the Apostles' Creed with his people, Mr. Layman [Lehman] said: "I would repeat the creed, but with an interpretation in my own mind."[144]

Without negative sanctions against such hypocrisy—hypocrisy elevated to a strategy of subversion—the conservatives could not save their Church. If they could not keep out Cedric Lehman, they could not keep out anyone willing to play mental games with the most minimal of Christian creeds. Lehman and those like him did not believe the creeds and confessions of the historic Church, Presbyterian or otherwise.

The task for their opponents was two-fold: (1) to identify what the liberals did believe as alien to Christianity; (2) to mobilize those who believed in the Westminster Confession to remove their enemies from their midst. The problem was therefore confession and sanctions. Lehman had thrown down the challenge to the Trinitarians by publicly confessing belief without believing what he was verbally confessing. It was a challenge to the conservatives to do something about it: the same challenge Henry van Dyke had issued after another New York ordination—his son's—in 1913. No one had taken up that challenge a decade earlier. Henry Sloane Coffin, by now a part-time professor of practical theology at Union Seminary, immediately issued another challenge just like van Dyke's:

> In the face of the action taken by the majority of the General Assembly, it is impossible for those of us who stand in the pulpits of the Presbyterian Church to remain silent, and I feel that I owe it to my own congregation and the Presbytery to state

---

144. Quoted in Nykamp, Presbyterian Power Struggle, p. 160.

plainly that if any action is taken which removes Dr. Fosdick from the pulpit of the First Church on account of his interpretation of the Christian Gospel, I cannot honestly be allowed to remain in the pulpit of the Madison Avenue Church, for I share fully his point of view.[145]

He said he agreed with Fosdick and rejected all five of the Doctrinal Deliverance's points. As for the error-free Bible, he said: "But its science, history, ethics and theology are no more inerrant than those of other ancient documents." The virgin birth is not essential; he, for one, had no idea how Jesus was conceived. (Let's see: if not by the Holy Spirit, then it might be. . . . I don't know; it's just too confusing.) Jesus was resurrected, but not with a material body. He did not die to "satisfy divine justice." No single interpretation suffices. Jesus opposed the literalism of the Pharisees. As for modernism, he said he did not know what that was. Here is what he did know: "If the latter point of view becomes authoritative in the Presbyterian Church there will be no room for the thinking men and women of our day and tomorrow." (As it has turned out, there is lots of room for thinking men and women: empty pews by the hundreds of thousands.)

Coffin announced his unwillingness to withdraw: ". . . I will not voluntarily withdraw from the Presbyterian ministry and leave the Church to those who appear to me to misconstrue its standards and repudiate its Protestant heritage. . . ."[146] In 1913, the year of van Dyke's challenge, Coffin had worked at the General Assembly to defer a direct confrontation, using what he called "parliamentary dodges" to circumvent "the enemy."[147] In 1924, he issued his own judicial challenge. No one would accept it. The risk was too high. Under Presbyterian law, anyone bringing a false charge against another Presbyterian would himself be publicly censured.[148]

---

145. "Assail Fosdick Ban as Assembly Ends," *New York Times* (May 25), p. 10.
146. Cited in Morgan Phelps Noyes, *Henry Sloane Coffin: The Man and His Ministry* (New York: Charles Scribner's Sons, 1964), p. 165. This book is copyrighted by Union Theological Seminary.
147. *Ibid.*, p. 109.
148. *The Book of Discipline*, II:14. *The Constitution of the Presbyterian Church in the United States of America* (Philadelphia: Presbyterian Board of Publication and Sabbath School Work, 1904), pp. 395–96.

After a decade of experience, Coffin became a crucial strategist of the liberal forces in the 1923-26 battle.[149] His reward was the presidency of Union (1926-45). His nephew and fellow Bonesman, William Sloane Coffin, later became pastor of the church that Rockefeller had built for Harry Emerson Fosdick, the Riverside Church. As the historians of the Rockefellers write: "It has been liberal not only in theology, but in every other sphere as well. . . ."[150] This was to be expected.

Machen Becomes a National Spokesman

In February, 1923, Macmillan published Machen's *Christianity and Liberalism*.[151] The book was an extension of his 1922 article, "Liberalism or Christianity?"[152] The publisher did not think it would sell well. Macmillan correctly identified the money-maker: Machen's *New Testament Greek for Beginners* (1922).[153] This book has gone through over 50 printings[154]—without the cost of a single revision. (Money in book publishing is rarely made with best-sellers; they are too rare. It is made with back-lists: books that have a steady market of a few thousand copies per year.) *Christianity and Liberalism* sold only 1,000 copies in 1923. In 1924, however, it sold 3,000 copies, largely as a result of the Fosdick controversy and Henry van Dyke's press release.[155]

Van Dyke Strikes Again

Beginning in October, 1923, Machen had been called to preach regularly at First Presbyterian Church in Princeton, a practice common in those days: allowing Princeton Seminary professors access to the pulpit. He gave several sermons on the division between liberals

---

149. Nykamp, Presbyterian Power Struggle, pp. 162-63.
150. Harr and Johnson, *Rockefeller Century*, p. 179.
151. D. G. Hart, *Defending the Faith: J. Gresham Machen and the Crisis of Conservative Protestantism in Modern America* (Baltimore, Maryland: Johns Hopkins University Press, 1994), p. 62.
152. *Princeton Theological Review*, 20 (Jan. 1922).
153. Hart, *Defending the Faith*, p. 66.
154. *Ibid.*, p. 142n.
155. *Ibid.*, p. 142.

and conservatives. On December 30, He preached a sermon against the practice of liberals of reinterpreting the creeds of the faith rather than denying them. He challenged their honesty—a theme that he had presented in *Christianity and Liberalism*.

The next day, van Dyke, who was a distant relative of Machen's—his "Uncle Henry"—now emeritus professor of English at Princeton University, sent a scathing message to the treasurer of the Session, and released it simultaneously to the press. He was leaving the presence of the congregation until Machen left. It was a masterful piece of rhetoric. If he could get away with this challenge to the authority of the office of teaching elder, the modernists were approaching institutional victory.

> Having had another Sabbath spoiled by the bitter, schismatic and unscriptural preaching of the stated supply of the First Presbyterian Church of Princeton (directly contrary to the spirit of the beautiful text) I desire to give up my pew in the church. The few Sabbaths that I am free from evangelical work to spend with my family are too precious to me to be wasted in listening to such a dismal, bilious travesty of the gospel. We want to hear about Christ, the Son of God and the Son of Man, not about Fundamentalists and Modernists, the only subject on which your stated supply seems to have anything to say, and what he says is untrue and malicious. Until he is done, count me out, and give up my pew in the church. We want to worship Christ, our Savior.[156]

What is mind-boggling is that Van Dyke gave a *New York Times* reporter the following explanation for his action: "I am not seeking for strife; I am seeking for peace."[157] I am aware of no more vitriolic rhetorical attack on any participant on any side during the Presbyterian conflict, 1869 to 1936. No one in the conservative camp could have gotten away with anything like this, surely no one in a leader-

---

156. Cited in Ned B. Stonehouse, *J. Gresham Machen: A Biographical Memoir* (Philadelphia: Westminster Theological Seminary, [1954] 1977), p. 357. The *New York Times* version varies slightly.

157. "Van Dyke Quits Pew at Anger at Sermon," *New York Times* (Jan. 4, 1924), p. 1.

ship position. His own followers would have turned against him. But nothing happened to van Dyke. No charges were filed against him. He did as he promised: he stayed away until Machen's term as stated supply ended in 1925, and Charles Erdman replaced him. Then van Dyke returned with fanfare in the liberal press.[158]

Van Dyke was a major figure in the Presbyterian Church. He was a graduate of both the College of New Jersey and Princeton Seminary. He had studied at the University of Berlin in 1878. He had begun his ministerial career as a pastor of the United Congregational Church in Newport, Rhode Island, 1879–1882. He had been pastor of New York City's Brick Church, 1882–1900, to which he was called back on two occasions for a year. He had been Briggs' most visible defender. A generation before Fosdick toured prestigious college campuses giving liberal sermons, van Dyke was preaching baccalaureate sermons at Harvard, Princeton, and Columbia.[159] He had been Moderator of the General Assembly in 1902, as his father had been in 1876. He had chaired the committee that wrote the Confessional Revision of 1903. He was world-famous as a best-selling author: poetry, short stories, travelogues, and biography.[160] He had served as Wilson's Ambassador to The Hague during World War I. He was a neighbor of John D. Rockefeller, Jr., on Mount Desert Island. He was a clearly member in good standing of the American Establishment. As a former preacher, a professor of English, and a best-selling author, he, more than any Presbyterian liberal, understood the uses of rhetoric in public. As his son wrote in 1935, "All through his days, Henry van Dyke was beset by reporters. He was almost invariably a dramatic figure."[161]

In 1926 the tide visibly swung against the conservatives, and once again, it had been Henry van Dyke who in late 1923 had issued the challenge, just as he had at his son's ordination in 1913. He had escaped Church sanctions then; he would escape them again. Although Fosdick received most of the attention, then and now, it was van Dyke, above all other participants in the Presbyterian conflict after

---

158. Stonehouse, *Machen*, p. 374.
159. Tertius van Dyke, *Henry van Dyke: A Biography* (New York: Harper & Bros., 1935), p. 184.
160. "Van Dyke, Henry," *Dictionary of American Religious Biography*, p. 483.
161. Van Dyke, *Van Dyke*, p. 262.

1893, who best understood the tactics of the conflict: judicial and rhetorical. He used inflammatory rhetoric in 1923 to test the limits of judicial resistance, just as his friend Briggs had done, 1876–1893. Unlike Briggs, van Dyke never encountered any resistance.[162]

He had said of Machen that "what he says is untrue and malicious." Thus began the rhetorical isolation of Machen and the conservatives. This was not merely a rhetorical tactic; it was also judicial. The Book of Discipline stipulated that contentious men are not to be trusted when they bring charges against their brethren:

> Great caution ought to be exercised in receiving accusations from any person who is known to indulge a malignant spirit toward the accused, or who is not of good character, or who is himself under censure or process, or who is personally interested in any respect in the conviction of the accused, or who is known to be litigious, rash, or highly impudent.[163]

It was important judicially for the modernists that their opponents be tarred and feathered well in advance with the rhetorical brush of malignancy, litigiousness, and/or bad character. There was no easy way for such accusations to be refuted. Presbyterian law specified no formal requirement for the accusers to prove their accusations in a Church court before such a reputation became judicially relevant. The accused merely had to be "known to indulge" in such spitefulness. Known by whom? By *everyone*, as in "everyone knows that." So, for the next decade, the modernists did what they could rhetorically to make their opponents' malignant spirit well known. To raise the issue of modernism was to risk becoming known as a malignant spirit. This would make it difficult for anyone so designated to gain a judg-

---

162. Woodrow Wilson once said of him that he was the only man he had ever known who could strut while sitting down. Macartney, *Making of a Minister*, p. 123. Van Dyke had helped deliver the only major loss in Wilson's career prior to his League of Nations fight: the 1906 battle over the proposed reorganization of Princeton's system of elitist dining clubs. Wilson had favored banning these clubs for lower-division students. This loss rankled Wilson; it led him to resign from Princeton in 1910 and run for Governor of New Jersey.

163. *Book of Discipline*, II:13. *Constitution*, p. 395.

ment against a modernist. Hart devotes an entire chapter in his biography of Machen to "A Question of Character," as well he should.[164]

Machen's Public Reputation in 1923

On December 30, 1923, Machen was not a major figure. Almost two decades earlier, he had survived a year of higher criticism's gauntlet in Germany: at Marburg and Göttingen. He had joined the Princeton faculty in 1906. He had been ordained in the Northern Church in 1914, a self-imposed delay of eight years. He had published in *Princeton Theological Review*, an in-house academic journal. He had only one academic book to his credit, *The Origin of Paul's Religion* (1921), a successful attempt on his part to match the scholarship of the German liberals he was trying to refute. The book was as scholarly—and almost as dry—as anything the Germans had published on the supposed Pauline revisions of Jesus' message. The book was not well known outside of academic theological circles, and, as is the case with most academic books, not very well known even within academic theological circles. As with every other known academic treatise written by an evangelical, it persuaded no liberal scholars to confess saving faith in Christ.[165] *Christianity and Liberalism* was in print in 1923 but not selling well. None of this had made him a national figure. Henry van Dyke's December 31 press release did. As Machen later commented, soon the newspaper reporters "were as thick as flies."[166]

From the day the secular press picked up the story of van Dyke's departure, the sales of *Christianity and Liberalism* took off. Van Dyke had catapulted Machen into the position of the premier academic spokesman, not only for conservative Presbyterianism, but for American fundamentalism in general. Prior to this, Machen had deferred to Macartney, who had been the driving force behind the petition against Fosdick in the May General Assembly. From this time forward, Machen's star waxed as Macartney's waned. When the final split came

---

164. Hart, *Defending the Faith*, ch. 6.
165. Academic reviewers were critical of the book's thesis, though not its technical scholarship. *Ibid.*, pp. 53–54.
166. Cited in *ibid.*, p. 66.

in the denomination in 1936, Macartney remained behind, his influence gone except as a symbol of surrender.

Christianity vs. Liberalism

In *Christianity and Liberalism*, Machen criticized the growing influence of liberal theology in America and, specifically, in the Presbyterian Church. His view of liberal theology was considerably different from any that had been publicly expressed previously. As he wrote: "The plain fact is that liberalism, whether it be true or false, is no mere 'heresy'—no mere divergence at isolated points from Christian teaching. On the contrary it proceeds from a totally different root, and it constitutes, in essentials, a unitary system of its own."[167]

The unmistakable implication, given this premise, is that liberal theologians, not being Christians in the creedal sense of the word, and not being Presbyterians in the Confessional sense, should have no part in the ordained ministry of the Presbyterian Church. While there may be a certain latitude in defining a "liberal theologian," if a man cannot accept wholeheartedly the ordination declaration of the Church, he should not hold a high position in it. This assertion was almost identical with Bryan's in 1922, although argued far more persuasively and logically.[168] Machen suggested voluntary departure as the honest action of the person involved. This, too, was Bryan's opinion. Machen's emphasis was on the doctrinal foundations of the faith, far more than the experiential: ". . . it is the very essence of 'conservatism' in the Church to regard doctrinal differences as no trifles but as matters of supreme import."[169] He made his position absolutely clear: ". . . it is highly undesirable that liberalism and Christianity should continue to be propagated within the bounds of the same organization. A separation between the two parties in the Church is the crying need of the hour."[170]

Machen was arguing that liberalism is not heresy; it is apostasy. This moved the debate from a matter of belief to a matter of judicial

---

167. Machen, *Christianity and Liberalism*, p. 172.
168. *Ibid.*, p. 164.
169. *Ibid.*, p. 161.
170. *Ibid.*, p. 160.

action. There was no way for Machen logically to refrain from calling for a series of heresy trials. Yet he did refrain, and so did his allies. This undermined the logic of his argument, as his critics repeatedly said in public, and as van Dyke had said in 1913. They understood: *no sanctions—no heresy*, let alone apostasy.

Machen's book made it plain that the issue dividing the churches was the issue of *supernaturalism vs. naturalism*. Modernism is a rival religion. The time has come, Machen said, to settle the issue within the churches. The time has come to fight: ". . . the really important things are the things about which men will fight."[171] For Machen, the issue was truth. If the Christians do not defeat modernism, modernism will defeat the Christians. "In the intellectual battle of the present day there can be no 'peace without victory'; one side or the other must win."[172]

His thesis demanded negative sanctions: either the Christians should expel the modernists or the modernists should expel the Christians. The issue was sanctions. But he refused to invoke sanctions. He invoked morality. An honest liberal would withdraw, he insisted.[173] But liberals are dishonest, he said, for they seek a unity that cannot be sustained.[174] There must be peace in the Church, he said, but a peace born of separation. "Nothing engenders strife so much as a forced unity, within the same organization, of those who disagree fundamentally in aim."[175] But the liberals refused to withdraw.

Then why shouldn't the conservatives withdraw? "Certainly it may come to that. If the liberal party really obtains full control of the councils of the Church, then no evangelical Christian can continue to support the Church's work." He should have said *ought to* rather than *can*. Most conservative Presbyterians did continue to support the Church's work long after Machen departed. But he understood that one aspect of the fight was financial: positive sanctions. "If a man believes that salvation from sin comes only through the atoning death of Jesus, then he cannot honestly support by his gifts and by his pres-

---

171. *Ibid.*, p. 2.
172. *Ibid.*, p. 6.
173. *Ibid.*, p. 165.
174. *Ibid.*, p. 162.
175. *Ibid.*, p. 167.

ence a propaganda which is intended to produce an exactly opposite impression. To do so would mean the most terrible bloodguiltiness which it is possible to conceive. If the liberal party, therefore, really obtains control of the Church, evangelical Christians must be prepared to withdraw no matter what it costs."[176] Conclusion: stop giving; cut off the flow of funds.

He revealed here the tremendous institutional weakness of the conservatives. *Liberals had no concept of bloodguilt.* If they could lie successfully and not get thrown out, they would inherit "the resources of the evangelical churches," as Machen put it.[177] To do this, all they had to do was use "equivocal language"[178]—a horrible thought for creedalist Machen, but a trifle to the liberals. Then, if the conservatives remained in the Church after it went liberal, they would be psychologically impotent: suffering from bloodguilt. The liberals would have nothing to fear from such guilt-ridden opponents.

What would mark bloodguiltiness? Remaining in a liberal Church. How did Machen define a Church's liberal status? Creedally, but not judicially. Here was his Waterloo: ". . . the creedal basis still stands firm in the constitutions of evangelical churches."[179] This was *word without deed*: a written Confession without judicial sanctions, profession without submission. Machen's definition surrendered his case. He would re-define the Church in 1936 to include sanctions, but by then it was too late: he was under the sanctions.

All that the liberals had to do to remove any threat to themselves and their plans would be to gain control over the courts. They would not have to alter the language of the Confession. They had been working toward the capture of the courts for over two decades. If successful, they could disarm the conservatives. The conservative hardliners might choose to stay in the Church, but then they would be playing an escalated crossed-fingers game: pretending that the Church was still judicially orthodox just because it was Confessionally unchanged. They would suffer a psychological defeat by playing this

---

176. *Ibid.*, p. 166.
177. *Ibid.*, p. 165.
178. *Ibid.*
179. *Ibid.*, p. 166.

game: bloodguiltiness. Meanwhile, the conservative soft-liners would not care. They had not cared very much from 1901 to 1922. The liberals had everything to gain through duplicity except, as Machen put it, "higher ground."[180]

Machen's condemnation fell on deaf ears; his opponents were evolutionists and situation ethicists, not Calvinists. Higher ground for them meant bureaucratic survival and ultimate inheritance: the survival of the fittest. But, as Machen was to learn, beginning on December 31, they were able to create the camouflage of moral high ground. That had been true ever since van Dyke's 1893 manifesto, *A Plea for Peace and Work*. It would continue to be true. They would vilify the conservatives for defending the Church, just as W. H. Griffith Thomas had written regarding Chinese missions in 1921. For a liberal, the conservatives' defense of the Doctrinal Deliverance of 1910 was inherently offensive: a serious breach of etiquette, an affront to the gospel. Such a defense deserved no rhetorical mercy, and received none.

Machen said that the conservatives must not withdraw too soon. "The reason is found in the trust which the churches hold. That trust includes trust funds of the most definite kind. And contrary to what seems to be the prevailing opinion, we venture to regard a trust as a sacred thing."[181] Theologically, this use of the language of sacredness was an error. The trust was sacred, but not the trust funds. The sacredness of the trust was derived from the sacraments. *The protection of the sacraments, not the protection of trust funds, was the sacred duty of the evangelicals.* The liberals wanted those funds. The funds were worth defending, but Machen used rhetorical language that deflected men's attention from the sacred judicial issue: the defense of the sacraments by those Church officers who had been given an oath-bound charge to defend them. This was the sacred aspect of the Presbyterian conflict that none of the leaders on any side ever acknowledged, 1869–1936.

Calvin had defined the true Church in terms of orthodox preaching and the sacraments, with the implication that discipline was a

---

180. *Ibid.*, p. 165.
181. *Ibid.*, p. 166.

third aspect of the definition, but Presbyterian conservatives had reduced this formula to only one: orthodox preaching, i.e., orthodoxy without sanctions.

The Absence of Negative Sanctions in 1923

There was a glaring practical problem in Machen's analysis: the Presbyterian Church's ecclesiastical unity had not been judicially enforced for over two decades. No one had compelled anyone to leave the Church by means of a heresy trial. The 1923 General Assembly was still months away when Machen's book appeared. When Machen wrote the original essay in 1921, Fosdick's famous sermon was a year away. No Presbyterian conservative had publicly called for the implementation of negative judicial sanctions since 1900. For that matter, neither did Machen. Nowhere in the book did he issue the only challenge that would have mattered covenantally: "Get out now while you still can or we will remove you one by one through a series of heresy trials that will not end until all of you are either gone from the midst of this Church or are publicly silent."

It was not just a matter of calling for the removal of apostate pastors. That would have been necessary but not sufficient to save the Presbyterian Church. *The judicial issue was excommunication, not mere removal from office.* If liberalism is a rival religion, then it is not enough to identify ordained men who have been unfaithful to their ordination vows to uphold the Westminster Confession and the catechisms. No Church can afford knowingly to have on its membership rolls those who profess a rival religion. This is especially true of a Church in which all communicant members vote, i.e., impose sanctions. Machen could not make a judicially plausible case for liberalism as a rival religion unless he called forthrightly, in principle, for the threat of a heresy trial to be imposed over every member who professed the liberal creed.

Machen steadfastly refused to call for heresy trials for anyone, let alone laymen. Instead, he challenged his opponents to leave. This was not simply naive on his part; it was evidence of his startling ignorance of his opponents' covenantal theology. He was facing believers in a rival religion: *the power religion*. It was not simply that they had rejected the judicial authority of the Bible and the Confession. It was that they were calling for the establishment of a comprehensive rival covenant. Theological liberalism, like political liberalism (right wing Whiggism and left wing Progressivism), calls for a covenantal transfer of sovereignty to autonomous man. This proposed transfer applies to all five areas: sovereignty to autonomous man, authority to autonomous man, law to autonomous man, sanctions to autonomous man, and the Church's inheritance to themselves.

Protecting the Sacraments

In his writings, Machen did not make clear the comprehensive claims of his opponents' religion. He described it as a rival religion, but he did not call for the excommunication of those who held it. He called only for them to resign from ordained office, not from the Church. As was true with all of his Confessional predecessors, Machen never dealt with this fundamental judicial issue: the judicial protection of the sacraments.

He excoriated the modern Church, not just Presbyterians: ". . . the Church of today has been unfaithful to her Lord by admitting great companies of non-Christian persons, not only into her membership, but into her teaching positions."[182] He reminded his readers on the next page that "liberalism is not Christianity."[183] This meant that non-Christians were participating in the Lord's Supper. What should be done about this? Machen was forthright: nothing. "We are not now speaking of the membership of the Church, but of its ministry, and we are not speaking of the man who is troubled by grave doubts and wonders whether with his doubts he can honestly continue his membership in the Church. For great hosts of such troubled souls the Church offers bountifully its fellowship and its aid; it would be a crime to cast them out."[184]

The Church, he said, is a place of fellowship and aid for troubled souls. *With this statement, Machen gave away the case for ecclesiastical orthodoxy.* The history of lawful worship teaches that it would be a violation of Church standards *not* to deny such people access to the Lord's Table. Paul was clear: anyone taking the Lord's Supper with

---

182. *Ibid.*, p. 159.
183. *Ibid.*, p. 160.
184. *Ibid.*, p. 163.

such doubts is risking sickness and even death at God's hands (I Cor. 11:29–30). The integrity of the Church is to be preserved by removing false religion from its midst. This includes apostate laymen.

To say that Machen surrendered the case for ecclesiastical orthodoxy is to make a very serious accusation against him. Nevertheless, in terms of what Calvin taught regarding the sacraments and the Church's responsibility to screen access to them, there can be no doubt that Machen had abandoned Calvin on this issue, and not only Calvin; he had abandoned Paul. Revoking lawful access to the sacraments is the judicial issue of formal excommunication, which is the fundamental issue of Church sanctions.

Calvin was adamant on the need to excommunicate people in order to protect the Lord's Table: "And here also we must preserve the order of the Lord's Supper, that it may not be profaned by being administered indiscriminately. For it is very true that he to whom its distribution has been committed, if he knowingly and willingly admits an unworthy person whom he could rightfully turn away, is as guilty of sacrilege as if he had cast the Lord's body to dogs. On this account, Chrysostom gravely inveighs against priests who, fearing the power of great men, dare exclude no one."[185] The context of his remarks was ethics: openly sinful living rather than false doctrine. The judicial principle is the same in either case: closing communion to those who have denied the faith, in word or deed. Not to do so is to commit sacrilege, Calvin warned.

The non-Christian is at risk when he takes the Lord's Supper, said Calvin, for "it is turned into a deadly poison for all those whose faith it does not nourish and strengthen. . . ."[186] Men "profane and pollute it by so receiving it. . . . Hence, by this unworthy eating they bring condemnation upon themselves."[187] Those who partake illegally come under the threat of God's historical sanctions. "Therefore, they are their own accusers; they bear witness against themselves and seal their

---

185. John Calvin, *Institutes of the Christian Religion* IV: XII:5, trans. Ford Lewis Battles, 2 vols., *Library of Christian Classics*, vol. XXI (Philadelphia: Westminster Press, [1559] 1960), I:1231–32.
186. *Ibid.*, IV:XVII:40, I:1417.
187. *Ibid.*

own condemnation."[188] Are those who are known to hold a false religion then to be permitted access to the Lord's Supper knowingly by the officers of the Church? Sadly, Machen said *yes*, for the thesis of *Christianity and Liberalism* is that liberalism is not Christian faith, yet liberal laymen are not to be excluded from the Lord's Table.

What Is a Presbyterian Layman?

Machen's problem was the problem of all Presbyterian government: *the Church's standards do not specify what a member in good standing must believe*. Answer 172 of the Larger Catechism states that a person who has doubts regarding "his being in Christ" still has lawful access to the Lord's Supper "that he may be further strengthened." Only the "ignorant and scandalous" are to be barred (A. 173). This specifically places greater weight on intellectual perception ("ignorance") than it does on personal assurance of salvation. Charles Hodge cited these passages in his essay rejecting Coit's claim that New School Presbyterian laymen had been ejected in 1837 because they refused to accept the Confession. Not so, said Hodge; no such obligation exists for laymen. "Nothing, therefore, can be plainer than that our Church requires nothing more than credible evidence of Christian character as the condition of Christian communion. Of that evidence the Church officers are to judge."[189] This is *membership by good works*. This is humanism. This view of Church membership eventually transferred the Church to humanists.

Communing members are voting members in Presbyterianism. The system depends judicially on the judgment of elders in screening ministerial candidates before laymen are allowed to vote to hire them. Because voting members do not have to affirm faith in the Confession, this places heavy emphasis on the top-down administrative screening of candidates. The bottom-up screening process by Presbyterian laymen has always been understood as being without judicially enforceable theological standards. Elders screen local church members;

---

188. *Ibid.*, I:1417–18.
189. Hodge, *Princeton Review* (1840); reprinted in Hodge, *Discussions on Church Polity* (New York: Charles Scribner's Sons, 1878), p. 220. The footnote incorrectly cites Question 147.

teaching elders also screen ministerial candidates; presbyteries screen ruling elders retroactively. Only after the presbytery identifies lawful candidates for the ministry can members vote to hire one. In short, because there is no formal judicial content to a Presbyterian member's oath, a system of government was constructed that places almost total official control in the hands of elders, which in fact has meant ministers and the seminary professors who have screened them.

Machen's Dilemma

This structure of authority had a crucial implication for the conservatives' strategy, 1923–25. Any attempt by Machen and his allies to appeal to laymen over the heads of ministers and seminary faculties was doomed in advance. The system of government had been constructed from the beginning to screen laymen out of the sanctioning process above the local congregation because they are under no oath-bound stipulations beyond those administered by their local elders. The Westminster Confession does not directly govern Presbyterian laymen; therefore, Presbyterian law does not allow them to govern above the local congregation. Their only meaningful power above the local congregation is economic: *the power of the purse*. It was this power that the Church's bureaucrats sought to remove or reduce whenever possible. Meanwhile, Machen and his allies built much of their strategy on an appeal to laymen.

Machen was trapped by Presbyterian law. He could not publicly confront the crucial covenantal issue: *written, judicially enforceable confessional standards for voting Church members as well as for elders*. He could not suggest a judicial distinction between communicant members and voting members. He could not suggest that voting members be required to profess their oath-bound allegiance to the Constitution of the Church before they are given the vote over elders. He could not suggest that voting members be placed under the stipulations of the Confession for the sake of the purity of the Church. To have suggested this would have meant breaking with Presbyterianism, in which no legal distinction exists between voting and non-voting members. In order to protect the highest offices of the Church from sanctions imposed by people who have taken no oath to uphold the Confession, Presbyterianism established a two-tiered eldership. Only ministers (teaching elders) were entitled to preach the word (WCF

XXVIII:2), administer the sacraments (WCF XXVII:4), and ordain new ministers.[190]

Machen was correct in his assertion that liberalism was a violation of ministerial confessional standards. It was a rival religion. But he refused to make this obvious and judicially necessary extension of his argument: voting members must also swear an oath to the Confession. That is, those who impose judicial sanctions (i.e., vote as God's ordained agents) through the authority of the Westminster Confession must first formally place themselves under the stipulations of that Confession. If a man is not by oath under God's covenant law, he cannot lawfully rule in terms of God's covenant law.

To have argued that voting members should be under the same stipulations as the officers would have exposed him as someone who had broken with Presbyterian law: an extremist. He was about to become the Church's chief extremist even without making this application of his argument regarding liberalism. So, he toned down his case against the curse of liberalism—not just rhetorically but judicially. He refused to blame laymen for being liberals, i.e., for having adopted anti-Christianity as he defined it. This argument implicitly denied the biblical basis of Church authority: from the layman to the officers—bottom-up responsibility. It denied that God makes His Church covenant by means of the members' oath-bound confessions, who in turn delegate to officers the formal authority to represent them. *It made the personal confession of the officers the judicial basis of the Church covenant, as if the Church derived its authority from God by way of the officers.* Yet the members could fire any or all of the officers at any time: the sovereignty of the purse. The officers could hardly excommunicate all of the members.

Machen steadfastly refused to invoke a theology that defended the Lord's Table from God's covenantal enemies. He adopted the position of nearly open communion in the name of historic Presbyterianism, for this was in fact historic Presbyterianism. Any local church member, Machen insisted, can gain lawful access to the communion table

---

190. *Manual for Church Officers and Members*, 4th ed. (n.p.: Office of the General Assembly by the Publication Department of the Board of Christian Education, 1930), p. 256.

irrespective of his doubts regarding the truth of Christianity. The member could be a liberal and still take communion. He could deny the Apostles' Creed and still take communion unless his local officers decided otherwise—and in the New York Presbytery, they probably wouldn't. There was no denominational way to prevent this. *There was no Presbyterian standard of personal confession for Church membership.* Machen was trapped by the original compromises and oversights of the Westminster Assembly. The Puritan Independents still exercised their ecclesiastical rule over him through the Westminster Confession.[191] Machen was left without ecclesiastical sanctions at the most fundamental level: the oath that establishes the Church covenant. Machen was forced to reduce the operational definition of the Church to a "fellowship," an "aid" society. With respect to local church membership, *Machen accepted the number-one tenet of liberalism's official doctrine of the Church*: a fellowship without judicial sanctions.

What Machen described was, judicially speaking, what the liberal Church historian Winthrop S. Hudson described in 1953 in his discussion of the loss of both the authority and the distinctiveness of the Protestant Church under liberalism: "The church could and should be a center of fellowship which would give visible expression to the fundamental unity of mankind. The problem was to get the people into the church so that the oneness of humanity—the brotherhood of man—might be made evident to the community at large. Discipline, of course, could be relaxed. An indiscriminate welcome into the fellowship of the church could be extended to all members of the community. The errant and the wayward need not be excluded from the fold." That meant a relaxation of Church discipline. "But the relaxation of discipline in itself would scarcely draw people into the church's fellowship."[192] The Church needed something to differentiate its mission from that of the world. When the older evangelical vision departed, something had to replace it.[193] Nothing did. That was Hudson's lament.

---

191. See Appendix C, below: section on "The Divines Gather, 1643–48."
192. Winthrop Hudson, *The Great Tradition of the American Churches* (New York: Harper & Bros., 1953), p. 214.
193. *Ibid.*, p. 215.

In the Northern Presbyterian Church of Machen's day, there was no longer any reliable guardian of the oath. But there would soon be a guardian of the bureaucracy.

Sanctions and Creed

In 1925, in a series of lectures in Grove City, Pennsylvania, Machen returned to this theme of Church membership as distinguished from ministerial ordination. In his lecture, "Faith and the Gospel," he tightened what had been a very loose definition of Church membership in *Christianity and Liberalism*. He identified the Church as "the visible representative in the world of the body of Christ; and its members are not merely seekers after God, but those who have already found; . . ."[194] But he reaffirmed his earlier statement that he was not much concerned about admitting to membership "men who are struggling with doubts and difficulties about the gospel," but rather those "who are perfectly satisfied with another gospel; . . ."[195]

This did not solve his dilemma. How can a Church member be lawfully removed from membership when he believes in "another gospel"? There must be confessional standards governing each member. Machen acknowledged that there must be "a limit beyond which exclusion must certainly be practiced; . . ."[196] But "such requirements ought clearly to be recognized as provisional; . . . That is one reason why we must refuse to answer, in any definite and formal way, the question as to the minimum doctrinal requirements that are necessary in order that a man may be a Christian."[197]

With this statement, Machen publicly affirmed what had always been true of Scottish and English Presbyterianism. He was no revolutionary; he was a conservative. He was just more open about the reality of Presbyterian Church membership. From the Council of Nicea onward, there had been a requirement for membership in most

---

194. Machen, *What Is Faith?* (Grand Rapids, Michigan: Eerdmans, [1925] 1974), p. 158.
195. *Ibid.*, pp. 158–59.
196. *Ibid.*, p. 159.
197. *Ibid.*

churches: the public affirmation of a creed. But Presbyterianism has never required this as a formal test of membership. Neither does Presbyterianism's mandated liturgy—there is none—involve a corporate affirmation of any creed. Such affirmations are allowed, but they are not required. Except for an implied oath of obedience at baptism, the person seeking membership in a Presbyterian Church has never had to meet any denominational test of his or her orthodoxy. A local congregation's session is in charge of formulating whatever standards it chooses. This means, *judicially* speaking, that Presbyterian Church membership has always been congregational-independent. The higher courts of the denomination have nothing to say about it. The Confession and the catechisms are silent on the matter of the formal content of the member's confession of faith. For a layman, there is no Presbyterian confession of faith. *There is only a Congregationalist confession of faith.* The judicial sanctions are exclusively local: top-down. But the economic sanctions are also local: bottom-up. The layman controls the purse strings. He who pays the piper calls the tune, especially if he also has the vote.

The ecclesiastical implications of this fact have rarely been recognized by conservative Presbyterians. The liberals have always understood these implications far better than the conservatives have. Because a candidate for Presbyterian Church membership is under no denominationally enforced formal creedal requirement, the judicial authority over him is the session of the local congregation. The teaching elder and ruling elders make the decision regarding the credibility and acceptability of the candidate's statement of faith. The Confession says nothing regarding minimal requirements of belief for either officers or members. Since 1729, the American Presbyterian Church has used the Confession as a screening device for its officers, but that has always been a separate judicial matter. The Confession does not mandate this. *The Confession is silent with respect to its own judicial authority.*

Once ordained, a liberal minister can work with the local ruling elders to water down his congregation's required confession for membership. As far as the Church's standards require, all the new member has to do is to promise to obey Christ. Furthermore, this requirement is given in the Larger Catechism, not the Confession. "Baptism is not to be administered to any that are out of the visible church, and so strangers from the covenant of promise, till they profess their faith in Christ, and obedience to him. . . ." (Larger Catechism, Answer 166). Problem: an Arian or a Unitarian can readily profess faith in Christ unless such faith is carefully defined, as the historical creeds have done. *There is no theological or judicial content in this mandatory confession.* A promise to obey means nothing apart from written laws and institutional sanctions, neither of which are mentioned in the Confession or catechisms. It should also be understood that the Larger Catechism has rarely (I believe never) been appealed to in American Presbyterian judicial cases; it has always been a judicially neglected document in American Presbyterianism. So, from the perspective of local church membership, Presbyterianism is not only congregational-independent; it is also Arian-Unitarian. *The lowest common denominator is the highest enforceable standard.* Anyone who doubts this should consider what happened to the Presbyterian Church, U.S.A, from 1936 to the revision of the Confession in 1967. (Those who doubt me after doing this should then consider what has happened since 1967.)

Because Machen saw his theological battle as exclusively clerical-Confessional—a war over Confessional standards for the eldership, and really only the teaching eldership—he neglected the issue of the historic membership creeds. But he had little choice; three centuries of Presbyterian law were behind his opponents: *creedless membership.* Creeds in other ecclesiastical traditions have served as screening devices for their members in the same way that longer confessional statements serve as screening devices for their ordained officers. Creeds and confessions are equally oath-bound statements of faith. The creed-bound oath provides access to the sacraments; the Confession-bound oath provides access to the offices that administer the sacraments. Without a creed to provide judicial content for the self-maledictory oath of Church membership, there can be no judicially binding predictable negative Church sanctions. *Without oath-bound negative Church sanctions over the laity, judicial authority passes to the lowest-common denominator confession of the members.* When this confession is theologically empty, the lowest confessional limit is the one enunciated by the capitalist villain in Frank Norris' Progressive-era novel, *The Octopus*: "All the traffic will bear!" Lower, ever lower went the limit.

Representation and Subordination

A promise to obey Christ raises the question of judicial representation: Who speaks in Christ's name? Is it the local session, the presbytery, the synod, or the General Assembly? This raises the issue of centralized authority. In the twentieth century, political centralization has been increasingly acceptable to laymen in their capacity as citizens. In their capacity as local church members, they could hardly resist the same centralization process in the churches.

The Presbyterian layman is oath-bound to obey Christ. But in every hierarchical Church, ordained officers are presumed to speak for Christ unless there is evidence to the contrary. The Presbyterian layman will generally obey his ecclesiastical superiors; very few are theologically equipped to resist, and none can successfully resist on his own authority. Yet Machen and his supporters appealed to conservative laymen as if laymen possessed operational authority in a denomination that allowed theological Unitarians access to both the pulpit and the pew. It was clear that conservative laymen would be outvoted. A Unitarian confession of faith—or worse—would become the creedal membership standard as time went on because the modernists had allies outside the camp: in education, the media, and culture. American public schools after 1830 had been increasingly based on a Unitarian confession. New members would bring these confessions into the Church when they joined. It was up to the local session to prevent these implicit Unitarians from gaining access to the congregational vote until they abandoned this outlook. But would the sessions do this?

Machen understood the common denominator problem. He warned against the quest to find "some greatest common denominator which shall unite men in different Christian bodies; for such a greatest common denominator is often found to be very small indeed."[198] But he offered no solution to this, **the central judicial dilemma of the Presbyterian conflict.** *Voting members in Presbyterian churches in the long run control access to the pulpit and also the flow of funds. Eventually, the confession of the remaining members will govern the confession of the officers.* If the members refuse to pull the officers up to their

---

198. Machen, *What Is Faith?*, p. 159.

level, then the officers will pull the members' confession down to theirs. In such cases, the steady exodus of the more confessionally orthodox members will continue. But there is no escape from the covenantal structure of sovereignty: institutional sovereignty in history flows from the bottom up, not from the top down, no matter what systems men construct in a futile attempt to reverse this process (Lev. 4).[199] Church officers are dual representatives of God and the members. Their confession of faith cannot permanently deviate significantly in theological and judicial content from the corporate confession of those who elect them.

Humanist political liberals have long understand this principle, which is why they have universally mandated compulsory or near-compulsory government-operated school systems and government-regulated private schools. They seek to shape the opinions of the children of their judicial masters. They offer "free" tuition to gain the cooperation of the now over-taxed parents. They invoke the politics of guilt and pity regarding the needs of poor parents in order to justify the taxation of all parents. The key to understanding the public schools is not the needs of the poor; rather, it is the need of elected representatives and their appointed, self-certified, tenured educational bureaucrats to control the opinions of future voters. This was the heart of the attack on Bryan, 1922–25. These "outside allies" of the theological liberals were (and still are) in control of the public schools. This has made the work of liberals inside the Church much easier.

Reading the Old Testament, Machen should have understood: God did not bring sanctions against Israel because her leaders were corrupt while the people were righteous. God imposed negative corporate sanctions because the corrupt majority had demanded rule by corrupt leaders (Isa. 1). The silent majority in Israel was not in opposition to its sinful rulers; it was in full agreement. So it would prove to be in the Presbyterian Church. This was Machen's primary strategic problem. He never publicly recognized this; he did not warn his followers. He did the opposite, blaming the crossed-fingers confessions of the ministers and dismissing as judicially far less relevant the liberal confessions of voting members. So, every time the liberals raised the

---

199. Gary North, *Leviticus: An Economic Commentary* (Tyler, Texas: Institute for Christian Economics, 1994), ch. 4.

stakes in the conflict, more of Machen's previous supporters removed themselves from his leadership. Year by year after 1924, battle by battle, they defected.

The issue was oath-invoked sanctions. Sanctions are inescapable concepts. It is not a question of "sanctions vs. no sanctions." It is a question of which sanctions enforced on which people by which representatives. Access to the sacraments (which are a means of God's sanctions) is covenantally dependent on a formal oath, either personally prior to baptism or representatively for infants through a parent who is a Church member. The issue of the sacraments is judicially tied to the unified issue of oaths and sanctions. None of this is visible in Machen's writings because none of this is mandated in Presbyterianism. Machen learned in 1936 who controlled the sanctions. But he suspected the answer in 1923: ". . . the forces opposed to the gospel are now almost in control."[200] Nevertheless, he remained a postmillennial optimist: "And another Reformation in God's good time will come."[201]

A Matter of Rhetoric

Machen, true to the Princetonian tradition of attacking bad ideas in public rather than those who hold them, refused to name names in *Christianity and Liberalism*. On page 128, he did quote one sentence from Fosdick's "Shall the Fundamentalists Win?" but that was the extent of his challenge. Had he done more, he might have been faced with bringing an accusation of heresy (actually, apostasy) against his opponents. This the Princetonians had not been willing to do even in Briggs' day. The Princetonians gave indications of being men who feared to be drawn into heresy trials and counter-trials. The Princetonians were thereby forced to wage a defensive war after 1869. In 1929, the Old School's remaining members lost control over the Seminary.[202]

---

200. Machen, *Christianity and Liberalism*, p. 179.
201. *Ibid.*, p. 178.
202. See Chapter 10, below.

Despite Machen's self-restraint, the liberals' reviews of *Christianity and Liberalism* focused on Machen's supposedly vituperative tone—a fact noted by Hart in his doctoral dissertation but not in his book.[203] Yet Henry van Dyke's press release had been a personal attack on an ordained minister; the liberals did not publicly criticize him. This was to be Machen's fate from this time forward: no matter what slander was made against Machen in public, Machen was always regarded as the initiator, the rhetorical bully.[204] While Briggs had been able to identify almost any conservative doctrine as theologically deviant and get away with it, 1876-1890, Machen could say almost nothing theologically orthodox and get away with it after 1923.

It was far too late for a call to offensive judicial action. The conservatives did not have the votes, as they would soon learn. They had not had the votes since 1913, when van Dyke successfully called their bluff by challenging them to launch a heresy trial against him. In 1921, Warfield in his last days had already supplied Machen with the Church's autopsy: rotten wood. Machen in 1936 delivered the Church's funeral oration. But he kept Warfield's autopsy to himself from 1921 until his death in 1937. Only his mother had shared in this knowledge.

Machen's mild rhetoric did him no good whatsoever in the rhetoric wars. Nolan R. Best, editor of the liberal *Continent* from 1910 until late 1924, when he resigned because the Board suppressed one of his editorials on the Fosick case,[205] accused Machen in 1923 of "so

---

203. Hart, "Doctor Fundamentalis": An Intellectual Biography of J. Gresham Machen, 1881-1937 (Ph.D. dissertation, Johns Hopkins University, 1988), p. 161. Cf. Hart, *Defending the Faith*, pp. 79-80.

204. This mythology is continued in Nykamp's dissertation. He sees the conservatives as using what was regarded as unacceptable negative rhetoric in the dispute, 1922-26. As a doctoral dissertation in the Speech Department, it reflects the author's acceptance of the liberal mythology regarding that era. He cites the modernists' continual cries of "foul!" when in fact the liberals' abusive rhetoric at key points in the battle matched or exceeded the conservatives' rhetoric. They and their inclusivist associates called the conservatives names, and the most effective name was "un-Christian." For them, there could not be a non-Christian inside any church, but "un-Christians" abounded.

205. *The Christian Work* (Dec. 13, 1924), p. 686. In this issue, Best debated Machen on the question: "Is the Teaching of Dr. Harry Emerson Fosdick Op-

totally lacking in the fundamental element of fidelity to facts" that the book was "simply an offense against the ninth commandment."[206] That is, he called Machen a liar. Yet it was Machen who gained the reputation of being a loose canon rhetorically. That, too, was part of the modernists' successful rhetorical attack on Machen.[207] They dismissed as unacceptable rhetoric what was in fact a theologically precise critique that had hit its targets. It was not his rhetoric that outraged his opponents; it was his theology—the reverse of Briggs' experience, whose rhetoric had ignited the firestorm of protest. Machen wanted to debate the theological issues.[208] His opponents wanted institutional peace without debate. As time went on, so did his allies.

Machen's Views on Church and State

It is important to understand that Machen never regarded himself as a fundamentalist, although he became the leading intellectual spokesman for American fundamentalism over the next decade and a half. He was an Old School Calvinist. He was a postmillennialist, although not a vociferous one. He was, however, a vociferous critic of premillennialism[209]—an old Princeton Seminary tradition prior to 1900.[210] Most fundamentalists were (and still are) premillennialists. He was a believer in God's absolute predestination; few fundamentalists were (or are).

---

posed to the Christian Religion?" Machen took the affirmative.

206. Best, "Professor Machen's Christianity and Liberalism," *The Continent* (Dec. 12, 1923), p. 629; cited in Hart, *Defending the Faith*, pp. 79–80.

207. As someone who has specialized in confrontational rhetoric for an entire career, let me say that Machen was a pussycat. Fosdick was the master of deliberately misleading confrontational rhetoric in the 1920's, not Machen. But Fosdick had a thin skin. He was incensed when Machen nailed him in public for what he had written. See Miller, *Fosdick*, p. 142. President Harry Truman's famous line is applicable: "If you can't stand the heat, get out of the kitchen."

208. Machen and Best debated the following issue in *Christian Work* (Dec. 13, 1924): "Is the Teaching of Dr. Harry Emerson Fosdick Opposed to the Christian Religion?"

209. Machen, *Christianity and Liberalism*, pp. 48–49.

210. Paul C. Kemeny, "Princeton and the Premillennialists: The Roots of the *mariage de conveniance*," *American Presbyterians*, 71 (Spring 1993).

He was also a nineteenth-century Whig liberal in his political and economic views, something not understood by some of those Calvinist Presbyterians who have claimed him as their spiritual father.[211] Like Robert Dabney, the Southern Presbyterian theologian and social philosopher, Machen was a believer in limited civil government, non-intervention in foreign policy (one view he shared with Bryan), and private charities rather than tax-financed institutions of coercive wealth redistribution. He opposed Prohibition as an unwarranted incursion into people's freedom of action by the civil government.[212] He testified before a joint Congressional committee in 1926 against the proposed U.S. Department of Education.[213] He opposed the proposed amendment to the Constitution, the child labor amendment of 1935.[214] He opposed military conscription.[215] He opposed the New Deal's Social Security legislation and its anti-gold standard monetary policy, which, he said, undermined contracts.[216] He opposed Bible reading or the teaching of morality in public schools, since he recognized that the teachers were predominantly atheistic, deistic, or liberal in their theological opinions.[217] Presumably, he would have opposed prayer in public school classrooms. This was a departure from the

---

211. The best example of this historical "blackout" concerning Machen's economic views is the book by Machen's former colleague, Church historian Paul Woolley, *The Significance of J. Gresham Machen Today* (Nutley, New Jersey: Presbyterian & Reformed, 1977). Woolley, who taught at Westminster Seminary for four decades, died in 1984. He was a political liberal in the New Deal tradition. I reviewed his book unfavorably in the *Journal of Christian Reconstruction*, 4 (Winter 1977-78).

212. Stonehouse, *Machen*, p. 387.

213. *Proposed Department of Education*, Congress of the United States, Senate Committee on Education and Labor, House Committee on Education (Feb. 25, 1926), pp. 95-108; reprinted in Machen, *Education, Christianity, and the State*, edited by John W. Robbins (Jefferson, Maryland: Trinity Foundation, 1987), ch. 7. Cf. Machen, "Shall We Have a Federal Department of Education?" *The Woman Patriot* (Feb. 15, 1926); reprinted in Machen, *Education*, ch. 6.

214. Machen, "A Debate About the Child Labor Amendment," *The Banner* (Jan. 4, 1935), pp. 15-16.

215. *Ibid.*, p. 15.

216. "Machen to Franklin Delano Roosevelt," *New York Herald Tribune* (Oct. 2, 1935); cited in Hart, *Defending the Faith*, p. 143.

217. Machen, "The Necessity of the Christian School" (1933); reprinted in Machen, *Education*, ch. 5.

opinion held by A. A. Hodge in the 1880's.[218] Hodge could still claim that the United States was a Christian nation, and that its public schools should reflect this fact. By Machen's day, such a claim was less believable. But he did not publicly reject tax-financed public education.[219] His Scottish common sense rationalism did allow for some degree of common ground in education, which alone might legitimize tax-funded schools.

Machen and Bryan

Compare his views with Bryan's. Bryan was a Populist, a believer in Big Government to help the Little People. At the 1923 General Assembly, he had challenged a modernist critic who had dismissed him as being wrong . . . again. Bryan knew this was an attack on his political career. He responded by an appeal to his political record: "Did you do more than I did to put across women's suffrage? Did you do more than I did to put across the election of Senators by direct vote of the people? Did you do more than I did to levy an income tax so that those who had the wealth would have to pay for it? There has not been a reform for twenty-five years that I did not support and I am now engaged in the biggest reform of my life. I am trying to save the Christian Church from those who are trying to destroy her faith."[220] He had lobbied successfully to get Wilson's Federal Reserve Act passed by Congress.[221] He went so far as to call it "the most remarkable currency measure we ever made."[222] He later concluded that this noble institution "has been captured by Wall Street," but he called only for its restructuring into an agency for the public interest, not for its abolition.[223] Predictably, he was a strong supporter of Prohibition; many pages of Koenig's biography of Bryan are devoted to this subject. At the 1923 General Assembly, he introduced a resolu-

---

218. A. A. Hodge, "Religion in the Public Schools," *New Princeton Review*, 3 (1887); reprinted in *The Journal of Christian Reconstruction*, 4 (Summer 1977).
219. Machen, *Christianity and Liberalism*, p. 14.
220. Koenig, *Bryan*, p. 614. See *New York Times* (May 23, 1923), p. 4.
221. *Ibid.*, pp. 526-27.
222. *Ibid.*, p. 527.
223. *Ibid.*, p. 616.

tion to require ministers and church teachers in every Presbyterian school, college, or seminary to subscribe to a total abstinence pledge.[224] It passed. This was his one victory, the *New York Times* reported on page 1 (May 23). Given the fact that Federal law made the sale and consumption of alcohol illegal, this was not much of a victory.

Conclusion

With the publication of Bryan's book, *In His Image*, followed by the *New York Times*' series of attacks on Bryan in February and March of 1922, followed by Bryan's response in late February, followed by Fosdick's response to Bryan in the *Times* and his challenge to the fundamentalists in "Shall the Fundamentalists Win?" followed by Macartney's and Machen's responses to Fosdick and the liberals, Presbyterianism's rhetorical floodgates had been opened after 22 years of visible peace and after 29 years of reduced rhetoric: the 1893 departure of Briggs and the new strategy of peace and work announced by van Dyke. The rhetoric of confrontation after 1922 escalated on both sides, inside and outside the denomination.

Fosdick's sermon had broken the peace of the Church, and not just the Presbyterians. The *New York Times* ran this story on page 4 of the same May 23 issue: "Baptists Face New Fight Over Creed. Want Fosdick Disciplined." A fundamentalist group at the national convention of the Northern Baptists was pressing the assembly to adopt a five-point creed comparable to the 1910 Doctrinal Deliverance, though somewhat more detailed. The previous year, the assembly had resisted, but the Fosdick case had made another attempt look worthwhile. The move failed. As it turned out in 1924, the Presbyterians, with the most rigorous confession in Protestantism, were only marginally better able to discipline Fosdick than the creedless Baptists were: no negative sanctions.

On May 25, the *Times* ran this story "Heaton Heresy Case Dropped by Bishop." This referred to a Ft. Worth pastor in the Episcopal Church who had publicly opposed the virgin birth as an essen-

---

224. *Ibid.*, p. 613.

tial doctrine. His bishop said the man was in the wrong, but he refused to prosecute because higher Church officials agreed with Rev. Heaton: no negative sanctions.

The camp of the Presbyterian conservatives was divided. There were fundamentalists, a few of whom were active social reformers, but most of whom were not, except on the alcohol issue. There were New School Calvinists and heirs of the Cumberland Church. They were no longer an identifiable voting bloc. Their seminaries hired higher critics. There were Old School Calvinists who looked to Princeton Seminary as their representative—academic leadership rather than organizational. What united these people confessionally? The five-point Doctrinal Deliverance of 1910.

The camp of the modernists was not divided on their most fundamental institutional goal, namely, the necessity of capturing and maintaining institutional power. They were united against negative sanctions imposed in the name of any creedal statement. Any attempt by the conservatives to "clean house" on modernists by means of creedal statements of any kind was going to receive well-organized opposition from this camp.

The liberals had a strategic institutional task to accomplish in 1922. It was the same task that had faced them from 1869 on: to move the politically correct civil concept of religious toleration into the Church, i.e., to make theological toleration ecclesiastically correct. Machen and the exclusivists challenged the legitimacy of this transfer, but only with respect to the ordained ministry of preaching. What had been regarded as sacrosanct in American politics and had served as plank number one of the American civil religion—*religious confessional neutrality*—became the battering ram of the liberals inside the churches: to break down the Westminster Confession's middle wall of partition between Progressive political liberalism outside the Church and Progressive theological liberalism inside. What every American Protestant except members of the tiny Calvinist denomination known as the Covenanters (the Reformed Presbyterian Church of North America) had long ago accepted by 1922—neutral civil government and civil religion—had captured the mainline churches. What had been the rallying cry of liberal Whigs in eighteenth-century politics was now being proclaimed by theological liberals as the new orthodoxy for Church politics.

Machen, as a nineteenth-century political liberal—a classic Presbyterian Whig—rejected this institutional transfer of Whig political principles. The Church is not the State, he insisted, nor is it bound by the same concept of religious toleration. He made this argument the foundation of his judicial distinction between Church and State: "The state is an involuntary institution; a man is forced to be a member of it whether he will or no. It is therefore an interference with liberty for the state to prescribe any one type of opinion or any one type of education for its citizens."[225] In contrast are churches: voluntary associations.[226] The Church is confessional. It must not tolerate those who declare a rival confession to exercise judicial authority.[227] Machen understood his task: to persuade his readers of the judicial and covenantal distinction between the confessional standards that govern the Church (a voluntary organization) and those governing the State (a geographically compulsory organization). The future of the Presbyterian Church, U.S.A., would be determined by how many votes he could rally in terms of this judicial distinction. The votes constituted sanctions. The crucial issue was sanctions.

---

225. Machen, *Christianity and Liberalism*, p. 168.
226. *Ibid.*
227. *Ibid.*, pp. 168–69.

THE AUBURN *AFFIRMATION* AND ITS AFTERMATH

> *Another attack has been made by the modernist "Affirmation" of one hundred and fifty ministers, for which by an active propaganda many more signatures have now been secured. The Affirmation does indeed employ Christian terminology; and, deceived by this terminology, there are no doubt Christian men among the signers. But the document itself is radically hostile to the Christian faith. It is directed (1) against the creedal character of the Presbyterian Church and (2) against the entire factual basis of Christianity.*
>
> J. Gresham Machen (1924)[1]

Machen's rhetoric against the majority signers of this document was indirect. By admitting that some of the *signers* were Christians, though deceived by propaganda, he was saying implicitly that the *designers* were not Christians and were deceivers. The document was "radically hostile to the Christian faith." This would be Machen's argument for the rest of his life. The *Affirmation* became the most important single piece of evidence in the conservatives' case that liberalism had infiltrated the Church.

This document, released to the public on December 26, 1923, was officially entitled *An Affirmation designed to safeguard the unity and liberty of the Presbyterian Church in the United States of America*, but it became popularly known as the Auburn *Affirmation*, since it had

---

1. Machen, "The Parting of the Ways—Part II," *The Presbyterian* (April 24, 1924), p. 7.

been published by a temporary group located in Auburn, New York.[2] It was 1,800 words long. Originally, it bore the names of 149 ministers; by the time of the General Assembly in 1924, this had reached a total of 1,274 ministers.[3] This was about 14 percent of the ministers in the denomination.[4] That was a large percentage, for few men in any organization are normally willing to take sides publicly in an ideological confrontation.

In its judicial aspect, the *Affirmation* challenged the authority of the General Assembly to make judicially binding decrees. It asserted that according to the Adopting Act of 1729, by which the American Presbyterian Church was created, no candidate for the Presbyterian ministry could be held to confess more than that the Westminster Confession contains "the system of doctrine taught in the Holy Scripture." To single out any particular sections of the Confession as "essentials" of the faith would not be legal without the confirmation of at least two-thirds of the Presbyteries. In short, a man could swear allegiance to all of the Confession, yet not be responsible for believing even one of the specifics. The *Affirmation* was a defense of crossed fingers. Its conclusion: the action of the 1923 Assembly which required every candidate for the ministry to answer in the affirmative to the five points was unconstitutional, and not in the spirit of Christian freedom (Article III). This argument, if upheld by the Church's courts, would have the effect of vindicating the New York Presbytery's decision in 1923 to ordain two candidates for the ministry, Henry P. Van Dusen[5] and Cedric Lehman. But the *Affirmation* was intended to be far more than a judicial document, and so it became.

---

2. Charles E. Quirk, "Origins of the Auburn Affirmation," *Journal of Presbyterian History*, 53 (Summer 1975). This was based on his comprehensive 550-page Ph.D. dissertation, whose title rivals its length: The "Auburn" *Affirmation*: A Critical Narrative of the Document Designed to Safeguard the Unity and Liberty of the Presbyterian Church in the United States of America in 1924 (University of Iowa, 1967).

3. Quirk, "Auburn" *Affirmation*, p. iii.

4. Herman C. Weber, *Presbyterian Statistics Through One Hundred Years, 1826-1926* (n.p.: The General Council, Presbyterian Church in the U.S.A., 1927), p. 89.

5. The name of Henry Van Dusen was to surface again and again in the years after the Presbyterian conflict, especially after 1945, when he became the

The *Affirmation* would become the touchstone for the Presbyterian modernists and the conservatives from 1924 to 1936. It became the representative statement of theological toleration: rejected by Machen and his followers; honored by the modernists. Machen and his allies repeatedly used the list of ministers who signed the *Affirmation* to judge the character of the Church's boards and commissions. But they never brought a formal accusation against anyone who had signed it. This proved fatal to their cause. In his challenge to the presbytery's court that put Machen on trial in 1935, Machen's lawyer made a series of futile attempts to introduce the *Affirmation* as evidence of bias on the part of several of his accusers. The court announced that the statute of limitations had run out on the *Affirmation*'s signers, and there could be no further complaints against this document or those who had signed it. Then the court found Machen guilty. So, once again, it was a question of sanctions. Who would impose those sanctions? Would it be the signers or the critics?

Preparation for Battle

The year 1923 was the year of preparation. The two sides recognized that the years of comparative peace and quiet, 1901–1921, were over. The rhetoric on both sides in 1922 had challenged men of good will and good judgment in the peace-seeking middle to choose sides. Now representatives of both sides began the task of mobilizing their troops.

---

president of Union Seminary. He became one of the prominent proponents of a creedless universal Christianity. His book, *World Christianity* (1947), presents an attack on the early creeds and councils of the Christian Church as schism-creating. "Lastly and most important, all the councils were singularly ineffective in their primary aim—to further Christian concord. Far from proving successful devices even for preserving such Christian unity as then existed, each of the so-called Seven Great Ecumenical Councils of the early centuries except one actually resulted in one or more major schisms." Henry P. Van Dusen, *World Christianity: Yesterday, Today, Tomorrow* (New York: Friendship Press, 1947), p. 76. Contrary to Van Dusen, the primary purpose of the councils and creeds was not to create concord *in general*; it was to create concord *by exclusion of error*. They sought *unity through the authority to screen prospective Church members and to excommunicate*.

The Conservatives

Clarence E. Macartney was the most prominent of the conservatives. He organized three large meetings late in the year. The first was held on October 30 in Broadway Presbyterian Church in New York City. The pastor was Walter Buchanan. Only conservatives were invited to attend. Macartney and Machen spoke. Macartney called the attendees to a fight. "They who love the gospel dare not sin by silence. . . . The eyes of the whole world are fixed on the Presbyterian Church."[6] This was indeed the case, at least in the United States. The media recognized that something of historic importance was going on inside the denomination.

Two more meetings were held in December. The first was held on December 10 in Macartney's Arch Street Church in Philadelphia. All 15 living ex-Moderators in the Church were invited. Of those who replied, one was conservative but hostile to exclusivism. Two were conservative but not enthusiastic about the meeting, one was addressing the meeting (Maitland Alexander), one was cautiously favorable, and three replied without favoring exclusivism. Four did not reply. This was not an auspicious beginning. Henry van Dyke (1902) was understandably not enthusiastic. His letter was rhetorically clever, however, praising the meeting if it would not (as he knew it would) "be divisive and exclusive, a beginning of theological word-battles and heresy-trials. . . ."[7] He released his letter to the press, just as he would release another letter at the end of the month that was critical of Machen's occupancy of the pulpit in First Presbyterian Church in Princeton. About 1,000 people attended the meeting.[8]

Rev. Buchanan called Presbyterians to "rally to our Standards." He immediately widened the call: "But the attack is broader than our own beloved church. It is an attack on all those who stand for the

---

6. "The Flag Goes Up in New York Presbytery," *The Presbyterian* (Nov. 8, 1923); cited in Delwyn G. Nykamp, A Presbyterian Power Struggle: A Critical History of Communication Strategies in the Struggle for Control of the Presbyterian Church, U.S.A., 1922-1926 (Ph.D. dissertation, Northwestern University, 1974), p. 193.

7. *Ibid.*, p. 195.

8. *Ibid.*, p. 197.

infallibility of the Holy Scriptures. It is an onslaught by modernism, skepticism, all essentially rationalist. . . . It is a time when all Trinitarians should rally to a common standard, not only Presbyterians, but Methodists, Baptists, Congregationalists, Disciples of Christ. . . ."[9] This was an acknowledgment of the existence of conservative theological ecumenism, though without a call for covenantal union. The conflict that had broken out within Presbyterianism was representative of a larger conflict.

Buchanan then asked the 31-year-old question that by 1923 had become purely rhetorical—a means of pointing out the dishonesty of the enemy: "How, I ask, can honest men stay in the ministry of the Presbyterian Church when they no longer believe her doctrines? Why do they not get out?"[10] There were three possible answers: (1) they were not honest; (2) they had a different standard of honesty; (3) nobody with any authority had forced them to leave. The third answer, institutionally speaking, was the only one that mattered. It was a question of sanctions. Like claim-jumpers in the Old West, liberals were not about to abandon the mother lode until the sheriff forced them to leave.

Maitland Alexander's speech was perhaps the most revealing of all the speeches ever given by a conservative throughout the entire conflict, both for what it said and what it avoided. He pointed out that in academic institutions, teachers are expected to defend the principles of the schools. Unpatriotic men are dismissed. The implication was clear though unstated: Why not in the Presbyterian Church? He returned to the familiar theme: Why don't they leave? "Social radicals can join the Rand School, and Germans can go to Germany. Why cannot those who are out of sympathy with the doctrines of the Reformed faith go where they will be welcomed?" But then he did what almost no other critic ever did: he said why not. He raised the crucial issue: the acceptance by the modernists of the positive benefits of the Presbyterian ministry. These men were illegal intruders bent on mischief,

---

9. "An Address Delivered at the Mass Meeting in the Interest of Historic Presbyterianism and Evangelism," *The Presbyterian* (Jan. 13, 1924), p. 7; *ibid.*, pp. 198–99.

10. *Ibid.*, p. 199.

comparable to guests in a home who criticize the owner and refuse to leave.

> No one would think of objecting to any criticism of our homes, if it is made from without. . . . But when a man enters our home, becomes a member of our family, eats our food, is furnished with clothing, receives money from our family funds, holds his social position by reason of residence there, bears our name, and then attacks our principles, criticises our food, but eats it, instills disloyalty into our children, uses his residence with us to obtain grounds for attacking us, ridiculing our most precious family traditions, what do we do? We ask him to quickly and peacefully withdraw.

No one ever put it better: logically and rhetorically. But he failed to answer the obvious next question: What if the invader refuses to withdraw? The head of a family would then have to impose negative sanctions. First, he would command that the invader leave. Second, he would call the police and have him ejected. But ever since McGiffert's departure in 1900, the critics had not been forcibly ejected. Here was the overwhelming problem facing the conservatives: *they did not have the votes*. They also did not have the will. So, the critics continued to sit at the table. Unless they were finally ejected, they would share in the inheritance. More than this: they would disinherit the lawful heirs.

Alexander then made a prediction that was unsupported bluster: "People are talking about a split in the Presbyterian Church. There will be no split. They are talking about the exodus of orthodox Presbyterians. There will be no exodus of *orthodox* Presbyterians. Our offensive and defensive programme is just beginning, and when the laity of the church is sufficiently aroused, and takes pains to ascertain the theological position of those who are called to our churches, there may be an exodus of those who, finding that they cannot lead the church into [the] modernistic position, will quietly withdraw with good wishes and thanks of those whom they leave behind."[11]

---

11. *Ibid.*, p. 204.

But there would a split in 1936. The orthodox Presbyterians did join a small exodus when their representative was de-frocked. They would call their tiny denomination the Presbyterian Church of America[12] until the PCUSA took them into civil court, and the court forced them to change the name on the basis of its closeness to the mother Church's name—a kind of trademark infringement. Then they changed the name to the Orthodox Presbyterian Church—exactly what Alexander had said would never happen. Nykamp is correct regarding Alexander's speech: "The plan was reasonable only in an exclusivist dream world but not in the world that they were struggling with."[13]

There was no "offensive programme." There was only a defensive program covered with offensive rhetoric (in both senses). The modernists were offended. The evangelical peace-seekers were offended. But there was no offense. An offense had to employ the negative sanction of heresy trials, just as Henry van Dyke had said in 1913. The conservatives did not have the votes to conduct heresy trials. *In a defensive operation, rhetoric is not an effective substitute for sanctions.*

Alexander forthrightly appealed to the laity. In Presbyterianism, the laity in local congregations had so little power and so little self-confidence that they were in no position to veto the decisions of the Church's highest courts. The combined authority of the seminary degree and presbyterial ordination was far too great. Presbyterian laymen were the ecclesiastical equivalent of the Italian Army.

Alexander knew the conservatives were losing: ". . . we are every year increasing the number of those who will vote to do away with our Presbyterian doctrines when we ordain young men from our seminaries as ministers who cannot honestly take their ordination vow. . . . We tolerate among the faculties of our theological seminaries men who have abandoned the Reformed doctrines of the confession. We give money to support this kind of teaching."[14] Here it was at long last: an admission that the conservative middle was financing the

---

12. The seceding Presbyterians in the South in 1973 adopted the name Presbyterian Church in America (not *of*).
13. *Ibid.*
14. *Ibid.*, p. 205.

modernists. *The issue was sanctions*: positive (money) and negative (those who vote against Presbyterian doctrines).

Then he came to the heart of the matter: the sanction of the vote. "Orthodoxy is indicted not so much by a verbal *profession of it* as by a *vote for it*."[15] At long last, somebody had raised the crucial issue: sanctions. This indictment became conservatism's grave marker because the conservatives could not get the votes. Nevertheless, whenever a man in the conservative camp defected—and virtually all of the leaders of the 1920's eventually did, including Macartney—he valiantly proclaimed his continuing adherence to his verbal proclamation of a rigorously written Confession: a Confession that no longer had any negative sanctions attached to it by the courts. Not one of them would admit the truth: *no sanctions–no oath*.

Alexander saw the other problem: the success of the modernists in infiltrating the boards and commissions of the denomination. "The pressure of the constituency of orthodox Presbyterianism should be exerted to make the machinery of the church in its personnel conform absolutely to our confessional requirements. The mere re-nomination of members of the boards *by themselves* to succeed *themselves*, should not be a guarantee of re-election."[16] *Should* and *should not*: by 1923, these were the suggestions of a minority without available sanctions. The words had become rhetorical rather than judicial. These boards had always been self-sustaining, i.e., self-sanctioning, and outside the normal hierarchy of Church sanctions.

Alexander went on, pointing out that the modernists used verbal duplicity, affirming the words of the Confession but not believing them. "Our most difficult task is to strip this system of 'new definitions' of its orthodox disguise. . . ."[17] In modern American Constitutional theory, this is called "original intent"—the search for the original intent of the Constitution's Framers. Liberals pay no attention to this theory in politics, either.[18]

---

15. *Ibid.*, p. 206.
16. *Ibid.*
17. *Ibid.*, p. 207.
18. The main defender of this theory, Robert Bork, did not receive confirmation by the U.S. Senate when President Reagan nominated him to the Supreme

This was not a program. It offered no plan to get from the reality of Church politics to the ideal of Old School ecclesiology. Nykamp is correct: "Moreover, not once did he identify the Church's constitutional judicial means that were designed to handle allegations of doctrinal deficiencies. . . . The flaw was fatal to Presbyterian exclusivism."[19] *The issue was sanctions.*

Another meeting was held on December 14 in New York. Ten thousand people were invited; 1,200 attended. Alexander delivered the same speech. There is no question that in a denomination of two million members, the conservatives could rally about a thousand of them to attend a rally in a large city. What they did not do was organize a campaign to do anything judicial. Their efforts would be limited to vote-getting at the annual General Assemblies. That tactic worked only once: in 1924.

The Modernists

Beginning in the summer of 1923, the modernists began to organize. They held no rallies. They issued no pamphlets until December. They avoided rhetoric in public.

Two weeks after the close of the 1923 General Assembly, Rev. Murray Shipley Howland of the Lafayette Avenue Presbyterian Church of Buffalo, New York, sent out a circular letter. He was a Union Seminary graduate in the fateful year of 1900—the year McGiffert left the Church but not the Seminary.[20] In the debate at the 1923 General Assembly over Bryan's proposal to cut funding of Presbyterian colleges that taught evolution, Howland was the first man to challenge him in debate.[21] Five upstate New York ministers signed the letter. They protested the Philadelphia Presbytery's overture against Fosdick. They opposed the five-point Declaration. This Declaration,

---

Court. Bork later wrote a Foreword to the 1990 reprint of Herbert Schlossberg's 1983 book, *Idols for Destruction.*

19. Nykamp, Presbyterian Power Struggle, pp. 208–209.

20. Two centuries after the formation of the denomination, the New York vs. Philadelphia confrontation was still going on. Union Seminary's "old boy network" made the liberals' defensive efforts far less expensive to organize. The liberals avoided the negative publicity of controversial public meetings.

21. *New York Times* (May 23, 1923), p. 1.

they said, would keep well-educated young men out of the Presbyterian ministry. They invited 68 ministers to attend a meeting in Syracuse, New York. Thirty-three ministers came to the June 19 meeting. So did elder Nolan Best, editor of *The Continent*, a liberal outlet. In good Presbyterian fashion, the group established four study committees: law and history, doctrinal statement, propaganda, and finance. They reported back the next day. The meeting decided to raise $7,500—a considerable war chest in 1923—to fund additional meetings ($2,500) and the publication of a final pamphlet ($5,000). They established a permanent conference committee to continue the work.[22]

Nine men worked on this committee: five Auburn Seminary graduates and four Union Seminary graduates.[23] Eight were pastors, and they served large congregations averaging 1,100 members. The main figure in the committee was Robert Hastings Nichols.[24] Most of these congregations made large donations to the boards of the Church.[25] The goal of $7,500 was never met; the committee raised $3,557. Of this, most came from ministers, and $2,500 from ministers in the New York Presbytery.[26]

The conference committee worked quietly for six months gathering materials to write the *Affirmation*. Nichols did much of the work, although two decades later he wrote that Henry Sloane Coffin was the main contributor.[27] A 1945 letter from one of his colleagues reminded Nichols that Nichols had done as much as Coffin, which Nichols admitted in his letter of reply.[28] The word "Affirmation" was suggested by George Black Stewart, president of Auburn Seminary. Coffin, Nichols later claimed, had suggested the remainder of the title.[29]

---

22. Quirk, "Auburn" *Affirmation*, pp. 87-90.
23. *Ibid.*, p. 91.
24. Cf. Nichols, *Fundamentalism in the Presbyterian Church* (Auburn, New York: Jacobs Press, 1925).
25. Quirk, "Auburn" *Affirmation*, p. 92.
26. *Ibid.*, p. 94.
27. Nichols, "Leader of American Presbyterianism," in *This Ministry*, edited by Reinhold Niebuhr (New York: Charles Scribner's Sons, 1945), p. 49; cited in *ibid.*, p. 101.
28. *Ibid.*, pp. 101-102.
29. *Ibid.*, p. 105.

Strategies

The Presbyterian conservatives were led this time by Old School ministers and Machen. Better put, they were *represented* by Old School spokesmen. The term "led" implies the presence of a plan governing a group, with coordination of that group. There was no plan. There was barely a group, if by "group" we mean an organized body. Will Rogers' famous quip in the 1930's is far more applicable to Presbyterian conservatives than it was to its designated target: "I belong to no organized political party. I am a Democrat." The conservative spokesmen had great visibility, for the Old School had always relied on the printed word to deliver the message. But the Old School had never learned the intricacies and disciplines of mobilization. Their leaders had always been scholars first and pastors second—a very distant second. Warfield was the archetype: he rarely attended a General Assembly and, after the advent of J. Ross Stevenson as president of Princeton Seminary, never attended a faculty meeting.[30] This was not just because his wife was an invalid in need of care; it was a mind-set.

The modernists, in contrast, were skilled masters of the Church's bureaucratic machinery. They had their spokesmen: van Dyke, Coffin, and now Fosdick, but they were not dependent on them in the way that conservatives were dependent on their spokesmen. The modernists clearly understood institutional sanctions; the conservatives may have vaguely understood, but by 1923 were barely able to organize to administer them. All that the modernists had to do to win was to delay the application of the negative sanction of de-frocking. With only one Old School seminary remaining, the modernists had time on their side, as Alexander had implied: "We are every year increasing the number of those who will vote to do away with our Presbyterian doctrines when we ordain young men from our seminaries as ministers who cannot honestly take their ordination vow." The modernists did not need an offense in 1923. They needed only a successful defense. But they needed a theological statement to counter the escalating rhetoric of the Old School. The *Affirmation* provided it.

---

30. Ned B. Stonehouse, *J. Gresham Machen: A Biographical Memoir* (Philadelphia: Westminster Theological Seminary, [1954] 1977), p. 219.

The Five Points of Modernism

The *Affirmation* was a modernist document. This was the assertion of Machen and the conservative exclusivists from the beginning, a theme to which Machen returned again and again. Nevertheless, the document was signed by some conservatives and was promoted as a representative Church document. The wording of this document was carefully structured to achieve the goal of bringing conservatives under the authority of the modernists, but the theology of the *Affirmation* matched the five points of modernism.

1. A Non-Sovereign God

The *Affirmation* could not openly reject the doctrine of the sovereignty of God, which is stated clearly in the Confession. The *Affirmation* was presented as a judicial document. Had it openly denied God's sovereignty, the organizers could not have persuaded conservative ministers to sign it. But it could undermine this Calvinist doctrine indirectly by challenging the doctrine of the virgin birth, just as Fosdick had done in "Shall the Fundamentalists Win?" How could this be accomplished? By lumping the five points of the Doctrinal Deliverance of 1910 and 1923, which included the virgin birth, under the rubric, "theories."

> Some of us regard the particular theories contained in the deliverance of the General Assembly of 1923 as satisfactory explanations of these facts and doctrines. But we are united in believing that these are not the only theories allowed by the Scriptures and our standards as explanations of these facts and doctrines of our religion, and that all who hold to these facts and doctrines, whatever theories they may employ to explain them, are worthy of all confidence and fellowship.

2. A Non-Authoritative Bible

The *Affirmation* also declared that "There is no assertion in the Scriptures that their writers were kept 'from error.' The Confession of Faith does not make this assertion...."

> With respect to the interpretation of the Scriptures the position of our church has been that common to Protestants. "The Supreme Judge," says the Confession of Faith, "by whom all controversies of religion are to be determined, and all decrees of

councils, opinions of ancient writers, doctrines of men, and private spirits, are to be examined, and in whose sentence we are to rest, can be no other but the Holy Spirit speaking in the Scripture" (Conf. I. x). Accordingly our church has held that the supreme guide in the interpretation of the Scriptures is not, as it is with Roman Catholics, ecclesiastical authority, but the Spirit of God, speaking to the Christian believer. Thus our church lays it upon its ministers and others to read and teach the Scriptures as the Spirit of God through His manifold ministries instructs them, and to receive all truth which from time to time He causes to break forth from the Scriptures.

So, the Bible has no "ecclesiastical authority." Only "the Spirit of God, speaking to the Christian believer" has authority. This removes propositional truth from the status of binding authority. It therefore removes the Bible from a system of Church sanctions, which must be based on adjudicable standards. What does the Confession say about the infallibility of the Bible? Nothing.

> There is no assertion in the Scriptures that their writers were kept "from error." The Confession of Faith does not make this assertion; and it is significant that this assertion is not to be found in the Apostles' Creed or the Nicene Creed or in any of the great Reformation confessions. The doctrine of inerrancy, intended to enhance the authority of the Scriptures, in fact impairs their Supreme authority for faith and life, and weakens the testimony of the church to the power of God unto salvation through Jesus Christ. We hold that the General Assembly of 1923, in asserting that "the Holy Spirit did so inspire, guide and move the writers of Holy Scripture as to keep them from error," spoke without warrant of the Scriptures or of the Confession of Faith. We hold rather to the words of the Confession of Faith, that the Scriptures "are given by inspiration of God, to be the rule of faith and life" (Conf. I, ii).

3. Impermanent Standards

If the Doctrinal Deliverance was simply a presentation of a particular group of "theories," then there are no binding theological standards in the Church. The *Affirmation* went beyond a critique of the General Assembly's authority. It denied the legitimacy of any attempt to elevate any summary doctrinal standards to binding judicial status in ordination—and if not in ordination, then surely in heresy trials, although this was not stated explicitly.

> The General Assembly of 1923 expressed the opinion concerning five doctrinal statements that each one "is an essential doctrine of the Word of God and our standards." On the constitutional grounds which we have before described, we are opposed to any attempt to elevate these five doctrinal statements, or any of them, to the position of tests for ordination or for good standing in our church.

4. No Negative Sanctions

The *Affirmation* rejected the General Assembly's right to bring sanctions against individuals: no binding authority, i.e., no oath-bound judicial sanctions.

> While it is constitutional for any General Assembly "to hear testimony against error in doctrine," (Form of Govt. XII, v), yet such testimony is without binding authority, since the constitution of our church provides that its doctrine shall be declared only by concurrent action of the General Assembly and the presbyteries. Thus the church guards the statement of its doctrine against hasty or ill-considered action by either General Assemblies or presbyteries. From this provision of our constitution, it is evident that neither in one General Assembly nor in many, without concurrent action of the presbyteries, is there authority to declare what the Presbyterian Church in the United States of America believes and teaches; and that the assumption that any General Assembly has authoritatively declared what the church believes and teaches is groundless. A declaration by a General Assembly that any doctrine is "an essential doctrine" attempts to amend the constitution of the church in an unconstitutional manner.

5. Ecumenism

The issue within the Church, the liberals insisted, was ecumenism: an open door to pastors of many persuasions, Fosdick in particular. But this open-door policy implied that all denominations should have open doors. This points to a day when all interdenominational walls will be knocked down, since the universal fellowship of Christians will breach all restraining walls. The *Affirmation* called for a "united testimony" and "fellowship with all."

> Finally, we deplore the evidences of division in our beloved church, in the face of a world so desperately in need of a united testimony to the gospel of Christ. We earnestly desire fellowship with all who like us are disciples of Jesus Christ. We hope that those to whom this Affirmation comes will believe that it is not the declaration of a theological party, but rather a sincere appeal, based on the Scriptures and our standards, for the preservation of the unity and freedom of our church, for which most earnestly we plead and pray.

The *Affirmation*'s position had at least three implications. First, a candidate for the eldership can affirm his belief in any of the five points, but lawfully hold so many mental reservations and "explanations" to himself as to make his affirmation virtually meaningless. Second, it indirectly supported Fosdick's position, since his qualifications concerning the virgin birth and Scriptural inerrancy would, under the *Affirmation*'s new dispensation, be tolerated. Finally, it implied that a more inclusive Church was possible, to such an extent that almost anyone who was willing to use orthodox language while maintaining unlimited personal reservations could be ordained.

Theological or Judicial?

The ire of the conservatives was guaranteed when such points of faith as the virgin birth and Christ's working of miracles were somehow only theories, for which other theories could just as easily be substituted. But the *Affirmation*, in good Presbyterian fashion, was presented in terms of Presbyterian law. This creates a problem for the historian: explaining the importance of the document. As Quirk noted in his dissertation, the constitutional issue was deemed relatively unimportant, although it takes up most of the space. Its theological statements drew the most fire from the critics.[31] The historians have trouble understanding this only because they are liberals. They are blind to the presence of theology whenever it is dressed in the swad-

---

31. Quirk, "Auburn" *Affirmation*, p. v.

dling clothes of liberalism. They perceive this theology as "common sense"—what I like to call common-sense New York rationalism, in contrast to Princeton's common-sense Scottish rationalism. The Auburn *Affirmation*, like Fosdick's famous sermon, was an intensely theological document. Its theology was modernism: all five points.

The Key Covenantal Issue: *Authority*

If the *Affirmation* had merely challenged the 1923 General Assembly decision on the grounds of strict legality, the document would never have attained the fame and importance that it ultimately received. The conservatives never would have spent so much energy in attacking the *Affirmation* and the philosophy that lay behind it. From the point of view of the liberals, on the other hand, it would not have been nearly so effective a piece of propaganda if it had been phrased in strictly legal terms. The legal points would buy them time; if they gained time, the theological points would buy them victory.

Machen realized the danger to the orthodox position that the *Affirmation*'s denial of scriptural infallibility presented, and he did not let the Affirmation pass unnoticed. In a letter cited on page 4 of the *New York Times* on January 10, 1924, he restated his "two religions in one Church" thesis, applying it to the "Affirmationists," calling the document "a deplorable attempt to obscure the issue. The plain fact is that two mutually exclusive religions are being preached from the pulpits of the Presbyterian Church." But on this point—his central theme—Machen was the equivalent of a general without visible troops. When the 1924 General Assembly met the following May, no action was taken on the issue of the theology of the *Affirmation*, and no minority voice was heard, although Bryan himself was a member of the Committee on Bills and Overtures that reviewed the document.[32] This called into question the theological authority of the Doctrinal Deliverances of 1910, 1916, and 1923.

---

32. Lefferts A. Loetscher, *The Broadening Church: a study of theological issues in the Presbyterian church since 1869* (Philadelphia: University of Pennsylvania Press, 1954). p. 120.

Judicial Authority

The judicial issue raised by the *Affirmation* was specific: a denial of the authority of the General Assembly to establish judicially binding pronouncements. There is no question judicially: for amendments to the Confession of Faith to be valid, two-thirds of the presbyteries had to vote for them, followed by a majority vote in the next General Assembly.[33] This was never attempted with the Doctrinal Deliverances of 1910, 1916, and 1923. The *Digest*, the compendium of Presbyterian law, declared in 1923 that "it does not appear that the Constitution ever designed that the General Assembly should take up abstract cases and decide on them, especially when the object appears to bring these decisions to bear on particular individuals not judicially before the Assembly."[34] Edwin Rian, in his book-long apology for the orthodox wing, was forced to admit in 1940 that the "weight of the law seems to be on the side of the 'Auburn Affirmation.' . . . It is altogether likely that the General Assembly does not have the power to bind the Presbyteries to 'any essential and necessary doctrines' unless the Presbyteries have so voted."[35] Machen, he pointed out, did not support the constitutionality of the five points just because the General Assembly voted to accept them, but because they were taught in the Bible itself.[36] This, of course, was the heart of Machen's dilemma: the courts were empowered to enforce the Bible, but the Bible had to be interpreted through the details of the Confession. Meanwhile, conservative members on the Church's courts in Machen's day had long since moved away from the Calvinism of the Confession to, at best, the five points of the 1910 Deliverance.

One reason why the judicial issue may have been ignored in 1924 is that the General Assembly, in its capacity as the supreme court, had

---

33. *The Form of Government*, XXIV:II. *The Constitution of the Presbyterian Church in the United States of America* (Philadelphia: Presbyterian Board of Publication and Sabbath School Work, 1904), pp. 389–90.

34. *Digest of the Acts and Deliverances of the General Assembly of the Presbyterian Church In the United States of America*, 2 vols. (Philadelphia: Office of the General Assembly, 1923), I:271.

35. Edwin H. Rian, *The Presbyterian Conflict* (Grand Rapids: Eerdmans, 1940), p. 43.

36. *Ibid.*, p. 42.

not heard a heresy case since 1894: the de-frocking of Henry Preserved Smith. While the General Assembly had repeatedly affirmed the five-point Deliverance of 1910, no presbytery had conducted a heresy trial in terms of its five points. Judicially, the five points seemed moot. They had served more as a rallying cry than binding terms of judicial action. They had always been rhetoric.

The conservatives did not challenge the *Affirmation*'s legal assertion, namely, that the General Assembly could not unilaterally require presbyteries to enforce the five points. The conservatives challenged only its theory regarding "theories." It was the Affirmation vs. the Deliverance: a battle over symbols in the technical theological sense—creeds—that were in fact not judicially enforceable by 1924. The real battle had shifted to "symbols" in the conventional definition: representative statements of philosophy, not binding creeds. The dilemma Machen faced was this: *no sanctions–no oath; no oath–no covenant*. Then what was the Presbyterian covenant? This would not be answered definitively until it became clear who would impose negative sanctions on whom.

The 1924 General Assembly: Fosdick, Part II

The battle for the Moderator's office was even more heated in 1924 than it had been in the previous year. Clarence E. Macartney ran against Charles Erdman. Erdman was a professor at Princeton Seminary. He had been one of the authors of *The Fundamentals*. He had signed the 1915 statement, "Back to Fundamentals."[37] He could not be challenged as a modernist. Because Erdman's attitude was favorable to the more inclusive Church, Machen decided not to support him, and the majority of the faculty agreed with Machen. In a private letter sent in March, Machen wrote of Erdman: "If he is a candidate, I sincerely hope that he may be defeated; for he is more dangerous because of his good, little commentaries which betoken his belief in the New Testament. Ecclesiastically I fear that he will simply be a catspaw for the Modernists, as he was in 1920 or thereabouts, when he favored the agnostic scheme of organic union."[38] J. Ross Stevenson, president of

---

37. *Ibid.*, p. 121.
38. Machen to Mrs. A. L. Barry (March 21, 1924), cited in Ronald Thomas

Princeton since 1914, was also a supporter of a more broadly based Church, and he favored Erdman as a consequence. Thus, he alienated himself from the major segment of the faculty which served beneath him. Macartney won, 464 to 446, a slim edge of 18 votes.[39] Beginning a year later, Erdman would get his revenge.

Once again, Fosdick's case was the center of attention. Fosdick was not actually present; he was in England delivering a lecture.[40] His defense attorney in the trial was a relatively young New York lawyer, John Foster Dulles. Because of the two phases of his public career—liberal internationalist and seemingly conservative nationalist—it is necessary to survey Dulles' life briefly.

John Foster Dulles

He was the son of Allen Macy Dulles, a professor at Auburn Seminary. He was a Princeton University graduate. His grandfather, John Foster, had served briefly as Secretary of State under Presbyterian Benjamin Harrison.[41] Foster's influence remained great after his term as Secretary. His biographer reveals that he was referred to by one highly placed State Department employee after 1893 as the "handy man."[42] He subsequently held positions with the Carnegie Endowment for International Peace and the American Red Cross. "In every administration from Benjamin Harrison's through Woodrow Wilson's, Foster never strayed far from the vortex of foreign policy decision making. . . . Foster moved easily through the halls of the State Department, corporate board rooms, and the offices of foreign legations in Washington. At times it proved difficult to distinguish his public service from his private practice, a matter that did not cause Foster any noticeable concerns."[43] He was able to arrange a diplomatic

---

Clutter, The Reorientation of Princeton Theological Seminary, 1900–1929 (Th.D. dissertation, Dallas Theological Seminary, 1982), p. 118.

39. *Ibid.*

40. Harry Emerson Fosdick, *The Living of These Days: An Autobiography* (New York: Harper and Bros., 1956), p. 169.

41. He replaced James G. Blaine, who resigned in 1892. Michael J. Divine, *John W. Foster: Politics and Diplomacy in the Imperial Era, 1873-1917* (Athens, Ohio: Ohio University Press, 1981), p. 49.

42. *Ibid.*, p. 86.

43. *Ibid.*, pp. 86-87.

office for his grandson at age 19: secretary of the Chinese delegation to the 1907 Hague Conference.[44] Dulles' uncle by marriage, Robert Lansing, had also been greatly influenced by his father-in-law Foster, and greatly assisted by him when Foster asked his friend Elihu Root[45] to get Lansing a job as Counsellor in the State Department in 1914.[46] A year later, Lansing became Secretary of State, replacing Bryan, who had resigned in protest against Wilson's barely concealed pro-England foreign policy. Under President Eisenhower in the 1950's, Foster's grandson would also serve as Secretary of State; meanwhile, his brother Allen ran the Central Intelligence Agency, and his sister Eleanor ran the Berlin desk of the State Department.[47] John Foster Dulles' wife was a first cousin of John D. Rockefeller, Jr. The Dulles family was a highly influential part of the American Establishment in 1924.

As Secretary of State, Dulles gained his reputation as a political conservative and nationalist, the inventor of the "brinkmanship" tactic against the Soviet Union. In fact, he had been a staunch liberal theologically all of his life and an outspoken internationalist until the late 1940's.[48] He served on the Board of Union Seminary in the 1940's, as well as a trustee for the Rockefeller Foundation and the Carnegie Foundation (chairman).[49] He had been a representative of the U.S. government at the Versailles Peace Conference in 1919.[50] He had been one of the founders of the Council of Foreign Relations in 1921. His grandfather had arranged for him to get a job with the prestigious Wall Street law firm, Sullivan & Cromwell, before the young man had earned his law degree.[51] He rose to senior partner in the 1930's,

---

44. *Ibid.*, p. 95.

45. The first man to hold the unofficial position of Chairman of the American Establishment.

46. *Ibid.*, p. 97.

47. Leonard Mosley, *Dulles: A Biography of Eleanor, Allen, and John Foster Dulles and Their Family Network* (New York: Dial, 1978), ch. 18.

48. A well-documented and highly critical book on this is Alan Stang, *The Actor: The True Story of John Foster Dulles, Secretary of State, 1953-1959* (Boston: Western Islands, 1968).

49. Mosley, *Dulles*, p. 190.

50. *Ibid.*, pp. 55-62.

51. Devine, *Foster*, p. 96.

earning a salary of $300,000 a year.[52] This was the equivalent in today's money of about $5 million a year. He attended the ecumenical World Conference on Church, Community, and State at Oxford in 1937. There he called for the eradication of war. He also called for greater freedom of trade with Nazi Germany, Fascist Italy, and Japan, but especially Germany.[53] This is understandable; he was involved in arranging numerous financial deals with the Nazi government prior to the outbreak of the War.[54] This policy of cooperating with the Nazis led to a revolt of the Sullivan & Cromwell staff in 1934, including his brother Allen; he backed down and closed the German branch offices.[55] But he continued to sell advice to his German clients.

In a 1942 speech, he called for the creation of a world federation, a first step in the creation of world government. He recommended a three-step program: the establishment of a common monetary system to succeed the Bank for International Settlements; an Executive Organ to charter commercial companies worldwide, and taxable by the Executive Organ; and a reduction of tariffs to zero for these chartered commercial companies.[56] "By these three initial steps we will have begun that dilution of sovereignty which all enlightened thinkers agree to be indispensable."[57] In 1948, he was a speaker at the founding meeting of the World Council of Churches.[58] Just before he became Eisenhower's Secretary of State, he was president of the Rockefeller Foundation (1950-51). When he took over as Secretary of State, he invited

---

52. Nancy Lisagor and Frank Lipsius, *A Law Unto Itself: The Untold Story of the Law Firm of Sullivan and Cromwell* (New York: Morrow, 1988), p. 6.

53. John Foster Dulles, "The Problem of Peace in a Dynamic World," *The Universal Church and the World of Nations* (London: George Allen & Unwin, 1938), pp. 162, 165-66.

54. Charles Higham, *Trading With the Enemy: An Exposé of The Nazi-American Money Plot, 1933-1949* (New York: Delacorte, 1983), pp. 22, 118, 139.

55. John Robinson Beal, *John Foster Dulles: A Biography* (New York: Harper & Bros., 1957), p. 84.

56. John Foster Dulles, "Toward World Order," *A Basis for the Peace to Come* (New York: Abingdon-Cokesbury, 1942), pp. 52-53.

57. *Ibid.*, p. 56.

58. Mark G. Toulouse, *The Transformation of John Foster Dulles: From Prophet of Realism to Priest of Nationalism* (Macon, Georgia: Mercer University Press, 1985), p. 196.

Democrat Paul Nitze into his office and told him that he was actually in agreement with the policies of President Truman and Secretary of State Dean Acheson; he just thought he could handle Congress better than Acheson had.[59] He was correct; he did. He fired Nitze for partisan political reasons, as he told him, but then asked him to find his own replacement.[60]

His father was a theological liberal, a defender of ecumenism.[61] As part of the modernist strategy—accepted at face value by one of his son's biographers[62]—Alan Macy Dulles always professed attachment to the moderate or inclusivist wing rather than to modernism. Bear in mind, however, that he had been the one public critic of Charles Briggs who said that Briggs had not gone far enough in his 1891 Inaugural Address. It was he who advised his son to get involved on the side of the modernists in the General Assembly of 1924.[63] He suggested that his son's main objective should be to secure time, for "time is on the side of the Liberals."[64] He wanted to de-fang the conservative wing, which was the most important plank in the defensive side of the modernists' strategy. "Let those who want testify to Fundamentals, and let the truth prevail; but why use force and excommunication and anathema in this day and generation? Cannot Fundamentalists win through the truth, without persecution and prosecution?"[65] In short, no further negative sanctions.

Presbyterian law mandated that a person offering formal judicial counsel in a Church court had to be an elder.[66] In the 1920's, Dulles

---

59. Mosley, *Dulles*, pp. 307–308.

60. *Ibid.*, p. 309. On Nitze's influence in American foreign policy, see David Callahan, *Dangerous Capabilities: Paul Nitze and the Cold War* (New York: Burlingame, 1990). His Rockefeller connection can be seen in the photo that appears in *The Rockefeller Foundation Annual Report, 1957*: a meeting of the Washington Center of Foreign Policy Research.

61. Alan Macy Dulles, *The True Church: A Historical and Scriptural Study* (New York: Revell, 1907), p. 58.

62. Michael A. Guhin, *John Foster Dulles: A Statesman and His Times* (New York: Columbia University Press, 1972), pp. 14–15.

63. *Ibid.*

64. Letter to J. F. Dulles, April 29, 1924; cited in *ibid.*, p. 15.

65. Letter to J. F. Dulles (April 29, 1924). *Ibid.*, p. 14.

66. *The Book of Discipline*, IV:26. *Constitution of the Presbyterian Church*, p.

was an elder in the Brick Church, pastored by his old Princeton classmate, Tertius van Dyke, whose father had been pastor there two decades earlier.[67] It was an important church, located on New York's Upper East Side, and has remained important. (In 1989, the funeral of Episcopalian John J. McCloy, a man known simply as "the Chairman"—of the American Establishment—was held there.)[68] Dulles had already become a very important layman. At the invitation of Speer in 1921, he served on the Federal Council of Churches' Commission on International Justice and Goodwill. He had provided legal advice regarding the Federal Council's incorporation. In 1923, the General Assembly of the Church named him to membership in the American section of the Universal Christian Conference on Life and Work. Throughout the 1920's, he worked on the denomination's Church Extension Committee.[69] In 1931, Rockefeller invited him to become part of the Laymen's Inquiry's work in Asia, which he refused because he could not afford to give up the time.[70] It is clear in retrospect that Dulles was uninterested in theology throughout his career. He was a moralist, a believer in doing good.[71]

He based his legal defense of Fosdick on the argument of the Auburn *Affirmation* that the General Assembly did not possess the authority to impose new tests of orthodoxy.[72] But he won the case on a technicality, one which rested on a train schedule for success. A few

---

399.
67. Toulouse, *Transformation*, p. 15.
68. Kai Bird, *The Chairman: John J. McCloy and the Making of the American Establishment* (New York: Simon & Schuster, 1992), p. 15. This unofficial but very real Chairmanship has been held by four people, each of whom has nurtured the career of his successor: Elihu Root, Henry L. Stimson, McCloy, and David Rockefeller, who replaced McCloy as Chairman of the Council on Foreign Relations. This was in 1970. *Ibid.*, p. 619. As early as the 1957, when McCloy was Chairman of Chase Manhattan Bank and Rockefeller worked under him, Bird writes: "It was plain for all to see that Rockefeller was a McCloy protégé." *Ibid.*, p. 457.
69. Toulouse, *Transformation*, p. 16.
70. *Ibid.*, pp. 16–17.
71. Testimony of his sister, Eleanor: *ibid.*, p. 8.
72. *Ibid.*, p. 19.

days after his victory in the Fosdick case, Dulles described in a letter to his father how he won:

> We succeeded in wresting control . . . away from the Fundamentalists (Bills and Overtures Committee) and I was almost daily in controversy with Bryan. . . . The Fundamentalists had a very well and closely organized machine and had the votes on us throughout the proceeding. The only way we were able to secure a victory was through getting the Judicial Commission to assume jurisdiction in the case of Fosdick and of the Philadelphia Overture, which I do not think they really had, and then when it came to a question of accepting or reviewing the decision of the Judicial Commission, the Fundamentalists were, for the first time, unable to hold their votes in line. The Judicial Commission's report came out Wednesday afternoon about five o'clock. A special train left that evening and all of the delegates had their tickets and mileage books in their pockets. A review would have meant a delay of several days, and that was the only thing in the world which prevented a review of the Judicial Committee's decision in the Fosdick and Philadelphia Overtures.[73]

What is significant is that Dulles thought he would lose if the Committee on Bills and Overtures would take up the case. A year earlier, however, this committee had voted 21 to one against the Philadelphia Presbytery's complaint against Fosdick.[74] Opinion in the General Assembly had changed dramatically since 1923. It would soon shift back again.

Fosdick's Convenient Retreat

In 1923, the General Assembly had directed the Presbytery of New York to investigate the complaint against Fosdick.[75] The New York Presbytery had complied with this request. It issued a statement

---

73. Letter from John Foster Dulles to Alan Macy Dulles (May 2, 1924), *Dulles Papers*, Box 6; cited in *ibid.*, p. 20. Cf. Guhin, *Dulles*, pp. 15-16.

74. D. G. Hart, "Doctor Fundamentalis": An Intellectual Biography of J. Gresham Machen, 1881-1937 (Ph.D. dissertation, Johns Hopkins University, 1988), p. 145.

75. Loetscher, *Broadening Church*, p. 121.

clearing Fosdick of any suspicion. The General Assembly's Judicial Commission then issued this statement: "If he can accept the doctrinal standards of our Church, as contained in the Confession of Faith, there should be no difficulty in receiving him. If he cannot, he ought not to continue to occupy a Presbyterian pulpit."[76] The Commission instructed the Presbytery of New York to have Fosdick take the oath of ordination of the Presbyterian Church if he wished to remain in a Presbyterian pulpit. The Assembly adopted this report overwhelmingly. All Fosdick had to do was declare loyalty to an oath the tried and true way: with his fingers crossed.

As it turned out, Fosdick refused to join the Presbyterian Church; he resigned from his pulpit in 1924, the same year he moved into his new summer home on his own island off the coast of Maine.[77] This was a tactical victory for the conservatives. Fosdick had been warned that the moment he came under the jurisdiction of the Church, his every utterance would be monitored by conservatives, who would immediately prosecute if he said anything liberal.[78] Given the fact that he had just delivered the 1924 Lyman Beecher lectures at Yale, published as *The Modern Use of the Bible* (1924), there was little doubt that he would be formally tried. He knew this, and so declined the invitation to another round of trials. Nevertheless, there had been no official criticism of any of the theological issues involved in the Fosdick case. The conservatives had not been able to get the 1910, 1916, and 1923 Deliverances ratified in a court, even though the General Assembly had served as the Church's supreme court from the beginning. The five points had not, so far, been judicially enforced by any lower court, serving only as a general statement of the policy of the particular Assemblies that had supported them. The assertion of the Auburn *Affirmation*, that these five points were not legal requirements for ordination, was as yet unchallenged in any lower court. Meanwhile, the highest court had again refused to try anyone. The Judicial Commission officially sided with the Auburn *Affirmation*, denying that the

---

76. *Ibid.*, p. 122.
77. Mouse Island. Fosdick, *Living of These Days*, p. 114.
78. *Ibid.*, p. 171.

General Assembly possessed the authority to tell the presbyteries what to enforce other than the Confession.[79] At the close of the Assembly, Coffin wrote to his congregation: "The General Assembly not only did not condemn Dr. Fosdick for any of his teaching but with a full account of his work before it, graciously invited him to enter the Presbyterian ministry. I do not see how a more happy and orderly decision could have been reached."[80]

Ironically, Fosdick later remarked in his autobiography, "all this fuss was about a statement in which, if I erred at all, I erred on the side of conservatism."[81] Yet once begun, there could be no turning back, at least not so far as the orthodox elements of the Church were concerned. Fosdick had become a symbol of a larger problem, the problem of apostasy within the Church. The Assembly had not suspended Fosdick. The president of Princeton University, Rev. John Grier Hibben, had actually called Fosdick "a great teacher and prophet of righteousness."[82] Fosdick had been invited into the denomination. Conservatives were unwilling to do the only thing that could have reversed the deterioration: launch a series of heresy trials. As Nykamp comments, "Many exclusivists were willing to exert boundless effort for almost anything except for a heresy trial."[83]

A year after his withdrawal, Fosdick pieced together a book from previous magazine articles, *Adventurous Religion*. It was a comprehensive, popularly written defense of modernism. Its chapter titles clearly reveal its theology. These included: "I Believe in Man," "On Being a Real Skeptic," "Evolution and Religion," "Tolerance," and "What Christian Liberals Are Driving At." He assured his readers, in the familiar rhetorical reversal of the liberals, that the true men of faith are the liberals. The liberal, he said, "is a liberal because he is more religious, not because he is less."[84] From Briggs to Fosdick, the liber-

---

79. Loetscher, *Broadening Church*, p. 123.
80. Cited in Bradley J. Longfield, *The Presbyterian Controversy: Fundamentalists, Modernists, and Moderates* (New York: Oxford University Press, 1991), p. 126.
81. Fosdick, *Living of These Days*, p. 152.
82. Cited in "Presbyterianism Assailed from Within," *The Presbyterian* (Sept. 20, 1923), p. 11; cited in Nykamp, Presbyterian Power Struggle, p. 151.
83. *Ibid.*, p. 185.
84. Harry Emerson Fosdick, *Adventurous Religion and Other Essays* (New

als' constant refrain was this: "We're better Christians than the fundamentalists are." They were allowed to get away with this by the press. But when the conservatives invoked the same argument against the liberals in the name of the historic Christian creeds, the liberals and their allies in the secular press pilloried them as narrow-minded Neanderthals. It was "heads, we win; tails, you lose." The rhetorical game was rigged.

One reason why this strategy worked was because the conservatives held back in their own polemical writings. They were afraid of becoming trapped in the tar baby of heresy trials. Machen set the pattern: he never attacked specific Presbyterian liberals by name or by citing chapter and verse from their published works. Neither did other conservative Presbyterians. They never produced a book or position paper titled, *The Case Against Fosdick*, any more than earlier Princetonians had produced *The Case Against Briggs*. Instead, they inveighed against no one in particular for holding opinions in general. The issue, however, was sanctions. By 1926, it was clear to everyone that the conservatives' refrain had become, "Sanctions have we none."

Rockefeller to the Rescue!

John D. Rockefeller, Jr., immediately intervened and offered to set Fosdick up as pastor of Park Avenue Baptist Church, where Rockefeller attended. This would be only an interim appointment. He proposed to Fosdick the opportunity to serve as pastor of what would become the most prominent liberal pulpit of that generation, the interdenominational Riverside Church, for which Junior subsequently donated $26 million—in today's money, around $400 million. Fosdick accepted the offer. The Riverside Church opened in 1930, and 6,000 people gathered at the "unveiling." As the Rockefeller biographers describe the event, "To symbolize the interdenominational spirit and its further reconciliation of religion and science, the tympanum arching the main portal contained the figures of non-Christian religious leaders and outstanding heroes of secular history, Confucius and Moses,

---

York: Association Press, 1926), p. 233.

Hegel and Dante, Mohammed and even the dread Darwin." Here is a description of the Riverside Church's neighborhood.

> The building itself was located a block away from the northern boundary of New York's leading university, Columbia (an institution that had been the recipient of numerous large gifts from the Rockefeller Foundation, the General Education Board, and the Laura Spelman Rockefeller Memorial Fund) and adjacent to Barnard College (to which Senior had given money half a century earlier, and in recognition of which Cettie [John D. Senior's wife] had been put on the first board of trustees). Across Claremont Avenue, which bounded Riverside Church on the east, was Union Theological Seminary, whose site Junior had helped to choose and whose 1922 endowment drive he had launched with a $1,083,333 gift, amounting to a quarter of its goal. Already one of the foremost divinity schools in the land, whose faculty would boast such formidable voices of modern Protestantism as Reinhold Niebuhr, Henry Pitney Van Dusen, and John C. Bennett, the Seminary's influence was to be greatly enhanced by its proximity to Riverside Drive and the other institutions the Rockefellers had helped to locate there.
>
> By the time of his death, Junior had contributed nearly $75 million to these developments, including $23 million to the Sealantic[85] Fund (the foundation he had established for his religious charities) "to strengthen and develop Protestant theological education" for a little more mortar in the edifice of the Protestant establishment he, more than any other individual, had made possible.[86]

These institutions included the National Council of Churches and the World Council of Churches, at 475 Riverside Drive, for which Rockefeller provided the initial capital. "Soon the fifteen-story Inter-

---

85. The name was a combination of Seal (for Seal Harbor, on Mount Desert Island, where the Rockefellers had their summer estate) and Atlantic, the ocean surrounding the harbor. It was established in 1938 and shut down in 1973. He made a huge donation of $20 million in 1954: *Washington Star* (Jan. 25, 1954).

86. Peter Collier and David Horowitz, *The Rockefellers: An American Dynasty* (New York: Holt, Rinehart and Winston, 1976), pp. 154–55.

church Center would rise on this plot as the headquarters of the principal Protestant denominations in America, their Home and Foreign Missions, and their National Council."[87] In the spring of 1954, the Rockefeller Foundation awarded $525,000 to Union for a program in advanced religious studies. A few months later, John D. Rockefeller, III, donated $250,000 to Union to endow a Harry Emerson Fosdick visiting professorship.[88] In short, Rockefeller took good care of his wounded.

Preparation for the 1925 General Assembly

The General Assembly of 1924 had not been able to identify Fosdick as someone outside the bounds of Presbyterian orthodoxy. There was a good reason for this. *By 1924, there was no judicially enforceable Presbyterian orthodoxy.*

In July, 1924, following the 1924 General Assembly, the Auburn committee dissolved. It transferred its funds to a new group, called the Correspondence Committee. The name was reminiscent of the intercolonial Committees of Correspondence created by Sam Adams in the 1770's. Thirty inclusivist pastors from across the United States joined to educate the Church regarding the issue of freedom. The group published three pamphlets in 1925, including one by Coffin, *Freedom in the Presbyterian Church* and one by Nichols, *Fundamentalism and the Presbyterian Church*.[89]

An editorial by David Kennedy, the editor of *The Presbyterian* (Sept. 4, 1924), charged that the Affirmationists had denied the authority of the Church's standards. One signer, Charles Candee, responded. He was a Princeton Seminary graduate. He challenged Kennedy to bring heresy charges against him. Kennedy refused.[90] Here it was again: a replay of van Dyke's 1913 challenge. For eleven years, no one had responded. Then, for one brief moment, someone accepted the challenge.

---

87. *Ibid.*, p. 155n.
88. *Washington Star* (Jan. 23, 1954).
89. Quirk, Auburn *Affirmation*, p. 260.
90. *Ibid.*, pp. 261–62.

Several weeks later, four men in the Madison, Wisconsin, Presbytery charged Affirmationist George Hunt with having violated his ordination oath. The presbytery's Moderator refused to preside; instead, he resigned. Two former Moderators also refused to preside. The presbytery then voted 21 to four to clear Hunt. The prosecution appealed to the Synod of Wisconsin, but the Synod's Judicial Commission declared that the evidence was insufficient.[91] This meant that in that synod, the *Affirmation* did not constitute heresy.

Early in 1925, Henry van Dyke once again offered himself as a candidate for a heresy trial, just as he had in 1913. "My liberal views are well known; my record is open. I cordially invite you to try me for heresy before a court of the church, if you dare."[92] Kennedy did not accept this challenge, either. Thus, it was clear that the conservatives did not have the ability to enforce their will. Their bluster was a bluff. The modernists called their bluff at the 1926 General Assembly. The decade-long rout of the conservatives would now begin.

Politics (Gasp!)

In January, 1925, Machen and seven other men formed what came to be called the Committee of Eight. They sent out a circular to over 1,000 men.[93] It called for more large meetings. It warned about modernism. It called for the selection at the presbytery level of loyal men to attend the 1925 General Assembly.

This circular brought great resistance throughout the denomination.[94] The Affirmationists replied with a document, *For Peace and Liberty*. It was signed by all 31 members of the Correspondence Committee.[95] Both sides were politicking by any standard: lining up supporters, publishing position papers, criticizing opponents. But what led to rhetorical outrage against the Committee of Eight was that its

---

91. *Ibid.*, pp. 262-64.
92. Letter to *The Presbyterian* (Feb. 12, 1925); cited in Nykamp, Presbyterian Power Struggle, p. 348.
93. *New York Times* (Jan. 5, 1925), p. 11; cited in Quirk, Auburn *Affirmation*, p. 265.
94. *Ibid.*, pp. 265-66.
95. *Ibid.*, p. 267.

circular called for presbyteries to send exclusivists to the 1925 General Assembly. This, it turned out, violated some unstated etiquette in the Church not to get involved visibly in ecclesiastical politics. Worse; the document had failed to state exactly how this kind of presbytery-level organizing and screening should be done. This was the classic mark of men untrained in Church politics trying to rally their troops. There was no careful planning along the lines of the Affirmationists. There was no plan at all. Writes Nykamp: "The contrast between this dramatic action and the long-planned, carefully prepared action of the inclusivists was to exclusivism's disadvantage."[96]

The modernists had a field day. Two liberal journals adopted the rhetoric of shocked horror by printing C. M. Hunter's "Shall We Politicize the Presbyteries?" He censured the Committee of Eight for its "lower motives." (The thought of the liberals' shock at politics is amusing; power through politics was their religion.) But the article got to the judicial heart of the matter: the failure of the exclusivists to press for trials. "Without giving any clue to the locality of these unknown apostates, they have made serious charges. They owe it to the church to publish the names of those ministers who are undermining the faith of thousands. We wish to know who they are and in what presbyteries. If they can tell us, we will publish their names. But if they are not produced, our readers will understand which of the Ten Commandments has been violated...."[97]

Here was the bedrock problem: Machen and his allies thought that political organizing to impose control from the top could result in victory, but the official locus of Church authority was in the presbyteries. The real locus of authority, however, was in the seminaries: the source of future ministers. The General Assembly legally could serve only as a final court for heresy cases appealed to its jurisdiction. But the 87 inclusivists had stated clearly in 1893 that they did not intend to abide by any precedent set there.[98] Each case was a one-time event in their eyes. If they stuck to this, the General Assembly would

---

96. Nykamp, Presbyterian Power Struggle, p. 334.
97. C. M. Hunter, *Presbyterian Banner* (Jan. 15, 1925); quoted in *The Presbyterian Advance* (Jan. 22, 1925), p. 18; cited in Nykamp, p. 339.
98. *Minutes of the General Assembly, 1893*, pp. 167–68.

have to try hundreds of cases, but the Briggs case had taken three Assemblies to settle. The Fosdick case had taken two, and had he subscribed to the Confession, who knows how many years the case would have absorbed? The costs of prosecution would have to be borne at the presbyterial level.

The denomination would grind to a halt if the modernists were willing to continue their resistance. Eventually, a peace-seeking majority will capitulate to one side or the other, usually the one that claims that all it wants is peace. In the case of the Presbyterian modernists, this meant peace to subvert, peace to steal the other side's inheritance, and peace to screen ministerial candidates early: at the seminary level.

The experience in the Madison Presbytery indicated how far the exclusivists would get at the local level: nowhere. But the substitution of a national election campaign for local trials was also futile. The fact that Machen and the others went public with a call for national Church politics indicated the extent of the lostness of their cause: they were going up against men whose religion was politics, men who had spent two decades mastering the techniques of vote-getting and evasion.

1925-26: The Visible Turning Point

The 1925 General Assembly sent out confusing signals. Although the participants did not know it at the time, the General Assembly was at another turning point. The outcome was probably decided by William Jennings Bryan, who once again contributed his efforts to a losing effort. A conservative, Lapsley McAfee, ran against moderate William O. Thompson, the retiring president of Ohio State University. Bryan unaccountably supported Thompson. This split the conservative vote. Then Thompson withdrew.[99] Erdman replaced Thompson as the moderates' candidate and won. Since it is possible, and indeed probable, for two-thirds or even three-quarters of the members of a given Assembly to be new representatives, at the time it was not certain whether this new body marked a change in the out-

---

99. Willard H. Smith, *The Social and Religious Thought of William Jennings Bryan* (Lawrence, Kansas: Coronado, 1975), p. 213.

look of the Church as a whole, or whether it was an abnormality, one which would be changed in 1926 and future Assemblies.

This session reviewed the case of the two New York licensees who had been approved by the presbytery, Van Dusen and Lehman, in 1923. A complaint had been lodged against the pair by a minority group within the New York Presbytery, and the complaint was based on doctrinal grounds. The two had refused to affirm their belief in the virgin birth; under the provisions of the new requirements for ordination advanced by the 1923 General Assembly, were these two eligible to serve in the Presbyterian ministry? This time the question could not be avoided. Both sides were ready to engage the battle. Once again, John Foster Dulles served as legal counsel for the liberals. He emphasized the authority of the local presbytery to decide who is and is not orthodox.[100] The decision of the Judicial Commission sustained the complaint; the Presbytery was at long last instructed to take appropriate action. The 1910 Deliverance was legally sustained. Understandably, the liberal faction was horrified. It would never be horrified again, however. It was time now for the conservatives to be horrified.

The Committee of Fifteen

Henry Sloane Coffin rose to inform the General Assembly that if this ruling was upheld, the liberals would leave the denomination. This was the equivalent of Arius standing in front of the Nicean Assembly and threatening to leave. Fat chance. If ever in Church history a man's obvious bluff should have been called, it was then. Coffin was holding only a pair of deuces, if that. The whole point of the modernist strategy for over three decades had been to stay in the Church until forced out, one by one. They had said so repeatedly. Coffin had said so. Yet Hart says the Assembly took the bluff seriously: "The threat of losing New York's considerable resources and the risk of depleting Presbyterian influence in the region forced leaders to reconsider their decision."[101] If he is correct, which I sincerely doubt, then

---

100. Toulouse, *Transformation*, p. 23.
101. D. G. Hart, *Defending the Faith: J. Gresham Machen and the Crisis of Conservative Protestantism in Modern America* (Baltimore, Maryland: Johns Hopkins

the Northern Presbyterian Church that day sold its soul for an unsecured promise of 30 pieces of silver. Bryan should have given a "Cross of Silver" speech.

The decision of the Judicial Committee put the New York Presbytery on trial. The *New York Times* reported that the liberals were fighting with their backs to the wall.[102] A formal protest was introduced by Rev. Joel Hayden of Chicago. For the Judicial Commission to insist that Presbyterian ministers believe in the virgin birth of Christ was nothing less than Roman Catholic tyranny. "By requiring such absolute conformity it restores those Roman Catholic theories of ecclesiastical authority, which it was the very purpose of Presbyterian Protestantism to overthrow."[103] Luther redivivus!

The protestors once again pointed to the fact that the 1923 Deliverance had not been approved by two-thirds of the presbyteries.[104] The focus of the Judicial Commission, like Presbyterian conservatives in general, had been on the 1923 Doctrinal Deliverance. No one on any side of the debate mentioned the obvious, namely, that the Westminster Confession mandated belief in the virgin birth: ". . . being conceived by the power of the Holy Ghost, in the womb of the virgin Mary, of her substance" (VIII:2). The conservatives had rested their case, not on the Westminster Confession, but on an unratified fundamentalist document of dubious authority. This tactic had only one year to go.

The *Times* referred repeatedly to "extreme conservatives." The phrase "extreme liberals" had not occurred in the secular press in half a century. Macartney was the leader of the "fighting Fundamentalists." The reporter continued: "It is pointed out that in order to maintain their victory the extreme Fundamentalists must now institute heresy trials or move to exscind rebellious presbyteries."[105] Macartney was specifically calling for this, should the New York Presbytery not con-

---

University Press, 1994), p. 117.
102. "Modernists See Presbyterian Split," *New York Times* (May 28, 1925), p. 1.
103. *Ibid.*, p. 8.
104. *Ibid.*
105. *Ibid.*, p. 8.

form to the Judicial Commission.[106] But the New York Presbytery was ready to go into the civil courts to defend its property, a dispute that could last two decades.[107] What broke the evangelicals' will to resist was not Coffin's threat that the New York Presbytery would pull out; it was his threat that they would not leave even if thrown out. The price of their departure would be decades of conflict.

They would not have to leave. The liberals and their allies had a plan, and Erdman was the key. He left the Moderator's chair and introduced a motion to appoint a Commission of Fifteen to study the spiritual condition of the Church and the causes for unrest. The *Times* reported that Erdman would do the appointing after the close of the General Assembly.[108] The motion carried easily. This would defer the day of institutional judgment for the liberals for another year. As things turned out, it deferred it permanently. The Committee of Fifteen was composed mainly of moderates. Mark Matthews, a fundamentalist from Seattle, was a member. Speer was a member.[109] No Auburn *Affirmation* signer was. Erdman's selection of moderates, however, assured a report favorable to the liberal wing, for all that the liberals were asking for—in 1925—was peace. Their battle cry had always been: "No further negative sanctions." The peace-seeking moderates believed them. The question was: On whose terms? At what price? That would not be absolutely clear until 1936.

Reporting on the Assembly's decision the following day, May 28, the *New York Times* reported: "Extreme fundamentalists and Liberals admitted that a definite break in the Church had been put off for a year pending the work of the special committee of fifteen. . . . If the committee of fifteen recommends that the next General Assembly reverse yesterday's action and this is adopted, the threatened schism will have been averted."[110] This is exactly what the Special Commission did.

---

106. *Ibid.*, p. 1.
107. *Ibid.*, p. 8.
108. *Ibid.*, p. 1.
109. Longfield, *Presbyterian Controversy*, pp. 156–57.
110. *New York Times* (May 28), p. 1.

To understand the nature of the crucial change that took place in the denomination over the next twelve months, we need to leap ahead to a few days prior to the 1926 General Assembly.

Controversies over Machen

When Erdman replaced Machen as the stated supply preacher at the First Presbyterian Church of Princeton in early 1925, van Dyke reappeared, as he had promised on the last day of 1923. This led to a hostile editorial in *The Presbyterian*, followed by a printed reply that was printed in two liberal journals, a reply written by Erdman that was a thinly veiled attack on Machen. This increased the antagonism between the Erdman and Machen.[111]

Events at Princeton Seminary overshadowed everything else during the year that the Committee of Fifteen was gathering its data. In May, 1926, shortly before the 1926 General Assembly met, the Seminary's Board of Directors voted to fill the empty Chair of Apologetics and Christian Ethics with the most controversial member of its faculty, Machen. He would replace William Brenton Greene. As might be expected, his continued opposition to liberal theology and his efforts to defeat Erdman's election in 1924 had alienated the inclusivists, whether pietists or modernists. Neither Erdman nor President Stevenson desired to see him in the apologetics department, since this involves the formal defense of the faith, but they were powerless to reverse the Directors' decision until the General Assembly met. They had a problem with precedent: not once in the history of the Seminary had a recommendation by the Board of Directors been overturned.

Another question had been raised at the April meeting of the New Brunswick Presbytery, the one to which the Seminary's members belonged. Very late in the meeting, when all but eight of the members had gone home, someone introduced a motion defending the Volstead Act (Prohibition). Machen voted against it. The Moderator then did something highly irregular: he asked if Machen wanted his vote recorded. Machen told him he did not. His biographer, Ned

---

111. Stonehouse, *Machen*, pp. 374–77.

Stonehouse, reprints a letter to Macartney in which he explained himself. Machen said he did not believe that "the Church in a corporate capacity, as distinguished from the activity of its members," should go "on record to such political questions."[112] He did not invoke nineteenth-century Whig liberalism, i.e., the denial of the Federal government's legitimate authority in this area. The Presbyterian Church at the General Assembly had repeatedly come out against the consumption of alcohol. The Progressives and the fundamentalists had been joined together in the Great Crusade against liquor for over a decade by 1926. General Assemblies had repeatedly taken a public stand on this issue. To take a public stand against Prohibition would have separated Machen from many of the fundamentalists who made up the bulk of his lay followers. Fundamentalist laymen worried a lot more about demon rum than demon higher criticism. Carry Nation had never swung her legendary axe in the Union Seminary library. This is probably why the Moderator had singled out Machen, forcing him into a corner: to undermine Machen's moral leadership.[113]

His vote was easily exploited as a sign of his personal intemperance, even though he was a non-drinker, since not everyone was aware of his personal habits. Such whispered slander was made even more plausible by the fact that his brother Arthur led an anti-Prohibition society.[114] This position was consistent with Machen's philosophy of nonintervention of the State into a citizen's personal affairs, something he had made quite explicit in the introduction to *Christian-*

---

112. Stonehouse, *Machen*, p. 384.

113. This divisive issue was one cause of the 1937 split between the 1936 seceders. In June of 1937, after the departure of the premillennial, fundamentalist, faction which became the Bible Presbyterian Church in 1938, the seceders began criticizing the fledgling Presbyterian Church of America as a "wet" church. Rev. J. Oliver Buswell, president of Wheaton College, sent such a letter to several local newspapers in Philadelphia. George P. Hutchinson, *The History Behind the Reformed Presbyterian Church, Evangelical Synod* (Cherry Hill, New Jersey: Mack, 1974), p. 236. The Bible Presbyterians in 1945 came out against gambling, movie attendance, social dancing, alcohol, and tobacco. *Ibid.*, p. 259n. These were the classic five points of American fundamentalism's social theory prior to the 1970's.

114. Clarence E. Macartney, *The Making of a Minister* (Great Neck, New York: Channel Press, 1961), p. 187.

ity and Liberalism. This philosophy was not made clear by opponents who wished to discredit his actions.

Hart believes that this vote cost him the chair of apologetics at Princeton.[115] So did Macartney, who said so at the time.[116] A month later at the 1926 General Assembly, Machen's nomination by the seminary was tabled. The Assembly then went on to adopt a resolution opposing any modification of the Volstead Act.

To this controversy was added a flap over the newly created League of Evangelical Students.[117] First, a Princeton delegation to the Students' Association of Middle-Atlantic Theological Seminaries in the fall of 1924 led to the students' decision to pull out. The Association had recommended that a Unitarian be admitted.[118] President Stevenson and student advisor Erdman agreed with this decision to pull out. Second, in 1925, six student bodies met to form a new group: The League of Evangelical Students. Its doctrinal statement was evangelical: affirmation of the virgin birth, the Trinity, Christ's substitionary atonement, and the resurrection.[119] The vote on the Princeton Seminary campus was exactly the two-thirds needed to bring the campus into the League. But Stevenson described the whole matter as having "stirred up antagonisms," and was "threatening the order and discipline of the Seminary...."[120]

Erdman had been hesitant about the new group, so the students voted him out as faculty advisor in the spring of 1925, a position he had held since 1907. They replaced him with Old Testament scholar Robert Dick Wilson.[121] The *New York Times* (April 6) invoked the pejorative rhetoric of the liberal wing, speaking of the "bitter attacks by the extreme Fundamentalists in the Presbyterian Church..."[122]

---

115. D. G. Hart, "J. Gresham Machen: The Politically Incorrect Fundamentalist," *Tabletalk* (March 1992), pp. 13-14.
116. *New York Times* (June 3, 1926), p. 4.
117. Stonehouse, *Machen*, pp. 377-80.
118. *Ibid.*, p. 377.
119. Clutter, Reorientation of Princeton, pp. 136-37.
120. *Ibid.*
121. Stonehouse, *Machen*, p. 378.
122. *Ibid.*, p. 379.

Machen was blamed at the time and subsequently.[123] In fact, a student, Joseph Schofield, later claimed responsibility for opposing Erdman.[124] The secretary of the Student Association later confirmed in writing to Erdman that Machen had nothing to do with the decision.[125] The newspapers, however, blamed Machen and his fundamentalist allies.[126] Note: these campus issues were considered media-worthy in 1926. The Presbyterian conflict was not some peripheral issue.

The Dividing Line: The Scopes Trial

The 1925 General Assembly had not been unified behind either faction of the Church, but this was not true of the 1926 Assembly. It was at this gathering that the inclusivist elements gained supremacy, never to relinquish their control of Church affairs.

What had taken place since 1925? Perhaps most important for the Presbyterian Church, U.S.A. in particular, and for the fundamentalist cause in general, was the humiliating defeat suffered by William Jennings Bryan at the Scopes "monkey trial" the previous July. No one has described it better than George Marsden in his book, *Fundamentalism and American Culture* (pp. 184–86). His account is an example of historical writing at its best. But because of copyright problems, I have decided not to cite it verbatim here, as I did in my original manuscript.

The trial in Dayton, Tennessee, was a symbolic event that captured in one week the drama of the preceding 50-year battle between fundamentalism and modernism. Dayton provided the culture-deciding moment of truth for both sides. Both sides suspected in advance that it might. Both sides were confident that the jury would convict Scopes; Tennessee's anti-evolution law was easy to interpret. The question was one of legitimacy, not law. Was the Tennessee law morally just? Was it even sane?

---

123. *Ibid.*, pp. 378–79. See also Stewart G. Cole's *History of Fundamentalism* (1931), pp. 126–27, and Norman F. Furniss, *The Fundamentalist Controversy* (1954), p. 139; cited in Clutter, p. 138.
124. Clutter, Reorientation, p. 139.
125. A. H. Wessels to Erdman (Nov. 8, 1926): *ibid.*, p. 140.
126. *Ibid.*, pp. 141–42. Clutter cites the *New York Times* (April 6, 1925), Philadelphia *Public Ledger* (April 6, 1925), *New York Herald Tribune* (April 6, 1925).

The trial was also the climax of what would turn out to be Bryan's final crusade, which he had entered into only four years before. Prior to 1921, he had tolerated evolutionary theory.[127] Bryan, the Great Commoner and Great Loser in American political history, had already described the battle over evolution as the greatest reform effort of his career.[128] At Dayton, he lost it.

As the incarnation of rural Populism, he fit perfectly into the liberals' stereotype of the fundamentalist: a rural or small town resident laboring to preserve the outmoded way of life of a day gone by. In the minds of urban humanists, Bryan was a living relic of an antediluvian age. Marsden is correct: "Mark Twain and H. L. Mencken in collaboration could hardly have scripted it better.... The central theme was, inescapably, the clash of two worlds, the rural and the urban."[129] On at least one point, the modernists were in full agreement with Karl Marx's *Communist Manifesto*, thereby conforming to Marxism's theory of the bourgeoisie: "the idiocy of rural life."[130]

Theological modernists were allied with humanists in their joint stand against rural fundamentalism and its organizational arms in the north. Most theological modernists in 1925 did not yet perceive that it was not humanism's hostility to fundamentalism as such that made this alliance possible, but rather humanism's commitment to urban life's erosion of all religions other than the secular religion of humanism. Fundamentalism fell first; then it was theological modernism's turn. The second stage of the erosion process became visible to a few theologically liberal observers within a decade. It became much clearer after 1960. But in 1925, a joint effort helped send fundamentalism into the wilderness for the next 50 years.

---

127. Lawrence W. Levine, *Defender of the Faith: William Jennings Bryan: The Last Decade, 1915-1925* (New York: Oxford University Press, 1965), p. 264.

128. Cited in Willard B. Gatewood, Jr., "Introduction," in Gatewood, ed., *Controversy in the Twenties: Fundamentalism, Modernism, and Evolution* (Nashville, Tennessee: Vanderbilt University Press, 1969), p. 21.

129. George M. Marsden, *Fundamentalism and American Culture: The Shaping of Twentieth Century Evangelicalism, 1870-1925* (New York: Oxford University Press, 1980), p. 185.

130. Karl Marx and Frederick Engels, *Manifesto of the Communist Party* (1848), in Marx and Engels, *Collected Works* (New York: International Publishers, 1976), vol. 6, p. 488.

Mencken, who was present at the trial (and who generally respected Machen, as his obituary of 1937 indicates),[131] described Bryan as a buffoon who hated the city, and who had at last been beaten by his urban foes. He had "lived too long, and descended too deeply into the mud, to be taken seriously hereafter by fully literate men, even of the kind who write school-books."[132] Mencken's assessment of Bryan soon was transferred to conservative Protestantism in general. Marsden writes:

> It would be an oversimplification to attribute the decline and the disarray of fundamentalism after 1925 to any one factor. It does appear, however, that the movement began in reality to conform to its popular image. The more ridiculous it was made to appear, the more genuinely ridiculous it was likely to become. The reason was simple. [Walter] Lippmann was correct that the assumptions of even the best of the fundamentalist arguments were not acceptable to the best educated minds of the twentieth century. Before 1925 the movement had commanded much respect, though not outstanding support, but after the summer of 1925 the voices of ridicule were raised so loudly that many moderate Protestant conservatives quietly dropped support of the cause rather than be embarrassed by association.
>
> The most solid evidence of the dramatic decline in fundamentalist influence is found in the two denominations where the controversies had been fiercest. From 1922 to 1925 fundamentalists were close to gaining control of the Northern Presbyterian and Northern Baptist groups. Suddenly in 1926 they were much weakened minorities. Perhaps members were simply tired of the acrimony of debate, and the national fundamentalist fad had played itself out. There is no sure explanation of the decline. The simplest explanation lies in the sordid and reactionary cultural image it had acquired.[133]

With the death of Bryan five days after the trial, the stage was set for the 1926 General Assembly. The most prominent fundamental-

---

131. See Appendix A, below.
132. Cited in Marsden, *Fundamentalism and American Culture*, p. 187.
133. *Ibid.*, p. 191.

ist—as distinguished from orthodox or Calvinistic—member of the Presbyterian Church would no longer be a participant. (What is rarely remembered is that while Darrow won the case in the court of public opinion, he lost the legal battle. The anti-evolution statute remained on the books in Tennessee and was still being enforced in the early 1960's.)[134]

I do not agree with Marsden that the conservatives were close to a victory, 1922-25. They could not convict Fosdick for heresy in 1924. The boards were in the hands of their enemies. So were the Executive Commission and its 1924 replacement, the General Council. But with respect to voting strength on issues that could not be successfully adjudicated—i.e., not brought to a conclusion—the conservatives did have the votes. This was a brief, institutionally irrelevant triumph of conservative symbols over modernist symbols. Problem: the crucial issue was sanctions.

The 1926 General Assembly

Three judicial decisions were made at this Assembly. First, the report of the special Committee of Fifteen was read and adopted. Second, Machen's appointment was not confirmed by the Assembly, but instead was postponed. Finally, a special committee was appointed to investigate Princeton Seminary.

The report of the Committee was significant. It condemned the view—Machen's thesis—that two exclusive religions existed within the Presbyterian Church. It also offered the opinion that the General Assembly, while permitted to make theological deliverances, cannot bind any future Assembly to abide by them unless they are formally ratified by two-thirds of the Presbyteries. This was the position of the *Affirmation*. The report was adopted by a heavy majority.[135]

Machen, again, was one of the few who realized what this could ultimately mean to his cause, that it was in complete disagreement with his conception of the Church. His thesis concerning the schizophrenic condition of American Protestantism and particularly of his denomination had been formally repudiated. It was too late to halt the

---

134. Levine, *Defender of the Faith*, p. 352n.
135. Loetscher, *Broadening Church*, pp. 130-32.

march of events; the tide was rolling against the orthodoxy of John Calvin and its adherents, yet even Rian, writing as late as 1940, could not seem to grasp the fact, for he wrote that "It is a matter of great sorrow that no attempt whatsoever was made at the time to bring individual signers of the 'Auburn Affirmation' to trial."[136] If such an attempt had been made, unquestionably it would have been buried in a deluge of protests. The Assembly of 1926 was not the Assembly of 1893. Neither were the presbyteries.

In refusing to act upon the appointment of Machen, the Assembly took a step unprecedented in the history of Princeton Seminary. It was evident from the beginning that he was not going to have an easy time of it. He was not present at the Assembly, and he became distressed as he read reports that were being sent to him. Stonehouse has written: "When he became aware that the opposition to his person might be made the occasion for an investigation of the Seminary," he was willing to resign from the post, except for the fact that at the time, a resignation would make it appear as if the conservatives feared an investigation. This, of course, was the case; they did fear such an investigation, but Machen concluded that if the opposition were aware of this fear, there could be no way to stop one.[137]

Machen's fears were justified by the subsequent action. A five-man committee was selected to study the causes of dissention at Princeton, and approval of Machen's appointment was to be withheld until the committee could report on its findings.

Erdman offered the *New York Times* one reason for the inaction on Machen's case, a story the *Times* began on page 1: "I have no personal feeling, and this is not a theological question. What is questioned is whether Dr. Machen's temper and methods are such as to qualify him for a chair in which his whole time will be devoted to defending the faith. . . . "[138] It would never be a theological question in the eyes of the bureaucrats. Stevenson agreed with Erdman's analysis when he said, "There is not a doctrinal difference in our faculty,

---

136. Rian, *Presbyterian Conflict*, p. 57.
137. Stonehouse, *Machen*, p. 388.
138. "Presbytery Votes Princeton Inquiry," *New York Times* (June 3, 1926), p. 4.

and there are no contentions about theological disagreements." But, he said, there are some "who believe that the time has come to make the differences clear. Their plea is that now is the time to draw lines in our Church. This election, I say, is involved in that situation."[139] Finally, Stevenson crystallized his position: "We are the agency of the combined old school and new school, and my ambition as President of the Seminary is to have it represent the whole Presbyterian Church and not any particular faction of it."[140] The ability of the Old School to reproduce even a shadow of its former self through seminary training—the key to survival in Presbyterianism—was coming to an end.

The dozen other Presbyterian seminaries were hostile to the Old School. Now the only seminary that still presented a somewhat united Old School front was going to become a reflection of the entire denomination. *This meant the death of the Old School in Northern Presbyterianism.* The Old School was being asked to show toleration. Meanwhile, the other seminaries could hire anyone they pleased, including modernists. This was the essence of the liberals' cry for toleration. It can easily be summarized: "You play ball with us, and we'll smash you in the face with the bat."

The arguments of Erdman and Stevenson, if taken together, are clearly self-contradictory. If the issue was neither personal nor theological, then what was the basis for the division of the factions? The solution to the confusion lies in the conception of theological agreement that Stevenson and Erdman held. If a man subscribed to the Westminster Confession as a system of doctrine, as every Presbyterian minister had to, then there was, in their eyes, undisputed theological agreement, at least as far as the administrative organs of the Church were concerned. Machen, on the other hand, insisted that if a man professed a belief in the Church standards, yet did not support them in his preaching, then his faith was not accounted to him as faith. Between these two conceptions of orthodoxy, no compromise was possible.

---

139. *Ibid.*
140. *Ibid.*

The Problem of Creeds

From an institutional standpoint, the Church must govern in terms of some set of standards, some statement of faith. It has always been the Protestant position that the Bible alone is the inspired and authoritative word of God. No human document is on a plane equal to the Bible. A creed, therefore, cannot be infallible. If a creed is not infallible, then it is open to alteration over time. Machen admitted this, but he was of the opinion that certain eras in Church history are not appropriate for making modifications in the historic creeds, and he believed that his era was such a period.

His theological opponents also chose not to modify the creeds in his day, probably because they realized that they had not yet completed the capture of the institutional hierarchies, denomination by denomination. They understood that they did not yet have the votes to make substantive changes in the Westminster Confession in Northern Presbyterianism in the 1920's. Prior to the revision of 1967, it was their tactic to claim that as long as a minister affirmed his faith in the words of the Confession, it was irrelevant that he maintained mental reservations, or that he preferred to define certain words or phrases in ways that were in outright opposition to the original meaning of the Confession. It was this tactic which outraged Machen and his allies.

The modernists placed little value on creeds and confessions. As historicists and ethical relativists, they believed that each age makes its own truth. Marsden writes: "It was part of the liberals' contention that the issues separating them from the fundamentalists were determined by social forces. As Shailer Mathews put it in *The Faith of Modernism*, 'the differences between the two types of Christians are not so much religious as due to different degrees of sympathy with the social and cultural forces of the day.' While the fundamentalists argued that the acceptance or rejection of unchanging truth was at issue, the modernists insisted that the perception of truth was inevitably shaped by cultural circumstances. By modernist definition fundamentalists were those who for sociological reasons held on to the past in stubborn and irrational resistance to the inevitable changes in culture."[141] Thus, it

---

141. Marsden, *Fundamentalism and American Culture*, p. 185.

did not bother them that anyone would voice his support of a 1647 document but not actually believe all of it. Machen could see where this would lead: to the capture of the Presbyterian Church by a minority theological faction that promoted a rival religion.

Denying the Theological Conflict

What mattered most to the modernist faction was power. They wanted to consolidate their power over the various institutions of the Church. Both Erdman and Stevenson proclaimed that their debate with Machen was not theological but organizational. They wanted no controversy. Controversy upsets people. It leads to reduced financial support for mediating institutions. Most of all, controversy forces each side to declare its first principles and its intentions. This forces underlying disputants out into the open prematurely. It was basic to the tactics of the modernists to rely on the argument of "institutional stability and peace," and later on, after they had more votes, the argument of "this is an administrative matter involving only failure to obey a lawful decision of an organization." In short, it was their deliberate tactic to hide the inescapable theological conflict and to emphasize the issues of institutional peace. After 1933, they emphasized obedience to the decisions of the institutional hierarchy. They converted questions of *theology* into questions of *power*. This is understandable, for twentieth-century liberalism is a worldview based on the capture and exercise of power. It is a theology of salvation by law: planning by formally educated elites.

Machen's opponents devoted their efforts to capturing the seats of power within the Church, while he and his supporters had divided interests. The great mass in the middle, the evangelicals, wanted to avoid conflict within the church. This placed them on the side of the modernists, who also wanted to avoid conflict, but for a different reason: they had not yet consolidated their power.

Stonehouse has recorded that "the appointment of this committee in the historical situation virtually guaranteed the reorganization of the institution. Machen foresaw this as the likely result."[142] The accu-

---

142. Stonehouse, *Machen*, p. 394.

racy of Machen's judgment was confirmed in developments within the Seminary and the Church itself. These developments were to influence the course of American Protestantism from that time forward.

Conclusion

The year 1926 marks the year in which the inclusivists, acting to defend the modernists, took control of the General Assembly. The modernists had controlled the executive since at least 1920. The reaction against the bad publicity of the Scopes trial transformed the Northern Presbyterian Church in 1926 as surely as it transformed the Northern Baptists.

What is important to recognize is that 1926 also marked the rise of the independent evangelical movement and the long decline of the mainline Protestant denominations in the North. Robert T. Handy, Church historian at Union Seminary, delivered a 1959 presidential address to the American Association of Church History. He called it, "The American Religious Depression, 1925–1935."[143] He was speaking as a spiritual heir of the denominational victors. The mid-1920's saw a decline in giving to foreign missions; complaints about this surfaced in 1926.[144] Membership in the PCUSA declined by 5 percent, 1926 to 1936; membership declined by 6.7 percent in the Protestant Episcopal Church in the same period.[145] What Handy failed to note was that after 1925, evangelicals departed or stayed away from mainline churches in droves. This era began a period of Church growth and parachurch growth that continues until today.[146] But inside the Presbyterian Church in 1926, these larger trends were not yet visible. What was visible was the defeat of the conservatives.

In the skirmishes between the orthodox party and the liberals within the Presbyterian Church, there were very few dedicated, self-conscious members in either camp. As is the case in any large organization, the goals and hopes of most members are more mundane than

---

143. *Church History*, 29 (1960), pp. 3–16.
144. *Ibid.*, p. 4.
145. Joel A. Carpenter, "Fundamentalist Institutions and the Rise of Evangelical Protestantism, 1929–1942," *ibid*, 49 (1980), p. 65.
146. *Ibid.*

ideology or theology. They want peace and fellowship. The ministers want a retirement program, opportunities to advance their careers, and institutional growth. The ministers take the attitude that since what they are doing is morally correct, they might as well enjoy growth. But then their vision becomes clouded. They confuse means and ends. They begin to conduct their lives on the assumption that whatever produces growth is morally correct, or at least preferable to the alternatives. Form—numerical growth—replaces substance: the declaration of a supernatural Gospel.

What the vast majority of Church leaders wanted after 1924 was peace. The liberals promised this to them, if only they could prevail on their orthodox colleagues to stop all the fighting. The liberals promised peace without negative sanctions. But there can never be peace without negative sanctions. At best, there can only be peace for those who control the sanctions. There will always be sanctions, whether or not there is peace.

Year by year, the conservative experientialists pressured the orthodox men to stop squabbling and get on with God's kingdom work, meaning Church growth and missions. Tract-passing or its Presbyterian equivalents (sermons, Sunday School materials, reprints of radio broadcasts) became more important to most members than the content of theological treatises or the opinions of seminary professors. After all, how much theology can go into a tract? They concluded that the level of theological discussion in the Church should not be raised above the theology of the tract, if such discussion might bring discord.

In 1924, Fosdick had been slapped on the wrist for his rhetorical attack on the conservatives. The message sent by the General Assembly was clear: the conservatives could not impose effective negative sanctions. The conservatives wanted peace at the price of Confessional purity. They wanted to avoid the necessity of imposing sanctions. The crucial issue was sanctions.

10

PRINCETON, PENSIONS, AND PEACE

> *Instead of making our theological seminaries merely centres of religious emotion, we shall make them battle-grounds of the faith, where, helped a little by the experience of Christian teachers, men are taught to fight their own battle, where they come to appreciate the real strength of the adversary and in the hard school of intellectual struggle learn to substitute for the unthinking faith of childhood the profound convictions of full-grown men.*
>
> J. Gresham Machen (1913)[1]

Machen issued this stirring call to intellectual battle in a lecture to the incoming Princeton students in 1912. But he should have added, "if they survive the ordeal." Machen's faith almost did not survive the academic ordeal of Germany in 1905-6. D. G. Hart blames Machen's spiritual crisis on Johns Hopkins University rather than Germany.[2] This argument has the marks of a younger historian's attempt to overcome one of the more easily documented theses of his most distinguished predecessor—in this case, Ned B. Stonehouse, whom he dismisses anonymously with the comment, "some have interpreted. . . ."[3] He thereby dismisses the obvious as peripheral: Machen's crisis came

---

1. Machen, "Christianity and Culture," *Princeton Theological Review*, 11 (Jan. 1913), p. 13.
2. D. G. Hart, *Defending the Faith: J. Gresham Machen and the Crisis of Conservative Protestantism in Modern America* (Baltimore, Maryland: Johns Hopkins University Press, 1994), p. 22.
3. *Ibid.*

in the middle of his academic year in Germany, not at Johns Hopkins. This crisis was precipitated in Germany, whether or not it had simmered at Princeton Seminary for three years and, even earlier, at Johns Hopkins.

In Germany, Machen had come under the influence of the eloquent liberal theologian, Wilhelm Herrmann, who also taught Karl Barth. Stonehouse called this section of his biography "Captivation by Herrmann."[4] Early in 1906, Machen wrote home: "For me to speak of the Christian ministry in one breath with myself is hypocrisy."[5] Stonehouse concluded that "one cannot doubt that the impact made by Liberalism especially in the person of Herrmann had precipitated it."[6] Stonehouse, a master scholar in Machen's own field of New Testament studies, recognized clearly what Hart fails to mention: that the chief battlefield of the war between Christianity and liberalism is New Testament studies, for it is here that the authenticity of God's revelation is most under attack. As Machen wrote to his older brother in early 1906, "In the field of the N.T., there is no place for the weakling. Decisiveness, moral and intellectual, is absolutely required. Any other kind of work is not merely useless (it might even be humbly useful in other fields), but is even perhaps harmful."[7] He did not write anything like this while he was at Johns Hopkins.

Presbyterian seminaries in that era indulged in a form of academic initiation, a suicidal practice that led irrevocably to the capture of all of them by the liberals: they sent their young candidates for their faculties to Germany to swim in the cesspool of theological liberalism for a year or two. About all the guidance the young men received before departing was a warning: "When you inhale, be sure to keep your mouth above water." Can you imagine Martin Luther insisting that every Lutheran scholar spend a year studying theology at the Vatican? But even this does not do justice to the degree of absurdity. Can you imagine Luther recommending that they study in Istanbul?[8]

---

4. Ned B. Stonehouse, *J. Gresham Machen: A Biographical Memoir* (Philadelphia: Westminster Theological Seminary, [1954] 1978), p. 105.

5. *Ibid.*, p. 115.

6. *Ibid.*, p. 116.

7. *Ibid.*, p. 122.

8. It is now nine decades since Machen went to Germany. Today, no one

Machen was a victim of this unofficial requirement. He refused ordination until 1914. This led him and Princeton into their game of "reinterpreting the founding document": a faculty position without ministerial ordination. Princeton accepted Machen's baptism by fire (or whatever) as valid; the faculty and Board conveniently ignored the fact that he had not yet sworn formal covenantal allegiance to the Westminster Confession, as required by the Seminary's rules. Only ordained Presbyterians took such an oath. "A mere technicality," Princeton had implicitly announced, adopting the liberals' view of founding documents. "We had our fingers crossed," they implicitly announced, a practice the liberals surely approved of. When Machen delivered his 1912 lecture to incoming students, he was still not ordained. Other young men did not survive the spiritual ordeal in Germany; Briggs is the premier example. Those who survived with their faith intact were hired by Princeton; those whose faith did not survive were hired by Union.

The Academic Vulnerability of Presbyterianism

Because of the strong emphasis that Presbyterians have always placed on a highly educated ministry, to the point of distinguishing "teaching elders" (seminary graduates) from "ruling elders" (laymen elected to office), the denomination was inherently vulnerable to long-term infiltration by those who were academically certified, especially by German universities, but not in agreement with the Westminster standards. Ruling elders were not full-time employees of a local congregation. They had little time to develop long-term strategies. Teaching elders, who might have been expected to uphold the doctrinal standards, were graduates of seminaries, and seminaries were being undermined.

The denomination recognized higher academic degrees as the main criteria for permanent positions, and the humanist world that granted

---

teaches at Westminster Seminary who does not have an advanced academic degree from a state-accredited university or humanist seminary. This means that every prospective faculty member is still required to "go to Germany." But it is far worse today. In 1905, they were not asked to earn a degree; they just had to attend.

such degrees was hostile to the orthodox faith. Thus, the lure of Harvard, Princeton (University), Yale, and the German theological swamps was too great, just as it has been too great for Christian colleges in the twentieth century. Academic prestige had been the golden calf for Presbyterians for three centuries, but the worship of this idol became an all-consuming lust after the secularization of higher education in America. So ingrained was this mind-set that even the Church established by Machen in 1936 incorporated the PCUSA's certification standards into its Form of Government:

> Because it is highly reproachful to religion and dangerous to the church to trust the holy ministry to weak and ignorant men, the presbytery shall admit a candidate to licensure only if he has received a bachelor of arts degree, or its academic equivalent, from an accredited college or university. He must also have completed at least two years of study in a theological seminary.[9]

This, despite the fact that it was Rockefeller's General Education Board that pioneered the accreditation system of American colleges—a modern priestly function if there ever was one—by establishing the operating model with the accreditation of American medical schools prior to 1920.[10] It is through academic accreditation that the humanists have enforced the secularization of America's privately funded colleges, despite the fact that private colleges are participants in an inherently decentralized system.[11] The regional accrediting agencies are private, yet they possess government-sanctioned monopoly power that dwarfs any-

---

9. *The Form of Government* (1941), in *The Standards of Government Discipline and Worship of The Orthodox Presbyterian Church* (Philadelphia: Committee on Christian Education, The Orthodox Presbyterian Church, 1965), p. 19.

10. John Ensor Harr and Peter J. Johnson, *The Rockefeller Century* (New York: Charles Scribner's Sons, 1988), pp. 79-81.

11. George Marsden's *Soul of the American University* needed a chapter on this topic. The book is silent about it. The book does include a chapter on academic freedom and the American Association of University Professors, a watchdog organization formed in 1913 in reaction to the firing of a humanist professor—a Princeton Seminary graduate—by Ethelbert Warfield, B. B. Warfield's brother, who served as the president of the Board of Trustees of Princeton Seminary in 1904. Warfield was president of Lafayette College at the time. George Marsden, *The Soul of the American University: From Protestant Establishment to Established Nonbelief* (New York: Oxford University Press, 1994), pp. 302-306.

thing ever prosecuted by the U.S. Department of Justice. Through them, the humanists have screened candidates for the Presbyterian ministry from Machen's era until today.

The old-boy network among the teaching elders of the PCUSA eroded the willingness of their fellow graduates to boot them out. Old friends from seminary, after all, were recognized as fellow "runners of the academic gauntlet." Besides, their own professors had graduated them. This was not quite the same as having baptized their theological views, but over time, this is what graduation from seminary came to mean. The seminary degree was, after 1893 (and probably from 1812 onward), very nearly the equivalent of ordination.

Warfield's Belated Warning

Warfield was the acknowledged intellectual leader of Old School Presbyterianism after 1890. He recognized the threat posed by seminary education, but he discussed this threat publicly only late in his career. He saw the seminary as a support institution, one with distinct limitations. "It is not the function of the seminary to give young men their entire training for the ministry. That is the concern of the presbytery; and no other organization can supersede the presbytery in this business. The seminary is only an instrument which the presbytery uses in training young men for the ministry. *An* instrument, not *the* instrument. The presbytery uses other instruments also in this work."[12] But no matter how hard he and other Calvinistic Presbyterians might proclaim the legitimate sovereignty of the presbytery, their rationalism and their respect for the institutions of higher (humanist) learning eventually undercut their own warnings. Over the decade prior to the time that he wrote this, Warfield had fought the move on the part of the pastoral faction at Princeton to modify the curriculum ever so slightly in the direction of practical theology. He had great faith in the "tradition once delivered": the Protestant scholasticism of Turretin by way of Charles Hodge.

---

12. Warfield, "The Purpose of the Seminary," *The Presbyterian* (Nov. 22, 1917); reprinted in *Selected Shorter Writings of Benjamin B. Warfield—I*, edited by John E. Meeter (Nutley, New Jersey: Presbyterian & Reformed, 1970), p. 374.

Credentials and Certification

The liberals had a difficult time in their capture of the Northern Presbyterians because of the rigorous orthodoxy of the Westminster standards. It took them six decades: 1875 to 1936. But Princeton Seminary could not withstand indefinitely the pressure of humanist education. It was not merely a question of the lack of numbers of Old School advocates. It was a much deeper problem than Church politics. Old School Presbyterianism was itself rationalistic in its apologetic methodology—its philosophical defense of the faith. Its apologetic was based on the belief in the existence of shared first principles of logic between the saved and the lost. This was essentially a form of *epistemological "inclusivism."* Warfield wrote: "All minds are of the same essential structure. . . ."[13] Because their minds have the same structure, unbelievers are subject to arguments for Christianity that appeal to a common human reason. It was this aspect of the apologetics of Princeton Seminary that Westminster Seminary philosopher-theologian Cornelius Van Til criticized for half a century as Princeton's weak link theologically.[14]

Warfield was a postmillennialist. He believed that the gospel of Christ will triumph on earth before Christ physically returns again at the final judgment. But what marked Warfield's eschatology was his reliance on human reason—the Old Princeton rationalist apologetic method—as the basis of this great revival. It is difficult for us to believe that anyone in the post-Darwin, or even post-Kant world could have believed in reason as *the* means of evangelism, but Warfield did.

> The part that Apologetics has to play in the Christianizing of the world is rather a primary part, and it is a conquering part. It is the distinction of Christianity that it has come into the world

---

13. Warfield, "Introduction to Francis R. Beattie's *Apologetics*" (1903); reprinted *Selected Shorter Writings of Benjamin B. Warfield—II* edited by John E. Meeter (Nutley, New Jersey: Presbyterian & Reformed, 1973), p. 103.

14. His criticisms of Charles Hodge's *Systematic Theology* appear under the heading "Less Consistent Calvinism," in his classroom syllabus, *Apologetics* (Westminster Theological Seminary, 1959), pp. 47ff. His criticisms of Warfield are found in his book, *A Christian Theory of Knowledge* (Nutley, New Jersey: Presbyterian & Reformed, 1969), ch. 8.

clothed with the mission to *reason* its way to its dominion. Other religions may appeal to the sword, or seek some other way to propagate themselves. Christianity makes its appeal to right reason, and stands out among all religions, therefore, as distinctively "the Apologetic religion." It is solely by reasoning that it has come thus far on its way to its kingship. And it is solely by reasoning that it will put all its enemies under its feet.[15]

The credentials of Christianity, said Warfield, are its logic. "It stands calmly over against the world with its credentials in its hands, and fears no contentions of men."[16] But these credentials collapsed in the 1920's in the face of Darwinism, post-Heisenberg science (1927–the present), and the triumph of secular humanism. The common-ground logic that Warfield proclaimed became an intellectual drawbridge over which humanists crossed Christianity's defensive moat and began to batter down its gates. Christianity's supposed credentials turned out to be humanism's credentials, both in principle (common-ground logic) and institutionally (seminary and university degrees).

Nineteenth-century Presbyterian Calvinists believed that their religion, once its basic premises were accepted, would lead inescapably to certain definite conclusions about God's relationship to man and the universe. They believed, as Warfield did, that *logic* is the foundation of systematic religion. Machen was an intellectual heir of this tradition. He wrote: "There is sometimes a salutary lack of logic which prevents the whole of a man's faith being destroyed when he has given up a part. But the true way in which to examine a spiritual movement is in its logical relations; logic is the great dynamic, and the logical implications of any way of thinking are sooner or later certain to be worked out."[17] It was his perception of this nineteenth-century Calvinism that led the skeptic Oliver Wendell Holmes, Sr., to write his poem, "The Wonderful One Hoss Shay," a mirror of nineteenth-

---

15. Warfield, "Introduction to Beattie's *Apologetics*," *op. cit.*, pp. 99–100.
16. *Ibid.*, p. 100.
17. Machen, *Christianity and Liberalism* (New York: Macmillan, 1923), pp. 172–73.

century Calvinism. The shay was a marvel of craftsmanship, but when one part of it broke, the whole thing collapsed.

Old Princeton's Apologetics

This rationalistic weakness of Princeton's apologetic methodology had been present from the beginning. In an informative introduction to the writings of several of the great Princeton theologians, Mark Noll offers a fine summary of the presuppositions—common-ground reasoning—of what has come to be called the Scottish common-sense philosophy. It was this which Van Til, using a consistently "presuppositionalist" apologetics in the tradition of Abraham Kuyper and especially Herman Bavinck, challenged from the earliest stages of his career. Noll writes:

> This approach laid great stress on the "common sense" of humankind. It argued that normal people, using responsibly the information provided by their senses, actually grasped thereby the real world. Furthermore, an exercise of the "moral sense," a faculty analogous in all important ways to physical senses, gave humans immediate knowledge about the nature of their own minds. And because all humans, humanity in *common*, were able to grasp the truth of the world in this way—in fact, could not live unless they took for granted that truth was available in this way—this *common sense* could provide the basis for a full-scale philosophy as well. . . . The Scottish philosophers regarded truth as a static entity, open equally to all people wherever they lived, in the present or past. They placed a high premium on scientific investigation. They were deeply committed to an empirical method that made much of gathering relevant facts into logical wholes. They abhorred "speculation" and "metaphysics" as unconscionable flights from the basic realities of the physical world and the human mind. And at least some of them assumed that this approach could be used to convince all rational souls of the truth of Christianity, the necessity of traditional social order, and the capacity of scientific methods to reveal whatever may be learned about the world.[18]

---

18. Mark Noll, "Introduction," in Noll, ed., *The Princeton Theology, 1812–1921* (Grand Rapids, Michigan: Baker, 1983), p. 31.

It should not be surprising to find that Machen spoke of the need of defending a "scientific theology."[19] His debt to the Old Princeton, including its partial commitment to experientialism, was great.[20] He saw himself as one of Warfield's heirs.

Two "nations" within the Church were unquestionably divided theologically: humanism vs. Christianity. They were not equally divided philosophically. Common-ground apologetics softened the radical intellectual distinction between the saved and the lost because rationalist apologetics failed to see that the incompatible *ethical* presuppositions created inescapable differences in men's interpretation of the facts and their use of logic.

An overestimation of the role of the intellect in challenging men to believe in Christ led to an overestimation of the skills imparted by higher education. This served in effect as *a bridge across the great divide over which theological liberals could pass*. The passport that got the humanists across the bridge was the seminary degree. It could be argued that it was a similar overestimation of the benefits of classical education which helped to undermine the Puritans in the seventeenth century.[21] Scottish Enlightenment rationalism also led Calvinistic Harvard down the path toward Unitarianism in the late eighteenth century.[22]

"Other Sanctions Have We"

From the invention of the university until the present, the Church has consented to a second, unofficial means of bringing judicial sanctions: the academic examination. Candidates for the highest Church offices in hierarchical churches have long been required by Church rules to run an academic gauntlet before they are eligible for

---

19. Machen, *Christianity and Liberalism*, p. 17.

20. On the Old Princeton and its theology of experience, see W. Andrew Hoffecker, *Piety and the Princeton Theologians* (Phillipsburg, New Jersey: Presbyterian & Reformed, 1981).

21. John Morgan, *Godly Learning: Puritan Attitudes towards Reason, Learning, and Education, 1560–1640* (Cambridge University Press, 1986).

22. Daniel Walker Howe, *The Unitarian Conscience: Harvard Moral Philosophy, 1805–1861* (Middletown, Connecticut: Wesleyan University Press, [1970] 1988), ch. 1.

ordination. This decision transferred Church authority—covenantal authority—to an institution that is not normally under the direct judicial authority of the Church. Even where the educational institution's charter places the Church in control, several layers of bureaucracy, in the Church and in the school, protect the instructors from direct judicial sanctions imposed by the Church. The legitimacy of such sanctions-thwarting procedures is defended by the doctrine of academic freedom.

A Shift in Legitimacy

In Presbyterianism, a series of seminary examinations has taken increased precedence over the single presbyterial examination as the means of screening access to the position of teaching elder, i.e., the gospel ministry. This shift in authority had taken place a century before Machen's day. The seminary had been invented to strengthen the faith of ministerial candidates after American colleges had capitulated to anti-Christian ideologies: Unitarianism, Transcendentalism, and secularism, i.e., the religion of humanity.[23] The seminary was to be a supplement to the university, which in turn had been a substitute for an apprentice system for training ministers. At each step, bureaucratic formalism and impersonalism replaced the personalism of apprenticeship. This has been a culture-wide phenomenon in the West since the early decades of the nineteenth century. It has accelerated rapidly with the spread of tax-funded education. But the Church established the pattern, beginning in the late eleventh century: the university.

The very existence of Princeton Seminary testified to the nature of the institutional compromise after 1812. In this sense, Machen's cause had been lost long before the 1920's. When the formal academic examination became the most important screening device for entrance into the ministry, the struggle for control over who would administer the examinations shifted from the presbyteries to the seminaries. Princeton was the last Northern Presbyterian seminary to depart from the Westminster Confession. It was the last bastion. But the battle had been lost in principle the day a seminary supplemented presbyterial

---

23. R. J. Rushdoony, *The Nature of the American System* (Fairfax, Virginia: Thoburn Press, [1965] 1978), ch. 6.

examinations with academic examinations. Seminaries from the beginning have been vulnerable to the shifting climates of academic opinion. A national seminary gained a degree of legitimacy that no single presbytery possessed. Yet this legitimacy was informal. Few rules governed it, and fewer sanctions.

The liberals understood the nature of this shift in legitimacy and screening from 1869 onward. The conservatives did not. Not even Machen recognized its full implications for ecclesiastical government. He was blinded, as were the Old Princeton traditionalists in general, by the myth of the primacy of the intellect. They did not recognize one of the dominant realities of modern times: the primacy of the intellect is manifested institutionally as the *primacy of the academic degree*. Their opponents took advantage of this blindness.

The 1923 Report on Seminary Education

I have found no statement of this blindness that surpasses the 1923 report of the Special Committee to Visit Theological Seminaries, which had been created by the 1922 General Assembly. This report was introduced at what was supposedly a conservative-dominated General Assembly. It called for a reconstruction of seminary education through the removal of all presbyterial authority in setting entrance requirements for students. It announced: "The most unfortunate feature of the entire system is that Presbyteries practically control the entrance requirements. In the earlier days a presbyterial examination may have served the purpose; it is no longer an acceptable or efficient method. That entire question might better be left to the Seminaries."[24] The report also called for a total restructuring, not just of seminary curricula, but of ministerial ordination itself. Ordination henceforth should require examinations in Christian education, psychology, philosophy, Christian sociology, and missions.[25] The move away from traditional theology was obvious, yet the report was accepted by the General Assembly.

There was also a recommendation regarding the control of seminaries by dual bodies, Trustees and Boards. The problem, said the

---

24. *Minutes of the General Assembly, 1923*, p. 231.
25. *Ibid.*, p. 235.

report, was that the seminaries had too many board members. This is not efficient—not in accord with modern standards of corporate control. "The corporation management of the present day is usually through a small body of men carefully selected for the purpose."[26] What was needed was centralization of control on a more permanent basis. The report called for a restructuring of seminary control: ". . . to reorganize by a combination of the functions of Trustees and Directors in one body elected for a definite term of ten years."[27] This was a dagger aimed at the heart of Princeton Seminary, which had a dual board system, yet as far as I have been able to determine, no one at Princeton commented on it publicly at the time. Within five years, the Princetonians understood. Too late.

This report created no sensation, no visible opposition. It seemed only to reinforce the long-term desire of seminaries to become autonomous from all Church authority. Here was one more move in the direction of theological liberalism, given the liberal make-up by 1923 of every Presbyterian seminary faculty except Princeton's. As the faculty of Princeton learned, 1926–29, this call for the judicial independence of seminaries had one major exception: Princeton.

Confession and Sanctions

Machen, faithful to Princeton's Scottish apologetics, saw the battle for the faith as primarily intellectual. "False ideas are the greatest obstacles to the reception of the gospel."[28] He focused on the Old School's revision of the third point of the biblical covenant model: propositional truth (not ethics). This had been the apologetic strategy of the Princetonians from the beginning in 1812. This was what lured them into accepting Charles Briggs' strategically brilliant offer in 1880 to co-publish *The Presbyterian Review*. They believed that the battle for Christianity could be won on the battlefield of ideas. Then they invited their mortal enemies onto the battlefield, forgetting that this was an explicitly Christian battlefield supposedly open only to Chris-

---

26. *Ibid.*, p. 227.
27. *Ibid.*
28. Machen, "Christianity and Culture," p. 7.

tian participants. This decision baptized higher criticism in the Presbyterian Church. From that time on, no Princetonian could ever publicly argue that higher criticism is methodologically heretical.

The Princetonians were strategically in error. This undermined their tactics. The "soft underbelly" of Presbyterian ecclesiology had always been sanctions, not stipulations. The problem was not a lack of propositional truth. The Presbyterian Church imposed on its ministers at the time of ordination a requirement to affirm faith in the most detailed and rigorous theological confession in Christendom. The problem was, once a man made this profession of faith, the Presbyterian Church had no predictable answer to the question: "Now what?"

The Confessionally rigorous Calvinists voluntarily surrendered to the Confessionally less rigorous Calvinists in 1758 and 1869. The public debate in these two instances was over stipulations, but since both sides professed allegiance to the same stipulations, the unspoken issue centered on sanctions. "How hard will the Old School push the New School to put their sanctions where their mouths are?" The answer in 1869: "Not very hard." By remaining in the Church after 1903, the Old School surrendered to the New School regarding a loosening of the Confession. The debate was subsequently about stipulations; Old School sanctions were a lost cause. Then both Old School and New School surrendered to the invading Cumberland Presbyterians in 1906. Old School, New School, and Cumberland Arminians surrendered to the modernists in 1936. The official issue still was sanctions, but in reality it was both stipulations and sanctions. The takeover was complete. The surrender on stipulations in 1967 was a mere formality: public ratification of a 31-year-old treaty of surrender.

There is a lesson here: *theology apart from sanctions is not theology; it is, as the Auburn Affirmation insisted, merely a theory.* Institutions do not persevere by theories alone. They also require sanctions to enforce their foundational theories. There can be no chain of command apart from sanctions. There can be no voice of authority institutionally without sanctions. Otherwise, no one would pay attention to that voice.

Legalism at Princeton

I define "legalism" as the self-conscious decision to break the intention of a rule in the name of the rule. It involves violating the spirit of a law by means of the letter of the law. It is one thing to ignore the letter of the law. That is antinomianism. It is quite another to use it against the obvious intent of the law-giver.

The Presbyterian Church's leaders in the first decade of the nineteenth century grew concerned over the fate of theological education at the College of New Jersey. The college was not producing enough ministerial candidates. It was also legally independent of Church control.[29] Princeton Seminary opened in 1812. Its founders were determined to keep the new seminary under Church control, rejecting the suggestion that the seminary be placed under the authority of the College,[30] despite the fact that 21 of the 23 members of the College's Board of Trustees were Presbyterians.[31] (Harvard in 1819 and Yale in 1822 established divinity schools as separate departments under the control of the respective college boards.)[32] When the General Assembly in 1811 designated Princeton Seminary as the Church's only seminary, it specified that every professor must be an ordained minister in the Presbyterian Church. Each had to swear that he would not teach anything opposed to the Church's Confession.[33] This meant that the seminary was under the authority of the General Assembly, and each faculty member was under the authority of the presbytery in which the seminary was located. The founders understood that he who teaches the next generation of ministers possesses the strongest judicial position in the denomination because of his control over the classroom and its powerful sanctions: grading and therefore graduation.

---

29. Mark A. Noll, *Princeton and the Republic, 1768–1822* (Princeton, New Jersey: Princeton University Press, 1989), p. 263.

30. Lefferts A. Loetscher, *Facing the Enlightenment and Pietism: Archibald Alexander and the Founding of Princeton Theological Seminary* (Westport, Connecticut: Greenwood Press, 1983), p. 128.

31. Noll, *Princeton*, p. 262.

32. Loetscher, *Facing the Enlightenment*, pp. 158–59.

33. George P. Hutchinson, *The History Behind the Reformed Presbyterian Church, Evangelical Synod* (Cherry Hill, New Jersey: Mack, 1974), p. 128.

Every Princeton Seminary professor by charter had to be under Church control. This was the clear intent of the founders.

Machen's Appointment

The extent of Princeton Seminary's later commitment to technical scholarship above the authority of the Church is best seen in Machen's appointment to a teaching position: instructor. He received the appointment in the fall of 1906. He was not ordained to the teaching eldership until June 23, 1914.[34] He was elevated to assistant professor in May, 1914, to begin in the fall of that year. The faculty was self-conscious about this, as Stonehouse's language indicates: "Acting on the background of Machen's licensure, the Faculty of the Seminary was not slow to recommend his election as Assistant Professor of New Testament in its report to the Board of Directors at its meeting during the first week of May, 1914."[35]

Notice the change in title: "instructor" to "assistant professor." The key was the word "professor." Only ordained men could be professors at Princeton Seminary. So, Machen had not been a professor, 1906–14; he had been merely an instructor. He had graded students, delivered lectures, and participated in faculty meetings. But he had never been a professor. He had possessed the authority to impose professorial sanctions on students, but without the professorial title. He had possessed the substance of judicial authority but not the form.

The faculty and Board of Directors had played a game with the language of charter. The founders had used the word "professor" to define a faculty member. The word "instructor," like the words "assistant professor," were additions many decades later. Such professional academic distinctions did not occur to the General Assembly of 1811. This is how the Old School professors got their way with the seminary's charter. Fifteen years after Machen's 1914 appointment, the modernists and their allies would also get their way with the charter.

Why had Machen waited so long to be ordained? Because he had doubts about the faith. Early in 1906, he had written a letter to his brother concerning his doubts concerning his faith. He also had

---

34. Stonehouse, *Machen*, p. 197.
35. *Ibid*., p. 202.

doubts about his worthiness to become a minister.[36] Nevertheless, Princeton wanted him, and wanted him badly. William Armstrong, his former mentor at Princeton, wrote to him on March 11. He knew of Machen's hesitancy to enter the ministry. He assured Machen that "you need have no hesitancy for fear of binding yourself for more than one year and for this there would be no necessity of ordination."[37]

The state of Machen's mind may be seen from his letter to his father on March 30: "How I envy the humble clerk, who at least has some employment in which he can engage with enthusiasm and without doubts and qualms of conscience!"[38] He said that he wished he could start a career in business, but it was too late for that. When he returned to the United States he visited his family's summer estate in Seal Harbor, Maine.[39] After he left Seal Harbor, he and his mother began an exchange of letters, unprecedented for their emotional intensity, arguing over his decision to return to Germany to study for several more years.[40] That summer, he finally decided to join the Princeton faculty. But, as his biographer writes, "It was not until the fall of 1913 that he attained such assurance and calm that he could undertake the first step looking toward ordination, that of being taken under care of presbytery, and could confidently and joyfully look toward ordination."[41]

Princeton set a precedent with Machen. It placed a man onto its faculty who was not only not ordained, but whose refusal to become ordained, at least in the early years,[42] was based on his own sense of religious doubt. There was no question about his academic credentials. He was a skilled linguist in Greek—one of the best students ever trained by that master of the classics, Johns Hopkins University's Basil S. Gildersleeve. He had spent a year in two German universities,

---

36. *Ibid.*, p. 113.
37. Armstrong to Machen (11 March 1906), *ibid.*, p. 121.
38. *Ibid.*
39. *Ibid.*, p. 135.
40. *Ibid.*, pp. 135–44.
41. *Ibid.*, p. 145.
42. Hart believes that he became more secure after 1910. Hart, *Defending the Faith*, p. 30.

even though he had not received a degree. That was sufficient, and always had been at Princeton. He had survived Princeton's soul-threatening but informal faculty eligibility initiation rite of the German academic gauntlet.[43] Therefore, the formal requirement of ministerial ordination was regarded by the Princeton faculty as optional. With this decision, the Old Princeton publicly announced its new operational ecclesiology: *judicial expediency for the sake of academic criteria*.

Princeton: The Old School's Last Bastion

The issues that divided Presbyterians regarding the fate of Princeton Seminary were the same ones that divided them in the other ecclesiastical battles. Princeton was committed legally to the Westminster Confession. From 1811 onward, its Plan committed the organization and its professors to the terms of the Westminster Confession and the Church's catechisms. Each professor also subscribed to this oath:

> I do solemnly promise and engage not to inculcate, teach, or insinuate anything which shall appear to me to contradict or contravene, either directly or impliedly, anything taught in the said Confession of Faith or Catechisms, nor to oppose any of the fundamental principles of Presbyterian Church government, while I remain a professor in this seminary.[44]

In 1870, the year following the reunion, the General Assembly adopted changes in the Plan of the seminary which greatly strengthened the power of the Board of Directors to fill its own vacancies and fix the salaries of the professors. The General Assembly had the power to veto the first of these powers, however.[45] More to the point, what the General Assembly of 1870 gave, a subsequent General Assembly could take away. Princeton, unlike Union, from its origin had been under the authority of the General Assembly.[46] And because Un-

---

43. Stonehouse, *Machen*, p. 42.
44. Cited in Edwin H. Rian, *The Presbyterian Conflict* (Grand Rapids, Michigan: Eerdmans, 1940), p. 62.
45. *Ibid.*
46. Lefferts A. Loetscher, *The Broadening Church: a study of theological issues in the presbyterian church since 1869* (Philadelphia: University of Pennsylvania

ion was still allowed to place men in the voting ministry of the Church, Union and its theological allies had thereby gained a potential stranglehold over Princeton which the Princetonians could not conceivably gain over Union.

J. Ross Stevenson

Stevenson was a graduate of McCormick Seminary, originally a Calvinist institution founded by Cyrus McCormick, the wealthy Old School Calvinist. He also had served as pastor of New York's Fifth Avenue Presbyterian Church. He was an inclusivist, deeply committed to Church union. He had been present at the World's Missionary Conference in Edinburgh in 1910 (as had Erdman),[47] "which inaugurated the modern ecumenical movement," according to John Mackay, Stevenson's liberal successor at Princeton.[48] There could be no doubt in 1914: he was an ecumenist—religiously committed, not just vaguely interested.

Lefferts Loetscher was the son of one of Princeton Seminary's faculty members—one of three praised by Henry van Dyke,[49] the other two being Erdman and Stevenson.[50] Loetscher summarizes the view of this power shift that was held by liberals in the Church, and for this reason it deserves reprinting:

> There was a feeling in some quarters that Princeton's place in the Church and in the religious world was not what it once had been. By the year 1913 the gradual divergence between the "historic Princeton position" and the emerging attitudes in the Church were threatening the seminary with partial isolation. Finally, after much deliberation, the Board of Directors elected to the presidency Dr. J. Ross Stevenson, distinguished pastor and active churchman with membership on numerous General Assembly and interdenominational boards and committees. The determining factor in his election was the desire that the seminary

---

Press, 1954), p. 69.
47. Stonehouse, *Machen*, p. 215.
48. *Ibid.*, p. 213.
49. *Ibid.*, p. 73.
50. Loetscher, *Broadening Church*, p. 139.

might, under his leadership, be brought into closer relationship with the Church as a whole.[51]

In 1938, Stevenson had been, in the words of John Mackay, "the chief representative of American Christianity in the city of Utrecht" at the founding of the organization that became, in 1948, the World Council of Churches.[52] Nevertheless, Loetscher describes Stevenson as follows: "His utterances, with lifelong consistency, attested his earnest evangelicalism and basic conservatism."[53] Loetscher's assessment of men such as Robert Speer, Erdman, and Stevenson always accentuated their supposedly innate conservatism and evangelicalism, but these men proved to be bureaucratic wedges for the liberals.

Stevenson was inaugurated in 1914 and immediately began taking a leading role in the Seminary's affairs. Previously, the president had been little more than a presiding officer at faculty meetings.[54] Stevenson was far more of an activist president than Patton had ever been. Like Woodrow Wilson, another activist who had succeeded Patton, Stevenson was determined to re-shape Princeton. He achieved his goal in 1929.

The League of Evangelical Students

As I mentioned in the previous chapter, a significant controversy between Stevenson and the faculty took place in 1924–25, the year after Stevenson had supported Erdman as Moderator of the General Assembly, while the faculty had supported Clarence Macartney. A Princeton delegation to the Students' Association of Middle-Atlantic Theological Seminaries in the fall of 1924 led to the students' decision to pull out. The Association had recommended that a Unitarian be admitted. The students of six campuses then created a new organization, the League of Evangelical Students. Most of the other Presbyterian seminaries in the Church refused to join the League. Even worse, in Stevenson's view, was the fact that the League allowed Bible Col-

---

51. *Ibid.*, p. 138.
52. Cited in Stonehouse, *Machen*, p. 213.
53. Loetscher, *Broadening Church*, p. 139.
54. Rian, *Presbyterian Conflict*, p. 66. Cf. Loetscher, *Broadening Church*, p. 138.

lege students to join. Stevenson raised the specter of "know-nothingism." He warned that "religion without sound learning must ultimately prove injurious to the Church." Here it was: the appeal to the educated ministry, meaning a *certified* ministry. That he could use such an argument pointed to the vulnerability of Machen's position and the position of conservative "scientific theologians" everywhere. The liberals used a kind of jiu-jitsu on the conservatives: they elevated certification over doctrine. It proved impossible after 1923 for the conservatives to counter this argument effectively, for they and their predecessors had already succumbed to it institutionally.

Second, Stevenson asked rhetorically, "shall this institution now be permitted to swing off to the extreme right wing so as to become an interdenominational Seminary for Bible School-premillennial-secession fundamentalism?"[55] Here again, a liberal could appeal rhetorically to what seemed to be a traditional theological heritage. Machen was outspokenly allied to premillennialists inside the Church,[56] although he was a postmillennialist,[57] and he was unquestionably becoming the intellectual spokesman of American fundamentalism, which by 1924 was overwhelmingly dispensational and separatist. Stevenson could make it appear as though the students, and therefore Machen and the Princeton Calvinists, were deviating from established Presbyterian traditions and adopting *extreme* right-wing traditions, which were the only right-wing traditions there were, liberal rhetoric indicated. (The more things change, the more they stay the same.)

Tactics and the Confession

Machen's dilemma was a dilemma which is still being sorted out in today's creedal churches. On the one hand, he stood for the Westminster Confession. On the other hand, he needed allies within the

---

55. Cited in Rian, *Presbyterian Conflict*, p. 70.
56. Machen, *Christianity and Liberalism*, pp. 48-49.
57. "Human institutions are really to be molded, not by Christian principles accepted by the unsaved, but by Christian men; the true transformation of society will come by the influence of those who have themselves been redeemed. . . . [I]t is not true that the Christian evangelist is interested in the salvation of individuals without being interested in the salvation of the race." *Ibid.*, pp. 158-59.

Church whose leaders no longer believed in the Confession's Calvinistic provisions. So, Machen invoked the Doctrinal Deliverance of 1910 to rally the troops. This creedal formulation was acceptable to antimodernists outside the Presbyterian tradition. He argued that it was necessary to cooperate with premillennialists within the Church,[58] yet on the next page, he also argued that it was and is necessary to separate ecclesiastically from Lutherans on the basis of differing views of the Lord's Supper, and also from Anglicans and Arminians. He was the spokesman for a conservative alliance, though not ecumenical union. An alliance is not an oath-bound covenant with judicial sanctions.

Consider his words concerning Roman Catholicism:

> Far more serious still is the division between the Church of Rome and evangelical Protestantism in all its forms. Yet how great is the common heritage which unites the Roman Catholic Church, with its maintenance of the authority of Holy Scripture and with its acceptance of the great early creeds, to devout Protestants to-day! We would not indeed obscure the difference which divides us from Rome. The gulf is indeed profound. But profound as it is, it seems almost trifling compared to the abyss which stands between us and many ministers in our own Church. The Church of Rome may represent a perversion of the Christian religion; but naturalistic liberalism is not Christianity at all.[59]

Machen faced a real problem. The original version of the Westminster Confession read: "There is no other head of the Church but the Lord Jesus Christ. Nor can the Pope of Rome, in any sense, be head thereof: but is that Antichrist, that man of sin, and son of perdition, that exalteth himself, in the Church, against Christ and all that is called God" (XXV:6). The Presbyterian Church had modified this section in 1903 to soften it. The new Church which he and his supporters founded in 1936 adopted a modified version of the modified version: "There is no other head of the Church but the Lord Jesus

---

58. *Ibid.*, pp. 48–49.
59. *Ibid.*, p. 52.

Christ. Nor can the Pope of Rome, in any sense, be head thereof."[60] They accepted the revised Confession—a change that above all other changes would have been rejected by virtually all Protestants in the Reformation. The doctrine that the Pope is the Antichrist was probably the only doctrine that was accepted by every Protestant group in the sixteenth century.

It is clear in retrospect that the Westminster Confession no longer functioned in Machen's day to bind the Church together, nor could it be used to purge the Church of heresy. Each side appealed to the Confession when it seemed appropriate or tactically useful. Neither side appealed to it when it wasn't. Thus, an odd situation developed: those who believed virtually all of the Confession joined with those who believed part of the Confession to do battle against those who believed virtually none of the Confession, but who proclaimed allegiance to the Confession, and who protested any clarifying additions to the Confession that might have made their subterfuge more difficult.

The Battle Over the Boards

In May of 1926, Machen was elected by the Board of Directors and confirmed by the Board of Trustees as professor of apologetics and ethics. A minority of Directors and Trustees immediately appealed the decision to the General Assembly, which was meeting that month.[61] That they would do so indicates that they perceived a major shift in the theological conditions within the Church since 1925. At the General Assembly, Machen's nomination was tabled in committee. Nothing like this had happened since the Briggs case. But this time, theology would not be mentioned. Never again would theology be mentioned by the sanctions-bringers as the basis of their actions. The theologians of "theology without sanctions" were now in control.

---

60. They were willing to adopt the "original, modified" version of the PCUSA, but they feared complications stemming from possible copyright infringement of the wording. As Prof. John Murray later said, "The Hebrews would not cooperate with the Samaritans."

61. Loetscher, *Broadening Church*, p. 141.

(In 1934, they would metamorphose into "sanctions without theology" theologians.)

A five-man committee was set up at the 1926 General Assembly by the Standing Committee on Theological Seminaries to investigate the "welfare of Princeton Seminary" and to attempt to "harmonize differences." Machen's appointment to the chair of apologetics was delayed until this committee reported back to the General Assembly. The committee visited Princeton during the interval between Assemblies, interviewing faculty members, students, and members of the Boards of Trustees and Directors. (The Church's senior bureaucrat after 1920, Stated Clerk Lewis Mudge, had been a member of the Board of Trustees from 1910.)[62] The report of the committee, adopted at the 1927 Assembly, invoked the language of van Dyke's 1893 modernist document, *A Plea for Peace and Work*. Describing Stevenson's faction as the minority, the report declared: "The minority believe in peace and work, the majority believe in controversy in defense of the truth, and work."[63] The real problem was not theological; it was administrative, the report concluded: "The root and source of the serious difficulties at Princeton, and the greatest obstacle to the removal of these difficulties, seem to be in the plan of government by two boards."[64]

From the point of view of the moderate and liberal wings, the conservative Board of Directors had to be thwarted, since the Board was in charge of all appointments to the faculty, the school's curriculum, and all other matters except financial, which was the responsibility of the Trustees. Therefore, any attempt to put Princeton under one Board of Control was a direct thrust at the conservative orthodoxy of Princeton Seminary.

The legal implication of the committee's report was that the Board of Trustees was really an organization equal in responsibility to the Board of Directors in the management of Princeton's affairs, a view which Machen would later challenge. But the legal implication

---

62. *Minutes of the General Assembly, 1945*, p. 99.
63. *Minutes of the General Assembly, 1927*, p. 97.
64. *Ibid.*, p. 131.

was only one aspect of the report. The other was far more revealing. The committee stated that the root of the problem was the division of control into two boards. In other words, *the problem was institutional and governmental, not theological.* This had been the standard argument of the liberals from the beginning: divisions were never admitted to be theological, but only institutional and personal ("unloving attitudes," "extremism"). The liberals had by this time gained an enormous advantage over their opponents. They had framed the terms of the debate.

Framing the Public Debate

Consider Erdman's response two years earlier to a hostile editorial in *The Presbyterian* (Jan. 15, 1925). The editorial had pointed out that Henry van Dyke had returned to Princeton's First Presbyterian Church now that Erdman was preaching there. Erdman replied in *The Presbyterian Advance* (Jan. 22, 1925). He presented the now-standard response whenever a conservative was pressured by even more conservative men to act more consistently according to his stated faith. He called his opponents unkind, unloving, and/or un-Christian. "Allow me to reply, that I repudiate your insinuations as unfounded, unwarranted, unkind and unchristian." Then he reiterated the now-familiar theme: "You intimate that a division exists in the seminary faculty. No such division exists on points of doctrine. Every member of the faculty is absolutely loyal to the standards of our church. The only division I have observed is as to spirit, methods or policies. This division would be of no consequence were it not for the unkindness, suspicion, bitterness and intolerance of those members of the faculty who are also editors of *The Presbyterian*." But Machen was the only faculty member who was a member of the editorial staff of *The Presbyterian*.[65]

Erdman was the Moderator of the 1925 General Assembly. Because of this, he had also been present at the meeting of the Standing Committee on Theological Seminaries. Machen replied in a printed pamphlet late in 1926. "According to the Chairman of the committee,

---

65. Rian, *Presbyterian Conflict*, pp. 73–74.

it had been asserted that I am spiritually unqualified to hold the post in question and teach good will to the students, that I am temperamentally defective, bitter and harsh in my judgments of others and implacable to brethren who do not agree with me."[66] Machen then pointed to the division within the faculty as the real reason for the committee's decision. He said that the division became clear in 1920 with the Plan of Organic Union, which Erdman and Stevenson had supported.[67] He denied that he had done anything "to introduce such unpleasant personalities into our relationships at Princeton."[68] Machen had also opposed Erdman's candidacy for Moderator at the 1924 General Assembly, supporting Macartney. Was this a crime, he asked rhetorically? If so, he stands convicted.[69] "Ever since 1920 Dr. Erdman had consistently favored an ecclesiastical policy to which the majority of his colleagues conscientiously opposed."[70] He quoted the Philadelphia *Public Ledger* of a speech by Erdman, who had said: "I want the constructive work of the Presbyterian Church to go on without interruption on account of any doctrinal controversy. . . ." This, concluded Machen, proves his "doctrinal indifferentism."[71] This position neglects the work of doctrine in salvation, since "only by persuading men to accept the blessed 'doctrine' or gospel can it save human souls."[72]

Then Machen got to Erdman's *Presbyterian Advance* article. He cited Erdman's phrase: ". . . the unkindness, suspicion, bitterness and intolerance of those members of the faculty who are also editors of *The Presbyterian*." That, Machen said, narrowed the field down to one man: Machen. He denied that he had in any way been responsible for anything written in *The Presbyterian* except for articles signed by him.[73] The newspapers had picked up the story that Machen had at-

---

66. Machen, *Statement* (Nov. 23, 1926), p. 5.
67. *Ibid.*, pp. 6–7.
68. *Ibid.*, p. 7.
69. *Ibid.*, p. 8.
70. *Ibid.*, p. 12.
71. *Ibid.*, p. 13.
72. *Ibid.*, p. 14.
73. *Ibid.*, p. 19.

tacked Erdman. He cited *The New York Herald Tribune* (Feb. 1, 1925) and *The Daily Princetonian* (Feb. 2, 1925).[74] Then Machen reiterated what he said throughout the period, and which his opponents, for rhetorical effect in order to subvert the denomination, always ignored: theology. "The difference of principle involves convictions which I cherish more than anything else in all the world and the consistent application of which I cannot relinquish for any personal consideration whatsoever. Dr. Erdman's letter placed the difference between us on the plane of personalities; my replies endeavored to place it again upon the plane which I always placed it—upon the plane of a conflict of principles."[75]

In any era, those who hold rigorously to a set of ideas or principles stand out as extremists. The bell-shaped curve always places true believers and true disbelievers at the extremities of the curve. "Extremist" was a word repeatedly used by Machen's critics to describe Machen's wing of the Church. A bell-shaped curve has two ends. Those at the other end—modernists—were never described as extremists. This indicates the extent to which the modernists and their allies in the press had already framed the terms of the debate. Once this is done by one's opponents, escape is very difficult.

When the stakes are not considered high, few people enjoy a fight. Few approve of a fighter. Machen was a fighter. What doomed him was his era. The theology of religious pluralism had been adopted by mainline American Protestantism by 1925. The Unitarianism of the public schools had been imparted to generations of students, who had learned their lessons well. Bryan's humiliation in Tennessee had hastened the process. Nevertheless, Machen called Princeton students to volunteer for a fight in a 1929 sermon.

> Paul was a great fighter because he was at peace. He who said, "Fight the good fight of faith," spoke also of "the peace of God which passeth all understanding"; and in that peace the sinews of his war were found. He fought against the enemies that were without because he was at peace within; there was an inner sanc-

---

74. *Ibid.*, p. 20.
75. *Ibid.*, p. 21.

tuary in his life that no enemy could disturb. There, my friends, is the great central truth.[76]

By then, his was visibly a lost cause at Princeton. There are few volunteers for lost causes.

Machen was not a great hater; he was a great fighter. He was a gentleman who would slice an enemy from throat to groin theologically, but who seemed to bear no personal animosity toward his decimated target. He was like a prosecuting attorney who does not hate the defendant, but dearly wants to see him convicted for crimes committed. Understandably, the ecclesiastical kidnappers who had been caught in the act were not going to oblige him by giving him added jurisdiction: a full professorship in apologetics. He was dangerous enough in the Department of New Testament.

Machen was correct: "At no time in this controversy have I indulged in any personally abusive language such as is found in the attack on me in *The Presbyterian Advance*."[77] What Machen faced was the *power of prior rhetoric*: his opponents charged the conservatives with telling lies, distorting facts, and generally committing breaches of rhetorical etiquette, when in fact it was they who were the prime perpetrators. They got away with it because they had successfully painted themselves as a besieged minority of peacemakers and seekers after tolerance. Machen was the victim of this rhetorical strategy, and he knew it: ". . . Dr. Erdman has done me the worst kind of injury that can be done to one man by another; he has impaired my good name in the community and throughout the Church at large."[78] This mythology has persevered. In 1974, a doctoral dissertation in speech was still promoting Erdman's line, asserting that Machen had a weak character. (Unlike Erdman, who would have had to respond publicly to Machen's withering logic without appearing to be a blithering id-

---

76. Machen, "The Good Fight of Faith," Sermon delivered in the Princeton Seminary chapel, March 10, 1929; printed in *The Presbyterian* (March 28, 1929), p. 8.
77. Machen, *Statement*, p. 21.
78. *Ibid.*, p. 22.

iot, the dissertation's author added that Machen's thought was also weak.)⁷⁹

Machen got to the political point late in the *Statement*: the publicity that had pictured Erdman as the victim of the faculty. This had appeared in the public press prior to his election as Moderator in 1925. The press picked up the twin stories: Erdman's access to the pulpit vacated by Machen—part of the normal rotation of this assignment, a fact not mentioned by the press—and the story of his removal as faculty advisor after he opposed the League of Evangelical Students.⁸⁰ In response, conservatives in the Presbytery of New Brunswick had started a committee to mail out press releases to counter what they regarded as false or misleading information.⁸¹ As Machen said, "We represent an unpopular cause, for which it is difficult to get a hearing."⁸² This existence of such a group indicates that the conservatives were becoming a little better organized.

"I am not a controversialist," Erdman had announced. "On the contrary," Machen replied, "he has shown himself, during his last few years, to be a controversialist of a very decided kind." Erdman had not directed his complaint about controversy to the signers of the Auburn *Affirmation* or doctrinal indifferentism. "But it is directed against men who defend the Christian faith."⁸³

Machen printed *Additional Statement*—"Printed, Not Published," it said on the cover—on December 18, 1926. He pointed out that Erdman's attack on the unnamed *Presbyterian* editors who were on the faculty of Princeton had to mean him. "In reply Dr. Erdman entered into certain explanations, the purport of which apparently was that he intended his attack in The Presbyterian Advance to be directed not

---

79. "Machen's intensity and complexity, and the weakness of his character and thought, make misreading him likely, if not inevitable." Delwyn G. Nykamp, A Presbyterian Power Struggle: A Critical History of Communication Strategies in the Struggle for Control of the Presbyterian Church, U.S.A., 1922-1926 (Ph.D. dissertation, Northwestern University, 1974), p. 88. I am torn between describing this sentence as supercilious or merely condescending.
80. Machen, *Statement*, p. 27.
81. *Ibid.*, p. 29.
82. *Ibid.*, p. 30.
83. *Ibid.*, p. 37.

against me but against some other member of the faculty."[84] But this information appeared in print in *The Presbyterian Advance* on Feb. 12, 1926. That, Machen did not have to say, was 13 months later. He reminded his readers that Erdman had fired the first shot, not only in *The Presbyterian Advance* but in two other newspapers. Also, he reminded them, "I have not engaged either first or last in any personal abuse of Dr. Erdman. . . ."[85]

The liberals who organized the campaign against the conservatives could not accept this explanation. An attack on a man's theology constituted, in their repeatedly stated public view, a personal attack. In contrast, Erdman's deeply personal attack on the unnamed Princeton faculty member's moral reputation was regarded by them as merely an accurate summary of the situation—fair play beyond question. They could not allow the issue to hinge on theology, for that would have meant allowing Machen and the conservatives to gain the high moral ground, not to mention legal leverage in Church courts. It would have allowed Machen to set the agenda, to frame the debate. They had to prevent this at all costs. To thwart him, they had to invoke personalities—converting an ecclesiastically legitimate judicial attack by the conservatives into an immoral personal attack.

Machen never fell into the trap of initiating personal attacks, as his predecessor Francis Patton had in his attack in 1874 on Swing. But despite Machen's clean hands, his opponents kept telling the press that there was a lot of suspicious dirt under his fingernails.

The 1927 General Assembly

At the 1927 General Assembly, Robert E. Speer was elected Moderator by acclamation. No Moderator had ever before been elected by acclamation.[86] He had only a token opponent.[87] A laymen, a bureau-

---

84. Machen, *Additional Statement*, p. 1.
85. *Ibid.*, p. 7.
86. William Joseph Watson, The Emergence of the Idea of Pluralism Within the Presbyterian Church in the U.S.A., 1890-1940 (Ph.D. dissertation, Yale University, 1988), p. 89.
87. W. Reginald Wheeler, *A Man Sent from God: A Biography of Robert E. Speer* (n.p.: Revell, 1956), p. 205.

crat, and a peace-keeping evangelical, Speer achieved what no other Presbyterian layman ever had: Moderator. It was a portent of things to come, not just in 1927 but for the next nine years. During the 1930's, his Rockefeller connection would lead him into the final stage of the Presbyterian conflict. He would become the last performer to play that indispensable role which had been played so effectively by a series of liberals since 1893: wounded lamb.

The question of the supplementary ordination clauses of 1910, 1916, and 1923 was reintroduced at the 1927 Assembly. A Special Commission appointed in 1925 reported back in 1927. Speer was a member.[88] This time, a final decision was reached. The authority of the five points was dismissed as not binding because every deliverance must be in "the exact language of the article as it appears in the Confession of Faith."[89] Furthermore, no subsequent Assembly is bound to uphold the decisions of a previous Assembly.[90] This report was adopted without debate.[91] Loetscher thought that this was a turning point in the Church's history since 1869: "It meant that moderate theological liberalism would have what it had unsuccessfully sought almost since the reunion, an acknowledged place in the Church's life and thought."[92] He was incorrect; 1920 had been the turning point. The 1927 General Assembly was merely the public acknowledgment of a liberal takeover of the Church's hierarchy that had taken place seven years earlier. It ratified the 1926 triumph.

No More Heresy Trials

But there was more to this report than what Loetscher indicated. It was the modernists' magna carta. It relieved them of their greatest fear: de-frocking by the General Assembly. The key passage was the section titled, "Authority of the General Assembly and the Function of Presbyteries in Regard to Licensure and Ordination." It asserted that the powers of the General Assembly are delegated by the presby-

---

88. Loetscher, *Broadening Church*, p. 133.
89. *Minutes of the General Assembly, 1927*, p. 81.
90. *Ibid.*, p. 80.
91. *Ibid.*, p. 58.
92. Loetscher, *Broadening Church.*, p. 135.

teries. These powers are specific and limited. "It follows that the powers of the General Assembly are numerated and defined; but the powers of Presbytery, being reserved powers, are not necessarily fully enumerated, nor strictly defined."[93] So far, so good. Next, "Licensure of probationers and ordination to the gospel ministry are the exclusive functions of the Presbytery. Whatever powers in this connection have been delegated to the General Assembly, the Assembly itself cannot do indirectly what it has no authority to do indirectly."[94] So far, still so good: the Assembly cannot ordain ministers. But there was more. The Assembly is the highest court, and has authority to interpret general deliverances "and apply the Constitution to specific judicial cases."[95] To use the analogy of baseball pitching, this was the long, slow curve. Then, seven pages later, came the fast break: the prohibition of post-ordination heresy trials by the General Assembly. I quote the passage verbatim because a summary would seem unbelievable. *The General Assembly may not lawfully revoke any man's ordination for any reason.* It can go as far as severing all connection with the offending presbytery (mass de-frocking?) that ordained him, but *once ordained, always ordained* as far as the General Assembly can legally say.

> When, however, complaint has been lodged against a Presbytery because it has, through its ministerial members, ordained a candidate alleged to be not qualified, and execution of the decision complained of has not been stayed by one-third of the members recorded as present when the decision was made, joining in complaint against the ordination, the complaint may be answered by the superior court, even by the General Assembly, unfavorably to the Presbytery's action, but this would not invalidate the ordination nor affect the official status of the newly endowed minister, nor annul the sacred rites already performed by him. The Presbytery may be disciplined for erroneous action, and there appears to be no limit to the authority of the General Assembly in dealing with a Presbytery that has proved to be contumacious, but the individual whom the Presbytery has ordained

---

93. *Minutes of the General Assembly, 1927*, p. 62.
94. *Ibid.*
95. *Ibid.*

constitutionally can not be reached by this process. If there has been no stay, and he has been invested with the office, the issue, so far as he is affected, is between the General Assembly and the Presbytery and is founded upon a complaint against the Presbytery, to which he is not even a party. The one proper method of proceeding against the newly ordained minister would be to prefer charges against him personally and the substantive charges should be based upon facts coming to the knowledge of the Presbytery subsequent to his ordination. For these he might, if convicted, be suspended or deposed, but the disposition of this case would not affect, technically, the complaint against the Presbytery called to account for ordaining him.[96]

The report continued: "It would not seem logical to infer that the General Assembly has been clothed with authority to revoke an ordination when the Presbytery itself does not possess this authority, or that the General Assembly can direct a Presbytery to do something by means which the Presbytery is forbidden to employ originally."[97] The commission made its position crystal clear: "Once a minister, always a minister. . . ."[98]

By unanimous vote, the General Assembly abandoned its authority to call into question any man's ordination for any reason. Even the presbytery was said to be limited—unlike the statement to the contrary seven pages earlier. Only upon the introduction of new material not available to the presbytery at the time of the person's ordination can a presbytery revoke this ordination. If one-third of the members of presbytery did not complain at the time of the ordination, which would annul it until a later date, an ordination is irrevocable. All authority to revoke it is lodged with the presbytery. Thus, once cleared by his presbytery regarding any accusation against him, the man cannot be tried by any higher court. This had been the modernists' number-one judicial goal since the 1870's: the prohibition of double jeopardy.

---

96. *Ibid.*, p. 69.
97. *Ibid.*, p. 70.
98. *Ibid.*, p. 68.

Notice this phrase: "The Presbytery may be disciplined for erroneous action, and there appears to be no limit to the authority of the General Assembly in dealing with a Presbytery that has proved to be contumacious. . . ." How, pray tell, can a presbytery be disciplined if its ordained ministers cannot be deposed from office? How can an entire presbytery be de-frocked by the General Assembly if none of its members can be de-frocked by the General Assembly?

Unless a subsequent General Assembly reversed this decision, the Presbyterian conflict had finally been settled judicially. But no one said publicly what this meant in terms of Church polity. The report had revoked Presbyterianism's system of appeals courts, with the General Assembly as the supreme court. The report announced a new ordination polity: regional autonomy. It created a truncated system of local courts. The initiating executive agency of ordination would henceforth also become the supreme court with respect to its ordinations. A presbytery would sit in final judgment of itself. This report mandated judicial paralysis: the end of negative sanctions above the presbytery level. It announced the end of hierarchy. Legally, the Church would now become a Presbyterian-Congregational hybrid, almost as the 1801 Plan of Union had prescribed. Yet this new polity had not been voted on by the presbyteries. It could not survive, given the Form of Government.

As it turned out, this new judicial order was merely temporary: a holding action to secure immunity from prosecution for the liberals, so that they would enjoy peace and toleration, giving them time to restructure Presbyterian law. That restructuring began in 1931 and took effect in 1934.

In 1936, the Presbytery of New Brunswick revoked Machen's ordination, and the General Assembly upheld this act. This was power religion in action. Things evolve, especially judicial standards.

Bait and Hook: The Pension Program

We come now to a topic that has never been mentioned in any published discussion of the Presbyterian conflict. This was the strategic role of the pension fund in the consolidation of bureaucratic power within the denomination. There are reasons for this previous silence. To discuss money as a primary motivation of godly men alienates the theologically faithful who prefer to view the Presbyterian conflict strictly in terms of theological controversy. Similarly, to discuss the strategic use of money and promises of money as part of a conspiratorial program of infiltration alienates the intellectual and spiritual heirs of the victors who successfully employed the strategy. Neither side wants to follow the money. It is time to do so, especially in the context of the 1927 General Assembly.

In 1908, the Church voted to create an Executive Commission to represent the General Assembly in between Assemblies. This was a major move in the direction of denominational centralization. The Executive Commission immediately began making plans to consolidate the boards, a strategy which was not completed until the 1924 General Assembly. In 1912, the Executive Commission had proposed the consolidation of the two boards that administered ministerial relief. The new board would be called the Ministerial Sustenation Fund. As part of this plan, the Executive Commission proposed the creation of a ministers' retirement fund "of not less than $10,000,000."[99] This was an enormous sum in 1912's pre-war purchasing power—in the range of $200 million in 1995 dollars. Motivated by this generous promise, the General Assembly voted to consolidate the two boards. The $10 million never materialized. The Church had established a $7 million fund by 1918, but with the post-war purchasing power of the dollar reduced considerably. Then the mini-depression of 1920–21 reduced the market value of this inadequate portfolio. Meanwhile, more ministers than ever before were approaching retirement age.[100] It was clear that a crisis was approaching: ". . . the deficit was becoming unmanageable."[101] A new round of promises became necessary.

Investing and Divesting

In 1924, the newly consolidated Board of Pensions introduced a plan for a replacement pension fund. The plan promised to raise $15 million in capital. This plan was voted for by the General Assembly. But the plan lacked a specific clause: the right of a minister to demit

---

99. *Minutes of the General Assembly, 1912*, p. 233.
100. R. Douglas Brackenridge and Lois A. Boyd, *Presbyterians and Pensions, 1717–1988* (Atlanta: John Knox Press, 1988), pp. 68–69.
101. *Ibid.*, p. 69.

the ministry or leave for any other reason and take his pension money with him. That is, *there was zero vesting*. The Pension Board had designed a system in which each participant's funds would be totally locked into the denomination until he retired on schedule. This omission became part of a 1928 overture by the Presbytery of Marion, which insisted that a minister should be allowed to collect his funds, plus 4 percent interest, "but shall sacrifice all benefits and payments that have been made on his behalf by salary paying organizations."[102] This was incorporated into the final plan in 1928. This was only partial vesting: a minimal 25 percent.

The Board of Pensions had announced to the 1927 General Assembly that as of April 1, 1927, the denomination's new pension program, the Service Pension Plan, had been in effect. A minister had until March 31, 1928, to sign up to obtain credit for his prior years of service. He had to pay in ten percent of his salary (15 percent if he had a manse) for that year in order to become eligible. This means that for ten percent of one year's income he would receive a retroactive retirement credit for his entire career. This was a very large piece of bait. This year would be a minister's "window of opportunity." The 1928 Foreword to the Service Pension Plan reminded readers of this past deadline.[103] But the Board in fact kept the window open beyond the deadline.[104]

To fund this extraordinary offer—unprecedented in the history of private pension funds—the Board of Pensions had to raise a huge amount of money. Preliminary work on this had begun in 1923, when the Assembly appointed a committee that included millionaires Frederick Weyerhauser and Richard Mellon. It also included publicist Will Hays, the former Postmaster General of the United States and then "motion picture czar" who ran the Hays Office.[105] The real work began in 1927. At that time, over $15 million in pledges were on record.[106] But pledges are easier to obtain than money. As of April 1,

---

102. *Minutes of the General Assembly, 1928*, p. 26.
103. *Ibid*., p. 250.
104. *Minutes of the General Assembly, 1929*, Part 2, *Reports of the Boards, Board of Pensions*, p. v.
105. Brackenridge & Boyd, *Pensions*, p. 72.
106. *Ibid*., p. 75.

1929, six months before the stock market crash, only $8.2 million had been collected.[107] That was the high point of pledge-collecting.

Those who had already retired by April 1, 1927, were not included in the new program. Almost 2,000 of these people were on the Presbyterian relief roles in May, 1928.[108] The Board regretfully announced that at some unstated future time (perhaps seven years), the Board would no longer fund these pre-1927 pensioners even partially, and annual support from the Board should be expected to drop until that time.[109] The Board implored the Church at large to do its duty and support these unfortunates.[110] As for the hoped-for $15 million, all of it "belongs absolutely to the men and women who were in active service of the Presbyterian Church on April 1, 1927."[111] The political implication: *those who no longer could impose ministerial judicial sanctions were not eligible for the bait.*

From 1928 on, a participating minister contributed 2.5 percent and his congregation contributed 7.5 percent. For this, the retired pensioner at age 65 would receive 1.25 percent of his average salary during his covered years.[112] At a salary of $1,200 a year (the minimum specified by many synods), times 35 years, the figure for lifetime income was $42,000. Multiplying this by .0125 gives $525 a year. The minimum guaranteed income was $600 a year.[113] A widow received half: a minimum of $300 a year, which would cease upon remarriage.[114] An orphan would receive $100 a year until maturity; then nothing.[115] The maximum income paid to a retired minister was $2,000 a year.[116]

---

107. *Minutes of the General Assembly, 1929, II, Board of Pensions Report*, p. 8.
108. *Ibid.*, II, *Pensions*, p. 3.
109. *Ibid.*, II, *Pensions*, p. 4.
110. *Ibid.*, II, *Pensions*, pp. 4–5.
111. *Ibid.*, II, *Pensions*, p. 5.
112. *Minutes of the General Assembly, 1928*, p. 251.
113. *Ibid.*, p. 252.
114. *Ibid.*, p. 256.
115. *Ibid.*, p. 257.
116. *Ibid.*, p. 252.

The minister's pension was minimally vested. Any minister who withdrew from the denomination had been warned in advance: he would receive his contributions of 2.5 percent, plus 4 percent interest on his money.[117] Whatever his local church had contributed, plus all the build-up of interest, stayed with the Pension Board. This was the denomination's hook. Rather than taking a salary increase of 7.5 percent and investing it, along with his 2.5 percent, a participating minister took his salary in a different form: a three-to-one "matching" grant. Financially, it made no difference to the congregation which way he chose to be compensated. It did make a difference in terms of control, however. He would not be so likely to leave the denomination if it would cost him three-quarters of his pension's equity. This turned out to be doubly true nine years later, in the middle of the depression.

The pension scheme was pure bait and hook. It worked. By the time of the 1928 General Assembly, over 7,000 ministers and Church workers were enrolled. This made participation in the plan the rule rather than the exception that it had been previously.[118] In 1926, only 2,500 ministers had been enrolled when it paid only $350 a year after 35 years of service.[119]

The 1936 General Assembly elected as its Moderator Rev. Henry B. Master, a Princeton Seminary graduate, who had served as the executive secretary of the Board of Pensions since 1919.[120] His presence at the podium was a visible reminder to the assembled ministers of just how much was at stake in a decision to walk out of the denomination alongside Machen.

Bait and Switch

The plan had been sold to the ministers with this guarantee: no minister would be forced to retire at age 65. Master had assured everyone in writing: "Our retirement plan provides a pension at the age of sixty-five IN ORDER TO PREVENT RETIREMENT."[121] Most min-

---

117. *Ibid.*, pp. 257–58.
118. Brackenridge and Boyd, *Pensions*, p. 76.
119. *Ibid.*, p. 70.
120. *New York Times* (May 29, 1936), p. 3.
121. Brackenridge and Boyd, *Pensions*, p. 74.

isters knew what the Board also knew, that after age 49, a man's opportunities dropped sharply. Larger congregations hired young ministers, so older men had to content themselves with demand from smaller churches offering reduced salaries. A decade later, the Board changed the rules: mandatory retirement at age 65. This engulfed the denomination in controversy.[122]

The monograph on the history of Presbyterian pension programs does not offer an explanation for this change. There are two obvious reasons: one economic, one theological. First, economics: if a man stopped paying into the fund at age 65 but received income from it, his portion of the fund would suffer a net outflow. The benefit to the older man was double income: pension plus salary. On the other hand, if the recipient was forced to retire, a younger man would replace him, and he would probably become a participant in the program. His contributions would flow in.

Second, theology: forcible retirement was a way to push older conservatives out of their pulpits. In 1937, Machen and the hard-line Calvinists were gone, but there were many older men in the denomination's pulpits who held very conservative theological views. These men would now have to resign from their pulpits at age 65 if they wanted to receive their pension income. In 1936, they had been forced to remain in the Church if they wanted to keep their pensions. The longer they had been in the Church, the more valuable their pensions were. So, older men who stayed behind, hoping to keep their jobs and their pensions, unlike Machen and his followers, who gave up both, now faced another decision: pension income or job, but not both at once. They had forgotten the rule of contracts: "The large print giveth, and the fine print taketh away." They had been warned in the *Minutes* that almost nobody ever read: "The right to alter and amend the above described Plan, as may be found to be to the general advantage of the Church, is reserved to the Board of Pensions of the Presbyterian Church in the U.S.A., such alterations and amendments to be effective only after approval of the General Assembly."[123] Legally, no commercial insurance company could have written in a clause like

---

122. *Ibid.*
123. *Minutes of the General Assembly*, 1928, p. 257.

this one. The Presbyterian Church could. This was power religion in action. Things evolve, especially pension guarantees.

In 1939, the Board of Pensions admitted to the denomination that the Board's assets had dropped by $12 million. These were "paper" losses, the Church was assured: a merely temporary fall in market value. The Board had invested 70 percent of its portfolio in railroad bonds and mortgages at something over 4 percent. Millions of dollars worth of these bonds and mortgages had gone into default. The Board then wound up owning a lot of depreciated real estate. The fund's managers then began switching more of the portfolio into stocks. Then came the 1937–38 stock market crash.[124]

The 1939 General Assembly was assured by a Pension Board official that the fund's reserves were actuarially sound. The attendees were also informed that in order to begin collecting their pensions, ministers would have to retire at age 65.[125] This was obviously doubletalk. If the fund's reserves were sound, why the change in retirement policy? The problem was admitted publicly at the 1940 General Assembly. The justification for the change in policy in 1939 was that the pension fund would not otherwise meet actuarial standards.[126] By 1940, the Board's reputation was very low.[127] At the 1941 General Assembly, ministers were told that, beginning in October of 1942, pension benefits would be reduced by ten percent.[128]

What saved the revised pension program was the inflation of World War II. This so reduced the pre-1940 value of the pension fund's legal obligations that the program survived on paper, i.e., on paper money. The hook had caught many fish; the bait now melted away.

Princeton Seminary

The 1926 committee to investigate Princeton presented its report, filling pages 87 to 134 of the *Minutes*. The committee also turned over

---

124. *Ibid.*, pp. 122–23.
125. *New York Times* (May 28, 1939), p. 19.
126. *Ibid.* (May 26, 1940), p. 21.
127. Brackenridge and Boyd, *Pensions*, p. 124.
128. *New York Times* (May 24, 1941), p. 34.

to the General Assembly a transcript of the hearings that was 800 pages long. The committee's conclusion was classically Presbyterian: another committee was recommended. Coming to that conclusion, however, did not require 47 pages plus 800 pages of hearings. The committee had to lay some groundwork, also called poisoning the well. For example, in dealing with the conflict between Erdman and Machen, in which Erdman had in print falsely implied that Machen was behind an editorial in *The Presbyterian* that was hostile to Erdman, the committee cited Machen's willingness to let the matter drop. "I do not believe that any desire on my part for personal vindication should be allowed to jeopardize the high interests with which this institution is entrusted. I do not, of course, mean that I shall necessarily agree with Dr. Erdman's ecclesiastical policies, with regard to which I must, of course, follow the dictates of my conscience. But I am ready and willing, with appreciation of the good offices of the Committee, to resume full personal friendly relations with Dr. Erdman."[129]

This statement presented a major problem for the committee. The modernists, from van Dyke's 1923 press release onward, had spent a great deal of space in the press painting Machen as a bitter, unyielding, un-Christian controversialist. This conciliatory statement by Machen undercut this image of his personality. This, in turn, would tend to remove the stigma of "malignant spirit" from the man, thereby removing from him the added judicial burden imposed by Presbyterian law on such people.[130] The committee could not allow this to go unchallenged, so, without citing any specific infraction on Machen's part, the report hastened to add:

> But the ensuing discussion left with the Committee the impression that the statement had been academic and defensive, rather than an overture toward reconciliation. Dr. Machen confesses no fault. He accepts no forgiveness and offers none. The

---

129. *Minutes of the General Assembly, 1927*, p. 98.
130. *The Book of Discipline*, II:13. *The Constitution of the Presbyterian Church in the United States of America* (Philadelphia: Presbyterian Board of Publication and Sabbath School Work, 1904), p. 395. See Chapter 8, above: subsection on "Van Dyke Strikes Again," pp. 505–508.

net effect of these personal conferences with the Faculty upon the minds of the Committee was an impression that no essential change had taken place in the mind of Dr. Machen. He still believes that there are serious differences in the doctrinal attitudes of the Faculty, and he is unwilling to trust the doctrinal loyalties of his colleagues. This obviously leaves much to be desired as a basis of brotherly relations.[131]

There is an implicit formula here: *doctrinal differences = unbrotherly relations*. This formula was promoted by the modernists, accepted hesitatingly by the conservative middle, and applied to the orthodox party.

The committee criticized the divided authority of the trustees and the directors, calling it "unwise and always likely to be a source of friction."[132] Since 1922, the charter designated only a Board of Trustees.[133] But the Board of Directors had existed since the original Plan of 1811, before the charter of incorporation, as the Assembly's agency of control.[134]

A report of the General Assembly in 1893, the year of Briggs' de-frocking, had specified that the property of the Seminary was governed by stipulations. The Seminary had come under the jurisdiction of the reunited Church in 1870 on the basis of a continuation of the Confession of Faith and Catechisms, "as these doctrines were understood and explained by the Old School General Assembly," and these "shall continue to be taught in the Seminary."[135] The donors had specified this provision. These gifts were made under stipulations that were a matter of civil law.[136] But the Trustees legally controlled these funds. The 1926 committee assured everyone that the Trustees would carry out this trust.[137] The committee met with the Trustees and ad-

---

131. *Minutes of the General Assembly, 1927*, pp. 98–99.
132. *Ibid.*, p. 102.
133. *Ibid.*, pp. 102–103.
134. *Ibid.*, p. 104.
135. *Ibid.*, p. 107.
136. *Ibid.*
137. *Ibid.*, pp. 108–109.

vised that they secure legal counsel on the matter of single-board control with respect to New Jersey law.[138]

The committee recommended that all the seminaries be placed under the jurisdiction of the General Assembly.[139] This, of course, did not include Union, which had pulled out a generation earlier, or Auburn, which had also pulled out. It assured the Assembly that "sacred trusts" existed between donors and seminaries, and that the wishes of donors would be upheld.[140]

Seven years later, a Barthian was on the faculty at Princeton as a visiting lecturer, and Emil Brunner himself was on the faculty in 1939. This was power religion in action. Things evolve, especially sacred trusts.

The committee recommended deferring all appointments to any faculty position until the next General Assembly.[141] This meant Machen and O. T. Allis, who was Machen's alter ego in the Old Testament department.

The committee referred back to the 1923 decision of the General Assembly to consolidate control over seminaries in one board per seminary. The Princeton boards had ignored it.[142]

The committee concluded that "The root and source of the serious difficulties at Princeton, and the greatest obstacle to the removal of these difficulties, seem to be in the plan of government by two boards."[143] Irreconcilable theological conflict is thus transformed into an administrative matter, and so it can be reconciled. (Thus might men of good will and advanced management training heal the breach between heaven and hell.)

Recommendations: (1) appoint another committee; (2) delay the appointments of Machen and also Allis, who had been appointed to the chair in Old Testament.[144]

---

138. *Ibid.*, p. 109.
139. *Ibid.*, p. 112.
140. *Ibid.*, p. 113.
141. *Ibid.*, p. 119.
142. *Ibid.*, p. 124.
143. *Ibid.*, p. 131.
144. *Ibid.*, p. 133.

The Assembly's vote to accept the report (503 to 323) revealed that there was no longer any institutionally significant opposition to the power religion. The commissioners rose and cheered.[145]

On the Defensive

It was clear that Machen and his supporters were now completely on the defensive. There was little that they could accomplish to halt the onrushing events. During the year between the 1927 and 1928 Assemblies, a petition was circulated asking the new Assembly to refrain from tampering with Princeton's system of government, and it eventually collected the signatures of some 11,000 ruling elders and 2,500 ministers.[146] It was presented to the 1928 Assembly, but judging from the events that followed, it had no effect.

Machen felt the sting of the rejection. He referred to it as "an indignity almost without precedent in the entire history of our Church."[147] There had been one such precedent: the rejection of Briggs' appointment in 1891 by the General Assembly. Briggs retained his appointment because Union pulled out from under the General Assembly's control. Princeton did not. Briggs was de-frocked in 1893 for heresy; Machen was de-frocked in 1936 for failure to obey.

Machen never received his appointment. For the first time in the history of Princeton, the Board's appointment was vetoed. The Board then decided to appoint a less controversial man, one with no reputation nationally, and with no teaching experience, either. He had earned a Princeton University Ph.D. in philosophy in 1927. He was a disciple of Geerhardus Vos, the least understood of the orthodox members of the faculty. In 1928, he was serving as a pastor in rural Indiana. All in all, it looked like a safe bureaucratic appointment, one that would not rock the boat. They appointed a man who, they believed, would shun public controversy: Cornelius Van Til. This call brought Van Til back into academia from a rural Indiana congrega-

---

145. Loetscher, *Broadening Church*, p. 145.
146. D. G. Hart, "Doctor Fundamentalis": An Intellectual Biography of J. Gresham Machen, 1881-1937 (Ph.D. dissertation, Johns Hopkins University, 1988), p. 294.
147. Machen, *Statement*, p. 1.

tion of 70 families.[148] In 1928, he had wanted only to be a pastor in the Christian Reformed Church.

Machen's Plea for Pluralism

In a pamphlet issued in December, 1927, Machen returned to a familiar theme. He pointed out that one member of the committee which the Board of Trustees had created to work out the reorganization was a signer of the Auburn *Affirmation*.[149] The presence of Affirmationists on any board, committee, or commission became a touchstone for Machen and his allies: proof of the theological unreliability of the group.

He began his defense with a summary of what the Seminary stood for: the accuracy of the Bible, the doctrinal authority of the Westminster Confession, and a rigorous intellectual defense of Christianity.[150] Its students are subjected to a rigorous academic program: ". . . we try to divest our students of the notion that there is any royal road to sacred learning. . . ."[151] They are required to study many viewpoints; the curriculum is not "unduly negative."[152]

In Chapter 2, he offered a brief history of the attack on Princeton. He blamed its president: ". . . the first important step was the coming of J. Ross Stevenson as president of the Seminary."[153] By naming Stevenson, Machen launched a last-ditch suicide mission, since no academic organization tolerates published attacks on its president from inside the system unless it is totally on the defensive. But Stevenson's associates had almost won by late 1927.

Machen insisted that Stevenson was opposed to Old School tradition at Princeton. Machen's tactical problem was that Stevenson had been president since 1914. Why, at this late date, was Machen com-

---

148. William White, *Van Til: Defender of the Faith* (Nashville: Thomas Nelson Sons, 1979), p. 71.
149. Machen, *The Attack Upon Princeton Seminary: A Plea for Fair Play* (Dec. 1927), p. 5.
150. *Ibid.*, pp. 6–11.
151. *Ibid.*, p. 12.
152. *Ibid.*, p. 13.
153. *Ibid.*, p. 16.

plaining? This is always the problem of the critic who tries to work within the system: he then finds it tactically difficult ever to appeal beyond the system. He argued that Stevenson could have resigned; instead, Stevenson had appealed to the General Assembly to consolidate the Trustees and the Board.[154] This pointed to the conservatives' problem since 1893: their opponents had no intention of resigning.

The Assembly should reverse this consolidation, Machen argued. There are other seminaries. They are liberal. Why should Princeton's message be muted? The conservatives "must be allowed to have at least one seminary that clearly and unequivocally represents their view."[155]

This was a theologically doomed argument that reflected an ecclesiastically doomed movement. He was arguing utter nonsense, given his theological commitment. He had argued that liberalism is a rival religion. But if he was correct, then on what basis should liberals be allowed to teach in seminaries inside the Church? Religious pluralism has no place in the Church; this had been Machen's argument from the beginning. His 1927 argument made as much sense as a principled defender of monogamy complaining that a married man ought to allow his wife to have her own home, keeping his concubines in another dwelling. The only monogamist who would invoke such an argument is a frantic wife whose husband is openly planning to put his concubines down the hall.

He predicted that if the reoarganization went through, Princeton would soon go modernist.[156] In one way, he was correct; in another, he was not. Princeton by 1933 had moved publicly toward neo-orthodoxy: Adolph Keller's Stone Foundation lectures.[157] In 1939, Emil Brunner was a guest faculty member. Princeton adopted what Van Til in 1947 would call the new modernism.

The liberals in 1929 were at last ready to reveal the fact that their commitment to pluralism had always been tactical, not principled. *They did not believe in pluralism; they believed in power.* They did not

---

154. *Ibid.*, pp. 16–17.
155. *Ibid.*
156. *Ibid.*, p. 36.
157. See below: section on "The New Princeton," pp. 638–41.

believe in equal time for orthodoxy in the councils of the Church; they believed in no time for orthodoxy. They wanted to confine orthodoxy to prayer closets. What they had said in print regarding the free expression of ideas, 1891 to 1926, was rhetoric for popular consumption. They had no intention of acting in terms of their rhetoric. Why should they?

The modernists were Progressives. Indeed, as Hofstadter says, "Progressivism can be considered from this standpoint as a phase in the history of the Protestant conscience, a latter-day Protestant revival. Liberal politics as well as liberal theology were both inherent in the response of religion to the secularization of society."[158] As Progressives, modernists believed in the use of force to change men and society. Most of all, they believed in using other people's money to achieve their goals. But they were wise. They understood that they could not be open about this use of force. So they adopted another strategy, very long term: the institutional suppression of rival views. Lester Frank Ward, who provided the Progressives with their sociological worldview,[159] had presented this strategy of institutional infiltration through ideological filtering as early as 1883. "Instill progressive principles, no matter how, into the mind, and progressive actions will result." But there is a problem: the reaction against coercion. "The attempt to change opinions by direct efforts has been frequently made. No one will deny that coercion applied to this end has been a signal failure." Then how should progressive people change unprogressive minds who hold unprogressive views? *By a systematic program of exclusion and censorship.* "The forcible suppression of the utterance or publication in any form of unwelcome opinions is equivalent to withholding from all undetermined minds the evidence upon which such views rest; . . ."[160] Conclusion: "It is simply that true views may as

---

158. Richard Hofstadter, *The Age of Reform: From Bryan to F.D.R.* (New York: Vintage, 1955), p. 152.

159. Henry Steele Commager, *The American Mind: An Interpretation of American Thought and Character Since the 1880's* (New Haven, Connecticut: Yale University Press, 1950), ch. 12.

160. Lester Frank Ward, *Dynamic Sociology; or Applied Social Science*, 2 vols. (New York: Appleton, [1883] 1907), II:547.

easily be created by this *method of exclusion* as false ones, which latter is the point of view from which this fact is regarded. The more or less arbitrary exclusion of error, *i.e.*, of false data, is to a great degree justifiable. . . . This, however, is the essence of what is here meant by education, which may be regarded as a systematic process for the manufacture of correct opinions."[161] No Whig pluralist illusions here!

The Presbyterian modernists were ready to put the final squeeze on the main source of what they regarded as the most dangerous theological ideas in the United States: Princeton Seminary. They fully understood that this was the point of entry of the most self-conscious, consistent, academically sophisticated alternative to theological modernism. They had to silence it, but without providing evidence of the coercive nature of this carefully planned, decades-old pincer movement. Machen knew they understood exactly what they were doing: "But the truth is that Princeton is being attacked not in spite of its success but because of it."[162]

His plea for fair play—allowing at least one Old School seminary out of a dozen[163]—was a cry of desperation. His commitment to Whig politics had at this point overcome his commitment to a pure Church. He had always previously insisted that Whig pluralism be confined to civil government. He had always understood that there could be no "equal time" for historic Calvinism in a Church that was dominated by anti-creedal modernists and both liberals and evangelicals who agreed with Speer's minimal-creed persuasion. Now he had proof. Even one-thirteenth time was too much for the likes of Erdman and Stevenson. There had to be a victory for one side or the other. By 1927, it was clear which side this would be. Machen must have known this, for he wrote: "The ecclesiastical machinery rolls smoothly on, and the Church proceeds to destroy that wherein its real safety rests."[164]

---

161. *Ibid.*, II:548.
162. Machen, *Attack*, p. 37.
163. Not counting Union and Auburn, which were outside the Church.
164. *Ibid.*

Machen's Judicial Protest

Just before the 1928 General Assembly convened at Tulsa, Oklahoma, Machen published a 35-page pamphlet stating legal objections to the proposed reorganization. This booklet, bearing the lengthy title of *Legal Opinion on Questions Involved in Proposed Reorganization of Princeton Theological Seminary*, was an attempt by Machen, Allis, and several attorneys to show that the reorganization, as proposed, was not constitutional according to Presbyterian Church law, and might well be counter to New Jersey state law. Several questions were considered, but the three main points concerned the powers of the Trustees, the right of the General Assembly to postpone the appointments of Machen and Allis, and the legal restrictions on the reorganization itself.

We need to examine the logic of his position, not because it convinced the Church's authorities, but because it didn't. Machen was following the tradition of judicial theology. He wanted to abide by the laws of the Church and the laws of the State of New Jersey. He wanted to abide by the Seminary's charter. He wanted to remain faithful to both the letter of the law and the spirit of the law. In short, he wanted to save Princeton Seminary from those whose goal was to subvert it. But his appeal to law fell on deaf ears. His liberal opponents wanted to capture something that did not belong to them—an oath-bound institution that still affirmed the terms of the oath. Those who affirmed it but did not believe it asked only one thing: "Who holds the hammer?" After 1925, they did. It was time to use it.

The liberals' governing principle was the capture of power. To achieve this at Princeton Seminary, they had to ignore the letter of the law and the intentions of those who had built the institution. They now moved from their earlier position of legalism—undermining the intent of the law by the letter of the law—to the exercise of raw power. This did not bother them in the slightest. After all, their spiritual cousins had already captured Princeton University under Woodrow Wilson and his successor, Rev. John Grier Hibben.[165]

---

165. Hibben was typical of the era. He was another supposed conservative

But Machen did not have clean hands in this matter. He had served as an instructor from 1906 to 1914, in obvious defiance of the intent of the founders of Princeton Seminary, who wanted only ordained men as teachers on the faculty. Old Princeton, in desperately short supply of competent teachers, had bent the rules. Like a branch pulled back and then released, this infraction snapped back and struck down its previous beneficiary.

The Fine Details of the Law

Machen's pamphlet surveyed three issues: the power of the Trustees, the approval of the nomination of professors, and the legality of the proposed reorganization. On the first issue, the power of the Trustees, the authors stated that the Assembly assumes a two-board control of the Seminary. This, they assert, is not the case: "The Trustees have no voice in the management of the Seminary at all . . . except so far as additional powers may be vested in them by the Plan; and such additional powers, if any, are *at most* a veto for financial reasons on certain expenditures on funds."[166] If the logic of the General Assembly concludes that this makes the Trustees a second board of control, then it must also take into account that a small part of the funds are held by the Assembly's Trustees, and therefore, "by the same token the Trustees of the General Assembly are a third board of control."[167] This technicality proved unimpressive to the General Assembly.

On the second question, the approval of the nomination of professors, the authors argued that the veto, logically, should be used during the same General Assembly meeting as the nomination to any chair is made, "otherwise the Seminary may be kept in a state of turmoil and

---

who had been voted for by the trustees in 1912, two years after Wilson's departure, in order to reverse or at least modify Wilson's reforms, but who then consolidated these reforms. Henry Wilkinson Bragdon, *Woodrow Wilson: The Academic Years* (Cambridge, Massachusetts: Belknap Press of Harvard University, 1967), pp. 405–407.

166. Machen, Allis, and Armstrong, *Legal Opinion on Questions Involved in Proposed Reorganization of Princeton Theological Seminary* (Baltimore, Maryland: Author's Printing, 1928), p. 6.

167. *Ibid.*, p. 7.

uncertainty indefinitely by postponing from year to year action on elections of professors."[168]

This had been Francis Patton's argument a generation earlier during the Briggs dispute. In the interest of academic freedom, he had said, let us limit the Assembly's right to veto any appointment to the next Assembly after the nomination.[169]

The pamphlet called attention to the hesitation of Auburn Seminary to enter the Presbyterian seminary system in 1871, precisely because of the vagueness of the Plan of Princeton Seminary concerning the veto power of the Assembly. In order to alleviate these fears, the Assembly had passed an amendment to Article III, Section I of the Plan, "apparently unanimously," that the veto would have to be applied at the General Assembly following the appointment.

Stevenson held another view, according to the pamphlet: a postponement is not a "failure to act." The authors took exception, however, claiming that a "'failure to act' plainly means 'failure to take final action.'"[170] Therefore, the actions of the 1926 and 1927 Assemblies were void, and both men were entitled to their chairs and pay, to be enforced by the Church courts.

It might appear as though Machen and Allis were motivated purely by personal interest to publish this attack, an action aimed merely at getting their back pay and offices. In light of their subsequent decisions to leave Princeton on doctrinal grounds, breaking contact with Princeton completely, it would seem more reasonable to assume that they were really trying to show that the whole matter of Princeton was being mishandled by the liberal faction in control of

---

168. *Ibid.*

169. Patton spoke before the General Assembly of 1891, the GA which followed Briggs' 1891 Inaugural Address. He said: "I am a professor. I have the prejudices of my class, and I tell you that, in the name of that class, I will protest against the right of an Assembly to hold the threat of veto over me a dozen years in succession. They have their chance once, and if they don't veto my appointment then, they ought not to have the chance four or five years hence. . . . I tell you it is in the interest of freedom. . . ." Cited in G. L. Prentiss, *The Union Theological Seminary in the City of New York: Its Design and Another Decade of its History* (Asbury Park, New Jersey: Pennypacker, 1899), pp. 123-24.

170. *Legal Opinion*, p. 14.

the General Assemblies' machinery. Machen, with financial support available to him outside of his capacity as a teacher—money that permitted him to publish the pamphlet—was hardly worried personally about the differences in pay scales between an assistant professor and full professor, except as a point of legal contention. In any case, as recently as 1926, he had been approached by Columbia Seminary, the Southern Presbyterian institution, to accept the chair in New Testament.[171] He would have been a plum on that far less distinguished faculty. He was not facing forced retirement.

The third and final issue, the legality of the proposed reorganization, affords additional insight into the hopelessness of the orthodox position. Appealing to Article I, Section 3 of the Plan of the Seminary, the authors asserted that to be legal, any alteration in the Plan must be approved by a unanimous vote if the proposed change is introduced at that Assembly. Otherwise, the specific recommendation cannot be voted on until the next General Assembly, at which time a majority decision can alter the Plan. At the 1927 meeting, W. O. Thompson introduced notice that "at the next meeting of the General Assembly to be convened in May, 1928, a resolution will be proposed for adoption abrogating the Plan of Princeton Theological Seminary." This was not a true proposal, in the authors' view, since it was not specific in regard to the changes to be made, and therefore to be legal, a unanimous vote had to be registered at the General Assembly of 1928.[172]

A Holding Action

These men were clearly fighting a holding action. At most, assuming the unreasonable hope that their thesis would be upheld in the hostile Assembly, the decision to reorganize Princeton could only be postponed for one year, since the opposition obviously had the votes, even if not a unanimous voice. Perhaps the defenders hoped for a change of heart on the part of the Assembly of 1928, since the constituency of the presbyteries might conceivably change, or the new

---

171. Stonehouse, *Machen*, p. 424.
172. *Legal Opinion*, pp. 22–24.

delegates might be more conservative. But this was an unrealistic hope, and, as it turned out, a useless one; the conservative camp became smaller at each succeeding Assembly.

Nevertheless, Machen had done everything he could judicially. He had repeated his familiar arguments about the need for a strong voice for historic Presbyterianism. This did no good on the floor of the Assembly. The 1928 Assembly voted to postpone the reorganization for one more year, asking the Board of Directors to try to compose the differences on the faculty in the intervening period.

The Defections Begin

The Seminary's Directors, probably seeing the inevitability of the 1929 General Assembly's action, reversed their traditionally impregnable orthodox stand, and voted, 17 to ten, to approve the report of the Committee of Eleven. Perhaps there was some thought that a useless fight against the Assembly, whose power in the matter was unquestioned, would do no good, and in fact might alienate the new board completely. Whatever the reason, the capitulation of the Directors made the final decision of the 1929 Assembly anti-climactic. At that Assembly, the debate over Princeton was allocated a total of 25 minutes of discussion time. Machen was allowed to speak for five minutes.[173] So much for three decades of pleas from the liberals for "fair play" and "toleration." The liberals now had the votes, and from that time on, they wasted no more time. There would now be negative sanctions.

The newly created board was composed of one-third of the members of the Directors, one-third on the old Board of Trustees, and one-third from the Church at large. Both Mudge and Speer were members.[174] The president's powers were also enlarged. This last decision emphasized a new trend; formerly, when out of power, liberals and moderates had pushed for decentralization of power. Now they began a process of centralization, with the conservatives making a new

---

173. Stonehouse, *Machen*, p. 439.
174. "New Board Pledges Seminary to Faith," *New York Times* (June 15, 1929), p. 15.

plea for tolerance and Christian freedom. The roles and arguments had reversed.

Once in power, the liberals were never to turn loose. *Their creed was power*, and they would defend it with far greater enthusiasm and commitment than the conservatives had defended the Westminster Confession. The conservatives' pleas for tolerance had no visible effect. The new doctrine of the liberal faction was straightforward from this point on: "In the name of institutional stability and peace—not doctrinal conformity—you must submit." The *Times* dutifully dismissed the critics as members of the "extreme conservative group."[175] Liberal rhetoric never changes. I am unaware of any case during the Presbyterian conflict when a liberal or mass media news outlet referred to the "extreme liberal group."

This has gone on ever since. Typical are the comments of Church historian Winthrop Hudson, in his supposedly neutral academic textbook: "Nowhere was the Fundamentalist case stated with more clarity and cogency than in Machen's writings, but his ill-tempered dogmatism in personal relationships and his determination to dominate the life of the seminary drove even staunchly conservative colleagues to make common cause with the Auburn 'Affirmationists.'"[176] He follows this remark with a description of the Baptist Bible Union, a fundamentalist organization of the same era. "Here too the bitter-spirited intransigence of the extremists caused some of the priminent early leaders of the movement to defect and work out a policy of coexistence with the liberals."[177] Extremists were everywhere in the 1920's, but only on the Right.

The first step in consolidating power at Princeton was to issue a lie to the press, which announced that the Board would "do nothing whatever to alter the distinctive doctrinal position which the seminary has maintained throughout its entire history."[178] Machen correctly dismissed this announcement as "meaningless." In this era, he said, the

---

175. *Ibid.*
176. Winthrop S. Hudson, *Religion in America* (New York: Charles Scribner's Sons, 1965), p. 270.
177. *Ibid.*
178. *Ibid.*

same words are given different meanings. Machen was correct. Four years later, the Seminary invited the Barthian socialist Adolph Keller to deliver the Stone lectures; a decade later, Emil Brunner was on the faculty.

Machen's Response: The Issue Is Doctrine

The new board assumed control of the Seminary in mid-June of 1929. Within days, Machen had challenged it as a deception. But he hastened to remove all traces of personal responsibility, another example of his rhetorically mild-mannered ways—ways guaranteed to lose the battle. "I do not mean to impugn the good faith of these gentlemen."[179] The *Times* quoted Machen as saying that the new board was not legally installed, but "If the new board of directors were legally in control of Princeton Seminary, I should resign my professorship at once."[180] Then he opened the challenge: "In any case I am convinced that the time has come for bold and definite action on the part of the evangelicals in the Presbyterian Church. It is evident that they can look for no tolerance or fairness from those who at present are in control of the ecclesiastical machinery. . . . The evangelicals must at once take steps to found a new seminary that shall continue the old Princeton tradition. . . ."[181]

He also hoped that the civil courts would clear up the illegalities at Princeton, since they were the last hope. But, "the evangelicals must not depend on the possibility of that." Machen had, by this time, given up hope in a successful civil suit. Stonehouse reports that Machen blamed himself for not having introduced a motion into the 1930 General Assembly to put the Seminary back under the old Plan, "and this on the understanding that the action taken in 1929 would inevitably result in legal chaos."[182] But this, too, would have been nothing more than an obstructionist tactic, which would have had no chance of doing more than temporarily deflecting the Assembly from the new path it was following.

---

179. "Charges Deception in Seminary Change," *ibid*. (June 17, 1929), p. 9.
180. "Machen Proposes a New Seminary," *ibid*. (June 18, 1929), p. 22.
181. *Ibid*.
182. Stonehouse, *Machen*, p. 441.

Professionally Naive Conservatives

The new Board of Directors immediately issued a ringing declaration which was designed to pacify those who wanted above all to be pacified.

> In the one hundred and seventeen years of its history, Princeton Seminary has stood with firm steadfastness for the propagation at home and abroad, and for the scholarly defense of evangelical Christianity as formulated in the Standards of the Presbyterian Church. In taking up the duties assigned to it by the General Assembly, the temporary Board of Directors feels that it has a sacred mandate from the Assembly to continue unchanged the historic policy of the Seminary and do nothing whatever to alter the distinctive traditional position which the Seminary has maintained throughout its entire history.[183]

The new Board of Directors now included two signers of the Auburn *Affirmation*.[184] Here was a strange way to affirm devotion to the Princeton tradition!

The battle over Princeton began a separation of sheep from goats, and also between the "about to be sheared" sheep and the "let's avoid the catastrophe" sheep. *The Presbyterian*, long the conservative outlet for Machen's wing, now switched editorial policy. Rev. Samuel G. Craig had resigned in 1929 in protest at interference with his editorials opposing the change at Princeton. Machen helped him by funding the creation of the Presbyterian & Reformed Publishing Co., which began publishing *Christianity Today*[185] in May of 1930. The investors at *The Presbyterian* hired William Courtland Robinson as editor. Robinson had been a director of Princeton and an opponent of the reorganization, but he would not admit the reality of what had happened. Robinson announced in the May 15 issue: "That which many predicted and which some of us feared has not taken place. . . . We cannot find a single happening during this year now closing to which a conservative could take serious exception."

---

183. Loetscher, *Broadening Church*, p. 147.
184. Stonehouse, *Machen*, p. 441.
185. Hart, "Doctor Fundamentalis," p. 295n.

The modernists had bided their time since 1900. They were not foolish. They could bide their time for another year or two. But the direction in which Princeton was headed was clear. Machen had predicted it, and the three professors who followed him to Westminster knew. So did Geerhardus Vos, C. W. Hodge, and Machen's old friend, "Army" Armstrong, who remained behind.[186]

Westminster Seminary

Four men on the faculty resigned: Machen; Robert Dick Wilson, the foremost orthodox Old Testament scholar in the English-speaking world; Old Testament scholar O. T. Allis, who had edited *Princeton Theological Review* for years; and Cornelius Van Til, the man who took Machen's place as Calvinism's leading orthodox apologist upon Machen's death. This group of four seceding professors became the nucleus around which a new seminary was built. Ironically, Princeton had just elected Allis to the Helena chair of Oriental and Old Testament Literature, and Van Til to the Stuart Professorship of Apologetics and Christian Ethics.[187]

Less than a month later, on July 18, 1929, a meeting was held in Philadelphia at which steps were taken to begin the new school, Westminster Theological Seminary, to be located in Philadelphia. This was a wise location, since the Philadelphia Presbytery had long been the leading conservative force in the Assemblies, and there was far more chance of having Westminster graduates being ordained there than in some other, less orthodox, presbytery. Westminster was opened in the fall of 1929, a month before the stock market crashed.

Van Til had resisted the call. He did not want to return to teaching. That summer, he took a pastorate in Spring Lake, Michigan. Allis went to Spring Lake to plead with him to join the faculty. He refused. Then, in August, came Machen and Ned B. Stonehouse. He refused. "We aren't called stubborn Dutchmen without cause," he later remarked.[188] But a month later, he showed up. He retired in 1972 and

---

186. Stonehouse, *Machen*, p. 450.
187. *Minutes of the General Assembly, 1930*, p. 40.
188. White, *Van Til*, p. 89.

remained close to the Seminary until his death in 1987: over 50 years of academic service from a man who wanted to be a rural pastor.

In his speech at the Seminary's opening exercises (Sept. 25, 1929), with 50 students enrolled, Machen invoked the memory of the Old Princeton: "No, my friends, though Princeton Seminary is dead, the noble tradition of Princeton Seminary is alive. Westminster Seminary will endeavor by God's grace to continue that tradition unimpaired; it will endeavor, not on a foundation of equivocation and compromise, but on an honest foundation of devotion to God's Word, to maintain the same principles that the old Princeton maintained."[189] Yet this was not really the case. Old Princeton had been Old School in its alignment. Westminster was less consistently Old School.

There would soon be a major change: the arrival of amillennial Dutch theologians from the Christian Reformed Church. Soon, R. B. Kuiper and Ned B. Stonehouse would be added to Westminster's faculty. The Old School Presbyterians remained at Princeton or retired after 1930. At Westminster, the tradition of Scottish common-sense apologetics was replaced by Van Til's presuppositionalism; Warfield's postmillennialism by Dutch amillennialism.

The New Princeton

Calvinists were no longer in control of Princeton's administration, and the outstanding orthodox voices had left the faculty. The last stronghold of orthodox Calvinism in the Presbyterian Church, U.S.A., had been broken up. Moderator John McDowell, in answering Machen's statements in the *New York Times*, had tried to soothe the conservatives of the Church when he wrote that "the board of trustees are on record to the effect that they desire no change in the historical theological position of Princeton Seminary relative to the standards of the Church."[190]

---

189. Machen, "Westminster Theological Seminary: Its Purpose and Plan" (1929), in *Studying the New Testament Today: New Testament Student*, edited by John H. Skilton (Philipsburg, New Jersey: Presbyterian & Reformed, 1974), p. 169.

190. "Machen Proposes a New Seminary," *New York Times* (June 18, 1929), p. 22.

Princeton, Pensions, and Peace 639

These last seven words, "relative to the standards of the Church," were qualifications that altered the surface implication of the statement, that no theological change was going to take place. Almost immediately, there was a decided shift over to the neo-orthodoxy of Barth and Brunner and a rejection of the Calvinist system by many of the new men on the faculty. While the departure of the four Calvinist professors hastened the shift, still it could not have been prevented for long, if only because new appointments to the chairs of theology would have been filled with those who held the new theology. The General Assembly was lost by the conservatives, and it was only a matter of time before the inclusivism would become a reality throughout the whole of the organization.

In 1932, Geerhardus Vos retired. In 1933, the prestigious Stone Foundation Lectures of Princeton Seminary featured a German theologian, Adolph Keller, who introduced the theology of Karl Barth to the students. In 1898, Abraham Kuyper, the soon-to-be Prime Minister of the Netherlands, had delivered his remarkable *Lectures on Calvinism* as his Stone Lectures.[191] Now, the students were told: "To Barth, as a Christian socialist, it seemed that the Church was lacking in the social courage to seek new manifestations of God's Spirit."[192] Why has the Spirit waited so long to manifest Himself? Does He change over time? The answer seems to be *yes*. God evolves, or at least His Spirit as manifested to man can reconstruct one age's firm morality to make a whole new moral world: process theology.

> . . . he [Barth] was confronted with a Christian conservatism which understood the facts of revelation as given historical data, that is to say, as so much divine capital consisting of transcendent facts and ethical commandments which had become the property of men and which they could treat in the same way as the facts and laws of a scientific system. This kind of Christianity felt itself to be in complete possession of salvation. In its false fundamentalistic assurance it had forgotten the dynamic character

---

191. Abraham Kuyper, *Lectures on Calvinism* (Grand Rapids, Michigan: Eerdmans, 1931).
192. Adolph Keller, *Religion and Revolution: Problems of Contemporary Christianity on the European Scene* (New York: Revell, 1934), p. 62.

of God's revelation, which lifts the Gospel beyond the possibility of being permanently posited by human experience and Christian knowledge and connotes a process of continual development.[193]

From this point of view, Karl Barth is strongly opposed to any canonized interpretation of the Bible, which defines once for all the meaning of the Word of God and prevents the Holy Spirit from using the written Word as a manifestation of God's will. When the Church tries to define once and forever what the authoritative interpretation of the Bible should be, it assumes an authority which it does not possess and identifies itself with the dynamic action of the Spirit. Karl Barth demands a free exegesis of the Bible, trusting in the spiritual power of the Word of God to explain itself and to remain eternally a critical, corrective power over against any man's purely individualistic interpretation of it. To any man in a truly listening and obedient attitude, the Bible explains itself.[194]

It should be clear what the faculty at Princeton was doing. Keller was challenging the orthodox party's view of the Confession as a fixed, binding standard of faith and action. He was substituting evolution for creedalism. This confirmed Machen's warnings. But Machen and his supporters still had a problem: to explain the proper use of the Confession, both theologically and institutionally, as a document which has relevance in every era. If Machen was unable to gather support for a purge of liberals in this, the most creedal of churches, because his supporters did not really accept the whole creed, then the effectiveness of a fixed creed as a tool of institutional administration and screening had been fatally compromised in the Presbyterian Church.

Princeton Seminary soon proved to be a lost cause.[195] Machen understood this in 1929. It was a lost cause because it no longer held to

---

193. *Ibid.*, pp. 61–62.
194. *Ibid.*, p. 66.
195. In his unpublished—and deservedly so—Ph.D. dissertation, W. J. Watson announces confidently: "Yet Princeton Seminary no more became a liberal institution after Machen left it than it had been a fundamentalist institution before." Watson, Idea of Pluralism, p. 159. True, Princeton had never been a fundamentalist institution; it had been Calvinist. But Barthianism is surely not conservative in relation to the Westminster Confession of Faith. Watson's theological assessment

the Confession. But if confessions need revision from time to time, by what standard, or by what procedure, could the revisors legitimately change the Confession without abandoning it? How can structure and change, law and application, be fused together in a creedal organization? How can changing historical circumstances not affect the application of biblical and creedal principles? But if circumstances change, then how is the overarching fixed truth of the creed going to be preserved in a new historical setting?

Machen knew that the problem still existed. He was still struggling to call his Church to reconfirm the creeds. But the 1647 document no longer motivated many men. The Confession needed revision, but how could it be revised without undermining it? Barthianism is a doctrine of evolution. How can creeds honor the fact of historical change without becoming Barthian-evolutionistic? More to the point, how could Calvinists who had accepted Lyell's chronology in defiance of the Confession's explicit chronology defend themselves from evolutionism, whether biological or Barthian?[196]

Conclusion

The Presbyterian conflict seemed to be resolved. First, Princeton was now to become more representative of the Church as a whole, more responsive to new trends in theology. "Relative to the standards of the Church," as McDowell had said, there would be no change in theology, because there were no longer any fixed theological standards in the Church. As the Church's theology drifted, Princeton's would follow closely; so, in relation to each other, there would be no

---

is clouded by his humanistic worldview, which led him to refer to Charles Briggs' opponents as "extreme reactionaries" (*ibid.*, p. 38). Such language is within the bounds of political correctness at Yale University.

196. Van Til answered Barth in a comprehensive fashion in the late 1940's—an answer based explicitly on the Creator-creature distinction. Prior to this, the followers of the Old Princeton tradition were ill-equipped to handle the practical and theoretical problems associated with creedal revision. Van Til's apologetics relied on God's decree and man's analogical reasoning as a creature: approaching a fixed, unchanging truth. Creedal revision is valid because covenant-keeping men improve their knowledge of God and His creation over time. God does not change, but covenant-keeping man's understanding of Him does.

change! It was all relative, so long as there is no fixed standard by which to measure change. Second, the orthodox party now had their own training center, Westminster Seminary, and while it was not a part of the Church, its professors were still Presbyterian ministers, and its graduates, if they so chose, might become Presbyterian ministers.

The Old School had always affirmed that theological seminaries should be under the authority of the Church.[197] Princeton Professor John de Witt in 1893 declared: "The Board of Directors of Princeton Seminary is as much the creature of the General Assembly as it has ever been. It is simply the agent of the Assembly to execute the Assembly's own 'plan.'"[198] The irony of Westminster Seminary would be that, as the last remaining seminary to defend the Old School's theology, it could do so only by defying and rejecting the Old School's tradition of Church control over seminary education.

In 1927, the General Assembly revoked its own authority to revoke the ordination of heretics. This decentralized power. The General Assembly also established a pension plan that would penalize any minister covered by this plan who then left the denomination. This centralized power. The 1927 General Assembly sent out mixed signals. It was traveling in opposite directions simultaneously. This could not continue indefinitely.

In 1931, the liberals, who were in complete control of the bureaucracy, recommended to the General Assembly a revision of the Form of Government. If passed by the presbyteries, this revision would radically restructure the Church. This proposed revision was debated for three years, but it received very little attention from the conservatives. Beginning in late 1932, another issue riveted the attention of the Church: foreign missions. The revision was approved by the presbyteries in 1934. It created a comprehensive system of negative sanctions. The crucial issue was sanctions.

---

197. Benjamin B. Warfield, "The One Hundred and Fourth General Assembly," *Presbyterian and Reformed Review*, 3 (1892), p. 531.
198. John de Witt, "Dr. Roberts' Article on Seminary Control," *ibid.*, 4 (1893), p. 125.

11

CONFLICT OVER FOREIGN MISSIONS

The missionary movement is the great religious movement of our day.

J. Gresham Machen (1913)[1]

In the three years following the reorganization at Princeton, there was relative calm within the Presbyterian Church, but trouble was brewing. It had been brewing for a long time. Church historian Sidney E. Mead discusses this trouble: missions.

> But during the last quarter of the nineteenth century and the opening years of the twentieth, real belief in the all-sufficiency of this kind of [world-converting] missions declined, at least among those of the top leadership in most of the large denominations. During this period enlightened theological professors hand in hand with "Princes of the Pulpit," responding to the impact of scientific thinking in the garb of evolution and to the deplorable economic and social conditions in the burgeoning industrial society, shaped the "new theology" and the "social gospel." Inevitably as their views came to prevail the conception of the work of the church underwent changes, and missions were metamorphosed from the simple task of winning converts to which, it was assumed, all else would be added, to the complex task of participating actively in social betterment and reconstruction.

---

1. Machen, "Christianity and Culture," *Princeton Theological Review*, 11 (Jan. 1913), p. 6.

Foreign missions, from being simple outposts of Christian evangelization, became outposts of the latest technological, medical, agricultural, and educational knowledge and practice being developed in the United States.[2]

Mead then asks a rhetorical question: "Why would the devoted medical missionary in Africa, China, or India be closely examined regarding his views on the Trinity of [*sic*: or] the Virgin Birth, or any other 'merely' theological views for that matter?" The missions agencies agreed. In 1921, W. H. Griffith Thomas had created a brief sensation with his public accusations regarding modernism on the mission field. In 1932, the long-smoldering crisis over missions would break out again.

Conservatives Are Squeezed Out

Meanwhile, the final consolidation of the boards and commissions of the Church took place in the three years after Princeton's reorganization: before the battle over foreign missions. Change was accelerating. For example, the 1929 General Assembly sent down an overture to the presbyteries that women be allowed to be ordained as elders: ruling and teaching. The overture failed: 170 to 108, with 7 not acting.[3] A parallel overture, allowing women to serve as ruling elders and deacons, passed: 158 to 118.[4] For the first time in Presbyterian history, women could lawfully speak in God's name in a Church court. Machen and the Old School had remained remarkably silent on this issue. They apparently did not see it as fundamental. They did not organize a protest.

At the 1930 General Assembly, Rev. Samuel G. Craig, editor of the newly formed conservative journal, *Christianity Today*, introduced

---

2. Sidney E. Mead, *The Lively Experiment: The Shaping of Christianity in America* (New York: Harper & Row, 1963), p. 119.

3. *Minutes of the General Assembly, 1930*, pp. 49–50. Women became eligible for the pastorate in the Church in 1956. John D. Krugler and David Weinberg-Kinsey, "Equality of Leadership: The Ordination of Sarah E. Dickson and Margaret E. Towner in the Presbyterian Church of the USA," *American Presbyterians*, 68 (Winter 1990), p. 244.

4. *Ibid.*, pp. 50–53.

a motion to take the question of Princeton's reorganization to the civil courts in New Jersey. He felt that because some private legal opinion deemed the Trustee's alteration of the charter illegal, the final test should come in legal action. This motion was soundly defeated. No further action was taken by the orthodox wing to challenge the reorganization.

That same year saw the trial of dispensational fundamentalist pastor Donald Grey Barnhouse. He was a minister in Philadelphia's Tenth Presbyterian Church. Barnhouse had announced from the pulpit that he would rather die than have a liberal preach in his pulpit. Pressured by the presbytery, he apologized, and his presbytery accepted his apology. The liberals in the presbytery did not; they appealed to the Synod of Pennsylvania, who ordered the presbytery to try him for breach of the ninth commandment and violation of his ordination vows. He was convicted.[5] The liberals had begun to employ negative sanctions with a vengeance. Barnhouse was only admonished mildly, but the conviction set an example, as convictions are supposed to. It seemed to persuade Barnhouse of the futility of protest. (In 1935, he went on a tour of Presbyterian foreign missions. When he returned, he published a generally favorable report in *The Presbyterian*. "I have every reason to believe that most of our missionaries hold to the historic truths of the Christian faith as expressed in the creedal statement of our denomination."[6]) The trial convinced Machen that conservative dissenters would be convicted if they spoke the truth about liberalism.[7]

---

5. D. G. Hart, "Doctor Fundamentalis": An Intellectual Biography of J. Gresham Machen, 1881-1937 (Ph.D. dissertation, Johns Hopkins University, 1988), pp. 291-93. Hart cites C. Allyn Russell, "Donald Grey Barnhouse: Fundamentalist Who Changed," *Church History*, 59 (1981), pp. 33-57.

6. *The Presbyterian* (Oct. 31, 1935), p. 5. Cited in James Alan Patterson, Robert E. Speer and the Crisis of the American Protestant Missionary Movement, 1920-1937 (Ph.D. dissertation, Princeton Theological Seminary, 1980), p. 163.

7. D. G. Hart and John Muether, *Fighting the Good Fight: A Brief History of the Orthodox Presbyterian Church* (Philadelphia: Committee on Christian Education and the Committee of the Historian of the Orthodox Presbyterian Church, 1995), p. 33.

In a long article in *Christianity Today* (May 1930), Machen continued to warn that modernism and Christianity are rival religions, and that they cannot be maintained for long in the same Church. He surveyed the history of the decline of orthodoxy within the Church: the 1906 union with the Cumberland Presbyterian Church, the widespread support for the Plan of Church Union in 1920, the Auburn *Affirmation* in 1923, the restructuring of Princeton Seminary in 1929. "The doctrinal drift is also practically in complete control of the agencies of public discussion," by which he meant denominational magazines. What to do about it? Face the facts; avoid paring down our ecclesiastical program; support *Christianity Today*; support Westminster Seminary; keep our banner flying in the Church's councils; avoid despair.[8] This is a program suited to a remnant on the distant fringes of authority, not a movement strong enough to threaten the imposition of negative institutional sanctions. (By 1935, he was openly calling his supporters a remnant.)[9]

Machen vs. Speer

Five months later, Machen again sounded the alarm in a long review of Robert E. Speer's book, *Some Living Issues*. Machen and Speer had exchanged long letters in 1929 regarding the Foreign Missions Board.[10] The problem was not just modernism; the problem more and more was the compromise with modernism by peace-seekers in the Church. Machen understood that there were three forces in the Church. In *Christianity and Liberalism* he had discussed two. But this was insufficient. In any confessional or ideological organization, the large, less committed middle will decide which way the organization goes. It will choose which shepherd to follow. Machen warned his followers of the institutional drift of the Church's center towards modernism. The mobilizing issue for Machen, as always, was the Auburn *Affirmation*. There were three possible responses to it, he said: oppose it, support it, or

---

8. Machen, "The Present Situation in the Presbyterian Church," *Christianity Today* (May 1930), p. 6.

9. He wrote: "The Christian remnant, at least so far as it is clearly aware of the great issue, is only a minority in the Church." Machen, "What May Be Learned from the 1935 General Assembly of the Presbyterian Church in the U.S.A.," *Independent Board Bulletin* (June 1935), p. 5.

10. Bradley J. Longfield, *The Presbyterian Controversy: Fundamentalists, Modernists, and Moderates* (New York: Oxford University Press, 1991), pp. 181–83.

delay making a judgment. Speer was taking the third option. This third position, Machen said, was the most dangerous to the life of the Church, for it allows men to believe that they are not very far down the road to unbelief when they are very far down that road.

> With regard to that issue, three positions are possible and are actually being taken today. In the first place, one may stand unreservedly for the old Faith and unreservedly against the indifferentist tendency in the modern Church; in the second place, one may stand unreservedly for Modernism and against the old Faith; and in the third place, one may ignore the seriousness of the issue and seek, without bringing it to a head, to preserve the undisturbed control of the present organization in the Church. It is this last attitude that is represented by the book now under review. Dr. Robert E. Speer certainly presents himself not as a Modernist but as an adherent of the historic Christian Faith; yet he takes no clear stand in the great issue of the day, but rather adopts an attitude of reassurance and palliation, according high praise and apparently far-reaching agreement to men of very destructive views....
>
> It is this palliative or reassuring attitude which, we are almost inclined to think, constitutes the most serious menace to the life of the Church today; it is in some ways doing more harm than clear-sighted Modernism can do. The representatives of it are often much farther from the Faith than they themselves know; and they are leading others much farther away than they have been led themselves. Obviously such a tendency in the Church deserves very careful attention from thoughtful men....
>
> But when it is considered, fairness demands that it should be considered not in its poorest, but in its best, representatives. That is our justification for occupying so much space with the present review. Dr. Robert E. Speer is perhaps the most distinguished and eloquent popular representative of what is commonly called the "middle-of-the-road" or pacifist position with regard to the great religious issue of the day.[11]

---

11. "Dr. Machen Surveys Dr. Speer's New Book," *Christianity Today* (Oct. 1930), p. 9.

This was an undisguised frontal assault against the most popular man in the denomination . . . and the most influential. Their confrontation would escalate in 1932, for Speer was still the head of the Board of Foreign Missions, where the maelstrom would appear. Machen would learn, 1932 to 1936, what Briggs learned in 1893: success or failure institutionally in the Presbyterian Church would be based on the middle group's assessment of the combatants' rhetoric. Speer avoided all confrontational rhetoric; Machen, as a defender of a shrinking minority position, could not do the same. A man in any public organization whose colleagues control the bureaucratic machinery as well as the legislature's votes can afford to be non-confrontational. A man with neither had better be ready for a long institutional battle if he chooses to be equally non-confrontational. This is what the liberals had decided when van Dyke had proposed the strategy in 1893. The fruits of their patience had already begun to bloom. Speer could afford to remain rhetorically bland in public. He had control of the machinery.

Machen's Academic Seclusion

In January, 1931, Machen began a series in Christianity Today titled, "Notes on Biblical Exposition." It continued for two years until the issue of foreign missions caught his attention. This series was a popular study of Paul's ministry. Rare was any reference in it to contemporary topics. It was as if Machen decided to pull back from the fray in order to write articles that could have been written a century earlier by any competent conservative theologian. Timelessness is surely a secondary goal for anyone who finds himself in the midst of a life-and-death struggle. The series seems to reflect a conscious decision on Machen's part to shift the precious resource of time—his and his readers'—away from the Presbyterian conflict and toward traditional Presbyterian academic affairs. Very few other articles by Machen appeared in the interim, yet Christianity Today had become the only outlet for the exclusivists. The major exception was his three-part article on "The Truth About the Presbyterian Church," which attacked the newly created Permanent Judicial Commission,[12] the secrecy of the Church's councils and courts,[13] and the proposed plan of union with the United Presbyterians.[14] That Machen, as the intellectual leader of the Old School forces, not to mention the intellectual leader of American fundamentalism, would go into what amounted to near-seclusion journalistically for almost two years seems odd in retrospect. His book, *The Virgin Birth of Christ*,[15] appeared in 1930, so it was not that he was too busy with a more important writing project.

The Calm Before the Storm

The 1931 General Assembly was, on the surface, an uneventful meeting. It offered testimony of a truce. In a feature article that appeared in the June 17, 1931, issue of *Christian Century*, John Ray Ewers observed: "The evangelical group, or the solid middle-of-the-road crowd, predominates. There seems to be no lunatic fringe.... It is essential to obtain this picture of this strong, dependable, middle-of-the-road crowd in order to understand the happenings in this assembly."[16]

The inclusivists' candidate for Moderator, Lewis S. Mudge, who was also the Stated Clerk of the Church, was elected narrowly. Commenting editorially on this fact, *Christianity Today* concluded that this near defeat was probably not due to any disfavor of Mudge personally, but to "the feeling that he had been put forward by the same group that has been virtually dictating the election of moderators as well as important appointments for a number of years." The editorial continued: "It seems to us, therefore, that the vote for moderator indicates that there are more in the Church than many had supposed who disapprove of those tendencies that have been in evidence in the Presbyterian Church in recent years."[17] The future seemed unsure, but not

---

12. Nov. 1931.
13. Dec. 1931.
14. Jan. 1932.
15. New York: Harper & Row.
16. John Ray Ewers, "Presbyterians in a Conservative Mood," *Christian Century* (June 17, 1931), p. 817.
17. *Christianity Today* (June 1931), p. 3.

necessarily foreboding. The summary view of the conservative journal on the 142nd General Assembly was fairly neutral: "As a whole it, perhaps, offers more warrant for encouragement on the part of conservatives than did the assemblies immediately preceding. This, however, is not saying a great deal."[18]

This was all an illusion. The General Council had introduced to the General Assembly a proposed revision of the Form of Discipline, the first major revision since 1884.[19] Discussions of the proposed revision would continue through 1934, when the presbyteries overwhelmingly voted for it: 190 to 13, with 11 abstentions.[20] In September of 1933, seven months before the change became law, Mudge initiated the first step in the purge of Machen and his allies. The institutional issue was the financial support of Church boards, particularly Foreign Missions. The judicial issue would be ecclesiastical submission. The theological issue would be liberalism: the Auburn *Affirmation* vs. the Westminster Confession of Faith.

At the 1931 Assembly a resolution supporting the Church's continuing participation in the Federal Council of Churches was passed, which included this ringing declaration: "A Central Agency like the Federal Council of Churches standing on the rock of Evangelical faith and the Deity of Christ and directly responsible to the Evangelical Churches of the United States is indispensable."[21] A year later, the General Council announced in the name of the General Assembly: "That we record our gratitude to God for the growing consciousness of Christian unity which has found expression through the Federal Council. We are conscious of the necessity of finding the mind of Christ in the field of moral and social issues which press upon all our churches."[22]

Centralization

The move toward greater centralization continued unabated. The liberals continued to extend their control over the Church's adminis-

---

18. *Ibid.*, p. 12.
19. *Minutes of the General Assembly, 1933*, p. 60.
20. *Minutes of the General Assembly, 1934*, pp. 184-85.
21. *Minutes of the General Assembly, 1931*, p. 105.
22. *Minutes of the General Assembly, 1932*, p. 275.

trative machinery. The newly created Permanent Judicial Commission, which by 1931 had become the highest court of appeal, had eight ministers and seven elders. Half of the ministers, Machen noted, had signed the Auburn *Affirmation*. Signers of the *Affirmation* also held high positions in the Board of Foreign Missions and the Board of Christian Education.[23] Yet only 14 percent of the ministers had signed it. Their heavy representation at the highest levels of Church authority was not a random distribution.

The centralization of judicial procedure within the Church was almost complete. Machen called the Permanent Judicial Commission "now practically the supreme doctrinal as well as disciplinary authority in the Church."[24] He did not yet recognize the magnitude of the shift: after 1931, there was no further need for a supreme doctrinal authority. The issue of doctrine never again became an official issue in the Northern Presbyterian Church's supreme court.

The 1932 Assembly, held in Denver, likewise saw the relative absence of doctrinal discussion. The much smaller United Presbyterian Church had submitted a plan of union to the 1930 General Assembly, and both denominations began to discuss this at their respective 1932 General Assemblies. The General Assembly did vote to merge in 1934, but the United Presbyterians voted against it. They were afraid of being swallowed by the larger Church.[25]

The move toward further centralization could not be stopped. An overture to dissolve the General Council (Presbytery of Steubenville) and another to reorganize it and strip it of its authority to "originate or put into operation any matter that has not been referred to it by

---

23. Machen, "The Truth About the Presbyterian Church: I. Modernism in the Judicial Commission," *Christianity Today* (Nov. 1931), pp. 5-6; "The Truth About the Presbyterian Church: II. Secrecy in Councils and Courts," *ibid.* (Dec. 1931), p. 7.

24. Machen, "Modernism in the Judicial Commission," *ibid.*, p. 5.

25. On J. Ross Stevenson's support of union and Machen's opposition, see Ki-Hong Kim, Presbyterian Conflict in the Early Twentieth Century: Ecclesiology in the Princeton Tradition and the Emergence of Presbyterian Fundamentalism (Ph.D. dissertation, Drew University, 1983), pp. 183-88. Union with the United Presbyterian Church did not come until 1958. Union with the PCUS (Southern Presbyterians) came in 1983, a decade after the departure of the conservatives from the PCUS into the Presbyterian Church in America.

the General Assembly" (Philadelphia North and 18 other presbyteries)[26] were answered in the negative by the Committee on Bills and Overtures.[27] In the *New York Times*, shortly after the Assembly ended, several ministers who had attended were quoted as saying that the Assembly had been a machine. These critics were not all disgruntled conservatives, and their criticisms were not along doctrinal lines. This time, the dissention was purely an administrative matter. One minister, Daniel Russell, who described himself as a conservative, attacked the Assembly outspokenly: "Of course, there is no longer any democracy in the General Assembly. That day has gone by. Democracy certainly has failed there." Rev. Nelson Chester could not agree that the whole Church was undemocratic, but he did agree that the Assembly had been a machine.[28]

Disputes: Doctrinal or Administrative?

The confusion between doctrinal disputes and administrative measures had been a paramount feature of Church government for ten years. By the end of 1932, this distinction was clearer. The new doctrinal orientation of the Church was in complete opposition to theological conservatism. A new controversy appeared which proved impossible to reconcile, and it eventually resulted in the secession of the conservatives.

The renewal of open warfare within the Church centered, as it had a decade earlier, around a prominent liberal member and a liberal document, with Machen leading the orthodox opposition against both. In the early 1920's, the issue had been, primarily, that of ordination, and the attention of the Church had focused on the case of Fosdick and the Auburn *Affirmation*. In the latter part of the decade, the controversy had centered around education, specifically Princeton. Now the battlefield shifted to the third element that made up the Church's program, missions. In 1921, W. H. Griffith Thomas had unleashed an attack on the missionary enterprise in China, charging

---

26. *Minutes of the General Assembly, 1932*, p. 30.
27. *Ibid.*, p. 107.
28. "Church Assembly Called a Machine," *New York Times* (June 14, 1932), p. 23.

Presbyterian missionaries with cooperation with modernist, and even atheistic, institutions. He had gained little support. Eleven years later, such a charge, introduced into a temporarily calm but supercharged atmosphere within the Church, provided a spark which ignited the final phase of the Presbyterian conflict.

Rumors of Theological War

For two decades, John D. Rockefeller, Jr., had employed denominationalist Speer and ecumenist John R. Mott.[29] Mott had headed numerous Rockefeller-funded religious organizations: the International Missionary Council, the International Missionary Agricultural Council, the Panama Conference on Christian Work in Latin America, the Committee on Cooperation in Latin America (along with Speer), the Committee on Benevolence, and the Committee on Social and Religious Surveys.[30] This final organization later became the Institute for Social and Religious Research (ISRR). As one historian has put it, "Standard Oil was Mott's organizational model. He incorporated the culture and methods of corporations into the missionary movement. Over the years, millions of Rockefeller dollars poured into Mott's pursuit of streamlined, efficient evangelism."[31] As early as 1910, Rockefeller sent Mott to China to help establish Peking Union Medical College.[32]

In the pre-World War I era, writes Schenkel, "Every Protestant leader—Speer included—was in a hurry, and the taint of Rockefeller money was not sufficient cause for qualms."[33] Speer became, in Schenkel's words, a "trusted associate" of Rockefeller's.[34] In 1920, Speer was elected president of the Federal Council of Churches, an

---

29. Albert F. Schenkel, *The Rich Man and the Kingdom: John D. Rockefeller, Jr., and the Protestant Establishment* (Minneapolis, Minnesota: Fortress Press, 1995), p. 127.

30. Gerard Colby with Charlotte Dennett, *Thy Will Be Done: The Conquest of the Amazon: Nelson Rockefeller and Evangelism in the Age of Oil* (New York: HarperCollins*Publishers*, 1995), chart, p. 45.

31. *Ibid.*, p. 33.

32. *Ibid.*

33. Schenkel, *Rich Man and Kingdom*, p. 129.

34. *Ibid.*, p. 99.

organization that Rockefeller's money helped start in 1908. Rockefeller was impressed with his work there: Speer seemed cautious.[35] Rockefeller was wise; in 1923, the Southern Presbyterian Church almost pulled out of the FCC, but Speer's plea before the General Assembly prevented it.[36]

The ISRR

In 1920, Rockefeller had joined and then bailed out of the Interchurch World Movement, with a combination of cash and loans forgiven. He had put $1.5 million of his own money into this venture, which then collapsed.[37] Two years after the collapse of the IWM, Rockefeller established the Institute for Social and Religious Research (ISRR). It inherited the research files of the IWM. Speer had advised him in 1920 about the kind of organization it should be: a research program to help the denominations carry out activities.[38] Raymond Fosdick had other ideas. He wanted the money used for social research. He wanted it to parallel the work of the Social Science Research Council, which was set up with Laura Spelman Rockefeller Memorial Fund money in 1923. The ISRR funded the famous Middletown research (Muncie, Indiana) conducted by Progressivist Robert Lynd, a former Union Seminary student, and his wife, Helen.[39] This study has been used ever since by liberals to flay the class divisions of American life. The ISRR Board disapproved of its class-division emphasis, and Rockefeller did not fund its publication; the book nevertheless became a best-seller.[40] From 1923 to 1928, Rockefeller donated

---

35. *Ibid.*, p. 148.
36. C. Gregg Singer, *The Unholy Alliance* (New Rochelle, New York: Arlington House, 1975), p. 59.
37. See Chapter 6, above: section on "The Interchurch World Movement, 1919–1921," pp. 392–403.
38. Schenkel, *Rich Man and Kingdom*, p. 149.
39. *Ibid.*, pp. 152–53.
40. *Ibid.*, pp. 153–54. Cf. Charles E. Harvey, "Robert S. Lynd, John D. Rockefeller, Jr., and *Middletown*," *Indiana Magazine of History*, 79 (Dec. 1983), p. 352. Lynd nevertheless subsequently served for years as the executive secretary to the Social Science Research Council, created by Beardsley Ruml, who had been on the Rockefeller payroll since the early 1920's. Harvey, "John D. Rockefeller, Jr., and the Social Sciences: An Introduction," *Journal of the History of Sociology*,

$1.35 million to the ISRR.[41] From its inception in 1921 until 1934, Mott was its president.[42]

Beginning in 1930, the ISRR funded the Laymen's Foreign Mission Inquiry, which represented the major denominations of American Christianity. Mott was a major influence in the Laymen's Inquiry. As chairman of the International Missionary Council, Mott had produced a world missions report in 1928-29 that had caught Rockefeller's attention.[43] Rockefeller had consulted fellow-Baptist Harry Emerson Fosdick regarding the study project, who had expressed doubts about Christian proselytizing done by Baptist missionaries.[44] He also consulted Speer, who objected to an independent agency's conducting the investigation.[45] He did not take Speer's advice. An independent group conducted the study. The members of the Laymen's Committee were not official spokesmen of their respective denominations. Rockefeller gave $363,000[46]—a large sum in the depression years.

The treasurer was James Miliken Speers, the vice-president of the Presbyterian Board of Foreign Missions.[47] He was a prominent merchant. He had also served in the IWM, first as its treasurer,[48] later as chairman of the Executive Committee when Mott resigned. Rockefeller and Raymond Fosdick then shut it down.[49] After it had shut down, an auditor complained to Rockefeller of the "criminal carelessness" of those handling the IWM's affairs.[50] In 1937, Speers served on the committee that produced the anti-capitalist economic report of the

---

IV (Fall 1982), p. 10.

41. *Ibid.*

42. *Addresses and Papers of John R. Mott*, 6 vols. (New York: Association Press, 1947), V:742.

43. C. Howard Hopkins, *John R. Mott: 1865–1955* (Grand Rapids, Michigan: Eerdmans, 1979), p. 681.

44. Schenkel, *Rich Man and Kingdom*, p. 156.

45. *Ibid.*

46. *Ibid.*, p. 157.

47. *Ibid.*

48. *Ibid.*, p. 138.

49. Charles E. Harvey, "Religion and Industrial Relations: John D. Rockefeller, Jr., and the Interchurch Movement, 1920-1921," *Research in Political Economy*, 4 (1981), p. 213.

50. Schenkel, *Rich Man and Kingdom*, p. 141.

Oxford Conference on Church, Community, and State.[51] Mott was chairman of that committee.[52] This conference was the pre-War prototype of what became the World Council of Churches in 1948. The name was proposed at the 1937 conference by liberal Presbyterian Samuel McCrea Cavert, the General Secretary of the Federal Council.[53] Cavert, Mott, and Robert E. Speer had served together on the General War-Time Commission in 1917.[54] My point is simple: the two leading lay figures on the Board of Foreign Missions, Speer and Speers, worked closely with the same group of dedicated modernists who created the World Council of Churches a decade and a half later. They were all closely associated with Rockefeller, who was the top donor to the World Council for two decades, 1939 to 1959.[55]

Toward the end of 1932, reports began to circulate that the conclusions reached by the group were highly biased against the traditional conception of missions, and conservatives in all denominations began to take alarm. On November 18, an official but incomplete report was published by the Appraisal Commission of the Laymen's Foreign Mission Inquiry. The next day, November 19, Mott delivered a speech at the Roosevelt Hotel. Mott referred to the "widespread discussion in progress due to reading of the inadequate press releases."[56] But he tried to put a good face on this. Discussion is healthy. He pointed to the report's "downright frankness and courage."[57] He thanked Rockefeller, "that splendid layman"—his full-time employer for over a decade—for his "vision, courageous initiative, generous cooperation, and wise counsel. . . ."[58] All of this was designed to produce "the liberation of greater lay forces and relating them to the

---

51. Peter H. Hobbie, "'Bringing Oxford Home': American Presbyterian Perceptions of the Oxford Conference on Church, Community, and State," *American Presbyterians*, 66 (Spring 1988), p. 29.

52. Hopkins, *Mott*, p. 687.

53. Samuel McCrea Cavert, *On the Road to Christian Unity: An Appraisal of the Ecumenical Movement* (New York: Harper & Bros., 1961), p. 24.

54. Hopkins, *Mott*, p. 525.

55. Schenkel, *Rich Man and Kingdom*, p. 192.

56. Mott, "Significance of the Appraisal of the Laymen's Foreign Mission Inquiry," *Addresses and Papers*, VI:323.

57. *Ibid.*, VI:325.

58. *Ibid.*

plans of the expanding Kingdom of Christ."[59] Here was the lifetime theme of layman John R. Mott: to extend God's kingdom through laymen. The report was ignored by most laymen, but it briefly aroused the fury of conservative pastors.

The Gauntlet Is Thrown Down

In the November 30 edition of *Christian Century*, an editorial appeared, "Is Modernism Ready?" The editorial praised the report of the Appraisal Commission, calling it "the most formidable critique" that had appeared in the hundred-year history of American missions. It warned prophetically: "A major battle looms on the horizon of Protestant Christianity. It is no academic battle of ideas, this time, though it will bring into play the whole ideology of both traditional and modern thought. But the basic functioning of organized Christianity is involved. When you touch the missionary enterprise you touch everything that goes by the name Christian. Is modernism ready to take over so fundamental a function as the long cherished enterprise of Christian missions?"

This time, the editorial stated, the liberal elements of the Christian churches were taking the initiative, putting the conservatives on the defensive. To date, said *Christian Century*, liberals had been a minority, and so had contented themselves with the status quo, not willing to challenge established institutions and programs of their denominations so long as conservatives left them in peace. "But that period of silent and uncritical acquiescence in the status quo has passed, and the Laymen's report is the signal that it has passed."

The editorial pointed to the decreasing number of qualified missionaries available to Protestant churches, blaming much of the drop on "the obsolescence of dogmatic orthodoxy." This had been a familiar theme of the liberals for a generation: orthodoxy is turning away bright young candidates for the ministry. The editorial then appealed to liberal churchmen to join in an attack on the conservative bastion of missions, since liberals were no longer minority participants. "Modernists are not now a minority in Protestant leadership. They are no longer merely tolerated in the churches. They represent the most ef-

---

59. *Ibid.*, VI:326.

fective influence in all the progressive communions. They cannot escape the responsibility that goes with numerical strength and accepted leadership. . . . Are modernists ready for the discharge of the responsibility which the commission, in making this report, has assumed on their behalf? Are they willing to take the consequences of the principles which the commission has laid down?"

As it turned out, modernists did not bother to concern themselves about such threatening consequences. They did not need to.

Pearl S. Buck Intervenes

The impact of this editorial would have been even greater had it not been dwarfed by a review of the Laymen's report in the preceding issue by the best-known American missionary, Pearl S. Buck. Her novel, *The Good Earth* (1931), had just won the Pulitzer Prize. Mrs. Buck had been sent to China with her husband under the auspices of the Board of Foreign Missions of the Presbyterian Church. Conservatives were aghast that someone representing their Church in the mission field could have written an article as unorthodox as this one. For six months, the controversy over missions within the Presbyterian Church would center around her. Then it shifted to Machen.

Mrs. Buck was enamored with the report, which was published in book form one month later under the name *Re-Thinking Missions*. "I have not read merely a report. I have read a unique book, a great book. . . . The first three chapters are the finest exposition of religion I have ever read."[60] Then she went on to offer her own critique of the missionary enterprise, insisting that missionaries in China had been far too concerned with preaching the message of salvation through Christ, rather than meeting the material needs of the people. Missionaries had, in her opinion, been isolating themselves from the Chinese community by laying such stress on the Christian gospel. "I am weary to death with this incessant preaching," she concluded. "It deadens all thought, it confuses all issues, it is producing in our Chinese church a horde of hypocrites. . . ."

---

60. Pearl S. Buck, "The Laymen's Mission Report," *Christian Century* (November 23, 1932), p. 1434.

This was too much for the conservatives. To call the traditional gospel of Christ into question, to put it on a level below that of material aid, was a challenge which could not go by without comment or action. Now the flood gates were opened, and three decades of pent-up feelings of bitterness, of disgust with the new theology, of frustration at being thwarted by the Church's administration, were released, and not just in the Presbyterian Church. Mrs. Buck found herself at the center of this protest.

Pearl Buck was known in Presbyterian circles as the wife of J. Lossing Buck, a Presbyterian missionary to China. She is described by Stonehouse as "Mrs. J. Lossing (Pearl) Buck."[61]

The books and articles on this phase of the Presbyterian conflict avoid a discussion of who Mrs. Buck really was during this period. She was a world-famous novelist, of course, but she would soon become much more. Yet in her autobiography, *My Several Worlds* (1954), she does not mention her role in the Presbyterian conflict. Regarding this aspect of her several worlds, her readers were not informed about who she had been, just as readers of books and dissertations about the Presbyterian conflict have not been informed about the world she entered into in 1932.

She returned from China in August, 1932, with her husband, who was on a missionary's sabbatical, and who enrolled in a Ph.D. program at Columbia University. In the month that she wrote her initial review of the Laymen's Report, November, 1932, she had begun an emotional relationship—though not adulterous—with her publisher at The John Day Company, Richard Walsh.[62] He asked her to marry him in early 1933.[63] Later that year, when she and her husband—his Ph.D. already completed!—returned to China, she announced to him that she intended to separate from him for a year.[64] (On their way

---

61. Ned B. Stonehouse, *J. Gresham Machen: A Biographical Memoir* (Philadelphia: Westminster Theological Seminary, [1954] 1978), p. 476.

62. Buck to Walsh, Nov. 4, 1932; cited in Theodore F. Harris (in consultation with Pearl S. Buck), *Pearl S. Buck: A Biography* (New York: John Day, 1969), p. 152.

63. *Ibid.*, p. 153.

64. *Ibid.*, p. 154.

back to China, they had visited Sidney and Beatrice Webb, the founders of the Fabian Society, at their English estate.)[65] She returned to the United States in 1934, divorced her husband *in absentia* in 1935 in the quick-divorce city of Reno, Nevada, and immediately married Walsh. Three decades later, she told her biographer, "I wasn't convinced—I never have been convinced—about marriage."[66] So much for her commitment to marriage and the mission field.

If this were the story of just another broken marriage covenant, it would not be worth mentioning. If Mrs. Buck-Walsh had been just another liberal, it would also not matter—Machen argued with a lot of them. But because of who Richard Walsh was, it does matter. He was not just an editor. He was the president of the company.[67] He was more than just the president of a book publishing firm. He has been described as one of three "family agents" of the Straight family.[68] That made all the difference.

I now must make a brief detour. The following material relates only peripherally to the Presbyterian conflict. It relates heavily to the American Establishment, modernist in its cultural commitment, for which Machen's theology was anathema. It was Progressive in its politics, for which Machen's Whig liberalism was anathema. Machen was up against an entrenched, well-funded machine, not just inside the Church but outside it. Pearl S. Buck went from the Presbyterian missions field in China straight into the Establishment. Through that Establishment, she gained access to the *New Republic*, for which she wrote Machen's obituary in 1937. The influence she wielded after 1932 was the result of her connection to the system of influence that directed elite public opinion in the United States in that era. To present a picture of what Machen was up against, I must spend a few pages describing the subsequent connections of Pearl S. Buck.

---

65. Pearl S. Buck, *My Several Worlds: A Personal Record* (New York: John Day, 1954), pp. 283–85. She does not mention her husband's presence.

66. Harris, *Pearl S. Buck*, p. 167.

67. Carroll Quigley, *Tragedy and Hope: A History of the World in Our Time* (New York: Macmillan, 1966), p. 936.

68. *Ibid.*, p. 940.

Straight into the Establishment

Willard and Dorothy Straight founded *The New Republic* in 1914 and retained ownership of it. It enjoyed Dorothy's financial support until 1953. This journal launched the foreign policy career of Walter Lippmann, who became the most influential columnist in America for the next half century.[69] Willard in 1914 was employed by J. P. Morgan & Co.[70] His big break in life had come while he was working in Korea as a reporter in his twenties in 1904. He had been recruited by E. H. Harriman, the multi-millionaire stockbroker and owner, since 1898, of the Union Pacific Railroad. Harriman was a close associate of William Rockefeller, John D. Sr.'s brother, who owned National City Bank (later called Citibank).

Harriman in 1904 was trying to create an around-the-world transportation system. He met Straight in Korea and hired him as his agent in the region. In 1906, Teddy Roosevelt invited Straight to the White House for a personal chat and then appointed him to be the U.S. Consul in Mukden in Manchuria—the only State Department representative north of the Great Wall.[71] Chernow describes Straight as "the most dashing, adventurous agent in Morgan history. . . ."[72] In 1910, when he came to Morgan headquarters, he was, in Chernow's words, "appalled at the way the House of Morgan bossed around the State Department." As Straight said, "It was not difficult to see where the real power lies in this country."[73]

Paralleling the Straight family's career, the Harriman family became one of the dominant influences in American life. Harriman's daughter in 1910 would begin funding the eugenics movement in America. His son Averell became one of the six "Wise Men" who dominated American foreign policy after World War I until the Vietnam War.[74] Averell's infusion of funds into the English private bank-

---

69. Ronald Steel, *Walter Lippmann and American Foreign Policy* (New York: Vintage, [1980] 1981), ch. 8.

70. Ron Chernow, *The House of Morgan: An American Banking Dynasty and the Rise of Modern Finance* (New York: Atlantic Monthly Press, 1990), p. 138.

71. *Ibid.*, p. 134.

72. *Ibid.*, p. 133.

73. *Ibid.*, p. 135.

74. Walter Isaacson and Evan Thomas, *The Wise Men: Six Friends and the World They Made* (New York: Simon & Schuster, 1986).

ing firm of Brown Brothers in 1930 and again in 1933 saved the prestigious but hard-pressed firm from bankruptcy and made him a partner in a re-named Brown Brothers, Harriman.[75] (Harriman's younger partner, Prescott Bush,[76] did well with the firm and also as a U.S. Senator; Prescott's son George had a decent career, too, though not with the bank.) Averell's much younger widow Pamela, formerly the daughter-in-law of Winston Churchill, was regarded as the most powerful woman in the Democratic Party until Hillary Clinton's husband was elected President in 1992. She raised $12 million for the Party in the 1980's, and had known and liked Clinton since 1980.[77] Beginning in early 1992, she had worked to win him the Party's nomination.[78] He succeeded. He appointed her U.S. Ambassador to France in 1993. So, from E. H. Harriman to his daughter-in-law, we see over nine decades of power-brokering in Washington.[79]

In 1911, Straight decided to marry America's richest heiress, orphan Dorothy Payne Whitney, worth $7 million at the time—in today's money, around $150 million. To persuade the Whitneys to allow her to marry below her station, he asked Roosevelt to intercede, which he did.[80] Straight died at the Paris Peace Conference in December of 1918, while assisting Wilson's agent, "Colonel" E. M. House. In 1919, Dorothy would help found the New School for Social Research, a liberal and sometimes radical university.[81]

The *New Republic* was one of the two most influential journals of opinion in the United States in the 1930's, the other being the *Nation*. Both had circulations of 30,000 to 40,000. In regard to the influence of the *New Republic*, it is useful to cite radical journalist I. F. Stone, who

---

75. Rudy Abramson, *Spanning the Century: The Life of W. Averell Harriman, 1891–1986* (New York: Morrow, 1992), pp. 198, 208.

76. *Ibid.*, p. 197.

77. Christopher Ogden, *Life of the Party: The Biography of Pamela Digby Churchill Hayward Harriman* (Boston: Little, Brown, 1994), p. 448.

78. *Ibid.*, p. 438.

79. In 1994, it was revealed that the Harriman family fortune had dwindled to $3 million. "Harriman Suit: Misconduct or Just Bad Luck Investing?" *New York Times* (Sept. 25, 1994).

80. Chernow, *House of Morgan*, p. 135.

81. *Ibid.*, p. 201.

published a review in the *Nation* (Oct. 21, 1939) of Felix Frankfurter's book, *Law and Politics* (1939). Frankfurter had been appointed to the U.S. Supreme Court the previous January. Frankfurter was a liberal: a member of House's "Inquiry" staff, which did the planning for the Paris peace conference in 1919,[82] a co-founder of the American Civil Liberties Union in 1920, and a Harvard Law School professor. After the election of Franklin Roosevelt in 1932, he became one of Roosevelt's most trusted scouts for recruiting talent to serve in the New Deal.[83] More to the point, he had been a *New Republic* staffer from its beginning in 1914. Ronald Steel writes: "He soon spread himself over the entire magazine, writing articles, furnishing legal advice, and joining in editorial conferences."[84] In his book review, Stone made this observation: "If I may be forgiven for speaking of *The Nation*'s weekly comrade-in-arms, the young men who started the *New Republic* were concerned not so much with influencing the masses as with influencing important men."[85] This, they surely achieved.

The world of the American Establishment was (and remains) a world in which very rich people have moved in very liberal circles, funding the activities of those who, on first glance—before you follow the money—are their mortal enemies. This world is a secure and pleasant one for those inside its protective boundaries. The funding that provides this security is part of the control exercised by the rich over the would-be weathermakers of the climate of public opinion. For example, when Mrs. Buck first aroused some mild displeasure from the missions board, Rockefeller wrote to one of his subordinates recommending that she be hired by the Riverside Church as a missionary should she be fired by the Presbyterians.[86] This did not become necessary. In 1937, when she published an obituary of Machen in *The New Republic*, she was part of the Straight publishing empire. That empire

---

82. Steel, *Lippmann*, p. 129.
83. *Ibid.*, p. 301.
84. *Ibid.*, p. 61.
85. Cited in James J. Martin, *American Liberalism and World Politics, 1931–1941*, 2 vols. (New York: Devin-Adair, 1964), I:2.
86. Schenkel, *Rich Man and Kingdom*, pp. 163–64.

was soon to be extended by the Straight family's heir, Michael, who at age 22 returned to the United States in 1938.[87] He was legally in control of *New Republic, Asia,* and *Theatre Arts*; he participated in the overseeing of the Museum of Modern Art. Richard Walsh and his wife ran *Asia* for him. Walsh was also president of the holding company of *New Republic*.[88]

To understand how the American Establishment has operated in the twentieth century, consider Georgetown University historian Carroll Quigley's discussion of the family connections of Dorothy Payne-Whitney-Straight-Elmhirst.

> She was the daughter of William C. Whitney, New York utility millionaire and the sister and co-heiress of Oliver Payne, of the Standard Oil trust. One of her brothers married Gertrude Vanderbilt, while the other, Payne Whitney, married the daughter of Secretary of State John Hay, who enunciated the American policy of the "Open Door" in China. In the next generation, three first cousins, John Hay ("Jock") Whitney, Cornelius Vanderbilt ("Sonny") Whitney, and Michael Whitney ("Mike") Straight, were allied in numerous public policy enterprises of a propagandist nature, and all three served in varied roles in the late New Deal and Truman administrations. In these they were closely allied with other "Wall Street liberals," such as Nelson Rockefeller.[89]

It is worth noting that Quigley taught history to Bill Clinton, who referred to him favorably in his July 16, 1992, Presidential nomination acceptance speech at the Democratic National Convention.

---

87. Straight was a communist at this time, and he passed what he says was unclassified information to a Soviet agent while serving as a speech writer for Roosevelt in 1939. He had been part of a Cambridge University secret society, the Apostles, which in his years was the recruiting ground for two of the Soviet Union's most highly placed spies, Guy Burgess and Anthony Blunt. He was part of that cell. Straight described all this and much more in his autobiography, *After Long Silence* (New York: Norton, 1983).

88. Quigley, *Tragedy and Hope*, p. 941.

89. *Ibid.*, pp. 938–39.

To an extent not sufficiently emphasized by Machen's biographers and others who have written about the Presbyterian conflict, Machen was challenging the American Establishment. Through his family's connections, Machen had spent his life close enough to the Establishment to know exactly what he was facing. He knew he was not involved in some cultural side-show peripheral to American civilization. But this was not the impression which readers obtained from Rian's *Presbyterian Conflict* (1940) and Loetscher's *Broadening Church* (1954), which until the 1980's constituted the little-known secondary sources of the Presbyterian conflict, itself nearly forgotten for five decades.

The Five Points of Modernism in Missions

Re-Thinking Missions was the full report of the Appraisal Commission, the summary volume, written by Harvard's W. E. Hocking, of a seven-volume set. In the first chapter, it replaced Christianity's exclusive claims with a vague reference to an undefined "supreme good": "Whatever its present conception of the future life, there is little disposition to believe that sincere and aspiring seekers after God in other religions are to be damned: it has become less concerned in any land to save man from eternal punishment than from the danger of losing the supreme good."[90] It began, in other words, with the fundamental presupposition of humanism: *there is no hell*.

The book re-stated the theology of modernism and applied it to missions. The book was an attempt to replace traditional missiology with a new theology. The report was a plea for understanding among religions in the face of the common enemy: "materialism, secularism, naturalism." "[T]he former opponents have become to this extent allied by the common task. It is not surprising if our missions make this realignment difficult, perhaps embarrassing; it compels a thorough re-analysis of the purpose of missions in reference to other faiths."[91]

---

90. *Re-Thinking Missions: A Laymen's Inquiry After 100 Years* (New York: Harper & Bros., 1932), p. 19.
91. *Ibid.*, p. 29.

Common faiths, common task: here was modernism's call to mission. If accepted, it would mean the end of missions.

1. The Non-Sovereignty of God

The original Christian missionary impulse was based on an attitude: the uniqueness of Christianity's God. The authors understood that "the friendly recognition of other faiths means to many Christians in the mission fields and at home an essential disloyalty, a compromise with error, and a surrender of the uniqueness of Christianity." This view of the world is dominionist: ". . . the conquest of the world by Christianity. . . ." In this older view, "There was one way of salvation and one only, one name, one atonement: this plan with its particular historical center in the career of Jesus must become the point of regard for every human soul."[92] Therefore, "those in the mission field who now face toward tolerance and association have their own qualms."[93] Missionaries ask this question: "If we fraternize or accept the fellowship of the alien faith, what becomes of the original hope that Christianity will bring the world under its undivided sway? If that objective is surrendered, has not the nerve of the mission motive itself been cut?"[94]

The authors clearly recognized the postmillennial impulse of Christian missions. This perspective had long been dominant, especially in Anglo-American missions.[95] In a very real sense, the world-conquering vision of Cecil Rhodes, Alfred Milner, and the Anglo-American alliance—which launched the Council on Foreign Relations in 1921—was a secular imitation of this older millennial outlook.[96] Rockefeller and the American Establishment had adopted this secularized postmillennial vision.

---

92. *Ibid.*, p. 35.
93. *Ibid.*, p. 36.
94. *Ibid.*
95. J. A. De Jong, *As the Waters Cover the Sea: Millennial expectations in the rise of Anglo-American missions, 1640–1810* (Kampen, Netherlands: Kok, 1970).
96. John Marlowe, *Milner: Apostle of Empire* (London: Hamish Hamilton, 1976); Carroll Quigley, *The Anglo-American Establishment* (New York: Books in Focus, 1981).

Christianity "is disposed to run out into action. It expects to be applied."[97] The authors viewed this viewpoint as one-sided. Christianity cannot afford "to leave to Buddhism or to Hinduism the arts of meditation."[98] "We would commend to the Christian Church a serious inquiry into the religious value of meditation. . . ."[99] The lure of Eastern mysticism for modernists was the promise of a non-cognitive encounter with an undefined, non-judgmental transcendence. It was an ancient lure.

"But perhaps the chief hope for an important deepening of self-knowledge on the part of Christendom is by way of a more thoroughgoing sharing of its life with the life of the Orient. Sharing may mean spreading abroad what one has"—notice the word *may*—"but sharing becomes real only as it becomes mutual, running in both directions, each teaching, each learning, each with the other meeting the unsolved problems of both."[100] There was no *may* associated with mutualism. Mutual sharing was the *only* way.

Then what is unique about Christianity? Only its particular group of doctrines. But its basic teachings are common in all religions. The Christian doctrine of a sovereign God is, for modernism, a non-sovereign doctrine.

2. The Non-Authority of the Bible

Re-Thinking Missions did not deal explicitly with the authority of the Bible except in relation to doctrines. This silence stands as a testimony to the irrelevance of the Bible to the missionary enterprise. Chapter 6, a two-section chapter, dealt with "Education: Primary and Secondary." Chapter 7, "Education: Higher," continued the theme. In none of these chapters is the Bible mentioned. The same is nearly true in the chapter on "Christian Literature."[101] It mentions Bible societies in a seven-line paragraph. "As the work of these Societies is outside the sphere of our Inquiry, we have made no investigation of them."[102]

---

97. *Re-Thinking Missions*, p. 45.
98. *Ibid.*
99. *Ibid.*
100. *Ibid.*, p. 46.
101. *Ibid.*, ch. 8.
102. *Ibid.*, p. 190.

Without the authority of the Bible to guide hierarchies as the sole source of fundamental law, there must be another source. In an evolutionary world, laws change. But what about hierarchies? We need a new set of hierarchies.

The problem with higher education in foreign missions, is "the lack of unity of administration."[103] "We are convinced that the only remedy for this condition is the establishment of centralized authority. . . . This proposal is identical in principle with that which this Commission is making in Chapter XIV for the reorganization of the administration of missions."[104] The Church ceases to speak authoritatively. It must be replaced by administrative agencies that operate efficiently. The gospel of efficiency replaces the gospel of Jesus Christ; Frederick W. Taylor replaces the Apostle Paul.[105]

3. Evolution: Doctrinal and Ethical

Missionaries need new doctrines and new ethical viewpoints. Christian doctrine must not be considered valid if it is static. To be relevant, doctrine must evolve with the times. Doctrine must become subordinate, as it was with Jesus, to "the realization and fulfillment of life."

> For years in most of these mission fields the message has been *doctrine-centered*, sometimes almost centered upon the use of phrases. The preaching, the Bible teaching and the Sunday school work with children has been to a very large extent built around theological conceptions. However effective this method may have been in the past, for the period now before us and for awakened minds, it is psychologically the wrong approach to begin with complicated abstract doctrines, dogmatically asserted. It runs counter to the well-tested methods in education now in

---

103. *Ibid.*, p. 178.
104. *Ibid.*, p. 179.
105. Daniel Nelson, *Frederick W. Taylor and the Rise of Scientific Management* (Madison: University of Wisconsin Press, 1980). Cf. Richard W. Reifsnyder, "Managing the Mission: Church Restructuring in the Twentieth Century," in *The Organizational Revolution: Presbyterians and American Denominationalism*, edited by Milton J Coalter, John M. Mulder, and Louis B. Weeks (Louisville, Kentucky: Westminster/John Knox Press, 1990), p. 57.

vogue throughout the world. The Christianity which is to convince and bring spiritual content to thoughtful and serious-minded persons in any part of the world today must put the emphasis where the founder of Christianity himself put it from the first, namely, upon the realization and fulfillment of life and upon those methods and processes and energies by which life can be brought to its divine possibilities. This does not mean in any sense that the interpretation of Christianity in ways that fit the intellectual needs of man's life is unimportant. It only means that stereotyped patterns of doctrine and static phrases which have gone dead should give place to a thoroughly vital message, expressed in the living forms of thought which convince and persuade the mind today.[106]

This is process theology. It sees "processes and energies" as the means by which life attains its "divine possibilities." The absolute Creator-creature distinction of Christian theology, including its assertion of the unique divinity of Jesus Christ—as distinct from His perfect humanity—is denied by these words. There is nothing divine in man, according to orthodox Christianity; divinity is an exclusive attribute of God.

The book made a frontal attack on orthodox Christianity when it stated that in the mission field, "Conformity is by no means desirable. Differences of thought and emphasis should be welcomed. They become tragic only when each one of those who disagree claims to be infallibly right. . . ."[107] Doctrinal rigidity hampers missionary activity. This had been Speer's message from the beginning of his career; it was also the message of modernism.

What is true of doctrine is also true of ethics. The early missionaries made a mistake in this regard, too, the Inquiry concluded. They believed that converts should pull out of their pagan culture and begin rebuilding their lives exclusively in terms of Christianity's laws and ethics. Our missionaries were "repelled by the external strangeness, the plural gods, the idols, the devious elements of superstition, fear,

---

106. *Re-Thinking Missions*, pp. 94-95.
107. *Ibid.*, p. 93.

baseness, priestly corruption." They told the new converts to abandon their pagan institutions. "This clean-breach method, experience has now amply shown mistaken." It required too heroic a break from local tradition.[108] It ignored the fact that there are many ways to God; we are all brothers in a common quest.

> But the central lesson they were slower to read, though they might have been led to it by their own faith that God has not anywhere left himself without a witness. It was hard for the missions to mix with their absorbing interest in rebirth a practical recognition that the surrounding religions were religions, and as such were ways to God. Their very compassion led them to hold these "false" religions responsible for the defects of oriental society and custom, the counterpart of an equally hasty social theory which made Christianity responsible for all the advantages they felt in western life. . . .
>
> But further, the mission is impelled by the requirements of simple truth. For after all, "we *are* brothers in a common quest, and the first step is to recognize it, and disarm ourselves of our prejudices."[109]

The proposed process of moral unification presented in *Re-Thinking Missions* was not based on progressive sanctification in terms of God's authoritatively revealed law and God's electing grace. It was based on the hope that moral platitudes that are already acceptable to all peoples can be used to reconstruct all societies. In this sense, the liberals appealed to a universal "right morality" in the same way that Warfield had appealed to a universal "right reason."[110] But like Warfield, who could never discover those universal principles of right reason that do, in fact, logically compel faith in the gospel, so the liberals have never found those universal moral principles that can serve as the foundation of a new world order. (Conclusion: power will have to

---

108. *Ibid.*, p. 30.
109. *Ibid.*, p. 31.
110. B. B. Warfield, "Introduction to Francis R. Beattie's *Apologetics*" (1903); reprinted in *Selected Shorter Writings of Benjamin B. Warfield—II*, edited by John Meeter (Nutley, New Jersey: Presbyterian & Reformed, 1973), p. 100.

suffice; the blue helmets of the United Nations will have to replace the golden rule.)

Noticeable also is the explicit attempt to distinguish Christian values from Western civilization. The liberals recognized that there was a very close relationship between the geographical origins of Christianity in the West and the coming of Western civilization. Max Weber had argued eloquently for the connection between the ethics of Protestantism and the origin of the institutions of Western rationalism, including capitalism.[111] They had to counter this argument, for to link Christianity and Western civilization would have made foreign missions seem like cultural wedges for a specific sort of religion with specific sorts of institutional consequences. This would not have been sufficiently liberal—sufficiently multi-cultural—in its vision. The idea that Christian ethics produces specific sorts of institutional products—the civilization of middle-class values—has been abhorrent to most evangelical liberal moralists. Their visions of order are anti-Western, as the rhetoric of the liberation theology (RIP) used to indicate.[112] Theological modernists are anti-Western and anti-middle class precisely because the middle-class West is the product of historic Christianity, and they are at war with historic Christianity.

4. No Negative Sanctions

The Inquiry recognized as crucial in Western missions the impulse for world dominion: the extension of Christendom. But fundamentalist missions, like fundamentalist evangelism, have had as their central motivation the salvation of souls from eternal negative sanctions. This has also been an important motivation in all Christian missionary enterprises. What, then, of the doctrine of hell in modern missions? *Re-Thinking Missions* was even more silent here than it was on the authority of the Bible.

---

111. Max Weber, *The Protestant Ethic and the Spirit of Capitalism*, translated by Talcott Parsons (New York: Charles Scribner's Sons, 1958). This book first appeared in German the form of a series of essays in a scholarly journal in 1904–1905, and first appeared in English in 1930.

112. Liberation theology fell out of favor when Gorbachev did. It became passé overnight. There is no negative sanction greater than this one in the theology of modernism.

The authors presented a brief history of missions to the orient. In the early days of missions to the orient, Protestants hoped to reap a harvest of souls: ". . . millions of souls, believed to be in danger of eternal death, might be given the opportunity of life; there was but one way, the way of Christ. There was need for haste."[113] The authors prudently did not challenge this vision of salvation from sin and eternal death. But they immediately substituted another vision, a vision of a new world order:

> Mingled with this concern for individuals, there was the appealing vision of the world-wide Church. It was well to have many centers from which local extensions might begin. Around this picture of the universal Christian community gathered obscurely all that we now think of as preparation for world unity in civilization. We know that to effect an understanding in religious matters is to pave the way for an understanding in other matters. The world must eventually become a moral unity: to this end, it was necessary that the apparent localism of Christianity should be broken down. It must not be thought of as solely the religion of the West. It was because Christianity is *not* western, but universally human, that it must be brought back to the Orient and made at home there.[114]

In short, the report moved from a discussion of hell to a discussion of social theory. This does not mean that the report had no concept of sanctions. Social theory is impossible without the concept of sanctions, both positive and negative. Missionaries are to bring positive sanctions only: in education,[115] literature,[116] medical missions,[117] agricultural missions,[118] industrial missions,[119] and women's interests and activities.[120] These positive sanctions must not be conceived as

---

113. *Re-Thinking Missions*, p. 8.
114. *Ibid.*
115. Chapters 6–7.
116. Chapter 8.
117. Chapter 9.
118. Chapter 10.
119. Chapter 11.
120. Chapter 12.

one-way activities: Western Civilization's suppression of Eastern Civilization. There must be interaction: mutual sharing.

5. Ecumenism

The quest today, the Inquiry announced, is for "world unity in civilization."[121] This, I hasten to add, was also the quest of Christ's Apostles. The difference between the two kingdoms, Christ's and Satan's, is the differing attitudes toward the sovereignty of God, the distinction between God and His creation, the relationship between God's law and dominion, and the nature of the new birth. Satan wants a one-world State; Christ proclaims a one-world, decentralized order.[122] Satan offers dominion through the exercise and pursuit of power; Christ offers dominion through ethical conformity to God and service to man.[123] But both religions are kingdom religions, and both proclaim the world-wide locus of the ethical struggle.

The authors of *Re-Thinking Missions* brought together in one place virtually all of the tenets of theological liberalism of that generation. Theirs was a secular postmillennial faith. They set forth the possibility of world-wide reconstruction. They claimed that they were calling for Christian reconstruction, but it was in fact a call for the absorption of existing Christian institutions by the forces of humanism. Nevertheless, this vision of conquest by the preaching of the gospel—the gospel of world unity—motivated the liberals of that generation. They saw the possibility of creating a new world order based on shared moral reference points.

Here is the familiar refrain of first-stage liberalism—before the excommunications by second-stage liberalism begin: all roads lead to the same God. We are all sons of our universal Father. Not sons the way Cain was a son—ready to kill his biological brother—but sons in the way that liberal preaching imagines men to be: men without permanent ethical differences to divide them institutionally. But revelational

---

121. *Ibid.*, p. 8.
122. Gary North, *Healer of the Nations: Biblical Blueprints for International Relations* (Ft. Worth, Texas: Dominion Press, 1987).
123. Gary North, *Dominion and Common Grace: The Biblical Basis of Progress* (Tyler, Texas: Institute for Christian Economics, 1987).

ethics divides men. Thus, the liberal is adamant: we must abandon all forms of God-revealed ("exclusivist") ethics.

The final call of the Commissioners, predictably, was for ecumenical consolidation:

> *The need of unity on a comprehensive scale.* The time has come for a plan of administrative unity on a comprehensive scale. In the homely but striking metaphor of a missionary leader in the Orient, the old model, which was once regarded as a marvel, will no longer sell. Possibly by making a few superficial improvements and introducing one or two new features it may be made to last a little longer. But certainly the wiser course is to undertake at once, in the light of experience and with a long look ahead, the construction of a new model designed to meet the needs of a new world.
>
> A careful study of the problem in its varied aspects has convinced the Commission that the efforts heretofore made in the direction of unity and coordination have produced few significant results, but we recognize great difficulties of effecting union on a large scale. Denominational loyalties are deeply embedded in emotional religious life, and have dominated missionary effort for more than a century. There are many other intricate and perplexing questions to be solved. We believe, nevertheless, that thoughtful Protestants will not [no?] longer insist upon imposing a particular theology and polity upon the Christians of Asia; that they will desire rather to encourage the followers of Christ in the Orient to develop their religious life and their religious organizations in harmony with their own conceptions and their own genius; and that to this end they will be willing to support a far wider and bolder policy of missionary cooperation and union than has heretofore been attempted.[124]

This was a call for "mission," but a wholly new form of mission. It was *a mission from the East to the West*. It was a call for world unity apart from God's revelation. It was a mission from Babylon to Jerusa-

---

124. *Re-Thinking Missions*, p. 318.

lem. It was another call for the top-down centralization of institutional life, another architect's vision of a new Tower of Babel.

You can guess what administrative change the Commission suggested, but just for the record I will allow the Commissioners to spell it out: "The Commission proposes, therefore, a single administrative unit for the foreign Christian enterprise in place of the complex, costly and duplicative machinery the existence of which is encumbering the great work that Christian good will is trying to do."[125] In short, what is needed is ecumenical unity and administrative consolidation and centralization. These goals were predictable. To make sure that nobody missed their point, the Commission offered a six-point summary of the "advantages":

> (1) A new view of the functions and responsibilities of the Christian Church: a call to wider allegiances, and a rebuke to un-Christian divisiveness.
>
> (2) An administrative basis, simple, adaptable, and economical.
>
> (3) Centralized disbursement, accounting, and audit of funds.
>
> (4) A body of creative leaders raised above the level of denominationalism.
>
> (5) Experimentation under expert guidance.
>
> (6) A united and coordinated front on the foreign field.[126]

After reading the Report, Rockefeller wrote ecstatically to the commissioners in August:

> The deep sympathy, broad grasp, keen penetration; the unquestioned faith in the fundamental, underlying, world-embracing significance of the spiritual values of true religion which these chapters reveal, coupled with the generous appreciation of all that is excellent and the courageous indication of defect and weaknesses, give assurance that this report if finished as it has

---

125. *Ibid.*, p. 319.
126. *Ibid.*, p. 322.

begun is destined to have an influence not only on the religious life of the world but on civilization itself far beyond anything that has ever been dreamed or hoped.[127]

Within three years, the Report had sunk without a trace in most denominations.[128] The foreign missions field had already begun to go through a series of radical changes, especially in Asia with Japan's invasion of Manchuria. Then came World War II, the post-war rise of nationalism, the national independence movements, the dissolution of the British and Dutch Empires (the last empire to fall was Portugal's—the least empire-like), the banning of foreign missionaries as agents of Western colonialism, and the rise of Communism. *Re-Thinking Missions* became a forgotten relic of the inter-war era of American theological modernism. But in 1932 and 1933, it created a minor sensation, revealing the wide theological diversity within American Protestantism.[129] It went through ten printings in six months.[130] It also led to the consummation of the Presbyterian conflict.

Official Reactions: Mild

The reactions of the official boards of missions of the various denominations were, to say the least, cautious. Methodists were the most wholeheartedly in support of the book. The General Council of the Presbyterian Church, while not rejecting the "constructive comments" on the machinery for selecting and training the candidates, rejected the doctrinal aspects of the report: "We cannot accept the interpretation placed by the Report upon the Christian message and the missionary objective. What is proposed is virtually a denial of evangelical Christianity. The Gospel cannot surrender its unique supremacy."[131]

The Board of Missions itself was not so clear-cut in its appraisal of the report. Quite naturally, it defended the validity of the mission

---

127. Cited in Schenkel, *Rich Man and Kingdom*, p. 160.
128. Patterson, Speer, p. 119.
129. Archibald G. Baker, "Reactions to the *Laymen's Report*," *Journal of Religion*, 13 (1933), pp. 379-98.
130. Colby and Dennett, *Thy Will Be Done*, p. 40.
131. Reprinted in *Christianity Today* (Dec. 1932), p. 19.

work it was sponsoring, claiming that it may not have been perfect, but certainly worthy of support. Board members never took a direct stand against the doctrinal issues that the report had raised, as the General Council had done, but instead limited themselves to a carefully worded statement that reaffirmed the Board's "abiding loyalty to the Evangelical basis of the missionary enterprise."[132] Its whole tone was neutral to an extreme. Only months later, after the furor had engulfed the Board, did it at last express disagreement with the book, a point noted by Machen the following June.[133]

A comment in *Christianity Today* summarized the positions of the various boards of the denominations, although directed specifically to the Presbyterian Church: "All officialdom seemed to be mobilizing its power to satisfy conservatives, on the one hand, by repeated evangelically-toned statements, and to satisfy modernists on the other hand, by doing nothing to disturb their presence on the mission field or in the boards at home."[134] The conservatives were given rhetoric; the liberals were given jobs.

The official responses of the bureaucrats in power could not hide the magnitude of the negative response, at least in the Presbyterian Church. Macartney spoke for the conservatives: "But in these 129,000 words, I can note just one mention of the word 'sin.' The omission is significant. Nor do I recall seeing a single mention of the Third Person of the Trinity, the Holy Spirit. . . ."[135] In the same issue of *Christianity Today*, the editor wrote: "It is safe to say that nothing has happened in recent years more fitted to divide the churches than the Laymen's missionary report." It would literally divide the Presbyterian Church, U.S.A., over the next three and a half years.

Mrs. Buck Strikes Again

The controversy had barely begun when Mrs. Buck added more fuel to the blaze by publishing a second article in the January, 1933,

---

132. *Ibid.*, p. 20.

133. Machen, "The Observations About the Assembly," *Christianity Today* (June 1931), p. 5.

134. *Ibid.*, p. 21.

135. Clarence E. Macartney, "'Renouncing Missions' or 'Modernism Unmasked,'" *Christianity Today* (Jan. 1933), p. 6.

issue of *Harper's Magazine*. This time, she expressed her own theological convictions, offering at the same time her personal critique of the mission system. If the first article had upset orthodox churchmen, this one was calculated to give them apoplexy.

It began with an attack on the mediocrity which she felt she saw in the missionaries in China, "ignorant . . . arrogant . . . superstitious" men in far too many cases, "who have taught superstitious creeds and theories and have made the lives of hungry-hearted people more wretched and more sad."[136] She made it clear, however, that she did not blame these men too much because, as she said, "I do not believe in original sin."[137]

Her statement of personal belief was so unorthodox that even the moderates in the Church would have to take exception: "Some believe in Christ as our father did. To some he is still the divine son of God, born of the virgin Mary, conceived by the Holy Spirit. But to many of us he has ceased to be that. Some of us do not know what he is, some of us care less. In this world of our life it does not matter perhaps what he is. . . . He was perhaps the best man who ever lived. But that is all he is."[138] As to the uniqueness of Christianity, she made herself unmistakably clear: "I do not believe that any religion is comprehensive enough to exclude all others."[139]

Speer Responds

Almost immediately after the publication of *Re-Thinking Missions*, Speer replied in *The Missionary Review of the World* (Jan. 1933). Later in the year, this long article became a short book, *"Re-Thinking Missions" Examined*. His published response is important, both for what it said and for what it did not say. It was also important for the way in which he said it.

By the mid-1930's, Speer was the chief representative of American Protestant denominational missions. With 1,305 Presbyterian mission-

---

136. Pearl S. Buck, "Is There a Case for Foreign Missions?" *Harper's* (Jan. 1933), p. 145.
137. *Ibid.*, p. 148.
138. *Ibid.*, p. 150.
139. *Ibid.*, p. 152.

aries in the field,[140] this should not be surprising. Only Mott had equal or greater name-recognition,[141] but Mott was an interdenominationalist. Speer was, too, but he tried to keep alive some sort of federalism until the unification could be consummated. He did not want to get too far ahead of those in the pews who wrote the checks. Speer's response to *Re-Thinking Missions* would reveal the degree of hostility or commitment of the American Protestant missions establishment to the ecumenism and secularism of Rockefeller's vision of missions.

Speer was a mild-mannered liberal who covered his theology with conservative phrases. Had his critics read Speer's 1910 Duff Lectures, *Christianity and the Nations*, they would have seen what their problem was: a liberal was running the Foreign Missions Board. There was one Christian doctrine, above all others, that he sought to de-emphasize or avoid altogether: hell. Speer avoided the topic like the plague. This was the common mark of a liberal. Had he not been a liberal, this would have been a very peculiar omission in the writings of the chief representative of Presbyterian foreign missions.

In his 1902 book, *The Principles of Jesus*, he included a brief chapter on "Jesus and Hell," which self-consciously befuddled the issue. "'The everlasting fire' is one of Jesus' own expressions. Does He mean 'everlasting' and does He mean 'fire'? He certainly does not mean material fire. Men long ago perceived that, but He does mean something of which our word 'fire' is the best metaphor, something utterly destructive of evil and impurity."[142] This narrows the question to what Jesus said, but there is more about hell in the Bible than what Jesus said. The Book of Revelation is quite clear: hell means material fire, or better put, the contents of hell, which includes the perfect, eternal, resurrected bodies of covenant-breakers, are dumped into a literal, physical fire at the final judgment. Bodily eternal fire matches

---

140. John R. Fitzmier and Randall Balmer, "A Poultice for the Bite of the Cobra: The Hocking Report and Presbyterian Missions in the Middle Decades of the Twentieth Century," in *The Diversity of Discipleship: The Presbyterians and Twentieth-Century Christian Witness*, edited by Milton J Coalter, John M. Mulder, and Louis B. Weeks (Louisville: Westminster/John Knox Press, 1991), p. 124.

141. Longfield, *Presbyterian Controversy*, p. 186.

142. Robert E. Speer, *The Principles of Jesus Applied to Some Questions of Today* (New York: Revell, 1902), p. 175.

bodily resurrection. "And death and hell were cast into the lake of fire. This is the second death. And whosoever was not found written in the book of life was cast into the lake of fire" (Rev. 20:14–15). As for eternity, Speer wrote, we just do not know what this means. "What those terms signify in the life that is beyond this, we shall not understand until we get there."[143] He pleaded ignorance. Nobody ever was de-frocked for pleading ignorance, and besides, Speer had never been ordained. He was immune to judicial action. Speer was a consummate producer of cotton candy prose: all sweetness and air. Nothing he ever wrote left visible traces a year later. He wrote dozens of volumes, yet rarely said anything of theological substance. For over four decades, he gave his readers long shrift.

There was an exception, however. In 1910, the year of the Edinburgh World Missionary Conference, he delivered the Duff Lectures on foreign missions. Here, he came close to saying what he really believed about hell. "The idea that the supreme missionary motive has been the desire to save the souls of the heathen from hell rests upon a very partial knowledge of missionary literature. . . . The epistles of Paul know nothing of it. He never once uses the word hell."[144] He adopted a version of Pelagianism, i.e., the denial of the consequences of original sin: ". . . we know that men are not to be judged as though all had seen the same light. No man is lost for not accepting a Savior of whom he has never heard."[145] He refused to discuss the obvious implication of this theology: it is the Christian missionary who necessarily sends heathens to hell, whatever it is, for he brings the message of redemption through faith in Jesus Christ alone, and thereby inflicts heathen souls with the deadly curse: no more excuses.

He also made his ecumenical vision clear: "I belong to the Presbyterian Church, but I have not the slightest zeal in seeking to have the Presbyterian Church extended over the non-Christian world."[146] He wanted ecumenical foreign missions. The West must not export de-

---

143. *Ibid.*
144. Robert E. Speer, *Christianity and the Nations* (New York: Revell, 1910), pp. 32–33.
145. *Ibid.*, p. 33.
146. *Ibid.*, p. 332.

nominationalism abroad: ". . . the Occidental character of our divisions makes it both unnecessary and inexpedient to export them to the mission field."[147] This implies ecumenism: "But the ideal of foreign missions is not realised by a federation of separate agencies. It contemplates a united Church, not a compact of separate units, but one corporate and manifested life."[148] This was happening abroad, he said. "It is showing the Church at home the possibility of union, not only of co-operation in work or of federation of separate Christian bodies, but of actual union."[149] "The missionary movement is teaching us also the duty of union."[150] What was wrong with non-Christian religions? Their lack of unity. "And yet once more, the non-Christian religions are inadequate to the social needs of men because every one of them denies the unity of mankind. . . . To be sure, 'The fatherhood of God and the brotherhood of man,' is a common phrase throughout the world, but both of these great conceptions are the contribution of the Christian revelation."[151] Little wonder that with these ideas, he became a trusted Rockefeller advisor as early as 1913 and remained such for two decades prior to *Re-thinking Missions*. What is astounding is that he could remain on the Presbyterian Church's payroll without at least a protest from conservatives.

Speer in late 1932 was trapped between the Rockefeller establishment, which he did not trust despite his participation on its fringes, and the Machen-Macartney wing of his own Church. He had to say something publicly. He rued what he called the "fresh ammunition" given by the Report to both fundamentalists and modernists. He was correct in one thing: the Report did not arouse much interest in missionary activity. It aroused interest only in the Report and discussions about the Report.[152] He had a bureaucrat's assessment of the Report: "Certainly this report has made our whole problem vastly more difficult for us. It has played directly into the hands of extrem-

---

147. *Ibid.*, p. 336.
148. *Ibid.*, p. 349.
149. *Ibid.*, p. 352.
150. *Ibid.*, p. 353.
151. *Ibid.*, p. 282.
152. Speer to William Miller, April 1, 1933; cited in Patterson, *Speer*, p. 99.

ists of both wings. I think we have seldom had a document which has had so good a purpose to promote unity and which has had so dire a result in making unity difficult."[153] Unity is indeed a good purpose; the question is: By what standard? It was this question that Speer had avoided answering throughout his career. This is what had long made him the modernists' wedge, second in importance only to W. H. Roberts during Roberts' lifetime; second to none after 1920.

Speer began his little book with some polite genuflecting to the Rockefeller machine, though without naming it: "Our first desire ought to be and is to express hearty appreciation of the purpose and spirit of this Inquiry and Report and of the unselfish devotion of time and effort which it represents."[154] The Inquiry was undertaken out of the "highest motives," the reader was assured.[155] Furthermore, "Let it be said at once that there ought to be no sensitiveness at all on the part of Missions and Boards with regard to their being passed under the severest criticism."[156] (This openness applied to criticism from those funded by the Rockefeller Foundation, not from Machen and his allies.) Speer alluded to the funding: "As a matter of fact, the financial response from the laymen was negligible and the Inquiry was carried through, not as a great and widespread movement of laymen, but by a very small and devoted group." How small? Fewer than half a dozen people.[157]

In Defense of Protocol

Speer referred to the "enormous publicity campaign" that had begun the previous September. This had violated the promised confidentiality of the Report, which the Boards of the various denominational missions organizations were pledged to honor until they received copies of the Report on November 18. They honored the pledge; the unnamed promoters did not. The Boards had to sit quietly "when

---

153. Speer to Frank Mason North, Jan. 17, 1933; cited in *ibid*.
154. Robert E. Speer, *"Re-Thinking Missions" Examined* (New York: Revell, 1933), p. 7.
155. *Ibid*.
156. *Ibid*., p. 8.
157. *Ibid*., p. 10.

their constituents were demanding why they made no explanation of their position under the flood of criticism. . . ."[158] Bureaucratic protocol had been violated—normally, a cardinal sin—in this case by Rockefeller interests, so Speer's criticism was muted. The main criticism is that the negative publicity from critics has "made it difficult to secure a fair consideration of the good elements in the Report."[159]

There was another problem. The various denominational missions boards had been told that they would appoint the commission that would make the Inquiry. But then the investigation was conducted "in complete independence of the Boards. . . ."[160] Another breach of protocol! This criticism appears under the subhead: "Who Was Responsible?" But Speer did not answer his own question, nor even refer to it again. That, too, showed great deference to the man who was behind it. Schenkel, in his study of Rockefeller's religious commitment, comments on the highly secretive aspect of the Inquiry's funding. "The commission officially completed its task with a public unveiling of its report at the Roosevelt Hotel on 13 January 1933. As usual, Rockefeller's name did not appear on the program. The extent of Rockefeller's role in the enterprise was not generally known, and he declined invitations, such as that of *Good Housekeeping* magazine, to comment on it."[161]

Reading the Report, Speer recognized "the high-mindedness of it, the beautiful literary statement. . . ."[162] (Perhaps if you have spent your adult life reading committee reports—and Presbyterian committee reports at that—the bureaucratic report known as *Re-Thinking Missions* might seem a literary delight.)

Then Speer got down to business. First, "The report suffers from a lack of adequate depth of background."[163] It left out a chapter on the history of missions for lack of space. It barely mentioned St. Paul. It

---

158. *Ibid.*, p. 12.
159. *Ibid.*
160. *Ibid.*, p. 13.
161. Schenkel, *Rich Man and Kingdom*, p. 162.
162. Speer, *"Re-Thinking Missions" Examined*, p. 14.
163. *Ibid.*, p. 16.

ignored the uplifting social ideas of early missionaries.[164] Second, the report was "exclusive and partisan."[165] Third, the Report "makes the grave error, which we must all seek to correct, of requiring that all shall be taken or none. This is unwise tactics. . . ."[166] It proposes to change the theological basis of missions.[167] It calls for a common, inter-religious quest for truth.[168]

Here Speer began to target the real problem: the Report's rejection of the Church's claims regarding the uniqueness of Christ and His claims. Machen would have agreed. But Machen would have called attention to the Bible's doctrine of Christ and redemption. Speer said: "For us, Christ is still *the* Way, not *a* way. . . ."[169] What, judicially and ethically speaking, is this Way? What about the doctrine of the substitutionary atonement? Speer did not mention this. What about the doctrine of hell? He did not mention this, either. Instead, he asked other rhetorical questions: "Are we really apprehending Him and His power? Are we willing to let God in Christ work supernaturally in us today?"[170] Power and supernatural personal encounter: here we find language that would appeal to two of the three factions inside the Presbyterian Church: liberals and experientialists.

The Unruffled Flow of Funds and Power

Then he got to the heart of the matter, bureaucratically speaking. The Report called for the centralization of funding and administration. But donors, Speer knew from experience, would not continue to give to such a centralized agency. He wrote what would become a prophetic statement: "One of the Commissioners on November 19 declared that donors had no right to act thus, that they should give their money and let the overhead body, which knows better than they do, spend it. There is truth in this, but only within limits."[171]

---

164. *Ibid.*, pp. 17–23.
165. *Ibid.*, p. 23.
166. *Ibid.*, p. 25.
167. *Ibid.*, pp. 26–29.
168. *Ibid.*, pp. 28–31.
169. *Ibid.*, p. 31.
170. *Ibid.*, p. 36.
171. *Ibid.*, p. 37.

Over the next three years, the Presbyterian Church would define these limits: inside the Presbyterian Church. Speer in 1933 was not about to assent to the transfer of what would, in 1934, become the declared and judicially enforceable sovereignty of Presbyterian boards over Presbyterian congregations' funds, to some interdenominational Board that would skip the middlemen, namely, denominational boards. "It is a mistake to think that in Christian missions or anywhere else centralized monopoly is a good thing."[172] Machen would be de-frocked in 1936 for saying the same thing, and then acting on it.

The Report, Speer said, was too critical of many missionaries, yet few were interviewed. It was wrong to criticize Asian missionaries for having tried to separate the Asians from traditional religion. It disparaged doctrinal evangelism.[173] But we are back to the same question: What is Christianity—doctrinally, judicially, and ethically? Speer did not say. For the next ten pages, his little book reported on "Some Excellent Recommendations" in the Report: social reform and—here one can detect the interest of Mr. Rockefeller—"For Better Commercial Representatives."[174]

Then came the big one—the number-one evil of the Report: "Of all these, the central and gravest issue must be faced. It is the dreadful peril of divisiveness with which this Report is charged."[175] Spoken like a true bureaucrat, a true seeker after interdenominational unity and peace. "It has sown discontent among the denominations which were not involved in the Inquiry, but all of whose work falls under the judgments of the Report."[176] The Report calls for a "new agency." "What a tragedy it would be if a movement which earnestly and fervently seeks for larger unity among the Churches should issue in a new and rival organization either within or outside of the Churches!"[177]

Speer was an ecumenist, though more of a federal ecumenist. He wanted to retain denominational distinctives, though not theological

---

172. *Ibid.*
173. *Ibid.*, pp. 38–47.
174. *Ibid.*, p. 57.
175. *Ibid.*, p. 59.
176. *Ibid.*
177. *Ibid.*

distinctives or polity, which did not concern him, and hadn't since his Student Volunteer Movement days.[178] But if doctrine and polity are not legitimate reasons for separateness, then what is? He never said, but money and tradition come to mind: tradition generates money.

Disturbing the Peace

Church historian William Hutchison, generally sympathetic to Speer, is persuaded by the evidence to admit: "In expanding on these points Speer frequently seemed quintessentially the politician—beholden to too many constituencies, too quickly falling back upon practical considerations in serious matters of principle."[179] This was not Machen's weakness. The problem was, Machen was facing a shrinking constituency.

Speer's defender, James Patterson, wrote his Princeton Seminary Ph.D. on Speer, using the resources of Princeton's Speer Library, refers to "Speer's vigorous criticisms of *Re-Thinking Missions.* . . ."[180] The rhetoric of a bureaucrat who seeks to avoid upsetting either source of his funding—Rockefeller on the left and devoted laymen on the right—is described as vigorous. Predictably, Patterson regards Machen's attacks on Speer as having the "appearance of a personal vendetta" for Speer's having participated directly in the reorganization of Princeton Seminary.[181]

The historiography written by the spiritual heirs of the winners reflects their inability to understand that for a Calvinist, theology is a life-and-death matter. They do not believe that without propositional truth based on a permanent standard over history and revealed in history, the drift down academic relativism's calm tributary leads to the waterfall of cultural nihilism. It leads to this: "Young people, regard-

---

178. He said in 1894, "We Presbyterians and Methodists have no business being apart on questions of doctrine and polity." Cited in Longfield, *Presbyterian Controversy*, p. 187.

179. William R. Hutchison, *Errand to the World: American Protestant Thought and Foreign Missions* (Chicago: University of Chicago Press, 1987), p. 170.

180. James A. Patterson, "Robert E. Speer, J. Gresham Machen and the Presbyterian Board of Foreign Missions," *American Presbyterians*, 64 (Spring 1986), p. 63.

181. *Ibid.*, p. 62.

less of their sexual orientation, need to understand the institutional power of heterosexism and the injustice that it perpetuates. As the church is called to speak a truthful word about sexuality, it does so in the name of God's call to justice—a call that invites gay and lesbian adolescents to explore the goodness of their sexuality within the community of God's people."[182]

Machen Responds

The reaction in conservative circles was immediate. Any semblance of unity within the Church was banished by the end of January. Orthodox men were up in arms—small-caliber, as always—and Machen soon led the attack, again in terms of the now rejected five-point Doctrinal Deliverance. In a proposed overture to the General Assembly, submitted to the New Brunswick Presbytery for ratification on January 24, 1933, he called for a policy of electing to the Board of Foreign Missions only those who subscribed to the five points.[183] This overture was made the order of the day for April 11.

Just before the presbytery meeting in April, Machen again went to the printing press, this time with a 110-page brief exposing what he believed were modernist tendencies in the Board of Foreign Missions. It criticized the Board on several accounts, but main ones included: an attack on the Laymen's Mission report which, Machen felt, had not been adequately repudiated by the Board; a criticism of Mrs. Buck's theological position; a criticism of "Modernist propaganda" from the Candidate Secretary's office; and, finally, a reference to the fact that there were two signers of the Auburn *Affirmation* on the Board.[184] We see, again, that the *Affirmation* had become Machen's touchstone of liberalism: proof of infidelity.

---

182. *Keeping Body and Soul Together: Sexuality, Spirituality, and Social Justice*, A Document Prepared for the 203rd General Assembly (1991) by the General Assembly Special Committee on Human Sexuality, p. 89, lines 3500–3501.

183. Stonehouse, *Machen*, pp. 475–76.

184. Machen, *Modernism and the Board of Foreign Missions of the Presbyterian Church in the U.S.A.* (Author, 1933). Reprinted in *Modernism and Foreign Missions: Two Fundamentalist Protests*, edited by Joel A. Carpenter (New York: Garland, 1988).

The Silence of the Board

The argument he had with the Board in regard to *Re-Thinking Missions* was its refusal to rebut unhesitatingly "this broadside of modernist unbelief," this "public attack against the very heart of the Christian religion."[185] Two Board members were actually a part of the original Laymen's Inquiry which appointed the Appraisal Commission: James Speers and Mrs. J. H. Findley. The Board's reply, too vague to be meaningful, seemed entirely unsatisfactory, and Machen described it in military terms: "Did ever a trumpet in time of battle, in a time when the very citadel of the Faith had been attacked, give forth a feebler sound?"[186] After reviewing Mrs. Buck's essay, he quipped, "One thing is certainly to be said for Mrs. Buck. She is absolutely clear. Her utterances are as plain as the utterances of our board are muddled."[187] What bothered Machen most was liberalism camouflaged by the terminology of Christianity. He resented the deception.

The principal question regarding Mrs. Buck, for Machen, was this: Why didn't the Board dismiss her? He said that the Board had two possible plans of action available to it: to eliminate her quietly, "without intensifying yet further the charge of intolerance which already rests upon the Christian Church," a course of action morally reprehensible but financially more profitable; or to dismiss her for cause, on the basis of doctrine.[188] He was wrong. There was a third possibility: do nothing. Be patient. Sit tight. Pray that the woman will resign and go away.

In the third section of the booklet, he referred to the Auburn *Affirmation*. He asked the fundamental question from the orthodox point of view: Are the signers of the *Affirmation* "fit persons to be employed by the great Boards of the Church for the responsible duty of saying to the world what the essential meaning of the Church is?"[189] The *Affirmation*, he went on, was a "typical Modernist document . . . typical in the deceptive way it uses general terms which

---

185. *Ibid.*, p. 6.
186. *Ibid.*, p. 8.
187. *Ibid.*, p. 15.
188. *Ibid.*, p. 16.
189. *Ibid.*, p. 22.

many interpret in a Christian sense, but which many interpret in a non-Christian sense."[190] Finally, he crystallized his position, a position which was later to lead to a division within Westminster Seminary's own Board of Trustees, and ultimately to a division within the Presbyterian Church: "A mighty conflict is on in the Presbyterian Church at the present time. On one side of the conflict are to be put believers in, and defenders of, the Word of God; on the other side are to be put not only the signers of the Auburn Affirmation themselves, but also those who are ready to make common cause, without protest, with the signers of the Affirmation in mission boards, in governing boards of theological seminaries, and in the courts and councils of the Church."[191]

He ended the booklet with many pages of documentation showing conclusively that the Church missionaries in China were in many cases cooperating with extremely liberal, and even pro-Communist, elements within that country.

Machen Debates Speer

On the day of the presentation of Machen's overture regarding the Foreign Missions Board, a public debate took place between Machen and Speer. Speer was normally an eloquent speaker.[192] The New Brunswick Presbytery invited Speer to speak, which he did, saying he did not wish to get involved in controversy. He refused to answer any of Machen's specific charges against the Board. He called for unity, for trust in the Board. "What we need today is not conflict and division among us who hold this common faith but a unified front against all that is opposed to Christ and His gospel."[193] This had been his theme since the day he addressed the 1901 General Assembly. He added: "If there is one missionary of our Board who is not faithful to the central message of our church the Board does not know of it."[194]

---

190. *Ibid.*, p. 23.
191. *Ibid.*, p. 24.
192. Machen's estimation: Machen, "Dr. Robert E. Speer and His Latest Book," *Christianity Today* (May 1933), pp. 15, 23.
193. Cited in Patterson, *Speer*, p. 151.
194. Quoted in *Christianity Today* (April 1933), p. 22. This article is a lengthy

The obvious question, then, was what of Mrs. Buck? Speer had to admit that she was not sound in the faith. "We recognize that these are impossible views to be held by any missionary in the Presbyterian Church in the U.S.A."[195] He did not elaborate, since he could not explain how she could remain on the Church mission field; he simply intimated that "there were facors in the case that could not be referred to publicly." This is a standard bureaucratic ploy: plead the need for secrecy. (Bureaucrats can never get enough secrecy.) But the Board had to do something about her, and it chose the easiest path.

Passing the Buck

Mrs. Buck would not affirm her commitment to anything resembling orthodox Christianity. Ironically, some of the Board's members in their private correspondence began to sound like the Confessionalists: they hoped she would voluntarily resign. This was the position of Charles Erdman, who was president of the Board that year.[196] The Board in this case imitated the conservatives: it refused to bring negative sanctions against her. Meanwhile, Machen wrote to her assuring her that his opposition to her was strictly theological, not personal.[197]

Late in April of 1933, Mrs. Buck provided the Board with its hoped-for solution when she resigned from the mission enterprise of the Presbyterian Church. Her resignation was accepted on May 1 "with deep regret." Machen called this conciliatory action on the part of the Board "fundamentally dishonest policy."[198] In her obituary on Machen in 1937, she wrote, "we had much the same fate. I was kicked out of the back door of the church and he was kicked out of the front one."[199] But she had not been kicked out. She had decided to divorce

---

summary of the debate by an anonymous correspondent.
195. *Ibid.*
196. Letter of Charles Erdman to Speer (March 25, 1933); Patterson, Speer, p. 153.
197. Pearl S. Buck, "A Tribute to Dr. Machen," *New Republic* (January 20, 1937), p. 355.
198. Machen, "Dr. Robert E. Speer and His Latest Book," *Christianity Today* (May 1933), p. 15.
199. Buck, "Tribute," p. 355.

her missionary husband, get out of China, and join her new husband and the American Establishment in New York City. She had resigned before a trial was even suggested; Machen had not.

The Fate of Machen's Overture

The New Brunswick Presbytery rejected Machen's overture regarding the Board, but on May 1, the same day that Mrs. Buck's resignation was accepted, the Philadelphia Presbytery accepted the overture, and on May 5, the Aberdeen Presbytery followed suit. In retrospect, it seems remarkable that the proponents of such a reform could have thought that this overture might gain the acceptance of the whole Church in 1933.

The overtures had been referred to the Standing Committee on Foreign Missions. The Committee asked the Philadelphia Presbytery to send a commissioner to defend the overture. None appeared. Machen then requested to speak. It was well known that he had written the overture. The Committee at first refused, since Machen was not a commissioner, but then relented. Members of the Board replied. The Committee then voted 45 to 2 against the overture. The majority report affirmed its confidence in the Board, and the General Assembly voted overwhelmingly to accept it.[200] Speer's biographer concludes: "Machen's decisive defeat at the General Assembly of 1933 marked a critical juncture in the course of fundamentalist dissent."[201]

Perhaps the most telling evidence of the nature of the response by the Board of Foreign Missions and the General Assembly which approved its report was the fact that in a 15-part report to the General Assembly, the discussion of the overtures' criticisms appeared in section 14. Section 1 is representative of the mind-set of the Board: correct procedure has been followed!

After a thorough examination of the Minutes of the Board for the last year, (1) We would record our satisfaction in the excel-

---

200. A summary of these events appeared in the next year's *Minutes*: *Minutes of the General Assembly, 1934*, p. 72. Normally, such important details as these never appear in the *Minutes*.

201. Patterson, Speer, p. 158.

lence with which the minutes are recorded and indexed, finding them to be truly a work of artistic quality perfect in their mechanics. (2) We express our conviction that if the church at large could know the conscientiousness and thoroughness and prayerfulness with which every matter was considered, as indicated by the Minutes, full confidence in the Board's ability and integrity would be established.[202]

First things first, after all. The minutes are complete! So, if anyone fails to find something objectionable in the records which the Board provides, this has to be because nothing is remiss.

And what was second in importance? Need anyone ask? The Treasurer's report.[203]

But what of the many theological objections? They were groundless, the Board announced. The General Assembly concurred. The acceptable proof was not judicial theology; rather, it was perceived character. "We know that Dr. Robert E. Speer stands absolutely true to the historic doctrinal position of the Presbyterian Church, and we would be remiss if we did not testify to our recognition that his entire life bears testimony to the supreme effort to extend the gospel to humanity across the world."[204] The battle was reduced to a question of representation, as major covenantal battles always must be. Men must choose sides; each side has a leader. In the battle between orthodoxy and modernism in Northern Presbyterianism, it boiled down to this choice: Machen or Speer. The respective leader's cloak would cover the actions of his subordinates. It was clear by 1933 whose cloak was the broadest. "The Assembly also expresses its thorough confidence in the members of the Board of Foreign Missions. . . ."[205]

Privately, Machen summarized his problem in getting the Board to take a stand. Van Til related to his biographer this recollection of Machen's account: "I write to the Board asking what it proposes to do about Pearl Buck. The Board writes back and says, 'Dr. Speer is a

---

202. *Minutes of the General Assembly, 1933*, p. 154.
203. *Ibid.*
204. *Ibid.*, p. 159.
205. *Ibid.*

very fine man.' I answer, 'I realize Dr. Speer is a very fine man but what I would like to know is what you plan to do about Pearl Buck's public pronouncements.' The Board writes me again and says, 'Machen, why are you so bitter?'"[206]

A Softening of Orthodox Resistance

In the mid-June edition of *Christianity Today* an editorial appeared which gave an indication of the battle to come within the orthodox camp itself. At the May General Assembly, the conservatives had announced the creation of an independent missions board. This might lead to negative Church sanctions. Samuel Craig, editor of the magazine, and also a member of the Board of Control at Westminster, began to move toward the fire escape: the Confession. "But, be the present majority [in the General Assembly] an actual majority or not, as long as the standards of the church remain as they are there is no reason why the present minority should not remain in the Church and continue its struggle in behalf of the grace of God. . . . The situation would be quite different if the standards of the Church were altered so as to be made to conform to the policies of the modernist-indifferentist party. In that case this minority would be bound to separate themselves from the organization known as the Presbyterian Church of the U.S.A. . . ." The implication here, of course, was that the Westminster Confession still had meaning within the Church, although in terms of application to specific judicial cases it was a dead letter.

The Problem of Creedalism

This returns us to the persistent problem of the function of creeds. The conservatives who chose to remain in the Church until they died continually reaffirmed that the reason why they could stay in the Church in good conscience is because it was still a creedal Church. But the Church of England also has a creed—the same creed it has had since the sixteenth century. Yet virtually no one would have been so naive in 1933 as to argue that either the Church of

---

206. Cited in William White, Jr., *Van Til: Defender of the Faith* (Nashville, Tennessee: Thomas Nelson, 1979), p. 106.

England or the Protestant Episcopal Church was in any way bound by that creed, or that even a strong minority of its clergy still held to it.

The Northern Presbyterian Church did not get around to altering its Confession until 1967. The Barthians, liberals, and followers of either of the Niebuhrs had long been content to play the same "mental reservations" game that had outraged Machen in 1923.[207] The old slogan applied well to Presbyterians after the 1930's: "Presbyterians can believe anything at all, and generally do." Eventually, they rewrote the Westminster Confession, but that was three decades after Machen's little band had been removed from the Church. Yet Craig and many others justified their continued subordination to the Church—and thereby appeared to justify the same decision by hundreds of thousands of Bible-believing laymen—on the basis of its commitment to the Confession.

Could Machen argue against them effectively? If it was wrong for the liberals to lie about their attachment to the Westminster Confession, why was it wrong for the conservatives who no longer believed in tenets such as predestination to make similar mental reservations? Was the Church a Confessional Church as far back as 1923? Machen had said *yes*, even though he probably knew that the Westminster Confession was unenforceable in the Church's courts—that there was no way that liberals could be convicted in a heresy trial. By 1924 there was no doubt, with the ordination of Henry P. Van Dusen by the New York Presbytery. Yet in 1923, Machen had written: "If the liberal party, therefore, really obtains control of the Church, evangelical Christians must be prepared to withdraw no matter what it costs. Our Lord has died for us, and surely we must not deny Him for the favor of men. But up to the present time such a situation has not yet appeared; the creedal basis still stands firm in the constitutions of evangelical churches."[208]

The creedal basis of the Presbyterian Church was not only *not* standing firm after 1924, it was unenforceable in the Church's courts.

---

207. Machen, *Christianity and Liberalism* (New York: Macmillan, 1923), pp. 162–65.
208. *Ibid.*, p. 166.

That was the significant test, at least for anyone who held the traditional view of Presbyterianism, namely, that the Church's hierarchy is essentially an appeals court system. But Machen had failed to lead God's people out of Egypt in the 1920's. By delaying his exodus, he was thereby affirming a view of creedalism which was not significantly different from Craig's and other of the "remainers" of 1936. The question of when the Church *really* departed from its creeds became a matter of personal conviction, and a lot of those men—indeed, the majority—who refused to come out in 1936 died as members in good standing in the Church. They just never seemed to get conviction. The "firm creedal foundation" that Machen praised in 1923 somehow looked just as firm to them in, say, 1950.

The Church Supports Missions

At the 1933 General Assembly, two reports came from the Standing Committee on Foreign Missions. The majority report asserted that the Board of Foreign Missions deserved "the wholehearted, unequivocal, and affectionate commendation of the church at large." The minority view stated that the criticisms that Machen had leveled at the Board were grounded in fact, and it recommended that the Assembly go on record as supporting the traditional gospel of Christ by electing a list of conservative candidates to the Board. The minority report was not permitted to circulate in written form; the majority position was. The majority report was also included in the memorial roll of those ministers who had died on the mission field during the year, so that a vote against the majority report was a vote against the memorial as well. While it had been customary to include the roll in the Committee's report, conservatives were incensed that the tradition had not been set aside to make way for a minority report. The full effect of the tactic is impossible to measure. The majority view undoubtedly had the votes to assume adoption by the Assembly, but conservatives felt that they had been insulted and thwarted.[209]

---

209. Reported in *Christianity Today* (April 1933), p. 22.

The Independent Board

Following approval of the report and before the Assembly adjourned, Rev. H. McAllister Griffiths announced the formation of a new missionary board, the Independent Board for Presbyterian Foreign Missions. It was not to interfere with missionaries already in the field, but it was to provide an outlet for those orthodox members of the Church who felt that their gifts to the regular Board were being misused. The first meeting of a tentative Independent Board was held on June 27, 1933, in Philadelphia. Officially organized on October 17, Machen was elected as its president.

That fall, Machen issued a protest against recent actions of the New Brunswick Presbytery in inserting into its rules for ordination a totally new requirement. All candidates for the ministry and all ministers already ordained who were transferring into the New Brunswick Presbytery had to be examined "as to their willingness to support the regularly authorized Boards and Agencies of the Presbyterian Church, U.S.A., particularly the Board of Foreign Missions." Machen opposed this on constitutional grounds, for such a requirement had neither been sanctioned by the General Assembly nor approved by a majority of the presbyteries, according to the rules of the Church. He also argued that men cannot be bound to statements concerning their future actions unless the constitution specifies these actions. Finally, he argued that the new requirement would transform a freewill offering into a tax, something clearly outside the bounds of the Church's authority to demand. In support of this assertion, Machen quoted from the report (approved) of the Joint Committee on Foreign Missions of 1870: "Especially free and responsible directly to Christ are all Christian people, in deciding through what agencies they will do their share of the work for missions." The Church, accordingly, could not demand funds from its membership, but would have to rely upon voluntary contributions of the laity, made in accordance with their own consciences. The decision as to where specific monies are to be allocated is in the hands of the laymen of the Church, not in the hands of the Church hierarchy.[210]

---

210. Machen, "Freedom in the Presbyterian Church," *Christianity Today* (Oct.

On October 24, 1933, Christian Reformed Church pastor R. B. Kuiper was installed as Professor of Practical Theology at Westminster Seminary. In his short inaugural speech, the text of which appeared in *Christianity Today* (Nov. 1933), Kuiper stated the principle which was to guide for the next three years those orthodox churchmen who allied themselves with Machen and his cause, that of Christian freedom: ". . . Christ's will as expressed in His Word is law for the Church, and His will alone. No man or group of men, no church council, has the right to subtract from the law of Christ or add to it. Rules and regulations made by the Church itself and not based directly upon the law of Christ may or may not be conducive to good order, but never may they bind the conscience. This is the great principle of Christian Liberty. . . ." That Machen had to go outside the denomination to recruit such a spokesman did not bode well for his cause.

The Appeal to Conscience

This challenge to the authority of the Church councils was to have an increasingly important role as the inclusivists cemented their control of the administrative machinery. In essence, the orthodox minority appealed to the Church's constitution, and ultimately to Christ's will. It is to Christ that the individual conscience is responsible, the Christ revealed in the pages of the New Testament by the Holy Spirit. Machen spoke for the minority a year later when he wrote a defense against formal charges brought against him by the presbytery: "I cannot, no matter what any human authority bids me to do, support a propaganda that is contrary to the gospel of Christ; I cannot substitute a human authority for the authority of the Word of God. . . ."[211] In short, the position of the orthodox wing could now be described in these terms: "'The Supreme Judge,' says the Confession of Faith, 'by whom all controversies of religion are to be determined, and all decrees of councils, opinions of ancient writers, doctrines of men, and private spirits are to be examined, and in whose

---

1933), p. 5.

211. Machen, *Statement to the Special Committee of the Presbytery of New Brunswick in the Presbyterian Church in the U.S.A. Which Was Appointed by the Presbytery at its Meeting on Tuesday, September 25, 1934...* (Author, 1935), p. 14.

sentence we are to rest, can be no other than the Holy Spirit speaking in Scripture' (Conf. I,x)."

These words, however, were not from Machen's pen, nor from the councils of the Philadelphia Presbytery, but from section I of the Auburn *Affirmation*. The *Affirmation* had been directed at the ecclesiastical determination of doctrine, while Machen and Kuiper were attacking administrative decisions that were out of accord with the traditional Presbyterian view of Scripture and Church law, or at least Old School traditions. The appeal in both cases was to Christian liberty. Even the wording was similar. Consider, for example, part IV of the *Affirmation*: "We do not desire liberty to go beyond the teachings of evangelical Christianity. But we maintain that it is our constitutional right and our Christian duty within these limits to exercise liberty of thought and teaching that we may more effectively preach the Gospel of Jesus Christ, the Savior of the World." Liberty of thought, constitutional right, Christian duty: these were the essentials of the Machen's position in 1933. Clearly, the positions of the two ideological factions were in the process of reversing themselves, each appropriating the other's arguments of a decade earlier—and a century earlier. It was the Old School that had booted out the New School in 1837 for its support of ecclesiastically independent foreign missions boards.

Machen insisted that the General Assembly did not possess the authority to hand down administrative fiats in advance. This had always been the liberals' position. The General Assembly is a lawful court, but each case had to be decided on its own merits.[212] The General Assembly may make general pronouncements, of course, "But these pronouncements have purely moral or persuasive force. Legally they have no more force than pronouncements of the humblest member of the Church."[213] What, then, of the Doctrinal Deliverances of 1910, 1916, and 1923? Machen still battled the theology of the *Affirmation*, but he now adopted its judicial foundation. The General Assembly in 1927 had expressly adopted the judicial view of the *Affirmation*—presbytery autonomy in ordination—but the judicial agents

---

212. *Ibid.*, p. 34.
213. *Ibid.*, p. 33.

of the General Assembly had now returned to the legislative theory of Deliverances, and then some. The General Assembly, if it supported these representatives, would threaten sanctions against everyone who disobeyed, ministers and members alike.

A Question of Authority

Machen announced in his 1934 *Statement*, "I CANNOT OBEY THE ORDER."[214] He appealed to the Constitution of the Church. "THOUGH DISOBEYING AN ORDER OF THE GENERAL ASSEMBLY, I HAVE A FULL RIGHT TO REMAIN IN THE PRESBYTERIAN CHURCH IN THE U.S.A. BECAUSE I AM IN ACCORD WITH THE CONSTITUTION OF THAT CHURCH AND CAN APPEAL FROM THE GENERAL ASSEMBLY TO THE CONSTITUTION."[215]

He could indeed appeal to the Church's Constitution, but all constitutions are interpreted by designated interpreters. His appeal was ultimately to a future General Assembly, for the General Assembly, acting in its capacity as the highest court, would authoritatively interpret the Constitution. Machen's days as a minister in the denomination were numbered.

Rev. John McDowell, the Moderator of the 1933 General Assembly, stood on the floor of a meeting of the conservative Chester Presbytery on September 26, 1933, and proclaimed that if a citizen of this country were to take an attitude against the Constitution of the United States, he would be expelled; similarly, if a minister in the Presbyterian Church could not support the constitution of the Church, he should get out.[216] This was the argument of the Portland Deliverance of 1892. Conservatives in 1933 saw themselves as the true constitutionalists, for they formally supported its written form: the Westminster Confession of Faith and the two catechisms. Each side claimed that the other was subverting the constitution. Nevertheless, McDowell's language was strikingly similar to that used by the Machen in 1923. If a man cannot agree with the Church, then he

---

214. *Ibid.*, p. 14.
215. *Ibid.*, p. 15.
216. Reprinted in *Christianity Today* (Oct. 1933), p. 16.

should voluntarily remove himself from the Church: such was the basis of both arguments. Because the theological orientation of the Church had changed, the positions of the two factions were reversed. Yet the arguments remained intact, and the written constitution was no different, but not for long. The Form of Discipline had been totally revised in 1931. In 1933 and 1934, the presbyteries voted to accept it. That final centralization of power would bring the Presbyterian conflict to a close.

Machen immediately wrote a formal protest. He surveyed the post-1869 history of Presbyterian foreign missions that showed that the General Assembly had always denied that assessments for foreign missions were mandatory.[217] He was correct; after 1936, his analysis was also correct. From 1933 to 1936, however, the hierarchy pretended that he was not correct and imposed an oath-bound commitment to the support of Presbyterian foreign missions as a convenient means of expelling its critics.

Machen observed in 1934 that the General Assembly had made a profession of obedience to the boards of the Church a condition of ordination. Support for the boards is voluntary, the directive said; nevertheless, local churches must not support unapproved agencies—the position of Old School Presbyterians in 1837. Machen ridiculed this argument: the General Assembly says the Church is voluntary, but if you do not obey, you must leave.

> "You may enter the Presbyterian Church in the U.S.A. or not as you please," says the General Assembly in effect; "but if you do you must leave your liberty behind. If you once enter you are our slaves. Henceforth support of whatever missionary program successive General Assemblies may set up is obligatory upon you, whether you think the program is right or wrong. If you think that the missionary program of any General Assembly is so wrong that you cannot conscientiously support it, then the only thing for you to do is to leave the Church."[218]

---

217. Machen, "Freedom in the Presbyterian Church," *Christianity Today* (Oct. 1933), pp. 5, 8.
218. Machen, *Statement to the Special Committee*, p. 24.

Yet this is exactly what Machen and his predecessors had been arguing since the Portland Deliverance of 1892, and before them, in 1838: conform or leave. "The essence of all religious liberty and ecclesiastical order," the 1838 *Pastoral Letter* declared, "is evidently involved in the principle, that when two parties in the same community cannot agree, the majority must govern; but if the minority cannot in conscience submit either to the measures, or the doctrines of the majority, it is their right and duty to separate, and form a different denomination."[219] But the shoe was now on the other foot. Machen invoked the same argument that liberals had been invoking since the 1893 General Assembly: "It is both the right and the duty of an individual in the Church to 'censure' and to disobey any actions of the General Assembly or of any other judicatory that are contrary to the Constitution of the Church."[220] The problem, however, is that majorities declare what the constitution is and says, in 1838 as well as in 1936.

Old School vs. Old School

Machen in 1935 wrote: "I disobeyed this purely arbitrary administrative order of the General Assembly on the ground that it was contrary to the Constitution of the Church, and that therefore my ordination pledge not only permitted but required me to disobey it. The only way to test the constitutionality of an action of the General Assembly is in the courts of the Church—beginning with the lowest court, the Presbytery."[221] Machen labeled the actions of the General Assembly in 1934 as the exercise of illegitimate authority. Yet a very similar exercise of authority was what the Old School had imposed through the General Assembly in 1837. The *Circular Letter* had announced:

> The General Assembly is vested by the constitution of our church with plenary power "to decide in all controversies respecting doctrine and discipline; to reprove, warn, or bear testi-

---

219. *Minutes of the General Assembly, 1838*, p. 48.
220. Machen, *Statement to the Special Committee*, p. 38.
221. *Christianity Today* (May 1935), p. 294.

mony against error in doctrine or immorality in practice, in any church, Presbytery, or Synod; to superintend the concerns of the whole church; to suppress schismatical contentions and disputations; and, in general, to recommend and attempt reformation of manners, and the promotion of charity, truth, and holiness, through all the churches under their care."[222]

What was the institutional issue that had called forth this 1837 assertion of authority? The General Assembly's obligation to defend the Church's boards. "To suffer Boards constituted by ourselves, pledged to adhere to our own standards, and responsible to our own judicatories, to languish while we sustain and strengthen societies over which we have no control, and which are gradually undermining at once our purity, and, of course, our real strength, while professing to add to our numbers, would manifestly be as unwise as it would be criminal in those who profess to love the Presbyterian Church, and to consider her as conformed, in her doctrine and order, to the apostolic model."[223]

There would be a difference, however. In 1837, the General Assembly threw out all of their opponents without a trial. They cleansed the denomination of a few representative theological troublemakers by removing tens of thousands of members: the people the troublemakers represented. They eliminated the shepherds they regarded as unreliable by sending them away, along with their sheep. In 1935 and 1936, there would be trials, almost all with foregone conclusions. At the conclusion of those trials, those shepherds declared guilty voluntarily departed and invited their sheep to accompany them. There were very few sheep who decided to follow. The excluded sheep and shepherds of 1837 had become the dominant force after the reunion of 1869. The victorious shepherds of 1837 became comparatively meek sheep after the reunion. The 1869 peace treaty between the two flocks delivered the ranch into the hands of the wolves in 1936. The spiritual heirs of both flocks were then consumed at the wolves' leisure.

---

222. *Minutes of the General Assembly, 1837*, p. 506.
223. *Ibid.*, p. 507.

A Question of Sanctions

Attacks on the Independent Board grew in intensity. Charges of unconstitutional behavior were leveled at the organizers and supporters of the body by the Church bureaucracy. In late 1933, Murray Forst Thompson, a member of both the Independent Board and the Pennsylvania Bar, published an answer to the critics within the Church. In a four-part argument, he put forth the following theses: (1) there is nothing in Church law forbidding the establishment of such a Board; (2) Church judicatories have no power to pass laws "binding the conscience" and penalizing supporters of the body; (3) nothing requires that a man support financially any Church body; (4) money can legally be given to organizations outside the Church. Since the Independent Board was outside the Church, and therefore not within its jurisdiction in the courts, Thompson concluded that nothing could be done to silence it. Then he, too, appealed to the doctrine of Christian Liberty: "The Confession of Faith declares that 'God alone is Lord of the conscience and hath left it free from the doctrines and commandments of men which are in anything contrary to His Work, or beside it, in matters of faith and worship' (XX:2). If the Constitution contained such restrictions, it would be contrary to the principles of Christian liberty and freedom of conscience set forth in the Holy Scriptures."[224]

There were two major flaws in his argument. First, unlike the Board itself, those inside the Church who were associated with the Independent Board could be silenced within the Church. Second, the Church may not have had the authority to bind the conscience, but it surely had the power to censure those who resisted its power. And so it did. The most independent agency of all, Union Seminary, gained its revenge.[225]

---

224. Murray Forst Thompson, "Have the Organizers of the Independent Board for Foreign Presbyterian Missions Violated the Law of the Presbyterian Church in the U.S.A.?" *Christianity Today* (Dec. 1933), p. 10.

225. In our day, the deteriorating, high-crime neighborhood in which Union is still located has gained its revenge. As Forrest Gump might say, "Liberalism is as liberalism does."

The magnitude of the Church's negative response does not seem to match the threat. The Independent Board had put only eleven missionaries in the field by 1936.[226] To say, as Roark does, that the Independent Board constituted an economic threat to the Board of Foreign Missions during a time of economic depression misses the point.[227] Something far more important than the statistical reality of the competition in 1936 for missionary candidates and missionary funds was at stake. What was at stake was a theological principle: *the flow of funds*. There was no more sacred principle for the liberals, as the final stage of the Presbyterian conflict revealed. And, in Machen's opinion, there was no clearer evidence of ecclesiastical tyranny than the judicial enforcement of this principle.

Conclusion

In the years following the reorganization of Princeton Seminary, the character of the Presbyterian Church, U.S.A., had continued on its path toward inclusivism. Doctrinal clarity became less and less an issue for Church leaders, leaving administrative authority rather than theological agreement the real basis of Church unity. Any challenge to this authority was seen by officialdom as dangerous to the Church.

The appeal to the Scriptures remained the fundamental plea of the orthodox camp, but it now included an appeal to the strict construction of the General Assembly's authority. The liberals had previously been the advocates of this same strict constructionism. Now, however, the liberal wing, along with those conservatives who favored a broader Church, were in control of the judicial machinery of the Church. They were no longer disposed to conform with the letter of the law and constitutional limitations. Denominational unity became an end in itself, far more important than strict adherence to Presbyterian law or tradition. Unity was point five of modernist covenant theology: ecumenism.

---

226. D. G. Hart, *Defending the Faith: J. Gresham Machen and the Crisis of Conservative Protestantism in Modern America* (Baltimore, Maryland: Johns Hopkins University Press, 1994), p. 157.

227. Dallas Roark, J. Gresham Machen and His Desire to Maintain a Doctrinally True Presbyterian Church (Ph.D. dissertation, Iowa State University, 1963), p. 218.

When orthodox Presbyterians began to disturb the external facade of Church unity, they placed themselves in a precarious position. The Church as a whole was tired of controversy, and sought peace and unity at all costs. The orthodox were also numerically weaker as a faction than their opponents had been in 1923, since the inclusivist conservatives were not acting as a buffer for the orthodox wing as they had done for the liberals. There was no sympathetic sentiment to shield them from the new majority. The extent of their weakness became unmistakably clear in 1934. They lost the vote for Moderator by 818 to 87. It had been 691 to 120 the year before.

Throughout 1934 and 1935, the Board of Foreign Missions kept issuing pamphlets defending its position against critics.[228] The Missions bureaucracy was feeling the heat of negative publicity. Negative publicity had been for two decades the only negative sanctions available to the conservatives, with the one exception of the resignation of Fosdick, a Baptist. But the Church's courts now began to apply negative sanctions against the critics. In 1936, the verbal critics would depart. There would not be many of them.

As for Rockefeller, there was one positive effect of *Re-Thinking Missions*. After 1932, he never again gave money to any denomination.[229] That went far to sever the Rockefeller connection from the churches. It is also worth noting that by 1975, missionaries sent out by denominations in the National Council of Churches supplied fewer than eight percent of American Protestant foreign missions.[230] In 1980, evangelical missions boards supplied 90 percent of the 35,000 career foreign missionaries sent from North America.[231] The criticisms made by Griffith Thomas in 1921 and Machen in 1933 were no longer relevant. Foreign missions (conservative), which require money, personal dedication, and a lifetime of hard work, had replaced foreign mission (liberal). Missions had indeed been re-thought by the liberals, and they decided to stay home. The positive sanctions of liberalism's mission were insufficient to motivate modernists to go onto the mis-

---

228. Patterson, Speer, p. 161.
229. Schenkel, *Rich Man and Kingdom*, p. 174.
230. Patterson, Speer, p. 194.
231. Carpenter, "Introduction," *Modernism and Foreign Missions*, p. [14].

sion field. Meanwhile, the positive sanctions of gospel missions were sufficient to motivate evangelicals to go. The crucial issue is sanctions.

Phase 5: Whose Inheritance?

12

INHERITANCE AND DISINHERITANCE

God alone is Lord of the conscience, and hath left it free from the doctrines and commandments of men, which are, in any thing, contrary to His Word; or beside it, in matters of faith or worship. So that, to believe such doctrines, or to obey such commands, out of conscience, is to betray true liberty of conscience: and the requiring of an implicit faith, and an absolute and blind obedience, is to destroy liberty of conscience, and reason also.

Westminster Confession of Faith (1647), XX:2

This section of the Confession had served New School Arminians in the 1830's and modernists after 1910 as the touchstone of liberty in the Church. The modernists had asserted in the Auburn *Affirmation* that the General Assembly had no authority to bind ordained men's consciences by deliverances. The General Assembly could at most serve as a final court of appeal, not a legislative body, in the area of Church law. Power lodged in the presbyteries. This had been affirmed by the 1927 General Assembly—the "Speer Assembly"—with the liberals completely in control.[1] The conservatives had maintained the opposite in their rejection of the Auburn *Affirmation*. "The whole history of the Church, as recorded in the Digest, shows that the Assembly alone is the final interpreter of the law," proclaimed the

---

1. *Minutes of the General Assembly, 1927*, p. 62.

editor of *The Presbyterian* in 1924.[2] This was true, but only with respect to specific lower court cases that had been appealed to it. Now the ecclesiastical positions would reverse.

The issue, as always, was sanctions. *The Presbyterian* had enunciated this most clearly in 1922, during the Fosdick case. "No nation, no constitutional church, or other body can afford to allow its constitution to be violated. Such violation is deadly. If it is not resisted, the constitutional body must collapse."[3] The words of the Constitution—the Westminster Confession—had not changed, but its interpretation after 1927 was open to any man holding any theological view, so long as his presbytery would ordain him. Negative sanctions would no longer be imposed by the General Assembly in terms of the Confession, but rather in terms of the flow of funds. The politics of Progressivism had at last gained control over the Presbyterian Church. The guiding principle of the politics of Progressivism is easy to state: *compulsory progressive change funded by other people's money.*

The Church's hierarchy argued in September, 1933, that the General Assembly had the authority to enforce ecclesiastical rules. They denied that there had been a shift with respect to matters of theology and belief. But, they insisted, toleration regarding theology is not the same thing as toleration of disobedience with respect to Church bureaucracies, namely, the requirement that congregations support the official boards of the Church. On this matter, there must be obedience.

The conservatives argued that the underlying issue was theological, since their opposition to the boards, especially Foreign Missions, was based on theological modernism within the boards and tolerance of modernism by the boards. This argument was dismissed by the

---

2. D. S. Kennedy, "An Affirmation of One Hundred and Fifty Liberal Ministers," *The Presbyterian* (Jan. 17, 1924), p. 9; cited in Ki-Hong Kim, Presbyterian Conflict in the Early Twentieth Century: Ecclesiology in the Princeton Tradition and the Emergence of Presbyterian Fundamentalism (Ph.D. dissertation, Drew University, 1983), p. 158.

3. "The Presbyterian Church a Constitutional Body," *The Presbyterian* (Nov. 9, 1922), p. 6; cited in Kim, *ibid.*, p. 151. A month later, he warned that schism might become necessary if the "vice and error" were not removed. "Honorable and Necessary Schisms" (Dec. 7, 1922), p. 4. Cited in *ibid.*, p. 152.

Church and its agencies. The Church in effect adopted a rule: "Ecclesiastical sanctions against ecclesiastical infractions." This meant that the General Assembly's executive agents were *announcing in advance* that those convicted by their presbyteries of membership in the Independent Board would automatically be convicted by the General Assembly. The General Assembly had thereby reverted to a functional legislative body. It had adopted the Old Princeton's ecclesiology[4] in order to stamp out Old Princeton's theology. A series of "non-heresy" trials began in 1935 because the 1934 General Assembly's General Council demanded that they begin.

Sanctions and the Transfer of Authority

There are two kinds of sanctions: positive and negative. The Church's positive judicial sanctions are applied in three ways: by the *sacraments*, which are the covenantal signs and seals of Church membership; by *ordination*, at which time judicial authority is simultaneously passed down from God and up through the Church's members; and by *laymen voting* in a local congregation. God and the members are jointly represented by the ordaining officers.[5] The Church's negative judicial sanctions are applied in three ways: exclusion from the communion table (excommunication); removal from the ministry or ruling eldership (suspension); removal from ruling eldership or getting fired by the congregation. The right hand of fellowship is removed in the first case; the authority imparted by ordination is removed in the second case; local representation or employment is removed in the third case.

Excommunication is under the authority of the local congregation's session; suspension is under the authority of the presbytery. The question for the Presbyterian Church, U.S.A., in the post-1900 phases of the Presbyterian conflict was this: Did the authority to impose these two sanctions reside *solely* in these two local authorities? Was this authority exclusive? Or was there an appeals system that could reverse the decision of a lower jurisdiction? Specifically, was

---

4. *Ibid.*, pp. 198–205.

5. On the two-way nature of ordination—upward and downward—including civil ordination, see Gary North, *Leviticus: An Economic Commentary* (Tyler, Texas: Institute for Christian Economics, 1994), ch. 4.

there double jeopardy protection? Could a person cleared by a lower court be subsequently convicted by a higher court? A preliminary answer came at the 1927 General Assembly in the midst of the controversy over Princeton Seminary. The locus of the authority to ordain ministers was declared to be lodged exclusively in the local presbytery. There could be no further appeal to a higher court.[6]

Meanwhile, control over Princeton Seminary was centralized. The General Assembly restructured it in 1929. So, there was a two-fold movement: authority downward to the presbyteries in matters of ordination; authority upward to the General Assembly in terms of control over Princeton's Board. The Old School would no longer be allowed to control the content of instruction in the last remaining Old School Seminary. It ceased to be an Old School seminary. At the same time, no one could rely on a synod or the General Assembly to remove men from office whose confessions were heretical. From 1927 onward, the modernists had gained their announced long-term goal: *no further negative sanctions.* In 1928–29, they took their first public action—the reorganization of Princeton—in terms of their unannounced long-term goal: *negative sanctions against Confessionalists.*

So much for *formal* sanctions. The fact is, they constitute only the maximum judicial limits of Church sanctions. The reality, as is true in any complex organization, is very different in operation. Not many people are ever excommunicated. Not many Church officers are ever removed from office. The effects of these formal sanctions are achieved representatively: as warnings to others of like mind and like will. But this assumes continuity through a system of judicial precedents. *If there are no binding judicial precedents, then the imposition of formal sanctions ceases to be representative.* The structure of authority in the organization will disintegrate if a determined opposition group knows that the authorities either cannot or will not systematically impose predictable sanctions, and knowing this, systematically defies authority. If the organization also funds its opponents, then the replacement of the existing leadership is assured.

So, the *operating* sanctions are not primarily formal. This constitutes a challenge for all those within the organization, as well as for

---

6. See Chapter 10, above: section on "The 1927 General Assembly," pp. 610–14.

historians seeking in retrospect to make sense of its actual operations. While the organization is supposed to do things "by the book"—point three: stipulations—many things are done without official reference to the book. It is here—beyond the book—that the history of any organization normally takes place. Publicly enforcing the book is a rare event except in times of turmoil and transition. The issue is sanctions.

There is a pattern to institutional change. First, if formal negative sanctions cannot be imposed at all, or if they must be imposed continually (not merely representatively) to maintain order, the organization is ripe for a takeover. Second, if sanctions are continually threatened but never imposed, the organization is in the final stages of a takeover. Third, the transition is publicly announced when there are neither threats nor systematic formal sanctions. Fourth, the takeover takes place when formal sanctions are imposed in terms of a different set of stipulations, either explicit or implicit. Fifth, the takeover is complete when no further formal sanctions must be imposed in order to gain compliance. This completes the transfer of the inheritance.

In the case of the Presbyterian conflict after 1900, we can date these five stages: (1) new stipulations, silence on negative sanctions (1903-1909); (2) threatened formal negative sanctions, but no imposition (1910-1925); (3) cessation of both threats and negative sanctions (1926-1933); (4) new *operational* stipulations, renewed negative sanctions (1934-36); (5) no further formal negative sanctions required (1936 to the present).

The Transformation of Presbyterian Law

In 1934, the revision of the Book of Discipline became law. A new phrase was introduced into Presbyterian law: administrative discipline.[7] The move to administrative law—what Harold Berman has identified as the seventh and most revolutionary legal revolution in Western history[8]—was now complete in the Northern Presbyterian

---

7. The text reads: "3. Administrative Discipline. . . . 4. Purpose of Administrative Discipline." *Book of Discipline*, I:2, 3. *Minutes of the General Assembly, 1934*, p. 145.

8. Harold J. Berman, *Law and Revolution: The Formation of the Western Legal Tradition* (Cambridge, Massachusetts: Harvard University Press, 1983), pp. 33-41.

Church. One further step remained: a public exhibition of this new authority.

Meanwhile, something had been removed: any reference to doctrine or the judicial standards of the Church. Under Chapter I, Section 6, "Purpose of Discipline," we read: "The purpose of discipline is to vindicate the authority and honor of Jesus Christ by the maintenance of the truth, the removal of scandal, the censure for offenses, the spiritual good of offenders, and the promotion of the purity and edification of the Church."[9] But as Pontius Pilate put it, "What is truth?" More to the point, where do we find it?

Part 7, "Subjects of Discipline," announced: "All baptized persons, being covenant members of the Church and under its care, are subject to administrative discipline, and entitled to the benefits thereof." This was a major innovation in Presbyterian law: *non-ordained members previously had been under the initiatory discipline only of the local congregation*. They were not members of the presbytery or higher courts, which were accessible only by oath (subscription to the Confession) and ordination. They could contest a local church court's judgment against them in the Church's higher courts, but the idea of administrative discipline on non-ordained members—discipline initiated on them from above the local congregation—had been utterly foreign to Presbyterianism. Since non-ordained members had taken no oath to uphold the Confession, they had not previously been under the initiatory authority of higher courts: presbyteries, synods, and the General Assembly. These courts could lawfully enforce the stipulations of the oath only on those who had taken the oath. All this changed judicially in 1934.

This is additional evidence of an unannounced but radical shift away from the Confession. *A formal oath-bound affirmation of the Confession was no longer a distinguishing mark of the structure of Northern Presbyterian law*. All members were now placed under the same system of administrative discipline, Confessional oath or not. The implicit content of the oath had therefore shifted: from adherence to the terms of the Confession to obedience to higher Church judicatories

---

9. *Minutes of the General Assembly, 1934*, p. 145.

irrespective of the Confession. Explicitly, the Confession was still invoked as one aspect of the Church's Constitution, along with the two catechisms, The Form of Government, The Book of Discipline, and The Directory for Worship.[10] In fact, *to get at the laymen administratively, the General Assembly implicitly had to abandon the Confession as the judicial basis of its administrative decisions.* It substituted maintenance of "the truth" as the binding administrative standard. Every Church member was henceforth obligated to obey the General Assembly's determination of the truth, irrespective of the Confession. *The Westminster Confession would never again be invoked as the basis of administrative discipline. It would no longer operationally provide the stipulations of the oath.* This confirmed what had been true for decades. The Confession had been a dead letter judicially since at least 1901, and functionally since Swing departed in 1874.

The General Council was explicit regarding the new order: every member has "an obligation to the faithful observance of those terms of communion and fellowship which cannot be set aside by any plea whatsoever."[11] Terms? What terms? By what oath of allegiance? "All church members and church officers can be held and must be held to the agreements which they have made."[12] Agreements? What agreements? By what oath of allegiance?

The document specified that Church officers had taken such an oath,[13] but it remained silent regarding members. All it said was that members had to obey.

The Steamroller Starts Rolling

On May 3, 1934, an informal meeting was held by certain members of the Independent Board for Presbyterian Foreign Missions and representatives of the Administrative Committee of the General Council of the Church, at the latter's request. Machen and the other Independent Board members were handed a typewritten statement which informed them that the General Council "was of the unani-

---

10. *Ibid.*, p. 73.
11. *Ibid.*
12. *Ibid.*, p. 74.
13. *Ibid.*

mous opinion that the Independent Board for Foreign Presbyterian Missions, in its organization and operation, is contrary to the fundamental principles of the Constitution of the Church." In September of 1933, before the presbyteries had ratified the new Form of Government, the Stated Clerk had notified the presbyteries of the General Council's new policy regarding the Independent Board.[14]

The organizers of the Board, in the opinion of the General Council, were "violating" their "ordination or membership vows, or both."[15] The Council, Machen was informed, was about to circulate this report and a printed argument supporting it to all commissioners of the forthcoming General Assembly, to take place in three weeks. When the members of the Council were asked if the Independent Board could have a copy of the brief against it in advance, they replied that this would be inconvenient, since it was already at the printers.[16] Thus, there was no opportunity for Machen and the other Board members to rebut the arguments against them until the General Assembly met. The scent of kangaroo court was in the air. This scent would soon get much stronger.

The targeted victims challenged the right of the General Council to engage in the publication of a document condemning the Independent Board members before they had the opportunity to plead their cases, individually, in the Church court system.[17] Their pleas went unheard, and the Council published its booklet, *Studies in the Constitution of the Presbyterian Church in the U.S.A.* During the General Assembly meeting, the Council distributed its specific recommendations for action on the Independent Board and its supporters just before lunch on the day the question was to be debated. There were

---

14. D. G. Hart, *Defending the Faith: J. Gresham Machen and the Crisis of Conservative Protestantism in Modern America* (Baltimore, Maryland: Johns Hopkins University Press, 1994), p. 152.

15. Machen, *Statement to the Special Committee of the Presbytery of New Brunswick in the Presbyterian Church of the U.S.A. Which was Appointed by the Presbytery at Its Meeting on Tuesday, September 25, 1934. . .* (Author, December 12, 1934), p. 6

16. *Ibid.*, p. 7.

17. Edwin H. Rian, *The Presbyterian Conflict* (Grand Rapids, Michigan: Eerdmans, 1940), pp. 151–52.

only a few hours available for Board members to prepare an adequate defense. Their rebuttal presented primarily the same arguments that Thompson had offered in his article on the Independent Board in 1933.[18] The chief one was that the Board was wholly outside the Church's structure, and therefore not subject to its jurisdiction. This soon proved to be irrelevant, since members of the Independent Board were inside the Church's structure and subject to its jurisdiction. That jurisdiction was now comprehensive.

The great purge could now begin.

The Great Purge

Studies in the Constitution filled pages 71 to 116 of the *Minutes*. It began by establishing the General Council's authority to deal with the issue at hand. In an "Introductory Note," it cited Chapter XXII, Section II of the new Form of Government, which authorized the General Council "to consider between annual meetings of the General Assembly cases of serious embarrassment or emergency concerning the benevolent and missionary work of the Church, and to provide direct methods of relief."[19] Then it identified the embarrassment-emergency: ". . . certain ministers and laymen of the Presbyterian Church in organizing within the denomination an 'Independent Board for Presbyterian Foreign Missions.'" That the document identified laymen as participants in the Board was judicially significant, not because the General Council necessarily contemplated action against them, but because the new Form of Government had revoked laymen's judicial immunity from prosecution by a presbytery. Laymen were now under the terms of a new implicit oath: obedience to the directives of the General Assembly.

What had been illegal under Presbyterian law for three centuries had now been authorized: *an administrative legal order that was initiated by the General Assembly.* Under the old system of courts, the General Assembly possessed no formal authority to serve as a legislative agency in the area of theology. The 1930 edition of *The Digest*,

---

18. Murray Forst Thompson, "Have the Organizers of the Independent Board for Presbyterian Foreign Missions Violated the Law of the Presbyterian Church in the U.S.A.?" *Christianity Today* (Dec. 1933).

19. *Minutes of the General Assembly, 1934*, p. 70.

under control of the liberals (e.g., Mudge), had carefully distinguished between the General Assembly's "legislative and administrative acts" and its authority as a supreme court. "When the General Assembly as a non-judicial body makes deliverances, they are entitled to great respect, but they are subject to modification or repeal at any time by a majority vote in the General Assembly."[20] Yet inevitably, supreme courts do legislate. They may choose not to admit this, but they do legislate. Judge-made law is new law. Supreme courts can reverse themselves, as the *Digest* affirmed in 1930.[21]

The conservatives had implicitly acknowledged this in their Deliverances of 1910, 1916, and 1923: they kept invoking them to prove that the Deliverances were still in effect. But they had never been in effect, judicially speaking: no sanctions. The liberals had protested, affirming adherence to the formal definition of the General Assembly as a court that had no authority to declare law apart from specific judicial cases. After 1934, this objection was no longer valid. It could not be invoked legitimately by Machen and his allies. *The revision of 1934 had transformed the Church into an administrative court*: a court that declares the law in advance, applies the law in specific cases, and enforces the law through its own bureaucratic agencies. The conservatives had set the judicial precedent in 1910, but had neither the will to prosecute individuals in the presbyteries nor the votes to get the Form of Government changed. In 1934, the liberals had both. They did not hesitate to implement negative sanctions.

The Flow of Funds

The restructured 1934 Form of Government, by extending the General Assembly's administrative authority to laymen, had in principle abandoned the Westminster Confession, which laymen were not required to subscribe to by oath. But if the Confession was no longer operationally the binding standard, what was? The answer soon became manifest: money—specifically, money for the boards. The boards' moral right to a stream of uncontested income had been chal-

---

20. *Digest of the Acts and Deliverances of the General Assembly of the Presbyterian Church In the United States of America*, 2 vols. (Philadelphia: Office of the General Assembly, 1930), I:288.
21. *Ibid.*, I:288–89.

lenged by the Independent Board. For the power religion, the flow of funds is sacred.

Studies in the Constitution explicitly affirmed the literally sacred nature of the flow of funds. After spending 50 pages on the history of independent missions agencies, which proved only that opinions about their legitimacy had varied, and there had, since 1869, always been congregational support for independent missions agencies, the General Council got to the point: money. Members are under a judicial obligation to support the boards of the Church financially. The sacramental nature of Presbyterian liberalism's power religion at last manifested itself in no uncertain terms:

> Missionary offerings are one of the ordinances enjoined in a particular church by the Constitution of the Presbyterian Church. The successive provisions of the Confession of Faith, the Form of Government, and the Directory for Worship, which have already been noted, make these missionary offerings just as really a part of the instituted worship of the Church as are prayer, preaching the Word of God, or the sacraments. A church member or an individual church that will not give to promote the officially authorized missionary program of the Presbyterian Church is in exactly the same position with reference to the Constitution of the Church as a church member or an individual church that would refuse to take part in the celebration of the Lord's Supper or any other of the prescribed ordinances of the denomination as set forth in Article VII of the Form of Government.[22]

The Form of Government, from the never-ratified Westminster Assembly version of 1645 until 1934, listed as ordinances the singing of psalms, reading the Bible, preaching, catechising, the sacraments, a collection made for the poor, and dismissing the people with a blessing. These appear under the section, *Of the Ordinances in a particular congregation.*[23] Three comments are in order. First, this list did not apply to higher levels of Church authority; these ordinances were ex-

---

22. *Minutes of the General Assembly, 1934*, p. 110.
23. *The Form of Presbyterial Church-Government* (1645), in *The Confession of Faith* (Publications Committee of the Free Church of Scotland, 1970), p. 404.

clusively congregational in application. Second, what about collections for the poor? The Church never had attempted to impose this as a requirement for ordination or continued membership, although it appears in the same section as the other local church ordinances. This is the only reference in the section to money; there is silence regarding other mandated collections. Third, the Form of Government did not have equal official authority to the Westminster Confession and the two catechisms, which required a two-thirds vote of the presbyteries to revise (not just a majority), and which are silent regarding collections made for the poor. The only explicit reference points for "ordinances" in the Confession are the marks of the Church: preaching and the sacraments (VII:6; cf. XXV:3). The obvious question: When in Presbyterian history had an oath to support financially the Church's boards been taken by Church officers, let alone its members? The answer: never, before or since.

Then the General Council, in the name of the General Assembly, drew a practical conclusion: "In designating missionary offerings as an ordinance, the Constitution of the Presbyterian Church specifically enjoins all church judicatories, all church officers, and all individual churches to guide, direct, and make effectual through the authorized agencies of the Church the missionary offerings of all church members to the same extent as they are enjoined to perform the same office with reference to any other ordinance of the Church."[24] This specified what Church courts were to do. But what if they meet resistance? The General Council was quite specific: *begin the trials*. The General Council issued its final warning to every member: quit the Independent Board or prepare for judicial action.

If this ordinance was mandatory, what about the others? Would the courts require special oaths of obedience regarding, for example, catechising children or psalm singing? What about special collections for the poor? Not one of these traditional Presbyterian issues was raised. What was raised was this:

> 2. That all ministers and laymen affiliated with the Presbyterian Church in the United States of America, who are officers, trustees or members of "The Independent Board for Presbyterian

---

24. *Minutes of the General Assembly, 1934*, pp. 110–11.

Foreign Missions", be officially notified by this General Assembly through its Stated Clerk, that they must immediately upon the receipt of such notification sever their connection with this Board, and that refusal to do so and a continuance of their relationship to the said Independent Board for Presbyterian Foreign Missions, exercising ecclesiastical and administrative functions in contravention of the authority of the General Assembly, will be considered a disorderly and disloyal act on their part and subject them to the discipline of the Church.

3. That Presbyteries having in their membership ministers or laymen who are officers, trustees or members of "The Independent Board for Presbyterian Foreign Missions", be officially notified and directed by this General Assembly through its Stated Clerk to ascertain from said ministers and laymen within ninety days of the receipt of such notice as to whether they have complied with the above direction of the General Assembly, and in case of refusal, failure to respond or non-compliance on the part of these persons, to institute, or cause to be instituted, promptly such disciplinary action as is set forth in the Book of Discipline.[25]

Presbyteries were instructed to initiate proceedings. In the Doctrinal Deliverance of 1910 and subsequently, presbyteries were instructed by the General Assembly to inquire as to ministerial candidates regarding their beliefs. That is, for men seeking ordination, the presbyteries were told to do their screening job. Not once did the General Assembly bring sanctions against any presbytery that failed to follow this order. The General Assembly also had not instructed presbyteries to bring sanctions against men already ordained. The presbyteries had no such authority; once ordained, only a trial could remove a man from office. In 1927, even this authority had been denied to the General Assembly by the General Assembly. But under the revised Book of Discipline, the General Assembly authorized presbyteries to impose sanctions on elders, deacons, and laymen alike.

The Assembly adopted the recommendations of the General Council, including the text of *Studies in the Constitution*. If Church courts were willing to enforce this directive, orthodox Presbyterians

---

25. *Ibid.*, pp. 115–16.

would have three choices: they could cease to support the Independent Board in any official capacity; they could continue to support it and risk disciplinary measures; or they could withdraw from the Church. Everything had changed in Presbyterian Church since the Scopes trial in 1925. What had been the administrative reality since the General Assembly of 1920 was now in full public view: the triumph of modernism.

Macartney registered a protest in *The Presbyterian*: "The action of the General Assembly was unjust and unconstitutional in that it amounted to a sentence upon ministers within the church without a hearing and without a trial."[26] The trials would soon begin. A year later, he decided to submit in silence, which he did until his retirement. Then he received his pension.

Jurisdiction Over Machen

Machen's opponents were masters of the ecclesiastical machinery. They had used this skill to defend themselves when the conservative forces technically had the votes. Now, knowing that the balance of power had shifted in their favor, they began to use the bureaucratic system to do to the orthodox wing what the conservatives should have done to them, beginning in 1913 at the latest. Unlike the conservatives, they had the bureaucratic skill and the votes to get their way. They also had the will.

On January 23, 1934, Machen submitted a request to the New Brunswick Presbytery that he be given permission to transfer to the Philadelphia Presbytery. Why he had waited so long to transfer remains a mystery. He had been teaching at Westminster Seminary in Philadelphia since the fall of 1929. His request was granted, and on March 5, 1934, the Philadelphia Presbytery voted 78 to 48 to accept him into the fellowship. Some of the members had wanted to question him concerning his attitude toward the official agencies of the Church, but this was ruled out of order, and Machen entered the jurisdiction of a far more conservative presbytery.[27]

---

26. Macartney, "Presbyterians, Awake," *The Presbyterian* (July 19, 1934), pp. 8-9.
27. Rian, *Presbyterian Conflict*, p. 171.

Shortly after he had entered the Philadelphia Presbytery, 44 Presbytery delegates filed a notice of complaint with the Synod of Pennsylvania, protesting his acceptance into the fellowship. This complaint was taken under consideration by the Committee on Judicial Business of the Synod, and it was recommended that a final decision as to the legality of Machen's presence within the Philadelphia body be postponed until the 1935 Synod meeting. This postponement, made in June, 1934, effectively silenced Machen's voice in both presbyteries, for it placed him in the category of a minister "in transit," and as such, he was not permitted to speak or to vote in the deliberations of any presbytery.

On June 13, Lewis S. Mudge, Stated Clerk of the General Assembly, informed Mr. Elmer Walker, Stated Clerk of the New Brunswick Presbytery, that Machen was still a member of the presbytery.[28] Two days earlier, he had informed the Pennsylvania Synod of his opinion. He informed the Synod that he would instruct the New Brunswick Presbytery to "take up the matter" of Machen's connection to the Independent Board.[29] On June 19, the Pennsylvania Synod voted to delay for a year any consideration of the protest against Machen.[30] This meant that the Synod avoided tangling with either Mudge or Machen. On June 26, the New Brunswick Presbytery passed a motion requiring Machen to state whether he was willing to sever all connections with the Independent Board, as the General Assembly had demanded. Machen sent a letter of protest to the presbytery: "Without prejudicing the question whether I am or am not still under the jurisdiction of the Presbytery of New Brunswick or whether, if I am still under the jurisdiction of that Presbytery, the Presbytery is warranted in addressing to me officially the inquiry contained in your letter, I desire to say, very respectfully, for the information of the Presbytery, that I have not severed my connection with the Independent Board for Presbyterian Foreign Missions, and that I regard the action of the

---

28. Letter to Machen from Elmer Walker, dated July 16, 1934. Reprinted in Machen, *Statement to the Special Committee*, p. 75.
29. A reprint of his letter appears in *Christianity Today* (Aug. 1934), p. 62.
30. *Ibid.*

General Assembly enjoining me to do so as being contrary to the Constitution of the Presbyterian Church in the U.S.A."[31]

In response to Machen's defiance of the mandate of the Assembly, a special committee was appointed by the Presbytery of New Brunswick to meet with Machen and to discuss with him the question of his membership on the Independent Board, and, should he remain uncooperative, to recommend disciplinary action at the next meeting of the Presbytery.

The question of Machen's membership in the Philadelphia Presbytery became a crucial point; if he was legitimately a part of the Philadelphia Presbytery, there was little chance of his being brought to trial immediately over the issue of the Independent Board, since the Philadelphia body was in the control of the orthodox forces. If, on the other hand, he was still legally under the jurisdiction of the New Brunswick Presbytery, it was likely not only that he would be placed on trial, but that the decision of the New Brunswick court would go against him.

Machen had little choice, under the circumstances, but to cooperate with the special committee until his jurisdictional status could be officially designated by the Synod of Pennsylvania. He did make a request, however, that he be permitted to bring a stenographer to the committee meeting. This request was denied by the committee. As the committee's chairman wrote to him, "We are not a committee of trial and could pass no judgment which would be binding in character." He called the meeting "a friendly and fraternal conference," in which Machen's interests would be "amply protected."[32] Machen subsequently declined to appear in person, and again he resorted to the printing press, sending a 98-page brief to the committee outlining his position concerning the Assembly's mandate.

The Issue of Christian Freedom

In it, Machen again proclaimed the doctrine of Christian freedom. He presented a five-point argument, with the body of the pamphlet

---

31. Letter to Elmer Walker from Machen, dated July 25, 1934. Machen, *Statement to the Special Committee*, p. 76.

32. Letter to Machen from D. Wilson Hollinger, dated October 24, 1934. Reprinted in *ibid.*, p. 83.

devoted to a defense of his basic five points: (1) that obedience to the command would mean supporting a foreign gospel; (2) that it would mean substituting a human authority for Christ's; (3) that it would mean acquiescence to a mandatory Church tax; (4) that all of these things are forbidden by the Bible; and (5) that he had a full right to remain in the Church in spite of his refusal to acquiesce.

The question of mandatory contributions to the official Church agencies was considered at length by Machen, since he believed that such a tax was an extreme infringement on the personal liberty of Church members.

The modernists in power in the Assembly appealed to the new Constitution of the Church, in order to support their demands that Machen and his supporters submit to administrative control. Again, the vital question for the hierarchy was not doctrine but administrative force. Their religion was the power religion.

What divided the two wings was in fact theology. The modernists believed in the theology of power and the bureaucratic machinery necessary to capture and enforce power. The conservatives who were willing to fight—and only a small group of them were willing to fight—believed in creedal religion, meaning the supernatural revelation of God to man in His Bible. Both sides had a covenant theology. Both sides appealed to provisions in the Church constitution and body of rules to attack and defend. But the conservatives were defending a written creed; their opponents were defending an implicit, unwritten creed: the doctrine of salvation through power. The conservatives saw the battle in terms of the moral requirements of an officially supernatural creed, while the liberals saw the battle in terms of the very heart of their religion, namely, conformity to the administrative decisions they were in a position to hand down. The liberals did not admit that the dividing issues were theological, meaning supernatural and creedal, for such an admission would have been contrary to the tenets of their religion.

The Issue of Hierarchical Authority

The 1934 General Assembly was caught in a dilemma of its own creation. If it denied completely the voluntary nature of contributions, it was tampering with a generally accepted principle of voluntarism within all Protestantism. If it did not assert this prerogative of the Assembly to direct all contributions, then its case against Machen and the Independent Board was unfounded. Its own pronouncements reflected this confusion: "As the judicatory of jurisdiction in all matters relating to missionary operations, it [the General Assembly] has never presumed to interfere with the rights or preferences of individual members to give their money or efforts to such missionary objects as they may choose. On the contrary, it has always maintained that the right to control the property of the members of the Church, to assess the amount of their contributions, or to prescribe how they shall dispose of their money, is utterly foreign to the spirit of Presbyterianism. Every contribution on the part of an individual member of the Church must be purely voluntary. . . . In maintaining, however, this personal freedom of individual members, in their contributions to the Church, the General Assembly has never recognized any inconsistency in asserting with equal force, that there is a definite and sacred obligation on the part of every member of the Presbyterian Church to contribute to those objects designated by the authorized judicatory of the denomination."[33] But this judicial dialecticism was merely formal. The hierarchy had decided to come down on the side of compulsion. "Pay up or get out!"

Perhaps it was true that the Assembly—the 1934 Assembly—could not see any inconsistency in its pronouncements, but Machen saw a glaring one, and he pointed it out for the benefit of the special committee: "What the General Assembly therefore says in effect (if we may use colloquial language) is: 'Support of the Boards is voluntary: don't you dare say that it is not voluntary; but, all the same, if you do not come right across with it we shall see that it will be the worse for you.'"[34]

In what was perhaps the key clause in the Assembly's mandate, it was asserted that "For any lower judicatory to assume the right of censuring the actions of a higher judicatory is a gross abuse of power on its part, and a nullification of the Constitution of the Church."[35]

---

33. Machen, *Statement to the Special Committee*, pp. 70–71. Cf. *Minutes of the General Assembly, 1934*, p. 113.

34. *Ibid.*, p. 24.

35. *Ibid.*, p. 38.

This provision was to play an important role in Machen's trial, for according to the clause, no lower Church court could challenge the legality of the mandate. Such a restriction deprived the lower courts of their judicial powers, making them merely administrative bodies implementing the decisions from above. Their functions as courts had been pre-empted. This is the true nature of all administrative law, and why it constitutes a revolution.[36]

Top-Down or Bottom-Up?

It is important to understand that it is here, in this concept of lawful authority, that we see the political conflict of the ages. From the days of the early Near Eastern dynastic tyrannies, the power religionists envisioned political authority as a top-down system.[37] In contrast to this perception, the Hebrew commonwealth was divided into tribes. The localism of such a decentralized structure was inescapable. Central power was limited. The king was limited by the priests. The priests could not permanently buy rural land belonging to tribe members (Lev. 25). Family members inherited leased family land after 50 years (the jubilee), thereby reducing the central power of the tribes (Lev. 25). The entire social system was based on an appeals court (Ex. 18), not a top-down administrative system. Peter knew that he had the moral authority to appeal to God as against the administrative decisions of men (Acts 5:29).

The social structure of the biblical holy commonwealth is a bottom-up law-order, with government beginning with self-government under God's law, and with all ultimate power coming from heaven. The battle between the power religionists and the judicial religionists in the Presbyterian Church reflected this fundamental difference in the concept of authority.

What had stymied the conservatives in their battle against the liberals in the early 1920's was the Presbyterian court system. The local presbyteries had enormous latitude. Without the vote of two-thirds of the presbyteries, no new creedal requirements could be imposed on

---

36. Berman, *Law and Revolution*, pp. 33–41.
37. Karl A. Wittfogel, *Oriental Despotism: A Comparative Study of Total Power* (New Haven, Connecticut: Yale University Press, 1957).

individual presbyteries. Thus, the local presbyteries had the authority to ordain heretics and apostates, and the New York Presbytery did it continually. This decentralized system worked against the conservatives, given the fact that they refused to press charges or discipline the New York Presbytery. In 1837, they had known better: they threw out four presbyteries in one shot. After 1869, they forgot.

The liberals took advantage of Presbyterian localism, 1910 to 1933. But once in power, they reversed the traditional decentralized administrative system. They knew in 1934 that the General Assemblies could not impose a new, liberal creed on the whole Church. They did not want to get into such a battle yet. There was no reason to place in jeopardy their recent consolidation of power; a battle over the Confession would have played into the hands of the conservatives. They opted instead for administrative decision-making. The overwhelming public support of the 1934 Form of Government showed there would be no significant resistance. They chose to avoid excommunicating men in terms of doctrine. They adopted a policy of excommunicating men for disobedience or disloyalty to the only god they believed was worth worshipping: *the process god who reveals himself in administrative power*. It was entirely consistent with their religion that they appealed continually to the moral necessity of conformity to the centralized apparatus of the Church's administrative machinery. After all they possessed the liberals' definition of holy eucharist: 50+ percent of the votes.

Machen would have none of it. "The issue in the Church is doctrinal to the core. . . . The gentlemen in control of the administrative machinery of the Church may go on using the old phrases—'no doctrinal issue,' 'purely administrative issue,' and the like—but those phrases are no longer convincing to the public. They might just as well be put on a phonograph record. Putting them on a phonograph record would be a good way to save 'overhead.'"[38] The issue in 1935 was the same as it had been in 1923: Christianity vs. modernism.[39]

---

38. Machen, "What May Be Learned from the 1935 General Assembly of the Presbyterian Church on the U.S.A.," *Independent Board Bulletin*, 1 (June 1935), p. 5.

39. *Ibid.*

McIntire vs. Speer

On January 15, 1935, Rev. Carl McIntire, then an unknown young minister, presented an Overture against the Board of Foreign Missions to his Presbytery of West Jersey, which voted with only one negative vote to accept it and send it to the General Assembly. On March 5, Robert E. Speer sent a reply. A committee sent by the Board, which included J. Ross Stevenson, spoke to the Presbytery for two hours on April 15. The Presbytery without debate then rescinded its previous vote, 51 to 38. In response, McIntire published a 96-page booklet, *Dr. Robert E. Speer, The Board of Foreign Missions of the Presbyterian Church in the U.S.A. and Modernism* (April 11, 1935). This booklet was a detailed refutation of Speer's March 5 reply. It constitutes the most detailed and documented criticism of Speer and the Board ever published.

Typical of how the liberals operated, and still operate, was Speer's response to McIntire's original accusation regarding a book by Winifred Kirkland, *The Way Of Discovery*, prepared as a series of talks at Fosdick's Riverside Church. The Board recommended it. On page 19, Mrs. Kirkland had written: "There has been only one human being brave enough to release within himself the full creative power of believing that God was his Father. But unless Jesus' method of making himself divine can be imitated, his achievement is a mockery rather than a challenge." McIntire had identified this as Unitarianism. He did not go far enough. The woman's statement was worse than Unitarianism; it was Arianism—the heresy against which orthodoxy was established at the Council of Nicea. The suggestion that Jesus became divine and that we can do the same was the essence of the Arian heresy. Such a suggestion denies the unique position of Jesus Christ as the co-eternal Son of God, the Creator of the universe (Col. 1:16). Yet the Board of Foreign Missions had publicly recommended this book. The obvious question was: Why? It was a question that Speer had to deflect without actually answering.

In response, Speer said that the book had never been recommended by the Board. It had merely been named in a flier prepared by the Women's Committees of the Boards of Foreign Missions and Home Missions, named "without comment for supplemental reading." (What if the book had been *Mein Kampf*, named "without comment for supplemental reading"?) Furthermore, "When attention was called to these two sentences the pamphlet was withdrawn by the Board of Foreign Missions."[40] McIntire then asked: "How can a Board withdraw a publication, recommend that publication jointly with the Board of National Missions, and still not be responsible for its recommendation and use?"[41] This was the proper question, but it convinced no one in power.

A familiar tactic long used by liberals' has been to recommend heresy and, when caught red-handed, withdraw the offensive document, plead ignorance and innocence, and wait for another opportunity. And why not? For a century, there have been no negative sanctions against anything that the conservatives did not spot, and there have been no negative sanctions against anything that they did spot, since the bureaucracy could immediately plead ignorance or the non-official status of the offending item. This is standard operating policy in every conservative-funded, liberal-run organization. When caught, the perpetrators always dismiss the document as "merely discussion documents" or "unofficial." This almost always works.

Speer then denied that the lady's pamphlet was Unitarianism.[42] His statement revealed a theological ignorance that is startling: either Speer's ignorance or the presbytery's, which accepted at face value his response. "To call this 'Unitarianism' is sheer irresponsibility."[43] Speer then went much further. He actually referred to biblical passages in defense of the idea that Jesus *made Himself* divine, although Speer refused to quote these passages verbatim. Here is one of the passages: "Therefore the Jews sought the more to kill him, because he not only had broken the sabbath, but said also that God was his Father, making himself equal with God" (John 5:18). The context indicates that "making" meant "asserting." Jesus did not construct His own divinity. Then he cited John 13:15: "For I have given you an example, that ye should do as I have done to you." The context of this statement was foot-washing. Then he cited I John 2:6: "He that saith he abideth in

---

40. Carl McIntire, *Dr. Robert E. Speer, The Board of Foreign Missions of the Presbyterian Church in the U.S.A. and Modernism* (1935), pp. 9–10.
41. *Ibid.*, p. 9.
42. *Ibid.*, p. 11.
43. *Ibid.*, p. 12.

him ought himself also so to walk, even as he walked." The context here was ethics, not ontology. Speer was deliberately misleading his readers. That a presbytery let him get away with such deliberate misrepresentation of Trinitarian theology—a defense of Arianism—indicates just how bad things were in 1935.

McIntire politely added this comment: "Surely this wresting of the Scriptures to support unscriptural truth is not the work of Dr. Speer. Yet it is his writing."[44] This was the rhetoric of non-confrontation.

Speer used the same back-peddling when trying to escape another hand grenade tossed by Mrs. Kirkland, in *Woman and Missions*: "What does the agony on Gethsemene reveal except that Jesus saw human existence so beautiful that he could not bear to leave it." McIntire said: "This is Modernism."[45] Surely, it was. This pamphlet was published, McIntire had said in his original Overture, by the Board of Foreign Missions. Speer responded: Not so, not so! False, false! "It is 'Published by the Women's Committees of the Boards of Missions of the Presbyterian Church in the U.S.A.' . . . [T]he Boards do not write it or censor its contents. . . ."[46] Yet it had been sent out by the Board of Foreign Missions. McIntire asked: If the Board is not responsible for its subcommittees, then who is? And so it went for another three pages: debate over the meaning of Mrs. Kirkland's statement. Speer supported the legitimacy of the statement, though he admitted that "steps have been taken to have more care exercised in the future."[47] That care never arrived. Instead, McIntire was excommunicated a year later—the only protesting minister in the Church to have received this ultimate negative sanction in 1936.

Also recommended in 1933 by the Board was James Hall Franklin's book *The Never Failing Light*. Hall wrote: "Truly the light was shining in dense spiritual darkness when Jesus began teaching men of all races, of all religions and all classes to look up to the Unseen as their Father and to practice love and brotherhood as the sum total of his requirements of his children." This is modernism, said McIntire.

---

44. *Ibid.*, p. 11.
45. *Ibid.*, p. 16.
46. *Ibid.*
47. *Ibid.*, p. 17.

To which Speer replied in his usual forthright manner: "This textbook has not been in some respects a satisfactory book. . . ."[48] Furthermore, the book was not published by the Board.[49] Recommended, yes, but not published. The same refrain came in response to E. Herman's *The Ministry of Silence and Meditation*, recommended in 1934: "Whether our ultimate intellectual conclusions be orthodox or heterodox matters comparatively little. . . ."[50] This was just one more pamphlet published by the Women's Committees of the Boards of National and Foreign Missions, said Speer.

McIntire had originally included a section on the Board's cooperative work with liberals in Christian colleges and universities in Asia. He had cited numerous liberal textbooks used in those schools. Speer replied: ". . . it was not known to the Board that these books were in the course at the time."[51] "The tract is not satisfactory to us but its writer is an ordained minister in the Church of Scotland. . . ."[52] "Cooperative work is not free from difficulties and limitations."[53] In short, "it's true, but so what?"

Van Til once said that the unbeliever is like a man standing in front of what he regards as a bottomless pit. He challenges the Christian to give him any fact that points to the existence of God. Every time the Christian presents him with such a fact, the unbeliever shovels it over his shoulder into the pit. "I demand more facts if I am to be persuaded." Such was Speer and the Presbyterian Church's leadership in 1935. There were not a sufficient number of facts on earth to persuade them of the presence of liberalism in the Foreign Missions Board. In 1936, they suspended from the ministry all those who continued to present such facts.

Neither Sticks Nor Stones

In February, 1935, Machen published an article in *The Independent Board Bulletin*, "Sham Orthodoxy versus Real Orthodoxy." He has-

---

48. *Ibid.*, p. 20.
49. *Ibid.*, p. 21.
50. *Ibid.*, p. 25.
51. *Ibid.*, p. 32.
52. *Ibid.*, p. 34.
53. *Ibid.*, p. 38.

tened to add, as he always did, a statement that none of this was personal. "I do not mean that those who engage in such a propaganda are engaging in any conscious misrepresentation. No doubt very many of them really think that they are orthodox." This implies that some of them knew full well they were not orthodox, and these men were indeed engaging in conscious misrepresentation. But to name them meant launching a heresy trial and risking a trial for slander or, in the now-familiar phrase, violating the ninth commandment. Machen was about to go on trial for insubordination. He was in no position to bring specific accusations against specific ministers. No conservative in the denomination had been in such a position since 1926.

Sham orthodoxy says this, Machen said: "We are opposed to *any* Modernism that *may* be in the Presbyterian Church in the U.S.A." Real orthodoxy says this: "We are opposed to *the* Modernism which *is* in the Presbyterian Church in the U.S.A. and which dominates its ecclesiastical machinery." To which any good inclusivist would have said: "Says you." And then followed this with: "Prove it." That is exactly what Henry van Dyke had said in 1913, when he challenged anyone to bring him to trial.

Sham orthodoxy says: "We hold that the peace of the Church may be restored by bringing together the warring elements now in the Church." Real orthodoxy says: "We hold that the peace of the Church may be restored only by elimination from the Church of that unbelief which now dominates its councils and by a return of the Church to an honest adherence to the Word of God." To which any informed conservative would have asked: "How can we eliminate unbelief without heresy trials?" Meanwhile, any reasonably intelligent inclusivist was saying: "There is a third way to restore peace: eliminate Machen and his followers from the Church." The wheels of administrative procedure had already begun to grind.

Machen then threw down the gauntlet to every conservative who would not stand with him, meaning virtually all of his better-known former supporters by mid-1935. He raised the issue of sanctions and orthodoxy: voting. "We hold that whether a man is a Modernist or not is determined by the way he votes in Presbytery and at the General Assembly; he is a Modernist, no matter what kind of sermons he preaches, if he votes with the Auburn Affirmationists and other Modernist[s] in the great issues of the day." This meant, definitionally speaking, that the overwhelming majority of the Presbyterian ministers was modernist. Machen offered a judicial definition of the modernist rather than homiletic, voting rather than preaching, sanctions rather than confession. Judicially, he was correct, as the Church proved after 1936. The Presbyterian Church had become judicially modernist by 1935. But this did not mean that the muddled middle was confessionally modernist in 1935.

Machen at last had arrived at the crucial understanding of ecclesiology and Confessionalism that had eluded the Old School since 1869: *the issue is sanctions*. By moving from an emphasis on confession to an emphasis on sanctions as the defining mark of both modernism and orthodoxy, Machen had reversed the Old School's official position, which had always identified personal confession and the theological content of preaching as the judicially defining marks of orthodoxy. He had said so himself a decade earlier: "The corporate witness-bearing of the Presbyterian Church is carried on especially through the pulpit."[54] Machen was now implying that those ministers who voted with modernists deserved to be de-frocked, for they were not truly orthodox. This is what Maitland Alexander had implied in December, 1923, in his speeches to the anti-*Affirmation* audiences.[55] It is significant that Machen wrote to Alexander on June 3, 1935, to tell him that "the Gideon-band method is the method to use in this fight. . . ."[56] But he knew that in this instance, Gideon would not put the Midianites to flight.

By 1935, Machen was standing firm, just as Luther had: "Here I stand; I can do no other." He was calling for a new Reformation. He had been doing this since 1923: "And another Reformation in God's good time will come."[57] He knew what this meant: expulsion from

---

54. Machen, "The Parting of the Ways—Part 1," *The Presbyterian* (April 17, 1924), p. 8.

55. See Chapter 9, above: section on "Preparation for Battle," pp. 536-44.

56. Cited in Hart, "Doctor Fundamentalis": An Intellectual Biography of J. Gresham Machen, 1881-1937 (Ph.D. dissertation, Johns Hopkins University, 1988), p. 319n.

57. Machen, *Christianity and Liberalism* (New York: Macmillan, 1923), p. 178.

the Church, not the reform of the Church. Warfield had told him in 1921: "You can't split rotten wood." This meant trouble. "But meanwhile our souls are tried."[58]

If orthodoxy means voting against the modernists, and modernists control the machinery and the Assemblies, then *orthodoxy means expulsion*. If orthodoxy cannot bring negative ecclesiastical sanctions, then it must experience negative ecclesiastical sanctions in order to maintain itself. If the test of orthodoxy is judicial as well as confessional, then orthodoxy must identify itself by pushing on the system until it loses institutionally. Orthodoxy cannot be neutral. It cannot sit on the sidelines. Orthodox men must imitate Briggs: escalate the rhetoric until either victory comes or expulsion follows.

A month after the 1935 General Assembly, another essay by Machen appeared in *The Independent Board Bulletin* (June). He continued both his rhetoric and his unwillingness to name names. The issue, he said, was the tolerance of modernism, as it had been since 1922. He equated tolerance with incompetence.

> What we hold is that every member of the Board of Foreign Missions of the Presbyterian Church in the U.S.A. has shown his incompetence to be a member of that Board by his tolerance of Modernism in the work of the Board. It is not a question of this missionary or that. It is not a question of this member of the Board or that. It is a question of the Board itself. In the long run, sound missionaries cannot proceed from an unsound Board. Sweet water cannot come from a bitter fountain. Make the Board sound, and in the long run the missionaries will be sound; make the Board unsound, as it is at present, and in the long run the missionaries will be unsound. That is true no matter what good missionaries may be found at present, even under that unsound Board, on the mission field.

Here we see the absolute futility of the Old School's position since 1869. Machen was unwilling to identify specific missionaries as modernists. In Presbyterianism, naming names brings risks of a court trial for the one who names them. Not naming names, however, guar-

---

58. *Ibid.*

antees that the present administration will continue unless, through pangs of conscience, the malefactor voluntarily resigns. The modernists moved quietly into the Church's bureaucracies, 1900 to 1913, and thought to themselves, "Sticks and stones may break my bones, but names will never hurt me." From the day in 1913 when Henry van Dyke publicly challenged any conservative to take him into the New York City Presbytery court for his beliefs, the conservatives were reduced to calling names at no one in particular. Without the willingness and the ability to impose negative sanctions on specific ordained ministers, the conservatives had neither sticks nor stones, and if they named names, sticks and stones would be transferred to their opponents for use in counter-trials. All that the conservatives had was rhetoric against modernist ideas in general, Church boards taken as collectives, and trends. The trends were all against them, as Machen well knew, and had known since his 1912 Seminary lecture on "Christianity and Culture."

Machen's Trial

The special committee ignored Machen's reasoned appeal. It brought back to the Presbytery of New Brunswick a list of specific charges against him, including violation of his ordination vows, and it called for Machen's formal trial before the court of the presbytery, with all proceedings closed to the public. When he heard that the trial was not to be open to the press, Machen went to the press to condemn this restriction. This bad publicity put pressure on the presbytery, which reversed itself and opened the hearing to reporters.[59] The trial began on February 14, 1935.

Some aspects of the trial bordered on the bizarre. The question of jurisdiction was technically at the heart of Machen's defense. Was he a member of the New Brunswick Presbytery? Machen said *no*. The presbytery said *yes*. The Synod of Pennsylvania had placed him in judicial limbo. His presbytery membership was now "in transit." But Mudge had told the New Brunswick Presbytery that Machen was under its jurisdiction. The New Brunswick Presbytery had filed charges

---

59. Rian, *Presbyterian Conflict*, p. 176.

against him. Machen's counsel, Rev. H. McAllister Griffiths (accompanied by Edwin H. Rian), argued that the presbytery had no jurisdiction. The argument came down to whether the Philadelphia Presbytery's clerk had sent a receipt of acceptance—a stub—to the New Brunswick Presbytery's clerk. The New Brunswick Presbytery's clerk insisted that he had not received the stub.[60] The trial continued.

Machen said nothing throughout the trial. Machen's defense counsel invoked the Auburn *Affirmation*. Some members of the court had signed it or were members of churches whose pastors had signed it. These men should not be sitting in judgment of Machen, his defense counsel argued repeatedly. Finally, court member Kuizenga appealed to the Moderator: "I think that this court is competent to decide that this is not a doctrinal controversy nor a doctrinal question, and that no remarks of this sort shall be allowed in this court."[61] He added that any reference to the Auburn *Affirmation* was out of order, since the time for anyone to issue a challenge had run out under the statute of limitations.[62]

Legally, Kuizenga was correct: there was a statute of limitations in the Church, and it had expired. There had been no negative sanctions on the *Affirmation*, 1923 to 1934. It was now time for other negative sanctions. In short, time had run out for the conservatives. The court ruled that Machen could not invoke either the *Affirmation* or theology as an aspect of his defense. This effectively ended his defense. But the trial continued, and the transcript fills over 400 double-spaced pages.

The unanimous final verdict of "guilty" was handed down on March 29. All charges against him were upheld. Machen "has been guilty of conduct contrary to the government and discipline of the church, unfaithful in maintaining the peace of the church, has been insubordinate to the lawfully constituted authorities of the church, has violated his ordination vows, has shown contempt of and rebellion against his superiors in the church, and has been guilty of a

---

60. Transcript, Machen Trial, p. 158.
61. *Ibid.*, pp. 63–64.
62. *Ibid.*, p. 64.

breach of his lawful promises."[63] The court took care to repeat the standard line: "Questions of doctrine have not entered into the case except as the Defendant has endeavored to make them an excuse and justification for his wilful disobedience of Church authority, and his disregard for his ordination vows."[64] Machen was suspended as a minister of the Presbyterian Church in the U.S.A., with execution of the sentence to be deferred until the case could be reviewed by the higher Church courts.

According to pre-1934 Northern Presbyterian law, suspension also involved excommunication. Suspension "is the sentence by which a Church member or officer is restrained from the exercise and enjoyment of all church privileges and rights. Its visible signs are exclusion from the Lord's Table and from the right of suffrage."[65] This defination was altered in 1934, but then the alteration was revoked on the following page. Suspension of laymen was defined as temporary excommunication, but "with respect to church officers, it is their temporary exclusion from the exercise of their office, and, at the discretion of the judicatory, from sealing ordinances also. . . . Indefinite suspension is the exclusion of an offender from sealing ordinances, or from his office, until he exhibits signs of repentance, or until, by his conduct, the necessity of the highest censure be made manifest."[66] The highest censure was excommunication.[67] This summary was immediately contradicted by the non-discretionary formula of suspension, which the judiciary had to announce publicly: ". . . do now declare you suspended from the communion of the Church (and from the exercise of your office)."[68] So, suspension after 1933 does seem to have invoked excommunication, even though the text of the actual statute said that excommunication was merely an option.

---

63. *Ibid.*, pp. 410–11.
64. *Ibid.*, p. 408.
65. *Manual for Church Officers and Members*, 4th ed. (n.p.: Office of the General Assembly by the Publication Department of the Board of Christian Education, 1930), p. 161.
66. *Minutes of the General Assembly, 1934*, pp. 162–63.
67. *Ibid.*, p. 163.
68. *Ibid.*, p. 162.

Machen commented on the trial after the decision of guilty had been handed down: "The special judicial commission of the presbytery of New Brunswick has simply condemned me without giving me a hearing. I am condemned for failing to obey a lawful order; but when my counsel offered to prove that the order that I had disobeyed was not lawful but unlawful the court refused to hear a word of argument. I am condemned for making false assertions about the modernism of the official board of foreign missions, but when my counsel offered to prove that those assertions were true the court would not hear a word of the evidence that we were perfectly ready to produce. It is not too much to say that a trial conducted in this fashion is nothing but a farce...."[69]

But it *was* too much to say. There was a Presbyterian statute of limitations; it had run out. Machen and the conservatives had accused the Foreign Missions Board of harboring heresy in general but no heretics in particular. Machen's accusation in *Christianity and Liberalism* was that modernism went beyond heresy; it was apostasy. Machen was like a man who keeps accusing an organization of promoting Communism, but then steadfastly refuses to identify anyone who teaches Communism. No organization can tolerate such accusations from members against its formally constituted agencies. Sooner or later, the accuser must identify specific violations. Machen had refused to do this, and nothing that his defense lawyer said during the trial indicated that he would introduce any specifics beyond someone's having signed the *Affirmation*. But Machen had said that some of the signers of the Auburn *Affirmation* were innocent through ignorance;[70] he just never said who was guilty. In the entire battle over foreign missions, no conservative had ever accused one liberal missionary on the field other than Mrs. Buck, who had resigned. Meanwhile, Robert Dick Wilson (1924) and Donald Grey Barnhouse (1935) had delivered first-hand clean bills of health. Machen's case was doomed to the ex-

---

69. *Christian Century* (April 17, 1935), p. 519.

70. "The Affirmation does indeed employ Christian terminology; and, deceived by this terminology, there are no doubt Christian men among the signers." Machen, "The Parting of the Ways—Part II," *The Presbyterian* (April 24, 1924), p. 7.

tent that it relied on his statement of conscience regarding the content of the Missions Board. His only hope was to attack the new legal order, an equally doomed defense: that new legal order had been voted on overwhelmingly by the presbyteries.

The decision of the court was upheld by the Synod of New Jersey, and the Synod of Pennsylvania upheld the complaint against Machen's acceptance into the Philadelphia Presbytery at the 1935 meeting, although the action was taken on extremely technical details of administration. The verdict to remove Machen from the Church's ministry was maintained.

An odd sidelight on the trial took place at the 1935 General Assembly, when a case came before the Permanent Judicial Commission involving two men who had been licensed by the Chester Presbytery, although they had refused to confirm their undivided allegiance to the official Church agencies. O. T. Allis was a member of this very conservative presbytery.[71] The Pennsylvania Synod had upheld the complainants, deciding against the two men, but the Permanent Judicial Commission reversed the Synod's ruling, and permitted the men to enter the Church. It affirmed the absolute sovereignty of presbyteries in licensing candidates for the ministry. "The principle of the Constitution is that a Presbytery in conformity to the Constitutional requirements is the sole judge regarding licensure and when a Presbytery is satisfied it may license."[72] In short, the mandate of the 1934 Assembly was judicially overturned. The Permanent Judicial Commission had reaffirmed the General Assembly's 1927 mandate.

This would have been a disaster to the modernists. The Commission had not properly interpreted the new revelation: sanctions would now be imposed; the liberals' orthodoxy from 1876 to 1933 had now evolved into its opposite. In between this General Assembly and the 1936 General Assembly, the Permanent Judicial Commission got the message . . . permanently. The steamroller rolled on, despite this reversal, which in retrospect proved to be a fluke.

Machen decided to take his case to the General Assembly. He knew by now that he would surely lose, but he believed he had an

---

71. *Minutes of the General Assembly, 1935*, p. 84.
72. *Ibid.*, p. 86.

obligation to continue the fight. On April 10, 1935, Machen wrote to Rev. J. R. McMahon:

> As for your comment, that I have "no chance," I am perfectly well aware of the fact that I have no chance of vindication from the courts of the Presbyterian Church in the U.S.A. I am very much less concerned about these courts than I am about maintaining my testimony to the gospel and being faithful to my ordination pledge when I became a minister in the Presbyterian Church in the U.S.A.[73]

Showdown at Westminster

All those Presbyterians who maintained their connections with the Independent Board were removed from the Church by their various presbyteries. This did not involve many of the Church's orthodox members, even those originally connected with Westminster Seminary. Some of these men were unwilling to give support to the Independent Board when it became clear that to do so would mean being cut out from the fellowship of the Church. Most notable of these was Samuel G. Craig, editor of *Christianity Today*, which had been the primary outlet for the orthodox wing since 1930. He resigned from the Board of Trustees of Westminster over this issue, since Machen felt it was incompatible for any who could not support the Independent Board and the possibility of creating a new Church upon expulsion to remain with Westminster. The faculty issued an ultimatum to the Trustees: support the Presbyterian Constitutional Covenantal Union—launched the previous June, which had as its fallback position the formation of a new Church—or else the faculty would resign. Allis, Machen's close friend since their seminary days, and a staunch orthodox advocate, resigned from his Chair at Westminster, and he was followed by 13 of the 28 trustees on January 7, 1936.[74]

The loss of Allis was very serious. He was the acknowledged successor to Robert Dick Wilson. He was 56 years old, but he lived to be

---

73. Machen archives, Westminster Theological Seminary, Philadelphia.
74. Rian, *Presbyterian Conflict*, pp. 98-99.

93, and he was productive right up until the end. His magnum opus, *The Old Testament: Its Claims and Critics*, was published in 1972, when he was 92. In 1936, he had not yet published his major books, *Prophecy and the Church* (1945), *The Five Books of Moses* (1949), *God Spake By Moses* (1951), and *The Unity of Isaiah* (1952). He was a giant not yet in his prime, and Machen had forced him out with an ultimatum: "them or us," meaning an independent seminary or an independent board of foreign missions.

What Machen had done by forcing Westminster's Board members to support the Independent Board was to force an ecclesiastical issue on what was supposed to be an independent seminary. The seminary had been established in order to remove it from ecclesiastical control by any Church. Machen violated his principle of an independent seminary board by forcing board members to give at least token acceptance to a completely separate organization, the Independent Board for Presbyterian Foreign Missions.

The great, grim irony of this decision was that in November, 1936, just two months before his death, the theological independents—fundamentalists in Presbyterian robes—voted Machen out of his long-term position as president of the Independent Board.[75] They became true to the name "Independent." Machen's successors then had to start a new foreign missions board under the auspices of the new denomination. But Allis and the others never returned.

Why had Machen done it? Consistency. He had shifted his definition of orthodoxy to include sanctions: voting. This included neutrality: not voting against modernism. He rejected all forms of neutrality with respect to the rival missions boards. It was time to be kicked out of the Church for principle. But by forcing Westminster's Board members to acknowledge the legitimacy of the Independent Board, he was forcing them either to get out of the Presbyterian Church or out of the seminary. Men who had stood by him for a long time decided to remove themselves from his direct influence. The fight for the Presbyterian Church had been lost, in his view; it had not been irrevocably lost in theirs. They were incorrect, but being forced by Machen to

---

75. *Ibid.*, pp. 241–42.

choose between Westminster Seminary or the Presbyterian Church gave them an excuse to leave the ecclesiastical battlefield.

By May, 1936, the lines were drawn between the most militant of the orthodox Presbyterians, and those who wished to remain in the Church.

Schism or Apostasy?

In his column in his new periodical, *The Presbyterian Guardian* (May 4, 1936), Machen chose as its title, "An Apostate Church?" He announced: "It is not schism to break away from an apostate church. Indeed it is schism to remain in an apostate church, since to remain in an apostate church is to separate from the true Church of Jesus Christ." The question at hand: Will the Permanent Judicial Commission uphold the Mandate of the 1934 and 1935 General Assemblies, thereby revealing the Church as apostate? He answered: "Yes." He was correct; the Commission did uphold the mandates, and the General Assembly sustained the Commission. His recommendation if this should happen: "We ought to separate at once from an apostate church organization...." He no longer capitalized the word "church" when referring to the Presbyterian Church. He had previously always done so.

On May 8, Macartney phoned Machen to offer his services as a defense attorney at the trial. Machen graciously turned down the offer in a long letter the next day. The issue was representation, he said. Macartney had decided to remain in the Church. Machen called its machinery apostate in his letter. Machen did not criticize Macartney for remaining behind; in fact he thanked him for all his support, but he said that if he (Machen) were to be lightly reprimanded—unlikely, he thought—then the press would ask Macartney to explain Machen's position. The press would confuse the two positions. He said he had to be represented by someone who agreed with him. He wanted a split: "I think that the evil which this Permanent Judicial Commission is doing will result in the great good of a separation of evangelical forces in the Presbyterian Church in the U.S.A. from an apostate ecclesiastical machine. But I cannot acquiesce in that evil for one moment.... If that Permanent Judicial Commission should acquit me, I should adopt every means of forcing the issue immediately in some other way. But that is a most unlikely contingency. . . ."[76]

Machen had finally come to the full realization that the covenantal issue in the denomination was sanctions. He decided to press his point by remaining in the Church until it imposed negative sanctions in terms of its apostate unofficial creed. The imposition of such sanctions would testify to the apostasy of the Church, he believed. He was correct; but this had been equally true in every year since 1901. The Old School had been unwilling to test the orthodoxy of the Church after 1900 by pressing for heresy trials. In fact, it had not initiated a trial against Briggs in 1876 (first Inaugural Address), 1881 (articles in *Presbyterian Review*), or 1889 (*Whither?*). The Old School had been unwilling to define covenantal orthodoxy in terms of sanctions because of the implicit understanding that undergirded the reunion of 1869: Old School standards of Confessional orthodoxy would not be used to initiate heresy trials. Only New School standards would be employed. After 1906, Cumberland Presbyterian Church standards would be employed, defined by the 1903 revision. After van Dyke's challenge in 1913, only van Dyke's standards would be employed, which meant no Confessional standards at all. After decades of wrangling, it came at last to this: Machen's standards vs. "Uncle Henry's."

Uncle Henry's prevailed.

The Presbyterian Church of America was formed on June 11, 1936. A remnant of 34 ministers and 17 ruling elders attended that original General Assembly meeting.[77]

The last front-page article devoted by the *New York Times* to the Presbyterian conflict appeared on June 15, 1936. In the extension on page 21, the *Times* reprinted much of Machen's June 14 sermon. Machen argued that Satan tempted Christ to worship him by offering Christ the opportunity to do great things for the world. This temptation is still offered to the Church. Just dip the battle flag's colors to

---

76. Machen to Macartney, May 9, 1935; reprinted in *Presbyterian Guardian* (Jan. 1962), p. 5.

77. D. G. Hart and John Muether, *Fighting the Good Fight: A Brief History of the Orthodox Presbyterian Church* (Philadelphia: Committee on Christian Education and the Committee of the Historian of the Orthodox Presbyterian Church, 1995), p. 37.

the enemy, and there will be no further trouble, Christians are assured. He applied this analogy to the Presbyterian Church, U.S.A. "It is an army 2,000,000 strong. Only it is an army no more. That dip of the colors made all the difference in the world."

Suspension and Appeal

The Presbyterian Church's *Digest* was a compendium of the judicial acts of the General Assembly. The first detailed *Digest* appeared in 1873, known as Moore's *Digest*. It summarized earlier short compendiums of 1820, 1850, 1856, and 1861. Moore issued two more: in 1886 and 1898. A *Supplement* for 1898 to 1907 was issued by William H. Roberts. The next edition appeared in 1922 (two volumes). Another appeared in 1930 (two volumes). There was a supplement in 1934 under Lewis S. Mudge. Two more volumes appeared in 1938.

Volume I of the 1938 edition published the appeals of several ministers who had been suspended by lower courts in 1936 because of their connection to the Independent Board. In each case, the Permanent Judicial Commission of the General Assembly upheld the convictions. Judicial Case No. 1 disposed of the appeals by H. McAllister Griffiths, Merrill T. MacPherson, Edwin H. Rian, Paul Woolley, and Charles J. Woodbridge, all of the Philadelphia Presbytery.[78] The Commission added: "It is to be noted that the charges against these appellants do not in any wise involve questions of faith or doctrine."[79] Judicial Case No. 2 upheld the suspension of Carl McIntire by the Synod of New Jersey. In addition, it formally excommunicated him—the only suspended minister singled out for this ultimate sanction.[80] Judicial Case No. 3 was the longest: the suspension of Machen.[81] Judicial Case No. 4 upheld the suspension of Arthur F. Perkins by the Synod of Wisconsin.[82] Judicial Case No. 5 upheld the admonition, a lesser

---

78. *Digest of the Acts and Deliverances of the General Assembly of the Presbyterian Church In the United States of America*, 2 vols. (Philadelphia: Office of the General Assembly, 1938), I:573-80.
79. *Ibid.*, I:575.
80. *Ibid.*, I:878-79.
81. *Ibid.*, I:871-78.
82. *Ibid.*, I:881-84.

offense than suspension, of J. Oliver Buswell, the president of Wheaton College.[83] Total: eight suspensions, one admonition.

By suspending the opposition's leaders, the Church ended all opposition from laymen on this issue. No Northern Presbyterian layman subsequently took up Machen's cause by joining the Independent Board, or if he did, no trace of his opposition has survived.[84] Some 4,200 laymen did agree with Machen and departed with him: about one-fifth of one percent of the denomination's membership.

Two ministers who were members of the Independent Board did avoid suspension. Henry W. Coray in the summer of 1934 had requested that his presbytery allow him to proceed to China as a missionary under the Independent Board. This would require the presbytery to leave his charge as pastor of the West Pittson Presbyterian Church in Pennsylvania. He asked to be released in October. The presbytery refused to release him. The presbytery warned him that if he left his charge, his name would be erased from the presbytery as having become an independent. Rather than trying him for insubordination, it merely erased his name.[85]

Wilbur M. Smith escaped suspension because his presbytery, the highly conservative Chester Presbytery, refused to bring him to trial. It adopted the minority report of the presbytery's Special Judicial Committee. In November, 1935, the Synod of Pennsylvania, through its Permanent Judicial Commission, instructed the Chester Presbytery to institute action against Smith. The General Assembly concurred.[86] He resigned from the Independent Board, with Machen's blessing, before they could bring him to trial.[87]

With the triumph of the liberals, the *Digest* no longer had a role to play. There was a supplemental booklet in 1939 and again in 1940 revising the *Digest*, but after that, the series was never again revised.

---

83. *Ibid.*, I:755–57.
84. Sun Oil Company's J. Howard Pew, the richest man in the Church, subsequently bankrolled a conservative tabloid, *The Presbyterian Layman*, for many years. He remained in the Church, part of the loyal opposition.
85. *Minutes of the General Assembly, 1936*, pp. 35–36.
86. *Ibid.*, pp. 37–40.
87. Wilbur M. Smith, *Before I Forget* (Chicago: Moody, 1971), pp. 116–17.

The End of the Battle

Machen had twice taken stands for institutional independency: Westminster Seminary and the Independent Board. That second stand backfired on him in November when a majority of the Independent Board voted to remove him as president, replacing him with Harold S. Laird. Laird was still the head of the Independent Board when he was unanimously elected Moderator of the 1939 Synod of the Bible Presbyterian Church.[88] Laird was not a Presbyterian pastor in 1936; he was pastor of an independent church. This was also true of the new vice president of the board, Merrill T. MacPherson.[89] From that point on, the Independent Board became openly committed to premillennialism, total abstinence from alcohol, and independency from any ecclesiastical control.[90] It remained so as of 1995; Carl McIntire was still its vice president, almost six decades after the event.[91]

Machen died six weeks later on January 1, 1937, in North Dakota. At his funeral, two men officiated, R. B. Kuiper and Edwin Rian.[92] Rian had also been one of the two men to defend him at his 1935 trial. Rian was the Secretary of the Committee on Home Missions and Church Extension as well as field secretary of Westminster Seminary. A decade later he returned to the Presbyterian Church, U.S.A. He became the secretary to James McCord, president of Princeton Seminary, in 1967, the year the Confession was revised. He served until 1982. The chief defender at Machen's trial was Griffiths, who would join the secession from Machen's church in 1937, becoming the Stated Clerk of the Bible Presbyterian Church in 1938.[93] In between, however, he became involved in a sexual scandal and withdrew from local church duties, although he was never charged formally by any Church court.[94] He retained his position on the Independent Board.

---

88. *A Brief History of the Bible Presbyterian Church And Its Agencies* (no publisher, no date, but probably published in 1968), p. 64.
89. George P. Hutchinson, *The History Behind the Reformed Presbyterian Church, Evangelical Synod* (Cherry Hill, New Jersey: Mack, 1974), p. 233.
90. *Ibid.*, p. 234.
91. Letterhead, March 6, 1995.
92. *Christian Beacon* (Jan. 7, 1937), p. 1.
93. *Brief History*, p. 60.
94. Charles G. Dennison, "Tragedy, Hope and Ambivalence: The History of

Machen had decided during the summer that a fight with the fundamentalists was coming. He emphatically renounced the term "fundamentalist" in a private letter that September.[95] The explosion came in the November meeting of the Independent Board. Machen was not re-elected as president. The deciding vote was cast by Griffiths.[96]

A Shattered Dream

At the 1937 General Assembly of the newly formed Presbyterian Church of America, Rev. Charles Woodbridge recounted the last weeks of Machen's life, and then made an assessment: his expulsion from the Independent Board had killed him. "Dr. Machen told some of us that this was the greatest blow he ever had to stand in his life." He continued: "Six weeks later came the journey to Bismarck. . . . The physician who attended Dr. Machen in his last hours attributed his death largely to the fact that some severe shock had left him in a weakened physical condition. Those of us who were closely associated with Dr. Machen during those last six weeks know what that shock was."[97] A similar story was related by his sister-in-law, Helen Woods Machen, who said that Machen had spoken with her by phone on the night of his dismissal: "They kicked me out as President, it's the hardest blow I've ever had yet, I'm done for now. . . . Now everything is in the hands of men who haven't the slightest notion of the issues at stake . . . everything I've worked for, loved and suffered for has been kicked out too. I feel it's the end for me, this time they've finished me."[98] The "they" were fundamentalists, not liberals.

The 1937 General Assembly marked the secession of McIntire, Buswell, and their premillennial followers, which included a Westminster Seminary second-year student, Francis Schaeffer, who then transferred to the newly established Faith Seminary. The official history of

---

the Orthodox Presbyterian Church, 1936–1962, Part 1," *Mid-America Journal of Theology*, 8 (Fall 1992), pp. 155–56.

95. *Ibid.*, p. 157.

96. *Ibid.*, pp. 157–58.

97. *New York Times* (June 3, 1937); cited in Dallas M. Roark, "J. Gresham Machen: The Doctrinally True Presbyterian Church," *Journal of Presbyterian History*, 43 (June 1965), p. 138.

98. Cited in Hart, *Defending the Faith*, pp. 164–65.

McIntire's Bible Presbyterian Church does not mention the premillennialists' 1936 takeover of the Independent Board. Prior to the 1937 assembly, Buswell had contacted the press and had identified the new denomination as a "wet" Church. It was obvious that he was laying the ground work for a secession.[99] When their candidate for Moderator, dispensationalist Milo Jamison (whose story of the crossed fingers gave me the title of this book), was defeated, they walked out. McIntire explained the reasons for his secession in his newspaper, the *Christian Beacon* (June 10, 1937). He wanted "a freer, more aggressive testimony, with the warmth of personal evangelism in it, as well as a careful teaching of the great system of doctrine set forth in the Scriptures."[100] Marsden is correct: the separatists who created the Bible Presbyterian Church in September of 1938 were heirs of the New School tradition,[101] but they were no longer New School Presbyterians; they were fundamentalists. New School Presbyterianism by 1937 no longer existed as an identifiable movement. Neither did Old School Presbyterianism.

McIntire wrote in 1944: "We must beware of extreme separation. We do not want to dry up like the Orthodox Presbyterian Church, or become a little, small group like the Reformed Episcopal Church."[102] But with the split between McIntire and the original Bible Presbyterian Church in 1956,[103] the Bible Presbyterian Church began its march into invisibility to the general public. In 1967, he wrote a book in which he claimed that only the Bible Presbyterian Church still maintained Machen's original commitment. He failed to mention

---

99. Hutchinson, *History*, p. 236.

100. Cited in *ibid.*, p. 237.

101. George M. Marsden, "The New School Heritage and Presbyterian Fundamentalism," *Pressing Toward the Mark: Essays Commemorating Fifty Years of the Orthodox Presbyterian Church*, edited by Charles G. Dennison and Richard C. Gamble (Philadelphia: Committee for the Historian of the Orthodox Presbyterian Church, 1986), p. 179. Cf. Marsden, "Perspective on the Division of 1937," *ibid.*

102. Cited in Hutchinson, *History*, p. 244.

103. It changed its name to the Columbus Synod of the Presbyterian Church, then to the Evangelical Presbyterian Church (1961), and then united with the Reformed Presbyterian Church in North America (General Synod) to become the Reformed Presbyterian Church, Evangelical Synod (1965).

Machen's removal from the Independent Board by McIntire's colleagues in 1936. "This is the denomination which has continued to join the issue in the struggle over the Auburn Affirmation, the reorganization of Princeton Seminary, the formation of the Independent Board for Presbyterian Foreign Missions, the ecclesiastical trials of 1936. . . ."[104] He dismissed the Orthodox Presbyterian Church as a defender of the Christian Reformed Church's tradition. It was run by the "group that wanted a different kind of church. . . ."[105]

The conflict, Woodbridge said, had been "independency versus historic Presbyterianism." And so it had. In self-defense, Machen had publicly adopted the New School's nineteenth-century theory of ecclesiastically independent ministries. That view led, step by step, to the destruction of the Old School in 1936.

Arthur F. Perkins

On the day Machen died, Rev. Arthur F. Perkins' funeral was held in Wisconsin. He died three days before Machen did. A year earlier he had been in good health. He was an even more obvious victim of the Presbyterian power religion. He had operated a summer camp for children in Wisconsin. He was a premillennialist Presbyterian pastor. He was also opposed to the modernists. He had made the mistake of charging young people $3.50 a week instead of the $12 charged by the presbytery's camp. This brought down the wrath of his presbytery, which announced:

> Your committee is of the opinion that the plans in process of promotion under the name of CRESCENT LAKE BIBLE FELLOWSHIP are quite unwise, unethical and divisive (as well as positively contrary to our vows as presbyters, looking toward the peace, unity and purity of the church).[106]

In vain did he protest that the camp was not a deliberately rival camp, just a place for children to have Bible studies and have fun. It

---

104. Carl McIntire, *The Death of a Church* (Collingswood, New Jersey: Christian Beacon Press, 1967), p. 165.

105. *Ibid.*, p. 164.

106. [Carrie Fenton], *A Costly Dream at Crescent Lake and Lake Lundgren* (Salem, Oregon: Panther, 1979), p. 59.

was non-denominational. It was not run through his local church. That, of course, was the liberals' whole point in the summer of 1936. He refused to close it, and he refused to resign from the Independent Board. For this he was suspended.[107] His health declined sharply after this.[108] He died in late December, possibly as the result of a seemingly minor head injury.[109]

The deaths of Machen and Perkins—one an Old School Presbyterian intellectual and the other a fundamentalist Presbyterian evangelist—are representative of the fate of conservative Northern Presbyterianism. But there was another representative figure: Clarence E. Macartney.

The Eloquent Preacher Who Shut Up

Macartney remained behind. He also remained silent. On March 8, 1939, an essay by him was published in the modernist periodical, *Christian Century*. It was titled "Warm Hearts and Steady Faith." The editor's subtitle announced: "Eighth Article in the Series 'How My Mind Has Changed in This Decade.'" He insisted that "I have experienced no emotional or intellectual change in the last ten years. Of course, I have had widening experiences, and perhaps here and there the emphasis has altered; but as regards what Coleridge called the 'constituent' doctrines of the faith, I am conscious of no change."[110] That he would quote Coleridge rather than the Westminster standards is revealing.

He then spent two pages reminiscing about his early years. Of his leadership in the fundamentalist controversy, he said only that there was "no bitterness in his spirit." He referred to many harsh letters he had received from liberals and modernists during the fight. But regard-

---

107. His defense attorney was Rev. Harry Rimmer, who was well-known as a fundamentalist Presbyterian author and speaker. Rimmer was a creationist, though a "gap theorist" in the *Scofield Reference Bible* tradition (Gen. 1:1–2). See Henry R. Morris, *History of Modern Creationism* (San Diego, California: Master, 1984), pp. 58, 88–92.

108. *A Costly Dream*, p. 60.

109. *Ibid.*, p. 95.

110. Clarence Edward Macartney, "Warm Hearts and Steady Faith," *Christian Century* (March 8, 1939), p. 315.

ing the theological and ecclesiastical issues he had raised for over a decade and a half, he was silent. He spoke only of his joy in preaching sermons and running his "Tuesday noon meeting for business men." He then cited James McCosh, the president of Princeton, in McCosh's evaluation of his brother-in-law's ministry, who "was not deep and metaphysical." McCosh said, "They go to hear him because they like to have their hearts warmed."[111] That was New School Presbyterianism in 1869. The problem was, it was now 1939.

He warned against the reduced unity of witness within denominations. He spoke of the "tragic expulsion" of Machen. He pled for the legitimacy of localism: "More and more, I despair of getting a united witness from churches which embrace in their point of view and preaching almost every religious opinion. Therefore I value less the whole ecclesiastical structure, and feel that more and more for the true witness to the gospel and the Kingdom of God we must depend upon the particular local church, the individual minister and the individual Christian."[112] This was the cry of despair of an outvoted old man at the end of a war—a surrender to Congregational polity in the name of localism. He neglected to deal with the obvious issue, *succession*, point five of the covenant. The question in 1939 was this: What will happen to the faithful local congregation's witness after the death or retirement of today's evangelical pastor? The curricula of the seminaries would determine that in Presbyterianism. That meant neo-orthodoxy. Emil Brunner was serving as a guest professor of systematic theology at Princeton at the time of the publication of Macartney's article. [113]

Macartney rejoiced in the swing away from "the extreme modernist position toward what may be described as the conservative position."[114] Here was the grand illusion of those who remained behind: that Barth, Brunner, and neo-orthodoxy were positive replacements for modernism, that they were not offering, in Van Til's subsequent phrase, a new modernism.[115] This illusion rested on a false assump-

---

111. *Ibid.*, p. 317.
112. *Ibid.*
113. *Brief History*, p. 22.
114. Macartney, "Warm Hearts," p. 318.
115. Cornelius Van Til, *The New Modernism: An Appraisal of the Theology of Barth and Brunner* (Philadelphia: Presbyterian and Reformed, 1947).

tion: that theological Progressivism's Kantian phenomenal realm of social gospel politics was inherently far more apostate than neo-orthodoxy's Kantian noumenal realm of personal encounter with a Christ who does not speak objective propositional truth in history. Both positions were equally opposed to the Christian doctrine that God has spoken definitively to man in the texts of the Bible in ways that can be categorized into such propositional statements as judicially binding creeds and confessions.

Macartney took a few mild swipes at the ecumenical movement, and then ended his essay with the doctrine of eternity. "In the last ten years I have emphasized more and more the doctrine of immortality and the future life." We have all, irrespective of our theologies, neglected "this great doctrine."[116] He never spoke a truer word. Had the conservatives in every denomination from 1869 onward screened every candidate for the eldership with questions regarding the reality of hell, the modernists would have had a heck of a time capturing the American churches. He was equally correct about this: "Certainly in the church today there seems to be a general conspiracy to keep silent about the future life. . . . The failure to sound the note of the future life has made much of our preaching secular and commonplace." But by 1939 his warning was too late by exactly seventy years.

A beaten general, he would never again launch another attack or participate in one. As one biographer says, after 1939, he concentrated on his preaching. He attended presbytery meetings only infrequently, making token appearances at best. "This was ironical, indeed, for the one who had been recognized as the unquestioned leader of the conservative forces within the church and a former moderator of the General Assembly."[117] On the contrary, there was nothing ironical about it. He fully understood the terms of surrender. He would collect his pension; for this, he would pay the required price: silence. Those who stayed behind with him also honored the agreement, as surely as Robert E. Lee's defeated troops honored his. Loetscher wrote in 1954: "The termination of the judicial cases in 1936 marked

---

116. Macartney, "Warm Hearts," p. 319.
117. C. Allyn Russell, "Clarence E. Macartney: Prince of the Pulpit," *Journal of Presbyterian History*, 52 (Spring 1974), p. 56.

the virtual cessation to date of theological controversy within the Church's judicatories. In spite of important internal diversities, the Church since 1936 has enjoyed the longest period of peace since the reunion of 1869."[118]

Henry van Dyke once contemptuously dismissed the conservatives: "They are not great theologians, but they have a tremendous sense of the value of real estate."[119] As they proved in 1936, his assessment was correct, but it was even more true of the liberals, whose theology was far more earth-bound. Liberals, after all, went to civil court to keep the local church property that the seceders had to leave behind. Nevertheless, one by one, the conservatives abandoned Machen and his ever-shrinking band of confessional die-hards. They kept their pulpits, but they lost the denomination.

In 1937, Robert E. Speer retired on his 70th birthday, the maximum age limit for secretaries of Church boards, as required by the General Assembly.[120] In 1938, Lewis Mudge, second academically behind Speer at Princeton University in 1889, retired from his position as Stated Clerk.[121] In 1956, Princeton Seminary named its magnificent new library building in honor of Speer.[122]

Conclusion

The theological issue in Machen's eyes after 1915 had always been simple: Christianity vs. liberalism. This meant *confession*. He chose to remain in the Church until a split was precipitated by the liberals. This meant *sanctions*. He knew by 1929 that there was no possibility that the Church would return to conservative evangelicalism, let alone

---

118. Lefferts A. Loetscher, *The Broadening Church: a study of theological issues in the presbyterian church since 1869* (Philadelphia: University of Pennsylvania Press, 1954), p. 155.

119. Cited in Tertius van Dyke, *Henry van Dyke: A Biography* (New York: Harper & Bros., 1935), p. 375.

120. W. Reginald Wheeler, *A Man Sent from God: A Biography of Robert E. Speer* (n.p.: Revell, 1956), p. 251.

121. *Minutes of the General Assembly, 1938*, p. 131.

122. The second library building, completed in 1994, bears the name of Henry R. Luce, founder of *Time, Life, Fortune,* and *Sports Illustrated*, and a member of Skull & Bones.

Calvinistic orthodoxy, in his lifetime. He had been warned by Warfield in 1921 that a split, even with the conservatives in the majority, could not save the Presbyterian Church. The rottenness of the wood had progressed too far. Dry rot—Prohibitionism plus modernism—had set in. The historic Calvinist faith of the Church no longer was respected, even in 1921. Warfield understood that history marches forward, that institutions rarely, if ever, can be persuaded to return to the traditional ways from which they have departed.

But it was not just confession and sanctions. It was also point two: *hierarchy* (representation). The modernists fully understood this principle. Hart writes: "Yet one of the curious features of the Presbyterian controversy is why the denomination devoted so much energy to silencing what was at best a small and peripheral movement."[123] There is nothing curious about it. The modernists needed a public sacrifice, one that would represent the death of the opposition. After 1925, Machen was the acknowledged intellectual spokesman of the entire American fundamentalist movement, as well as the Old School, the only intellectual of the historical Protestant tradition that seriously threatened modernist scholarship. The modernists understood what every power-seeking bully knows from grade school days: if you can beat to a pulp your most prominent opponent in full public view, throwing him and his followers off the playground and stealing all of their marbles, you will have no further trouble with the other boys. You can then extort a percentage of their marbles on a regular basis by rigging the rules. Either they play by your rules or they are kept off the playground by your associates. Most boys want access to the playground far more than they want to keep all of their marbles. By 1967, however, Presbyterian conservatives had completely lost their marbles.

The liberals did not have any commitment to be gentle, fair, or considerate of Machen's wing of the Church. There was nothing moderate about them, once they had gained power. Tolerance then meant toleration of this transfer of control. The liberals had played the game of "mental reservation" with the word "toleration," just as they had

---

123. Hart, *Defending the Faith*, p. 157.

with the Westminster Confession. In 1934, the first game ended. The second game did not end until the Confessional revision of 1967. In 1936, through the imposition of sanctions, the Presbyterian Church was made safe, in Malcolm Muggeridge's marvelous phrase, for moderate men of all shades of opinion.[124]

What no doubt bothered Machen was that so many of his former spiritual colleagues remained behind in the Church. Confrontation by confrontation, the ranks had thinned: the 1926 General Assembly, Princeton's 1929 reorganization, the 1933 Independent Board. Men refused to acknowledge what he had warned them all in 1923: if the liberals captured the Church, it would be immoral to remain inside. His conservative and orthodox former supporters had not gone into print calling him an extremist in 1923 or thereafter, but they refused to leave with him. They demonstrated by their refusal to depart that they had not really believed him when he wrote that refusal to leave "would mean the most terrible bloodguiltiness which it is possible to conceive."[125]

In 1922, in the aftermath of W. H. Griffith Thomas' accusations that the foreign mission field had been infiltrated by modernists, an Old School member of the Presbyterian Foreign Missions Board, John Fox, wrote a letter to Speer. His goal was to provoke Speer to a stronger public stand against modernism. He made this observation: "What a man will not fight for, what he will not part with his best friend for, when necessary, has usually a slighter and slighter hold on his mind."[126] No better epitaph than this exists for the evangelical wing of the Presbyterian Church, U.S.A. Theology had lost its hold on the minds of good men. Yet in Fox's case, his personal epitaph was different. Just before he died, he called Henry Sloane Coffin to his bedside[127]—his old opponent, the president of Union Seminary, the

---

124. Malcolm Muggeridge, *Chronicles of Wasted Time, Chronicle I: The Green Stick* (New York: Morrow, 1973), p. 168.

125. Machen, *Christianity and Liberalism*, p. 166.

126. Fox to Speer, June 22, 1922; cited in James Alan Patterson, Robert E. Speer and the Crisis of the American Protestant Missionary Movement, 1920–1937 (Ph.D. dissertation, Princeton Theological Seminary, 1980), p. 133.

127. Morgan Phelps Noyes, *Henry Sloane Coffin: The Man and His Ministry* (New York: Charles Scribner's Sons, 1964), p. 85.

living incarnation of both theological liberalism and successful bureaucratic strategy in the Presbyterian Church. This, too, was representative of what happened to the Old School in Northern Presbyterianism, 1922 to 1936. It died, leaving the liberals in control over succession. The liberals inherited the Old School's institutional legacy, and the New School's as well. They had achieved their long-term goal.

But history moves forward, and succession continues. The heirs of the modernists have seen their inheritance dissipate since 1965: the steady shrinking of mainline Presbyterianism and the other mainline Protestant denominations, and their expulsion from the American Establishment for non-payment of dues. In the power religion of democracy, covenant renewal is by voting. Mainline Protestantism can no longer deliver the votes. The Christian Right can.

Not believing in the infallibility of the Scriptures, the liberals paid no attention to the Psalms, especially this one: "And he gave them their request; but sent leanness into their souls" (Ps. 106:15). They gained the inheritance through deception. "Bread of deceit is sweet to a man; but afterwards his mouth shall be filled with gravel" (Prov. 20:17). Negative sanctions have come. The crucial issue is sanctions.

Addendum

For over three decades, I have been asked a question by members of the Orthodox Presbyterian Church: "What if Machen had lived?" For an OPC member in the 1960's, though far less so today, this question was analogous to the one asked of historians, especially by Southerners, in the generation after the Civil War: "What if Lincoln had lived?" The professionally correct answer is: "Nobody knows." The theologically correct answer is: "His death was predestined before the foundation of the world." We cannot know what Machen would have accomplished or what those around him would have accomplished. But we can be fairly certain regarding what he would not have accomplished: launching the new Reformation that he had long prayed for.

We do know what Machen had accomplished by the time of his death. First, he had served as an academic spokesman for conservative academic Protestantism, which was about to enter a wilderness period that lasted for a generation. Those few fundamentalists who knew about him, 1924 to 1936, respected his stand for the Bible and against modernism, but they knew little or nothing about his Calvinism or his views on apologetics, politics, and economics. They were vaguely in agreement with his theology, but his mind-set was basically opposed to fundamentalist pietism, as his 1913 essay on "Christianity and Culture" had indicated. He was no pietist, no withdrawer from culture.

Second, he had been the creator of a tiny Calvinist denomination. But his leadership role here had not been primarily as a builder but as a defender of a besieged theological tradition. He was a Moses who led a Remnant out of Egypt. Was he prepared to serve as a Joshua? Few men can do both; the number of Martin Luthers in history is limited.

Third, he had been trained to be a scholar, not an administrator. He had founded Westminster Seminary. He would have been forced to work hard to keep Westminster afloat economically. He and John Murray were the last of the Old School theologians in 1937. Murray would have taught systematic theology. Van Til would have taught apologetics. Machen might have taught a few courses in New Testament, but Stonehouse was fully capable, if not more capable. Machen's job would have been clear: to raise the money to supply the next generation of OPC pastors. There would have been little time to write another book as scholarly as *The Origin of Paul's Religion* or *The Virgin Birth of Christ*.

Fourth, the denomination would have looked to him for general leadership, but how successful he would have been as a denominational organizer and builder is unknown. He had not been trained to do such a thing. His expulsion from the Independent Board's Board had made it clear that Presbyterian fundamentalists would not tolerate his personal leadership in building a new denomination.

Meanwhile, his opponents were also about to enter into their wilderness journey, though in far greater outward comfort. They were about to become passé. Barth would be answered by Van Til in the late 1940's; it is unlikely that Machen's Old School Scottish rationalism was fit for that task. As for Harry Emerson Fosdick, he had to content himself with being theologian for the *Reader's Digest* and serving as John the Baptist for Norman Vincent Peale. Lesson: God is not mocked.

CONCLUSION TO PART 3

At present we are inarticulate; we know the riches of the gospel; we wonder at those who have it already at hand and yet are content instead with the weak and beggarly elements. When will God raise up the man of His choice to give His message powerfully to the world? We cannot say. But the truth is not dead, and God has not deserted His church. Behind all the darkness and perplexity of the present time we can discern, on the basis of the promises of God, the dawn of a better day. There may come a time, sooner than we can tell, when again we cry in the church, as every redeemed soul cries even now: 'The old things are passed away; behold they are become new.'

J. Gresham Machen (1923)[1]

With these words, Machen ended his sermon, "The Present Issue in the Church." It was delivered on December 30, 1923, while he was serving as stated supply (not pastor) in the First Presbyterian Church of Princeton. It was the fifth in a series that ended the year. It was the sermon that persuaded Henry van Dyke to write his famous press release, thereby catapulting Machen into the national spotlight.

That generation of Americans soon received an answer to Machen's question: "When will God raise up the man of His choice to give His message powerfully to the world?" It did not, however, see the brighter day that he hoped might soon dawn. It saw even greater darkness. But great darkness allows bright lights to shine more powerfully.

Machen recognized his problem in 1923: the growing theological darkness had not received a matching increase in the light that was necessary to dispel it. He knew that one man could not supply it. As

---

1. Machen, "The Issue in the Church" (1923); reprinted in Machen, *God Transcendent*, edited by Ned Bernard Stonehouse (Carlisle, Pennsylvania: Banner of Truth Trust, [1949] 1982), p. 51.

a representative, he could lead others, but the Church relies on the division of labor to achieve her God-mandated task (I Cor. 12). Machen in 1923 stood almost alone in the professional world of academic theology, and as time passed, the ranks of those who stood with him thinned.

This was a culture-wide problem for American Protestantism. In his book-long academic Jeremiad, liberal Church historian Winthrop Hudson in 1953 chronicled the loss of vision and dedication of American Protestantism after 1900. He scorned the fundamentalists as backward-looking anachronisms, but he recognized that liberalism had failed. The peak years for American Protestantism, even in the cities, was 1900 to 1920.[2] Yet throughout this period, the churches, and especially Church colleges, were becoming secular, increasingly indistinguishable from the general intellectual milieu around them.[3] There was an intellectual retreat, as well as a loss of Church discipline.[4] In this sense, theological modernism surrendered intellectually to political and humanistic modernism.[5]

This did not apply to Princeton Seminary. It still defended late-eighteenth-century or, at best, early nineteenth-century Scottish common-sense philosophy. It was out of date, both theologically and epistemologically, and proud of it. Had it not been for the presence of Vos on the faculty, the Princeton of Machen's era could proclaim, echoing Charles Hodge, that "a new idea never originated in this Seminary."[6] But the Old Princeton, like the Old School, had not reproduced itself. When this happens, a movement dies. This is what happened to the Old Princeton in 1929. The postmillennialism of Princeton was replaced by amillennialism at Westminster.[7] The

---

2. Winthrop Hudson, *The Great Tradition of the American Churches* (New York: Harper & Bros., 1953), p. 195.
3. *Ibid.*, pp. 197–98.
4. *Ibid.*, p. 217.
5. *Ibid.*, p. 218.
6. Cited in A. A. Hodge, *The Life of Charles Hodge, Professor in the Theological Seminary Princeton N. J.* (New York: Charles Scribner's Sons, 1880), p. 521.
7. The premillennialism of Carl McIntire's Faith Seminary was a New School heritage. The postmillennialism of John Murray was not evident until his lectures on Romans 11 in 1964 and the publication of the second volume of his

Princeton apologetic was never taught at Westminster; it was replaced by Van Til's presuppositionalism and (later) Robert Knudsen's Dooyeweerdianism.[8] These developments were imports from the Christian Reformed Church. Although Machen loved to say that Princeton's tradition lived on at Westminster, this was no longer the case after 1936. Princeton had failed to reproduce. Something had to replace it.

The Old Princeton

Throughout the nineteenth century, defenders of Old School Presbyterianism were firmly entrenched at Princeton Seminary and were dominant in the Philadelphia Presbytery. At the beginning, the founders' social vision had been shaped by the older aristocratic, hierarchical worldview, as had the Westminster standards. Nineteenth-century America did not prove to be favorable to such an aristocratic outlook. Democratic theory rapidly replaced the older aristocratic legacy in the Jacksonian era, beginning in the late 1820's.[9] But this shift did not affect the fundamental legacy of the U.S. Constitution, which can fairly be described as right-wing Enlightenment thought: decentralist, voluntarist, and anti-State power—Jackson's ideology. This was the social thought of Adam Smith and the Scottish Enlightenment, from which was born Scottish common-sense realism, the philosophy of Princeton Seminary. It was easy—natural, one might say—for Princeton to be associated loosely and unofficially with the social thought of independent capitalism.

The ideal of the independent capitalist had never been absent in the Scotch-Irish communities in the Carolinas. It remained powerful

---

Epistle to the Romans in 1965. His classroom notes on eschatology in the senior systematics course appeared to be amillennial. I audited both courses at the same time and was struck by the incongruity.

8. Knudsen did not write much, and his influence on campus was quite limited. Herman Dooyeweerd was a Dutch legal theorist and philosopher. See Dooyeweerd, *In the Twilight of Western Thought* (Philadelphia: Presbyterian & Reformed, 1960); *A New Critique of Theoretical Thought*, 4 vols. (Philadelphia: Presbyterian & Reformed, 1953-58).

9. Paul Johnson, *The Birth of the Modern: World Society, 1815-1830* (New York: HarperCollins*Publishers*, 1991), pp. 929-42.

in the Southern Presbyterian Church after the split from the Northern Presbyterians and long after the Civil War. The premier Old School theologian in the South, Robert L. Dabney, ended his academic career teaching political economy at the University of Texas.[10] The South was never enamored with the economic ideal of the urban colossus. It was the Southern Presbyterian Church that nurtured J. Gresham Machen, even though he lived in urban Baltimore. Machen's social outlook was that of nineteenth-century liberalism: the independent capitalist ideal, although modified by a the ideal of the Southern gentleman. That vision had departed from the America of the 1920's. As George Marsden says, "J. Gresham Machen was an anomaly in that era."[11]

An Anomaly

Something had happened to undermine that earlier version of Scottish liberalism. Three things, actually: historicism, Darwinism, and industrialism-urbanism. The urban growth in the midwestern United States had been unprecedented. In 1830, Chicago was a village of 50 people. In 1900, it was a city of well over 1.5 million.[12] The Progressive movement after 1890 transformed the older Whig liberalism into a new liberalism: centralist, compulsory, and statist. The State was progressively regarded as the primary implement of social transformation and salvation. When the individualistic social Darwinism of Herbert Spencer and William Graham Sumner was replaced by the corporate social Darwinism of Lester Frank Ward and the Progressives, the older liberalism went into decline.

The failure of Old School Presbyterianism to respond effectively to these challenges points to a serious deficiency: the Old School did not possess a biblically integrated world-and-life view. Their apolo-

---

10. His favorite economics text was J. B. Say's. Thomas Cary Johnson, *The Life and Letters of Robert Lewis Dabney* (Richmond, Virginia: Presbyterian Committee of Publication, 1903), p. 445. Say, the modern mythology goes, was refuted by John Maynard Keynes. He wasn't.

11. George M. Marsden, "J. Gresham Machen, History, and Truth," *Westminster Theological Journal*, 42 (Fall 1979), p. 157.

12. Jack Lessinger, *Regions of Opportunity* (New York: Times Books, 1986), p. 36.

getic was a hybrid: Scottish theology of 1646 and Scottish philosophy of 1776. The first tradition was explicitly Calvinist; the second was implicitly Unitarian. When the intellectual world abandoned Scottish common-sense rationalism in the wake of Darwinism and all the other Darwin-based ism's of the twentieth century, this left the Old School with neither a common-ground apologetic method nor a convincing social theory. The new rationalism was not the static rationalism of either idealism or empiricism, where one could appeal either to fixed logic or to objective facts. The new rationalism was the historicism of nationalism, Marxism, Darwinism, and Progressivism, where the laws of society and thought change with the environment, and so do the historically relevant facts. Common-sense rationalism was dismissed as passé—a death sentence in the worldview of the new rationalism.

The New School and the evangelicals did not take the Confession's Calvinism seriously, although they may have been vaguely content with the economics of Adam Smith. They were willing to risk a fight for neither. Presbyterian modernists took neither tradition seriously. They were willing to challenge both—intellectually in the early stages, institutionally after 1933. This left the Old School without steadfast allies within the vast majority of the Presbyterian Church. By 1936, Machen's worldview, like the world that had produced it, was gone with the wind.

Machen was a Calvinist. From at least 1660, Calvinism in the Anglo-American religious universe had been regarded by the intellectual leaders as a threat to common sense. It places God fully in control of everything, yet it insists that man is fully responsible for his own sin. This alone would have made Machen an anomaly.

Western Civilization changed institutionally after the Industrial Revolution. It changed intellectually after Darwin. The second half of the nineteenth century was the turning point of this transformation. The old theological world had begun to crumble: a more comfortable intellectual world that was confident regarding a presumed harmony between the Bible and natural science, the Bible and historical evidence, morality and prosperity,[13] religion and civilization. All of this

---

13. In 1889, the faculty of the University of Texas asked Dabney to deliver

was being called into question. This loss of faith offered a challenge: the opportunity to offer a systematically biblical alternative to the dying hybrid. The Old School did not respond to this challenge. It stuck with the worldview and methodology of the dying hybrid, and did so in the name of Calvinism. Losing this unique opportunity, it also lost the war for orthodoxy within Northern Presbyterianism.

The Theological Issue: Propositional Truth in History

God has spoken in history. What He has said is true for all time and beyond time. This does not negate the fact that He has revealed Himself in history, by word and deed. The problem men face is that they are time-bound creatures of God. They must make sense of the past in terms of permanent truths, yet these truths were revealed to men in history.

This is the problem of orthodox theology: systematic theology (permanent propositional truth) and biblical theology (historically revealed truth).[14] It is the problem of creedal revision in Church history: making something that is mostly true propositionally even more true. It is the problem of personal responsibility: in relation to permanent standards, but also in relation to one's own time. As time goes on, more is given because more has been learned. To whom much is given, much is expected (Luke 12:47–48).

Old Princeton emphasized systematic theology from the its founding in 1812. Its critics in the early twentieth century pointed out that the faculty paid too little attention to the problems of biblical theology.[15] Biblical theology was regarded by liberals as the child of histori-

---

the commencement discourse. Dabney selected this subject: "Religion and Morality, the Indispensable Supports for Political Prosperity." Johnson, *Dabney*, p. 448. The address is reprinted in Dabney, *Discussions*, vol. 3, *Philosophical*, edited by C. R. Vaughan (Harrisonburg, Virginia: Sprinkle, [1892]), pp. 536–50. It appears just before the chapter on "The Standard of Ordination." This is a long-dead world, at the University of Texas, surely, but also in the Southern Presbyterian Church.

14. Richard Gaffin, "Systematic Theology and Biblical Theology," in *The New Testament Student and Theology*, edited by John H. Skilton (n.p.: Presbyterian & Reformed, 1976), ch. 3.

15. Gerald Birney Smith, Shirley Jackson Case, and D. D. Luckinbill, "Theological Scholarship at Princeton," *American Journal of Theology*, 17 (1913), pp. 95,

cal criticism. In an era dominated by the myth of evolution—in nature and in history—this was a telling criticism. The era after Darwin but before World War II worshipped the historical method, even though there was no agreement about what constituted this method. Princeton's emphasis on systematic theology made its task that much more difficult. It needn't have been.

There was one man who might have made a significant difference in the battle against modernism, a man whose contributions were ignored by all sides, although his office was within walking distance of Warfield's and then Machen's: Geerhardus Vos. He joined the faculty of Princeton in 1893 to fill the newly created chair in Old Testament biblical theology—the same year that Briggs was suspended from the ministry because of his inaugural address for Union's chair in biblical theology. A member of the Christian Reformed Church, he was not directly involved in the Presbyterian conflict. He remained at Princeton until his retirement in 1932. He avoided rhetoric in his writings. He surely was not a skilled stylist.[16] Yet it was in his writings that the biblical alternative to modernism appeared: a thoroughly orthodox alternative to the relativistic biblical theology of the higher critics. Vos understood that there need be no contradiction between systematic theology and biblical theology, between definitive truth and history.

His intellectual heir, Cornelius Van Til, demonstrated throughout his career at Westminster Seminary that there is an irreconcilable logical contradiction between humanism's version of systematic theology—static rationalism—and its version of biblical theology: historical process. As Van Til put it, the fixed logic of Parmenides cannot be shown to relate in any way to Heraclitus' historical flux. It is only the fixed revelation of God in history—the Bible—that can reconcile logic and history.

Vos was not assigned to teach apologetics, although his discoveries offered a way out for the Old School's apologists. They did not un-

---

100; cited in D. G. Hart, "Doctor Fundamentalis": An Intellectual Biography of J. Gresham Machen, 1881-1937 (Ph.D. dissertation, Johns Hopkins University, 1988), p. 101.

16. Transitional sentences were rarely used by Vos, nor were headings, subheadings, and other aids to readers.

derstand the magnitude of what Vos was getting at. They did not appropriate for their own battles his monumental discoveries regarding the progress of revelation in the Old Testament, or as he called it, "the history of special revelation."[17] He was the most original theologian that Princeton ever had on its faculty, but his colleagues ignored the high-caliber ammunition that he kept turning out, year after year. Here was a man with a Ph.D. in Arabic studies who had taught everything from Greek grammar to systematic theology at Calvin Seminary (1888–1893),[18] yet he remained on the sidelines. His wife, author of the deservedly famous *Child's Story Bible*, is the only Vos most Old School heirs have ever read.[19] The Old School labored in vain to overcome the most effective intellectual challenge of the then-confident humanists: the irreconcilability of the supposedly evolutionary historical process and the ideal of Calvinist systematic theology—fixed propositional truth.

Without widespread institutional faith in fixed propositional truth, on what judicial basis can anyone be lawfully excluded from the Church? Only on the basis of institutional convenience. It was convenient in 1936 for the deniers of fixed propositional truth to remove Machen from their midst.

Personalism: The Neglected Alternative

It is a commonplace observation that most heresies are illegitimate extensions of some biblical truth. A similar observation should be made about the Old School in general and Princeton Seminary in particular. Its great strength was its unswerving commitment to the integrity of the Bible. Its great weakness was its equally unswerving commitment to eighteenth-century rationalism as a means of defending the Bible. Princeton's defense of the faith indulged in a myth: the primacy

---

17. Richard B. Gaffin, "Introduction," *Redemptive History and Interpretation: The Shorter Writings of Geerhardus Vos*, edited by Gaffin (Phillipsburg, New Jersey: Presbyterian and Reformed, 1980), p. xiv.

18. *Ibid.*, p. x.

19. Melvin Vos, Geerhardus' grandson, told me in 1963 that the family received virtually all of its book royalty income from his grandmother's book, almost nothing from his grandfather's books.

of the intellect. It imitated the educational bureaucracy created by medieval scholastics. It abandoned the biblical model: apprenticeship.

Apprenticeship vs. Credentialism

Presbyterian Church rules have always required candidates for the ministry to have a college degree and a seminary degree; only special exceptions were allowed (such as in Briggs' case, who never graduated from college or seminary).[20] Had the Old School adopted apprenticeship for the training of its ministerial candidates, the Western frontier of the United States might not have fallen to the Methodists, Baptists, Disciples of Christ, and Cumberland Presbyterians after 1800. Had the Old School used the apprenticeship system, the aura of credentialism might not have engulfed the denomination. The impersonalism of the educational establishment replaced the personalism of the apprenticeship system. Responsibility became impersonal—a system of formal examinations—rather than personal: one on one.

One thing is certain: it would have been far more difficult for the liberals to have executed their strategy of subversion had the Presbyterian Church not operated colleges and seminaries. From the beginning of the university system in the late middle ages, the college has been the equivalent of a gigantic sign on the front of the Church: "Come and get us!" Heretics, apostates, and humanists have taken advantage of this offer very seriously for nine centuries. The commitment to neutral academic methodology inherent in every institution of higher learning makes it easy for subversives to pick it off. Wrap a subversive hidden agenda in the swaddling clothes of common-ground rationalism, and it can pass through every known academic barrier. Wolves in sheepskin invade the flock. The crucial authority granted to such institutions by the Church, the State, and the professions hands over to virtually autonomous bureaucrats the ideological future of the organizations that have substituted an earned degree for on-the-job appren-

---

20. Another example was the conservative leader, Mark A. Matthews. Robert K. Churchill, *Lest We Forget: A Personal Reflection on the Formation of The Orthodox Presbyterian Church* (Philadelphia: Committee of the Historian of the Orthodox Presbyterian Church, [1986]), p. 24.

ticeship. To capture the robes of authority—black robes or white smocks—a movement needs only to capture the universities.

The problem with this strategy is that the movement will then succumb to the universities. The means of subversion become the end of subversion. A civilization that transfers to scholars dressed in black academic robes the authority to screen its future leaders has handed itself over to the bureaucrats who run every known system of formal education. The academic bureaucrats who control who gets into and out of the classroom will eventually re-create society in their own image. It happens every time: in Pharaonic Egypt, in Mandarin China, and in the modern world. When an organization authorizes written examinations as a substitute for on-the-job training as its preferred method for screening future employees, its bureaucratization becomes as inevitable as anything social theory can postulate.

Sanctions affect performance. If you create a system of rewards and punishments, those participating under these sanctions will shape their behavior to maximize their return, given whatever constraints the system imposes. You get what you pay for. If you tell young men that entry into the ministry is based on passing written exams in institutions of higher education, they will spend most of their time and effort mastering the techniques necessary for passing the exams. The churches must select candidates from a limited supply of survivors. Problem: there is no evidence showing that passing written exams prepares men to pastor churches. There is considerable evidence based on actual Church growth rates that these skills are inversely related: the greater the skill in passing formal exams, the less the skill in pastoring. Additionally, there is a positive correlation between the ability to pass written exams and political liberalism. As Ladd and Ferree concluded in 1982, based on a detailed survey of the opinions of 1,112 members of American seminary faculties, "Those who teach in schools of religion and theology resemble fairly closely a larger community of *academic humanists* of which they are a part."[21] Of those responding, 50 percent or more described themselves as politically liberal. The Epis-

---

21. Everett Carll Ladd and G. Donald Ferree, Jr., "The Politics of American Theology Faculty," *This World*, 2 (Summer 1982), p. 84.

copalians were the highest: 78 percent. Then came Methodists (69 percent) and Presbyterians (63 percent). The only faculties below 50 percent were Southern Baptists (32 percent), other Baptists (17 percent), and Pentecostals (7 percent).[22] Conclusion: to avoid producing liberal pastors, take great care to send students to low-prestige educational institutions. This is not a Presbyterian-type conclusion.

Those students who seek access to a seminary education must first prove themselves skilled at passing collegiate exams designed and imposed by politically correct liberals, atheists, feminists, and New Age mystics on the college campus. The issue, as always, is sanctions. *The Church's preliminary screening process is placed in the hands of the Church's mortal enemies. This has been going on for nine centuries.* You get what you pay for, and hierarchical churches pay ministerial candidates for passing academic exams. The operational rule is: "Those who baptize infants have been academically certified by liberals." So, hierarchical churches get their choice: liberalism or stagnation in the early stage; liberalism with stagnation in the middle stage; liberalism with contraction in the final stage. The Presbyterian Church, U.S.A., is now in the final stage.

The enemies of the Church are clever. They search for weak points and attack them, even as a pack of wolves attacks stragglers in a herd of deer. The targeted animal kicks for a while, but it is doomed. *The weak point in churches that baptize infants is their intellectual pride.* "Our ministers have more academic degrees from humanist-accredited universities than yours do," they brag. There are two possible responses: (1) "They're a lot more liberal, too." (2) "You don't have very many churches to employ them, and the ones you have are tiny." This is the inevitable result of substituting seminary education for pastoral apprenticeship: a choice between the prevailing climate of academic opinion and growth.

The Question of Positive Sanctions

Throughout this book, I have stressed the question of negative sanctions. Without them, it is impossible to police the boundaries of

---

22. "Theology Faculty: How They Compare," *ibid.*, p. 72.

any organization. But negative sanctions are not sufficient. Eternity is more than the lake of fire; it is also the New Heaven and New Earth. The two realms are equally ultimate in terms of duration, but not in terms of influence. Grace is not equally ultimate with sin; it is far greater. This is the message of the Bible, from Genesis 3 to Revelation 22.

Machen and the Old School faced a problem. It is the problem faced by every movement: how to persuade people to accept your ideas and your program rather than someone else's. Although the language of marketing is foreign to ecclesiastical etiquette, marketing is surely a form of persuasion. The Old School had a marketing problem. They never solved it.

As theologians, the Old School approached the problem as if persuasion were primarily intellectual. The assumption of the primacy of the intellect can be found in the writings of Charles Hodge, Warfield, and Machen. It was the bedrock presupposition of the Old Princeton's apologetics. But it is not a biblical presupposition. Grace is comprehensive; it encompasses reason, but it is not confined to it or defined primarily in terms of it. This is why the sacraments are equally ultimate with preaching as a mark of the Church. This is why Calvin said that the sacrament of the Lord's Supper should be taken "very often, and at least once a week."[23] Yearly communion he dismissed "as a veritable invention of the devil, whoever was instrumental in introducing it."[24]

The benefits of salvation are more than intellectual. The blessings of grace are more than doctrinal. Yet the Old School saw progress in history as primarily doctrinal. They chose not to present their case for orthodoxy in terms other than intellectual-doctrinal. The problem is, only a few churches in history have ever been extensively doctrinal in their appeal; Presbyterianism is the most notable. Within Presbyterianism, the Old School was the most self-consciously doctrinal. This led to the creation of a movement that did not offer effective motivational appeals outside of the narrow confines of doctrine.

---

23. John Calvin, *Institutes of the Christian Religion* (1559), IV:XVII:43. Ford Lewis Battles translation (Philadelphia: Westminster Press, 1960), p. 1421.

24. *Ibid.*, IV:XVII:46, p. 1424.

There is a rule in scientific advertising: "Lead with the benefits; follow with the features." List the features only to prove the benefits. The public is not interested in features that cannot be translated into benefits. This is as true of the Church-going public as any other identifiable market. The tendency is for manufacturers to focus on the features and assume that the potential buyers will see the benefits. This is the engineer's illusion. He thinks that the features are the benefits. The public does not care about features unless these features bring benefits.

There are benefits to good theology, a doctrine of the escape from hell being high on the list. This was a promise that was easier to sell in Machen's day than in ours, and surely easier in Warfield's day. But Baptists can promise this, too. What was the **Unique Service Proposition**—the USP—of Old School Presbyterianism? What was the one great benefit that was the exclusive monopoly, or close to it, of Old School Presbyterianism? The Old School Presbyterian leaders, being theologians, answered: *rigorous Confessional theology*. The general public yawned. So did the Presbyterian public. (They still do.)

Machen kept raising the costs. As with anything else, the higher the cost, the less is demanded. Machen priced Old School Presbyterianism out of the market. He did not come up with a benefit other than rigorous theology, for which there is always a narrow market. He was trying to sell a theological-institutional system to two million laymen and 9,500 ordained teaching elders when he could not sell it to the minority faction on the faculty of Princeton Seminary or to anyone on the faculty of Princeton University, the Northern Presbyterian Church's most prestigious institution after 1900.

The liberals promised two major benefits: institutional peace and missionary activity. The evangelical majority in the Church wanted both. Their ability and willingness to grasp the subtleties of theology were limited. The larger the Church, the more limited this ability and willingness. The higher the ecclesiastical stakes, the less interested the majority became. *The higher the stakes, the higher the costs.* They wanted orthodoxy, but they wanted it cheap. The evangelicals were unwilling to pay the escalating price. When Machen and his colleagues began to speak of hundreds of heretics in Presbyterian pulpits, the specter of never-ending heresy trials loomed before them, with General Assembly having to hear each one on appeal, probably several times. They did not suspect that the Presbyterian system would accommodate wholesale de-frockings. The liberals had insisted that this was not judicially possible in Presbyterianism. The conservatives did not learn differently until 1935, when the liberals began the process. This information came too late for the conservative middle to respond. They learned the price of peace under liberalism: silence regarding theology and regular financial assessments from local congregations, i.e., *closed mouths and open wallets*.

What are the benefits of theological orthodoxy? What are the benefits that extend beyond the intellectual pleasures of considering in detail the Westminster Confession of Faith? What are the practical benefits? Liberals insisted there are none. Conservatives thought there may be some, but not enough to recommend heresy trials except in exceptional cases—rhetorically exceptional. What Machen lacked —what the Old School lacked—was a theory of covenantal sanctions in history that connects Confessional faithfulness, moral holiness, and cultural triumph in history. Machen hinted at this relationship in his 1913 essay, "Christianity and Culture," but he did not elaborate.[25] He did not show how adherence to ever-more rigorous confessions can lead to Church growth. He did not attempt to argue, let alone prove, that improved Church confessions can and will lead to greater corporate wealth, happiness, and external benefits. He did not discuss Christendom as the cultural manifestation of orthodoxy. As a nineteenth-century Whig liberal, he denied the covenantal relationship between Church creeds and political life. How, then, was he going to persuade two million Presbyterians to pay the costs of an unending stream of heresy trials? He wasn't. He didn't.

Machen's Last Stand

Machen had initiated a break with the denomination on doctrinal grounds. His justification was simple: it is immoral to require God-fearing Christians to subsidize ecclesiastical institutions that have been captured by liars and subtle manipulators who no longer believe even

---

25. Machen, "Christianity and Culture," *Princeton Theological Review*, 11 (Jan. 1913).

the five minimal points of the 1910 Doctrinal Deliverance, let alone the Westminster Confession. The result of his efforts was the creation of a Church which was in the Old School Confessional tradition, but whose membership was vastly smaller than the old denomination's. Its size, of course, meant little to him, just so long as its theological content was sound.

This act of separation began a chain of events which continued to break the conservatives into smaller and smaller fragments, with each new denomination frequently more in conflict with its neighbor than with the original denomination. Ministers and laymen have drifted into such independent bodies in considerable numbers, choosing whichever fine points of Calvinist and dispensational theologies that have seemed logical to them.

The conflict between individual belief and group standards has been resolved by the creedal churches only by denying the legitimacy of existing larger denominations, often by totally rejecting all formal structures linking individual denominations. Reformed Christians—or any other group of Christians—have yet to discover an acceptable *permanent* point midway between a broadly based, but less doctrinally demanding, Church organization, and a doctrinally explicit Protestant local church of few members. The churches, to this extent, are still grappling with the humanists' inescapable dilemma, unity vs. diversity. Rushdoony has observed: "Every philosophy of autonomous man from the Greeks to the present has foundered on the problem of the one and the many, universality and particularity. If the one be affirmed as the ultimate reality, the individuals are swallowed up in the whole. If the many be affirmed, then reality is lost in endless particularity and individuality, and no binding concept has any reality. Thus, the one and the many are in perpetual tension."[26] How, then, can Christians escape this dualism which faces autonomous man?

The doctrinal conflicts within American Presbyterianism, from the inception of the Church until the present, serve as eloquent foot-

---

26. Rousas J. Rushdoony, *Intellectual Schizophrenia: Culture, Crisis, and Education* (Philadelphia: Presbyterian and Reformed, 1961), p. 10.

notes to this inescapable dilemma for men who are not governed by the Bible and by God's Spirit. The tradition of denominational division is not merely the heritage of Luther, but of the fundamental dichotomy of Western thought. There has yet to be a resolution of the conflicts between the authority of conscience and the authority of the institutional Church.

Institutional Purity and Peace

Machen tried to resolve the conflicts by calling for a defensive alliance with premillennialists, Anglicans, Lutherans, and even Roman Catholics.[27] This did not deal with the issue which was to divide the newly created Orthodox Presbyterian Church: How to resolve such differences *institutionally*? It was not enough to have fellowship across denominational traditions; the problem facing the Church was the problem of personal subordination to an institution which is governed by a written confession and written rules of discipline. Which confession? Which rules?

What can be said of Machen's role in the developments in modern American Protestantism? Pearl S. Buck pointed to the age-old institutional problems of cooperation, compromise, and conscience in her assessment of his efforts in the concluding remarks of her obituary on his earthly journey: "Of course what he did not realize was that he could never have lived in a church. As soon as it had become an entity he would have had to compromise with this opinion or that, or more impossible still to him, with a majority opinion, and he would have had to break again with them all. One might say that death was merciful to him, except I have an idea he enjoyed his wars."[28]

Murray Forst Thompson, Machen's old colleague, told me in the spring of 1984 that Mrs. Buck's assessment was incorrect. Machen was tired of the squabbling, he had told Thompson in 1936, and was anxious to get the new denomination into operation. But even if he had lived, the squabbles would have continued. There was no escape. He

---

27. Machen, *Christianity and Liberalism* (New York: Macmillan, 1923), pp. 48ff.
28. Pearl S. Buck, "A Tribute to Dr. Machen," *New Republic* (January 20, 1937), p. 355.

had established a new organization, and problems of cooperation face the members of all organizations. He had never gone into print with any guidelines concerning the biblical way to reconcile the legitimate authority of the human conscience and the legitimate authority of God's monopolistic institution, the Church. The problem is always the sin of autonomy. The divisiveness of the self-professed autonomous conscience is always a problem for institutions. At the same time, the implicit tyranny of the self-professed autonomous institution is always a problem for consciences—at least for ethically unseared consciences.[29]

Principle or Power?

It must be admitted, however, that problems of conscience are less visible in organizations that are not founded on ethical, ideological, or philosophical standards—organizations such as the Northern Presbyterian Church after 1936. In such organizations, the overriding issue is *power*: how to attain it and how to maintain it. Under such circumstances, questions of principle are translated into questions of power. People raise questions of principle only insofar as questions of principle are relevant to the attaining and maintaining of power.

Machen's view had always been straightforward: maintaining fundamental principle is more important than maintaining short-run institutional power, for it is out of adherence to God's principles that God's elect attain eternal power under God. His opponents in the Presbyterian Church, U.S.A., least of all Mrs. Buck, could never understand his position.

What stands out in the history of the capture of the Northern Presbyterian Church is the unwillingness of the Bible-believing wing of the Church to stand for principle and fight: seminary by seminary, ordination by ordination, heresy trial by heresy trial. They had the votes after 1869, but they seldom used them. They did not understand the requirements of the theological warfare of their day, nor did they

---

29. "Now the Spirit speaketh expressly, that in the latter times some shall depart from the faith, giving heed to seducing spirits, and doctrines of devils, speaking lies in hypocrisy, having their conscience seared with a hot iron" (I Tim. 4:1-2).

understand the costs of a long-term battle. Their opponents did recognize the nature of the battle and the costs involved. They also understood that if they carefully used their opponent's short-sightedness, they could gain time to impose their strategy. What was this tactic for gaining time? *Avoiding premature conflicts.* They understood their opponents well: the conservatives wanted institutional peace at virtually any price, especially after 1900. By the time that the Bible-believing forces woke up to the danger that faced them, all but one of their seminaries had been captured, as had the New York Presbytery.

The conservatives were content to accept the language of orthodoxy rather than the substance. The liberals have used this blindness on the part of conservatives to their own advantage for well over a century. As long as words sound biblical and Bible-honoring, the fight-avoiding conservatives are willing to keep quiet in the name of toleration.

What can we legitimately conclude? The situation in the large mainline Protestant churches in 1940 is accurately summarized by Church historian Sidney E. Mead. "'Fundamentalism' in America was a movement that tried, among other things, to recall these denominations to theological and confessional self-consciousness. It was defeated in the major denominations, not so much by theological discussion as by effective political manipulation of denominational leaders to sterilize this new 'divisive' element."[30] Those who remained behind became institutionally sterile: no spiritual heirs.

Theological liberalism steadily manifested itself in the affairs of the Church. Consider the overwhelming support given by the General Assembly to the creation of something like the United Nations Organization, beginning in May, 1941, four years before the UN was created. (The influence of John Foster Dulles was crucial in this early support; he was a strong internationalist prior to 1948.)[31] In every year but one, 1946 to 1990, the General Assembly annually promoted

---

30. Sidney E. Mead, *The Lively Experiment: The Shaping of Christianity in America* (New York: Harper & Row, 1963), p. 114.

31. Mark G. Toulouse, "Working Toward Meaningful Peace: John Foster Dulles and the Federal Council of Churches, 1937–1945," *Journal of Presbyterian History*, 61 (Winter 1983).

the work of the UN.³² In 1947, eleven years after the de-frocking of Machen, two decades before the 1903 Westminster Confession was revised, the General Assembly voted its approval of the following position: "We believe that the ultimate goal for World Organization should be Federal World Government. The success of the United Nations is an important step toward this end."³³ Once in the hands of power religionists, the proclamation of the Northern Presbyterian Church's political commitments preceded the proclamation of its confessional commitment.

After 1936, creed-affirming conservatives went along quietly with the liberals, since the Confession was left formally intact. The substance or content of the Confession had long since been compromised into institutional irrelevance, but those who held the religion of cultural irrelevance (pietism) did not take great offense. "The Confession, the Confession," they proclaimed, imitating the Israelites in Jeremiah's day, who proclaimed, "the temple, the temple" (Jer. 7:4). In 1967 the Confession was changed, yet the remnant of the conservatives still remained silent. Their religion was the escapist religion, and their long-standing alliance with the power religion could not be broken without abandoning escapism—in other words, without either a fight or a public exodus. They did not want either in 1903, 1906, 1926, 1929, 1934, 1936, or 1967. They do not want either today. The Church was not split cleanly in 1936, and it cannot be split cleanly today. You cannot split rotten wood.

Wolves and Sheep

Early in his career, Machen had recognized the tendency toward theological drift within the denomination. In 1915, a year after his ordination, he wrote a letter to his mother describing his fears. I quote from his letter in Chapter 14.³⁴ Above all, he wrote, he resented the deceptiveness of the liberals, and the fact that the New York Presbytery kept ordaining known unbelievers. "I do not mean to use harsh

---

32. Robert F. Smylie, "The Presbyterian Church and the United Nations: An Overview," *American Presbyterians*, 68 (Summer 1990), p. 73.
33. *Minutes of the General Assembly, 1947*, p. 209. Cited in *ibid.*, p. 78.
34. Section: "Dry Rot Had Set in Early," p. 862.

phrases in a harsh way, and my language must be understood to be Biblical. But men like McGiffert and William Adams Brown at Union Seminary are perfectly clear about the enormous gulf that separates their religion from orthodox Protestantism—just about as clear about it as Dr. Warfield is. Why then do they try to deceive the simple-minded people in the Church? That is the real ground of my quarrel with them."[35]

He recognized where the votes were in the denomination: "The mass of the Church here is still conservative—but conservative in an ignorant, non-polemic, sweetness-and-light kind of way which is just meat for wolves." That is to say, the conservatives were unwilling to defend what they believed by imposing negative sanctions. They would indeed become meat for wolves.

The Religion of Pluralism

The 1934 enactment by the General Assembly regarding the flow of funds marked the penultimate judicial act of the liberals' capture of the Presbyterian Church. The final act was the Permanent Judicial Commission's 1936 decision to sustain suspensions of the handful of ministers who had disobeyed the 1934 declaration. They had challenged the theology of the flow of funds.

The supporters of the 1934 declaration insisted that it was not in any way a theologically based decision; it was strictly administrative. This presumes that Church administration can be separated from theology. Administration is strictly a matter of obedience, they insisted, but in this case, obedience supposedly had nothing to do with theology, especially the theology of those running and serving under the Foreign Missions Board. Although they were never quite so crass about it, the liberals meant this: *obedience has everything to do with power and money*. But, they pretended, as all defenders of pluralism must pretend, that covenantal law can be (and should be) separated from theology. This had been the refrain of every pluralist from Roger Williams to John Dewey.

---

35. Cited by Ned B. Stonehouse, *J. Gresham Machen: A Biographical Memoir* (Philadelphia: Westminster Theological Seminary, [1954] 1977), p. 221.

Machen and his supporters knew better with respect to ecclesiastical law, although all of them believed the theology of pluralism with respect to civil law. What undermined Machen philosophically was that the precepts of American civil pluralism, which he defended throughout his career, had seeped into the Church. Vainly did he protest that the Church's status as a voluntary institution separated it from the civil pluralism of American society. He did not recognize that pluralism is as theocratic as all the other theories of covenantal government. It cannot be hedged in by rival theologies of separation. There is no neutrality. The Princeton apologetic affirmed neutrality. Van Til's apologetic denied it, but Machen was not a follower of Van Til; he was merely his employer. Machen was defending the Church against well-organized forces that had adopted a consistent pluralism that proclaimed: "no negative institutional sanctions against rival theological theories." He was using a natural law-based apologetic methodology that had been undermined by Lyell's time frame a generation before the reunion of 1869. He kept appealing to a common ethics. There was no common ethics, for there was no common theology, just as he had said in *Christianity and Liberalism*. He kept telling the liberals that they should withdraw if they did not believe the Westminster Confession. That is, he kept telling power religionists that they should cease their quest for power. The fact was, there was no common morality. There was no common theology. But there was a common administrative hierarchy. In 1936, a de-frocked Machen withdrew.

Ever since the Briggs trial, the liberals had maintained that the General Assembly had no authority to announce binding theological positions. It had the authority to try cases, but not to announce in advance any theological position. The liberals had attempted to maintain a distinction between a supreme court and a legislative body.[36]

---

36. This convenient judicial fiction began breaking down in American civil law as soon as John Marshall became Chief Justice of the U.S. Supreme Court. The power to declare the law retroactively is in fact the power to declare the law in advance. Only a certain embarrassed silence on this matter, coupled with the traditional Constitutional distinction between the legislative and judicial branches, has maintained the legal fiction in American civil law. The Constitution's Framers did not understand what the doctrine of judicial review could do to their hoped-for tripartite separation. Marshall was later to teach Jefferson and Madison a long series of lessons in Constitutional theory.

This was an imported legal concept based on the U.S. Constitution. Ever since 1910, they had declared that the General Assembly could not enforce the Doctrinal Deliverance of 1910. But, they hastened to add in 1934, the General Assembly had not only the authority but the duty to uphold the administrative authority of the ecclesiastical hierarchy. The Church had voted overwhelmingly to restructure its rules in 1934. Now these rules would be enforced—in a non-doctrinal way, of course. Machen and his allies recognized the nature of the sham, but this did them no institutional good. They could not persuade the experientialist majority of the truth of their position, namely, that the 1934 declaration was the liberals' means of sweeping the more vocal theological conservatives from their midst.

The declaration equating the financial support of the Church's mission boards with participation in the sacrament of the Lord's Supper was a theological declaration of awesome proportions. It was a break, at the very least, with all of Protestant Church history, and in fact a break with all of Church history. But the fiction of "administration, not theology" was central to the liberals' theology: their long-term denial of the judicial, institutional relevance of all theology, i.e., sanctions—point four of their covenant model. In 1936, they demonstrated their commitment to "theology without negative ecclesiastical sanctions" by imposing negative ecclesiastical sanctions. Somehow, their apologists—sometimes referred to as theologically neutral professional Church historians—have failed to see the irony of all this. The modernists were like the Jewish leaders in Jesus' day, crying out against Jesus' critical public comments against the religious establishment. Similar counter-measures were adopted by both establishments.

The Price of Peace

By 1920, Presbyterian modernists concluded that they would henceforth be able to dominate the denomination's bureaucracies as successfully as they had dominated all but one of the theological seminaries: Princeton. They would be required to pay no price except the price they had been paying for a generation: *patient institutional infiltration*, a skill that their theological peers had demonstrated masterfully in several other denominations by the end of World War I.[37]

The conservative, "peace at any reasonable price" leaders of the denominations wanted to pay a low price. They believed all too often that the only price that they would have to pay was institutional: a less rigorous confession, the presence of more leaders within the denomination who really did not believe even this watered-down confession, and the departure of contentious hard-liners who refused to pay the theological price. The price they actually paid, in denomination after denomination, was exceedingly high: the surrender of theological leadership to men who held an explicitly rival faith, modernism.

The Presbyterians were a case in point. The ranks of those pastors who were willing to stand up and fight, even if the cost was their eventual dismissal from the denomination they sought to defend, were steadily thinned out as the risk of their de-frocking increased. The personal price of peace kept getting higher, until the only way to avoid paying it was to break ranks with Machen and join the "loyal opposition" within the denomination. A majority of these once-vociferous conservatives could not bring themselves to become disloyal to those who had captured the denomination's machinery. They kept proclaiming their loyalty to the "true Church," defined as the "Church of the Westminster Confession," when in fact hardly anyone in the denomination still believed in that Confession, and nobody was ready to enforce it judicially in the Church's courts.

The comforting presence of the Westminster Confession and its two catechisms as polished antiques in the denomination's local prayer closets served as salve for many conservative consciences. The liberals were content to allow traditionalists to go quietly into those little local museums and worship there in peace and obscurity, just so long as they remained quiet upon their return to the denomination's institutional seats of power. After all, God's Church is supposed to be a place of peace and quiet, almost everyone agreed. Assuming that they

---

37. C. Gregg Singer, *The Unholy Alliance* (New Rochelle, New York: Arlington House, 1975), chaps. 1–3.

were not accompanied by judicial sanctions, these Confessional antiques meant little or nothing to the liberals. Yet even stripped of all institutional sanctions, they meant everything to the conservatives who remained. After 1936, the liberals were giving up nothing very valuable in their eyes in order to keep the conservatives quiet and their funds flowing upward, and the conservatives were willing to give up everything else, including the future even of the Confessional museum itself, just so long as the liberals allowed it to remain open until that generation died off.

In 1967, the 1903 Westminster Confession was officially supplemented in order to make it conform to the tenets post-1964 of American political liberalism.[38] First, there is the family of man: "God has created the peoples of the earth to be one universal family."[39] ("Cain, your mother and I think you and Abel should set up a neighborhood home church. You can both be ministers.") It attacked "enslaving poverty in a world of abundance," and then announced: "The church cannot condone poverty. . . ." (A grammar book would have helped here. Of course the Church can condone poverty; the question is: Should it?) Poverty is caused, among other factors, by "the rapid expansion of populations."[40] The revision called for "peace, justice, and freedom among nations. . . ." It invoked the language of near-pacifism and internationalism in the "search for cooperation and peace. . . . This search requires that the nations pursue fresh and responsible relations across every line of conflict, even at risk to national security, to reduce areas of strife and to broaden international understanding." All nations are equal before God: "Although nations may serve God's

---

38. On the revision of the Confession, see Edward A. Downey, Jr., *A Commentary on the Confession of 1967 and An Introduction to "The Book of Confessions"* (Philadelphia: Westminster Press, 1968). For a critique of Downey's book, see Edmund P. Clowney, "The Broken Bands," in *Scripture and Confession: A Book About Confessions Old and New*, edited by John H. Skilton (Nutley, New Jersey: Presbyterial & Reformed, 1973), ch. 7.

39. "The Confession of 1967," 9:44; in *The Constitution of the United Presbyterian Church in the United States of America, Part I: Book of Confessions*, 2nd ed. (Philadelphia: Office of the General Assembly of the United Presbyterian Church in the United States of America, 1970).

40. *Ibid.*, 9:46.

purposes in history, the church which identifies the sovereignty of any one nation or any way of life with the cause of God denies the Lordship of Christ and betrays its calling."[41] ("December 8, 1941. Dear Mr. Churchill: the Presbyterian Church wishes to express its deep concern regarding the intemperance of your recent remarks before the House of Commons regarding the motivation of Germany and Chancellor Hitler. Your rhetorical contrast between Christian civilization and barbarism was especially objectionable. A copy of our specific objections is enclosed.") As for foreign *mission* (rarely called *missions* in liberal circles), "The Christian finds parallels between other religions and his own and must approach all religions with openness and respect."[42] (I wonder what the parallel might be between Christianity and Hinduism's practice of pressuring widows to be burned alive on their husbands' funeral pyres. The practice is called "suttee," and is derived from the Sanskrit word for "faithful wife." But I digress.) Then there is the traditional bugaboo of modern intellectuals, *alienation*, in this case regarding sex. There is great confusion about sex today because of, among other things, "the pressures of urbanization. . . ." In the midst of this confusion, the Church comes under the judgment of God whenever "it withholds the compassion of Christ from those caught in the moral confusion of our time."[43] ("Of course we believe in the Seventh Commandment, but. . . .") What is needed is a greater commitment to "responsible freedom" in marital affairs. (Questions: Freedom to do what? Responsible to whom? For how long? For how much per month until she remarries?) The revision of 1967 reveals the working out of one of the most powerful motivations of modern theological liberalism, the desire to be up to date: "trendier than thou." Had the Confession been revised a decade later, it might have included a section calling on God's people to eat more natural whole grain foods and less red meat.[44]

---

41. *Ibid.*, 9:45.
42. *Ibid.*, 9:42.
43. *Ibid.*, 9:47.
44. If you think I am exaggerating, read Ronald J. Sider, *Rich Christians in an Age of Hunger* (Downers Grove, Illinois: Inter-Varsity Press, 1977), pp. 42-45. He discusses the benefits of abstaining from beef in order to free up more grain to

Simultaneously, the most judgmental antique in the Presbyterian prayer closet, the Larger Catechism, was thrown out as junk. "Get rid of this clutter; people keep tripping over it!" By 1967, there were few mourners remaining to bewail the loss.[45] There was no mass exodus of those who had long claimed that their continuing presence within the denomination was justified by the continuing presence of the historic Presbyterian creeds and confessions.[46]

In 1936, Samuel G. Craig and others who had originally stood with Machen decided to abandon ship when public support for Machen's Independent Board for Presbyterian Foreign Missions rather than the denomination's missions board became grounds for excommunication. Later that year, when Machen and his associates were at last booted out of the Church, the bulk of their former supporters remained on board the theologically sinking ship, almost as secret well-wishers may have remained on board *H.M.S. Bounty*, watching Captain Bligh and his loyal supporters sail away in their little open boat.[47] Bligh's shipboard well-wishers chose to forget who was now captain of the *Bounty* and what its mission would soon become. The difference is, those who mutinied against the Confession's Calvinist theology took control of the whole fleet, while those who had resisted them wound up stranded in the cultural equivalent of Pitcairn Island.

---

feed poor people in the Third World.

45. It was restored at the time of the reunion with the Southern Presbyterians in 1983.

46. The behind-the-scenes figure in this resistance movement was Presbyterian layman and Sun Oil Company billionaire, J. Howard Pew, who died in 1973. The main public personality was Henrieta C. Mears, who guided an evangelical group headquarted unofficially at Hollywood's First Presbyterian Church from the mid-1930's through the late 1950's. Richard C. Halverson, Chaplain of the U.S. Senate, 1981 to 1994, was one of her disciples. Karen M. Feaver, "The Soul of the Senate," *Christianity Today* (Jan. 9, 1995), p. 27. So was Bill Bright, founder of Campus Crusade for Christ.

47. Bligh has had a bad press for two centuries. The sexually debauched mutineers have been made heroes. A revisionist account is Richard Hough, *Captain Bligh and Mr. Christian: The Men and the Mutiny* (New York: Dutton, 1973).

Machen's Legacy

Machen's faith was a nineteenth-century faith which had run its course both epistemologically[48] and institutionally. Most of his supporters, Calvinists and fundamentalists, held a twentieth-century evangelical faith which only recently has visibly begun to run its course intellectually and institutionally.[49] *What was required was a total theological, ecclesiastical, and cultural reconstruction.* This was Warfield's implicit point to Machen in 1921 when he called the denomination rotten wood. The preliminary theological and philosophical foundations of such a reconstruction were laid at Machen's own Westminster Seminary by the man he hired to teach apologetics, Cornelius Van Til, who dynamited the foundations of the Princeton apologetic.[50]

Machen left behind something of very great long-term significance: the philosophical foundations of a new Calvinism, Van Til's, which Machen may not have fully understood.[51] One thing is clear: he did recognize that Van Til's system was different. Van Til criticized the Old Princeton apologetic as a compromise with paganism. At the end of his first year at Westminster, he submitted his resignation. Machen refused it.[52] Van Til years later related the story of a train trip

---

48. "Epistemology" asks the question: "What can we know, and how can we know it?"

49. James Davison Hunter, *Evangelicalism: The Coming Generation* (Chicago: University of Chicago Press, 1987).

50. Gary North, *Political Polytheism: The Myth of Pluralism* (Tyler, Texas: Institute for Christian Economics, 1989), ch. 3.

51. William White, Jr., *Van Til: Defender of the Faith, An Authorized Biography* (Nashville, Tennessee: Nelson, 1979), p. 99. Greg L. Bahnsen disagrees, but if he is correct, then Van Til was not the revolutionary thinker that Van Til's followers have generally imagined. Bahnsen has emphasized continuity over discontinuity in the transition from the Old Princeton to the New Westminster. I believe that there was far more discontinuity than his essay conveys. Greg L. Bahnsen, "Machen, Van Til, and the Apologetical Tradition of the OPC," in *Pressing the Mark: Essays Commemorating Fifty Years of the Orthodox Presbyterian Church*, edited by Charles G. Dennison and Richard C. Gamble (Philadelphia: Committee for the Historian of the Orthodox Presbyterian Church, 1986), ch. 17. See Darryl G. Hart, "The Princeton Tradition in the Modern World and the Common Sense of J. Gresham Machen," *Westminster Theological Journal*, 46 (1984), pp. 1–25.

52. Robert L. Atwell, "The Heritage of the Orthodox Presbyterian Church,"

with Machen to Grand Rapids. Van Til had offered then to resign, but Machen replied: "You mustn't. At this stage, I couldn't afford to lose even a janitor."[53]

Machen's spiritual heirs need the memory of his valiant fight as both an inspiration and a warning: an inspiration because of his courage, and a warning because of the seeming futility of his decision to fight a battle that he could not win, theologically or institutionally, with the resources at his disposal. Machen's was a lost cause institutionally, but it was not a lost cause theologically and historically. He believed this with all his heart until the day he died. So should all those who call themselves his spiritual heirs.

We should not forget what has happened to the winners. After 1965, the Presbyterian Church, U.S.A., and the Presbyterian Church, U.S. (Southern Presbyterians), began a long decline in membership. In 1965, the two denominations had a total of 4.25 million members. In 1990, the now-unified denomination had 2.85 million. If the same rate of decline continues, the denomination will not exist in the middle of the twenty-first century.[54]

Machen on the Good Fight

Machen delivered a chapel sermon to the students of Princeton Seminary on March 10, 1929, a few months before he led a small exodus of faculty members and students to the newly created Westminster Seminary. It was titled, "The Good Fight of Faith." He called the students into battle. Of Paul, he said: "Fortunately, he was a great fighter; and by God's grace he not only fought, but he won." We know he won because his doctrine of grace was adopted by Augustine and the Protestant Reformers.[55] This was how Old School Presbyteri-

---

New Horizons (May–June 1981), p. 4. Rev. Atwell attended the first General Assembly of the Church in 1936, and later served as a member of Westminster Seminary's Board of Trustees.

53. Related to me by George Hutchinson, to whom Van Til told the story.

54. "Presbyterians and the Mainline Decline," *Christianity Today* (Sept. 13, 1993), p. 39. This was a review of the seven-volume study, *The Presbyterian Presence: The Twentieth-Century Experience*, edited by Milton J Coalter, John M. Mulder, and Louis M. Weeks (Westminster/John Knox Press).

55. Machen, "The Good Fight of Faith," *The Presbyterian* (March 28, 1929),

ans had always seen the battle: as theological. They defined victory in terms of the progress of doctrine in history.

Machen saw his enemies as theological enemies. They proclaim, he summarized: ". . . let us hold to a Person and not to a dogma; let us sink small doctrinal differences and seek the unity of the church of Christ; let us drop doctrinal accretions and interpret Christ for ourselves; let us look for our knowledge of Christ, not to ancient books, but to the living Christ in our hearts; let us not impose Western creeds on the Eastern mind; let us be tolerant of opposing views."[56] This view is in harmony with the naive fundamentalist slogan, which few fundamentalists really believe: "No creed but Christ, no law but love." But Machen's enemies were not fundamentalists; they were modernists. Their creed was the denial of the legitimacy of creeds. Their law was situation ethics: the evolving law of Darwin's universe. By 1991, the spiritual heirs of Machen's enemies proposed this for consideration by the 203rd General Assembly: "Young people, regardless of their sexual orientation, need to understand the institutional power of heterosexism and the injustice that it perpetuates. As the church is called to speak a truthful word about sexuality, it does so in the name of God's call to justice—a call that invites gay and lesbian adolescents to explore the goodness of their sexuality within the community of God's people."[57] It was little more than half a century's journey from theological perversion to sexual perversion. Machen had seen it coming: "God save us from the deadly guilt of consenting to the presence as our representatives in the church of those who lead Christ's little ones astray. . . ."[58]

Machen fought a theological battle. He lost that battle, for it was more than theological. It was institutional. Words without institutional sanctions could not win it. They never can. His opponents had

---

p. 6.
56. *Ibid.*, p. 7.
57. *Keeping Body and Soul Together: Sexuality, Spirituality, and Social Justice*, A Document Prepared for the 203rd General Assembly (1991) by the General Assembly Special Committee on Human Sexuality, p. 89, lines 3500–3501.
58. Machen, "Good Fight," p. 7.

control over the machinery of sanctions, not just negative sanctions but also positive. Machen by 1929 was well aware of this. To follow him was to abandon many of the Presbyterian Church's positive sanctions.

> . . . you will have the opposition, not only of the world, but increasingly, I fear, of the church. I cannot tell you that your sacrifice will be light. No doubt it would be noble to care nothing whatever about the judgment of our fellowmen. But to such nobility I confess that I for my part have not quite attained, and I cannot expect you to have attained it. I confess that academic preferments, easy access to great libraries, the society of cultured people, and in general the thousand advantages that come from being regarded as respectable people in a respectable world—I confess that these things seem to me to be in themselves good and desirable things. Yet the servant of Jesus Christ, to an increasing extent, is being obliged to give them up.[59]

Through his pen and his preaching, but mostly his pen, Machen gained leadership over a shrinking, confused, besieged, betrayed, and dispirited army. That army had suffered a series of defeats extending back, ultimately, to 1865. Its officers after 1869 were not prepared to fight a protracted conflict. But this was exactly what Machen was calling them to—very late in the battle. This is what God calls His people to throughout history. There are no volunteers, the Calvinist insists. All covenant-keepers are unwilling draftees initially.

Machen's Social Immunity

Machen could not be bought off: not with money, prestige, or the promise of career advancement. Machen was an independently wealthy bachelor. This economic independence made him a force to be reckoned with. But his immunity was not merely financial; it was not merely spiritual; it was also social. He had lived among the super-rich all of his life, and their world held no fascination for him. His followers had no first-hand awareness of this world. His biographers

---

59. *Ibid.*

know of its geographical existence, but they show no understanding of its social implications, both for Machen and the elite that opposed him, most notably Henry van Dyke.

His family was rich enough to own property inside the archetypal enclave of America's financial elite, Mount Desert Island in Maine. They bought it before this became economically prohibitive. As William Hutchison has described it, "On Mount Desert, year after year, Browns and Peabodys of the religious establishment vacationed with Eliots, Rockefellers, and Peppers—that is, with education, business, and political leadership."[60] Years later, Union Seminary professor and ecumenist William Adams Brown reminisced about the time he spent there.[61] George Marsden hints at its existence and importance: "The major university founders, such as White [Cornell], Gilman [California, Johns Hopkins], Angell [Michigan], and Eliot [Harvard], kept in close touch and sometimes vacationed in the same vicinity in Maine."[62] The man known in the 1950's as the Chairman of the American Establishment, John J. McCloy, spent his middle-class youth on the island prior to World War I, where his mother was the favored hairdresser of the elite.[63] From that crucial geographical entry point,[64] he made the personal contacts that led to his becoming the most influential private citizen in the United States, and presumably the world, from 1949 to at least 1970, and possibly into the early 1980's.[65] *Geography has consequences.* (We could use detailed studies of

---

60. William R. Hutchison, "Protestantism as Establishment," in Hutchison, ed., *Between the Times: The Travail of the Protestant Establishment in America, 1900–1960* (New York: Cambridge University Press, 1989), p. 10. Peter Collier and David Horowitz, *The Rockefellers: An American Dynasty* (New York: Holt, Rinehart and Winston, 1976), p. 147.

61. William Adams Brown, *A Teacher and His Times* (New York: Charles Scribner's Sons, 1940), pp. 144–55.

62. George Marsden, *The Soul of the American University: From Protestant Establishment to Established Nonbelief* (New York: Oxford University Press, 1994), p. 196.

63. Kai Bird, *The Chairman: John J. McCloy and the Making of the American Establishment* (New York: Simon & Schuster, 1992), pp. 30, 54–55.

64. And from Harvard Law School.

65. Alan Brinkley, "Minister Without Portfolio," *Harper's* (Feb. 1983).

the well-connected residents of the three island enclaves of the American Establishment: prior to World War II, Mount Desert and Jekyll [Georgia];[66] beginning in the early 1930's and accelerating after 1945, Jupiter, located in Florida's Hobe Sound.[67])

Locking Out the Riff-Raff

Because nobody else is going to tell you about this, please allow me a few extra paragraphs, even though the material is extraneous to the Presbyterian conflict; it is not extraneous to the mind-set of the senior members of the Establishment. It was this mind-set that Machen, as a nineteenth-century Whig liberal and democrat, rejected completely. He had seen it first-hand.

Mount Desert Island was the prototype Establishment enclave. In 1910, the year that he served as foreman of the grand jury in New York, Rockefeller bought a 104-room granite mansion there, importing tiles from the Great Wall of China.[68] He used Mount Desert Island as his first great experiment in permanently sequestering property away from the free market, which develops properties aimed for sale to middle-class buyers. He and his elite neighbors were concerned about "overdevelopment."[69] This is an elitist code word for "real estate sales to the upper middle class." They created an association and donated 5,000 acres to it; then they gave it to the Federal government. President Wilson used executive authority in 1916 to create a special monument; in 1919,

---

66. This was where the secret meeting—first names only—was held in 1910 to plan the Federal Reserve System. This important meeting is rarely mentioned in history textbooks. See Thomas W. Lamont, *Henry P. Davidson* (New York: Harper & Bros., 1933), pp. 96–101; Nathaniel Wright Stephenson, *Nelson W. Aldrich: A Leader in American Politics* (Port Washington, New York: Kennikat, [1930] 1971), ch. 24: "Jekyll Island"; Thibaut de Saint Phalle, *The Federal Reserve: An Intentional Mystery* (New York: Praeger, 1985), p. 49. See the oblique reference to this conference by one of the participants, Paul Warburg, in his authoritative history, *The Federal Reserve System: Its Origin and Growth*, 2 vols. (New York: Macmillan, 1930), II:58.

67. "Millionaires Find Resort Is Too Rich For Their Blue Blood," *Wall Street Journal* (Feb. 1, 1995).

68. Collier and Horowitz, *Rockefellers*, p. 97.

69. John Ensor Harr and Peter J. Johnson, *The Rockefeller Century* (New York: Charles Scribner's Sons, 1988), p. 199.

Congress passed a law making it Lafayette National Park. Junior bought more land and donated it to the government; this is now Acadia National Park.[70]

He and his heirs have repeated this lock-out, using tax-deductible money, to remove prime real estate from the market in wilderness areas surrounding elite enclaves. This raises the value of the remaining properties, and it secures an insulated social world for them. The area around Jackson Hole, Wyoming, is one of the prime areas where the Rockefellers own large tracts. This area has long been the focus of a Rockefeller-inspired lock-out, beginning in 1919.[71] Land values there reflect this: astronomical. But the original model was Mount Desert Island. The Rockefeller family biographers say of Junior's role: "Very shortly, he became a towering figure, the greatest ally the National Park Service ever had."[72] The assistance was mutual. The National Park Service provides the authority to keep the rest of us out of these areas on a permanent basis.

This program to seal off wilderness areas from development had its origins in the special role of wilderness in the coming of age for the sons of the rich. It is one of the three ordeals of youth and early manhood: the wilderness summer (wealthy scion Teddy Roosevelt is the most famous exemplar); the academy (Exeter, Groton, etc.), and military service in wartime (again, Roosevelt the "Rough Rider" is most famous).[73] Mount Desert Island has been a big part of this.[74] Nelson Aldrich, as part of the Old Money Establishment, is quite forthright about its political implications: "The social religion of Nature, which began with rich kids going outdoors for their health, ends in political action against the market—the condo developers, the shopping-mall impresarios, the army of entrepreneurs whom Old Money (and not Old Money) alone imagines despoiling Arcadia."[75] This pro-

---

70. *Ibid.*
71. *Ibid.*, pp. 201–211.
72. *Ibid.*, p. 198.
73. Nelson Aldrich, Jr., *Old Money: The Mythology of America's Upper Class* (New York: Knopf, 1988), ch. 5: "Three Ordeals."
74. *Ibid.*, pp. 164, 166.
75. *Ibid.*, p. 169.

gram of removing land from exposure to market forces is now a worldwide religious-political effort, in the name of conservation, and elitist money is behind it in a pump-priming fashion.[76] Government money accounts for far more, however: forfeited revenues that the sale of government-owned land could produce, as well as land-management expenses borne by the government. What is being conserved is the lifestyle of the rich and famous.

The economics of the environmental movement points to an interest group that is more permanent and far better organized politically than part-time nature-lovers who backpack along the John Muir Trail during one memorable summer vacation at age 19. Economist Thomas Sowell, who grew up in rural North Carolina and urban Harlem during the Great Depression and war years,[77] has put his insightful finger on the problem: the non-rich have too much money in the aggregate for the minority rich to compete against successfully. The non-rich are foreclosing on the rich because they have more money. "There are infinitely more of them, and real estate dealers and developers would rather get $10 million from 10,000 people than get $1 million from one millionaire."[78]

> In the natural course of economic events, the non-rich would end up taking more and more land and shore away from the rich. Spectacular homes with spectacular views would be replaced by mundane apartment buildings with only moderately pleasant vistas. A doctor or movie mogul who can now walk the beach in front of his house in splendid isolation would be replaced by whole families of ordinary grubby mortals seeking a respite from the asphalt and an occasional view of the sunset.
>
> The climax of the story is when the affluent heroes are rescued by the government. In the old days, this used to be the cavalry, but nowadays it is more likely to be the zoning board or

---

76. A detailed study of this is found in Larry Abraham and Franklin Saunders, *The Greening* (Atlanta, Georgia: Soundview, 1993).

77. Sowell, *Black Education: Myths and Tragedies* (New York: David McKay, 1972).

78. Sowell, *Pink and Brown People and Other Controversial Essays* (Stanford, California: Hoover Institution Press, 1981), p. 104.

the coastal commission. They decree that the land cannot be used in ways that would make it accessible to the many, but only in ways accessible to the few. Legal phrasing is of course more elaborate and indirect than this, but that is what it all boils down to. This is called "preserving the environment" (applause) from those who would "misuse" it (boos).[79]

Machen did not participate in the Establishment, even though he owned property in its midst. The Establishment offered no allure to him. He had no desire to pursue membership in any inner ring.[80] The Establishment could offer him no meaningful positive sanctions. Negative sanctions also did not terrify him. The economic threat of forfeiting an academic chair, pulpit, or pension was no threat to him. But, as he learned after 1929, in the midst of the Great Depression, such an economic threat held considerable terror for most pastors, especially men with families and the promise of a pension.

Conclusion

The problem Machen faced was this: how to devise a successful strategy that would reverse the stalemate psychology that had engulfed Old School Presbyterianism even before the 1869 reunion. He failed in this task. He and his dwindling band of followers did not win the battle to reform the Presbyterian Church. It is my contention that the institutional war had surely been lost by 1906 at the latest, and probably as early as 1869. The Old School surrendered in three stages: first to the New School (1869), then to the Arminians from the Cumberland Presbyterian Church (1906), and only late in the struggle to the modernists (1920's). The modernists inherited the Church in 1936 because of a series of prior theological and institutional surrenders. These surrenders paralleled a series of political surrenders by old Whig liberalism during the same era: the rise of Progressivism.

In 1925, Machen wrote a long, highly critical review essay on Fosdick's book, *The Modern Use of the Bible* (1924). He ended the essay

---

79. *Ibid.*
80. C. S. Lewis, "The Inner Ring" (1944), in *The Weight of Glory and Other Addresses* (New York: Macmillan, 1980), pp. 93-105.

with this postmillennial vision: "But this is not the first period of decadence through which the world has passed, as it is not the first period of desperate conflict in the Church. God still rules, and in the midst of the darkness there will come in His good time the shining of a clearer light. There will come a great revival of the Christian religion; and with it will come, we believe, a revival of true learning: the new Reformation for which we long and pray may well be accompanied by a new Renaissance."[81]

A renaissance is a re-birth. Machen wanted a re-birth of Christian scholarship undergirded by a civilization-wide spiritual re-birth. His vision was not shared by many of his allies in 1925: pastors or laymen, Calvinists or fundamentalists. He understood that the war for Christ is the war to re-establish Christendom, but he focused his energies on narrower defensive tasks throughout his career: defending the Bible from modernist scholars in *The Origin of Paul's Religion* and *The Virgin Birth of Christ*, defending the common believer's faith from popular modernism, defending Princeton Seminary from the inclusivists, and defending the Presbyterian Church from wolves in sheep's clothing. He lost every battle.

He fought with the rusty and discarded weapons of Old School Presbyterianism: a seventeenth-century Confession of Faith that was no longer believed; a pair of catechisms that no one had ever appealed to in the General Assembly's court; seventeenth-century Protestant scholastic theological categories—Turretin's six loci—whose latest update was Charles Hodge's 1873 *Systematic Theology*;[82] an apologetic methodology based on Scottish common-sense realism, which twentieth-century, post-Kantian philosophy had long since abandoned as naive; a version of creationism based on the acceptance of Lyell's geological time scale in opposition to the Confession; a critique of biblical higher criticism based on the common-ground methodology of lower

---

81. Machen, "The Modern Use of the Bible," *Princeton Theological Review*, 23 (1925), p. 81.

82. This still is the case in 1995: there has been no Presbyterian Calvinist systematic theology to replace Hodge's *Systematic Theology* unless we consider Louis Berkhof's 1939 *Systematic Theology*, a dry-as-dust catalogue of doctrinal opinions of obscure Continental theologians. Berkhof substitutes quotations in Dutch for Hodge's quotations in Latin.

criticism; a recovery of the teaching ministry based on a non-existent plan to reform seminary education rather than a revival of pastoral apprenticeship; a version of postmillennialism devoid of biblical law and its appropriate sanctions; and the ideal of Christendom which proclaimed the legitimacy of nineteenth-century Whig political economy, i.e., common-ground political humanism. He was an academic man trying to stop a juggernaut based on deception and subversion. He was trying to overcome the combined efforts of modern philosophy, modern science, and modern politics. He was battling the American Establishment, which was heavily funded by John D. Rockefeller, Jr.[83]

Machen's defense of Presbyterian orthodoxy was hampered by his intellectual defense of the faith: a nineteenth-century version of rational Calvinism, Scottish common-sense realism, i.e., empiricism. His allies were less rigorous methodologically than he was. Had he won, his victory would have resulted in a major setback for Christianity. Machen's apologetic approach was defective. His loss of that skirmish was essential for the overall progress and ultimate victory of God's people, in time and on earth, before Christ's Second Coming.

When Machen left the Presbyterian Church, not one established Presbyterian leader or spokesman joined the exodus. The only name anyone might have recognized was Dulles. It belonged to Joseph Welsh Dulles, who was not a famous Dulles. Machen left behind a denomination of two million members, 9,500 ministers, and enormous wealth. Seven months later, he was dead.

What did Machen leave behind to his successors? A model of the stalwart defender who stands and fights against seemingly impossible odds. A commitment to scholarship at the highest level, yet also a commitment to the techniques of popular mobilization: lectures, rallies, pamphlets, simple books, magazine essays, radio addresses—high-

---

83. For references to half a dozen letters between Machen and Junior, see D. G. Hart, *Defending the Faith: J. Gresham Machen and the Crisis of Conservative Protestantism in Modern America* (Baltimore, Maryland: Johns Hopkins University Press, 1994), p. 190, note 2. These letters related to Machen's participation in worship services and projects of the Mount Desert Parish Church. He even preached occasionally at the church. *Ibid.*, p. 85. The Establishment knew exactly who he was.

tech for his day—and even testimony before the U.S. Congress on major issues. But above all else, his willingness to hire Cornelius Van Til and keep him on the faculty of Westminster Seminary despite the fact that Van Til was working hard to destroy his students' faith in the compromised apologetic tradition of Old Princeton. Van Til substituted the absolute Creator/creature distinction[84] and the doctrine of the Trinity—the one and the many, equally ultimate—for common-ground rationalism and the humanist myth of neutrality as the basis of Christian apologetics[85] and systematic theology.[86] This constituted the laying of the necessary foundation for the new Reformation and new renaissance Machen so strongly believed are coming. God's positive sanctions will eventually come to the Church that remains faithful to Jesus Christ, he believed. For Machen's postmillennial eschatology, the crucial issue for the Church was sanctions—positive sanctions, not negative.

---

84. This is not to say that the Princetonians had ignored this. Machen was strong in his affirmation of the distinction in *Christianity and Liberalism*, pp. 62-63. But they had not made it the starting-place in their apologetics.

85. Van Til, *The Defense of the Faith*, 3rd ed. (Phillipsburg, New Jersey: Presbyterian & Reformed, 1967).

86. Van Til, *An Introduction to Systematic Theology*, vol. 5 of *In Defense of the Faith* (Phillipsburg, New Jersey: Presbyterian & Reformed, [1961] 1978).

Part 4

THE STRATEGY OF SUBVERSION

Honesty, despite all that can be said and done, is not a trifle, but one of the weightier matters of the law. Certainly it has a value of its own, a value quite independent of consequences. But the consequences of honesty would in the case now under discussion not be unsatisfactory; here as elsewhere honesty would probably prove to be the best policy. By withdrawing from the confessional churches—those churches that are founded upon a creed derived from Scripture—the liberal preacher would indeed sacrifice the opportunity, almost within his grasp, of so obtaining control of those confessional churches as to change their character. The sacrifice of that opportunity would mean that the hope of turning the resources of the evangelical churches into the propagation of liberalism would be gone. But liberalism would certainly not suffer in the end. There would at least be no more need of using equivocal language, no more need of avoiding offense. The liberal preacher would obtain the full respect of his opponents, and the whole discussion would be placed on higher ground. All would be perfectly straightforward and above-board.

J. Gresham Machen (1923)[*]

---

[*] Machen, *Christianity and Liberalism* (New York: Macmillan, 1923), p. 165.

INTRODUCTION TO PART 4

It is our duty not to withdraw from the Presbyterian Church. Christian honor requires us to remain.

Henry van Dyke (1893)[1]

Like Shakespeare's Brutus, van Dyke was an honorable man. So were they all honorable men. Unlike Brutus and his colleagues, however, they won.

Van Dyke announced a new rhetorical strategy for his liberals in 1893 manifesto, *A Plea for Peace and Work*. He could see what was going to happen to Briggs. He knew that Briggs' confrontational rhetoric had been the cause of his imminent defeat. He was determined that it should not happen again. Because of Henry Preserved Smith's public commitment to Briggs, he followed Briggs out the door in 1894. McGiffert left under fire in 1900. But by then van Dyke was ready for the next phase, beginning with creedal revision and a new hymnal, which became realities in 1903. For a decade longer, soft words triumphed. Meanwhile, he became the best-known literary figure in Presbyterianism. The outside world gave him great respect. Then, in 1913, van Dyke threw down a verbal gauntlet: he came to the defense of his son, as a good father is expected to. He came with a challenge: "Try me for heresy if you dare." No one dared. A decade later he escalated the rhetoric again by releasing to the press his letter to the treasurer of the session at First Presbyterian Church of Princeton: "I'm leaving until Machen leaves." He left. He got away with it. In 1933, in the year of his death, he led the Church to another revision of the hymnal. It had all been so easy. And every summer, he refreshed himself among the scions of the American Establishment on Mount Desert Island.

In van Dyke's words and van Dyke's life we see the grand strategy of theological liberalism. It began with a willingness to moderate liber-

---

1. Van Dyke, *The Bible As It Is* (New York: Session, 1893), p. 29.

alism's image for the sake of public opinion. Liberals, led by van Dyke, sought to create a pair of public images, positive and negative: a band of good men doing good works who were being assailed by right-wing extremists who were hampering good works for the sake of antiquated dogmas. This imagery was adopted by the modernists' allies: the humanist, Progressive media, which reinforced the message from what appeared to be independent sources.

The conservatives were caught in a pincer movement between two wings of the same modernist army: inside and outside. Unless the conservatives were willing to adopt Machen's two-religions model, they would never understand that their mortal enemies had launched a systematic, carefully coordinated strategic pincer movement against them. They would not understand that the pagans outside the Church were merely echoing the contrived imagery established by the pagans inside the Church. (Pagans launched the rhetorical attack in 1922 on Bryan.) This is why *Christianity and Liberalism* was so important as a statement of the conservatives' position. It was an affront to the liberals then; it is an affront to them today. Most of the conservatives failed to take it seriously then, and most of them fail to take it seriously today.[2]

Machen's analysis was the conservatives' equivalent of van Dyke's *Plea for Peace and Work*. It provided a diagnosis of the problem: two irreconcilable religions in the same Church. It also provided a prognosis: not good. In 1936, both the diagnosis and the prognosis proved accurate.

The liberals had a systematic, comprehensive, consistent strategy. The conservatives did not. The liberals had tactics that were integrated into their strategy. The conservatives did not. The liberals had the advantage of being part of a self-confident Progressive movement that saw itself as the wave of the future. The conservatives did not. The Progressives' eschatology was a secularized postmillennialism.[3] With the exception of the Princetonians, American conservative Christian-

---

2. See Preface, above: section on "Hart Attack," pp. xxxiii–xxxvi.
3. Jean B. Quandt, "Religion and Social Thought: The Secularization of Postmillennial Thought," *American Quarterly*, 25 (Oct. 1973).

ity after 1865 had become premillennial or amillennial: without cultural hope in this, the "Church Age."[4]

You can't beat something with nothing. Strategically, the conservatives had next to nothing. The liberals had a great deal. Most of all, they had the climate of respectable intellectual opinion on their side. They were historicists in an era of historicism. They were social reform Darwinists in an era of social reform Darwinism (post-1890). They were dogmatically anti-dogmatic, in an era of dogmatic anti-dogmaticism. They were for ecclesiastical pluralism in an age of political pluralism. Their spiritual accomplices outside the Church controlled the major institutions of higher learning, and the Presbyterian Church required its ministerial candidates to graduate from these institutions. Above all, they were men who had rejected the doctrine of hell in a culture increasingly dominated by an educated elite that had rejected the doctrine of hell. The crucial issue was sanctions.

---

4. James H. Moorhead, "The Erosion of Postmillennialism in American Religious Thought, 1865-1925," *Church History*, 53 (March 1984).

13

THEOLOGY, STRATEGY, TACTICS

We remember that our Church has been twice rent asunder by issues which have been recognized shortly afterward as unnecessary. We dread the possibility of having such a painful experience repeated in our own time. We are persuaded that the great body of the Church, laymen and ministers, have little sympathy with the extremes of dogmatic conflict, and are already weary of the strife of tongues, and are longing for peace and united work.

A Plea for Peace and Work (1893)[1]

It is to be noted that the charges against these appellants do not in any wise involve questions of faith or doctrine.

Digest . . . of the General Assembly (1938)[2]

Briggs was de-frocked officially for heresy in 1893. Machen was de-frocked officially for non-heresy in 1936. In each case, sanctions were applied in terms of a theology. The conservatives' theology was a theology of ultimate sanctions: heaven and hell. The liberals' theology was a theology of temporal sanctions: the flow of funds. The

---

1. Reprinted in *The Presbyterian Enterprise: Sources of American Presbyterian History*, edited by Maurice W. Armstrong, Lefferts A. Loetscher, and Charles A. Anderson (Philadelphia: Westminster Press, 1956), pp. 253–54.

2. *Digest of the Acts and Deliverances of the General Assembly of the Presbyterian Church In the United States of America*, 2 vols. (Philadelphia: Office of the General Assembly, 1938), I:575.

liberals constructed and then executed a comprehensive strategy based on their theology. It was a strategy of subversion. It is time to evaluate the liberals' strategy: what it was and why it worked.

Offense and Defense

Every successful strategy has both an offensive and defensive aspect, but one aspect will be emphasized more than the other in any given historical situation. Neither the Old School nor the New School had an offensive strategy after the reunion of 1869. They had defense only, and not much of that after 1900.

In 1869, the Old School had a substantial numerical majority over the New School in membership, ministers, and churches. This did them no good. The Old School adopted a primarily defensive strategy after the Swing case in 1874. Its leaders chose to concentrate on only one aspect of the conflict: formal theology. They wrote theological essays and a few books that were critical of modernism. This, they hoped (and no doubt prayed), would keep the Presbyterian Church from drifting into liberalism. The Old School had no visible offensive strategy of its own. It was limited institutionally to whatever the New School was willing to support, which after the McCune trial in 1878 was not very much. *The Church rarely brought formal covenant lawsuits against modernists.* To become successful, the Old School had to devise a comprehensive offensive strategy. It never did.[3] They lacked a secondary institutional strategy after 1900 other than writing articles and holding public meetings (1922-1925). They were attacked by the modernists' allies outside the gates and were undermined by modernists within. They lost. Step by step, they surrendered the Presbyterian Church to its enemies until such time as a last-ditch defensive effort could only result in the defeat of the defenders.

The New School also employed a primarily defensive strategy. This strategy had six stages. (1) From 1869 to 1878: go along with the Old School's numerical majority by pursuing two pastors, David Swing and William McCune. But McCune's problem was his repudia-

---

3. For a discussion of a possible strategy, see the Conclusion to Part 2, above: section on "The Ordination Examination," pp. 298-301.

tion of denominationalism and infant baptism, not liberalism as such. He was an evangelical ecumenist, not a modernist.[4] (2) From 1879 to 1890: keep the Old School from interfering with both evangelism and the peace of the Church; refuse to bring heresy accusations against modernists. (3) From 1891 to 1900: keep the modernists from becoming so rhetorically forthright in their rejection of conservative evangelicalism that the New School's effective control over the Church's machinery would become an embarrassment. (4) From 1901 to 1921: maintain the peace of the Church. (5) From 1922 to 1925: assert control through the General Assembly. (6) From 1926 to 1933: defer the major confrontation that Machen was demanding. (7) From 1934 to 1936: consent to the imposition of Church sanctions, but in the name of peace—a defensive reaction. This meant isolating Old School members and their fundamentalist and traditionalist evangelical allies. In June of 1936, the New School quietly surrendered.

The liberals had a comprehensive strategy: subversion. This strategy was both offensive and defensive.

Capturing the Robes

American liberals adopted a culture-wide offensive strategy after 1865, a long-term strategy of institutional infiltration and capture. Three institutions were the primary targets of this strategy: the college, the judiciary, and the Church. I have called this strategy capturing the robes.[5] These three institutions have long possessed enormous influence in American life. All three are marked publicly by the wearing of black robes on formal occasions. Robes were the medieval world's mark of judicial sovereignty. The liberals' strategy has worked exceptionally well. They have captured the nation.[6]

---

4. Lefferts A. Loetscher, *The Broadening Church: a study of theological issues in the presbyterian church since 1869* (Philadelphia: University of Pennsylvania Press, 1954), p. 16.

5. Gary North, *Backward, Christian Soldiers?* (Tyler, Texas: Institute for Christian Economics, 1984), ch. 7.

6. This strategy of subversion was employed throughout the West. It has worked everywhere, even in religiously and culturally isolated nations such as Portugal.

In the institutional struggle for the control of the churches, liberal humanists became known as modernists. What was the nature of the liberals' ecclesiastical strategy? It was primarily offensive. It was also conspiratorial. What do I mean by "conspiracy"? The word comes from two Greek words meaning "breathe together." A conspiracy is an organized effort to steal a rival movement's institutions through a strategy of misrepresentation, infiltration, and money—preferably money supplied by those people whose authority is being undermined.

There are two parts to a successful offensive conspiratorial strategy: external and internal. *First,* there is a frontal assault intellectually and financially from outside the targeted organization or organizations. This assault challenges the legitimacy of the presuppositions and actions of the targeted organization. *Second,* there is simultaneously a systematic, coordinated program of subversion from within. Subversives who hold the views and goals of the institution's enemies "outside the walls" enter the targeted organization as if they were in agreement with the ideals of the intended victims. They have a hidden agenda. Their agenda is to conquer from within. They seek to gain positions of authority within the targeted organization. They spend decades to gain access to these positions. Theirs is a long-range strategy.[7] Those people who are committed to a long-term plan have a great advantage over enemies with a short-range mentality.

How did this offensive strategy apply to the Northern Presbyterian Church? A good example comes from the 1940's, a few years after the end of the struggle surveyed by this book. Nathaniel Weyl,

---

7. The institutional model is the Jesuit Order. The oath-bound solidarity, discipline, and fixity of purpose that marked the Jesuits from 1534 to 1965 is unmatched by any other organization that I am aware of. Yet even the Jesuits succumbed to the modernists' strategy of subversion. The collapse took place in a two-year period: 1965–1966. See Malachi Martin, *The Jesuits: The Society of Jesus and the Betrayal of the Roman Catholic Church* (New York: Simon & Schuster, 1987). It is one of the remarkable facts of Western history that the Jesuits' founder, Ignatius of Loyola, and John Calvin studied at the same time (1528) at the same small college at the huge (40,000 students) University of Paris, the College of Montaigu. Erasmus had studied there a generation earlier.

in later years a conservative author and scholar, describes an offer he received while still in college.

> ... when I was the leader of the radical movement on the Columbia University campus, I was invited to become an honorary member of the Atheists' Club at adjacent Union Theological Seminary. I asked rather naively how an honorable man could accept an appointment to the ministry if he didn't believe in God. The reply was that the pulpit provided a captive audience, a position of authority and a regular salary—all most useful to socialist and Communist propagandists. I declined the invitation.[8]

What we need to understand is this: *the modernists' primary offensive strategy was theological, not organizational.* This is what has not been recognized by the standard histories of the Presbyterian conflict. The historians have accepted the modernists' word that they were not concerned with theology, only with "mission." The historians have not recognized that *modernism is a theology disguised as a program or mere methodology.* The modernists employed this disguise to advance their theology. In their dedicated commitment to a uniquely covenantal theology, they mirrored the Old School: the five points of modernism.

The modernists systematically imported alien theological ideas into the Church, but they disguised these ideas. They defended this alien theology by means of two arguments: (1) the supposed consistency of modernism with the underlying ethical meaning of the doctrines of the Church, though of course not with the specific terminology of the Confession and catechisms; (2) an appeal to the (autonomous) scientific spirit of the age. The first claim was a lie because the second claim was true. They used the language of orthodoxy in order to destroy the substance of orthodoxy.

Their secondary offensive strategy was organizational: infiltrating the seminaries, boards, and bureaucracies of the Church. They were wolves in sheep's clothing who came to replace the shepherds and steal both the sheep and the sheepfold. The shepherds on duty before

---

8. Nathaniel Weyl, *Karl Marx: Racist* (New Rochelle, New York: Arlington House, 1979), p. 67.

1922 did not clearly identify the secondary aspect of the modernists' offensive strategy, and so they did not take effective steps to defeat it.

The modernists also had a defensive strategy: to avoid excommunication. They appealed to the institutionally dominant New School members in terms of a plea for peace, for the open investigation of the Bible, for toleration, for evangelism, and for unity. They also resorted to an appeal to academic freedom for the Church's seminaries. This defensive strategy was what the public saw. It concealed the quiet, offensive strategy of bureaucratic infiltration except in the case of a few controversial appointments to seminary positions, which became public matters.

The Modernists' Five Steps to Victory

Presbyterian modernists were committed to a theological strategy: to overturn the judicial authority of the Bible by means of an appeal, first, to the categories of biblical higher criticism and, second, to a specific form of biblical theology based on higher criticism. This approach asserted that (1) the historical claims of the Bible's existing texts regarding dates and authorship cannot be supported by the internal textual evidence of the dates and authorship, and (2) historical evidence contemporary (supposedly) to the texts also throws doubts on the texts' dating.

The presupposition of the modernist approach to the Bible is that the Bible is subject to the same form of literary and textual criticism that every other text is. In fact, modern literary criticism was originally derived from the techniques of higher criticism. The modernists were understandably alert to the limits of history. Their alertness was an outgrowth of their worldview: the substitution of historical process for God's absolute decree. They understood that the subversion of the denomination would take a long time.

The Five Steps: Strategy and Tactics

The modernists had a five-point covenant theology.[9] The structure of this theology established the requirements of their institutional

---

9. See Chapter 1, above: section on "The Five Points of Modernism," pp. 70-81.

strategy. It is crucial to recognize that modernism was a theology more than an institutional program. Modernism's theology drove its strategy, not vice-versa.

First, there had to be a substitution of a new doctrine of God in the name of Calvinist orthodoxy. This could be done through emphasizing some aspects of the Bible's doctrine of God and neglecting others. But what had to be eliminated from liberal Christianity was the doctrine of God's absolute sovereignty. The undermining of this doctrine was accomplished by numerous appeals to the New School's tradition of experientialism and experientialism's dual emphasis: evangelism and cooperation. Calvinism's God was re-defined by the modernists as the God of merciful inclusion rather than the God of covenantal exclusion, the God of grace rather than the God of wrath. The premier mark of such exclusiveness is the presence of negative sanctions: in eternity and history. As a tactic, the modernists could appeal to the traditionally loose interpretations and language of the New School as a means of undermining the authority of the Old School's view. Tactically, they could operate under the umbrella of operational Arminianism, invoking the memory of New School men such as Albert Barnes, in order to shield themselves from censure from the formal Calvinism of the Old School. They could wait patiently to come out from under this umbrella until they felt confident that they had the votes to shield Kant's noumenal god from Calvin's.

Second, there had to be a challenge to the judicial authority of the Bible: higher criticism. Undermining the judicial authority of the Old Testament had begun very early: a seventeenth-century reaction against Puritanism.[10] This worldview was being extended in the nineteenth century through German higher criticism. The modernists' primary long-run tactic was to encourage young scholars to go to German universities for graduate study, and then return to teach in the seminaries. One member per faculty was sufficient; the seminary's entire faculty would then be forced to defend the legitimacy of higher

---

10. Henning Graf Reventlow, *The Authority of the Bible and the Rise of the Modern World* (London: SCM Press, [1980] 1984), Part II.

criticism as an academic method in order to justify the presence of that single higher critic on the faculty.

A subordinate tactic was to create a jointly published journal, *The Presbyterian Review*, sanctioned by the denomination, which would act as a conduit for higher criticism. This journal would not initially have to endorse higher criticism. It would only have to provide a forum for debate, with higher criticism therefore acting as an equal participant theologically. The approach would be to focus the debate on the question of *methodology* rather than theology, i.e., the question of the more productive way to "mine the resource" of God's word. For this approach to work, the journal would necessitate getting Old School defenders of inerrancy to participate, although this would be necessary only at the beginning. This was an appropriate tactic to use against the Old School: publishing in scholarly journals was an Old School tradition. Once the major representatives of the Old School had accepted the legitimacy of the public debate, it would prove nearly impossible for them to shut it off. They would already have "baptized" the methodology as academically and theologically legitimate. How could they make a court case out of this methodology, given their prior participation? As a byproduct, the journal might recruit new men.[11]

Third, there had to be a challenge to the judicial legitimacy of the denomination's confessional standards. The tactic here was simple: force a public embarrassment or at least acknowledgment that the denomination no longer was willing to enforce certain points in the Confession and the catechisms. Even better, prove that the best representatives in the Old School had publicly deviated from the standards without having been called to account, and without their ever having called for a formal revision of the standards. It would then be possible to extrapolate from these precedents: "If the Old School can abandon certain points without fear of sanctions, why not the New School?" Modernists could continue to hide under the New School's umbrella.

---

11. *Presbyterian Review*'s biggest catch for the modernists was Henry Preserved Smith of Lane Seminary. See Loetscher, *Broadening Church*, p. 34.

Fourth, there had to be a challenge to the legitimacy of the Church's courts. It would not be sufficient to show that the courts had not previously been willing to defend the Confession's standards on some points. It was necessary to show that the courts should not impose sanctions at all regarding "technical or methodological" disputes. This tactic could be successful only after a sufficient number of modernist graduates of seminaries had been ordained and were sitting on Presbyterian courts. The courts would then refuse to convict. To make this stand, the General Assembly had to be undermined as the denomination's supreme court: too many ruling elders voted at the General Assembly, and they did not share the New York Presbytery's views on ordination.

Fifth, the Confessionalists would have to be cut off from the institutional inheritance. This took place definitively in 1936, and continued, congregation by congregation, until 1967, when the Westminster Confession was formally revised. This strategy required some means of protecting against an exodus of pastors and donors. The modernists adopted two major tactics. First, they gained control over the national pension fund in 1927: any pastor leaving the denomination would lose his pension. The other major tactic was keeping ownership of Church property: seceders would lose the property.

Strategy and Tactics: Details

The modernists adopted a strategy that was consistent with their worldview. They adopted tactics that were both consistent with their strategy and applicable to changing conditions. They were able to employ this strategy from within the Northern Presbyterian Church because of the institutional and theological opening made available to them by the Presbyterian union of 1869, after which the Confessional rigor of the Old School could no longer be enforced by all of the presbyteries. It is my suggestion that variants of this modernist strategy were employed successfully in every denomination in the United States until the 1970's, when the Missouri Synod Lutherans slowed it down dramatically, and in the 1980's, when the Southern Baptist Convention reversed it.

The fundamental strategy of the modernists has been to destroy the legitimacy of conservative, traditional denominations. This is a theological strategy. Legitimacy is central; it is point one of the five-point organizational model: legitimacy, authority, legality, sanctions, and inheritance. Without legitimacy, no organization can long survive. Since American Protestant churches have long denied the legitimacy of invoking political power to defend theology, the modernists had only to undermine their rivals' confidence in the their own standards. These standards were both theological and institutional.

Modernists targeted the intellectual leadership of the churches with an attack on traditional theology. They targeted laymen differently: not with an explicitly theological appeal, but rather practical. They appealed to the benefits of Church growth through institutional peace. This appeal was also seemingly ethical: an appeal to their opponents' sense of fair play. Simultaneously, from outside the ecclesiastical camp, modernists and humanists delivered a relentless intellectual attack on the fundamental confession of the conservatives: faith in the Bible as the infallible word of God. From inside the camp, the modernists always adopted the role of wounded lambs: the institutionally abused. Only when they had taken control of a denomination's judicial hierarchy did they adopt a new role: wounded water buffaloes.

The attack began with theology and later extended to Church courts: standards and sanctions. We must understand their strategy and their tactics. To do this, we must first understand the broad outlines of their theology.

Theology

There is no permanent plan of God that provides coherence to the universe.

There is no inerrant and permanent verbal revelation of God to man.

There must therefore be a reliable word of man in order to provide coherence in the universe.

This word is evolving: "dynamic," "progressive," "process-oriented," "dialectical," and therefore *relative* over time.

Creeds are men's verbal representations of a symbolic (zero fixed content) representation of God, rather than men's verbal approximations of God's permanent word.

The essence of the Church's ministry is concern for mankind rather than the defense of the integrity of God's word.

The unity of God must be reflected in the unity of man.

The unity of man must be reflected in the unity of man's institutions.

Any institutional disunity must be smoothed over dialectically, until such time as the forces of unity can purge out the non-pluralistic elements.

Strategy: From Outside the Camp

Undermine the sense of legitimacy among a targeted denomination's leaders.

Use the higher criticism of the Bible as a means of challenging the legitimacy of conservative denominations: "defenders of childish myths."

Use the latest findings of humanist scholarship, especially Darwinism, to attack the conservative Church as out of touch with reality.

Establish standards of academic certification that conform to those taught in institutions controlled by secular humanists or theological modernists.

Produce a continuing barrage of propaganda from the "neutral" secular media exposing the targeted group as foolish, old-fashioned, and unfair. (The classic example of this strategy is what the press, national and international, did to William Jennings Bryan at the Scopes trial in 1925.)

Strategy: From Inside the Camp

The overall strategic goal is the attainment of institutional control of the targeted Church's educational and judicial institutions.

Target seminaries first: you indoctrinate[12] the next generation of ministers, plus your enemies pay your salary. Also, an educational institution is inherently co-operative: financing and recruiting force a broader base of supporters, meaning less theologically rigorous donors.

Target denominational colleges (same reasons).

Emphasize certification by Establishment humanist institutions of higher learning as the preferred (later, required) criteria for service in denominational institutions of higher learning.

---

12. Pour doctrine into.

Emphasize educational credentials for the highest Church positions. (A liberal and ecumenical bias dominates formal education generally, as does the doctrine of academic freedom, which can be transferred to other institutions.)

Infiltrate the centralized agencies within the Church: your enemies will then pay your salary.

Recruit bright or popular young people.

Recruit wealthy or powerful laymen through offers of prestige positions or the promise of future influence.

Infiltrate the Church's publishing outlets.

Create new publishing outlets within the Church.

Avoid institutional confrontations initially.

Co-operate with other denominations or ecclesiastical groups. Ecumenists inside all groups can then support each other.

Rely on other people's money at every stage, if possible.

Tactics

Adopt the Bible's language to advance the cause of the unification of man.

Resist calls for creedal discipline. Invoke toleration ("pluralism").

Emphasize the benefits of practical religion: healing the sick, feeding the hungry, etc.

Place shared concern for mankind on a par (and then above) "divisive" concern for creeds or doctrines.

Repeat pleas for peace whenever the creedalists begin to organize their forces.

Implement all procedural protections against charges of heresy. Issue warnings concerning the high costs of such a fight, including institutional sanctions to be imposed on people who bring unprovable accusations.

Conduct all battles against enemies in terms of institutional criteria, not creeds: toleration, peace, and (in the final stages) obedience to hierarchical authority.

Master the Church's bureaucratic machinery. Quietly place your allies in these permanent bureaucratic positions.

Academic Freedom: Escaping Negative Sanctions

In every institution, the ultimate earthly authority over operations is possessed by those who finance these operations. Even in covenantal institutions, he who pays the piper calls the tune. If the tunes do not please the payers, they can stop paying. Yet every institution is staffed by pipers who prefer to call their own tunes while being supported by the listeners. *The pipers prefer the payers to sit quietly and listen to the pipers' officially sanctioned tunes.* (Applause is optional.) If there is one universal law of bureaucracy, this is it. Those who pay pipers need to be perpetually on guard against every institutional roadblock against their authority to call the tune.

In the history of the West, the most successful of all such roadblocks has been the ideology known as academic freedom. It has been successful because the pipers of academia have persuaded everyone that they are in fact priests: in principle beyond any negative sanctions except those imposed by their own members. The primary key to extending their control has been the substitution of academic certification for apprenticeship as the means of entry into the professions: first and foremost, the Church's bureaucratic hierarchies; secondarily, the State's. This has been true since the late eleventh century.[13] The secondary key has been the re-definition of occupations as professions: State-regulated occupations. The self-anointed priests of academia thereby gain control over access to employment by Church and State.

The Church established this pattern by uncritically accepting the claims of the academic pipers: first with the college and then with the theological seminary (1808 onward). The Church transferred the initial sanctioning process from ordained Church officers to the academic pipers. Marsden points out that in the United States in the 1870's, "the revolutionary trend toward universities, elective courses, separation of disciplines, and academic freedom (on the premise that there might be more than one variety of truth) was just beginning."[14]

---

13. The University of Bologna, devoted to a revival of Roman law, was the original model for the secularization of Western education. Harold J. Berman, *Law and Revolution: The Formation of the Western Legal Tradition* (Cambridge, Massachusetts: Harvard University Press, 1983), pp. 123–27.

14. George M. Marsden, *Fundamentalism and American Culture: The Shaping of Twentieth-Century Evangelicalism, 1870–1925* (New York: Oxford University

With the exception of the ideal of academic freedom, these trends did not even begin to touch Princeton Seminary until 1906, the year that over a thousand Cumberland Presbyterian congregations began entering the PCUSA, and also the year that both Machen and Charles Erdman joined the faculty. But academic freedom of the faculty from the General Assembly had been entrenched at Princeton since 1870. Any newly appointed professor who avoided a veto by the General Assembly at the next GA meeting could not again be challenged by a GA in that particular academic office.

A Most Successful Lie

The ideology of academic freedom rests on a lie: the idea that the professor's pursuit of truth is sovereign, irrespective of the intent of those who finance this pursuit. This lie is undergirded by another lie: that truth exists independently of the hierarchical authority associated with biblical covenantalism. That is to say, there is supposedly some self-existing, religiously neutral, universal system or methodology of truth that exists apart from the self-revelation of God in the Bible. Academic freedom rests, in short, on the myth of religious neutrality.

Schlossberg has identified the two supposed sources of this independently existing truth: history and nature. He calls them idols of history and idols of nature.[15] There is one valid alternative to these twin idols: the absolute authority of the Bible. Most conservatives refuse to accept this alternative. This is why the conservative critic of higher education, Russell Kirk, could not escape the academic rot he so deplored.[16] He wrote: "For no proverb is truer than this: 'The man who pays the piper calls the tune.'"[17] But he did not apply this principle to higher education. He did not identify the family as the lawful primary tune-caller in education, with the Church as a secondary

---

Press, 1980), p. 14.

15. Herbert Schlossberg, *Idols for Destruction: Christian Faith and Its Confrontation with American Society* (Westchester, Illinois: Crossway, [1983] 1993), p. 11.

16. Russell Kirk, *Decadence and Renewal in the Higher Learning: An Episodic History of American University and College Life since 1953* (South Bend, Indiana: Gateway, 1978).

17. Russell Kirk, *The Intemperate Professor* (Baton Rouge: Louisiana State University Press, 1965), p. 31.

agent, and the State as a completely illegitimate interloper. He recognized that "If you take the king's shilling, you must fight the king's battles."[18] But he did not call for the total abolition of taxpayer-funded education. He also accepted the definition of academic freedom provided by the humanist editor of *Collier's Encyclopedia*, W. T. Couch:

> "Academic freedom," says a distinguished editor, W. T. Couch, "is the principle designed to protect the teacher from hazards that tend to prevent him from meeting his obligations in the pursuit of truth." This is the best definition of the idea that I have come upon.[19]

On the contrary, academic freedom is the ideology of self-anointed would-be academic priests: a technique employed to escape the lawful authority of Church, State, and family—the God-ordained covenantal institutions that in our day support educators financially and culturally. "The pursuit of truth" is the verbal smoke screen they use to camouflage their real intentions: to gain the authority to define truth as a pursuit—an evolutionary or dialectical process, mainly academic—and thereby gain priestly status. The marks of their priestly status are the black academic robe and the Ph.D. degree.

Non-Covenanted Screening Agents

Who has operational authority over education: Church, State, or family? The economic answer is simple: in order to maximize income, whoever provides the funding is *sovereign economically*. Whoever is *sovereign judicially* must meet the demand of those who pay the bills.[20] Higher education has always rejected both of these principles of sovereignty. Faculty members insist on controlling the system, no matter who is legally in charge, and no matter what the bill-payers desire.[21]

---

18. *Ibid.*, p. 37.
19. Russell Kirk, *Academic Freedom: An Essay in Definition* (Chicago: Regnery, 1955), p. 1. I worked with Couch in the summer of 1963. I was not impressed.
20. This is not equally true of covenantal institutions, e.g., the family, but schools are not covenantal institutions, i.e., established by a lawful self-maledictory oath before God.
21. Henry Manne [MANee], "The Political Economy of Modern Universi-

This was also true of nineteenth-century theological seminaries: the first graduate schools in America.

The problem with a seminary is that it trains candidates for the preaching ministry. A seminary screens access to ordination. It can be outside the ecclesiastical chain of command, yet its authority to accept men as students and to graduate only some of them makes it functionally part of the system. In Presbyterianism, the seminary becomes the most important part, for its professors possess great though informal authority, and its graduates inherit denominational authority over time.

No Presbyterian seminary was ever under extensive ecclesiastical authority, not even Princeton, which was the most subordinate of all the seminaries. The reunion of 1869 did lead to the establishment of veto power over new faculty appointments by the General Assembly. The denomination had only until the next General Assembly meeting to veto any professorial appointment. After that meeting ended, the professor was safe for the remainder of his academic career, even if subsequently de-frocked. By continuing to extend the positive sanction of institutional acceptability to Union Seminary after its secession in 1892, the denomination transferred its inheritance to the mortal enemies of both Calvinism and the Westminster Confession. This transfer was completed in 1936.

The presbyteries continued to demand judicial sovereignty over ordination, but they were not functionally sovereign, since the Presbyterian tradition of an educated ministry mandated seminary education for candidates except in special circumstances. The presbyteries successfully resisted control by the General Assembly, yet in doing so, they transferred the authority to impose preliminary sanctions—academic sanctions—to theologically and judicially independent seminaries. This was inherently an affirmation of academic autonomy.

To some extent, every nineteenth-century Presbyterian seminary faculty hid behind the medieval robe of academic freedom—autonomy from Church interference—yet seminaries existed only because they were the delegated screening agents for the presbyteries. In order to

---

ties," in Anne Husted Burleigh, ed., *Education in a Free Society* (Indianapolis: Liberty Fund, 1973).

defend its covenantal standards, the Presbyterian Church would have had to abandon all traces of the self-serving professorial ideology known as academic freedom. The presbyteries would have had to monitor the doctrines taught in every Presbyterian college and seminary classroom, with the General Assemblies ready to try cases of theological deviance by any faculty member. Except in the 1890's, the Church was unwilling to do this.

Note: those who have written the book-length histories of the Presbyterian conflict, as well as the history of just about everything else, are the salaried beneficiaries of the academic screening system, and rarely even think to criticize it. It deserves criticism.[22] This system has delivered money, prestige, and enormous power into their hands. The universally accepted ideology of academic freedom and its visible sign, the academic robe, have led to the triumph of self-certified humanism in every accredited academic institution of higher learning in the West. This should alert churches to the covenantal threat posed by academic freedom and academic robes, but it rarely does.

The Soft Underbelly[23]

Beginning with the founding of Andover Seminary in 1808, the theological seminary became the soft underbelly of conservative American Christianity. After 1875, a tiny handful of dedicated and highly educated modernists began to exploit this weakness. Briggs was their front man after Baptist C. H. Toy retreated under fire. Briggs lost the battle, but his associates won the war. He remained at Union Seminary to instruct the next generation of Presbyterian ministers. So did his de-frocked colleague, Henry Preserved Smith. So did his "quit just before being de-frocked" colleague Arthur C. McGiffert, who later became Union's president.

Nothing was done by the denomination's officers to strengthen the defenses of the Presbyterian seminary system. In 1936, Machen learned just how easily the seminaries could have been defended after

---

22. Robert A. Nisbet, *The Degradation of the Academic Dogma: The University in America, 1945–1970* (New York: Basic Books, 1971); Nisbet, "The Permanent Professors: A Modest Proposal," in Nisbet, *Tradition and Revolt: Historical and Sociological Essays* (New York: Random House, 1968), ch. 12.

23. Winston Churchill's phrase regarding what he believed was the military weak point of the Axis powers: Mediterranean Europe.

1870. By this time, he was in charge of his own seminary, Westminster Seminary, an institution legally as independent as Union Seminary had been before 1870 and after 1891, but with this crucial difference: the doors to the Presbyterian Church's pastorates were effectively closed to Westminster's graduates after 1936. The Presbyterian Church, U.S.A., removed its positive sanctions from Westminster Seminary. The majority Calvinists could have done the same thing after 1869. The modernists in 1936 understood ecclesiastical sanctions, having spent over six decades evading them and then overcoming them. The Calvinists of the Northern Presbyterian Church never did understand how to employ negative sanctions. As a result, they fought for what was a lost cause after 1869.

Strategies must be adjusted in order to work in different organizational environments. The liberals have been successful in every system of ecclesiology. The Congregationalists fell first, in the mid-nineteenth century; then came the Episcopalians and the Disciples of Christ in the late nineteenth; the Methodists in the early twentieth; the Northern Baptists, and the Northern Presbyterians by the mid-1930's; and all but the Missouri Synod Lutherans (so far) and Wisconsin Synod Lutherans since then. Even the Jesuits fell in the mid-1960's. Only the Southern Baptists have reversed the process, and it took a systematic plan to do it.

To understand why the Presbyterian liberals' strategy was successful, we must first recognize the four types of Protestant Church government. I argue that Presbyterianism is uniquely vulnerable to the strategy of subversion, for its system of government corresponds closest to the modern liberal's preferred form of government: bureaucracy.

Three Views of Church Government

There are four basic systems of Church government: prelacy, episcopacy, independency, and Presbyterianism. Traditional Presbyterian theologians have generally combined prelacy and episcopacy, dismissing prelacy and not mentioning episcopacy,[24] but this is analytically

---

24. See Robert L. Breckenridge, "Presbyterian Government: Not a Hierarchy, but a Commonwealth" (1843), in *Paradigms in Polity*, edited by David W. Hall and Joseph H. Hall (Grand Rapids, Michigan: Eerdmans, 1994), p. 507.

incorrect. The fundamental practical question of authority in any system of government is this: "To whom do I report?" This is the question of *lawful hierarchy*. I begin my discussion of the four systems with this question: To whom does an ordained officer report?

Prelacy is marked by a hierarchical government in which bishops serve: (1) as regional pastors to local pastors; (2) as superior pastors to subordinate pastors in ecclesiastical orders whose institutional boundaries are occupational rather than geographical, i.e., religious orders. A supreme bishop can more easily settle the turf disputes that prelacy generates with its system of ecclesiastical orders. For example, an offense-oriented international order such as the Jesuits would be institutionally impossible to maintain outside of prelacy. Without its own bishop to protect it from any bishop other than the Pope, the power of a cross-boundary ecclesiastical order would be eroded by objections from bishops whose territories had been invaded.

Episcopacy also has bishops. The bishop serves as a regional pastor to local pastors. He helps the pastor to settle disputes within the local congregation. He provides advice regarding what should be done to extend the work of the local church. He exercises a veto, but one subject to formal appeal.

Both prelacy and episcopacy at the upper levels provide some degree of initiatory authority, although far less so in episcopacy than in prelacy, because of the differing nature of authority structures over the bishops.

To whom do the bishops report? The decisions of episcopal bishops are judged by a synod composed of other bishops and laymen who represent local congregations. The system is based on personal authority held in check by corporate authority; this corporate authority is not limited to bishops. Representatives of local churches share

---

James Bannerman referred to three systems, "the Episcopalian or Prelatic, the Presbyterian, and the independent systems." Bannerman, *The Church of Christ*, 2 vols. (Edinburgh: Banner of Truth Trust, [1869] 1960), II:260. Thomas Witherow criticized prelacy's centralized tyranny (Church of England) and independency's capacity for localized tyranny, but he never referred to episcopacy. Witherow, *The Apostolic Church: Which Is It?* (Edinburgh: Publication Committee of the Presbyterian Church of Scotland, [1856] 1967), pp. 14–15; 59–66. *Paradigms in Polity* reprints the first section on pages 37–38.

judicial authority in the highest council. Final sovereignty is not lodged in any person or any ecclesiastical order.

In prelacy, bishops are judged only by other bishops. Prelacy requires a supreme bishop, or at least one who is "first among equals." Because official authority is personal, prelacy is far more capable of initiating projects from the top than other forms of hierarchical Church order are.

Independency is marked by a senior local officer, the pastor, who is a member of the congregation and who has no higher individual or association above him beyond the local congregation. He is technically "first among equals" in the local government, but his visibility and audibility place him in a unique position. The pastor who cannot exert informal control over his officers will eventually quit or be fired.

Each of these three systems is bureaucratic, for each has ultimate authority lodged in a corporation, but all three have strong elements of personalism, since an individual is responsible for initial decision-making, subject to a corporate or personal (i.e., papal) veto.

The Presbyterian System

Presbyterianism, in contrast, is far more impersonal organizationally. Its personalism is judicially local. On the local level, the pastor or teaching elder is "first among equals," for he belongs to his presbytery, not to the local congregation. He is ordained by other teaching elders, and he alone has the right to ordain other ministers. "Ruling elders are not to take part in the ordination of ministers."[25] (The physical act of laying on hands in ordination is optional; prayer is deemed sufficient.)[26] In this sense, the minister is judicially separate from ruling elders, who are elected by the local congregation, not the presbytery. Nevertheless, the system asserts the equality of elders: "Whether in Session, Presbytery, Synod, or General Assembly, all el-

---

25. *Manual for Church Officers and Members*, 4th ed. (n.p.: Office of the General Assembly by the Publication Department of the Board of Christian Education, 1930), p. 256.
26. *Ibid.*, p. 288.

ders are on an equality."[27] Paraphrasing George Orwell, all Presbyterian elders are equal, but some are more equal than others.

The local congregation cannot impose judicial sanctions on the pastor, except the sanction of dismissal, which is extreme and rarely resorted to. This sanction is more economic than judicial. All decision-making above the congregational level is corporate rather than individual: committees of pastors and lay (ruling) elders. No individual speaks for a presbytery, synod, or General Assembly with the same degree of judicial and personal authority that a pastor speaks for a local congregation. Committees and permanent Church boards possess most of whatever power exists in American Presbyterianism to initiate projects outside of local congregations. American Presbyterianism has no doctrine of personal representation above the local congregation.[28]

Yet personal representation is an inescapable concept. In any organization, there must be a "first among equals." God makes some men responsible for others. There are always few leaders and lots of followers. Too many cooks will spoil the ecclesiastical soup as predictably as any other kind of soup. Leaders possess greater authority and greater responsibility. Leadership at the national level will generally fall into the hands of one or two spokesmen for each of three identifiable institutions: seminaries, the larger churches, and one or two of the permanent national boards. We can classify the three major groupings as intellectual leaders, pastoral leaders, and bureaucratic leaders. Occasionally, a nationally known figure without institutional ties may appear, the obvious example being William Jennings Bryan in the first half of the 1920's, but this is rare.[29]

---

27. *Ibid.*, p. 230.

28. If modern Presbyterianism had an accountable representative for each presbytery or regional synod who answered to the regional synod, but who was empowered to act in its name between synod meetings, Presbyterianism would become episcopal. In some Calvinist denominations, there used to be a special office of superintendent, which was similar to a bishop's role in episcopacy. See "Superintendent," *Cyclopaedia of Biblical, Theological, and Ecclesiastical Literature*, 12 vols. (New York: Harper & Bros, 1894), X:32.

29. It is worth noting that when Bryan ran for Moderator of the General Assembly in 1923, a period of comparative strength for conservatives, he lost.

The intellectuals voice the technical details of rival theological viewpoints. The large-church pastors voice the practical applications of the rival theological viewpoints. The bureaucratic leaders implement the practical applications of the rival theological viewpoints. The intellectuals battle in print, so the records of their battles survive. In the 1880's, Charles A. Briggs battled Princetonians A. A. Hodge and B. B. Warfield. In the early 1920's, Machen had no rival Presbyterian theologian to match him; he battled the whole theological world of liberal American Protestantism, and he did so virtually by himself. The major pastoral representatives were the two most famous American pastor-preachers of their day: Clarence E. Macartney, who initially sided with Machen, against Harry Emerson Fosdick. Both of them wrote.

The key figure was a layman and a bureaucrat: Robert E. Speer, the head of the Foreign Missions Board. While Speer was a prolific author,[30] he is not remembered for his writing, which is understandable: his writing is remarkably unmemorable. His writing style reflected his bureaucratic commitment; there is nothing unique about anything he wrote. He is remembered because he wielded great institutional authority, and because his side won.

The Centralization of Power

What the history of Northern Presbyterianism reveals is that the Old School's representatives, mainly theologians, were progressively impotent to change Church affairs in the 1880–1900 era, and at the mercy of the informal decisions of the bureaucrats after 1906. As power was steadily centralized in the national boards after 1900, and especially after the restructuring of the Church's government in 1908, the impetus favored those aspects of Church life that are pleasing to bureaucrats: numerical growth, institutional stability, personal cooperation, and public peace. Why was power centralized nationally? Because the pastors of large congregations have very similar institutional

---

30. His biographer lists 54 volumes, 25 pamphlets, 64 articles, and 69 published addresses and sermons. James Alan Patterson, Robert E. Speer and the Crisis of the American Protestant Missionary Movement, 1920–1937 (Ph.D. dissertation, Princeton Theological Seminary, 1980), pp. 197–210.

goals for their own churches that bureaucrats have for the denomination. Only those rare large-church pastors who prefer theology to growth will side with Calvinism's theology of exclusivism.[31] Leading pastors tended to side with the Church's bureaucrats, deferring the details of administration to them and thereby transferring great authority to them. Large-church pastors represented the other pastors, who acquiesced to this transfer.

There is a basic rule in life: *power flows to those who will take full responsibility*. In an officially bureaucratic system, this will inevitably be bureaucratic leaders. But there is an inherent problem with bureaucracy: very few bureaucrats want to take full responsibility. So, power flows to those few bureaucrats who make deals, manipulate others, and do it behind closed doors. *The heart of a bureaucracy is its secrecy*.[32]

This creates a problem for historians, who are supposed to confine themselves to written records. They tend to pay attention to what articulate representatives have written, not what consummate bureaucrats have done behind the scenes. When participants destroy copies

---

31. Calvinism in its postmillennial version—the common version in nineteenth-century Presbyterianism—is not inherently exclusivist numerically, since it preaches worldwide evangelism and triumph. But until the days of expansion come, Calvinism is operationally the most exclusivist theology in Christendom. It teaches that God predestines the few to salvation and lets the many perish. It teaches that Christ did not die for all men in an eternal salvation sense; He died only for the elect.

32. Max Weber commented on this feature of bureaucracy as long ago as the World War I era. "This superiority of the professional insider every bureaucracy seeks further to increase through the means of *keeping secret* its knowledge and intentions. Bureaucratic administration always tends to exclude the public, to hide its knowledge and action from criticism as well as it can. Prussian church authorities now threaten to use disciplinary measures against pastors who make reprimands or other admonitory measures in any way accessible to third parties, charging that in doing so they become 'guilty' of facilitating a possible criticism of the church authorities. . . . This tendency toward secrecy is in certain administrative fields a consequence of their objective nature: namely, wherever power interests of the given structure of domination *toward the outside* are at stake, whether this be the case of economic competitors of a private enterprise or that of potentially hostile foreign polities in the public field." Max Weber, *Economy and Society: An Outline of Interpretive Sociology*, edited by Guenther Roth and Claus Wittich (New York: Bedminster, [c. 1917] 1968), p. 992.

of their correspondence, as J. Ross Stevenson did, it makes the historian's work that much more difficult. This is equally true for contemporaries. They do not see what is really going on organizationally.

Appeals Court vs. Central Planning

Presbyterian government, as with all forms of government, is hierarchical. What is unique about Presbyterianism is that its higher assemblies were originally designed to function primarily as appeals courts. Nineteenth-century Presbyterianism was a bottom-up system of government, not top-down. Its system of appeals courts reflected the heart of original Presbyterian government. This was the conclusion of Rev. Thomas Witherow of Belfast in his 1856 defense of Presbyterianism, *The Apostolic Church: Which Is It?* "In the Apostolic Church there was recognized the privilege of appeal and the right of government. This privilege is not only admitted, but it is one of the most distinguishing principles of Presbyterianism."[33] He referred to Wardlow's defense of ecclesiastical independency:

> "Independency," says Dr. Wardlow, "is the *competency* of every distinct Church to manage, *without appeal*, its own affairs. This is an ingenious mode of disguising the most repulsive feature of the system. Very few would deny that a Church is competent to manage its own affairs in such a way as to obviate the necessity of appeal; but what we assert is, that, when the Church lacks the necessary wisdom and discretion to do so, appeal among Independents is not permitted, the injured is deprived of redress, and power, for which the possessor is irresponsible to man, degenerates into tyranny when it is unwisely exercised, and there is nothing to keep it in check."[34]

Presbyterian General Assemblies and synods were never designed to be initiating agencies. Presbyterianism has always implicitly recognized that non-profit, bureaucratic agencies find it difficult for central managers to initiate and then oversee the details of large projects. Sociologist Georg Simmel wrote in 1908: "The higher official often lacks

---

33. Witherow, *Apostolic Church*, p. 69.
34. *Ibid.*, p. 65.

the knowledge of technical details or of the actual objective situation. The lower official usually moves in the same circle of tasks during all his life, and thus gains a specialized knowledge of his narrow field that a person who rapidly advances through the various stages does not possess. Yet, the decisions of such persons cannot be executed without that knowledge of detail."[35] Central managers must limit themselves to announcing the organization's general goals, establishing the criteria of successful performance, and imposing appropriate sanctions: rewards and punishments. They cannot carry out their grand designs without generating voluntary and active support at the lower levels of the organization. Central management cannot tell its subordinates exactly what needs to be done in particular cases. The old example is correct: if you assign two men to swat a fly, one to give the orders and the other to swat the fly, the fly will die of old age. There is always something lost—information and motivation—between central management and lower management.

The Limits on Knowledge

No institution's chain of command is perfect. The institution's sanctions, both positive and negative, which are necessary for establishing and maintaining control by the top, never quite fit the ends desired at the top. Exhaustive knowledge of specific details is required at the top for complete control. But exhaustive knowledge is an illegitimate goal for a creature. The knowledge possessed by those at the bottom is diverse, specialized, and constantly fluctuating. This information cannot be transmitted to the top without adding confusion and removing precision. There is "noise" generated by the channels of communication. The primary task of the founders of an organization is to design an institution in which (1) the organization does not subsequently deviate from its foundational goal; (2) the really important information that keeps the organization both faithful and flexible is not lost in the noise; (3) the value of the organization's output is maximized, using ordinary inputs, both human and inanimate; (4) mo-

---

35. Simmel, "Superordination and Subordination" (1908), in *The Sociology of Georg Simmel*, translated and edited by Kurt H. Wolff (New York: Free Press, [1950] 1964), p. 290.

tivation focuses on whatever is most important for both survival and fidelity to the original goals; (5) the organization remains flexible enough to respond to new conditions. This is extremely difficult to do. The old slogan about the British Navy is on target: "An organization designed by geniuses to be run by morons."

A free-market profit management system achieves these ends by means of the profit-and-loss statement. Senior managers have this vital numerical and quantitative tool of evaluation. A non-profit bureaucracy, unlike profit-seeking management, does not operate in terms of a competitive market. It does not have a profit-and-loss statement.[36] Therefore, bureaucracies cannot operate for very long as anything more than agencies with the veto. They are not entrepreneurial, i.e., seeking out new areas of service and new sources of funds. They are traditional: trying to keep the institutional ship afloat, moving slowly along a familiar route. Initiative has to remain at the local level. Members of any senior bureaucracy who forget this must then face the grim reality of the observation made by Lamennais, the early nineteenth-century French conservative social theorist: "Centralization induces apoplexy at the center and anemia at the extremities."[37] This institutional reality is what brought down the Soviet Union in 1991.

Presbyterian government in its original form reflected this. Primary initiative was left at the level of the local congregation. While the denomination's central government declared its Confession and heard judicial appeals and expressed general goals, Presbyterian General Assemblies were not effective initiating agencies. Those who ran the modern bureaucracy in between General Assemblies became very effective initiators, but at the price of ecclesiastical liberty.

The Confession as Constitutional Law

If liberty is to be maintained, how can a Presbyterian denomination resist the centrifugal pressures of independency? How can the

---

36. Ludwig von Mises, *Bureaucracy* (New Haven, Connecticut: Yale University Press, 1944). See Chapter 14, below: section on "Three Management Systems," pp. 847–49.

37. Cited in Robert A. Nisbet, *The Sociological Tradition* (New York: Basic Books, 1966), p. 115.

organizational unity of the wider Church be conformed to the diverse needs and skills of local congregations? How can the congregation or pastor be policed without destroying local initiative? The answer is simple: *by means of the Confession and catechisms of the Presbyterian Church*. These documents provide objective standards by which candidates for the eldership—both ruling elders and teaching elders (ministers)[38]—are screened *and subsequently monitored*. This second phase is crucial, as the Confessionalists learned too late in the Presbyterian conflict. These documents serve as standards by which the decisions of local congregations can be evaluated by an appeals court.

What was the original theory behind Presbyterian government? First and foremost, it rested on the public confession that the Bible provides permanent fundamental law to judge the content of the creeds. Chapter I of the Westminster Confession of Faith is "*Of the Holy Scripture.*" It is the longest chapter in the Confession. Section 1 says that God has revealed Himself in history through His written word: "Therefore it pleased the Lord, at sundry times, and in divers manners, to reveal Himself, and to declare His will unto His Church; . . . to commit the same wholly unto writing: . . ." *The Bible is the Church's fundamental law*. Section 8 says of the two testaments, "being immediately inspired by God, and, by His singular care and providence, kept pure in all ages, are therefore authentical; so as, in all controversies of religion, the Church is finally to appeal to them."

Second, the Westminster Confession and, in theory if rarely in practice, the Larger and Shorter Catechisms, provide the Presbyterian Church with constitutional law: its articles of incorporation. Third, the Form of Government provides the by-laws of this constitution.[39] Fourth, subsequent court decisions, including the highest court, the General Assembly, serve as legal precedents.[40] All of these features

---

38. Witherow believed that these are different departments of the same offices: *Apostolic Church*, p. 67; cf. p. 75, where he lamented the "disparity among teaching and ruling elders among Presbyterians. . . ."

39. *The Constitution of the Presbyterian Church in the United States of America* (Philadelphia: Presbyterian Board of Publication and Sabbath School Work, 1904).

40. *Digest of the Acts and Deliverances of the General Assembly of the Presbyterian Church In the United States of America.*

must be assumed to be judicially coherent with each other, or else no level of Presbyterian Church government possesses legitimacy. Any successful attack on an existing establishment within a Presbyterian denomination has to begin with an attack on some aspect of this integrated judicial structure. The existing establishment must be made to appear illegitimate because of its violation of the coherence of this structure.

A successful attack cannot rest here. The modernist attack in the Presbyterian Church, U.S.A., eventually carried out a full-scale alteration of the entire structure, culminating in 1967 with the alteration of the Westminster Confession. But this attack did not begin with a frontal assault on the Bible or the Church's Confession. It had begun nine decades earlier with a process of chipping away at both the Bible and the Confession, which created doubts long before modernists launched their successful attack in the 1920's.

The modernists had a strategy. First, the Bible must be challenged, though not all of it, and not all at once. Doubt comes in bits and pieces, and this is sufficient if your opponents have defended a "total package" view of the Bible's infallibility and integrity.

Next, doubts must be raised regarding some details of the Confession. Calling into question the objective authority of the Westminster Confession is inherently an attack on the Presbyterian system of government. Without the judicial authority of the Confession, one of two things must take place: (1) local congregations become independent of the denomination's central government; (2) the central government becomes tyrannical and theologically arbitrary by invoking a different standard. The Confession therefore serves as the keystone in the Presbyterian system of checks and balances. The problem is, there has been no agreement regarding what is actually affirmed through subscription—stricter vs. looser subscription—nor about the proper locus of enforcement of the Confession's provisions.

Confession: Subscription and Revision

Confessions are human artifacts. No confession can be elevated to equality with the Bible in an orthodox Church. To do so would divinize the creed or confession. Creeds are imperfect. Creeds must be supplemented by confessions as times and concerns change. A creed that is never changed and never supplemented is abandoned to the realm of the past; it becomes a museum piece or an icon that is invoked for tradition's sake. The progress of confessions in history is a mark of theological progress. So, the question arises: How to preserve the authority of a confession, if wholesale changes threaten it or no changes whatsoever also threaten it? Here is the dilemma: if the confessions are never revised because of men's fear of reducing the confessions' authority, the confessions will eventually lose authority, for they will become out of date.

Only the Bible possesses timeless authority, according to the Westminster Confession. So, if Presbyterian courts neglect to enforce the Confession and the two catechisms because they are perceived to be out of date, then the documents will eventually lose their authority. A confession that does not speak to fundamental theological issues of the day becomes irrelevant. Without revisions, the omissions and errors of the past become permanent. The inheritance remains incomplete.

Institutionally, a denomination that requires 100 percent subscription to a confession has either committed suicide or will abandon the confession unofficially. All confessions are imperfect. Thus, to require complete subscription is to prevent official confessional revision. The revisions will come anyway, i.e., the confession will be abandoned, but not openly. If no one inside the denomination is allowed to disagree, how can there ever be discussions regarding a needed revision? This is the paradox of confessionalism.

The Presbyterian Church recognized the existence of this paradox. In 1729, the New England group—the "low Church" wing—made it clear that there had to be a resolution to the problem. The Adopting Act of 1729 was the result. All candidates for the eldership had to subscribe to the Westminster Confession and catechisms in general, but then publicly admit any doubts before ordination. The ordaining presbytery would then take up the matter.[41] Both the discussion of the issue and the resulting screening process were to be public. If a presbytery ordained the man, he became a "point of entry" for the new idea. If the synod or General Assembly let this ordination stand, it was admitting that the new idea was, in the words of the Adopting

---

41. Loetscher, *Broadening Church*, p. 2.

Act, in accord with the "essential and necessary articles, good forms of sound words and systems of Christian doctrine. . . ."[42] The presbytery had the initial authority to test new ideas through the ordination procedure. If not overruled, this decision stood. The presbytery "baptized" the new idea into the covenant theology of the Confession.

Revising the Confession

How to preserve judicial authority through constitutional amendment and by the revision of legal precedents: here is a major dilemma of Constitutional government, both civil and ecclesiastical. The dilemma is more obvious with respect to Presbyterian government than with any other form of Church government. A Presbyterian system must take active institutional steps to ensure that its courts exercise the veto, or else it fragments into independency or centralizes into bureaucratic tyranny. One of the steps in legitimizing the veto is to revise the Westminster Confession periodically in order to make it conform more closely to the Bible before major challenges to orthodoxy appear. This is mandatory so that a continual process of screening prior to men's ordination and their subsequent exclusion (heresy trials) can take place in terms of a *widely* agreed-upon and *actively* agreed-upon profession of faith. When the Confession ceases to be revised as institutional bulwark against attacks on orthodoxy, local courts' confidence in the Presbyterian process of inclusion (ordination) and exclusion (heresy trials) inevitably falters. Candidates for the office of teaching elder will not be thoroughly examined, and heresy trials will cease. It was this problem—the dilemma of frozen Confessional authority in a changing world—that undermined Presbyterian Calvinists after the Swing case in 1874. It was the problem that confronts every system of government:

1. Identifying the final sovereignty

2. Speaking authoritatively in the name of this final sovereignty

3. Specifying the stipulations of this permanent authority

---

42. "The Adoption Act of 1729," reprinted in *Presbyterian Enterprise*, p. 31.

4. Enforcing these stipulations

5. Revising these stipulations to meet the organization's new responsibilities

The Authority of the Presbytery

Here is the key jurisdictional point. *The presbytery had the authority and therefore the responsibility to impose sanctions*: the positive sanction of ordination or the negative sanction of a refusal to ordain. If it failed in its task by ordaining someone whose confession was too deviant, this positively sanctioned individual could later be brought before a higher institutional authority. Furthermore, no one who had been ordained was legally beyond the sanctions of his presbytery. If, after his ordination, he changed his mind about any aspect of the Westminster Confession or the catechisms, and said so publicly, he could be disciplined. The problem was, there was nothing in the Adopting Act that required him to make his new confession public in a presbytery meeting, as he was required to do at the time of his ordination examination. So, a personal strategy of concealment was legally possible. It would take a public confession on his part to warn the presbytery. But where would this confession be more likely to take place? In the pulpit? In a seminary classroom? On the floor of presbytery? Or in a published document?

As it turned out, to become actionable, a Confession-denying confession by an ordained Presbyterian minister almost always had to appear in a published document. The Presbyterians are marked, more than any other denomination in Christendom, by three features: a detailed formal Confession, committees, and printed literature. The Presbyterian system unofficially adopted a rule: "If it isn't in print, it isn't judicable."

The modernists prior to 1900 faced a threat: "publish and perish." The printed word became the primary battlefield of the Presbyterian conflict up until 1893. After Briggs' de-frocking in 1893, the boards and agencies of the Church became the primary battlefields, and not a shot was fired. The conservatives offered no visible resistance. In 1922, the public battlefield again became the printed word, but by this time, the war was over in the bureaucracy. This meant that the visible battle after 1922 would be fought between representatives who had command of the printed word, yet the outcome of the war had already been determined. The war of the words was like fireworks overhead; the battle had been decided in the bureaucratic trenches by 1920.

Double Jeopardy

There was another problem, one rarely discussed by the participants or by Church historians: the problem of double jeopardy. The prohibition against a second trial for a man declared innocent is a fundamental principle of the common law. Does this judicial principle apply equally to ecclesiastical law and family law? Are the human rights (immunities from the State) that are protected by common law against double jeopardy more fundamental than the grants of privilege associated with Church membership and ordination or family membership? The churches have remained silent on these questions, but they have all concluded in practice that double jeopardy is legal.

If a presbytery initially clears a man, on what judicial basis can a higher court reverse this decision? Only one way: by ignoring the protection afforded to a civil defendant by the civil judicial rule prohibiting double jeopardy. Protection against double jeopardy is not a universal principle of Christian covenantal jurisprudence—civil, ecclesiastical, and familial. It is exclusively civil. A higher Church court possesses the lawful authority to reverse a presbytery's declaration of "not guilty." This means that the presbytery's trial is without final binding authority. Presbyterianism has rejected protection against double jeopardy. So have all other hierarchical Church traditions.

Even if the synod or General Assembly later de-frocked the entire presbytery—this has never happened—the presbytery's original declaration of "not guilty" would still stand if protection against double jeopardy were a universal judicial principle. The General Assembly actually adopted such a view in 1927.[43] But Presbyterianism does not regard the presbytery as a kind of grand jury: an investigative body that recommends prosecution but does not try cases. The presbytery is a judicial body that declares guilt or innocence, but its declaration is not final.

---

43. See Chapter 10, above: subsection on "No More Heresy Trials," pp. 611-14.

Nineteenth-century Presbyterian conservatives ignored the civil judicial principle of protection from double jeopardy. Charles Briggs had his presbytery's declaration of innocence reversed by the General Assembly in 1893. This system was immediately challenged by liberal Henry van Dyke. "It is an encouragement of perpetual strife, and a thing unheard of even in criminal courts where they do not make any profession of religion."[44] He ignored the obvious: *a presbytery is not just a court; it is also an executive agency*. It ordains ministers. If it also possessed final authority in refusing to de-frock them, it would become a judge of its own prior decisions. It would sit in judgment of itself. *To this extent, it would become autonomous, destroying the hierarchical authority of Presbyterianism*. This is not true of a local civil court, which is not an initiating (executive) agency. No organization can delegate both initiating authority and final appeals authority to its lowest court and still retain its character as a hierarchical organization.

Conflicts over Turf

Corporate bodies that are not officially represented by one identifiable individual have great difficulty in initiating anything.[45] This is why local organs in original Presbyterianism must initiate almost everything. Because of the paralyzing effects of the "turf" conflicts and personal rivalries that are inevitable within any corporate structure, a Presbyterian court's primary function is to apply the veto and settle disputes that have been appealed to it. The veto is a negative sanction.

Because of the high costs of gathering information in any large organization, disputes tend to be confined within subdivisions. Most information in life is generated and evaluated locally.[46] Modern communications theory has discovered that the farther away judges are from a project's point of initiation, the more subject they are to institutional "noise."

---

44. Henry van Dyke, *The Bible As It Is* (New York: Session, 1893), p. 17.
45. The Church is represented in heaven by Jesus Christ. He delegates authority to the institutional Church.
46. F. A. Hayek, "The Use of Knowledge in Society" (1945), in Hayek, *Individualism and Economic Order* (Chicago: University of Chicago Press, 1948), ch. 4.

When every case is appealed to a higher court, the organization faces breakdown. This is what has happened to the civil court system in the United States.[47] To preserve institutional order, disputes must be contained locally. Nowhere can this be seen with greater clarity than in India during Britain's rule after 1860. It was the genius of the British Empire in India that a thousand young men in their twenties could control a huge and diverse population scattered across a huge area. Few of them lived long enough to retire. (The interesting but neglected fact is that by 1860, they were very often sons of poor country parsons.) As Drucker puts it, "These untrained, not very bright, and totally inexperienced youngsters ran districts comparable in size and population to small European countries. And they ran them practically all by themselves with a minimum of direction and supervision from the top."[48] They imposed this control with only a relative handful of troops to enforce their local decisions. They had to do this by persuasion, with only the threat of military sanctions, for there were not sufficient troops to enforce every decision by every administrator. To call in the troops was considered a failure.[49] Similarly, to call in a higher court is considered a failure by almost any bureaucracy. Bureaucracies seek to contain disputes.

Presbyteries Delegated Their Responsibility

The presbyteries had a built-in tendency to ordain every seminary graduate. Why was there nearly automatic ordination, at least regarding theological confession? First, a seminary had sanctioned his academic performance. Who was going to challenge this? Second, if every individual with a complaint against a newly ordained minister had appealed to the next higher court, the Presbyterian system would have broken down. The denomination would never have grown large, because of the high cost of adjudicating endless disputes. *The desire for growth mandated an etiquette hostile to appeals by critics in the presby-*

---

47. Macklin Fleming, *The Price of Perfect Justice* (New York: Basic Books, 1974).

48. Peter F. Drucker, *Management: Tasks, Responsibilities, Practices* (New York: Harper & Row, 1974), p. 404.

49. *Ibid.*, p. 405.

tery. Presbyteries took the seminary's word for a graduate's orthodoxy. Third, a local presbytery wanted as much autonomy as it could maintain. The way to gain this autonomy was to avoid two things: appeals up the chain of command and intervention initiated from above. One way to preserve the illusion of presbyterial autonomy in ordination matters was to transfer responsibility to a legally independent agency that had no control over the presbytery: the seminary. Fourth, the denomination was chronically short of graduates of Presbyterian seminaries. The presbyteries were under pressure to ordain candidates. (Note: a chronic shortage is the product of below-market pricing. The word "shortage" should always be mentally accompanied by the phrase "at the price offered.")

By saying *yes* to the confession of a candidate for the teaching eldership who had been graduated by a seminary, the presbytery transferred the cost of organizing any court appeal to "malcontents." A malcontent was defined institutionally as anyone who disrupted his presbytery. Few elders wanted to be identified as malcontents. So, a modernist who had already been screened by a seminary was safe until he "went denominational" with his beliefs, i.e., until he went into print. Printed documents cross jurisdictional boundaries more readily than any other form of incriminating evidence.[50] This meant that modernists could pick and choose their battlefields and their timing. *This transferred the offense into their hands*. When they stayed out of print, they could operate safely under the umbrella of their presbyteries or their seminary employers. As an overture from the Nashville Presbytery put it in 1916, in the midst of a major Church dispute over the liberal ordination policies of the New York Presbytery, "it is not only discourteous and unwarranted, but also unchristian and subversive of proper discipline, for one Presbytery to assert that the ministers of another Presbytery or Presbyteries are untrue to their ordination vows."[51] As for the validity of the charges, the New York Presbytery insisted that complaints by other presbyteries had been

---

50. An audio cassette tape crosses boundaries today, but this is a post-1960 phenomenon.

51. *Minutes of the General Assembly, 1916*, p. 59.

made "on the basis of misleading newspaper records."[52] Why so much fuss, the presbytery implied, just because three ordained candidates had refused to affirm the virgin birth of Christ?[53]

Does this mean that presbyteries normally seek to cover up theological deviations by those within its jurisdiction? Yes, as surely as they cover up moral deviations.[54] This is another result of every bureaucracy's desire for secrecy. Any public discussion of deviant ideas or deviant behavior within its jurisdiction calls into question the bureaucracy's wisdom in allowing at least one of the disputants into the system. Other bureaucracies may start prying into the operations of the first one. This threatens the first bureaucracy's authority to police itself. It threatens turf.

In the case of a denomination without an objective confession to serve as the institutional standard, one of two things will begin to take place: (1) the central government will become increasingly dependent on local authorities to police the system, which leads to fragmentation ("the confusion of tongues"); or (2) local governments will become increasingly subjected to a central government that is operating arbitrarily from a distance. The Northern Presbyterian Church was headed in the first direction until 1922, when conservatives sounded the alarm in response to a crucial printed document, a sermon by Harry Emerson Fosdick. After 1930, it moved in the second direction,

---

52. *Ibid.*, p. 130.
53. *Ibid.*, p. 131.
54. When a Presbyterian pastor is found to have committed adultery, one approach for his presbytery is to persuade him to resign quietly and take a church in another presbytery. This strategy is called, "Not with our wives, you don't!" Part of my library on Puritan history belonged to a pastor in just this situation. He decided to leave the pastorate instead of moving. He sold his library. With the rise of civil lawsuits against churches and presbyteries, this tendency to cover up has escalated. Public ecclesiastical sanctions can subsequently cost a church millions of dollars in legal fees and judgments. The same conservative presbytery to which the adulterous pastor belonged also had a member who was a suspected homosexual. When the local government's case against him lost in civil court on a technicality, he privately threatened a lawsuit against the presbytery if it brought charges against him. The man taught in a local high school. The presbytery kept him on its rolls. He should have been excommunicated for threatening a civil lawsuit. But no one wants a lawsuit, which is why I'm not naming names. You will have to take my word for all this.

when the modernist-inclusivist alliance at the top took steps to isolate and then purge the conservative critics.

With respect to disciplining heresy, it is very expensive for someone in one presbytery to gather incriminating evidence against someone in another presbytery. *Critics within a presbytery are unlikely to cooperate openly with critics in another presbytery, even though those outside share their concern.* Elders knows this informal rule; to break this rule is a breach of etiquette. Every organization has formal rules and unofficial etiquette, and a breach of etiquette, even in the name of the formal rules, carries unofficial but very real penalties. Those critics who violate it begin their campaign from an institutionally tainted starting point. They face an uphill battle, even if they come in the name of the Church's Confession. Thus, judicial cases that go up the Presbyterian appeals court are rarely theological disputes between an individual or congregation in one presbytery and someone in another. If critics within a presbytery remain silent about abuses, there is little likelihood that critics across presbyterial boundaries will complain to the General Assembly.

In prelacy or episcopacy, a bishop may be willing to confront another bishop, face to face, first in private and then in public, in order to deal with a problem in the other bishop's territory. He sees the problem as a personal threat to his own authority, especially if the problem is theological or institutional, since the problem may spread into his own jurisdiction. He defends his own turf in the name of some higher principle, and the etiquette of the organizational structure allows this. A cross-boundary dispute can easily be initiated by a bishop in the name of some higher principle. This is not the case in Presbyterianism. Because Presbyterianism has no person with the official authority to initiate such a confrontation across jurisdictions, there is little likelihood that a Presbyterian elder will do this with anyone outside his presbytery's boundary except in strictly personal conflicts. A layman will never do it.

First Among Equals

I have already referred to this feature of government. We need to consider it in greater detail. The seminary professor becomes a dominant force within Presbyterianism because of Presbyterianism's traditional emphasis on a formally trained ministry. His authority is wholly unofficial, so it is extremely difficult to identify its operations or oppose it judicially. Every ministerial candidate is forced to go through a preliminary screening process: seminary. Thus, the academic screeners inevitably become a dominant force within an organization—the presbytery—that limits itself mostly to screening and vetoing. The presbytery's role in training ministers inevitably declined when the seminary's role increased. Going under care of presbytery became a formality. The seminary's faculty became the primary screeners. They did so in terms of formal academic criteria, not pastoral criteria.

Princeton's B. B. Warfield in 1917 warned against the growing authority of the theological seminary at the expense of presbyterial authority in the training of ministers, but this warning came more than a century too late.[55] But this aspect of Presbyterianism's unofficial pecking order explains why Machen, as the most famous Presbyterian seminary professor, could successfully initiate the counter-attack against the organized forces opposing Calvinism.

There is another aspect of this unofficial hierarchy of influence: *teaching elders over ruling elders.* Teaching elders are screened by "accredited professionals": first by seminary professors, then by a presbytery's examining committee. Pastors are deferred to as possessors of greater authority by ruling elders, who have been screened only by local church members and the presbytery. The teaching elder becomes unofficially dominant over the ruling elder in the Church's higher courts, even though "one elder–one vote" is the official rule. To offset this influence, ruling elders can conceivably exercise the veto at the presbytery, synod, or General Assembly level, since their votes count as heavily as the votes of teaching elders. But this power is never exercised autonomously by ruling elders as a voting bloc. Both their self-confidence and their experience are low. As for initiating anything against the suggestion of the combined witness of seminary professors and teaching elders, there is little likelihood that ruling elders will

---

55. Benjamin B. Warfield, "The Purpose of the Seminary," *The Presbyterian* (Nov. 22, 1917); reprinted in *Selected Shorter Writings of Benjamin B. Warfield—I*, edited by John E. Meeter (Nutley, New Jersey: Presbyterian & Reformed, 1970), p. 374.

attempt it. The price is too high. Their pain is guaranteed, while their likelihood of success is almost zero. So, ruling elders become, at best, the swing vote. This was the situation in the 1923 General Assembly, when the ruling elders voted for the reaffirmation of the 1910 Doctrinal Deliverance. The teaching elders were evenly divided, and the employees of the boards were opposed.

If a seminary drifts into heresy, there is little that can be done about it within a presbytery except to appeal to a higher court and refuse to ordain graduates of the seminary. The presbytery cannot do very much to improve the seminary, which is not under its authority; the presbytery's only response is defensive: exclusion of its graduates. If the seminary is legally independent of the denomination, things become even more difficult for its outside critics. This institutional reality became crucial in the Presbyterian conflict. The Presbytery of New York, dominated by Union Theological Seminary and its graduates, became modernism's primary "point of entry" into the denomination, a kind of theological Ellis Island. Union Seminary was legally independent rather than under the authority of the denomination after it withdrew from the Presbyterian Church in 1892 in response to the General Assembly's veto of Charles Briggs as Union's professor of biblical theology. It had no Church authority over it, yet it remained the primary training institution for candidates for the ministry in New York. After 1900, conservative ruling elders within the New York Presbytery were locally powerless to remove these graduates once they had been ordained as teaching elders.

The Presbyterian structure makes it very difficult for those outside a presbytery to take action against a man who is being shielded by his own presbytery. Only in the most notorious cases, where the offender had gone into print with his views, could those outside break the "protective coating" of the New York Presbytery's shell. The best analogy that I can think of is biological: the diseased cell. If the body's antibodies cannot isolate the diseased cell and kill it, the "rogue cell" will infect and transform all the others. The New York Presbytery became the biological equivalent of a lentivirus: very slow working but ultimately fatal to its host.

Presbyterian Leadership

The leadership of Presbyterianism has included theological scholars, yet the form of government of American Presbyterianism does not even mention the office of scholar. Function very early replaced form. While a ruling elder in theory has equal voting authority with a teaching elder, in fact teaching elders dominate the Presbyterian governmental structure at all levels. While a teaching elder in theory has equal voting authority with a seminary professor, in fact the interests of seminary professors have long dominated those presbyteries in which the seminaries operate. The operational hierarchy of Presbyterianism is this: seminary professors > teaching elders > ruling elders > members. The basis of the professors' authority is Presbyterianism's traditional insistence on an educated ministry, meaning a formally educated and officially certified teaching eldership.

Local church members finance the entire structure. Here is the great paradox of all hierarchical denominations: *money flows from the bottom to the top, while power flows from the top to the bottom.* Presbyterianism, being Protestant, acknowledges formally that individuals possess final governmental authority—the right to transfer their memberships to other denominations or local congregations—but, governmentally speaking, power flows downward. Members rarely transfer to a rival denomination, and when they do, they usually do so as individuals rather than as members of organized protest groups. Most of those who pay the pipers generally remain content to listen to whatever tunes the pipers choose to play. This was true of the Presbyterianism hierarchy, 1869 to 1936. This is why the semi-independent tune-writers, i.e., seminary professors, always become the functional high priests of Presbyterianism.

Eventually, listeners cease to pay the pipers. The decline in membership of the mainline American denominations has accelerated since the end of World War II,[56] especially after 1970.[57] Old members rarely

---

56. Dean Kelley, *Why Conservative Churches Are Growing* (New York: Harper & Row, 1977).

57. See the citations in Bradley J. Longfield, *The Presbyterian Controversy: Fundamentalists, Modernists, and Moderates* (New York: Oxford University Press, 1991), p. 3.

leave except by death, but replacements rarely arrive except by birth (and then leave during college). Attrition is eroding the domains of the lordly pipers. But this is a long, drawn-out process. Rarely do listeners revolt. They just leave: by death, by letter of transfer, or by just wandering away.

In nineteenth-century Presbyterianism, theologians were usually employed by the seminaries. Orthodox theologians were caught between the traditional academic ideology of academic freedom and the centuries-old reality of infiltration by covenant-breakers: beginning in the institutions of higher learning and spreading through the entire society. They refused to break with the ideology of academic freedom. They placed the supposedly neutral domain of scholarship above the Westminster Confession of Faith—not openly but operationally. They placed the seminaries beyond the negative sanctions of the Church. This doomed orthodox Calvinism within the Presbyterian Church, U.S.A., just as it has doomed every other Presbyterian denomination that has not become a separatist ghetto without a college attached to it. The formula for non-separatist Presbyterianism is: Presbyterian Church + Presbyterian college + Presbyterian seminary + time = liberalism. The formula for separatist Presbyterianism is: Presbyterian Church − Presbyterian college + Presbyterian seminary + time = liberalism or pietism. What happened in the Presbyterian Church, U.S.A., from 1869 to 1936, conforms to the first formula.

Overcoming the Strategy of Subversion

The conservatives in both the Old School and the New School adopted a defensive strategy after 1900. First, it was defensive intellectually. It allowed the intellectual leaders of a rival confession to establish the terms of public discourse. It was in this sense reactionary. This was the conservatives' crucial strategic error. In intellectual matters, as in moral matters, a defensive stance leads to surrender on the installment plan. To take anything except the moral and intellectual high ground is to experience a lifetime of making apologies. Apologizing is not what apologetics is all about.

Second, the New School initially possessed the instruments of legitimate judicial authority, but they failed to use these instruments effectively and continuously. In 1900, Presbyterian conservatives had visible control, but they refused to press their advantage in the

Church's courts. In 1936, they lost. Those who did not join the tiny exodus became silent onlookers.

The liberals' strategy of subversion could not be defeated by using short-range tactics or through a primarily defensive strategy. It could not be defeated by building thicker walls around the camp, for this produces a ghetto, not an army on the march. *A successful defense requires a systematic offense*: an assault against the enemy's worldview outside the camp, as well as a systematic policing of the ranks inside the camp. It requires the imposition of negative sanctions: inside and outside. It requires an ideological and financial assault outward—called missions—and constant ideological housecleaning inward. This is a full-time war.

The strategy of subversion is inappropriate for Christianity. We are not to be wolves in sheep's clothing, nor are we to be sheep in wolves' clothing. We must be completely open about our goal: *the conquest of the hearts and minds of everyone on earth by the comprehensive gospel of Jesus Christ.*[58] This gospel is public. "The high priest then asked Jesus of his disciples, and of his doctrine. Jesus answered him, I spake openly to the world; I ever taught in the synagogue, and in the temple, whither the Jews always resort; and in secret have I said nothing. Why askest thou me? ask them which heard me, what I have said unto them: behold, they know what I said" (John 18:19-21).

The capture of the Presbyterian Church, U.S.A., is a classic case of the successful implementation of the two-fold strategy of subversion: offensive and defensive. The shepherds who were on duty did not recognize what was happening to them until it was too late. The conspirators then removed from active duty a few representative shepherds who were willing to resist. The other shepherds meekly conformed for the sake of remaining officially on duty. The pay was good, and the uniforms were impressive: the robes of authority. By 1937, there was only a symbolic role for conservative shepherds. They had been penned in by the wolves.

---

58. Kenneth L. Gentry, Jr., *The Greatness of the Great Commission: The Christian Enterprise in a Fallen World* (Tyler, Texas: Institute for Christian Economics, 1990).

Conclusion

The Scottish-American Presbyterian court system has always officially rested on three assumptions. *First*, the primary responsibility for initiating a Church lawsuit lies at the local level, either with the congregation (lay members and ruling elders) or the presbytery (teaching elders and ruling elders). *Second*, the Westminster Confession of Faith and its two catechisms serve as the Constitution of the Church. The Bible is fundamental law, but it must always be interpreted in court cases by means of the Constitution. *Third*, in order to preserve both the theological integrity and the unity of the Church, courts at every level must impose negative sanctions on those elders, especially teaching elders, who refuse to preach and adjudicate in terms of the Church's Constitutional-Confessional standards.

The Presbyterian Church, U.S.A., failed to abide by assumptions two and three after 1900. By making it almost impossible for individuals to bring formal charges against a minister from outside a presbytery's boundaries, the traditional Presbyterian court system made it nearly impossible for critics of modernism to dislodge those who gave verbal profession to the Confession once and then repudiated it for the remainder of their careers.

The problem was sanctions, or lack thereof. Once ordained, a man was almost immune to formal negative sanctions unless he made a contentious public display of his disagreement with the Church or its Confession. The decisive issue was *contentiousness*. The Church's operational sin of sins was contention: disturbing the peace of the Church. The winners in the struggle for control of the Church would be those who worked quietly, not those whose rhetoric was most powerful. But principled men cannot remain silent in the face of opposition to their most cherished beliefs and institutions. The rhetoric would eventually escalate. When it came to rhetoric, Presbyterians were the most confrontational of the main religious traditions in America.[59]

---

59. Delwyn G. Nykamp, A Presbyterian Power Struggle: A Critical History of Communication Strategies in the Struggle for Control of the Presbyterian Church, U.S.A., 1922–1924 (Ph.D. dissertation, Northwestern University, 1974), pp. 53–58.

The Northern Presbyterian Church could not contain the contradictory theological forces that waged war for control of the denomination. The result was a series of splits: in 1741, 1838, and 1936.

There is a familiar slogan in America which applies the symbolism of an opera to the affairs of life: "It ain't over until the fat lady sings." The fat lady would sing only when one side or the other gained control over the Church's courts *and then systematically began to impose negative sanctions*. The crucial issue was sanctions.

14

MONOPOLY RETURNS AND THE FLOW OF FUNDS

The power position of a fully developed bureaucracy is always great, under normal conditions overtowering. The political "master" always finds himself, vis-à-vis the trained official, in the position of a dilettante facing the expert.

Max Weber (1917)[1]

Weber (1864–1920) wrote these words sometime after the publication of *The Protestant Ethic and the Spirit of Capitalism* in 1905 and before his death in 1920. A social theorist or historian would be hard-pressed to find a passage this short that better describes the political and institutional crisis of the twentieth century: the accelerating triumph of bureaucracy.

As early as 1909, Weber argued that our century is the most bureaucratic era since the days of the pharaohs. The spread of bureaucracy seems unstoppable. "The technical superiority of the bureaucratic mechanism stands unshaken, as does the technical superiority of the machine over the handworker. . . . The problem which besets us now is not: how can this evolution be changed?—for that is impossible, but: what will come of it?"[2]

---

1. Weber, *Economy and Society: An Outline of Interpretive Sociology*, edited by Guenther Roth and Claus Wittich (New York: Bedminster, [c. 1917?] 1968), p. 991. Reprinted in *From Max Weber: Essays in Sociology*, edited by H. H. Gerth and C. Wright Mills (New York: Oxford University Press, 1946), p. 232.

2. Weber, reprinted in J. P. Mayer, *Max Weber and German Politics* (London: Faber & Faber, 1956), pp. 126, 127. See Gary North, "Max Weber: Rational-

Two Social Models

The premier model for modern bureaucratic civilization has been the Church by way of the university. But the university is not an ecclesiastical model. Its system of rewards and concerns is much narrower than we find in an ecclesiastical system. When we think of the Church, we think of something larger and more complex than a university. The university is a classic bureaucracy; the Church has bureaucratic elements, but it is more than a bureaucracy.

The university system originally was episcopal: no supreme Pontiff; a separate corporation with legal autonomy, marked by the wearing of robes of authority; semi-autonomous and specialized academic departments led by commanding personalities; funding in part from below (students) and in part from above (Church and wealthy donors). But a university is not inherently episcopal, for as knowledge grows and specialization advances, there can be no equivalent of an academic archbishop. The head of a university becomes a peace-seeking, fund-raising, critic-challenging agent of the faculty. He acts in the name of the trustees, but he will normally be an agent of the faculty.[3]

As Christian colleges grew more autonomous from the Church and more academically specialized during the nineteenth century, they began to resemble the Presbyterian hierarchy far more than any other ecclesiastical system. The heart of both the modern college and Presbyterianism is *judicial impersonalism*: the committee as a way of life. The committee exists to enhance the operations of the system. The system is personal only at the local level. The teacher at his lectern is analogous to the preacher in his pulpit, although the teacher has more autonomy because (1) his listeners (students) cannot fire him, and (2) he is protected by the doctrine of academic freedom and even tenure. Above both of these employees is a system of bureaucracy in which collegiate authority is greater than anyone's personal authority.

---

ism, Irrationalism, and the Bureaucratic Cage," in North, ed., *Foundations of Christian Scholarship: Essays in the Van Til Perspective* (Vallecito, California: Ross House, 1976), ch. 8.

3. Henry Manne, "The Political Economy of Modern Universities," in Anne Husted Burleigh, ed., *Education in a Free Society* (Indianapolis, Indiana: Liberty Fund, 1973), pp. 116–18.

846

The Enlightenment's Two Wings

In the seventeenth century, the culture of Northern Europe began to be secularized, beginning with the philosophers: in physics, political theory, and economic theory. Isaac Newton's Unitarian vision of a universe under the rule of mathematical law was a powerful one. Nevertheless, with respect to Enlightenment social theory in the eighteenth century, it was the Church's organization that supplied the models. There were two models. The Jesuit order, with its system of top-down control, supplied the model for the Continental Enlightenment, especially the French Enlightenment (left wing). The Presbyterian Church, with its bottom-up system of appeals courts, supplied the model for the Anglo-American Enlightenment (right wing). The culmination of this viewpoint can be found in the Scottish Enlightenment: Adam Ferguson and Adam Smith. Edmund Burke was influenced by the social evolutionism of Ferguson and Smith, and his political theory reflects this, especially in his *Reflections on the Revolution in France* (1790).

For two centuries, the battle for the minds of men all over the world was fought between the ideal of the French Revolution and the ideal of the Anglo-American capitalist order. With the collapse of the economies of the Soviet Union and Eastern Europe in the late 1980's, and the fall of the Soviet Union in August of 1991, the ideal of the French Revolution is dead. It took two centuries for the world to make up its mind. Being pragmatic, men have now made their choice against full collectivism. Capitalism clearly delivers the goods.

Social Darwinism's Two Models

What has this to do with the Presbyterian conflict? Everything. Two decades after the publication of Darwin's *Origin of Species*, a debate within the Anglo-American camp broke out. Social Darwinism came in two forms: the free market version and the scientific planning version. The free market version prevailed among intellectuals and literate people in the first phase of the debate, which paralleled the second phase of the Presbyterian conflict. After 1890 and escalating after 1900, the central planning version prevailed.[4]

---

4. Gary North, *The Dominion Covenant: Genesis*, 2nd ed. (Tyler, Texas: Institute for Christian Economics, 1987), Appendix A: "From Cosmic Purposelessness to Humanistic Sovereignty."

Christians were left out of this debate, as they had been left out ever since the late seventeenth century. The general public has trusted no appeals to the Bible or the historic creeds of the Church as the foundation of social order. Christians therefore have had to choose which version of social Darwinism they preferred for the social order: the Whig version (decentralist, free market) or the Progressive version (centralist, bureaucratic).

The Old School, whose apologetic method invoked Scottish common-sense rationalism (empiricism), adopted the Whig tradition. The modernists, who affirmed evolutionary science as their intellectual model (scientific planning), adopted the Progressive version. The New School could not make up its mind. Its members preferred not to think about such matters. New School leaders called for simple evangelism. Theirs was the pietist tradition. They would decide which tradition would win, but they would not provide their own.

I. *The Economic Theory of Monopoly*

It is time to survey some basic economic theory of institutions. (No snoring, please.)

Three Management Systems

In 1944, Ludwig von Mises wrote *Bureaucracy*, a short book analyzing management in relationship to ownership. There are two forms of management, he argued: bureaucratic management and profit management. Profit management is based on the free market: private ownership, open entry, competition, and the profit-and-loss system. Consumers are sovereign in the profit-management system. They can buy or not, as they decide. Access to the consumer's money is based on satisfying his wants. In contrast, bureaucratic management is based on coercion: the ability to gain access to funds apart from meeting consumer demand in a free market. The State taxes those under its authority. Politicians allocate funds to various bureaucracies. These bureaucracies are dependent on the centralized collecting of funds. They do not meet consumer demand.[5]

---

5. Mises, *Bureaucracy* (New Haven, Connecticut: Yale University Press, 1944).

The two systems lead to different operations. Both profit managers and bureaucratic managers seek autonomy, but the profit manager cannot escape the consumer without calling on civil government to establish a monopoly for his firm. Unless the State grants him a monopoly—protection from his competitors—he faces competitors who seek to gain a share of any above-market profits he may be experiencing. The bureaucratic manager does not face such a degree of competition. The State establishes his monopoly in advance: a sphere of lawful jurisdiction in which his word, while not final, is authoritative. Thus, the bureaucrat's strategy for autonomy is based on persuading the politicians who legally are superior to him not to interfere with the day-to-day operations under his jurisdiction, and fund everything without much question—preferably, without any question.

The profit manager wishes to escape his competitors so that consumers will have to buy on his terms. Unless the State intervenes, he is rarely able to achieve this goal, and never for very long. The bureaucratic manager wishes to escape the politicians' negative sanctions, while retaining their positive sanctions: more money, wider jurisdiction, and (above all) a growing number of employees under him.[6] The manager rises professionally in terms of the number of employees under him—one of Parkinson's famous laws: the law of the rising pyramid.[7] (The most famous of these laws is: "Work expands so as to fill the time available for its completion.")[8]

Both systems rely on the flow of funds. They differ in the way that they gain continuing access to the flow of funds. The profit manager must serve the consumers (or provide the illusion that he is serving them). The bureaucratic manager must serve the politicians who in turn seek to control the consumers.

---

6. Thomas Sowell, *Knowledge and Decisions* (New York: Basic Books, 1980), p. 142.

7. C. Northcote Parkinson, *Parkinson's Law: And Other Studies in Administration* (Boston: Houghton Mifflin, 1957), ch. 1.

8. *Ibid.*, p. 2.

There is a third management system: non-profit management.[9] Non-profit organizations are somewhere in between, possessing neither political compulsion nor profit-seeking owners. The model is the disestablished Church. No one compels someone to join a local church, nor are its members compelled to pay tithes to a local congregation. The Church depends on charity, mainly from its members. While there is competition—local church vs. local church—there is no profit-and-loss statement.

The non-profit organization's manager must serve the donors, but usually through intermediaries. In the Presbyterian Church, the primary intermediaries are local church sessions and the General Assembly.[10] The number-one institutional goal of a Church board was to seek ways of establishing a nearly automatic pass-through from the donors to the board, either directly or through whatever bureaucratic agency represented the General Assembly.

Success Indicators

The crucial task of those who redesigned the Church's new structure in 1908 was to devise a system of success indicators that was consistent with the Church's non-profit legal status and consistent with the Church's goals. This was not done. The liberals did not want it done, and the conservatives had no idea that it should be done. Had it been done, when this new structure was imposed, the performance of those under this system of success indicators should have been monitored continuously to make certain that the bureaucrats were not using the system to attain goals—personal goals and institutional goals—other than those specified by the Church's officers. The employees should not have been allowed to use the letter of the law to thwart the spirit of the law. This is the problem of sanctions.

---

9. Richard C. Cornuelle, *Reclaiming the American Dream* (New York: Random House, 1966), ch. 5.

10. In the case of the Board of Foreign Missions, there was another agency, the women's missionary society.

Men seek positive sanctions. They seek to avoid negative sanctions. The question is: Can a man gain positive sanctions without imposing negative sanctions on others?

If life were a zero-sum game, such as a game of chance, every winner would produce at least one loser. But life is not a zero-sum game. There can be co-winners. The division of labor is productive (I Cor. 12). Marriage is a good example. Two people, male and female, working together are more productive than they are when they work apart. Biology, if not misdirected by legalized or even compulsory abortion (as in Communist China)[11] produces an equal number of males and females, or close to it: more males are born, but more of them die in infancy. The human race survives and grows—a blessing: "Lo, children are an heritage of the LORD: and the fruit of the womb is his reward. As arrows are in the hand of a mighty man; so are children of the youth. Happy is the man that hath his quiver full of them: they shall not be ashamed, but they shall speak with the enemies in the gate" (Ps. 127:3-5).

Beating the System

The institutional problem comes when men seek to advance their own ends at the expense of those who pay them and fund their activities rather than by serving the interests of those who fund them. Every system of rewards can be distorted in this way. The system is set up in terms of one set of goals—goals that are difficult to specify and difficult to integrate with each other—but the success indicators can be misused. Consider the grading system in school. It is established in order to pressure students to compete, work hard, and learn more. But it can be misused, such as by the practice of "studying for the test." Instead of learning the material for the sake of knowledge, the student studies whatever will enable him to score higher on a formal examination. Or consider profit in a business. The profit system is supposed to guide the producer in meeting the demands of customers. But in the short run, a producer can sometimes make

---

11. Michael Parks, "Peking Moving to Curb Killing of Baby Girls," *Los Angeles Times* (April 17, 1984); Nicholas D. Kristof, "A Mystery of China's Census: Where Have All the Girls Gone?" *New York Times* (June 17, 1991).

money by cheating the customer. In short, every system of rewards and punishments (sanctions) can be misused by sinful man. Systems should be designed with negative feedback mechanisms that thwart cheaters.

The incentives of the system very often reward people in ways not suspected by those who originally designed the system. The problem is this: those who benefit from the system have an incentive to become masters of the system. It is easier for them to beat the system than for part-time supervisors to police the system. The full-time bureaucrat is in a far better position to beat the system than the politician is. If the bureaucrat has tenure, and the politician does not, the revolving door effect of politics tends to keep the politicians ignorant of the ways in which the bureaucratic system is rigged to benefit those who run it and are employed by it.[12] *The personal payoff for gaining accurate information about the system is not symmetrical.* Those inside the system have greater incentives to master it than those who are outside, who are not nearly so focused. This leads us back to Weber's original comment: "The power position of a fully developed bureaucracy is always great, under normal conditions overtowering. The political 'master' always finds himself, vis-à-vis the trained official, in the position of a dilettante facing the expert."

So much for economic theory. Now we must apply it.

II. Applying the Economic Theory of Monopoly

Presbyterian Government

Presbyterians have never developed a theory of Presbyterian bureaucracy. This is a great irony, since it is Presbyterianism, more than any other ecclesiastical system, that has provided the operational bureaucratic model for the non-socialist West. A Western bureaucracy is impersonal rather than patrimonial. It is a system of offices to be competitively earned rather than inherited or appointed by a monarch. Access to bureaucratic posts is officially based on such criteria as performance on examinations, not (theoretically) personal contacts.[13]

---

12. This is the strongest technical argument against term limits for politicians in a government that provides Civil Service protection for bureaucrats.
13. Weber, *Economy and Society*, pp. 998–1001.

The Presbyterian emphasis on an educated ministry has produced the same outlook that marks bureaucracy.

Competing Claims to Funds

The Presbyterian system of government, developed in the first half of the seventeenth century, has never suggested a systematically Presbyterian structure for hierarchical control over Church boards. Yet the boards in the twentieth century became the driving force of Presbyterianism above the congregational level.

The local congregation has the initial claim on funds because they are generated from within the congregation except in the case of Church extensions: home missions. Above the congregational level, the boards have the next claim on these funds. This is why they are the secondary driving force. No agency above the local congregation has a legal claim on these funds, so the moral claim becomes fundamental. In the twentieth century, no presbytery, synod, or General Assembly has possessed a moral claim on these funds equal to the boards, especially the missions boards. The boards come in the name of the heathen and the downtrodden, or in the name of the retired minister or missionary. The appeal is to personalism. In fund-raising, no appeal is more powerful. Entire systems of fund-raising have been developed in terms of such appeals. A photograph of some starving waif is going to generate more net income than a reproduction of an organizational chart. The presbytery, synod, and General Assembly come to the donors in the name of the Church as a whole—an amorphous, unfocused, appeal to fund an impersonal system. In the language of modern fund-raising, they ask prospective donors to pay for envelopes and stamps. They cannot expect to rival the service boards in terms of fund-raising. Because there is no compulsion in Presbyterian fund-raising, the local congregation and the charitable boards will usually receive the lion's share of the funds, in that order.

Two Forms of Sovereignty

Judicial sovereignty is one thing. Economic sovereignty is another. In non-compulsory organizations, economic sovereignty predominates. He who legally manages an organization is dependent on the flow of funds. He has judicial sovereignty, but he does not have economic sovereignty. The General Assembly possesses judicial sovereignty over the Church's boards. In fact, only in rare cases, usually marked by a scandal, will the judicial sovereignty of a General Assembly overcome the economic sovereignty of a Church board. It is clear why the boards seek to gain a voice in whatever bureaucratic agency represents the General Assembly.

Even though a Church bureaucrat can be fired, his sovereignty is greater within his sphere of authority than the sovereignty of a civil bureaucrat protected by Civil Service laws within his sphere. In relation to the General Assembly, a Presbyterian bureaucrat possesses far more sovereignty than the civil servant possesses in relation to a politician. The typical politician will probably be in office next year. The typical attendee of a General Assembly probably will not be. Politicians possess legal sovereignty over taxing as well as spending; they can therefore redirect the flow of funds more easily than a General Assembly can. A Church board receives donations directly from individuals and congregations. If it can also gain a predictable annual budget from the General Assembly as part of an impersonal, bureaucratic budgeting process conducted before and outside the annual meeting of the General Assembly, the board has thereby locked in the flow of funds.

Scandals occasionally shake the foundations (temporarily) of civil government bureaucracies. The bureaucracies themselves may be accused of malfeasance. Such institution-wide scandals are unheard of in Church bureaucracies. They happen, of course; they are rarely made public when discovered, and they are rarely discovered. The Church's system of rewards is different from the State's. Politicians in the minority party can capitalize on civil bureaucratic scandals. They have an incentive to expose them. But a denomination is not supposed to be political. There are no formally structured rival political parties in a Church. Interest groups are informal and unofficial; they will do whatever they can to avoid the label of "party" or "political." The example of Machen's Committee of Eight in 1925 is representative. Because they tried to organize a national voting bloc to send conservatives to the 1925 General Assembly, they were successfully pilloried by the well-organized, deeply political modernists. So, scandals are covered up whenever possible by denominations. No one inside the denomination has an incentive to publicize them if, like the pregnant

Virgin Mary, they can be put away privately. Scandals are seen as the result of individual sinners, not an organized conspiracy. This outlook works to the advantage of organized ecclesiastical conspiracies.

The only way for political "dilettantes" to change a bureaucracy even temporarily is for them to cut its funding while they are re-writing the bureaucracy's rules. A cut in funding alone catches the attention of the bureaucrats. But short of a major scandal or a denomination-wide economic setback, Church boards' budgets are never cut by the General Assembly.

Preserving the Flow of Funds

The preservation of the flow of funds is the central goal of Church boards. No other goal has equal merit in the eyes of the bureaucrats who are part of the boards. Because the boards are nearly unassailable in public, the boards' incentives—success indicators—can be manipulated over time by the senior officials to meet the desires and hidden agendas of these semi-autonomous officials and their employees. The potential for misusing the board's formal success indicators is very great. The more time that the same self-appointing, tenured group has to manipulate the organization's formal success indicators, the more likely that the manipulation will take place. To imagine that this will not take place as time goes on is to imagine that original sin is no longer a factor in organizations.

Robert E. Speer led the Board of Foreign Missions from 1891 to 1937. As he proved in 1936, he was immune from criticism. His critics were not.

What was the formal success indicator for the Board of Foreign Missions? A numerical success indicator tends to become the dominant one in every bureaucracy, since it is easy to compare numerical performance, year by year. (Example: a student's grade point average.) The Mission Board's primary success indicator was numerical: the number of missionaries sent into the field. The Board was very successful: over 1,300 missionaries in 1935. The more important goal, Machen said, was to send theologically orthodox missionaries into the field. But it is much easier to compare raw numbers than confessions of faith. Speer had the raw numbers; meanwhile, Machen was unwilling to accuse any missionary of a crossed-fingers confession. It was obvious who would win that institutional dispute. Scandal was then re-defined: going public with the suggestion of a scandal.

The Quest for Ecclesiastical Monopoly Returns

The late nineteenth century was the great era of monopolies in American business, at least in Americans' perception of United States manufacturing. John D. Rockefeller, Sr.'s Standard Oil Company was the archetype: either as a model of efficiency or as a demon. The last great example of trust building came in January, 1901, the first month of the twentieth century, when J. P. Morgan created the United States Steel Corporation by organizing a group of hard-pressed steel manufacturers who bought the spectacularly price-competitive Carnegie Steel Corporation for $480 million, with $300 million in 5% per annum bonds going to Andrew Carnegie personally.[14] This made Carnegie the richest man on earth (since kings could not liquidate their wealth, converting it into money). Under President Theodore Roosevelt (1901–1909), the trust-busting era began. It accelerated under his successor, William Howard Taft. It has never been reversed.

To make this process palatable to big business, the Federal government offered a stick as well as a carrot: government regulation, meaning Federal price floors, meaning *barriers to entry that would protect existing corporate interests*. In public, the directors of big business deplored the government's trust-busting activities; in private, they encouraged it and financed those politicians, such as Senator Nelson Aldrich, who promoted it.[15] Those who had already established control over huge markets preferred protective regulation to open competition. This is the mind-set of every successful monopolist.

---

14. Harold C. Livesay, *Andrew Carnegie and the Rise of Big Business* (Boston: Little, Brown, 1975), pp. 187–88.

15. Gabriel Kolko, *The Triumph of Conservatism: A Reinterpretation of American History, 1900–1916* (New York: Free Press, [1963] 1977). On Aldrich —godfather of the Federal Reserve System, father-in-law of John D. Rockefeller, Jr., and grandfather of Nelson Aldrich Rockefeller—see Nathaniel Wright Setevenson, *Nelson W. Aldrich: A Leader in American Politics* (Port Washington, New York: Kennikat, [1930] 1971); Nelson W. Aldrich, Jr., *Old Money: The Myth of America's Upper Class* (New York: Knopf, 1988), ch. 1.

The monopolist seeks a situation where his suppliers compete against each other, while no one is allowed to compete against him in his role as supplier. He reduces his output and raises his prices, thereby gaining monopoly returns.[16] The economic goal of monopolists is the control over the upward flow of funds from the consumer. They claim *a legal right to the consumers' money*, not through open competition but through legislation against competitive interlopers—all in the name of the public good. To gain this control, monopolists give up some of their decision-making rights to the State and also the right to supply consumers outside of the production and pricing boundaries agreed to by the other members of the monopoly. In short, they give up their *judicial sovereignty* over the property they own in order to gain *economic sovereignty* over consumers.

An Ecclesiastical Monopoly

This is exactly what the modernists in the Presbyterian Church sought from 1874 onward. First, they sought control over the theological seminaries: the source of supply for candidates to the ministry. Second, they sought control over the Church's boards and permanent committees. Finally, in 1934, they demanded a monopoly over the distribution of funds by local congregations. They sought to exclude all rivals to these funds. The upward and outward flow of congregational funds had to be funneled through the official boards and committees of the Church. This was said to be the judicial equivalent of the Lord's Supper. The fact is, the modernists cared far more about the flow of funds than they cared about the Lord's Supper. The General Assembly announced no rules regarding the Lord's Supper; it announced very explicit rules regarding the flow of funds. Control over the Lord's Supper was the decision of the local congregations; it was never an issue in any of the competing theological camps. Control over money (economic sanctions) was the fundamental issue for liberals, and very important for conservatives. As Machen put it in 1923,

---

16. The best studies of this process remain Fritz Machlup's *The Political Economy of Monopoly* (1952) and *The Economics of Sellers' Competition: Model Analysis of Sellers' Conduct* (1952), both published by Johns Hopkins University Press, Baltimore, Maryland.

this control was a sacred trust.[17] The question was: Whose confession would determine who would exercise this trust?

As good Progressives, modernists publicly proclaimed the freedom of belief. They were free-thinkers—not in the Robert Ingersoll mode of outright atheism but in the Harry Emerson Fosdick and Henry Sloane Coffin mode: faith in the indeterminate god of the evolutionary process. They refused to be bound by the terms of the Westminster Confession or by the opinions of the conservative majority of the laity in the denomination. With respect to the flow of funds, they were also Progressives: they demanded centralized control. To achieve these twin goals—confessional independence and economic monopoly—they had to control the twin pipelines: into the pulpits and into congregational treasuries.

If modernists could not control the supply of candidates to the ministry, then local congregations would be able to hire men who agreed theologically with the members. This would bring an element of competition that the modernists did not want to face. This would also transfer excessive judicial sovereignty to local congregations. Presbyterianism proclaims a system of balanced judicial sovereignty: presbyteries control ordination; congregations control hiring and firing. (There is a third but unofficial element of control: certification by seminaries.) Ministers belonged to their regional presbyteries, not to their local congregations. The congregations, however, did have financial control. They did have the right to hire and fire their ministers. They had the authority to set ministerial salaries. Thus, congregations retained *economic sovereignty*. The presbytery could control only the supply of ministers. All sides in the Presbyterian conflict understood what this meant: *denominational monopoly returns for any group could be attained through control over ordination.*

The modernists knew that the typical local church member was more conservative than they were. Thus, modernists had to gain control over the machinery of certification: the seminaries. They had long enjoyed the advantage here: even before the 1869 reunion, it had been

---

17. Machen, *Christianity and Liberalism* (New York: Macmillan, 1923), p. 166.

considered important for candidates to seminary faculties to attend a German university for at least a year. This running of the German gauntlet undermined the Calvinism of candidates for the teaching positions. The experience had come close to undermining Machen's Calvinism; he had refused ordination from 1906 until 1914.

Machen had thoroughly enjoyed the intellectual challenge of German theological education, despite its effects on his faith. He had not accepted its philosophical premises, but he respected the vigor and discipline of German scholars.[18] He understood the eroding effects of both Darwinism and higher criticism. But as a scholar and as a representative of the Old Princeton, he could not bring himself to break from the old Presbyterian tradition of an educated ministry, which in his mind—and the minds of most Presbyterians—meant a formally educated, *bureaucratically (academically) certified* ministry. He believed in the eventual triumph of logic in human affairs. He wrote that "the true way in which to examine a spiritual movement is in its logical relations; logic is the great dynamic. . . ."[19] He deeply believed in higher education. He knew what devastating results German theological training was having on his contemporaries, yet he could not break with the idea that a young man with a bachelor's degree, a seminary degree, and no experience in the ministry could still benefit from studying humanism from humanists. He seems not to have recognized that his personality was unique; he possessed a psychological defense against humanism that few young men ever enjoy.

The other Presbyterian screening device was the possession of an advanced degree from a secular college. The prestigious colleges and universities after 1900 were controlled by secularists: the allies of the modernists outside of ecclesiastical boundaries. The modernists needed to do nothing here except sit tight.

By 1920, the modernists had control in all of the Presbyterian seminaries except Princeton. But they also had to control ordination: presbyterial exams. In the first phase of their strategy, they had to cut off questions from conservative members of the presbyterial ordina-

---

18. Ned B. Stonehouse, *J. Gresham Machen: A Biographical Memoir* (Philadelphia: Westminster Theological Seminary, [1954] 1977), pp. 104–12.
19. Machen, *Christianity and Liberalism*, p. 173.

tion committees regarding the details of the Confession or the five points of the Doctrinal Deliverance of 1910. Beginning in September, 1933, the General Council mandated a new question for all presbyterial exams: "Are you willing to support the boards of this Church?" Anyone answering in the negative could not be ordained. A candidate's free thought theologically was not regarded as a valid reason to oppose his ordination; his free thought on matters of denominational agency financing was prohibited.

After 1936, the modernists' monopoly could not be broken by either local ordination or independent parachurch agencies. It could only be broken through competition from outside the denomination: an exodus by ministers and members. To reduce this competition, the modernists used two threats: loss of pension benefits for ministers who departed and loss of local church property for congregations that departed. This second goal had to be enforced by the State. The State obliged. With only three exceptions, local church properties remained in the PCUSA.[20] To complete the process, the PCUSA sued in civil court in 1937 to force the Presbyterian Church of America to change its name—a kind of trademark infringement litigation. The denomination had previously proposed the name when considering union in 1932 with the United Presbyterians.[21] The secular courts upheld the larger denomination in 1938; in February, 1939, the new denomination changed its name to the Orthodox Presbyterian Church.[22]

The Iron Law of Cartels: Breakdown

The ecumenical movement was the ultimate hoped-for means of the modernists to restrict the exodus of its members. If every mainline denomination had joined the ecclesiastical cartel, this would have

---

20. The three were: Leith, North Dakota; Portland, Maine; and Branchton, Pennsylvania. *The Orthodox Presbyterian Church 1936-1986*, edited by Charles G. Dennison (Philadelphia: Committee for the Historian of the Orthodox Presbyterian Church, 1986), pp. 70, 163, 224. The Leith church later suffered a setback. Its attorney had not filed the papers correctly. A decade later, after having paid off all but a few hundred dollars of its mortgage, the congregation lost the property to the PCUSA presbytery, and had to buy it again. *Ibid.*, p. 70.

21. "News of the Church: The Proposed 'Presbyterian Church of America,'" *Christianity Today* (Jan. 1932), p. 19.

22. Edwin H. Rian, *The Presbyterian Conflict* (Grand Rapids, Eerdmans, 1940), pp. 233–34.

forced Church members to remain inside a confessionally modernist organization if they wanted the traditional higher Church or mid-Church (Presbyterian) liturgy of most hierarchical churches. The only other ecclesiastical options would have been local Bible churches and conservative Baptist churches: low Church liturgies.[23]

Ecumenism stalled. There are many reasons, but economically speaking, the main one was the concern over the division of the flow of funds and power. Those who controlled the denominational hierarchies in 1940 had established successful cartels by defeating the conservatives in their denominations. They were at the top of the flow of funds. To unite with other denominations' bureaucracies would have forced them to share an unknown portion of these funds and power with other bureaucrats. They were not convinced that in terms of money, power, and prestige, this was a good idea. The United Presbyterians had hesitated to join the PCUSA in 1934. It was not until 1958 that the union was consummated. This reluctance was shared by the officials in the other mainline denominations. The ecclesiastical leaders never broke down the liturgical and jurisdictional barriers, nor did they overcome the problem faced by the members of any incipient cartel, namely, the threat of giving up control over funds without being sure what the post-cartelization distribution of funds would be.

Every cartel eventually breaks down because its members cheat on the agreement or because its customers discover new sources of supply or substitutes. Firms quietly offer goods and services on terms more favorable than those agreed to publicly by the members of the cartel. Customers depart. The monopoly breaks down. It either lowers its prices or sees its markets shrink. This is the iron law of all cartels that are not protected by the threat of State violence. The modernist ecclesiastical cartel has been breaking down visibly since at least 1960, accelerating after 1965.

---

23. One mark of these low Church liturgies is the "altar call" at the end of each service: the minister asks people to come forward to accept Christ publicly. The altar call is the lineal descendent of the "anxious bench," an invention of Charles G. Finney. See Winthrop S. Hudson, *Religion in America* (New York: Charles Scribner's Sons, 1965), pp. 143–44. It was Finney's New School evangelism techniques and theology that had led to the division of the Presbyterian Church in 1837.

This breakdown had already begun in Machen's day. First, the old modernism was replaced by the new modernism: neo-orthodoxy. The Progressives and the old modernists had been believers in Kant's phenomenal realm: the techniques of scientific planning. Neo-orthodoxy represented the triumph of Kant's noumenal realm over Kant's phenomenal realm. Barth's faith in a self-authenticating and liberating but non-rational Christ-event or a Christ-encounter of the individual was substituted for faith in the liberating effects of the social gospel. *Heilsgeschichte* overcame mere *historie*. This switch in theology to neo-orthodoxy began at Princeton Seminary in the early 1930's, at the point of the triumph of the old modernism in the denomination.[24]

Second, younger members in the Church, when they reached the late teens or early twenties, departed into secularism, evangelicalism, or cults. Henry P. Van Dusen, ten years after his ordination by the New York Presbytery had provoked a storm of protest from conservatives, was an associate professor of systematic theology at Union. (He later became its president.) In his book, *The Plain Man Seeks for God* (1933), he lamented the failure of the older liberalism. "In seeking to save religious belief from annihilation by the accepted thought-forms of the secular world, it has become a pallid reflection of the secular philosophy. . . . Youth's verdict is sound: 'Religion has become an elective in the university of life.'"[25] His warning was echoed that same year by John C. Bennett, who in 1963 succeeded Van Dusen as the president of Union. "The most important fact about contemporary American theology is the disintegration of liberalism."[26] Yet the modernists of 1910 had insisted that without the religion of modernism, young members would leave the Church. While younger members are leaving, older members are also departing: into the jurisdiction of the absolute Monopolist of the universe.[27] New members

---

24. The owl of Minerva flies only at dusk, wrote Hegel.
25. Henry P. Van Dusen, *The Plain Man Seeks for God* (New York: Charles Scribner's Sons, 1933), p. 25.
26. John C. Bennett, "After Liberalism—What?" *Christian Century* (1933), p. 1403; cited in Robert T. Handy, "The American Religious Depression, 1925–1935," *Church History*, 29 (1960), p. 10.
27. I cannot resist the temptation: a soul proprietorship.

are not being recruited at rates sufficient to offset the departing members.

Millions of people outside the churches have accepted modernism's dogma—which is humanism's dogma—that it really does not matter in eternity what men have believed in history about God, man, law, sanctions, and time. If it does not matter, then why join any Church and be forced to share a portion of one's income with those who have proclaimed the modernist dogma of the irrelevance of dogma? Better to eat, drink, and be merry—preferably through credit card debt—for tomorrow we die.

Dry Rot Had Set in Early

Machen wrote to his mother in 1915, his first year as an attendee at a General Assembly:

> Dreadful things seem to be going on at the General Assembly, the "liberal" candidate for moderator having been elected by a large majority. Of course a good many brethren did not know how bad he is. He posed as a "moderate conservative." But I fear the Union Seminary men, with their deceitful phrases, and their contempt for the Christian faith, will go quite unmolested. I trust the Southern Church will keep quite separate. If things get much worse in the North, I should hardly like to continue making contributions to the foreign missions fund, for example, of the Northern Church. Our Southern Board may continue to provide for the preaching of the gospel, and it will be well for those who believe in the gospel to have some faithful administrators of their funds. The mass of the Church here is still conservative—but conservative in an ignorant, non-polemic, sweetness-and-light kind of way which is just meat for the wolves.[28]

By the time that Machen wrote this letter, a few weeks after the 1915 General Assembly, the theological drift he described was far advanced. He knew that the Southern Presbyterian Church was still Calvinistic, that its foreign missions board was still basically orthodox.

---

28. Machen to his mother, summer, 1915; cited in Stonehouse, *Machen*, p. 221.

He admitted in private in 1915 what he announced in public in 1933: he had deep suspicions regarding the Board of Foreign Missions. He knew in 1915 that Union Seminary had gone modernist, that those who ran for General Assembly moderator as "moderate conservatives" were operational representatives of the modernists, and that the conservatives were too naive to do anything about the drift into liberalism. While this drift was temporarily slowed in the General Assembly from 1923 until 1925, it accelerated rapidly after the Scopes trial in the summer of 1925. There was no way to reverse it after that.

Machen's concern was valid in 1915: the Board of Foreign Missions was indeed the representative ecclesiastical agency that had fallen to those who were opponents of Calvinism. There were reasons for this, most notably Speer's ecumenical vision. Union Seminary was officially outside the Church's authority after 1892; the Board of Foreign Missions was not.

Why was the Board of Foreign Missions so vulnerable to subversion? There are numerous possible answers: (1) the minimal theological confessions of the sources of the funding (laymen); (2) the board's sources of recruits; (3) the leadership of Speer; (4) the non-denominational impulse of those involved in foreign missions, both domestically and abroad; (5) administrative centralization, especially unified budgeting; (6) the great distances involved if North American presbyteries were made the locus of jurisdiction.

Foreign Missions and Ecumenism

David Dawson has surveyed the development of Presbyterian missions philanthropy. (He calls this *mission*, not *missions*. Conservatives support missions; liberals support mission. The official change in Presbyterian terminology came in 1958.)[29]

---

29. In 1958, the year of the union between the United Presbyterian Church and the PCUSA, the new denomination adopted a new term, the "General Mission Program." Dawson writes: "This was the beginning of a new era of unified administration, mirroring developments in other areas of society, in which all 'mission' (defined much more broadly) would be addressed through a centralized interpretation and administration." David G. Dawson, "Mission Philanthropy, Selected Giving and Presbyterians, Part II," *American Presbyterians*, 69 (Fall 1991), p. 211.

In 1800, a Permanent Mission Fund was established by the General Assembly, but most money after 1810 was funneled through the American Board of Commissioners for Foreign Missions, a joint Presbyterian-Congregational board, which was established in 1810, and also through the American Home Missionary Society after 1826.[30] Joint-venture missions drew the wrath of the Old School in the 1830's. In 1831, the Synod of Pittsburgh established the Western Foreign Missionary Society. In 1837, the General Assembly created the Board of Foreign Missions.[31]

The 1869 reunion brought consolidation. Presbyteries were reduced from 259 to 165. The missions agencies merged. Seven specialized boards were created to consolidate the work of the two churches' boards. The size of the individual boards shrank.[32] The work of the boards increased. This increased the responsibilities of the permanent secretaries of the boards. They became lobbyists for their boards.[33] The most famous such member after 1891 was Speer. The Church's officials hoped that consolidation of finances would make budgeting more predictable. Local churches were encouraged to send money to the boards. This request rarely worked.[34] Nondenominational ministries competed effectively for Presbyterians' money.

In the early 1870's, Presbyterian women began establishing local missionary societies. This was a major factor in the expansion of foreign missions of the Church.[35] Reifsnyder writes: "Although technically subordinate to the church boards, these women's societies largely managed their own affairs, raising their own money and determining where it would be spent."[36] Between 1880 and 1890, giving to missions doubled to $890,000.[37] Gifts from these societies tended to be

---

30. Dawson, "Mission Philanthropy, Selected Giving and Presbyterians, Part I," *ibid.*, 68 (Summer 1990), p. 122.
31. *Ibid.*
32. Richard W. Reifsnyder, "Presbyterian Reunion, Reorganization and Expansion in the Late 19th Century," *ibid.*, 64 (Spring 1986), p. 29.
33. *Ibid.*, p. 30.
34. *Ibid.*, p. 31.
35. *Ibid.*, p. 32.
36. *Ibid.*
37. *Ibid.*

designated for specific missionaries or children in missions schools.[38] Dawson allows an 1879 primary source document to draw a sexist (and accurate) observation for him: "Christian women always want to be brought into immediate contact with the object of their beneficence," which includes receiving "stirring letters" from the recipients.[39] After the reunion, women's giving was heavily weighted (designated) to independent missionaries and missions organizations. Of the $7.8 million raised through women's Thank Offerings, 1869–1876, only $114,500 reached the General Assembly.[40] (A parallel influence, of even greater impact, took place in the United Presbyterian Church in the 1880's: the Women's General Missionary Society.[41] In the Southern Presbyterian Church in the late nineteenth century, new missionaries were sent out largely through the support of women's missions societies, which, along with Sunday schools, contributed one-third of the missions funding.[42])

This development placed considerable economic sanctions over missionaries into the hands of women's organizations, i.e., laymen. These sanctions were less direct than in local congregational giving, but more direct than in missionary giving through a board. Women's societies were not authorized to screen candidates in terms of theology. Yet access to free money always involves screening. The question is: What was the most likely basis of this screening? Without documentary evidence to the contrary, I surmise: a one-time interview plus a lifetime of letters. The candidate for a foreign mission field had only to appear once before a group of women, give a 20-minute speech about the great challenge of the missionary endeavor broadly conceived, and introduce his wife. If he received a promise of support, he could depart in peace, probably for the rest of his life. There would be no further interviews or reviews. So long as he continued to send inspirational letters back to his missionary sponsoring group, he would forever remain "that nice young man with the lovely wife."

---

38. Dawson, "Mission Philanthropy, Part I," *ibid.*, p. 123.
39. *The Foreign Missionary* (Sept. 1879), p. 115; cited in *ibid.*, p. 124.
40. *Ibid.*
41. Dawson, "Mission Philanthropy, Part II," *ibid.*, pp. 204–205.
42. *Ibid.*, p. 207.

This is the problem of the lowest common theological denominator. The ecclesiastically unofficial confession of women would become the screening standard in the absence of presbytery sanctions.

The General Assembly in 1871 set up a General Assembly Benevolence Committee to promote giving to all eight GA boards. (An identical move was made for the eight boards in the United Presbyterian Church in 1871.)[43] The GA adopted a unified budget in 1874 for the agencies, with each receiving a fixed percentage of the undesignated gifts. Result: "It seemed to have had no impact on designations."[44] The GA and the benevolence societies were caught in a dilemma that never faded: if they wanted to maximize giving, they had to allow designated giving. Any attempt to centralize and bureaucratize the collection and disbursement of funds reduced total donations. People generally prefer to give to people rather than organizations.[45] Not until the 1950's did officials in the PCUSA discourage designated giving. In the 1960's, this policy became official, yet even today, the issue still divides the denomination.[46] Dawson points out that "virtually every individual Presbyterian and every congregation participate in designations in one form or another."[47]

The Collegiate Awakening

After 1886, the largest source of recruits for Protestant American missions was the cooperative parachurch movement in general and John R. Mott in particular. His theological confession shaped American foreign missions, and a lower common denominator confession did not exist in the evangelical community.

The 1890's saw a Collegiate Awakening. Methodist Mott and his friend and associate Speer became the major figures in Protestant foreign missions in this period. They recruited a generation of college men to serve on the foreign missions field. These recruits came

---

43. *Ibid.*, p. 204.
44. Dawson, "Mission Philanthropy, Part I," *ibid.*, p. 124.
45. A basic rule of all fund-raising letters: say "I," not "we." "We-we" letters pull significantly lower returns.
46. Dawson, "Mission Philanthropy, Part II," *ibid.*, p. 223.
47. *Ibid.*, p. 222.

through the Student Volunteer Movement (SVM), founded in 1888,[48] and the foreign missions arm of the YMCA, both of which were led by Mott for over three decades in the 1890-1920 era.[49] From at least the 1890's, he regarded his own work as an ecumenical ministry. "The unifying of the Christian organizations of the student world is not an end in itself. It is but a preparation for a larger work in the world."[50] He believed in "the strategic importance of the colleges and universities" in "the spiritual conquest of the world."[51] He was not alone in his views. The centrality of non-denominational, non-creedal, non-ecclesiastical student ministries was proclaimed by Presbyterian layman and ex-President of the United States, Benjamin Harrison: "But now in many, perhaps most, of the great universities and colleges the students are dependent upon volunteer agencies for such instruction in the Word of God as they receive. There is no agency so efficient, none so free in action, as the Christian College Association. It is within—it is not an intruder; it unites all, of every name."[52]

It was during this period when the number of candidates for the Presbyterian ministry moved steadily upward from fewer than 100 per 100,000 members per year in the late 1870's to over 150 in the early 1890's, with a steady fall after 1896 to fewer than 75 at the turn of the century. (After World War I, this figure fell to slightly over 50.)[53]

---

48. Eldon G. Ernst, *Moment of Truth for Protestant America: Interchurch Campaigns Following World War I* (American Academy of Religion & Scholars' Press, 1974), p. 18.

49. Senior secretary, Intercollegiate YMCA: 1890-1915; General Secretary, YMCA: 1915-1928. Chairman, Student Volunteer Movement, 1888-1920. Honorary General Secretary, World's Student Christian Federation: 1895-1897; General Secretary, 1897-1920; Chairman, 1920-1928. C. Howard Hopkins, *John R. Mott, 1865-1955* (Grand Rapids, Michigan: Eerdmans, 1979), p. 800, "positions held."

50. John R. Mott, *Strategic Points in the World Conquest: The Universities and Colleges as Related to the Progress of Christianity* (New York: Revell, 1897), p. 22.

51. *Ibid.*, p. 23.

52. *Ibid.*, p. 6.

53. Herman C. Weber, *Presbyterian Statistics Through One Hundred Years, 1826-1926* (n.p.: The General Council, Presbyterian Church in the U.S.A., 1927), chart, p. 100.

Moody and Mott

Mott had received his calling in July, 1886, in the sixth year of Dwight L. Moody's summer conferences held at his Mount Hermon conference grounds in Northfield, Massachusetts. This one was unique, however: it was a month-long foreign missions conference aimed at college students. By the end of that conference, Mott had emerged as the leader of the student group.[54] Moody became Mott's personal model for the devoted life.[55] In 1887, Speer arrived at Northfield, where his life was equally transformed.[56]

There were three aspects of Moody's ministry that are not widely known by those who know of his reputation as the greatest evangelist of his day. Gundry's biography discusses all three. These features became very important for the subsequent development of the world interdenominational missions movement. First, Moody was never ordained. He was a lay evangelist.[57] He believed that the theological confessions of simple Christians constituted the bedrock of theology; beyond this minimal common denominator, he was not too concerned personally. This was especially true late in his career, when he would invite such modernists as Henry Drummond and William Rainey Harper to speak at his Northfield conferences.[58] His most famous student disciples, Mott and Speer, also were never ordained. Thus, they could not easily come under pressure from theological conservatives in their respective denominations regarding confessional standards, which applied only to ordained men.

Second, Moody hesitated to preach on the doctrine of hell. He believed in it, but he rarely preached it.[59] "Terror never brought a man in yet," he proclaimed.[60] On this point, Mott, Speer, and the

---

54. Hopkins, *Mott*, pp. 24–30.
55. *Ibid.*, p. 28.
56. Robert E. Speer, *D. L. Moody: An Address to the Northfield Schools* (Founder's Day address, 1931), p. 11.
57. Stanley L. Gundry, *Love Them In: The Proclamation Theology of Dwight L. Moody* (Chicago: Moody Press, 1976), p. 166.
58. It was at the 1887 student conference that Moody brought in Drummond, who openly espoused liberalism. *Ibid.*, p. 213. This was the first Northfield conference attended by Speer.
59. *Ibid.*, pp. 96–101.
60. *Ibid.*, p. 99.

modernists agreed completely. Moody's premillennial pietism, however, did not sink into the thinking of his collegiate missionaries, especially Mott, who became a defender of the social gospel.

A third feature of Moody's last days was important for subsequent developments in the lives of his liberal disciples. Moody grew weary of the infighting between modernists and conservatives. In 1899, less than a year before his death, he criticized the modernist-conservative debate. His strongest words were against the conservatives. "Instead of fighting error by emphasis of truth, there has been too much 'splitting of hairs,' and only too often an unchristian bitterness. This has frequently resulted in depleted churches, and has opened the way for the entrance of still greater errors. Under these conditions, the question of the authorship of the individual books of the Bible has become of less importance than a knowledge of the teaching of the Bible itself; the question of the two Isaiahs less urgent than a familiarity with the prophecy itself."[61] This was also Speer's recommendation: reduce confrontation by ignoring the dividing issues. This meant, in practice, that conservatives had a moral obligation to remain politely silent while liberals taught higher criticism in denominational colleges, seminaries, magazines, and pulpits.

There was a fourth aspect worth mentioning: the Rockefeller connection. Until Moody's death in 1899, Rockefeller Senior was a financial supporter of Moody's ministry.[62]

Mott was a liberal. His liberalism can be seen in his recommended reading list for laborers. Half a dozen of Shakespeare's plays (unnamed), Bishop Butler's *Analogy*, Sir Henry Maine's *Village Communities*, Boswell's *Johnson*, and Blackstone's *Commentaries*: these are conventional enough, although the four tedious volumes of Blackstone seem inappropriate for anyone who is not a late-eighteenth-century lawyer. He rounded out this brief list with Alfred Wallace's *Natural Selection* (in 1858, Wallace propounded evolution through

---

61. Moody, "To Stir Up the Churches and Convert Christians," *Detroit Journal* (April 1899), cited in *ibid.*, p. 212.

62. Gerard Colby with Charlotte Dennett, *Thy Will Be Done: The Conquest of the Amazon: Nelson Rockefeller and Evangelism in the Age of Oil* (New York: HarperCollins*Publishers*, 1995), p. 15.

natural selection, word of which forced Darwin to go into print to get at least partial credit for the discovery)[63] and Benjamin Kidd's *Social Evolution*.[64] These two books were openly Darwinian. Kidd was a defender of social planning. He called for national legislation to "raise the position of the lower classes *at the expense of the wealthier classes. All future progressive legislation must apparently have this tendency. It is almost a conditio sine qua non of any measure that carries us a step forward in our social development.*"[65] Free market economics is obsolete. "It has served its end in the stage of evolution through which we have passed; . . ."[66] Religion, including Christianity, was defined by Kidd as a belief in the supernatural which provides non-rational sanctions that pressure individuals to subordinate their interests to social interests, "in the general interests of the evolution which the race is undergoing."[67] The book is insufferably dull, highly dated, and long forgotten. Mott's suggestion that it was of the same importance as Shakespeare, or even Bishop Butler, testifies to Mott's hidden political agenda.

Ecumenism in the Church

The gradual centralization of the Church's agencies paralleled the growth of ecumenical foreign missions. While there is always tension between the one and the many, as occasional disagreements between Mott and Speer over the role of denominations illustrated, these two developments complemented each other institutionally. This was possible because of the de-emphasis on theology that was inherent in both developments. The denominational agencies wanted theological peace intradenominationally so as not to interrupt the flow of funds. The interdenominational organizations wanted theological peace inter-

---

63. Arnold C. Brackman, *A Delicate Arrangement: The Strange Case of Charles Darwin and Alfred Russel Wallace* (New York: Times Books, 1980).
64. *Addresses and Papers of John R. Mott*, 6 vols. (New York: Association Press, 1947), VI:499.
65. Benjamin Kidd, *Social Evolution*, rev. ed. (New York: Putnam's, [1898] 1921), p. 249.
66. *Ibid.*, p. 253.
67. *Ibid.*, p. 111.

denominationally for the same reason. The cause of Christ is greater than theological fine points, Christians were told, and the cause of Christ was therefore seen as ecumenical. This was especially true of foreign missions, where the cultural contrast between paganism and Christianity was stark. Reifsnyder has described the results:

> A significant byproduct of the expansion of the denominational machinery in support of the evangelical cause was a shift in theological focus. Precise doctrinal formulation became less important to a new generation challenged by the scope of the work before them. Whereas prior to the Civil War denominational machinery, particularly in the Old School, was designed to preserve doctrinal truth, now theological precision was sacrificed to insure that the broadest possible consensus would be maintained for denominational work.
>
> The boards and agencies naturally tended to encourage this commitment to "the work" as a basis for national denominational unity and identity. They provided a focus for the church's crusade to create a Christian America and thus they sought to appeal to a broad constituency. Promoting the Presbyterian work of their boards was more likely to secure broad loyalty and support than trying to define theologically what it meant to be Presbyterian. This is not to say that doctrine was ignored. But the reorganization and the eagerness of the church to promote mission expansion by the latest means accelerated the theological shift to a focus on Christ rather than the Calvinistic distinctives.[68]

The motivation of the boards paralleled the motivation of the experientialists and the modernists. This was to prove fatal to Old School Presbyterianism in 1936.

Interdenominational Foreign Missions from 1900 to 1906

Paralleling the SVM in the first decade was the Forward Movement, another interdenominational ministry that gained support in the Presbyterian Church. This movement emphasized local Church

---

68. Reifsnyder, "Presbyterian Reunion," p. 35.

support of specific missionaries. The General Assembly backed it from 1902 on. So did the Board of Foreign Missions. This is not surprising. The director of the Presbyterian Church's branch of Forward Movement was a layman, David McConaughy, who had been general secretary of the YMCA in Philadelphia in 1895 and had served as the Y's first American secretary to India.[69] In 1902, he, Speer, Mott, and a few others organized a prayer circle that met annually: "Quiet Day."[70] They would meet together each year until only Mott was left; his last meeting was in 1951.[71] (During and after World War I, McConaughy became one of the two most important fund-raisers employed by the Presbyterian Church,[72] the author of the denomination's book on giving, *In Account with the Silent Partner*.[73])

The Laymen's Missionary Movement was another interdenominational missions organization. It sprang from the Haystack Commemoration held in 1906 in New York City. The first meeting was held at the Henry Sloane Coffin's Fifth Avenue Presbyterian Church.[74] It soon became a major source of missionary giving to the cooperating denominations, of which the Presbyterian Church was one. It quadrupled donations. It appealed to businessmen to make designated offerings.[75]

There were many of these interdenominational missions movements.[76] These movements encouraged designated giving to mission stations. A local church supported one station or one missionary. Each station had two budgets: the primary one from the Board of Foreign Missions and a secondary one from its supporting churches or individuals. The Board wanted the money to be sent through the Board, if possible. The growth of independent sources of income would threaten the control of the Board over its missionaries. Would

---

69. Hopkins, *Mott*, pp. 67–68.
70. *Ibid.*, pp. 214–15.
71. *Ibid.*, p. 700.
72. *Minutes of the General Assembly, 1917*, p. 58; *Minutes of the General Assembly, 1920*, p. 245.
73. *Minutes of the General Assembly, 1918*, p. 59.
74. Ernst, *Moment of Truth*, p. 19.
75. Dawson, "Mission Philanthropy, Part I," p. 126.
76. Ernst, *Moment of Truth*, pp. 20–22.

the rise of these independent parachurch missionary funding societies threaten Board control? Not if they sent the money through the boards. The president of the Forward Movement understood this concern and did his best in 1905 to gain support of the boards of the denominations by issuing this Board-pleasing scenario: "The tendency will be more and more for churches to turn over their missionary obligations to societies, for societies to turn it over to boards, for boards to turn it over to Executive Committees, and Executive Committees to Secretaries; so that, in the last result, the chief responsibility for the great work will rest on the shoulders of a dozen men."[77] Only if the independent societies cooperated would this be true. Only those nondenominational societies formally committed to such centralization would receive the formal approval of the boards.

Mott and Speer

In 1906, the SVM held its fifth United States-Canadian convention. The preparatory service began with a speech by Mott. It was followed by a speech by Speer.[78] This pattern did not change. Fourteen years later, the eighth international convention was held. It was led off by a prayer by J. Ross Stevenson, the president of Princeton Seminary. It was followed by a speech by Mott. This was followed by an address by Speer.[79] These addresses were followed by speeches from S. Earl Taylor, who, along with Mott,[80] was leading John D. Rockefeller Jr.'s short-lived ecumenical project, the Interchurch World Movement,[81] and from Sherwood Eddy, Mott's long-time assistant in the YMCA.[82] Some 6,000 students were in attendance at the 1920 meet-

---

77. Francis Wayland, *The Forward Movement Handbook* (1905), cited in Dawson, "Mission Philanthropy, Part I," p. 127.

78. *Students and the Modern Missionary Crusade* (New York: Student Volunteer Movement for Foreign Missions, 1906), pp. 3-15.

79. *North American Students and World Advance*, edited by Burton St. John (New York: Student Volunteer Movement for Foreign Missions, 1920), pp. 16-34.

80. Mott resigned from the Executive Committee in April, 1920. Hopkins, *Mott*, p. 621.

81. See Chapter 6, above: section on "The Interchurch World Movement, 1919-1921," pp. 392-403.

82. *North American Students*, pp. 37-56.

ing.[83] By 1920, Eddy had joined the Socialist Party and had come out in favor of the diplomatic recognition of the Soviet Union by the United States. Later that year, Mott threatened to resign from the YMCA if Eddy was fired, thus saving Eddy's position of leadership in the missionary movement.[84]

Eddy's ideas were representative of the more radical members of the next generation of SVM members, who led a revolt against Mott at the 1920 convention. The social gospel of the 1920's was far more radical than the earlier version.[85] Yet Mott and Speer remained as the visible intermediaries between mainline Protestant missions and social gospel radicalism until their deaths. Speer served as president of the Federal Council of Churches, 1920–24.

By 1906, Mott and Speer had become the dominant figures of American Protestant foreign missions. Through the SVM, they had supplied almost 3,000 missionaries sent out by 50 denominations, from 1888 to January 1, 1906.[86] Of these 826 went to China, 275 went to Japan, and 624 went to India, Burma, and Ceylon.[87] In addition, the SVM sponsored missions classes; over 12,000 students had attended by 1906.[88] From the beginning, it was an ecumenical operation. This, Mott said, was one of its great contributions. "Uniting as it does so many of the future leaders of the Church who have spent from four to seven years in the most intimate spiritual fellowship and united Christian service in student life, it is not strange that this should be true."[89]

---

83. Mott, "The World Opportunity," *ibid.*, p. 17.

84. Hopkins, *Mott*, pp. 621–22. Eddy was not only a socialist, he was an ethical relativist. "I regard morality as a spirit rather than rules," he proclaimed in his autobiography, *A Pilgrimage of Ideas or The Re-education of Sherwood Eddy* (New York: Farrar & Rinehart, 1934), p. 264.

85. William McGuire King, "The Emergence of Social Gospel Radicalism: The Methodist Case," *Church History*, 50 (Dec. 1981).

86. Mott's estimate in 1906 was 2,953 missionaries sent out by the SVM alone. This did not count the YMCA and other Mott-related organizations. Between 1902 and 1906, exactly 1,000 were sent out. Mott, "The First Two Decades of the Student Volunteer Movement," *Students and the Missionary Crusade*, p. 42.

87. *Ibid.*, p. 43.

88. *Ibid.*, p. 46.

89. *Ibid.*, p. 52.

Mott was a proponent of these social gospel.[90] According to his reminiscences, this influence came after the 1910 Edinburgh World Missionary Conference.[91] But ecumenism had always been present in his thinking. Mott and Speer had not spent their time recruiting Calvinists and what would later become known as fundamentalists. They had recruited "the best and the brightest" of American colleges.

While it would be misleading to blame the rise of Chinese and Japanese socialism entirely on Mott, Speer, and their recruits, there is no doubt that Protestant missionaries from the United States and Britain were the source of socialist ideas among Chinese intellectuals, who had been taught in missionary schools. This influence began in the 1890's, paralleling the recruiting activities by Mott and Speer.[92] The rise of socialism in both China and Japan prior to 1907 came as a result of English and American Protestant missionaries. As Martin Bernal comments (favorably), "The United States was undoubtedly the Western nation most responsible for introducing socialism to China."[93] It was missionaries—evangelicals or "low church" missionaries, as Bernal calls them—who accomplished this. The same was true in Japan.[94] The old-line missionaries in China were conservatives, most notably those recruited by the China Inland Mission. The new ones, recruited in the United States through the SVM and the YMCA, tended to be liberals.[95]

Liturgy vs. Ecumenism

There is more to the failure of liberal ecumenism than the churches' failure to establish a cartel. Liturgy also has played a major

---

90. Hopkins, *Mott*, pp. 622–33.
91. *Addresses and Papers*, VI:522.
92. Martin Bernal, *Chinese Socialism to 1907* (Ithaca: Cornell University Press, 1976), ch. 2, a study of the China-based English-language newspaper, *The Review of the Times*, whose influence for socialism began in the 1890's.
93. *Ibid.*, p. 8.
94. *Ibid.*, p. 9.
95. Joel A. Carpenter, "Introduction," in *Modernism and Foreign Missions: Two Fundamentalist Protests*, edited by Carpenter (New York: Garland, 1988), p. [3]. On the YMCA as liberal in spirit, see C. Howard Hopkins, *History of the YMCA in North America* (New York: Association Press, 1951).

role. Men are emotionally committed to traditional liturgies. What they grew up with they tend to regard as the preferable liturgical standard. There are exceptions, of course. A religious experience later in life in a Church with a different liturgy can move a person out of his original commitment. Usually this will be a lower Church liturgy designed to produce such experiences. The older liturgy will be regarded in retrospect as too narrow, too cold, or too formal: "stifling the spirit." But apart from such a conversion experience, or the acceptance of a spouse's liturgical preferences, most people remain content with the liturgy they grew up with if they remain in a local church at all.

Liturgy is the greatest single barrier to ecumenism. Church members look upon another tradition's liturgy and shudder. "If I wanted to be a [Lutheran, Episcopalian, Baptist, etc.], I'd have joined a [Lutheran, Episcopal, Baptist, etc.] Church!" On the one hand, the presence of a familiar liturgy keeps men from departing, even in the face of a major shift in theology in the pulpit. The liberals in Presbyterianism and the other mainline churches could be confident that if they were careful to avoid the rhetoric of confrontation, their parishioners would rarely defect. Liturgy would keep them in their pews until death did them part. This proved to be the case. On the other hand, this very liturgical commitment has kept ecumenists from being able to consummate Church union except with other denominations with the same liturgical tradition. For example, the Presbyterians never succeeded in joining with the Episcopalians, although this was attempted. The Episcopalians would not "move down" liturgically.

There is also the social phenomenon of denominationalism. I think of the remark of the well-educated Presbyterian minister in the movie *A River Runs Through It*. He dismissed Methodists sometime around 1935 as "Baptists who can read." There is a sense of cultural and social superiority that a higher liturgy Church member has. There is also a sense of spiritual superiority that the lower Church liturgy member has. Neither is willing to move downward into the void, which is where he sees rival ecclesiastical organizations sliding.

Rent-Seeking Monopolies: Sacraments and Money

I have argued elsewhere that it is the historian's task to seek answers to two fundamental questions: (1) How did a man or organization celebrate the sacraments? (2) Where did the money come from and go?[96] In the case of Presbyterian liberals, the answer to both questions is the same. For them, collecting the money was the equivalent of taking the sacraments. They actually announced this in 1934 —something that few if any other liberals have ever been willing to do. This had been their implicit theory of the sacraments from the first stirrings of Presbyterian liberalism in the mid-1870's until the takeover in 1936. It 1934, they made it explicit. The experientialists went along with this.

The economic mark of the Church's authority is its collection of tithe, just as the economic mark of the State's authority is the taxation of those within its jurisdiction.[97] Churches do not believe this regarding their authority, although they do believe it with respect to the State's authority. They do not make the right to vote in local church elections conditional on the payment of ten percent of a family head's net income.[98] The crucial institutional question in both Church and State is this one: *Which level of the hierarchical structure possesses the designated authority to collect money from the individual?* The answer to this question will determine the degree of centralization within the organization. In all hierarchical churches, this authority lodges in the local congregation. In all modern states, it lodges in the central government. The goal of twentieth-century political and theological liberalism has been to centralize the money-collection machinery and the law-making authority.

The local congregation is not regarded as possessing the right to demand the tithe as a condition of membership. Because of this, there has always been a debate over ministries outside the control of the Church. There has also been a debate over the claims of Church agencies higher up the chain of command. In Presbyterianism prior to 1936, the Church's higher levels were supported, voluntarily or involuntarily, by the lower levels, i.e., by money collected from congrega-

---

96. Gary North, *Political Polytheism: The Myth of Pluralism* (Tyler, Texas: Institute for Christian Economics, 1989), p. 553.

97. Gary North, *Tithing and the Church* (Tyler, Texas: Institute for Christian Economics, 1994).

98. *Ibid.*, ch. 3.

tions and individuals. The local congregation was not compelled to support the higher levels. Even today, a member is not compelled to support his local congregation. This has led to endless debates over who has primary claim to the donated money. In the 1830's, the Old School denied the legitimacy of the claims of missionary agencies that were outside the denomination. The New School affirmed this legitimacy. In the 1930's, the roles reversed, with this addition: those in control of the agencies were either liberals or the functional representatives of liberals.

Presbyterianism before 1934 had been judicially silent regarding any Church agency's legal or moral claim on money collected by the local congregation. The ordinances of a Church were local; this idea extended back to the Form of Presbyterial Church-Government (1645), *Of the Ordinances in a particular Congregation*: psalm-singing, preaching, the reading of the Bible, sacraments, a collection taken for the poor, and a closing blessing. This *entrenched localism* is why the history of the Presbyterian Church has been marked by interminable appeals for money from the agencies as well as local congregations.

The 1934 directive did not specify sanctions to be imposed against any member or congregation that refused to pay, nor could it: the tradition of charitable voluntarism was too deeply ingrained in the Presbyterian Church's history. The hierarchy could not legally coerce payments into their boards' coffers. The hierarchy could, however, impose restrictions on the outflow of funds. This was a classic assertion of monopoly: *a monopoly cannot legally compel payments upward, but it can legally prohibit payments outward*. The monopolist announces: "If you buy, you must buy from us!" The General Assembly announced: "If you give, you must give only to those controlled by us!" Economists call such activities *rent-seeking*.[99] Machen called them tyrannical, the mark of apostasy.

The directive did specify sanctions against members or congregations that paid money to rival boards outside the denomination. This really meant sanctions against ministers who recommended giving

---

99. James M. Buchanan, Robert D. Tollison, and Gordon Tullock, *Toward a Theory of the Rent-Seeking Society* (College Station: Texas A & M University Press, 1981).

money elsewhere. There was no way that a Church court would prosecute laymen in this matter unless they became extremely vocal, which was unlikely within Presbyterianism. Ministers made the public pronouncements. The liberals' goal was to set a judicial precedent with ministers.

The culmination of this process of bureaucratic rent-seeking came in 1936. It was a well-established Presbyterian tradition by then. It had begun in the early nineteenth century with the Old School's denial of legitimacy for gifts by Presbyterians to interdenominational missions. It reappeared in the late nineteenth century and escalated after 1906: the effects of the Cumberland reunion. The liberals' war was won in the trenches of the Church's bureaucracies, where there are very few easily accessible records. The liberals knew how to fight that war; the conservatives never had a clue as to what was going on until it was way too late. They came under the liberals' negative sanctions.

Conclusion

The Presbyterian Church, U.S.A., was like a large, poorly guarded bank with a vault full of cash and mortgages. If it remained unguarded, it was going to be robbed, sooner or later. It remained unguarded. But the eventual robbers were not one-shot lone gunmen or midnight safe-crackers. They were more like embezzlers. They were after a flow of funds. This process of redirecting the flow of funds would go on for a long time. They used the embezzled funds to buy up shares in the bank until they owned a controlling interest in it. Then they kicked the original managers off the Board. The Church's General Assembly meeting was like an annual corporation meeting of a very large firm: open to the shareholders but rarely controlled by them. Unlike corporate shareholders, however, the attendees at the General Assembly could not sell their shares short.

These professional embezzlers had a working arrangement with the bank examiners on the outside. Modernists inside the churches had a working relationship with Progressives outside the churches. There would be no public criticism from the outside; there would be only acclamation. "A fine bank, well run, and getting better all the time."

The problem has come in our day: the Presbyterian Bank's capital is running out. New banks in town are attracting the old bank's depositors. Unlike the Presbyterian Bank, the Episcopal Bank, the Methodist Bank, and the other Mainline Banks of America, these new banks are independent, well-managed, and must be taken over one at a time. They also offer higher rates of interest to depositors. This makes it tough on professional embezzlers. The negative sanction of consumer rejection has made itself felt. The crucial issue is sanctions.

CONCLUSION TO PART 4

And the lord commended the unjust steward, because he had done wisely: for the children of this world are in their generation wiser than the children of light (Luke 16:8).

They soon forgat his works; they waited not for his counsel: But lusted exceedingly in the wilderness, and tempted God in the desert. And he gave them their request; but sent leanness into their soul (Psalm 106:13-15).

Modernists inside the Presbyterian Church successfully captured the robes of authority and the reigns of power within two generations of Rev. David Swing's departure from the denomination in 1874. They had a systematic world-and-life view and a strategy and tactics to match. They were self-conscious about who they were and who their enemies were. They took a long-run perspective, especially after the de-frocking of Charles Briggs in 1893. They were willing to work quietly and systematically in the protective shadows of the Church's bureaucracies for three decades, until Harry Emerson Fosdick in 1922 challenged Bryan in the *New York Times* and Bryan's allies in his sermon, "Shall the Fundamentalists Win?"

Their victory in 1936 was part of a series of ecclesiastical victories, beginning with the capture of Congregationalism in the mid-nineteenth century. The Presbyterian conflict was the latest of several such conflicts—Congregational, Episcopalian, Methodist, Disciples of Christ, and Northern Baptists—which ended by 1940 with the triumph of the liberals. A generation later, a similar victory took place in the Southern Presbyterian Church. The Presbyterian reunion of 1983, North and South, was the liberals' version of the reunion of 1869. It was the capstone of a century of Presbyterian ecumenical efforts. But it did not reverse the post-1965 contraction of liberal Presbyterianism.

To make their strategy work, the liberals had to establish beachheads within the Presbyterian Church, safety zones in which they could build legitimacy for their movement and develop a program for capturing the institutional inheritance of the Calvinists. They found havens in the colleges, the seminaries, and the permanent boards and bureaucracies of the Church. They also achieved dominance early in the New York Presbytery. They took advantage of the Presbyterian system's weaknesses. They used a plea for peace and work in place of formal theology to take advantage of Presbyterianism's system of semi-autonomous Church boards. From 1876 to 1929, they used the secular dogma of academic freedom to take advantage of Presbyterianism's commitment to a formally educated ministry. They used the protection of the New York Presbytery to articulate their theology and their reform programs to take advantage of Presbyterianism's system of operational immunity for local presbyteries. They sought protection and salaries in the semi-automomous havens from heresy-hunting that had been created by New School Presbyterians after the reunion of 1869.

After 1920, they reversed their strategy. They had achieved dominance in the largest and most prestigious boards by 1920. They consolidated the boards into four large ones in 1924, which had been their goal since 1906. This delivered all of the boards into their hands. They suppressed Princeton Seminary's academic freedom in 1929. In 1931, they re-wrote the Form of Government to centralize the General Council's power over the presbyteries; this was ratified by the presbyteries in 1934. In short, they adopted the Old School's institutional structure of 1838, but they replaced the Old School's Calvinism with an open-ended theological confession, liberalism's version of Judaism's *shawmah Israel*: "Hear, O Israel. There is, at the most, one God."

The Owl of Minerva

With the death of Machen on New Year's Day, 1937, American fundamentalism and American Calvinism lost their only nationally known academic spokesman. This seemed to seal the liberals' triumph. For the next decade, no nationally known intellectual articulated conservative Protestantism. Billy Graham's appearance on the scene in 1949 offered a challenge to the Protestant Establishment, but Graham was then an outsider. He did not seem to be much of a threat. When John D. Rockefeller, Jr., died in 1960, the Protestant Establishment seemed all but immovable, seated securely as the functional Levites in the gates of public authority. But the owl of Minerva flies at dusk, and when it does, those below should cover their heads.

Protestant ecumenism stalled in the 1950's. It did not come close to achieving its long-heralded goal. The ecumenical ideal became increasingly utopian as the mainline denominations began to scramble for new members and more money after 1960. The goal of putting together a New Ecclesiastical Order was placed on the back burner at a low setting; preserving each denomination's existing flow of funds went to the front burner. The practical positive sanction of the flow of funds proved more powerful as a guiding light than the ecumenical vision. The bright promise of 475 Riverside Avenue began to fade, along with the whole neighborhood, and today it is barely visible. Colorado Springs is where the Protestant action is today, not New York City.

The ecclesiastical decline that began to set in as early as 1925 came on the heels of modernism's greatest public relations victory: the humiliation of William Jennings Bryan in Dayton, Tennessee. Handy's 1960 essay, "The American Religious Depression, 1925–1935,"[1] was a scholarly lament from the point of view of mainline Protestantism. But this era of decline launched a period of Church growth and parachurch growth that continues until today.[2] The ecclesiastical Seven Sisters never consolidated their monopoly; meanwhile, new, independent, and "theologically incorrect" competitors appeared on the scene. This is the fate of every rent-seeking cartel: it always breaks down in the face of new competition. Putting this in the language of modern business, the Seven Sisters have lost market share. In the area of foreign missions—the Presbyterian battleground in 1935—liberalism barely registers in the "others" category.

The quest for monopoly returns is a dead end. Those who indulge in it are doomed to disappointment. The ecumenical impulse is just one more discarded dream of monopoly rent-seekers, another example of "buy high, sell low."

---

1. *Church History*, 29 (1960), pp. 3–16.
2. Joel A. Carpenter, "Fundamentalist Institutions and the Rise of Evangelical Protestantism, 1929–1942," *ibid*, 49 (1980), p. 65.

Conclusion

The liberals adopted a strategy: a strategy of subversion. It was remarkably successful in the mainline Protestant denominations, 1875 to 1940. In one century, from 1875 to 1975, liberals pushed fundamentalists out of the major denominations and into the fringes of cultural irrelevance, where the fundamentalists actually preferred to dwell, just like John the Baptist: beyond the Jordan.[3] But by accomplishing this in the name of Progressive principles, the liberals also pushed the mainline Protestant churches into irrelevance at the other end of the wilderness.[4] The mainline churches are perceived by the public as just one more rent-seeking cartel among many, just one more voice favoring high-tax political reform. Increasingly, the secular authorities have begun to perceive that these Levites can no longer deliver the political sacraments: votes. So, the civil authorities have ceased inviting representatives of the Seven Sisters into the gates of the city. They invite them onto the parade review stand only on special ceremonial occasions, and only if Billy Graham is not available.

"Bread of deceit is sweet to a man; but afterwards his mouth shall be filled with gravel" (Prov. 20:17). Gravel has become their reward, their sanction. The crucial issue is sanctions.

---

3. Then came another Jordan, Hamilton, who invited fundamentalists to vote for Jimmy Carter in 1976. They came, a lot of them voted for him, and then they voted for Ronald Reagan and against Carter in 1980 after Carter proved no different from all the others. "Trust me," he had said in 1976. "Not this time," they replied in 1980.

4. Winthrop Hudson, *The Great Tradition of the American Churches* (New York: Harper & Bros., 1953).

CONCLUSION

The rise of this modern naturalistic liberalism has not come by chance, but has been occasioned by important changes which have recently taken place in the conditions of life. The past one hundred years have witnessed the beginning of a new era in human history, which may conceivably be regretted, but certainly cannot be ignored, by the most obstinate conservatism. The change is not something that lies beneath the surface and might be visible only to the discerning eye; on the contrary it forces itself upon the attention of the plain man at a hundred points. Modern inventions and the industrialism that has been built upon them have given us in many respects a new world to live in; we can no more remove ourselves from that world than we can escape from the atmosphere that we breathe.

But such changes in the material conditions of life do not stand alone; they have been produced by mighty changes in the human mind, as in turn they themselves give rise to further spiritual changes. The industrial world of to-day has been produced not by blind forces of nature but by the conscious activity of the human spirit; it has been produced by the achievements of science. The outstanding feature of recent history is an enormous widening of human knowledge. . . . No department of knowledge can maintain its isolation from the modern lust of scientific conquest; treaties of inviolability, though hallowed by all the sanctions of age-long tradition, are being flung ruthlessly to the winds.

J. Gresham Machen (1923)[*]

---

[*] Machen, *Christianity and Liberalism* (New York: Macmillan, 1923), pp. 2–3.

CONCLUSION

Liberty first. And why? Because without liberty there is no true orthodoxy. A man cannot be taught to believe and think right without liberty. Orthodoxy must flourish in an air of freedom. . . . That is the position of a conservative.

Henry van Dyke (1891)[1]

In the second place, a true Christian Church will be radically intolerant. . . . Now, a church is a voluntary association. No one is compelled to be a member of it; and no one is compelled to be one of its accredited representatives. It is, therefore, no interference with liberty to insist that those who do choose to be its accredited representatives shall not use the vantage ground of such a position to attack that for which the church exists.

J. Gresham Machen (1933)[2]

How much theological diversity could be tolerated by the Northern Presbyterian Church and still remain Presbyterian? Van Dyke answered: "more." Forty-two years later, a few months before van Dyke died, Machen answered: "less." The Presbyterian Church sided with van Dyke in 1936. It decided that the important issue was not theology; it was the flow of funds. Nevertheless, that view reflected an implicit theology: Progressivism. Theological modernism was the same as political modernism with respect to their central confession: *a self-certified, self-appointed, self-perpetuating administrative elite's legitimate control over other people's money*—other people being the majority, which affirms a rival confession.

---

1. Cited in Tertius van Dyke, *Henry van Dyke: A Biography* (New York: Harper & Bros., 1935), p. 129.
2. Machen, "The Responsibility of the Church in Our New Age," *Annals of the American Academy of Political Science*, 165 (Jan. 1933), p. 8.

The conservatives who remained behind, for whatever reasons, acted as though they believed that Machen had been incorrect. They acted as though there were not two rival religions battling for control over the assets of the Presbyterian Church. Modernists had always known better, but they could not have gained control over the flow of funds had they admitted publicly what they knew to be true. They wisely affirmed the opposite until they had gained control over the administrative and judicial arms of the Church. Then the purge began.

Those Unitarians who had kept going into print to prod Presbyterian modernists to "come clean" and pull out of a Church that mandated a ministerial oath to a Calvinist Confession of Faith were as naive as the conservatives who stayed behind after 1936. These Unitarian critics had misunderstood the central tenet of the shared ideal of theological modernism and political modernism. The issue was not confession; the issue was power. The issue was not the theological content of the ministerial oath; the issue was sanctions.

Covenantalism

The fundamental ecclesiastical issue in the Presbyterian conflict was covenantalism. This is true of every Church conflict, but historic Presbyterianism's claim to be the defender of covenant theology placed covenantal issues somewhat more visibly at the center of the battle. Nevertheless, covenant theology had yet to be precisely defined in Machen's day, contrary to the mythology of covenant theologians. There was no formal Confessional definition of the details of the Church covenant. There was (and is) no covenant theology of the baptism oath in official Presbyterianism.

This put the Calvinists in the denomination at a distinct disadvantage, not just theologically but also strategically. They did think covenantally with respect to formal sovereignty (God's), formal authority (infallible Bible), and law (Confession and catechisms), but not with respect to sanctions (law without sanctions as mere opinion) and succession (academic training). They did not understand after 1892 that full-time monitoring and policing of what was taught in all of the seminaries was crucial to the future of the Church. They did not acknowledge the implications of the screening process for ordination: the sanctions began in college, continued through seminary, and only at the very end of the process became a matter of presbyterial authority. This screening process had unofficially transferred authority to those outside presbyterial authority: academic faculties. The Calvinists' confusion with regard to this unofficial operational authority (point two) to impose academic sanctions (point four) to authorize succession (point five) doomed their cause. The modernists did understand: after Union Seminary withdrew from Church authority in 1892, its graduates retained equal access to ordination (positive sanctions) and therefore to succession.

Three Covenant Theologies

Covenant theology is not simply theological doctrine—point three, stipulations—as the Old School preferred to define it. Rather, it was all five points of the covenant: sovereignty, authority, law, sanctions, and succession. The Presbyterian conflict was a long battle over the sovereignty of God (how comprehensive?), the authority of the Bible (how reliable?), the stipulations of the Westminster Confession of Faith (how binding?), Church sanctions (locus of?), and Church growth (ecumenism?). But the crucial institutional issue was point four: sanctions. If sanctions could not be imposed by the Calvinists, they would be imposed by a rival faction operating in terms of a rival system of covenant theology. Sanctions are an inescapable concept. It is never a question of "sanctions vs. no sanctions." It is always a question of which sanctions. As Lenin asked: "Who, whom?"

There were three rival groups in Northern Presbyterianism, 1869–1936: Old School Calvinism, New School Calvinism-evangelicalism (fundamentalism after 1910), and liberalism disguised as New School Calvinism until about 1913, after which the disguise was abandoned. This means that three rival religions battled for control: judicial religion, experiential religion, and power religion. Each group had its own version of the covenant. Only one version could win institutionally. Had the Old School Calvinists understood this, they would not have joined with the New School in 1869, but only Charles Hodge and eight others at the General Assembly understood this at the time. After 1869, they could do little about it institutionally, despite their numerical majority in the first decade. They had lost their will to resist. After 1869, the Old School Calvinists, denying the very concept of chance, never had one.

The judicialists had a concept of ecclesiastical law: a comprehensive Confession of faith invoked by ministerial oath, but not invoked by members. What they did not have was a means of enforcing this view on the Church at large. Members were not bound by the Confession, for they took no oath. After 1875, judicialists never again initiated heresy trials. Strong on theology, they were weak on negative sanctions.

The conservative evangelicals understood almost nothing about the implications of the covenant. They did not think in a self-consciously covenantal fashion. They knew only that they did not want the Presbyterian Church to enforce the expressly Calvinistic stipulations of the Westminster Confession, and the Church never did. The heresy trials of the 1890's were conducted in terms of common-ground doctrines that were shared with fundamentalism in general. After 1900, the conservatives did not enforce the modified Confession (1903) or the new lowest-common-denominator Confession (the 1910 Doctrinal Deliverance). They did not believe that all of the terms of the oath should be enforced, and they had the votes to enforce their view by vetoing attempts by the judicialists to bring formal heresy trials. The majority evangelicals substituted another concept of law: *peace unless rhetorically provoked*. This view prevailed from 1879 (after the 1878 McCune trial) until 1934. Weak on theology, they were weak on negative sanctions.

The liberals understood the implications of their covenant theology. They knew that only one party could win, but they had to pretend they didn't. Instead, they called publicly for the imported political doctrine of pluralism, i.e., religious toleration—Whig political liberalism in ecclesiastical robes—until they had sufficient votes to enforce their view of the covenant. Their view of the covenant substituted process theology for inerrancy in all five points prior to their victory: sovereignty (evolving god, evolving mankind), authority (historicism's Bible), law (situation ethics), sanctions (open debate), and succession (open-ended). But, like all Progressive evolutionists, they abandoned their open-ended process theology once they came into power. They substituted a new form of inerrency: sovereignty (majority rule), authority (unquestioned submission), law (executive-administrative), sanctions (the flow of funds), and succession (winners take all). The only confession they bothered to enforce after 1933 was ministerial confession of faith in point two: hierarchy. In 1934, they officially elevated the collection of money to the judicial equivalent of a sacrament: *the flow of funds*. They consolidated the Church's machinery in terms of this view from 1931 to 1934. From 1934 to 1936, they imposed it, with the assent of the inclusivist evangelicals.

The decline of Presbyterianism's flow of funds after 1965 testifies to the truth of Machen's original contention: the Church is a voluntary institution. The boards of the Presbyterian Church can enforce their claims on the laity's flow of funds, if at all, only within the boundaries of the denomination. In 1910, modernists insisted that if the Presbyterian Church did not change its theology, bright young men would not join. The Church did change its theology—several times: to modernism, realism, Barthianism, and. . . ? (Evolution at work!) But the bright, secularized young men and women have continued to depart.[3] The modernists' social theology of 1910 grew feeble and had retired by 1940. Such is the age-old problem of conforming to the spirit of the age. All such spirits are mortal. They grow feeble; then they need catheters; then they die. Point five of the covenant cannot be evaded: succession. Those confessing a modified confession, either openly or with crossed fingers, will inherit. Confessions cannot remain simultaneously relevant and static. Only the Bible possesses this unique status.

Defending the Church

The traditional marks of the institutional Church are preaching, the sacraments, and discipline. Each of the three major groups within Presbyterianism had its own emphasis in the defense of the marks of the Church.

Calvinism

Old School Calvinists placed most of their emphasis on preaching. The problem was, they had to establish a means of securing the orthodoxy of preaching. With the establishment in 1812 of Princeton Theological Seminary, the Old School unofficially transferred initial

---

3. Bradley J. Longfield, *The Presbyterian Controversy: Fundamentalists, Modernists, and Moderates* (New York: Oxford University Press, 1991), Epilogue.

authority over the content of theology from the local presbytery to a national seminary. The sanctions became primarily academic. Prior to the publication of Hodge's *Systematic Theology*, the ability to read Latin was more important than any other academic skill for entrance into the Presbyterian ministry, since Princeton used Turretin's Latin textbook as its text. Given the fact of most Americans' minimal ability with foreign languages, this policy drastically narrowed the base from which to recruit pastors. This negative sanction over Presbyterian ordination served as a positive sanction for Baptist and Methodist ordination. They took full advantage of it, on a scale never before seen in home missions.

The Old School did formally proclaim the presbytery as the court of initial access to the teaching ministry, but this did little good after 1900. The presbyteries were operationally free to ordain whomever they pleased without a serious threat of hierarchical negative sanctions. The New York Presbytery ordained a series of creed-denying (not just Confession-denying) candidates. From the General Assembly of 1892 until 1936, the Old School appealed to confessional morality: if a man does not believe the Confession, he should leave. But after the Confessional revision of 1903, no Calvinists left the denomination. That judicially sealed their cause's doom. When, in late 1936, the defrocked Machen at last announced in an editorial that the 1903 revisions had been "compromising amendments," "highly objectionable," a "calamity," and "a very serious lowering of the flag,"[4] he implicitly admitted to having crossed his own fingers at his ordination in 1914. He had labored under too great a burden for conducting a successful ecclesiastical campaign. He had never admired the standards—the "flag"—to which he had rallied his troops. Five weeks after he made this belated assessment, he was dead.

The sacraments were not explicitly discussed by Old School Presbyterians as being tied to propositional truth, so they did not become a focus of debate. None of the three groups regarded the sacraments as invoking God's sanctions in history. None saw the Lord's Supper as a covenant renewal celebration. None saw the Church's role in guard-

---

4. Machen, *Presbyterian Guardian* (Nov. 28, 1936), pp. 69–70.

ing this public invocation of God's sacramental sanctions as judicially relevant. Thus, the Old School did not proclaim the covenantal link between propositional truth in the pulpit and the judicial ramifications of the oath-bound sacraments. The only systematic defense of the Lord's Supper in Presbyterianism was offered by the local congregation and the local presbytery: closed communion, i.e., baptized Church members only. Nevertheless, the Larger Catechism did relate the sacrament of baptism to obedience. A Presbyterian Church member was understood as having professed faith in Christ and having promised to obey, i.e., a confession honoring hierarchy. "Baptism is not to be administered to any that are out of the visible church, and so strangers from the covenant of promise, till they profess their faith in Christ, and obedience to him. . ." (A. 166). The modernists understood this covenantal principle of hierarchy, which is why, at the General Assembly of 1934, they formally equated local congregations' donations to the Church's official boards with the Lord's Supper. *For liberals, the flow of funds up the hierarchy was the equivalent of the blood of Christ.* They demanded sacramental obedience, so defined. Machen refused to give it, and this led to his de-frocking.

Ultimately, the Presbyterian structure of government passes local judicial sovereignty into the hands of communing members, who can hire and fire pastors, and who can decide to donate money or not. Yet the members' confession of faith was always formally devoid of theological content. Membership standards were imposed by the local church's session. No denomination-wide membership standards existed. In New York City, these standards were minimal. A modernist layman would have no problem in confessing a theologically empty oath; modernist ministers confessed such judicial language continually. At the level of the local congregation, the lowest common denominator increasingly prevailed. When the catechizing of children was not strongly recommended by a local congregation's session, the lowest common denominator fell very low indeed, though never so low as the theological confession of Henry van Dyke or Henry Sloane Coffin.

The Old School Calvinists delivered their votes by proxy to the New School Calvinists after 1869. They had returned to the smaller fold on their opponents' terms. Legitimacy would henceforth flow downward from New School abolitionism to fill the void of Old

School adiaphorism. Presbyterial sanctions were operationally in the hands of New School Calvinists in all but a handful of presbyteries, from 1869 onward. This meant that Old School Calvinists had to gain the support of non-Calvinists in order to enforce denominational discipline. The one exception was Patton's pursuit of Swing in 1874. The defense of the Presbyterian Church would not be made by an appeal to the Westminster Confession. Charles Hodge had recognized this in 1869. His was a voice crying in the wilderness.

Patton was a major participant in the Presbyterian conflict, the mirror image of Henry van Dyke, who survived Patton by four months. He was the hard-liner after the reunion, the one Old School theologian who brought formal negative sanctions against a liberal in a Church court. Yet he began a quiet retreat after he became president of Princeton University in 1888. He refused to purge the university of its liberal faculty members; so, in 1902, they purged him. (Negative sanctions are inescapable concepts.) They paid him a small fortune to leave quietly, and he did. He chose as his successor the man he had hired, who had said nothing good about him, and who had engineered the purge: Woodrow Wilson. Finally, in 1926, the year of the liberals' takeover of the General Assembly, he openly repudiated the Old School tradition on inerrancy. In *Fundamental Christianity*, he announced: "Concerning now the inspiration of the Scripture, you cannot on that account assume that it is errorless. . . . Nor have we any right to substitute the word 'inerrancy' for 'inspiration' in our discussion of the Bible unless we are prepared to show from the teaching of the Bible that inspiration means inerrancy—and that, I think, would be difficult to do."[5] His career, more than anyone else's, incarnates the demise of Old School Calvinism, just as van Dyke's incarnates the triumph of modernism.

Conservative Evangelicalism

The evangelicals may have been formally committed to Calvinism, but, as in the cases of William Jennings Bryan and Billy Sunday, this commitment never affected anything they wrote or said in public.

---

5. Francis L. Patton, *Fundamental Christianity* (New York: Macmillan, 1926), pp. 162–63.

They became increasingly dominant numerically after the arrival of the Cumberland Presbyterians in 1906. Their view of the content of preaching was significantly less rigorous that the Calvinists' view. Their official view of the sacraments was the same as the Old School's: rarely mentioned. Their view of discipline after McCune was de-frocked in 1878 was that only rhetorical confrontation of the most severe kind was worth the price of a long, drawn-out judicial proceeding. The war would therefore be won by that faction which could successfully present itself as the injured party, the victim of un-Christian rhetoric.

Liberalism-Modernism

Modernism was hostile to any screening of the Church in terms of the Westminster Confession. Modernists announced another standard: peace, toleration, and work. This meant peace and toleration for them while they worked to subvert the enforcement mechanism undergirding the Westminster standards. Preaching was never regarded by modernists as an operational mark of the Church. This left only the sacraments and Church discipline as the operational marks.

The sacraments created no problem for the modernists. The sacraments were seen as traditional rituals, not covenantal. Operationally, this was equally true of all the Presbyterian factions. The sacraments were never invoked by anyone until 1934, when the modernists invoked them in the name of the flow of funds. Modernists also downplayed all discipline above the presbyterial level until 1934; then they announced the authority of the General Assembly over presbyteries—the very thing they had denied since the days of Charles Briggs. In 1934, they were defending the Church's right to collect funds, not the theological content of preaching. They defended what they believed to be most important.

What the modernists accomplished judicially and institutionally was the substitution of the lowest common confession of the non-ordained Church member for the theological content of the ministerial oath. To be baptized, i.e., to become a member, a person (or his adult representative) only had to vow "faith in Christ, and obedience to him. . ." (Larger Catechism, A. 166). Even this minimal proclamation was not formally required by any Presbyterian judicial document to take place in a public ceremony. No statement of theological faith was required of members by any Presbyterian judicial document.

The member's *implicit* oath at the time of his baptism or his reception by letter of transfer had neither judicial content nor theological content. What did it mean to obey Christ? The Confession did not say. The member's vow was always the absolute minimal vow in the Church. This vow, in the hands of the modernists after 1933, became the modernists' mandated vow for all ministers and all laymen: the promise to obey Christ's representatives (point two). Thus, the Presbyterian conflict ended when the modernists succeeded in substituting a new ministerial oath for the Confessional vow: *the common member's oath of allegiance*. The lowest-common-denominator oath in Presbyterianism triumphed at its highest judicial level: the General Assembly. It was not that the content of the 1729 ministerial vow was abandoned publicly; that did not take place until 1967. But in terms of Church sanctions, the original ministerial vow ended in 1936.

A Matter of Strategy

There is no way that any organization can sustain a series of inconclusive, unresolved battles at its highest level, year after year. This is why the honoring of judicial precedents is mandatory for institutional survival. There has to be an agreed-upon settling of specific divisive issues. Any group within an organization that refuses to be bound by past court decisions has made a decision: (1) to paralyze, by endless appeals and trials, the leadership's ability to impose sanctions, (2) to capture the institution because of their opponents' lack of will to impose escalating sanctions, or (3) to destroy it by means of continuing paralysis if it cannot be captured. Gandhi's techniques of nonviolent but active resistance against British rule are the classic modern examples of this strategy. They were successfully adopted by Martin Luther King and Chicago radical Saul Alinsky.[6]

These techniques rest on a fundamental assumption: *the action is the reaction*. If there is no reaction from the leadership, the initiators

---

6. Saul D. Alinsky, *Rules for Radicals: A Practical Primer for Realistic Radicals* (New York: Vintage, 1972); *Reveille for Radicals* (New York: Vintage, 1969).

of institutional change escalate the confrontation. When at last there is a reaction, as there must be if the organization is to survive the challenge and the paralysis it brings, the strategy of the challengers is to make the leaders pay a very heavy price: in the press, among the organization's constituency, and in the organization's bank account.

The Moral High Ground

The success of this strategy rests on a crucial assumption: the resisters must be perceived as operating from the moral high ground. As the master strategist Saul Alinsky wrote, "*All effective actions require the passport of morality.*"[7] Therefore, it is imperative for the targets of the strategy of non-violent non-cooperation to respond with a counter-appeal based on a superior morality. If the resisters can be identified successfully by the representative leadership of the organization as willful subversives of a legitimate moral order, the resisters' strategy of non-cooperation will fail. The resisters will be seen as destroyers, not men with a valid moral cause. Their institutional support will dry up. Then they can be surgically removed.

Most members understand that any organization has the right and obligation to remove destroyers from its midst. Its leaders can and must act on behalf of the membership to remove a cancer from the organization. But to complete this operation, there must be a will to resist on the part of the leaders, as well as a strategy of persuasion to mobilize the membership. Above all, *there must be an agreed-upon moral standard to appeal to as the basis of the imposition of sanctions.* Only then can the defensive sanctions successfully be applied.

By the 1920's, the conservatives had been crossing their fingers for over two generations on the issue of the six-day creation. They refused to admit this publicly, but they in fact regarded the Confession's statement—and therefore Genesis 1—as "just another theory" of origins. This opened the door to Lyell's chronology, and from there to Darwin's process theology. *They opened the door to Progressivism.* Also, ever since 1876, they had not successfully shown that higher criticism of the Bible as a methodology of moral evolutionism was the ideologi-

---

7. Alinsky, *Rules for Radicals*, p. 44. Emphasis in the original.

cal foundation of an attack on the Church and Christendom. They refused to conduct heresy trials except for flagrant heresy expressed flagrantly. They were not willing to resist, thereby revealing a lack of moral fervor and commitment: *moral mid-ground*. By the 1920, the conservatives no longer occupied the moral high ground. They were vulnerable.

Meanwhile, the liberals had worked diligently since 1893 to define a new moral high ground: peace, toleration, and work. Briggs' rhetoric of confrontation had belied his commitment to peace, and for this he had been de-frocked in 1893. A few months before the 1893 General Assembly, Henry van Dyke was able to replace Briggs as the leader of the Presbyterian modernists when he and his 234 colleagues issued *A Plea for Peace and Work*. A successful realignment of what defined the moral high ground was crucial for the success of the modernists' strategy. Once accomplished—and by 1913, it was accomplished—the modernists pursued a three-part propaganda campaign: (1) the identification of the imposition of Church sanctions as the moral low ground (a counter-affirmation of presbyterial autonomy); (2) the identification of the Doctrinal Deliverance of 1910 as a mere theory (a counter-affirmation of theological relativism); (3) the identification of the General Assembly as a court whose decisions are strictly past-oriented, not establishing precedents (a counter-affirmation of non-cooperation).

The modernists adopted low-profile tactics that matched their strategy after 1900. Nykamp is correct regarding the 1922 to 1926 period, i.e., the Bryan phase and its aftermath: "Although inclusivists held many major Church offices, initial victories went to exclusivists." But these victories were not institutional; they were rhetorical: form without substance. "Inclusivists then used sophisticated, carefully engineered campaigns that employed public and private communications media to acquire support from a majority of the Church populace. Exclusivists thundered judgments about their opponents in mass rallies. The more subtle, quieter strategy of inclusivism won; exclusivism was excluded from the Presbyterian Church."[8] And every other mainline Church as well.

---

8. Delwyn G. Nykamp, A Presbyterian Power Struggle: A Critical History

The Demise of Whiggery

The spirit of the age ("climate of opinion") was against the conservatives after 1900. Darwinism's process theology had eroded the judicial foundations of the older Protestant worldview, not just in the Presbyterian Church but throughout American society.[9] So had early Unitarianism's program of creedless public education.[10] For that matter, the very creedlessness of the U.S. Constitution (Article VI, Section III: no religious test oaths) seemed to justify the legitimacy of social cooperation under a common-ground, non-creedal, non-sectarian, even non-Christian civil covenant. The Presbyterian conservatives, as nineteenth-century political Whigs, accepted this conclusion, since the philosophical origins of both the U.S. Constitution and the Princeton apologetic were the same: Scottish common-sense realism (John Witherspoon by way of his former student, James Madison).[11]

As a Whig liberal, Machen argued for a judicial distinction between Church and State based on the traditional Whig distinction between voluntarism and involuntarism. The Church is voluntary, he said, and therefore bound by its own laws to enforce ministerial oaths. But the liberals could rely on the spirit of the age to undermine men's confidence in Machen's argument. They could rely on the visible success of creedless peace and work in civil affairs and modern education. It would take a monumental program of re-education for the conservatives to persuade Church members that heresy trials, systematic searching for Confessional deviation, and literally decades of conflict were the necessary price of theological purity. Who on earth was *that* committed to theological purity during the Progressive era? Nobody, including the Old School, none of whom called for heresy trials after

---

of Communication Strategies in the Struggle for Control of the Presbyterian Church, U.S.A., 1922-1926 (Ph.D. dissertation, Northwestern University, 1974), p. 2.

9. Henry F. May, *Protestant Churches and Industrial America* (New York: Harper Torchbooks, [1949] 1967), ch. 5.

10. Lawrence Cremin, *The Transformation of the School: Progressivism in American Education, 1876-1957* (New York: Vintage, 1964), Part 1.

11. Gary North, *Political Polytheism: The Myth of Pluralism* (Tyler, Texas: Institute for Christian Economics, 1989), Part 3.

Patton pressured Swing out of the denomination. Christian theology seemingly had been shown to be irrelevant to civil affairs and modern education. Not one President of the United States had ever been a conservative evangelical.[12] "Why all the fuss over the details of theology?" the liberals asked rhetorically. Meanwhile, the crossed fingers of the conservatives, even including Machen—his refusal to support the six-day creation,[13] as well as his secret rejection of some of the 1903 revisions—had undermined their will to resist. With crossed fingers, it is difficult to cast the first stone.

Lying for a Good Cause

Difficult, but not impossible. One man who mastered the art of stone-casting with crossed fingers was Lefferts Loetscher, whose history of the Presbyterian conflict still shapes the debate. Historians make mistakes, but there are times when an historian with an agenda will deliberately mislead his readers. The more skilled the historian, the more likely that a major error of interpretation is a form of subtle deception. Loetscher, a power religionist and a defender of power religionists, was a skilled deceiver for the sake of his cause. In his assessment of Machen's ecclesiology, he cited Machen's insistence that the Church is a voluntary institution. Then he commented: "In constitution, though of course not in purpose, he likened the Church to a political club. This was good Anabaptist doctrine and might even pass for Congregationalism, but it certainly was not Presbyterianism. The Presbyterian conception of the Church is organic. Presbyterian doctrine is that normally people are born into the Church."[14]

---

12. Garfield was a Disciple of Christ, i.e., a Cambellite. He had prepared to become a minister in his youth, but had gone into politics instead. By 1881, a few months before his assassination, he had become a theological liberal. W. W. Wasson, *James A. Garfield: His Religion and Education* (Nashville: Tennessee Book Co., 1952), pp. 120-21.

13. D. G. Hart, *Defending the Faith: J. Gresham Machen and the Crisis of Conservative Protestantism in Modern America* (Baltimore, Maryland: Johns Hopkins University Press, 1994), pp. 96-99.

14. Lefferts A. Loetscher, *The Broadening Church: a study of theological issues in the presbyterian church since 1869* (Philadelphia: University of Pennsylvania Press, 1954), p. 117.

He assumed that his readers had little or no understanding of theology or history—generally, a safe assumption. He figured that he could fool them, which he did. So, he lied. Let us examine his lie more carefully. He said, "Presbyterian doctrine is that normally people are born into the Church." This statement implies that Presbyterians believe in Church membership through procreation and baptism, not through evangelism and baptism. Operationally, it may seem this way: Presbyterian evangelism is generally regarded as one step ahead of Episcopalian evangelism, which is one step ahead of Eastern Orthodox evangelism.[15] But theologically, such a summary is not only nonsense; in the context of Machen's battle, it is preposterous. The final battle in the Presbyterian conflict (1933-36) was officially a battle over foreign missions. (Unofficially, it was a battle over inheritance.) The foreign missions field is where most Church members are brought into the Church through conversion and voluntary confession, not by birth. The fact is, Presbyterianism rests, and has always rested, on the doctrine of a Church covenant sealed judicially by baptism, which is seen as a voluntary covenant: invoked either by an adult on his own behalf or on behalf of his infant. As the premier Presbyterian historian of his day, Loetscher knew this. He simply ignored it for the sake of discrediting Machen.

Second, Loetscher deliberately ignored the context of Machen's point in the passages he cited: the judicial distinction between subservience to civil government, which is involuntary, and to Church government, where membership is confessional and voluntary.[16] If there is any single principle of government that has united American Protestants in their confession of faith in political pluralism, it is this one. There was nothing especially Congregational about Machen's distinction, let alone Anabaptist (the Presbyterians' dreaded A-word!); it is as Presbyterian a distinction as might be imagined, though not uniquely so. More than this; this same judicial distinction has been the founda-

---

15. Presbyterian D. James Kennedy's Evangelism Explosion is the common-ground version; the publishers would not accept his original Calvinistic version, as he told me several years ago.

16. Machen, *Christianity and Liberalism* (New York: Macmillan, 1923), pp. 168-69, 171.

tion of the entire tradition of Whig political liberalism, as well as the humanism of the American Civil Liberties Union: the separation of Church and State.

Loetscher was dishonest. He was also one of the most respected American Church historians in the guild. He got away with this subterfuge at Machen's expense. Four decades ago reviewers should have pointed out his deception. They refused. Winners not only write the histories and screenplays, they also write the book reviews.

Confession and Confrontation

The strategy of the modernists in the Northern Presbyterian Church—avoiding a frontal assault after 1893—was only temporary. They reversed it in 1922; or, more to the point, Harry Emerson Fosdick reversed it. They reversed their call for judicial toleration in 1931 when they initiated a revision of the Form of Government. They could not maintain their creedal silence forever; they would eventually confess the power religion and enforce its claims. They expected to win in the end. The "end" was defined as the day that they could make a public confession of their true faith, confident that they could control the courts and impose negative sanctions on those who might protest. The issue was sanctions. When modernism's fat lady finally sang, she would have her foot on her opponent's neck. Until she did, there would be no song.

Eventually, men confess their true faith, even men who do not expect to win. This is an important theological point. Men's ability to remain confessionally lukewarm is drastically limited. They cannot always remain silent. Rushdoony has called this the phenomenon of necessary confession. "Confession is a necessary aspect of man's psychology and nature. Man was created by God to be a confessing creature, to confess God in all his activities, research, study, and science. In every area, man makes a religious confession in all that he does and is. Man's life is a confession before the world of the faith and purpose which govern his heart. Man's life is also a continual confession before God and to God. Every thought and motive is naked and open before God. . . . For the unregenerate, the God of Scripture is a prying God who must be barred from the mind of man. His resentment against such sovereign power is intense. His thoughts are his totally private property, and he will not allow to God title over a single thought."[17]

Covenant-breaking man's problem is guilt. "The sinner refuses to confess his sins to God and to acknowledge his guilt, and he refuses to confess Christ in his daily life and motives, but he does not thereby escape *the need for confession*. Where men refuse to make a godly confession, they will make an ungodly one. They will confess with their lives, thoughts, and deeds, their rebellion against God, and they will confess with their mouth their sins with a bravado or in spite of themselves."[18]

One by one, from Briggs to Speer to Macartney, they "came clean." They finally admitted where their hearts were, meaning where their dreams were. Their hearts were not with the Westminster Confession *and a system of Church courts that would enforce it*. Machen was more forthright than his opponents and even his colleagues, and because of this verbal forthrightness, he progressively alienated the majority of his fellow Presbyterians. He believed in consistent confession, continual confession, a life based on confession. His confession? The 1788 Whig revision of the Westminster Confession. Most of it, anyway.[19] And he never invoked ecclesiastical sanctions.

The Institutional Costs of Policing Confessions

The problem for Machen and his initial supporters was that most Presbyterian conservatives did not want institutional trouble. They knew about the effects of modernism in theory, but they did not want to admit that their Church had been infiltrated and captured at the top by 1920. They did not want to go through the agonies associated with a series of long, drawn-out heresy trials. They would have had to begin with a majority of the members of the New York Presbytery, one by one. Representatives from other presbyteries would have had to attend the ordination meetings of the New York Presby-

---

17. R. J. Rushdoony, *Revolt Against Maturity: A Biblical Psychology of Man* (Fairfax, Virginia: Thoburn Press, 1977), p. 274.

18. *Ibid.*, pp. 274-75.

19. Not the six-day creation (IV:1), not the Pope as the antichrist (XXV:6), and not lawful oaths as ethically mandatory (XXII:3).

tery, and any suspected modernist would then have been challenged by means of complaints from other presbyteries to the General Assembly. Wholesale excommunications of existing New York Presbytery members would have been necessary. But such trials require proof, and proof is expensive, embarrassing, and difficult for outsiders to collect. Prudent modernists recognized by 1893 what was required for a successful capture of a major denomination—their avoidance of confrontational rhetoric—and they were willing to wait to "go public" with even a mild version of their underlying religious faith.

It is said that the price of liberty is eternal vigilance. This is dead wrong. *The price of liberty is eternal sanctions.* There can be no long-term liberty for any society that denies the doctrine of hell. The fear of God is the beginning of wisdom, including political and economic wisdom. Men should fear God, if not for liberty's sake, then for their eternal state.

God created heaven and hell to serve as preliminary "holding areas" for the eternal state: the new heavens and new earth, and the lake of fire (Rev. 20:14–15). His people are to enforce His law with positive and negative sanctions in history, especially negative sanctions: the price of purity. Few bureaucracies are ever willing to pay this price, and those that do generally do so out of fear: a challenge from another bureaucracy. Because of their understanding of the paralysis of bureaucracies, the modernists eventually took over the mainline denominations, one by one. The modernists' strategy in the Northern Presbyterian Church was clear: say nothing outrageous in public, write nothing outrageous, build up an institutional power base, preach toleration when challenged, and plan a takeover which will forever remove toleration for those Presbyterians who might seek to apply the orthodox creeds by means of judicial sanctions.

There were time limits, however. Men cannot keep silent forever. The question was: When to speak out? Which side would speak out first? Which side would persevere in a systematic campaign of confession—confession unto confrontation, confession unto institutional victory: the modernists or the conservatives?

Confessional Progress, Sanctions, and *Adiaphora*

The rhetorical offensive began outside the Church: in the pages of the *New York Times*, beginning in January, 1922. Bryan's political threat was too great: returning the content of taxpayer-funded education to the taxpayers. The *Times* launched a multi-pronged attack on Bryan.

This led to Fosdick's March 12 attack in the *Times*, then to his May 22 sermon, "Shall the Fundamentalists Win?" This in turn produced an institutional reaction: Macartney's 1923 overture from the Philadelphia Presbytery. It also led to Machen's published protest, *Christianity and Liberalism* (1923). The initiative had come from modernists outside the Presbyterian Church. Then it shifted to a modernist inside the Church.

In the most important sermon of his career—the one he preached on December 30, 1923, which led to Henry van Dyke's departure from the congregation and his December 31 press release—Machen offered a rhetorical speculation that no Protestant theologian has ever answered clearly, yet which must be answered by someone, sometime. It is a mark of the breakdown of both theology and ecclesiology in the twentieth century that the question has never been dealt with by those who have lost almost every ecclesiastical battle. It is the question of confessional revision. Machen said: "Formerly, when men had brought to their attention perfectly plain documents like the Apostle's Creed or the Westminster Confession or the New Testament, they either accepted them or else denied them. Now they no longer deny, but merely 'interpret.' Every generation, it is said, must interpret the Bible or the Creed in its own way. But I sometimes wonder just how far this business of interpretation will go."[20]

Machen was an honest man, as his critics freely admitted, so this passage reveals self-delusion on a major scale. He did not recognize how far Princeton Seminary had gone in the convenient-interpretation game. The Westminster Confession, not to mention Genesis 1, leaves no doubt about the doctrine of creation: God created the world out of nothing "in the space of six days" (IV:1). This, to use Machen's words, is "perfectly plain." A man can either accept this plain teaching or deny it. But men—most notably, the two greatest systematic theologi-

---

20. Machen, "The Issue in the Church" (1923), in *God Transcendent*, edited by Ned B. Stonehouse (Carlysle, Pennsylvania: Banner of Truth Trust, [1949] 1982), p. 45.

ans on the Princeton faculty, Charles Hodge and Warfield—chose to deny it by interpreting it to mean something radically different from what the plain teaching explicitly says. Six days does not mean six days, they insisted; it means an indeterminate time period. How long a time period? Answer (unstated): "Whatever amount of time is needed to legitimize our latest refusal to confront modern uniformitarian geology." They bowed to the chronology of James Hutton by way of Charles Lyell, and then hoped and prayed that no one would wind up as Lyell did late in his career: a disciple of Charles Darwin. Machen himself remained profoundly mute on the creation-evolution debate. Yet it was this great public debate in Dayton, Tennessee, that sealed the fate of the orthodox wings in the Northern Presbyterian and Northern Baptist churches after 1925.[21] Machen did not overcome the problem of his own crossed fingers.

The 1903 Revision in 1936

Machen announced in 1923: "Every generation, it is said, must interpret the Bible or the Creed in its own way." His Westminster colleague John Murray also affirmed this; Murray taught systematic theology at Westminster Seminary for over 35 years. He wrote: "Unless we maintain that the tradition established in the church from the early fourth century until the seventeenth was a mistake, there can be no gainsaying of the demand that creedal confession must keep pace with the challenge of heresy."[22] Machen argued late in 1936 that confessions can be revised, but that his era was not a safe era for revision.[23] Nevertheless, his new denomination accepted two of the revisions of 1903: rejecting the Confession's assertion that the Pope is the antichrist (XXV:6) and rejecting the last trace of the Puritans' theocratic worldview, i.e., which identified as a sin a man's refusal to swear a lawful oath to a lawful authority (XXII:3).[24] To this extent,

---

21. As mentioned in Chapter 7, Bryan was an age-day creationist.

22. John Murray, "The Theology of the Westminster Confession of Faith," in *Scripture and Confession: A Book About Confessions Old and New*, edited by John H. Skilton (Nutley, New Jersey: Presbyterian & Reformed, 1973), p. 126.

23. Machen, "The Creeds and Doctrinal Advance," *ibid.*, p. 156.

24. *Minutes of the Second General Assembly of the Presbyterian Church of America* (Nov. 12-14, 1936), p. 13.

they acknowledged that Henry van Dyke and his colleagues had been correct and the Westminster Divines had been incorrect. They acknowledged that they had needed modernists to make it institutionally possible for Calvinists to get closer to the truth.

The Puritans and most other Protestants, as well as the Catholic Church, had assumed that the State is an oath-bound covenantal institution under God. Thus, both Church and State can lawfully compel from anyone under their authority the presentation of sworn testimony in their courts. Certain Anabaptist groups have denied that an oath to the State is valid; rather, they say, it is a sin to take such an oath. Calvin had opposed this position, arguing that such an oath can be valid.[25] The Puritans had taken this one step farther, saying that it is a sin not to swear. They had in mind courtroom testimony as a witness who calls upon God as a witness. So did Calvin, who wrote that "swearing means to call upon God as a witness. . . ."[26] The Puritans included loyalty oaths made to the prince; so did Calvin.[27]

Why, then, the 1936 revision? Machen's Church did not say, any more than the parent Church had said in 1903. But it is obvious why: to strip the last traces of theocracy out of the Confession in an attempt to make the Confession conform to modern political pluralism. Along with 1646's Confessional statements went 1647's supporting Bible verses, but no Presbyterian assembly has substituted new ones, nor has anyone thought it necessary to do so. The political Anabaptism of Roger Williams had at long last triumphed in Presbyterianism in 1903, which became, symbolically, the Calvinists' mid-winter flight from Boston into the wilderness of Rhode Island. From this Confessional wilderness Presbyterianism has not yet emerged.

Even in 1936 (and today), no Presbyterian Calvinist minister has had the courage to demand a revision of the Confession with respect to the six-day creation, despite the fact that no Calvinist Presbyterian

---

25. John Calvin, *Brief Instruction for Arming All the Good Faithful Against the Errors of the Common Sect of the Anabaptists* (1544), in *Treatises Against the Anabaptists and Against the Libertines*, Benjamin Wirt Farley, editor (Grand Rapids, Michigan: Baker, 1982), ch. 4.
26. *Ibid.*, p. 94.
27. *Ibid.*, p. 104.

seminary professor is willing to defend the Confession in print on this point. Crossed fingers remain crossed.

We have yet to see a conservative defender of theological orthodoxy write a treatise on confessional progress and revision. As Machen put it in his sermon, "I sometimes wonder just how far this business of interpretation will go." Interpreting away personally inconvenient portions of a confession is a convenient option for men who have ceased to believe those portions. If the Church allows such crossed-fingers revisions, then how secure—how authoritative—is the original confession? If a section of the Westminster Confession of Faith is not worth defending through the imposition of ecclesiastical sanctions, how binding is the ministerial oath on anyone's conscience? If it is binding on the conscience, how can it possibly be revised by those who have sworn belief in it? But if it is not binding on the conscience, what is wrong with interpreting it into oblivion?

This is the great unanswered dilemma of creedal progress: the one area of progress that Protestants of all eschatological persuasions are forced by their history to admit there is in history; otherwise, the Protestant Reformation was an illegitimate schism. If a man states that he does not believe a passage in a confession, and if he is nevertheless ordained to office, those who ordained him are inevitably saying that with respect to the confession—the ministerial covenantal oath—the passage is either part of the *adiaphora* of the Christian faith (things indifferent) or else something not yet sorted out ecclesiastically ("But we're working on it!").[28]

All sides argued that, with reference to the their oath-bound affirmations of the Westminster Confession, conscience was at stake. All sides prevaricated. All sides crossed their fingers. Conscience was a very small tributary of a far larger river. Consciences were quieted by means of the Jesuitical game of reinterpretation and re-definition. ("Are you a priest?" asked the English inquisitor to a Jesuit. "I am not

---

28. Eschatology is such a thing in modern Calvinism: historic premillennialism, amillennialism, postmillennialism, and dispensational premillennialism cannot possibly be reconciled. Yet American Presbyterianism, unlike conservative Lutheranism, has relegated these differences to the realm of theological speculation beyond the reach of ecclesiastical sanctions: things indifferent.

a priest," he replied, while thinking to himself, "of Apollo.") What was at stake was inheritance: jobs, real estate, libraries, and the denomination's reputation. And, we should also add, full pension vesting after 35 years of service in the pulpit.

The Question of Strict Subscription

From 1729 until today, American Presbyterianism has never required absolutely strict subscription to the Confession. It could not, for that would elevate the Confession to equality with the Bible, the only unchanging source of truth. Presbyterians have always acknowledged that the Confession is flawed in relation to the Bible. The Bible is sovereign over the Confession. Thus, strict subscription has always meant stricter subscription, not absolute subscription.

Stricter than what? There is the rub. Byron Snapp, a strict confessionalist, in reviewing Longfield's *Presbyterian Controversy*, writes of exceptions to the Confession: "If Scripture supports these doctrinal exceptions, then our standards must change to conform to God's word."[29] *But standards do not change on their own initiative. People must work to change them.* Yet if everyone with the authority to change the standards is required to express his complete agreement with the standards, in the name of the unchanging Bible, then the standards can no more be legally changed by "truly confessional" (TC) men than the Bible can. To announce the need to alter the standards is to invite de-frocking—the problem faced by the liberals. This is why they demanded immunity from negative sanctions for their writings.

This is the unsolved dilemma of strict subscription. The result of this dilemma is crossed fingers. Snapp writes that without strict subscription, "presbyteries may begin to receive men who believe that women ought to be ordained to the office of elder." Quite true. As evidence, I offer the fact that Machen and his allies remained virtually silent in print on this issue in 1929 and 1930 when the proposal to ordain women as ruling elders and deacons was sent down to the presbyteries by the General Assembly. The decision to ordain women was then passed by a vote of 158 to 118. This did not require a two-thirds

---

29. Byron Snapp, *Presbyterian Witness*, 8 (Summer 1994), p. 10.

vote, because the Confession did not explicitly limit the office of elder to men. The conservatives did not believe this issue was worth fighting about, either before or after the vote. Yet many of these men were strict subscriptionists. Since the Confession did not speak directly to the issue of women elders—in mid-seventeenth-century England, this ecclesiastical problem did not exist—they were faced with defending the non-ordination of women by an appeal to the Bible. But by 1929, nothing could be successfully defended by the conservatives by an appeal to the Bible, even if the Confession spoke clearly to the issue. Thus, *the Confession operationally took precedence over the Bible in the Church's courts*, at least when its silence helped the liberal cause.

Here is the perpetual dilemma of strict subscription: whenever the Confession cannot in practice be changed, it operationally takes precedence over the Bible in judicial affairs. It has to. *Anything that is elevated as equal to the changeless Bible will inevitably take precedence over the Bible.* The question then becomes one of power: Which group, all members of which crossed their fingers at the time of ordination and/or subsequently, can gain control of the judicial machinery, i.e., the voice of ecclesiastical authority?

We can see this principle of substitution at work in the post-Old Covenant era. The New Testament has superior interpretive authority over the Old Testament in Christianity. The Talmud's authority over the Old Testament in Judaism is equally true.[30] Only the Karaites, a tiny Jewish sect hated by Orthodox Jews, reject the Talmud for the Torah, and their rejection of the Talmud is total.

On the other hand, if the Confession can legally be changed, then absolute subscription becomes an impossible position to defend. Men are allowed to change their minds and still remain in the pastorate. The institutional question remains the same, however: How to capture the judicial machinery that establishes the operational limits of how tight or loose a subscription is enforceable?

Here is the institutional dilemma of a confession: *the larger the denomination, the lower the common confessional denominator.* Charles

---

30. Jacob Neusner, *Judaism and Scripture: The Evidence of Leviticus Rabbah* (Chicago: University of Chicago Press, 1986), p. xi.

Hodge referred to this confessional problem in 1858. "We could not hold together a week, if we made the adoption of all its propositions a condition of ministerial communion. . . . [I]t is not only difficult but impossible to frame a creed as extended as the Westminster Confession, which can be adopted in all its details by the ministry of any large body of Christians. . . ."[31] The greater the growth, the lower the confessional minimum. The traditional mark of success—growth—apparently leads to confessional surrender. This is the dilemma of Presbyterianism and every other known ecclesiastical system. No denomination has solved it yet. We see growing churches whose leaders have abandoned the original confession through crossed fingers. We see shrinking or stagnant churches that have lost touch with reality whenever a social problem has appeared—abortion comes to mind—that the confession does not mention. Finally, we see local church splits, which in the Southern Baptist tradition are known as home missions programs.

Hodge was adamant against absolute subscription. "Are we living in a false show? Are we pretending to adopt a principle of subscription, which in fact we neither act on for ourselves, nor dream of enforcing on others?"[32] With respect to the Confession's defense of the enforcement of the Church's theology by the civil magistrate, the American Presbyterian Church officially rejected this, despite the words of the Confession, from 1729 until the revision of the Confession in 1788, when the offending passages were officially removed. "It cannot be denied, therefore, that the church understood the adoption of the Westminster Confession as not involving the adoption of every position in that book."[33] "The principle that the adoption of the Confession of Faith implies the adoption of all the propositions therein contained, is not only contrary to the plain, historical meaning of the words which the candidate is required to use, and the mind of the church in imposing a profession of faith, but the principle is impracti-

---

31. "The General Assembly," *Princeton Review* (July 1858), p. 561.
32. Charles Hodge, "Adoption of the Confession of Faith," *ibid.* (Oct. 1858), p. 670.
33. *Ibid.*, p. 682.

cable. It cannot be carried out without working the certain and immediate ruin of the church."[34]

So, there are stricter subscriptionists and looser subscriptionists, but there are no absolute subscriptionists in Presbyterianism. This is why an appeal to the Confession resolves nothing permanently. There is no permanent Confession that is beyond revision; there are therefore no permanently resolved Confessional questions. The Church is always moving forward. Progressive sanctification is always at work. So is heresy. The parallel wars go on: (1) old errors vs. new truths; (2) new errors vs. old truths. In the case of the Presbyterian Church after 1900, those who held old errors gave their votes by proxy to those who held new errors in order to suppress those who held old truths. "The enemy of my enemy is my friend"—until the day we have eliminated our common enemy.

Meanwhile, charismatic churches are growing everywhere.[35]

There can be no question about this: the Westminster Confession is incomplete. *The Confession is silent regarding the authority and judicial uses of the Confession.* For example, it contains no section describing the proper procedure for making amendments to it. The fact that the Westminster Assembly never addressed the obvious question of the judicial authority of the Confession and catechisms is indicative of the ecclesiastical problem. This has left Presbyterianism open-ended confessionally. No appeal to the 1647 or subsequent versions of the Confession can resolve this question: Exactly how open-ended? This is what has led to the problem of crossed fingers in Presbyterianism, generation after generation.

A Retreat from History

The Presbyterian conflict was a conflict over history and the Church's role in it. When the General Assembly allowed George

---

34. *Ibid.*, p. 685.
35. If this represents the early stages of another Great Awakening, high Churchmen will probably miss out again, just as they did after 1797. The demand for high Church liturgy and mid-Church confessionalism is low. The demand for entertainment is high. The trinitarian confession basic to ecclesiastical success today is drums, guitar, and electronic keyboard.

Bourne's de-frocking on a technicality in 1818, the Old School began a long retreat from relevance in history. The Old School was joined in this retreat by New School experientialists in 1869. The pietism of the New School steadily undermined what little remained of the Old School's original theological commitment to cultural transformation. By Machen's day, not much remained.

The Old School had a theology: (1) sovereign God, (2) authoritative Bible, (3) moral law of God, (4) doctrine of final judgment, and (5) postmillennial eschatology. It never officially surrendered this theology. The Old School disappeared with Machen's death, but it had clung to that theology in public.

Prior to the reunion of 1869, the Old School had an ecclesiastical system that mirrored this theology prior to the reunion: (1) legitimate Church, (2) hierarchical court system, (3) Westminster Confession of Faith, (4) binding ministerial oaths, and (5) a seminary system. But their faith wavered on point one after 1864: legitimate Church. Their neutrality on chattel slavery had undermined their confidence in the legitimacy of their forced expulsion of the New School in 1837. So, they surrendered to the New School in 1869. By 1910, they had consented to a new ecclesiastical system: (1) legitimate Church (New School's), (2) a toothless hierarchy, (3) the five-point fundamentalist Doctrinal Deliverance, (4) crossed fingers (the 1903 revision), and (5) one seminary out of a dozen, not counting Union.

The Old School surrendered in 1869. They continued to surrender after the Swing case in 1874. Initiative passed to the New School because legitimacy (sovereignty) had passed to the New School. *After 1900, initiative passed to the modernists.* Why? First, because equal legitimacy had passed to the modernists. Despite the expulsion of Briggs and Smith, and the near-expulsion of McGiffert, the modernists gained legitimacy equal to the other two schools. The Church's conservative leadership refused to conduct a continuing series of heresy trials against all those who voiced Briggs' opinions without his rhetoric. Union Seminary continued to train candidates for the Presbyterian ministry. The issue was not theology; the issue was sanctions. Because the conservatives refused to impose negative sanctions on the modernists, the modernists were allowed to seek positive sanctions wherever they could. They sought and found such sanctions in the boards and bureaucracies of the Church.

Sources of Additional Legitimacy

Judicially, the modernists gained legitimacy by default: the refusal of conservatives to impose negative sanctions. This does not explain the comprehensive nature of the modernists' victory. You can't beat something with nothing. What was the "something" that the modernists had that the conservatives did not?

What they had was support from the outside. Sometimes this was financial, as the Rockefeller connection indicates. But more money flowed to Rockefeller in 1919 than ever flowed from Rockefeller. He hired Speer on part-time basis. The support they received from the outside was not primarily or even secondarily financial; it was cultural.

What the modernists enjoyed was the intellectual climate of opinion. Not the opinion prevailing in places like Dayton, Tennessee; rather, places like New York City; Cambridge, Massachusetts; and New Haven, Connecticut. There was a drastic split between the older Protestant culture and the new humanism. The new humanism did not have the numbers, but it had the self-confidence. It had, in short, a compelling sense of five things: its own legitimacy, authority, law, sanctions, and destiny. In its own eyes, it was the wave of the future. And so compelling was that vision that its enemies became persuaded, at least with respect to American culture. Fundamentalism's premillennialism added to this sense of inevitable replacement: the eschatological substitution of new heirs in history.

There was a victory. There was a surrender. The modernists had a vision of victory. The conservatives, with few exceptions, had a vision of surrender. This made all the difference.

Modernisms' Two Branches

The modernists had a long-term goal: to replace the heirs. They used deception when necessary, confrontational rhetoric when necessary, and infiltration continually. They relied on their knowledge of their opponents' weaknesses to sustain them. The Old School was all theology and no sanctions after 1874. They did not want a confrontation in the courts. The New School had even less theology. They also did not want a confrontation. When provoked by Briggs, they acted to remove him from their presence ecclesiastically. Then they allowed him and his equally modernist colleagues to teach candidates for the ministry. They could have refused to ordain Union's graduates, but they pulled back from this decision after 1897.

In the United States, a new priesthood was substituted for the minister after the Civil War: the professor. But what did the professor profess? Darwinism. He professed a new evolutionistic cosmology, a new evolutionistic philosophy, and a new evolutionistic ethics. He was a new voice of authority.

For D.G. Hart to speak of theological modernism, 1885 to 1935, as if it had not been part of the warp and woof of political and cultural modernism is to ratify the legitimacy of pietism's retreat from relevance in history. It is another attempt to segregate the institutional Church from the world around it. It is to attribute to the opponents of orthodoxy the pietists' view of the institutional Church: a cultural ghetto with little or no impact on the society around it. It is to attribute to the modernists' voice of authority—Darwinism—the same cultural and political irrelevance that pietists attribute to the Bible. It is, in short, to break with Machen.

This is not to say that this theory of the distinction between two different modernisms—cultural and theological—does not have a long tradition. It was Machen's own forthrightness in calling attention to the status of theological modernism as a separate religion that challenged the thesis of the two modernisms. If theological modernism was a rival religion—a religion in conformity to the climate of humanist opinion—then what else could it have been except cultural modernism? Machen knew of the intimate connections of the two branches of modernism, both philosophically and personally. He had studied at Johns Hopkins. He lived among the elite of the American Establishment every summer: Mount Desert Island. He had testified to Congress. He knew. But there are those among the ranks of his spiritual heirs who still sing the old song: theological modernism had only the loosest connections to cultural modernism. "Church is Church, and society is society, and rarely the twain do meet."

In pietistic churches, this is true. So, the pietist-humanist alliance continues: humanists establish the destination and drive the bus; pietists' taxes pay for the bus and most of the gas, but nonetheless, they sit dutifully in the back. "No back seat drivers here! That's not our responsibility. We must render unto Caesar the things that are Caeser's.". More to the point, they render unto Seizer. They supply Seizer's flow of funds.

J. Gresham Machen had the right enemies. The liberals hated him. They had good cause. He publicly called into question their well-orchestrated subterfuge by which they were stealing the ecclesiastical inheritance built up by generations of of faithful Chrtistians. The successors of the winners have written the textbooks. They continue the mythology established by their spiritual predecessors. Norman Furniss in 1954 labeled Machen "chronically disputative."[36] Ernest Sandeen in 1970 referred to his "perverse obstinacy" as a movement leader.[37] Both authors' remarks were published by prestigious academic publishers. To the victors belong the spoils.

Answers to My Original Questions

I listed numerous questions in the Foreword. It is time to summarize my answers.

What are the tell-tale signs that your Church is moving away from orthodoxy toward theological liberalism? First, an emphasis on Church growth over the Church's confession. If the program of Church growth does not include explicit institutional means of implementing the confession along with the growth, then the sell-out is underway.

Second, an emphasis on academic respectability over the Church's confession. Evidence: the denominational college and the seminary where most of the ministerial candidates attend no longer teach the Church's historic confession in a *required course for graduation* for students who are members of the Church and for all students receiving scholarship aid of any kind from the institution. This means that there must be full-cost tuition from everyone else. There is no good reason for the absence of such a required course in any denominational organization that provides certified training; hence, there has to

---

36. Norman L. Furniss, *The Fundamentalist Controversy, 1918–1931* (New Haven, Connecticut: Yale University Press, 1954), p. 35.
37. Ernest R. Sandeen, *The Roots of Fundamentalism: British and American Millenarianism, 1800–1930* (Chicago: University of Chicago Press, 1970), p. 257.

be a bad reason from the point of view of orthodoxy. The school is headed for "broad Churchism," which is the first step toward liberalism. If either the college or the seminary teaches any form of higher criticism, the battle is as good as lost. The same is true of any aspect of Darwinism, the reigning theology of our age. If the seminary does not teach explicitly against higher criticism and Darwinism in required classes, and if the college does not teach against both of these ideas in the religion major and the philosophy major, and against Darwin in the biology and geology departments, the intellectual and cultural battles will continue to be lost by Christianity.

What are the most vulnerable and undefended parts of your Church? Its oaths and their enforcement through sanctions. First, if communicant members are not required to affirm belief in the Apostles' Creed or one of the more complex early Church creeds, the lowest common denominator principle will ultimately undermine the entire denomination. A corporate verbal re-affirmation of this oath should be built into the denomination's required liturgy, and *always required prior to the application of a sacrament*. Second, if ministers are not required to affirm a far more detailed confession of faith, the Church will drift toward the lowest common denominator confession.

Now I will get very specific. First, every member of the faculty of the denominational college or seminary must re-affirm the Church's detailed confession of faith at the end of every school term, or else his next year's contract is null and void. Any personal objections to any aspect of the confession must also be made in writing each year. These exceptions must be made available to the public. The employment contract must specify this. Tenure is out of the question. The mere existence of academic tenure is *prima facie* evidence of a sell-out. Second, every member of every permanent commission and board, as well as every bureaucratic employee with executive authority, must annually re-affirm belief in the full ministerial confession. This must be in writing. Any personal exceptions to the confession must also be put in writing. Copies of these exceptions must be available on request to any voting Church member in the denomination.

What are the catch phrases of those who are actively infiltrating your Church or selling it out? "If we require such detailed confessions of members and ministers, we will never have Church growth." "Heresy trials never do any good." "Christianity has always made room for a wide range of opinions." "We must not be so narrow that we exclude good people from joining." "The Church is here to help people, not drive them away." "We will lose our young people if we emphasize this doctrine." "The Bible is not a textbook of [ ]." "The Bible is a book of spiritual principles, not a book of science." "Science has proven this to be incorrect." "Truth is unified: the Bible is not in opposition to science. [We must therefore reinterpret the Bible]." "We cannot hire the best faculty with confessional requirements this narrow." "Academic freedom." "God is a God of love, not of judgment." "Personal religious experience is more important than creeds are." "Heart religion is more important than head religion." And, at the final stage of the takeover: "Jesus was a great teacher." All of this is abetted by those inside the Church who proclaim some variant of this one: "No creed but the Bible, no law but love."

What was the strategy of subversion that proved successful in the most spectacular Protestant takeover in modern American history? Their public strategy was to use conservative biblical phrases as a cover for importing alien religious categories into the Church. When challenged, the modernists said that their ideas were the true Christianity; orthodoxy was the pretender. They pleaded for tolerance. Their private strategy was silence: infiltrate the boards and bureaucracies quietly. They evaded negative sanctions until they were in control of the courts; then they imposed them with a vengeance. Their definition of tolerance proved to be highly selective: tolerance for those who quietly accepted the Church boards' moral claim on their money.

How did the modernists' accomplices outside the Church cooperate with infiltrators inside to undermine and then capture the Church? The media identified the modernists' critics as narrow-minded, intolerant, confrontational, and bitter. At the same time, the media portrayed the "true meaning" of Christianity as in being accord with whatever the liberals were teaching. Whenever a modernist was caught red-handed and booted out, he was immediately employed by modernists outside. *The liberals took care of their wounded.* This reduced the personal risk of becoming a subversive, lowering its cost, thereby increasing the supply of subversion.

What was the bait that the subversives used to hook to the Presbyterian Church? Bait: for candidates for the ministry, there was the promise of employment. Hook: earn college and seminary degrees. Bait: for those seeking employment by the colleges and seminaries, there was the promise of near tenure for life. Hook: earn an advanced academic degree in a secular institution. Bait: for ministers, there was a heavily subsidized retroactive pension. Hook: the loss of three-quarters of the pension fund's assets upon resigning prematurely. Bait: for the laymen, there was the promise of participation in a growing Church with a large missions outreach. Hook: toleration of heresy.

Which deeply rooted Presbyterian ideals led to the institutional defeat of those who held them? First and by far the most important covenantally, the absence of any theological content in the member's confession of faith: the lowest common denominator. Second, the absence in the Confession of Faith of any statement regarding its own authority: how to use it, enforce it, and amend it to preserve the purity of the Church. Third, an educated ministry, meaning men in possession of advanced academic degrees. Colleges and universities have been deeply influenced by secularism in all known cases, from the University of Paris to the present: Greek rationalism/irrationalism, Newtonian rationalism/reductionism, Adamic (Ferguson and Smith) common-sense rationalism, Kantian rationalism/irrationalism. The seminaries have also been easily infiltrated: the requirement that all faculty members first attend "German" institutions of higher learning. Fourth, the ideal of near-autonomy for presbyteries, which led to the New York Presbytery situation: a safe-haven entry-point for liberals.

What never works in any program to reform a Church's hierarchy? A call from outside the hierarchy for the hierarchy to change its policies unless this call is accompanied by a budget cut or the threat of a budget cut if these policies are not changed. It is far more effective to cut the budget now and promise to restore it later than to threaten a budget cut in the future. This gets the bureaucrats' attention faster.

What terrifies the infiltrators in the early stages of their invasion? A requirement for employment that they must publicly affirm their unqualified belief in the doctrine of hell (Luke 16:19–31), and the doctrine of the lake of fire (Rev. 20:14–15). The price of liberty is eternal sanctions.

What terrifies them after they have completed the takeover at the top? Budget cuts or (even better) the abolition of the national boards and bureaucracies that employ them. Decentralization terrifies them. Having to raise their own funds terrifies them. The heart of liberalism's goal, both secular and theistic, is this confession: *elitist-directed evolutionary change financed by other people's money.*

Why does the liberals' strategy of subversion always backfire on them in the next generation, or even sooner? People will not commit themselves strongly to a voluntary organization whose creed and goals cannot easily be readily distinguished from other institutions.[38] The more that the humanists inside the Church re-position the Church to reflect respectable humanist opinion outside the Church, the more that outsiders see no compelling reason to join the Church, and the more that its youth see no compelling reason to return after college or marriage. The Church, structurally, was designed by God to be on the offensive: a light to the world. When it loses this light because it is no brighter than the world, it no longer has a unique service proposition to offer. Attrition then takes over. Salt without savor is fit only for grinding underfoot.

What was the institutional and theological legacy of the Presbyterian reunion of 1869? The Old School moved from rigorous Confessionalism to less rigorous Confessionalism. It moved from a willing-

---

38. Winthrop Hudson, *The Great Tradition of the American Churches* (New York: Harper & Bros., 1953).

ness to conduct heresy trials to a greatly reduced willingness. It moved from intolerance regarding Arminian theology to toleration.

Why did the Northern Presbyterian Church cease all heresy trials after 1900? The New School was unwilling even to threaten such trials except when provoked by confrontational rhetoric. The modernists ceased employing such rhetoric until 1922, by which time it proved impossible to prosecute heresy trials successfully.[39] This eliminated the pressure on liberals that had created the conservative backlash in the 1890's. After 1903, the Confession had been watered down to such an extent that the Old School had been repudiated. They had to compromise with the 1903 revisions in order to remain in the Church. They refused to leave, just as the modernists refused to leave. They had to play the game of crossed fingers, just as the liberals did. This undermined their confidence in the appropriateness of Church sanctions. It strengthened the liberals, whose strategy of subversion was obviously working.

What was the theological strategy of the liberals after 1900? They switched from a public emphasis on the benefits of biblical higher criticism—Briggs' strategy—to an emphasis on peace, work, and toleration: van Dyke's strategy. They argued that the Presbyterian tradition allows freedom of thought. They emphasized the practical benefits of liberalism: making this a better world (with other people's money). They repositioned liberty of thought as the moral high ground, to replace confessional orthodoxy.

What was the institutional strategy of the liberals after 1900? They steadily infiltrated the Church's boards and commissions. They continued to infiltrate the seminaries. Men such as Henry Sloane Coffin mastered the intricacies of parliamentary procedure. They defied the conservatives sporadically after 1913, but only in the name of a higher good, i.e., freedom of thought and tolerance.

---

39. Fosdick was removed on a technicality: he had never been ordained as a Presbyterian minister. He was offered the opportunity to remain in his pulpit if he submitted to ordination. He refused.

What is the proper role of historic creeds and confessions in the life of the Presbyterian Church? The creeds—shorter than the confessions—should establish a church's institutional boundaries. Communicant membership should be by confession of faith in the creed. This should not be voting membership, however, lest the lowest common denominator principle be subsidized. Voting membership should require more: affirmation of the full Confession. *Those given the right to impose ecclesiastical sanctions in terms of a confession must be under those sanctions and confession.* Detailed confessions serve as Constitutional law documents of the respective denominations. This law is always subject to the fundamental law of the Bible. Confessions establish boundaries for Church officers, and should also establish boundaries for voting communicant members. Those who lawfully impose Presbyterian Church sanctions—voting in a local election is such a sanction—should be governed by an oath to the Westminster Confession and both catechisms. To argue otherwise is to relegate the standards for voting membership to *adiaphora*.

Because there are no formal creedal standards for Presbyterian laymen, this led to a constant lowering of the lowest common denominator. The low common denominator of the layman's creed at first triumphed over the ministerial Confession: from Calvinism to Arminianism. But after 1925, the judicially unenforceable five-point Doctrinal Deliverance of 1910 left the laymen confessionally more rigorous than most graduates of the seminaries, which were increasingly modernist: old modernism (Progressivism) or new modernism (neo-orthodoxy). Rhetoric and infiltration by 1926 had decided which confessional standard would triumph, either: (1) the laymen's presumed but unspecified Arminian-experiential creed; (2) the officers' institutionally unenforceable judicial Calvinist Confession; or (3) modernism. The modernists in 1934 controlled the judicial machinery. They imposed negative sanctions in terms of their supposedly creedless five-point creed. (See above: p. 180.)

Why did the Presbyterian Church, U.S.A., abandon its Confession as the means of screening its leadership? New School members and fundamentalists were most interested in Church growth and evangelism. They did not see the great value of the Confession, let alone the two judicially ignored catechisms, in screening ministerial candidates. New School members did not regard the benefits of screening by means of the details of the Confession—the Old School's tradition—as offsetting the costs of full-time screening: acrimonious trials, long presbytery examinations, and the difficulty of mastering the Confession. Conservatives were unwilling to affirm the Confession in the important areas of origins (no six-day creationism), canon (lower criticism), and eternal sanctions (no non-elect infants). This also undermined their confidence in the use of the Confession as a screening device. This was the problem of crossed fingers.

What was the importance of seminary education in the liberals' capture of the Presbyterian Church? The seminary replaced informal apprenticeship after 1812. It was added onto the requirement of college, i.e., mastery of Latin. Prior to the 1870's, seminaries screened the number of ministerial candidates by requiring fluency in Latin, Greek, Hebrew, and systematic theology, thereby making additional screening far more perfunctory at the final level. Presbyteries moved from reliance on the content of theology—what ministerial candidates actually professed—to formal academic certification: where they received their training. Presbyteries deferred unofficial responsibility for evaluating theological competency to academic theologians. These theologians themselves were expected to experience the gauntlet of higher education, especially German higher education. Not that they had to graduate from a German university; they merely had to attend for a year or two. This was usually sufficient to undermine their faith in the Confession's view of Scripture. The liberals succumbed to the rationalist methodologies of the Germans; the conservatives had long since succumbed to the rationalist methodology of the Scots. The professors molded students in their own images over a three-year training period. After one year in office, each faculty member became immune to removal from that office by the General Assembly. It was far easier to capture the seminaries than the General Assembly. It was also more profitable. Infiltrators were paid by the seminaries.

What was the theological legacy of Princeton Seminary? Princeton was stricter-Confessional, rigorously academic, rationalist in the Scottish empiricist (facts-based) tradition, postmillennial in eschatology, and confident in traditional systematic theology (Turretin's seventeenth-century *loci*). The Princetonians believed in public theological debate, especially in academic journals. This led them into the disastrous trap of co-publishing with Union Seminary *The Presbyterian Review*, which allowed higher criticism to enter the Church as merely one more legitimate, intellectually neutral methodology among others. The Princetonians assumed the primacy of the intellect—at the very least, rational thought as first among equals. But this meant, in the final analysis, *the primacy of the formal academic degree.* Princeton was the last Northern Presbyterian seminary to succumb to modernism, but it had succumbed in principle to the methodology of modernism by 1881, as *The Presbyterian Review* proves.

What was the theological legacy of Union Seminary? Union was New School until the 1890's, when it publicly went modernist. It was always committed to open inquiry. It stressed practical theology: evangelicalism before 1890, Progressive political activism after 1900. It became the most important Presbyterian seminary in the United States, and probably the most important seminary anywhere. Its faculty after 1900 represented the American Protestant Establishment. It was committed to the toleration of everything except orthodoxy.[40]

What compromises in strategy was Machen forced to make, and why? He had to accept the Doctrinal Deliverance of 1910 as the best means of testing a minister's theological orthodoxy. The Church's conservatives had long since abandoned the Westminster Confession as a test of orthodoxy. They had abandoned too much of it by 1900 and most of it after 1906. Machen kept referring to the authority of the Westminster Confession, but he had no hope of ever seeing it enforced judicially. This forced him into a common-ground alliance with Arminians in the Church and outside.

---

40. Union's Harry F. Ward was the most politically radical seminary professor in America—and probably in the world. On Ward, see C. Gregg Singer, *The Unholy Alliance* (New Rochelle, New York: Arlington House, 1975), pp. 357–59.

Why did people who initially "talked conservative" wind up going along with liberal Church leaders? The cost of remaining with Machen grew too high. At each stage, Machen forced a confrontation with entrenched modernists and their majority experientialist allies, and each time he lost. This narrowed the range of his supporters, and it steadily guaranteed his ultimate institutional defeat. Most people will not commit to a movement which they regard as institutionally doomed. The positive sanctions offered by the Church for silence were great: jobs, peace, a building, and a pension plan. The negative sanctions were great, especially after 1934: unemployment during the Great Depression.

Why did others who "talked Calvinistic" wind up going along with liberal Church leaders? For the same reasons as the conservatives, but with this added element: Machen's demands on them pressed them ever more tightly. They formally confessed adherence to the same Confession. There is always the temptation to dismiss as too radical, and therefore dangerous to a successful extension of the common faith, that person who is closest to you ideologically, but who is taking the implications that you hold in common to ever-more costly conclusions. "Stand up and stand firm," Machen implored, but they much preferred to stand pat.

Did Machen's tactics destroy the Old School Presbyterian tradition? Yes. The Dutch-American Calvinist tradition replaced it in the Orthodox Presbyterian Church after 1936 because of the problem of hiring academically qualified candidates for Westminster Seminary's faculty. John Murray alone defended something resembling the Old School system, but he did not clearly articulate its postmillennialism.[41] The New School tradition was also either dead or severely paralyzed by 1936. Fundamentalism had replaced the New School tradition after 1910. The Bible Presbyterian Church in 1938 was more fundamentalist than New School, tolerating anti-covenantal dispensationalism in

---

41. His postmillennialism appears in his book, *The Epistle to the Romans*, 2 vols. (Grand Rapids: Eerdmans, 1965), II:91–103.

the name of tolerating historic premillennialism. It launched no reforming crusades comparable to the New School's attack on slavery.

How was a Baptist, John D. Rockefeller, Jr., involved in the Presbyterian conflict? He understood the power of money in a world that was moving into moral relativism. He saw the long-term potential for funding ministers' educations.[42] He believed in modernism, which meant point five: ecumenism. His money financed ecumenism from 1910 onward, when the ecumenists were slowly gaining control over the Presbyterian Church's trust funds, properties, agencies, and tithes. He provided funding for liberals in the Presbyterian Church, most notably the liberal Baptist who resigned from it under fire in 1924: Harry Emerson Fosdick. He funded the mailing of Fosdick's famous sermon. He was equally ready to take care of Mrs. Buck after 1932, but her book royalties and movie royalties rolled in, and she re-married very well, so she did not need his assistance. He also funded Robert E. Speer throughout the period, though not on a full-time basis. Rockefeller armed the infiltrators and took care of the wounded when necessary. Finally, he funded criticism of biblical orthodoxy from outside the Presbyterian camp: a crucial aspect of the liberals' capture of the Church.

What Was to Be Done?

What went wrong? Why were the liberals able to capture the Northern Presbyterian Church in 1936? It goes back to 1646.

Problems

The Westminster Assembly failed to explain judicially what the ecclesiastical authority of its own documents should be. The Assembly failed to address this fundamental covenantal question: What is the judicial basis of both ordination and local church membership? That is, what oath is mandatory for officers? What oath is mandatory of members? Because Presbyterianism did not deal with the issue of the oath-bound confession of faith in its foundational documents, the

---

42. The Sealantic Fund.

problem of stricter subscription vs. looser subscription was never resolved. This problem plagued American Presbyterianism from 1729 on: New Side (New York Synod) vs. Old Side (Philadelphia Synod); later, Old School vs. New School; finally, conservatives vs. modernists.

Second, the pre-1869 Old School sank on the shoals of *adiaphora*—specifically, the issue of chattel slavery. Refusing to deal with this social, economic, and political issue exegetically, circumstances after 1861 forced the Old School to deal with it defensively in terms of politics, both civil and ecclesiastical. In a weakened psychological condition, 1864-1869, it succumbed to the lure of one more reconciliation with its twice-divorced ex-spouse. The Old School Presbyterian tradition never did come up with a detailed exegetical solution to the question of chattel slavery. Westminster Seminary's Scot, John Murray, as late as 1957 was still unwilling to condemn it biblically.[43]

Third, the Church never did establish the judicial and institutional basis of its control over the content of education, either in its colleges or its seminaries. The chain of command was more informal than formal. Presbyterian higher education was tied judicially more to the Prussian doctrine of academic freedom than to Confessional authority. The educational boards were almost completely independent of the General Assembly. They became self-appointing entities. This self-appointing, self-perpetuating feature became the model for the other Church boards.

Fourth, the boards of the Church were never integrated judicially into the Church's structure of presbyterial authority. A recognition of the problem of integrating the boards into Presbyterian government went back to the days of the division of 1838. Citing Presbyterianism's regulative principle of formal Church worship, James Thornwell had rejected the degree of independence given to the boards by the General Assembly, an authority not authorized by the Bible. He wanted smaller boards that were directly responsible to the General Assembly, not large legally independent boards with near-permanent

---

43. John Murray, *Principles of Conduct: Aspects of Biblical Ethics* (Grand Rapids, Michigan: Eerdmans, 1957), pp. 100-102.

executive committees that barely answered to the General Assembly. These boards were "virtually self-appointed."[44] They employed full-time fund-raisers who spoke at local congregations. Robert Breckenridge agreed, and went even further. He said that pastors should raise the funds as part of ordinary worship.[45] This would have transferred the power of the purse back to local congregations. Thornwell's next suggestion would have made it far more difficult for liberals ever to have captured the Presbyterian Church. He recommended placing authority for home missions and foreign missions with the presbyteries. This way, he said, the boards would not send out Pelagians and Arminians.[46] Little did he suspect that by 1900, semi-Pelagians would have been orthodox compared to those missionaries who were actually being sent out. He had spotted the weak link: the inability of the boards to screen out heretics. But the key question still remained: *Why would the presbyteries initially fail to screen out any heretics who would then be sent out by the boards?*

Charles Hodge disagreed. In 1860, in a debate with Thornwell in front of the General Assembly, Hodge defended the existing system of boards, rejecting Thornwell's application of the regulative principle to the details of Church government, as distinguished from formal worship.[47] Calvin had been speaking of baptism when he wrote: "*First, whatever is not commanded, we are not free to choose.*"[48] So, Hodge concluded, Thornwell's view of the regulative principle was too narrow; unless the Bible says not to create a new office, the Church is allowed to create it. Thornwell was teaching "hyper-hyper-hyper High Church Presbyterianism." To which Thornwell replied that Hodge was teaching "no, *no*, NO Presbyterianism, no *no*, NO Churchism."[49]

---

44. Ernest Trice Thompson, *Presbyterians in the South*, 3 vols. (Richmond, Virginia: John Knox Press, 1973), I:511.

45. *Ibid*.

46. *Ibid*, I:512.

47. Charles Hodge, *Discussions in Church Polity* (New York: Charles Scribner's Sons, 1878), p. 133.

48. John Calvin, "Form of Administering the Sacraments," in *Selected Works of John Calvin: Tracts and Letters*, Henry Beveridge, translator (Grand Rapids, Michigan: Baker, [1849] 1983), vol. 2, *Tracts*, p. 118.

49. *Ibid.*, I:515.

Their rhetoric had descended to the level of rival schoolboys on a playground. Hodge's view prevailed, and it ultimately led the Church into liberalism. When the majority should not have listened to him, it did; when it should have listened to him (the 1869 reunion), it didn't. Once again, the much-praised and rarely specified Presbyterian regulative principle had failed in practice to regulate anything. There was no agreement by two of Presbyterianism's greatest theologians on what it actually meant. In this respect, little has changed since 1860. (Without an afterthought, American Presbyterians use organs in their churches today, but from the Westminster Assembly to Thornwell, there were those who denied their use in the name of the regulative principle.[50] Dabney allowed musical instruments in worship, but he opposed the organ as being uniquely papist. Adopt an organ, he said, and you are headed into popery.[51] Any Presbyterian minister who holds such a view today is regarded by his peers as a harmless eccentric, unless he presses the issue in his presbytery, in which case he is regarded as a troublemaking crank. One thing is certain: he has a very small congregation if he has any congregation at all.)

In an article published in January, 1861, as the South was seceding from the Union, Thornwell got the last, judicially accurate word against Hodge: "The Board, therefore, seems to us to be an organization within the Church, occupying the place and exercising the powers which belong to her own judicatories."[52] But this did not go far enough analytically. Why should a supreme court, i.e., the General Assembly, establish and supervise executive administrative agencies? This confusion of supreme executive authority and supreme judicial authority in one organization has been the organizational Achilles' heel of Presbyterianism from the beginning. It concentrates both final judicial authority and supreme executive authority at the top of an impersonal bureaucratic system. *Power concentrated means power exercised, and eventually it becomes power captured by power religionists.*

---

50. *Ibid.*, II:429.
51. *Ibid.*, II:430.
52. Thornwell, *Collected Writings*, IV:240; cited in *ibid.*, I:515.

The General Assembly did not appoint new trustees for Church boards on a regular basis. The boards in effect could grant a board member a kind of tenure for good behavior: tenure as far as the General Assembly was concerned. This tenure extended to all those hired by, or sent out by, these boards. (The advent of Civil Service protection for employees of the Federal government, which began in the 1880's, paralleled the development of the Presbyterian Church boards in the same era.) This near immunity to dismissal enabled modernists to infiltrate the boards, which were almost as autonomous functionally as the seminaries. The two biggest boards, Foreign Missions and Home Missions, sent out ordained men, yet the boards did not police the confessions of these men. The boards were not empowered to do so, which made employment by the boards a safe haven, Confessionally speaking, for liberals. Presbyterian foreign missions were closely associated with the post-1886 collegiate parachurch missions movement that was led by Mott and Speer. Liberals became the dominant force in this collegiate movement: YMCA, SVM, etc.

Fifth, there was the Presbyterian problem of the voice of authority in between General Assembly meetings. Silence for 51 weeks each year became less acceptable as the Church grew ever-larger, more complex, and wealthier. After 1906, the liberals worked for three decades to create permanent agencies that spoke in the name of the GA, and which would gain enormous influence over each GA, whose attendees were mostly first-timers. The elected officials who served as GA attendees faced what all politicians face: the expertise of the permanent bureaucracy. They surrendered.

Sixth, the Presbyterian Church never found a way to deal with the heresy of the New York Presbytery. Those outside the New York Presbytery found it almost impossible to control heretics under its jurisdiction before 1900, and completely impossible after 1900. The defensive mentality of presbyteries resists all criticisms from outsiders, and this puts pressure on minority critics inside, who can solve their problems only by going "over the head" of the presbytery to "outsiders." This meant that a heretic had to go into print in order for those outside his presbytery to bring effective negative sanctions against him.

Seventh, the General Assembly had become a legislative assembly that sat in judgment of itself. This is the essence of administrative law:

legislator, judge, and jury. The structure of the General Assembly played into the hands of the modernists, who transformed Presbyterian law in the same way that they transformed civil law: through top-down administrative law courts.

Solutions

First, the solution to the Westminster Confession was the addition of another chapter on ecclesiastical oaths: for ordination and for membership. There also needed to be a section on the locus of authority in policing these oaths: local to national. This required that Confessional affirmation had to be dealt with: stricter vs. looser. Synods should have automatically reviewed the ordination of every elder who offered an exception to the Confession. This requirement, of course, would either have paralyzed the court system or led to automatic approval unless the Confession had been modified occasionally to meet shifting theological opinion. But there was no other way: either the Confession is revised or the courts jam up or elders play the game of crossed fingers. In any case, the Church's true confession will change over time.

Second, the solution to the problem of *adiaphora* always is exegesis: searching the whole of the Scriptures for the judicial foundations of social theory and policy.

Third, control over higher education had to be returned to the presbyteries by way of agencies controlled by them, not by the General Assembly. Any denomination that does not have a permanent committee of laymen and ministers who monitor the textbooks and lecture notes of the denominational college and seminary has surrendered to liberalism in advance. This committee on educational standards must not be appointed; it must be elected every two or three years: one minister and one layman (not necessarily a ruling elder) per synod or presbytery (depending on the size of the denomination), but not elected by the General Assembly, which is too easily controlled by the boards. The Presbyterian Church did not have such a committee—the only national committee it really needed.

This committee had to have the authority, subject to a veto only by the General Assembly, to cut the denomination's financial support of the suspect institution by up to 5 percent per year, a cut not to be restored until the committee's academic recommendation is implemented. The rule is: *no sanctions*–no oath; no oath–no covenant. Committee members should have been encouraged to consult with outside specialists in the various academic fields, whether or not they were members of the denomination.

Fourth, all national Presbyterian boards should have been turned over by the General Assembly to the presbyteries. These boards were executive agencies operating under the jurisdiction of a supreme court. This created a hybrid system of bureaucratic authority, judicial and executive, that always leads directly into the tyranny of administrative law—the judicial revolution that is undermining the West. The boards should have been appointed, funded, and policed by the presbyteries, which do lawfully initiate because they ordain men to local office. The General Assembly should have remained a supreme court. Each board member on every board would have been appointed by his presbytery, with rotating synodical representation to keep boards no larger than a dozen members per board. A board member would have been limited to a three-year term. The boards' membership should have been replaced annually: one-third of the board's officers every year. No board should have been allowed to recommend successor members. No synod would have been allowed to appoint a new member if any other synod had not sent a member during the same term. The Stated Clerk should have been removed from his ex officio position on every board. No board should have been under the administrative control of the General Assembly. Power must be decentralized to preserve freedom. The General Assembly should have relinquished all control over the boards.

Public choice economic theory informs us of one reality of original sin: whenever a bureaucracy gets access to a nearly guaranteed stream of income, its members seek their individual goals first and the bureaucracy's autonomous goals second. The goals of those supplying the funds are, at best, a distant third. This is why the flow of funds is so important to bureaucrats. They change their behavior only in response to a reduction in the flow of funds: negative sanctions. *The only way to control the spread of bureaucracy is to de-fund it.* There is no other way for dilettantes (us) to control experts (them). There is no other permanent solution to the steady transfer of power from the laity to the central bureaucracy. Conclusion: missions should be local or presbyterial, the latter on a matching-fund basis. The local church sends out missionaries, and the presbytery matches funds using some fixed formula.

Fifth, who speaks for the General Assembly in between meetings? There was no clear answer. Scottish Presbyterianism had a preliminary answer: the superintendent. This pastoral office prevailed in Scottish Presbyterianism during the "Second Episcopacy" of 1662–1690.[53] What if, alongside presbyteries, synods, and General Assemblies, there had been a hierarchical system of superintendents, one for each presbytery and synod, each one subject to the veto of his presbytery or synod? All would have been ultimately responsible to the General Assembly, itself made up of ruling elders and teaching elders. What if each superintendent had possessed the authority to investigate the rumors of heresy within his own jurisdiction? What if he had been able to sit down with another superintendent and discuss with him, as a man possessing equal authority, the goings-on inside the other man's jurisdiction? What if a superintendent had possessed the authority to examine the classroom instruction of any seminary professor within his jurisdiction? Then it would not have required the lonely stand of some courageous individual in another presbytery—a man not possessing the authority of an entire presbytery—to have called public attention to the theologically unsound condition of the New York Presbytery. Machen performed this service to the denomination in the 1920's, but by then it was too late. He stood increasingly alone, an anomaly: a Presbyterian who believed that the Westminster Confession should be honored verbally, though not enforced through heresy trials.

There was no such judicial representative above the congregational level. But there must be operational continuity in any organization; the larger the organization, the more imperative this continuity. People understand this with respect to civil authority, but they are less willing to admit that ecclesiastical authority is equally in need of personal continuity. *Functional authority in Presbyterianism unceremoniously moved from the infrequent gatherings of corporate judicial assem-*

---

53. Geddes MacGregor, *Corpus Christi: The Nature of the Church According to the Reformed Tradition* (Philadelphia: Westminster, 1958), pp. 80n–81n.

blies to the permanent corporations of the Church. This silent transfer of functional authority accelerated after the centralization of 1908. The judicial continuity of the Presbyterian Church was increasingly provided by its permanent commissions and boards, which were represented by men who were first among equals. The most influential Presbyterian representative of all after 1920 was Robert E. Speer. His advent to the robes of power came at the General Assembly of 1927.

The office of superintendent was abandoned early by the Scottish Church, never reaching American shores. Not to have a spokesman is to adopt a mode of independency, e.g., the Southern Baptist Convention. To have a spokesman is to adopt either prelacy or episcopacy. Spokesmen there are in Presbyterianism. Machen was one. Macartney was one. So were van Dyke, Coffin, and Speer. But they are informal spokesmen and therefore not subject to a formal veto, since their words carry no official authority.

Sixth, how to enable critics in one presbytery to overcome the defensive mind-set of another presbytery? The defensive mentality of presbyteries led them to protect deviants in their midst from criticisms by those outside the presbytery. This was another example of Presbyterianism's absence of personalism above the congregational level. I have no idea how this problem can be solved within the framework of Presbyterian government without a superintendent. So far, no solution has even been discussed publicly.

Seventh, General Assembly meetings should have been divided into two completely separate sessions: first as a court of appeals; second as a policy-initiating body. The judicial session should have come first; if it ran out of time, there would have been no legislative session that year. Everything done in either session should have been subject to a veto by the presbyteries.[54] The presbyteries should have put the General Assembly's legislative authority on a very short chain. No decision not approved by two-thirds of the authorized delegates at a General Assembly (not just at a particular session) would have been considered valid. A majority vote by all the attendees (not just those

---

54. On the judicial session, see Appendix B, below: section on "A Technical Solution to Confessional Revision," pp. 970–72.

in attendance at a poorly attended session), but not a two-thirds majority, should have automatically triggered an overture to be sent down to the presbyteries for a final vote. Until approved by the over half of the presbyteries, the proposed legislation should have been put on hold. No five-point Doctrinal Deliverances, no 14-point Social Deliverances, no authorizations of money for the Federal Council of Churches, no calls for a League of Nations, unless approved by two-thirds of the delegates or by over half of the presbyteries. In short, *no national voice of authority on issues not authorized by those represented.* The presbyteries had delegated vast authority to the seminaries and the General Assembly, which was an open invitation to liberals: "Come and get us!" They did.

Finally, there was one other solution: keep the denomination so small that screening by an intimate network of pastors keeps out liberals. This has been the only workable long-term Presbyterian solution so far. Baptists and charismatics think it is just the right solution for solving Presbyterian conflicts. For that matter, so do the liberals in mainline Presbyterianism. It reduces competition.

Conclusion

The Presbyterian conflict began in 1721 and escalated through the First Great Awakening, which split the denomination in 1741. In this initial phase of the conflict, the debate was over the role of "experience vs. confession" as the true mark of saving faith. This crucial theological debate was never resolved. The Church reunited in 1758. The debate re-surfaced again in the 1820's as a result of the Second Great Awakening. To this was added another dividing issue: slavery. The Church split again in 1837, and each of the factions subsequently divided over slavery and the Civil War.

The second phase of the conflict began with the reuniting of the Northern Church in 1869: the authority issue, Bible and Confession. From this point on, the division was a three-way split. The third phase, beginning in 1901, was a time of visible peace; it was during this phase that the Westminster Confession was revised and the liberals captured the administrative machinery of the Church. It was a conflict over legitimate standards and the rule of law. The fourth phase was the debate over legitimate sanctions, 1922 to 1933. The fifth phase was the final one: the decision regarding who would inherit the assets of the Presbyterian Church. It ended inside the Church in 1936. It ended outside the Church when the civil courts decided in 1938 that the separating Presbyterian Church of America could not retain its name, which was the property of the Presbyterian Church in the U.S.A. What had begun in 1721 as a debate over strict subscription ended in 1939 in a battle over trademark rights.

Presbyterianism has two enormous chinks in its judicial armor. *First, at the bottom*: the absence of any denomination-wide creed for communicant members, who are also voting members. (Prior to the Civil War, donors who were not members had the vote when calling a pastor[55]—a true judicial nightmare.) This system of judicial representation places authority into the hands of those who are not formally covenanted to the Church in terms of judicially explicit and enforceable theological stipulations. There is no Presbyterian personal confession beyond faith in Christ and a willingness to obey Him; there has been none since 1647. Those who are not under an oath with theological content can lawfully hire and fire the Church's voices of judicial authority: elders. *Second, at the top*: the fusion of legislative, executive, and final judicial authority in the same organization, the General Assembly. The institution which establishes policy and executes policy sits as its own judge over policy. This is the essence of administrative law. It is also the essence of tyranny.

This dualism of initiating authority cannot persist indefinitely. One or the other must become supreme: the oath-less member or the supreme bureaucracy. From 1934 to 1936, the issue was finally resolved when the supreme administrative law court announced its formal initiating authority over all presbyteries, which in turn announced their newly acquired executive authority over all members. The lowest-common-denominator confession proved to be the confession of the liberals who had captured control over the General Assembly's unified executive and judicial machinery. Nevertheless, what took place in this brief, consummating period had always been implied by the General Assembly's triple authority: executive, legislative, and judicial. What changed judicially in 1934 was that the communi-

---

55. Thompson, *Presbyterians in the South*, I:518–19.

cant members were at last brought under the General Assembly's authority despite the absence of any oath on their part. This destroyed the intermediary courts' layers of judicial authority that had been built into Presbyterianism in order to insulate the authority of teaching elders from the decisions of communicant members. In order to get at the communicant members' wallets—the flow of funds—the new judicial order commandeered the initiating authority of the presbyteries. We could also say that in order to commandeer the initiating authority of the presbyteries, the new legal order extended its authority over communicant members. Presbytery's rights went the way of state's rights: gone with the wind. So did member's rights.[56]

The Presbyterian conflict had implications far beyond the four walls of the institutional Church. It was more than a conflict over theology narrowly defined. It was a battle for the soul of what was a Protestant nation when the conflict began in 1721, though not when it ended in 1936. To understand how high the stakes were, consider the words of George Santayana in 1913: "The present age is a critical one and interesting to live in. The civilization characteristic of Christendom has not yet disappeared, yet another civilization has begun to take its place."[57] One year later, World War I broke out, and by its end in 1918, the ideal of Christendom was gone. For the first time since the days of King Saul, the kings had departed,[58] and so had the long-fading ideal of Christendom. The triumph of Renaissance-Enlightenment civilization was complete. Humanistic civil covenants would now be administered and enforced in the West. The fourth stage of the Presbyterian conflict began in 1922, after this culture-wide succession had taken place. The power religionists' strategy of subversion had worked well inside the Church, just as it had worked well outside the Church, as Machen and his allies would soon learn.

---

56. Paralleling these developments were analogous developments in American civil law.

57. Cited in Henry F. May, *The End of American Innocence: A Study of the First Years of Our Own Time, 1912-1917* (Chicago: Quadrangle, [1959] 1964), two pages prior to the Introduction.

58. In the classic aphorism of Egypt's King Farouk, a British puppet who was deposed in the early 1950's, "There are but five kings left in the world: the King of England, and the kings of jacks, hearts, diamonds, and spades."

In 1908, the year of the administrative restructuring of the Presbyterian Church, Woodrow Wilson wrote this regarding legitimate government: "Each part of the government loses force and prestige in proportion as it ceases to give, and give publicly, conclusive reasons for what it is doing and for what it is declining to do."[59] That assessment, perhaps more than any other, stands as the tombstone which was waiting in reserve for the Presbyterian Church, U.S.A. The modernists' strategy of subversion has always rested on *bureaucratic secrecy*—the creation of a shadow government and a shadow confession. Decade by decade, the Presbyterian Church's hierarchy has offered its bureaucratic explanations for each successive outrage, from its financial support of Rockefeller's Interchurch World Movement in 1919 to its support of Communist Angela Davis in 1971 to its financial support of the RE-imagining Conference in 1993. The denomination is aging[60] and shrinking. The bureaucracy's post-scandal explanations fall on fewer and fewer ears.

The Angela Davis case is representative. In 1971, the denomination's Council on Church and Race donated $10,000 to her legal defense fund. In 1970, the gifts from the churches to the General Assembly's General Mission fund totaled $24.6 million. In 1972, gifts had dropped to $22.6 million. In 1973, they had dropped to $20.3 million. Meanwhile, giving to the congregations rose from $368.8 million (1971) to $373.2 million (1972) to $410.5 million (1973). The members applied negative sanctions to the bureaucracy, not to their local congregations. Membership dropped by 100,000 each year, from 3 million in 1971 to 2.8 million in 1973.[61] It has continued to drop. Presbyterians continue vote with their wallets and their feet. Such is the fate of administrative law. It creates apoplexy at the center and anemia at the extremities. (And what became of Miss Davis? She was awarded the

---

59. Woodrow Wilson, *Constitutional Government in the United States* (New York: Columbia University Press, [1908] 1961), p. 110.

60. Some 13 percent of PCUSA members are in the 18–34 age group, compared with 36 percent nationally. A third are age 65 or older, almost double the percentage of older Americans. *National & International Religion Report* (July 10, 1995), p. 5.

61. John R. Fry, *The Triviliazation of the United Presbyterian Church* (New York: Harper & Row, 1975), p. 50.

Lenin Peace Prize in 1979. She ran as Vice President of the United States on the Communist Party ticket in 1980 and 1984. She was expelled by the Party in 1992. In 1995, she was named to what is probably the most prestigious academic position at the University of California, Santa Cruz: the tenured Presidential Chair. She never earned a Ph.D. Lesson: the Left takes care of its own.)[62]

A Final Word

In the spring of 1963, about the time I completed my B.A. thesis on the Presbyterian conflict, Dallas Roark completed his Ph.D. dissertation on Machen. In the Conclusion, he offered this assessment: "The judgment of time has validated the conclusion that Machen exaggerated the extent of liberalism within the Presbyterian Church."[63] This was not time's judgment; it was Roark's. Nothing in his dissertation had prepared the reader for his assessment, and I can think of nothing of denomination-wide significance that has happened since 1936 that would validate it. The revised Confession of 1967 surely did not. Neither did the "RE-imagining 1993" conference. But those of us who write conclusions to monographs are frequently tempted sorely to make judgments more sweeping than our circumscribed theses warrant, if only to justify the enormous commitment of our time and effort. I, too, will now succumb to this temptation.

The question facing Christians today is this: *Will there be a resurrection of Christendom?* Few of Machen's heirs believe in the possibility of such a resurrection; few believed in 1937. Some of them believe not only that it will not be resurrected; it should not be resurrected.[64] I believe that Christendom can, will, and ought to be resurrected, though next time without kings, and also without a U.S. Department of Education. This is my confession. It was also Machen's.

---

62. Jeffrey Hart, "Angela Davis: Academic Fraud," *Conservative Chronicle* (April 26, 1995). p. 25.

63. Dallas Roark, J. Gresham Machen and His Desire to Maintain a Doctrinally True Presbyterian Church (Ph.D. dissertation, Iowa State University, 1963), p. 215.

64. Gary North, *Westminster's Confession: The Abandonment of Van Til's Legacy* (Tyler, Texas: Institute for Christian Economics, 1991).

APPENDIXES

Appendix A

H. L. MENCKEN'S OBITUARY OF MACHEN

"Dr. Fundamentalis"[1]

The Rev. J. Gresham Machen, D. D., who died out in North Dakota on New Year's Day, got, on the whole, a bad press while he lived, and even his obituaries did much less than justice to him. To newspaper reporters, as to other antinomians, a combat between Christians over a matter of dogma is essentially a comic affair, and in consequence Dr. Machen's heroic struggles to save Calvinism in the Republic were usually depicted in ribald, or, at all events, in somewhat skeptical terms. The generality of readers, I suppose, gathered thereby the notion that he was simply another Fundamentalist on the order of William Jennings Bryan and the simian faithful of Appalachia. But he was actually a man of great learning, and, what is more, of sharp intelligence.

What caused him to quit the Princeton Theological Seminary and found a seminary of his own was his complete inability, as a theologian, to square the disingenuous evasions of Modernism with the fundamentals of Christian doctrine. He saw clearly that the only effects that could follow diluting and polluting Christianity in the Modernist manner would be its complete abandonment and ruin. Either it was true or it was not true. If, as he believed, it was true, then there could be no compromise with persons who sought to whittle away its essential postulates, however respectable their motives.

---

1. Baltimore *Evening Sun* (January 18, 1937), 2nd Section, p. 15.

Thus he fell out with the reformers who have been trying, in late years, to convert the Presbyterian Church into a kind of literary and social club, devoted vaguely to good works. Most of the other Protestant churches have gone the same way, but Dr. Machen's attention, as a Presbyterian, was naturally concentrated upon his own connection. His one and only purpose was to hold it [the Church] resolutely to what he conceived to be the true faith. When that enterprise met with opposition he fought vigorously, and though he lost in the end and was forced out of Princeton it must be manifest that he marched off to Philadelphia with all the honors of war.

II

My interest in Dr. Machen while he lived, though it was large, was not personal, for I never had the honor of meeting him. Moreover, the doctrine that he preached seemed to me, and still seems to me, to be excessively dubious. I stand much more chance of being converted to spiritualism, to Christian Science or even to the New Deal than to Calvinism, which occupies a place, in my cabinet of private horrors, but little removed from that of cannibalism. But Dr. Machen had the same clear right to believe in it that I have to disbelieve in it, and though I could not yield to his reasoning I could at least admire, and did greatly admire, his remarkable clarity and cogency as an apologist, allowing him his primary assumptions.

These assumptions were also made, at least in theory, by his opponents, and thereby he had them by the ear. Claiming to be Christians as he was, and of the Calvinish persuasion, they endeavored fatuously to get rid of all the inescapable implications of their position. On the one hand they sought to retain membership in the fellowship of the faithful, but on the other hand they presumed to repeal and reenact with amendments the body of doctrine on which that fellowship rested. In particular, they essayed to overhaul the scriptural authority which lay at the bottom of the whole matter, retaining what coincided with their private notions and rejecting whatever upset them.

Upon this contumacy Dr. Machen fell with loud shouts of alarm. He denied absolutely that anyone had a right to revise and sophisticate Holy Writ. Either it was the Word of God or it was not the Word of God, and if it was, then it was equally authoritative in all its details, and had to be accepted or rejected as a whole. Anyone was free to reject it, but no one was free to mutilate it or to read things into it that were not there. Thus the issue with the Modernists was clearly joined, and Dr. Machen argued them quite out of court, and sent them scurrying back to their literary and sociological *Kaffeeklatsche*. His operations, to be sure, did not prove that Holy Writ was infallible either as history or as theology, but they at least disposed of those who proposed to read it as they might read a newspaper, believing what they chose and rejecting what they chose.

III

In his own position there was never the least shadow of inconsistency. When the Prohibition imbecility fell upon the country, and a multitude of theological quacks, including not a few eminent Presbyterians, sought to read support for it into the New Testament, he attacked them with great vigor, and routed them easily. He not only proved that there was nothing in the teachings of Jesus to support so monstrous a folly; he proved abundantly that the known teachings of Jesus were unalterably against it. And having set forth that proof, he refused, as a convinced and honest Christian, to have anything to do with the dry *jehad*.

This rebellion against a craze that now seems so incredible and so far away was not the chief cause of his break with his ecclesiastical superiors, but it was probably responsible for a large part of their extraordinary dudgeon against him. The Presbyterian Church, like the other evangelical churches, was taken for a dizzy ride by Prohibition. Led into the heresy by fanatics of low mental visibility, it presently found itself cheek by jowl with all sorts of criminals, and fast losing the respect of sensible people. Its bigwigs thus became extremely jumpy on the subject, and resented bitterly every exposure of their lamentable folly.

The fantastic William Jennings Bryan, in his day the country's most distinguished Presbyterian layman, was against Dr. Machen on the issue of Prohibition but with him on the issue of Modernism. But Bryan's support, of course, was of little value or consolation to so intelligent a man. Bryan was a Fundamentalist of the Tennessee or barnyard school. His theological ideas were those of a somewhat backward child of 8, and his defense of Holy Writ at Dayton during the Scopes trial was so ignorant and stupid that it must have given

Dr. Machen a great deal of pain. Dr. Machen himself was to Bryan as the Matterhorn is to a wart. His Biblical studies had been wide and deep, and he was familiar with the almost interminable literature of the subject. Moreover, he was an adept theologian, and had a wealth of professional knowledge to support his ideas. Bryan could only bawl.

IV

It is my belief, as a friendly neutral in all such high and ghostly matters, that the body of doctrine known as Modernism is completely incompatible, not only with anything rationally describable as Christianity, but also with anything deserving to pass as religion in general. Religion, if it is to retain any genuine significance, can never be reduced to a series of sweet attitudes, possible to anyone not actually in jail for felony. It is, on the contrary, a corpus of powerful and profound convictions, many of them not open to logical analysis. Its inherent improbabilities are not sources of weakness to it, but of strength. It is potent in a man in proportion as he is willing to reject all overt evidences, and accept its fundamental postulates, however unprovable they may be by secular means, as massive and incontrovertible facts.

These postulates, at least in the Western world, have been challenged in recent years on many grounds, and in consequence there has been a considerable decline in religious belief. There was a time, two or three centuries ago, when the overwhelming majority of educated men were believers, but that is apparently true no longer. Indeed, it is my impression that at least two-thirds of them are now frank skeptics. But it is one thing to reject religion altogether, and quite another thing to try to save it by pumping out of it all its essential substance, leaving it in the equivocal position of a sort of pseudo-science, comparable to graphology, "education," or osteopathy.

That, it seems to me, is what the Modernists have done, no doubt with the best intentions in the world. They have tried to get rid of all the logical difficulties of religion, and yet preserve a generally pious cast of mind. It is a vain enterprise. What they have left, once they have achieved their imprudent scavenging, is hardly more than a row of hollow platitudes, as empty as [of] psychological force and effect as so many nursery rhymes. They may be good people and they may even be contented and happy, but they are no more religious than Dr. Einstein. Religion is something else again—in Henrik Ibsen's phrase, something far more deep-down-diving and mudupbringing, Dr. Machen tried to impress that obvious fact upon his fellow adherents of the Geneva Mohammed. He failed—but he was undoubtedly right.

Appendix B

HOW TO IMMUNIZE PRESBYTERIANISM

> *Modern liberalism in the Church, whatever judgment may be passed upon it, is at any rate no longer merely an academic matter. It is no longer a matter merely of theological seminaries or universities. . . . At the theological seminaries and universities, however, the roots of the great issue are more clearly seen than in the world at large; among students the reassuring employment of traditional phrases is often abandoned, and the advocates of a new religion are not at pains, as they are in the Church at large, to maintain an appearance of conformity to the past. But such frankness, we are convinced, ought to be extended to the people as a whole. Few desires on the part of religious teachers have been more harmfully exaggerated than the desire to "avoid giving offense."*
>
> J. Gresham Machen (1923)[1]

It is time for me to give offense (again). It is time for me to say what is wrong structurally with American Presbyterianism, a system of Church government that did not provide the defenders of the Westminster Confession with the weapons they needed to defend the Church against its mortal enemies, once the Church grew large enough and wealthy enough to be worth capturing. The evolution of Presbyterianism from Calvinism to Arminianism to liberalism was ac-

---

1. Machen, *Christianity and Liberalism* (New York: Macmillan, 1923), pp. 17–18.

companied by Church growth. There were institutional reasons for this.

The typical Presbyterian Calvinist will insist that Church growth, liberalism, and Presbyterian government are not inextricably linked. This pattern in Church history is not a uniquely Presbyterian problem, he says. He has a good point: Church growth and theological liberalism have accompanied each other in other denominational traditions. But the question remains: Why did the most theologically rigorous Protestant confessional tradition succumb to Arminianism and then to liberalism? Other ecclesiastical traditions did not have Calvinist confessions to defend them. Presumably, their theological defenses were weaker than Presbyterianism's. Nevertheless, one by one, Presbyterian denominations have gone liberal except when they started small and have stayed small.

The reason has to be institutional. We know this because the various Presbyterian Churches' confessions have remained intact for decades after the liberals' conquest was functionally complete. Formal Presbyterian confessions have lagged behind pulpit confessions by at least a generation. These rigorous formal confessions could not overcome Presbyterianism's structural weaknesses. Why not?

It is this question that Presbyterian Calvinists have steadfastly resisted dealing with in print. The fact that they refuse to address it in print indicates that they are afraid to mention it, for fear of being labeled anti-Presbyterian when they propose institutional solutions. Instead of proposing structural reforms, they take the easy way out. They recommend policies that are guaranteed to keep the Church small. This implicitly hands over the world to non-Presbyterians. The non-Presbyterian world, of course, appreciates this indirect subsidy.

Conservative Presbyterian denominations eventually become divided between Confessionalists and Church growth advocates. In our era, the Confessionalists regard the Church growth people as touchy-feelie sell-outs, while the Church growth people regard the Confessionalists as nit-picking, low-pension losers. Liturgically, the war between two extremes is a debate over the psalm book vs. the overhead projector.[2] Each side wishes the other would just go away.

---

2. Two centuries ago, the psalm book had no musical notation. Today, the

Once this division appears, the Confessionalists always lose control of the denomination. There are no known exceptions. The lure of large churches, large pensions, and assistants who do most of the marriage counselling prevails. The Church growth people concentrate on what they do best: growing their churches by whatever works. The Confessionalists concentrate on what they do best: overwhelming one-time visitors with unfamiliar theology. In Presbyterian government, votes count. The Church growth people eventually gain more votes. The Confessionalists then have three choices: (1) spend their lives being outvoted at General Assembly; (2) quit attending General Assembly; or (3) leave to form a new denomination, which will subsequently divide at least once—the Machen-McIntire phenomenon. In the two (or more) new groups, the cycle then begins anew.

The problem is point two of the biblical covenant model: representation/authority. Presbyterians like to pretend that all votes are equal. This is an old Whig belief, and it has always flourished in the face of the facts. Twentieth-century modernists have known better: elite core groups provide direction for the voters. The elite core groups in Presbyterianism have not changed significantly for over four centuries: ordained men who possess advanced academic degrees issued by non-Presbyterian institutions ("doctors")—John Calvin is the classic example—and pastors of large congregations. Over the last century, the former have had a tendency to go liberal; the latter have had a tendency to go pietistic, i.e., non-controversial. To these two groups has been added a third in the twentieth century: senior bureaucrats in the permanent denominational boards. These three groups have become the operational models of success in Presbyterianism.

Young men seeking to enter the Presbyterian ministry must first go through the screening process controlled by the first group. The doctors, not the presbyteries, impose the sanctions. If the students survive, they are then forced to seek jobs. Who has jobs to offer? Hardly anyone; we are talking about Presbyterians, not Baptists. But if there are any jobs available, they will be offered by the remaining two elite groups: pastors of large congregations and senior bureaucrats. The small-congregation Confessional preachers have only this to say: "Sil-

---

overhead projector songs have no musical notation.

ver and gold have we none, and not many Federal Reserve Notes, either." Men respond to positive sanctions. They can see who has positive sanctions to offer. They can also see who doesn't.

Dust-Eating as a Way of Institutional Life

Let us go back to what happened in the United States after 1800. The Baptists and the Methodists captured America west of the Allegheny Mountains. They accomplished this because, first, they did not require their ministers to attend college or seminary. Second, they adopted circuit-riding: a pastor was a pastor of several churches at once. Elders ran the local churches in between pastoral visits. Both of these practices were foreign to Presbyterianism and the other Calvinist denominations. What Paul did with the churches he planted, so also did the Methodists and Baptists in the Western United States, 1800 to 1860.

Very early, American Calvinists made an implicit decision: to allow the Baptists and Methodists to take over the nation's ecclesiastical tradition in preference to abandoning the principle of the academically certified minister and the two-office view of the eldership: ruling and teaching. Presbyterians preferred (and still prefer) to see eternally lost people go to hell rather than modify these two Presbyterian distinctives. Presbyterians would also rather see Baptists take over a society rather than modify these two distinctives. Presumably, they would rather see sinners become Arminian Baptists or charismatics rather than see them go to hell, but these are the only options available to most sinners. The third option, namely, that most sinners will be converted to Presbyterianism, is institutionally impossible because of the academic lag time between the increased demand for ministers and the supply thereof.

Having made this decision in the late eighteenth century, Presbyterians went a step further in the nineteenth: requiring the members of their seminary faculties first to run the gauntlet in humanistic institutions. Unofficially, they required all candidates for seminary faculty positions to study in Germany. Later, after Johns Hopkins University set the pattern for graduate education by importing German academic humanism, Presbyterians allowed these candidates to substitute an advanced degree from an American humanist institution in place of spending a year or two in a German university. In the twentieth century, Presbyterians have required their colleges' faculty members to earn a Ph.D. from a humanist-accredited secular university. The key word here is *accredited*. Every candidate for high teaching authority must first be accredited by humanists. Also, the Church's teaching institutions are accredited by humanists: colleges and seminaries. The surrender to Rockefeller's system of collegiate accreditation is as ingrained today as it was in Machen's day:

> Because it is highly reproachful to religion and dangerous to the church to trust the holy ministry to weak and ignorant men, the presbytery shall admit a candidate to licensure only if he has received a bachelor of arts degree, or its academic equivalent, from an accredited college or university. He must also have completed at least two years of study in a theological seminary.[3]

Presbyterians from the very beginning self-consciously made a decision to conform to the academic standards of their mortal enemies. In the twentieth century, they have voluntarily placed their institutions of higher learning under the judicial authority of liberal humanists: accrediting boards dominated by people who espouse the same liberalism that Machen called a rival religion. This is an open admission on the part of Calvinist Presbyterians that theologically liberal humanists, not Christians, and surely not Calvinists, know what is best in education. The first principle of Presbyterian ordination is the requirement that the Presbyterian Church crawl on its belly, serpent-like, eating the dust of death—humanism's dust. Yet for me to say this, even after what I have demonstrated in this book regarding the surrender of the Presbyterian Church to the liberals, will outrage the professional dust-eaters who run the institutions of Presbyterian higher learning. Meanwhile, most Presbyterian laymen will shrug their shoulders and say, "Well, that's just the way it is. It has always been this way." Yes, it has, but this does not make it right.

This mental attitude—this self-conscious surrender to humanist academic dust-eating—is what led to the transfer of the United States

---

3. *The Form of Government* (1941), in *The Standards of Government Discipline and Worship of The Orthodox Presbyterian Church* (Philadelphia: Committee on Christian Education, The Orthodox Presbyterian Church, 1965), p. 19.

into the hands of the pietist-humanist alliance. It led to the abandonment of the ideal of Christendom. It led to the idea of trickle-down knowledge: from the humanists to the Church. "Truth, Lord," Presbyterians have said in this century to humanist academics, "yet the dogs eat the crumbs which fall from their masters' table."

Christians have self-consciously and forthrightly insisted in the twentieth century that God will deliver history progressively into the hands of covenant-breakers. Nowhere outside of Eastern Orthodoxy has this pessimism been more devastating than in Presbyterianism. Presbyterians know that the only thing that can reverse the covenant-breakers' present visible control over this world is a massive Christian revival. They also know that in past revivals, Presbyterianism has not kept up with the local church-planting activities of Arminian Baptists and Methodists, who have a different concept of the eldership. In a widespread revival, the demand for local churches and elders grows more rapidly than the supply of pastors who have survived four years in a humanist-accredited university and three years in a humanist-accredited Presbyterian (i.e., ecclesiastically independent) seminary. While the Baptists are busy planting churches, the Presbyterians are busy writing term papers.

Today, there are about six billion people on earth. The vast majority of them will go to hell unless a revival comes very soon. If, by the sovereign grace of God, a great revival does come, Presbyterianism, Episcopalianism, Lutheranism, and all the other hierarchical Church traditions that require humanist-certified ministers will be dwarfed by the explosion of growth of Arminian Baptist and charismatic churches. Baptists and charismatics can ordain ministers to keep up with demand. Because of Presbyterianism's term-paper-based ordination requirements, Presbyterians implicitly announce to the lost: "Our ministers are humanist-certified, as God prefers that all ministers should be; therefore, you must go either to hell or to an Arminian church around the corner. God cares far more about ministers with degrees from humanist-accredited universities than He cares for the souls of the lost, and we Presbyterians honor this ultimate concern. We have our priorities correct. We always have."

Am I exaggerating? I challenge you: without writing to the Church's national board of home missions, can you identify three skid row rescue missions anywhere in the United States that are run by Calvinistic Presbyterian churches? (Frankly, I doubt that the board of home missions can name three.) When you think "rescue mission," do you think Presbyterian Church or Salvation Army? When you think "creeping liberalism," do you think Presbyterian Church or Salvation Army? When you think "academically certified preachers," do you think Presbyterian Church or Salvation Army?

A worldwide revival will put an Arminian church on just about every corner. Calvinistic Presbyterians know this. They do not pray for revival because to pray for revival is to pray for the engulfing of Presbyterianism by Arminian independents. Psychologically, very few Christians can pray regularly and fervently for the visible defeat of their own denominational tradition by another denominational tradition. They prefer instead to believe that God has predestined every church tradition to cultural defeat and, if they are amillennialists, maybe even to persecution by covenant-breakers. They mutter to themselves: "You're no better than we are. You're going to fail, too!" So, they decide that true revival is impossible in history, that Jesus will inevitably return to a spiritually dark world in which covenant-breakers rule supreme. Presbyterian Calvinists believe that God has condemned billions upon billions of souls to the agonies of eternal torment for the sake of preserving a humanist-accredited Presbyterian ministry—a ministry that has gone liberal without exception in every large Presbyterian denomination, unlike the Southern Baptists, who merely went Arminian. It is far easier for Calvinists to accept the idea of the eschatologically predestined cultural failure of Christianity in history than it is for them to pray that God will send showers of blessing that will multiply Arminian Baptists like weeds and Presbyterians like prize rose bushes: magnificent but rare.

The only technique that has kept Presbyterian ministers as a group from going theologically liberal has been to keep Presbyterian denominations tiny, so that the ministers can more easily screen out theologically lax ministerial candidates. Because its members do not expect the denomination to grow, the Church's presbyteries resist the urge to ordain lots of ministerial candidates. "We run a tight ship around here: lean and mean." To the Baptists, this sounds more like "slim and grim." These Presbyterian denominations are sometimes smaller in national membership than a pair of First Baptist Church congregations in two large Southern cities. This has produced an outlook hostile to the idea of mass revival, even if such a revival alone can lead to the salvation of the souls of over five billion people. This outlook must change if Presbyterianism is to remain true to its own confession:

> Q. 191. *What do we pray for in the second petition?*
>
> A. In the second petition, (which is, *Thy kingdom come,*) acknowledging ourselves and all mankind to be by nature under the dominion of sin and Satan, we pray, that the kingdom of sin and Satan may be destroyed, the gospel propagated throughout the world, the Jews called, the fulness of the Gentiles brought in; the church furnished with all gospel-officers and ordinances, purged from corruption, countenanced and maintained by the civil magistrate; that the ordinances of Christ may be purely dispensed, and made effectual to the converting of those yet in their sins, and the confirming, comforting, and building up of those that are already converted: that Christ would rule in our hearts here, and hasten the time of his second coming, and our reigning with him for ever: and that he would be pleased so to exercise the kingdom of power in all the world, as may best conduce to these ends. (Larger Catechism.)

When was the last time you heard this prayer or anything remotely like it prayed from the pulpit of a Presbyterian Church? My guess: the next time will be the first.

Structural Reform

Without structural reform, Presbyterianism will never break out of its cultural despair, a despair born of academic dust-eating. Good intentions are not enough. The Old School had good intentions in 1908. That did them no good when they consented to the bureaucratization of the Church. I realize that no Presbyterian will take seriously all of my recommendations in this appendix. I doubt that any Presbyterian leader will take seriously even a majority of them. These recommendations are designed to hold in check centralized power, which I believe is a goal basic to Presbyterian government. While every generation of Presbyterian leaders voices its affirmation of Presbyterianism's system of checks and balances, every generation seems to centralize power. Those employed by the national boards want checks and money orders far more than checks and balances.

There is an anomaly here. I think this anomaly comes from a refusal of Presbyterians to examine the prevailing system of Presbyterian Church government in terms of one overarching task: *follow the money*. They do not analyze Church structures in terms of their sources of funding. That surely was the case during the Presbyterian conflict. Here is the rule: *the agency that writes the paychecks holds the institutional hammer*. For example, if local churches write the paychecks to the missionaries, then they are in control of missions. If a presbytery writes the checks, it is in control. If a denominational Church board writes the checks, then it is in control. Similarly, if a local congregation pays its minister to train an apprentice minister, then the local church is in control of screening candidates for ordination. If a presbytery pays the minister to train the candidate, then it is in control of the screening process. If a seminary pays faculty members to train candidates for ordination, then it is in control of the screening process.

"Follow the money" is a very simple principle to understand; it is just not easy for Presbyterians to believe. Even those few who believe it refuse to act upon it. They do not have the votes to change the system, so they shrug their shoulders and pretend that the funding of the system does not shape it. Warning: *when Presbyterian Calvinists play "let's pretend," Presbyterian inclusivists play "let's take over."*

If Presbyterians ever become serious about immunizing the Church from a takeover by those who do not believe in the Westminster standards, there are ways to achieve this. Here is a two-part rule for the reform of Presbyterian government: (1) match ordination vows with judicial sanctions; (2) match judicial responsibility with money (economic sanctions). This may sound easy, but it has revolutionary implications.

Membership: Communicant

Who gets access to the Lord's Supper in Presbyterianism? Presbyterianism's foundational documents are virtually silent on this. No explicit theological profession is required for local church membership. There is no denomination-wide standard. Local congregational sessions determine who gets access. This may be by giving a testimony of conversion. When it is, back the local church goes to experientialism and away from Calvin's standards: confession of faith and a scandal-free life. Or this may be by the recitation of answers found in a catechism. When it is, back the local church goes to a modified version of Roman Catholicism's confirmation: the sacrament of baptism without the sacrament of the Lord's Supper. Undergirding this delay in the case of children is some version of what the Baptists call "the age of accountability."

When discussing communicant membership, Presbyterians must deal with baptism. Baptism is by covenantal oath. An oath to what? Presbyterianism does not say, other than an unspecified, zero-content faith in Jesus and a promise to obey Him. The baptismal oath should be taken in terms of one of the historic Church's creeds. Why? *Because Presbyterians are not Donatists*. They renounce the Anabaptist doctrine of re-baptism. Presbyterians affirm that the baptisms imposed by all creedally orthodox churches are valid. God's covenantal sanctions are the same, so the confessional stipulations of the oath should be the same. Whatever minimum Trinitarian confession validates an acceptable baptism outside Presbyterianism should also validate baptism inside Presbyterianism. Presbyterian baptism should therefore be by one of the common oaths of Christendom, e.g., Apostles' Creed or Nicene Creed. This creed must be affirmed by the person being baptized or by the person speaking as his judicial agent, i.e., a parent.

Membership: Voting

The communicant member should not automatically be given the right to vote. He is not formally under the sanctions of the Westminster Confession. He has sworn no oath to it. He should therefore not be allowed to impose judicial sanctions in terms of it. *People who impose covenantal sanctions should also be under these sanctions*. If a local church member is not by oath consigned under the stipulations that govern the imposition of Church sanctions, then he should not impose Church sanctions. If he cannot be deprived of his authority to impose sanctions for publicly denying or compromising the stipulations enforced by these sanctions, he should not be allowed to exercise them.

This seems obvious to me, but it has not been obvious to the Presbyterians who have compiled the rule books. Presbyterian communicant members who have not sworn allegiance to the Westminster standards are allowed to vote for or against ruling elders. When ordained by a presbytery, these ruling elders are instructed to govern in terms of the Westminster standards. But those communicant members who impose periodically the congregation's sanctions on these ruling elders are not under any obligation to honor the Westminster standards. They can impose final judicial sanction on those whose governing is not to their liking: "You're fired."

When searching for the locus of real institutional authority, always follow the money. Voting members hire and fire teaching elders. They have the authority to impose the supreme economic sanction: "You're fired."

In Presbyterianism, only sporadically and unpredictably is oath-bound judicial authority closely matched to economic authority, either at the local level or at the level of the Church's boards. *This is the supreme unsolved problem with Presbyterian government.* First, Presbyterian voting members are not by oath consigned to the Westminster Confession and its two catechisms. Second, Presbyterian voting members can refuse to pay their tithes and still retain the vote. He who pays the piper calls the tune. In Presbyterianism, those who control all of the economic sanctions (check-writers) and also the final local judicial sanctions (voters) are not formally under the stipulations of the Westminster Confession. They are under sanctions imposed by the session, but they control who gets on the session. Their confession is institutionally sovereign, but their confession is not explicitly Presbyterian. They control final local judicial authority.

This is why Presbyterian Churches again and again have moved from Calvinism to experientialism to Arminianism to liberalism. Oaths count. So do votes. *Calvinism's rigid theology is not judicially protected by an equally rigid representative oath.* The lowest common denominator eventually triumphs. The Westminster Confession of Faith is watered down in practice. An antique copy of the Confession may remain in the local church's library, but nobody is required to read it or enforce discipline in terms of it.

Membership: Presbytery

Judicial sovereignty in Presbyterianism is officially lodged in the presbytery, but the presbytery has never been acknowledged as having a moral or legal claim on anyone's money. This system is inherently schizophrenic: a division between judicial sovereignty and economic sovereignty. The non-oath-bound local church members have all of the economic sovereignty and the lion's share of the judicial sovereignty. This dual sovereignty is manifested in the words: "You're fired." He who pays the piper calls the tune.

Every member of the presbytery must take an oath of allegiance to the Westminster standards and the denomination's Form of Government. This is standard in Presbyterianism. But this oath is not deemed sufficient for teaching elders. An extra-Confessional standard is also imposed. This extra-Confessional standard was the wedge that the liberals used to gain entrance into the Church: a seminary degree.

The presbyteries of the PCUSA officially transferred the preliminary ordination sanctions to the faculties of the seminaries, including Union, which was outside the Church after 1892. This unofficially transferred primary sovereignty over ordination from the presbyteries to the seminaries. The presbyteries remained mute about this transfer of primary sovereignty, but the liberals fully understood the nature of the transfer. They began targeting the seminaries. They learned how to pass written examinations, especially exams in German. This strategy was completely successful. In 1929, they captured Princeton, the last bastion. The likes of Machen, Allis, Wilson, Van Til, and Vos proved helpless to stop it. If they proved helpless, who wouldn't?

Calvinists believe that a ministerial apprentice cannot learn the skills needed to be a successful minister by studying first-hand with a successful minister, but must instead be trained for at least four years in college by atheists and those certified academically by atheists, followed by three years in a seminary staffed by men with advanced academic degrees who have never served in a pastorate. This belief was crucial to the replacement of Presbyterians, Episcopalians, and Congregationalists by Baptists and Methodists in the United States, 1800–1860.

Here is a judicial solution. Every candidate for the teaching eldership must pass an examination or series of examinations, including (at the discretion of the presbytery) a period of apprenticeship with a minister under the direct authority of the presbytery, but no outside institutional requirements may be imposed. The presbytery must maintain exclusive, monopolistic control over the sanctions governing the ordination of every candidate. It may not lawfully delegate any aspect of the screening process to an outside agency, e.g., a seminary. This means that the seminary system must be deprived of its positive judicial sanction—the special blessing of the presbyteries—and its negative judicial sanction: the ability to veto a candidate's eligibility for ordination.

Every fifth year, every minister in the presbytery must take the presbytery's series of written examinations required of the candidates. This honors the principle that everyone who imposes sanctions must be under the same sanctions. This keeps the exams honest, and it monitors the belief system and intellectual competence of all ministers. If the exams are not worth imposing on every minister, they are not worth imposing on any minister. If they are "cram and forget" exams, they are irrelevant to the ministry. Such exams are little more than disguised subsidies to further the expansion of Arminian culture. Drop them.

Funding

Each lower unit of Church government must tithe to the next higher unit. Why? Because the flow of funds must match the flow of authority. This process must begin with voting members of the local congregation (self-government). Any unit of government can lawfully solicit more money than the tithe from individual members or congregations, but there is no automatic funding for any agency of government beyond the tithe of the next lower unit. This honors the principle of the tithe. This principle keeps central government small. Here is an unbreakable defensive rule:

> *To lodge both money and judicial authority in a permanent, oath-bound agency of government is to invite a takeover of that agency. Conclusion: if any agency is lawfully entitled to exercise significant judicial authority, keep it poor.*

The enforcement of this rule keeps power-seekers from gaining power with other people's money. Power-seekers are rarely able to fund their own projects. They always seek funding by their enemies. The best way to screen out liberal power religionists is to prevent them from gaining automatic institutional access to conservatives' money.

Meetings Should Settle Disputes

The hierarchical appeals court system in Exodus 18 was civil. To the extent that Exodus 18 is a valid guide for Church government, it serves as a testimony against legislative authority. Israel's civil courts applied God's law; they did not write it. There is no indication that they were required to meet automatically, although this might have been allowed for predictability's sake. They settled problems that could not be settled by a lower court. The Jerusalem Council (Acts 15) was called to deal with a problem. It was not an annual meeting.

Parkinson's law teaches that work expands so as to fill time allotted for its completion. This law applies to all scheduled meetings. The best way to reduce the number of meetings and the length of meetings is to specify in advance what kind of work must be accomplished: *no issue to be settled–no meeting.*

A court should only meet when there is a case to decide or a dispute to be resolved that lower courts find too difficult. If a Presbyterian Church court is also believed to be a legislative assembly, then the two functions—judicial and legislative—had better be clearly distinguished in Church law and procedure, and the meetings should be held separately, if not in separate weeks, then (to save transportation costs) at least on separate days.

When there is a problem to solve, hold a meeting to solve that problem. Then adjourn the meeting. Any meeting that becomes a scheduled fellowship event for good old boys has moved from being God's earthly high court to a something resembling a Rotary Club meeting. Save the fellowship meetings for heaven. A Church court that is assembled to do anything except solve an existing problem will eventually become a problem. When it does, there will be a host of power-seekers who offer to sell their services to the court on a full-time basis to head off problems before they start. That is when the Church's problems really start.

There are no free lunches and no free courts. Lower courts that call for a special appeals court session must be willing to fund the special session. The assessment of court costs should be made on a pro-rated basis at a fixed percentage: the larger the tithe income (but not gifts and offerings) received by the lower court (presbytery or synod), the larger its share of the special court's expenses. With greater blessing comes greater responsibility (Luke 12:47–48): the principle of the tithe. Those lower courts that refuse to pay their pro-rated share of the special session cannot vote at the session meeting: *no money–no vote.* Finally, if it is known in advance that there will not be enough representatives to constitute a quorum, do not hold the meeting.

National Church Spokesmen

The General Assembly of the Presbyterian Church, U.S.A., fell to the liberals because Presbyterians expected someone to represent the Church nationally, and this had to be the General Assembly. But the General Assembly was not in session 51 weeks out of each year. So, the infiltrators proposed a permanent Executive Commission (after 1924, a General Council) to function as a bishopric. But no Presbyterian would say the dreaded B-word. The Executive Commission was a layer of bureaucracy that was ripe to be picked off by the liberals. As with the U.S. Presidency, which proposes the annual budget which the Constitution explicitly says is the responsibility of the House of Representatives to pass, so it was with the Executive Commission: it absorbed a judicially sovereign agency's operational authority. The tail thereafter wagged the dog.

Except during the annual General Assembly meeting, it must be either bishops or silence: take your pick. If your vote is against bishops, and the General Assembly has not spoken on a topic, then every inquiry should be answered by a form letter: "This issue has not been addressed by the denomination or the General Assembly." (I suggest that this form letter already exists with respect to one hot-potato issue: abortion.)

The Church does not need a lot of people on a national staff to send out such form letters. The Stated Clerk can do this easily. All he needs is an executive secretary, someone to answer the phone, and a computerized data base on the past decisions of the General Assembly. It does not take a supercomputer or a large staff to print out form letters.

Ask yourself: What are all those people doing back there, anyway? Where is all that money going? Why?

Denominational Colleges

The General Assembly must create institutional means of policing the denomination's institutions of higher learning. Here is a starting point: every course that assigns a book that was not published by the denomination's press must include a printed outline written by the professor who assigned it. It must refute in detail the theological errors or omissions in the book's assumptions. Every student must be given such an outline for each assigned book or assigned journal article at the beginning of the course: *no outlines–no course.* I know of no better way for a Church to monitor the real-world theological commitment of its academic employees.

I can think of nothing that will gain more resistance by the professorial class. "Those narrow-minded Bible-thumpers will know exactly what I'm actually teaching their children! This must be stopped, and stopped now!" *Sanction*: for each one-semester course offered without the outline(s), the denomination cuts 1 percent of this year's financial support to the institution next year. If your denomination refuses to do this, or something equally painful for those professors who resist, your denomination is being sold out. It will take the infiltrators no more than two generations to capture it.

If you are personally unwilling to suggest this in writing to someone who is in authority, you are part of the sell-out process. When you get stonewalled—count on it—you must then take your suggestion to someone in authority over the stonewaller. If you hear the phrase "academic freedom," you will know that the sell-out is in progress. If you hear the phrase, "The faculty will all quit if we do this," you will know that you have identified the soft underbelly of the infiltrators—and, if nothing is done, this will remain the soft underbelly of orthodoxy. If they all quit, orthodoxy wins this round. If some department cannot be replaced, drop that major for the time being. *Better to have no academic major than a department run by liberal infiltrators.* (Do you really believe this? Those who now run your denomination's college or seminary probably do not.) Lutheran liberals quit in the mid-1970's when they left the Missouri Synod's Concordia Seminary to established Seminex.[4] It

---

4. Seminary in Exile.

sounded like a non-prescription sleeping pill, and academically, it was. It went out of existence within a few years.

If you refuse to take such action, please don't complain when Billy-Bob or Jenny Sue comes home from the denominational college with a purse full of condoms (especially in Billy-Bob's purse).

Here is another solution to the problem of higher education, although too utopian to be realistic. However, it is what is really needed. The solution to education is negative sanctions: the formal abolition of both academic freedom and tenure. Those who pay the professorial pipers must call the tune. In practice, this means that the professors, not a board of laymen, should own the academic institutions. The board should not be expected to be able to exercise authority over specialists, i.e., a faculty. Dilettantes cannot control experts. So, the faculty must learn to meet the market: tuitions, donations, and contracts from information buyers. There is only one sure way to learn this: to become an owner. Faculties should own the schools on a profit-seeking basis.[5]

What is there that inherently makes higher education a non-profit venture? Only tradition. Faculties prefer low-risk ventures which they secretly control, but without the responsibilities of ownership. Academic accrediting agencies enforce this tradition. But why should Calvinists ever seek to be accredited academically by modernists? (Ask the Board of Trustees of your own denomination's seminary, which is, I assure you, academically accredited by modernists. They have gone to the accreditation agencies with this message: "We come in the name of the absolutely sovereign Judge of history to beg you to accredit us. We'll call you Christians if you'll call us scholars.")

Seminaries

The operational authority of the academic degree in Presbyterianism can be seen to the original Form of Presbyterial Church-Government (1645), which was never formally adopted by either the Westminster Assembly or the Church of Scotland. The document referred

---

5. Henry Manne, "The Political Economy of Modern Universities," in *Education in a Free Society*, edited by Anne Husted Burleigh (Indianapolis, Indiana: Liberty Fund, 1973).

to a Church office not mentioned in the Bible: doctor. It announced: "A teacher, or doctor, is of most excellent use in schools and universities; as of old in the schools of the prophets, and at Jerusalem, where Gamaliel and others taught as doctors" (*Teacher or Doctor*). Problem: the school of prophets granted no academic degrees, and Gamaliel was a Pharisee. Gamaliel's school was indeed the model, and that baleful influence has undermined every hierarchical Western denomination, as surely as it helped undermine Old Covenant Israel.

The school of the prophets was personal. The prophets had apprentices who served them and learned on the job. Jesus operated such a school. There were no formal entry requirements. There were no degrees required to get in or granted upon leaving. There were no committee-approved catalogues. There were no textbooks written by pagan authors. But Athens since the late eleventh century has conquered the New Jerusalem as surely as Babylon conquered the Old Jerusalem. *Apprenticeship is the biblical model, not the school of Gamaliel by way of the University of Paris.*

To reduce the power of seminaries in their unofficial but universal quest to become the ordaining agents, presbyteries must not discriminate against ministerial candidates who have had no formal education. This would destroy the certification difference between teaching elders and ruling elders. This has been too radical a step for Presbyterians, who equate formal education with ministerial education. Thus, Presbyterianism has steadily gone liberal whenever higher education has gone liberal, i.e., constantly.

Solutions

Technology is now about to undermine the monopoly enjoyed by Athens. A CD-ROM disc contains up to 250,000 pages of fully indexed material.[6] It costs less than $2 each to produce 1,000 CD-ROM disks, once the electronic material is put onto a master disk. The library problem is all but solved technologically. When the Internet can link students and teachers around the world for a few dollars per hour, and with the price of telephone time steadily dropping, the

---

6. In 1996, this is expected to rise to 2.5 million pages.

problem of the classroom is all but solved. Wait until fiber optics arrives. Then television will link these classrooms.

Here is a simple reform program for the curriculum of Calvinist seminaries. Teach Calvin's *Institutes* as the required text in a three-year course in systematic theology. Forget about Charles Hodge; John Calvin was better, especially on the doctrine of creation. Second, teach the Westminster Confession of Faith and the Larger Catechism. Here is the rule: nobody graduates who does not have a thorough working knowledge of the content and historical background of Calvin and the Confession. Nobody graduates who cannot use the Bible to defend Calvin's *Institutes* and the Confession. To graduate, each student must pass at least one week of written exams on the *Institutes* and the Westminster documents. Presbyterian seminaries should produce masters of the foundational documents of Presbyterianism.

Such a curriculum has never been attempted by any Presbyterian seminary in history. There is one thing that all Calvinist seminaries have avoided like the plague: Calvin's *Institutes*. Dead German theologians—that's the thing! Practical theology—that's the thing! Or courses in Greek that 80 percent of the students have forgotten three years after graduation. Academic tradition must be upheld. It is time to reform Calvinist seminaries by forcing all graduates to master Calvin's theology. Students need three years of Calvin. Anyone who would attempt such a reform would wind up as Morton Smith did, when he required his students at Reformed Theological Seminary to master the Westminster Confession: unemployed. If you think Calvinist seminaries are ready to teach Calvin, think again. Why should they start now? There is no market for Calvin in American Christianity. There hasn't been since the Second Great Awakening, when the seminary was invented. It would break too much tradition to start teaching Calvin at this late date.

Of course, I could be wrong. Send for a copy of your favorite Calvinist seminary's catalogue. Go through the course listings. Look for a required course on Calvin's *Institutes*. Look for a required course on one of the historic Calvinist confessions. I don't mean a full year's course in each, which would not be nearly enough. I mean just one semester per course, i.e., two required courses out of 30 in a typical three-year curriculum. Send me a photocopy when you find them. But if you don't find them, stop sending that seminary any donations.

Otherwise, you will continue to finance something other than Calvinism-Presbyterianism. Your seminary will continue to use your money to train ministers for non-Presbyterian pulpits. When it comes to the ecclesiology of their graduates, Presbyterian seminaries have their students sing only one hymn for three years: "Just as I am." John Witherspoon's rule governing the College of New Jersey still holds: "Every question about forms of church government is so entirely excluded that . . . if they [the students] know nothing more of religious controversy than what they have learned here, they have that Science wholly to begin."[7]

These are technical solutions. They will not solve the more fundamental problem, which is an institutional conflict over the true nature of the seminary's mission. Laymen do not understand this truth: every Presbyterian seminary lives a dual existence. Like a bigamist, the seminary seeks to operate two households. To one wife, it declares: "We train ministers; send us money." To the other wife—like Rachel, the beloved wife—it declares: "We train Christian scholars; send us academically certified young men." This dual institutional role—ministerial screening center and graduate school of theology—cannot be successfully achieved by a single institution, especially with a faculty screened by the humanist university rather than the pastorate. The seminary hires as faculty members men whose only calling in life has been to write graduate school term papers and then articles for the seminary's in-house academic journal. It places these men in charge of training young men with no practical leadership experience, who need to be taught how to wage the war of faith in the trenches: local churches. But how are they actually taught this unique skill? By writing term papers.

Conservative Presbyterian seminaries in the twentieth century have trained their students to reject the conclusions of dead German theologians. Meanwhile, Presbyterian congregations are filled with followers of C. I. Scofield. The typical Presbyterian layman's problem is not the *historie/heilsgeschichte* dualism of Karl Barth; it is the his-

---

7. Cited in Leonard Trinterud, *The Forming of an American Tradition: A Re-examination of COLONIAL PRESBYTERIANISM* (Salem, New Hampshire: Ayer, [1949] 1978), p. 256.

tory/Rapture dualism of Hal Lindsey. The pastor is rarely afflicted by the mindlessness of the Christ-event of neo-orthodoxy; he is afflicted by the mindlessness of some updated version of Edgar Whisnant's *88 Reasons Why the Rapture is in 1988*. Amillennialists indulged themselves with Harold Camping's *1994?* in 1993 and 1994. The underlying message is the same: long-term missionary activities cannot change this world for the better; the Great Commission is the Great Impossible Dream.

This leads us to the question of missions.

Missions

Presbyterians since 1812 have pretended against overwhelming evidence that their seminary graduates are equipped both ministerially and scholastically. Yet since 1812, we have seen the results of such self-delusion: small Calvinist churches, larger Arminian churches, shrinking liberal churches, and ever-more liberal colleges and seminaries, all labeled "Presbyterian." Presbyterian Calvinist scholarship has fallen on hard times in our day, but Presbyterian home missions—except for the Arminian Cumberland Presbyterians—fell on hard times much earlier: about 1797.

The first attempt to overcome the failure of Presbyterian home missions was the Plan of Union with the Congregationalists in 1801; that lasted until 1837. It split the Church. Then, in 1857–58, came the secondary revival that converted Charles Briggs. That revival did not survive the Civil War. Then, in the late 1880's and 1890's, came the Collegiate Great Awakening under Robert E. Speer and John R. Mott, which was foreign missions-oriented. In each case, the immediate result was the erosion of Calvinism.

What went wrong? *A failure to match ordinational authority with money*. The presbytery ordains the minister, so the presbytery should send him out, either to the home missions field or the foreign missions field. Judicial authority and economic authority are matched. The presbytery retains both sanctions. Simple, isn't it? Nothing judicially anti-Presbyterian about this! Yet it is utterly opposed to the American Presbyterian tradition. This is why the American Presbyterian Church has never solved the problem of missions: from 1801 to right now.

From 1801 until the split in 1837, Arminians short-circuited the Church's system of authority by establishing parachurch ministries. The Confessionalists responded by creating church missions boards, which became nearly autonomous. The anti-Confessionalists saw the opportunity: access to other people's money and control over whoever represented the Church on the missions field. The liberals steadily took over the Foreign Missions Board under Robert E. Speer after 1890.

This is the age-old Presbyterian problem of government: the addition of layers of bureaucracy that are outside the formal structure of authority, i.e., from the local congregation to the General Assembly and back to the presbyteries. *To discover who really has the authority, follow the money.* Authority flows with money, and most of the missions money since 1870 has flowed directly to the ministers who are under the authority of the boards, or directly to the boards, or from the General Assembly to the boards.

Should fund-raising for missions be centralized? Only if the intention of the Church is to repeat the experience of Old School Presbyterianism.

My proposed system does contain an anomaly. What happens when the missionary establishes a local presbytery? He joins that presbytery, but his funding comes from his home presbytery. This was the problem the PCUSA faced: liberal missionaries in the field under presbyteries too far away to monitor them. Without making the missionary into a bishop, how can the home presbytery allocate his authority? As a man being funded from the initiating presbytery but under the authority of the foreign presbytery? Does this break the rule of matching funding with judicial authority? Yes, it does. This is Presbyterianism's price for not having bishops. But if the Church's solution to this problem is to create national boards that both fund and monitor the missionaries, Presbyterian missions will again go liberal. The board will break the presbytery's operational authority as surely as a foreign presbytery will. Better for the funding presbytery to trust the foreign presbytery's judgment rather than to trust a centralized national missions board's judgment. The foreign presbytery is a far better agent than the national board to monitor what the missionary is doing. It has a direct interest in suppressing heresy, an interest that a national missions board has to a far lesser degree. *Keep judi-*

cial authority local. Let presbyteries deal with presbyteries. Centralized missions boards muddy the waters of authority. This is why they eventually muddy the theological waters.

National Boards

Here are a few general rules that should govern all national Presbyterian boards:

Presbyteries or synods should elect one-third of the trustees to each of the boards every year: one representative per presbytery or synod. No board of trustees should be larger than 12 people. That was as large a group as Jesus managed, and there was a ringer even in that carefully screened group. Large boards always fall under the domination of one person. Keep boards small and under control of the presbyteries and synods.

No trustee may be paid from funds generated by the board. His salary and expenses are paid by the synod or presbytery that elected him. He reports back to his synod or presbytery. He is a judicial agent of his synod or presbytery, not an independent agent.

Do not allow existing trustees to nominate successor trustees. Stop the "old boy network" before it begins.

All employees of the boards must annually re-affirm their commitment to the Church's confessional standards. They must note in writing any personal exceptions. These exceptions must be made public.

No employee of any board may serve as a trustee of any other board or of his own board. Separate the paychecks from the vote.

The board must raise all of its funding each year through direct appeals. No overall budget guarantee may be given to any board of the Church by any agency of the Church, especially the General Assembly.

To which a Presbyterian with any experience with Church boards will respond: "Fat providence." Or, citing John Wayne: "That'll be the day."

Robert's Rules of Order

If any level of Church government becomes so complex or so divided by factions that it needs Robert's Rules of Order to operate, that unit of government should be immediately downsized through a budget cut.

A Technical Solution to Confessional Revision

How can the Presbyterian Church deal with this problem? How can those desiring revision be given an opportunity to express their views in preparation for a vote to revise?

If sanctions are automatically imposed by a presbytery's court for an ordained man's subsequent reversal of opinion, those who want to revise the Confession on any point will never have the votes to do so. How could they even identify themselves as desiring a revision without identifying themselves as doubters in the Confession? In such a case, Confessional revision would take place only through starting a new denomination: Protestantism's notorious splintering effect. But if a candidate is lawfully ordained in spite of his rejection of portions of the Confession, what is to be done about a presbytery such as the New York Presbytery of 1891 or 1913? As Machen asked: How far will this go?

There is an institutional solution to this dilemma. It is judicial rather than legislative, as Presbyterian assemblies officially are. It is a two-stage process. First, allow any person who has been convicted of heresy by the General Assembly to appeal his conviction to the presbyteries immediately following that General Assembly. He does so in the following manner. He proposes what he regards as a true statement of the doctrine. Meanwhile, he remains suspended from office and possibly excommunicated. He is guilty until declared innocent by a two-thirds vote of the presbyteries.

In stage one of the appeal, the General Assembly automatically sends down the man's overture to the presbyteries, calling for a vote on whether to begin the revision process. There must be a majority vote by the presbyteries to begin the process. If they vote against beginning the revision process, the heretic's conviction stands. Obviously, most convictions will stand.

Second, if a simple majority of the presbyteries vote to begin debating a revision of the Confession on the disputed point (and no other), the next General Assembly automatically must send down the convicted man's proposed revision of the creed according to the language originally suggested by him.

There is now a major institutional problem. If the presbyteries vote to revise the Confession, those who disagree with this change are no longer in agreement with the new version. On the other hand, if they vote to leave the Confession as it is, those voting to change it have now identified themselves as being in agreement with the convicted heretic. There is no neutrality possible. The stipulations governing the oath must be enforced, unless new stipulations are imposed. In the latter case, the new stipulations must be enforced. The oath has changed.

Here is one way to sort it out. The final vote in each presbytery is taken by means of a letter of resignation from each person actually voting. Each elder who decides that this is worth voting on drops his letter of resignation into a box. These letters are retained by the presbytery.

At the end of the year, when the votes of the presbyteries are tallied, the change either passes or is rejected. Each person voting on the losing side nationally has his letter of resignation accepted by his presbytery. He is no longer a presbytery officer or a voting member of a local congregation. He is no longer by oath consigned to Presbyterian office.

Those who do not want to risk voting—the famous 80 percent—are assumed to agree with the standards, whatever the outcome. They really do not care one way or the other—not enough to risk their ordination. *Those who really do care will determine the outcome of the election, as it should be.* Those who want the privilege of re-writing the Confession's standards must place themselves under the standards that they say they believe in. So must those who wish to defend the old Confession. If anyone cares enough about the issue to impose sanctions (the vote) in the revision process, he must pay the price for having lost.

Such a system would keep the General Assembly from becoming a final court of appeal. This decentralizes power. The GA can be vetoed by the presbyteries, but only at high institutional cost and high risk for those who take part in the actual voting.

Risky, isn't it? So is taking a covenantal oath. But this system of Confessional revision would retain the characteristic legal feature of the General Assembly as a court of appeal rather than a legislative body.

If there has not been a heresy trial in your denomination in a generation, there had better be a good reason: not one person has been suspected of being heretical. The larger the denomination, the truer this is. Respect the 10-80-10 rule: ten percent of the ministers will be liberals compared to the Church's operational (i.e., enforced by sanctions) confession. The Church had better find out how liberal.

Conclusion

An 18-year-old Presbyterian who has been catechized faithfully and has been trained in a Christian school is better trained theologically than nine-tenths (or more) of those Baptist and Methodist pastors who restructured religion in the United States, 1800 to 1860. So, why not ordain him if he wants to be a minister? Because he is too young? Charles Spurgeon was ordained at age 19. By the time he was 20, he had 500 people regularly attending his weekly prayer meetings. (Poor lad; he never went to college. Crippled for life!) Because he is too inexperienced? Then apprentice him. Because he has not yet been certified by academic humanists? Does this answer really impress you? It doesn't impress the Mormons, who yearly send thousands of young men on bicycles into the highways and byways of the world to knock on doors, and who have built a huge organization through this practice.

Presbyterians are the people of the catechism. They catechize their children for years. Then, when the child is fully conversant with the details of the Christian faith, Presbyterian parents send him off to a humanist institution of higher learning to educate him and certify him as educated, where he is taught a worldview absolutely foreign to the catechism. If a young man survives this ordeal and still seeks ordination, he will be asked to spend three more years training in some seminary (not necessarily a Calvinist one), none of which in this century has required that all of its graduates take a class in Calvin's *Institutes*, let alone read half a dozen of Calvin's commentaries. He will be taught to become a minister by men whose only institutionally fixed requirement for employment as teachers is their possession of a Ph.D.

or Th.D. degree issued by a humanist institution of higher learning—men who probably have never spent so much as a year in the pastorate. Then, new degree fresh in hand, he will probably be ordained by a presbytery that has never seen him before the day he takes his one-hour oral exam.

If the prayer of welcome into the presbytery were honest, it would go something like this:

> Having survived at least four years of training by state-certified humanists who are clearly on the road to perdition, and having survived three years of additional training by men certified by those same perdition-bound humanists, and having survived this afternoon's written exams in Greek and Hebrew, which you will now be allowed to forget, just as the rest of us have forgotten, except for the two men in this presbytery who examined you, and having passed your one-hour oral exam, which you could have done at age 18 if you had memorized the Larger Catechism, we now welcome you into the bonds of fellowship in this presbytery. As your token of covenantal authority, we have presented you with a copy of *Robert's Rules of Order*, which you had better master if you intend to have any influence in these meetings over the next three and a half decades. Amen.

This ministerial screening system is so utterly self-defeating that only the best-educated, humanist-certified Protestants in history could have devised it. There has to be a better way.

Appendix C

THE STRANGE LEGACY OF
THE WESTMINSTER ASSEMBLY

And when they brought out the money that was brought into the house of the LORD, Hilkiah the priest found a book of the law of the LORD given by Moses. And Hilkiah answered and said to Shaphan the scribe, I have found the book of the law in the house of the LORD. And Hilkiah delivered the book to Shaphan. And Shaphan carried the book to the king, and brought the king word back again, saying, All that was committed to thy servants, they do it. And they have gathered together the money that was found in the house of the LORD, and have delivered it into the hand of the overseers, and to the hand of the workmen. Then Shaphan the scribe told the king, saying, Hilkiah the priest hath given me a book. And Shaphan read it before the king. And it came to pass, when the king had heard the words of the law, that he rent his clothes. And the king commanded Hilkiah, and Ahikam the son of Shaphan, and Abdon the son of Micah, and Shaphan the scribe, and Asaiah a servant of the king's, saying, Go, enquire of the LORD for me, and for them that are left in Israel and in Judah, concerning the words of the book that is found: for great is the wrath of the LORD that is poured out upon us, because our fathers have not kept the word of the LORD, to do after all that is written in this book (II Chron. 34:14–21).

Israel had lost the law of God and had forgotten its details. Covenant-breakers had ruled over them in terms of different laws. This is not so remarkable as it sounds. Christians today have almost equally short memories because they are not interested in Church history, which they allow humanists and liberals to write for them.

Very few Presbyterians know much about Presbyterian Church history. This includes Presbyterian pastors. They have not been told that the Presbyterian foundational documents were written mainly by Anglicans who had never been inside a Presbyterian Church. They do not know that Scottish Presbyterian Church government has never been conducted in terms of the judicial documents officially printed by the Scottish Presbyterian Church, which in fact have no legal status. They are unaware of the origin of the Westminster Assembly: called into existence by politicians who were in the midst of what is known as the English Civil War, and who needed someone to show them how, in the absence of bishops, to ordain chaplains to serve the armed forces, so that the military could defeat a King who favored bishops. The politicians' ecclesiastical goal was this: "Weak King–no bishops." Their political goal was this: "No bishops–weak King." The Westminster Assembly was a wartime gathering whose fate would be sealed, in England at least, by the military first, the politicians second, and the Church third.

Oliver Cromwell

The Assembly was dependent on the success of one man above all others: Oliver Cromwell. If he lost on the battlefield, they might literally lose their heads. In his hands was the future of Puritanism in England and, to a lesser extent, Scotland. He was the central figure. Yet in the neo-Puritan movement, pioneered by the British Isles' Banner of Truth Trust in the early 1960's, Cromwell's name is rarely mentioned except in passing (very fast passing). This, too, may seem strange. But it is not strange at all, for the Banner of Truth suffers from the problems that faced the Puritan movement after the restoration of Charles II to the throne in 1660. It has neither an army nor any political influence. It has adopted post-1660 Puritan theology, which excludes politics as *adiaphora* (things indifferent to the faith), ignoring the fact that Puritan covenant theology originally included civil government as one of the four forms of oath-bound covenantal government: personal, ecclesiastical, familial, and civil.[1]

---

1. Richard Baxter divided his *Christian Directory* (1673) into these four

Today, on both sides of the Atlantic, the spiritual heirs of the Westminster Assembly affirm the radical Whigs' secular ideal of universal religious toleration, an ideal that appalled every member of the Westminster Assembly, an idea affirmed only by one man in that era, Roger Williams, whose 1644 book was ordered burned by the Parliament that had called the Assembly into existence. Nevertheless, it was Cromwell who first brought religious toleration for non-Anglican Protestants in England, a fact ignored at the time by the New England Puritans and forgotten ever since by spiritual heirs of the Westminster Assembly. This horrified the Assembly's members. All but five of them had opposed Cromwell's ecclesiastical ideal—independency—and the Assembly's great work was undermined in England because of the immediate political results of that ideal.

To make sense of these anomalies, and several more that we will get to shortly, we must first consider the origin of the Westminster Assembly.

The End of the Old Order

The Arminian Archbishop William Laud had attempted in the spring of 1637 to impose Anglicanism on Scotland, something that James I had also attempted to do before his death in 1625, but had failed to accomplish. Laud would also fail, and great was the failure thereof. The Scots refused to accept Laud's new worship service book. A Scottish rebellion began on July 23, 1637, when a group of young women at the St. Giles Church in Edinburgh broke up the services led by the local bishop. Resistance to both the Archbishop and the King escalated throughout 1638. That a group of unordained young women launched the Presbyterian revolt that brought on the English Civil War—better described as the Premature Revolution—is, on the face of it, a wee bit peculiar.

Charles I invaded Scotland in the spring of 1639. His army lost. He was forced to sign a truce, but it soon became clear that the peace would not last long. The next year, he called Parliament into session to raise money to fight a looming war. Parliament met in April, 1640.

---

covenantal units of government.

Not having been called into session since 1629, Parliament refused his request for money. The King dissolved Parliament in May, 1640: the Short Parliament.

The Scots invaded that summer. They won the war in August and settled into the six northern counties. They imposed daily monetary penalties until a permanent settlement could be arranged. The King did not have the money. He therefore consented to another Parliamentary election in November, 1640. With the Scots tying down what remained of the King's forces, the "Presbyterians" (anti-prelates) did well in the election. The King settled with the Scots in late 1641.[2] He never found a way to settle with his new Parliament, which executed him in 1649, and sat until Oliver Cromwell replaced it in 1653: the Long Parliament.

In between the two 1640 Parliaments, Archbishop Laud had imposed a system of 17 new Church laws aimed at strengthening the bishops and the King. One law damned to hell anyone who would oppose the King. Clergymen also had to swear an oath never to change the Church of England. The Church voluntarily abandoned this oath after the Scots won, but by then it was too late for episcopacy.[3] Laud had tried to repair a weakened dam to resist a tidal wave. The tidal wave struck in November, 1640.

When Parliament assembled, it immediately arrested the long-persecuting Archbishop. The system of Church courts and civil sanctions that had been imposed by the bishops was now abolished—as it turned out, forever. But no one could be sure of that in late 1640. In January, 1643, prelacy was abolished.[4] But, as in the case of Geneva over a century earlier, abolishing the bishops created a judicial vacuum. Geneva's civil council had filled the absent bishop's social func-

---

2. David Stevenson, *The Scottish Revolution, 1637-1644: The Triumph of the Covenanters* (New York: St. Martin's, 1973), ch. 7.

3. Michael A. R. Graves and Robin H. Silcock, *Revolution, Reaction and the Triumph of Conservatism: English History, 1558-1700* (Auckland: Longman Paul, 1984), p. 293.

4. Benjamin Breckinridge Warfield, "The Westminster Assembly and Its Work" (1908), in *The Westminster Assembly and Its Work* (Grand Rapids, Michigan: Baker, [1931] 1991), p. 10.

tion with Calvin.[5] Parliament needed more than one man to replace national episcopacy.

The exercise of monopolistic ecclesiastical power through civil government still existed as a social ideal. It had existed for over a millennium. Historian William Haller writes of the pre-1644 era in England: "Practically everybody agreed that there could be but one true religion and that the church should be maintained by the state. The continuance of ordered society was as yet inconceivable without the Christian church, and the church was inconceivable except as a single comprehensive institution uniform in faith and worship."[6] The one exception was Roger Williams, but no one in 1643 knew about him outside of the Massachusetts Bay Colony and Rhode Island. Four years later, they could imagine alternatives—many alternatives.

At the beginning of 1645—the year in which Cromwell gained military supremacy—Parliament executed Laud. His King was executed four years later. James I's phrase, "No bishop–no king," proved to be quite accurate in the 1640's.

Root, Branch, and Synod

Some 15,000 petitioners in London signed what became known as the "root and branch petition," which was submitted to Parliament on December 11, 1640.[7] It called for the complete abolition of episcopacy, with "its dependencies, roots and branches."[8] On January 12, Parliament received a similar petition from 11 counties signed by

---

5. R. J. Rushdoony, "Calvin in Geneva: The Sociology of Justification by Faith," *Politics of Guilt and Pity* (Fairfax, Virginia: Thoburn Press, [1970] 1978), p. 271. This essay was originally published in the *Westminster Theological Journal.*

6. William Haller, *The Rise of Puritanism* (New York: Columbia University Press, 1938), p. 6.

7. Larry Jackson Holley, The Divines of the Westminster Assembly: A Study of Puritanism and Parliament (Ph.D. dissertation, Yale University, 1979), p. 15.

8. "The Root and Branch Petition," in *The Puritan Revolution: A Documentary History*, edited by Stuart E. Prall (Garden City, New York: Anchor, 1968), p. 97. See also the collection of Parliamentary documents related to the Westminster Assembly in David Hall, "Parliamentary Background of the Assembly," in *To Glorify and Enjoy God*, edited by John L. Carson and David W. Hall (Edinburgh: Banner of Truth Trust, 1994), p. 269.

14,000 people.⁹ But Parliament did not respond. The King still had the power to dissolve it, and the members were unwilling to take action on these petitions. In May, Cromwell and other Independents introduced a bill to abolish the episcopacy. Parliament debated it in June, but did not pass the bill.¹⁰ The majority still believed in a national Church under the general authority of the State, but they did not know what to substitute for episcopacy. They leaned toward Presbyterianism to the extent that they understood it. Over the next four years, they would help create it. Then they would abandon it.

The root-and-branch petition revealed that there were some in Parliament who were willing to disrupt the traditional ecclesiastical order. But the critics of episcopacy had a problem: almost everyone in Christendom believed in the necessity of a civil government covenanted under God and ruled by a godly civil magistrate. But if not episcopacy, then what? No one was sure.

Apocalyptic Expectations

Since the days of Foxe's *Book of Martyrs* (*Acts and Monuments of These Latter and Perillous Days*, 1563), there had been an almost universal belief in England that Protestants, under a godly king and (said the Anglican bishops) a godly episcopacy, would rout the Antichrist, meaning the Roman Church.¹¹ This apocalyptic expectation was appropriated by the Puritans in the late 1630's and early 1640's, but the saving agent would be a reformed Church, not the Church of Archbishop Laud. They believed that this could be accomplished speedily, if only the true Church could be substituted for Laud's brand of Anglicanism.

Parliament called into existence the Westminster Assembly in mid-1643 in earnest and apocalyptic expectation that this Assembly would speedily provide the theological and judicial framework for the true Church to fulfill the Book of Revelation. Parliament wanted reform, and wanted it fast. But reform did not come fast. These great

---

9. Holley, Divines, p. 22.
10. *Ibid.*, pp. 32–34.
11. William M. Lamont, *Godly Rule: Politics and Religion, 1603–60* (London: Macmillan, 1969), chaps. 1–3.

expectations of creating a godly people and a godly social order were dashed within two years, and smashed as an ideal within a decade. Writes William Lamont: "The disenchantment of 1645 can only be understood against the background of the inflated hopes of 1641."[12]

In July, 1641, Parliament passed and the King signed an act that abolished the Church's Court of High Commission, which had possessed the authority to impose corporal and financial punishments.[13] When the King in August, 1641, agreed not to disband Parliament as his price to get Parliament to allocate the funds to pay off the resident Scottish army, Parliament began to consider calling a synod of theologians to advise them regarding Church reform. It took over a year and a half even to get them assembled.[14]

Synod: Yes or No?

In late December, 1641, Parliament voted to imprison 12 bishops, members of the House of Lords.[15] In January, the King marched troops to Parliament and tried to arrest five members of the House of Commons. This attempt failed. The King then withdrew and left London.[16] The next month, though preparing for war with Parliament's forces, the King signed Parliament's act that forbade all temporal power to bishops, meaning their right to serve in the House of Lords.[17] But the King resisted every attempt by Parliament to call a synod, and his cooperation was needed to legalize the act. When Parliament threatened an ultimatum to the King in June, 1642, one section of which insisted on the synod, the King resisted.[18] The Civil War broke out in July, and this further delayed their plans to call the Assembly.[19] The bill to call it passed in November, 1642.

---

12. *Ibid.*, p. 108.
13. Wayne Renwick Spear, Covenanted Uniformity in Religion: The Influence of the Scottish Commissioners upon the Ecclesiology of the Westminster Assembly (Ph.D. dissertation, University of Pittsburgh, 1976), p. 29.
14. Holley, Divines, chaps. 2, 3.
15. *Ibid.*, p. 56.
16. Spear, Covenanted Uniformity, p. 43.
17. This was the Clerical Disabilities Act: *ibid.*, p. 29.
18. Holley, Divines, p. 77.
19. *Ibid.*, p. 82.

The King had insisted that the Assembly be appointed by the Church.[20] Parliament knew that this would guarantee episcopacy. Instead, Parliament appointed the attendees. The representatives of the House of Commons from each county appointed two attendees per county.[21] Then the House of Lords was allowed to appoint 14 more.[22]

To gain legitimacy for both the Assembly and Parliament's right to convoke it without the King's permission, Parliament had to make sure that the Assembly was truly representative. Also, Parliament could not interfere excessively in its operations.[23] The pro-Presbyterian group exercised effective control over 40 percent of Parliament's 51 committees that dealt with religion.[24] Parliament formally summoned the Assembly on June 24, 1643. The King's victories over Parliament's military forces came in the following month. So, there is no substantial evidence that the Assembly was a payoff to the Scots for joining the war against the King.[25]

By then, Parliament had no doubts about the need to abolish episcopacy. In its July 12 ordinance (it was not technically a law, since the King had not signed it) to form the Assembly, Parliament identified the Church's system of bishops as "evil."[26]

The Divines Gather, 1643–48

The Assembly's Divines were above-average clerics.[27] Twenty-five had been cathedral clergy. Thirteen had been royal chaplains.[28] Their educational attainments were high: 87 percent had a bachelor's degree, 85 percent had a master's degree, 37 percent had a bachelor of divinity, and a quarter had a doctor of divinity.[29] This, in a Church of

---

20. *Ibid.*, p. 96.
21. *Ibid.*, pp. 151–53.
22. *Ibid.*, p. 159.
23. *Ibid.*, pp. 118–27.
24. *Ibid.*, p. 132.
25. *Ibid.*, p. 137.
26. "An Ordinance Calling for the Assembly," *Glorify and Enjoy*, p. 292.
27. For brief biographies, see Holley, *Divines*, Appendix XX.
28. *Ibid.*, p. 237.
29. *Ibid.*, p. 167.

10,000 ministers[30] in which illiterate pastors were common. For example, only half of the congregations in Norfolk and Suffolk had pastors who could read.[31] Half of the Divines had published at least one book, mostly since 1641.[32]

When in attendance, the delegates were paid four shillings a day by the government.[33] Parliament appointed 121 ministers and 30 laymen: 20 lords and ten commoners drawn from Parliament itself. As the years dragged on, fewer and fewer attended; they had difficulty assembling a quorum of 40 after 1645.[34]

The Factions

Among the attendees were four Scottish ministers and two laymen, plus three scribes.[35] Not being English, the Scots did not have a vote in the Assembly, but they were influential.[36] They were not merely representatives of the Scottish Church but of the Scottish nation itself, as Treaty Commissioners for the Solemn League and Covenant between the two nations, which had not been ratified at the time the Assembly opened. They arrived on September 15, 1643, ten days before England ratified the Solemn League and Covenant. They met with the Assembly only as private men without a vote; they met with Parliament separately and directly, as national agents.[37] The fact is, as John R. de Witt has commented, "what is often considered to be the quintessentially Presbyterian gathering was in fact not a presbyterian assembly at all. Rather, it was an English body whose clerical members were all Puritans and ministers in the Church of England, who had been episcopally ordained."[38] One of the Scottish attendees,

---

30. *Ibid.*, p. 160.
31. *Ibid.*, p. 167.
32. *Ibid.*, p. 206. For a 36-page bibliography, see *ibid.*, Appendix XIX.
33. "An Ordinance for Calling the Assembly," *Glorify and Enjoy*, p. 293.
34. Spear, Covenanted Uniformity, pp. 60–61.
35. For biographies, see *ibid.*, pp. 92–106.
36. Peter Toon, *Puritans and Calvinism* (Swengel, Pennsylvania: Reiner, 1973), pp. 57, 62. See also Spear, Covenanted Uniformity.
37. Warfield, *Westminster Assembly*, pp. 31–34.
38. John Richard de Witt, "The Form of Church Government," in *Glorify and Enjoy*, p. 146.

Robert Baillie, later wrote: "You know this is no proper Assembly, but a meeting called by the Parliament. . . ."[39]

The Assembly met at Westminster Abbey in London. At least five Independents were in attendance, balancing the four non-voting Scots. All five had lived in Holland during Laud's reign.[40] Between these two small factions at each end of the ecclesiastical spectrum—one of them not voting—the battle would be fought . . . interminably, from Parliament's point of view. Here were well over a hundred fully convicted Puritan theologians and ministers who made their livings talking, usually to a passive audience that did not talk back. This many God-convicted men in one assembly guaranteed a very long assembly, though neither they nor Parliament suspected this in mid-1643. It met for almost 1,200 meetings for almost five years.[41] While they were meeting, the first modern political revolution was taking place around them.

The Debates Begin

The Assembly first came together on July 1, 1643. It leaned strongly toward the Presbyterian position, but the Independents succeeded in delaying the development of a recommended system of Church government for many months. The Assembly debated endlessly. The Presbyterians probably thought that debate would persuade the Independents. If so, they were naive. The debates went on. The Scottish attendees complained of this endless delay.[42] The majority could have ended debate, but they allowed it to continue. This delay would seal the fate of English Presbyterianism.

The Presbyterians wanted a State Church with ministerial control over ordination and excommunication. Parliament wanted the power to appoint the ministers; some members wanted no excommunication at all (the Erastian party).[43] The Independents wanted local church

---

39. Cited in *ibid.*, p. 147.
40. Holley, *Divines*, p. 170. These were Bridge, Nye, Goodwin, Burroughs, and Simpson.
41. Edwin S. Gaustad, *Liberty of Conscience: Roger Williams in America* (Grand Rapids, Michigan: Eerdmans, 1991), p. 59.
42. William Haller, *Liberty and Reformation in the Puritan Revolution* (New York: Columbia University Press, 1955), pp. 115-16.
43. Lamont, *Godly Rule*, pp. 113-21.

autonomy and civil toleration for Protestant churches. There was no middle ground.

The five Independents appealed to Parliament and went into print in January, 1644, with *An Apologeticall Narration*.[44] This was a self-conscious decision to appeal to the general public in a matter affecting both Church and State. The battle of the theological pamphlets had begun in earnest in 1641, accelerated rapidly in 1642 when the war began (paralleled by the initial appearance of political pamphlets),[45] and would soon become a flood.[46] This pamphlet war was unprecedented in the history of man. Writers appealed to people who could legally vote in civil elections, yet tens of thousands of those who read the pamphlets did not have the vote. They would demand the vote within three years.[47] Some of these non-voters wrote their own pamphlets. The Church could no longer control the range of theological opinion. The State would soon no longer be able to control the range of political opinion.[48]

Among the growing army of pamphleteers in 1644 was Roger Williams, who had come to England in 1643, just as the Assembly opened. He wanted to secure a charter for Rhode Island and a printer for his writings.[49] He achieved both goals. In mid-July, 1644, two weeks after the crucial battle of Marston Moor, at which Cromwell defeated the King's troops, Williams' publisher released his *Bloudy*

---

44. Reprinted in William Haller, *Tracts on Liberty in the Puritan Revolution, 1638-1647*, 3 vols. (New York: Octagon, [1934] 1979), II:305-39. For Haller's commentary, see volume 1, ch. 6.

45. Margaret A. Judson, *The Crisis of the Constitution: An Essay in Constitutional and Political Thought in England, 1603-1645* (New Brunswick, New Jersey: Rutgers University Press, [1949] 1988), p. 9. Cf. ch. 10: "The Issues Become Clear."

46. For a list of the pamphlet responses of attendees of the Assembly, see Haller, *Tracts*, I:51. For a list of replies by Independents, see *Tracts*, I:52.

47. A. S. P. Woodhouse, ed., *Puritanism and Liberty: Being the Army Debates (1647-9)* (Chicago: University of Chicago Press, [1951] 1965).

48. Christopher Hill, *The World Turned Upside Down: Radical Ideas During the English Revolution* (New York: Viking, 1972); Hill, *Puritanism and Revolution: Studies in Interpretation of the English Revolution of the 17th Century* (New York: Schocken, 1958).

49. Gaustad, *Liberty of Conscience*, pp. 57-58.

Tenent of Persecution, for cause of Conscience, pleading for toleration of all sects. He was safely en route back to Rhode Island when it appeared. Parliament promptly ordered it burned.[50] It has become one of the two most famous pamphlets of that era. But Parliament did not burn John Milton's *Areopagitica*, another plea for toleration published that year, which is the other famous pamphlet.

The flood of pamphlets on both sides soon destroyed the old system of licensed publications. The King had tried to control publishing through licensing before 1642; Parliament tried in 1643;[51] but neither side was successful.[52] While the Westminster Assembly was debating the fine points of Puritan theology, the political theory of English Protestantism was beginning to unravel in full public view.

Presbyterian Worship and Order

The pamphlets in 1644 put pressure on the Assembly to get something completed and approved by Parliament. The Assembly hurried—by its standards—to finish the Directory of Publick Worship: from late May to November. Nothing in the Directory of Publick Worship was uniquely Presbyterian. The final committee had been made up of Independents and Presbyterians,[53] so the Directory was a compromise document.

The Directory prescribed a detailed list of liturgical requirements, including the outline of an introductory prayer that fills three small-print pages. This prayer would, before the conclusion of the service, be followed by two more. Prayers on fast days at the Westminster Assembly lasted from one to two hours.[54] It was also Scottish practice in that era to begin the service with a half hour of reading from the Bible.[55] Sermons lasted well over an hour. There was also psalm singing. It is not surprising that the Puritans rejected Calvin's insistence

---

50. *Ibid.*, p. 85.
51. Haller, *Liberty and Reformation*, p. 134.
52. *Ibid.*, p. 139.
53. William Maxwell Hetherington, *History of the Westminster Divines* (Edmondton, Canada: Still Water Revival Books, [1856] 1991), p. 179.
54. Iain Murray, "The Directory for Public Worship," *Glorify and Enjoy*, p. 186.
55. *Ibid.*, p. 177.

on weekly communion: not enough time. Scottish Presbyterian worship, as with Puritan worship generally,[56] was marathon worship. It reflected the Scottish landscape: only the most hardy could survive.[57]

One section raised questions for the future: "The ignorant and the scandalous are not fit to receive the sacrament of the Lord's Supper."[58] This meant that the Church would control access to the sacraments in a State Church. This alienated those who, following Swiss physician Thomas Erastus (1524-83), believed that the sacrament is a sanction and a means of discipline, and who refused to allow the Church on its own authority to close communion to anyone. Despite opposition from Parliament's Erastians, Parliament approved the document in January, 1645.[59] It was received by the Scottish Parliament and the Scottish Church the next month. But because the document was written to overcome the objections of the Independents, including politicians in Parliament, it was only loosely and mildly Presbyterian; nevertheless, it became a foundational though unofficial document for Scottish Presbyterianism. It was never officially ratified.

Church Government

Also in February, 1645, the General Assembly of the Church of Scotland voted to accept a modified version of the Westminster Assembly's Propositions Concerning Church Government and Ordination of Ministers,[60] known later in Scottish Presbyterian circles as the

---

56. John Cotton, when preaching in England's city of Boston, would preach for two hours in the morning, conduct two hours of questions and answers, and then do it again with new material in the afternoon. Yet his church was the best-attended parish church in England. Carl Bridenbaugh, *Vexed and Troubled Englishmen, 1590-1642* (New York: Oxford University Press, [1967] 1976), p. 296.

57. We are not among the survivors, including those who call for a return to the Westminster standards without understanding what they were expressly designed to achieve liturgically.

58. *The Directory for the Publick Worship of God*, in *The Confession of Faith* (Publications Committee of the Free Presbyterian Church of Scotland, 1970), p. 394. Notice that it says "the ignorant," not "the heretical." The assumption of the primacy of the intellect undergirds this rule: the exclusion of baptized minors and, by logical extension, the retarded and the senile.

59. Haller, *Liberty and Reformation*, p. 216.

60. Reprinted in Spear, *Covenanted Uniformity*, Appendix B.

Form of Presbyterial Church-Government.[61] Because the Confession of Faith was still over a year in the future when the Assembly finished this document, there was no mention in it of verbal subscription to any Confession, either by members or ministers. This was to have enormous importance for the history of Presbyterianism, most notably during America's Presbyterian conflict. This was the issue of the binding oath of allegiance. Neither the Form of Government nor the Confession of Faith ever said what the role of the oath is. Neither announced what the role of the Confession is. Such an announcement would have tied Parliament's hands, and Parliament was clearly unwilling to have its hands tied. It had arrested Laud in 1640 for having imposed such an oath, even though he had revoked it before Parliament assembled. It executed him in January, 1645, the month before the Scottish Assembly ratified the Form of Government. The Westminster Assembly in 1645 was not going to get Parliament to accept a comparable oath of allegiance to the Form of Government when no Confession of Faith existed. By the time the Confession was submitted, Cromwell and the Independents controlled Parliament.

The Form of Government did not say exactly how local church officers should gain their office. It said only that "Christ hath appointed" them (*Of the Officers of the Church*). The Church is allowed (though not necessarily required by the Bible) to be governed by Assemblies: congregational, classical (i.e., presbyteries), and synodical (*Of Church-Government, and the several sorts of assemblies for the same*). There was not one word about a required statement of faith in the section on ministerial ordination, despite the fact that the 12-part section is called, *Concerning the Doctrinal Part of Ordination of Ministers*. This is one of the strangest features in the history of Presbyterianism.

In *The Rules for Examination are these*, we are told that the prospective candidate must read the original biblical languages. If he is found deficient in this, he must be examined to see if "he hath skill in logick and philosophy." He must write an essay in Latin. He must be familiar with "authors in divinity." No authors are mentioned. All of

---

61. *Confession of Faith*, p. 396.

the specifics of ordination were exclusively formal; nothing theologically substantive appears anywhere in the document.[62]

Parliament Resists

The English Parliament never did ratify this document. In late summer, 1645, Parliament did authorize the Ordination of Ministers.[63] In March, 1646, Parliament voted to decree a modified form of Presbyterianism throughout the land. The Scottish commissioners complained that the system did not allow presbyteries to bring judgments on congregations under their jurisdiction; the presbyteries were advisory only[64]—rather like the Westminster Assembly was for Parliament. Then Parliament's Presbyterian faction introduced legislation to suppress blasphemy and heresy, which was not adopted until May, 1648, when there was no possibility of enforcing it.[65]

In early spring, 1646, a conflict broke out between Parliament and the Assembly over excommunicable sins. For all sins not listed by Parliament, Parliament demanded that provincial lay commissioners, functioning as bishops, determine who was subject to local congregational discipline. Parliament refused to accept the Assembly's full list of sins. The Assembly protested: Church elders alone should have this authority. Parliament then voted the Assembly guilty of breach of privilege, a serious offense. Parliament demanded that the Assembly prove that Church courts are autonomous from the State. Parliament wanted to retain the authority to sanction the elders: an Erastian State Church, with Parliament on top.[66] The Assembly wanted a Puritan State Church, with the elders autonomous from the State, and with the State compelled by law to enforce their judgments: Church on top. This was never sorted out to either authority's satisfaction. Parliament backed off from its high-handed demands after the King surren-

---

62. *The Form of Presbyterial Church-Government and of Ordination of Ministers*, in *Confession of Faith*, pp. 397–416.
63. Iain Murray, *The Reformation of the Church* (London: Banner of Truth Trust, 1965), p. 205.
64. Toon, *Puritans and Calvinism*, p. 63.
65. Haller, *Liberty and Reformation*, p. 217.
66. De Witt, "Form of Government," *Glorify and Enjoy*, pp. 158–60.

dered to the Scots in May.[67] Parliament then directed the Assembly to get on with the writing of the Confession of Faith.

Chapter XXX of the Confession embodies the Presbyterian view, but it was never accepted by Parliament.[68] The divisive issue was Church sanctions: Who has the right to impose them?[69] By 1646, there was no doubt regarding who would make this decision: Oliver Cromwell and his associates.

This Man Cromwell

Oliver Cromwell was a military genius. His most significant innovation came as a result of his insight into the weakness of cavalry tactics in his day. After a victorious cavalry charge, the victors pursued their defeated victims, or else stopped, dismounted, and collected booty from the bodies. A victorious cavalry officer could get only one effective charge out of his forces. Cromwell taught his men to stay in the saddle and stay in formation after a charge. Using this tactic, his cavalry brought victory to Parliament's forces at the battle of Marston Moor on July 2, 1644. Parliament's army of about 27,000 men defeated the King's army of 18,000,[70] turning what initially appeared to be a defeat into a stunning victory.[71] The royalists lost between 3,000 and 7,000 men (estimates vary), while Parliament's army lost 300.[72] Cromwell followed that victory with four more years of victories.

Cromwell was an ecclesiastical Independent. He rejected the Anglican Church's system of bishops, but he also rejected Presbyterianism. He was a member of Parliament. At first, he served militarily under the Earl of Manchester, an Englishman of such strong Presbyterian sentiments that he had been appointed one of the Parliamentary

---

67. John de Witt, *Jus Divinum: The Westminster Assembly and the Divine Right of Church Government* (Kampen, Holland: Kok, 1969), pp. 225-26.

68. De Witt, "Form of Government," *Glorify and Enjoy*, p. 162. For a detailed treatment of these debates, see de Witt, *Jus Divinum*.

69. Spear, Covenanted Uniformity, p. 124.

70. Maurice Ashley, *Oliver Cromwell and the Puritan Revolution* (New York: Collier, 1958), p. 63.

71. Antonia Fraser, *Cromwell: The Lord Protector* (New York: Knopf, 1974); pp. 120-29.

72. *Ibid.*, pp. 128-29.

lay delegates to the Westminster Assembly.[73] Initially, there was no friction between Cromwell and Manchester. Then, in early 1644, with the entry of the Scots into the Civil War on the side of Parliament, Scotsman Lawrence Crawford arrived. He became a major-general in Manchester's army. He believed that the Solemn League and Covenant, ratified by Scotland in August, 1643, and by Parliament the following month, should be enforced: a State Church. For him, this meant a Presbyterian Church. His presence led to a falling out between Manchester and Cromwell.[74]

Cromwell and the Scots

In the Solemn League and Covenant, both the Scottish and English Parliaments agreed that they would preserve "the reformed religion in the Church of Scotland, in doctrine, worship, discipline, and government, against our common enemies," and called for the reform of religion in England and Ireland "in doctrine, worship, discipline, and government, according to the word of GOD, and the example of the best reformed Churches; . ." (Sec. I). This, in the eyes of the Scots, meant the establishment of Presbyterianism as the State-enforced religion of the British Isles with no toleration for other churches. They had pressured Parliament for something like this as early as April, 1641.[75] They were so determined on this point that in April, 1643, they sent two commissioners to the King offering to join his side against Parliament if the King would agree to impose Presbyterianism on England. He rejected their offer; he preferred to seek aid from the Irish, in return for religious toleration.[76] At that point, the Scots offered their aid to Parliament.

It was clear that the Scots had a not-so-hidden agenda in all this: *Presbyterian supremacy by force of arms.* The Solemn League and Covenant added that "incendiaries, malignants, or evil instruments, by hindering the reformation of religion, dividing the king from his people,

---

73. Robert S. Paul, *The Lord Protector: Religion and Politics in the Life of Oliver Cromwell* (Grand Rapids, Michigan: Eerdmans, [1955] 1964), pp. 72–73.
74. *Ibid.*, pp. 73–75.
75. Holley, *Divines*, p. 30.
76. *Ibid.*, p. 104.

or one of the kingdoms from another," who opposed this covenant would "be brought to publick trial, and receive condign punishment, as the degree of their offences shall require or deserve, or the supreme judicatories of both kingdoms respectively, or others having power from them for that effect, shall judge convenient" (Sec. IV).

This punishment clause, in the eyes of the Independents, justified the execution of the King in 1649. He had become the malignant, evil instrument who was hindering the reformation of religion. The Scots, however, by then had switched sides: officially in the name of the Solemn League and Covenant and the Scottish National Covenant; unofficially because the King, an inveterate liar, was in the Scots' custody as a captive in late 1648, and to get back in power, he had sworn to use his authority to impose Presbyterianism on England.

Cromwell disagreed with the Presbyterian view of Church government and the Scottish interpretation of the Solemn League and Covenant. The victory at Marston Moor provided him with the Parliamentary influence he needed to be given his own army, the New Model Army, which was formed in 1645. This army was dominated by Independents. They were led spiritually by chaplains who were Independents, not ordained by any hierarchical church. The men listened to sermons that emphasized spiritual liberty and the necessity of a conversion experience.[77] Haller writes, "the triumph of the army confirmed the break-up of ecclesiastical order so that every resulting particle or fragment of the church as a whole, whether parish congregation or gathered flock, was left actually independent of every other and a law to itself."[78] Cromwell's victory over the King at the battle of Naseby on June 14, 1645, made it clear that the ecclesiastical goals of the Scots at the Westminster Assembly would not be achieved in England. The Civil War, militarily, was over, unless the Scots should intervene on the side of the King. They did: in 1647. Cromwell defeated them, too. That doomed Presbyterianism in Cromwellian England, 1649–58. (The refusal of English Presbyterians to accept the

---

77. Haller, *Liberty and Reformation*, ch. 6.
78. *Ibid.*, p. 219.

Confession of Faith as confessionally binding after 1662 doomed English Presbyterian in post-Cromwellian England.)

The Confession of Faith

The Westminster Confession of Faith was not handed to Parliament until December, 1646. The Parliament demanded Scripture proofs. These were supplied in April, 1647. In August, the Scottish General Assembly ratified it. The Larger and Shorter Catechisms were never ratified by Parliament; the Scottish General Assembly ratified them in July.

The final form of the Confession was never approved by Parliament. The Confession was renamed *Articles of the Christian Religion*, and several chapters were not approved: XXX, *Of Church Censures*; XXXI, *Of Synods and Councils*; and Section 4 of Chapter XX, *Of Christian Liberty*. That is, the *Articles* were not Presbyterian. They were accepted by the House of Commons in 1649, but they were never granted the force of law.[79] In short, having spent almost five years struggling to hammer out the basis of the reform of the Church of England, the Westminster Assembly had accomplished nothing judicially relevant in England. It did, however, establish what became an unofficial Church tradition for the Scots: a mild form of Presbyterianism that had been written by English theologians and modified to deal with the objections, first, of ecclesiastical Independents in the Assembly (July of 1643 to April of 1645) and, second, the demands of a Parliament increasingly controlled by Independents (1645 to 1648). On December 6, 1648, Col. Pride, in Cromwell's absence, marched on Parliament, ejected about 40 members of Presbyterian persuasion, leaving 80 members in power. This was Pride's Purge; it removed Presbyterianism from what came to be known as the Rump Parliament. Cromwell, upon his arrival in London that evening, said he had not approved Pride's action but accepted it gladly.[80]

In 1649, the year Parliament accepted the *Articles*, it beheaded the King. This attacked the covenantal foundation of Scottish Presbyteri-

---

79. Toon, *Puritans and Calvinism*, p. 59.
80. Fraser, *Cromwell*, pp. 269-70; Paul, *Lord Protector*, pp. 181-82.

anism, which had declared in *The National Covenant* (1639): ". . . we perceive, that the quietness and stability of our religion and kirk doth depend upon the safety and good behaviour of the King's Majesty, as upon a comfortable instrument of God's mercy granted to this country, for the maintaining of his kirk, and ministration of justice amongst us; . . ."[81] Scotland re-covenanted with Charles II when he arrived from the Continent in June, 1650, and swore an oath to the covenant.[82] His oath turned out a decade later to be as worthless as his father's similar promises had been. Cromwell invaded Scotland and defeated Charles II's forces.[83] Under Parliament (1649-53), and then under Cromwell's Protectorate (1653-58), followed by the Restoration of Charles II (1660), the accession of James II (1685), the Glorious Revolution (1688), and the arrival of William III (1689), the State Church of Scotland would not be protected in the way those signatories had imagined in 1639. That covenantal world of State Church monopoly was over in Anglo-American politics.

A Transformed Scottish Legacy

The Westminster Assembly had intended to complete its ecclesiastical work with the Directory for Church Government, but this document was never ratified by Parliament or the Scottish Church.[84] It has been forgotten since the eighteenth century.[85] The Form of Presbyterial Church-Government and the Directory of Church Government were not formally acknowledged by the Presbyterian Church as judicially authoritative until 1921, in the era of modern ecumenism.[86] The Free Presbyterian Church, formed in 1843, had acknowledged them, but only as "regulations," not as "tests,"[87] i.e., oath-bound subscriptions.

---

81. *The Confession of Faith of the Church of Scotland*, in *Confession of Faith*, p. 349.
82. Graves and Silcock, *Revolution, Reaction*, p. 422.
83. *Ibid.*, pp. 422-23.
84. Spear, Covenanted Uniformity, p. 245.
85. *Ibid.*, p. 327.
86. *Ibid.*, pp. 329-30.
87. *Ibid.*, p. 328.

The bizarre nature of the history of Presbyterianism should by now be obvious. Its strictly liturgical (1644) and ecclesiastical (1645) documents were co-designed by what would today be called Congregationalists. The five Independents did not withdraw from the Westminster Assembly until April, 1645.[88] Work on the Confession of Faith began the month after the Independents departed.[89] The Confession was designed by the Presbyterians to overcome resistance by their opponents in the Parliament. As it turned out, this self-restraint proved useless. The English Parliament never accepted the ecclesiastical sections of the Confession.

Other oddities of the five-year effort of the Assembly are also worth mentioning. Scotland's Solemn League and Covenant (1643) had been signed in preparation for entry into a war against the King, whose safety the 1639 National Covenant had promised to uphold. Scotland became a military ally of Cromwell and the Independents, who rose to power and then destroyed the judicial basis of the Scottish National Covenant: first by executing the King; second, by imposing Protestant religious toleration on the realm, including Scotland. As it turned out, a group of Englishmen established the foundational documents of Scottish Presbyterianism. In 1648, the year after the Assembly completed the annotated Confession, England went to war with Scotland.

The Scottish Church did not formally ratify the Westminster Assembly's documents on Church government. In any case, these documents were only vaguely Presbyterian, and even those sections that can be regarded as Presbyterian are merely authorized, not defended as expressly biblical.[90] While the General Assembly of 1647 accepted the Directory of Church Government, this had to be ratified in 1648. By 1648, there was little possibility of England's adopting the documents. The Scottish Church dropped the matter, although it ratified the Confession of Faith and the two catechisms. After 1649, the Scottish Church's General Assembly could no longer publish its acts: under

---

88. Haller, *Liberty and Reformation*, p. 217.
89. Toon, *Puritans and Calvinism*, p. 57.
90. Spear, Covenanted Uniformity, pp. 337–43.

Cromwell, then under Charles II and James II. Only in 1688, after the Glorious Revolution, did the Scottish Church regain its independence. But in that year, it re-ratified only the Westminster Confession of Faith.[91] In practice, the Form of Presbyterial Church-Government did serve as a *de facto* rule, but it was far less Presbyterian than earlier Church rules. The Church had downgraded its standards in 1647 for the sake of a compromise document. Spear sees this as evidence of the Scottish Church's good faith in signing the Solemn League and Covenant.[92] This may help to explain what they did in 1647. It does not explain why they put up with it after 1688.

Two generations later, Scotland would not be known so much for its Presbyterianism as for its common-sense rationalism (unitarian), whose empiricist methodology would be adopted by Presbyterian theologians, and for its world-famous empiricist skeptic, David Hume. In 1787–88, American Presbyterians voted to remove the section of the Confession authorizing the civil magistrate to call a synod like the Westminster Assembly. Had this view of civil authority prevailed earlier, the Church International would not have the Nicene Council, and Presbyterians would not have the Westminster Confession of Faith.

From State Church to Protestant Sect

Free speech became dominant in the New Model Army, which was formed in 1645. Cromwell continued to defeat the King's forces, bringing the day of political judgment closer to the Presbyterians. Let us review the history briefly. In 1646, the Westminster Assembly submitted the Westminster Confession. Parliament had the Assembly add supporting Bible proof texts. In May, 1647, Parliament officially received the amended Confession, but by that time, Cromwell and the Independents were dominant militarily. In late 1647, the defeated King made an alliance with the Scots.[93] In 1648, Parliament was in the hands of Cromwell's supporters. A Scottish army invaded England in

---

91. *Ibid.*, pp. 324–26.
92. *Ibid.*, p. 347.
93. Haller, *Liberty and Reformation*, pp. 314, 319.

July, 1648, hoping to put the King back on the throne. This army was completely defeated by Cromwell by October,[94] and with it, English Presbyterianism.

The English Presbyterians had been trapped by the decision of the Scottish Presbyterians to defend the King and a Throne-Church theocratic order, which had been affirmed by the language of the Solemn League and Covenant (Sec. VI). English Presbyterians could impose Church unity only by force, but the only significant force available was Cromwell's New Model Army, which opposed Presbyterianism.[95] Haller writes: "The advance of the army under Cromwell's leadership meant the final defeat of the work of the Westminster Assembly."[96] He concludes: "The English people were never again to be united in a visible church of any sort."[97] After the Restoration, English Presbyterianism refused to accept the Westminster Confession of Faith as binding, and in 1719, the denomination went unitarian.

This historical reality made American Presbyterianism an ecclesiastical structure very different from Scottish Presbyterianism in 1645. The eighteenth-century English Whig ideal of religious toleration had been long preceded by the Puritan Independents' ideal of religious toleration, at least for non-Catholics. The Presbyterian Church of Scotland in 1643 had been a State Church, with the Church dominant over the State.[98] All Presbyterians in the 1640's assumed the legitimacy of this arrangement. The State was expected to back up the pastors. The civil magistrate, said the Confession, has the duty "to take order that unity and peace be preserved in the Church, that the truth of God be kept pure and entire, that all blasphemies and heresies be suppressed, all corruptions and abuses in worship and discipline prevented or reformed, and all the ordinances of God duly settled, administered, and observed" (XXIII:3). But Cromwell would not en-

---

94. Fraser, *Cromwell*, pp. 242–61.
95. Haller, *Liberty and Reformation*, p. 319.
96. *Ibid.*, p. 341.
97. *Ibid.*, p. 355.
98. Jane Lane, *The Reign of King Covenant* (London: Robert Hale, 1956), provides a hostile account, but one based on the judicial reality of Church authority over civil authority.

force this under the Protectorate, and surely Charles II and, after 1684, his quasi-Papist brother James II would not. Yet Scotland was under the King's authority. Negative sanctions against theological deviance would henceforth be exclusively ecclesiastical—something that no Presbyterian would have imagined in 1646. Religious toleration, beginning surely with the defeat of the Scottish army in 1648, steadily became the ideal of Anglo-Scottish-American Presbyterianism.

After 1647, the Presbyterians had a monumental problem. The Church's foundational documents had been written to gain the acceptance of a civil assembly that included non-Presbyterians—as time went on, a growing number of non-Presbyterians. The documents did not fit together. The Form of Presbyterial Church-Government (1645) had no required statement of faith, i.e., no theological stipulations. It required no oath from Church officers or members. The Confession of Faith (1647) also did not mention Church oaths. It did not specify how its own stipulations were to apply judicially. The burning question should have been this: What was the covenantal relationship between these two completely separate documents? But no one in authority asked it in 1648, and no one in authority has asked it since.

Conclusion

The Westminster Assembly was both political and ecclesiastical, for there was no separation of Church and State in the seventeenth century outside of Rhode Island. The Assembly's politically assigned task in 1643 was to hammer out a religious settlement, in an era in which a three-way revolution would be fought over ecclesiology: Independents, Presbyterians, and Anglicans. By the end of the Assembly, there was no agreement about theology, either. In 1643, England was Calvinistic; the Arminian bishops were gone. By 1648, when the bulk of the Assembly's work was completed, England was a confessional cacophony: Calvinists, Arminians, Socinians (unitarians), experientialists, ranters, ravers, and all points in between. In just five years, while the Assembly debated the fine points of Calvinism, Calvinism's near-monopoly disappeared in England. After Charles II returned to the throne in 1660, Calvinism faded away except in the Empire's outposts: Scotland and North America.

The Westminster Assembly's assigned task was to provide advice for Parliament for reforming the Church of England. What it actually accomplished was to formalize Scottish Presbyterianism. It was asked by Parliament to suggest Church government reforms. "Doctrinal matters lay wholly in the background."[99] What it actually accomplished was the production of the most comprehensive theological confession in Protestant history, but with very few specifics on Church government. Parliament rejected the Assembly's handful of suggested ecclesiastical reforms, yet ratified its theological system. Then it refused to legislate this theological system. A year after the completion of the annotated version of the Confession in 1647, England went to war with Scotland, whose national Church was the only immediate ecclesiastical beneficiary of the Assembly's work, which in turn had sent representatives to the Assembly as a result of the 1643 treaty between two nations. Finally, in 1660, after the Puritan political revolution had ended in total failure, Charles II ascended to the throne, re-established bishops in 1661, who then, with Parliament's assent, re-imposed Anglicanism's Thirty-nine Articles of Religion. So, in the final analysis, Parliament had allocated money to an elite group of intellectuals for five years to complete what they had expected to be about a six-month wartime project, which was followed by a war between the former allies.

All things considered, the Westminster Assembly can be described fairly as a representative government project, a model of what politicians can achieve with the public's money. It achieved the opposite of everything Parliament had announced as its goals.

---

99. Warfield, *Westminster Assembly*, p. 12.

Appendix D

FRANCIS SCHAEFFER AND
THE PRESBYTERIAN CONFLICT

Because Francis Schaeffer became an intellectual spokesman for American fundamentalism, conservative evangelicalism, and a handful of Calvinists with the publication of his book, *The God Who Is There* (1968), it is necessary to review his role in the divisions of 1936 and 1937. This experience shaped his subsequent career.

In June of 1936, Schaeffer had completed his first year of seminary at Westminster. He joined the exodus with Machen. One year later, Schaeffer departed from the newly formed Presbyterian Church of America. He followed Carl McIntire. He completed his third year of seminary at McIntire's newly created Faith Seminary.[1] He was ordained in the Bible Presbyterian Church in 1938.[2] He participated in that Church's 1938 revision of the Chapter XXXIII of the Westminster Confession of Faith to make it an explicitly premillennial document.[3] The Bible Presbyterians also revised the Confession to return

---

1. This school went bankrupt in 1995, leaving a debt of over $1 million. It had invested in a Ponzi scheme known as New Era Philanthopy, a name similar to the Presbyterian liberals' fund-raising organization, 1919 to 1923: the New Era Movement.

2. See photo in *A Brief History of the Bible Presbyterian Church And Its Agencies* (no publisher, no date, but probably published in 1968), p. 63.

3. *The Constitution of the Bible Presbyterian Church* (Collingswood, New Jersey: Independent Board for Presbyterian Home Missions, 1959), p. 41. The fact that the Bible Presbyterian Church's Constitution was published by the Independent Board of Presbyterian Home Missions testifies to the continuing commitment of the Church to independency.

to the 1903 revision with respect to infants who die: ". . . with regard to the salvation of those dying in infancy we do not regard our Confession as teaching or implying that any who die in infancy are lost."[4] The Presbyterian Church of America had adopted the Confession's original statement the year before.

He was a dedicated ecclesiastical separatist and fundamentalist in 1937. In 1942, he wrote the following in a paper presented to the Bible Presbyterian Synod: "Let no one of us forget that our Separatist position is not an arbitrary thing; it is doctrinal. If one should ask for a single word that would show our stand against the evils of this day, the word would be Separatist; and it should be for we are Separatists." He went on to reaffirm his commitment to the premillennialism of the Bible Presbyterian Church: "We can say with pride that we are the first Reformed group to say formally by our creed that we believe in the premillennial Second Coming of our Lord."[5] He made his commitment clear: "We believe this doctrine with all of our heart."[6]

McIntire's Independent Board for Presbyterian Foreign Missions sent Schaeffer to Switzerland in 1947.[7] McIntire's name is absent from Mrs. Schaeffer's various accounts of their lives, but he was a dominant force in Schaeffer's early career. Because of Schaeffer's break with McIntire in 1956, when he stayed with the Evangelical Presbyterians rather than McIntire's Bible Presbyterians, he was not subsequently regarded as a fundamentalist in McIntire's mold, but he never abandoned his premillennialism. No one who would not sign a premillennial statement of faith could become a staff member at L'Abri.[8] He also never abandoned his separatism. In the early 1970's, when the Orthodox Presbyterian Church and Schaeffer's Reformed Presbyterian Church, Evangelical Synod, were seriously discussing the possibil-

---

4. *Ibid.*, p. 45.

5. Cited in George P. Hutchinson, *The History Behind the Reformed Presbyterian Church, Evangelical Synod* (Cherry Hill, New Jersey: Mack, 1974), p. 254.

6. *Ibid.*, p. 255.

7. Edith Schaeffer, *The Tapestry: The Life and Times of Francis and Edith Schaeffer* (Waco, Texas: Word, 1981), p. 246.

8. I applied in 1970; I was sent a copy of this statement of faith. I could not sign it.

ity of reuniting, it was Schaeffer's vocal opposition against this reunion, more than anyone else's, that killed the plan.⁹ The Orthodox Presbyterians voted for the merger in 1975, but the RPCES voted against it. Schaeffer had helped split the Church in 1937, and he never retreated from this decision. His decision stuck.

Christianity and Civilization

His premillennialism undergirded all of his apologetic work. This is why his film series and his book, *How Should We Then Live?*, never attempted to answer his crucial question. The book and film were devoted to the chronicling of the surrender of Christendom as a civilization and the rise of humanism as the result. He ended with a warning: there are only two choices available to man today: the Bible or an "imposed order."¹⁰ In his tenth film, he made this even clearer: the imposed order will be run by a humanist elite.

He called for a return to the Bible, not as a utilitarian solution to cultural problems, but as a moral requirement. "It means the acceptance of Christ as Savior and Lord, and it means living under God's revelation."¹¹ But as a consistent premillennialist, he had never accepted the theocratic ideal of Christendom for the era prior to the millennium. The best that Christians can legitimately hope for, he said, is minority status. *"Such Christians do not need to be a majority in order for this influence on society to occur."*¹²

This made no sense, given his eschatology. His book and his film series surveyed the systematic growth of religious self-consciousness on the part of non-Christians in the West: their dedication to removing every trace of Christian influence. The series began with a section on the persecution of Christians by the Roman Empire. There is no doubt as to what he privately thought must come: something far

---

9. This is the opinion of Charles Dennison, historian of the OPC, and George Hutchinson, author of the history of the RPCES. Personal telephone conversations: March 14, 1995.

10. Francis A. Schaeffer, *How Should We Then Live? The Rise and Decline of Western Thought and Culture* (Westchester, Illinois: Crossway, 1976), p. 252.

11. *Ibid.*

12. *Ibid.*

worse for the Church, namely, the Great Tribulation.[13] But he was not willing to admit forthrightly to his film audience and to his readers that this was the underlying eschatological presupposition of his life's work. This was why his work was not a call to explicitly Christian social action but a survey of what the Church has given up; not an explicitly biblical blueprint for social and cultural reconstruction but a cataloguing of Christendom's surrender and hand-wringing disguised as an intellectual's cultural critique; not a call for the progressive establishment of God's kingdom on earth in history but a program of religious common-ground anti-abortion politics—yet somehow in the name of a non-utilitarian Christianity.

Apologetics and Civilization

Schaeffer took Van Til's apologetic method, which Van Til had taught him at Westminster, and the philosophy of Gordon Clark, which was a common-ground rationalistic system, and reworked them into a partially presuppositional, partially Clarkian-logical hybrid. Never did he footnote Van Til in any of his books.[14] For that matter, neither did he footnote Clark. When asked in 1968, "Where did your husband get all this?" Mrs. Schaeffer offered a long, rambling disquisition about his discussions with "existentialists, logical positivists, Hindus, Buddhists, liberal Protestants, liberal Roman Catholics, Reformed Jews and atheistic Jews, Muslims, members of occult cults, and people of a wide variety of religions and philosophies, as well as atheists of a variety of types." This went on for two pages.[15]

The hybrid nature of his apologetic method made it difficult for him to come to grips with the idea of the common ground between believer and unbeliever. Van Til argued that the common ground or point of contact is the image of God in man. Covenant-breaking man knows that he is a covenant-breaker. Clark argued that it is common

---

13. He was not a dispensationalist, i.e., a believer in the pre-Tribulation rapture of the Church. In historic premillennialism, the Church is said to go through the Great Tribulation just prior to the Second Coming.

14. Van Til wrote a critical paper on Schaeffer's apologetic method in the late 1960's. It is scheduled to be republished on the CD-ROM version of his collected works.

15. Edith Schaeffer, *L'Abri* (London: Norfolk, 1968), pp. 226–27.

logic: the principle of non-contradiction. Schaeffer was more Clarkian than Vantillian. This made him more susceptible to the idea that Christians might have a positive influence on non-Christians even though Christians must remain as minority participants. Somehow, Christians can argue their way into the dialog. Van Til, as an amillennialist, had no illusions in this regard. He expected increasing persecution for the Church as each side becomes increasingly consistent with its presuppositions. This is certainly more consistent with Schaeffer's premillennial belief that the Great Tribulation lies ahead of us, and the Church will go through it. Historic premillennialists generally share this eschatological belief with amillennialists.

Calvinism and Civilization

In his five-volume *Complete Works,* published in 1982, there is no discussion of his Calvinism; he kept this a secret from his fundamentalist audiences. Schaeffer's followers were systematically misled throughout his public, published career regarding what he really believed. I think it is safe to say that it was not an oversight on Schaeffer's part that he neglected to reprint his 1976 pamphlet defending infant baptism in his *Complete Works.* This pamphlet had been published by an obscure local publisher long after Schaeffer had become the nation's best-selling evangelical philosopher-critic.[16]

Among Protestants, Calvinist Presbyterians have historically been more committed to the goal of building a Christian civilization than other Protestants have been. That Schaeffer was a Presbyterian is not surprising. That he refused to discuss his Calvinism in his writings is surprising. He wrote as if he believed that common-ground logic would not only persuade non-Christians to stop being so evil, it would even persuade Arminians. With respect to developing a believable critique of evil, this strategy may have been correct: covenant-breaking men recognize covenant-breaking when they see it (Rom. 2:14–15). With respect to gaining support for a positive reconstruction of an evil society, this assumption was not correct: covenant-breaking men rebel against the truth and adopt evil alternatives (Rom. 1:18–22).

---

16. Francis Schaeffer, *Baptism* (Wilmington, Delaware: Trimark Publishers, 1976).

They rebel against the truth. This is why Schaeffer's suggestion that Christians can have a positive social influence as time goes on, despite their perpetual minority status, makes no sense biblically.

Calvinism is a consistent, comprehensive world view. This is what a positive program of social reconstruction requires. Schaeffer never attempted to develop such a positive Christian alternative. He may have known that "you can't beat something with nothing," but his eschatology persuaded him that Christians cannot legitimately expect to beat paganism.

Succession: C. Everett Koop

The only nationally visible result of Schaeffer's social philosophy was the public career of his co-author (*Whatever Happened to the Human Race?*), C. Everett Koop, who was appointed in 1981 by President Reagan to serve as the Surgeon General of the United States. Koop in 1987 used his high office to recommend a program of compulsory sex education in the schools, beginning as early as kindergarten[17] and for public school instruction on how to use condoms.[18] Under questioning, Dr. Koop admitted that as Surgeon General, he would have to recommend abortion as one way of dealing with the unborn children of mothers with AIDS.[19] By the spring of 1987, Koop was self-consciously in retreat from his earlier Christian position. With respect to the abortion issue, he commented: "I've written all that I have to write on that issue. There are other, bigger things that I should turn my attention to as surgeon general: Where this country is and where it's going in health care."[20] He had openly adopted ethical neutrality as his social theology. In an interview with

---

17. *Washington Post* (March 24, 1987), "Health Focus."

18. I wrote at the time, "Koop has become a kind of bureaucratic condom himself: Preaching a prophylactic solution to a world facing a religious crisis. He has betrayed his trust." Gary North, "Koop's Condom Argument Has a Hole in It," *A.L.L. About Issues* (May–June 1987), p. 48; published by the American Life League.

19. "Koop suggests abortion as option for AIDS carriers," *Washington Times* (March 25, 1987).

20. "The Still-Crusading Koop Keeps the Moralizing Quiet," *Insight* (March 16, 1987). This is published by the conservative *Washington Times*.

the politically liberal *Washington Post*, he announced: "I am the surgeon general of the heterosexuals and the homosexuals, of the young and the old, of the moral and the immoral, the married and the unmarried. I don't have the luxury of deciding which side I want to be on."[21] He neglected the obvious: he had the luxury of resigning his office in protest. To do so, however, he would have had to abandon the national sex-education program which he had personally recommended.

Then, in the fall of 1987, without much media attention, he admitted that condoms really are not much protection for homosexual contacts.[22] But in 1988, the government sent a copy of a popularized version of his 1986 report on AIDS to every household in the United States: *Understanding AIDS: A Message from the Surgeon General*. Half of page 4 is devoted to the condom solution: ". . . the use of condoms is recommended to help reduce the spread of AIDS." Under "risky behavior," the report lists "Unprotected sex (without a condom) with an infected person." "Safe behavior" is described as: "Not having sex. Sex with one mutually faithful, uninfected partner. Not shooting drugs" (p. 3). Notice the reference to "partner" rather than "spouse."

In his 1991 autobiography, he bewailed the fact that his 1986 report had been criticized by the religious right. He felt, he said, "a profound sense of betrayal by those on the *religious* right who took me to task."[23] His sense of betrayal was reciprocated by the religious conservatives whose organized support alone had allowed Reagan's appointment of Koop to get through the hostile U.S. Senate in 1981. His sense of betrayal immediately pushed him closer to the political left. "First, I needed to capitalize on my new alliance with the moderates and liberals to continue to get the message on AIDS to each American citizen."[24] This alliance was never broken during his term as

---

21. *Washington Post* (March 24, 1987), "Health Focus." This is what he had said publicly from the beginning: *ibid*. (Oct. 2, 1981).
22. "Koop Warns on Risk of AIDS in Condom Use," *Los Angeles Times* (Sept. 22, 1987).
23. C. Everett Koop, *Koop: The Memoirs of America's Family Doctor* (New York: Random House, 1991), p. 216.
24. *Ibid*., p. 217.

Surgeon General. It is understandable why, prior to the 1988 Presidential election, Democrats Jesse Jackson, Al Gore, and Michael Dukakis all offered to keep him if they won; Republican candidate George Bush did not.[25]

Bush, the victor in 1988, did not appoint Koop to the office he wanted, Secretary of Health and Human Services (welfare). This disappointed Koop because he had wanted to create a program for universal health insurance coverage that would "at last provide health insurance to the 37 million Americans who live in that fearful world of the uninsured."[26] Bush's Democrat successor presented such a compulsory plan in 1993. Koop publicly supported it. President Clinton, he told the press, has "accomplished more in health reform in the past few months than all four of his living predecessors put together."[27] This compulsory health insurance plan was not passed by Congress, despite the fact that the President's party controlled both houses, nor was any substitute program passed. The President had promised to make support for his compulsory health insurance plan the key issue in the 1994 Congressional elections, but after its defeat in early 1994, he neglected to do so in the campaign that fall. The Democrats went on to lose both houses of Congress, their biggest defeat in four decades.

Conclusion

In 1984, the year before he died, Schaeffer had cried out against what he called *The Great Evangelical Disaster*.[28] Yet he had baptized the intellectual foundations of this disaster. He was a Calvinist who never wrote about his Calvinism; a Presbyterian who concealed his essay on infant baptism from his non-Presbyterian readers; a post-tribulation premillennialist who believed that prior to the Second Coming of Christ to establish an earthly millennium, the Church would inevitably go through the Great Tribulation; an historian who lamented the decline of Christendom, but who explicitly rejected the

---

25. *Ibid.*, p. 308.
26. *Ibid.*, p. 312.
27. Alan Clymer, "First Lady Rebuts Health Plan Critic," *New York Times* (Sept. 21, 1993), p. A18.
28. Westchester, Illinois: Crossway Books.

inherently theocratic ideal of Christendom; and a promoter of a non-utilitarian Christianity who nevertheless suggested that the non-Christian world might someday listen to minority-status Christians, making them an influence for good, despite the fact that such minority influence could come only to the extent that Christianity becomes utilitarian for covenant-breakers. It is no wonder that his son Franky, who produced his father's movies, has left Protestantism to join the Eastern Orthodox Church, and has renounced all Christian social activism. Theological schizophrenia is difficult to live with.[29]

In *The Great Evangelical Disaster*, Schaeffer warned against what he called the spirit of accommodation with the world. He pointed to the history of evangelical academia, where bright students went off to the finest universities and were captured by the secularism of the classroom, to return to the evangelical colleges "where what they present in their classes has very little that is distinctively Christian."[30] He called this academic infiltration, as indeed it is. But what did he offer in its place? A critique of humanism, no matter how skillful, is not sufficient; there must be a Christian alternative. You can't beat something with nothing. But Schaeffer never suggested a methodology by which such an alternative might be developed.

---

29. For a detailed critique of Schaeffer's theological schizophrenia, see Gary North, *Political Polytheism: The Myth of Pluralism* (Tyler, Texas: Institute for Christian Economics, 1989), ch. 4. See also David Chilton and Gary North, "Apologetics and Strategy," *Christianity and Civilization*, 4 (1983), pp. 116-31: "Francis Schaeffer's *A Christian Manifesto*."

30. Francis Schaeffer, *The Great Evangelical Disaster* (Westchester, Illinois: Crossway, 1984), p. 119.

Appendix E

WINNERS AND LOSERS

Ask, and it shall be given you; seek, and ye shall find; knock, and it shall be opened unto you (Matthew 7:7).

On Friday, September 15, 1995, I celebrated. First, I had enough money in my checking account to cover the check I wrote to the Internal Revenue Service to pay my quarterly income tax bill. Second, I had finished all but the final proofing of the index of *Crossed Fingers* after about a hundred hours of work on it. So, it was time to celebrate. I took my wife out to the local Barnes & Noble bookstore that opened last month. She sat and read an R. C. Sproul book that she had smuggled in; I shopped.

By the providence of God, my eyes lighted on the blue spine of a book, *The Churching of America, 1776–1990*, by Finke and Stark. I pulled it down. I opened it. I skimmed sections. And I marveled. There, before my very eyes, was the mother lode that I had been looking for since mid-September, 1962.

Crossed Fingers was finished. Should I begin a re-write? The index was finished. Should I risk having to re-index the entire book? I would call that approach mad—Stark raving mad. My solution: add a few footnotes retroactively and write another appendix. As I always say: "When you've written a book over a thousand pages long, what's an extra appendix among friends?"

What Hath Sociology Wrought?

Finke and Stark are sociologists. (Beware of sociologists bearing gifts, I usually say.) They are sociologists who understand free market economics, especially the economics of cartels. This is extremely rare among sociologists. They also are well-versed in American religious history. Finally, they write in clear, straightforward English. This is simply astounding.

They have presented the statistical and historical evidence that validates the following themes in *Crossed Fingers*:

> 1. The connection between seminary education and ecclesiastical liberalism in the nineteenth century.
>
> 2. The coming of liberalism as the beginning of ecclesiastical stagnation and then decline.
>
> 3. The shortage of ministers (at the price offered) in the hierarchical denominations.
>
> 4. The failure of hierarchical denominations on the American frontier as the result of 1-3.
>
> 5. The long decline of mainline Protestant denominations after 1920.
>
> 6. The ecumenical movement as a cartel.
>
> 7. The Rockefeller connection.

Obviously, I wish someone had written the book in 1961 and I had read it in the summer of 1962. It would have saved me a lot of time. I would have gone down fewer rabbit trails. But better late than never.

Finke and Stark have not been bowled over by the standard historiography of American Church history. They recognize that those who have dominated this academic field have shared a common worldview since at least the 1920's: theological liberalism and ecumenism. The historians have interpreted American Protestant Church history as the growth of theological liberalism in the churches, with fundamentalism supposedly confined to small, isolated groups, mostly in the rural South. They write:

> For most historians, religion means theology, and therefore the history of American religion is the history of religious ideas. There is nothing wrong with writing histories of ideas, of course. But when historians trace the history of American religious ideas they nearly always adopt (at least implicitly) a model of intellec-

tual progress. Their history is organized on the basis of showing how new religious ideas arose and were progressively refined. Moreover, the standards against which refinement is usually judged are entirely secular—parsimony, clarity, logical unity, graceful expression, and the like. One never encounters standards of theological progress or refinement based on how effectively a doctrine could stir the faithful or satisfy the heart. As a result, the history of American religious ideas always turns into an historical account of the march toward liberalism. That is, religious ideas always become more refined (i.e., better) when they are shorn of mystery, miracle, and mysticism—when an active supernatural realm is replaced by abstractions concerning virtue.[1]

Success and Failure

To be successful, argue Finke and Stark, a religious movement must do two things: comfort the soul and motivate its adherents to a higher standard of performance than the average person is willing to commit.[2] This is not what mainline denominational liberalism offers. Instead, it offers theological refinement. In American religious history, "theological refinement is the kind of progress that results in organizational bankruptcy."[3]

Men want a religion that offers rewards for sacrifice. "People seek a religion that is capable of miracles and that imparts order and sanity to the human condition."[4] Men are asked to pay costs in the here and now in order to receive greater rewards "elsewhere and later."[5]

I would add that theological liberalism denies or de-emphasizes the elsewhere and later aspect: beyond the grave. Then where and when will payday arrive? In its social gospel aspect, "later" refers to life on earth. Liberalism secularized traditional postmillennial eschatology, which had faded by 1900. This left the liberals as near monopolists

---

1. Roger Finke and Rodney Stark, *The Churching of America, 1776–1990: Winners and Losers in Our Religious Economy* (New Brunswick, New Jersey: Rutgers University Press, [1992] 1994), pp. 4–5.
2. *Ibid.*, p. 5.
3. *Ibid.*
4. *Ibid.*, p. 275.
5. *Ibid.*

regarding the historical continuity between today's sacrifice and tomorrow's rewards. But when this liberal optimism faded in the economic pessimism of the 1930's, and especially in the economic optimism and "Philistinism" of middle-class America's post-War boom, it was replaced by Norman Vincent Peale's individualistic power of positive thinking and by neo-orthodoxy's noumenal individualistic encounter theology, which hardly any of its adherents have ever encountered. Liberalism went bland; it also visibly went bankrupt organizationally after 1965.

The decline of America's mainline denominations did not begin in the 1960's. It was far along by 1812.[6] Most academic commentators have blamed the decline of the 1960's on too little modernism or on too much secularization.[7] But they and their predecessors had contributed to this process of secularization, as the authors show. Those whose theology had caused the crisis now proclaimed that the churches needed more of the same. And so they got it, such as the Presbyterians' Confessional revision of 1967 or the Angela Davis incident in 1971. So, the pews emptied further. They continue to empty.

On page 232, the authors offer a table showing the relationship between ecumenism and denominational growth. In 1932, a survey was taken that showed the extent of denominational acceptance or resistance to ecumenism. The most hostile large denomination was Missouri Synod Lutheranism: 89.5 percent rejected ecumenism. Yet from 1916 to 1926, this denomination had experienced the highest net growth: over 50 percent. The next highest groups were the other Lutherans, excluding only the United Lutherans: 60 percent rejection. These groups experienced the second largest rate of growth, over 45 percent. And so it went, down to the Evangelical Synod, in which 10 percent rejected ecumenism (lowest), and which had suffered a 22.6 percent decline in membership (largest). The Northern Presbyterians were, as usual, right in the middle: about 21 percent rejected ecumenism, and growth had been an anemic 1.4 percent. This was in contrast

---

6. *Ibid.*, p. 249.
7. *Ibid.*

to the Southern Presbyterians, who rejected ecumenism by almost 53 percent, and which had enjoyed an 11 percent growth rate.[8]

Price Competition and Market Share

If there is a testable law in economic theory, it is this one: *at a lower price, more will be demanded, other things being equal.*[9] The story of the demise of Calvinism in America is the story of above-market pricing.

Calvinism was dominant in the United States in 1790: Congregationalism, Presbyterianism, and Episcopalianism. A century later, Arminianism was dominant. I have already dealt with this transformation, using E. S. Gaustad's *Atlas of American Religion* (1962) as my source.[10] Finke and Stark have used other primary sources to reach similar conclusions. There were fewer than 5,000 Methodists in 1776.[11] There were 65 Methodist congregations averaging 75 members. Membership per congregation was similar among the Baptists and Presbyterians.[12] The percentage of Church members in the colonies was generally about 20 percent. The highest was in South Carolina: 31 percent (white members). The lowest was in Vermont: 9 percent. Massachusetts and New York were around 20 percent. Pennsylvania was high: 26 percent.[13] The vast majority of America's population in 1776 was outside the authority of the churches.

New England was overwhelmingly Congregational: 63 percent. This was by law: Congregationalism was an established Church. Taxes supported the ministers. This would remain true in Massachusetts until 1833. (At that time, Horace Mann's public school system replaced Congregationalism as Massachusetts' established Church.) The ecclesiastical results of this subsidy were these: upper class, well-paid pastors;

---

8. *Ibid.*, p. 232.

9. Of course, other things in history are never equal.

10. See Introduction to Part 2, above: section on "The Second Great Awakening," pp. 108–12.

11. Specifically, 4,921. *Ibid.*, p. 25. The rely on the *Minutes of the Annual Conference of the Methodist Episcopal Church.*

12. *Ibid.*, p. 26.

13. *Ibid.*, p. 27.

a highly educated ministry; creeping liberalism (Harvard College went Unitarian in 1805); and an inability to compete outside of the region. Congregational home missions efforts were impotent. When the Plan of Union of 1801 created joint home missions outside of New England, most of the newly formed Congregationalist congregations joined the Presbyterian Church.[14] What Adam Smith had predicted in 1776 had come true: the State's infusion of funds had reduced the clerical recipients' ability to compete.[15]

(A similar strategy was used by the modernists a century later: the Federal Council of Churches' control over radio air time through the government's Federal Communications Commission, which in the mid-1920's imposed a requirement that all radio stations set aside free time for public service broadcasting. The religious FCC persuaded the newly created national radio networks to allow only FCC representatives to fill these free time slots. Then the religious FCC persuaded the national networks to sell commercial air time only to FCC-linked pastors. The evangelicals could not crack this cartel, not even Charles E. Fuller's "Old-Fashioned Revival Hour," which was limited to buying air time on local stations. When the National Religious Broadcasters—the evangelicals' organization—in 1960 persuaded the government's FCC to authorize payments for public interest time slots, the National Council's radio cartel collapsed. Liberals could not compete with those evangelical ministries that had been built up on local radio stations for three decades through donations from the audience. The same sequence was repeated on television.[16] There was another factor: technology. The tape recorder, first used by Hitler in the early 1940's to broadcast simultaneous speeches across Germany, was pioneered on commercial radio by Bing Crosby, beginning in 1947. Crosby hated rehearsals and hated doing his radio show three times for three of the four time zones. The audio tape made it possible for evangelical ministers to buy air time from lots of local stations. Technological breakthroughs—videotape and satellite broadcasting—per-

---

14. *Ibid.*, p. 74.
15. Adam Smith, *Wealth of Nations*, Cannan edition (Modern Library, 1937), pp. 741–42; cited in *ibid.*, p. 52.
16. *Ibid.*, pp. 218–23.

formed the same cartel-busting feat in the 1970's. Once again, it was reliance on State coercion that doomed the liberals.)

The Congregationalist-Presbyterian Plan of Union was a cartel: restricting denominational competition on the frontier between Presbyterians and Congregationalists. It failed because suppliers from outside the cartel met the growing demand. The Methodists and the Baptists were not participants in the agreement.[17] The Presbyterians and Episcopalians tried to keep out interlopers by controlling public real estate. In Buffalo, New York in 1818, the Presbyterians controlled the court house on Sunday; the Episcopalians controlled the school house.[18] The Methodists and Baptists had to build their own buildings. Then they filled them.

The American Home Missionary Society was one of the parachurch ministries that caused such dissention between Old School and New School Presbyterians in the 1820's and 1830's. The authors point out that this organization was a response to the price-competitive Methodists and Baptists, whose pastors served free of charge or close to it. The AHMS raised funds to help finance well-paid and well-educated missionaries from the hierarchical churches to evangelize frontier regions that were in the middle of the Second Great Awakening. But price competition on the frontier was fierce. "The Congregationalists, Presbyterians, and Episcopalians could not sustain churches in these areas without home missions subsidies, if for no other reason than that they depended on a well-educated and well-paid clergy."[19] In the 1830's, an urban Presbyterian or Congregationalist pastor was paid anywhere from $1,000 a year to $3,000.[20] Meanwhile, a Methodist circuit rider was officially paid $100, but very often they were paid even less by the organization.[21] They were the Protestant Jesuits. Of the first 700 circuit riders, almost half died before age 30, 199 of them within the first five years of service.[22]

---

17. *Ibid.*, p. 63.
18. *Ibid.*
19. *Ibid.*, p. 65.
20. *Ibid.*, p. 82
21. *Ibid.*, p. 81.
22. *Ibid.*, p. 153.

By 1850, the 65 Methodist congregations of 1776 had grown to 13,300: 2.6 million members—over one-third of the churched population. The Baptists had risen from 16.9 percent to 20.5 percent. The Episcopalians had fallen from 15 percent of the churched population to 3.5 percent. The Presbyterians had fallen from 19 percent to 11.6 percent.[23] So desperate were the Calvinist denominations that they often persuaded town councils to outlaw camp meetings as disturbances of the peace in the early 1800's.[24] They called on the State to defend their oligopoly. This did not work; in fact, it weakened them. It made them organizationally flabby.

I have stated in this book that the word "shortage" should not be used apart from the qualification "at some price." The price of entry into Calvinist pulpits was advanced education: grammar school Latin above all, followed by college, and after 1808 (Congregationalism) and 1812 (Presbyterianism), theological seminary. This price of entry was a cost. As costs rise, the quantity supplied falls. Fewer men will pay the cost. They must be lured by future compensation to justify their present expenditure. This created a shortage of qualified ministers. Well-educated pastors could demand high wages, but only from prosperous eastern and urban congregations. Actual demand for such high-priced pastors, as registered in the total number of calls from all churches, necessarily fell. Calls from tiny churches were numerous on the Western frontier, meaning *calls at low prices*. Who would meet this demand? Baptist and Methodist laymen-turned-pastors.

The Presbyterians did keep pace proportionally: the number of members in relation to the total population. They had not enjoyed State establishment. They could compete more successfully than Congregationalists and Episcopalians, who fell permanently into insignificance numerically. Meanwhile, Baptists and Methodists increased their share of the population, as more Americans than ever before joined local churches.[25] In 1776, about 17 percent of Americans were local church members. By 1860, it was 37 percent. In 1906, it was 50 per-

---

23. *Ibid.*, pp. 55–56.
24. *Ibid.*, pp. 101–102.
25. *Ibid.*, p. 72.

cent. In 1926, it was 56 percent. In 1980, it was about 62 percent.[26] Although the standards for membership have declined since 1776, those churches that have held their members to standards that are more in conflict with the secularism of the prevailing culture have grown, avoiding the decline suffered by liberal mainline denominations.

Seminaries and Liberalism

When the innovative Methodist missionary Francis Asbury died in 1816, there was no Methodist college. In 1847, Methodists started a seminary. By 1880, there were 11 Methodist theological seminaries, 44 colleges and universities, and 130 women's schools.[27] There was also liberalism: New School Methodism. Centralization proceeded apace after 1850; so did the beginnings of Unitarianism in the denomination. So did personal wealth, pew rentals, and other signs of creeping social legitimacy.[28] These developments led to a split in 1860: the creation of Free Methodism.[29]

Liberalism led to a decline in the number of Methodists as a percentage of the overall population ("market share"),[30] which peaked for Methodism in 1850. The Baptists overtook them in sheer numbers in 1906.[31] But the market share of the Northern Baptists, with their seminary training and higher salaries, declined side by side, though at a slightly lower rate, from 1850 to 1926.[32] It was the Southern Baptists that provided the growth.[33]

By the time the Methodists opened their first seminary, the mainline denominations had turned out 6,000 ministers.[34] Yet the replacement of the original Big Three denominations was visible to all by

---

26. *Ibid.*, p. 15.
27. *Ibid.*, p. 154.
28. *Ibid.*, p. 150.
29. *Ibid.*, pp. 151–52.
30. *Ibid.*, p. 145.
31. *Ibid.*
32. *Ibid.*, chart, p. 171.
33. *Ibid.*, chart, p. 149.
34. *Ibid.*, p. 77.

1847. Meanwhile, the Congregationalists had gone Unitarian. As the authors note, "religious doctrine often seems to become accommodated and secularized whenever it is delivered into the control of intellectuals."[35] It happened to the Methodists, too. The entry point was the seminary by way of German graduate schools.[36]

Rural Ecumenism and the Rockefeller Connection

Throughout the first half of the twentieth century, modernists actively pursued the goal of consolidating rural churches. This was part of the larger ecumenical movement. The initial organizational impulse for this began with a 1908 government project promoted by Teddy Roosevelt: the Commission on Country Life. This was the same year that the Federal Council of Churches came into existence. The report of the Commission was published in 1909. It recommended the creation of an agricultural extension service, initiation of government research projects in America's land grant colleges and universities, and the inclusion of home economics courses and agriculture courses in America's high schools.[37] This was necessary, the report said, because America's rural communities were declining rapidly. The government had to do something soon, in the report's words, to "unite the interests of education, organization and religion into one forward movement for rebuilding of rural life."[38]

The work of the Commission was taken over by Kenyon L. Butterfield, president of the Massachusetts Agricultural College, a leading member of the Commission. In 1921, Butterfield was a co-founder of the Institute of Social and Religious Research. The ISRR had just been created by Raymond Fosdick in his capacity as Rockefeller's lawyer. It inherited the field reports of the Interchurch World Movement, which Fosdick had just shut down.[39] Under Butterfield, the ISRR promoted what Finke and Stark call the myth of the country church

---

35. *Ibid.*, p. 158.
36. *Ibid.*
37. *Ibid.*, p. 202.
38. Cited in *ibid.*
39. See Chapter 6, above: section on "The Interchurch World Movement, 1919–1921," pp. 392–403.

crisis.[40] This myth rested on two assumptions: (1) cities were growing while rural areas were declining; (2) all denominations were being forced to close some country congregations and subsidize others. This perspective had been stated clearly in a 1911 essay by Presbyterian minister Warren Wilson in the *American Journal of Sociology*.[41] But the story was entirely fabricated. The evidence did not support the myth, and its statistically competent promoters knew this.[42] First, rural population was not shrinking: 41 million (1890), 51 million (1920), 57 million (1940). As a percentage of the total U.S. population, rural population was shrinking, but this is not the same as saying that rural population was shrinking. Finke and Stark therefore conclude: "Consequently, the closure of rural churches could not have been the result of a decline in the potential church population."[43]

Wilson's proposed solution to the non-existent problem—non-existent for Bible-believing Arminian churches—was Church unity: ecumenism. He was in charge of the Presbyterian Church's rural surveys, conducted from 1911 to 1913. In the report on Ohio rural churches, published by the Presbyterian Church's (i.e., Wilson's) Department of Country Life (probably published in 1912 or 1913; there is no date), this bit of ecumenical ecclesiology appeared: "The Survival of the Fittest. . . . The large Church is the more efficient working Force. Small, weak churches would fare better if combined."[44] This became a constant theme for the next half century.

Saving Faith in Sociology

Finke and Stark rely heavily on an article by James H. Madison, published in 1986 in the *Journal of American History*. Madison reports that in 1912, at a the quadrennial meeting of the Federal Council of Churches,[45] a dozen men committed to rural ecumenism met in But-

---

40. *Ibid.*, p. 207.
41. *Ibid.*, pp. 207–208.
42. *Ibid.*, p. 214.
43. *Ibid.*, p. 208.
44. Reproduced in James H. Madison, "Reformers and the Rural Church, 1900–1950," *Journal of American History*, 73 (1986), p. 651.
45. Where Shailer Mathews was elected president.

terfield's hotel room. They proposed that the denominations create research departments to conduct huge statistical surveys of rural churches. Their model was the Presbyterian Church's Department of Church and Country Life, part of the Board of Home Missions.[46] Its founder and director was Wilson, a Union Seminary graduate and a Columbia University Ph.D. in sociology.[47] Following Wilson's lead, conservationist promoter Gifford Pinchot and Charles Otis Gill issued a report through the Federal Council in 1913 that announced: "With the whole world turning to combined or cooperative action as the basis of efficiency, the program of the country church continues to deal wholly with individuals, and hence remains defective and one-sided."[48] (In that same year, the Presbyterian Church shut down the Department of Church and Country Life.[49] This was one year after the Church had cut funding for socialist Charles Stelzle's urban social activities.[50]) In 1915, the Federal Council's Conference on Church and Country Life was regarded as sufficiently important by President Woodrow Wilson to warrant delivering the closing address of the conference. The other Presbyterian Wilson, Warren, also spoke.[51]

By 1912, faith in sociological surveys was widespread in liberal theological circles. Charles E. Hayward had written as early as 1900: "The sociological movement is born of God, and is destined to be the mightiest power behind the Gospel the world has ever known."[52] In retrospect, Rockefeller's similar enthusiasm for the Interchurch World Movement's surveys in 1920 was not unique.

In 1920, the IWM published two volumes of guidelines for organizing rural churches to meet standards of efficiency. "Rural churches are dying," it announced.[53] Reform was needed. To revitalize fading

---

46. *Ibid.*, p. 652.
47. *Ibid.*, p. 649.
48. Cited in *ibid.*, p. 652
49. *Ibid.*, p. 653.
50. See Chapter 6, above: section on "Alliances vs. the Broadening Church," p. 361.
51. *Ibid.*, pp. 632–33.
52. Charles Hayward, *Institutional Work for the Country Church* (1900), p. 32, cited in *ibid.*, p. 647.
53. Cited in *ibid.*, p. 635.

rural Church leadership, pastors had to be paid more. After the report was issued, one of its directors announced that the minimal salary should be $1,200 a year, plus a free parsonage. Every church needed an organ, a well-equipped kitchen, and a moving picture projector.[54] To accomplish this, small churches would have to merge into large non-denominational community churches.

This was one more example of the liberals' cartel mentality. The liberals' hoped-for cartel was breaking down before it was even imposed, mimicking the Calvinist's would-be cartel on the frontier a century earlier. Price competition was still at work; so were creedal competition and liturgical competition. Fundamentalist interlopers kept invading the market. In 1914, John Hargreaves had predicted in the *American Journal of Sociology* that within ten years, community churches would be everywhere. In 1926, the reality was different: 301 federated congregations out of 167,864 congregations.[55]

A series of Rockefeller-funded reports, like their predecessors, promoted the myth of the death of country churches. But what was dying after 1900 was mainline denominational presence in rural areas, not the rural Church. Nevertheless, a stream of these reports continued through the 1950's, all making the same grim forecasts, all calling for ecumenism as the cure.[56] Finke and Stark write:

> How could the reformers have been mistaken about the "fact" that rural churches were closing left and right? It depends on what kind of churches one counts. If we confine our attention to the mainline churches, Wilson's comments are not only accurate but prophetic. Between 1916 and 1926 the Presbyterian Church in the U.S.A. lost 826 churches (-8.5 percent), the Congregationalists dropped 872 (-14.8 percent), the Disciples lost 748 (-8.9 percent, and the Methodist Episcopal Church lost 3,185 (-10.9 percent). Many, if not most, of these losses were country and village churches.

---

54. *Ibid.*, p. 660.
55. Finke and Stark, *Churching of America*, p. 212.
56. Madison, pp. 664–65.

But if we broaden our view to take in the entire landscape of rural American religion, the picture looks very different. Between 1916 and 1926 there was a *net increase* of 4,667 in the total number of American churches. The number of Lutheran and Catholic churches increased by 2,746, but this can account for only a modest part of the gain in churches. Given that the mainline churches mentioned above had lost 5,631 congregations, more than ten thousand new churches were needed to reach the new total. If the mainline was declining, someone else must have been quickly gaining. In addition to the Southern Baptists, who gained 1,178 churches, the "someones" included the Assemblies of God (+553 percent), Church of God (Cleveland, Tenn.) (+442 percent), Christian and Missionary Alliance (+169 percent), Church of the Nazarene (+577 percent), Churches of Christ (+656 percent), Free Will Baptists (+274 percent), the Pentecostal Holiness Church (+60 percent), and the Salvation Army (+310 percent).[57]

There was a hidden agenda behind the liberals' stream of deliberately misleading reports: consolidation. During World War I, Wilson was a faculty member at Columbia Teachers College. His colleague was Mabel Carney. This school was the central institution for progressive education during the Progressive era. The faculty in Wilson's day included John Dewey, Edward L. Thorndike, and William H. Kirkpatrick,[58] all of whom were leaders in the progressive education movement.[59] Wilson and Carney promoted rural consolidation of the churches and also the schools.[60] Carney's educational program was an extension of the General Education Board's long-term plan to create a system of public schools throughout the South and rural areas. This plan succeeded with the schools, which were funded by taxation and subject to political control. It failed with the churches.

---

57. Finke and Stark, *Churching of America*, p. 208.
58. Lawrence A. Cremin, *The Transformation of the School: Progressivism in American Education, 1876-1957* (New York: Vintage, [1961] 1964), pp. 172-73.
59. See the chapters on all three in R. J. Rushdoony, *The Messianic Character of American Education: Studies in the History of the Philosophy of Education* (Nutley, New Jersey: Craig Press, 1963).
60. Madison, p. 644.

The liberals knew that they had to overcome the national influence of rural, conservative areas, where saving faith in Jesus Christ was dominant, not saving faith in sociology. They viewed the revivalism and emotionalism of rural churches as a mere "backwash," to cite Edmund Brunner,[61] whom Wilson had recommended when he turned down the directorship of the ISRR's town and country survey program.[62] Their media efforts culminated in the Scopes trial in 1925.

Conclusion

Finke and Stark end their book with this key rhetorical question: "When hell is gone, can heaven's departure be far behind?"[63] The denial of hell—point four of the biblical covenant model, sanctions—is the primary confession of covenant-breaking modern man. This denial has been theological modernism's most important doctrine, just as it has been modern science's.[64]

The decline of conservatism in Presbyterianism was intimately connected to the unwillingness of conservatives to screen access to the pulpit and the ministry in terms of the doctrine of hell. By the 1920's, those ministers who had rejected the doctrine of hell had ceased to be interested in preaching the Westminster Confession's way of salvation. The Presbyterian Church conformed to Finke and Stark's suggestion.

The authors also draw an inference from the history of American religion. If we view improvements in theology as inherently liberal improvements (as good liberals believe this must be), their conclusions seem consistent with the data. "In this book the history of American religion is the history of human actions and human organizations, not the history of ideas (refined or otherwise). But this is not to say that we regard theology as unimportant. To the contrary, we shall argue repeatedly that religious organizations can thrive only to the extent that they have a theology that can comfort souls and motivate sacrifice. In a sense, then, we are urging an underlying model of religious

---

61. Cited in Finke and Stark, *Churching of America*, p. 238.
62. Madison, p. 655.
63. Finke and Stark, *Churching of America*, p. 249.
64. Gary North, *Is the World Running Down? Crisis in the Christian Worldview* (Tyler, Texas: Institute for Christian Economics, 1988), ch. 2.

history that is the exact opposite of that based on progress through theological refinement. We shall present compelling evidence that theological refinement is the kind of progress that results in organizational bankruptcy."[65]

If they are correct, then for Calvinist theology to do more than survive in tiny denominations, Calvinists must find a way to match any proposed theological refinements with both the comforting of souls and the sacrificial motivation of the laity. Problem: it is easy—confessionally, financially, and liturgically—to be a member of a Calvinist denomination. The denomination calls upon its pastors (and their wives) to do most of the sacrificing. In this sense, Calvinism long ago adopted what would become the ecclesiastical legacy of post-Vatican II Roman Catholicism: high academic standards and low pay for ministers, but hardly anything demanded from the laity. Roman Catholicism began an historically unprecedented rapid decline in 1966, the year after Vatican II ended: declines in attendance, giving, and new priests and nuns.[66] This does not bode well for Calvinism.

---

65. Finke and Stark, *Churching of America*, p. 5.
66. *Ibid.*, pp. 259–61.

Scripture Index

Genesis
1:1   60, 71

Exodus
18   125, 960

Leviticus
10:1-7   288n
25   726
25: 44-46   125, 131, 132

Numbers
3:6-9   42
3:10   42

Deuteronomy
8:17   47
8:18   48
31:9-13   42

Joshua
24:13   48

I Kings
18:40   6

II Chronicles
34:14-21   974

Nehemiah
8:13   42

Psalms
2   xlii-xliii
106:13-15   881
106:15   756
127:3-5   850

Proverbs
13:22   48
20:17   756, 884
127:3-5   850

Jeremiah
7:4   775
15:10-11   xi

Ezekiel
13:10   49

Daniel
2:37-45   159
8   159

Matthew
10:28   40
16:19   44

18:15-18	125		12:19	41
20:16	45			
27:62-64	30		**I Corinthians**	
28:18-20	92, 114		3:12-15	74
			11:29-30	43, 515
Mark			12	758
7:10	158		15:45	148
Luke			**II Corinthians**	
4:18-21	125		3:3	203
9:62	xxx		3:12-15	74
12:47-48	44, 764, 960		5:17-18	74
14:28-30	xxx			
16:18	881		**Galatians**	
16:22-28	40		1:6-11	286
16:28	41			
20:37	158		**Ephesians**	
24:27	158		2:8-9	45
24:44	158			
			Philippians	
John			2:12	74
1:12	45			
2:6	729		**Colossians**	
3:36	40		1:16	728
5:18	729			
13:15	729		**I Timothy**	
18:19-21	841		1:10	124
			4:1-2	773n
Acts				
5:29	726		**James**	
15	960		1:22-24	xxx
			2:10	225
Romans				
2:14-15	38		**I Peter**	
9:10-13	228		4:17	52
9:11-13	55			

I John
2:3-4   52

Revelation
20:14   45
20:14-15   41, 78, 79, 301, 904

Index

abolitionism
    "Arminianism" &, 288
    Bourne case, 123–27
    Old School, 128, 130–36, 338
    post-war General Assembly, 133–34
    Progressivists' roots, 327
    revivalism &, 112
    "rights of man," 288
    Unitarian, 113, 125, 135
    Wilberforce, William, 129
    see also slavery
abortion, 229, 850, 911, 961
academic freedom, 812–17, 840, 882, 927, 962
accreditation, 585, 951, 963
Act of Uniformity (1662), 100
action & reaction (strategy), 896–97
Adam, 148, 215
Adams, Herbert, 312
Adams, William, 138, 140
adiaphora, 128, 130–38, 338, 927
administrative law
    Berman's warning, 711
    centralization, 337
    executive independence, 313
    Form of Government (1934), 711–13, 723
    General Assembly's power, 930–31, 936–37
    Machen's suspension, 315
    overrides presbyteries, 724–25
    theology of power, 723
Adopting Act (1729), 199, 260, 369, 535
adultery, 88, 835n
advertising, xxvi, 769
alchemy (Isaac Newton), 105
Aldrich, Nelson (Senator), 855
Alexander, Maitland, 538–42, 733
Alinsky, Saul D., 896–97
Allis, O. T., 158n, 631, 637, 739–40
Althusius, Johannes, xlvii–xlviii
American Revolution, 105–8
amillennialism, 638, 953, 967
amnesia of the South, 128
Anabaptists, 24, 900, 907
Anderson, Walter, 445
Andover Seminary, 131–32, 194, 816
Antichrist, 979
antinomianism, 53, 595
apologetics
    Greene, 337–38
    Machen, 593, 777, 792–93

neutrality, 777
Old School (dualism), 761
Princeton Seminary, 174–75, 195, 589–90, 593–94, 761, 793
Princeton University, 184
Princeton's Chair of Apologetics, 603–4
Schaeffer, 1002–3
Warfield, 587–88
see also Van Til
apostasy, 24, 510–11, 741–42
Apostles (Cambridge University), 664n
Apostles' Creed, 493, 503, 520
Appomattox, 128
apprenticeship, 765–67, 958–59, 964
arbitrary law enforcement, 12–13
Arianism (Speer defends), 727
Arminianism
abolitionism &, 288
Bryan, 462
conservative, 90–91
missions (1801–37), 968
misusing words, 287
revivalism, 950, 952–53
works in salvation, 89
Arminius, Jacob, 54–55
Armstrong, William, 166–67
Athanasius, 38
atheists' club (Union Seminary), 804
Athens, 964
atonement, 89, 317–18 (see also salvation, soteriology)
Auburn *Affirmation*
authority issue, 549
conscience, 545–46, 697–98
crossed fingers, 535
deceivers and deceived, 534
escaped sanctions, 549
five points of modernism, 545-48
judicial issue, 550
liberty, 697–98, 707
Machen on, 534, 549, 625, 687–89, 737
number of signers, 535
proof of infiltration, 534
statute of limitations, 735–37
"theories," 545
toleration, 536
Augustine, 224, 450
authority
appeals court system, 725
Bible or history, 150
bottom-up, 524, 727
Church bureaucrat's, 853–54
conscience vs. Church, 710–11, 771–73 (see also conscience)
debates over, 149
economic & judicial, 967
flow of funds (see flow of funds: authority, sovereignty)
follow the money, 968
General Assembly (see General Assembly: authority)
inerrancy &, 149–50
mixed signals, 710
money &, 957, 959
poverty &, 959
power &, 47
presbytery, 830–31
reform needed, 959
robes (see robes)
sanctions, 127, 149, 594
schizophrenic (1927–33), 710

self-authenticating, 150
seminaries, 564, 591–93
source of, 149–50
top-down (tyranny), 725
voice of (representation), 930
Westminster Confession's, 912
autonomy, 47, 435, 514, 772–73
awakening (collegiate), 866–67

Bacon, Benjamin, 162–63
bait & hook, 614–18, 919
bait & switch, 618–20
Bank of England, 335
Banner of Truth Trust, 975
baptism
    Anabaptists, 24, 956
    communicant, 956
    creed &, 24, 956
    Donatism, 23–24, 956
    halfway covenant, 101–2
    oath, 24–25, 522, 956
    oath-sign, 956
    Presbyterian, 901
    sacrament, 43
Baptists, 109–10, 162, 531, 876, 950, 952, 972, 1014–17
Barnes, Albert, 198, 283, 291, 806
    Arminian, 116–17, 121
    Modernists' appeal to, 120–21, 283
    reunion (1870), 120
    trials, 117–18
    Union Director, 198
Barnhouse, Donald Grey, 423, 645, 738
Barrows, Elijah, 132
Barth, Karl, 50n, 88, 204, 334, 639–41, 750, 861, 996

Bartlett, Dr. (biting dog story), 255–56
Beck v. Bell, 447
Becker, Carl, xiv
Beecher, Willis, 174–75
Bennett, John C., 475, 861
Berman, Harold, 711
Best, Nolan, 527, 543
Bible
    attack on (see higher criticism)
    Auburn *Affirmation*, 546
    authority, 149–50, 157
    autographs, 218–19
    Briggs on, 216–221
    creeds &, 100, 827–28, 910
    Darwinism vs., 149
    equality with = inferior to, 910
    fundamental law, 150, 826
    higher criticism (see higher criticism)
    higher critics (Presbyterian), 157
    historicism &, 154–57
    infallible?, 5, 266 (see also higher criticism, inerrency)
    inspiration of, 157 (see also higher criticism)
    Jesus' view, 158
    law & flux (solution to), 154
    precedence over, 910
    presuppositions, 164–68
    Re-Thinking Missions, 667–68
    Revised Version (1881), 163–64
    slavery (Old School), 123–25, 129, 134, 290
    social order, 847

symbols, 160
Unitarians, 135
Westminster Confession, 56–57, 157, 195
Bible Presbyterian Church, 20, 1000
Bible Union of China, 411
biblical theology, 160, 762–63
Big Bang, 79, 226n
Birth of a Nation, 187
bishops, 298, 321, 818–19, 836, 961, 977–78, 980
Bligh, Captain, 782
bloodguilt, 511–12
Board of Foreign Missions
  anti-Doctrinal Deliverance, 499
  defense of, 691–93, 705
  ecumenical, 870–71
  funding of, 863–66
  Machen attacks, 687–89, 691–93
  McIntire's booklet (1935), 727–30
  model of independent board, 313
  Re-Thinking Missions, 677
  success indicators manipulated, 854–55
  why so vulnerable to liberalism, 863
  see also Buck, missions, Speer
boards
  annual confession requirement, 917
  anti-conservative (1923), 499
  authority, 930
  chain of command, 927–30
  Church hierarchy, 364, 852
  consolidation, 363–64, 409, 423–24, 644, 882
  flow of funds, 366–68, 853, 716–17, 852–55
  histories of (none), xlv
  Hodge vs. Thornwell, 928–29
  inclusivists, 425
  institutional goal, 849, 854
  missions (see Board of Foreign Missions)
  monitoring, xlv, 849–51
  not integrated into government, 852, 927–30
  presbyteries &, 932–33, 968–69
  Princeton Seminary, 603–5, 622–23, 626, 630–35
  reform of, 932, 969
  reorganization (1908), 363–68
  representation, 934
  rules, 969–70
  self-appointed, 541, 928
  success indicators, 849–51
  tenure, 930
  weak theology, 425
Bohr, Niels, 378
Book of Discipline, 508
Bourne, George, 123–27, 129, 145
Bowden, Henry, xxxi
Bowne, Borden P., 275
Brandeis, Louis, 446
Breckenridge, Robert, 119–20, 928
Briggs, Charles Augustus
  academic degrees (none), 169
  American Presbyterianism (1885), 203
  anti-boundaries, 204
  anti-Calvinism, 208

anti-Confession, 222, 224–25
anti-creation, 222, 224
anti-creeds, 236, 243
anti-hierarchy, 235–36
anti-Pauline, 205
anti-sanctions, 198–99, 230
bad faith, 232
Bible's errors, 216–21, 242
Biblical Study (1883), 202–3, 217
certitude, 202, 204
"civil war," 249
claims immunity, 260
cleared by Presbytery, 257
confession (1906), 280
Confession vs. Confession, 261, 315
Confessional revision, 176, 206
Congregationalism, 236
conversion, 168–69
covenant theology, 207–8
creation, 222
defenders, 266
de-frocked (1893), 264
dialecticism, 211–16
doctrine, 212
double jeopardy, 265
ecclesiology, 236
ecumenism, 215, 235, 276–81
employment at Union, 198
evolutionist, 223–24
experientialism, 169–70, 204
five points of modernism, 208–38
Fosdick &, 477
front man, 816
German theology, 226
hell, 227–35

heretical, 205, 208, 253
higher criticism, 200–2, 216 20, 241–44
hounding, 255–56
immunity, 191, 244
importance, 207
Inaugural Address (1891), 239–44, 252–54
infants, 227–30
irenical?, 211, 221, 239, 241, 251
Jahveh, 213
judicial strategy, 220
Kantian, 212, 214
lies, 231–32, 237–38
Love, 280
lower criticism, 165
McGiffert &, 269
messianic rhetoric, 197
modernism as *Zeitgeist* (spirit of age), 280
modernism's five points, 208–38
mysticism, 204, 212
New York Presbytery clears, 191, 261–62
Orwellian newspeak, 279–80
patriarchs, 241
Patton &, 255
point man, 177, 200, 249–50
Presbyterian Review, 261 (see also *Presbyterian Review*)
process theology, 316
progress, 238
ratchet (heresy), 250, 260
reason, 204, 243
Reformers as higher critics, 217–18
rhetoric (see Briggs' rhetoric)

rights, not toleration demanded, 260
Roman Catholicism, 246
second defense, 260-62
sense of destiny, 197, 249
strategy of subversion, 178-79
subscription, 260-61
tactics, 198, 219
theology of (five points), 207-38
theology the real threat, 180
truth, 204, 212
victory in 1900?, 345
Whither? (1889), 207, 239
Briggs case (no precedent), 266
Briggs' rhetoric
    cause of de-frocking, 179-80
    deception, 208, 215, 224, 237-38, 280
    escalating (1883-1909), 202-5, 250-51
    forces a decision on Church, 257
    Inaugural Address (1891), 241-44
    modern critics (mild), 245
    personal attacks, 239
    three stages, 281-82
    Union Seminary's assessment, 247
British Navy, 825
broad Church, 361-62
Brookings Institution, 485-86
Brookings, Robert, 485-86
Brown, William Adams, 229, 248, 253, 787
Brunner, Emil, 751
Bryan, Charles, 458
Bryan, William Jennings
    anti-Darwinism motion (1923), 497, 500-1
    anti-elite, 335
    anti-eugenics, 453-56
    archetype fundamentalist, 83
    Arminian, 462
    attacks on, 431-42, 470
    cross of gold, 457-58
    "Cross of Silver," 567
    Cumberland Presbyterian Church, 458
    Darrow &, 461
    Darwinism in Presbyterian Colleges, 501
    death of, 463, 574-75
    democracy, 459
    fair fight called for, 427, 439
    fear of water, 458
    five-toed horse, 457
    Fosdick &, 476
    General Assembly (1925), 565
    humanism of, 459-60
    In His Image, 428-29, 456, 531
    income, 457
    leadership, 820
    liberal ministers, 427
    loser, 458
    "medieval" (Fosdick), 476
    Mencken's description, 574, 944-45
    Moderator candidate (lost), 496-97
    neutrality doctrine, 439
    New York Times, 427-28, 436-37, 904-5
    not six-day creation, 461
    one victory (anti-liquor), 530
    politics of, 329, 529-30
    politics of plunder, 460, 468

Populist, 329, 457, 469, 530, 573
public schools, 436–41, 467–69
radical, 458–60, 530
rhetoric, 457
Scopes trial, 572–74
social gospel leaders, 459
sorcerer's apprentice, 468
state legislatures, 430
Unitarian public schools defended, 440
Buck, Pearl S., 422, 658–60, 663–64, 677–78, 688, 690–91, 772
Buck v. Bell, 446–47
Buckley, William F., 376n
budget (Executive Commission), 367, 399–403
Bureau of Social Hygiene, 377
bureaucracy
apprenticeship vs., 765–67
budget cuts, 919–20
capture of, 321–22
chain of command, 968
Church & State, 350
Church as model, 845, 851–52
competitors, 848
control over, 313, 854
credentials, 766
de-fund, 932
democracy vs., 333
dominant, 844
Executive Commission (1908), 313, 344, 366–67, 399–403
explanations of scandals, 938
flow of funds, 848–49, 932–33
foundations, 380
impersonal, 845, 851
information non-symmetrical, 851
law of, 812
management, 823–24, 848
Mises on, 847–48
modernism, 904
non-profit organizations, 849
paralysis of, 904
rent-seeking, 879, 883
reorganization (1908), 313, 365, 849
reorganization (1923–24), 501–2
responsibility-avoiding, 822
sanctions, 851, 919–20
secrecy, 822–23
shadow, 367
teacher's immunity, 845
university as model, 845
Weber on, 844
Burke, Edmund, 846
Bush, George, 375, 662
Bush, Prescott, 662
Buswell, J. Oliver, 744, 747
Butler, Charles, 240–41
Butler, Nicholas Murray, 431–32

Cain, 673
Calvin, John
church membership, 47n
Church's marks, 42–43
excommunication, 44n, 515–16
Institutes, 965
Lord's Supper weekly, 768
Loyola &, 803n
sacrament, 52–53
State oaths, 907
Calvinism
anti-"common sense," 761
atonement, 85

central doctrines, 89
Church (marks of), 42–43, 891–94
comprehensive worldview, 55
exclusivist, 371
five points, 54–56
four-point, 65, 353–54, 356, 425
"iron thing," 146
judicial representation, 148
oath &, 957
Old School Presbyterianism, 89
particular redemption, 355
Progressives &, 327–8
Trinitarian, 89
capitalist ideal, 759–60
Carnegie Steel, 855
Carnell, Edward, 232n, 233n
Carney, Mabel, 1021
cartels, 859–62, 883, 1020
Carter, Jimmy, 137, 884n
castor oil, 147
casuistry, 105
catechisms, 21, 23, 25, 351–52, 972
Catholic Church (see Roman Catholicism)
cease-fire, xx
censorship, 627–28
centralization (see administrative law, bureaucracy)
cesspool (German education), 583
chain of command, 499, 594, 824, 927, 959, 968
Chalmers, Thomas, 232
charity, 443–44, 455

Charles I, 976, 980, 990, 991, 992–93
Charles II, 100, 993
Chautauqua, 433–34
checks, 955
chef analogy (historicism), 153
Chesterton, G. K., xii, xv, 447
China, 409–14, 422–23, 653, 659–60, 689, 850, 875
Christendom
  abandoned, 135, 137, 138, 937
  Bryan &, 468
  lost in World War I, 937
  Machen's view, 770
  radical Republicans, 135
  resurrection of, 939
  Schaff's ecumenism, 234–35
  to humanism, il
Christian Century, xvii, 344, 354, 657–58
Christian Reformed Church, 356
Christian Right, 755
chronology: Egypt vs. Bible, 159
Church
  apostate, 24, 325
  authority, 877
  Briggs on, 235–37
  bureaucracy's model, 845
  conscience &, 770–73
  definition, 1923, 513
  dilemma, 771
  discipline, 102–3
  divisions, 1720's, 99
  ecumenism, 859–62
  education &, 765–67
  Enlightenment's models, 846
  established, 440
  excommunication, 709–10

fellowship, 520
fragmentation, 771
fundamental law, 150, 155
government, xvi–xvii
government structures, xvi–xvii, 817–27
growth, xvii, 581, 883, 911, 916, 948–49, 1011–16
growth vs. confession, 911
hierarchy (see chain of command, hierarchy, representation)
kingdom &, 5
liturgy, 876
lowest common denominator (see lowest common denominator)
marks of, 42–43, 52, 895–96
membership, 11–12, 47, 87, 101, 521, 922, 955–57
New England, 440
non–profit, 849
oath (see oath)
political club (Machen), 900
politics, 564
reform, 919–20
rural, 1017–22
sanctions (see sanctions)
scandals, 853–54
screening & colleges, 767
sovereignty of, 5
splits, 911
State &, 901–2, 978, 979, 996
tax-funded, 440
toleration (see tolerance)
two nations inside, 590
voluntary, 887, 891
vulnerability, 917
wages, 1014–15

Church Union (1920), 403–7
circuit riders, 1014
citizenship, 86
Civil Service, 853, 930
Clark, Gordon, xv–xvi
Clarke, John, 433–34
Clarke, William, 192–93
classical civilization, xiii–xiv
Cleveland, Grover, 186, 328–29, 339, 457, 460
climate of opinion, 316, 799, 899, 915
Clinton, Bill, 665
Coffin, Henry Sloane
    Auburn *Affirmation*, 543
    challenge to try him (1923), 503–4
    Edinburgh Conference, 373
    family background, 374
    Fox's deathbed, 754–55
    Laymen's Missionary Movement, 872
    ordination in 1900, 304
    predecessor, 303
    strategist, 504–5
    victory in 1924, 559
    "we won't leave!," 504, 568
    "we will leave!," 566
Coffin, William, 504
College of New Jersey, 107–8
College of Wooster, 496–97
colleges, 765–66, 962–63
Collins, Anthony, 163
Columbia Seminary, 270–74, 632
Columbia Teachers College, 1021
Columbia University, 431, 473, 659
Committee of Eight, 563–64

Committee of Fifteen, 566–68, 575
common ground (see apologetics, methodology)
Common Market, 395
confession
   adiaphora problem, 908–9
   Arian, 523
   authority of, 828
   baptism &, 956
   Briggs, 250
   Congregational, 522
   conscience, 908–9
   content of, 522–23
   crossed fingers (see crossed fingers)
   debate over, 4
   defined, 8n
   faculty &, 917
   formal act vs. content, 27
   hidden, 314
   institutional standard, 835
   laymen, 522, 524
   lowest common denominator, 359, 362–63, 523, 893, 896, 910–11
   mental reservations, 578
   neutrality-pluralism, 532
   oath, 43
   official vs. unofficial, 315
   progressive, 206, 908
   protection, 11
   psychologically necessary, 902–3, 904
   ramp, 30
   revision, 5, 30–31, 155–56, 891, 931
   role of, 5, 922
   sanctions, 315, 503, 523
   speed limit analogy, 156
   true faith, 902
   Unitarian, 524
   unity, 524
   see also Westminster Confession
conflict & sanctions, 6
Congregationalism, 99, 111–12, 117, 119, 236
Conklin, E. G., 451–53
conscience
   Auburn *Affirmation*, 545–46, 697–98
   autonomy &, 772-73
   Church &, 710–11, 771–73
   creedal progress, 908
   liberals', 341, 773
   oath &, 908–9
   Westminster Confession, 57–58, 707, 908
consecration & culture, 35–36
conservatism
   Arminian, 90–91
   Calvinist, 90
   ignoring the Confession, 314
   judicial strategy, 322–24
   see also strategy: conservative
conservatives
   buffer, 705
   caring for wounded, 296
   Church (marks of), 894–95
   control over courts, 319
   creationism, 897
   crossed fingers, 897, 923
   defensive strategy, xl–xli, 540, 542, 544, 624, 632–32, 799
   heresy trials, 388, 903–4
   ignorant, 776
   judicial strategy, 322–24

leadership, 544
legal precedents, 320
marbles, 754
moral mid-ground, 897–98
naive, 636
offense-less (1923), 540
political involvement, xxi
post-Cumberland, 370–71
rallies (1923), 537, 542
rhetoric, 461, 540, 734
rhetoric only, 540, 734
rhetorical gestures, 323
sacraments, 895
sanctions, 539, 560, 889
short-sighted, 773–74
shrinking forces, 540
six-day creation (see creationism)
social action, xxi
spokesmen, not leaders, 544
stalemate mentality, xli
surrender by, 779, 791
tasks in 1923, 503
Ten Commandments, 320
time ran out (1935), 735
unorganized, 544
votes (insufficient), 539, 541
Whigs, 320
will to resist, 266, 269–76, 326, 383–84, 539, 568, 897, 900
women elders, 407–8, 644, 909–10
conspiracy history, xlii–xliii
conspiracy (modernism), 803
constitutionalism
    checks & balances, 330
    debate, 5
    hidden, 312–13
    oath, 899

    United States, 13–14, 106
    Westminster Confession, 825–27
    Wilson on, 312
contention, 508, 842
contractualism, xlvii–xlviii
controversy, 45, 579
cook analogy (historicism), 153
Coray, Henry, 744–75
cosmic personalism, 148–49, 153
Cotton, John, 986n
Couch, W. T., 814
Council on Foreign Relations, 553
counterfeiting, xxxvi
covenant
    civil, 106
    debate over, 889
    defined, xxviii, 85–88
    five points (see five points of covenantalism)
    history, xlii, xlvii
    lawsuit, 384–86
    marriage, 86
    model, 53–54
    oath, 54, 85, 551
covenantalism (see five points of covenantalism)
Covenanters, 532
Craig, James, 252
Craig, Samuel, 636, 644–45, 693, 740, 782
creatio ex nihilo, 224–26
creationism
    age-day (Hodge), 61
    authority &, 149
    battle over law, 149
    Briggs vs., 224
    crossed fingers, 897

law &, 149, 226
Machen, 900, 905–6
no defenders, 370
Princeton, 223, 226, 301, 905–6
process theology vs., 226, 897 (see also process theology)
public schools, 441, 467
Westminster Confession, 223–24
credentialism, 765–67
creed
apostasy &, 24
baptism &, 24, 956
Bible vs?, 100
Briggs vs., 236, 243
Church growth, xvii
church membership, 521
Church of England, 693
confession &, 8n, 827
evolution &, 75–77
experiential religion's view, 53
fallible, 578
gnosticism &, 51
illusion of, 694–95
judicial religion, 53
limited, 31
Lord's Supper, 43
Machen's dilemma, 512, 693–94
oath, 523
organization, 27
politics &, 770
power religion's view, 53
process vs., 75
progress, 156
purpose of, 536n
revision, 298, 827–28
role of, 922

sanctions &, 199, 492, 695
Swing's view, 181–82
see also confession
Cromwell, Oliver
Banner of Truth, 975
episcopacy, 979
failure of, xlviii
Independent, 989
military genius, 989
Rump Parliament, 992
toleration of religion, 976, 994
victories, 991
Crosby, Bing, 1013
Cross, John, 4
crossed fingers
Auburn *Affirmation*, 535
conservatives, 346, 584, 596–98, 892, 906, 923
counter effects of, 325–26
inheritance &, 326
Jamison's account, 19
Lehman (1923), 503
Machen (1903 revision), 892, 906–7
modernists, 326
New School vs. Old School, 357
Old School (1903), 354–58
orthodox Church, 512
paralysis &, 91
presbyteries, 370
reducing (3 ways), 297–99
strict subscription, 909
today (creationism), 907–8
Union Seminary, 245
universal practice, 19–20, 297
Crossed Fingers
background of, xxiv–xxv, xxvii–xxx

goals of, xix–xx, xxx–xxxiv,
  li, 20
monograph, x–xi
questions, xxi–xxiv
strategy manual, xx
theme, xviii–xix, xxxi–xxxvi
Crunden Robert, 327–28
culture, 35, 49
Cumberland Presbyteries, 358-
  59, 363
Curtis, Edward, 252, 275

Dabney, Robert, 139, 271, 760,
  761n–762n, 929
Darrow, Clarence, 438, 573
Darwin, Charles
  anti-charity, 454
  Galton &, 454
  isms, 761
  Lyell, 62
  politics &, 330
Darwinism
  Bible vs., 149
  Bryan vs., Chapter 7, 497
  eugenics, 442–46
  free market (social), 326, 327
  higher criticism, 192–93
  historicism, 152–53, 761
  joint idols, 151
  laws against, 429–30
  Nietzsche &, 463
  public schools, 467–68
  reform (social), 326–27, 846–
    47
  social gospel &, 80
  time frames, 301
  triumph, 915
  two forms, 67–68

  undermined Protestantism,
    899
Davidson, A. B., 201
Davidson, Samuel, 200
Davis, Angela, 938–39
Day, Thomas, 283
decentralization, 420–22
deconstruction, 153
decree, 214
democracy, 294
  anti-oath, 324
  bluegrass (Kentucky educa-
    tion), 429–30
  Bryan's faith in, 459
  bureaucracy vs., 333
  Church & State, 325
  elite, 332
  evolution issue, 332, 432
  General Will, 316–17, 332
  method, 325
  modernism's god, 316
  New York Times vs. 432
  open-ended, 324n, 332
  reigning religion, 294
Democratic Party, 328–29, 377,
  458
dialecticism, 211–216, 481, 724
Digest (church law), 743–44
discipline in Church, 712 (see
  also sanctions)
dispensationalism, 118n, 137
division of labor, 850
divorce, 86, 87
Dixon, Thomas, 168
Doctrinal Deliverance (1910)
  dead letter, 390
  five points, 369, 567
  Fosdick case, 498, 558

fundamentalist, 23, 370, 372
no sanctions, 716
ordination candidates only, 719
re-enacted periodically, 389, 716
renounced (1927), 611
rhetoric, 551
Social, 371–72
unenforceable, 558
doctrine
below certification, 601
central to Old School, 768–69
Church growth &, 767–72
denied regarding discipline (liberals), 736
Machen on Princeton, 635
Presbyterian conflict (Machen), 726, 735, 776
Re-Thinking Missions, 668–69
Speer denigrates, 345–46
dogma, 34, 170, 251
dominion, 28–29, 46, 49
Donatism, 23–24, 956
Dort (Synod), 54
double jeopardy, 265, 613, 710, 831–32
doubt (methodological), 169
doubt (rhetorical), 202
doubt (strategy), 827
dry rot, 862–63
dualism, xiv
Duhem, Pierre, 434–35
Dulles, Alan, 252, 552, 553, 555
Dulles, Eleanor, 553
Dulles, John Foster, xxi, 552–57, 566, 774
Dulles, Joseph Welsh, 793
Durant Will, xxvi, 77–78

dust-eating, 950–54

Earp, Wyatt, 339n
Eastern mysticism (missions), 667
ecclesiology (see Church)
ecumenism
alliance only (Machen), 602
Auburn *Affirmation*, 547–48
basis of unity?, 80–81
breakdown, 860–61
Briggs, 276–81
bureaucracies' agenda, 400, 407
cartel, 859–62
church growth &, 1011–12
Church Union (1920), 403–7
Committee on Church Cooperation (1903), 407
"ecumenical" (1900) 305
Edinburgh Conference, 373
flow of funds problem, 860
foreign missions &, 305–6
Interchurch World Movement, 393, 400
liturgy vs., 876
modernism, 80
New School, 117
New York Conference (1900), 305–6
Princeton Seminary vs., 64
Re-Thinking Missions, 673–74
Rockefeller money, 391
Schaff, Philip, 234–35
stalled, 1950's, 883
theology vs., 870–71
threat to (1933), 704–5
World War I, 391–92
Eddy, Sherwood, 873–74
Edinburgh Conference, 373

education
    accreditation, 466, 963
    assault on, 465
    catechism vs., 972
    certification over doctrine, 601
    chain of command, 927
    compulsory, 437, 525
    denominational colleges, 962–63
    dust-eating, 950–54
    ecumenical bridge (degree), 590
    Establishment, 440–41
    flow of funds, 433–34, 436–41, 465
    General Education Board, 465–67, 585
    Old School's faith in, 590
    politics of plunder, 438–40
    presbyterial control, 931–32
    public schools' true goal, 525
    Puritans, 439–40
    Riley on, 464–65
    South, 467
    vulnerability, 917, 923, 927
    see also academic freedom, seminaries
Egypt (chronology), 159
Eisenhower, Dwight, xxi
elders
    hierarchy of power, 839
    two-tier, 22–23, 584, 819–20, 958–59, 964
    weakness of ruling elders, 837–38
    women, 407–8, 644, 909–10
elect infant, 63
electron, xiv
Elijah, 6

elite, 47, 68, 326, 332, 435–36, 438, 579, 949
Ely, Richard T., 312, 459
emotion, 98 (see also experiential religion)
empty pews, 504
Enlightenment, 337, 759, 846
entropy, 79
environmentalism, 788–91
episcopacy, 817–19
Episcopal Church, 276, 337, 531, 876
equal time, 92, 173–74, 628 (see also pluralism)
Erastianism, 988
Erastians, 983, 986
Erdman, Charles
    Committee of Fifteen, 568
    inclusivist, 551
    Machen &, 551, 569, 576, 605–7, 609–10, 621
    Moderator in 1925, 565–66
Erikson, Kai, 299n
Esau, 55, 228, 317
eschatology
    amillennialism, 638
    fundamentalism, 914
    Princeton's, 63–64
    Progressivism's, 349–50, 798–99
    social gospel, 1010
    unresolved, 908n
    see also amillennialism, postmillennialism, premillennialism
Establishment
    Bryan's threat, 468
    Buck, Pearl, 660

eugenics, 442–49
 families, 664
 islands, 787–88
 liberal, 663
 Machen &, 488, 665
 Machen vs., 791
 public schools, 440–41
 Skull & Bones, 376
 Straight family, 661–64
 van Dyke, 382, 507
ethics
 apologetics &, 590
 power religion, 47
 rival views, 323–24
 sin, 225–26
 situation, 75, 226, 232, 326
 Westminster Confession, 57–58
etiquette, 232, 513, 564, 833–34, 836
eugenics
 abandoned, 453
 charity as bad, 443–44
 Nordic supremacy, 442–46
 Progressivism, 445–56
 sterilization, 452
evolution
 changing law, 221
 doctrine, 668–69
 ethics, 669–71
 higher criticism &, 74
 highest truth, 332
 history & nature, 152–53, 221–22
 religion's, 456
 see also Darwin, Darwinism
evolutionism
 anti-democracy, 432
 Barthianism, 639–41
 elite directs, 435–36, 438 (see also planning)
 final judgment, 22–22, 77, 224
 flow of funds, 436–41
 higher criticism &, 159–60
 Kentucky debate, 431–36
 Kidd, Benjamin, 870
 law, 149
 Princeton Seminary, 223, 236
 progress, 435
 public schools, 429–41
 relativism, 221–22
 religion &, 456
 Woodrow case, 270–74
examinations, 333–34, 590–91, 959 (see also ordination)
exclusivism, 16, 81, 308, 371
excommunication
 administrative power, 726
 authority, 709–10
 creed &, 26
 experientialism &, 27
 final judgment &, 318
 judicial issue, 514
 modernists deny, 318
 "obedience, not theology," 726
 organizations &, 26
 suspension &, 736–37
 theology &, 318, 726
 ultimate negative sanction, 44
 see also sanctions
Executive Commission, 313, 344, 366–67, 399–403, 409, 615, 961
experience, 85, 88, 101, 147, 204
experiential religion
 accountability, 28

alliance with power religion, 775
antinomian, 53
anti-confession, 25–26
anti-culture, 49
anti-power, 49
anti-responsibility, 28, 49–50
Briggs, 168–70
church membership, 87
confessions as acts, 27–28
cultural irrelevance, 31
excommunication &, 27
gnosticism, 50–51
Greene attacks, 98
halfway covenant, 101–2
liberals &, 16, 18
Machen on, 26
naive, 25–26
New England, 100–2
New School, 3, 292
New Side, 3, 117
peace-seeking, 18, 31, 49, 581
peace terms, 94
pietism, 16
propositional truth, 50
secularization &, 113
separatist or inclusivist, 51
summary, 16
tracts, 581
see also pietism
expulsion (New School), 119–20
"extreme" conservatives, 567, 568, 571, 601, 607, 634, 641n, 681–82

Fabian Society, 660
faith (marks of), 5
Faith Seminary, 999
fat lady, 843, 902

fatherhood of God, 215, 673, 681
Federal Council of Churches
   Erdman &, 386
   Presbyterian Church, Progressivism, 347, 371–72, 650
   Roberts &, 349–50
   Rockefeller &, 336
   social creed, 347
   Speer &, 347
   Stevenson &, 386
federal theology, 148
feeling, 98
feelings, 85, 86–87
Ferguson, Adam, 151
final judgment
   escape from (modernism), 222–23
   infant damnation, 227–30
   intermediate state, 230–31, 233
   Larger Catechism, 301–2
   redemption, 318
   rival views, 324
   see also hell
Finke, Roger, 1008–23
Finney, Charles, 111–12, 118–19
first among equals (pastor), 819, 820, 836–38
First Great Awakening, 104
five points of covenantalism, 889–91
   Bible, 53–54
   Calvinism, 54–56
   evangelicalism/fundamentalism, 64–66
   missions (modernism), 666–75
   modernism, 66, 70–81, 208–238, 478–82, 545–48, 805–8
   Princeton Seminary, 60–64

Westminster Confession, 56–60
flag, 892
flat earth, 432, 441
flow of funds
  authority, xx, 401, 877, 959
  away from liberalism, xx
  boards, 853, 854
  bureaucracy, 932–33
  church structure, 955
  competing claims, 852
  control, 522
  declining, 891
  ecumenism, 860
  Executive Commission (1920), 401, 403
  Form of Government (1934), 716–20, 724, 878–79
  General Assembly, 853
  Machen's view, 511
  management systems, 848–49
  missions, 696, 704, 864–66, 872–73
  moral claim on money, 878
  oath, 700
  politics of plunder, 439–40
  power &, 518, 839
  power religion, 717
  public schools, 433–34, 436–41
  rent-seeking monopolies, 876–79
  restructuring (1908), 366–68
  sacrament, 890, 893
  sacramental, 716–20
  sacred principle (liberals), 704
  sanctions, 800, 878
  theology (liberals), 776, 800–1
  voluntary, 852

follow the money, 339–40, 663, 876, 955, 968
Foreword Movement, 871–72, 873
forgery (Bible), 159
formula, 840
Fosdick, Harry Emerson
  anti-Apostles' Creed, 492
  anti-Calvinist, 472
  anti-creeds, 493
  anti-hell, 472
  Bible & Koran, 480
  Briggs' ploy, 476–77
  Bryan &, 476
  cleared by NY Presbytery, 557–58
  continuing revelation, 480
  creative power, 47–48
  creeds without sanctions, 492
  Dulles &, 556–57
  five points of modernism, 479–82
  fundamentalists &, 478
  higher criticism, 477
  income, 474–75
  influence, 471–72
  invited to join Church, 558–59
  John the Baptist to Peale, 756
  Lee, Ivy, 491
  "liberals are more religious," 559
  lie about Rockefeller's backing, 484
  Lippmann &, 493–94
  Machen &, 527n
  memorial services, 474
  modernism's five points, 478–82

oath, 558
Peale &, 756
positive thinking, 472
rhetoric, 477, 482–83, 559–60, 904–5
Rockefeller Foundation, 473
ruling elders vs., 498–99
sanctions, 491–92, 708
science, 480–81
"Shall the Fundamentalists Win?", 478–84, 488, 491
suicide attempt (student), 472
symbol of apostasy, 559
tolerance, 491–92
train schedule, 557
"vegetarian meat packer," 493
virgin birth, 479
Fosdick, Raymond
  "bag man," 379
  career, 484–86
  Rockefeller's agent, 340, 376–77, 379, 654
  theology of, 487
  Wilson &, 473
Foster, John, 552–53
Foulkes, William, 392–93, 498
foundations, 380
Fox, John, 359–60, 369, 385, 754–55
Frankfurter, Felix, 663
Frelinghuysen, Theodore, 104
French Revolution, 15–16, 151, 288, 846
fund-raising, 852
fundamentalism
  defeat of, 774
  Doctrinal Deliverance of 1910, 370, 372
  Fosdick vs., 478

ghetto phenomenon, 8
history/God, 137
Machen &, 6–7
Prohibition, 570
Riley, W. B., 464
sanctions, 481
Scopes trial, 572–75
Southern Presbyterian, 136
surrender of, 914
Fundamentals (1910–15), 387–88

Galton, Francis, 442, 454
Gamaliel, 478, 964
Gandhi, M., 896
gap theory, 60
Garfield, James A., 900n
Garrison, William Lloyd, 125–26
Gates, Frederick, 379–80
Gaustad, E. S., 109m 477, 478n
genealogies adjusted, 175
General Assembly
  administrative law, 423–24, 715–16, 930–31, 936–37 (see also administrative law)
  attendees, 853
  Auburn *Affirmation*, 547, 549–51
  authority, 360, 368–69, 423–24, 549–51, 642, 698–704, 710, 716, 723–26
  calm (1931–32), 649–53
  Church agencies &, 313
  covenant voice, 325
  division of 1837, 285–89
  Doctrinal Deliverance (see Doctrinal Deliverance)
  double jeopardy argument, 265
  flow of funds, 853 (see also flow of funds)

Fox's protest (1906), 359–60
General Council preparations (1923), 501–2
inclusivists' victory, 1926, 580
initiation, 423–24, 825
legislative, 323, 709, 777–78
Machen's thesis condemned, 575
machine, 652
meetings: judicial, legislative, 934–35
missions &, 691, 695, 866
"moderates" in 1915, 862–63
modernists' theory, 777–78
Old School (1837), 701–2
Portland Deliverance (1892), 258–59
Princeton &, 576–77, 595, 598–99, 642
Prohibition, 571
records of, 501
representation, 321–22, 325, 930, 933–34
representatives, 961
seminary graduates (1895–97), 276
sovereignty, 853
spokesmen, 960
Supreme Court, 259, 264, 320, 323, 360, 368–69, 550–51
truth, 713
turning point (1925–26), 565–77
United Nations, 774–75
veto by presbyteries, 934–35
veto power over seminary appointments, 254–55
General Council, 423–24, 501–2, 650, 651–52, 676, 713, 718

General Education Board, 465–67, 585
General Will, 316–17, 332
Geneva, 977
Germany, 152, 160, 164, 226, 582–85, 923
ghetto (fundamentalism), 8
Gildersleeve, Basil, 598
Gilman, Daniel, 311, 375n
Gladden, Washington, 161, 257
Glorious Revolution, 995
gnosticism, 49, 50–51
golden calf, 585
government (see Church: government structures, State)
grace, 52, 318, 768
grading, 850
graduate school, 184–85
Graham, Billy, 7–8, 882
Grant, Madison, 442–45, 449, 451
Great Awakenings (see First Great Awakening, Second Great Awakening)
Great Awakening (collegiate), 866–67
Green, Ashbel, 108
Green, W. H., 176–77, 254
Greene, William Brenton
  Broad Churchism, 361–62
  heart and head, 98
  social theories, 337–38
Griffin, Leland, 202, 281
Griffith Thomas, W. H., 410–11, 413, 652–53
Griffiths, H. McAllister, 696, 735, 744, 746
Grotius, Hugo, xlviii
growth (see church: growth)

guilt, 317, 903

halfway covenant, xxix, 101–2
Hall, John, 302–3
Hamilton, Alexander, 14
Handy, Robert, 580
Harper, William Rainey, 252, 257, 413, 433, 465
Harriman, Averell, 375n
Harriman, E. H., 661
Harriman, Pamela, 662
Harrison, Benjamin, 306, 552, 867
Hart, D. G., xxxiii–xxxiv, xxxvi, 566, 582–83, 753
Harvard, 162, 184
Harvey, Charles, 340
Hayek, F. A., 299
Hays, Will, 616
Hearst, William Randolph, 7
hell
    Briggs, 226–35
    denial of, 77–80
    evangelicals, 65
    excommunication &, 318
    holding area, 904
    intermediate state, 230–35
    intolerant, 41
    Jesus on, 40
    Larger Catechism, 231, 301–2
    liberty &, 904
    Machen on, 40
    modernism vs., 70, 77–80
    ordination exam, 301–2, 751
    orthodoxy, 40
    rejection, 799
    Re-Thinking Missions, 665, 671–72
    sanctions, 40–41
    screening device, 751, 920
    Speer, 679–80
    torture, 41
    Westminster Confession, 41–42
    see also final judgment
Henry, Carl, 7
Henry, Patrick, 1
Heraclitus, 153, 154
heresy
    Briggs reverses definitions, 279–80
    challenge, 562–63
    closet, 218
    continual, 770
    costs, 293, 298, 565
    early Church, xiii–xiv
    endless, 899
    failure in 1924, 563
    Machen, 510, 514
    New York Presbytery, 903–4
    operational definition (resources), 299
    peace, 182–83
    policing, 836
    presbyteries, 369
    Princeton vs., 526
    progress of heresy trials, 912
    renounced, 1927, 611–14
    shadow government, 310
    Smith, W. Robertson, 201
    statute of limitations, 249
    tree of orthodoxy, 293
    trials (see heresy trials)
    tyranny, xiii
    Union's rejection of, 248
    see also Briggs, McGiffert
heresy trials
    Candee's challenge (1924), 562

Coffin's challenge (1923), 504–5
costs of, 269–70, 293, 299, 565, 904
covenant lawsuit, 384
endless, 565, 769–70
illegal (1927), 611–14
last attempt (1924), 563
no convictions (1830's), 117–21
Old School avoids, 232, 560
paralysis-inducing, 565
precedents?, 296–97, 564
"putting them behind us," 345
reunion's unstated agreement, 742
risk for the accuser, 504, 508
Snowden's challenge (1916), 388
tree of orthodoxy, 293
Van Dyke's challenge (1913), 382–84
Van Dyke's challenge (1924), 563
Hibben, John Grier, 559, 629
hierarchy
budget cuts, 919–20
Church, 818–19
phase two, 4–5
Presbyterianism, 524–26, 837
see also representation
high ground (see moral high ground)
higher criticism
academic debate, 195
America, 192–94
autographs, 218–19
biblical theology &, 805
Briggs &, 200–2, 216–19, 241–44
Church sanctions, 161
claims, 157–58
Clarke, William Newton, 192–93
Darwinism, 192–93
doubt (methodology of), 169
"equal time," 92, 173–74, 628
evolution &, 74
evolutionism &, 159–60
fallible authors, 216
five points of modernism (point three), 72–74
God's word to man's word, 203
Green on, 176–77
historicism &, 72–75
history of, 192–94, 200–1, 282
legitimate by 1890, 252–53
methodology, 72–73, 158–59, 160, 164–69, 172, 174, 897–98
"naval campaign," 161
New Scholarship &, 185
origin, 806
Presbyterian Review, 172–77
presupposition, 167
Princetonians vs., 155, 173
Reformers?, 216–18
Reventlow on, xxix
sanctions, 200–1
slavery, 135
Van Til, Cornelius, 168
Wellhausen, Julius, 192
see also Briggs
Hill, William, ix
historians, xliv, 41, 251–52, 429, 455, 686–87, 778, 816, 916
historicism
chef analogy, 153

Darwinism, 152–53, 761
higher criticism, 72–73
law & change, 151–54
McGiffert, 268–69
modernism, 67
nationalism, 154, 761
Old School, 154–57, 761
history, ix–xi, xlii–xlvi, 1009–10
Hitler, Adolph, xxxix–xl, li, 447–48
Hocking, W. E., 665
Hodge, A. A.
    Briggs vs., 213
    Christian nation, 530
    infants, 228
    Presbyterian Review, 171–72
    theistic evolutionist, 223
Hodge, Charles
    anti-reunion, 143, 291
    Church boards, 928–29
    church membership (good works), 517
    Constitutional History, 113
    creation, 60–61
    division of 1837, 99, 285
    German education, 164
    humanism of, 517
    most difficult project, ix
    old ideas, 758
    slavery, 132, 133
    subscription, 911–12
    Systematic Theology, 209, 310
    What is Darwinism? (1874), 222
Hodge, Edward, 354
Hofstadter, Richard, xxxv, 627
Holmes, Oliver Wendell, 446–47, 588–89

holy commonwealth, 104–5, 725–26
Hoover, Herbert, 488n
Howland, Murray, 542
Hudson, Winthrop, 109, 110m, 520, 758
humanism, xviii, 51, 152, 337, 573
Hutchinson, George, x
Hutchison, William, xix–xx, 200, 686
Hutton, James, 906
Huxley, Thomas, 311, 442
hymnal, 374

ideal type, 36
idols, 150–51, 813
immunity, 188–89
imputation, 52, 148, 316, 317
Independent Board, 696–704
    attacks on, 703
    Craig &, 693
    flow of funds, 704
    founding, 693, 696
    General Council, 714–15
    laymen, 744
    Machen ousted, 745–46
    purge of, 715–20
    "resign!," 719
    sanctions begin, 713–15
    vulnerable, 703
    Westminster Seminary &, 739–41
inerrancy, 149–50, 157–58, 220–21
infanticide, 210
infants, 157, 227–30, 353, 355
information & systems, 824–25,

832–33
Ingersoll, Robert, 193–94
inheritance, 5, 81, 227, 326
Institute for Social & Religious
    Research, 654–55
institutional history, xliii–xlvi
intellect (see apologetics)
Interchurch World Movement,
    392–403, 654, 655, 1017
intermediate state, 230–34, 243
irrelevance, 31
islands (Establishment), 787–88
Israel, 525, 725–26

Jackson, Andrew, 759
Jacob, 55, 228
Jameson, J. Franklin, 312
Jamison, Milo, 19–20, 747
Japan, 875
Jefferson, Thomas, 14
Jekyll Island, 787–88
Jesuits, 803n, 817, 846
Jesus, 158, 318 (see also atonement)
Jews, 59
Jim Crow laws (South), 128, 137
jobs to offer, 949–50
Johns Hopkins University,
    xxxvi, 184–85, 311
Judaism, 910
judicial religion
    all or nothing, 53
    covenant defined, 88
    creedal, 53
    Greene defends, 98
    peace terms, 94
    sanctions, 52
    slow learning, 30
    summary, 16

    theology of, 52
Jupiter Island, 788
justice, 152

Kant, 212, 214
Keller, Adolph, 626, 639–40
Kentucky, 431–36, 468
Keynes, John Maynard, xlviii
Kidd, Benjamin, 326, 870
King, Martin L., 896
kingdom of God, 59–60, 80–81
King, McKenzie, 490n
Kingsley, Charles, 450
Kirk, Russell, 813–14
Kline, Meredith, xxviii
Koop, C. Everett, 1004–6
Koran, 480
Kuhn, Thomas, 202
Kuiper, R. B., 697
Ku Klux Klan, 187
Kuyper, Abraham, 639

Lane Seminary, 267, 268
Lansing, Robert, 553
Larger Catechism, 782
Latin, 108, 209–10, 310, 892,
    923, 987
Laud, William, 976–78
law
    administrative (see administrative law)
    arbitrary enforcement, 12, 320
    casuistry, 105
    Church, 319–21
    creationism &, 149, 226
    evolutionism &, 149, 319
    history &, 151–54
    humanistic, 152
    knowledge of, 149

modernism vs. conservatism, 319–24
natural, 154
precedents, 188, 319–20, 322, 710, 896
predictability, 11, 320
process, 226
protection of weak, 10, 12
rule of, 320–21
sanctions &, 11, 120, 145
speed limits, 10, 12
undermining, 321
Westminster Confession, 57–58
laymen, 517–18, 712–13, 715, 747, 865
Laymen's Inquiry, 655–58, 683 (see also *Re-Thinking Missions*)
Laymen's Missionary Movement, 872
League of Evangelical Students, 601
League of Nations, 395, 408, 417
Lee, Ivy, 483–84, 488–91
left, 15–16
legalism, 595–98, 629–30
legitimacy
    Church government, 827
    modernism, 913–14
    New School, 145, 893–94, 913
    Old School, 127, 145, 913
    phase one, 4
    Princeton Seminary (1865), 134–35
    undermining, 808–9
    Westminster Assembly, 981
Lehman, Cedric, 502–3
Levites, xxxiv, 42, 884
liberalism (theological)
    churches, xx
    "equal time," 92, 173–74, 628
    failure (1933), 861
    formula, 840
    Hutchinson's analysis, xix–xx
    Machen on, 514
    peaked in 1959, xxi
    pietist alliance, 18
    power religion, 514
    range of beliefs, 91–92
    sacraments, 22, 31
    sacred cow (public education), 468
    scientific ideal, 92
    Scottish, 760–61
    signs of, 916–17
    strategy, 802–5
    strategy (gnostic), 51
    summary, 16
    see also modernism, modernists, power religion
liberation theology, 671
liberty, 887, 904
Lincoln, Abraham, 141
Lippmann, Walter, 493–94, 661
Lipscomb, David, 136n
liturgy, 876
Livingston, William, 106n
Locke, John, xlviii
Loetscher, Lefferts
    apologist for liberalism, xxxii
    Briggs, 249
    misrepresented Machen, 900–2
    turf-protection, 253
Log College, 311
Longfield, Bradley, 356–57
Lord's Supper
    creed &, 43
    General Assembly, 856

Machen on, 515–16, 519
Stoddard, 102–3
Lovett, Robert, 376n
lower criticism, 62–63, 164–66, 167–68
lowest common denominator
confession, 359, 362–63, 523, 893, 896, 910–11
Cumberland reunion, 359
gets ever-lower, 298, 362
highest enforceable standard, 523
historic creeds: minimum, 917
large denominations. 910–11
membership standards, 893
New School, 142
oath, 896, 919
Old School's challenge (1906), 362–63
Presbyterian Church, 359, 362–63, 893, 922
sanctions define, 359
Loyola, Ignatius of, 803n
Luce, Henry R., 375n
Ludlow Massacre, 489–90
Luther, Martin, 216, 583
Lutheranism, xvii, 177, 808, 817
Lyell, Charles, 61–62, 777, 792, 906
Lynd, Robert, 654

Macartney, Clarence E.
abuse from liberals, 495–96
anti-Fosdick, 494–95, 498, 509
archetype conservative Calvinist, 83–84
beaten general, 751
call to battle, 537
Christian Century essay, 749

Machen &, 742
Moderator (1924), 502
Re-Thinking Missions, 677
surrender of, 749–52
waning star (1924–), 509
Wilson's career, 187
Machen, J. Gresham
abandoned by allies, 525, 754, 757
accomplishments, 755–56
accusations by, xxxiv
affirmation of confession, 309
alliance, not ecumenism, 602, 722
alone in 1923, 757
anomaly, 760–62
apologetics, 593, 777, 792–93
apologetics chair, 569–71, 576, 603–4, 624
apostate Church, 325
apostate liberalism, 510–11
appealed to common ethics, 777
appealed to laymen, 518, 524
appointment, 584, 596–98
archetype Old School, 84
Auburn *Affirmation*, 534, 549, 625, 688–89, 735, 737
battle flag dipped, 743
better day coming, 757
bloodguilt issue, 512
Board of Foreign Missions, 687–89, 691–93
"boot me," 315
Buck &, 688, 772
bully?, 527
call to fight, 607–8
called a liar, 527–28
capitalist ideal, 760

career, pre–1924, 508–9
categories (2 or 3), 16–17, 646–48
Christendom, 770, 939
Christian freedom, 723
Christianity & Liberalism, 505, 509–16, 527, 798
Church as a helpful fellowship, 515–16
Church as a political club, 900–2
Church is unsound, 1
Church membership, 514–15, 521
Church Union (1920), 405–6
Church & State, 533
classification scheme, 17–18, 35–37
coercion, 1934, 725
Committee of Eight, 563–64
compromised strategy, 924
compulsory funding, 696
concern in 1915, 862–63
Confession, 512, 752
confessional interpretation, 905
confessional revision, 30
contentious?, 508–9
controversy, 45
creedal Church, 308
creedal revision, 346, 906
creeds & politics, 770
critics, 239, 576–77
Cross (hatred of), 470
crossed fingers, 596–98, 892, 906
crossed fingers problem, 309
culture and faith, 35
darkness, 757

death, 746–47, 755
defeat, 346, 691, 792
defenseless, 314–15
defensive battle (Princeton), 624
defines Church, 520–21
dilemma, 29, 314, 550, 601–2, 924
doctrinal battle, 315, 602, 635, 726, 735, 776, 785
dogma, 34
education, 440–41
enemies, 916
Erdman &, 551, 569, 576, 605–7, 609–10, 621
eschatology, 528
Establishment &, 488, 665, 791
exclusionary Church, 95, 308
excommunication of liberals?, 514, 517
experientialists, 25
factions analyzed, 16–17
faith of, 783
fighter, 608
flow of funds (1923), 512
Fosdick &, 527n
fundamentalism's spokesman, 601
fundamentalist?, 6, 528
General Assembly vs. conscience, 697–99
Germany, 582–83, 597–98, 858
giving offense, 947
good fight, 784
Greene &, 339
Hart vs., xxxiii–xxxiv
hearing, 722–23
hell, 40
heresy trials, 510

higher education, 858
historians' view, 634
honest liberals, 796
ignorance of liberal ethics, 514
independency, 745–46
industrialism, 886
infallible Bible, 308
institutional strategy, 315
intolerance, 887
investigating committee, 621–22
job offers, 632
last days of his life, 946
last stand, 770–71
legacy, 784, 793–94
legal arguments, 629–32
liberal scorn, 470
liberalism as apostate, 510–11
liberals' argument, 701
liberals' consciences, 341
libraries, 786
Loetscher on, 901–2
logic, 858
lost cause, 608, 784
Macartney &, 741–42
member's oath, 518–20
membership by good works, 517, 520, 521–22
membership (presbytery), 735
Mencken on, 942–46
ministerial oath, 309
missions, 643, 862
Moderator contest, 551–52
modernism summarized, 35–37, 785
Mount Desert Island, 597, 787
national figure overnight (1924), 509
New School, 143–44

new seminary, 635
"no chance," 739
no heresy trials demanded, 511, 514, 727, 731
no names, 526, 560, 734, 737, 738
oaths, 309, 314, 324
offense-less, 314
officers of the Church, 309
Old Princeton, 638
Old School, 924–25
open communion, 519
ordination, 309, 584, 630
Origin of Paul's Religion, 509, 756
orthodoxy & voting, 731–32, 740
Paul's religion, 205
"Peace, peace," 1, 36
persuasion, 768
pluralism in seminaries, 625–28
pluralisms, 777
politics of, 528–29
polygamy of the soul, 308
positive sanctions, 786
postmillennial, 526, 601, 791–92
precedents, 325
primacy of intellect (degree), 592, 593
Prohibition vote, 570–71
pronunciation, xii
propositional truth, 593–94
purge at Westminster, 740–41
raising costs to followers, 769, 779, 925
remnant (language), 646
renaissance (hope in), 792

Re-Thinking Missions, 677, 687-89
review of Speer, 646–47
revision of 1903 (evils of), 892, 906–7
rhetoric, 239, 608, 648
Roman Catholicism, 602–3
rusty weapons, 792–93
sacraments (no defense), 513, 515–17, 519–20, 526
sacred trust funds, 513
salvation, 308
sanctions, 514, 519–20, 551, 732, 770
schism, 741–42
"schismatic preaching" (van Dyke), 506
scientific theology, 590, 601
seclusion (1931–32), 648–49
self-defense, 737
seminaries, 582
sham orthodoxy, 731–32
silence at his trial, 735
six-day creation, 900, 905–6
skipped over Church's history (1906–20), xli
social immunity, 786–88
Speer &, 647–48, 689–90, 693
spiritual crisis of, 582–83, 596–97
spokesman, 6–7, 601, 753
Statement to Special Committee (1934), 722–23
Stevenson &, 625–26
strategy, 29–30, 315, 518, 525, 564, 791
subscription to Confession, 308
surrenders case, 515

system of doctrine (Confession), 308
tax-funded schools, 530
theistic evolution, 462
thesis condemned (1926), 575–76
tolerance, 734
transfer of presbytery membership, 720–22, 734–35
trapped by Presbyterian law, 518
trial of, 735–39
true faith, 34
trust funds, 513
two religions, 510–11, 549, 575, 776, 915
van Dyke &, 505–6, 509, 757
Van Til &, 783–84, 793–94
victory, 31
Virgin Birth of Christ, 649, 756
vituperative tone?, 527
voluntarism, 700–1
voluntary Church, 887, 900–1
voting defines orthodoxy, 732
voting members, 518
Waterloo, 512
wealth, 791
weapons, 792–93
weary, 772–73
what to do (1930)?, 646–47
Whig, 324–25, 332, 337, 529–30, 533, 628, 770, 777, 793, 899, 900
withdrawal of conservatives (1923), 511, 513, 694
withdraws of liberals, 510, 511, 777
wolves & sheep, 776

women ruling elders, 407–8, 909–10
worldview, 761
MacPherson, Merrill, 744
Madison, James, 899
Madison Presbytery, 563
mailing lists, 491
majority, 701
management, 823–25, 847–49
Mann, Horace, 112, 440, 468
marbles, 754
marriage, 86, 87
marriage analogy (reunion), 289–90
Marsden, George, 311–12, 572, 573, 574, 578, 812
Marshall, John, 777n
Marston, Moor, 989, 991
Marx, Karl, 573
Masada, 30
Massa, Mark, 171, 174, 250, 251
Mateer, Horace, 497
Mather, Cotton, xvii, 103, 105
Mathews, Shailer, 70–81, 145, 160, 410–11, 459, 578
Maurice, F. D., 450
McCloy, John J., 556, 787
McConaughy, David, 872
McCormick, Cyrus, 180–81
McCosh, James
    Confessional revision, 206
    Macartney quotes, 750
    Patton &, 184
    theistic evolutionist, 184, 222, 450
McCune, William, 183, 296
McDowell, John, 638, 641, 699
McGiffert, A. C., 2, 268–69, 293
McIntire, Carl

    excommunicated, 744
    Machen &, 747–48
    Schaeffer &, 999
    self-justification, 748
    separatist, 747
    Speer &, 727–30
Mead, Sidney, 439, 643–44, 774
meaning, 79–80
mechanism, 150–51
medievalism, 279, 434–35, 441, 452, 476
meetings, 960–61
Mein Kampf, 221
Mellon, Richard, 616
membership (Church)
    administrative discipline, 712–13
    confession, 524
    Continental Calvinism, 101–2
    creedless, 523
    local (pre-1934), 712–13
    lowest common denominator, 922
    Machen's views, 514-15, 521
    oath, 11–12, 936
    standards, 516–17, 518, 519
    voting, 11, 518, 922, 936
Mencken, H. L., 463, 574, 942-46
Merriam, Charles, 68–69, 378
Methodists, 109, 110–11, 275, 876, 950, 1014–17
methodology, 73, 114, 164–69, 172, 195, 312, 334
Miller, Samuel, 140
Milner, Alfred, 666
mind (leap of being), 326
minister
    certified, 108

College of New Jersey, 107–8
education, 22
exams, 766–67
income, 475
statistics, 335, 359
Westminster Confession, 21
see also ordination
Minutes of the General Assembly, xlix–xlvii, 349, 500–1
miracles, 1010
Mises, Ludwig, 847–48
mission (liberal term), 666, 674–75, 705
missions
    Board (see Board of Foreign Missions)
    Briggs on, 235
    candidates, 866–67
    China, 410–11
    decentralized by Speer (1921), 420–22
    disclaimers, 728–30
    division of 1837, 286
    dominionist, 666, 673
    Eastern mysticism, 667
    ecumenism, 305–6, 673–75, 871
    Edinburgh Conference of 1910, 373
    evangelicals dominate (1980), 705
    final conflict, 901
    Foreword Movement, 871–72, 873
    fund-raising, 864–66, 872–73, 968
    General Assembly &, 866
    great awakening, 1880's, 313
    Griffith Thomas, 410–11, 413
    history of, 717, 967–68
    interdenominational, 717, 871–75 (see also parachurches)
    Laymen's Inquiry (see Laymen's Inquiry)
    liberals, 1932, 657
    Machen in 1915, 862
    Mead's analysis, 643–44
    mission, 671–72, 781
    mission vs., 863
    Old School, 121–23
    postmillennial, 666, 673
    presbyteries &, 967–69
    pro-Fosdick, 499
    procedure is flawless, 691–92
    self-defense, 691–92, 705
    success indicator, 854
    vulnerable, 863
    women's societies &, 864–66
    see also *Re-thinking Missions*
Missouri Synod Lutheranism, xvii
Mitchell, John, xliv
mobs, 339
moderates, xx
Moderators invited to speak, 537
modernism
    administrative law, 337, 723, 931 (see also administrative law)
    agenda-setting, 145, 297
    allies outside Church, 456–57, 525, 798, 879
    anti-controversy, 589
    anti-precedent, 319, 322
    antinomian, 75
    appeal to Barnes, 120–21
    Auburn *Affirmation* (see Auburn *Affirmation*)

authority (1933), 704
backfires, 920
bait & hook, 919
bear market, xxi
benefits promised, 769
Bible, 72–75
Briggs publicly affirms, 280
bureaucracy &, 331–32, 904
capturing seminaries, 296
caring for wounded, 295
cartel, 859–62, 883, 1020
central assertion, 438
certification over doctrine, 601
Chinese missions, 410–11 (see also China)
Church growth &, 948–49
Church (Marks of), 895–89
compulsory schools, 525
confession (also Progressivism's), 887
confessional indeterminacy, 115
conscience, 341
consistency, 808
courts, 512
covenant, 889–90
covenant theology, 208, 723
creed of, 269, 723
Darwinism, 66, 438
deception, xxxiv, xxxvi
democracy, 316, 324
described, 66–67, 92
disintegration, 861
divisions, 438
doctrine, 76
doctrine of God, 806
dogma, 799, 862
ecumenism, 66, 80–81, 235, 392–403, 704–5, 883

equal time doctrine, 92, 173–74, 628
eschatology, 798
ethics, 512–13 (see situation ethics)
eucharist, 727
exclusion of rivals, 81, 84, 192
experientialism, 88, 169
faith of, xxxv, 269, 857
final judgment, 318, 492 (see also hell)
five points, 66, 70–81, 208–238, 478–82, 545–48
five steps, 805–8
flow of funds, xx, 704, 776–77, 800, 887–88, 890
formalism, 115
Fosdick, 499
framed the debate, 607
free thought, 857
freedom of inquiry, 198–99
fundamentalists defined, 578
goals, xxxvi, 82, 461, 579, 613, 914–16
god, 316, 318, 333, 341
"government, not theology," 605
heart of, 235
hell, 77–80, 318, 799
hell & excommunication, 318
higher criticism, 72–74, 805, 806–7
higher ground = survival, 513
historicism, 67
history/God, 137
honor, 263
humanism &, 525, 573
hypocrisy, 503
immunity period, 188–89

Index 1059

institutional heart, 235
judicial strategy, 321
language, 804
lay doctrine, 78
legitimacy, 913–14
loose construction, 704
low profile tactics, 898
Machen's misunderstanding, 341
Machen's summary of, 785
Machen's thesis, 510
magna carta (1927), 611–14
Mencken on, 945
missions (1932), 657–58
missions publications, 728–30
misusing words, 287
monopoly, 859
moral high ground, 898
neo-orthodoxy &, 861
no rallies, 542
obedience, 735–36, 776–77 (see also administrative law)
other people's money, 337, 403, 437, 438–41, 887, 920
outside support, 798–99, 803, 914, 918–19
patience, 538, 779
peace & work, 898
peace terms, 93–94
personalism, 115
"personalities, not theology," 607, 622
phrases, 918
pincer movement, 798
pluralism, 304, 626–27, 890
positioning, 496
positive sanctions, 913
power religion, 627, 634, 723
preaching, 895

process theology, 71–72, 73–74, 226, 316, 323, 897
progress in history, 72
Progressive Movement, xxxv, 313, 324, 327–28, 336, 627, 847, 857
propaganda campaign, 898
power religion, 634
Princeton &, 628
public sacrifice, 754
radio cartel, 1013
reform, 93, 324
relativism, 75
religion & science, 456
representation, 316, 341
Re-Thinking Missions, 235, 665–76
rhetoric (see Briggs' rhetoric, rhetoric)
Roman Catholicism, xii, 280–81
sacrament, 893, 895
salvation by power, 723
sanctions, 492, 544, 778
science & religion, 456
secrecy, 938
secularization of, 758
self-confidence, 914
seminaries, 856–58, 923
situation ethics (see situation ethics)
social reform, 93
sociological explanations, 578
sovereignty of God, 72, 79
sovereignty of the people, 315
stages, 767
stealing the inheritance, 227
strategy (see strategy: modernism)

surrender to secularism, 758
tactics, xl–xli, 326, 774, 811
theological & secular, 66
theology of, 316, 341, 723, 800, 804, 809–10
theology, not methodology, 804
tide of, 269
tolerance, 80, 492, 532, 634, 708–9, 754
"true orthodoxy," 73, 279
two branches, xxv, 627, 798–99, 914–16, 918–19
umbrella, 806
unified, 915
victory of, xiii
vituperative, 526
whirl is king, xiii
Zeitgeist (Briggs), 280
see also liberalism, power religion
modernists
    accomplices (see modernism: two branches)
    agenda-setting, 297
    alliance with New School, 310
    appealed to Barnes case, 120–21
    breakdown of cartel, 859–62
    care of wounded, 918–19
    crossed fingers, 326
    Form of Government (1934), 902
    goals of, 81–82, 461, 613, 679, 914–16
    honor, 258
    immoderate after 1933, 753
    intruders, 538–39
    judicial strategy, 321–24

    magna carta (1927), 611–14
    monopoly (quest for), 856–59
    moral high ground strategy, 898
    other people's money, 258 (see also other people's money)
    positive sanctions (bureaucracy), 914
    public burnt offering (1936), 753
    ready to fight, 1936, 360
    rhetoric (see Briggs' rhetoric, rhetoric)
    "sticks & stones," 734
    "victims of verbal abuse" ploy, 496
    what they fear most, 920
    withdraw from Church?, 258–59, 341, 511, 538–39
    "wounded lambs" ploy, 492, 611, 809
money (see flow of funds, follow the money, other people's money)
Monnet, Jean, 395
monopoly, 851–60, 883
Moody, Dwight, 375, 868–69
moral high ground, 897–98
moralism, 136
Morgan, Edmund, xxix
Morgan, J. P., 661, 855
Mormons, 972
Morris, Henry, 463–64
Mott, John R.
    Edinburgh Conference, 373
    leadership, 867
    liberalism of, 869–70
    Moody &, 868

Index 1061

New York Conference (1900),
   305–6
  Rockefeller &, 381, 653
  social gospel, 875
  Speer &, 305, 873, 875
  two questions, 306
  visionary in 1900, 305
Mount Desert Island
  Machen, 597, 787, 915
  McCloy, John, 787
  model, 788–89
  van Dyke's home, 382
  van Dyke's last sermon, 318n
Mudge, Lewis, 649, 721, 752
Murray, John, 756, 925, 927
Museum of Art, 374

Naseby, Battle of, 991
National Park Service, 788–89
nationalism, 154
natural law, 154
nature, 151, 153, 435
Nazis, xxxix–xl, 445, 447–48, 554
neo-evangelicalism, 7–8
neo-orthodoxy, 147, 334, 861
  (see also Barth)
neutrality, 175, 195, 211, 439,
  532
New England Puritans, 87–88,
  439–40
New Era Movement, 393,
  397–99, 403
New Model Army, 991, 995
New Republic, 660–61, 663
New School
  alliance with modernists, 310
  anti-sanctions, 120, 282–83
  Confession &, 114, 922–23
  conservative?, 143–44

  crossed fingers, 357
  ecclesiology, 144
  ended in 1936, 747
  expelled, 119–20
  experientialism, 3, 115, 145,
    292
  glorifying God, 114
  Great Commission, 114
  heresy trials, 120–21, 143, 310
  legitimacy, 145, 893–94, 913
  lies, 291
  lowest common denominator,
    142
  McIntire, Carl, 747–48
  misusing words, 289
  ordination exam, 300
  parachurches, 119, 122, 147
  poison (experientialism), 147
  pre-1857, 127
  Progressivism &, 327–28
  radical Republicans, 135, 144
  Reconstruction of South, 144
  revivals &, 95, 117
  sanctions, 120, 129–30, 143–44,
    894
  slavery, 127, 129–30, 143–44
  strategy, 801–2, 840–41
  theology, 144
  umbrella, 121, 283, 347, 834,
    906
  worship, 114
New Side, 87, 113, 117
New York Presbytery
  Cincinnati Presbytery vs.
    (1916), 385
  clears Briggs, 191, 257, 261–62
  Fosdick case, 498, 502, 556–58
  heresy trials, 903–4
  higher criticism, 382

immune, 930
lentivivus, 838
point of entry, 838
"rogue cell," 838
under siege (1925), 567–68
virgin birth, 368, 385, 502
New York Times
  anti–democracy, 432
  Bryan's article, 427–28
  Bryan's motion on Darwinism (1923), 501
  eugenics, 455
  front page, 1
  rhetoric, 567
  science & religion, 456
Newton, Isaac, 105, 330, 846
Newtonianism
  Awakenings, 112
  Darwinism replaces, 328–31
  eighteenth century, 105, 846
  idol of nature, 150–51
  social theory, 846
  Wilson vs., 328–9
Nicea, 38, 727
Nichols, Robert, xxvii, 543
Nietszche, F., 463
Nisbet, Robert A., xxxvii, 151, 317, 435
Nitze, Paul, 555
Nixon, Richard, xliv
noise, 824
Noll, Mark, 282
non–profit management, 849
Nordic supremacy, 442–46
Nykamp, Delwyn, 540, 532, 564, 609n, 898

oath
administrative law &, 712–13, 936–37
baptism, 24–25, 522, 956
centrality of, xxviii
Church member, 519, 936
confession & oath-renewal, 43
conscience &, 908–9
conservatives, 314
content (judicial), 314
covenant, xxviii, 551
covenantal, 85
creeds, 523
crossed fingers, 297
dead letter, 313–14
democratic, 324
flow of funds, 700
Fosdick, 558
hell, 41–42
judicial content, 314
laymen, 712–13, 715, 956
lowest common denominator, 896, 919
Machen on, 309, 324
members', 517–18, 519–20, 712–13, 919, 956
membership, 11–12, 21, 517, 936, 956–57
office, 25
Princeton Seminary, 584
renewal, 43
sacraments &, 917
sanctions, xxviii, 9, 21, 43, 314, 357, 383, 541
solutions to problem, 93n
State, 906–7

stipulations, 43
test, 106n
Westminster Confession, 58, 906, 925-26, 987
Olbricht, Thomas, 192-94
old money, 789
Old School
abolitionism as *adiaphorum*, 128, 130-36, 338
academic disputation, 189 (see *Presbyterian Review*)
alliance, 1906-, 362
anti-abolition, 126
appearance of arbitrariness, 195
Bible on abolitionism, 123-25
Bourne case, 123-29, 145
Confessional revision, 195, 353-57 (see Westminster Confession: revision)
credentialism, 765-67
crossed fingers, 346, 354-58
death of, 577, 747, 748, 755
defensive, 302, 351
dilemma, 296-97
division of 1837, 288
ecclesiology matched theology, 913
emasculated, 135
failed to reproduce, 758
failure to repent, 291-92
General Assembly (1837), 701-2
hierarchy, 147
high Church, 114
historicism &, 154-57
isolated, 1865, 139
last bastion (Princeton), 598-99

Latin, 892
legitimacy lost, 127, 134
lost cause, xxv, xxxvii, 170
"love of God," revision, 354-55
marketing problem, 768-70
neutrality on slavery, 127, 130
no strategy, 189
officers, 21-23
Old School vs., 701-2, 877
ordination exam strategy, 299-302, 751
parachurch ministries, 121-22, 877-78
particular redemption, 354
Patton's career, 894
preaching, 22-23, 891-92
primacy of intellect, 592, 768
progress as doctrinal, 768, 784-85
rationalistic, 587, 768 (See also apologetics, methodology)
resistance ends (1903), 356
retreats, 23
reunion moves, 1862, 138
reversed with New School, 122, 701-2, 748 (see also parachurches)
ruling elders (see elders)
sacraments, 22, 892-93
sanctions, 742-43
scholars, 544
slavery (see abolitionism, *adiaphora*, Bourne, slavery)
Southern, 133
spent force by 1890, 245
stalemate psychology, xli, 791
strategy, 801, 840
subordinate, 1869, 291

subscription to Confession, 116
suicide, 363
surrender, 115, 123, 135, 140–41, 791, 913
survival, 1920's, 334
swallowed, 291
task of, 154–57
theology of, 913
unique service proposition, 769
weaknesses, xxxviii
Whigs, 324–25, 847
women ruling elders, 644, 909–10
worship, 114
Old vs. New, 3–4, 104, 117
ordinances, 717–18, 878
ordination
    Baptist, Methodist, 892
    "club" mentality, 389
    Congregational (1927), 611–14
    control over, 857–59
    degree (academic), 585, 594, 958
    exams, 299–302, 333–34, 594
    immunity after, 842
    malcontents' role, 834
    Mott & Speer, 868
    oath, 313–14, 958
    obedience to boards, 700
    permanent (1927), 611–14
    prayer of welcome, 973
    presbyterial, 192
    representation, 315–16
    screening, 191, 333–34, 857, 888–89
    seminaries &, 191, 586, 958
    two-office eldership, 819, 958

weak sanctions afterward, 594
Westminster Assembly, 986–87
women, 407–8, 644, 909–10
organization, 824–25, 896
organization as metaphor, 151
Orthodox Presbyterian Church
    accredited colleges, 951
    name change, 859
    numbers, 743, 744
    revision of 1903, 906–7
orthodoxy
    benefits, 770
    Briggs' argument, 179, 279–80
    Calvin on, 513–14
    conservatives on, 514
    expulsion (1936), 733
    Machen's definition, 730–32, 740
    price of, 769–70
    sanctions &, 120, 199, 514–15, 732–33
    unenforceable by 1924, 562
Osborn, Frederick, 449
Osborn, Henry F., 442, 442n, 448–49, 449–50, 453
other people's money, 258, 335–37, 403, 438–41, 708, 887, 920, 959
owl of Minerva, 883

Palmer, Benjamin, 136
pamphlet, x
pamphlet war, 984–85
parachurches, 121–23, 147, 286, 364, 717, 877–78, 883, 1014
Parker, Alton, 329
Parkinson's law, 848, 960
Parliament

Archbishop Laud, 977–78
Church reform, 979–80
episcopacy substitution pamphlet wars, 985
problem, 977–78, 979
root & branch petition (1640), 978–79
taxes, 976–77
Westminster Assembly, 979, 980–81, 984
Patterson, Paige, xvi (note)
Patton, Francis
academic freedom defended, 631n
Briggs' appointment, 255
capitulation, 894
denounced as outsider, 182
dual role, 180
McCormick's man, 180–81
point man, 180
Princeton University, 183–87
Swing case, 180–83
theistic evolutionist, 222
Paul the apostle, 205
peace
competing definitions, 94, 565
experientialism, 18, 27
goal after 1924, 581
heresy trials, 182–83, 564–65
issue after 1900, 293
modernist tactic, 496, 565, 579
quest for, 581
price of, 49, 568, 770, 778–83
separation, 511
terms of (all sides), 93–94
van Dyke, 263, 506
victory &, 511
"peace, peace," 1, 17–18, 28, 36, 196

pension fund, 614–20
Pentateuch, 157–58
Perkins, Arthur, 744, 748–49
Permanent Judicial Commission, 651, 738, 741
personalism, 819–21
persuasion, 768–70
Pew, J. Howard, 360
phases, 4–6
Philadelphia Overture, 495
philosophy, xiv
pietism
defined, 17
experientialism, xviii, 16
fundamentalism, 16
humanist alliance, 915
irrelevance, 775
Presbyterian, 16
Presbyterian Church, 913
South, post-1865, 135–37
Pilate, Pontius, 712
pincer movement, 798
pipers, 398, 468, 522, 812, 839, 957, 958
Plan of Union, 1801, 286, 1014
planning as an ideology, 326, 331, 579
pluralism
Church & State, 777
"equal time," 92, 173–74, 628
Machen's appeal to (Princeton), 625–28
modernists' illusion, 626–27, 890
no negative sanctions, 304
theocratic ideal, 777
voluntary Church, 901
Westminster Confession (1788), 106

Whiggery, 899
poison (experientialism), 147
politics
    Church, 564
    mailing lists, 458
    plunder, 439, 460, 468
    see also Progressivism, State, Whigs
Pontier, Alan, 212
Pope, 353, 602–3, 906
Popper, Karl, 153n
population control, 449, 455
Populism, 329, 335–36, 457, 460, 469 (see also Bryan)
Portland Deliverance (1892), 258–59, 532, 699
positive thinking, 472
postmillennialism, 63–64, 482, 526, 798–99, 822n
power
    center, 343
    centralized, 929
    flow of funds &, 776, 839
    modernists' respect for, 340, 579
    obedience &, 776
    paychecks &, 955
    pluralism, 776–78
    Prohibition, 393
    responsibility &, 822
power religion
    alliance with experientialists, 775
    anti-creedal, 53
    antinomian, 53
    autonomy, 47
    confessions &, 27
    conscience &, 773
    democracy, 294
    ethics &, 47
    flow of funds (sacred), 717
    knowledge &, 46
    Machen's blindness, 777
    man's experience, 50
    peaceful coexistence, 30
    sacramental, 717
    salvation by knowledge, 46
    salvation by law, 579
    sanctions, 48
    sovereignty, 46–47
    strategy (see strategy: modernism)
    summary, 16
    toleration &, 48
    top-down, 725
    wealth, 48
power-seekers, 959, 960
prayer closets, 779–80
precedents, 188, 226, 296–97, 319–21, 322, 710, 896
predestination, 90 (see also sovereignty: God)
predictability (legal), 320
predictable nature, 153
prelacy, 817–19
premillennialism
    Bible Presbyterians, 20
    Machen's dilemma, 6, 602
    Presbyterian conservatives, 66
    social gospel vs., 14
    two forms, 64n
Prentiss, G. L., 255, 257
Presbyterian Church, U.S.A.
    academic freedom, 927
    academic vulnerability, 584–90
    administrative law (see administrative law)
    Adopting Act (1729), 199, 369

aging, 938
American Revolution, 105–7
apostate?, 25
appeals courts, 823, 842, 846, 960–61
apprenticeship, 958–59, 964
Arian membership confession, 522–23
"bank," 878–79
baptism, 522–23, 901
boards, 331, 364, 852, 927–31, 928–29 (see also boards)
bureaucracy, 331, 350, 821–22
calm (1931), 649–50
center of power, 344
centralization, 331, 349, 398, 501–2, 650–52, 684–85, 821–22
Church's marks, 42–43, 52, 891–94
Church Union (1920), 403–7
colleges, 962–63
Committee of Fifteen, 566–68, 575
confession had changed, 313–15
Congregationalist membership, 521–22
Constitution of, 5
contentiousness as major sin, 842
core groups, 949
courts, 512, 726, 842
credentialism, 765
Creedal revision, 694
creedalism (illusion), 693–95
Digest, 743–44
discipline & truth, 712
division of 1837, 285–86

doctor, 964
dry rot, 862–63
ecumenism, 403–7
elders, 837–38, 839, 958
evangelism, 901
excommunication, 709–10 (see also double jeopardy)
Executive Commission, 313, 344, 366, 399–403
factions, 1923, 531
Federal Council (see Federal Council of Churches)
final stage, 767, 784
flow of funds (see flow of funds)
follow the money (see follow the money)
foreign missions (see missions)
Form of Government (1934), 711–20, 724, 878–79
four-point Calvinism, 353–54, 356
front page, 1–2
fundamental law, 155
General Assembly (see General Assembly)
General Council, 423–24, 650–52
government documents, 993
growth & liberalism, 947–50
heresy trials renounced, 611–14
ideals (vulnerable), 919
inclusive (1903), 371
Interchurch World Movement, 392–403, 654
jobs to offer, 949–50
judicial precedents, 319–21
laymen screened out, 518

League of Nations, 408
legitimacy, 913
localism, 726, 750, 878
lowest common denominator, 359, 362–63, 523, 893
majority, 701
members, 712–13, 839–40, 878–79
members' oath, 11, 21, 712–13, 889, 893, 895–96, 936
membership, 11–12, 516–17, 518, 519, 521–23, 712–13, 893, 955–59
ministerial shortage, 950
ministerial statistics, 335, 867
"ministers forever," 27, 611–14
ministers' incomes, 475
Minutes, xlvi–xlvii, 500–1
New Era Movement, 393, 397–99, 403
New York Times, 1
non-Calvinist, 1903, 122
oaths (see oaths)
ordinances, 717–18
ordination (see ordination)
ordination of women, 407–8, 644, 909–10
parachurch ministries, 121–23, 147, 286, 364
peak membership, 1925, 580
pension fund, 614–20
Permanent Judicial Commission, 651, 738, 741
perversion, 785
piper & tune (members), 522
prayer closets, 779–80, 782
precedents (see precedents)
property and secession, 752, 859

reform (1931–33), 650, 700
regulative principle, 928
RE-imagining, 2n, 938
reorganization (1908), 363–68
reorganization (1923–24), 501–2
representation, 365–66, 933–34
restructured (1908), 363
reunion (see reunion of Church)
revivalism, 952
sacramental ministry, 21–22
sanctions (see sanctions)
Scottish Enlightenment, 846
sell-out, xvii
seminaries, 584–93 (see also seminaries)
shadow government, 309–10, 313
shrinking, 784
silent majority, 525
sin = contentiousness, 842
small by design (splinters), 935, 948, 953–54
social gospel, 336, 361
sound or unsound? (Machen), 1
Southern (see Southern Presbyterian Church)
special interest group, 8
spokesman, 365–66, 933–34
Stated Clerk, 348–50
statute of limitations, 735, 737
success indicators, 849–51
superintendent, 933–34
testimony, xviii
tombstone (1908), 938
trademark, 859
turf conflicts, 832–36

two questions, 20
United Nations &, 774–75
voting members, 11, 517–26, 956–57
vulnerability, 584–90, 919
Presbyterian conflict
"administrative, not theology" (1936), 776–78
alignments, 143
American Civilization &, 937
categories, 46
central dilemma (members' confession), 524
conservatives' ignorance, 774
covenantal, xlvii, 888–91
dating, 2–3
debate over hell, 41
de-escalation (1900), 283–84
doctrinal or administrative?, 735–36, 776
end of (members' oath), 896
historians, 251–52
issues, xxxviii
major event, 488
McGiffert, 2
microcosm, xxv
ministers suspended, 744
oath, xxviii
phases, 2–6, 935–36
pietism, 913
preaching only?, 44–45
problems, 926–31
reversed positions, 698, 699–700
Rockefeller &, 926
sacraments, 21–22, 44
sanctions, xxxviii–xxxix, 6, 9, 190–92, 525
solutions to, 931–35

standards &, 9
subscription, 3–4, 13
two issues, 44
see also General Assembly, ordination
Presbyterian Review, 171–74, 176–77, 193–95, 261, 593, 807
Presbyterianism
academic model, 845
Achilles' heel, 929
Anglo-American, 996–97
apostasy defined, 24
appeals court system, 823, 846, 960–61
baptism, 24, 901
bottom-up, 823–24
bureaucracy, 321, 851
catechism, 972
chinks in armor (2), 936
committee: way of life, 845
confession: Arian, 523
covenant, 901 (see also five points of the covenant)
creeds &, 521
dead letter (oaths), 314
defining characteristics, 314
dust-eating, 950–54
English, 99–100, 261, 996
eschatological pessimism, 952
government system, 819–27
hell, 41–42
high priests, 839
ideals, 919
ignorance of history, ix
impersonalism (judicial), 819, 845
intellectual condition, x–xi
leadership, 839–40) see also representation)

localism, 725, 878
oaths, 21, 24
Old vs. New, 3–4, 87, 117
open-ended confessionally, 912
pecking order, 837, 839, 949–50
personalism, 819–21, 934
presbyters (see presbyteries)
printed literature, 830
reform, 954–55
representation (see representation)
rescue missions (few), 952–53
sacramental, 20–25
"soft underbelly" = sanctions, 594
Southern (see Southern Presbyterian Church)
standards of evidence (Fosdick), 500
unresolved problem (government), 957
vulnerability, 936
weaknesses, 947–48
worship, 985–86
presbyteries
academic freedom, 816
authority of, 830–31
autonomy, 892, 919
care of, 837
cover-ups, 835
critics in, 834, 836
defensive, 934
delegate responsibility, 833–34
discipline, 613–14
disrupting, 298
education (control over), 931–32
exams, 310–11, 959
insiders vs. outsiders, 182
malcontents, 834
missions boards &, 967–69
national boards &, 932
no claim on money, 957–58
old-boy networks, 182
prayer of welcome, 973
rights, 937
sanctions, 815, 830, 958–59
seminaries &, 310, 592, 923, 958
sovereign (1935), 738
surrender of sovereignty, 958
veto of General Assembly, 934–35
Presidents, 900
Pressler, Paul, xvi (note)
Pride's Purge, 992
priesthood
modern, 37, 42, 43
Old Testament, 42
professors, 915
science, 75
Princeton Theological Seminary
apologetics, 174–75, 589–90, 593–94, 761, 764–65
Boards, 593, 603–5, 622–23, 626, 630–32
capitalism, 759
chair of apologetics, 575–77
Church Union division, 406
Confessional interpretation, 905
control over (1929), 710
creationism, 60–61, 223–24, 226, 301
crossed fingers (faculty ordination), 584, 596–98

curriculum battle (1914), 387, 586
defections, 633–34
defenders, 636
faculty (1812), 595–96
faculty oath, 584, 595–96
failed to reproduce, 758–59
five points, 60–64
General Assembly &, 576–77, 595, 598–99, 642
graduates (1914), 334, 386
inerrency, 218–19
infants, 63, 228
interpreting the charter, 596
investigation, 620–24
judicial expediency (Machen), 598
last bastion, 598–99
League of Evangelical Students, 571
legacy (theological), 924
legal issues, 629–32
legalism, 595–98, 629–30
legitimacy after 1865, 134–35
Machen's appointment, 596–98
Machen's ordination, 584, 596
modernist attack, 628
neutrality, 777
no trials, 526
old ideas, 758
Old School, 60
ordination required, 584, 595
post-1929, 639–41
predestination, 60
Presbyterian Review (see *Presbyterian Review*)
propositional truth (faith in), 593
Protestant scholasticism, 209–10
rationalism, 764–65
report of 1923, 592–93
resigners, 637
reunion, 1869, 142
slavery issue, 134–35
Stevenson (see Stevenson, J. Ross)
strategy, 172–74, 194–95
systematic theology, 762–63
tactics, 170–77
theological legacy, 60–64, 923–24
Vos, 758, 763–64
weakness (rationalism), 764–65
Westminster Seminary &, 758–59
Princeton University, 183–87, 282, 364
procedure, 324
process theology, 71–72, 79, 226, 316, 323, 639–40, 668–69
professor, 845
progress, 72, 156, 238, 768
Progressivism
  Calvinism &, 327–28
  class theory, xlviii
  confession (also modernism's), 887
  democracy, 331–32
  Democratic Party, 329, 457–58
  election of 1912, 458, 460
  elite, 335
  eschatology of, 349–50, 482, 798
  evolutionism &, 432, 897
  eugenics, 445–46
  Hofstadter on, xxxv, 627

liberal religion, 627
masters of procedure, 324
modernism &, xxxv, 313, 324, 327–28, 336, 627, 847, 857
new liberalism, 760
other people's money, 258, 335–36, 708, 887
politics of, 708
Populism &, 335–36, 460
Prohibition, 570
secularization, 627
social science, 322
statist, 760
strategy, 335
Ward &, 326
Wilson as incarnation, 327
worldview, 331–32
Prohibition, 136, 570, 944
prophets (school of), 964
propositional truth (see truth)
Protestant Reformed Church, 356
Protestant Scholasticism, 208–10, 237
public relations, 488–89
Puritanism, 101–2, 148, 439–40 (see also New England Puritanism, Westminster Assembly)

Quakers, 129, 282
Quigley, Carroll, 664–65

racism, 442–46
radical Republicans, 135
radio, 1013
ratchet, 189, 250, 260
rationalism, xv
Reagan, Ronald, 884n

recipe, 153
Reconstruction, 144
redemption, 45
Reece Committee, 378
reform, 326–28
Reformed Episcopal Church, 337, 748
regulation, 855
regulative principle, 928–29
RE-imagining conference, 2n
relativism, 153, 268–69
remnant, 1, 646
rent-seeking, 878, 879
rescue missions, 952–53
representation
 atonement, 317–18
 basis of, 316–17
 Briggs, 345
 bureaucracy, 365
 Calvinist theology, 148
 Church officers, 148–49, 523–24
 equal votes (Whig illusion), 949
 first among equals, 820, 836–38
 future (modernists), 324
 General Assembly, 930, 933–34
 heresy &, 188
 hierarchy, 148–49, 364, 524–26
 history, 148
 imputation &, 317–18
 Machen & Macartney, 741–42
 modernism, 188, 315–18, 321–22, 934
 national, 961
 ordination, 315–16

Presbyterian, 365–66, 524–26, 820-21, 933–34
   sanctions &, 149, 710
   Speer &, 821
   spokesmen, 960
   strategies, 319–24
   Weber's view, 333
   see also hierarchy
responsibility, 49
Re-Thinking Missions, 235, 658, 665–76
reunion of Church (1869)
   Barnes' congregation, 120
   Civil War & unity, 138–41
   continuity (name), 290–93
   experientialism, 147
   heretics, 142
   marriage analogy, 289–90
   sanctions &, 141–42
   vote, 143
   revision of Confession (see Westminster Confession: revision)
revivalism
   anti-denominational, 391
   Arminianism &, 950, 952–53
   First Great Awakening, 104
   missions, 967
   New School, 95, 111, 117
   Presbyterian government &, 952
   "save America," 391
   Second Great Awakening, 109–12
rhetoric
   agenda-setting, 297
   anti-Macartney, 495–96
   avoiding controversy, 252, 263–64, 266, 283, 295–96
   Briggs' (see Briggs' rhetoric)
   Butler's, 431–32
   conservatives, 323, 429, 461
   conservatives as heretics, 266
   de-escalating, 283–84
   "defenders of the peace" ploy, 496
   Doctrinal Deliverance of 1910, 551
   escalating, 531–32, 842 (see also Briggs' rhetoric)
   Fosdick's, 477, 482–83, 559–60
   Machen's, 608, 648
   modernism, 284, 496, 527
   New School resistance to, 292–93, 296
   persuasion, 202
   rigged game, 560
   sanctions &, 540
   stages of, 202, 281–82
   van Dyke, 264, 506–7, 797
   see also Briggs' rhetoric
Rhode Island, 984–85
Rhodes, Cecil, 666
Rian, Edwin, xxv, xxxii, xxxvi, 735, 744, 746
Riefsnyder, Richard, 864, 871
Riley, William Bell, 464–67
Rimini, Robert, 112
Riverside Church, 505, 560–61
Roark, Dallas, xlvii, 704, 939
Robert's Rules of Order, 25, 970, 973
Roberts, William H., 348–50, 401–2, 682
Robertson, Pat, 137
robes, 323, 802–5, 816, 845, 881
Robespierre, M., 151
Robinson, William, 636

Rockefeller Foundation, 379n, 554
Rockefeller, John D., Jr.
   connection, 340, 488, 705
   denominations (1932), 705
   ecumenical movement, 391
   ends support of eugenics, 445, 449
   Federal Council of Churches &, 336
   follow the money, 340
   Fosdick's rescuer, 560–61
   funding of modernism, 340, 391
   General Education Board, 465–67, 585–86
   Graham &, 8
   grand jury, 377
   Harvey's assessment, 340
   higher education, 465–67
   Interchurch World Movement, 393–96, 654
   Laymen's Inquiry, 655, 656, 683
   Mott, 381, 653
   Mount Desert Island, 788–89
   Osborns &, 449
   population control, 449
   Presbyterian conflict, 926
   Re-Thinking Missions, 675–76, 683
   Speer &, 417–18, 653–54, 655
   Union Seminary, 475
   World Council of Churches, 656
Rockefeller, John D., Sr., 379-80 410, 465, 489
Rogers, Will, 544

Roman Catholicism, 236, 277, 279–80, 280–81, 567, 602
Rome, xiv
Roosevelt, Franklin, 460
Roosevelt, Teddy, 306, 661, 662, 855
root & branch petition, 978–79
Root, Elihu, 490n, 553
Rotary Club, 960
rotten wood, xviii–xix
Rousseau, J. J., 151–52, 316–17
ruling elders, 22–23, 119, 351, 499, 517–18
Ruml, Beardsley, 378–79, 654n
rural life, 457, 573
Rushdoony, Rousas J.
   confession, 902–3
   gnosticism described, 51
   humanistic law, 152
   one-many problem (Church), 771
   open universe, 152
   process, 71
   revivalism, 391
Russell, Jeffrey Burton, xxvii, 434n

sacraments
   apostasy &, 24
   defense of, 513
   Donatism, 23–24, 956
   Eastern Church, 53
   Erastians, 986
   flow of funds, 716–20, 778, 877
   judicial religion, 52
   Lord's Supper, 955–56
   Machen on, 526
   majority vote (liberalism), 726

military oath, 52
modernism, 31, 294, 726, 895
no defense of, 513–17, 519–20
oath &, 52, 526, 917
Old School, 892–93
Presbyterian conflict, 21–22, 44
Presbyterian doctrine, 20–25
sacred, 513
sanctions, 43
voting (civil), 294
Western Church, 52
salvation, 45–46, 116–17, 317 (see also atonement, soteriology)
sanctification, 74, 79, 198, 225, 230–31, 317
sanctions
    absence of (1900–23), 514–15
    academic, 590–91, 767
    academic freedom, 591, 812–17
    Auburn *Affirmation*, 536
    authority &, 127
    avoiding, 75, 198–99, 390
    bait & (pensions), 617
    behavior, 766
    boards, 364
    Briggs vs., 198–200, 230
    Church, 709
    Church covenant, 519–20
    confession, 315, 351, 503, 521–23
    conflict &, 6
    creeds &, 199, 492
    Cumberland reunion, 359
    defining marks (Machen, 1935), 732
    Doctrinal Deliverance, 390
    education, 963
    exclusion/inclusion, 95, 390
    excommunication (see ex-communication)
    final judgment, 40–41, 77–80, 318 (see also final judgment, hell)
    flow of funds (see flow of funds)
    formal, 710–11
    Fosdick on, 491–92, 708
    hell, 40–41, 77–80, 231 (see also final judgment, hell)
    heresy &, 510
    higher criticism, 161, 200–1
    incentives, 851
    inclusion/exclusion, 95
    inescapable concept, 256–57, 526
    informal, 710–11
    invaders, 539
    jobs to offer, 949–50
    judicial religion, 52
    key factor, xxxviii–xxxix
    last time, 268
    law & 11, 120, 145
    legitimacy (seminary), 591–92
    liberty &, 904
    lowest common denominator, 359
    mark of authority, 128
    members, 878–79
    membership, 12
    missions, 672
    modernism, 75, 144, 190–92, 778
    moral standard, 897
    New School, 120, 144, 894
    oath, xxvii, 9, 21, 43, 314, 357, 383, 541

Old School, 357–59, 732, 742–43
operating, 711
organization, 9
orthodoxy &, 541, 731–32
phase four, 5
political, 441
positive, 284, 709, 767–70, 786
precedents, 188, 710 (see also precedents)
Presbyterian, 258–59
Presbyterian conflict, 525
presbytery, 830
representative, 149, 710
reunion, 1869, 141
rhetoric &, 540
rival views, 318
sacraments, 43
seminaries, 590–93, 816–17
"soft underbelly," 594
statute of limitations, 188–89
"sticks & stones," 734
stipulations &, 21, 594
subscription (see subscription)
success indicators, 849
suspension, 736–37
take over, 711
theology &, 142, 594, 800–1
theory of growth &, 770
Union Seminary, 815
victory &, 494, 770
votes, 541, 732–33, 956–57
Westminster Assembly, 9, 59
Westminster Confession, 25
whose?, 256, 526, 743
Sanger, Margaret, 455
Sanhedrin, 30
Santayana, George, 937
Satan, 148

scandal, 853–84, 855
Schaeffer, Francis, 747, 999–1004, 1006–7
Schaff, Philip, 206, 233–35, 278, 305
Schlossberg, Herbert, xliii, 813
scholasticism (see Protestant scholasticism)
school of prophets, 963
science ideal, 73–75, 92, 105, 223–24
Scopes trial, 438, 461–64, 572–75
Scotland, 976–77, 990–91, 993, 996
Scottish philosophy, 589–90, 759–62 (see also apologetics, common ground, methodology)
secession, 357–58, 743
Second Great Awakening, 109–12, 972, 1014–15
secrecy, 331, 822–23, 938
secularization, 101, 113
Seligman, E. R. A., 441
seminaries
    academic freedom, 812–17, 840, 882, 927
    America's first grad schools, 311
    anti-Old School, 577
    Calvin ignored, 965
    capture of, 295
    catalogues, 334
    dead German theologians, 965, 966
    degrees, 586
    dual functions, 966
    dust-eating Christians, 950–54
    exams, 333–34, 592–93

faculty, 583
Germany &, 950-51
importance to liberals, 923
infiltration, 584, 840
lax, 334
legitimacy conferred, 590-91
liberal, 626
locus of authority, 564
Machen's plea, 626
Methodist, 1016-17
modernism's strategy, 856-58, 923
Old School swamped, 334
ordination, 191, 310-11, 834-35
ordination &, 834-35
politics of, 766-67
presbyteries &, 310, 923
professors, 836-37
reform, 963-67
report on (1923), 591-92
roots of conflict (Machen), 947
ruling elders, 23
sanctions, 191, 816-17
sanctions on, 191, 592-93
screening, 333-34, 591-92, 815, 888
"soft underbelly," 816
sovereignty over presbyteries, 958
succession, 888-89
suicide in Germany, 583
surrender of, 334
transformation, 185
vulnerability, 584-90
Warfield's view, 586
Seminex, 962
separation, 78, 81, 94, 511, 771
Seven Sisters, xxvii, 883, 884

shadow government, 309-10, 313
Shedd, W. G. T., 223, 229, 253
sheep, xxxvi, 841
Shenckel, Albert, xxv (note)
silent majority, 525
Simmel, Georg, 823-24
sin, 225-26, 677, 678
situation ethics, 75, 226, 232, 261, 326
six-day creation, 897 (see also creationism)
Skull & Bones, 375-76
slavery
  adiaphora, 131-35, 927
  higher criticism, 135
  legitimacy of Old School lost cause, 913
  major issue, 290
  Murray's view, 927
  New School, 127
  neutrality on, 913
  no repentance, 291-92
  Old School, 290, 913, 927 (see also abolitionism, *adiaphora*, Bourne)
  reunion, 140
  South's psychology, 137
  see also abolitionism
Slosser, Bob, 137
Smith, Adam, xlviii, 846
Smith, Henry P., 267-68, 295
Smith, Morton, 965
Smith, W. Robertson, 173, 174, 200-1, 257
Smith, Wilbur, 744
Smyth, E. C., 275
Snapp, Byron, 909
social action, xxi

Social Darwinism (see Darwinism)
social gospel
  Bryan &, 459
  Coffin's book, 374
  Darwinism &, 80
  Deliverance of 1910, 371–75
  eschatology, 1010
  Federal Council of Churches, 331
  Greene vs., 337–39
  Ingersoll, Robert, 194
  Mott, 875
  planning, 331–32
  Presbyterian Church &, 336
  Presbyterians, 361
social order, 847
social theory, 338
socialism, 361, 874, 875
sociology, xix, xxvii, 337–39
Socrates, 46
soteriology, 116–17, 148 (see also atonement, salvation)
Southern Baptist Convention, xvi, 808
Southern Presbyterian Church, 135–37, 270–74, 327
sovereignty
  boards, 852–53
  budgeting, 367
  ecclesiastical, 5
  economic, 814–15, 958
  economic & judicial, 852–53
  God's, 54–55, 56, 60–61, 64–65, 71–72, 75, 212, 214
  hell &, 79
  judicial & economic, 856, 958
  modernism, 72
  oath-less members, 958

  Old School Calvinism, 89
  schizophrenic, 958
  seminaries, 958
  Westminster Confession, 56
Sowell, Thomas, 790–91
Spaulding, Frank, 441
species, 326
speed limits, 10–11, 12–13, 156
Speer, Robert E.
  archetype inclusivist, 84
  author, 821
  Buck, Pearl, 690
  bureaucrat, 346–48, 415, 685
  Bushnell's disciple, 418
  crucial figure, 316, 415, 419, 422
  debater, 415
  decentralization tactic (1921), 420–22
  doctrinal trifles, 345
  Duff lectures, 679
  ecumenism, 415, 680–81
  fatherhood of God, 681
  Federal Council, 415, 417, 653–54
  flow of funds, 684–85
  Fox challenges, 754
  Fundamentals, 419
  Jesus made Himself divine, 728–29
  layman, 316
  League of Nations, 417
  liberal, 679–81
  Machen &, 647–48, 689–90, 693
  Machen's book review, 646–47
  McIntire &, 727–30
  Moderator, 415, 610–11

Mott &, 873, 875
Mudge &, 415
new world order, 416–17
Pelagian, 680
premillennialist, 415
pro-Prohibition, 416
Re-Thinking Missions, 681–87
retirement, 753
Rockefeller &, 417–18, 653–54, 655
theology vs. growth, 419–20
water–carrier for liberals, 348
World War I crusade, 416
wounded lamb role, 611
Speers, James, 655–56, 688
Spencer, Herbert, 326
spirit of the age, 891, 899
Spurgeon, Charles, 972
stalemate mentality, xli
Standard Oil, 855
standards, 5, 9, 76–77
Stark, Rodney, 1008–23
State
    biological predestinator, 447
    Church &, 901–2, 978, 979, 996
    Newton to Darwin (Wilson), 328–32
    oath-bound, 907
    Progressivism, 326–27, 760
    see also Whigs
state's rights, 128
statute of limitations, 735, 737
Stearns, Jonathan, 140–41, 146
Stelzle, Charles, 361
Stephens, Alexander H., 128
sterilization, 444, 446–49, 452, 456
Stevenson, Adlai, 472

Stevenson, J. Ross, 577, 599-601, 625–26, 823
Stewart brothers, 387, 409
"sticks & stones," 734
Stimson, Henry, 376n, 490n
stipulations, 21, 594
Stoddard, Lothrop, 444
Stoddard, Solomon, 87–88, 102-3
Stone, I. F., 663
Straight family, 661–64
strategy
    conservatives, xx, 517–18, 526–28, 593–94, 801–2, 840–41
    failure, 791, 841
    judicial, 321–24
    legal, 321
    liberal's gnosticism, 51
    Machen's, 29–30, 924
    modernism, 902
    moral high ground, 897–98
    New School, 801–2
    non–cooperation, 897
    offense & defense, xl–xliii, 841
    Old School, 145, 187–89, 801
    representation, 319–24
    subversion, xlii
    three factions, 36
    "vegetarian," 493
    verbal subversion (1837), 286–89
strategy (modernism)
    action is reaction, 896–97
    avoiding harsh rhetoric, 331, 842
    Bible vs. Bible, 157, 827 (see also higher criticism)

capture of Church courts, 512–13
"capturing the robes," 802–5
care of the wounded, 295
colleges, 765–66, 962–63
Confession vs. Confession, 179, 827
conspiratorial, 803–4
delay, 555, 565, 568, 637
doubt (Bible, Confession), 827
five steps, 805–8
flow of funds, 856–57 (see also flow of funds)
Gandhi's model, 896
goals, 321, 856
hidden agenda (capture), 803
immunity for heresy (two years), 188–89
infiltrate boards, 918
inheritance, 326
institutional, 921
monopoly, 856–59
new (1900–), 331, 340–41
offensive & defensive, 841
outside/inside, 524, 798, 803, 810–11
patience, 48, 555, 565, 568, 637
plea for peace, 48
precedent, 188
Presbyterian Review (see *Presbyterian Review*)
Progressives, 335
ratchet of heresy, 189
representation, 318–24
reversed (Southern Baptists), 817
revised (1900–), 340
rhetoric (1883–1922), 797 (see also Briggs' rhetoric)
rhetoric (1922–25), 429, 431, 433–36, 441, 449–52, 476–77, 531, 574, 902, 904–5
sanctions (avoiding), 190, 805, 812–17
sanctions (imposing), 190
secrecy, 331
seminaries, 304, 856
subversion, xlii, 262, 323–24, 503, 765–66, 841, 920
success of, 817
summary of, 809–11
targets of, 809
theological, 804, 921
toleration (pluralism), 532
"try me!" 413, 562–63
undermine churches' legitimacy, 807–8
victory, 145
Strong, Dennis, xxvii
Stuart, Moses, 132
stub, 735
Student Volunteer Movement, 415, 420, 867, 873–74
Studies in Constitution (1933), 714–15, 716–20
subscription
 Briggs on, 199, 260–61
 church & State, 13–15
 Confession over Bible, 910
 crossed fingers, 909
 early Presbyterian, 3–4
 Hodge on, 911–12
 no final resolution, 912
 revision of Confession, 827–30
 speed limits, 10–11, 12–13
 strict vs. loose, 8–15
 stricter vs. looser, 909–12

Westminster Confession, 931, 987
success indicators, 854
Sullivan & Cromwell, 553–54
Sumner, William G., 326, 375n
superintendent, 933
Supreme Court of U.S., 777n
"survival of fittest," 326, 463, 513
suspension of ministers, 736–37
Sutton, Ray, xxviii
SVM (see Student Volunteer Movement)
Swing, David, 180–83, 894, 913
symbols, 160
systematic theology, 160, 209, 762–64

tactics
    bait & hook, 919
    liberals, 266, 420, 429, 807, 811
    Princeton's, 170–77
    seminaries (see seminaries)
    Westminster Confession &, 602–3
Taft, Robert A., 376n
Taft, William H., 375, 446, 855
takeover, 711
Talmud, 910
teacher, 845
Tennent, Gilbert, 119
Tennent, William, 311
tenure (academic), 917
termites, xix
theocracy, 104, 106, 907
theology
    biblical, 763
    conservatives' (heaven & hell), 800

covenant (see covenant's five points)
evolving, 641–42
history of, 1009–10
implicit, 37
important, 38
liberal, 800, 809–10
process (see process theology)
"scientific" (Machen), 590
systematic, 160, 209, 761–64
tyranny &, xii
without sanctions, 594
Thompson, Murray, 703, 772–73
Thornwell, James, 136, 927–28, 929
tithe, 877–78, 957, 959, 960
tolerance
    Auburn *Affirmation*, 536
    Briggs, 260
    Cromwell, 994
    denial to orthodox, 904
    ecclesiastical, 42
    end of (1934), 753–54
    Fosdick &, 491–92
    Fosdick's sermon, 478
    "mental reservation," 753–54
    modernism, 80, 634, 708–9
    neutrality, 211, 532
    plea for, 80, 634
    post-1900, 284
    power religion, 48
    van Dyke, 262–63
    Whig ideal, 976
tomb of Jesus, 30
tortoise, 138
torture, 41
Toy, C. H., 161–63, 257, 295, 816

trademark, 859
traditionalism, 179
train schedule, 557
trifles, 345, 483
Trinity, 38
Truman, Harry, 527n
truth, 546, 593–94, 712, 713,
    762–64, 813
tuition, 916
TULIP, 54–55
turf conflicts, 832–36
turf-protection, 253, 267, 836
Turrentin, F., 310, 792
tyranny, xli

umbrella, 121, 283, 347, 806, 834
Union Theological Seminary
    atheists' club, 804
    Barnes on the Board, 120
    Briggs' Inaugural Address
        (1891), 240–48
    crossed fingers, 245
    divided over Briggs, 252–53
    faculty pledge, 245
    founding, 198
    leaves Church, 259
    legacy (theological), 924
    sanctions, 815
    shelter, 198
    subversive, 245
    theological legacy, 924
    turf-protection, 253
Unitarianism
    abolitionism &, 112–13, 135
    English Presbyterianism, 100
    members' confession, 524
    naive, 888
    public education, 440, 899
    Scottish philosophy &, 590

United Nations, 187, 774–75
United Presbyterian Church,
    xv–xvi, 649, 651, 860, 865, 866
United States Steel, 855
unity threatened, 704–5
university (episcopal structure),
    845
University of California, 311
urbanization, 760

Van Dusen, Henry, 502, 535,
    566, 861
van Dyke, Henry
    ambassador, 381, 507
    anti-Calvinist, 352, 382
    anti-hell, 353
    anti-heresy trials, 262, 382,
        537
    archetype modernist, 82–83
    attacks Machen, 506–7, 527,
        757, 797
    Briggs' defender, 507
    challenge to de-frock him,
        382–83, 563, 797
    confessional revision, 352, 507
    double jeopardy, 832
    Erdman &, 569
    Establishment, 507
    honor, 263, 797
    hymnal revision, 353
    last sermon, 318
    liberty of belief, 887
    lie, 352
    literature, 381
    McCosh &, 223
    Moderator, 353
    Mount Desert Island, 507
    Patton &, 894
    process theology, 318

rhetoric, 264, 506-7, 797
sets agenda (1893), 262-63
strategist, 507, 798
strategy, 797-98, 800
tactical master, 507-8
Wilson &, 187
withdraw?, 797
van Dyke, Tertius, 382, 556
Van Til, Cornelius
  apologetics, 175
  apologetics chair, 624-25
  bottomless pit analogy, 730
  higher criticism, 168
  humanism's dualism, 763
  Machen &, 783-84, 793-94
  reconstruction, 783
  Vos &, 763
  Westminster Seminary &, 637-38
vegetarians, 493
victory, 511, 914
virgin birth, 368, 385, 479-80, 502, 504, 545, 566-67, 649, 678
Virginia, 446
Vos, Geerhardus, 63, 758, 763-64
voting, 294, 295n, 518, 539, 732-33
voting as sacrament, 31, 294
voting Church members, 11

wages (ministerial), 1014-15, 1020
Walsh, Richard, 659, 660
Ward, Harry F., 924n
Ward, Lester F.,
  elite, 332, 439
  method of exclusion, 627-28
  Progressivism, 67-69, 326
Warfield, Benjamin B.

  apologetic, 587-88
  Cumberland union, 358
  eschatology, 587-88
  lower criticism, 62-63, 164-66
  methodology, 175
  postmillennial, 587
  Presbyterian Review, 172, 176
  right reason, 670
  rotten wood, 753
  sanctions, 259
  seminaries, 586, 837
  theistic evolution, 175, 223
  time frame, 301
Warfield, Ethelbert, 585n
weak links, 303
wealth, 48
Webb, Sidney, 660
Weber, Max
  bureaucracy, 333, 844
  death of meaning, 80
  democracy, 333
  ideal type, 35
  Protestantism, 671
  science's treadmill, 75
  secrecy, 822n
Wellhausen, Julius, 192
Wescott & Hort, 165
Westminster Assembly
  Civil War, 985
  Cromwell &, 975-76, 979, 995-96
  debates, 983-85
  divided, 9
  education, 981-82
  excommunicable sins, 988
  factions, 982-83
  Form of Government, 986-88, 993
  government project, 998

legacy of confusion, 9
legitimacy, 981
pamphlet war, 984–85
Parliament creates, 979, 980–81, 997
Parliament &, 986, 988–89, 992–93, 994, 997–98
Scotland &, 996–97
worship, 985–86
Westminster Confession
  administrative discipline vs., 712–13
  attack on, 179, 807
  authority (silence), 25, 522, 912, 919, 926–27, 997
  Barnes abandoned, 118
  Bible &, 56–57, 150, 157, 195, 909, 910
  Church & State, 996
  Congregational influence, 994
  conscience, 57–58, 707, 908
  Constitution, 842
  Constitutional law, 155–56, 825–27
  creationism, 223–24
  dead letter, 713
  elect infants, 65, 227–29
  election doctrine, 58
  exclusivist, 92, 370
  experience?, 87
  five points, 56–60
  fundamental law?, 155
  hell, 41–42
  ignored by conservatives, 314
  immunity, 199
  imputation, 317
  indifferentism, 314
  judicial representation, 317
  kingdom, 59–60
  law (moral), 57–58
  laymen, 518
  minister, 20–21
  museum piece, 144, 351, 779–80
  New School, 922–23
  no test of orthodoxy, 362–63
  oath, 20, 21, 25, 58, 517–18, 926–27, 931
  officers (see elders)
  Orthodox Presbyterian Church, 906–7
  over Bible, 910
  post-1933, 713
  prayer closets, 779
  predestination, 58
  Princetonians vs., 62
  revision, 30, 155–56, 176, 206, 829–30, 906–8, 970–72
  revision (1903), 64–65, 88, 122, 351–57, 892, 906
  revision (1967), 208–9, 780–82
  revision procedure, 970–72
  revisions by OPC (1936), 346
  sacramental, 20–22
  sanctification, 317
  sanctions, 59
  Scotland &, 994–95
  screening device, 370, 640
  silence of, 912
  sovereignty of God, 56
  subscription, 3, 4, 8–15, 828–30, 909–12, 931, 987
  succession, 59–60
  tactics &, 602–3
  theocratic, 907
  virgin birth, 480, 567
  women elders, 909–10
Westminster Seminary

independent, 740
Princeton &, 637–38, 642, 758–59
purge by Machen, 739–41
sanctions against, 817
Weyerhauser, Frederick, 616
Weyl, Nathaniel, 803–4
Whigs
    American, 14, 107n
    conservatives, 320
    demise of, xlviii, 899–902
    Machen (see Machen: Whig)
    natural law, 107
    Newton &, 330
    Old School, 324–25, 337, 339, 847
    pluralism, 899–900
    toleration, 976
    votes are equal, 949
    Wilson rejects, 330
whirl, xiii
Whitefield, George, 104
Whitehead, A. N., xxvii
Whitney, Dorothy, 662
Wilberforce, William, 129
will to resist, 266, 269–76, 326, 383–84, 539, 568, 897, 900
Willard, Samuel, 351
Williams, Roger, 907, 976, 978, 984–85
Wilson, J. M., 69–70
Wilson, Rev. Joseph, 133, 348n
Wilson, Robert Dick, 422–23, 571, 637
Wilson, Warren, 1018, 1019, 1021
Wilson, Woodrow
    anti-whig, 328–9

Congressional Government, 312
Constitutional Government, 329–31
    Darwin, 330
    defeat at Princeton, 508n
    doubt-free, 344
    Fosdick, Raymond, 489
    government, 312–13, 938
    Johns Hopkins University, 312
    Lee, 489
    Machen family, 343–44
    political shifts, 329
    Princeton University, 186–87
    Progressive, 327–28
    racist, 187
    shifting views, 328–9
    two governments, 312–13
    Whigs, 328–30
    Woodrow case, 274
Wishart, Charles, 496–97
Witherow, Thomas, 818n, 822
Witherspoon, John, 106, 364, 899, 966
wolves, 766, 767, 775–76, 841
women's societies, 864–66
Woodbridge, Charles, 744, 746, 748
Woodrow, James, 270–74
Woolley, Paul, 744
words, 287, 289
World Alliance for International Friendship, 408
World Council of Churches, 656
World War I, 391–92
worship, 114
wounded (care of), 295, 296,

562, 663, 919, 939
wounded lambs role, 492, 611, 809
Wright, G. Ernest, 214

Yale, 111, 162–63, 184, 252, 275, 375, 441, 641n
YMCA, 411, 867, 872

HELPFUL SUGGESTIONS FOR BOOK REVIEWERS

This is a large book. Most reviewers will not want to read all of it. This is especially true of those reviewing it for the secular press.

Here is the basic approach that all professional but hard-pressed reviewers adopt in such situations. First, read the flyleaf and back cover copy. Second, read the Table of Contents. Third, see if there are chapter conclusions. More than this is generally considered optional.

Because this book is large, you can tip your cap to scholarly objectivity by mentioning that there is a great deal of useful material here, especially in the footnotes. This is safe; hardly anyone actually reads footnotes. (You might also mention that they really are footnotes, not endnotes. People who learned to read after 1965 have rarely encountered such odd phenomena.)

You will be writing for editors who would be alienated by the book's thesis, as well as its style, should they read it. They won't, of course. But it is quite possible that some outraged, theologically correct soul will write to your editor and demand an accounting for an even-handed review, let alone a favorable one. So, you need to add some clearly identifiable signal flares. For those of you who have never read a book review by that consummate book reviewer and destroyer of academic reputations, the English historian A. J. P. Taylor, I have added some useful brief phrases that may help.

"This book would have destroyed the author's academic reputation, had he ever had one." [A variant of one of Taylor's better lines.]

"It's a shame that the author isn't employed by a college or university, so that he could be dismissed."

"Compared to *Crossed Fingers*, Cotton Mather's *Magnalia* is a model of Enlightenment objectivity."

"The author is a modern-day Oliver Cromwell with a word processor—and a lot more warts."

"Rush Limbaugh with a catechism."

"A book written for people who think *The Bell Curve* wasn't sufficiently controversial."

"A book written for people whose trigger fingers move when they read."

"The author writes with all the subtlety of a finger jabbing your eye. Your left eye."

"Reading this book is like sitting in a movie theater next to someone who has seen the film three times and keeps whispering loudly what's going to happen next."

"*Crossed Fingers* is to historical scholarship what iron pyrite is to gold mining."

"He must be channeling for Westbrook Pegler." [Note: for readers in the advanced AARP set.]

"Col. McCormick would have loved this guy. So would Cyrus." [Note: only for the cognoscenti.]

"Orosius on uppers!" [Note: historical journals only.]

"What can you expect from someone who summarizes liberal theology in three words: 'Let us prey'?"

"Here is an author who will never be quoted out of context by a hostile reviewer. There is no need. What he writes in context is utterly outrageous."

ABOUT THE AUTHOR

Gary North received his Ph.D. in American history from the University of California, Riverside, in 1972.

He is the author of approximately three dozen books in the fields of economics, history, and theology. His first book, *Marx's Religion of Revolution*, appeared in 1968. His *Introduction to Christian Economics* appeared in 1973, the year he began writing a multi-volume economic commentary on the Bible, which now covers Genesis, Exodus (three volumes), and Leviticus. He was the general editor of the Biblical Blueprints Series (1986–87), a 10-volume set, for which he wrote four of the books.

Beginning in 1965, his articles and reviews have appeared in over three dozen newspapers and periodicals, including the *Wall Street Journal*, *Modern Age*, *Journal of Political Economy*, *National Review*, and *The Freeman*.

He edited the first fifteen issues of *The Journal of Christian Reconstruction*, 1974–81. He edited a *festschrift* for Cornelius Van Til, *Foundations of Christian Scholarship* (1976). He edited two issues of *Christianity and Civilization* in 1983: *The Theology of Christian Resistance* and *Tactics of Christian Resistance*. He edited *Theonomy: An Informed Response* (1991).

He is the editor of the monthly financial newsletter, *Remnant Review*. He writes two bi-monthly Christian newsletters, *Biblical Economics Today* and *Christian Reconstruction*, published by the Institute for Christian Economics.

He lives in Tyler, Texas, with his wife and four children.

WHAT IS THE ICE?

by Gary North, President, ICE

The Institute for Christian Economics is a non-profit, tax-exempt educational organization which is devoted to research and publishing in the field of Christian ethics. The perspective of those associated with the ICE is straightforwardly conservative and pro-free market. The ICE is dedicated to the proposition that biblical ethics requires full personal responsibility, and this responsible human action flourishes most productively within a framework of limited government, political decentralization, and minimum interference with the economy by the civil government.

For well over half a century, the loudest voices favoring Christian social action have been outspokenly pro-government intervention. Anyone needing proof of this statement needs to read Dr. Gregg Singer's comprehensive study, *The Unholy Alliance* (Arlington House Books, 1975), the definitive history of the National Council of Churches. An important policy statement from the National Council's General Board in 1967 called for *comprehensive economic planning*. The ICE was established in order to *challenge* statements like the following:

> Accompanying this growing diversity in the structures of national life has been a growing recognition of the importance of competent planning within and among all resource sectors of the society: education, economic development, land use, social health services, the family system and congregational life. It is not generally recognized that an effective approach to problem solving requires a comprehensive planning process and coordination in the development of all these resource areas.

The *silence* from the conservative denominations in response to such policy proposals has been deafening. Not that conservative church members agree with such nonsense; they don't. But the conservative denominations and associations have remained silent because they have convinced themselves that *any* policy statement of any sort regarding social and economic life is *always* illegitimate. In short, there is no such thing as a correct, valid policy statement that a church or denomination can make. *The results of this opinion have been universally devastating.* The popular press assumes that the radicals who do speak out in the name of Christ are representative of the membership (or at least the press goes along with the illusion). The public is convinced that to speak out on social matters in the name of Christ is to be radical. *Christians are losing by default.*

The ICE is convinced that conservative Christians must devote resources to create alternative proposals. There is an old rule of political life which argues that "You can't beat something with nothing." We agree. It is not enough to adopt a whining negativism whenever someone or some group comes up with another nutty economic program. We need a comprehensive alternative.

Society or State

Society is broader than politics. The State is not a substitute for society. *Society encompasses all social institutions*: church, State, family, economy, kinship groups, voluntary clubs and associations, schools, and non-profit educational organizations (such as ICE). Can we say that there are no standards of righteousness — justice — for these social institutions? Are they lawless? The Bible says no. We do not live in a lawless universe. But this does not mean that the State is the source of all law. On the contrary, God, not the imitation god of the State, is the source.

Christianity is innately decentralist. *From the beginning, orthodox Christians have denied the divinity of the State.* This is why the Caesars of Rome had them persecuted and executed. They denied the operating presupposition of the ancient world, namely, the legitimacy of a divine rule or a divine State.

It is true that modern liberalism has eroded Christian orthodoxy. There are literally thousands of supposedly evangelical pastors who have been compromised by the liberalism of the universities and seminaries they attended. The popularity, for example, of Prof. Ronald Sider's *Rich Christians in an Age of Hunger*, co-published by Inter-Varsity Press (evangelical Protestant) and the Paulist Press (liberal Roman Catholic), is indicative of the crisis today. It has sold like hotcakes, and it calls for mandatory wealth redistribution by the State on a massive scale. Yet he is a professor at a Baptist seminary.

The ICE rejects the theology of the total State. This is why we countered the book by Sider when we published David Chilton's *Productive Christians in an Age of Guilt-Manipulators* (sixth printing, 1996). Chilton's book shows that the Bible is the foundation of our economic freedom, and that the call for compulsory wealth transfers and higher taxes on the rich is simply *baptized socialism*. Socialism is anti-Christian to the core.

What we find is that laymen in evangelical churches tend to be more conservative theologically and politically than their pastors. But this conservatism is a kind of *instinctive conservatism*. It is *not* self-consciously grounded in the Bible. So the laymen are unprepared to counter the sermons and Sunday School materials that bombard them week after week.

It is ICE's contention that *the only way to turn the tide in this nation is to capture the minds of the evangelical community*, which numbers in the tens of millions. We have to convince the liberal-leaning evangelicals of the biblical nature of the free market system. And we have to convince the conservative evangelicals of the same thing, in order to get them into the social and intellectual battles of our day.

In other words, *retreat is not biblical*, any more than socialism is.

By What Standard?

We have to ask ourselves this question: *"By what standard?"* By what standard do we evaluate the claims of the socialists and interventionists? By what standard do we evaluate the claims of the secular free market economists who reject socialism? By what standard are we to construct intellectual alternatives to the humanism of our day? And by what standard do we criticize the social institutions of our era?

If we say that the standard is "reason," we have a problem: Whose reason? If the economists cannot agree with each other, how do we decide who is correct? Why hasn't reason produced agreement after centuries of debate? We need an alternative.

It is the Bible. The ICE is dedicated to the defense of the Bible's reliability. But don't we face the same problem? Why don't Christians agree about what the Bible says concerning economics?

One of the main reasons why they do not agree is that the question of biblical economics has not been taken seriously. Christian scholars have ignored economic theory for generations. This is why the ICE devotes so much time, money, and effort to studying what the Bible teaches about economic affairs.

There will always be some disagreements, since men are not perfect, and their minds are imperfect. But when men agree about the basic issue of the starting point of the debate, they have a far better opportunity to discuss and learn than if they offer only "reason, rightly understood" as their standard.

Services

The ICE exists in order to serve Christians and other people who are vitally interested in finding moral solutions to the economic crisis of our day. The organization is a *support ministry* to other Christian ministries. It is non-sectarian, non-denominational, and dedicated to the proposition that a moral economy is a truly practical, productive economy.

The ICE produces several newsletters. These are aimed at intelligent laymen, church officers, and pastors. The reports are non-technical in nature. Included in our publication schedule are these monthly and bi-monthly publications:

Biblical Economics Today (6 times a year)
Christian Reconstruction (6 times a year)
Biblical Chronology (12 times a year)

Biblical Economics Today is a four-page report that covers economic theory from a specifically Christian point of view. It also deals with questions of economic policy. **Christian Reconstruction** is more action-oriented, but it also covers various aspects of Christian social theory. *Biblical Chronology* deals with studies in the chronology of the Bible as they relate to the reconstruction of ancient history.

The purpose of the ICE is to relate biblical ethics to Christian activities in the field of economics. To cite the title of Francis Schaeffer's book, "How should we then live?" How should we apply biblical wisdom in the field of economics to our lives, our culture, our civil government, and our businesses and callings?

If God calls men to responsible decision-making, then He must have *standards of righteousness* that guide men in their decision-making. It is the work of the ICE to discover, illuminate, explain, and suggest applications of these guidelines in the field of economics. We publish the results of our findings in the newsletters.

The ICE sends out the newsletters free of charge. Anyone can sign up for six months to receive them. This gives the reader the opportunity of seeing "what we're up to." At the end of six months, he or she can renew for another six months.

Donors receive a one-year subscription. This reduces the extra trouble associated with sending out renewal notices, and it also means less trouble for the subscriber.

There are also donors who pledge to pay $15 a month. They are members of the ICE's *"Reconstruction Committee."* They help to provide a predictable stream of income which finances the day-to-day operations of the ICE. Then the donations from others can finance special projects, such as the publication of a new book.

The basic service that ICE offers is education. We are presenting ideas and approaches to Christian ethical behavior that few other organizations even suspect are major problem areas. *The Christian world has for too long acted as though we were not responsible citizens on earth*, as well as citizens of heaven. ("For our conversation [citizenship] is in heaven" [Philippians 3:20a].) *We must be godly stewards of all our assets*, which includes our lives, minds, and skills.

Because economics affects every sphere of life, the ICE's reports and surveys are relevant to all areas of life. Because *scarcity affects every area*, the whole world needs to be governed by biblical requirements for *honest stewardship* of the earth's resources. The various publications are wide-ranging, since the effects of the curse of the ground (Genesis 3:17-19) are wide-ranging.

What the ICE offers the readers and supporters is an introduction to a world of responsibility that few Christians have recognized. This limits our audience, since most people think they have too many responsibilities already. But if more people understood the Bible's solutions to economic problems, they would have more capital available to take greater responsibility — and prosper from it.

Finances

There ain't no such thing as a free lunch (TANSTAAFL). *Someone has to pay for those six-month renewable free subscriptions.* Existing donors are, in effect, supporting a kind of intellectual missionary organization. Except for the newsletters sent to ministers and teachers, we "clean" the mailing lists each year: less waste.

We cannot expect to raise money by emotional appeals. We have no photographs of starving children, no orphanages in Asia. We generate ideas. *There is always a very limited market for ideas, which is why some of them have to be subsidized by people who understand the power of ideas - a limited group, to be sure.* John Maynard Keynes, the most influential economist of this century (which speaks poorly of this century), spoke the truth in the final paragraph of his *General Theory of Employment, Interest, and Money* (1936):

> . . . the ideas of economists and political philosophers, both when they are right and when they are wrong, are more powerful than is commonly understood. Indeed, the world is ruled by little else. Practical men, who believe themselves to be quite exempt from any intellectual influences, are usually the slaves of some defunct economist. Madmen in authority, who hear voices in the air, are distilling their frenzy from some academic scribbler of a few years back. I am sure that the power of vested interests is vastly exaggerated compared with the gradual encroachment of ideas. Not, indeed, immediately, but after a certain interval; for in the field of economic and political philosophy there are not many who are influenced by new theories after they are twenty-five or thirty years of age, so that the ideas which civil servants and politicians and even agitators apply to current events are not likely to be the newest. But, soon or late, it is ideas, not vested interests, which are dangerous for good or evil.

Do you believe this? If so, then the program of long-term education which the ICE has created should be of considerable interest to you. What we need are people with a *vested interest in ideas*, a *commitment to principle* rather than class position.

There will be few short-term, visible successes for the ICE's program. There will be new and interesting books. There will be a constant stream of newsletters. There will educational audio and video tapes. But the world is not likely to beat a path to ICE's door, as long as today's policies of high taxes and statism have not yet produced a catastrophe. We are investing in the future, for the far side of humanism's economic failure. *This is a long-term investment in intellectual capital.* Contact us at: *ICE., Box 8000, Tyler, TX 75711.*

Westminster's Confession:
The Abandonment of Van Til's Legacy
by Gary North

In October, 1990, the long-promised book by the faculty of Westminster Theological Seminary finally appeared: *Theonomy: A Reformed Critique*. In response comes *Westminster's Confession*. It is both a negative and a positive statement. Theonomists believe that "you can't beat something with nothing." It is not enough to demonstrate that someone is wrong: you must also show what is correct.

Cornelius Van Til made this principle the bedrock application of his apologetic method. It was not enough to demonstrate that his opponents' systems of thought were internally inconsistent; he also showed why Christianity is the **only** logical alternative. But he left an incomplete legacy. He refused to offer an explicitly biblical alternative to the natural law theory that he had refuted. His system created a judicial vacuum.

Into that vacuum have come two rival factions: the political pluralists and the theonomists. The battle is now engaged.

Westminster Seminary's problem for a generation – indeed, Calvinistic American Presbyterianism's problem for two centuries – has been to justify a commitment to modern religious and political pluralism in terms of the Westminster confession's judicial standards. The faculty has been double-minded on this point: Proclaiming their commitment to Van Til's apologetic method, they have simultaneously denied the idea that the Bible is the bearer of biblical blueprints or judicial frameworks for society. In short, they have abandoned any ideal of a Christian society, i.e., Christendom itself.

This is Westminster's social and cultural confession – a theologically negative confession, proclaiming in the name of the original Westminster Assembly what society ought not to be, but never daring to suggest what it should be. In contrast, *Westminster's Confession* offers a positive confession. It offers a biblical alternative. It restores the vision of Christendom.

385 pp., indexed, hardback, $14.95
Institute for Christian Economics, P.O. Box 8000, Tyler, Texas 75711

Political Polytheism: The Myth of Pluralism
by Gary North

"Who is LORD over the United States" A Christian citizen knows the answer: Jesus Christ. But if this really is the true answer, grounded firmly on the Bible, then why is it that so few Christians are willing to proclaim this fact publicly, and why is it that no Christian political candidate dares mention it? There is a reason: the theology of political pluralism, the dominant public theology in our day.

Political pluralism is not simply a political philosophy; it is a theology. It is America's civil religion. This theology teaches that there must never be a nation that identifies itself with any religion. Well, not quite. The nation of Israel is grudgingly allowed to do so, as are the Islamic nations. But no nation is ever supposed to identify itself as Christian. "A Christian nation is self-contradictory!"

So we are told. but who tells us? Secular humanists who are dedicated to wiping out all political opposition. Also, Christian teachers who teach in tax-supported schools. Also, professors in Christian colleges who attended either state universities or secular humanist private universities, which are the only accredited universities in the United States that grant the Ph.D. degree. Also, the U.S. Constitution.

This is the problem. God-fearing Christian Americans have been told that the Constitution teaches the absolute separation of Church and State. They have been told correctly. But what they have not been told is precisely where it says this. It does not say this in the first Amendment. The First Amendment says only that Congress shall make no law regarding religion or the free exercise thereof. So, where does the Constitution prohibit a Christian America? In a section that has been ignored by scholars for so long that it is virtually never discussed – the key provision that transformed America into a secular humanist nation. But it took 173 years to do this: from 1788 until 1961. *Political Polytheism* discusses this crucial provision in detail. It presents a new vision of politics, a vision self-consciously tied to the Bible.

795 pp., indexed, hardback, $22.50
Institute for Christian Economics, P.O. Box 8000, Tyler, Texas 75711

The Greatness of the Great Commission: The Christian Enterprise in a Fallen World
by Kenneth Gentry

"Save Souls, Not Cultures!" This has been the motto of twentieth-century evangelism. Having encountered heavy resistance to the prophets' message of comprehensive revival and restoration in history, modern evangelical Christianity has abandoned the prophets. Unlike Jonah, who grew weary of life in the belly of a whale, modern evangelicalism has not only grown accustomed to the Church's cultural irrelevance today, it has actually proclaimed this pathetic condition as God's plan for the "Church Age." But is it? Not according to Jesus' instructions to His Church: the discipling (putting under God's discipline) of all nations (Matthew 28:19-20).

Paul makes it clear that the progressive expansion of Jesus' kingdom in history will continue until all things are under His dominion, on earth, before He returns physically to judge the world (I Corinthians 15:25-26). This was David's message, too (Psalm 110:1-2).

This book presents a biblical case for God's salvation and restoration in history. Sin is comprehensive; God's healing grace is no less comprehensive. Wherever sin reigns today, there God speaks to sinful man and offers a way of escape (I Corinthians 10:13). To argue that the Great Commission does not include every aspect of today's cultures – all of Satan's kingdom – is to argue that there is no way of escape in many areas of life.

The war between God's kingdom (civilization) on earth and Satan's kingdom (civilization) on earth is total, encompassing every aspect of life. The Great Commission calls the Church (in this "Church Age") to make a full-scale attack on modern humanist civilization, but always in terms of a positive message and practical program: a better way of life in every area of life. This is the greatness of the Great Commission. It must not be narrowed to exclude culture from God's special grace.

184 pp., indexed, paperback, $9.95; hardback, $25.00
Institute for Christian Economics, P.O. Box 8000, Tyler, TX 75711

That You May Prosper: Dominion By Covenant
by Ray R. Sutton

In the history of Christianity there has never been a theologian who has explained to anyone's satisfaction just what the Biblical covenant is. We have heard about "covenant theology" since Calvin's day, but can anyone tell us just what Calvin said the covenant is, how it works, and what common features are found in every Biblical covenant? Can anyone describe just exactly what the seventeenth-century Puritans had in mind when they used the word? They couldn't.

Have you read anywhere that the covenant is an inescapable concept, that it is never a question of "covenant vs. no covenant," that it is always a question of whose covenant? Has anyone explained how all societies have imitated the Bible;s covenant model, or how Satan has adapted a crude imitation of the Biblical covenant?

Until Ray Sutton cracked the code of the Bible's covenant structure in late 1985, no one had gone into print with a clear, Biblically verifiable model of the covenant – or if anyone did, no trace of his work has survived. Covenant theologians have never adopted it.

You can check this for yourself. Read any book dealing with the Biblical covenant. See if it explains: (1) the structure of the covenant; (2) the uses of the covenant model in Bible history; (3) the application of the same covenant model in Bible texts, Old and New Testaments; (4) the history of the covenant's impact in the West; and (5) the continuing authority and importance of the Biblical covenant in modern life: church, state, family, business, etc.

Utilizing careful and detailed Biblical exposition, and practical and lucid Biblical application, Sutton shows just how God desires for us to obtain our promised victory. But he not only shows us all the hows of the covenant, he shows us all the whats, whens, wheres, and whys as well.

Whether your interest is theological or practical, philosophical or personal, sociological or devotional, *That You May Prosper* is certain to be an eye-opening contribution to your Christian walk.

366 pp., indexed, bibliography, hardback, $15.95
Institute for Christian Economics, P.O. Box 8000, Tyler, Texas 75711

Phase 3: Whose Legality?
1901 — Founding conference, National Federation of Churches
1902 — Woodrow Wilson becomes president of Princeton U.
        Patton becomes president of Princeton Seminary
1903 — Westminster Confession revised (universal love of God)
        Establishment of the Committee on Church Cooperation
1906 — Cumberland Presbyterians arrive (1,100 congregations)
        J. Gresham Machen joins Princeton's faculty
        Charles Erdman joins Princeton's faculty
1908 — Federal Council of Churches (FCC) begins; led by Roberts
        Presbyterian Church reorganized; Executive Commission begins
1910 — GA's Doctrinal Deliverance (fundamentalist)
        GA's Social Deliverance (social gospel)
        Edinburgh conference on world missions
        Rockefeller leads the New York City grand jury
        Wilson elected Governor of New Jersey
1912 — Wilson elected President of the United States
1913 — Patton resigns as president of Princeton Seminary
        Van Dyke's challenge: "Initiate a heresy trial against me!"
1914 — J. Ross Stevenson replaces Patton
        Machen becomes Assistant Professor; then is ordained
1918 — Council on Organic Church Union established by GA
1919 — Interchurch World Movement (IWM) begins
        New Era Movement begins in PCUSA: centralized fund-raising
1920 — Rockefeller joins IWM
        Speer becomes president of Federal Council (to 1924)
        Presbyteries vote not to join Church Union
        Presbyteries vote not to ordain women elders (129 to 125)
        GA votes to pay Presbyterian Church's share of IWM's bills
1921 — W. H. Griffith Thomas on liberalism in foreign missions
        Speer re-structures authority over foreign missionaries
        Lewis Mudge becomes Stated Clerk (to 1938)

Phase 4: Whose Sanctions?
1922 — William Jennings Bryan's *New York Times* attack on Darwinism
        Harry E. Fosdick's sermon, "Shall the Fundamentalists Win?"
1923 — Machen's *Christianity and Liberalism* published
        GA calls for unification of seminaries' boards
        GA calls for New York Presbytery's trial of Fosdick
        Auburn *Affirmation* signed by 149 ministers
        Van Dyke's attack on Machen's preaching
1924 — Auburn *Affirmation* published (over 1,200 eventually sign)
        General Council replaces Executive Commission (GA)

1863 — Lincoln's Emancipation Proclamation
1864 — Northern Old School condemns slavery as a sin
    Reunion: Southern New School/Old School (PCUS)
1865 — Civil War ends
    Republican radicals take over GA's of both schools in North
1866 — Briggs receives "light" of higher criticism in Germany
1868 — James McCosh becomes president of Princeton U.

Phase 2: Whose Authority?
1869 — Reunion: Northern Old School/New School (PCUSA)
1870 — Reunion Assembly in Albert Barnes' church
1871 — Darwin's *Descent of Man*
1874 — Rev. David Swing resigns under fire from Francis Patton
    Charles Hodge's *What Is Darwinism?*
    Union Seminary hires Briggs
1876 — Briggs' first inaugural address
    W. Robertson Smith is brought to trial in Scotland
    Johns Hopkins University opens
1878 — Rev. William McCune convicted of heresy (ecclesiology)
1880 — *Presbyterian Review* begins publication: joint venture
1881 — Essays on higher criticism in *Presbyterian Review*: pro & con
1882 — General Assembly's Deliverance against higher criticism;
    no action
1884 — W. H. Roberts becomes Stated Clerk (to 1920)
1885 — Briggs' *American Presbyterianism*
1888 — Patton becomes president of Princeton U.
    B. B. Warfield joins Princeton Seminary's faculty
1889 — Briggs' *Whither?*
    Debate over Confessional revision
    Robert E. Speer and John R. Mott: missions recruiting
        (students)
1891 — Briggs' second inaugural address
    Speer joins Foreign Missions Board (to 1937)
1892 — Trial of Briggs begins (New York Presbytery)
    Doctrinal Deliverance by General Assembly (Portland, Oregon)
    Union Seminary leaves the denomination
1893 — Henry van Dyke's *Plea for Peace and Work* manifesto
    Briggs convicted of heresy by GA
1894 — Henry Preserved Smith convicted of heresy by GA
1896 — College of New Jersey becomes Princeton U.
1900 — A. C. McGiffert leaves Church under fire
    Ecumenical Conference on Foreign Missions, New York City